新 約 全 書

THE BOOKS OF THE NEW TESTAMENT

新約全書

THE BOOK OF THE NEW TESTAMENT

新約

The New Testament

現代英文譯本/現代中文譯本（修訂版）
TODAY'S ENGLISH VERSION/TODAY'S CHINESE VERSION
(Revised Editions)

聯合聖經公會
United Bible Societies

新約
現代英文譯本／現代中文譯本（修訂版）

THE NEW TESTAMENT
Today's English Version / Today's Chinese Version (Revised Editions)

TEV/TCV240DI Series 2001 – 22M

ISBN 962 293 525 7	TEV/TCV240DI	Trade Ed
ISBN 962 293 533 8	TEV/TCV240DI	Tourist Ed (HK)
ISBN 962 293 534 6	TEV/TCV240DI	Tourist Ed (Macau)
ISBN 962 293 535 4	TEV/TCV243DI	Trade Ed (Hard Cover)

馬太福音
MATTHEW

INTRODUCTION

The Gospel according to Matthew tells the good news that Jesus is the promised Savior, the one through whom God fulfilled the promises he made to his people in the Old Testament. This good news is not only for the Jewish people, among whom Jesus was born and lived, but for the whole world.

Matthew is carefully arranged. It begins with the birth of Jesus, describes his baptism and temptation, and then takes up his ministry of preaching, teaching, and healing in Galilee. After this the Gospel records Jesus' journey from Galilee to Jerusalem and the events of Jesus' last week, culminating in his crucifixion and resurrection.

This Gospel presents Jesus as the great Teacher, who has the authority to interpret the Law of God, and who teaches about the Kingdom of God. Much of his teaching is gathered by subject matter into five collections:

(1) the Sermon on the Mount, which concerns the character, duties, privileges, and destiny of the citizens of the Kingdom of heaven (chapters 5-7);

(2) instructions to the twelve disciples for their mission (chapter 10);

(3) parables about the Kingdom of heaven (chapter 13);

(4) teaching on the meaning of discipleship (chapter 18); and

(5) teaching about the end of the present age and the coming of the Kingdom of God (chapters 24-25).

Outline of Contents

簡 介

馬太福音指示我們：耶穌就是上帝應許賜給人類的拯救者。藉着他，上帝實現了在舊約中向自己的子民許下的諾言。這福音不但是給猶太人的，也是給全世界的人。

本書的編排十分週密，從耶穌降生開始，說到他受洗、受試探、傳道、施教，和在加利利一帶醫治病人，然後記述耶穌從加利利上耶路撒冷途中的經歷和最後一週發生的事件，最後是他被釘十字架和復活。

本福音書所寫的耶穌是一位偉大的導師。他有權柄解釋上帝的律法；他教導有關上帝主權的真理。他的教導按內容可歸納爲五大類：

一、山上寶訓—論天國了民的品位、責任、權利，和前途（第五至七章）。

二、十二使徒的使命（第十章）。

三、關於天國的比喻（第十三章）。

四、關於作門徒的意義（第十八章）。

五、關於今世的終結和上帝主權的實現（第二十四、二十五章）。

提要

The Ancestors of Jesus Christ
(Luke 3.23-38)

1 This is the list of the ancestors of Jesus Christ, a descendant of David, who was a descendant of Abraham.

2-6aFrom Abraham to King David, the following ancestors are listed: Abraham, Isaac, Jacob, Judah and his brothers; then Perez and Zerah (their mother was Tamar), Hezron, Ram, Amminadab, Nahshon, Salmon, Boaz (his mother was Rahab), Obed (his mother was Ruth), Jesse, and King David.

6b-11From David to the time when the people of Israel were taken into exile in Babylon, the following ancestors are listed: David, Solomon (his mother was the woman who had been Uriah's wife), Rehoboam, Abijah, Asa, Jehoshaphat, Jehoram, Uzziah, Jotham, Ahaz, Hezekiah, Manasseh, Amon, Josiah, and Jehoiachin and his brothers.

12-16From the time after the exile in Babylon to the birth of Jesus, the following ancestors are listed: Jehoiachin, Shealtiel, Zerubbabel, Abiud, Eliakim, Azor, Zadok, Achim, Eliud, Eleazar, Matthan, Jacob, and Joseph, who married Mary, the mother of Jesus, who was called the Messiah.

17So then, there were fourteen generations from Abraham to David, and fourteen from David to the exile in Babylon, and fourteen from then to the birth of the Messiah.

The Birth of Jesus Christ
(Luke 2.1-7)

18This was how the birth of Jesus Christ took place. His mother Mary was engaged to Joseph, but before they were married, she found out that she was going to have a baby by the Holy Spirit. 19Joseph was a man who always did what was right, but he did not want to disgrace Mary publicly; so he made plans to break the engagement privately. 20While he was thinking about this, an angel of the Lord appeared to him in a dream and said, "Joseph, descendant of David, do not be afraid to take Mary to be your wife. For it is by the Holy Spirit that she has conceived. 21She will have a son, and you will name him Jesus–because he will save his people from their sins."
22Now all this happened in order to make

耶穌基督的家譜
（路 3 · 23-38）

1 耶穌的家譜如下：
耶穌基督是大衞的後代，大衞是亞伯拉罕的後代。

2 亞伯拉罕生以撒，以撒生雅各，雅各生猶大和他的兄弟。3 猶大跟塔瑪生法勒斯和謝拉，法勒斯生希斯崙，希斯崙生亞蘭，4 亞蘭生亞米拿達，亞米拿達生亞順，拿順生撒門，5 撒門跟喇合生波阿斯，波阿斯跟路得生俄備得，俄備得生耶西，6 耶西生大衞王。

大衞跟烏利亞的妻子生所羅門，7 所羅門生羅波安，羅波安生亞比雅，亞比雅生亞撒，8 亞撒生約沙法，約沙法生約蘭，約蘭生烏西雅，9 烏西雅生約坦，約坦生亞哈斯，亞哈斯生希西家，10 希西家生瑪拿西，瑪拿西生亞們，亞們生約西亞。11 以色列族被擄到巴比倫期間，約西亞生約雅斤和他的兄弟。

12 被擄到巴比倫以後，約雅斤生撒拉鐵，撒拉鐵生所羅巴伯，13 所羅巴伯生亞比玉，亞比玉生以利亞敬，以利亞敬生亞所，14 亞所生撒督，撒督生亞金，亞金生以律，15 以律生以利亞撒，以利亞撒生馬但，馬但生雅各，16 雅各生約瑟，就是馬利亞的丈夫。那被稱為基督的耶穌是從馬利亞生的。

17 這樣算起來，從亞伯拉罕到大衞共十四代，從大衞到以色列人被擄到巴比倫也是十四代，從被擄到基督的誕生又是十四代。

耶穌基督的誕生
（路 2 · 1-7）

18 耶穌基督誕生的經過是這樣的：他的母親馬利亞已經跟約瑟訂了婚，但是在成婚以前，馬利亞知道自己已經由聖靈懷了孕。19 她的未婚夫約瑟為人正直，但又不願意公開羞辱她，卻有意要秘密解除婚約。20 他正在考慮這事，主的天使在夢中向他顯現，說：「大衞的後代約瑟，不要怕，儘管娶馬利亞作妻子，因為她懷的孕是由聖靈來的。21 她將要生一個兒子，你要給他取名叫耶穌，因為他將拯救他的子民脫離他們的罪。」
22 這一切事的發生是要應驗主藉着先知所

come true what the Lord had said through the prophet, 23"A virgin will become pregnant and have a son, and he will be called Immanuel" (which means, "God is with us.")

24So when Joseph woke up, he married Mary, as the angel of the Lord had told him to. 25But he had no sexual relations with her before she gave birth to her son. And Joseph named him Jesus.

Visitors from the East

2 Jesus was born in the town of Bethlehem in Judea, during the time when Herod was king. Soon afterward, some men who studied the stars came from the East to Jerusalem 2and asked, "Where is the baby born to be the king of the Jews? We saw his star when it came up in the east, and we have come to worship him."

3When King Herod heard about this, he was very upset, and so was everyone else in Jerusalem. 4He called together all the chief priests and the teachers of the Law and asked them, "Where will the Messiah be born?"

5"In the town of Bethlehem in Judea," they answered. "For this is what the prophet wrote:
6'Bethlehem in the land of Judah,
　　you are by no means the least of the
　　　　leading cities of Judah;
for from you will come a leader
　　who will guide my people Israel.' "

7So Herod called the visitors from the East to a secret meeting and found out from them the exact time the star had appeared. 8Then he sent them to Bethlehem with these instructions: "Go and make a careful search for the child; and when you find him, let me know, so that I too may go and worship him."

9-10And so they left, and on their way they saw the same star they had seen in the East. When they saw it, how happy they were, what joy was theirs! It went ahead of them until it stopped over the place where the child was. 11They went into the house, and when they saw the child with his mother Mary, they knelt down and worshiped him. They brought out their gifts of gold, frankincense, and myrrh, and presented them to him.

12Then they returned to their country by another road, since God had warned them in a dream not to go back to Herod.

The Escape to Egypt

13After they had left, an angel of the Lord appeared in a dream to Joseph and said, "Herod will be looking for the child in order to kill him. So get up, take the child and his mother and escape to Egypt, and stay there until I tell you to leave."

說的話：23「有童女將懷孕生子，他的名字要叫以馬內利。」（「以馬內利」的意思就是「上帝與我們同在」。）

24 約瑟一醒過來，就照着主的天使所吩咐的去做，跟馬利亞成婚；25但是在她生孩子以前沒有跟她同房。孩子出生，約瑟就給他取名叫耶穌。

東方的訪客

2 希律作王的時候，耶穌誕生在猶太的伯利恆。有幾個星象家從東方來到耶路撒冷；2他們問：「那出生要作猶太人的王的在哪裏？我們在東方看見了他的星，特地來朝拜他。」

3 希律王聽了這話，着急不安；整個耶路撒冷的人也同樣不安。4希律就召集了所有的祭司長和民間的經學教師，問他們：「基督該誕生在甚麼地方？」

5 他們回答：「在猶太的伯利恆，因為先知曾這樣寫着：

6 猶大地區的伯利恆啊，
　　你在猶大諸城邑中並不是最小的；
　　因為有一位領袖要從你那裏出來，
　　他要牧養我的子民以色列。」

7 於是，希律暗地裏召見從東方來的星象家，向他們查問那顆星出現的準確日子，8然後吩咐他們前往伯利恆，說：「你們去，仔細尋找那小孩子，找着了就來向我報告，我也好去拜他。」

9 聽了這話，他們就走了。這時候，他們在東方看見的那顆星又出現，並且在前頭引導他們，一直來到小孩子出生地方的上面才停住。10他們看見那顆星，真是歡欣快樂。11他們進了屋子，看見小孩子和他的母親馬利亞，就俯伏朝拜這孩子，然後打開寶盒，拿出黃金、乳香、沒藥等禮物獻給他。

12 在夢中，上帝指示他們不要回去見希律，於是他們從另一條路回自己的家鄉去。

逃往埃及

13 他們走了以後，主的天使在約瑟的夢中顯現，說：「起來！帶着小孩子和他的母親逃往埃及，住在那裏，直到我吩咐你離開；因為希律要搜索這孩子，要殺害他。」

14Joseph got up, took the child and his mother, and left during the night for Egypt, 15where he stayed until Herod died. This was done to make come true what the Lord had said through the prophet, "I called my Son out of Egypt."

The Killing of the Children

16When Herod realized that the visitors from the East had tricked him, he was furious. He gave orders to kill all the boys in Bethlehem and its neighborhood who were two years old and younger–this was done in accordance with what he had learned from the visitors about the time when the star had appeared.

17In this way what the prophet Jeremiah had said came true:

18"A sound is heard in Ramah,
  the sound of bitter weeping.
Rachel is crying for her children;
  she refuses to be comforted,
  for they are dead."

The Return from Egypt

19After Herod died, an angel of the Lord appeared in a dream to Joseph in Egypt 20and said, "Get up, take the child and his mother, and go back to the land of Israel, because those who tried to kill the child are dead." 21So Joseph got up, took the child and his mother, and went back to Israel.

22But when Joseph heard that Archelaus had succeeded his father Herod as king of Judea, he was afraid to go there. He was given more instructions in a dream, so he went to the province of Galilee 23and made his home in a town named Nazareth. And so what the prophets had said came true: "He will be called a Nazarene."

The Preaching of John the Baptist

(Mark 1.1-8; Luke 3.1-18; John 1.19-28)

3 At that time John the Baptist came to the desert of Judea and started preaching. 2"Turn away from your sins," he said, "because the Kingdom of heaven is near!" 3John was the man the prophet Isaiah was talking about when he said,

"Someone is shouting in the desert,
  'Prepare a road for the Lord;
  make a straight path for him to travel!'"

4John's clothes were made of camel's hair; he wore a leather belt around his waist, and his food was locusts and wild honey. 5People came to him from Jerusalem, from the whole province of Judea, and from all over the country near the Jordan River. 6They confessed their sins, and he baptized them in the Jordan.

7When John saw many Pharisees and

14於是，約瑟動身，連夜帶着孩子和他的母親逃往埃及，15住在那裏，直到希律死了。這事是要應驗主藉着先知說的話：「我從埃及把我的兒子召出來。」

屠殺嬰兒

16希律發現自己受了星象家的愚弄，非常惱怒，就按照他向星象家打聽到那顆星出現的時期，派人把伯利恆和附近地區兩歲以內的男孩子都殺掉。

17這事應驗了先知耶利米所說：

18在拉瑪聽見了
  號咷大哭的聲音。
蕾潔爲着孩子們哀哭，
  不肯接受安慰，
  因爲他們都死了。

從埃及回來

19希律死了以後，在埃及，主的天使在約瑟的夢中顯現，20說：「起來！帶着小孩子和他的母親回以色列地，因爲那些想殺害這孩子的人已經死了。」21於是約瑟動身，帶着小孩子和他的母親回以色列去。

22約瑟因爲聽見亞基老繼承他父親希律作猶太王，不敢到那裏去。後來，主又在約瑟的夢中指示他，他就避開加利利地區，23在叫拿撒勒的城定居下來。這就應驗了先知所說的話：「他要稱爲拿撒勒人。」

施洗者約翰傳道

（可1·1—8；路3·1—18；約1·19—28）

3 那時，施洗者約翰來到猶太的曠野傳道。2他說：「悔改吧，因爲天國快實現了！」3約翰就是先知以賽亞所說的那個人；他說：

在曠野有人呼喊：
爲主準備他的道路，
修直他要走的路徑！

4約翰穿着駱駝毛的衣服，腰間繫着皮帶；吃的是蝗蟲和野蜜。5羣衆從耶路撒冷、猶太全境，和約旦河一帶來到他跟前。6他們承認自己的罪，約翰就在約旦河爲他們施洗。

7約翰看見許多法利賽人和撒都該人也來

Sadducees coming to him to be baptized, he said to them, "You snakes–who told you that you could escape from the punishment God is about to send? [8]Do those things that will show that you have turned from your sins. [9]And don't think you can escape punishment by saying that Abraham is your ancestor. I tell you that God can take these rocks and make descendants for Abraham! [10]The ax is ready to cut down the trees at the roots; every tree that does not bear good fruit will be cut down and thrown in the fire. [11]I baptize you with water to show that you have repented, but the one who will come after me will baptize you with the Holy Spirit and fire. He is much greater than I am; and I am not good enough even to carry his sandals. [12]He has his winnowing shovel with him to thresh out all the grain. He will gather his wheat into his barn, but he will burn the chaff in a fire that never goes out."

The Baptism of Jesus
(Mark 1.9-11; Luke 3.21-22)

[13]At that time Jesus arrived from Galilee and came to John at the Jordan to be baptized by him. [14]But John tried to make him change his mind. "I ought to be baptized by you," John said, "and yet you have come to me!"

[15]But Jesus answered him, "Let it be so for now. For in this way we shall do all that God requires." So John agreed.

[16]As soon as Jesus was baptized, he came up out of the water. Then heaven was opened to him, and he saw the Spirit of God coming down like a dove and lighting on him. [17]Then a voice said from heaven, "This is my own dear Son, with whom I am pleased."

The Temptation of Jesus
(Mark 1.12-13; Luke 4.1-13)

4 Then the Spirit led Jesus into the desert to be tempted by the Devil. [2]After spending forty days and nights without food, Jesus was hungry. [3]Then the Devil came to him and said, "If you are God's Son, order these stones to turn into bread."

[4]But Jesus answered, "The scripture says, 'Human beings cannot live on bread alone, but need every word that God speaks.'"

[5]Then the Devil took Jesus to Jerusalem, the Holy City, set him on the highest point of the Temple, [6]and said to him, "If you are God's Son, throw yourself down, for the scripture says,

'God will give orders to his angels about you;
    they will hold you up with their hands,
        so that not even your feet will be hurt on
        the stones.' "

[7]Jesus answered, "But the scripture also says, 'Do not put the Lord your God to the test.' "

要求受洗，就對他們說：「你們這些毒蛇！上帝的審判快要到了，你們以爲能夠逃避嗎？[8]要用行爲證明你們已經悔改。[9]不要自以爲亞伯拉罕是你們的祖宗就可以逃避審判。我告訴你們，上帝能夠拿這些石頭爲亞伯拉罕造出子孫來！[10]斧頭已經擱在樹根上了，凡不結好果子的樹都要砍掉，丟在火裏。[11]我用水給你們施洗，表示你們已經悔改；但是，在我以後來的那一位要用聖靈和火給你們施洗。他比我偉大多了，我就是替他提鞋子也不配。[12]他手裏拿着簸箕，要揚淨穀物，把麥子收進倉庫；至於糠秕，他要用永不熄滅的火燒掉。」

耶穌受洗
（可 1 · 9—11；路 3 · 21—22）

[13]那時候，耶穌從加利利往約旦河太見約翰，要請他施洗。[14]約翰想要改變他的主意，就說：「我應當受你的洗禮，你反而來找我！」

[15]可是耶穌回答他：「現在就這樣做吧，因爲這樣做是實行上帝的要求。」於是約翰答應了。

[16]耶穌一受了洗，從水裏出來，天爲他開了；他看見上帝的靈好像鴿子降下來，落在他身上。[17]接着，從天上有聲音說：「這是我親愛的兒子，我喜愛他。」

耶穌受試探
（可 1 · 12—13；路 4 · 1—13）

4 接着，耶穌被聖靈帶到曠野去，受魔鬼試探。[2]禁食四十晝夜後，耶穌餓了。[3]那試探者上前對他說：「既然你是上帝的兒子，命令這些石頭變成麵包吧！」

[4]耶穌回答：「聖經說：『人的生存不僅是靠食物，而是靠上帝所說的每一句話。』」

[5]魔鬼又帶耶穌到聖城，讓他站在聖殿頂的最高處，[6]對他說：「既然你是上帝的兒子，你跳下去；因爲聖經說：

上帝要爲你吩咐他的天使；
他們要用手托住你，
使你的腳不至於在石頭上碰傷。」

[7]耶穌回答：「可是聖經也說：『不可試探主—你的上帝。』」

8Then the Devil took Jesus to a very high mountain and showed him all the kingdoms of the world in all their greatness. 9"All this I will give you," the Devil said, "if you kneel down and worship me."

10Then Jesus answered, "Go away, Satan! The scripture says, 'Worship the Lord your God and serve only him!' "

11Then the Devil left Jesus; and angels came and helped him.

Jesus Begins His Work in Galilee
(Mark 1.14-15; Luke 4.14-15)

12When Jesus heard that John had been put in prison, he went away to Galilee. 13He did not stay in Nazareth, but went to live in Capernaum, a town by Lake Galilee, in the territory of Zebulun and Naphtali. 14This was done to make come true what the prophet Isaiah had said,

15"Land of Zebulun and land of Naphtali,
   on the road to the sea, on the other side
      of the Jordan,
   Galilee, land of the Gentiles!
16The people who live in darkness
   will see a great light.
On those who live in the dark land of death
   the light will shine."

17From that time Jesus began to preach his message: "Turn away from your sins, because the Kingdom of heaven is near!"

Jesus Calls Four Fishermen
(Mark 1.16-20; Luke 5.1-11)

18As Jesus walked along the shore of Lake Galilee, he saw two brothers who were fishermen, Simon (called Peter) and his brother Andrew, catching fish in the lake with a net. 19Jesus said to them, "Come with me, and I will teach you to catch people." 20At once they left their nets and went with him.

21He went on and saw two other brothers, James and John, the sons of Zebedee. They were in their boat with their father Zebedee, getting their nets ready. Jesus called them, 22and at once they left the boat and their father, and went with him.

Jesus Teaches, Preaches, and Heals
(Luke 6.17-19)

23Jesus went all over Galilee, teaching in the synagogues, preaching the Good News about the Kingdom, and healing people who had all kinds of disease and sickness. 24The news about him spread through the whole country of Syria, so that people brought to him all those who were sick, suffering from all kinds of diseases

---

8 最後，魔鬼帶耶穌上了一座很高的山，把世上萬國和它們的榮華都給他看。9魔鬼說：「如果你跪下來拜我，我就把這一切都給你。」

10 耶穌回答：「撒但，走開！聖經說：『要拜主—你的上帝，惟獨敬奉他。』」

11 於是，魔鬼離開了耶穌，天使就前來伺候他。

耶穌開始在加利利傳道
（可1‧14-15；路4‧14-15）

12 耶穌聽見約翰被關在監獄裏，就避開，到加利利去。13他沒有在拿撒勒住下，卻去住在迦百農。那城在西布倫和拿弗他利地區，靠近加利利湖。14這是要應驗先知以賽亞的話：

15 西布倫地和拿弗他利地，
   沿海的路，約旦河的那邊，
   外邦人的加利利！
16 住在黑暗中的人
   要看見大光；
   住在死蔭之地的人
   有光要照亮他們。

17 從那時開始，耶穌宣講信息說：「悔改吧，因為天國快實現了！」

耶穌呼召四漁夫
（可1‧16-20；路5‧1-11）

18 耶穌沿加利利湖邊走着，看見兩個打魚的兄弟，西門（別號彼得）和他的弟弟安得烈，正在湖裏撒網打魚。19耶穌對他們說：「來跟從我！我要使你們成為得人的漁夫。」20他們立刻丟下了魚網，跟從耶穌。

21 耶穌再往前走，看見另外兩個兄弟—西庇太的兒子雅各和約翰；他們跟父親一起在船上整理魚網。耶穌呼召他們，22他們立刻捨了船，辭別父親，跟從耶穌。

耶穌的教導和治病
（路6‧17-19）

23 耶穌走遍加利利全境，在各地方的會堂裏教導人，宣講天國的福音，治好民間各樣的疾病。24他的名聲傳遍了敍利亞，因此那裏的居民把患各種疾病、受各樣痛苦的人；例如被鬼附身的、顛癇的、癱瘓的，都帶到

and disorders: people with demons, and epileptics, and paralytics–and Jesus healed them all. [25]Large crowds followed him from Galilee and the Ten Towns, from Jerusalem, Judea, and the land on the other side of the Jordan.

The Sermon on the Mount
(Luke 6.20-26)

5 Jesus saw the crowds and went up a hill, where he sat down. His disciples gathered around him, [2]and he began to teach them:

True Happiness
(Luke 6.20-23)

[3]"Happy are those who know they are
    spiritually poor;
    the Kingdom of heaven belongs to them!
[4]"Happy are those who mourn;
    God will comfort them!
[5]"Happy are those who are humble;
    they will receive what God has promised!
[6]"Happy are those whose greatest desire is
    to do what God requires;
    God will satisfy them fully!
[7]"Happy are those who are merciful to others;
    God will be merciful to them!
[8]"Happy are the pure in heart;
    they will see God!
[9]"Happy are those who work for peace;
    God will call them his children!
[10]"Happy are those who are persecuted
    because they do what God requires;
    the Kingdom of heaven belongs to them!

[11]"Happy are you when people insult you and persecute you and tell all kinds of evil lies against you because you are my followers. [12]Be happy and glad, for a great reward is kept for you in heaven. This is how the prophets who lived before you were persecuted.

Salt and Light
(Mark 9.50; Luke 14.34-35)

[13]"You are like salt for the whole human race. But if salt loses its saltiness, there is no way to make it salty again. It has become worthless, so it is thrown out and people trample on it.

[14]"You are like light for the whole world. A city built on a hill cannot be hid. [15]No one lights a lamp and puts it under a bowl; instead it is put on the lampstand, where it gives light for everyone in the house. [16]In the same way your light must shine before people, so that they will see the good things you do and praise your Father in heaven.

他跟前來，他一一治好了他們。[25]成羣的人從加利利、十邑、耶路撒冷、猶太，和約旦河對岸一帶來跟隨他。

山上寶訓

5 耶穌看見一大羣人，就上山；坐了下來，他的門徒環繞在他左右。[2]他開始教導他們。

論福
（路6‧20—23）

3 「承認自己靈性貧乏的人多麼有福啊；
    他們是天國的子民！
4 「為罪惡悲傷的人多麼有福啊；
    上帝要安慰他們！
5 「謙和的人多麼有福啊；
    他們要承受上帝所應許的產業！
6 「渴望實行上帝旨意的人多麼有福啊；
    上帝要充分地滿足他們！
7 「以仁慈待人的人多麼有福啊；
    上帝也要以仁慈待他們！
8 「心地純潔的人多麼有福啊；
    他們要看見上帝！
9 「促進和平的人多麼有福啊；
    上帝要稱他們爲兒女！
10 「爲了實行上帝的旨意而受迫害的人多
    麼有福啊；
    他們是天國的子民！

11 「當別人因爲你們跟從我而侮辱你們，迫害你們，說各樣壞話毀謗你們，你們多麼有福啊。[12]要歡喜快樂，因爲在天上將有豐富的獎賞爲你們保存着；從前的先知也同樣受過人的迫害。」

鹽和光
（可9‧50；路14‧34—35）

13 「你們是人類的鹽。鹽若失掉了鹹味，就無法使它再鹹。它已成爲廢物，只好丟掉，任人踐踏。

14 「你們是世界的光。建造在山上的城是無法遮蓋起來的。[15]沒有人點亮了燈去放在斗底下，一定是放在燈臺上，好照亮全家的人。[16]同樣，你們的光也該照在人面前，讓他們看見你們的好行爲，來頌讚你們在天上的父親。」

Teaching about the Law

17"Do not think that I have come to do away with the Law of Moses and the teachings of the prophets. I have not come to do away with them, but to make their teachings come true. 18Remember that as long as heaven and earth last, not the least point nor the smallest detail of the Law will be done away with–not until the end of all things.*a* 19So then, whoever disobeys even the least important of the commandments and teaches others to do the same, will be least in the Kingdom of heaven. On the other hand, whoever obeys the Law and teaches others to do the same, will be great in the Kingdom of heaven. 20I tell you, then, that you will be able to enter the Kingdom of heaven only if you are more faithful than the teachers of the Law and the Pharisees in doing what God requires.

Teaching about Anger

21"You have heard that people were told in the past, 'Do not commit murder; anyone who does will be brought to trial.' 22But now I tell you: if you are angry*b* with his other you will be brought to trial, if you call your brother 'You good-for-nothing!' you will be brought before the Council, and if you call your brother a worthless fool you will be in danger of going to the fire of hell. 23So if you are about to offer your gift to God at the altar and there you remember that your brother has something against you, 24leave your gift there in front of the altar, go at once and make peace with your brother, and then come back and offer your gift to God.

25"If someone brings a lawsuit against you and takes you to court, settle the dispute while there is time, before you get to court. Once you are there, you will be turned over to the judge, who will hand you over to the police, and you will be put in jail. 26There you will stay, I tell you, until you pay the last penny of your fine.

Teaching about Adultery

27"You have heard that it was said, 'Do not commit adultery.' 28But now I tell you: anyone who looks at a woman and wants to possess her is guilty of committing adultery with her in his heart. 29So if your right eye causes you to sin, take it out and throw it away! It is much better for you to lose a part of your body than to have your whole body thrown into hell. 30If your right hand causes you to sin, cut it off and throw it away! It is much better for you to lose one of your limbs than to have your whole body go off to hell.

a the end of all things; *or* all its teachings come true.
b you are angry; *some manuscripts have* if without cause you are angry.

論法律

17「不要以為我來的目的是要廢除摩西的法律和先知的教訓。我不是來廢除,而是來成全它們的眞義。18我實在告訴你們,只要天地存在,法律的一點一畫都不能廢掉,直到萬事的終結①。19所以,那違犯誡命中最小的一條,並且敎別人也這樣做的,在天國裏要成爲最微小的。相反地,那遵守法律,並且敎別人也同樣遵守的,在天國裏要成爲最偉大的。20我告訴你們,你們一定要比經學敎師和法利賽人更忠實地實行上帝的旨意才能夠進天國。」

論發怒

21「你們聽過,古人曾被禁戒:『不可殺人;殺人的應受裁判。』22但是我告訴你們,向弟兄動怒的②,也應受裁判;罵弟兄爲『廢物』的,得上法庭;罵弟兄爲『蠢東西』的,逃不了地獄的火刑。23因此,你在祭壇前要獻供物給上帝的時候,要是想起有弟兄對你不滿,24你就該把供物留在祭壇前,立刻去跟他和解,然後再回來把供物獻給上帝。

25「假如有人要控告你,把你拉上法庭,你該趁着還沒有到法庭之前跟他和解。不然,等到進了法庭,他就要把你交給法官,法官把你交給法警,關進監獄。26我告訴你,你得坐牢,等到你繳清罰款的最後一文錢。」

論姦淫

27「你們聽過古時候有這樣的敎訓說:『不可姦淫。』28但是我告訴你們,看見婦女而生邪念的,已在心裏姦污她了。29假如你的右眼使你犯罪,把它挖出來,扔掉!損失身體的一部分比整個身體陷入地獄要好得多。30假如你的右手使你犯罪,把它砍下來,扔掉!損失肢體之一比整個身體下地獄要好得多。」

①「直到萬事的終結」或譯「直到法律所敎導的一切都實現」。
②「向弟兄動怒的」有些古卷加「無緣無故……」。

Teaching about Divorce

(Matthew 19.9; Mark 10.11-12; Luke 16.18)

31"It was also said, 'Anyone who divorces his wife must give her a written notice of divorce.' 32But now I tell you: if a man divorces his wife for any cause other than her unfaithfulness, then he is guilty of making her commit adultery if she marries again; and the man who marries her commits adultery also.

Teaching about Vows

33"You have also heard that people were told in the past, 'Do not break your promise, but do what you have vowed to the Lord to do.' 34But now I tell you: do not use any vow when you make a promise. Do not swear by heaven, for it is God's throne; 35nor by earth, for it is the resting place for his feet; nor by Jerusalem, for it is the city of the great King. 36Do not even swear by your head, because you cannot make a single hair white or black. 37Just say 'Yes' or 'No'–anything else you say comes from the Evil One.

Teaching about Revenge

(Luke 6.29-30)

38"You have heard that it was said, 'An eye for an eye, and a tooth for a tooth.' 39But now I tell you: do not take revenge on someone who wrongs you. If anyone slaps you on the right cheek, let him slap your left cheek too. 40And if someone takes you to court to sue you for your shirt, let him have your coat as well. 41And if one of the occupation troops forces you to carry his pack one mile, carry it two miles. 42When someone asks you for something, give it to him; when someone wants to borrow something, lend it to him.

Love for Enemies

(Luke 6.27-28, 32-36)

43"You have heard that it was said, 'Love your friends, hate your enemies.' 44But now I tell you: love your enemies and pray for those who persecute you, 45so that you may become the children of your Father in heaven. For he makes his sun to shine on bad and good people alike, and gives rain to those who do good and to those who do evil. 46Why should God reward you if you love only the people who love you? Even the tax collectors do that! 47And if you speak only to your friends, have you done anything out of the ordinary? Even the pagans do that! 48You must be perfect–just as your Father in heaven is perfect.

論休妻

（太19‧9；可10‧11—12；路16‧18）

31「又有這樣的教訓說：『凡要休棄妻子的，必須寫休書給她。』32但是我告訴你們，除非妻子不貞，丈夫不能休棄她。因爲，要是妻子再嫁，他等於使妻子犯了姦淫；而娶她的男人也算犯了姦淫。」

論發誓

33「你們又聽過古人的教訓說：『不可違背誓言；在主面前所發的誓必須履行。』34但是我告訴你們，你們根本不可以發誓。不可指天發誓，因爲天是上帝的寶座；35不可指地發誓，因爲地是上帝的腳凳；也不可指着耶路撒冷發誓，因爲它是大君王的城；36甚至不可指着自己的頭發誓，因爲你無法使自己的一根頭髮變黑或變白。37你們說話，是，就說是，不是，就說不是，再多說便是出於那邪惡者。」

論報復

（路6‧29—30）

38「你們聽過有這樣的教訓說：『以眼還眼，以牙還牙』39但是我告訴你們，不可向欺負你們的人報復。40有人打你的右臉，連左臉也讓他打吧！有人拉你上法庭，要你的內衣，連外衣也給他吧！41假如有人③强迫你替他背行李走一里路，跟他走兩里吧！42有人向你要東西，就給他；有人向你借些甚麼，就借給他。」

論愛仇敵

（路6‧27—28；32—36）

43「你們又聽過這樣的教訓說：『愛你的朋友，恨你的仇敵。』44但是我告訴你們，要愛你們的仇敵，並且爲迫害你們的人禱告。45這樣，你們才可以作天父的兒女。因爲，天父使太陽照好人，同樣也照壞人；降雨給行善的，也給作惡的。46假如你們只愛那些愛你們的，上帝又何必獎賞你們呢？就連稅棍也會這樣做！47假如你們只向朋友打招呼，那又有甚麼了不起呢？就連異敎徒也會這樣做！48你們要完全，正像你們的天父是完全的。」

③「有人」或譯「有佔領軍的軍人」。

Teaching about Charity

6 "Make certain you do not perform your religious duties in public so that people will see what you do. If you do these things publicly, you will not have any reward from your Father in heaven.

2"So when you give something to a needy person, do not make a big show of it, as the hypocrites do in the houses of worship and on the streets. They do it so that people will praise them. I assure you, they have already been paid in full. ³But when you help a needy person, do it in such a way that even your closest friend will not know about it. ⁴Then it will be a private matter. And your Father, who sees what you do in private, will reward you.

Teaching about Prayer

(Luke 11.2-4)

5"When you pray, do not be like the hypocrites! They love to stand up and pray in the houses of worship and on the street corners, so that everyone will see them. I assure you, they have already been paid in full. ⁶But when you pray, go to your room, close the door, and pray to your Father, who is unseen. And your Father, who sees what you do in private, will reward you.

7"When you pray, do not use a lot of meaningless words, as the pagans do, who think that their gods will hear them because their prayers are long. ⁸Do not be like them. Your Father already knows what you need before you ask him. ⁹This, then, is how you should pray:

'Our Father in heaven:
  May your holy name be honored;
10 may your Kingdom come;
  may your will be done on earth as it is
    in heaven.
11 Give us today the food we need.ᶜ
12 Forgive us the wrongs we have done,
    as we forgive the wrongs that others
    have done to us.
13 Do not bring us to hard testing,
    but keep us safe from the Evil One.'ˣ

14'If you forgive others the wrongs they have done to you, your Father in heaven will also forgive you. ¹⁵But if you do not forgive others, then your Father will not forgive the wrongs you have done.

Teaching about Fasting

16"And when you fast, do not put on a sad face as the hypocrites do. They neglect their

---

c we need; *or* for today, *or* for tomorrow.
x *Some manuscripts add* For yours is the kingdom, and the power, and the glory forever. Amen.

論施捨

6 「你們要小心，不可在別人面前炫耀自己的虔誠，故意讓別人看見。這樣做的話，你們就不能從天父獲得獎賞。

2 「所以，你施捨的時候，不可大吹大擂，像那些偽善的人在會堂或街道上所做的，為要得到別人的誇獎。我告訴你們，他們這樣做已經得了所能得到的報償。³ 你施捨的時候，別讓左手知道右手所做的，⁴ 這應該是一件隱密的事。這樣，那位看得見你在隱密中做事的天父一定會獎賞你。」

論禱告

（路 11.2—4）

5 「你禱告的時候，不可像偽善的人，喜歡在會堂裏或十字路口站着禱告，故意讓別人看見。我告訴你們，他們這樣做已經得了所能得到的報償。⁶ 你禱告的時候，要進你的內室，關上門，向在隱密中的天父禱告。那位看得見你在隱密中做事的天父一定會獎賞你。

7 「你們禱告的時候，不可像異教徒那樣重複沒有意義的話。他們以為只要長篇大論，上帝就會垂聽。⁸ 不可像他們那樣。在你們祈求以前，你們的天父已經知道你們所需要的。⁹ 因此，你們要這樣禱告：

  我們在天上的父親，
  願人都尊崇你的聖名；
10 願你在世上掌權；
  願你的旨意實現在地上，
  如同實現在天上。
11 賜給我們今天所需的④飲食。
12 饒恕我們對你的虧負，
  正如我們饒恕了虧負我們的人。
13 不要讓我們遭受承擔不起的考驗；
  要救我們脫離那邪惡者的手。⑤

14 「你們若饒恕別人的過錯，你們的天父也會饒恕你們；¹⁵你們若不饒恕別人的過錯，你們的天父也不會饒恕你們的過錯。」

論禁食

16 「你們禁食的時候，不可像偽善的人；

---

④「今天所需的」或譯「明天所需的」。
⑤有些較晚的抄本有「因為國度、權柄、榮耀都屬於你，直到永遠。阿們。」

appearance so that everyone will see that they are fasting. I assure you, they have already been paid in full. [17]When you go without food, wash your face and comb your hair, [18]so that others cannot know that you are fasting–only your Father, who is unseen, will know. And your Father, who sees what you do in private, will reward you.

Riches in Heaven
(Luke 12.33-34)

[19]"Do not store up riches for yourselves here on earth, where moths and rust destroy, and robbers break in and steal. [20]Instead, store up riches for yourselves in heaven, where moths and rust cannot destroy, and robbers cannot break in and steal. [21]For your heart will always be where your riches are.

The Light of the Body
(Luke 11.34-36)

[22]"The eyes are like a lamp for the body. If your eyes are sound, your whole body will be full of light; [23]but if your eyes are no good, your body will be in darkness. So if the light in you is darkness, how terribly dark it will be!

God and Possessions
(Luke 16.13; 12.22-31)

[24]"You cannot be a slave of two masters; you will hate one and love the other; you will be loyal to one and despise the other. You cannot serve both God and money.

[25]"This is why I tell you: do not be worried about the food and drink you need in order to stay alive, or about clothes for your body. After all, isn't life worth more than food? And isn't the body worth more than clothes? [26]Look at the birds: they do not plant seeds, gather a harvest and put it in barns; yet your Father in heaven takes care of them! Aren't you worth much more than birds? [27]Can any of you live a bit longer[d] by worrying about it?

[28]"And why worry about clothes? Look how the wild flowers grow: they do not work or make clothes for themselves. [29]But I tell you that not even King Solomon with all his wealth had clothes as beautiful as one of these flowers. [30]It is God who clothes the wild grass–grass that is here today and gone tomorrow, burned up in the oven. Won't he be all the more sure to clothe you? What little faith you have! [31]"So do not start worrying: 'Where will my food come from? or my drink? or my clothes?'

d live a bit longer; or grow a bit taller.

他們裝出一副苦相，故意蓬頭垢面，好讓別人看出他們正在禁食。我告訴你們，他們這樣做已經得了所能得到的報償。[17]你禁食的時候，要梳頭洗臉，[18]不要讓別人看出你是在禁食，只讓那位在隱密中的天父知道；看得見你在隱密中做事的天父一定會獎賞你。」

論天上的財寶
（路12·33—34）

[19]「不可爲自己積聚財寶在地上，因爲有蟲蛀，也會生銹，又有盜賊破門進來偷竊。[20]要爲自己積聚財寶在天上；那裏沒有蟲蛀，不會生銹，也沒有盜賊進來偷竊。[21]你的財寶在哪裏，你的心也在那裏。」

身體的燈
（路11·34—36）

[22]「眼睛好比身體的燈。如果你的眼睛好，全身就光明；[23]如果你的眼睛壞，全身就黑暗。同樣，如果你裏頭的光變成黑暗，那黑暗該是多麼可怕呀！」

上帝和財物
（路16·13；12·22—31）

[24]「沒有人能夠伺候兩個主人。他要不是厭惡這個，喜愛那個，就是看重這個，輕看那個。你們不可能同時作上帝的僕人，又作錢財的奴隸。

[25]「所以我告訴你們，不要爲了生活上所需的飲食，或者身上所穿的衣服操心。難道生命不比飲食重要，身體不比衣服重要嗎？[26]你們看天空的飛鳥：牠們不種不收，也不存糧在倉裏，你們的天父尚且飼養牠們！你們豈不比鳥兒更貴重嗎？[27]你們當中又有誰能夠藉着憂慮多活幾天[e]呢？

[28]「爲甚麼要爲衣服操心呢？看看野地的百合花怎樣生長吧！它們既不工作又不縫衣；[29]可是我告訴你們，甚至像所羅門王那樣的榮華顯赫，他的衣飾也比不上一朵野花那樣的美麗。[30]野地的花草今朝出現，明天枯萎，給扔在火爐裏焚燒，上帝還這樣打扮它們，他豈不更要賜衣服給你們嗎？你們的信心太小了！[31]所以，不要爲我們吃甚麼、

[e]「多活幾天」或譯「多長高幾寸」。

³²(These are the things the pagans are always concerned about.)

Your Father in heaven knows that you need all these things. ³³Instead, be concerned above everything else with the Kingdom of God and with what he requires of you, and he will provide you with all these other things. ³⁴So do not worry about tomorrow; it will have enough worries of its own. There is no need to add to the troubles each day brings.

Judging Others
(Luke 6.37-38, 41-42)

7 "Do not judge others, so that God will not judge you, ²for God will judge you in the same way you judge others, and he will apply to you the same rules you apply to others. ³Why, then, do you look at the speck in your brother's eye and pay no attention to the log in your own eye? ⁴How dare you say to your brother, 'Please, let me take that speck out of your eye,' when you have a log in your own eye? ⁵You hypocrite! First take the log out of your own eye, and then you will be able to see clearly to take the speck out of your brother's eye.

⁶"Do not give what is holy to dogs–they will only turn and attack you. Do not throw your pearls in front of pigs–they will only trample them underfoot.

Ask, Seek, Knock
(Luke 11.9-13)

⁷"Ask, and you will receive; seek, and you will find; knock, and the door will be opened to you. ⁸For everyone who asks will receive, and anyone who seeks will find, and the door will be opened to those who knock. ⁹Would any of you who are fathers give your son a stone when he asks for bread? ¹⁰Or would you give him a snake when he asks for a fish? ¹¹As bad as you are, you know how to give good things to your children. How much more, then, will your Father in heaven give good things to those who ask him!

¹²"Do for others what you want them to do for you: this is the meaning of the Law of Moses and of the teachings of the prophets.

The Narrow Gate
(Luke 13.24)

¹³"Go in through the narrow gate, because the gate to hell is wide and the road that leads to it is easy, and there are many who travel it. ¹⁴But the gate to life is narrow and the way that leads to it is hard, and there are few people who find it.

喝甚麼,或穿甚麼操心;³²這些事是不信的人所追逐的。你們的天父知道你們需要這一切東西。³³你們要先追求上帝主權的實現,遵行他的旨意,他就會把這一切都供給你們。³⁴因此,你們不要為明天憂慮,明天自有明天的憂慮;一天的難處一天擔當就夠了。」

不評斷別人
(路 6 · 37—38,41—42)

7 「不要評斷人,上帝就不審斷你們。²因為,你們怎樣評斷人,上帝也要照樣審斷你們;你們用甚麼量器來量,上帝也要用同樣的量器量給你們。³你為甚麼只看見弟兄眼中的木屑,卻不管自己眼中的大樑呢?⁴你眼中有大樑,怎能對弟兄說『讓我來去掉你眼中的木屑』呢?⁵你這偽善的人,先把自己眼中的大樑移去,才能看得清楚怎樣把弟兄眼中的木屑挑出來。

⁶「不要把神聖的東西丟給狗,牠們會轉過頭來咬你們;不要把珍珠扔給豬,牠們會把珍珠踐踏在腳底下。」

祈求,尋找,敲門
(路11 · 9—13)

⁷「你們祈求,就得到;尋找,就找到;敲門,就給你們開門。⁸因為凡祈求的,就得到;尋找的,就找到;敲門的,門就開了。⁹你們當中有誰,兒子要麵包,卻給他石頭?¹⁰要魚,卻給他蛇?¹¹你們雖然邪惡,還曉得拿好東西給自己的兒女,你們在天上的父親豈不更要把好東西賜給向他祈求的人嗎?

¹²「所以,你們要別人怎樣待你們,就得怎樣待別人;這就是摩西法律和先知教訓的真義。」

窄門
(路13 · 24)

¹³「你們要從窄門進去;因為那通向滅亡的門是寬的,路是好走的,朝著這方向走的人很多。¹⁴那通向生命的門是多麼窄,路是多麼難走,找到的人也很少。」

A Tree and Its Fruit
(Luke 6.43-44)

15"Be on your guard against false prophets; they come to you looking like sheep on the outside, but on the inside they are really like wild wolves. 16You will know them by what they do. Thorn bushes do not bear grapes, and briers do not bear figs. 17A healthy tree bears good fruit, but a poor tree bears bad fruit. 18A healthy tree cannot bear bad fruit, and a poor tree cannot bear good fruit. 19And any tree that does not bear good fruit is cut down and thrown in the fire. 20So then, you will know the false prophets by what they do.

I Never Knew You
(Luke 13.25-27)

21"Not everyone who calls me 'Lord, Lord' will enter the Kingdom of heaven, but only those who do what my Father in heaven wants them to do. 22When the Judgment Day comes, many will say to me, 'Lord, Lord! In your name we spoke God's message, by your name we drove out many demons and performed many miracles!' 23Then I will say to them, 'I never knew you. Get away from me, you wicked people!'

The Two House Builders
(Luke 6.47-49)

24"So then, anyone who hears these words of mine and obeys them is like a wise man who built his house on rock. 25The rain poured down, the rivers flooded over, and the wind blew hard against that house. But it did not fall, because it was built on rock.
26"But anyone who hears these words of mine and does not obey them is like a foolish man who built his house on sand. 27The rain poured down, the rivers flooded over, the wind blew hard against that house, and it fell. And what a terrible fall that was!"

The Authority of Jesus
28When Jesus finished saying these things, the crowd was amazed at the way he taught. 29He wasn't like the teachers of the Law; instead, he taught with authority.

Jesus Heals a Man
(Mark 1.40-45; Luke 5.12-16)

8 When Jesus came down from the hill, large crowds followed him. 2Then a man suffering from a dreaded skin disease came to him, knelt down before him, and said, "Sir, if you want to, you can make me clean."

e MAKE ME CLEAN: *This disease was considered to make a person ritually unclean.*

樹和果子
（路6‧43—44）

15「你們要提防假先知。他們來到你們面前，外表看來像綿羊，裏面卻是凶狠的豺狼。16你們能夠從他們的行為認出他們。荊棘不能結葡萄，蒺藜也不能結無花果。17好樹結好果子；壞樹結壞果子。18好樹不結壞果子；壞樹也不結好果子了。19不結好果子的樹都得砍下，扔在火裏。20所以，從他們的行為，你們能夠認出假先知來。」

我不認識你們
（路13‧25—27）

21「不是每一個稱呼我『主啊，主啊』的人都能進天國；只有實行我天父旨意的才能進去。22在末日來臨的時候，許多人要對我說：『主啊，主啊，我們曾奉你的名傳上帝的信息，也曾奉你的名趕許多鬼，行許多奇蹟。』23那時候，我要公然地告訴他們：『我從不認識你們；你們這些作惡的，走開吧！』」

兩種基礎
（路6‧47—49）

24「所以，所有聽我這些話而實行的，就像一個聰明人把房子蓋在磐石上；25縱使風吹，雨打，水沖，房子也不倒塌，因為它的基礎立在磐石上。26可是，那聽見我這些話而不實行的，就像一個愚蠢的人把房了蓋在沙土上，27一遭受風吹，雨打，水沖，房子就倒塌了，而且倒塌得多麼慘重！」

耶穌的權威
28耶穌講完了這些話，羣眾對他的教導都感到十分驚奇；29因為耶穌跟他們的經學教師不同，他的教導帶有權威。

耶穌治好痲瘋病人
（可1‧40—45；路5‧12—16）

8 耶穌從山上下來，成羣結隊的人跟着他。2有一個痲瘋病人來見他，向他下拜，說：「主啊，只要你肯，你能使我潔

3Jesus reached out and touched him. "I do want to," he answered. "Be clean!" At once the man was healed of his disease. 4Then Jesus said to him, "Listen! Don't tell anyone, but go straight to the priest and let him examine you; then in order to prove to everyone that you are cured, offer the sacrifice that Moses ordered."

Jesus Heals a Roman Officer's Servant
(Luke 7.1-10)

5When Jesus entered Capernaum, a Roman officer met him and begged for help: 6"Sir, my servant is sick in bed at home, unable to move and suffering terribly."

7"I will go and make him well," Jesus said.

8"Oh no, sir," answered the officer. "I do not deserve to have you come into my house. Just give the order, and my servant will get well. 9I, too, am a man under the authority of superior officers, and I have soldiers under me. I order this one, 'Go!' and he goes; and I order that one, 'Come!' and he comes; and I order my slave, 'Do this!' and he does it." 10When Jesus heard this, he was surprised and said to the people following him, "I tell you, I have never found anyone in Israel with faith like this. 11I assure you that many will come from the east and the west and sit down with Abraham, Isaac, and Jacob at the feast in the Kingdom of heaven. 12But those who should be in the Kingdom will be thrown out into the darkness, where they will cry and gnash their teeth." 13Then Jesus said to the officer, "Go home, and what you believe will be done for you."

And the officer's servant was healed that very moment.

Jesus Heals Many People
(Mark 1.29-34; Luke 4.38-41)

14Jesus went to Peter's home, and there he saw Peter's mother-in-law sick in bed with a fever. 15He touched her hand; the fever left her, and she got up and began to wait on him.

16When evening came, people brought to Jesus many who had demons in them. Jesus drove out the evil spirits with a word and healed all who were sick. 17He did this to make come true what the prophet Isaiah had said, "He himself took our sickness and carried away our diseases."

The Would-Be Followers of Jesus
(Luke 9.57-62)

18When Jesus noticed the crowd around him, he ordered his disciples to go to the other side

---

淨。」3耶穌伸手摸他，說：「我肯，你潔淨吧！」他的痲瘋立刻消除，潔淨了。4於是耶穌對他說：「不要把這件事告訴人，要直接去見祭司，讓他替你檢查，然後按照摩西的規定獻上祭物，向大家證實你已經潔淨了。」

耶穌治好羅馬軍官的僕人
（路7‧1—10）

5耶穌來到迦百農，有一個羅馬軍官來迎接他，求他幫助，6說：「主啊，我的僕人患了癱瘓病，躺在家裏，非常痛苦。」

7耶穌說：「我去醫治他。」

8軍官回答：「主啊，你親自到舍下來，我不敢當；只要你吩咐一聲，我的僕人就會好的。9就像在我上面有指揮我的長官，下面有受我指揮的兵士；我命令這一個人去，他就去，命令那一個人來，他就來，對我的奴僕說『做這件事』，他就去做。」

10耶穌聽見這話，非常詫異，對跟從他的人說：「我實在告訴你們，像這樣的信心，我在以色列人當中，從來沒有遇見過。11我告訴你們，將有許許多多的人從東從西前來，跟亞伯拉罕、以撒、雅各一起在天國坐席。12那些本來可以成為天國子民的人，反而要被驅逐到外面的黑暗裏；在那裏，他們要哀哭，咬牙切齒。」13然後耶穌向那軍官說：「回家去吧，照你的信心給你成全！」

他僕人的病就在那時刻好了。

耶穌治好許多病人
（可1‧29—34；路4‧38—41）

14耶穌來到彼得的家，看見他岳母正發高燒，躺在牀上。15耶穌一摸她的手，熱就退了，她立刻起來接待耶穌。

16傍晚的時候，有人帶了許多被鬼附身的人來見耶穌。耶穌只用一句話就把鬼都趕走，又治好了所有的病人。17他這樣做正應驗了先知以賽亞所說的：

「他背負了我們的軟弱，
擔當了我們的疾病。」

要跟從耶穌的人
（路9‧57—62）

18耶穌看見許多人圍繞着他，就吩咐門徒

of the lake. [19]A teacher of the Law came to him. "Teacher," he said, "I am ready to go with you wherever you go."

[20]Jesus answered him, "Foxes have holes, and birds have nests, but the Son of Man has no place to lie down and rest."

[21]Another man, who was a disciple, said, "Sir, first let me go back and bury my father."

[22]"Follow me," Jesus answered, "and let the dead bury their own dead."

Jesus Calms a Storm
(Mark 4.35-41; Luke 8.22-25)

[23]Jesus got into a boat, and his disciples went with him. [24]Suddenly a fierce storm hit the lake, and the boat was in danger of sinking. But Jesus was asleep. [25]The disciples went to him and woke him up. "Save us, Lord!" they said. "We are about to die!"

[26]"Why are you so frightened?" Jesus answered. "What little faith you have!" Then he got up and ordered the winds and the waves to stop, and there was a great calm.

[27]Everyone was amazed. "What kind of man is this?" they said. "Even the winds and the waves obey him!"

Jesus Heals Two Men with Demons
(Mark 5.1-20; Luke 8.26-39)

[28]When Jesus came to the territory of Gadara on the other side of the lake, he was met by two men who came out of the burial caves there. These men had demons in them and were so fierce that no one dared travel on that road. [29]At once they screamed, "What do you want with us, you Son of God? Have you come to punish us before the right time?"

[30]Not far away there was a large herd of pigs feeding. [31]So the demons begged Jesus, "If you are going to drive us out, send us into that herd of pigs."

[32]"Go," Jesus told them; so they left and went off into the pigs. The whole herd rushed down the side of the cliff into the lake and was drowned.

[33]The men who had been taking care of the pigs ran away and went into the town, where they told the whole story and what had happened to the men with the demons. [34]So everyone from the town went out to meet Jesus; and when they saw him, they begged him to leave their territory.

Jesus Heals a Paralyzed Man
(Mark 2.1-12; Luke 5.17-26)

9 Jesus got into the boat and went back across the lake to his own town.[f] [2]where

f HIS OWN TOWN: Capernaum (see 4.13).

渡湖到對岸去。[19]有一個經學教師來見他，對他說：「老師，你無論到哪裏去，我都要跟從你。」

[20]耶穌說：「狐狸有洞，飛鳥有窩，可是人子連枕頭的地方都沒有。」

[21]另外有一個門徒對耶穌說：「主啊，請讓我先回去埋葬我的父親。」

[22]耶穌說：「你儘管跟從我，讓死人去埋葬他們的死人吧！」

耶穌平息風浪
（可 4・35—41；路 8・22—25）

[23]耶穌上了船，他的門徒跟着他去。[24]忽然，一陣暴風襲擊湖面，浪濤掩蓋了船，耶穌卻睡着了。[25]門徒到他跟前，喊醒他，說：「主啊，救救我們，我們快沒命啦！」

[26]耶穌回答：「為甚麼這樣害怕？你們的信心太小了！」於是他起來，斥責風和浪，風浪就平靜了。

[27]大家非常驚奇，彼此說：「這個人究竟是誰，連風和浪都聽從他！」

治好兩個被鬼附身的人
（可 5・1—20；路 8・26—39）

[28]耶穌到湖對岸的加大拉地區，遇見兩個從墓穴出來的人。這兩個人被鬼附身，十分凶狠，因此沒有人敢走這條路。[29]他們見了耶穌，立刻喊着說：「上帝的兒子，你為甚麼要干擾我們？時機未到你就來折磨我們嗎？」

[30]剛好，附近有一大羣豬在吃東西。[31]鬼就央求耶穌：「如果你要趕我們出去，就打發我們進豬羣裏面去吧。」

[32]耶穌說：「去吧！」鬼就出來，進入豬羣；整羣的豬衝下山崖，竄入湖中，都淹死了。

[33]放豬的人就逃進城去，把這件事的始末和被鬼附身的人所遭遇的向大家報告。[34]全城的人都出來看耶穌，他們見到了，就要求他離開他們的地區。

耶穌治好癱瘓病人
（可 2・1—12；路 5・17—26）

9 耶穌上船，渡過了湖，回到他自己的城。[2]有人抬着一個躺在牀上的癱瘓病人到

some people brought to him a paralyzed man, lying on a bed. When Jesus saw how much faith they had, he said to the paralyzed man, "Courage, my son! Your sins are forgiven."

3Then some teachers of the Law said to themselves, "This man is speaking blasphemy!"

4Jesus perceived what they were thinking, and so he said, "Why are you thinking such evil things? 5Is it easier to say, 'Your sins are forgiven,' or to say, 'Get up and walk'? 6I will prove to you, then, that the Son of Man has authority on earth to forgive sins." So he said to the paralyzed man, "Get up, pick up your bed, and go home!"

7The man got up and went home. 8When the people saw it, they were afraid, and praised God for giving such authority to people.

Jesus Calls Matthew
(Mark 2.13-17; Luke 5.27-32)

9Jesus left that place, and as he walked along, he saw a tax collector, named Matthew, sitting in his office. He said to him, "Follow me."

Matthew got up and followed him.

10While Jesus was having a meal in Matthew's house,g many tax collectors and other outcasts came and joined Jesus and his disciples at the table. 11Some Pharisees saw this and asked his disciples, "Why does your teacher eat with such people?"

12Jesus heard them and answered, "People who are well do not need a doctor, but only those who are sick. 13Go and find out what is meant by the scripture that says: 'It is kindness that I want, not animal sacrifices.' I have not come to call respectable people, but outcasts."

The Question about Fasting
(Mark 2.18-22; Luke 5.33-39)

14Then the followers of John the Baptist came to Jesus, asking, "Why is it that we and the Pharisees fast often, but your disciples don't fast at all?"

15Jesus answered, "Do you expect the guests at a wedding party to be sad as long as the bridegroom is with them? Of course not! But the day will come when the bridegroom will be taken away from them, and then they will fast.

16"No one patches up an old coat with a piece of new cloth, for the new patch will shrink and make an even bigger hole in the coat. 17Nor does anyone pour new wine into used wineskins, for the skins will burst, the wine will pour out, and the skins will be ruined. Instead, new wine is poured into fresh wineskins, and both will keep in good condition."

g in Matthew's house; or in his (that is, Jesus') house.

他面前來。耶穌看出他們的信心,就對癱瘓病人說:「孩子,放心吧,你的罪蒙赦免了!」

3 有幾個經學教師心裏想:「這個人說了狂妄的話!」

4 耶穌知道他們在想些甚麼,就問:「你們為甚麼懷着邪惡的念頭呢?5 對這個人說『你的罪蒙赦免』容易,或是說『起來走』容易呢?6 我要向你們證明,人子在地上有赦罪的權。」於是他對癱瘓病人說:「起來,拿起你的牀,回家去吧!」

7 那個人就起來,回家去了。8 看見的人都驚奇害怕;他們頌讚上帝,因為他把這樣的權賜給人。

馬太蒙召
(可 2 · 13—17;路 5 · 27—32)

9 耶穌離開那裏再往前走,看見了一個收稅的,名叫馬太,坐在稅關上。耶穌對他說:「來跟從我!」

馬太就起來,跟從了他。

10 耶穌在馬太家裏吃飯的時候,許多稅棍和壞人也來了,跟耶穌和他的門徒一起吃飯。11 有些法利賽人看見了,就對耶穌的門徒說:「為甚麼你們的老師跟稅棍和壞人一起吃飯呢?」

12 耶穌聽見了這話就說:「健康的人用不着醫生,有病的人才用得着。13 聖經說:『我要的是仁慈,不是牲祭。』你們去研究這句話的意思吧!因為我來的目的不是要召好人,而是要召壞人。」

禁食的問題
(可 2 · 18—22;路 5 · 33—39)

14 有一次,施洗者約翰的門徒來問耶穌:「我們和法利賽人常常禁食,你的門徒卻不禁食,為甚麼呢?」

15 耶穌回答:「新郎還在婚宴的時候,賀喜的客人會悲傷嗎?當然不會。可是日子將到,新郎要從他們當中被帶走,那時候他們就要禁食了。

16「沒有人拿新布去補舊衣服,因為新的補釘會扯破那舊衣服,使裂痕更大。17 也沒有人拿新酒裝在舊皮袋裏。這樣做的話,皮袋會脹破,酒漏掉,連皮袋也損壞了。要把新酒裝在新皮袋裏;那麼,兩樣就都保全了。」

The Official's Daughter and the Woman Who Touched Jesus' Cloak

(Mark 5.21-43; Luke 8.40-56)

18While Jesus was saying this, a Jewish official came to him, knelt down before him, and said, "My daughter has just died; but come and place your hands on her, and she will live."

19So Jesus got up and followed him, and his disciples went along with him.

20A woman who had suffered from severe bleeding for twelve years came up behind Jesus and touched the edge of his cloak. 21She said to herself, "If only I touch his cloak, I will get well."

22Jesus turned around and saw her, and said, "Courage, my daughter! Your faith has made you well." At that very moment the woman became well.

23Then Jesus went into the official's house. When he saw the musicians for the funeral and the people all stirred up, 24he said, "Get out, everybody! The little girl is not dead—she is only sleeping!" Then they all started making fun of him. 25But as soon as the people had been put out, Jesus went into the girl's room and took hold of her hand, and she got up. 26The news about this spread all over that part of the country.

Jesus Heals Two Blind Men

27Jesus left that place, and as he walked along, two blind men started following him. "Have mercy on us, Son of David!" they shouted.

28When Jesus had gone indoors, the two blind men came to him, and he asked them, "Do you believe that I can heal you?"

"Yes, sir!" they answered.

29Then Jesus touched their eyes and said, "Let it happen, then, just as you believe!" 30and their sight was restored. Jesus spoke sternly to them, "Don't tell this to anyone!"

31But they left and spread the news about Jesus all over that part of the country.

Jesus Heals a Man Who Could Not Speak

32As the men were leaving, some people brought to Jesus a man who could not talk because he had a demon. 33But as soon as the demon was driven out, the man started talking, and everyone was amazed. "We have never seen anything like this in Israel!" they exclaimed.

34But the Pharisees said, "It is the chief of the demons who gives Jesus the power to drive out demons."

會堂主管的女兒和患血崩的女人

(可 5.21-43；路 8.40-56)

18 耶穌正在向約翰的門徒說這些話的時候，有一個猶太會堂的主管來見他，在他面前跪下，說：「我的女兒剛死了，求你去為她按手，使她再活過來。」

19 耶穌起來，跟着他去；耶穌的門徒也一起去。

20 有一個女人患了十二年血崩；她走到耶穌背後，摸了一下他外袍的衣角。21她心裏想：「只要我摸到他的衣角，我一定會得醫治。」

22 耶穌轉過身來，看見她，就對她說：「孩子，放心吧，你的信心救了你！」就在那時候，那個女人的病好了。

23 耶穌來到那主管的家，看見出殯的吹鼓手和亂哄哄的人羣，24就對他們說：「你們都出去，這孩子沒有死，她只是睡着了！」

大家都譏笑他。25這羣人被趕出去以後，耶穌進女孩子的臥室，拉着她的手，她就起來。26這消息傳遍了整個地區。

治好兩個盲人

27 耶穌離開那地方，再往前走。有兩個盲人跟着他，喊着說：「大衛之子啊，可憐我們吧！」

28 耶穌進了屋子，兩個盲人來到他面前，他就問他們：「你們信我能做這件事嗎？」

他們回答：「主啊，我們信。」

29 於是，耶穌摸他們的眼睛，說：「照你們的信心成全你們吧！」30他們的視覺便恢復了。耶穌鄭重地吩咐他們：「不要把這事告訴任何人！」

31 可是，他們一出去就把耶穌的事傳遍那一帶地方。

治好啞巴

32 他們出去的時候，有人把一個被鬼附身的啞巴帶到耶穌面前來。33鬼一被趕出去，那個人就開口講話了。大家都很驚訝，說：「在以色列，我們從沒見過這樣的事。」

34 可是，法利賽人說：「他是靠着鬼王來趕鬼的。」

Jesus Has Pity for the People

35Jesus went around visiting all the towns and villages. He taught in the synagogues, preached the Good News about the Kingdom, and healed people with every kind of disease and sickness. 36As he saw the crowds, his heart was filled with pity for them, because they were worried and helpless, like sheep without a shepherd. 37So he said to his disciples, "The harvest is large, but there are few workers to gather it in. 38Pray to the owner of the harvest that he will send out workers to gather in his harvest."

The Twelve Apostles

(Mark 3.13-19; Luke 6.12-16)

10Jesus called his twelve disciples together and gave them authority to drive out evil spirits and to heal every disease and every sickness. 2These are the names of the twelve apostles: first, Simon (called Peter) and his brother Andrew; James and his brother John, the sons of Zebedee; 3Philip and Bartholomew; Thomas and Matthew, the tax collector; James son of Alphaeus, and Thaddaeus; 4Simon the Patriot, and Judas Iscariot, who betrayed Jesus.

The Mission of the Twelve

(Mark 6.7-13; Luke 9.1-6)

5These twelve men were sent out by Jesus with the following instructions: "Do not go to any Gentile territory or any Samaritan towns. 6Instead, you are to go to the lost sheep of the people of Israel. 7Go and preach, 'The Kingdom of heaven is near!' 8Heal the sick, bring the dead back to life, heal those who suffer from dreaded skin diseases, and drive out demons. You have received without paying, so give without being paid. 9Do not carry any gold, silver, or copper money in your pockets; 10do not carry a beggar's bag for the trip or an extra shirt or shoes or a walking stick. Workers should be given what they need.

11"When you come to a town or village, go in and look for someone who is willing to welcome you, and stay with him until you leave that place. 12When you go into a house, say, 'Peace be with you.' 13If the people in that house welcome you, let your greeting of peace remain; but if they do not welcome you, then take back your greeting. 14And if some home or town will not welcome you or listen to you, then leave that place and shake the dust off your feet. 15I assure you that on the Judgment Day God will show more mercy to the people of Sodom and Gomorrah than to the people of that town!

耶穌關懷人民

35 耶穌周遊各市鎮鄉村，在各會堂裏教導人，宣講天國的福音，並治好民間的各種疾病。36當他看見一羣羣的人，動了惻隱之心；因爲他們孤苦無助，像沒有牧人的羊羣一般。37於是，他對門徒說：「要收成的很多，但是收割的工人太少。38你們要祈求農場的主人，派工人來收割他的農作物。」

十二使徒

(可 3 · 13—19；路 6 · 12—16)

10耶穌召集他的十二個門徒在一起，賜給他們驅逐邪靈和醫治各種疾病的權力。2以下是十二個使徒的名字：第一個是西門（別號彼得），還有他的弟弟安得烈，西庇太的兒子雅各，雅各的弟弟約翰，3腓力，巴多羅買，多馬，收稅的馬太，亞勒腓的兒子雅各，達太，4激進黨的西門，還有那出賣耶穌的加略人猶大。

十二使徒的使命

(可 6 · 7—13；路 9 · 1—6)

5 耶穌差遣這十二個人出去，吩咐他們：「不要到外邦人的地區，也不要進撒馬利亞人的城市。6你們要到以色列人中迷失的羊羣那裏去。7所到的地方要宣講：『天國快實現了！』8你們要醫治病患，叫死人復活，潔淨痲瘋病人，趕鬼。你們白白地得，也要白白地給。9錢袋裏不要帶金、銀、銅幣；10出門不要帶旅行袋或兩件內衣，也不要帶鞋子和手杖。因爲工人得到供應是應該的。

11「你們到一個市鎮或鄉村時，先打聽那裏有誰願意接待你們，就住在他家裏，直到你們離開那地方。12你們進了一家，就說：『願你們平安。』13如果這家的人歡迎你們，你們爲他們求的平安就會臨到這家。如果他們不歡迎你們，就收回你們的祝福。14那不歡迎你們、不聽你們話的家或城，你們就離開那裏，把腳上的塵土踩掉。15我實在告訴你們，在審判的日子，所多瑪和蛾摩拉所遭受的懲罰比那地方所受的要輕呢！」

Coming Persecutions
(Mark 13.9-13; Luke 21.12-17)

16"Listen! I am sending you out just like sheep to a pack of wolves. You must be as cautious as snakes and as gentle as doves. 17Watch out, for there will be those who will arrest you and take you to court, and they will whip you in the synagogues. 18For my sake you will be brought to trial before rulers and kings, to tell the Good News to them and to the Gentiles. 19When they bring you to trial, do not worry about what you are going to say or how you will say it; when the time comes, you will be given what you will say. 20For the words you will speak will not be yours; they will come from the Spirit of your Father speaking through you.

21"People will hand over their own brothers to be put to death, and fathers will do the same to their children; children will turn against their parents and have them put to death. 22Everyone will hate you because of me. But whoever holds out to the end will be saved. 23When they persecute you in one town, run away to another one. I assure you that you will not finish your work in all the towns of Israel before the Son of Man comes.

24"No pupil is greater than his teacher; no slave is greater than his master. 25So a pupil should be satisfied to become like his teacher, and a slave like his master. If the head of the family is called Beelzebul, the members of the family will be called even worse names!

Whom to Fear
(Luke 12.2-7)

26"So do not be afraid of people. Whatever is now covered up will be uncovered, and every secret will be made known. 27What I am telling you in the dark you must repeat in broad daylight, and what you have heard in private you must announce from the housetops. 28Do not be afraid of those who kill the body but cannot kill the soul; rather be afraid of God, who can destroy both body and soul in hell. 29For only a penny you can buy two sparrows, yet not one sparrow falls to the ground without your Father's consent. 30As for you, even the hairs of your head have all been counted. 31So do not be afraid; you are worth much more than many sparrows!

Confessing and Rejecting Christ
(Luke 12.8-9)

32"Those who declare publicly that they belong to me, I will do the same for them before my Father in heaven. 33But those who reject me publicly, I will reject before my Father in heaven.

將來的迫害
（可13.9—13；路21.12—17）

16「要留意！我派遣你們出去，正像把羊送進狼羣中。你們要像蛇一樣機警，像鴿子一樣溫馴。17當心，有人要拘捕你們，帶你們上法庭，在他們的會堂裏鞭打你們。18為了我的緣故，你們將被帶到統治者和君王面前受審問，向他們和外邦人見證福音。19你們被審問的時候，不要擔心說甚麼或怎樣對答；那時候，上帝會指示你們該說的話。20因為你們所說的，不是自己的話，而是你們天父的靈藉着你們說的。

21「兄弟要出賣兄弟，置他們於死地；父親也要這樣對待兒女；兒女要跟父母作對，並且害死他們。22為了我，大家要憎恨你們；但是那忍耐到底的人必然得救。23他們在這城裏迫害你們，就逃到另一城去。我告訴你們，你們還沒有走遍以色列的城市，人子就要來臨。

24「學生不高過老師，奴僕不高過主人。25因此，學生的遭遇跟老師一樣，奴僕的遭遇跟主人一樣，也該滿足了。如果一家的主人被叫作鬼王別西卜，家裏其他的人豈不是要受更大的凌辱嗎？」

不要怕
（路12.2—7）

26「所以，不要怕人，一切隱藏的事都會被揭發，祕密的事也會被洩露。27我在暗中所告訴你們的，你們要在光天化日之下說出來；你們私下聽到的話，也要當眾宣佈。28那只能殺害肉體、卻不能殺滅靈魂的，不用害怕；要懼怕的是上帝，只有他能把人的肉體和靈魂都投進地獄。29兩隻麻雀固然用一個銅錢就買得到，但是你們的天父若不許可，一隻也不會掉在地上。30至於你們，連你們的頭髮也都數過了。31所以，不要怕，你們比許多麻雀要貴重多了！」

宣認基督
（路12.8—9）

32「那在人面前認我的，我在我天父面前也要認他；33那在人面前不認我的，我在天父面前也不認他。」

Not Peace, but a Sword
(Luke 12.51-53; 14.26-27)

34"Do not think that I have come to bring peace to the world. No, I did not come to bring peace, but a sword. 35I came to set sons against their fathers, daughters against their mothers, daughters-in-law against their mothers-in-law; 36your worst enemies will be the members of your own family.

37"Those who love their father or mother more than me are not fit to be my disciples; those who love their son or daughter more than me are not fit to be my disciples. 38Those who do not take up their cross and follow in my steps are not fit to be my disciples. 39Those who try to gain their own life will lose it; but those who lose their life for my sake will gain it.

Rewards
(Mark 9.41)

40"Whoever welcomes you welcomes me; and whoever welcomes me welcomes the one who sent me. 41Whoever welcomes God's messenger because he is God's messenger, will share in his reward. And whoever welcomes a good man because he is good, will share in his reward. 42You can be sure that whoever gives even a drink of cold water to one of the least of these my followers because he is my follower, will certainly receive a reward."

The Messengers from John the Baptist
(Luke 7.18-35)

11 When Jesus finished giving these instructions to his twelve disciples, he left that place and went off to teach and preach in the towns near there.

2When John the Baptist heard in prison about the things that Christ was doing, he sent some of his disciples to him. 3"Tell us," they asked Jesus, "are you the one John said was going to come, or should we expect someone else?"

4Jesus answered, "Go back and tell John what you are hearing and seeing: 5the blind can see, the lame can walk, those who suffer from dreaded skin diseases are made clean,h the deaf hear, the dead are brought back to life, and the Good News is preached to the poor. 6How happy are those who have no doubts about me!"

7While John's disciples were leaving, Jesus spoke about him to the crowds: "When you went out to John in the desert, what did you expect to see? A blade of grass bending in the wind? 8What did you go out to see? A man dressed up in fancy clothes? People who dress like that live in palaces! 9Tell me, what did you

h MADE CLEAN: See 8.2.

不是和平，而是刀劍
（路12．51-53；14．26-27）

34「不要以為我是帶和平到世上來的；我並沒有帶來和平，而是帶來刀劍。35我來是要使兒子反對他的父親，女兒反對她的母親，媳婦反對她的婆婆。36人的仇敵就是自己家裏的人。

37「那愛父母勝過愛我的，不配跟從我；那愛子女勝過愛我的，不配跟從我；38那不肯背起自己的十字架跟着我腳步走的，也不配跟從我。39那想保存自己生命的，反要喪失生命；那為着我失掉生命的，反要得到生命。」

論獎賞
（可9．41）

40「誰接待你們就是接待我；接待我就是接待差我來的那一位。41為了某人是上帝的使者而接待他的，一定會分享使者所得的獎賞；為了某人是義人而接待他的，也一定會分享義人的獎賞。42我實在告訴你們，無論是誰，就算拿一杯冷水給門徒中最微小的一個喝，只因那個人是我的門徒，一定會得到獎賞。」

施洗者約翰的門徒來見耶穌
（路7．18-35）

11 耶穌指示十二個門徒的話說完了，就離開那地方，繼續到附近各村鎮教導人和傳福音。

2 施洗者約翰在監獄裏聽見了關於基督的工作，就派他的門徒去見耶穌，3 問他：「你就是約翰所說將要來臨的那一位，或是我們還要等待另一位呢？」

4 耶穌回答：「你們回去，把你們所聽到、所看到的，報告約翰，5 就是：失明的看見，跛腳的行走，痲瘋的潔淨，耳聾的聽見，死人復活，窮人聽到福音。6 那對我不疑惑的人多麼有福啊！」

7 約翰的門徒走了以後，耶穌向羣眾談起約翰說：「你們從前到曠野去找約翰的時候，想看的是甚麼呢？是看被風吹動的蘆葦嗎？8 你們究竟出去做甚麼呢？是看衣著華麗的人嗎？穿這種衣服的人是住在王宮裏。9 那麼，你們出去看甚麼呢？看先知嗎？是

go out to see? A prophet? Yes indeed, but you saw much more than a prophet. [10]For John is the one of whom the scripture says: 'God said, I will send my messenger ahead of you to open the way for you.' [11]I assure you that John the Baptist is greater than anyone who has ever lived. But the one who is least in the Kingdom of heaven is greater than John. [12]From the time John preached his message until this very day the Kingdom of heaven has suffered violent attacks,[i] and violent men try to seize it. [13]Until the time of John all the prophets and the Law of Moses spoke about the Kingdom; [14]and if you are willing to believe their message, John is Elijah, whose coming was predicted. [15]Listen, then, if you have ears!

[16]"Now, to what can I compare the people of this day? They are like children sitting in the marketplace. One group shouts to the other, [17]'We played wedding music for you, but you wouldn't dance! We sang funeral songs, but you wouldn't cry!' [18]When John came, he fasted and drank no wine, and everyone said, 'He has a demon in him!' [19]When the Son of Man came, he ate and drank, and everyone said, 'Look at this man! He is a glutton and wine drinker, a friend of tax collectors and other outcasts!' God's wisdom, however, is shown to be true by its results."

The Unbelieving Towns
(Luke 10.13-15)

[20]The people in the towns where Jesus had performed most of his miracles did not turn from their sins, so he reproached those towns. [21]"How terrible it will be for you, Chorazin! How terrible for you too, Bethsaida! If the miracles which were performed in you had been performed in Tyre and Sidon, the people there would have long ago put on sackcloth and sprinkled ashes on themselves, to show that they had turned from their sins! [22]I assure you that on the Judgment Day God will show more mercy to the people of Tyre and Sidon than to you! [23]And as for you, Capernaum! Did you want to lift yourself up to heaven? You will be thrown down to hell! If the miracles which were performed in you had been performed in Sodom, it would still be in existence today! [24]You can be sure that on the Judgment Day God will show more mercy to Sodom than to you!"

Come to Me and Rest
(Luke 10.21-22)

[25]At that time Jesus said, "Father, Lord of heaven and earth! I thank you because you have shown to the unlearned what you have

i has suffered violent attacks; *or* has been coming violently.

的,可是我告訴你們,他比先知還大。[10]他就是聖經上所提到的那一位。上帝說:『看吧,我要差遣我的使者作你的前驅;他要為你開路。』[11]我實在告訴你們,在人間沒有比約翰更偉大的人,但是在天國裏,最微小的一個都要比約翰偉大呢![12]從施洗者約翰開始傳道到今天,天國遭受到猛烈的攻擊⑦,強暴的人企圖奪取它。[13]到約翰為止,所有先知的書和摩西的法律都講論到天國的事;[14]如果你們願意接受他們所說的預言,約翰就是那要來的以利亞了。[15]有耳朵的,都聽吧!

[16]「至於這世代的人,我要拿甚麼來比擬呢?他們正像在街上玩耍的孩子,其中的一羣向另一羣喊說:[17]『我們為你們奏婚禮樂曲,你們不跳舞!我們唱喪禮哀歌,你們也不哭泣!』[18]約翰來了,不吃不喝,大家說:『他有鬼附身!』[19]人子來了,也吃也喝,大家卻說:『他是酒肉之徒,跟稅棍和壞人交朋友!』但是,上帝的智慧是從他智慧的果子彰顯出來的。」

不信的城
(路10・13─15)

[20]那時,耶穌譴責曾經看見他行過許多神蹟的城市,因為那些地方的人沒有悔改。[21]他說:「哥拉汛哪,你要遭殃了!伯賽大啊,你要遭殃了!我在你們當中行過的神蹟要是行在泰爾和西頓,那裏的人早就披麻蒙灰,表示他們已棄邪歸正了。[22]我實在告訴你們,在審判的日子,泰爾和西頓所遭受的懲罰比你們所受的要輕呢![23]至於你,迦百農啊,你要把自己捧上天嗎?你會給摔進地獄去!我在你們那裏行過的神蹟要是行在所多瑪,它今天一定還存在着![24]我再告訴你們,在審判的日子,所多瑪所遭受的懲罰比你們所受的要輕呢!」

到我這裏來
(路10・21─22)

[25]那時候,耶穌說:「我父,天地的主,我感謝你;因為你向聰明、有學問的人所隱

⑦「天國遭受到猛烈的攻擊」或譯「天國一直猛進着」。

hidden from the wise and learned. 26Yes, Father, this was how you were pleased to have it happen.

27"My Father has given me all things. No one knows the Son except the Father, and no one knows the Father except the Son and those to whom the Son chooses to reveal him.
28"Come to me, all of you who are tired from carrying heavy loads, and I will give you rest. 29Take my yoke and put it on you, and learn from me, because I am gentle and humble in spirit; and you will find rest. 30For the yoke I will give you is easy, and the load I will put on you is light."

The Question about the Sabbath
(Mark 2.23-28; Luke 6.1-5)

12Not long afterward Jesus was walking through some wheat fields on a Sabbath. His disciples were hungry, so they began to pick heads of wheat and eat the grain. 2When the Pharisees saw this, they said to Jesus, "Look, it is against our Law for your disciples to do this on the Sabbath!"
3Jesus answered, "Have you never read what David did that time when he and his men were hungry? 4He went into the house of God, and he and his men ate the bread offered to God, even though it was against the Law for them to eat it–only the priests were allowed to eat that bread. 5Or have you not read in the Law of Moses that every Sabbath the priests in the Temple actually break the Sabbath law, yet they are not guilty? 6I tell you that there is something here greater than the Temple. 7The scripture says, 'It is kindness that I want, not animal sacrifices.' If you really knew what this means, you would not condemn people who are not guilty; 8for the Son of Man is Lord of the Sabbath."

The Man with a Paralyzed Hand
(Mark 3.1-6; Luke 6.6-11)

9Jesus left that place and went to a synagogue, 10where there was a man who had a paralyzed hand. Some people were there who wanted to accuse Jesus of doing wrong, so they asked him, "Is it against our Law to heal on the Sabbath?"

11Jesus answered, "What if one of you has a sheep and it falls into a deep hole on the Sabbath? Will you not take hold of it and lift it out? 12And a human being is worth much more than a sheep! So then, our Law does allow us to help someone on the Sabbath." 13Then he said to the man with the paralyzed hand, "Stretch out your hand."

藏的事,卻向沒有學問的人啓示出來。26是的,天父啊,這樣的安排都是出於你的美意!

27「我父親已經把一切都給我了。除了我父親,沒有人認識兒子;除了兒子和兒子所願意啓示的人,也沒有人認識父親。
28「來吧,所有勞苦、背負重擔的人都到我這裏來!我要使你們得安息。29你們要負起我的軛,跟我學,因爲我的心柔和謙卑。這樣,你們就可以得到安息。30我的軛是容易負的;我的擔子是輕省的。」

安息日的問題
(可2·23—28;路6·1—5)

12不久以後,耶穌在一個安息日經過麥田。他的門徒餓了,就摘了一些麥穗來吃。2有些法利賽人看見了,對耶穌說:「你看,你的門徒做了在安息日不准做的事!」
3耶穌回答:「大衞和他的隨從在飢餓的時候做了甚麼,你們沒有念過嗎?4他走進上帝的聖殿,他跟他的隨從吃了獻給上帝的供餅;那是違法的(因爲那種餅只有祭司才可以吃)。5難道你們沒有念過摩西的法律所記載的?每逢安息日,祭司在聖殿裏都破壞了安息日的規矩,可是他們不算犯罪。6我告訴你們,這裏有比聖殿更重要的。7聖經上說:『我要的是仁慈,不是牲祭。』假如你們眞正明白這話的意思,你們就不會把無辜的人定罪。8因爲人子是安息日的主。」

治好手枯萎的病人
(可3·1—6;路6·6—11)

9耶穌離開了那地方,到猶太人的會堂去。10在那裏有一個人,他的一隻手枯萎了。有些人想找耶穌的錯處,就問他:「在安息日治病是不是違法的?」

11耶穌回答:「假如你們當中有人有一隻羊,這隻羊在安息日掉進坑裏去,怎麼辦呢?他不把羊拉上來嗎?12人比羊貴重多了!所以,在安息日行善是法律所允許的。」13於是,耶穌對那人說:「把手伸直!」

He stretched it out, and it became well again, just like the other one. 14Then the Pharisees left and made plans to kill Jesus.

God's Chosen Servant

15When Jesus heard about the plot against him, he went away from that place; and large crowds followed him. He healed all the sick 16and gave them orders not to tell others about him. 17He did this so as to make come true what God had said through the prophet Isaiah:
18"Here is my servant, whom I have chosen,
 the one I love, and with whom I am
  pleased.
I will send my Spirit upon him,
 and he will announce my judgment
  to the nations.
19He will not argue or shout,
 or make loud speeches in the streets.
20He will not break off a bent reed,
 nor put out a flickering lamp.
He will persist until he causes justice to
 triumph,
21and on him all peoples will put their hope."

Jesus and Beelzebul
(Mark 3.20-30; Luke 11.14-23)

22Then some people brought to Jesus a man who was blind and could not talk because he had a demon. Jesus healed the man, so that he was able to talk and see. 23The crowds were all amazed at what Jesus had done. "Could he be the Son of David?" they asked.

24When the Pharisees heard this, they replied, "He drives out demons only because their ruler Beelzebul gives him power to do so."

25Jesus knew what they were thinking, and so he said to them, "Any country that divides itself into groups which fight each other will not last very long. And any town or family that divides itself into groups which fight each other will fall apart. 26So if one group is fighting another in Satan's kingdom, this means that it is already divided into groups and will soon fall apart! 27You say that I drive out demons because Beelzebul gives me the power to do so. Well, then, who gives your followers the power to drive them out? What your own followers do proves that you are wrong! 28No, it is not Beelzebul, but God's Spirit, who gives me the power to drive out demons, which proves that the Kingdom of God has already come upon you.

29"No one can break into a strong man's house and take away his belongings unless he first ties up the strong man; then he can plunder his house.

30"Anyone who is not for me is really against

他一伸手，手就復原，跟另一隻手一樣。14法利賽人出去，計劃對付耶穌，要殺害他。

上帝所揀選的僕人

15 耶穌聽到這消息，就離開那裏，許多人跟着他。他治好了他們所有的疾病，16吩咐他們不要把消息張揚出去。17這正應驗了先知以賽亞所說的：

18 看哪，他是我所揀選的僕人；
 我鍾愛他，喜歡他。
 我要把我的靈賜給他；
 他要向萬民宣告我的審判。
19 他不爭辯，不喧嚷，
 也不在大街上叫喊。
20 壓傷的蘆葦，他不折斷；
 將熄的燈火，他不吹滅。
 他要堅持正義，直到正義得勝。
21 全世界的人民
 都要把希望寄託於他！

耶穌和別西卜
（可 3 · 20－30；路11 · 14－23）

22 當時，有人把一個被鬼附身、又瞎又啞的人帶到耶穌面前來。耶穌治好他，使他又能夠說話，也能夠看見。23羣眾都很驚奇，說：「難道他就是那大衛之子嗎？」

24 法利賽人聽見這話就說：「他會趕鬼，無非是靠鬼王別西卜罷了。」

25 耶穌知道他們在想些甚麼，就對他們說：「任何國家自相紛爭，必然衰敗；一城一家自相紛爭，也必然破碎。26如果撒但驅逐撒但，就是自相紛爭，他的國又怎能站立得住呢？27如果我趕鬼是靠別西卜，那麼，你們的子弟趕鬼，又是靠誰呢？你們的子弟要證明你們是錯的！28如果我靠上帝的靈趕鬼，這就證明上帝已經在你們當中掌權了。

29「有人能進武士的家搶奪他的財物嗎？除非先把武士綁起來才能搶他的家。

30「那不跟我同道的，就是反對我的；不

me; anyone who does not help me gather is really scattering. [31]For this reason I tell you: people can be forgiven any sin and any evil thing they say;*j* but whoever says evil things against the Holy Spirit will not be forgiven. [32]Anyone who says something against the Son of Man can be forgiven; but whoever says something against the Holy Spirit will not be forgiven–now or ever.

A Tree and Its Fruit
(Luke 6.43-45)

[33]"To have good fruit you must have a healthy tree; if you have a poor tree, you will have bad fruit. A tree is known by the kind of fruit it bears. [34]You snakes–how can you say good things when you are evil? For the mouth speaks what the heart is full of. [35]A good person brings good things out of a treasure of good things; a bad person brings bad things out of a treasure of bad things.

[36]"You can be sure that on the Judgment Day you will have to give account of every useless word you have ever spoken. [37]Your words will be used to judge you–to declare you either innocent or guilty."

The Demand for a Miracle
(Mark 8.11-12; Luke 11.29-32)

[38]Then some teachers of the Law and some Pharisees spoke up. "Teacher," they said, "we want to see you perform a miracle."

[39]"How evil and godless are the people of this day!" Jesus exclaimed. "You ask me for a miracle? No! The only miracle you will be given is the miracle of the prophet Jonah. [40]In the same way that Jonah spent three days and nights in the big fish, so will the Son of Man spend three days and nights in the depths of the earth. [41]On the Judgment Day the people of Nineveh will stand up and accuse you, because they turned from their sins when they heard Jonah preach; and I tell you that there is something here greater than Jonah! [42]On the Judgment Day the Queen of Sheba will stand up and accuse you, because she traveled all the way from her country to listen to King Solomon's wise teaching; and I assure you that there is something here greater than Solomon!

The Return of the Evil Spirit
(Luke 11.24-26)

[43]"When an evil spirit goes out of a person, it travels over dry country looking for a place to rest. If it can't find one, [44]it says to itself, 'I will go back to my house.' So it goes back and finds the house empty, clean, and all fixed up. [45]Then it goes out and brings along seven other spirits even worse than itself, and they come and live

j evil thing they say; *or* evil thing they say against God.

跟我一起收聚的，便是拆散的。[31]所以，我告訴你們，人所犯一切的罪和所說一切褻瀆的話都可得到赦免；但是褻瀆聖靈的人不能得到赦免。[32]邪說話冒犯人子的，可以得到赦免；但是褻瀆聖靈的，無論今世來世，都不能得到赦免。」

果樹和果子
（路6‧43—45）

[33]「果樹好，果子就好；果樹壞，果子也壞。從果子可以認出果樹的好壞。[34]你們這些毒蛇，你們原是邪惡的，怎能說出好話來呢？因為心裏所充滿的，口就說了出來。[35]好人從他積存的善發出善來；壞人從他積存的惡發出惡來。

[36]「我告訴你們，在審判的日子，每人所說的閒話句句都要交帳。[37]因為，上帝要用你自己的話來宣告你有罪，也要用你自己的話來宣告你無罪。」

求神蹟
（可8‧11—12；路11‧29—32）

[38]當時，有幾個經學教師和法利賽人來對耶穌說：「老師，我們希望你顯個神蹟給我們看。」耶穌說：[39]「這時代的人多麼邪惡、多麼不忠！你們竟要求我顯神蹟！不，除了先知約拿的神蹟，再也沒有別的神蹟給你們看了。[40]約拿曾經在大魚的肚子裏三天三夜，人子也要在地的深處三天三夜。[41]在審判的日子，尼尼微人要站起來控告你們這一代的人，因為他們聽見約拿的宣道就棄邪歸正了。我告訴你們，這裏有比約拿更重大的事呢！[42]在審判的日子，南方的女王要站起來控告你們這一代的人，因為她長途跋涉來聽所羅門王智慧的話。我告訴你們，這裏有比所羅門更重大的事呢！」

邪靈回來
（路11‧24—26）

[43]「邪靈離開了所附的人，走遍乾旱地區，尋找棲息的地方，都找不到，[44]就說：『我要回原來的屋子去。』他回去後，發現屋子還空着，而且打掃得又乾淨又整齊。[45]於是他又出去，帶回七個比他更邪惡的靈來，

there. So when it is all over, that person is in worse shape than at the beginning. This is what will happen to the evil people of this day."

Jesus' Mother and Brothers
(Mark 3.31-35; Luke 8.19-21)

46Jesus was still talking to the people when his mother and brothers arrived. They stood outside, asking to speak with him. 47So one of the people there said to him, "Look, your mother and brothers are standing outside, and they want to speak with you."[k]

48Jesus answered, "Who is my mother? Who are my brothers?" 49Then he pointed to his disciples and said, "Look! Here are my mother and my brothers! 50Whoever does what my Father in heaven wants is my brother, my sister, and my mother."

The Parable of the Sower
(Mark 4.1-9; Luke 8.4-8)

13 That same day Jesus left the house and went to the lakeside, where he sat down to teach. 2The crowd that gathered around him was so large that he got into a boat and sat in it, while the crowd stood on the shore. 3He used parables to tell them many things.

"Once there was a man who went out to sow grain. 4As he scattered the seed in the field, some of it fell along the path, and the birds came and ate it up. 5Some of it fell on rocky ground, where there was little soil. The seeds soon sprouted, because the soil wasn't deep. 6But when the sun came up, it burned the young plants; and because the roots had not grown deep enough, the plants soon dried up. 7Some of the seed fell among thorn bushes, which grew up and choked the plants. 8But some seeds fell in good soil, and the plants bore grain: some had one hundred grains, others sixty, and others thirty."

9And Jesus concluded, "Listen, then, if you have ears!"

The Purpose of the Parables
(Mark 4.10-12; Luke 8.9-10)

10Then the disciples came to Jesus and asked him, "Why do you use parables when you talk to the people?"

11Jesus answered, "The knowledge about the secrets of the Kingdom of heaven has been given to you, but not to them. 12For the person who has something will be given more, so that he will have more than enough; but the person who has nothing will have taken away from him even the little he has. 13The reason I use parables in talking to them is that they look, but do not see, and they listen, but do not hear or

k Some manuscripts do not have verse 47.

跟他住在一起。那個人後來的景況比從前更壞了。這邪惡時代的人的處境也是這樣。」

耶穌的母親和兄弟
（可 3·31—35；路 8·19—21）

46 耶穌還在跟羣衆說話的時候，他的母親和兄弟來了。他們站在外面，想要跟他說話。47有人告訴耶穌：「喂，你的母親和兄弟站在外面，要跟你說話呢！」

48 耶穌回答：「誰是我的母親？誰是我的兄弟？」49於是他指着他的門徒說：「你們看，這些人就是我的母親，我的兄弟！50凡實行我天父旨意的，就是我的兄弟、姊妹，和母親。」

撒種的比喻
（可 4·1—9；路 8·4—8）

13 同 一 天，耶穌離開了家，到湖邊去。他坐下。2一大羣人集合到他跟前來，所以他上了一條船，坐下；羣衆傍着水邊站着。3他就用比喻向他們講解許多事情。

他說：「有一個撒種的出去撒種。4他撒的時候，有些種子落在路旁，鳥兒飛來把它們吃掉了。5有些落在淺土的石地上，因爲土壤不深，很快就長苗；6但太陽一出來，幼苗給曬焦了；又因爲根不夠深，就枯乾了。7有些落在荊棘中，荊棘長起來，把幼苗擠住了。8另外有些種子落在好土壤裏，長大結實，收成有一百倍的，有六十倍的，也有三十倍的。」

9 於是耶穌說：「有耳朵的，都聽吧！」

比喻的目的
（可 4·10—12；路 8·9—10）

10 門徒來見耶穌，問他：「爲甚麼你對羣衆講話都用比喻呢？」

11 耶穌回答：「關於天國奧祕的知識已經賜給了你們，沒有給他們。12因爲那已經有的，要給他更多，讓他豐足有餘；那沒有的，連他所有的一點點也要奪走。13爲了這緣故，我用比喻對他們講；因爲他們視而不

understand. [14]So the prophecy of Isaiah applies to them:

'This people will listen and listen, but not understand;
they will look and look, but not see,
[15]because their minds are dull,
and they have stopped up their ears
and have closed their eyes.
Otherwise, their eyes would see,
their ears would hear,
their minds would understand,
and they would turn to me, says God,
and I would heal them.'

[16]"As for you, how fortunate you are! Your eyes see and your ears hear. [17]I assure you that many prophets and many of God's people wanted very much to see what you see, but they could not, and to hear what you hear, but they did not.

Jesus Explains the Parable of the Sower
(Mark 4.13-20; Luke 8.11-15)

[18]"Listen, then, and learn what the parable of the sower means. [19]Those who hear the message about the Kingdom but do not understand it are like the seeds that fell along the path. The Evil One comes and snatches away what was sown in them. [20]The seeds that fell on rocky ground stand for those who receive the message gladly as soon as they hear it. [21]But it does not sink deep into them, and they don't last long. So when trouble or persecution comes because of the message, they give up at once. [22]The seeds that fell among thorn bushes stand for those who hear the message; but the worries about this life and the love for riches choke the message, and they don't bear fruit. [23]And the seeds sown in the good soil stand for those who hear the message and understand it: they bear fruit, some as much as one hundred, others sixty, and others thirty."

The Parable of the Weeds

[24]Jesus told them another parable: "The Kingdom of heaven is like this. A man sowed good seed in his field. [25]One night, when everyone was asleep, an enemy came and sowed weeds among the wheat and went away. [26]When the plants grew and the heads of grain began to form, then the weeds showed up. [27]The man's servants came to him and said, 'Sir, it was good seed you sowed in your field; where did the weeds come from?' [28]'It was some enemy who did this,' he answered. 'Do you want us to go and pull up the weeds?' they asked him. [29]'No,' he answered, 'because as you gather the weeds you might pull up some of the wheat along with them. [30]Let the wheat and the

見,聽而不聞,又不明白。[14]以賽亞的預言正應驗在他們身上;他說:

這人民聽了又聽,卻不明白;
看了又看,卻看不見。
[15]因為他們心智閉塞,
塞住了耳朵,閉上了眼睛。
不然,他們的眼睛就會看見,
耳朵也會聽見,
心裏領悟,回心轉意,
我就治好他們。

[16]「但是你們是有福的!因為你們的眼睛看得見,耳朵聽得見。[17]我實在告訴你們,有許多先知聖賢要看你們所看見的,卻沒有看到;要聽你們所聽見的,也沒有聽到。」

解釋撒種的比喻
(可4.13-20;路8.11-15)

[18]「所以,你們要明白這撒種比喻的意思。[19]那聽了天國的信息卻不明白的人正像撒在路旁的種子,那邪惡者來到,把撒在他心田裏的信息都奪走了。[20]那撒在石地上的種子是指人聽了信息,立刻樂意接受,[21]只是扎根不深,不能持久,一旦為了信息而遭遇患難或迫害,立刻放棄。[22]那撒在荊棘中的種子是指人聽了信息以後,生活的憂慮和財富的誘惑窒息了信息的生機,無法結出果實。[23]那撒在好土壤裏的種子是指人聽了信息,並且領悟了;他結出果實,收成有一百倍的,有六十倍的,有三十倍的。」

稗子的比喻

[24]耶穌向他們講另一個比喻:「天國好比有人把好的種子撒在田裏。[25]大家睡覺的時候,敵人來了,把稗子撒在麥子中間,就走了。[26]到了麥子長大結穗的時候,稗子也出現了。[27]莊主的僕人前來說:『主人,你撒在田裏的是好種子,這些稗子究竟從哪裏來的呢?』[28]他回答:『這是敵人幹的。』他們就問:『你要我們去把稗子拔掉嗎?』[29]他說:『不必啦!因為你們拔除稗子的時候,恐怕連麥子也拔掉了。[30]讓麥子跟稗子一

weeds both grow together until harvest. Then I will tell the harvest workers to pull up the weeds first, tie them in bundles and burn them, and then to gather in the wheat and put it in my barn.' "

The Parable of the Mustard Seed
(Mark 4.30-32; Luke 13.18-19)

31Jesus told them another parable: "The Kingdom of heaven is like this. A man takes a mustard seed and sows it in his field. 32It is the smallest of all seeds, but when it grows up, it is the biggest of all plants. It becomes a tree, so that birds come and make their nests in its branches."

The Parable of the Yeast
(Luke 13.20-21)

33Jesus told them still another parable: "The Kingdom of heaven is like this. A woman takes some yeast and mixes it with a bushel of flour until the whole batch of dough rises."

Jesus' Use of Parables
(Mark 4.33-4)

34Jesus used parables to tell all these things to the crowds; he would not say a thing to them without using a parable. 35He did this to make come true what the prophet had said,
"I will use parables when I speak to them;
I will tell them things unknown since the creation of the world."

Jesus Explains the Parable of the Weeds
36When Jesus had left the crowd and gone indoors, his disciples came to him and said, "Tell us what the parable about the weeds in the field means."

37Jesus answered, "The man who sowed the good seed is the Son of Man; 38the field is the world; the good seed is the people who belong to the Kingdom; the weeds are the people who belong to the Evil One; 39and the enemy who sowed the weeds is the Devil. The harvest is the end of the age, and the harvest workers are angels. 40Just as the weeds are gathered up and burned in the fire, so the same thing will happen at the end of the age: 41the Son of Man will send out his angels to gather up out of his Kingdom all those who cause people to sin and all others who do evil things, 42and they will throw them into the fiery furnace, where they will cry and gnash their teeth. 43Then God's people will shine like the sun in their Father's Kingdom. Listen, then, if you have ears!

The Parable of the Hidden Treasure
44"The Kingdom of heaven is like this. A man happens to find a treasure hidden in a

起長吧;收割的時候,我會吩咐收割的工人先拔掉稗子,捆起來燒掉,然後收聚麥子,儲藏在我的倉庫裏。』」

芥菜種的比喻
(可4.30-32;路13.18-19)

31 耶穌對他們講另一個比喻:「天國好比一粒芥菜種子,人把它種在田裏。32這種子比其他一切的種子都小,等它長起來卻比任何蔬菜都大;它成為一棵樹,連飛鳥也在它的枝子上搭窩。」

麵酵的比喻
(路13.20-21)

33 耶穌講了另一個比喻:「天國好比麵酵,一個女人拿來放在四十公升的麵裏,使全團麵都發起來。」

使用比喻
(可4.33-34)

34 耶穌用比喻對羣眾講述這一切;除了用比喻,他就不對他們說甚麼。35他這樣做正應驗了先知所說過的話:「我要用比喻向他們講述,把創世以來隱藏的事告訴他們。」

解釋稗子的比喻
36 耶穌離開羣眾,進屋子裏去。門徒又來問他:「請告訴我們,田裏的稗子這個比喻是甚麼意思?」

37 耶穌說:「那撒好種子的是人子;38田地是這個世界;好種子是屬於天國的人;稗子是屬於那邪惡者的人;39撒稗子的敵人就是魔鬼;收割的時候是今世的末了;收割的工人是天使。40到了今世的末了,作惡的人要像稗子一樣被拔出來,扔在火裏焚燒。41人子要差遣他的天使,把他國度裏那些使人犯罪和一切作惡的人都抓起來,42扔在火爐裏。在那裏,他們要哀哭,咬牙切齒。43那時候,義人在天父的國度裏,將好像太陽發射光輝。有耳朵的,都聽吧!」

寶藏的比喻
44「天國好比財寶藏在田裏。有人發現了,就把它掩蓋起來,然後很高興地把自己

field. He covers it up again, and is so happy that he goes and sells everything he has, and then goes back and buys that field.

The Parable of the Pearl

45"Also, the Kingdom of heaven is like this. A man is looking for fine pearls, 46and when he finds one that is unusually fine, he goes and sells everything he has, and buys that pearl.

The Parable of the Net

47"Also, the Kingdom of heaven is like this. Some fishermen throw their net out in the lake and catch all kinds of fish. 48When the net is full, they pull it to shore and sit down to divide the fish: the good ones go into the buckets, the worthless ones are thrown away. 49It will be like this at the end of the age: the angels will go out and gather up the evil people from among the good 50and will throw them into the fiery furnace, where they will cry and gnash their teeth.

New Truths and Old

51"Do you understand these things?" Jesus asked them.

"Yes," they answered.

52So he replied, "This means, then, that every teacher of the Law who becomes a disciple in the Kingdom of heaven is like a homeowner who takes new and old things out of his storage room."

Jesus Is Rejected at Nazareth

(Mark 6.1-6; Luke 4.16-30)

53When Jesus finished telling these parables, he left that place 54and went back to his home town. He taught in the synagogue, and those who heard him were amazed. "Where did he get such wisdom?" they asked. "And what about his miracles? 55Isn't he the carpenter's son? Isn't Mary his mother, and aren't James, Joseph, Simon, and Judas his brothers? 56Aren't all his sisters living here? Where did he get all this?" 57And so they rejected him.

Jesus said to them, "A prophet is respected everywhere except in his hometown and by his own family." 58Because they did not have faith, he did not perform many miracles there.

The Death of John the Baptist

(Mark 6.14-29; Luke 9.7-9)

14 At that time Herod, the ruler of Galilee, heard about Jesus. 2"He is really John the Baptist, who has come back to life," he told his officials. "That is why he has this power to perform miracles."

所有的都變賣了，去購買那塊田。」

珍珠的比喻

45「天國又好比一個商人尋找貴重的珍珠。46當他發現了一顆極貴重的珍珠，就去賣掉他所有的一切，來購買那顆珍珠。」

撒網的比喻

47「天國又好比魚網撒在湖裏，捕捉各樣的魚類。48網一滿，漁夫把它拉上來，坐在岸上把魚兒分開，揀好的放在桶裏，壞的扔掉。49今世的末了也要這樣：天使要出去，從好人中把壞人分別出來，50投進火爐。在那裏，他們要哀哭，咬牙切齒。」

新的和舊的

51耶穌問他們：「這些話你們都明白嗎？」

他們回答：「都明白。」

52耶穌說：「這麼說來，每一個經學教師成為天國的門徒，就像一家的主人從他的庫房裏搬出新和舊的東西來。」

耶穌在拿撒勒被厭棄

（可6．1-6；路4．16-30）

53耶穌講完了這些比喻，離開那地方，54回到自己的家鄉。他在會堂裏教導人；聽見的人都很驚訝，說：「他從哪裏得到這樣的智慧？他還行神蹟呢！55這個人不是那木匠的兒子嗎？他的母親不是馬利亞嗎？雅各、約瑟、西門，和猶大不都是他的弟弟嗎？56他的妹妹們不都住在我們這裏嗎？他這一切本領究竟從哪裏來的呢？」57於是他們厭棄他。

耶穌對他們說：「先知在本鄉本家外都受人尊重。」58因為他們不信，他在那裏沒有行很多神蹟。

施洗者約翰的死

（可6．14-29；路9．7-9）

14 那時候，加利利的希律王聽到了耶穌的事，2就對臣下說：「這個人一定是施洗者約翰復活了，才會有能力行這些神蹟。」

3For Herod had earlier ordered John's arrest, and he had him tied up and put in prison. He had done this because of Herodias, his brother Philip's wife. 4For some time John the Baptist had told Herod, "It isn't right for you to be married to Herodias!" 5Herod wanted to kill him, but he was afraid of the Jewish people, because they considered John to be a prophet.

6On Herod's birthday the daughter of Herodias danced in front of the whole group. Herod was so pleased 7that he promised her, "I swear that I will give you anything you ask for!"

8At her mother's suggestion she asked him, "Give me here and now the head of John the Baptist on a plate!"

9The king was sad, but because of the promise he had made in front of all his guests he gave orders that her wish be granted. 10So he had John beheaded in prison. 11The head was brought in on a plate and given to the girl, who took it to her mother. 12John's disciples came, carried away his body, and buried it; then they went and told Jesus.

Jesus Feeds Five Thousand
(Mark 6.30-44; Luke 9.10-17; John 6.1-14)

13When Jesus heard the news about John, he left there in a boat and went to a lonely place by himself. The people heard about it, and so they left their towns and followed him by land. 14Jesus got out of the boat, and when he saw the large crowd, his heart was filled with pity for them, and he healed their sick.

15That evening his disciples came to him and said, "It is already very late, and this is a lonely place. Send the people away and let them go to the villages to buy food for themselves."

16"They don't have to leave," answered Jesus. "You yourselves give them something to eat!"

17"All we have here are five loaves and two fish," they replied.

18"Then bring them here to me," Jesus said. 19He ordered the people to sit down on the grass; then he took the five loaves and the two fish, looked up to heaven, and gave thanks to God. He broke the loaves and gave them to the disciples, and the disciples gave them to the people. 20Everyone ate and had enough. Then the disciples took up twelve baskets full of what was left over. 21The number of men who ate was about five thousand, not counting the women and children.

Jesus Walks on the Water
(Mark 6.45-52; John 6.15-21)

22Then Jesus made the disciples get into the boat and go on ahead to the other side of the lake, while he sent the people away. 23After

---

3 原來，希律爲了他的兄弟腓力的妻子希羅底的緣故下令逮捕約翰，把他綁起來關在監獄裏。4因爲約翰屢次指責希律：「你不可佔有希羅底作妻子。」5希律想殺他，但是怕人民，因爲他們都認爲約翰是先知。

6 希律生日那一天，希羅底的女兒在賓客面前跳舞，很得希律的歡心。7希律就對她發誓說：「無論你要求甚麼，我都願意給你。」

8 女兒受母親的指使，要求說：「請立刻把施洗者約翰的頭放在盤子裏給我！」

9 王感到非常爲難，可是他已經在賓客面前發了誓，只好命令照她所求的給她。10於是希律差人到監獄裏去，斬了約翰的頭，11放在盤子裏，給了希羅底的女兒；女兒把它交給母親。12約翰的門徒來，把屍體領去，埋葬了，然後把這件事告訴耶穌。

耶穌使五千人吃飽
（可6．30-44；路9．10-17；約6．1—13）

13 耶穌聽到這消息，就上船，離開那裏，獨自到偏僻的地方去。羣衆知道了，從各城鎮走路跟着他。14耶穌上岸，看見這一大羣人，動了惻隱的心，治好他們的疾病。

15 傍晚的時候，門徒來見耶穌，對他說：「天晚了，這裏又是偏僻的地方，請叫羣衆散開，讓他們自己到附近村莊去買食物。」

16 耶穌回答：「不用叫大家散開；你們給他們吃吧。」

17 門徒說：「我們這裏只有五個餅和兩條魚。」

18 耶穌說：「拿來給我。」19於是，他吩咐羣衆坐在草地上，然後拿起五個餅和兩條魚，舉目望天，感謝上帝，擘開餅，遞給門徒，門徒又分給羣衆。20大家都吃，而且都吃飽了。門徒把剩下的碎屑收拾起來，裝滿了十二個籃子。21吃的人數，除了婦女和孩子，約有五千。

耶穌在水上行走
（可6．45—52；約6．15—21）

22 事後，耶穌立刻催門徒上船，先渡過對岸，等他遣散羣衆。23羣衆散了以後，他獨

sending the people away, he went up a hill by himself to pray. When evening came, Jesus was there alone; 24and by this time the boat was far out in the lake, tossed about by the waves, because the wind was blowing against it.

25Between three and six o'clock in the morning Jesus came to the disciples, walking on the water. 26When they saw him walking on the water, they were terrified. "It's a ghost!" they said, and screamed with fear.

27Jesus spoke to them at once. "Courage!" he said. "It is I. Don't be afraid!"

28Then Peter spoke up. "Lord, if it is really you, order me to come out on the water to you."

29"Come!" answered Jesus. So Peter got out of the boat and started walking on the water to Jesus. 30But when he noticed the strong wind, he was afraid and started to sink down in the water. "Save me, Lord!" he cried.

31At once Jesus reached out and grabbed hold of him and said, "What little faith you have! Why did you doubt?"

32They both got into the boat, and the wind died down. 33Then the disciples in the boat worshiped Jesus. "Truly you are the Son of God!" they exclaimed.

Jesus Heals the Sick in Gennesaret
(Mark 6.53-56)

34They crossed the lake and came to land at Gennesaret, 35where the people recognized Jesus. So they sent for the sick people in all the surrounding country and brought them to Jesus. 36They begged him to let the sick at least touch the edge of his cloak; and all who touched it were made well.

The Teaching of the Ancestors
(Mark 7.1-13)

15 Then some Pharisees and teachers of the Law came from Jerusalem to Jesus and asked him, 2"Why is it that your disciples disobey the teaching handed down by our ancestors? They don't wash their hands in the proper way before they eat!"

3Jesus answered, "And why do you disobey God's command and follow your own teaching? 4For God said, 'Respect your father and your mother,' and 'If you curse your father or your mother, you are to be put to death.' 5But you teach that if people have something they could use to help their father or mother, but say, 'This belongs to God,' 6they do not need to honor their father.[l] In this way you disregard God's command, in order to follow your own teaching. 7You hypocrites! How right Isaiah was when he prophesied about you!

l their father; some manuscripts have their father or mother.

自上山禱告；到晚上還留在那裏。24這時候，船離岸已經很遠，遇着逆風，在波浪中顛簸。25天快亮的時候，耶穌在湖上朝着門徒走來。26門徒看見他在湖面上走，非常驚駭，說：「是鬼魂！」他們都害怕得叫起來。

27耶穌立刻對他們說：「放心，是我，不要怕！」

28彼得說：「主啊，如果是你，叫我在水上走，到你那裏去！」

29耶穌說：「來！」彼得就從船上下去，在水上朝着耶穌走過去。30但是他一看到風勢猛烈，心裏害怕，開始往下沉，就喊叫：「主啊，救我！」

31耶穌立刻伸手拉住他，說：「你的信心太小了，為甚麼疑惑呢？」

32他們上了船，風就停了。33船上的門徒都向他下拜，說：「你真是上帝的兒子。」

治好革尼撒勒病人
（可 6．53-56）

34他們渡過了湖，在革尼撒勒登岸。35那裏的人一認出是耶穌就派人出去，把附近地區的病人都帶到耶穌的面前來。36他們要求耶穌讓病人只摸一摸他外袍的衣角；所有摸着的人都得到醫治。

祖先的傳統
（可 7．1-13）

15 有幾個法利賽人和經學教師從耶路撒冷來見耶穌，問他：2「為甚麼你的門徒不遵守我們祖先的傳統？他們吃飯以前並沒有按照規矩洗手！」

3 耶穌回答：「為甚麼你們為着遵守傳統，卻違背了上帝的命令呢？4上帝說：『要孝敬父母』；又說：『咒罵父母的，必須處死。』5你們偏偏說，要是有人對父母說：『我已經把奉養你們的當供物獻給上帝了』，6他就用不着孝敬父母。你們拿傳統來抵消上帝的話。7假冒為善的人哪，以賽亞指着你們所發的預言是多麼正確啊！他說：

上帝這樣說：

8'These people, says God, honor me with their words,

but their heart is really far away from me.
9It is no use for them to worship me,

because they teach human rules as though they were my laws!' "

The Things That Make a Person Unclean
(Mark 7.14-23)

10Then Jesus called the crowd to him and said to them, "Listen and understand! 11It is not what goes into your mouth that makes you ritually unclean; rather, what comes out of it makes you unclean."

12Then the disciples came to him and said, "Do you know that the Pharisees had their feelings hurt by what you said?"

13"Every plant which my Father in heaven did not plant will be pulled up," answered Jesus. 14"Don't worry about them! They are blind leaders of the blind; and when one blind man leads another, both fall into a ditch."

15Peter spoke up, "Explain this saying to us."

16Jesus said to them, "You are still no more intelligent than the others. 17Don't you understand? Anything that goes into your mouth goes into your stomach and then on out of your body. 18But the things that come out of the mouth come from the heart, and these are the things that make you ritually unclean. 19For from your heart come the evil ideas which lead you to kill, commit adultery, and do other immoral things; to rob, lie, and slander others. 20These are the things that make you unclean. But to eat without washing your hands as they say you should–this doesn't make you unclean."

A Woman's Faith
(Mark 7.24-30)

21Jesus left that place and went off to the territory near the cities of Tyre and Sidon. 22A Canaanite woman who lived in that region came to him. "Son of David!" she cried out. "Have mercy on me, sir! My daughter has a demon and is in a terrible condition."

23But Jesus did not say a word to her. His disciples came to him and begged him, "Send her away! She is following us and making all this noise!"

24Then Jesus replied, "I have been sent only to the lost sheep of the people of Israel."

25At this the woman came and fell at his feet. "Help me, sir!" she said.

26Jesus answered, "It isn't right to take the children's food and throw it to the dogs."

---

8 這人民用唇舌尊敬我，
他們的心卻遠離我。
9 他們竟把人的規例當作我的命令；
他們敬拜我都是徒然！」

使人不潔淨的東西
（可 7‧14-23）

10 耶穌召集羣眾到他面前，對他們說：「你們要聽，也要明白！11 那從人嘴裏進去的東西不會使人不潔淨；那從人嘴裏出來的才會使人不潔淨。」

12 後來門徒告訴耶穌：「法利賽人聽見了你這話，很不服氣，你知道嗎？」

13 耶穌回答：「凡不是我天父所栽種的植物都要連根拔除。14 不要理他們吧！他們是瞎子在作嚮導；瞎子給瞎子領路，兩個人都會跌進坑裏去。」

15 彼得說：「請你向我們解釋這比喻的意思。」

16 耶穌說：「你們到現在還是跟別人一樣不明白嗎？17 難道你們不曉得，一切從人嘴裏進去的東西，到了肚子裏，然後又排泄出來？18 但是從嘴裏出來的是出自內心，那才會使人不潔淨。19 因為從人心裏出來的有種種惡念；這些惡念指使他犯凶殺、淫亂、通姦、偷盜、撒謊、毀謗等罪。20 這一切才真的會使人不潔淨。至於不先洗手吃飯那一類的事是不會使人不潔淨的。」

一個女人的信心
（可 7‧24-30）

21 耶穌離開那地方，避到泰爾和西頓附近地區去。22 當地的一個迦南女人來見他，喊着說：「主啊，大衛之子，可憐我吧！我的女兒被鬼附着，痛苦不堪。」

23 耶穌一句話也不回答。門徒上來求他，說：「請叫她走開！她跟着我們，一路喊叫呢！」

24 耶穌回答：「我奉差遣只去尋找以色列人中迷失的羊。」

25 那女人一聽見這話，就在他的腳前下拜，說：「主啊，請幫助我！」

26 耶穌說：「拿兒女的食物給小狗吃是不對的。」

27"That's true, sir," she answered, "but even the dogs eat the leftovers that fall from their masters' table."

28So Jesus answered her, "You are a woman of great faith! What you want will be done for you." And at that very moment her daughter was healed.

Jesus Heals Many People

29Jesus left there and went along by Lake Galilee. He climbed a hill and sat down. 30Large crowds came to him, bringing with them the lame, the blind, the crippled, the dumb, and many other sick people, whom they placed at Jesus' feet; and he healed them. 31The people were amazed as they saw the dumb speaking, the crippled made whole, the lame walking, and the blind seeing; and they praised the God of Israel.

Jesus Feeds Four Thousand
(Mark 8.1-10)

32Jesus called his disciples to him and said, "I feel sorry for these people, because they have been with me for three days and now have nothing to eat. I don't want to send them away without feeding them, for they might faint on their way home."

33The disciples asked him, "Where will we find enough food in this desert to feed this crowd?"

34"How much bread do you have?" Jesus asked.

"Seven loaves," they answered, "and a few small fish."

35So Jesus ordered the crowd to sit down on the ground. 36Then he took the seven loaves and the fish, gave thanks to God, broke them, and gave them to the disciples; and the disciples gave them to the people. 37They all ate and had enough. Then the disciples took up seven baskets full of pieces left over. 38The number of men who ate was four thousand, not counting the women and children.

39Then Jesus sent the people away, got into a boat, and went to the territory of Magadan.

The Demand for a Miracle
(Mark 8.11-13; Luke 12.54-56)

16Some Pharisees and Sadducees who came to Jesus wanted to trap him, so they asked him to perform a miracle for them, to show that God approved of him. 2But Jesus answered, "When the sun is setting, you say, 'We are going to have fine weather, because the sky is red.' 3And early in the morning you say, 'It is going to rain, because the sky is red and dark.' You can predict the weather by

27那女人說:「是的,主啊,可是小狗也吃主人桌上掉下來的碎屑呢!」

28於是耶穌說:「婦人,你的信心好大呀!照你所要的,給你成全吧!」她的女兒就在那時候好起來了。

治好各種病人

29耶穌離開那地方,來到加利利湖邊。他上了山,坐下。30一大羣人又來找他,並帶來跛腳的、失明的、殘疾的、啞巴的,和許多患其他疾病的人,安置在耶穌腳前;耶穌一一治好他們。31那羣人看見了啞巴的說話,殘疾的復原,跛腳的走路,失明的看見,都非常驚奇,也都讚美以色列的上帝。

耶穌使四千人吃飽
(可8.1—10)

32耶穌叫門徒來,對他們說:「我很體貼這一羣人,他們跟我在一起已經三天,現在沒有甚麼可吃的了。我不願意叫他們餓着回去,恐怕會在路上暈倒。」

33門徒說:「在這偏僻的地方,我們哪裏去找足夠的食物給這一大羣人吃飽呢?」

34耶穌問他們:「你們有多少餅?」

他們回答:「七個餅和幾條小魚。」

35耶穌吩咐羣衆坐在地上,36拿起那七個餅和幾條小魚,感謝上帝,擘開,遞給門徒;門徒又分給羣衆。37大家都吃,而且吃飽了。門徒收拾剩餘的碎屑,裝滿了七個籃子。38吃飽的,除了婦女和孩子,有四千人。

39於是耶穌遣散羣衆,然後上船,往馬加丹地區去。

求神蹟
(可8.11—13;路12.54—56)

16有幾個法利賽人和撒都該人來見耶穌,想陷害他,所以要求他顯個神蹟,證明他所做的是出於上帝。2耶穌說:「傍晚,你們說:『明天一定是晴天,因爲天邊有紅霞。』3早晨,你們說:『今天會有風雨,因

looking at the sky, but you cannot interpret the signs concerning these times!^m ⁴How evil and godless are the people of this day! You ask me for a miracle? No! The only miracle you will be given is the miracle of Jonah."

So he left them and went away.

The Yeast of the Pharisees and Sadducees
(Mark 8.14-21)

⁵When the disciples crossed over to the other side of the lake, they forgot to take any bread. ⁶Jesus said to them, "Take care; be on your guard against the yeast of the Pharisees and Sadducees."

⁷They started discussing among themselves, "He says this because we didn't bring any bread."

⁸Jesus knew what they were saying, so he asked them, "Why are you discussing among yourselves about not having any bread? What little faith you have! ⁹Don't you understand yet? Don't you remember when I broke the five loaves for the five thousand men? How many baskets did you fill? ¹⁰And what about the seven loaves for the four thousand men? How many baskets did you fill? ¹¹How is it that you don't understand that I was not talking to you about bread? Guard yourselves from the yeast of the Pharisees and Sadducees!"

¹²Then the disciples understood that he was not warning them to guard themselves from the yeast used in bread but from the teaching of the Pharisees and Sadducees.

Peter's Declaration about Jesus
(Mark 8.27-30; Luke 9.18-21)

¹³Jesus went to the territory near the town of Caesarea Philippi, where he asked his disciples, "Who do people say the Son of Man is?"

¹⁴"Some say John the Baptist," they answered. "Others say Elijah, while others say Jeremiah or some other prophet."

¹⁵"What about you?" he asked them. "Who do you say I am?"

¹⁶Simon Peter answered, "You are the Messiah, the Son of the living God."

¹⁷"Good for you, Simon son of John!" answered Jesus. "For this truth did not come to you from any human being, but it was given to you directly by my Father in heaven. ¹⁸And so I tell you, Peter: you are a rock, and on this rock foundation I will build my church, and not even death will ever be able to overcome it. ¹⁹I will give you the keys of the Kingdom of heaven;

爲天色暗紅。』你們很會觀察天色，卻不會洞察這個時代的徵兆⑧！⁴這時代的人竟是那麼邪惡、淫亂！你們要求神蹟嗎？除了約拿的神蹟，你們再也看不到別的神蹟了。」

耶穌說完，就離開他們走了。

法利賽人和撒都該人的酵母
（可 8‧14—21）

⁵ 門徒渡湖到對岸，忘了帶餅。⁶耶穌告訴他們：「你們要小心，要提防法利賽人和撒都該人的酵母。」

⁷ 門徒彼此議論：「他說這話是因爲我們沒有帶餅吧。」

⁸ 耶穌知道他們在說些甚麼，就問他們：「你們爲甚麼在討論沒有帶餅的事呢？你們的信心太小了！⁹竟然到現在還不明白！難道你們忘記了我曾把五個餅分給五千人吃飽的事嗎？當時還剩下多少籃的碎屑呢？¹⁰還有那七個餅給四千人吃飽，你們又收拾了多少籃的碎屑呢？¹¹爲甚麼還不明白我不是跟你們談餅的事？你們要提防法利賽人和撒都該人的酵母！」

¹² 門徒這才明白耶穌並不是要他們提防那餅裏的酵母，而是要提防法利賽人和撒都該人的教訓。

彼得認耶穌爲基督
（可 8‧27—30；路 9‧18—21）

¹³ 耶穌到了凱撒利亞‧腓立比的境內；在那裏他問門徒：「一般人說人子是誰？」

¹⁴ 他們回答：「有的說是施洗者約翰；有的說是以利亞；也有的說是耶利米或其他先知中的一位。」

¹⁵ 耶穌問他們：「那麼，你們說我是誰？」

¹⁶ 西門‧彼得回答：「你是基督，是永生上帝的兒子。」

¹⁷ 耶穌說：「約翰的兒子西門，你眞有福了；因爲這眞理不是人傳授給你的，而是我天上的父親向你啓示的。¹⁸我告訴你，你是彼得，是磐石；在這磐石上，我要建立我的教會，甚至死亡的權勢也不能勝過它。¹⁹我要給你天國的鑰匙，你在地上所禁止的，在

---

m Some manuscripts do not have the words of Jesus in verses 2-3.

⑧有些古卷沒有「傍晚……時代的徵兆」。

what you prohibit on earth will be prohibited in heaven, and what you permit on earth will be permitted in heaven."

20Then Jesus ordered his disciples not to tell anyone that he was the Messiah.

Jesus Speaks about His Suffering and Death
(Mark 8.31-9.1; Luke 9.22-27)

21From that time on Jesus began to say plainly to his disciples, "I must go to Jerusalem and suffer much from the elders, the chief priests, and the teachers of the Law. I will be put to death, but three days later I will be raised to life."

22Peter took him aside and began to rebuke him. "God forbid it, Lord!" he said. "That must never happen to you!"

23Jesus turned around and said to Peter, "Get away from me, Satan! You are an obstacle in my way, because these thoughts of yours don't come from God, but from human nature."

24Then Jesus said to his disciples, "If any of you want to come with me, you must forget yourself, carry your cross, and follow me. 25For if you want to save your own life, you will lose it; but if you lose your life for my sake, you will find it. 26Will you gain anything if you win the whole world but lose your life? Of course not! There is nothing you can give to regain your life. 27For the Son of Man is about to come in the glory of his Father with his angels, and then he will reward each one according to his deeds. 28I assure you that there are some here who will not die until they have seen the Son of Man come as King."

The Transfiguration
(Mark 9.2-13; Luke 9.28-36)

17 Six days later Jesus took with him Peter and the brothers James and John and led them up a high mountain where they were alone. 2As they looked on, a change came over Jesus: his face was shining like the sun, and his clothes were dazzling white. 3Then the three disciples saw Moses and Elijah talking with Jesus. 4So Peter spoke up and said to Jesus, "Lord, how good it is that we are here! If you wish, I will make three tents here, one for you, one for Moses, and one for Elijah."

5While he was talking, a shining cloud came over them, and a voice from the cloud said, "This is my own dear Son, with whom I am pleased–listen to him!"

6When the disciples heard the voice, they were so terrified that they threw themselves face downward on the ground. 7Jesus came to

---

天上也要禁止；你在地上所准許的，在天上也要准許。」

20 於是，耶穌吩咐門徒千萬不要告訴任何人他就是基督。

耶穌預言自己的受難和死
（可 8．31－9．1；路 9．22－27）

21 從那時候開始，耶穌清楚地指示門徒說：「我必須上耶路撒冷去，在長老、祭司長，和經學教師手下遭受許多苦難，並且被殺害，第三天將復活。」

22 彼得拉耶穌到一邊，勸阻他，說：「不！主啊，這事絕不可臨到你身上！」

23 耶穌轉身對彼得說：「撒但，走開！你是我的絆腳石；因為你所想的不是上帝的想法，而是人的想法。」

24 於是，耶穌對門徒說：「如果有人要跟從我，就得捨棄自己，背起他的十字架來跟從我。25因為那想救自己生命的，反要喪失生命；那為着我喪失生命的，反要得到生命。26一個人就是贏得了全世界，卻賠上了自己的生命，有甚麼益處呢？沒有！他能夠拿甚麼去換回自己的生命呢？27人子將要在他父親的榮耀中，跟他的天使一起來臨。那時候，他要按照各人的行為施報應。28我鄭重地告訴你們，站在這裏的人，有的在他們死以前會看見人子來到他們當中掌權。」

改變形像
（可 9．2－13；路 9．28－36）

17 六天後，耶穌帶着彼得以及雅各和約翰兩兄弟悄悄地上了一座高山。2在他們面前，耶穌的形像變了：他的面貌像太陽一樣明亮，衣服也像光一樣潔白。3忽然，三個門徒看見摩西和以利亞在跟耶穌講話。4彼得對耶穌說：「主啊，我們在這裏真好！你若願意，我就在這裏搭三座帳棚，一座給你，一座給摩西，一座給以利亞。」

5 彼得正說這話的時候，一朵燦爛的雲彩籠罩了他們；有聲音從雲中出來，說：「這是我親愛的兒子，我喜愛他。你們要聽從他！」

6 門徒聽見這聲音，非常害怕，都俯伏在地上。7耶穌走過來，拍他們，說：「起

them and touched them. "Get up," he said. "Don't be afraid!" [8]So they looked up and saw no one there but Jesus.

[9]As they came down the mountain, Jesus ordered them, "Don't tell anyone about this vision you have seen until the Son of Man has been raised from death."

[10]Then the disciples asked Jesus, "Why do the teachers of the Law say that Elijah has to come first?"

[11]"Elijah is indeed coming first," answered Jesus, "and he will get everything ready. [12]But I tell you that Elijah has already come and people did not recognize him, but treated him just as they pleased. In the same way they will also mistreat the Son of Man."

[13]Then the disciples understood that he was talking to them about John the Baptist.

Jesus Heals a Boy with a Demon
(Mark 9.14-29; Luke 9.37-43a)

[14]When they returned to the crowd, a man came to Jesus, knelt before him, [15]and said, "Sir, have mercy on my son! He is an epileptic and has such terrible attacks that he often falls in the fire or into water. [16]I brought him to your disciples, but they could not heal him."

[17]Jesus answered, "How unbelieving and wrong you people are! How long must I stay with you? How long do I have to put up with you? Bring the boy here to me!" [18]Jesus gave a command to the demon, and it went out of the boy, and at that very moment he was healed.

[19]Then the disciples came to Jesus in private and asked him, "Why couldn't we drive the demon out?"

[20]"It was because you do not have enough faith," answered Jesus. "I assure you that if you have faith as big as a mustard seed, you can say to this hill, 'Go from here to there!' and it will go. You could do anything!"[n]

Jesus Speaks Again about His Death
(Mark 9.30-32; Luke 9.43b-45)

[22]When the disciples all came together in Galilee, Jesus said to them, "The Son of Man is about to be handed over to those [23]who will kill him; but three days later he will be raised to life."

The disciples became very sad.

---

[n] *Some manuscripts add verse 21:* But only prayer and fasting can drive this kind out; nothing else can (*see Mk 9.29*).

來，不要怕！」[8]他們抬頭一看，只見耶穌，其他的人都不見了。

[9] 他們下山的時候，耶穌吩咐他們：「在人子沒有從死裏復活以前，千萬不要把所看見的異象告訴人。」

[10] 於是門徒問耶穌：「為甚麼經學教師說以利亞必須先來呢？」

[11] 耶穌回答：「以利亞是要先來準備一切。[12]可是我告訴你們，以利亞已經來過，人卻不認識他，反而任意對待他。同樣，人子也將受他們的虐待。」

[13] 門徒們這才明白耶穌這話是指着施洗者約翰說的。

治好被鬼附身的孩子
（可 9‧14-29；路 9‧37-43）

[14] 他們回到羣眾那裏的時候，有一個人上來，跪在耶穌面前，[15]說：「主啊，求你可憐我的兒子！他患了癲癇病，很痛苦，時常跌在火裏或水裏。[16]我帶他去見你的門徒，可是他們不能治好他。」

[17] 耶穌說：「你們這時代的人多麼沒有信心，多麼腐敗啊！我還得在你們這裏多久呢？還得容忍你們多久呢？把孩子帶到這裏來！」[18]於是耶穌責備那鬼；鬼一出來，孩子的病立刻好了。

[19] 事後，門徒私下來問耶穌：「為甚麼我們不能把那鬼趕出去呢？」

[20] 耶穌回答：「因為你們的信心不夠。我實在告訴你們，假如你們有像一粒芥菜種子那麼大的信心，就是對這座山說：『從這裏移到那裏！』它也會移過去。沒有任何事情是你們不能做的。[⑨]」

耶穌再預言自己的死
（可 9‧30-32；路 9‧43-45）

[22] 門徒都集合在加利利的時候，耶穌對他們說：「人子將被交在人手裏，[23]他們要殺害他，但第三天他將復活。」

門徒聽了非常憂愁。

[⑨] 有些古卷加21節「至於這一種鬼，只有靠禁食、禱告才趕得出去。」

Payment of the Temple Tax

24When Jesus and his disciples came to Capernaum, the collectors of the Temple tax came to Peter and asked, "Does your teacher pay the Temple tax?"

25"Of course," Peter answered.

When Peter went into the house, Jesus spoke up first, "Simon, what is your opinion? Who pays duties or taxes to the kings of this world? The citizens of the country or the foreigners?"

26"The foreigners," answered Peter.

"Well, then," replied Jesus, "that means that the citizens don't have to pay. 27But we don't want to offend these people. So go to the lake and drop in a line. Pull up the first fish you hook, and in its mouth you will find a coin worth enough for my Temple tax and yours. Take it and pay them our taxes."

Who Is the Greatest?
(Mark 9.33-37; Luke 9.46-48)

18At that time the disciples came to Jesus, asking, "Who is the greatest in the Kingdom of heaven?"

2So Jesus called a child to come and stand in front of them, 3and said, "I assure you that unless you change and become like children, you will never enter the Kingdom of heaven. 4The greatest in the Kingdom of heaven is the one who humbles himself and becomes like this child. 5And whoever welcomes in my name one such child as this, welcomes me.

Temptations to Sin
(Mark 9.42-48; Luke 17.1-2)

6"If anyone should cause one of these little ones to lose his faith in me, it would be better for that person to have a large millstone tied around his neck and be drowned in the deep sea. 7How terrible for the world that there are things that make people lose their faith! Such things will always happen–but how terrible for the one who causes them!

8"If your hand or your foot makes you lose your faith, cut it off and throw it away! It is better for you to enter life without a hand or a foot than to keep both hands and both feet and be thrown into the eternal fire. 9And if your eye makes you lose your faith, take it out and throw it away! It is better for you to enter life with only one eye than to keep both eyes and be thrown into the fire of hell.

The Parable of the Lost Sheep
(Luke 15.3-7)

10"See that you don't despise any of these little

繳納聖殿稅

24 耶穌和門徒來到迦百農的時候,有幾個徵收聖殿稅的人來見彼得,問他:「你們的老師付不付聖殿稅呢?」

25 彼得回答:「當然付。」

彼得進屋子去的時候,耶穌先問他:「西門,誰向這世上的君王繳納關稅或人頭稅,是本國的公民呢?還是外國人呢?你的意見如何?」

26 彼得說:「是外國人。」耶穌說:「那麼,本國的公民可以免稅了。27但是我們不要冒犯這班人。你到湖邊釣魚,把釣上的第一條魚拿來,打開牠的口,你會發現一個錢幣;這錢足夠繳納你和我的聖殿稅,你就拿去給他們吧。」

誰最偉大
(可 9.33—37;路 9.46—48)

18那時候,門徒來問耶穌:「在天國裏誰最偉大?」

2 耶穌叫了一個小孩子來,讓他站在他們中間,3 說:「我實在告訴你們,除非你們回轉,變成像小孩子一樣,你們絕不能成為天國的子民。4像這個小孩子那樣謙卑的,在天國裏就是最偉大的。5為了我而接待這樣一個小孩子的,就是接待我。」

引人犯罪
(可 9.42—48;路17.1—2)

6 「無論誰使信徒中一個微不足道的人離棄我,倒不如用大磨石拴在他的脖子上,把他淹死在深海。7 這世界竟有使人離棄我的事,多麼悲慘啊!這樣的事固然會發生,但是那造成這種事的人要遭殃了!

8 「如果你的一隻手或一隻腳使你犯罪,把它砍下來,扔掉。缺手缺腳而得永恆的生命,比手腳齊全而被扔進永不熄滅的烈火中好多了。9如果你的一隻眼睛使你犯罪,把它挖出來,扔掉。只有一隻眼而得永恆的生命,比雙眼齊全被扔進地獄的火裏好多了。」

迷羊的比喻
(路15.3—7)

10 「你們要小心,不可輕看任何一個微不

ones. Their angels in heaven, I tell you, are always in the presence of my Father in heaven.*o*

12"What do you think a man does who has one hundred sheep and one of them gets lost? He will leave the other ninety-nine grazing on the hillside and go and look for the lost sheep. 13When he finds it, I tell you, he feels far happier over this one sheep than over the ninety-nine that did not get lost. 14In just the same way your*p* Father in heaven does not want any of these little ones to be lost.

When Someone Sins

15"If your brother sins against you,*q* go to him and show him his fault. But do it privately, just between yourselves. If he listens to you, you have won your brother back. 16But if he will not listen to you, take one or two other persons with you, so that 'every accusation may be upheld by the testimony of two or more witnesses,' as the scripture says. 17And if he will not listen to them, then tell the whole thing to the church. Finally, if he will not listen to the church, treat him as though he were a pagan or a tax collector.

Prohibiting and Permitting

18"And so I tell all of you: what you prohibit on earth will be prohibited in heaven, and what you permit on earth will be permitted in heaven.

19"And I tell you more: whenever two of you on earth agree about anything you pray for, it will be done for you by my Father in heaven. 20For where two or three come together in my name, I am there with them."

The Parable of the Unforgiving Servant

21Then Peter came to Jesus and asked, "Lord, if my brother keeps on sinning against me, how many times do I have to forgive him? Seven times?"

22"No, not seven times," answered Jesus, "but seventy times seven,*r* 23because the Kingdom of heaven is like this. Once there was a king who decided to check on his servants' accounts. 24He had just begun to do so when one of them was brought in who owed him millions of dollars. 25The servant did not have

足道的人。我告訴你們,在天上,他們的天使常常侍立在我天父的面前。⑩

12「你們試想,假如一個人有一百隻羊,其中的一隻迷失了,難道他不留下那九十九隻在山野間、去尋找那隻迷失的羊嗎?13我告訴你們,他找到了這一隻迷失的羊一定非常高興,比他有那九十九隻沒有迷失的羊高興多了!14同樣,你們的天父⑪不願意任何一個微不足道的人迷失。」

對待犯過錯的弟兄

15「假使你的弟兄得罪你⑫,你就去見他,指出他的錯誤;只是要在他跟你單獨在一起的時候才這樣做。假如他聽了你的勸告,你便贏得你的弟兄。16假使他不聽,你就約請其他一兩個人一起去;這樣,每一句指責的話都有兩三個人可以作證。17如果他仍然不聽,就把這件事的始末向教會報告。他對教會也不聽從的話,你就把他當作外人或稅棍看待好了。」

禁止和准許

18「所以,我告訴你們,你們在地上所禁止的,在天上也要禁止;你們在地上所准許的,在天上也要准許。

19「我再告訴你們,你們在地上,如果有兩個人同心合意地祈求,無論求甚麼,我的天父一定為你們成全。20因為,凡有兩三個人奉我的名聚集的地方,我就在他們中間。」

不饒恕人的惡僕的比喻

21那時候,彼得來問耶穌:「主啊,我的弟兄得罪我,我該饒恕他幾次呢?七次夠嗎?」

22耶穌說:「不是七次,而是七十個七次⑬。23因為天國好比以下的故事:有一個君王要跟他的臣僕結帳。24他開始算帳的時候,有人把一個欠了他好幾萬塊金幣的臣僕帶到他面前來。25因為這個人沒有錢還

---

o Some manuscripts add verse 11: For the Son of Man came to save the lost (see Lk 19.10).
p your; some manuscripts have my.
q Some manuscripts do not have against you.
r seventy times seven; or seventy-seven times.

⑩有些古卷加11節「因為人子來的目的是要拯救失喪的人」。
⑪「你們的天父」另有些古卷作「我的天父」。
⑫「你的弟兄得罪你」另有些古卷作「你的弟兄犯罪」。
⑬「七十個七次」或譯「七十七次」。

enough to pay his debt, so the king ordered him to be sold as a slave, with his wife and his children and all that he had, in order to pay the debt. ²⁶The servant fell on his knees before the king. 'Be patient with me,' he begged, 'and I will pay you everything!' ²⁷The king felt sorry for him, so he forgave him the debt and let him go.

²⁸"Then the man went out and met one of his fellow servants who owed him a few dollars. He grabbed him and started choking him. 'Pay back what you owe me!' he said. ²⁹His fellow servant fell down and begged him, 'Be patient with me, and I will pay you back!' ³⁰But he refused; instead, he had him thrown into jail until he should pay the debt. ³¹When the other servants saw what had happened, they were very upset and went to the king and told him everything. ³²So he called the servant in. 'You worthless slave!' he said. 'I forgave you the whole amount you owed me, just because you asked me to. ³³You should have had mercy on your fellow servant, just as I had mercy on you.' ³⁴The king was very angry, and he sent the servant to jail to be punished until he should pay back the whole amount."

³⁵And Jesus concluded, "That is how my Father in heaven will treat every one of you unless you forgive your brother from your heart."

Jesus Teaches about Divorce
(Mark 10.1-12)

19 When Jesus finished saying these things, he left Galilee and went to the territory of Judea on the other side of the Jordan River. ²Large crowds followed him, and he healed them there.

³Some Pharisees came to him and tried to trap him by asking, "Does our Law allow a man to divorce his wife for whatever reason he wishes?"

⁴Jesus answered, "Haven't you read the scripture that says that in the beginning the Creator made people male and female? ⁵And God said, 'For this reason a man will leave his father and mother and unite with his wife, and the two will become one.' ⁶So they are no longer two, but one. No human being must separate, then, what God has joined together."

⁷The Pharisees asked him, "Why, then, did Moses give the law for a man to hand his wife a divorce notice and send her away?"

⁸Jesus answered, "Moses gave you permission to divorce your wives because you are so hard to teach. But it was not like that at the time of creation. ⁹I tell you, then, that any man who divorces his wife for any cause other than her unfaithfulness, commits adultery if he marries some other woman."

債，王就下令把他賣了作奴隸，連同他的妻子、兒女，和一切所有的也得賣掉，好償還債務。²⁶那僕人在王面前跪下來，哀求說：『請寬容我吧！我一定會把一切債務都還清的。』²⁷王動了慈心，免了他的債，並且把他釋放了。

²⁸「那個僕人出來後，遇見一個一起當差的同伴。這個同伴欠他幾塊錢，他就抓住他，招住他的喉嚨，說：『把欠我的錢還給我！』²⁹他的同伴跪下來，哀求他說：『請寬容我吧，我一定會還清的！』³⁰但是他不肯，反而把他下在監獄裏，等他還清欠款。³¹其他的同伴看見這事的經過都很悲憤；他們去見王，把這事的始末向他報告。³²於是王叫那個僕人來，對他說：『你這個惡奴，只因你向我要求，我免了你所有的債，³³你不該寬容你的同伴，像我寬容你一樣嗎？』³⁴王十分忿怒，把他關進監獄裏受刑，等他還清全部的債。」

³⁵耶穌說：「如果你們各人不肯從心裏饒恕弟兄，我的天父也要這樣對待你們。」

有關休妻的教導
（可10·1—12）

19 耶穌講完了這些話，離開加利利，回約旦河對岸的猶太地區去。²一大羣人跟着他，他就在那裏治好了他們的病人。

³有些法利賽人來見耶穌，想陷害他，問他：「我們的法律准許丈夫用任何理由休棄妻子，對嗎？」

⁴耶穌回答：「你們沒有念過這段經文嗎？『太初，創造主造男人又造女人。』上帝說：⁵『因此，人要離開父母，跟妻子結合，兩個人成為一體。』⁶既然這樣，夫妻不再是兩個人，而是一體。所以，上帝所配合的，人不可拆開。」

⁷法利賽人問他：「那麼，為甚麼摩西給我們一條誡命，說丈夫給妻子一張休書就可以休棄她呢？」

⁸耶穌回答：「摩西准許你們休妻，是因為你們心腸太硬；但在創世之初並不是這樣的。⁹我告訴你們，除非妻子不貞，任何人休棄妻子，再去跟別的女人結婚，就是犯了姦淫。」

10His disciples said to him, "If this is how it is between a man and his wife, it is better not to marry."

11Jesus answered, "This teaching does not apply to everyone, but only to those to whom God has given it. 12For there are different reasons why men cannot marry: some, because they were born that way; others, because men made them that way; and others do not marry for the sake of the Kingdom of heaven. Let him who can accept this teaching do so."

Jesus Blesses Little Children
(Mark 10.13-16; Luke 18.15-17)

13Some people brought children to Jesus for him to place his hands on them and to pray for them, but the disciples scolded the people. 14Jesus said, "Let the children come to me and do not stop them, because the Kingdom of heaven belongs to such as these."

15He placed his hands on them and then went away.

The Rich Young Man
(Mark 10.17-31; Luke 18.18-30)

16Once a man came to Jesus. "Teacher," he asked, "what good thing must I do to receive eternal life?"

17"Why do you ask me concerning what is good?" answered Jesus. "There is only One who is good. Keep the commandments if you want to enter life."

18"What commandments?" he asked.

Jesus answered, "Do not commit murder; do not commit adultery; do not steal; do not accuse anyone falsely; 19respect your father and your mother; and love your neighbor as you love yourself."

20"I have obeyed all these commandments," the young man replied. "What else do I need to do?"

21Jesus said to him, "If you want to be perfect, go and sell all you have and give the money to the poor, and you will have riches in heaven; then come and follow me."

22When the young man heard this, he went away sad, because he was very rich.

23Jesus then said to his disciples, "I assure you: it will be very hard for rich people to enter the Kingdom of heaven. 24I repeat: it is much harder for a rich person to enter the Kingdom of God than for a camel to go through the eye of a needle."

25When the disciples heard this, they were completely amazed. "Who, then, can be

---

10 門徒說：「既然丈夫和妻子的關係是這樣，不結婚倒好。」

11 耶穌回答：「這樣的教導並不是人人都能接受的，只有得到上帝特別恩賜的人才能接受。12因為人不結婚的理由很多：有些人是生來不適於結婚的；有些人是人為的原因不能結婚；另有些人是為了天國的緣故而不結婚。能夠接受這教導的人就接受吧！」

祝福小孩子
（可10·13—16；路18·15—17）

13 有人帶着小孩子來見耶穌，要請耶穌給他們按手禱告；門徒卻責備那些人。14可是耶穌說：「讓小孩子到我這裏來，不要阻止他們，因為天國的子民正是像他們這樣的人。」

15 於是，耶穌給他們按手，然後離開那地方。

青年財主
（可10·17—31；路18·18—30）

16 有一次，有人來見耶穌，說：「老師，我該做些甚麼善事才能夠得到永恆的生命呢？」

17 耶穌回答：「你為甚麼問我關於『善』的事呢？只有一位是善的。如果你要得到永恆的生命，就應該遵守誡命。」

18 他就問：「哪些誡命呢？」

耶穌說：「不可殺人；不可姦淫；不可偷竊；不可作假證；19要孝敬父母；要愛鄰人，像愛自己一樣。」

20 那青年回答：「這一切誡命我都遵守了，還要做些甚麼呢？」

21 耶穌說：「如果你要達到更完全的地步，去賣掉你所有的產業，把錢捐給窮人，你就會有財富積存在天上；然後來跟從我。」

22 那青年一聽見這話，垂頭喪氣地走開了，因為他非常富有。

23 於是，耶穌告訴他的門徒：「我實在告訴你們，有錢人要成為天國的子民多難哪！24我再告訴你們，有錢人要成為上帝的子民，比駱駝穿過針眼還要困難！」

25 門徒聽見這話，十分驚訝，就問：「這

saved?" they asked.

26Jesus looked straight at them and answered, "This is impossible for human beings, but for God everything is possible."

27Then Peter spoke up. "Look," he said, "we have left everything and followed you. What will we have?"

28Jesus said to them, "You can be sure that when the Son of Man sits on his glorious throne in the New Age, then you twelve followers of mine will also sit on thrones, to rule the twelve tribes of Israel. 29And everyone who has left houses or brothers or sisters or father or mother or children or fields for my sake, will receive a hundred times more and will be given eternal life. 30But many who now are first will be last, and many who now are last will be first.

The Workers in the Vineyard

20 "The Kingdom of heaven is like this. Once there was a man who went out early in the morning to hire some men to work in his vineyard. 2He agreed to pay them the regular wage, a silver coin a day, and sent them to work in his vineyard. 3He went out again to the marketplace at nine o'clock and saw some men standing there doing nothing, 4so he told them, 'You also go and work in the vineyard, and I will pay you a fair wage.' 5So they went. Then at twelve o'clock and again at three o'clock he did the same thing. 6It was nearly five o'clock when he went to the marketplace and saw some other men still standing there. 'Why are you wasting the whole day here doing nothing?' he asked them. 7'No one hired us,' they answered. 'Well, then, you go and work in the vineyard,' he told them.

8"When evening came, the owner told his foreman, 'Call the workers and pay them their wages, starting with those who were hired last and ending with those who were hired first.' 9The men who had begun to work at five o'clock were paid a silver coin each. 10So when the men who were the first to be hired came to be paid, they thought they would get more; but they too were given a silver coin each. 11They took their money and started grumbling against the employer. 12'These men who were hired last worked only one hour,' they said, 'while we put up with a whole day's work in the hot sun—yet you paid them the same as you paid us!' 13'Listen, friend,' the owner answered one of them, 'I have not cheated you. After all, you agreed to do a day's work for one silver coin. 14Now take your pay and go home. I want to

樣說來，有誰能得救呢？」

26 耶穌注視着他們，說：「人是不能，但在上帝，事事都能。」

27 這時候，彼得開口說：「你看，我們已經撇下一切來跟從你了，我們將得到甚麼呢？」

28 耶穌對他們說：「我告訴你們，在將來的新時代裏，人子坐在他榮耀寶座上的時候，你們跟從我的人要坐在十二個寶座上，來審判以色列的十二個支族。29無論誰，為了我的緣故撇下了他的房屋、兄弟、姊妹、父母、兒女，或田地的，都要得到百倍的酬報，並且要得到永恆的生命。30但是，有許多在先的，將要居後，居後的，將要在先。」

葡萄園工人的比喻

20 「天國好比下面的故事：有一個葡萄園主清早出去，雇工人到他的葡萄園工作。2他約定照常例每天給他們一塊銀幣，然後打發他們到葡萄園工作。3上午九點鐘左右，他再到市場去，看見有些人站在那裏，無所事事，4就對他們說：『你們也進葡萄園工作吧，我會給你們公道的工資。』5他們就去了。後來，中午十二點鐘和下午三點鐘，他又出去，照樣雇了一些工人。6下午將近五點鐘，他又到市上去，看見還有些人站在那裏，就問他們：『為甚麼整天站在這裏無所事事呢？』他們回答：7『因為沒有人雇用我們。』他就對他們說：『那麼，你們也進葡萄園工作吧。』

8 「傍晚的時候，園主對領班說：『把工人都叫來，分發工資給他們，從最後進來的先付，到首先進來的付完為止。』9那些五點鐘才來工作的，每個人領了一塊銀幣。10輪到那些最早來工作的人來領工資，他們以為一定會多得些，可是每一個人也只領到一塊銀幣。11他們領到之後，就埋怨主人：12『這些最後進來的人只做了一小時的工，我們卻整天在烈日下勞作，而你付給他們的竟跟付給我們的一樣！』13園主回答他們當中的一個人：『朋友，我並沒有佔你便宜。你不是同意每天一塊銀幣的工資嗎？14拿你

give this man who was hired last as much as I gave you. 15Don't I have the right to do as I wish with my own money? Or are you jealous because I am generous?' "

16And Jesus concluded, "So those who are last will be first, and those who are first will be last."

Jesus Speaks a Third Time about His Death
(Mark 10.32-34; Luke 18.31-34)

17As Jesus was going up to Jerusalem, he took the twelve disciples aside and spoke to them privately, as they walked along. 18"Listen," he told them, "we are going up to Jerusalem, where the Son of Man will be handed over to the chief priests and the teachers of the Law. They will condemn him to death 19and then hand him over to the Gentiles, who will make fun of him, whip him, and crucify him; but three days later he will be raised to life."

A Mother's Request
(Mark 10.35-45)

20Then the wife of Zebedee came to Jesus with her two sons, bowed before him, and asked him for a favor.

21"What do you want?" Jesus asked her.

She answered, "Promise me that these two sons of mine will sit at your right and your left when you are King."

22"You don't know what you are asking for," Jesus answered the sons. "Can you drink the cup of suffering that I am about to drink?"

"We can," they answered.

23"You will indeed drink from my cup," Jesus told them, "but I do not have the right to choose who will sit at my right and my left. These places belong to those for whom my Father has prepared them."

24When the other ten disciples heard about this, they became angry with the two brothers. 25So Jesus called them all together and said, "You know that the rulers of the heathen have power over them, and the leaders have complete authority. 26This, however, is not the way it shall be among you. If one of you wants to be great, you must be the servant of the rest; 27and if one of you wants to be first, you must be the slave of the others– 28like the Son of Man, who did not come to be served, but to serve and to give his life to redeem many people."

的錢回家去吧！我要給那最後進來的跟給你的一樣，15難道我無權使用自己的錢嗎？爲了我待人慷慨，你就嫉妒嗎？』」

16 於是耶穌說：「這樣，那些居後的，將要在先，在先的，將要居後。」

耶穌第三次預言自己的死
（可10・32—34；路18・31—34）

17 耶穌上耶路撒冷去的時候，把他的十二個門徒帶到一邊，一面走一面告訴他們：18「你們要知道，我們現在上耶路撒冷去，人子將被出賣給祭司長和經學教師；他們要判他死刑，19然後把他交給外邦人。他們要戲弄他，鞭打他，把他釘十字架；但第三天，他將復活。」

母親的請求
（可10・35—45）

20 西庇太的妻子帶着兩個兒子來見耶穌，向他下拜，請求一件事。

21 耶穌問她：「你要甚麼？」

她回答：「求你答應，在你作王的時候，讓我這兩個兒子，一個坐在你的右邊，一個坐在你的左邊。」

22 耶穌說：「你們不知道你們在要求些甚麼。我將要喝的苦杯，你們能喝嗎？」

他們回答：「我們能！」

23 耶穌告訴他們：「你們固然要喝我的苦杯，可是我沒有權決定誰要坐在我的左右。這些座位，我父親爲誰預備就給誰。」

24 其他十個門徒聽見這樣的請求，對這兩兄弟非常惱怒。25耶穌把他們叫到面前來，對他們說：「你們知道，這世上的人有執政者管轄他們，有領導者支配他們。26可是，你們卻不是這樣。你們當中誰要作大人物，誰就得作你們的僕人；27誰要居首，誰就得作你們的奴僕。28正像人子一樣，他不是來受人侍候，而是來侍候人，並且爲了救贖衆人而獻出自己的生命。」

Jesus Heals Two Blind Men

(Mark 10.46-52; Luke 18.35-43)

29As Jesus and his disciples were leaving Jericho, a large crowd was following. 30Two blind men who were sitting by the road heard that Jesus was passing by, so they began to shout, "Son of David! Have mercy on us, sir!"

31The crowd scolded them and told them to be quiet. But they shouted even more loudly, "Son of David! Have mercy on us, sir!"

32Jesus stopped and called them. "What do you want me to do for you?" he asked them.

33"Sir," they answered, "we want you to give us our sight!"

34Jesus had pity on them and touched their eyes; at once they were able to see, and they followed him.

The Triumphant Entry into Jerusalem

(Mark 11.1-11; Luke 19.28-40; John 12.12-19)

21 As Jesus and his disciples approached Jerusalem, they came to Bethphage at the Mount of Olives. There Jesus sent two of the disciples on ahead 2with these instructions: "Go to the village there ahead of you, and at once you will find a donkey tied up with her colt beside her. Untie them and bring them to me. 3And if anyone says anything, tell him, 'The Master^s needs them'; and then he will let them go at once."

4This happened in order to make come true what the prophet had said:

5"Tell the city of Zion,

Look, your king is coming to you!

He is humble and rides on a donkey

and on a colt, the foal of a donkey."

6So the disciples went and did what Jesus had told them to do: 7they brought the donkey and the colt, threw their cloaks over them, and Jesus got on. 8A large crowd of people spread their cloaks on the road while others cut branches from the trees and spread them on the road. 9The crowds walking in front of Jesus and those walking behind began to shout, "Praise to David's Son! God bless him who comes in the name of the Lord! Praise be to God!"

10When Jesus entered Jerusalem, the whole city was thrown into an uproar. "Who is he?" the people asked.

11"This is the prophet Jesus, from Nazareth in Galilee," the crowds answered.

治好兩個盲人

（可10‧46─52；路18‧35─43）

29 他們離開耶利哥的時候，一大羣人跟着耶穌走。30有兩個盲人坐在路旁，一聽見耶穌經過，就大聲喊叫：「主啊，大衛之子，可憐我們吧！」

31 大家責備他們，不許他們作聲；可是他們更加高聲喊叫：「主啊，大衛之子，可憐我們吧！」

32 耶穌停下來，叫他們過來，問說：「你們要我為你們做甚麼？」

33 他們回答說：「主啊，請你使我們的眼睛能夠看見！」

34 耶穌動了惻隱的心，摸他們的眼睛；他們立刻能夠看見，就跟從了耶穌。

光榮進耶路撒冷

（可11‧1─11；路19‧28─40；約12‧12─19）

21 他們走近耶路撒冷，到了橄欖山地區的伯法其。耶穌派遣兩個門徒先走，2吩咐他們：「你們到前面的村莊去。你們會立刻看見一匹驢和一匹小驢拴在一起；把牠們解開，牽來給我。3如果有人對你們說甚麼，就告訴他：『主⑭要用牠們』，他會立刻讓你們把牠們牽來。」

4 這件事是要實現先知所說的：

5 去告訴錫安城的兒女：

看哪，你們的君王來了！

他謙遜地騎在驢背上，

騎在小驢的背上。

6 兩個門徒依照耶穌的話做了。7他們把驢和小驢牽了來，把自己的衣服搭在驢背上，然後請耶穌騎上去。8羣眾中有許多人把自己的衣服鋪在路上，也有些人拿樹上砍下的樹枝鋪在路上。9前行後隨的人羣大聲呼喊：「頌讚歸於大衛之子！願上帝賜福給奉主名來的那位！頌讚歸於至高的上帝！」

10 耶穌進耶路撒冷的時候，全城都騷動起來。有人問：「這個人到底是誰？」

11 羣眾回答：「他是加利利省拿撒勒的先知耶穌。」

---

s The Master; or Their owner.

⑭「主」或譯「牠們的主人」。

Jesus Goes to the Temple
(Mark 11.15-19; Luke 19.45-48; John 2.13-22)

12Jesus went into the Temple and drove out all those who were buying and selling there. He overturned the tables of the moneychangers and the stools of those who sold pigeons, 13and said to them, "It is written in the Scriptures that God said, 'My Temple will be called a house of prayer.' But you are making it a hideout for thieves!"

14The blind and the crippled came to him in the Temple, and he healed them. 15The chief priests and the teachers of the Law became angry when they saw the wonderful things he was doing and the children shouting in the Temple, "Praise to David's Son!" 16So they asked Jesus, "Do you hear what they are saying?"

"Indeed I do," answered Jesus. "Haven't you ever read this scripture? 'You have trained children and babies to offer perfect praise.' "

17Jesus left them and went out of the city to Bethany, where he spent the night.

Jesus Curses the Fig Tree
(Mark 11.12-14, 20-24)

18On his way back to the city early next morning, Jesus was hungry. 19He saw a fig tree by the side of the road and went to it, but found nothing on it except leaves. So he said to the tree, "You will never again bear fruit!" At once the fig tree dried up.

20The disciples saw this and were astounded. "How did the fig tree dry up so quickly?" they asked.

21Jesus answered, "I assure you that if you believe and do not doubt, you will be able to do what I have done to this fig tree. And not only this, but you will even be able to say to this hill, 'Get up and throw yourself in the sea,' and it will. 22If you believe, you will receive whatever you ask for in prayer."

The Question about Jesus' Authority
(Mark 11.27-33; Luke 20.1-8)

23Jesus came back to the Temple; and as he taught, the chief priests and the elders came to him and asked, "What right do you have to do these things? Who gave you such right?"

24Jesus answered them, "I will ask you just one question, and if you give me an answer, I will tell you what right I have to do these things. 25Where did John's right to baptize come from: was it from God or from human beings?"

耶穌潔淨聖殿
（可11‧15—19；路19‧45—48；約2‧13—22）

12耶穌進了聖殿，把所有在聖殿裏做買賣的人趕出去。他推倒了兌換銀錢的人的桌子和販賣鴿子的人的凳子，13對他們說：「聖經記載，上帝說：『我的聖殿要作禱告的殿』，你們卻把它變成賊窩！」

14有失明的和跛腳的到聖殿裏來找耶穌；他就治好他們。15祭司長和經學教師看見耶穌所行的許多奇蹟，又聽見兒童在聖殿裏呼喊：「頌讚歸於大衛之子！」就很惱怒。

16他們問耶穌：「你聽見他們在喊些甚麼嗎？」

耶穌回答：「聽到了。聖經上所說『你使兒童和嬰兒發出完美的頌讚』這句話，你們沒有念過嗎？」

17於是耶穌離開他們，出城到伯大尼去，在那裏過夜。

詛咒無花果樹
（可11‧12—14，20—24）

18第二天一早，在回城裏去的路上，耶穌餓了。19他看見路旁有一棵無花果樹，就走上前去，卻找不到甚麼，只有葉子。因此他指着樹說：「你永遠不會再結果子！」那棵無花果樹立刻枯乾了。

20門徒看到這情形，大感驚奇。他們問：「這棵樹為甚麼會立刻枯乾了呢？」

21耶穌回答：「我鄭重地告訴你們，如果你們信而不疑，我對這棵無花果樹所做的，你們也做得到。不但這樣，你們甚至能夠對這座山說：『起來，投到海裏去！』也一定會實現。22只要有信心，你們在禱告中所求的一切都會得到。」

質問耶穌的權柄
（可11‧27—33；路20‧1—8）

23耶穌進了聖殿，正在教導人的時候，祭司長和猶太人的長老來見他，問他：「你憑甚麼權柄做這些事？是誰給你這權柄？」

24耶穌回答他們：「我先問你們一句話，如果你們回答我，我就告訴你們我憑甚麼權柄做這些事。25約翰施洗的權是從哪裏來的？是從上帝還是從人來的呢？」

They started to argue among themselves, "What shall we say? If we answer, 'From God,' he will say to us, 'Why, then, did you not believe John?' ²⁶But if we say, 'From human beings,' we are afraid of what the people might do, because they are all convinced that John was a prophet." ²⁷So they answered Jesus, "We don't know."

And he said to them, "Neither will I tell you, then, by what right I do these things.

The Parable of the Two Sons
²⁸"Now, what do you think? There was once a man who had two sons. He went to the older one and said, 'Son, go and work in the vineyard today.' ²⁹'I don't want to,' he answered, but later he changed his mind and went. ³⁰Then the father went to the other son and said the same thing. 'Yes, sir,' he answered, but he did not go. ³¹Which one of the two did what his father wanted?"

"The older one," they answered.

So Jesus said to them, "I tell you: the tax collectors and the prostitutes are going into the Kingdom of God ahead of you. ³²For John the Baptist came to you showing you the right path to take, and you would not believe him; but the tax collectors and the prostitutes believed him. Even when you saw this, you did not later change your minds and believe him.

The Parable of the Tenants in the Vineyard
(Mark 12.1-12; Luke 20.9-19)
³³"Listen to another parable," Jesus said. "There was once a landowner who planted a vineyard, put a fence around it, dug a hole for the wine press, and built a watchtower. Then he rented the vineyard to tenants and left home on a trip. ³⁴When the time came to gather the grapes, he sent his slaves to the tenants to receive his share of the harvest. ³⁵The tenants grabbed his slaves, beat one, killed another, and stoned another. ³⁶Again the man sent other slaves, more than the first time, and the tenants treated them the same way. ³⁷Last of all he sent his son to them. 'Surely they will respect my son,' he said. ³⁸But when the tenants saw the son, they said to themselves, 'This is the owner's son. Come on, let's kill him, and we will get his property!' ³⁹So they grabbed him, threw him out of the vineyard, and killed him.

⁴⁰"Now, when the owner of the vineyard comes, what will he do to those tenants?" Jesus

他們開始彼此爭辯起來，說：「我們該怎樣回答呢？如果我們說『從上帝那裏來的』，他會說：『那麼你們為甚麼不相信約翰呢？』²⁶如果我們說『從人那裏來的』，恐怕羣眾會對付我們，因為他們都相信約翰是個先知。」²⁷於是他們回答耶穌：「我們不知道。」

耶穌對他們說：「那麼，我也不告訴你們我憑著甚麼權柄做這些事。」

兩個兒子的比喻
²⁸耶穌又說：「另有一個比喻，我想知道你們的看法。某人有兩個兒子，他對老大說：『孩子，你今天到葡萄園去工作吧。』²⁹他回答：『我不去。』可是後來他改變了主意，就去了。³⁰父親也對老二說同樣的話。老二回答：『好的，爸爸，我就去。』可是並沒有去。³¹這兩個兒子究竟哪一個遵照了父親的意思呢？」

他們說：「那大兒子。」

耶穌說：「我鄭重地告訴你們，稅棍和娼妓要比你們先成為上帝國的子民。³²因為施洗者約翰來了，他指示你們應當走的正路，你們不信他；可是稅棍和娼妓倒信了他。你們看見了仍然沒有改變心意，還是不信他。」

壞佃戶的比喻
（可12‧1-12；路20‧9-19）
³³耶穌又說：「你們再聽另一個比喻吧！有一個園主開墾了一個葡萄園，周圍用籬笆圍著，在園中挖了一個榨酒池，蓋了一座守望台，然後把葡萄園租給佃戶，自己出外旅行去了。³⁴到了葡萄成熟的季節，他打發奴僕去向佃戶收取他應得的分額。³⁵佃戶揪著他的奴僕，毆打了一個，殺了一個，又用石頭砸了另一個。³⁶園主又差派其他的奴僕去，人數比先前的更多；佃戶照樣對付了他們。³⁷最後，園主差派自己的兒子去。他想：『他們總該尊重我的兒子。』³⁸可是佃戶看見那兒子的時候，彼此說：『這個人是園主的繼承人，來吧，我們殺掉他，就可以奪取他的產業！』³⁹於是他們揪住他，把他推出園外，殺掉了。

⁴⁰「這樣，葡萄園主回來的時候，他要怎

asked.

41"He will certainly kill those evil men," they answered, "and rent the vineyard out to other tenants, who will give him his share of the harvest at the right time."

42Jesus said to them, "Haven't you ever read what the Scriptures say?

'The stone which the builders rejected as worthless
   turned out to be the most important of all.
This was done by the Lord;
   what a wonderful sight it is!'

43"And so I tell you," added Jesus, "the Kingdom of God will be taken away from you and given to a people who will produce the proper fruits."*t*

45The chief priests and the Pharisees heard Jesus' parables and knew that he was talking about them, 46so they tried to arrest him. But they were afraid of the crowds, who considered Jesus to be a prophet.

The Parable of the Wedding Feast
(Luke 14.15-24)

22 Jesus again used parables in talking to the people. 2"The Kingdom of heaven is like this. Once there was a king who prepared a wedding feast for his son. 3He sent his servants to tell the invited guests to come to the feast, but they did not want to come. 4So he sent other servants with this message for the guests: 'My feast is ready now; my steers and prize calves have been butchered, and everything is ready. Come to the wedding feast!' 5But the invited guests paid no attention and went about their business: one went to his farm, another to his store, 6while others grabbed the servants, beat them, and killed them. 7The king was very angry; so he sent his soldiers, who killed those murderers and burned down their city. 8Then he called his servants and said to them, 'My wedding feast is ready, but the people I invited did not deserve it. 9Now go to the main streets and invite to the feast as many people as you find.' 10So the servants went out into the streets and gathered all the people they could find, good and bad alike; and the wedding hall was filled with people.

11"The king went in to look at the guests and saw a man who was not wearing wedding clothes. 12'Friend, how did you get in here with-

t Some manuscripts add verse 44: Whoever falls on this stone will be cut to pieces; and if the stone falls on someone, it will crush him to dust (see Lk 20.18).

樣處置那些佃戶呢？」

41 他們說：「他一定會凶狠地殺掉這些壞人，把葡萄園轉租給那些能按時交租的佃戶。」

42 耶穌對他們說：「聖經上的話你們沒有念過嗎？

泥水匠所丟棄的這塊石頭
已成為最重要的基石。
這是主的作為，
是多麼奇妙啊！」

43 耶穌又說：「所以，我告訴你們，上帝要把他的國從你們當中奪走，賜給那些能結果子的人。（44誰跌在這塊石頭上，誰就粉身碎骨；這塊石頭掉在誰的身上，也要把誰砸爛。⑮）」

45 祭司長和法利賽人聽見耶穌講這些比喻，知道耶穌是指著他們說的，46就想逮捕他。但是他們怕群眾，因為群眾承認耶穌是先知。

喜宴的比喻
（路14・15—24）

22 耶穌又用比喻對他們說：2「天國好比一個國王為自己的兒子預備婚宴。3他派遣僕人去催促他所邀請的客人來參加婚宴，可是他們不願意來。4他再派遣另一批僕人出去，吩咐他們告訴客人：『我的筵席已經擺好了，公牛和肥畜都宰了，一切俱備，請你們來赴宴。』5可是，那些被邀請的客人還是不加理會，各忙各的：一個到田裏去，一個去看自己的鋪子，6其餘的抓住那些僕人，拳打腳踢，把他們殺了。7國王大為震怒，派兵去除滅那些凶徒，燒毀他們的城市。8然後他對僕人說：『我的筵席已經擺好，但是先前所邀請的人不配享受。9現在你們到大街上去，把碰到的人都請來赴宴。』10於是僕人到街上去，把看到的人，無論好壞都請來，使喜堂上坐滿了客人。

11「國王出來會客的時候，看見一個人沒有穿喜宴的禮服，12就問他：『朋友，你到

⑮有些古卷沒有這節。

out wedding clothes?' the king asked him. But the man said nothing. 13Then the king told the servants, 'Tie him up hand and foot, and throw him outside in the dark. There he will cry and gnash his teeth.' "

14And Jesus concluded, "Many are invited, but few are chosen."

The Question about Paying Taxes
(Mark 12.13-17; Luke 20.20-26)

15The Pharisees went off and made a plan to trap Jesus with questions. 16Then they sent to him some of their disciples and some members of Herod's party. "Teacher," they said, "we know that you tell the truth. You teach the truth about God's will for people, without worrying about what others think, because you pay no attention to anyone's status. 17Tell us, then, what do you think? Is it against our Law to pay taxes to the Roman Emperor, or not?"

18Jesus, however, was aware of their evil plan, and so he said, "You hypocrites! Why are you trying to trap me? 19Show me the coin for paying the tax!"

They brought him the coin, 20and he asked them, "Whose face and name are these?"

21"The Emperor's," they answered.

So Jesus said to them, "Well, then, pay to the Emperor what belongs to the Emperor, and pay to God what belongs to God."

22When they heard this, they were amazed; and they left him and went away.

The Question about Rising from Death
(Mark 12.18-27; Luke 20.27-40)

23That same day some Sadducees came to Jesus and claimed that people will not rise from death. 24"Teacher," they said, "Moses said that if a man who has no children dies, his brother must marry the widow so that they can have children who will be considered the dead man's children. 25Now, there were seven brothers who used to live here. The oldest got married and died without having children, so he left his widow to his brother. 26The same thing happened to the second brother, to the third, and finally to all seven. 27Last of all, the woman died. 28Now, on the day when the dead rise to life, whose wife will she be? All of them had married her."

29Jesus answered them, "How wrong you are! It is because you don't know the Scriptures or God's power. 30For when the dead rise to life, they will be like the angels in heaven and will not marry. 31Now, as for the dead rising to life:

這裏來怎麼不穿禮服呢？』那個人一言不答。13國王就吩咐侍從：『把他的手腳都綁起來，扔到外面的黑暗裏。在那裏，他要哀哭，咬牙切齒。』」

14最後，耶穌說：「被邀請的人多，但被選上的人少！」

納稅給凱撒的問題
（可12·13-17；路20·19-26）

15法利賽人出去，彼此商議要怎樣從耶穌的話找把柄來陷害他。16他們差派自己的徒弟，會同希律黨黨徒去見耶穌，問他：「老師，我們知道你是誠實人；不管人怎麼想，你總是忠實地把上帝的道教導人，因為你不看情面。17請告訴我們你的想法：向羅馬皇帝凱撒納稅是否違背我們的法律呢？」

18耶穌知道他們的惡意，就說：「假冒為善的人哪，為甚麼想陷害我？19拿一個納稅用的銀幣給我看吧！」

他們給他一個銀幣。20耶穌問他們：「這上面的像和名號是誰的？」

21他們回答：「是凱撒的。」

於是耶穌對他們說：「那麼，把凱撒的東西給凱撒，把上帝的東西給上帝。」

22他們聽見這話，十分驚訝，就離開他走了。

復活的問題
（可12·18-27；路20·27-40）

23同一天，有些不相信復活這回事的撒都該人來見耶穌，問他：24「老師，摩西教導我們，一個人死了，沒有孩子，他的弟弟必須娶寡嫂為妻，替哥哥傳宗接代。25從前，我們這裏有兄弟七人，老大結了婚，死了，沒有孩子，留下寡婦給他弟弟；26老二、老三也是這樣，一直到老七，情形相同。27最後，那個女人也死了。28請問，既然他們都娶過她，在復活的日子，她算是哪一個的妻子呢？」

29耶穌回答他們：「你們錯了！你們不明白聖經，也不知道上帝的權能。30在死人復活的時候，他們要跟天上的天使一樣，也不娶也不嫁。31關於死人復活的事，你們沒有

haven't you ever read what God has told you? He said, ³²'I am the God of Abraham, the God of Isaac, and the God of Jacob.' He is the God of the living, not of the dead."

33When the crowds heard this, they were amazed at his teaching.

The Great Commandment
(Mark 12.28-34; Luke 10.25-28)

34When the Pharisees heard that Jesus had silenced the Sadducees, they came together, 35and one of them, a teacher of the Law, tried to trap him with a question. 36"Teacher," he asked, "which is the greatest commandment in the Law?"

37Jesus answered, " 'Love the Lord your God with all your heart, with all your soul, and with all your mind.' 38This is the greatest and the most important commandment. 39The second most important commandment is like it: 'Love your neighbor as you love yourself.' 40The whole Law of Moses and the teachings of the prophets depend on these two commandments."

The Question about the Messiah
(Mark 12.35-37; Luke 20.41-44)

41When some Pharisees gathered together, Jesus asked them, 42"What do you think about the Messiah? Whose descendant is he?"

"He is David's descendant," they answered.

43"Why, then," Jesus asked, "did the Spirit inspire David to call him 'Lord'? David said,

44'The Lord said to my Lord:
    Sit here at my right side
    until I put your enemies under your feet.'

45If, then, David called him 'Lord,' how can the Messiah be David's descendant?"

46No one was able to give Jesus any answer, and from that day on no one dared to ask him any more questions.

Jesus Warns against the Teachers of the Law and the Pharisees
(Mark 12.38-39; Luke 11.43, 46; 20.45-46)

23 Then Jesus spoke to the crowds and to his disciples. 2"The teachers of the Law and the Pharisees are the authorized interpreters of Moses' Law. 3So you must obey and follow everything they tell you to do; do not, however, imitate their actions, because they don't practice what they preach. 4They tie onto people's backs loads that are heavy and hard to carry,

念過上帝告訴你們的話嗎？³²上帝說：『我是亞伯拉罕的上帝，以撒的上帝，雅各的上帝。』這意思是說，上帝是活人的上帝，不是死人的上帝。」

33 羣衆聽到這樣的教訓，都覺得驚奇。

最大的誡命
（可12‧28-34；路10‧25-28）

34 法利賽人聽見耶穌堵住了撒都該人的口，就聚集在一起。³⁵其中一個法律教師想用一個問題來陷害耶穌。³⁶他問：「老師，在摩西法律當中，哪一條誡命是最重要的？」

37 耶穌說：「『你要全心、全情、全意愛主─你的上帝。』³⁸這是第一條最重要的誡命。³⁹第二條也一樣重要：『你要愛鄰人，像愛自己一樣。』⁴⁰摩西全部的法律和先知的教訓都是以這兩條誡命爲根據的。」

有關基督的問題
（可12‧35-37；路20‧41-44）

41 法利賽人聚集在一起的時候，耶穌問他們：⁴²「你們對基督的看法怎樣？他是誰的子孫呢？」

他們回答：「他是大衞的子孫。」

43 耶穌說：「那麼，爲甚麼聖靈感動大衞稱呼他爲『主』呢？大衞說：

44 主對我主說：
    你坐在我的右邊，
    等我使你的仇敵屈服在你腳下。

45 如果大衞稱他爲『主』，基督又怎麼會是大衞的子孫呢？」

46 沒有人能夠說一句話來回答耶穌的問題。從那天起，沒有人敢再向他提出難題了。

譴責經學教師和法利賽人
（可12‧38-39；路11‧43，46；20‧45-46）

23 耶穌對羣衆和他的門徒說：²「經學教師和法利賽人站在摩西的地位上解釋法律，³你們要遵從他們的教訓，但是不要模仿他們的行爲；因爲他們只會說，不會做。⁴他們捆紮難背的重擔擱在別人的肩膀上，自己卻不肯動一根手指頭去減輕他們的負

yet they aren't willing even to lift a finger to help them carry those loads. ⁵They do everything so that people will see them. Look at the straps with scripture verses on them which they wear on their foreheads and arms, and notice how large they are! Notice also how long are the tassels on their cloaks!ᵘ ⁶They love the best places at feasts and the reserved seats in the synagogues; ⁷they love to be greeted with respect in the marketplaces and to have people call them 'Teacher.' ⁸You must not be called 'Teacher,' because you are all equal and have only one Teacher. ⁹And you must not call anyone here on earth 'Father,' because you have only the one Father in heaven. ¹⁰Nor should you be called 'Leader,' because your one and only leader is the Messiah. ¹¹The greatest one among you must be your servant. ¹²Whoever makes himself great will be humbled, and whoever humbles himself will be made great.

Jesus Condemns Their Hypocrisy
(Mark 12.40; Luke 11.39-42, 44, 52; 20.47)

13"How terrible for you, teachers of the Law and Pharisees! You hypocrites! You lock the door to the Kingdom of heaven in people's faces, but you yourselves don't go in, nor do you allow in those who are trying to enter!ᵛ

15"How terrible for you, teachers of the Law and Pharisees! You hypocrites! You sail the seas and cross whole countries to win one convert; and when you succeed, you make him twice as deserving of going to hell as you yourselves are!

16"How terrible for you, blind guides! You teach, 'If someone swears by the Temple, he isn't bound by his vow; but if he swears by the gold in the Temple, he is bound.' ¹⁷Blind fools! Which is more important, the gold or the Temple which makes the gold holy? ¹⁸You also teach, 'If someone swears by the altar, he isn't bound by his vow; but if he swears by the gift on the altar, he is bound.' ¹⁹How blind you are! Which is the more important, the gift or the altar which makes the gift holy? ²⁰So then, when a person swears by the altar, he is swearing by it and by all the gifts on it; ²¹and when he swears by the Temple, he is swearing by it and by God, who lives there; ²²and when someone swears by heaven, he is swearing by God's throne and by him who sits on it.

---

u TASSELS ON THEIR CLOAKS: *These tassels were worn as a sign of devotion to God (see Nu 15.37-41).*

v *Some manuscripts add verse 14:* How terrible for you, teachers of the Law and Pharisees! You hypocrites! You take advantage of widows and rob them of their homes, and then make a show of saying long prayers! Because of this your punishment will be all the worse! *(see Mk 12.40).*

擔。⁵他們無論做甚麼事都是給人看的。他們佩戴大經文袋，又加長衣裳的繸子；⁶他們喜歡宴會上的首座和會堂裏的特別座位；⁷他們喜歡人家在公共場所向他們致敬問安，稱呼他們『老師』。⁸其實，你們不應該被稱爲『老師』；因爲你們彼此都是同道，只有一位是你們的『老師』。⁹你們不要稱呼地上的任何人爲『父親』，因爲你們只有一位在天上的『父親』。

¹⁰「你們也不應該被稱爲『導師』，因爲你們惟一的『導師』就是基督。¹¹你們當中誰是最偉大的，誰就得作你們的僕人。¹²上帝要把自高的人降爲卑微，又高舉甘心自卑的人。」

譴責僞善的人
（可12‧40；路11‧39—42，44，52；20‧47）

13「你們這班僞善的經學教師和法利賽人要遭殃了！你們當着人家的面把天國的門關起來，自己不進去，也不讓想進去的人進去！⑭

15「你們這班僞善的經學教師和法利賽人要遭殃了！爲了說服一個人入敎，你們不惜走遍天涯海角，等他皈依之後，你們卻把他塑造得比你們加倍的壞，比你們更該受地獄的刑罰。

16「你們這班瞎眼的嚮導要遭殃了！你們說：『如果有人指着聖殿發誓，可以不算數；如果指着聖殿裏的金子發誓，就必須遵守。』¹⁷你們這些瞎眼的傻子！試問金子重要呢？還是使金子成爲聖物的聖殿重要呢？¹⁸你們又說：『如果有人指着祭壇發誓，可以不算數；如果指着祭壇上的供物發誓，就必須遵守。』¹⁹你們這班瞎子啊！究竟供物重要呢？還是使供物成聖的祭壇重要呢？²⁰要知道，人指着祭壇發誓就是指着祭壇和壇上的一切供物發誓；²¹指着聖殿發誓就是指着聖殿和住在裏面的上帝發誓；²²指着天發誓就是指着上帝的寶座和坐在上面的上帝發誓。

---

⑭有些古卷加14節「你們這班僞善的經學敎師和法利賽人要遭殃了！你們佔寡婦的便宜，呑沒她們的家產，卻在人面前表演長篇的禱告，所以你們一定會受更嚴厲的懲罰！」

23"How terrible for you, teachers of the Law and Pharisees! You hypocrites! You give to God one tenth even of the seasoning herbs, such as mint, dill, and cumin, but you neglect to obey the really important teachings of the Law, such as justice and mercy and honesty. These you should practice, without neglecting the others. 24Blind guides! You strain a fly out of your drink, but swallow a camel!

25"How terrible for you, teachers of the Law and Pharisees! You hypocrites! You clean the outside of your cup and plate, while the inside is full of what you have gotten by violence and selfishness. 26Blind Pharisee! Clean what is inside the cup first, and then the outside will be clean too!

27"How terrible for you, teachers of the Law and Pharisees! You hypocrites! You are like whitewashed tombs, which look fine on the outside but are full of bones and decaying corpses on the inside. 28In the same way, on the outside you appear good to everybody, but inside you are full of hypocrisy and sins.

Jesus Predicts Their Punishment
(Luke 11.47-51)

29"How terrible for you, teachers of the Law and Pharisees! You hypocrites! You make fine tombs for the prophets and decorate the monuments of those who lived good lives; 30and you claim that if you had lived during the time of your ancestors, you would not have done what they did and killed the prophets. 31So you actually admit that you are the descendants of those who murdered the prophets! 32Go on, then, and finish up what your ancestors started! 33You snakes and children of snakes! How do you expect to escape from being condemned to hell? 34And so I tell you that I will send you prophets and wise men and teachers; you will kill some of them, crucify others, and whip others in the synagogues and chase them from town to town. 35As a result, the punishment for the murder of all innocent people will fall on you, from the murder of innocent Abel to the murder of Zechariah son of Berechiah, whom you murdered between the Temple and the altar. 36I tell you indeed: the punishment for all these murders will fall on the people of this day!

Jesus' Love for Jerusalem
(Luke 13.34-35)

37"Jerusalem, Jerusalem! You kill the prophets and stone the messengers God has sent you! How many times I wanted to put my arms around all your people, just as a hen

23「你們這班偽善的經學教師和法利賽人要遭殃了!你們連調味的香料,如薄荷、大茴香、小茴香等物都獻上十分之一給上帝,但是法律上真正重要的教訓,如正義、仁慈、信實,你們反而不遵守。這些重要的教訓才是你們所必須實行的,至於其他的,也不可忽略。24瞎眼的嚮導啊,你們從飲料中濾出一隻小蚊子,卻把一頭駱駝吞下去!

25「你們這班偽善的經學教師和法利賽人要遭殃了!你們把杯盤的外面洗得乾乾淨淨,裏面卻盛滿了貪慾和放縱。26瞎眼的法利賽人哪!先洗淨杯子的裏面,外面也就乾淨了。

27「你們這班偽善的經學教師和法利賽人要遭殃了!你們好像那粉刷了的墳墓,外面好看,裏面卻全是死人的骨頭和腐爛的東西。28同樣,外表看起來你們十分公正,內心卻裝滿着虛偽和邪惡。」

預言他們將受的刑罰
(路11·47—51)

29「你們這班偽善的經學教師和法利賽人要遭殃了!你們替先知築墳,為聖賢修墓,30而且說:『如果我們生活在祖先的時代,我們絕不至於像他們那樣殺害先知。』31可見你們已經承認自己就是那些殺害先知的人的子孫。32你們儘管做下去,去完成你們祖宗的暴行吧!33毒蛇和毒蛇的子孫哪!你們怎能逃脫地獄的刑罰呢?34你們聽吧,我要派遣先知、哲人,和教師到你們這裏來,有的要被你們殺害,有的要被你們釘十字架,有的要在你們的會堂裏受鞭打,從一個地方被趕到另一個地方。35這樣,一切殺戮無辜的懲罰要落在你們身上一就是從無辜的亞伯,直到你們在聖殿和祭壇之間所殺的巴拉加的兒子撒迦利亞的血債為止。36我實在告訴你們,這些懲罰都要歸給這一時代的人。」

為耶路撒冷哀哭
(路13·34—35)

37「耶路撒冷啊,耶路撒冷啊,你殺了先知,又用石頭打死上帝差派到你這裏來的使者!我多少次要保護你的子女,像母雞把小

gathers her chicks under her wings, but you would not let me! [38]And so your Temple will be abandoned and empty. [39]From now on, I tell you, you will never see me again until you say, 'God bless him who comes in the name of the Lord.' "

Jesus Speaks of the Destruction of the Temple
(Mark 13.1-2; Luke 21.5-6)

24 Jesus left and was going away from the Temple when his disciples came to him to call his attention to its buildings. [2]"Yes," he said, "you may well look at all these. I tell you this: not a single stone here will be left in its place; every one of them will be thrown down."

Troubles and Persecutions
(Mark 13.3-13; Luke 21.7-19)

[3]As Jesus sat on the Mount of Olives, the disciples came to him in private. "Tell us when all this will be," they asked, "and what will happen to show that it is the time for your coming and the end of the age."

[4]Jesus answered, "Watch out, and do not let anyone fool you. [5]Many men, claiming to speak for me, will come and say, 'I am the Messiah!' and they will fool many people. [6]You are going to hear the noise of battles close by and the news of battles far away; but do not be troubled. Such things must happen, but they do not mean that the end has come. [7]Countries will fight each other; kingdoms will attack one another. There will be famines and earthquakes everywhere. [8]All these things are like the first pains of childbirth.

[9]"Then you will be arrested and handed over to be punished and be put to death. Everyone will hate you because of me. [10]Many will give up their faith at that time; they will betray one another and hate one another. [11]Then many false prophets will appear and fool many people. [12]Such will be the spread of evil that many people's love will grow cold. [13]But whoever holds out to the end will be saved. [14]And this Good News about the Kingdom will be preached through all the world for a witness to all people; and then the end will come.

The Awful Horror
(Mark 13.14-23; Luke 21.20-24)

[15]"You will see 'The Awful Horror' of which the prophet Daniel spoke. It will be standing in the holy place." (Note to the reader: understand what this means!) [16]"Then those who are

雞聚集在翅膀下一樣。可是你們不願意！[38]瞧吧，你們的殿宇將成爲人煙絕跡的荒場。[39]我告訴你們，你們從此再也見不到我，一直到你們說：『願上帝賜福給奉主名而來的那位！』」

預言聖殿的毀滅
（可13‧1－2；路21‧5－6）

24 耶穌從聖殿出來，正要離開，門徒們來到他面前，指着聖殿的建築給他看。[2]耶穌對他們說：「你們不是都看見這些建築嗎？我實在告訴你們，這地方的每一塊石頭都要被拆下來，沒有一塊石頭會留在另一塊上面。」

災難和迫害
（可13‧3－13；路21‧7－19）

[3]耶穌在橄欖山上坐着；門徒們私下來問他：「請告訴我們，這事甚麼時候會發生呢？你的來臨和世界的終局有甚麼預兆呢？」

[4]耶穌回答：「你們要當心，不要受人愚弄。[5]因爲有許多人要假冒我的名來，說：『我是基督』，因而愚弄了許多人。[6]你們會聽見附近打仗的風聲和遠方戰爭的消息。你們不用害怕，這種事必然發生，但這不是說歷史的終點已經到了。[7]一個民族要跟另一個民族爭戰，一個國家要攻打另一個國家；到處會有饑荒和地震。[8]這一切事情的發生正像產婦陣痛的開始一樣。

[9]「那時候，你們要被逮捕，受酷刑，被殺害。爲了我的緣故，天下的人都要憎恨你們。[10]許多人要放棄他們的信仰，彼此出賣，彼此仇視。[11]許多假先知要出現，迷惑人心。[12]因爲邪惡氾濫，許多人的愛心會漸漸冷淡了。[13]但是，堅忍到底的人必然得救。[14]天國的福音先要傳遍天下，向全人類作見證，然後歷史的終局才會臨到。」

大災難
（可13‧14－23；路21‧20－24）

[15]「你們看見先知但以理所說的那『毀滅性的可憎之物』站在神聖地方的時候（讀者必須領會這句話的含意），[16]住在猶太地區

in Judea must run away to the hills. [17]Someone who is on the roof of a house must not take the time to go down and get any belongings from the house. [18]Someone who is in the field must not go back to get a cloak. [19]How terrible it will be in those days for women who are pregnant and for mothers with little babies! [20]Pray to God that you will not have to run away during the winter or on a Sabbath! [21]For the trouble at that time will be far more terrible than any there has ever been, from the beginning of the world to this very day. Nor will there ever be anything like it again. [22]But God has already reduced the number of days; had he not done so, nobody would survive. For the sake of his chosen people, however, God will reduce the days.

[23]"Then, if anyone says to you, 'Look, here is the Messiah!' or 'There he is!'–do not believe it. [24]For false Messiahs and false prophets will appear; they will perform great miracles and wonders in order to deceive even God's chosen people, if possible. [25]Listen! I have told you this ahead of time.

[26]"Or, if people should tell you, 'Look, he is out in the desert!'–don't go there; or if they say, 'Look, he is hiding here!'–don't believe it. [27]For the Son of Man will come like the lightning which flashes across the whole sky from the east to the west.

[28]"Wherever there is a dead body, the vultures will gather.

The Coming of the Son of Man
(Mark 13.24-27; Luke 21.25-28)

[29]"Soon after the trouble of those days, the sun will grow dark, the moon will no longer shine, the stars will fall from heaven, and the powers in space will be driven from their courses. [30]Then the sign of the Son of Man will appear in the sky; and all the peoples of earth will weep as they see the Son of Man coming on the clouds of heaven with power and great glory. [31]The great trumpet will sound, and he will send out his angels to the four corners of the earth, and they will gather his chosen people from one end of the world to the other.

The Lesson of the Fig Tree
(Mark 13.28-31; Luke 21.29-33)

[32]"Let the fig tree teach you a lesson. When its branches become green and tender and it starts putting out leaves, you know that summer is near. [33]In the same way, when you see all these things, you will know that the time is

的,該逃到山上避難;[17]在屋頂上的,不要下到屋子裏去拿東西;[18]在農場的,也不要回家拿外衣。[19]在那些日子裏,懷孕的女人和哺育嬰兒的母親都苦了![20]你們要懇求上帝不讓這些事在冬天或安息日發生。[21]因為那些日子的災難是創世以來未曾有過的,將來也絕不會再有。[22]要是上帝沒有縮短那些災難的日子,沒有人能夠存活。但是為了他所揀選的子民,上帝會縮短那些日子的。

[23]「如果有人對你們說:『瞧,基督在這裏!瞧,基督在那裏!』不要相信他。[24]因為假基督和假先知將出現,他們要行大的神蹟奇事來迷惑人;可能的話,甚至迷惑上帝所揀選的子民。[25]記住!我已經預先警告你們了。

[26]「如果有人告訴你們:『瞧,基督在曠野!』你們不要出去;或者說:『瞧,基督在屋子裏!』你們也不要相信。[27]因為人子來臨的時候會像閃電一樣,一剎那間,從東到西橫掃天空。

[28]「屍首在哪裏,禿鷹也會聚在那裏。」

人子的來臨
(可13‧24—27;路21‧25—28)

[29]「那些災難的日子一過去,太陽就要變黑,月亮不再發光,星星從天上墜落,太空的系統也都要搖動。[30]那時候,人子來臨的記號要在天際出現。地上萬族萬民都要哀哭;他們要看見人子充滿着能力和榮耀駕着天上的雲降臨。[31]號角的聲音要大響,他要差遣天使到天涯海角,從世界的這一頭到世界的那一頭,召集他所揀選的子民。」

無花果樹的教訓
(可13‧28—31;路21‧29—33)

[32]「你們要從無花果樹學一個教訓。當枝子呈現嫩綠的顏色,長出新葉的時候,你們知道夏天就要到了。[33]同樣,你們看見這一

near, ready to begin.ʷ ³⁴Remember that all these things will happen before the people now living have all died. ³⁵Heaven and earth will pass away, but my words will never pass away.

No One Knows the Day and Hour
(Mark 13.32-37; Luke 17.26-30, 34-36)

36"No one knows, however, when that day and hour will come–neither the angels in heaven nor the Son;ˣ the Father alone knows. ³⁷The coming of the Son of Man will be like what happened in the time of Noah. ³⁸In the days before the flood people ate and drank, men and women married, up to the very day Noah went into the boat; ³⁹yet they did not realize what was happening until the flood came and swept them all away. That is how it will be when the Son of Man comes. ⁴⁰At that time two men will be working in a field: one will be taken away, the other will be left behind. ⁴¹Two women will be at a mill grinding meal: one will be taken away, the other will be left behind. ⁴²Watch out, then, because you do not know what day your Lord will come. ⁴³If the owner of a house knew the time when the thief would come, you can be sure that he would stay awake and not let the thief break into his house. ⁴⁴So then, you also must always be ready, because the Son of Man will come at an hour when you are not expecting him.

The Faithful or the Unfaithful Servant
(Luke 12.41-48)

45"Who, then, is a faithful and wise servant? It is the one that his master has placed in charge of the other servants to give them their food at the proper time. ⁴⁶How happy that servant is if his master finds him doing this when he comes home! ⁴⁷Indeed, I tell you, the master will put that servant in charge of all his property. ⁴⁸But if he is a bad servant, he will tell himself that his master will not come back for a long time, ⁴⁹and he will begin to beat his fellow servants and to eat and drink with drunkards. ⁵⁰Then that servant's master will come back one day when the servant does not expect him and at a time he does not know. ⁵¹The master will cut him in piecesʸ and make him share the fate of the hypocrites. There he will cry and gnash his teeth.

---

w the time is near, ready to begin; or he is near, ready to come.
x Some manuscripts do not have nor the Son.
y cut him in pieces; or throw him out.

切現象就知道時候快到了⑰，就在門口了。³⁴你們要記住：這一代的人還沒有都去世以前，這一切事就要發生。³⁵天地要消失，我的話卻永不消失。」

那日那時沒有人知道
（可13‧32—37；路17‧26—30，34—36）

36「至於那要臨到的日子和時間，沒有人知道；天上的天使不知道，兒子也不知道⑱，只有父親知道。³⁷人子的來臨要像挪亞時代所發生的事一樣。³⁸洪水沒有來以前，人照常吃喝嫁娶，直到挪亞進入方舟那一天；³⁹他們糊裏糊塗，洪水來了，把他們都沖走。人子的來臨也是這樣。⁴⁰那時候，兩個人在田裏工作，一個被接去，另一個留下；⁴¹兩個女子在推磨，一個被接去，另一個留下。⁴²所以，要警醒，因為你們不知道主要在哪一天來臨。⁴³要記住這一點：一家的主人要是知道小偷晚上甚麼時候要來，他一定會警醒，不讓小偷破門而入。⁴⁴所以，你們也應該隨時準備好，因為人子要在你們料想不到的時間忽然來臨。」

可靠和不可靠的僕人
（路12‧41—48）

45「那麼，誰是又可靠又機智的僕人呢？就是受主人指派來管理其他僕人、按時分配糧食的那一個人。⁴⁶主人回來的時候，看見這僕人這樣忠於職守，這僕人是多麼有福啊！⁴⁷我實在告訴你們，主人要派他管理所有的產業。⁴⁸但是，如果他是一個壞僕人，他會在心裏盤算，『也許主人不會那麼早回來』，⁴⁹於是動手毆打其他的夥伴，跟酒徒吃喝玩樂。⁵⁰可是在他料想不到的日子，在他不知道的時間，主人回來了。⁵¹主人要重重地責打他⑲，使他跟假冒為善的人一同受刑罰；在那裏，他要哀哭，咬牙切齒。」

---

⑰「時候快到了」或譯「他就要來了」。
⑱有些古卷沒有「兒子也不知道」。
⑲「要重重地責打他」或譯「要把他趕出去」。

The Parable of the Ten Young Women

25 "At that time the Kingdom of heaven will be like this. Once there were ten young women who took their oil lamps and went out to meet the bridegroom. ²Five of them were foolish, and the other five were wise. ³The foolish ones took their lamps but did not take any extra oil with them, ⁴while the wise ones took containers full of oil for their lamps. ⁵The bridegroom was late in coming, so they began to nod and fall asleep.

⁶"It was already midnight when the cry rang out, 'Here is the bridegroom! Come and meet him!' ⁷The ten young women woke up and trimmed their lamps. ⁸Then the foolish ones said to the wise ones, 'Let us have some of your oil, because our lamps are going out.' ⁹'No, indeed,' the wise ones answered, 'there is not enough for you and for us. Go to the store and buy some for yourselves.' ¹⁰So the foolish ones went off to buy some oil; and while they were gone, the bridegroom arrived. The five who were ready went in with him to the wedding feast, and the door was closed.

¹¹"Later the others arrived. 'Sir, sir! Let us in!' they cried out. ¹²'Certainly not! I don't know you,' the bridegroom answered."

¹³And Jesus concluded, "Watch out, then, because you do not know the day or the hour."

The Parable of the Three Servants
(Luke 19.11-27)

¹⁴"At that time the Kingdom of heaven will be like this. Once there was a man who was about to leave home on a trip; he called his servants and put them in charge of his property. ¹⁵He gave to each one according to his ability: to one he gave five thousand gold coins, to another he gave two thousand, and to another he gave one thousand. Then he left on his trip. ¹⁶The servant who had received five thousand coins went at once and invested his money and earned another five thousand. ¹⁷In the same way the servant who had received two thousand coins earned another two thousand. ¹⁸But the servant who had received one thousand coins went off, dug a hole in the ground, and hid his master's money.

¹⁹"After a long time the master of those servants came back and settled accounts with them. ²⁰The servant who had received five thousand coins came in and handed over the other five thousand. 'You gave me five thousand coins, sir,' he said. 'Look! Here are another five thousand that I have earned.' ²¹'Well done, you good and faithful servant!'

十個少女的比喻

25 「 在那日，天國好比以下的故事：有十個少女手裏拿着油燈，出去迎接新郎。² 其中五個是愚笨的，五個是聰明的。³ 愚笨的帶了燈，卻沒有預備足夠的油；⁴ 聰明的帶了燈，另外又帶幾瓶油。⁵ 新郎來遲了，少女們都打盹，睡着了。

⁶ 「 到了半夜，有人呼喊：『新郎到啦，你們都出來迎接他！』⁷ 十個少女都醒過來，挑亮她們的燈。⁸ 那時候，愚笨的對聰明的說：『請分一點油給我們吧，因為我們的燈快要熄滅了。』⁹ 那些聰明的回答說：『不行，我們的油實在不夠分給你們，你們自己到鋪子裏去買吧。』¹⁰ 愚笨的少女去買油的時候，新郎到了。那五個有準備的少女跟新郎一起進去，同赴婚宴，門就關上了。

¹¹ 「 其他的少女隨後也到了。她們喊着：『先生，先生，請給我們開門！』¹² 新郎回答：『我根本不認識你們。』」

¹³ 耶穌說：「 所以，你們要警醒，因為你們並不知道那日子、那時間會在甚麼時候來臨。」

三個僕人的比喻
(路19．11—27)

¹⁴ 「 天國又好比以下的故事：有一個人要出外旅行，他叫僕人來，把產業交給他們。¹⁵ 他按照他們各人的才幹，一個給了五千塊金幣，一個給了兩千，一個給了一千，然後動身走了。¹⁶ 那領五千塊金幣的，立刻去做生意，另外賺了五千。¹⁷ 同樣，那領兩千塊金幣的，另外也賺了兩千。¹⁸ 可是那領一千塊金幣的，出去，在地上挖了一個洞，把主人的錢埋起來。

¹⁹ 「 過了許久，那幾個僕人的主人回來，跟他們結帳。²⁰ 那領五千塊金幣的進來，帶來了另外的五千，說：『主人，你給我五千塊金幣，你看，我另外賺了五千。』²¹ 主人說：『很好，你這又好又可靠的僕人！你在

said his master. 'You have been faithful in managing small amounts, so I will put you in charge of large amounts. Come on in and share my happiness.' ²²Then the servant who had been given two thousand coins came in and said, 'You gave me two thousand coins, sir. Look! Here are another two thousand that I have earned.' ²³'Well done, you good and faithful servant!' said his master. 'You have been faithful in managing small amounts, so I will put you in charge of large amounts. Come on in and share my happiness!' ²⁴Then the servant who had received one thousand coins came in and said, 'Sir, I know you are a hard man; you reap harvests where you did not plant, and you gather crops where you did not scatter seed. ²⁵I was afraid, so I went off and hid your money in the ground. Look! Here is what belongs to you.' ²⁶'You bad and lazy servant!' his master said. 'You knew, did you, that I reap harvests where I did not plant, and gather crops where I did not scatter seed? ²⁷Well, then, you should have deposited my money in the bank, and I would have received it all back with interest when I returned. ²⁸Now, take the money away from him and give it to the one who has ten thousand coins. ²⁹For to every person who has something, even more will be given, and he will have more than enough; but the person who has nothing, even the little that he has will be taken away from him. ³⁰As for this useless servant–throw him outside in the darkness; there he will cry and gnash his teeth.'

The Final Judgment

31"When the Son of Man comes as King and all the angels with him, he will sit on his royal throne, ³²and the people of all the nations will be gathered before him. Then he will divide them into two groups, just as a shepherd separates the sheep from the goats. ³³He will put the righteous people at his right and the others at his left. ³⁴Then the King will say to the people on his right, 'Come, you that are blessed by my Father! Come and possess the kingdom which has been prepared for you ever since the creation of the world. ³⁵I was hungry and you fed me, thirsty and you gave me a drink; I was a stranger and you received me in your homes, ³⁶naked and you clothed me; I was sick and you took care of me, in prison and you visited me.' ³⁷The righteous will then answer him, 'When, Lord, did we ever see you hungry and feed you, or thirsty and give you a drink? ³⁸When did we ever see you a stranger and welcome you in our homes, or naked and clothe you? ³⁹When did we ever see you sick or in prison, and visit you?' ⁴⁰The King will reply, 'I tell you, whenever you did this for one of the least

小數目上可靠，我要委託你經管大數目。進來分享你主人的喜樂吧！』²²那領兩千塊金幣的進來，說：『主人，你給我兩千塊金幣，你看，我另外賺了兩千。』²³主人說：『很好，你這又好又可靠的僕人，你在小數目上可靠，我要委託你經管大數目。進來分享你主人的喜樂吧！』²⁴這時候，那領一千塊金幣的僕人也進來，說：『主人，我知道你是個嚴厲的人；沒有栽種的地方，你要收割，沒有撒種的地方，你也要收聚。²⁵我害怕，就把你的錢埋在地下。請看，你的錢就在這裏。』²⁶他的主人說：『你這又壞又懶的僕人！旣然你知道我在沒有栽種的地方也要收割，沒有撒種的地方也要收聚，²⁷你就該把我的錢存入銀行，等我回來的時候，可以連本帶利一起收回。²⁸你們把他的金幣拿過來，給那個有一萬塊金幣的。²⁹因為，那已經有的，要給他更多，讓他豐富有餘；而那沒有的，連他所有的一點點也要奪走。³⁰至於這個無用的僕人，把他趕到外面的黑暗裏去；在那裏，他要哀哭，咬牙切齒。』」

最後的審判

31「在人子作王、天使跟他一起來臨的時候，他要坐在榮耀的寶座上；³²地上萬民都要聚集在他面前。他要把他們分為兩羣，好像牧羊人從山羊中把綿羊分別出來一樣。³³他要把綿羊放在右邊，山羊放在左邊。³⁴然後，王要對他右邊的人說：『蒙我父親賜福的人哪，你們來吧！來承受從創世以來就為你們預備的國度。³⁵因為我餓了，你們給我吃，渴了，你們給我喝；我流落異鄉，你們收留我；³⁶我赤身露體，你們給我穿；我害病，你們照顧我；我坐牢，你們來探望我。』³⁷那時候，那些義人要回答：『主啊，我們甚麼時候看到你餓了，給你吃？渴了，給你喝？³⁸甚麼時候看到你流落異鄉而收留你？看到你赤身露體而給你穿？³⁹我們甚麼時候看到你害病或坐牢而去探望你呢？』⁴⁰王要回答：『我鄭重地告訴你們，旣然你們為我的跟從者中最微小的一人做，就

important of these followers of mine, you did it for me!'

41"Then he will say to those on his left, 'Away from me, you that are under God's curse! Away to the eternal fire which has been prepared for the Devil and his angels! 42I was hungry but you would not feed me, thirsty but you would not give me a drink; 43I was a stranger but you would not welcome me in your homes, naked but you would not clothe me; I was sick and in prison but you would not take care of me.' 44Then they will answer him, 'When, Lord, did we ever see you hungry or thirsty or a stranger or naked or sick or in prison, and we would not help you?' 45The King will reply, 'I tell you, whenever you refused to help one of these least important ones, you refused to help me.' 46These, then, will be sent off to eternal punishment, but the righteous will go to eternal life."

The Plot against Jesus
(Mark 14.1-2; Luke 22.1-2; John 11.45-53)

26 When Jesus had finished teaching all these things, he said to his disciples, 2In two days, as you know, it will be the Passover Festival, and the Son of Man will be handed over to be crucified."

3Then the chief priests and the elders met together in the palace of Caiaphas, the High Priest, 4and made plans to arrest Jesus secretly and put him to death. 5"We must not do it during the festival," they said, "or the people will riot."

Jesus Is Anointed at Bethany
(Mark 14.3-9; John 12.1-8)

6Jesus was in Bethany at the house of Simon, a man who had suffered from a dreaded skin disease. 7While Jesus was eating, a woman came to him with an alabaster jar filled with an expensive perfume, which she poured on his head. 8The disciples saw this and became angry. "Why all this waste?" they asked. 9"This perfume could have been sold for a large amount and the money given to the poor!"

10Jesus knew what they were saying, and so he said to them, "Why are you bothering this woman? It is a fine and beautiful thing that she has done for me. 11You will always have poor people with you, but you will not always have me. 12What she did was to pour this perfume on my body to get me ready for burial. 13Now, I assure you that wherever this gospel is preached all over the world, what she has done will be told in memory of her."

是為我做！』

41「然後，王要對在他左邊的人說：『走開！受上帝詛咒的人哪，你們離開我吧！進到那為魔鬼和他的爪牙所預備永不熄滅的火裏去！42因為我餓了，你們沒給我吃，渴了，你們沒給我喝，43我流落異鄉，你們沒收留我；赤身露體，你們沒給我穿；我害病或坐牢，你們沒照顧我。』44這時候，他們要說：『主啊，我們甚麼時候看到你飢餓，或口渴，或流落異鄉，或赤身露體，或害病，或坐牢，而竟沒幫助你呢？』45王要回答：『我鄭重地告訴你們，既然你們沒為最微小的一人做，就是沒為我做。』46這樣的人要受永遠的刑罰。至於那些義人，他們會得到永恆的生命。」

殺害耶穌的陰謀
(可14‧1—2；路22‧1—2；約11‧45—53)

26 耶穌講完了這段話，就對門徒說：2「你們知道，再過兩天就是逾越節，人子將被出賣，被釘在十字架上。」

3那時候，祭司長和民間的長老在大祭司該亞法的府邸裏聚會，4一同計劃要秘密地逮捕耶穌，把他殺死。5可是他們說：「我們不可在節期中進行這事，免得激起民眾的暴動。」

在伯大尼受膏
(可14‧3—9；約12‧1—8)

6耶穌在伯大尼那患痲瘋病的西門家裏；7有一個女人帶來一隻玉瓶，盛滿了珍貴的香油膏。耶穌在吃飯的時候，那女人把香油膏倒在耶穌頭上。8門徒看見這事，很不高興，說：「為甚麼這樣浪費？9這香油膏可以賣不少錢來救濟窮人呢！」

10耶穌知道了，就對他們說：「何必為難這女人呢？她為我做了一件美好的事。11因為常有窮人跟你們在一起，但是我不能常與你們在一起。12她把這香油膏倒在我身上是為我的安葬做準備。13我實在告訴你們，普天之下，這福音無論傳到甚麼地方，人人都要述說她所做的事，來記念她。」

Judas Agrees to Betray Jesus

(Mark 14.10-11; Luke 22.3-6)

14Then one of the twelve disciples–the one named Judas Iscariot–went to the chief priests 15and asked, "What will you give me if I betray Jesus to you?" They counted out thirty silver coins and gave them to him. 16From then on Judas was looking for a good chance to hand Jesus over to them.

Jesus Eats the Passover Meal with His Disciples

(Mark 14.12-21; Luke 22.7-13, 21-23; John 13.21-30)

17On the first day of the Festival of Unleavened Bread the disciples came to Jesus and asked him, "Where do you want us to get the Passover meal ready for you?"

18"Go to a certain man in the city," he said to them, "and tell him: 'The Teacher says, My hour has come; my disciples and I will celebrate the Passover at your house.' "

19The disciples did as Jesus had told them and prepared the Passover meal.

20When it was evening, Jesus and the twelve disciples sat down to eat. 21During the meal Jesus said, "I tell you, one of you will betray me."

22The disciples were very upset and began to ask him, one after the other, "Surely, Lord, you don't mean me?"

23Jesus answered, "One who dips his bread in the dish with me will betray me. 24The Son of Man will die as the Scriptures say he will, but how terrible for that man who will betray the Son of Man! It would have been better for that man if he had never been born!"

25Judas, the traitor, spoke up. "Surely, Teacher, you don't mean me?" he asked.

Jesus answered, "So you say."

The Lord's Supper

(Mark 14.22-26; Luke 22.14-20; 1 Corinthians 11.23-25)

26While they were eating, Jesus took a piece of bread, gave a prayer of thanks, broke it, and gave it to his disciples. "Take and eat it," he said; "this is my body."

27Then he took a cup, gave thanks to God, and gave it to them. "Drink it, all of you," he said; 28"this is my blood, which seals God's covenant, my blood poured out for many for the forgiveness of sins. 29I tell you, I will never again drink this wine until the day I drink the new wine with you in my Father's Kingdom."

30Then they sang a hymn and went out to the Mount of Olives.

猶大同意出賣耶穌

（可14‧10—11；路22‧3—6）

14耶穌的十二使徒中，有一個加略人猶大；他去見祭司長，15說：「如果我把耶穌交給你們，你們願意給我甚麼？」他們拿三十塊銀幣給他。16從那時候起，猶大找機會要出賣耶穌。

和門徒同進逾越節晚餐

（可14‧12—21；路22‧7—13、21—23；約13‧21—30）

17除酵節的第一天，門徒來問耶穌：「你要我們在哪裏爲你預備逾越節的晚餐？」

18耶穌回答：「你們進城去見某某人，對他說：『老師說：我的時機快到了；我要和我的門徒在你家裏守逾越節。』」

19門徒就依照耶穌的吩咐去安排逾越節的晚餐。

20傍晚，耶穌與十二使徒坐席。21用飯的時候，耶穌說：「我告訴你們，你們當中有一個人要出賣我。」

22他們非常憂愁，一個一個地問他：「主啊，不是我吧？」

23耶穌回答：「跟我一起在盤子裏蘸餅吃的那個人要出賣我。24正如聖經所說，人子要受害，可是那出賣人子的人有禍了！這個人沒有出生倒好！」

25出賣耶穌的猶大也開口問：「老師，不是我吧？」耶穌說：「你自己說了。」

主的晚餐

（可14‧22—26；路22‧14—20；林前11‧23—25）

26他們吃飯的時候，耶穌拿起餅，先獻上感謝的禱告，然後擘開，分給門徒，說：「你們拿來吃；這是我的身體。」

27接着，他拿起杯，向上帝感謝後，遞給他們，說：「你們都喝吧；28這是我的血，是印證上帝與人立約的血，爲了使眾人的罪得到赦免而流的。29我告訴你們，我絕不再喝這酒，直到我與你們在我父親的國度裏喝新酒的那一天。」

30他們唱了一首詩，就出來，到橄欖山去。

Jesus Predicts Peter's Denial
(Mark 14.27-31; Luke 22.31-34; John 13.36-38)

31Then Jesus said to them, "This very night all of you will run away and leave me, for the scripture says, 'God will kill the shepherd, and the sheep of the flock will be scattered.' 32But after I am raised to life, I will go to Galilee ahead of you."

33Peter spoke up and said to Jesus, "I will never leave you, even though all the rest do!"

34Jesus said to Peter, "I tell you that before the rooster crows tonight, you will say three times that you do not know me."

35Peter answered, "I will never say that, even if I have to die with you!"

And all the other disciples said the same thing.

Jesus Prays in Gethsemane
(Mark 14.32-42; Luke 22.39-46)

36Then Jesus went with his disciples to a place called Gethsemane, and he said to them, "Sit here while I go over there and pray." 37He took with him Peter and the two sons of Zebedee. Grief and anguish came over him, 38and he said to them, "The sorrow in my heart is so great that it almost crushes me. Stay here and keep watch with me."

39He went a little farther on, threw himself face downward on the ground, and prayed, "My Father, if it is possible, take this cup of suffering from me! Yet not what I want, but what you want."

40Then he returned to the three disciples and found them asleep; and he said to Peter, "How is it that you three were not able to keep watch with me for even one hour? 41Keep watch and pray that you will not fall into temptation. The spirit is willing, but the flesh is weak."

42Once more Jesus went away and prayed, "My Father, if this cup of suffering cannot be taken away unless I drink it, your will be done." 43He returned once more and found the disciples asleep; they could not keep their eyes open.

44Again Jesus left them, went away, and prayed the third time, saying the same words. 45Then he returned to the disciples and said, "Are you still sleeping and resting? Look! The hour has come for the Son of Man to be handed over to the power of sinners. 46Get up, let us go. Look, here is the man who is betraying me!"

耶穌預言彼得不認他
（可14‧27—31；路22‧31—34；約13‧36—38）

31 後來，耶穌對門徒說：「今天晚上，你們都要為我的緣故離棄我；因為聖經說：『上帝要擊殺牧人，羊羣就分散了。』32但是我復活以後，要比你們先到加利利去。」

33 彼得對耶穌說：「即使其他的人都離棄你，我絕不離棄你！」

34 耶穌對彼得說：「我告訴你，今天晚上，雞叫以前，你會三次不認我。」

35 彼得回答：「即使我必須跟你同死，我也絕不會不認你！」

其他的門徒也都這樣說。

在客西馬尼園的禱告
（可14‧32—42；路22‧39—46）

36 耶穌和門徒來到一個地方，名叫客西馬尼；他對他們說：「你們在這裏坐，我去那邊禱告。」37於是他帶着彼得和西庇太的兩個兒子一起去。他開始憂愁難過，38對他們說：「我的心非常憂傷，幾乎要死。你們在這裏，跟我一起警醒吧！」

39 他稍往前走，俯伏在地上，禱告說：「我的父親哪，若是可以，求你不要讓我喝這苦杯！可是，不要照我的意思，只要照你的旨意。」

40 他回到那三個門徒那裏，發現他們都睡着了，就對彼得說：「你們不能跟我一起警醒一個鐘頭嗎？41要警醒禱告，免得陷入誘惑。你們心靈固然願意，肉體卻是軟弱的。」

42 第二次耶穌再去禱告說：「父親哪，若是這苦杯不可離開我，一定要我喝下，願你的旨意成全吧！」43他再回到門徒那裏，看見他們又睡着了；他們連眼睛也睜不開。

44 耶穌再離開他們，第三次去禱告，所說的跟先前的一樣。45然後他又回到門徒那裏，說：「你們還在睡覺、還在休息嗎？看哪，人子被出賣在罪人手中的時候到了。46起來，我們走吧！看哪，那出賣我的人來了！」

The Arrest of Jesus

(Mark 14.43-50; Luke 22.47-53; John 18.3-12)

47Jesus was still speaking when Judas, one of the twelve disciples, arrived. With him was a large crowd armed with swords and clubs and sent by the chief priests and the elders. 48The traitor had given the crowd a signal: "The man I kiss is the one you want. Arrest him!"

49Judas went straight to Jesus and said, "Peace be with you, Teacher," and kissed him.

50Jesus answered, "Be quick about it, friend!"z

Then they came up, arrested Jesus, and held him tight. 51One of those who were with Jesus drew his sword and struck at the High Priest's slave, cutting off his ear. 52"Put your sword back in its place," Jesus said to him. "All who take the sword will die by the sword. 53Don't you know that I could call on my Father for help, and at once he would send me more than twelve armies of angels? 54But in that case, how could the Scriptures come true which say that this is what must happen?"

55Then Jesus spoke to the crowd, "Did you have to come with swords and clubs to capture me, as though I were an outlaw? Every day I sat down and taught in the Temple, and you did not arrest me. 56But all this has happened in order to make come true what the prophets wrote in the Scriptures."

Then all the disciples left him and ran away.

Jesus before the Council

(Mark 14.53-65; Luke 22.54-55, 63-71; John 18.13-14, 19-24)

57Those who had arrested Jesus took him to the house of Caiaphas, the High Priest, where the teachers of the Law and the elders had gathered together. 58Peter followed from a distance, as far as the courtyard of the High Priest's house. He went into the courtyard and sat down with the guards to see how it would all come out. 59The chief priests and the whole Council tried to find some false evidence against Jesus to put him to death; 60but they could not find any, even though many people came forward and told lies about him. Finally two men stepped up 61and said, "This man said, 'I am able to tear down God's Temple and three days later build it back up.'"

62The High Priest stood up and said to Jesus,

耶穌被捕

（可14．43—50；路22．47—53；約18．3—12）

47 耶穌還在說話的時候，十二使徒之一的猶大來了。有一大羣人帶着刀棒跟他一起來；他們是祭司長和民間的長老派來的。48那出賣耶穌的人先給他們一個暗號，說：「我去親誰，誰就是你們所要的人，你們就抓他。」

49 猶大立刻走到耶穌跟前，說：「老師，你好！」然後親了他。

50 耶穌說：「朋友，你想做的，趕快做吧⑳！」

於是，那些人上前，抓住耶穌，把他綁起來。51跟耶穌在一起的人當中，有一個拔出刀來，向大祭司的奴僕砍去，把他的一隻耳朵削掉。52耶穌對他說：「把刀收起來！因爲凡動刀的，一定在刀下喪命。53難道你不知道我可以向我父親求援，而他會立刻調來十二營多的天使嗎？54如果我這樣做，聖經上所說、事情必須這樣發生的那些話又怎能實現呢？」

55 接着，耶穌向那一羣人說：「你們帶着刀劍棍棒出來抓我，把我當作暴徒嗎？我天天坐在聖殿裏教導人，你們並沒有下手。56不過，這一切事情的發生都是要實現先知在聖經上所說的話。」

這時候，所有的門徒都離棄他，逃跑了。

在議會受審

（可14．53—65；路22．54—55，63—71；約18．13—14，19—24）

57 那些抓了耶穌的人把耶穌帶到大祭司該亞法的府邸去。在那裏，經學教師和長老正在聚會。58彼得遠遠地跟着耶穌，到了大祭司的院子。彼得進院子去，跟警衞坐在一起，要看這事怎樣了結。59祭司長和全議會設法找假證據控告耶穌，要置他於死地，60雖然有很多人誣告他，但是找不出證據來。最後，有兩個人上前指稱：61「這個人說過：『我能夠拆毀上帝的聖殿，三天內又把它重建起來。』」

62 大祭司站起來，問耶穌：「這些人對你

---

z Be quick about it, friend!; or Why are you here, friend?

⑳「你想做的，趕快做吧」或譯「你來做甚麽」。

"Have you no answer to give to this accusation against you?" 63But Jesus kept quiet. Again the High Priest spoke to him, "In the name of the living God I now put you under oath: tell us if you are the Messiah, the Son of God."

64Jesus answered him, "So you say. But I tell all of you: from this time on you will see the Son of Man sitting at the right side of the Almighty and coming on the clouds of heaven!"

65At this the High Priest tore his clothes and said, "Blasphemy! We don't need any more witnesses! You have just heard his blasphemy! 66What do you think?"

They answered, "He is guilty and must die."

67Then they spat in his face and beat him; and those who slapped him 68said, "Prophesy for us, Messiah! Guess who hit you!"

Peter Denies Jesus
(Mark 14.66-72; Luke 22.56-62; John 18.1b-18, 25-27)

69Peter was sitting outside in the courtyard when one of the High Priest's servant women came to him and said, "You, too, were with Jesus of Galilee."

70But he denied it in front of them all. "I don't know what you are talking about," he answered, 71and went on out to the entrance of the courtyard. Another servant woman saw him and said to the men there, "He was with Jesus of Nazareth."

72Again Peter denied it and answered, "I swear that I don't know that man!"

73After a little while the men standing there came to Peter. "Of course you are one of them," they said. "After all, the way you speak gives you away!"

74Then Peter said, "I swear that I am telling the truth! May God punish me if I am not! I do not know that man!"

Just then a rooster crowed, 75and Peter remembered what Jesus had told him: "Before the rooster crows, you will say three times that you do not know me." He went out and wept bitterly.

Jesus Is Taken to Pilate
(Mark 15.1; Luke 23.1-2; John 18.28-32)

27 Early in the morning all the chief priests and the elders made their plans against Jesus to put him to death. 2They put him in chains, led him off, and handed him over to Pilate, the Roman governor.

的控告，你沒有甚麼答辯嗎？」63耶穌默不作聲。大祭司再一次對他說：「我指着永生上帝的名命令你發誓告訴我們，你是不是基督、上帝的兒子？」

64 耶穌回答：「這是你說的。但是我告訴你們，此後，你們要看見人子坐在全能者的右邊，駕着天上的雲降臨！」

65 大祭司一聽見這話，撕裂了自己的衣服，說：「他侮辱了上帝！我們再也不需要證人了。你們都聽見他侮辱了上帝；66你們認為怎樣？」

他們回答：「他該死！」

67 他們吐口水在他臉上，又用拳頭打他。那些打他耳光的人68說：「基督啊，你是個先知！說說看，是誰打你？」

彼得不認耶穌
（可14·66-72；路22·56-62；約18·15-18, 25-27）

69 彼得在外面的院子裏坐着；有大祭司的一個婢女走過來，說：「你也是跟那加利利人耶穌一夥的。」

70 彼得在大家面前否認了。他說：「我不知道你在說些甚麼」，71然後走出去，到了院子的門口。又有一個婢女看見了他，向站在那裏的人說：「這個人跟拿撒勒的耶穌是同夥的。」

72 彼得再次否認，發誓說：「我根本不認識那個人！」

73 過了一會兒，旁邊站着的人上來，對彼得說：「你跟他們確是一夥的；你的口音把你露出來了。」

74 彼得再一次賭咒說：「我不認識那個人。如果我說的不是實話，上帝會懲罰我！」

就在這時候，雞叫了。75彼得這才想起耶穌的話：「雞叫以前，你會三次不認我。」他就走出去，痛哭起來。

耶穌被解交彼拉多
（可15·1；路23·1-2；約18·28-32）

27 清早，所有的祭司長和猶太人的長老商議，要處死耶穌。2他們把耶穌綁起來，押走，交給羅馬總督彼拉多。

The Death of Judas

(Acts 1.18-19)

3When Judas, the traitor, learned that Jesus had been condemned, he repented and took back the thirty silver coins to the chief priests and the elders. 4"I have sinned by betraying an innocent man to death!" he said.

"What do we care about that?" they answered. "That is your business!"

5Judas threw the coins down in the Temple and left; then he went off and hanged himself.

6The chief priests picked up the coins and said, "This is blood money, and it is against our Law to put it in the Temple treasury." 7After reaching an agreement about it, they used the money to buy Potter's Field, as a cemetery for foreigners. 8That is why that field is called "Field of Blood" to this very day.

9Then what the prophet Jeremiah had said came true: "They took the thirty silver coins, the amount the people of Israel had agreed to pay for him, 10and used the money to buy the potter's field, as the Lord had commanded me."

Pilate Questions Jesus

(Mark 15.2-5; Luke 23.3-5; John 18.33-38)

11Jesus stood before the Roman governor, who questioned him. "Are you the king of the Jews?" he asked.

"So you say," answered Jesus. 12But he said nothing in response to the accusations of the chief priests and elders.

13So Pilate said to him, "Don't you hear all these things they accuse you of?"

14But Jesus refused to answer a single word, with the result that the Governor was greatly surprised.

Jesus Is Sentenced to Death

(Mark 15.6-15; Luke 23.13-25; John 18.39–19.16)

15At every Passover Festival the Roman governor was in the habit of setting free any one prisoner the crowd asked for. 16At that time there was a well-known prisoner named Jesus Barabbas. 17So when the crowd gathered, Pilate asked them, "Which one do you want me to set free for you? Jesus Barabbas or Jesus called the Messiah?" 18He knew very well that the Jewish authorities had handed Jesus over to him because they were jealous.

19While Pilate was sitting in the judgment hall, his wife sent him a message: "Have nothing to do with that innocent man, because in a dream last night I suffered much on account of him."

20The chief priests and the elders persuaded

猶大的死

（徒1‧18—19）

3 出賣耶穌的猶大看見耶穌被定罪，後悔了，就把三十塊銀幣拿去還給祭司長和長老，4 說：「我犯了罪，出賣了無辜者的命！」他們回答：「那是你自己的事，跟我們有甚麼關係？」

5 猶大把錢丟在聖殿裏，走出去，上吊自殺。

6 祭司長把錢撿起來，說：「這是血錢，把它放在奉獻箱裏是違法的。」7 商議的結果，他們同意拿這錢去購買陶匠的一塊地皮，作為埋葬異鄉人的墳地。8 因此，到今天人家還叫這塊地為「血田」。

9 這件事的經過實現了先知耶利米說過的話：「他們拿了三十塊銀幣，就是以色列人同意為他付出的價錢，買了陶匠的地皮；10這是依照主所命令我的。」

在彼拉多面前受審

（可15‧2—5；路23‧3—5；約18‧33—38）

11 耶穌站在總督面前，總督問他：「你是猶太人的王嗎？」

耶穌回答：「這是你說的。」12祭司長和長老對他的控告，他一概不回答。

13 於是彼拉多對他說：「你沒聽見他們控告你這許多事嗎？」

14 耶穌仍然一句話也不回答；彼拉多非常詫異。

被判死刑

（可15‧6—15；路23‧13—25；約18‧39—19‧16）

15 每逢逾越節，總督照慣例為羣眾釋放一個他們所要的囚犯。16那時，剛好有一個出了名的囚犯叫做〔耶穌〕巴拉巴。17所以，羣眾聚集的時候，彼拉多問他們：「你們要我為你們釋放哪一個呢？〔耶穌〕巴拉巴呢？還是那稱為基督的耶穌？」18彼拉多明明知道他們是出於嫉妒才把耶穌交給他的。

19 彼拉多開庭審判的時候，他的夫人派人來告訴他說：「那無辜者的事，你不要管，因為我昨晚在夢中為他吃盡苦頭。」

20 祭司長和長老挑唆民眾，他們就要求彼

the crowd to ask Pilate to set Barabbas free and have Jesus put to death. 21But Pilate asked the crowd, "Which one of these two do you want me to set free for you?"

"Barabbas!" they answered.

22"What, then, shall I do with Jesus called the Messiah?" Pilate asked them.

"Crucify him!" they all answered.

23But Pilate asked, "What crime has he committed?"

Then they started shouting at the top of their voices: "Crucify him!"

24When Pilate saw that it was no use to go on, but that a riot might break out, he took some water, washed his hands in front of the crowd, and said, "I am not responsible for the death of this man! This is your doing!"

25The whole crowd answered, "Let the responsibility for his death fall on us and on our children!"

26Then Pilate set Barabbas free for them; and after he had Jesus whipped, he handed him over to be crucified.

The Soldiers Make Fun of Jesus
(Mark 15.16-20; John 19.2-3)

27Then Pilate's soldiers took Jesus into the governor's palace, and the whole company gathered around him. 28They stripped off his clothes and put a scarlet robe on him. 29Then they made a crown out of thorny branches and placed it on his head, and put a stick in his right hand; then they knelt before him and made fun of him. "Long live the King of the Jews!" they said. 30They spat on him, and took the stick and hit him over the head. 31When they had finished making fun of him, they took the robe off and put his own clothes back on him. Then they led him out to crucify him.

Jesus Is Crucified
(Mark 15.21-32; Luke 23.26-43; John 19.17-27)

32As they were going out, they met a man from Cyrene named Simon, and the soldiers forced him to carry Jesus' cross. 33They came to a place called Golgotha, which means, "The Place of the Skull." 34There they offered Jesus wine mixed with a bitter substance; but after tasting it, he would not drink it.

35They crucified him and then divided his clothes among them by throwing dice. 36After that they sat there and watched him. 37Above his head they put the written notice of the accusation against him: "This is Jesus, the King of the Jews." 38Then they crucified two bandits with Jesus, one on his right and the other on his left.

拉多釋放巴拉巴,把耶穌處死。21可是總督問他們說:「這兩個人當中,你們要我釋放哪一個呢?」

他們回答:「巴拉巴!」

22 彼拉多問他們:「那麼,我該怎樣處置那稱為基督的耶穌呢?」

他們都喊:「把他釘十字架!」

23 彼拉多問:「他做了甚麼壞事呢?」

他們更大聲喊叫:「把他釘十字架!」

24 彼拉多看那情形,知道再說也沒有用,反而可能激起暴動,就拿水在羣衆面前洗手,說:「流這個人的血,罪不在我,你們自己承擔吧!」

25 羣衆異口同聲說:「他的血債由我們和我們的子孫承擔!」

26 於是彼拉多釋放巴拉巴給他們,又命令把耶穌鞭打了,然後交給人去釘十字架。

兵士戲弄耶穌
(可15‧16—20;約19‧2—3)

27 彼拉多的兵士把耶穌帶進總督府;全隊集合在他周圍。28他們剝下耶穌的衣服,給他穿上一件深紅色的袍子,29又用荊棘編了一頂冠冕給他戴上,拿一根藤條放在他的右手,然後跪在他面前戲弄他,說:「猶太人的王萬歲!」30他們又向他吐口水,拿藤條打他的頭。31他們戲弄完了,把他身上的袍子剝下,再給他穿上自己的衣服,然後帶他出去釘十字架。

耶穌被釘十字架
(可15‧21—32;路23‧26—43;約19‧17—27)

32 他們出來的時候,遇見一個古利奈人,名叫西門,就強迫他背耶穌的十字架。33他們來到一個地方,叫各各他,意思就是「髑髏岡」。34他們拿了攙着苦膽的酒給耶穌喝;耶穌嘗了,卻不肯喝。

35 於是,他們把耶穌釘在十字架上,又抽籤分了他的衣服,36然後坐在那裏看守他。37他們在他頭上方安了一面罪狀牌,牌上寫着:「這是耶穌,猶太人的王。」38他們又把兩個暴徒同釘在十字架上,一個在他右邊,一個在他左邊。

39People passing by shook their heads and hurled insults at Jesus: 40"You were going to tear down the Temple and build it back up in three days! Save yourself if you are God's Son! Come on down from the cross!"

41In the same way the chief priests and the teachers of the Law and the elders made fun of him: 42"He saved others, but he cannot save himself! Isn't he the king of Israel? If he will come down off the cross now, we will believe in him! 43He trusts in God and claims to be God's Son. Well, then, let us see if God wants to save him now!"

44Even the bandits who had been crucified with him insulted him in the same way.

The Death of Jesus
(Mark 15.33-41; Luke 23.44-49; John 19.28-30)

45At noon the whole country was covered with darkness, which lasted for three hours. 46At about three o'clock Jesus cried out with a loud shout, *"Eli, Eli, lema sabachthani?"* which means, "My God, my God, why did you abandon me?"

47Some of the people standing there heard him and said, "He is calling for Elijah!" 48One of them ran up at once, took a sponge, soaked it in cheap wine, put it on the end of a stick, and tried to make him drink it.

49But the others said, "Wait, let us see if Elijah is coming to save him!"

50Jesus again gave a loud cry and breathed his last.

51Then the curtain hanging in the Temple was torn in two from top to bottom. The earth shook, the rocks split apart, 52the graves broke open, and many of God's people who had died were raised to life. 53They left the graves, and after Jesus rose from death, they went into the Holy City, where many people saw them.

54When the army officer and the soldiers with him who were watching Jesus saw the earthquake and everything else that happened, they were terrified and said, "He really was the Son of God!"

55There were many women there, looking on from a distance, who had followed Jesus from Galilee and helped him. 56Among them were Mary Magdalene, Mary the mother of James and Joseph, and the wife of Zebedee.

The Burial of Jesus
(Mark 15.42-47; Luke 23.50-56; John 19.38-42)

57When it was evening, a rich man from Arimathea arrived; his name was Joseph, and he also was a disciple of Jesus. 58He went into

---

39 從那裏經過的人侮辱耶穌，搖着頭，40說：「你這想拆毀聖殿、三天內把它重建起來的！你若是上帝的兒子，救救自己，從十字架上下來吧！」

41 祭司長、經學教師，和長老也同樣地譏笑他，說：42「他救了別人，卻不能救自己！他不是以色列的王嗎？要是他現在從十字架上下來，我們就信他！43他倚靠上帝，自稱為上帝的兒子；好吧，現在讓我們看看上帝要不要來救他！」

44 連跟他同釘的暴徒也同樣辱罵他。

耶穌的死
（可15‧33-41；路23‧44-49；約19‧28-30）

45 中午的時候，黑暗籠罩大地，約有三小時之久。46到了下午三點鐘左右，耶穌大聲呼喊：「以利！以利！拉馬撒巴各大尼？」意思是：「我的上帝，我的上帝，你為甚麼離棄我？」

47 旁邊站着的人，有些聽見了，說：「他在呼喚以利亞呢！」48其中有一個人立刻跑過去，拿一塊海綿，浸在酸酒裏，然後綁在藤條上，要讓他喝。

49 其他的人說：「等着，我們看以利亞會不會來救他！」

50 耶穌又大喊一聲，氣就斷了。

51 這時候，懸掛在聖殿裏的幔子，從上到下裂成兩半。大地震動，巖石崩裂，52墳墓也被震開了，許多已經死了的聖徒都復活起來。53他們離開了墳墓，在耶穌復活以後進聖城；在那裏有許多人看見了他們。

54 看守耶穌的軍官和兵士看見了地震和所發生的一切事，都非常害怕，說：「他真的是上帝的兒子！」

55 那裏還有好些婦女從遠處觀看，她們是從加利利跟着耶穌來服事他的。56其中有抹大拉的馬利亞、雅各和約瑟的母親馬利亞，和西庇太兩個兒子的母親。

耶穌的安葬
（可15‧42-47；路23‧50-56；約19‧38-42）

57 傍晚的時候，有一個亞利馬太的財主來了；他名叫約瑟，也是耶穌的門徒。58他去

the presence of Pilate and asked for the body of Jesus. Pilate gave orders for the body to be given to Joseph. 59So Joseph took it, wrapped it in a new linen sheet, 60and placed it in his own tomb, which he had just recently dug out of solid rock. Then he rolled a large stone across the entrance to the tomb and went away. 61Mary Magdalene and the other Mary were sitting there, facing the tomb.

The Guard at the Tomb

62The next day, which was a Sabbath, the chief priests and the Pharisees met with Pilate 63and said, "Sir, we remember that while that liar was still alive he said, 'I will be raised to life three days later.' 64Give orders, then, for his tomb to be carefully guarded until the third day, so that his disciples will not be able to go and steal the body, and then tell the people that he was raised from death. This last lie would be even worse than the first one."

65"Take a guard," Pilate told them; "go and make the tomb as secure as you can."

66So they left and made the tomb secure by putting a seal on the stone and leaving the guard on watch.

The Resurrection

(Mark 16.1-10; Luke 24.1-12; John 20.1-10)

28After the Sabbath, as Sunday morning was dawning, Mary Magdalene and the other Mary went to look at the tomb. 2Suddenly there was a violent earthquake; an angel of the Lord came down from heaven, rolled the stone away, and sat on it. 3His appearance was like lightning, and his clothes were white as snow. 4The guards were so afraid that they trembled and became like dead men.

5The angel spoke to the women. "You must not be afraid," he said. "I know you are looking for Jesus, who was crucified. 6He is not here; he has been raised, just as he said. Come here and see the place where he was lying. 7Go quickly now, and tell his disciples, 'He has been raised from death, and now he is going to Galilee ahead of you; there you will see him!' Remember what I have told you."

8So they left the tomb in a hurry, afraid and yet filled with joy, and ran to tell his disciples.

9Suddenly Jesus met them and said, "Peace be with you." They came up to him, took hold of his feet, and worshiped him. 10"Do not be afraid," Jesus said to them. "Go and tell my brothers to go to Galilee, and there they will see me."

見彼拉多，要求收殮耶穌的身體；彼拉多就吩咐把耶穌的身體交給他。59約瑟把身體領了去，用乾淨的麻紗包裹起來，60安放在他自己的墓穴裏；這墓穴是他最近才從巖石鑿成的。他又把一塊大石頭滾過來，堵住墓門，然後離開。61抹大拉的馬利亞和另一個馬利亞面對着墳墓坐着，守在那裏。

墳墓的守衛

62第二天，就是預備日的後一天，祭司長和法利賽人一起去見彼拉多，說：63「大人，我們記得那個騙子還活着的時候曾經說過：『三天後我要復活。』64所以，請你下令嚴密守護墳墓，一直到第三天，他的門徒就不能把他偷走，然後去告訴人家『他從死裏復活了』，這樣的謊言要比先前的更糟！」

65彼拉多對他們說：「你們帶守衛去，盡你們所能，好好地把守墳墓！」

66於是他們去了，在石頭上加了封條，封住墓口，留下守衛把守。

耶穌復活

(可16・1―10；路24・1―12；約20・1―10)

28過了安息日，星期日黎明的時候，抹大拉的馬利亞跟另一個馬利亞一起到墳地去看。2忽然有強烈的地震，主的天使從天上降下來，把石頭滾開，坐在上面。3他的容貌像閃電，他的衣服像雪一樣潔白。4守衛們驚嚇得渾身發抖，像死人一般。

5那天使向婦女們說：「不要害怕，我知道你們要找那被釘十字架的耶穌。6他不在這裏，照他所說的，他已經復活了。你們過來，看安放他的地方。7你們趕快去告訴他的門徒：『他已經從死裏復活了，他要比你們先到加利利去；在那裏，你們會見到他！』要記住我告訴你們的話。」

8婦女們就急忙離開了墳地，又驚訝又極歡喜，跑去告訴他的門徒。

9忽然，耶穌在路上出現，對她們說：「願你們平安！」她們上前，抱住他的腳拜他。10耶穌對她們說：「不要害怕，去告訴我的弟兄，叫他們到加利利去；在那裏，他們會見到我。」

The Report of the Guard

11While the women went on their way, some of the soldiers guarding the tomb went back to the city and told the chief priests everything that had happened. 12The chief priests met with the elders and made their plan; they gave a large sum of money to the soldiers 13and said, "You are to say that his disciples came during the night and stole his body while you were asleep. 14And if the Governor should hear of this, we will convince him that you are innocent, and you will have nothing to worry about."

15The guards took the money and did what they were told to do. And so that is the report spread around by the Jews to this very day.

Jesus Appears to His Disciples

(Mark 16.14-18; Luke 24.36-49; John 20.19-23; Acts 1.6-8)

16The eleven disciples went to the hill in Galilee where Jesus had told them to go. 17When they saw him, they worshiped him, even though some of them doubted. 18Jesus drew near and said to them, "I have been given all authority in heaven and on earth. 19Go, then, to all peoples everywhere and make them my disciples: baptize them in the name of the Father, the Son, and the Holy Spirit, 20and teach them to obey everything I have commanded you. And I will be with you always, to the end of the age."

守衛的報告

11 婦女們還在趕路的時候，有些把守墳墓的兵士回城裏去，向祭司長報告所發生的一切事。12祭司長和長老一起商量後，拿一大筆錢給兵士們，13對他們說：「你們要說，耶穌的門徒們在夜間來了，趁着你們睡覺的時候把他的身體偷走了。14要是總督知道了這件事，我們會出面說話，擔保你們沒事。」

15 兵士接受了錢，照他們所吩咐的做了。這謠言到今天還在猶太人當中流傳着。

耶穌付託使命

（可16・14-18；路24・36-49；約20・19-23；徒1・6-8）

16 十一個門徒到了加利利，到耶穌吩咐他們去的那座山上。17他們一見到耶穌，就都向他下拜；可是還有人心裏疑惑。18耶穌走近他們，對他們說：「上帝已經把天上和人間所有的權柄都賜給我了。19所以，你們要去，使萬國萬民都作我的門徒，奉父、子、聖靈的名給他們施洗，20並且教導他們遵守我所給你們的一切命令。記住！我要常與你們同在，直到世界的末日。」

馬可福音
MARK

INTRODUCTION

The Gospel according to Mark begins with the statement that it is "the Good News about Jesus Christ, the Son of God." Jesus is pictured as a man of action and authority. His authority is seen in his teaching, in his power over demons, and in forgiving people's sins. Jesus speaks of himself as the Son of Man, who came to give his life to set people free from sin.

Mark presents the story of Jesus in a straightforward, vigorous way, with emphasis on what Jesus did, rather than on his words and teachings. After a brief prologue about John the Baptist and the baptism and temptation of Jesus, the writer immediately takes up Jesus' ministry of healing and teaching. As time goes on, the followers of Jesus come to understand him better, but Jesus' opponents become more hostile. The closing chapters report the events of Jesus' last week of earthly life, especially his crucifixion and resurrection.

The two endings to the Gospel, which are enclosed in brackets, are generally regarded as written by someone other than the author of *Mark*.

Outline of Contents

簡 介

馬可福音記述有關上帝的兒子耶穌基督的好消息。它告訴我們,耶穌既重實踐且具有權威。他的權威可從他的教導、制伏邪靈的能力,和赦罪的權柄看出。耶穌自稱「人子」;他到世上來的目的是要服事人類,並且爲拯救人類而犧牲自己的生命。

馬可以簡潔有力的文筆記述耶穌的事蹟,把重心放在他的工作方面,而不是他的言論和教導。作者先以簡短的篇幅敍述施洗者約翰的傳道以及耶穌的洗禮和受試探,接着報導耶穌的治病和教導,又記述耶穌的門徒如何逐漸地認識他,而反對的力量也如何不斷增長。末後的幾章寫耶穌在世最後一週的事,特別是關於他被釘十字架和復活的經過。

一般學者認爲,本書的兩段結語(用〔〕符號表明的)不是出自馬可的手筆,而是其他作者加上的。

提要

The Preaching of John the Baptist

(Matthew 3.1-12; Luke 3.1-18; John 1.19-28)

1 This is the Good News about Jesus Christ, the Son of God.[a] [2]It began as the prophet Isaiah had written:

"God said, 'I will send my messenger ahead
    of you
to open the way for you.'

[3]Someone is shouting in the desert,
'Get the road ready for the Lord;
make a straight path for him to travel!'"

[4]So John appeared in the desert, baptizing and preaching.[b] "Turn away from your sins and be baptized," he told the people, "and God will forgive your sins." [5]Many people from the province of Judea and the city of Jerusalem went out to hear John. They confessed their sins, and he baptized them in the Jordan River.

[6]John wore clothes made of camel's hair, with a leather belt around his waist, and his food was locusts and wild honey. [7]He announced to the people, "The man who will come after me is much greater than I am. I am not good enough even to bend down and untie his sandals. [8]I baptize you with water, but he will baptize you with the Holy Spirit."

The Baptism and Temptation of Jesus

(Matthew 3.13-4.11; Luke 3.21-22; 4.1-13)

[9]Not long afterward Jesus came from Nazareth in the province of Galilee, and was baptized by John in the Jordan. [10]As soon as Jesus came up out of the water, he saw heaven opening and the Spirit coming down on him like a dove. [11]And a voice came from heaven, "You are my own dear Son. I am pleased with you."

[12]At once the Spirit made him go into the desert, [13]where he stayed forty days, being tempted by Satan. Wild animals were there also, but angels came and helped him.

Jesus Calls Four Fishermen

(Matthew 4.12-22; Luke 4.14-15; 5.1-11)

[14]After John had been put in prison, Jesus went to Galilee and preached the Good News from God. [15]"The right time has come," he said, "and the Kingdom of God is near! Turn away from your sins and believe the Good News!"

[16]As Jesus walked along the shore of Lake Galilee, he saw two fishermen, Simon and his

---

a *Some manuscripts do not have* the Son of God.
b John appeared in the desert, baptizing and preaching; *some manuscripts have* John the Baptist appeared in the desert, preaching.

施洗者約翰傳道

(太 3 ・ 1―12 ; 路 3 ・ 1―18 ; 約 1 ・ 19―28)

1 上帝的兒子①，耶穌基督的福音是這樣開始的。 [2]先知以賽亞在他的書上記載：

上帝說：
看吧，我要差遣我的使者；
他要作你的前驅，為你開路。

[3]在曠野有人呼喊：
為主準備他的道路，
修直他要走的路徑！

[4]果然，約翰在曠野出現，為人施洗，並且宣講②：「你們要悔改，接受洗禮，上帝就赦免你們的罪。」[5]羣衆從猶太各地和全耶路撒冷到約翰跟前來。他們承認自己的罪；約翰就在約旦河裏為他們施洗。

[6]約翰穿着駱駝毛的衣服，腰間繫着皮帶；吃的是蝗蟲和野蜜。[7]他宣講：「在我以後要來的那一位比我偉大多了，我就是蹲下去替他脫鞋子也不配。[8]我用水給你們施洗，他卻要用聖靈給你們施洗。」

耶穌受洗和受試探

(太 3 ・ 13―4 ・ 11 ; 路 3 ・ 21―22 ; 4 ・ 1―13)

[9]過了不久，耶穌從加利利的拿撒勒來，約翰就在約旦河為他施洗。[10]耶穌一從水裏上來就看見天開了，聖靈像鴿子降在他身上。[11]從天上有聲音傳下來，說：「你是我親愛的兒子，我喜愛你。」

[12]聖靈立刻催促耶穌到曠野去。[13]他在那裏四十天，受撒但試探；他和野獸在一起，但是有天使伺候他。

耶穌呼召四漁夫

(太 4 ・ 12―22 ; 路 4 ・ 14―15 ; 5 ・ 1―11)

[14]約翰被關進監獄以後，耶穌到加利利去，宣講上帝的福音。[15]他說：「時機成熟了，上帝的國快實現了！你們要悔改，信從福音。」

[16]耶穌沿着加利利湖邊走，看見兩個打魚的—西門和他的弟弟安得烈—在湖上撒網打

---

①有些古卷沒有「上帝的兒子」。
②「果然，約翰在曠野出現，為人施洗，並且宣講」有些古卷作「施洗者約翰果然在曠野出現，宣講」。

brother Andrew, catching fish with a net. [17]Jesus said to them, "Come with me, and I will teach you to catch people." [18]At once they left their nets and went with him.

[19]He went a little farther on and saw two other brothers, James and John, the sons of Zebedee. They were in their boat getting their nets ready. [20]As soon as Jesus saw them, he called them; they left their father Zebedee in the boat with the hired men and went with Jesus.

A Man with an Evil Spirit
(Luke 4.31-37)

[21]Jesus and his disciples came to the town of Capernaum, and on the next Sabbath Jesus went to the synagogue and began to teach. [22]The people who heard him were amazed at the way he taught, for he wasn't like the teachers of the Law; instead, he taught with authority.

[23]Just then a man with an evil spirit came into the synagogue and screamed, [24]"What do you want with us, Jesus of Nazareth? Are you here to destroy us? I know who you are—you are God's holy messenger!"

[25]Jesus ordered the spirit, "Be quiet, and come out of the man!"

[26]The evil spirit shook the man hard, gave a loud scream, and came out of him. [27]The people were all so amazed that they started saying to one another, "What is this? Is it some kind of new teaching? This man has authority to give orders to the evil spirits, and they obey him!"

[28]And so the news about Jesus spread quickly everywhere in the province of Galilee.

Jesus Heals Many People
(Matthew 8.14-17; Luke 4.38-41)

[29]Jesus and his disciples, including James and John, left the synagogue and went straight to the home of Simon and Andrew. [30]Simon's mother-in-law was sick in bed with a fever, and as soon as Jesus arrived, he was told about her. [31]He went to her, took her by the hand, and helped her up. The fever left her, and she began to wait on them.

[32]After the sun had set and evening had come, people brought to Jesus all the sick and those who had demons. [33]All the people of the town gathered in front of the house. [34]Jesus healed many who were sick with all kinds of diseases and drove out many demons. He would not let the demons say anything, because they knew who he was.

魚。[17]耶穌對他們說：「來跟從我！我要使你們成為得人的漁夫。」[18]他們立刻丟下魚網，跟從了他。

[19]再走不遠，耶穌看見西庇太的兒子雅各和他的弟弟約翰；他們在船上整理魚網。[20]耶穌一呼召他們，他們就把父親和雇工留在船上，跟從了耶穌。

一個污靈附身的人
（路 4·31—37）

[21]他們來到迦百農城；安息日一到，耶穌進會堂教導人。[22]聽見耶穌教導的人都很驚奇，因為他的教導滿有權威，和一般經學教師不同。

[23]這時候，有一個污靈附身的人來到會堂，喊着說：[24]「拿撒勒的耶穌，你為甚麼干擾我們？你是來除滅我們的嗎？我知道你是誰；你是上帝的聖者！」

[25]耶穌命令污靈：「住口，快從這人身上出來！」

[26]污靈使那人猛烈地抽瘋，大叫一聲，然後離開那人。[27]大家驚訝不已，竊竊私議：「這是怎麼一回事？真是聞所未聞的道理！他居然有權柄指揮污靈，而污靈也服從他！」

[28]於是，耶穌的名聲很快地傳遍了加利利地區。

耶穌治好許多病人
（太 8·14—17；路 4·38—41）

[29]他們離開會堂，到西門和安得烈的家去；雅各和約翰也一道去。[30]西門的岳母正發高燒，躺在牀上；耶穌一到，他們就把她的病情告訴耶穌。[31]耶穌去看她，拉着她的手，扶她起來。她的熱退了，就起來接待他們。

[32]傍晚，太陽下山的時候，有些人把害各種病和被鬼附身的人都帶到耶穌跟前來；[33]全城的人也來了，聚集在門前。[34]耶穌治好許多患各種病症的人，也趕走許多鬼。他不准鬼說話，因為他們知道他是誰。

Jesus Preaches in Galilee
(Luke 4.42-44)

35Very early the next morning, long before daylight, Jesus got up and left the house. He went out of town to a lonely place, where he prayed. 36But Simon and his companions went out searching for him, 37and when they found him, they said, "Everyone is looking for you."

38But Jesus answered, "We must go on to the other villages around here. I have to preach in them also, because that is why I came."

39So he traveled all over Galilee, preaching in the synagogues and driving out demons.

Jesus Heals a Man
(Matthew 8.1-4; Luke 5.12-16)

40A man suffering from a dreaded skin disease came to Jesus, knelt down, and begged him for help. "If you want to," he said, "you can make me clean."c

41Jesus was filled with pity,d and reached out and touched him. "I do want to," he answered. "Be clean!" 42At once the disease left the man, and he was clean. 43Then Jesus spoke sternly to him and sent him away at once, 44after saying to him, "Listen, don't tell anyone about this. But go straight to the priest and let him examine you; then in order to prove to everyone that you are cured, offer the sacrifice that Moses ordered."

45But the man went away and began to spread the news everywhere. Indeed, he talked so much that Jesus could not go into a town publicly. Instead, he stayed out in lonely places, and people came to him from everywhere.

Jesus Heals a Paralyzed Man
(Matthew 9.1-8; Luke 5.17-26)

2 A few days later Jesus went back to Capernaum, and the news spread that he was at home. 2So many people came together that there was no room left, not even out in front of the door. Jesus was preaching the message to them 3when four men arrived, carrying a paralyzed man to Jesus. 4Because of the crowd, however, they could not get the man to him. So they made a hole in the roof right above the place where Jesus was. When they had made an opening, they let the man down, lying on his mat. 5Seeing how much faith they had, Jesus said to the paralyzed man, "My son, your sins are forgiven."

6Some teachers of the Law who were sitting there thought to themselves, 7"How does he

c MAKE ME CLEAN: *This disease was considered to make a person ritually unclean.*
d pity; *some manuscripts have anger.*

在加利利傳道
（路 4．42-44）

35 第二天一早，天還沒亮，耶穌就起來，離開屋子，到一個偏僻的地方去，在那裏禱告。36西門和他的同伴出去找他；37找到了，他們就說：「大家都在找你呢！」

38 耶穌說：「我們到附近的村莊去吧，我也必須在那些地方傳道，因為這正是我來的目的。」

39 於是，耶穌走遍加利利全境，在各會堂裏傳道，並且趕鬼。

耶穌治好痲瘋病人
（太 8．1-4；路 5．12-16）

40 有一個痲瘋病人來到耶穌跟前，跪下來求他，說：「只要你肯，你能夠使我潔淨。」

41 耶穌動了惻隱之心③，伸手摸他，說：「我肯，你潔淨吧！」42他身上的痲瘋立刻離開他，他就潔淨了。43耶穌立刻把他送走，並鄭重地囑咐，44說：「不要告訴任何人；直接去見祭司，讓他檢查，然後按照摩西的規定獻上祭物，向人證明你已經潔淨了。」

45 可是這個人一出去，到處宣揚這件事，以致耶穌不能再公然進城，只好住在城外偏僻的地方；羣眾仍然從各地方來找他。

耶穌治好癱瘓病人
（太 9．1-8；路 5．17-26）

2 過了幾天，耶穌又回到迦百農；他在家的消息傳開了。2許多人聚集，屋裏擠滿了人，連門前也沒有空地。耶穌向他們講道的時候，3有四個人抬着一個癱瘓病人來見耶穌。4因為人多，他們無法把他抬到耶穌面前。於是在耶穌所在之處的屋頂上拆開一個洞，然後把病人，連同他所躺臥的褥子，縋了下去。5耶穌看見這些人的信心，就對那癱瘓病人說：「孩子，你的罪蒙赦免了。」

6 有幾個經學教師坐在那裏，心裏議論說：7「這個人竟敢說狂妄的話！除了上

③「動了惻隱之心」另有些古卷作「心裏很生氣」。

dare talk like this? This is blasphemy! God is the only one who can forgive sins!"

8At once Jesus knew what they were thinking, so he said to them, "Why do you think such things? 9Is it easier to say to this paralyzed man, 'Your sins are forgiven,' or to say, 'Get up, pick up your mat, and walk'? 10I will prove to you, then, that the Son of Man has authority on earth to forgive sins." So he said to the paralyzed man, 11"I tell you, get up, pick up your mat, and go home!"

12While they all watched, the man got up, picked up his mat, and hurried away. They were all completely amazed and praised God, saying, "We have never seen anything like this!"

Jesus Calls Levi
(Matthew 9.9-13; Luke 5.27-32)

13Jesus went back again to the shore of Lake Galilee. A crowd came to him, and he started teaching them. 14As he walked along, he saw a tax collector, Levi son of Alphaeus, sitting in his office. Jesus said to him, "Follow me." Levi got up and followed him.

15Later on Jesus was having a meal in Levi's house.e A large number of tax collectors and other outcasts was following Jesus, and many of them joined him and his disciples at the table. 16Some teachers of the Law, who were Pharisees, saw that Jesus was eating with these outcasts and tax collectors, so they asked his disciples, "Why does he eat with such people?"

17Jesus heard them and answered, "People who are well do not need a doctor, but only those who are sick. I have not come to call respectable people, but outcasts."

The Question about Fasting
(Matthew 9.14-17; Luke 5.33-39)

18On one occasion the followers of John the Baptist and the Pharisees were fasting. Some people came to Jesus and asked him, "Why is it that the disciples of John the Baptist and the disciples of the Pharisees fast, but yours do not?"

19Jesus answered, "Do you expect the guests at a wedding party to go without food? Of course not! As long as the bridegroom is with them, they will not do that. 20But the day will come when the bridegroom will be taken away from them, and then they will fast.

21"No one uses a piece of new cloth to patch up an old coat, because the new patch will shrink and tear off some of the old cloth, making an even bigger hole. 22Nor does anyone

e in Levi's house; or in his (that is, Jesus') house.

帝,誰有赦罪的權呢?」

8 耶穌立刻看穿他們在轉些甚麼念頭,就對他們說:「你們為甚麼有這種想法呢? 9對這病人說『你的罪蒙赦免了』容易呢?還是說『起來,拿起你的褥子走』容易呢? 10我要向你們證明人子在地上有赦罪的權柄。」於是他對那癱瘓病人說: 11「我吩咐你,起來,拿起你的褥子,回家去吧!」

12 那個人起來,立刻拿起褥子,在大家注視下走出去。大家非常驚奇,頌讚上帝說:「我們從來沒有見過這樣的事!」

耶穌呼召利未
(太9·9-13;路5·27-32)

13 耶穌再到加利利湖邊,一大羣人聚集在他身邊,他就教導他們。 14他再往前走的時候,看見一個收稅的,就是亞勒腓的兒子利未,坐在稅關上。耶穌對他說:「來跟從我!」利未就起來,跟從了他。

15 以後耶穌在利未家裏吃飯,有許多稅棍和壞人也跟着他;當中有好些人跟耶穌和他的門徒同席吃飯。 16有些經學教師和法利賽人看見耶穌跟壞人和稅棍一起吃飯,就質問他的門徒:「他為甚麼跟稅棍和壞人一起吃飯呢?」

17 耶穌聽見了,就說:「健康的人用不着醫生,有病的人才用得着。我來的目的不是要召好人,而是要召壞人。」

禁食的問題
(太9·14-17;路5·33-39)

18 有一次,施洗者約翰的門徒和法利賽人正在禁食。有人來問耶穌:「為甚麼施洗者約翰以及法利賽人的門徒禁食,你的門徒卻不禁食?」

19 耶穌回答:「新郎還在婚宴上的時候,賀喜的客人會禁食嗎?只要新郎跟他們在一起,他們就不禁食。 20可是日子將到,新郎要從他們當中被帶走,那時候他們就要禁食了。

21「沒有人拿新布去補舊衣服,如果這樣做,新的補釘會撕破舊衣服,使裂痕更大。 22也沒有人拿新酒裝在舊皮袋裏,這樣做的

pour new wine into used wineskins, because the wine will burst the skins, and both the wine and the skins will be ruined. Instead, new wine must be poured into fresh wineskins."

The Question about the Sabbath
(Matthew 12.1-8; Luke 6.1-5)

23Jesus was walking through some wheat fields on a Sabbath. As his disciples walked along with him, they began to pick the heads of wheat. 24So the Pharisees said to Jesus, "Look, it is against our Law for your disciples to do that on the Sabbath!"

25Jesus answered, "Have you never read what David did that time when he needed something to eat? He and his men were hungry, 26so he went into the house of God and ate the bread offered to God. This happened when Abiathar was the High Priest. According to our Law only the priests may eat this bread–but David ate it and even gave it to his men."

27And Jesus concluded, "The Sabbath was made for the good of human beings; they were not made for the Sabbath. 28So the Son of Man is Lord even of the Sabbath."

The Man with a Paralyzed Hand
(Matthew 12.9-14; Luke 6.6-11)

3 Then Jesus went back to the synagogue, where there was a man who had a paralyzed hand. 2Some people were there who wanted to accuse Jesus of doing wrong; so they watched him closely to see whether he would cure the man on the Sabbath. 3Jesus said to the man, "Come up here to the front." 4Then he asked the people, "What does our Law allow us to do on the Sabbath? To help or to harm? To save someone's life or to destroy it?"

But they did not say a thing. 5Jesus was angry as he looked around at them, but at the same time he felt sorry for them, because they were so stubborn and wrong. Then he said to the man, "Stretch out your hand." He stretched it out, and it became well again. 6So the Pharisees left the synagogue and met at once with some members of Herod's party, and they made plans to kill Jesus.

A Crowd by the Lake

7Jesus and his disciples went away to Lake Galilee, and a large crowd followed him. They had come from Galilee, from Judea, 8from Jerusalem, from the territory of Idumea, from the territory on the east side of the Jordan, and from the region around the cities of Tyre and Sidon. All these people came to Jesus because they had heard of the things he was doing. 9The crowd was so large that Jesus told his disciples

話，新酒會脹破舊皮袋，酒和皮袋都會損壞。所以，新酒要裝在新皮袋裏！」

安息日的問題
（太12‧1—8；路6‧1—5）

23 有一個安息日，耶穌經過麥田。他的門徒們跟他同行；他們一邊走，一邊摘取一些麥穗。24於是法利賽人對耶穌說：「你看，你的門徒做了在安息日不准做的事！」

25 耶穌回答：「大衛在需要食物的時候做了甚麼事，你們沒有念過嗎？他跟他的隨從餓了，26就進上帝的聖殿，吃了獻給上帝的供餅。這事發生在亞比亞他當大祭司的時候。根據我們的法律，只有祭司才可以吃這餅；可是大衛自己吃了，又分給他的隨從吃。」

27 於是耶穌說：「安息日是為人而設的；人不是為安息日而生的。28所以，人子也是安息日的主。」

治好手枯萎的病人
（太12‧9—14；路6‧6—11）

3 耶穌又進會堂；那裏有一個人，他的一隻手枯萎了。2有些人在窺伺，要看耶穌在安息日治不治病，好控告他。3耶穌對那手枯萎的病人說：「站到前面來」，4然後問大家：「關於安息日，我們的法律是怎樣規定的？做好事還是壞事？救命還是害命？」

大家一聲不響。5耶穌怒目環視左右，心裏為這些人悲傷，因為他們的心腸剛硬。於是他對那病人說：「把手伸直！」那人一伸手，手就復原了。6那些法利賽人從會堂出來後立刻和希律黨人商量要怎樣對付耶穌，殺害他。

湖邊的羣眾

7 耶穌和門徒們離開那裏到加利利湖邊去，一大羣人跟着他。他們是從加利利、猶太、8耶路撒冷、以土買、約旦河對岸等地區以及泰爾和西頓附近的城市來的。這一大羣人來找耶穌是因為他們聽見耶穌所做的一切事。9人太多了，耶穌吩咐門徒替他準備

to get a boat ready for him, so that the people would not crush him. 10He had healed many people, and all the sick kept pushing their way to him in order to touch him. 11And whenever the people who had evil spirits in them saw him, they would fall down before him and scream, "You are the Son of God!"

12Jesus sternly ordered the evil spirits not to tell anyone who he was.

Jesus Chooses the Twelve Apostles
(Matthew 10.1-4; Luke 6.12-16)

13Then Jesus went up a hill and called to himself the men he wanted. They came to him, 14and he chose twelve, whom he named apostles. "I have chosen you to be with me," he told them. "I will also send you out to preach, 15and you will have authority to drive out demons."

16These are the twelve he chose: Simon (Jesus gave him the name Peter); 17James and his brother John, the sons of Zebedee (Jesus gave them the name Boanerges, which means "Men of Thunder"); 18Andrew, Philip, Bartholomew, Matthew, Thomas, James son of Alphaeus, Thaddaeus, Simon the Patriot, 19and Judas Iscariot, who betrayed Jesus.

Jesus and Beelzebul
(Matthew 12.22-32; Luke 11.14-23; 12.10)

20Then Jesus went home. Again such a large crowd gathered that Jesus and his disciples had no time to eat. 21When his family heard about it, they set out to take charge of him, because people were saying, "He's gone mad!"

22Some teachers of the Law who had come from Jerusalem were saying, "He has Beelzebul in him! It is the chief of the demons who gives him the power to drive them out."

23So Jesus called them to him and spoke to them in parables: "How can Satan drive out Satan? 24If a country divides itself into groups which fight each other, that country will fall apart. 25If a family divides itself into groups which fight each other, that family will fall apart. 26So if Satan's kingdom divides into groups, it cannot last, but will fall apart and come to an end.

27"No one can break into a strong man's house and take away his belongings unless he first ties up the strong man; then he can plunder his house.

28"I assure you that people can be forgiven all their sins and all the evil things they may say./ 29But whoever says evil things against the

一條小船，免得人羣擁擠他。10因爲他治好了許多病人，所有患病的人都擠向前來，要摸他。11那些被污靈附身的人一看見他，就俯伏在他面前，喊說：「你是上帝的兒子！」

12耶穌嚴厲地囑咐他們不可說出他是誰。

耶穌揀選十二使徒
（太10·1—4；路6·12—16）

13耶穌上了一座山，把他所要的人都召集到跟前。他們來了，14耶穌選出十二個人，稱他們爲使徒，又對他們說：「我揀選你們，要你們常跟我在一起，也要差遣你們出去傳道；15你們將有趕鬼的權。」

16耶穌所揀選的十二個人是：西門（耶穌又給他取名彼得），17西庇太的兒子雅各和雅各的弟弟約翰（耶穌又給他們取名半尼其，意思是「性如暴雷的人」），18安得烈，腓力，巴多羅買，馬太，多馬，亞勒腓的兒子雅各，達太，激進黨的西門，19和後來出賣耶穌的加略人猶大。

耶穌和別西卜
（太12·22—32；路11·14—23；12·10）

20耶穌回到家裏；一大羣人又聚攏來，以致他和門徒連吃飯的時間也沒有。21耶穌家裏的人知道了這種情形，出來要阻止他，因爲有人說：「他發瘋了！」

22有些從耶路撒冷下來的經學教師說：「他被別西卜附身！他是靠鬼王趕鬼的！」

23耶穌把這些人叫到跟前來，用比喻對他們說：「撒但怎能驅逐撒但呢？24一個國家自相紛爭，那國家必然站立不住。25一個家庭自相紛爭，那家庭也必然破碎。26這樣看來，假如撒但的國度自相紛爭，它就站立不住，終必滅亡。

27「沒有人能夠進武士的家，奪取他的財物；他必須先把武士綁起來才能夠洗劫他的家。

28「我實在告訴你們，人所犯一切的罪和所說一切褻瀆的話都可得到赦免；29但是褻瀆聖靈的人永遠得不到赦免，因爲他所犯的

f evil things they may say; or evil things they may say against God.

Holy Spirit will never be forgiven, because he has committed an eternal sin." 30(Jesus said this because some people were saying, "He has an evil spirit in him.")

Jesus' Mother and Brothers
(Matthew 12.46-50; Luke 8.19-21)

31Then Jesus' mother and brothers arrived. They stood outside the house and sent in a message, asking for him. 32A crowd was sitting around Jesus, and they said to him, "Look, your mother and your brothers and sisters are outside, and they want you."

33Jesus answered, "Who is my mother? Who are my brothers?" 34He looked at the people sitting around him and said, "Look! Here are my mother and my brothers! 35Whoever does what God wants is my brother, my sister, my mother."

The Parable of the Sower
(Matthew 13.1-9; Luke 8.4-8)

4 Again Jesus began to teach beside Lake Galilee. The crowd that gathered around him was so large that he got into a boat and sat in it. The boat was out in the water, and the crowd stood on the shore at the water's edge. 2He used parables to teach them many things, saying to them:

3"Listen! Once there was a man who went out to sow grain. 4As he scattered the seed in the field, some of it fell along the path, and the birds came and ate it up. 5Some of it fell on rocky ground, where there was little soil. The seeds soon sprouted, because the soil wasn't deep. 6Then, when the sun came up, it burned the young plants; and because the roots had not grown deep enough, the plants soon dried up. 7Some of the seed fell among thorn bushes, which grew up and choked the plants, and they didn't bear grain. 8But some seeds fell in good soil, and the plants sprouted, grew, and bore grain: some had thirty grains, others sixty, and others one hundred."

9And Jesus concluded, "Listen, then, if you have ears!"

The Purpose of the Parables
(Matthew 13.10-17; Luke 8.9-10)

10When Jesus was alone, some of those who had heard him came to him with the twelve disciples and asked him to explain the parables. 11"You have been given the secret of the Kingdom of God," Jesus answered. "But the others, who are on the outside, hear all things by means of parables, 12so that,

'They may look and look,

是永遠的罪。」（ 30耶穌說這話是因爲有人說：「他是污靈附身的。」）

耶穌的母親和兄弟
（太12‧46—50；路8‧19—21）

31 這時候，耶穌的母親和兄弟來了；他們站在外面，託人告訴耶穌，說他們要見他。32有一羣人圍坐在耶穌身邊；他們告訴他：「喂，你的母親和兄弟在外面，要找你呢！」

33 耶穌說：「誰是我的母親？誰是我的兄弟？」34他環視坐在他周圍的人，說：「你們看，這些人就是我的母親，我的兄弟！35凡實行上帝旨意的人就是我的兄弟、姊妹，和母親。」

撒種的比喻
（太13‧1—9；路8‧4—8）

4 耶穌又在加利利湖邊教導人。因爲聚集在他周圍的羣衆非常擁擠，他只好上了一條船，坐下。船在湖上，羣衆沿湖岸站着。2耶穌用比喻教導他們許多事，在教導中對他們說：

3「你們留心聽啊！有一個撒種的出去撒種。4他撒的時候，有些種子落在路旁，鳥兒飛來把它們吃掉了。5有些落在淺土的石地上，種子很快就長苗，因爲土壤不深，6太陽一出來，就把幼苗曬焦了，又因爲根不夠深，枯乾了。7有些落在荊棘中，荊棘長起來，把幼苗擠住了，不能結出果實。8有些種子落在好的土壤裏，長大成熟，結實纍纍，有的收成三十倍，有的六十倍，有的一百倍。」

9 耶穌又說：「有耳朵的，都聽吧！」

比喻的目的
（太13‧10—17；路8‧9—10）

10 耶穌獨自一人的時候，有些聽過他講論的人跟十二使徒一起來見他，要求他解釋這些比喻的意思。11耶穌說：「上帝國的奧祕已經給了你們；至於外界的人，他們所聽到的一切都是藉着比喻。12正像聖經所說：

他們看了又看，卻看不見，

yet not see;
they may listen and listen,
    yet not understand.
For if they did, they would turn to God,
    and he would forgive them.'"

Jesus Explains the Parable of the Sower
(Matthew 13.18-23; Luke 8.11-15)

13Then Jesus asked them, "Don't you understand this parable? How, then, will you ever understand any parable? 14The sower sows God's message. 15Some people are like the seeds that fall along the path; as soon as they hear the message, Satan comes and takes it away. 16Other people are like the seeds that fall on rocky ground. As soon as they hear the message, they receive it gladly. 17But it does not sink deep into them, and they don't last long. So when trouble or persecution comes because of the message, they give up at once. 18Other people are like the seeds sown among the thorn bushes. These are the ones who hear the message, 19but the worries about this life, the love for riches, and all other kinds of desires crowd in and choke the message, and they don't bear fruit. 20But other people are like seeds sown in good soil. They hear the message, accept it, and bear fruit: some thirty, some sixty, and some one hundred."

A Lamp under a Bowl
(Luke 8.16-18)

21Jesus continued, "Does anyone ever bring in a lamp and put it under a bowl or under the bed? Isn't it put on the lampstand? 22Whatever is hidden away will be brought out into the open, and whatever is covered up will be uncovered. 23Listen, then, if you have ears!"

24He also said to them, "Pay attention to what you hear! The same rules you use to judge others will be used by God to judge you–but with even greater severity. 25Those who have something will be given more, and those who have nothing will have taken away from them even the little they have."

The Parable of the Growing Seed

26Jesus went on to say, "The Kingdom of God is like this. A man scatters seed in his field. 27He sleeps at night, is up and about during the day, and all the while the seeds are sprouting and growing. Yet he does not know how it happens. 28The soil itself makes the plants grow and bear fruit; first the tender stalk appears, then the head, and finally the head full of grain. 29When the grain is ripe, the man

聽了又聽，卻不明白；
不然，他們回心轉意，
上帝就饒恕他們。」

解釋撒種的比喻
（太13‧18—23；路8‧11—15）

13耶穌又問他們：「你們不明白這比喻嗎？那麼，你們怎能明白其他的比喻呢？ 14撒種的人撒的是上帝的信息。 15有些人好像落在路旁的種子；他們一聽了信息，撒但立刻來了，把撒在他們心裏的信息奪走。 16另有些人好像落在石地上的種子；他們一聽了信息立刻樂意接受， 17可是信息在他們心裏扎根不深，不能持久，一旦爲了信息遭遇患難或迫害，立刻放棄。 18再有些人好像撒在荊棘中的種子；他們聽了信息， 19可是生活的憂慮、財富的誘惑，以及其他各種慾望紛紛而來，窒息了這信息的生機，無法結出果實。 20但是，有些人好像撒在好土壤裏的種子；他們聽了信息，領受了，並結出果實，有的收成三十倍，有的六十倍，有的一百倍。」

斗底下的燈
（路8‧16—18）

21耶穌又說：「有誰點了燈，拿來放在斗底或牀下？他豈不是要把它放在燈臺上嗎？ 22任何隱藏的事總會被張揚出來；任何掩蓋的事也會被揭露出來。 23有耳朵的，都聽吧！」

24他又告訴他們：「要留心你們所聽的！你們用甚麼量器來量，上帝也要用同樣的量器來量給你們，甚至要多給你們。 25那有的，要給他更多；沒有的，連他所有的一點點也要奪走。」

種子長大的比喻

26耶穌繼續說：「上帝的國好像一個人撒種在地上。 27他晚上睡覺，白天起來，那種子發芽生長，怎麼會這樣，他不知道。 28土壤自然而然地使植物生長，結實，先發芽，然後吐穗，最後穗上結滿子粒。 29農作物成熟，他立刻用鐮刀收割，因爲收成的時候到

starts cutting it with his sickle, because harvest time has come.

The Parable of the Mustard Seed
(Matthew 13.31-32, 34; Luke 13.18-19)

30"What shall we say the Kingdom of God is like?" asked Jesus. "What parable shall we use to explain it? 31It is like this. A man takes a mustard seed, the smallest seed in the world, and plants it in the ground. 32After a while it grows up and becomes the biggest of all plants. It puts out such large branches that the birds come and make their nests in its shade."

33Jesus preached his message to the people, using many other parables like these; he told them as much as they could understand. 34He would not speak to them without using parables, but when he was alone with his disciples, he would explain everything to them.

Jesus Calms a Storm
(Matthew 8.23-27; Luke 8.22-25)

35On the evening of that same day Jesus said to his disciples, "Let us go across to the other side of the lake." 36So they left the crowd; the disciples got into the boat in which Jesus was already sitting, and they took him with them. Other boats were there too. 37Suddenly a strong wind blew up, and the waves began to spill over into the boat, so that it was about to fill with water. 38Jesus was in the back of the boat, sleeping with his head on a pillow. The disciples woke him up and said, "Teacher, don't you care that we are about to die?"

39Jesus stood up and commanded the wind, "Be quiet!" and he said to the waves, "Be still!" The wind died down, and there was a great calm. 40Then Jesus said to his disciples, "Why are you frightened? Do you still have no faith?"

41But they were terribly afraid and began to say to one another, "Who is this man? Even the wind and the waves obey him!"

Jesus Heals a Man with Evil Spirits
(Matthew 8.28-34; Luke 8.26-39)

5 Jesus and his disciples arrived on the other side of Lake Galilee, in the territory of Gerasa. 2As soon as Jesus got out of the boat, he was met by a man who came out of the burial caves there. This man had an evil spirit in him 3and lived among the tombs. Nobody could keep him tied with chains any more; 4many times his feet and his hands had been tied, but every time he broke the chains and smashed the irons on his feet. He was too strong for anyone to control him. 5Day and night he wandered among the tombs and through the hills, scream-

了。」

芥菜種的比喻
（太13．31－32，34；路13．18－19）

30 耶穌問：「我們說上帝的國像甚麼呢？我們用甚麼比喻來說明它呢？31上帝的國好比一粒芥菜種子，是世上最小的種子。有人把它種在地裏，32過些時候，它長大起來，比各種蔬菜都大；它長出大枝，飛鳥也在它的蔭下搭窩。」

33 耶穌用許多類似的比喻向羣眾講道，照他們所能明白的教導他們。34他總是用比喻對他們講論；但是他單獨跟門徒在一起的時候，就向門徒解釋一切。

耶穌平息風浪
（太8．23－27；路8．22－25）

35 當天晚上，耶穌對門徒說：「我們渡湖到對岸去吧。」36於是他們離開羣眾。耶穌已經在船上等着，門徒上了船就帶着他走；另有別的船隻同行。37湖上忽然颳起大風，波浪沖擊，浪花打進小船，船幾乎灌滿了水。38當時耶穌在船尾，靠着枕頭睡着了。他們叫醒他，說：「老師，我們快死啦，你不在乎嗎？」

39 耶穌起來，命令風：「靜下來！」又吩咐浪：「停止！」風就停住，湖面平靜下來。40於是他對門徒說：「為甚麼膽怯，你們還沒有信心嗎？」

41 他們就非常恐懼，彼此說：「這個人究竟是誰，連風浪也聽從他！」

耶穌治好污靈附身的人
（太8．28－34；路8．26－39）

5 他們到加利利湖的那一邊，屬於格拉森人的地區。2耶穌一下船就遇見一個從墓穴出來的人；這個人被污靈附着，3一向住在墳地裏，沒有人能夠控制他，用鐵鍊也鎖不住他。4多少次用腳鐐手銬鎖住他，他卻打碎腳鐐，扭斷手銬。沒有人有夠大的力氣制伏他。5他日夜在墳地和山野間大喊

ing and cutting himself with stones.

6He was some distance away when he saw Jesus; so he ran, fell on his knees before him, 7and screamed in a loud voice, "Jesus, Son of the Most High God! What do you want with me? For God's sake, I beg you, don't punish me!" 8(He said this because Jesus was saying, "Evil spirit, come out of this man!")

9So Jesus asked him, "What is your name!"

The man answered, "My name is 'Mob'–there are so many of us!" 10And he kept begging Jesus not to send the evil spirits out of that region.

11There was a large herd of pigs near by, feeding on a hillside. 12So the spirits begged Jesus, "Send us to the pigs, and let us go into them." 13He let them go, and the evil spirits went out of the man and entered the pigs. The whole herd–about two thousand pigs in all–rushed down the side of the cliff into the lake and was drowned.

14The men who had been taking care of the pigs ran away and spread the news in the town and among the farms. People went out to see what had happened, 15and when they came to Jesus, they saw the man who used to have the mob of demons in him. He was sitting there, clothed and in his right mind; and they were all afraid. 16Those who had seen it told the people what had happened to the man with the de-mons, and about the pigs.

17So they asked Jesus to leave their territory.

18As Jesus was getting into the boat, the man who had had the demons begged him, "Let me go with you!"

19But Jesus would not let him. Instead, he told him, "Go back home to your family and tell them how much the Lord has done for you and how kind he has been to you."

20So the man left and went all through the Ten Towns, telling what Jesus had done for him. And all who heard it were amazed.

Jairus' Daughter and the Woman Who Touched Jesus' Cloak
(Matthew 9.18-26; Luke 8.40-56)

21Jesus went back across to the other side of the lake. There at the lakeside a large crowd gathered around him. 22Jairus, an official of the local synagogue, arrived, and when he saw Jesus, he threw himself down at his feet 23and begged him earnestly, "My little daughter is very sick. Please come and place your hands on her, so that she will get well and live!"

24Then Jesus started off with him. So many people were going along with Jesus that they

大叫，又拿石頭擊打自己。

6 他遠遠地看見耶穌，連忙跑過來，跪在耶穌面前，7 大聲說：「至高上帝的兒子耶穌，你爲甚麼來干擾我呢？我指着上帝求求你，不要折磨我！」（8 他講這話是因爲耶穌已經吩咐他說：「污靈，從那人身上出來！」）

9 耶穌問他：「你叫甚麼名字？」

他回答：「我名叫『大羣』，因爲我們數目衆多！」10他再三地哀求耶穌不要趕他們離開那地方。

11 在附近山坡上剛好有一大羣豬在吃東西；12污靈就央求耶穌，說：「把我們趕進豬羣，讓我們附在豬裏面吧。」13耶穌准了他們；污靈就從那人身上出來，進了豬羣；整羣的豬（約兩千隻）衝下山崖，竄入湖裏，都淹死了。

14 放豬的人都逃跑了；他們往城裏和周圍的鄉村去報告這消息。大家都出來要看看究竟發生了甚麼事。15他們到耶穌那裏，看見那個從前被鬼羣附着的人坐着，穿好了衣服，神智清醒，就很害怕。16看見這事經過的人把發生在被鬼附身那人身上和豬羣的事告訴了大家。17他們就要求耶穌離開他們的地區。

18 耶穌上船的時候，那個曾被鬼附身的人來求耶穌說：「請讓我跟你去。」

19 耶穌不答應，卻告訴他：「你回家去，告訴親友，主怎樣以慈愛待你和他爲你所做的事。」

20 那個人走了，開始在十邑地區傳揚耶穌在他身上所做的事；聽見的人沒有不驚奇的。

葉魯的女兒和患血崩的女人
（太9‧18-26；路8‧40-56）

21 耶穌又坐船渡過湖的那邊；在湖邊有一大羣人聚集到他跟前。22當地一個會堂主管名叫葉魯，也來了。他一看見耶穌就俯伏在他腳前，23懇切地求他：「我的小女兒病重垂危，請你來爲她按手，治好她，救她一命！」

24 耶穌就跟他一起去。好些人跟着他走，

were crowding him from every side.

25There was a woman who had suffered terribly from severe bleeding for twelve years, 26even though she had been treated by many doctors. She had spent all her money, but instead of getting better she got worse all the time. 27She had heard about Jesus, so she came in the crowd behind him, 28saying to herself, "If I just touch his clothes, I will get well."

29She touched his cloak, and her bleeding stopped at once; and she had the feeling inside herself that she was healed of her trouble. 30At once Jesus knew that power had gone out of him, so he turned around in the crowd and asked, "Who touched my clothes?"

31His disciples answered, "You see how the people are crowding you; why do you ask who touched you?"

32But Jesus kept looking around to see who had done it. 33The woman realized what had happened to her, so she came, trembling with fear, knelt at his feet, and told him the whole truth. 34Jesus said to her, "My daughter, your faith has made you well. Go in peace, and be healed of your trouble."

35While Jesus was saying this, some messengers came from Jairus' house and told him, "Your daughter has died. Why bother the Teacher any longer?"

36Jesus paid no attention tog what they said, but told him, "Don't be afraid, only believe." 37Then he did not let anyone else go on with him except Peter and James and his brother John. 38They arrived at Jairus' house, where Jesus saw the confusion and heard all the loud crying and wailing. 39He went in and said to them, "Why all this confusion? Why are you crying? The child is not dead–she is only sleeping!"

40They started making fun of him, so he put them all out, took the child's father and mother and his three disciples, and went into the room where the child was lying. 41He took her by the hand and said to her, *"Talitha, koum,"* which means, "Little girl, I tell you to get up!"

42She got up at once and started walking around. (She was twelve years old.) When this happened, they were completely amazed. 43But Jesus gave them strict orders not to tell anyone, and he said, "Give her something to eat."

Jesus Is Rejected at Nazareth
(Matthew 13.53-58; Luke 4.16-30)

6 Jesus left that place and went back to his hometown, followed by his disciples. 2On the Sabbath he began to teach in the syna-

g paid no attention to; *or* overheard.

擁擠他。

25那地方有一個女人患了十二年的血崩，26看過許多醫生，受盡許多痛苦，耗盡所有的家產；可是她的病不但沒有起色，反而一天比一天沉重。27她聽見過耶穌的事，所以雜在人羣中，走到耶穌背後，摸他的衣裳，28心裏想：「我一摸他的衣裳，一定得醫治。」

29她的血崩立刻止住，感覺到身上的病已經好了。30耶穌立刻知道有能力從自己身上出來，就在人羣中轉過頭來，說：「誰摸了我的衣裳？」

31他的門徒回答：「你看，這麼多人擁擠着你，爲甚麼問誰摸你呢？」

32於是耶穌環視左右，要知道是誰摸他。33那女人知道發生在自己身上的事，就戰戰兢兢地跪在耶穌腳前，把實情都說出來。34耶穌對她說：「孩子，你的信心救了你。平安地回去吧，你的病痛消除了。」

35耶穌還在說這話的時候，有人從會堂主管的家裏趕來，告訴葉魯：「你的女兒已經死了，何必再麻煩老師呢？」

36耶穌不理會④他們所說的話，對會堂主管說：「不要怕，只要信！」37於是他帶彼得、雅各，和雅各的弟弟約翰一道去，不許別人跟着。38他們來到會堂主管的家，耶穌看見大家亂成一團，號咷大哭。39耶穌進去對他們說：「你們爲甚麼大哭大嚷呢？孩子並沒有死，只是睡着了。」

40他們都譏笑他，耶穌就把他們趕出去，只讓孩子的父母和他的三個門徒跟他進女孩子的臥室。41他拉着女孩子的手，對她說：「大利大，古米！」意思就是：「小女孩，我吩咐你，起來！」

42女孩子立刻起來行走（那時她已經十二歲）。這事使大家非常驚訝！43耶穌鄭重地囑咐他們不要向她宣揚，又吩咐給孩子一些東西吃。

拿撒勒人厭棄耶穌
（太13．53-58；路4．16-30）

6 耶穌離開那地方，回到自己的家鄉；他的門徒也跟他一起來。2到了安息日，

④「耶穌不理會」或譯「耶穌聽到」。

gogue. Many people were there; and when they heard him, they were all amazed. "Where did he get all this?" they asked. "What wisdom is this that has been given him? How does he perform miracles? ³Isn't he the carpenter, the son of Mary, and the brother of James, Joseph, Judas, and Simon? Aren't his sisters living here?" And so they rejected him.

⁴Jesus said to them, "Prophets are respected everywhere except in their own hometown and by their relatives and their family."

⁵He was not able to perform any miracles there, except that he placed his hands on a few sick people and healed them. ⁶He was greatly surprised, because the people did not have faith.

Jesus Sends Out the Twelve Disciples
(Matthew 10.5-15; Luke 9.1-6)

Then Jesus went to the villages around there, teaching the people. ⁷He called the twelve disciples together and sent them out two by two. He gave them authority over the evil spirits ⁸and ordered them, "Don't take anything with you on the trip except a walking stick–no bread, no beggar's bag, no money in your pockets. ⁹Wear sandals, but don't carry an extra shirt." ¹⁰He also told them, "Wherever you are welcomed, stay in the same house until you leave that place. ¹¹If you come to a town where people do not welcome you or will not listen to you, leave it and shake the dust off your feet. That will be a warning to them!"

¹²So they went out and preached that people should turn away from their sins. ¹³They drove out many demons, and rubbed olive oil on many sick people and healed them.

The Death of John the Baptist
(Matthew 14.1-12; Luke 9.7-9)

¹⁴Now King Herod*ʰ* heard about all this, because Jesus' reputation had spread everywhere. Some people were saying, "John the Baptist has come back to life! That is why he has this power to perform miracles."

¹⁵Others, however, said, "He is Elijah."

Others said, "He is a prophet, like one of the prophets of long ago."

¹⁶When Herod heard it, he said, "He is John the Baptist! I had his head cut off, but he has come back to life!" ¹⁷Herod himself had ordered John's arrest, and he had him tied up

ʰ KING HEROD: *Herod Antipas, ruler of Galilee.*

他在會堂裏教導人。許多人聽見他的話都很驚訝,說:「這個人從哪裏得到這本領呢?誰給他這種智慧呢?他居然還能夠行神蹟! ³他豈不是一個木匠?他不就是馬利亞的兒子,雅各、約瑟、猶大,和西門的哥哥嗎?他的妹妹們不是都住在我們這裏嗎?」於是他們厭棄他。

⁴ 耶穌對他們說:「先知在本鄉、本族、本家外都受人尊重。」

⁵ 因此,他在自己的家鄉沒有行甚麼神蹟,只是給一些病人按手,治好他們。⁶對於這些人的不信,他非常詫異。

耶穌派遣十二使徒
(太10.5—15;路9.1—6)

耶穌繼續在附近各村莊教導人。⁷他召集十二使徒,派遣他們兩個兩個地出去。他賜給他們驅逐污靈的權柄,⁸同時吩咐他們說:「在旅途上除了一根手杖,甚麼東西都不用帶;不帶食物,不帶旅行袋,口袋裏也不帶錢,⁹只穿一雙鞋子,也不需要兩件內衣。」¹⁰他又對他們說:「當你們到了一個地方,哪一家願意接待你們,就住在那裏,直到你們離開那地方。¹¹無論到甚麼地方,如果當地的人不接待你們,也不聽你們的話,你們就離開那地方,把腳上的塵土也踩掉,表示對他們的警告。」

¹² 他們就出去傳道,勸人悔改。¹³他們又趕走許多鬼,用油塗抹許多病人,治好了他們的疾病。

施洗者約翰的死
(太14.1—12;路9.7—9)

¹⁴ 關於耶穌的一切事希律王都聽到了,因為耶穌的名聲傳遍各地方。有人說:「他是施洗者約翰復活了,所以具有行神蹟的能力。」

¹⁵ 有人說:「他是以利亞。」

也有人說:「他是個先知,像古時的先知之一。」

¹⁶ 希律聽見了這些話,卻說:「他是那個被我砍了頭的施洗者約翰,他復活了!」¹⁷希律曾下令逮捕約翰,把他綁起來,關在

and put in prison. Herod did this because of Herodias, whom he had married, even though she was the wife of his brother Philip. [18]John the Baptist kept telling Herod, "It isn't right for you to marry your brother's wife!"

[19]So Herodias held a grudge against John and wanted to kill him, but she could not because of Herod. [20]Herod was afraid of John because he knew that John was a good and holy man, and so he kept him safe. He liked to listen to him, even though he became greatly disturbed every time he heard him.

[21]Finally Herodias got her chance. It was on Herod's birthday, when he gave a feast for all the top government officials, the military chiefs, and the leading citizens of Galilee. [22]The daughter of Herodias[i] came in and danced, and pleased Herod and his guests. So the king said to the girl, "What would you like to have? I will give you anything you want." [23]With many vows he said to her, "I swear that I will give you anything you ask for, even as much as half my kingdom!"

[24]So the girl went out and asked her mother, "What shall I ask for?"

"The head of John the Baptist," she answered.

[25]The girl hurried back at once to the king and demanded, "I want you to give me here and now the head of John the Baptist on a plate!"

[26]This made the king very sad, but he could not refuse her because of the vows he had made in front of all his guests. [27]So he sent off a guard at once with orders to bring John's head. The guard left, went to the prison, and cut John's head off; [28]then he brought it on a plate and gave it to the girl, who gave it to her mother. [29]When John's disciples heard about this, they came and got his body, and buried it.

Jesus Feeds Five Thousand
(Matthew 14.13-21; Luke 9.10-17; John 6.1-14)

[30]The apostles returned and met with Jesus, and told him all they had done and taught. [31]There were so many people coming and going that Jesus and his disciples didn't even have time to eat. So he said to them, "Let us go off by ourselves to some place where we will be alone and you can rest a while." [32]So they started out in a boat by themselves to a lonely place.

[33]Many people, however, saw them leave and knew at once who they were; so they went from all the towns and ran ahead by land and arrived at the place ahead of Jesus and his disciples.

---

i The daughter of Herodias; *some manuscripts have* His daughter Herodias.

監獄裏。希律這樣做是爲了討好希羅底，因爲希律娶了他兄弟腓力的妻子希羅底。[18]約翰屢次指責他：「你佔了你兄弟的妻子是不對的！」

[19]因此希羅底對約翰懷恨在心，想要殺他，可是不能如願。[20]希律怕約翰，知道他是一個正直聖潔的人，要保護他。希律每次聽了約翰的講論，都非常不安，不過他仍然喜歡聽他談論。

[21]希羅底所等待的機會終於到了。希律生日的那一天，他舉行宴會招待政府的顯要、文武官員，和加利利民間的領袖。[22]席間，希羅底的女兒[⑤]出來跳舞；希律和賓客都賞心悅目。於是王對她說：「無論你向我求甚麼，我都給你。」[23]接着他又發誓：「無論你求甚麼，就是我江山的一半，我也給你！」

[24]那女孩子出去問她的母親：「我應該求甚麼呢？」

她的母親回答：「施洗者約翰的頭。」

[25]女孩子立刻回來見王，請求說：「求王立刻把施洗者約翰的頭放在盤子裏，給我！」

[26]王聽見這個請求，非常苦惱；可是他已經在賓客面前發誓，不願意拒絕女孩子的請求。[27]於是他立刻命令侍衛去拿約翰的頭來。侍衛出去，到監獄裏，斬下約翰的頭，[28]放在盤子裏，帶回給希羅底的女兒；女兒拿去交給母親。[29]約翰的門徒聽見這消息，就來把約翰的屍體領走，葬在墳墓裏。

耶穌使五千人吃飽
（太14・13—21；路9・10—17；約6・1—13）

[30]使徒們回來見耶穌，把他們所做所傳的一切都向他報告。[31]因爲來來往往的人太多，耶穌和門徒連吃飯的時間也沒有，所以耶穌對他們說：「你們來，跟我私下到偏僻的地方去休息一會兒。」[32]於是他們坐船出發，悄悄地到偏僻的地方去。

[33]可是，好些人看見他們離開，立刻認出他們。羣衆就從各城鎮出來，爭先恐後地趕路，比耶穌和門徒先到了那地方。

---

⑤「希羅底的女兒」另有些古卷作「他的女兒希羅底」。

34When Jesus got out of the boat, he saw this large crowd, and his heart was filled with pity for them, because they were like sheep without a shepherd. So he began to teach them many things. 35When it was getting late, his disciples came to him and said, "It is already very late, and this is a lonely place. 36Send the people away, and let them go to the nearby farms and villages in order to buy themselves something to eat."

37"You yourselves give them something to eat," Jesus answered.

They asked, "Do you want us to go and spend two hundred silver coins/ on bread in order to feed them?"

38So Jesus asked them, "How much bread do you have? Go and see."

When they found out, they told him, "Five loaves and also two fish."

39Jesus then told his disciples to make all the people divide into groups and sit down on the green grass. 40So the people sat down in rows, in groups of a hundred and groups of fifty. 41Then Jesus took the five loaves and the two fish, looked up to heaven, and gave thanks to God. He broke the loaves and gave them to his disciples to distribute to the people. He also divided the two fish among them all. 42Everyone ate and had enough. 43Then the disciples took up twelve baskets full of what was left of the bread and the fish. 44The number of men who were fed was five thousand.

Jesus Walks on the Water

(Matthew 14.22-33; John 6.15-21)

45At once Jesus made his disciples get into the boat and go ahead of him to Bethsaida, on the other side of the lake, while he sent the crowd away. 46After saying good-bye to the people, he went away to a hill to pray. 47When evening came, the boat was in the middle of the lake, while Jesus was alone on land. 48He saw that his disciples were straining at the oars, because they were rowing against the wind; so sometime between three and six o'clock in the morning, he came to them, walking on the water. He was going to pass them by,k 49but they saw him walking on the water. "It's a ghost!" they thought, and screamed. 50They were all terrified when they saw him.

Jesus spoke to them at once, "Courage!" he said. "It is I. Don't be afraid!" 51Then he got into the boat with them, and the wind died down. The disciples were completely amazed, 52because they had not understood the real

j SILVER COINS: *A silver coin was the daily wage of a rural worker (see Mt 20.2).*
k pass them by; *or* join them.

34耶穌一登岸,看見這一大羣人,動了惻隱的心,因為他們好像沒有牧人的羊羣。他開始教導他們許多事。35傍晚的時候,門徒來見他,對他說:「天晚了,這裏又是偏僻的地方,36請叫大家散開,讓他們自己到附近村莊買食物吃。」

37 耶穌說:「你們給他們吃吧。」

他們問:「你要我們去買兩百塊銀子的餅來給他們吃嗎?」

38 耶穌對他們說:「去看看你們一共有多少個餅?」

他們查過後說:「五個餅和兩條魚。」

39 耶穌吩咐門徒叫羣眾一組一組地坐在青草地上。40大家坐下來,有一百個人一組的,有五十個人一組的。41耶穌拿起五個餅和兩條魚,舉目望天,感謝上帝,然後擘開餅,遞給門徒,門徒就分給大家。同樣,他把兩條魚也分了。42大家都吃,而且都吃飽了。43門徒把剩下的餅和魚裝滿了十二個籃子。44吃飽的人數,男人就有五千。

耶穌在水上行走

(太14·22-33;約6·16-21)

45這事以後,耶穌立刻催他的門徒上船,先到對岸的伯賽大去,等他遣散羣眾。46他送走了他們就上山禱告。47傍晚時分,船已經開到湖中,耶穌還自己一個人留在岸上。48他看見門徒搖船非常辛苦,因為船逆着風走。天快亮的時候,耶穌在湖上朝着他們走來,想要從他們旁邊走過去⑥。49他們看見他在水上走,以為是鬼魂,就都驚喊起來;50因為他們看見他,都非常驚慌。

耶穌立刻對他們說:「放心吧,是我,不要怕!」51於是他上了船,和他們在一起,風就停了。他們又驚奇又困惑,52因為還沒有了解分餅這件事的意義;他們的思想

⑥「想要從他們旁邊走過去」或譯「想要加入他們」。

meaning of the feeding of the five thousand; their minds could not grasp it.

Jesus Heals the Sick in Gennesaret
(Matthew 14.34-36)

53They crossed the lake and came to land at Gennesaret, where they tied up the boat. 54As they left the boat, people recognized Jesus at once. 55So they ran throughout the whole region; and wherever they heard he was, they brought to him the sick lying on their mats. 56And everywhere Jesus went, to villages, towns, or farms, people would take their sick to the marketplaces and beg him to let the sick at least touch the edge of his cloak. And all who touched it were made well.

The Teaching of the Ancestors
(Matthew 15.1-9)

7 Some Pharisees and teachers of the Law who had come from Jerusalem gathered around Jesus. 2They noticed that some of his disciples were eating their food with hands that were ritually unclean–that is, they had not washed them in the way the Pharisees said people should.

3(For the Pharisees, as well as the rest of the Jews, follow the teaching they received from their ancestors: they do not eat unless they wash their hands in the proper way; 4nor do they eat anything that comes from the market unless they wash it first.*l* And they follow many other rules which they have received, such as the proper way to wash cups, pots, copper bowls, and beds.*m*)

5So the Pharisees and the teachers of the Law asked Jesus, "Why is it that your disciples do not follow the teaching handed down by our ancestors, but instead eat with ritually unclean hands?"

6Jesus answered them, "How right Isaiah was when he prophesied about you! You are hypocrites, just as he wrote:

'These people, says God, honor me with their words,

but their heart is really far away from me.

7It is no use for them to worship me,

because they teach human rules

as though they were my laws!'

8"You put aside God's command and obey human teachings."

9And Jesus continued, "You have a clever way of rejecting God's law in order to uphold your own teaching. 10For Moses commanded,

l anything that comes from the market unless they wash it first; or anything after they come from the market unless they wash themselves first.
m Some manuscripts do not have and beds.

遲鈍。

治好革尼撒勒病人
（太14・34—36）

53他們渡過了湖，在革尼撒勒靠岸，把船拴好。54他們一從船上出來，羣眾立刻認出耶穌。55於是他們走遍那地方，聽到耶穌在哪裏，就把患病的人用褥子抬到他那裏。56耶穌無論到鄉下，到城裏，或是到村莊去，羣眾都把病人放在街市上，要求耶穌讓病人僅僅摸一摸他外袍的衣角；所有摸着的人都得醫治。

祖先的傳統
（太15・1—20）

7 法利賽人和從耶路撒冷來的一些經學教師一起來見耶穌。2他們看見耶穌的門徒當中有人用不潔淨的手吃飯一就是沒有像法利賽人那樣先洗手。

3 原來法利賽人和一般猶太人都拘守祖先的傳統，若不照規定先洗手就不吃飯；4從街上買來的東西若不先洗過也不吃⑦。他們還拘守許多其他傳統的規例，好比怎樣洗杯子，洗鍋子，洗銅器和牀舖⑧等等。

5 因此法利賽人和經學教師們問耶穌：「為甚麼你的門徒不遵守祖先的傳統，竟用不潔淨的手吃飯呢？」

6 耶穌說：「以賽亞指着你們這班假冒為善的人所說的預言是對的；他說：

上帝這樣說：

這人民用唇舌尊敬我，

他們的心卻遠離我。

7 他們竟把人的規例當作我的命令；

他們敬拜我都是徒然！」

8 耶穌說：「你們拘守人的傳統，而放棄了上帝的命令。」

9 他又說：「你們技巧地拒絕上帝的命令，為的是要拘守傳統。10摩西命令你們：

⑦「從街上買來的東西不先洗過也不吃」或譯「他們從街上回來，若不先洗手，就不吃任何東西」。
⑧有些古卷沒有「牀舖」。

'Respect your father and your mother,' and, 'If you curse your father or your mother, you are to be put to death.' [11]But you teach that if people have something they could use to help their father or mother, but say, 'This is Corban' (which means, it belongs to God), [12]they are excused from helping their father or mother. [13]In this way the teaching you pass on to others cancels out the word of God. And there are many other things like this that you do."

The Things That Make a Person Unclean
(Matthew 15.10-20)

[14]Then Jesus called the crowd to him once more and said to them, "Listen to me, all of you, and understand. [15]There is nothing that goes into you from the outside which can make you ritually unclean. Rather, it is what comes out of you that makes you unclean."[n]

[17]When he left the crowd and went into the house, his disciples asked him to explain this saying. [18]"You are no more intelligent than the others," Jesus said to them. "Don't you understand? Nothing that goes into you from the outside can really make you unclean, [19]because it does not go into your heart but into your stomach and then goes on out of the body." (In saying this, Jesus declared that all foods are fit to be eaten.)

[20]And he went on to say, "It is what comes out of you that makes you unclean. [21]For from the inside, from your heart, come the evil ideas which lead you to do immoral things, to rob, kill, [22]commit adultery, be greedy, and do all sorts of evil things, deceit, indecency, jealousy, slander, pride, and folly— [23]all these evil things come from inside you and make you unclean."

A Woman's Faith
(Matthew 15 21-28)

[24]Then Jesus left and went away to the territory near the city of Tyre. He went into a house and did not want anyone to know he was there, but he could not stay hidden. [25]A woman, whose daughter had an evil spirit in her, heard about Jesus and came to him at once and fell at his feet. [26]The woman was a Gentile, born in the region of Phoenicia in Syria. She begged Jesus to drive the demon out of her daughter. [27]But Jesus answered, "Let us first feed the children. It isn't right to take the children's food and throw it to the dogs."

[28]"Sir," she answered, "even the dogs under the table eat the children's leftovers!"

[n] *Some manuscripts add verse 16:* Listen, then, if you have ears! *(see 4.23).*

『要孝敬父母』；又規定：『咒罵父母的，必須處死。』[11]你們偏偏說，要是有人把奉養父母的東西當作『各耳板』（意思是獻給上帝的供物），[12]他就不必奉養父母。[13]你們這樣做，等於拿你們傳授給別人的傳統來抵消上帝的話。你們還做了許多類似的事。」

使人不潔淨的東西
（太15．10—20）

[14]耶穌再一次召集羣衆到他面前，對他們說：「你們大家都要聽我的話，也要明白。[15]那從外面進到人裏面的不會使人不潔淨；相反地，那從人裏面出來的才會使人不潔淨。[⑨]」

[17]耶穌離開羣衆進屋子裏的時候，門徒問他這個比喻的意思。[18]耶穌對他們說：「你們也跟他們一樣不明白嗎？你們不曉得嗎？那從外面進到人裏面去的不會使他不潔淨；[19]因爲從外面進去的不是到他心裏去，而是到他的肚子裏，然後排泄出來。」（耶穌是指一切食物都是潔淨的。）

[20]他繼續說：「那使人不潔淨的是從人裏面出來的。[21]因爲從裏面，就是從人心裏出來的有種種惡念；這些惡念指使他去犯通姦、偷盜、凶殺、[22]淫亂、貪心、邪惡、詭詐、放蕩、嫉妒、毀謗、驕傲、狂妄等罪。[23]這一切的邪惡都是從人裏面出來而眞正使人不潔淨的。」

一個女人的信心
（太15．21—28）

[24]耶穌離開那地方，到泰爾地區去。他住進一家人家，不願意有人知道，卻隱藏不住。[25]立刻有一個女人，她的女兒被污靈附着，聽見耶穌的事就來見他，跪在他腳前。[26]這女人是一個外國人，生在敍利亞的腓尼基。她求耶穌把她女兒身上的鬼趕出去。[27]耶穌對她說：「先讓兒女吃飽吧。拿兒女的食物扔給小狗吃是不對的。」

[28]那女人回答：「是的，主啊，可是桌底下的小狗也吃孩子剩下的碎屑呀！」

[⑨]有些古卷加16節「有耳朵的，都聽吧！」

29So Jesus said to her, "Because of that answer, go back home, where you will find that the demon has gone out of your daughter!"

30She went home and found her child lying on the bed; the demon had indeed gone out of her.

Jesus Heals a Deaf-Mute

31Jesus then left the neighborhood of Tyre and went on through Sidon to Lake Galilee, going by way of the territory of the Ten Towns. 32Some people brought him a man who was deaf and could hardly speak, and they begged Jesus to place his hands on him. 33So Jesus took him off alone, away from the crowd, put his fingers in the man's ears, spat, and touched the man's tongue. 34Then Jesus looked up to heaven, gave a deep groan, and said to the man, *"Ephphatha,"* which means, "Open up!"

35At once the man was able to hear, his speech impediment was removed, and he began to talk without any trouble. 36Then Jesus ordered the people not to speak of it to anyone; but the more he ordered them not to, the more they told it. 37And all who heard were completely amazed. "How well he does everything!" they exclaimed. "He even causes the deaf to hear and the dumb to speak!"

Jesus Feeds Four Thousand People

(Matthew 15.32-39)

8 Not long afterward another large crowd came together. When the people had nothing left to eat, Jesus called the disciples to him and said, 2"I feel sorry for these people, because they have been with me for three days and now have nothing to eat. 3If I send them home without feeding them, they will faint as they go, because some of them have come a long way."

4His disciples asked him, "Where in this desert can anyone find enough food to feed all these people?"

5"How much bread do you have?" Jesus asked.

"Seven loaves," they answered.

6He ordered the crowd to sit down on the ground. Then he took the seven loaves, gave thanks to God, broke them, and gave them to his disciples to distribute to the crowd; and the disciples did so. 7They also had a few small fish. Jesus gave thanks for these and told the disciples to distribute them too. 8-9Everybody ate and had enough–there were about four thousand people. Then the disciples took up seven baskets full of pieces left over. Jesus sent the people away 10and at once got into a boat

---

29耶穌對她說:「憑着這句話,你可以回家去了;鬼已經從你女兒身上出去了!」

30於是那女人回家,看見女兒躺在牀上;鬼已經離開了她。

耶穌治好一個聾啞的人

31 耶穌離開泰爾附近地區,經過西頓,從十邑境界回到加利利湖。32有人把一個耳聾舌結的人帶到耶穌面前,請耶穌為他按手。33耶穌把他從人羣中領出來,帶到一邊,用自己的手指頭探進他的耳朵,又用口水擦在他的舌頭上。34耶穌抬頭望天,深深地歎了一口氣,對那個人說:「以法大!」意思就是「張開」!

35 那個人的耳朵立刻開了,舌頭也鬆了,他就開口說話,毫無困難。36耶穌吩咐大家千萬不要向人提起這件事;可是他越是叮嚀,他們越熱心傳揚。37所有聽見的人都非常驚奇;他們說:「他所做的事都好極了!他甚至叫聾子聽見,叫啞巴說話!」

耶穌使四千人吃飽

(太15.32—39)

8 過了不久,另外一大羣人聚集在一起。他們沒有甚麼可吃的了;耶穌叫門徒來,對他們說:2「我很替這一羣人擔心;因為他們跟我在一起已經三天,現在沒有甚麼可吃的了。3如果我叫他們餓着肚子回家,他們會在路上暈倒,因為他們有的是從遠方來的。」

4 他的門徒就問他:「在這偏僻的地方,我們哪裏去找足夠的食物給這許多人吃飽呢?」

5 耶穌問他們:「你們有多少個餅?」他們回答:「七個。」

6 耶穌吩咐羣眾坐在地上,然後拿起那七個餅,感謝上帝,擘開,遞給門徒,門徒就分給大家。7他們還有幾條小魚;耶穌獻上感謝,吩咐門徒也分給大家。8-9大家都吃,而且吃飽了;吃的人數約有四千。門徒收拾吃剩的碎屑,一共裝滿了七個籃子。耶穌遣散羣眾,10立刻和門徒上船往大瑪努他

with his disciples and went to the district of Dalmanutha.

The Pharisees Ask for a Miracle
(Matthew 16.1-4)

11Some Pharisees came to Jesus and started to argue with him. They wanted to trap him, so they asked him to perform a miracle to show that God approved of him. 12But Jesus gave a deep groan and said, "Why do the people of this day ask for a miracle? No, I tell you! No such proof will be given to these people!"

13He left them, got back into the boat, and started across to the other side of the lake.

The Yeast of the Pharisees and of Herod
(Matthew 16.5-12)

14The disciples had forgotten to bring enough bread and had only one loaf with them in the boat. 15"Take care," Jesus warned them, "and be on your guard against the yeast of the Pharisees and the yeast of Herod."

16They started discussing among themselves· "He says this because we don't have any bread."

17Jesus knew what they were saying, so he asked them, "Why are you discussing about not having any bread? Don't you know or understand yet? Are your minds so dull? 18You have eyes–can't you see? You have ears–can't you hear? Don't you remember 19when I broke the five loaves for the five thousand people? How many baskets full of leftover pieces did you take up?"

"Twelve," they answered.

20"And when I broke the seven loaves for the four thousand people," asked Jesus, "how many baskets full of leftover pieces did you take up?"

"Seven," they answered.

21"And you still don't understand?" he asked them.

Jesus Heals a Blind Man at Bethsaida

22They came to Bethsaida, where some people brought a blind man to Jesus and begged him to touch him. 23Jesus took the blind man by the hand and led him out of the village. After spitting on the man's eyes, Jesus placed his hands on him and asked him, "Can you see anything?"

24The man looked up and said, "Yes, I can see people, but they look like trees walking around."

25Jesus again placed his hands on the man's eyes. This time the man looked intently, his eyesight returned, and he saw everything clearly. 26Jesus then sent him home with the order,

地區去。

法利賽人求神蹟
（太16‧1－4）

11 有些法利賽人來見耶穌，跟他辯論。他們想陷害他，要求他顯個神蹟，證明他所行的是出於上帝。12耶穌深深地歎息，說：「這時代的人為甚麼要求神蹟呢？我實在告訴你們，這時代的人是不配看神蹟的！」

13 他就離開他們，又上船渡過湖的對岸。

法利賽人和希律的酵母
（太16‧5－12）

14 門徒忘了多帶餅，船上只有一個餅，沒有別的食物。15耶穌警告他們：「要謹慎，要提防法利賽人的酵母和希律的酵母。」

16 他們紛紛議論說：「他說這話是因為我們沒有餅吧。」

17 耶穌知道他們在想些甚麼，就問他們：「你們為甚麼討論沒有餅這件事呢？難道你們還不領悟、還不明白嗎？你們的頭腦是那麼遲鈍嗎？18你們有眼睛卻看不見嗎？有耳朵卻聽不到嗎？你們不記得19我擘開五個餅給五千人吃這件事嗎？你們把吃剩的碎屑裝滿多少籃呢？」

他們回答：「十二籃。」

20 耶穌又問：「當我擘開七個餅給四千人吃，你們又裝滿了多少籃的碎屑呢？」

他們回答：「七籃。」

21 於是耶穌問他們：「那麼，你們還不明白嗎？」

治好伯賽大的盲人

22 他們來到伯賽大，有人領一個盲人到耶穌跟前，要求耶穌摸他。23耶穌牽着盲人的手，帶他到村子外面去，先吐口水在他的眼睛上，然後按手在他身上，問他說：「你看得見東西嗎？」

24 他抬起頭來看，說：「我看見人，他們好像一棵棵的樹，走來走去。」

25 耶穌又把手放在他的眼上。這回盲人定睛一看，視覺恢復了，每一樣東西都看得清清楚楚。26耶穌叫他回家，又吩咐他說：

"Don't go back into the village."

「不要再進村子去。」

Peter's Declaration about Jesus
(Matthew 16.13-20; Luke 9.18-21)

27Then Jesus and his disciples went away to the villages near Caesarea Philippi. On the way he asked them, "Tell me, who do people say I am?"

28"Some say that you are John the Baptist," they answered; "others say that you are Elijah, while others say that you are one of the prophets."

29"What about you?" he asked them. "Who do you say I am?"

Peter answered, "You are the Messiah."

30Then Jesus ordered them, "Do not tell anyone about me."

Jesus Speaks about His Suffering and Death
(Matthew 16.21-28; Luke 9.22-27)

31Then Jesus began to teach his disciples: "The Son of Man must suffer much and be rejected by the elders, the chief priests, and the teachers of the Law. He will be put to death, but three days later he will rise to life." 32He made this very clear to them. So Peter took him aside and began to rebuke him. 33But Jesus turned around, looked at his disciples, and rebuked Peter. "Get away from me, Satan," he said. "Your thoughts don't come from God but from human nature!"

34Then Jesus called the crowd and his disciples to him. "If any of you want to come with me," he told them, "you must forget yourself, carry your cross, and follow me. 35For if you want to save your own life, you will lose it; but if you lose your life for me and for the gospel, you will save it. 36Do you gain anything if you win the whole world but lose your life? Of course not! 37There is nothing you can give to regain your life. 38If you are ashamed of me and of my teaching in this godless and wicked day, then the Son of Man will be ashamed of you when he comes in the glory of his Father with the holy angels."

9 And he went on to say, "I tell you, there are some here who will not die until they have seen the Kingdom of God come with power."

The Transfiguration
(Matthew 17.1-13; Luke 9.28-36)

2Six days later Jesus took with him Peter, James, and John, and led them up a high

彼得認耶穌為基督
（太16‧13—20；路9‧18—21）

27 耶穌和門徒往凱撒利亞‧腓立比附近的村莊去。在路上，他問他們：「一般人說我是誰？」

28 他們回答：「有的說是施洗者約翰；有的說是以利亞；也有的說是先知中的一位。」

29耶穌又問他們：「你們呢？你們說我是誰？」

彼得回答：「你是基督。」

30 於是，耶穌吩咐他們千萬不要把他的身份告訴任何人。

耶穌預言自己的受難和死
（太16‧21—28；路9‧22—27）

31 耶穌開始教導門徒說：「人子必須遭受許多苦難，被長老、祭司長，和經學教師棄絕，被殺害，三天後將復活。」32他把這些事說得清清楚楚。彼得就把耶穌拉到一邊，要勸阻他。33耶穌轉過身來，看看門徒，責備彼得說：「撒但，走開！你所想的不是上帝的想法，而是人的想法。」

34 於是，耶穌叫羣眾和門徒都到他跟前來，告訴他們：「如果有人要跟從我，就得捨棄自己，背起他的十字架來跟從我。35因為那想救自己生命的，反要喪失生命；那為我和福音喪失生命的，反要得到生命。36一個人就是贏得了全世界，卻賠上了自己的生命，有甚麼益處呢？沒有！37他能夠拿甚麼來換回自己的生命呢？38在這淫亂和邪惡的時代裏，如果有人以我和我的教訓為恥，人子在他父親的榮耀中、和他的聖天使一起來臨的時候，也要以他為恥。」

9 耶穌又對他們說：「我鄭重地告訴你們，站在這裏的人，有的會在他死以前看見上帝的主權帶着能力實現。」

改變形像
（太17‧1—13；路9‧28—36）

2 六天後，耶穌帶着彼得、雅各，和約

mountain, where they were alone. As they looked on, a change came over Jesus, [3]and his clothes became shining white–whiter than anyone in the world could wash them. [4]Then the three disciples saw Elijah and Moses talking with Jesus. [5]Peter spoke up and said to Jesus, "Teacher, how good it is that we are here! We will make three tents, one for you, one for Moses, and one for Elijah." [6]He and the others were so frightened that he did not know what to say.

[7]Then a cloud appeared and covered them with its shadow, and a voice came from the cloud, "This is my own dear Son–listen to him!" [8]They took a quick look around but did not see anyone else; only Jesus was with them.

[9]As they came down the mountain, Jesus ordered them, "Don't tell anyone what you have seen, until the Son of Man has risen from death."

[10]They obeyed his order, but among themselves they started discussing the matter, "What does this 'rising from death' mean?" [11]And they asked Jesus, "Why do the teachers of the Law say that Elijah has to come first?"

[12]His answer was, "Elijah is indeed coming first in order to get everything ready. Yet why do the Scriptures say that the Son of Man will suffer much and be rejected? [13]I tell you, however, that Elijah has already come and that people treated him just as they pleased, as the Scriptures say about him."

Jesus Heals a Boy with an Evil Spirit
(Matthew 17.14-21; Luke 9.37-43a)

[14]When they joined the rest of the disciples, they saw a large crowd around them and some teachers of the Law arguing with them. [15]When the people saw Jesus, they were greatly surprised, and ran to him and greeted him. [16]Jesus asked his disciples, "What are you arguing with them about?"

[17]A man in the crowd answered, "Teacher, I brought my son to you, because he has an evil spirit in him and cannot talk. [18]Whenever the spirit attacks him, it throws him to the ground, and he foams at the mouth, grits his teeth, and becomes stiff all over. I asked your disciples to drive the spirit out, but they could not."

[19]Jesus said to them, "How unbelieving you people are! How long must I stay with you? How long do I have to put up with you? Bring the boy to me!" [20]They brought him to Jesus.

As soon as the spirit saw Jesus, it threw the boy into a fit, so that he fell on the ground and

翰,悄悄地上了一座高山。就在他們面前,耶穌的形像變了,[3]他的衣服變成潔白光亮;世上沒有人能夠把布漂得那麼潔白。[4]三個門徒忽然看見以利亞和摩西在跟耶穌講話。[5]彼得對耶穌說:「老師,我們在這裏真好!讓我們搭三座帳棚,一座給你,一座給摩西,一座給以利亞。」[6]彼得和其他的人都很害怕,不知道該說甚麼才好。

[7]有一朵雲彩籠罩了他們。忽然,從雲裏有聲音傳出來,說:「這是我親愛的兒子,你們要聽從他!」[8]他們連忙向四周張望,卻看不見有別的人,只有耶穌和他們在一起。

[9]他們下山的時候,耶穌吩咐他們:「人子沒有從死裏復活以前,千萬不要把所看見的告訴任何人。」

[10]他們遵照耶穌的吩咐,只是彼此討論說:「從死裏復活是甚麼意思呢?」[11]他們又問耶穌:「為甚麼經學教師說以利亞必須先來呢?」

[12]耶穌回答:「以利亞的確要先來重整一切;然而,聖經上為甚麼又說人子必須受苦難和被棄絕呢?[13]我告訴你們,以利亞已經來了,他們卻任意對待他,正如聖經所說有關他的話。」

治好被鬼附身的兒童
(太17·14-21;路9·37-43)

[14]他們回到其他門徒那裏的時候,看見一大羣人圍着他們,有些經學教師正在跟他們辯論。[15]羣衆一看見耶穌都非常詫異;大家跑上去迎接他。[16]耶穌問門徒:「你們在跟他們辯論些甚麼?」

[17]人羣中有一個人說:「老師,我帶了我的兒子來看你;因為他有啞巴鬼附身,不能說話。[18]每當鬼襲擊他,就把他摔倒在地上,使他口吐白沫,咬緊牙關,渾身僵硬。我請求你的門徒趕走這鬼,可是他們無能為力。」

[19]耶穌對他們說:「你們這時代的人是多麼沒有信心哪!我還得在你們這裏多久呢?還得容忍你們多久呢?把孩子帶到我這裏來!」[20]他們就把他帶來。

那鬼一看見耶穌,立刻使孩子劇烈地抽

rolled around, foaming at the mouth. [21]"How long has he been like this?" Jesus asked the father.

"Ever since he was a child," he replied. [22]"Many times the evil spirit has tried to kill him by throwing him in the fire and into water. Have pity on us and help us, if you possibly can!"

[23]"Yes," said Jesus, "if you yourself can! Everything is possible for the person who has faith."

[24]The father at once cried out, "I do have faith, but not enough. Help me have more!"

[25]Jesus noticed that the crowd was closing in on them, so he gave a command to the evil spirit. "Deaf and dumb spirit," he said, "I order you to come out of the boy and never go into him again!"

[26]The spirit screamed, threw the boy into a bad fit, and came out. The boy looked like a corpse, and everyone said, "He is dead!" [27]But Jesus took the boy by the hand and helped him rise, and he stood up.

[28]After Jesus had gone indoors, his disciples asked him privately, "Why couldn't we drive the spirit out?"

[29]"Only prayer can drive this kind out," answered Jesus; "nothing else can."

Jesus Speaks Again about His Death
(Matthew 17.22-23; Luke 9.43b-45)

[30]Jesus and his disciples left that place and went on through Galilee. Jesus did not want anyone to know where he was, [31]because he was teaching his disciples: "The Son of Man will be handed over to those who will kill him. Three days later, however, he will rise to life."

[32]But they did not understand what this teaching meant, and they were afraid to ask him.

Who Is the Greatest?
(Matthew 18.1-5; Luke 9.46-48)

[33]They came to Capernaum, and after going indoors Jesus asked his disciples, "What were you arguing about on the road?"

[34]But they would not answer him, because on the road they had been arguing among themselves about who was the greatest. [35]Jesus sat down, called the twelve disciples, and said to them, "Whoever wants to be first must place himself last of all and be the servant of all." [36]Then he took a child and had him stand in front of them. He put his arms around him and said to them, [37]"Whoever welcomes in my name one of these children, welcomes me; and whoever welcomes me, welcomes not only me but

瘋，倒在地上打滾，口吐白沫。[21]耶穌問他的父親：「他害這病有多久了？」

他回答：「從小就有了。[22]鬼多次想殺滅他，把他扔進火裏，推下水裏。但是你若能做甚麼，求你憐憫我們，幫助我們！」

[23]耶穌說：「是的，你若能！有信心的人，甚麼事都能。」

[24]孩子的父親立刻大聲喊：「我信，但是我的信心不夠，求你幫助我！」

[25]耶穌看見羣衆圍攏上來，就嚴厲地命令那污靈：「你這聾啞鬼，我命令你從這孩子身上出來，不准你再進去！」

[26]那鬼大叫一聲，使孩子猛烈地抽了一陣瘋，那出來了。孩子好像死人一樣，大家都說：「他已經死了！」[27]但是耶穌拉着他的手，幫他起來，他就站起來。

[28]耶穌一進到屋子裏，門徒們就暗地問他：「爲甚麼我們不能把那鬼趕走呢？」

[29]耶穌說：「只有靠禱告才能夠趕走這種鬼，此外沒有別的方法。」

耶穌再預言自己的死
（太17・22—23；路9・43—45）

[30]他們離開了那地方，經過加利利。耶穌不願意任何人知道他的行蹤，[31]因爲他正在教導門徒。他說：「人子將被交在人手裏；他們要殺害他，死後第三天，他將復活。」

[32]可是他們不明白這話的意思，卻又不敢問他。

誰最偉大
（太18・1—5；路9・46—48）

[33]他們來到迦百農，進屋子後耶穌問他的門徒：「你們在路上爭論些甚麼？」

[34]他們都不作聲，因爲一路上他們在爭論誰最偉大。[35]耶穌坐下，叫十二使徒到他面前，對他們說：「誰要居首，誰就得居後，作大衆的僕人。」[36]於是他找一個小孩子來，叫他站在他們中間，又抱起他，對他說：[37]「爲了我而接待這樣一個小孩子的，就是接待我。接待我的，不僅僅是接待我，

also the one who sent me."

Whoever Is Not against Us Is for Us
(Luke 9.49-50)

38John said to him, "Teacher, we saw a man who was driving out demons in your name, and we told him to stop, because he doesn't belong to our group."

39"Do not try to stop him," Jesus told them, "because no one who performs a miracle in my name will be able soon afterward to say evil things about me. 40For whoever is not against us is for us. 41I assure you that anyone who gives you a drink of water because you belong to me will certainly receive a reward.

Temptations to Sin
(Matthew 18.6-9; Luke 17.1-2)

42"If anyone should cause one of these little ones to lose faith in me, it would be better for that person to have a large millstone tied around the neck and be thrown into the sea. 43So if your hand makes you lose your faith, cut it off! It is better for you to enter life without a hand than to keep both hands and go off to hell, to the fire that never goes out.o 45And if your foot makes you lose your faith, cut it off! It is better for you to enter life without a foot than to keep both feet and be thrown into hell.p 47And if your eye makes you lose your faith, take it out! It is better for you to enter the Kingdom of God with only one eye than to keep both eyes and be thrown into hell. 48There 'the worms that eat them never die, and the fire that burns them is never put out.'

49"Everyone will be purified by fire as a sacrifice is purified by salt.

50"Salt is good; but if it loses its saltiness, how can you make it salty again?

"Have the salt of friendship among yourselves, and live in peace with one another."

Jesus Teaches about Divorce
(Matthew 19.1-12; Luke 16.18)

10Then Jesus left that place, went to the province of Judea, and crossed the Jordan River. Crowds came flocking to him again, and he taught them, as he always did.

2Some Pharisees came to him and tried to trap him. "Tell us," they asked, "does our Law allow a man to divorce his wife?"

---

o Some manuscripts add verse 44: There 'the worms that eat them never die, and the fire that burns them is never put out' (see verse 48).
p Some manuscripts add verse 46: There 'the worms that eat them never die, and the fire that burns them is never put out' (see verse 48).

也是接待差我來的那一位。」

反對或贊同
（路9‧49—50）

38約翰對耶穌說：「老師，我們看見有人藉著你的名趕鬼，我們就禁止他，因為他不跟我們同夥。」

39耶穌說：「不要禁止他；因為沒有人會藉著我的名行神蹟，又馬上轉過來說壞話攻擊我。40因為不反對我們就是贊同我們。41我實在告訴你們，無論誰，只因為你們是屬於基督而給你們一杯水，一定會得到獎賞。」

引人犯罪
（太18‧6—9；路17‧1—2）

42耶穌說：「無論誰使信徒中任何一個微不足道的人離棄我，倒不如用大磨石拴在他的脖子上，把他沉到海底去。43如果你的一隻手使你犯罪，把它砍掉！缺了一隻手而得永恆的生命，比雙手齊全下地獄、落在永不熄滅的烈火裏好多了。⑩45如果你的一隻腳使你犯罪，把它砍掉！缺了一隻腳而得永恆的生命，比雙腳齊全被扔進地獄裏好多了。⑪47如果你的一隻眼睛使你犯罪，把它挖出來！缺了一隻眼睛而進入上帝國，比雙眼齊全被扔進地獄裏好多了。48在那裏，蟲子不死，烈火永不熄滅。

49「每一個人都要被火鍛鍊，像用鹽醃一樣。50鹽本是好的，可是它若失掉鹹味，怎能使它再鹹呢？你們要有鹽的作用，彼此和睦相處。」

有關休妻的教導
（太19‧1—12；路16‧18）

10耶穌離開那地方來到猶太地區，渡過約旦河。羣眾又聚集到他那裏，他就照常教導他們。

2 有些法利賽人來見耶穌，想陷害他，問他：「請告訴我們，我們的法律准許丈夫休棄妻子嗎？」

---

⑩有些古卷加44節「在那裏，蟲子不死，烈火永不熄滅。」
⑪有些古卷加46節「在那裏，蟲子不死，烈火永不熄滅。」

3Jesus answered with a question, "What law did Moses give you?"

4Their answer was, "Moses gave permission for a man to write a divorce notice and send his wife away."

5Jesus said to them, "Moses wrote this law for you because you are so hard to teach. 6But in the beginning, at the time of creation, 'God made them male and female,' as the scripture says. 7And for this reason a man will leave his father and mother and unite with his wife,*q* 8and the two will become one.' So they are no longer two, but one. 9No human being must separate, then, what God has joined together."

10When they went back into the house, the disciples asked Jesus about this matter. 11He said to them, "A man who divorces his wife and marries another woman commits adultery against his wife. 12In the same way, a woman who divorces her husband and marries another man commits adultery."

Jesus Blesses Little Children
(Matthew 19.13-15; Luke 18.15-17)

13Some people brought children to Jesus for him to place his hands on them, but the disciples scolded the people. 14When Jesus noticed this, he was angry and said to his disciples, "Let the children come to me, and do not stop them, because the Kingdom of God belongs to such as these. 15I assure you that whoever does not receive the Kingdom of God like a child will never enter it." 16Then he took the children in his arms, placed his hands on each of them, and blessed them.

The Rich Man
(Matthew 19.16-30; Luke 18.18-30)

17As Jesus was starting on his way again, a man ran up, knelt before him, and asked him, "Good Teacher, what must I do to receive eternal life?"

18"Why do you call me good?" Jesus asked him. "No one is good except God alone. 19You know the commandments: 'Do not commit murder; do not commit adultery; do not steal; do not accuse anyone falsely; do not cheat; respect your father and your mother.'"

20"Teacher," the man said, "ever since I was young, I have obeyed all these commandments."

21Jesus looked straight at him with love and said, "You need only one thing. Go and sell all you have and give the money to the poor, and you will have riches in heaven; then come and

3 耶穌反問：「摩西的命令是怎樣說的？」

4 他們回答：「摩西准許丈夫寫一張休書給妻子，就可以休棄她。」

5 耶穌對他們說：「摩西給你們寫下這一條誡命是因為你們的心腸太硬。6 可是太初，在創世的時候，上帝造人，有男的有女的；7 因此人要離開父母，跟妻子結合⑫，8 兩個人成為一體。既然這樣，夫妻不再是兩個人，而是一體。9 所以，上帝所配合的，人不可拆開。」

10 他們回到屋子裏的時候，門徒又問起這件事。11耶穌告訴他們：「任何男人休棄妻子，再去跟別的女人結婚，就是犯姦淫，辜負了妻子；12妻子若離棄丈夫，再去跟別人結婚，也是犯姦淫。」

耶穌祝福小孩子
（太19‧13—15；路18‧15—17）

13 有些人帶着小孩子來見耶穌，請耶穌摸他們；門徒卻責備那些人。14耶穌看見了就生氣，對門徒說：「讓小孩子到我這裏來，不要阻止他們，因為上帝國的子民正是像他們這樣的人。15你們要記住，凡不像小孩子一樣來接受上帝主權的人，絕不能成為他的子民。」16於是他抱起小孩子，一個一個地摸他們，給他們祝福。

財主的難題
（太19‧16—30；路18‧18—30）

17 耶穌剛上路，有一個人跑過來，跪在他面前，問他：「良善的老師，我該做甚麼才能夠得到永恆的生命呢？」

18 耶穌問他：「你為甚麼稱我為良善的呢？除上帝一位以外，再也沒有良善的。19你一定曉得這些誡命：『不可殺人；不可姦淫；不可偷竊；不可作假證；不可欺詐；要孝敬父母。』」

20 那個人回答：「老師，這一切誡命我從小就都遵守了。」

21 耶穌定睛看他，心裏很喜愛他，就說：「你還缺少一件。去賣掉你所有的產業，把錢捐給窮人，你就會有財富積存在天上；然

---

q Some manuscripts do not have and unite with his wife.

⑫有些古卷沒有「跟妻子結合」。

follow me." 22When the man heard this, gloom spread over his face, and he went away sad, because he was very rich.

23Jesus looked around at his disciples and said to them, "How hard it will be for rich people to enter the Kingdom of God!"

24The disciples were shocked at these words, but Jesus went on to say, "My children, how hard it is to enter the Kingdom of God! 25It is much harder for a rich person to enter the Kingdom of God than for a camel to go through the eye of a needle."

26At this the disciples were completely amazed and asked one another, "Who, then, can be saved?"

27Jesus looked straight at them and answered, "This is impossible for human beings but not for God; everything is possible for God."

28Then Peter spoke up, "Look, we have left everything and followed you."

29"Yes," Jesus said to them, "and I tell you that those who leave home or brothers or sisters or mother or father or children or fields for me and for the gospel, 30will receive much more in this present age. They will receive a hundred times more houses, brothers, sisters, mothers, children, and fields–and persecutions as well; and in the age to come they will receive eternal life. 31But many who are now first will be last, and many who are now last will be first."

Jesus Speaks a Third Time about His Death
(Matthew 20.17-19; Luke 18.31-34)

32Jesus and his disciples were now on the road going up to Jerusalem. Jesus was going ahead of the disciples, who were filled with alarm; the people who followed behind were afraid. Once again Jesus took the twelve disciples aside and spoke of the things that were going to happen to him. 33"Listen," he told them, "we are going up to Jerusalem where the Son of Man will be handed over to the chief priests and the teachers of the Law. They will condemn him to death and then hand him over to the Gentiles, 34who will make fun of him, spit on him, whip him, and kill him; but three days later he will rise to life."

The Request of James and John
(Matthew 20.20-28)

35Then James and John, the sons of Zebedee, came to Jesus. "Teacher," they said, "there is something we want you to do for us."

36"What is it?" Jesus asked them.

後來跟從我。」22那個人一聽見這話，臉色變了，垂頭喪氣地走了，因爲他很富有。

23 耶穌環視左右的門徒，對他們說：「有錢人成爲上帝國的子民是多麼難哪！」

24 門徒對他這話感到驚奇；但是耶穌又說：「孩子們哪，要成爲上帝國的子民是多麼難哪！25有錢人要成爲上帝國的子民，比駱駝穿過針眼還要難！」

26 這時候，門徒更爲驚訝，彼此對問：「這樣說來，有誰能得救呢？」

27 耶穌定睛看他們，說：「人是不能，上帝則不然；因爲在上帝，事事都能。」

28 彼得接着發言：「你看，我們已經撇下一切來跟從你了。」

29 耶穌對他們說：「是的，我實在告訴你們，凡是爲我或爲福音撇下了房屋、兄弟、姊妹、父母、兒女，或田地的，30必定在今世收穫更多。他將得到百倍的房屋、兄弟、姊妹、母親、兒女，或田地，並且要遭受迫害；而在來世，他將得到永恆的生命。31可是，許多在先的將要居後，居後的將要在先。」

耶穌第三次預言自己的死
（太20・17—19；路18・31—34）

32 他們在上耶路撒冷去的路上，耶穌走在前頭。門徒心懷戒懼；其他跟着的人也都害怕。耶穌再一次把十二使徒帶到一邊，告訴他們將要發生在他身上的事。33他說：「看吧，我們現在上耶路撒冷去。人子將被出賣給祭司長和經學教師；他們要判他死刑，然後把他交給外邦人。34他們要戲弄他，向他吐口水，鞭打他，並殺害他；三天後，他將復活。」

雅各和約翰的要求
（太20・20—28）

35 西庇太的兒子雅各和約翰來見耶穌，說：「老師，我們有一個請求，希望你能答應。」

36 耶穌問：「要我爲你們做甚麼？」

37They answered, "When you sit on your throne in your glorious Kingdom, we want you to let us sit with you, one at your right and one at your left."

38Jesus said to them, "You don't know what you are asking for. Can you drink the cup of suffering that I must drink? Can you be baptized in the way I must be baptized?"

39"We can," they answered.

Jesus said to them, "You will indeed drink the cup I must drink and be baptized in the way I must be baptized. 40But I do not have the right to choose who will sit at my right and my left. It is God who will give these places to those for whom he has prepared them."

41When the other ten disciples heard about it, they became angry with James and John. 42So Jesus called them all together to him and said, "You know that those who are considered rulers of the heathen have power over them, and the leaders have complete authority. 43This, however, is not the way it is among you. If one of you wants to be great, you must be the servant of the rest; 44and if one of you wants to be first, you must be the slave of all. 45For even the Son of Man did not come to be served; he came to serve and to give his life to redeem many people."

Jesus Heals Blind Bartimaeus
(Matthew 20.29-34; Luke 18.35-43)

46They came to Jericho, and as Jesus was leaving with his disciples and a large crowd, a blind beggar named Bartimaeus son of Timaeus was sitting by the road. 47When he heard that it was Jesus of Nazareth, he began to shout, "Jesus! Son of David! Have mercy on me!"

48Many of the people scolded him and told him to be quiet. But he shouted even more loudly, "Son of David, have mercy on me!"

49Jesus stopped and said, "Call him."

So they called the blind man. "Cheer up!" they said. "Get up, he is calling you."

50So he threw off his cloak, jumped up, and came to Jesus.

51"What do you want me to do for you?" Jesus asked him.

"Teacher," the blind man answered, "I want to see again."

52"Go," Jesus told him, "your faith has made you well."

At once he was able to see and followed Jesus on the road.

---

37 他們回答:「當你坐在榮耀的寶座上時,請讓我們跟你坐在一起,一個在你右邊,一個在你左邊。」

38 耶穌對他們說:「你們不知道所求的是甚麼。我要喝的苦杯,你們能喝嗎?我要受的洗禮,你們能受嗎?」

39 他們回答:「我們能!」

耶穌說:「我要喝的杯,你們固然要喝,我要受的洗禮,你們固然要受,40但是誰可以坐在我的左右,卻不是我能決定的。這些座位,上帝爲誰預備,就賜給誰。」

41 其他十個門徒聽見這事,對雅各和約翰很不滿。42因此,耶穌把他們都召集到他跟前來,對他們說:「你們知道,世上那些被認爲是統治者的有權管轄人民,領袖也有權支配人民。43但是,你們卻不是這樣。你們當中誰要作大人物,誰就得作你們的僕人;44誰要居首,誰就得做大衆的奴僕。45因爲人子不是來受人侍候,而是來侍候人,並且爲了救贖衆人而獻出自己的生命。」

治好盲人巴底買
(太20 · 29-34;路18 · 35-43)

46 他們來到耶利哥。當耶穌與他的門徒和一大羣人離開耶利哥的時候,有一個盲人—底買的兒子巴底買,坐在路旁討飯。47他一聽說是拿撒勒的耶穌,就喊說:「大衛之子耶穌啊,可憐我吧!」

48 許多人責備他,叫他不要作聲。可是他更大聲喊叫:「大衛之子啊,可憐我吧!」

49 耶穌就站住,說:「叫他過來。」

他們就對盲人說:「你放心,起來,他叫你呢!」

50 盲人馬上扔掉外衣,跳起來,走到耶穌跟前。

51 耶穌問他:「你要我爲你做甚麼?」

盲人回答:「老師,我要能看見!」

52 耶穌說:「去吧,你的信心治好你了。」

盲人立刻能看見,就跟隨着耶穌走了。

The Triumphant Entry into Jerusalem
(Matthew 21.1-11; Luke 19.28-40; John 12.12-19)

11 As they approached Jerusalem, near the towns of Bethphage and Bethany, they came to the Mount of Olives. Jesus sent two of his disciples on ahead ²with these instructions: "Go to the village there ahead of you. As soon as you get there, you will find a colt tied up that has never been ridden. Untie it and bring it here. ³And if someone asks you why you are doing that, say that the Master[r] needs it and will send it back at once."

⁴So they went and found a colt out in the street, tied to the door of a house. As they were untying it, ⁵some of the bystanders asked them, "What are you doing, untying that colt?"

⁶They answered just as Jesus had told them, and the crowd let them go. ⁷They brought the colt to Jesus, threw their cloaks over the animal, and Jesus got on. ⁸Many people spread their cloaks on the road, while others cut branches in the field and spread them on the road. ⁹The people who were in front and those who followed behind began to shout, "Praise God! God bless him who comes in the name of the Lord! ¹⁰God bless the coming kingdom of King David, our father! Praise be to God!"

¹¹Jesus entered Jerusalem, went into the Temple, and looked around at everything. But since it was already late in the day, he went out to Bethany with the twelve disciples.

Jesus Curses the Fig Tree
(Matthew 21.18-19)

¹²The next day, as they were coming back from Bethany, Jesus was hungry. ¹³He saw in the distance a fig tree covered with leaves, so he went to see if he could find any figs on it. But when he came to it, he found only leaves, because it was not the right time for figs. ¹⁴Jesus said to the fig tree, "No one shall ever eat figs from you again!"

And his disciples heard him.

Jesus Goes to the Temple
(Matthew 21.12-17; Luke 19.45-48; John 2.13-22)

¹⁵When they arrived in Jerusalem, Jesus went to the Temple and began to drive out all those who were buying and selling. He overturned the tables of the moneychangers and the stools of those who sold pigeons, ¹⁶and he would not let anyone carry anything through the Temple

r the Master; or its owner.

光榮進耶路撒冷
（太21．1—11；路19．28—40；約12．12—19）

11 耶穌和門徒走近耶路撒冷，到了橄欖山的伯法其和伯大尼。耶穌打發兩個門徒先走，²吩咐他們說：「你們到前面的村子去。你們一進去，就會看見一匹沒有人騎過的小驢拴在那裏。你們把牠解開，牽到這裏來。³如果有人問你們：『為甚麼做這事？』你們就告訴他：『主⑬要用牠，用後會立刻把小驢送回來。』」

⁴他們去了，看見路旁有一匹小驢被拴在門外。他們正在解開繩子的時候，⁵有些站在那裏的人問他們：「你們為甚麼解開小驢？」

⁶他們就照耶穌所吩咐的回答，那些人就讓他們牽走小驢。⁷他們把小驢牽到耶穌那裏，把他們的衣裳搭在驢背上，耶穌騎了上去。⁸有許多人用他們的衣裳鋪在路上，也有些人拿田野裏砍來的樹枝鋪在路上。⁹前行後隨的人喊着說：「頌讚上帝！願上帝賜福給那位奉主名而來的！¹⁰願上帝賜福給那將要臨到的我們祖宗大衛的國度！頌讚歸於至高的上帝！」

¹¹耶穌到了耶路撒冷，進聖殿去，各處察看一下。因為天已晚了，他就和十二使徒出城到伯大尼去。

詛咒無花果樹
（太21．18—19）

¹²第二天，他們從伯大尼回城；在路上，耶穌餓了。¹³他看見前面不遠的地方有一棵無花果樹，長滿了葉子，就走過去，想看看樹上有沒有果子。他到了樹前，只看見葉子，因為那時候不是結無花果的季節。¹⁴耶穌對着那棵樹說：「從今以後，再不會有人吃你的果子！」

他的門徒都聽見了這話。

耶穌潔淨聖殿
（太21．12—17；路19．45—48；約2．13—22）

¹⁵他們到了耶路撒冷，耶穌一進聖殿就把所有在聖殿裏作買賣的人都趕出去。他推倒兌換銀錢的人的桌子和販賣鴿子的人的凳子，¹⁶也不准任何人扛抬雜物在聖殿的院子

⑬「主」或譯「牠的主人」。

courtyards. 17He then taught the people: "It is written in the Scriptures that God said, 'My Temple will be called a house of prayer for the people of all nations.' But you have turned it into a hideout for thieves!"

18The chief priests and the teachers of the Law heard of this, so they began looking for some way to kill Jesus. They were afraid of him, because the whole crowd was amazed at his teaching.

19When evening came, Jesus and his disciples left the city.

The Lesson from the Fig Tree
(Matthew 21.20-22)

20Early next morning, as they walked along the road, they saw the fig tree. It was dead all the way down to its roots. 21Peter remembered what had happened and said to Jesus, "Look, Teacher, the fig tree you cursed has died!"

22Jesus answered them, "Have faith in God. 23I assure you that whoever tells this hill to get up and throw itself in the sea and does not doubt in his heart, but believes that what he says will happen, it will be done for him. 24For this reason I tell you: When you pray and ask for something, believe that you have received it, and you will be given whatever you ask for. 25And when you stand and pray, forgive anything you may have against anyone, so that your Father in heaven will forgive the wrongs you have done."[s]

The Question about Jesus' Authority
(Matthew 21.23-27; Luke 20.1-8)

27They arrived once again in Jerusalem. As Jesus was walking in the Temple, the chief priests, the teachers of the Law, and the elders came to him 28and asked him, "What right do you have to do these things? Who gave you such right?"

29Jesus answered them, "I will ask you just one question, and if you give me an answer, I will tell you what right I have to do these things. 30Tell me, where did John's right to baptize come from: was it from God or from human beings?"

31They started to argue among themselves: "What shall we say? If we answer, 'From God,' he will say, 'Why, then, did you not believe John?' 32But if we say, 'From human beings...'" (They were afraid of the people, because everyone was convinced that John had been a prophet.) 33So their answer to Jesus was, "We don't know."

---

s *Some manuscripts add verse 26: If you do not forgive others, your Father in heaven will not forgive the wrongs you have done (see Mt 6.15).*

穿來穿去。17他教導他們說:「聖經記載上帝的話說:『我的聖殿要作萬民禱告的殿』,你們卻把它變成賊窩!」

18 祭司長和經學教師聽見這話,就想法子要殺害耶穌。但是他們怕他,因為群眾都欽佩他的教導。

19 傍晚,耶穌就和門徒到城外去。

從無花果樹得教訓
(太21 · 20—22)

20 第二天一早,耶穌和門徒又從那條路經過,看見那棵無花果樹連根都枯死了。21彼得記起這事的經過,就對耶穌說:「老師,你看,你所詛咒的無花果樹枯死了。」

22 耶穌回答他們:「對上帝要有信心!23我鄭重地告訴你們,你們若對這座山說:『起來,投到海裏去!』只要心裏不疑惑,確信所說的一定實現,這事就會為你們實現。24所以,我告訴你們,你們禱告,無論求甚麼,相信是得着了,就會得到你們所求的。25你們站着禱告的時候,先要饒恕得罪你們的人;這樣,你們的天父也會饒恕你們的過錯。⑭」

質問耶穌的權柄
(太21 · 23—27;路20 · 1—8)

27 他們又來到耶路撒冷。耶穌在聖殿裏行走的時候,祭司長、經學教師,和長老來見他,28問他說:「你憑甚麼權柄做這些事?誰給你權柄做這些事呢?」

29 耶穌回答:「我先問你們一句話,如果你們回答我,我就告訴你們我憑甚麼權柄做這些事。30告訴我,約翰施洗的權是從哪裏來的?是從上帝還是從人來的?」

31 他們開始爭辯起來,說:「我們應該怎樣回答呢?如果我們說『從上帝那裏來的』,他會說:『那麼,你們為甚麼不相信約翰呢?』32如果我們說『從人那裏來的』,恐怕人民會對付我們,因為他們都相信約翰是先知。」33於是他們回答耶穌:「我們不知道。」

⑭有些古卷加26節「如果你們不饒恕別人,你們的天父也不會饒恕你們。」

Jesus said to them, "Neither will I tell you, then, by what right I do these things."

The Parable of the Tenants in the Vineyard
(Matthew 21.33-46; Luke 20.9-19)

12 Then Jesus spoke to them in parables: "Once there was a man who planted a vineyard, put a fence around it, dug a hole for the wine press, and built a watchtower. Then he rented the vineyard to tenants and left home on a trip. ²When the time came to gather the grapes, he sent a slave to the tenants to receive from them his share of the harvest. ³The tenants grabbed the slave, beat him, and sent him back without a thing. ⁴Then the owner sent another slave; the tenants beat him over the head and treated him shamefully. ⁵The owner sent another slave, and they killed him; and they treated many others the same way, beating some and killing others. ⁶The only one left to send was the man's own dear son. Last of all, then, he sent his son to the tenants. 'I am sure they will respect my son,' he said. ⁷But those tenants said to one another, 'This is the owner's son. Come on, let's kill him, and his property will be ours!' ⁸So they grabbed the son and killed him and threw his body out of the vineyard.

⁹"What, then, will the owner of the vineyard do?" asked Jesus. "He will come and kill those tenants and turn the vineyard over to others. ¹⁰Surely you have read this scripture?

'The stone which the builders rejected as worthless

turned out to be the most important of all.
¹¹This was done by the Lord;

what a wonderful sight it is!'"

¹²The Jewish leaders tried to arrest Jesus, because they knew that he had told this parable against them. But they were afraid of the crowd, so they left him and went away.

The Question about Paying Taxes
(Matthew 22.15-22; Luke 20.20-26)

¹³Some Pharisees and some members of Herod's party were sent to Jesus to trap him with questions. ¹⁴They came to him and said, "Teacher, we know that you tell the truth, without worrying about what people think. You pay no attention to anyone's status, but teach the truth about God's will for people. Tell us, is it against our Law to pay taxes to the Roman Emperor? Should we pay them or not?"

¹⁵But Jesus saw through their trick and answered, "Why are you trying to trap me? Bring a silver coin, and let me see it."

耶穌對他們說：「那麼，我也不告訴你們我憑甚麼權柄做這些事。」

壞佃戶的比喻
（太21・33—46；路20・9—19）

12 耶穌又用比喻教導他們。他說：「有一個人開墾了一個葡萄園，周圍用籬笆圍着，在園裏挖了一個榨酒池，蓋了一座守望臺，然後把葡萄園租給佃戶，自己出外旅行去了。²到了收葡萄的季節，他打發一個奴僕去向佃戶收他應得的分額。³佃戶揪着那奴僕，毆打他，叫他空手回去。⁴園主又打發另一個奴僕去；他們打破了他的頭，並且侮辱他。⁵園主再打發一個奴僕去，他們把他殺了。他們又同樣地對付了許多人，有的打，有的殺。⁶園主只剩他最疼愛的兒子。最後他打發他去見佃戶，心想：『他們一定會尊敬我的兒子。』⁷可是那些佃戶彼此商議說：『這個人是園主的繼承人，來吧，把他殺了，他的產業就歸我們了！』⁸他們就抓住那兒子，殺了他，把屍體拋出葡萄園外。」

⁹於是耶穌問：「這樣，葡萄園主要怎麼辦呢？他一定來殺滅這些佃戶，把葡萄園轉租給別人。¹⁰你們沒有念過這段經文嗎？

泥水匠所丟棄的這塊石頭

已成為最重要的基石。
¹¹這是主的作為，

在我們眼中是多麼奇妙啊！」

¹²因為猶太人的領袖知道耶穌講的比喻是指責他們的，就想要逮捕他。可是他們怕羣眾，只好離開他走了。

納稅給凱撒的問題
（太22・15—22；路20・19—26）

¹³有些法利賽人和希律黨徒奉命來見耶穌，想從他的話找把柄來陷害他。¹⁴他們對他說：「老師，我們知道你是誠實的人；你不管人怎麼想，也不看情面，總是忠實地把上帝的道教導人。請告訴我們，向羅馬皇帝凱撒納稅是不是違背我們的法律？我們納還是不納？」

¹⁵耶穌看穿他們的詭計，就說：「你們為甚麼想陷害我？拿一個銀幣給我看吧！」

16They brought him one, and he asked, "Whose face and name are these?"

"The Emperor's," they answered.

17So Jesus said, "Well, then, pay to the Emperor what belongs to the Emperor, and pay to God what belongs to God."

And they were amazed at Jesus.

The Question about Rising from Death
(Matthew 22.23-33; Luke 20.27-40)

18Then some Sadducees, who say that people will not rise from death, came to Jesus and said, 19"Teacher, Moses wrote this law for us: 'If a man dies and leaves a wife but no children, that man's brother must marry the widow so that they can have children who will be considered the dead man's children.' 20Once there were seven brothers; the oldest got married and died without having children. 21Then the second one married the woman, and he also died without having children. The same thing happened to the third brother, 22and then to the rest: all seven brothers married the woman and died without having children. Last of all, the woman died. 23Now, when all the dead rise to life on the day of resurrection, whose wife will she be? All seven of them had married her."

24Jesus answered them, "How wrong you are! And do you know why? It is because you don't know the Scriptures or God's power. 25For when the dead rise to life, they will be like the angels in heaven and will not marry. 26Now, as for the dead being raised: haven't you ever read in the Book of Moses the passage about the burning bush? There it is written that God said to Moses, 'I am the God of Abraham, the God of Isaac, and the God of Jacob.' 27He is the God of the living, not of the dead. You are completely wrong!"

The Great Commandment
(Matthew 22.34-40; Luke 10.25-28)

28A teacher of the Law was there who heard the discussion. He saw that Jesus had given the Sadducees a good answer, so he came to him with a question: "Which commandment is the most important of all?"

29Jesus replied, "The most important one is this: 'Listen, Israel! The Lord our God is the only Lord.[t] 30Love the Lord your God with all your heart, with all your soul, with all your mind, and with all your strength.' 31The second most important commandment is this: 'Love your neighbor as you love yourself.' There is no

t The Lord our God is the only Lord; or The Lord is our God, the Lord alone.

16 他們給他一個銀幣,耶穌問:「這上面的像和名號是誰的?」

他們回答:「是凱撒的。」

17 耶穌說:「那麼,把凱撒的東西給凱撒,把上帝的東西給上帝。」

他們聽了這話,對他非常驚訝。

復活的問題
(太22・23-33;路20・27-40)

18 有些不相信復活這回事的撒都該人來見耶穌。19 他們說:「老師,摩西為我們立法:『如果一個人死了,留下妻子,沒有孩子,他的弟弟必須娶寡嫂為妻,替哥哥傳宗接代。』20 曾經有兄弟七人:老大結了婚,死了,沒有留下孩子;21 老二娶了寡嫂,也死了,沒有留下孩子;老三也一樣。22 七個兄弟都娶過那個女人,都死了,都沒有留下孩子。最後那個女人也死了。23 這樣,在復活的日子,他們從死裏復活時,這個女人算是誰的妻子呢?因為兄弟七個都娶過她。」

24 耶穌回答他們:「你們錯了,為甚麼呢?因為你們不明白聖經,也不知道上帝的權能。25 他們從死裏復活的時候,要跟天上的天使一樣,也不娶也不嫁。26 關於死人復活的事,你們沒有念過摩西書上所記載那荊棘燃燒的故事嗎?上帝對摩西說:『我是亞伯拉罕的上帝,以撒的上帝,雅各的上帝。』27 意思是說,上帝是活人的上帝,不是死人的上帝。你們完全錯了!」

最大的誡命
(太22・34-40;路10・25-28)

28 有一個經學教師聽見他們的辯論,覺得耶穌給撒都該人的回答很好,就上來向耶穌提出一個問題:「誡命中哪一條是第一重要的?」

29 耶穌回答:「第一是:『以色列啊,你要聽!主─我們的上帝是惟一的主。30 你要全心、全情、全意、全力愛主─你的上帝。』31 第二是:『你要愛鄰人,像愛自己一

other commandment more important than these two."

32The teacher of the Law said to Jesus, "Well done, Teacher! It is true, as you say, that only the Lord is God and that there is no other god but he. 33And you must love God with all your heart and with all your mind and with all your strength; and you must love your neighbor as you love yourself. It is more important to obey these two commandments than to offer on the altar animals and other sacrifices to God."

34Jesus noticed how wise his answer was, and so he told him, "You are not far from the Kingdom of God."

After this nobody dared to ask Jesus any more questions.

The Question about the Messiah
(Matthew 22.41-46; Luke 20.41-44)

35As Jesus was teaching in the Temple, he asked the question, "How can the teachers of the Law say that the Messiah will be the descendant of David? 36The Holy Spirit inspired David to say:

'The Lord said to my Lord:
Sit here at my right side
until I put your enemies under your feet.'
37David himself called him 'Lord'; so how can the Messiah be David's descendant?"

Jesus Warns against the Teachers of the Law
(Matthew 23.1-36; Luke 20.45-47)

A large crowd was listening to Jesus gladly. 38As he taught them, he said, "Watch out for the teachers of the Law, who like to walk around in their long robes and be greeted with respect in the marketplace, 39who choose the reserved seats in the synagogues and the best places at feasts. 40They take advantage of widows and rob them of their homes, and then make a show of saying long prayers. Their punishment will be all the worse!"

The Widow's Offering
(Luke 21.1-4)

41As Jesus sat near the Temple treasury, he watched the people as they dropped in their money. Many rich men dropped in a lot of money; 42then a poor widow came along and dropped in two little copper coins, worth about a penny. 43He called his disciples together and said to them, "I tell you that this poor widow put more in the offering box than all the others. 44For the others put in what they had to spare of their riches; but she, poor as she is, put in all she had–she gave all she had to live on."

樣。』沒有其他的誡命比這些更重要的了。」

32 那經學教師對耶穌說:「老師,你說得對!正像你所說的,上帝是惟一的,他以外沒有別的。33以全心、全意、全力愛上帝,又愛鄰人,像愛自己一樣。這比在祭壇上獻燒化祭和其他的祭物給上帝重要得多了。」

34 耶穌看出他的回答滿有智慧,就對他說:「你離上帝的國不遠了。」

從此以後,沒有人敢再向耶穌問難。

有關基督的問題
(太22.41-46;路20.41-44)

35 耶穌在聖殿裏教導人的時候提出一個問題:「經學教師怎麼能說基督是大衛的子孫呢?36大衛曾受聖靈的感動說:

主對我主說:
你坐在我的右邊,
等我使你的仇敵屈服在你腳下。
37大衛自己稱他為『主』,基督又怎麼會是大衛的子孫呢?」

要提防經學教師
(太23.1-36;路20.45-47)

羣眾都喜歡聽耶穌講論。38在教導他們的時候,他說:「要提防經學教師;他們喜歡穿長袍招搖過市,喜歡人家在公共場所向他們致敬問安,39又喜歡會堂裏的特別座位和宴會上的首座。40他們吞沒了寡婦的家產,然後表演長篇的禱告。他們一定受到更嚴厲的懲罰!」

寡婦的奉獻
(路21.1-4)

41 耶穌坐在聖殿庫房的對面,看大家怎樣投錢在奉獻箱裏。很多有錢人投進許多錢;42後來一個窮寡婦上來,投進兩個小銅板,約等於一文錢。43耶穌把他的門徒都叫過來,對他們說:「我實在告訴你們,這個窮寡婦所投進奉獻箱的比其他的人都多。44別人是從他們的財富中捐出有餘的;可是她已經很窮,卻把自己全部的生活費用都獻上了。」

Jesus Speaks of the Destruction of the Temple (Matthew 24.1-2; Luke 21.5-6)

13 As Jesus was leaving the Temple, one of his disciples said, "Look, Teacher! What wonderful stones and buildings!"

2 Jesus answered, "You see these great buildings? Not a single stone here will be left in its place; every one of them will be thrown down."

Troubles and Persecutions (Matthew 24.3-14; Luke 21.7-19)

3 Jesus was sitting on the Mount of Olives, across from the Temple, when Peter, James, John, and Andrew came to him in private. 4 "Tell us when this will be," they said, "and tell us what will happen to show that the time has come for all these things to take place."

5 Jesus said to them, "Watch out, and don't let anyone fool you. 6 Many men, claiming to speak for me, will come and say, 'I am he!' and they will fool many people. 7 And don't be troubled when you hear the noise of battles close by and news of battles far away. Such things must happen, but they do not mean that the end has come. 8 Countries will fight each other; kingdoms will attack one another. There will be earthquakes everywhere, and there will be famines. These things are like the first pains of childbirth.

9 "You yourselves must watch out. You will be arrested and taken to court. You will be beaten in the synagogues; you will stand before rulers and kings for my sake to tell them the Good News. 10 But before the end comes, the gospel must be preached to all peoples. 11 And when you are arrested and taken to court, do not worry ahead of time about what you are going to say; when the time comes, say whatever is then given to you. For the words you speak will not be yours; they will come from the Holy Spirit. 12 Men will hand over their own brothers to be put to death, and fathers will do the same to their children. Children will turn against their parents and have them put to death. 13 Everyone will hate you because of me. But whoever holds out to the end will be saved.

The Awful Horror (Matthew 24.15-28; Luke 21.20-24)

14 "You will see 'The Awful Horror' standing in the place where he should not be." (Note to the reader: understand what this means!) "Then those who are in Judea must run away to the hills. 15 Someone who is on the roof of a house must not lose time by going down into the house to get anything to take along. 16 Someone

預言聖殿的毀滅

（太24‧1—2；路21‧5—6）

13 耶穌從聖殿出來的時候，他的一個門徒對他說：「老師，你看，這是多大的石頭，多宏偉的建築！」

2 耶穌說：「你們在欣賞這些偉大的建築嗎？這地方的每一塊石頭都要被拆下來，沒有一塊石頭會留在另一塊上面。」

災難和迫害

（太24‧3—14；路21‧7—19）

3 耶穌在橄欖山上，面對聖殿坐着。彼得、雅各、約翰，和安得烈私下來問他：4「請告訴我們，幾時會發生這事？這一切發生的時候會有甚麼預兆呢？」

5 耶穌告訴他們說：「你們要當心，不要受人愚弄。6 有許多人要假冒我的名來，說：『我就是基督』，因而愚弄了好些人。7 不要為了附近打仗的風聲和遠方戰爭的消息驚慌。這些事必然發生；但這不是說歷史的終局已經到了。8 一個民族要跟另一個民族爭戰；一個國家要攻打另一個國家；到處會有地震和饑荒。這些事的發生正像產婦陣痛的開始一樣。

9「你們自己要當心，因為人家要逮捕你們，交給法庭。你們要在會堂上受鞭打；為了我的緣故，站在統治者和君王面前，為福音作證。10 但是福音必須先傳給萬民。11 當他們逮捕你們，把你們帶到法庭的時候，不要事先憂慮說甚麼；到那時候，上帝指示甚麼，你們就說甚麼；因為你們所說的不是自己的話，而是聖靈藉着你們說的。12 那時候，人要出賣親兄弟，置他們於死地，父親對兒女也是這樣；兒女也要跟父母作對，置他們於死地。13 為了我，大家要憎恨你們。但是堅忍到底的人必然得救。」

大災難

（太24‧15—28；路21‧20—24）

14「你們要看見那『毀滅性的可憎之物』站在它不應該站的地方（讀者必須領會這句話的含意）。那時候，住在猶太的，該逃到山上避難；15 在屋頂的，不要下來，也不要到屋子裏去拿任何東西。16 在農場的，不要回

who is in the field must not go back to the house for a cloak. 17How terrible it will be in those days for women who are pregnant and for mothers with little babies! 18Pray to God that these things will not happen in the winter! 19For the trouble of those days will be far worse than any the world has ever known from the very beginning when God created the world until the present time. Nor will there ever be anything like it again. 20But the Lord has reduced the number of those days; if he had not, nobody would survive. For the sake of his chosen people, however, he has reduced those days.

21"Then, if anyone says to you, 'Look, here is the Messiah!' or, 'Look, there he is!'–do not believe it. 22For false Messiahs and false prophets will appear. They will perform miracles and wonders in order to deceive even God's chosen people, if possible. 23Be on your guard! I have told you everything ahead of time.

The Coming of the Son of Man
(Matthew 24.29-31; Luke 21.25-28)

24"In the days after that time of trouble the sun will grow dark, the moon will no longer shine, 25the stars will fall from heaven, and the powers in space will be driven from their courses. 26Then the Son of Man will appear, coming in the clouds with great power and glory. 27He will send the angels out to the four corners of the earth to gather God's chosen people from one end of the world to the other.

The Lesson of the Fig Tree
(Matthew 24.32-35; Luke 21.29-33)

28"Let the fig tree teach you a lesson. When its branches become green and tender and it starts putting out leaves, you know that summer is near. 29In the same way, when you see these things happening, you will know that the time is near, ready to begin.u 30Remember that all these things will happen before the people now living have all died. 31Heaven and earth will pass away, but my words will never pass away.

No One Knows the Day or Hour
(Matthew 24.36-44)

32"No one knows, however, when that day or hour will come–neither the angels in heaven, nor the Son; only the Father knows. 33Be on watch, be alert, for you do not know when the time will come. 34It will be like a man who goes away from home on a trip and leaves his servants in charge, after giving to each one his own work to do and after telling the door-

家拿外衣。17那些日子裏，懷孕的女人和哺育嬰兒的母親就苦了！18你們要懇求上帝不讓這些事在冬天發生。19因爲那些日子的災難是從上帝創世以來未曾有過的，將來也不會再有。20要是主沒有縮短那些災難的日子，沒有人能夠存活。但是，爲了他所揀選的子民，他已經縮短那些日子了。

21「如果有人對你們說：『瞧，基督在這裏！基督在那裏！』不要相信他。22因爲假基督和假先知將出現；他們要行神蹟奇事，盡其所能來欺騙上帝所揀選的子民。23你們要當心！我已經預先把這一切事都告訴你們了。」

人子的來臨
（太24‧29～31；路21‧25～28）

24「那些災難的日子過去以後，太陽要變黑，月亮不再發光，25星星要從天上墜落，太空的系統也都要搖動。26那時候，人子要出現，充滿着大能力和榮耀駕雲降臨。27他要差天使到天涯海角，從世界的這一頭到世界的那一頭，召集他所揀選的子民。」

無花果樹的教訓
（太24‧32-35；路21‧29-33）

28「你們要從無花果樹學教訓。當枝子呈現嫩綠的顏色，長出新葉的時候，你們知道夏天就要到了。29同樣，你們看見這一切的現象就知道時候快到了⑮，就在門口了。30你們要記住，這一代的人還沒有都去世以前，這一切事就要發生。31天地要消失，我的話卻永不消失。」

那日那時沒有人知道
（太24‧36-44）

32「至於那要臨到的日子和時間，沒有人知道；天上的天使不知道，兒子也不知道，只有父親知道。33你們要留心，要警醒，因爲你們不知道那時刻甚麼時候臨到。34正像一個人出外遠行，把家務交給僕人管理，分配每一個人的工作，又吩咐門房當心門戶。

---

u the time is near, ready to begin; or he is near, ready to come.

⑮「時候快到了」或譯「他就要到了」。

keeper to keep watch. [35]Watch, then, because you do not know when the master of the house is coming—it might be in the evening or at midnight or before dawn or at sunrise. [36]If he comes suddenly, he must not find you asleep. [37]What I say to you, then, I say to all: Watch!"

The Plot against Jesus
(Matthew 26.1-5; Luke 22.1-2; John 11.45-53)

14 It was now two days before the Festival of Passover and Unleavened Bread. The chief priests and the teachers of the Law were looking for a way to arrest Jesus secretly and put him to death. [2]"We must not do it during the festival," they said, "or the people might riot."

Jesus Is Anointed at Bethany
(Matthew 26.6-13; John 12.1-8)

[3]Jesus was in Bethany at the house of Simon, a man who had suffered from a dreaded skin disease. While Jesus was eating, a woman came in with an alabaster jar full of a very expensive perfume made of pure nard. She broke the jar and poured the perfume on Jesus' head. [4]Some of the people there became angry and said to one another, "What was the use of wasting the perfume? [5]It could have been sold for more than three hundred silver coins[v] and the money given to the poor!" And they criticized her harshly.

[6]But Jesus said, "Leave her alone! Why are you bothering her? She has done a fine and beautiful thing for me. [7]You will always have poor people with you, and any time you want to, you can help them. But you will not always have me. [8]She did what she could; she poured perfume on my body to prepare it ahead of time for burial. [9]Now, I assure you that wherever the gospel is preached all over the world, what she has done will be told in memory of her."

Judas Agrees to Betray Jesus
(Matthew 26.14-16; Luke 22.3-6)

[10]Then Judas Iscariot, one of the twelve disciples, went off to the chief priests in order to betray Jesus to them. [11]They were pleased to hear what he had to say, and promised to give him money. So Judas started looking for a good chance to hand Jesus over to them.

Jesus Eats the Passover Meal with His Disciples
(Matthew 26.17-25; Luke 22.7-14, 21-23; John 13.21-30)

[12]On the first day of the Festival of Unleavened Bread, the day the lambs for the

v SILVER COINS: See 6.37.

[35]所以，你們要警醒，因為你們不知道主人甚麼時候回來，也許傍晚，也許半夜，也許天亮以前，也許日出以後。[36]假如他忽然回來，別讓他發現你們在睡覺。[37]我對你們講的話也是對大家講的：你們要警醒！」

殺害耶穌的陰謀
（太26・1—5；路22・1—2；約11・45—53）

14 逾越節和除酵節的前兩天，祭司長和經學教師陰謀要祕密逮捕耶穌，把他處死。[2]他們說：「我們不要在節期中下手，免得激起民眾的暴動。」

耶穌在伯大尼受膏
（太26・6—13；約12・1—8）

[3] 耶穌在伯大尼那患痲瘋病的西門家裏。正在吃飯的時候，有一個女人帶來一隻玉瓶，裏面盛滿很珍貴的純哪噠香油膏。她打破玉瓶，把香油膏倒在耶穌頭上。[4] 有些在座的人很不高興，彼此議論說：「這樣浪費香油膏有甚麼意思？[5] 這香油膏可以賣三百多塊銀子，拿這錢來救濟窮人多好！」因此他們對那女人很生氣。

[6] 可是耶穌說：「由她吧！何必為難她呢？她為我做了一件美好的事。[7] 因為常有窮人跟你們在一起，願意的話，你們隨時可以救濟他們，可是我不能常與你們在一起。[8] 她已盡所能的做了；她把這香油膏倒在我身上是為我的埋葬先做準備。[9] 我實在告訴你們，普天之下，福音無論傳到甚麼地方，人人都要述說她所做的事，來記念她。」

猶大同意出賣耶穌
（太26・14—16；路22・3—6）

[10] 耶穌的十二使徒中，有一個加略人猶大；他去見祭司長，要把耶穌出賣給他們。[11]他們聽見猶大這麼說，喜出望外，答應給他錢。從那時起，猶大找機會要出賣耶穌。

耶穌和門徒同進逾越節晚餐
（太26・17—25；路22・7—14，21—23；約13・21—30）

[12] 除酵節的第一天，就是宰逾越節羔羊的

Passover meal were killed, Jesus' disciples asked him, "Where do you want us to go and get the Passover meal ready for you?"

13Then Jesus sent two of them with these instructions: "Go into the city, and a man carrying a jar of water will meet you. Follow him 14to the house he enters, and say to the owner of the house: 'The Teacher says, Where is the room where my disciples and I will eat the Passover meal?' 15Then he will show you a large upstairs room, fixed up and furnished, where you will get everything ready for us."

16The disciples left, went to the city, and found everything just as Jesus had told them, and they prepared the Passover meal.

17When it was evening, Jesus came with the twelve disciples. 18While they were at the table eating, Jesus said, "I tell you that one of you will betray me—one who is eating with me."

19The disciples were upset and began to ask him, one after the other, "Surely you don't mean me, do you?"

20Jesus answered, "It will be one of you twelve, one who dips his bread in the dish with me. 21The Son of Man will die as the Scriptures say he will; but how terrible for that man who will betray the Son of Man! It would have been better for that man if he had never been born!"

The Lord's Supper

(Matthew 26.26-30; Luke 22.14-20; 1 Corinthians 11.23-25)

22While they were eating, Jesus took a piece of bread, gave a prayer of thanks, broke it, and gave it to his disciples. "Take it," he said, "this is my body."

23Then he took a cup, gave thanks to God, and handed it to them; and they all drank from it. 24Jesus said, "This is my blood which is poured out for many, my blood which seals God's covenant. 25I tell you, I will never again drink this wine until the day I drink the new wine in the Kingdom of God."

26Then they sang a hymn and went out to the Mount of Olives.

Jesus Predicts Peter's Denial

(Matthew 26.31-35; Luke 22.31-34; John 13.36-38)

27Jesus said to them, "All of you will run away and leave me, for the scripture says, 'God will kill the shepherd, and the sheep will all be scattered.' 28But after I am raised to life, I will go to Galilee ahead of you."

29Peter answered, "I will never leave you, even though all the rest do!"

那一天,門徒來問耶穌:「你要我們到哪裏去為你預備逾越節的晚餐呢?」

13 於是,耶穌派了兩個門徒,吩咐他們說:「你們進城去,會遇見一個人拿着一瓶水,你們就跟着他。14他進哪一家,你們就問那家的主人:『老師說:我要和我的門徒吃逾越節晚餐的那間客房在哪裏?』15他會帶你們看樓上一間佈置好了的大房間;你們就在那裏替我們預備吧。」

16 兩個門徒出去,進了城,所遇見的每一件事正像耶穌告訴他們的;他們就在那裏預備逾越節的晚餐。

17 傍晚,耶穌和十二使徒來了。18他們坐下吃飯的時候,耶穌說:「我告訴你們,你們當中,跟我一起吃飯的,有一個人要出賣我。」

19 他們非常憂愁,一個一個地問他:「不是我吧?」

20 耶穌回答:「是你們十二人當中的一個;那跟我一起在盤子裏蘸餅吃的就是。21正如聖經所說,人子將要受害;可是那出賣人子的人有禍了!這個人沒有出生倒好!」

主的晚餐

(太26·26—30;路22·14—20;林前11·23—25)

22 他們吃飯的時候,耶穌拿起餅,先獻上感謝的禱告,然後擘開餅,分給門徒,說:「你們吃;這是我的身體。」

23 他又拿起杯,向上帝感謝後,遞給他們;他們都喝了。24耶穌說:「這是我的血,是印證上帝與人立約的血,為眾人流的。25我告訴你們,我絕不再喝這酒,直到在上帝的國度裏喝新酒的那一天。」

26 他們唱了一首詩,就出來,到橄欖山去。

耶穌預言彼得不認他

(太26·31—35;路22·31—34;約13·36—38)

27 耶穌對他們說:「你們都要離棄我,因為聖經說:『上帝要擊殺牧人,羊羣就分散了。』28但是我復活以後,要比你們先到加利利去。」

29 彼得說:「即使別人都離棄你,我也不離棄你!」

30Jesus said to Peter, "I tell you that before the rooster crows two times tonight, you will say three times that you do not know me."

31Peter answered even more strongly, "I will never say that, even if I have to die with you!"

And all the other disciples said the same thing.

Jesus Prays in Gethsemane
(Matthew 26.36-46; Luke 22.39-46)

32They came to a place called Gethsemane, and Jesus said to his disciples, "Sit here while I pray." 33He took Peter, James, and John with him. Distress and anguish came over him, 34and he said to them, "The sorrow in my heart is so great that it almost crushes me. Stay here and keep watch."

35He went a little farther on, threw himself on the ground, and prayed that, if possible, he might not have to go through that time of suffering. 36"Father," he prayed, "my Father! All things are possible for you. Take this cup of suffering away from me. Yet not what I want, but what you want."

37Then he returned and found the three disciples asleep. He said to Peter, "Simon, are you asleep? Weren't you able to stay awake for even one hour?" 38And he said to them, "Keep watch, and pray that you will not fall into temptation. The spirit is willing, but the flesh is weak."

39He went away once more and prayed, saying the same words. 40Then he came back to the disciples and found them asleep; they could not keep their eyes open. And they did not know what to say to him.

41When he came back the third time, he said to them, "Are you still sleeping and resting? Enough! The hour has come! Look, the Son of Man is now being handed over to the power of sinners. 42Get up, let us go. Look, here is the man who is betraying me!"

The Arrest of Jesus
(Matthew 26.47-56; Luke 22.47-53; John 18.3-12)

43Jesus was still speaking when Judas, one of the twelve disciples, arrived. With him was a crowd armed with swords and clubs and sent by the chief priests, the teachers of the Law, and the elders. 44The traitor had given the crowd a signal: "The man I kiss is the one you want. Arrest him and take him away under guard."

45As soon as Judas arrived, he went up to Jesus and said, "Teacher!" and kissed him. 46So

30 耶穌對彼得說：「我實在告訴你，今夜雞叫兩遍以前，你會三次不認我。」

31 彼得用更堅決的口氣說：「即使我必須跟你同死，我也絕不會不認你！」

其他的門徒也都這樣說。

在客西馬尼園的禱告
（太26・36—46；路22・39—46）

32 他們來到一個地方，名叫客西馬尼；耶穌對門徒說：「你們在這裏坐，等我去禱告。」

33 於是他帶着彼得、雅各、約翰一起去。他開始悲痛難過，34對他們說：「我的心非常憂傷，幾乎要死。你們留在這裏，警醒吧！」

35 他往前走幾步，俯伏在地上，祈求上帝說，若是可以，不使他經歷這個痛苦。36他求說：「阿爸，我的父親哪，你凡事都能。求你把這苦杯移去；可是，不要照我的意思，只要照你的旨意。」

37 他回來，發現三個門徒都睡着了；他對彼得說：「西門，你在睡覺嗎？你不能警醒一個鐘頭嗎？」38他又說：「要警醒禱告，免得陷入誘惑。你們心靈固然願意，肉體卻是軟弱的。」

39 他又走過去，仍然用同樣的話禱告。40然後他再回到門徒那裏，看見他們還是睡着。他們睜不開眼睛，也不知道對他說甚麼話好。

41 耶穌第三次回來，對他們說：「你們還在睡覺，還在休息嗎？夠了，時間到了，人子就要被出賣在罪人手中了。42起來，我們走吧！看哪，那出賣我的人來了！」

耶穌被捕
（太26・47—56；路22・47—53；約18・2—12）

43 耶穌還在說話的時候，十二使徒之一的猶大來了。有一羣人帶着刀棒跟他一起來；他們是祭司長、經學教師，和長老派來的。44那出賣耶穌的預先給他們一個暗號，說：「我去親誰，誰就是你們所要的人。你們抓住他，嚴密看守，把他帶走。」

45 猶大一到，立刻走到耶穌跟前，叫聲：「老師！」又親他。46於是他們下手抓住耶

they arrested Jesus and held him tight. [47]But one of those standing there drew his sword and struck at the High Priest's slave, cutting off his ear. [48]Then Jesus spoke up and said to them, "Did you have to come with swords and clubs to capture me, as though I were an outlaw? [49]Day after day I was with you teaching in the Temple, and you did not arrest me. But the Scriptures must come true."

[50]Then all the disciples left him and ran away.

[51]A certain young man, dressed only in a linen cloth, was following Jesus. They tried to arrest him, [52]but he ran away naked, leaving the cloth behind.

Jesus before the Council

(Matthew 26.57-68; Luke 22.54-55, 63-71; John 18.13-14, 19-24)

[53]Then Jesus was taken to the High Priest's house, where all the chief priests, the elders, and the teachers of the Law were gathering. [54]Peter followed from a distance and went into the courtyard of the High Priest's house. There he sat down with the guards, keeping himself warm by the fire. [55]The chief priests and the whole Council tried to find some evidence against Jesus in order to put him to death, but they could not find any. [56]Many witnesses told lies against Jesus, but their stories did not agree.

[57]Then some men stood up and told this lie against Jesus: [58]"We heard him say, 'I will tear down this Temple which men have made, and after three days I will build one that is not made by men.'" [59]Not even they, however, could make their stories agree.

[60]The High Priest stood up in front of them all and questioned Jesus, "Have you no answer to the accusation they bring against you?"

[61]But Jesus kept quiet and would not say a word. Again the High Priest questioned him, "Are you the Messiah, the Son of the Blessed God?"

[62]"I am," answered Jesus, "and you will all see the Son of Man seated at the right side of the Almighty and coming with the clouds of heaven!"

[63]The High Priest tore his robes and said, "We don't need any more witnesses! [64]You heard his blasphemy. What is your decision?"

They all voted against him: he was guilty and should be put to death.

[65]Some of them began to spit on Jesus, and they blindfolded him and hit him. "Guess who hit you!" they said. And the guards took him and slapped him.

穌。[47]站在旁邊的人當中,有一個人拔出刀來,向大祭司的奴僕砍去,削掉了他的一隻耳朵。[48]耶穌對他們說:「你們帶着刀棒出來抓我,把我當暴徒嗎?[49]我每天在聖殿裏教導人,常與你們一起,你們並沒有抓我。然而,聖經的話必須實現。」

[50]這時,所有的門徒都離棄他,逃跑了。

[51]有一個青年,身上只披着一塊麻布,跟在耶穌背後。他們抓他,[52]可是他丟下那塊布,赤着身子逃跑了。

在議會受審

(太26‧57—68;路22‧54—55,63—71;約18‧13—14, 19—24)

[53]他們把耶穌帶到大祭司的府邸;所有的祭司長、長老,和經學教師都聚集在那裏。[54]彼得遠遠地跟着耶穌,一直到大祭司府邸的院子裏,混在警衞當中坐着,烤火取暖。[55]祭司長和全議會想盡方法找證據控告耶穌,置他於死地,可是找不出任何證據。[56]好些人出面誣告他,可是他們的證詞都不相符。

[57]後來有幾個人站起來,作假證控告耶穌說:[58]「我們聽見他說:『我要把這座人手建造的聖殿拆了,三天內建另一座不是人手建造的聖殿。』」[59]就連這個控告,他們所說的也互相矛盾。

[60]於是大祭司在大家面前站起來,問耶穌:「他們對你的控告,你沒有甚麼答辯嗎?」

[61]耶穌緘口,一言不發。大祭司再問他:「你是不是基督,是那位該受稱頌的上帝的兒子?」

[62]耶穌回答:「我是!你們都要看見人子坐在全能者的右邊,駕着天上的雲降臨!」

[63]大祭司撕裂自己的衣服,說:「我們再也不需要證人了![64]你們聽見他說侮辱上帝的話了。你們說該怎麼辦呢?」

他們都判定他有罪,應該處死。

[65]有些人向他吐口水,又蒙着他的眼睛,用拳頭打他,問他:「猜猜看,是誰打你?」那些警衞也拉着他,用巴掌打他。

Peter Denies Jesus

(Matthew 26.69-75; Luke 22.56-62; John 18.15-18, 25-27)

66Peter was still down in the courtyard when one of the High Priest's servant women came by. 67When she saw Peter warming himself, she looked straight at him and said, "You, too, were with Jesus of Nazareth."

68But he denied it. "I don't know ... I don't understand what you are talking about," he answered, and went out into the passageway. Just then a rooster crowed.w
69The servant woman saw him there and began to repeat to the bystanders, "He is one of them!" 70But Peter denied it again.

A little while later the bystanders accused Peter again, "You can't deny that you are one of them, because you, too, are from Galilee."

71Then Peter said, "I swear that I am telling the truth! May God punish me if I am not! I do not know the man you are talking about!"

72Just then a rooster crowed a second time, and Peter remembered how Jesus had said to him, "Before the rooster crows two times, you will say three times that you do not know me." And he broke down and cried.

Jesus before Pilate

(Matthew 27.1-2, 11-14; Luke 23.1-5; John 18.28-38)

15 Early in the morning the chief priests met hurriedly with the elders, the teachers of the Law, and the whole Council, and made their plans. They put Jesus in chains, led him away, and handed him over to Pilate. 2Pilate questioned him, "Are you the king of the Jews?"

Jesus answered, "So you say."
3The chief priests were accusing Jesus of many things, 4so Pilate questioned him again, "Aren't you going to answer? Listen to all their accusations!"
5Again Jesus refused to say a word, and Pilate was amazed.

Jesus Is Sentenced to Death

(Matthew 27.15-26; Luke 23.13-25; John 18.39-19.16)

6At every Passover Festival Pilate was in the habit of setting free any one prisoner the people asked for. 7At that time a man named Barabbas was in prison with the rebels who had committed murder in the riot. 8When the crowd gathered and began to ask Pilate for the usual favor, 9he asked them, "Do you want me to set free for you the king of the Jews?" 10He knew very well that the chief priests had handed

w Some manuscripts do not have Just then a rooster crowed.

彼得不認耶穌

（太26‧69-75；路22‧56-62；約18‧15-18，25-27）

66 那時候，彼得還留在下面的院子裏。有大祭司的一個婢女走過來，67看見彼得在烤火，就定睛瞧着他，說：「你也是跟拿撒勒的耶穌一夥的。」

68 彼得否認說：「我不知道，也不懂得你在說些甚麼。」說着，他就避到前院。就在這時候，雞叫了。

69 一會兒，那個婢女又看見他，再對站在旁邊的人說：「這個人是他們一夥的！」70彼得又否認了。

又過了一會兒，那些站在旁邊的人再次指着彼得說：「你沒有辦法否認你是他們一夥的，因爲你也是加利利人！」

71 彼得就賭咒說：「我不認識你們所講的那個人！如果我說的不是實話，上帝會懲罰我！」

72 就在這時候，雞第二遍叫了；彼得這才記起耶穌對他說過的話：「雞叫兩遍以前，你會三次不認我。」彼得就忍不住哭起來。

在彼拉多面前受審

（太27‧1-2，11-14；路23‧1-5；約18‧28-38）

15 第二天一早，祭司長匆忙地跟長老、經學教師，和全議會商議，定好了他們的計劃。他們把耶穌綁起來，押走，交給彼拉多。2彼拉多問他：「你是猶太人的王嗎？」

耶穌回答：「這是你說的。」

3 祭司長控告耶穌許多事，4彼拉多就再盤問耶穌說：「你看，他們控告你這許多罪狀，你不答辯嗎？」

5 耶穌仍然一言不發；彼拉多非常詫異。

被判死刑

（太27‧15-26；路23‧13-25；約18‧39-19‧16）

6 每逢逾越節，彼拉多都照民衆的要求釋放一個囚犯。7剛好有一個人名叫巴拉巴，跟一些在暴亂中殺人的叛徒關在一起。8當羣衆集合，要求彼拉多按照慣例爲他們辦這件事的時候，9彼拉多問他們：「你們要我爲你們釋放猶太人的王嗎？」10其實彼拉多明明知道，祭司長是出於嫉妒才把耶穌解來

Jesus over to him because they were jealous.

11But the chief priests stirred up the crowd to ask, instead, that Pilate set Barabbas free for them. 12Pilate spoke again to the crowd, "What, then, do you want me to do with the one you call the king of the Jews?"

13They shouted back, "Crucify him!"

14"But what crime has he committed?" Pilate asked.

They shouted all the louder, "Crucify him!"

15Pilate wanted to please the crowd, so he set Barabbas free for them. Then he had Jesus whipped and handed him over to be crucified.

The Soldiers Make Fun of Jesus
(Matthew 27.27-31; John 19.2-3)

16The soldiers took Jesus inside to the court-yard of the governor's palace and called together the rest of the company. 17They put a purple robe on Jesus, made a crown out of thorny branches, and put it on his head. 18Then they began to salute him: "Long live the King of the Jews!" 19They beat him over the head with a stick, spat on him, fell on their knees, and bowed down to him. 20When they had finished making fun of him, they took off the purple robe and put his own clothes back on him. Then they led him out to crucify him.

Jesus Is Crucified
(Matthew 27.32-44; Luke 23.26-43; John 19.17-27)

21On the way they met a man named Simon, who was coming into the city from the country, and the soldiers forced him to carry Jesus' cross. (Simon was from Cyrene and was the father of Alexander and Rufus.) 22They took Jesus to a place called Golgotha, which means "The Place of the Skull." 23There they tried to give him wine mixed with a drug called myrrh, but Jesus would not drink it. 24Then they crucified him and divided his clothes among themselves, throwing dice to see who would get which piece of clothing. 25It was nine o'clock in the morning when they crucified him. 26The notice of the accusation against him said: "The King of the Jews." 27They also crucified two bandits with Jesus, one on his right and the other on his left.x

29People passing by shook their heads and hurled insults at Jesus: "Aha! You were going to tear down the Temple and build it back up in three days! 30Now come down from the cross and save yourself!"

31In the same way the chief priests and the

x *Some manuscripts add verse 28:* In this way the scripture came true which says, "He shared the fate of criminals" *(see Lk 22.37).*

交給他的。

11 可是祭司長煽動羣衆,竟要求彼拉多為他們釋放巴拉巴。12彼拉多再次問羣衆:「那麼,你們所稱為猶太人的王那人,我該怎樣處置呢?」

13 他們再大聲喊叫:「把他釘十字架!」

14 彼拉多問:「他做了甚麼壞事呢?」

他們更大聲喊叫:「把他釘十字架!」

15 彼拉多為了討好羣衆,就釋放巴拉巴給他們,又命令把耶穌鞭打了,然後交給人去釘十字架。

兵士戲弄耶穌
(太27‧27—31;約19‧2—3)

16 兵士把耶穌帶進總督府的院子裏,集合了全隊。17他們給耶穌穿上一件紫色的袍子,又用荊棘編了一頂冠冕,給他戴上,18然後向他致敬,說:「猶太人的王萬歲!」19他們又用藤條打他的頭,向他吐口水,跪下來拜他。20戲弄完了,他們剝下他紫色的袍子,再給他穿上自己的衣服,然後帶他出去釘十字架。

耶穌被釘十字架
(太27‧32—44;路23‧26—43;約19‧17—27)

21 在途中,他們遇見一個人,名叫西門,剛從鄉下進城,他們強迫他替耶穌背十字架(西門是古利奈人,是亞歷山大和魯孚的父親)。22他們把耶穌帶到一個地方,叫各各他,意思就是「髑髏岡」。23在那裏,他們拿沒藥調製的酒給耶穌喝,但是耶穌不喝。24於是他們把耶穌釘在十字架上,又抽了籤,把他的衣服分了。25早上九點鐘的時候,他們把耶穌釘十字架。26他的罪狀牌上寫着:「猶太人的王。」27同時他們又把兩個暴徒跟耶穌一起釘十字架,一個在他右邊,一個在他左邊。⑩

29 從那裏經過的人侮辱耶穌,搖着頭說:「哼,你這要拆毀聖殿、三天內把它重建起來的!30現在從十字架上下來,救救自己吧!」

31 祭司長和經學教師也同樣譏笑他,彼此

⑩有些古卷加28節「這樣,聖經上所說『他被列在罪犯中』的話應驗了。」

teachers of the Law made fun of Jesus, saying to one another, "He saved others, but he cannot save himself! 32Let us see the Messiah, the king of Israel, come down from the cross now, and we will believe in him!"

And the two who were crucified with Jesus insulted him also.

The Death of Jesus
(Matthew 27.45-56; Luke 23.44-49; John 19.28-30)

33At noon the whole country was covered with darkness, which lasted for three hours. 34At three o'clock Jesus cried out with a loud shout, *"Eloi, Eloi, lema sabachthani?"* which means, "My God, my God, why did you abandon me?"

35Some of the people there heard him and said, "Listen, he is calling for Elijah!" 36One of them ran up with a sponge, soaked it in cheap wine, and put it on the end of a stick. Then he held it up to Jesus' lips and said, "Wait! Let us see if Elijah is coming to bring him down from the cross!"

37With a loud cry Jesus died.

38The curtain hanging in the Temple was torn in two, from top to bottom. 39The army officer who was standing there in front of the cross saw how Jesus had died.y "This man was really the Son of God!" he said.

40Some women were there, looking on from a distance. Among them were Mary Magdalene, Mary the mother of the younger James and of Joseph, and Salome. 41They had followed Jesus while he was in Galilee and had helped him. Many other women who had come to Jerusalem with him were there also.

The Burial of Jesus
(Matthew 27.57-61; Luke 23.50-56; John 19.38-42)

42-43It was toward evening when Joseph of Arimathea arrived. He was a respected member of the Council, who was waiting for the coming of the Kingdom of God. It was Preparation day (that is, the day before the Sabbath), so Joseph went boldly into the presence of Pilate and asked him for the body of Jesus. 44Pilate was surprised to hear that Jesus was already dead. He called the army officer and asked him if Jesus had been dead a long time. 45After hearing the officer's report, Pilate told Joseph he could have the body. 46Joseph bought a linen sheet, took the body down, wrapped it in the sheet, and placed it in a tomb which had been dug out of solid rock. Then he rolled a large stone across the entrance to the tomb. 47Mary Magdalene and Mary the mother of Joseph

y had died; *some manuscripts have* had cried out and died.

說:「他救了別人,卻不能救自己! 32基督,以色列的王啊,現在從十字架上下來,讓我們看看,我們就相信!」

跟耶穌同釘十字架的人也同樣辱罵他。

耶穌的死
(太27‧45—56;路23‧44—49;約19‧28—30)

33 中午的時候,黑暗籠罩大地,約有三小時之久。34到了下午三點鐘,耶穌大聲喊:「以羅伊,以羅伊,拉馬撒巴各大尼?」意思是:「我的上帝,我的上帝,你為甚麼離棄我?」

35 旁邊站着的人有些聽見了,說:「你聽,他在呼喚以利亞!」36有一個人跑過去,把浸着酸酒的海綿綁在藤條上,送到耶穌的嘴邊,說:「等一下,我們看以利亞會不會來放他下來!」

37 耶穌大喊一聲,就斷了氣。

38 懸掛在聖殿裏的幔子,從上到下裂成兩半。39站在十字架前的一個軍官,看見耶穌喊叫和⑫死的情形,就說:「這個人真是上帝的兒子!」

40 還有些婦女從遠處觀看;其中有抹大拉的馬利亞,又有小雅各和約瑟的母親馬利亞,以及撒羅米。41耶穌在加利利的時候她們就跟隨他,服事他。還有其他好些婦女是跟耶穌一起來耶路撒冷的。

耶穌的安葬
(太27‧57—61;路23‧50—56;約19‧38—42)

42-43傍晚的時候,亞利馬太人約瑟來了;他是一個受人尊敬的議員,一向盼望上帝主權的實現。那天是預備日(就是安息日的前一天)。約瑟大膽去見彼拉多,向他要求收殮耶穌的身體。44彼拉多聽見耶穌已經死了,頗覺得驚奇。他把軍官叫來,問他耶穌是不是已經死了很久⑬。45既然從軍官那裏得到報告,彼拉多就把耶穌的身體給了約瑟。46約瑟買了麻紗,把耶穌的身體取下來,用麻紗包好,安放在一個從巖石鑿成的墓穴裏,又把一塊石頭滾過來,堵住墓門。47抹大拉的馬利亞和約瑟的母親馬利亞都守

⑫有些古卷沒有「喊叫和」。
⑬有些古卷沒有「很久」。

were watching and saw where the body of Jesus was placed.

The Resurrection

(Matthew 28.1-8; Luke 24.1-12; John 20.1-10)

16 After the Sabbath was over, Mary Magdalene, Mary the mother of James, and Salome bought spices to go and anoint the body of Jesus. ²Very early on Sunday morning, at sunrise, they went to the tomb. ³⁴On the way they said to one another, "Who will roll away the stone for us from the entrance to the tomb?" (It was a very large stone.) Then they looked up and saw that the stone had already been rolled back. ⁵So they entered the tomb, where they saw a young man sitting at the right, wearing a white robe–and they were alarmed.

⁶"Don't be alarmed," he said. "I know you are looking for Jesus of Nazareth, who was crucified. He is not here–he has been raised! Look, here is the place where he was placed. ⁷Now go and give this message to his disciples, including Peter: 'He is going to Galilee ahead of you; there you will see him, just as he told you.'"

⁸So they went out and ran from the tomb, distressed and terrified. They said nothing to anyone, because they were afraid.

AN OLD ENDING TO THE GOSPEL²

Jesus Appears to Mary Magdalene

(Matthew 28.9-10; John 20.11-18)

[⁹After Jesus rose from death early on Sunday, he appeared first to Mary Magdalene, from whom he had driven out seven demons. ¹⁰She went and told his companions. They were mourning and crying; ¹¹and when they heard her say that Jesus was alive and that she had seen him, they did not believe her.

Jesus Appears to Two Followers

(Luke 24.13-35)

¹²After this, Jesus appeared in a different manner to two of them while they were on their way to the country. ¹³They returned and told the others, but these would not believe it.

Jesus Appears to the Eleven

(Matthew 28.16-20; Luke 24.36-49; John 20.19-23; Acts 1.6-8)

¹⁴Last of all, Jesus appeared to the eleven disciples as they were eating. He scolded them, because they did not have faith and because

z *Some manuscripts and ancient translations do not have this ending to the Gospel (verses 9-20).*

耶穌復活

（太28‧1—8；路24‧1—12；約20‧1—10）

16 安息日一過，抹大拉的馬利亞、雅各的母親馬利亞，和撒羅米買了香料，要去抹耶穌的身體。² 星期天一清早，太陽剛出來，她們就往墳地去。³⁻⁴ 在路上，她們心裏盤算着：「有誰能幫我們把墓門口的石頭滾開呢？」（因為那是一塊大石頭）。可是她們抬頭一看，石頭已經給滾開了。⁵ 她們走進墓穴，看見一個青年坐在右邊，身上穿着白色的長袍；她們都很驚慌。

⁶ 那青年說：「不用驚慌；我知道你們在找那位被釘十字架的拿撒勒人耶穌。他不在這裏，他已經復活了！看，這是他們安放他的地方。⁷ 你們快去告訴他的門徒，尤其是彼得，說：『他要比你們先到加利利去，在那裏，你們可以見到他，正像他告訴過你們的。』」

⁸ 她們又驚訝又恐懼，立刻逃離墓穴，飛奔而去。她們沒有把這事告訴任何人，因為她們害怕。

‧有些古卷另附下列諸段‧
耶穌向抹大拉的馬利亞顯現

（太28‧9—10；約20‧11—18）

〔⁹ 星期天早晨，耶穌復活後，首先向抹大拉的馬利亞顯現（耶穌曾從她身上趕出七個鬼）。¹⁰ 她去告訴那些跟從耶穌的人；他們正在悲傷哭泣。¹¹ 他們聽見耶穌復活和馬利亞已經看見了他的這些報告，卻不相信。

向兩個門徒顯現

（路24‧13—35）

¹² 這事以後，耶穌以另一種形像向兩個正往鄉下去的門徒顯現。¹³ 這兩個人回來告訴其他的門徒，他們還是不相信。

向十一使徒顯現

（太28‧16—20；路24‧36—49；約20‧19—23；徒1‧6—8）

¹⁴ 最後，耶穌向正在吃飯的十一使徒顯現。他責備他們；因為他們既缺少信心又頑

they were too stubborn to believe those who had seen him alive. [15]He said to them, "Go throughout the whole world and preach the gospel to all people. [16]Whoever believes and is baptized will be saved; whoever does not believe will be condemned. [17]Believers will be given the power to perform miracles: they will drive out demons in my name; they will speak in strange tongues; [18]if they pick up snakes or drink any poison, they will not be harmed; they will place their hands on sick people, and these will get well."

Jesus Is Taken Up to Heaven
(Luke 24.50-53; Acts 1.9-11)

[19]After the Lord Jesus had talked with them, he was taken up to heaven and sat at the right side of God. [20]The disciples went and preached everywhere, and the Lord worked with them and proved that their preaching was true by the miracles that were performed.]

ANOTHER OLD ENDING[a]

[[9]The women went to Peter and his friends and gave them a brief account of all they had been told. [10]After this, Jesus himself sent out through his disciples from the east to the west the sacred and everliving message of eternal salvation.]

a Some manuscripts and ancient translations have this shorter ending to the Gospel in addition to the longer ending (verses 9-20).

固,不信他復活後看見過他的人所報告的。[15]他對他們說:「你們要到世界各地去,向全人類傳福音。[16]信而接受洗禮的,必然得救;不信的,要被定罪。[17]信的人有行這些神蹟的能力:他們會奉我的名趕鬼,說新的靈語,[18]用手拿蛇,喝了有毒的東西也不受傷害,按手在病人身上,病就好了。」

耶穌被接升天
(路24‧50-53;徒1‧9-11)

[19]主耶穌向他們說了這些話後,被接到天上去,坐在上帝的右邊。[20]門徒出去,到處傳福音;主與他們同工,藉着所行的神蹟,證明他們所傳的道是真實的。]

• 另有些古卷有下列結語 •

[[9]那些婦女去見彼得和他的朋友,把所聽到的都向他們報告。[10]事後,耶穌親自差遣他的門徒,從東到西,傳佈那神聖、不朽、使人獲得永恆拯救的信息。]

路加福音
LUKE

INTRODUCTION

The Gospel according to Luke presents Jesus as both the promised Savior of Israel and as the Savior of all people. *Luke* records that Jesus was called by the Spirit of the Lord to "bring the good news to the poor," and this Gospel is filled with a concern for people with all kinds of need. The note of joy is also prominent in *Luke*, especially in the opening chapters that announce the coming of Jesus, and again at the conclusion, when Jesus ascends to heaven. The story of the growth and spread of the Christian faith after the ascension of Jesus is told by the same writer in the book of *Acts*.

Parts 2 and 6 (see the outline below) contain much material that is found only in this Gospel, such as the stories about the song of the angels and the shepherds' visit at the birth of Jesus, Jesus in the Temple as a boy, and the parables of the Good Samaritan and the Lost Son. Throughout the Gospel great emphasis is placed on prayer, the Holy Spirit, the role of women in the ministry of Jesus, and God's forgiveness of sins.

Outline of Contents

Introduction 1.1-4
Birth and childhood of John the Baptist and of Jesus 1.5-2.52
The ministry of John the Baptist 3.1-20
The baptism and temptation of Jesus 3.21-4.13
Jesus' public ministry in Galilee 4.14-9.50
From Galilee to Jerusalem 9.51-19.27
The last week in and near Jerusalem 19.28-23.56
The resurrection, appearances, and ascension of the Lord 24.1-53

簡 介

路加福音告訴我們：耶穌是上帝應許賜給以色列人的拯救者，也是全人類的救主。路加記載耶穌受主的靈呼召「向貧窮人傳佳音」（４.１８），而這佳音充滿著對人類各種需要的關懷。本書處處洋溢著喜樂的氣氛，尤其是頭幾章有關耶穌的降生和最後他升天的報導。至於耶穌升天後福音的傳揚和擴展，本書作者在使徒行傳有詳細的記述。

第二部分和第六部分（參閱提要）所包括的材料，如伯利恆郊外天使的歌聲、牧羊人朝拜聖嬰、童子耶穌在聖殿裏，和好撒馬利亞人以及仁慈的父親的故事等，只見於本福音書。本書特別注重禱告、聖靈、婦女對耶穌工作的協助、上帝赦罪的恩典，和基督的普世使命。

提要

1. 序言（１.１-４）
2. 施洗者約翰和耶穌的降生及童年（１.５-２.52）
3. 施洗者約翰的工作（３.１-20）
4. 耶穌的洗禮和受試探（３.21-４.13）
5. 耶穌在加利利的工作（４.14-９.50）
6. 從加利利到耶路撒冷（９.51-19.27）
7. 最後一週在耶路撒冷和附近（19.28-23.56）
8. 主的復活、顯現，和升天（24.1-53）

1 Dear Theophilus:
Many people have done their best to write a report of the things that have taken place among us. [2]They wrote what we have been told by those who saw these things from the beginning and who proclaimed the message. [3]And so, Your Excellency, because I have carefully studied all these matters from their beginning, I thought it would be good to write an orderly account for you. [4]I do this so that you will know the full truth about everything which you have been taught.

The Birth of John the Baptist Is Announced

[5]During the time when Herod was king of Judea,[a] there was a priest named Zechariah, who belonged to the priestly order of Abijah. His wife's name was Elizabeth; she also belonged to a priestly family. [6]They both lived good lives in God's sight and obeyed fully all the Lord's laws and commands. [7]They had no children because Elizabeth could not have any, and she and Zechariah were both very old.

[8]One day Zechariah was doing his work as a priest in the Temple, taking his turn in the daily service. [9]According to the custom followed by the priests, he was chosen by lot to burn incense on the altar. So he went into the Temple of the Lord, [10]while the crowd of people outside prayed during the hour when the incense was burned. [11]An angel of the Lord appeared to him, standing at the right side of the altar where the incense was burned. [12]When Zechariah saw him, he was alarmed and felt afraid. [13]But the angel said to him, "Don't be afraid, Zechariah! God has heard your prayer, and your wife Elizabeth will bear you a son. You are to name him John. [14]How glad and happy you will be, and how happy many others will be when he is born! [15]John will be great in the Lord's sight. He must not drink any wine or strong drink. From his very birth he will be filled with the Holy Spirit, [16]and he will bring back many of the people of Israel to the Lord their God. [17]He will go ahead of the Lord, strong and mighty like the prophet Elijah. He will bring fathers and children together again; he will turn disobedient people back to the way of thinking of the righteous; he will get the Lord's people ready for him."

[18]Zechariah said to the angel, "How shall I know if this is so? I am an old man, and my wife is old also."

[19]"I am Gabriel," the angel answered. "I stand in the presence of God, who sent me to speak to you and tell you this good news. [20]But you have not believed my message, which will

a JUDAED: *The term here refers to the whole land of Palestine.*

序言

1 提阿非羅閣下：
已經有好些人從事寫作，報導在我們當中所發生的事。[2]他們的報導是根據那些從開始就親眼看見這些事，並且曾經傳佈這信息的人所敍述的。[3]這一切我都從頭仔細查考過了，所以我想按照次序向你報告，[4]目的是讓你知道你所學的道是正確的。

預言施洗者約翰的出生

[5]希律王統治猶太的時候，有一個祭司，名叫撒迦利亞，是屬於亞比雅祭司一班的；他的妻子叫伊利莎白，也是亞倫家族的後代。[6]在上帝眼中，他們兩個都是正直的人，嚴謹地遵守主一切的誡命和條例。[7]他們沒有孩子；因為伊利莎白不能生育，而兩人都已經老了。

[8]有一天，撒迦利亞值班，在上帝面前執行祭司的職務。[9]按照祭司慣例，抽籤的結果，他得以進入主的聖殿上香。[10]他上香的時候，民眾在外面禱告。[11]忽然，有主的天使站在香壇右邊向他顯現；[12]撒迦利亞看見了，驚惶害怕。[13]可是那天使對他說：「撒迦利亞，不要怕！上帝垂聽了你的禱告；你的妻子伊利莎白要給你生一個兒子，你要替他取名叫約翰。[14]你要歡喜快樂；許多人也要為他的誕生而喜樂。[15]在主的眼中，他將是一個偉大的人物。淡酒烈酒，他都不可喝；在母胎裏，他①就要被聖靈充滿。[16]他要帶領許多多以色列人歸回主－－他們的上帝。[17]他要作主的前驅，堅強有力，像先知以利亞一樣。他要使父親和兒女重新和好，使悖逆的人回頭，走上義人明智的道路；他要幫助人民來迎接主。」

[18]撒迦利亞對天使說：「我憑甚麼知道這事呢？我已經老了；我妻子也上了年紀。」

[19]天使說：「我是侍立在上帝面前的加百列；我奉派向你傳話，報給你這喜訊。[20]但是，因為你不相信我所說、在時機成熟時會

①「在母胎裏，他」或譯「他一出母胎」。

come true at the right time. Because you have not believed, you will be unable to speak; you will remain silent until the day my promise to you comes true."

21In the meantime the people were waiting for Zechariah and wondering why he was spending such a long time in the Temple. 22When he came out, he could not speak to them, and so they knew that he had seen a vision in the Temple. Unable to say a word, he made signs to them with his hands.

23When his period of service in the Temple was over, Zechariah went back home. 24Some time later his wife Elizabeth became pregnant and did not leave the house for five months. 25"Now at last the Lord has helped me," she said. "He has taken away my public disgrace!"

The Birth of Jesus Is Announced

26In the sixth month of Elizabeth's pregnancy God sent the angel Gabriel to a town in Galilee named Nazareth. 27He had a message for a young woman promised in marriage to a man named Joseph, who was a descendant of King David. Her name was Mary. 28The angel came to her and said, "Peace be with you! The Lord is with you and has greatly blessed you!"

29Mary was deeply troubled by the angel's message, and she wondered what his words meant. 30The angel said to her, "Don't be afraid, Mary; God has been gracious to you. 31You will become pregnant and give birth to a son, and you will name him Jesus. 32He will be great and will be called the Son of the Most High God. The Lord God will make him a king, as his ancestor David was, 33and he will be the king of the descendants of Jacob forever; his kingdom will never end!"

34Mary said to the angel, "I am a virgin. How, then, can this be?"

35The angel answered, "The Holy Spirit will come on you, and God's power will rest upon you. For this reason the holy child will be called the Son of God. 36Remember your relative Elizabeth. It is said that she cannot have children, but she herself is now six months pregnant, even though she is very old. 37For there is nothing that God cannot do."

38"I am the Lord's servant," said Mary; "may it happen to me as you have said." And the angel left her.

Mary Visits Elizabeth

39Soon afterward Mary got ready and hurried off to a town in the hill country of Judea. 40She went into Zechariah's house and greeted Elizabeth. 41When Elizabeth heard Mary's

---

實現的那些話，你將變成啞巴，直到我的應許實現的那一天才能說話。」

21 這時候，大家等待着撒迦利亞，不明白他為甚麼在聖殿裏耽擱這麼久。22到了他出來，不能跟他們說話，大家才曉得他在聖殿裏看見了異象。他不能說話，只好打手勢向大家示意。

23 在聖殿裏供職的日期一滿，撒迦利亞就回家去。24過了不久，他的妻子伊利莎白果然懷了孕，五個月之久沒有出門。25她說：「主終於這樣厚待我，除掉了我在公眾面前的羞辱。」

預告耶穌誕生

26 在伊利莎白懷孕的第六個月，上帝差遣天使加百列到加利利一個叫拿撒勒的城去，27要傳話給一個童女，名叫馬利亞；這童女已經跟大衞家族一個名叫約瑟的男子訂了婚。28天使到她面前，說：「願你平安！你是蒙大恩的女子，主與你同在！」

29 馬利亞因為天使這話，十分驚惶不安，反覆思想這問安的含意。30天使對她說：「馬利亞，不要害怕，因為上帝施恩給你。31你要懷孕生一個兒子，要給他取名叫耶穌。32他將成為偉大的人物，他要被稱為至高上帝的兒子。主－上帝要立他繼承他祖先大衞的王位。33他要永遠作雅各家的王，他的王權無窮無盡！」

34 馬利亞對天使說：「我還沒有出嫁，這樣的事怎麼能發生呢？」

35 天使回答：「聖靈要降臨到你身上；至高上帝的權能要庇蔭你。因此，那將誕生的聖嬰要被稱為上帝的兒子。36看你的親戚伊利莎白，她雖然年老，人家說她不能生育，可是她現在已經有了六個月的身孕。37因為在上帝沒有一件事是做不到的。」

38 馬利亞說：「我是主的婢女；願你的話成就在我身上。」於是天使離開了她。

馬利亞訪伊利莎白

39 不久，馬利亞動身，急忙往山區去，到了猶大一個城。40她進了撒迦利亞的家，向伊利莎白請安。41伊利莎白一聽見馬利亞的

greeting, the baby moved within her. Elizabeth was filled with the Holy Spirit ⁴²and said in a loud voice, "You are the most blessed of all women, and blessed is the child you will bear! ⁴³Why should this great thing happen to me, that my Lord's mother comes to visit me? ⁴⁴For as soon as I heard your greeting, the baby within me jumped with gladness. ⁴⁵How happy you are to believe that the Lord's message to you will come true!"

Mary's Song of Praise

⁴⁶Mary said,

"My heart praises the Lord;
⁴⁷   my soul is glad because of God my Savior,
⁴⁸   for he has remembered me, his lowly servant!
   From now on all people will call me happy,
⁴⁹   because of the great things the Mighty
       God has done for me.
   His name is holy;
⁵⁰   from one generation to another
       he shows mercy to those who honor him.
⁵¹He has stretched out his mighty arm
     and scattered the proud with all
       their plans.
⁵²He has brought down mighty kings from
     their thrones,
     and lifted up the lowly.
⁵³He has filled the hungry with good things,
     and sent the rich away with empty hands.
⁵⁴He has kept the promise he made to our
     ancestors,
     and has come to the help of his servant
     Israel.
⁵⁵He has remembered to show mercy to
     Abraham
     and to all his descendants forever!"

⁵⁶Mary stayed about three months with Elizabeth and then went back home.

The Birth of John the Baptist

⁵⁷The time came for Elizabeth to have her baby, and she gave birth to a son. ⁵⁸Her neighbors and relatives heard how wonderfully good the Lord had been to her, and they all rejoiced with her.

⁵⁹When the baby was a week old, they came to circumcise him, and they were going to name him Zechariah, after his father. ⁶⁰But his mother said, "No! His name is to be John."

⁶¹They said to her, "But you don't have any relative with that name!" ⁶²Then they made signs to his father, asking him what name he would like the boy to have.

⁶³Zechariah asked for a writing pad and wrote, "His name is John." How surprised they all were! ⁶⁴At that moment Zechariah was able

問安,腹中的胎兒就跳動了。伊利莎白被聖靈充滿,⁴²高聲呼喊:「你是女子中最蒙福的;你所懷的胎兒也是蒙福的!⁴³我主的母親前來探望我,我怎麼敢當呢?⁴⁴我一聽見你問安的聲音,我腹中的胎兒就歡喜跳躍。⁴⁵確信主傳給她的信息必定實現的女子多麼有福啊!」

馬利亞的尊主頌

⁴⁶馬利亞說:
我心尊主為大;
⁴⁷我靈以上帝──我救主為樂;
⁴⁸因為他顧念他卑微的婢女。
從今以後,萬民將稱我有福,
⁴⁹因為大能的上帝為我成全了大事。
他的名神聖;
⁵⁰他向敬畏他的人廣施仁慈,
代代無窮。
⁵¹他伸出權能的手臂,
驅除狂傲者心中一切的計謀。
⁵²他把強大的君王從寶座上推下去;
他又抬舉卑微的人。
⁵³他使飢餓的人飽餐美食,
叫富足的人空手回去。
⁵⁴⁻⁵⁵他向我們的祖先信守諾言,
扶助他的僕人以色列。
他顧念亞伯拉罕,向他大施仁慈,
並且及於他的後裔,直到永遠!
⁵⁶馬利亞跟伊利莎白住了約三個月,然後回家。

施洗者約翰的出生

⁵⁷伊利莎白分娩的日子到了,生了一個兒子。⁵⁸她的鄰居和親戚聽見了主賜給她這樣大的恩慈,都跟她一同歡喜。

⁵⁹孩子出生滿一星期,他們來為他行割禮,並想沿用他父親的名字叫他撒迦利亞。⁶⁰可是他母親說:「不行!他要叫約翰。」

⁶¹親友對她說:「你親族中並沒有叫這名字的。」⁶²他們就向他的父親打手勢,問他要給孩子取甚麼名字。

⁶³撒迦利亞要了一塊寫字板,寫上:「他的名字是約翰。」大家都非常驚訝。⁶⁴就在

to speak again, and he started praising God.
⁶⁵The neighbors were all filled with fear, and
the news about these things spread through all
the hill country of Judea. ⁶⁶Everyone who heard
of it thought about it and asked, "What is this
child going to be?" For it was plain that the
Lord's power was upon him.

Zechariah's Prophecy

⁶⁷John's father Zechariah was filled with the
Holy Spirit, and he spoke God's message:
⁶⁸"Let us praise the Lord, the God of Israel!
>   He has come to the help of his people and
>   has set them free.
⁶⁹He has provided for us a mighty Savior,
>   a descendant of his servant David.
⁷⁰He promised through his holy prophets
>   long ago
⁷¹   that he would save us from our enemies,
>   from the power of all those who hate us.
⁷²He said he would show mercy to our ancestors
>   and remember his sacred covenant.
⁷³⁻⁷⁴With a solemn oath to our ancestor
>   Abraham
>   he promised to rescue us from our enemies
>   and allow us to serve him without fear,
⁷⁵so that we might be holy and righteous
>   before him
>   all the days of our life.

⁷⁶"You, my child, will be called a prophet of
>   the Most High God.
>   You will go ahead of the Lord
>   to prepare his road for him,
⁷⁷to tell his people that they will be saved
>   by having their sins forgiven.
⁷⁸Our God is merciful and tender.
>   He will cause the bright dawn of salvation to
>   rise on us
⁷⁹   and to shine from heaven on all those who
>   live in the dark shadow of death,
>   to guide our steps into the path of peace."

⁸⁰The child grew and developed in body and
spirit. He lived in the desert until the day when
he appeared publicly to the people of Israel.

The Birth of Jesus
(Matthew 1.18-25)

2   At that time Emperor Augustus ordered a
   census to be taken throughout the Roman
Empire. ²When this first census took place,
Quirinius was the governor of Syria. ³Everyone,
then, went to register himself, each to his own
hometown.

這時候,撒迦利亞又能夠說話了,他就開口
頌讚上帝。⁶⁵鄰居都很驚訝。這消息傳遍了
全猶太山區;⁶⁶聽見的人都在想:「這孩子
將會成為怎樣的人物呢?」因為顯然有主的
權能與他同在。

撒迦利亞的預言

⁶⁷ 約翰的父親撒迦利亞被聖靈充滿,就傳
達上帝的信息,說:
⁶⁸ 讓我們歌頌主—以色列的上帝!
>   他眷顧他的子民,釋放了他們。
⁶⁹ 他從他的僕人大衛家中,
>   為我們興起了一位全能的救主。
⁷⁰ 古時候,他藉著聖先知們說過:
⁷¹ 他要拯救我們脫離敵人,
>   擺脫一切恨惡我們的人的權勢。
⁷² 他要向我們的祖宗大施仁慈,
>   並記住他神聖的約。
⁷³⁻⁷⁵他應許我們的先祖亞伯拉罕,
>   立誓要拯救我們擺脫仇敵,
>   使我們一生一世,
>   坦然無懼地在他面前,
>   以聖潔和正直事奉他。
⁷⁶ 我的孩子啊,
>   你要被稱為至高上帝的先知。
>   你要作主的前驅,為他預備道路;
⁷⁷ 要告訴他的子民:
>   由於他們的罪蒙赦免,
>   他們將獲得拯救。
⁷⁸ 我們的上帝慈悲柔和;
>   他使救恩的曙光照耀我們,
⁷⁹ 又從高天光照
>   一切生活在死亡陰影下的人,
>   引導我們走上和平的道路。
⁸⁰ 孩子漸漸長大,身心強健。他住在曠
野,一直到他在以色列人中公開活動的時
候。

耶穌誕生
(太 1 · 18—25)

2   那時候,羅馬皇帝奧古斯都頒佈命令,
   要羅馬帝國的人民都辦理戶口登記。
² 這頭一次的戶口登記是在居里扭任敍利亞
總督的時候。³ 大家都回本鄉去辦理登記。

4Joseph went from the town of Nazareth in Galilee to the town of Bethlehem in Judea, the birthplace of King David. Joseph went there because he was a descendant of David. 5He went to register with Mary, who was promised in marriage to him. She was pregnant, 6and while they were in Bethlehem, the time came for her to have her baby. 7She gave birth to her first son, wrapped him in cloths and laid him in a manger–there was no room for them to stay in the inn.

The Shepherds and the Angels

8There were some shepherds in that part of the country who were spending the night in the fields, taking care of their flocks. 9An angel of the Lord appeared to them, and the glory of the Lord shone over them. They were terribly afraid, 10but the angel said to them, "Don't be afraid! I am here with good news for you, which will bring great joy to all the people. 11This very day in David's town your Savior was born–Christ the Lord! 12And this is what will prove it to you: you will find a baby wrapped in cloths and lying in a manger."

13Suddenly a great army of heaven's angels appeared with the angel, singing praises to God:

14"Glory to God in the highest heaven,
    and peace on earth to those with whom he
      is pleased!"

15When the angels went away from them back into heaven, the shepherds said to one another, "Let's go to Bethlehem and see this thing that has happened, which the Lord has told us."

16So they hurried off and found Mary and Joseph and saw the baby lying in the manger. 17When the shepherds saw him, they told them what the angel had said about the child. 18All who heard it were amazed at what the shepherds said. 19Mary remembered all these things and thought deeply about them. 20The shepherds went back, singing praises to God for all they had heard and seen; it had been just as the angel had told them.

Jesus Is Named

21A week later, when the time came for the baby to be circumcised, he was named Jesus, the name which the angel had given him before he had been conceived.

Jesus Is Presented in the Temple

22The time came for Joseph and Mary to perform the ceremony of purification, as the Law of Moses commanded. So they took the child to

4 約瑟也從加利利的拿撒勒城往猶太去，到了大衞的城，叫伯利恆；因為約瑟屬於大衞的宗族，5他要跟他訂了婚的馬利亞一起登記。馬利亞已經有了身孕，6當他們在伯利恆的時候，她的產期到了，7生下頭胎兒子，用布包起來，放在馬槽裏，因為客棧裏沒有地方讓他們住。

牧羊人和天使

8 在伯利恆郊外，有些牧羊人夜間露宿，輪流看守羊羣。9主的天使向他們顯現；主的榮光四面照射他們，他們就非常驚惶。10可是天使對他們說：「不要害怕！我有好消息告訴你們；這消息要帶給萬民極大的喜樂。11今天，在大衞的城裏，你們的拯救者——主基督已經誕生了！12你們會看見一個嬰兒，用布包着，躺在馬槽裏；那就是要給你們的記號。」

13 忽然，有一大隊天軍跟那天使一起出現，頌讚上帝說：

14 願榮耀歸於至高之處的上帝！
    願和平歸給地上他所喜愛的人！

15 天使離開他們回天上去的時候，牧羊人彼此說：「我們進伯利恆城去，看主所告訴我們那已經發生了的事。」

16 於是他們急忙趕去，找到了馬利亞、約瑟，和躺在馬槽裏的嬰兒。17牧羊人看見以後，把天使所說關於嬰兒的事告訴大家。18聽見的人對牧羊人的話都很驚訝。19馬利亞卻把這一切事牢記在心裏，反覆思想。20牧羊人回去，為他們所聽見所看到的事讚美歌頌上帝，因為所發生的事跟天使所告訴他們的相符。

取名耶穌

21 八天後，嬰兒行割禮的日子到了，就為他取名叫耶穌；這名字是他未成胎以前天使替他取的。

奉獻給主

22 按照摩西法律的規定，潔淨的日期滿了以後，約瑟和馬利亞帶小孩子上耶路撒冷

Jerusalem to present him to the Lord, [23]as it is written in the law of the Lord: "Every first-born male is to be dedicated to the Lord." [24]They also went to offer a sacrifice of a pair of doves or two young pigeons, as required by the law of the Lord.

[25]At that time there was a man named Simeon living in Jerusalem. He was a good, God-fearing man and was waiting for Israel to be saved. The Holy Spirit was with him [26]and had assured him that he would not die before he had seen the Lord's promised Messiah. [27]Led by the Spirit, Simeon went into the Temple. When the parents brought the child Jesus into the Temple to do for him what the Law required, [28]Simeon took the child in his arms and gave thanks to God:

[29]"Now, Lord, you have kept your promise,
and you may let your servant go in peace.
[30]With my own eyes I have seen your salvation,
[31] which you have prepared in the presence of all peoples:
[32]A light to reveal your will to the Gentiles
and bring glory to your people Israel."

[33]The child's father and mother were amazed at the things Simeon said about him. [34]Simeon blessed them and said to Mary, his mother, "This child is chosen by God for the destruction and the salvation of many in Israel. He will be a sign from God which many people will speak against [35]and so reveal their secret thoughts. And sorrow, like a sharp sword, will break your own heart."

[36-37]There was a very old prophet, a widow named Anna, daughter of Phanuel of the tribe of Asher. She had been married for only seven years and was now eighty-four years old.[b] She never left the Temple; day and night she worshiped God, fasting and praying. [38]That very same hour she arrived and gave thanks to God and spoke about the child to all who were waiting for God to set Jerusalem free.

The Return to Nazareth

[39]When Joseph and Mary had finished doing all that was required by the Law of the Lord, they returned to their hometown of Nazareth in Galilee. [40]The child grew and became strong; he was full of wisdom, and God's blessings were upon him.

The Boy Jesus in the Temple

[41]Every year the parents of Jesus went to Jerusalem for the Passover Festival. [42]When Jesus was twelve years old, they went to the festival as usual. [43]When the festival was over,

[b] was now eighty-four years old; or had been a widow eighty-four years.

去，要把他奉獻給主。[23]這是依照主的法律所寫：「頭胎的男孩都要奉獻給主。」[24]他們也要依照主的法律所規定的，獻上一對斑鳩或兩隻小鴿子作祭品。

[25]當時，在耶路撒冷有一個人，名叫西面。他是敬畏上帝的義人，一向盼望以色列得到拯救。聖靈與他同在；[26]他得到聖靈的啟示，知道自己在離世以前會看見主所應許的基督。[27]由於聖靈的感動，他來到聖殿。這時候，耶穌的父母剛抱著孩子耶穌進來，要履行法律所規定的事。[28]西面把孩子抱在懷裏，頌讚上帝說：

[29]主啊，你已實現了你的應許；
如今可讓你的僕人平安歸去。
[30]我已親眼看見你的拯救，
[31]就是你為萬民所預備的：
[32]他要成為啟示外邦的亮光，
成為你子民以色列的榮耀。

[33]孩子的父母對西面所說關於孩子的事覺得驚訝。[34]西面給他們祝福，並且向孩子的母親馬利亞說：「這孩子被上帝揀選，是要使以色列中許多人滅亡，許多人得救。他要成為許多人毀謗的對象，[35]並因此揭露了這些人心底的意念。憂傷要像利劍刺透你的心。」

[36]有一個女先知，名叫安娜，是亞設支族法內力的女兒。她已經很老了，曾結過婚，跟丈夫一起生活了七年，[37]以後寡居，現在已經八十四歲[②]。她沒有離開過聖殿，日夜敬拜上帝，禁食、禱告。[38]正在這時候，她也來了，頌讚上帝，並且向所有期待上帝來救贖耶路撒冷的人宣講這孩子的事。

回拿撒勒

[39]約瑟和馬利亞按照主的法律履行了一切所規定的事，就回加利利，到他們的本鄉拿撒勒去。[40]孩子漸漸長大，健壯而有智慧；上帝的恩寵與他同在。

孩童耶穌在聖殿

[41]耶穌的父母每年都上耶路撒冷守逾越節。[42]耶穌十二歲的時候，他們照例前往守節。[43]節期完了，他們動身回家，孩童耶穌

[②]「以後寡居，現在已經八十四歲」或譯「已經寡居八十四年」。

they started back home, but the boy Jesus stayed in Jerusalem. His parents did not know this; [44]they thought that he was with the group, so they traveled a whole day and then started looking for him among their relatives and friends. [45]They did not find him, so they went back to Jerusalem looking for him. [46]On the third day they found him in the Temple, sitting with the Jewish teachers, listening to them and asking questions. [47]All who heard him were amazed at his intelligent answers. [48]His parents were astonished when they saw him, and his mother said to him, "Son, why have you done this to us? Your father and I have been terribly worried trying to find you."

[49]He answered them, "Why did you have to look for me? Didn't you know that I had to be in my Father's house?" [50]But they did not understand his answer.

[51]So Jesus went back with them to Nazareth, where he was obedient to them. His mother treasured all these things in her heart. [52]Jesus grew both in body and in wisdom, gaining favor with God and people.

The Preaching of John the Baptist
(Matthew 3.1-12; Mark 1.1-8; John 1.19-28)

3 It was the fifteenth year of the rule of Emperor Tiberius; Pontius Pilate was governor of Judea, Herod was ruler of Galilee, and his brother Philip was ruler of the territory of Iturea and Trachonitis; Lysanias was ruler of Abilene, [2]and Annas and Caiaphas were High Priests. At that time the word of God came to John son of Zechariah in the desert. [3]So John went throughout the whole territory of the Jordan River, preaching, "Turn away from your sins and be baptized, and God will forgive your sins." [4]As it is written in the book of the prophet Isaiah:

"Someone is shouting in the desert:
'Get the road ready for the Lord;
make a straight path for him to travel!
[5]Every valley must be filled up,
every hill and mountain leveled off.
The winding roads must be made straight,
and the rough paths made smooth.
[6]The whole human race will see God's salvation!' "

[7]Crowds of people came out to John to be baptized by him. "You snakes!" he said to them. "Who told you that you could escape from the punishment God is about to send? [8]Do those things that will show that you have turned from your sins. And don't start saying among yourselves that Abraham is your ances-

卻逗留在耶路撒冷；他的父母不知道這事，[44]以為他在同行的人羣中，走了一天的路程才開始在親友當中尋找他。[45]他們找不到他，就回耶路撒冷去找。[46]三天後，他們才在聖殿裏找到他。他正坐在猶太教師們中間，邊聽邊問；[47]所有聽見他的人都驚奇他的聰明和對答。[48]他的父母看見他，覺得很驚異。他的母親對他說：「孩子，為甚麼你這樣待我們？你父親和我非常焦急，到處找你呢！」

[49]耶穌回答：「為甚麼找我？難道你們不知道我必須在我父親的家裏③嗎？」[50]可是他們都不明白他這話的意思。

[51]於是，耶穌和他們回拿撒勒去，事事都順從他們。他母親把這一切事都珍惜地記在心裏。[52]耶穌的身體和智慧一齊增長，深得上帝和人的喜愛。

施洗者約翰的傳道
（太3‧1-12；可1‧1-8；約1‧19-28）

3 羅馬皇帝提庇留在位第十五年，龐修‧彼拉多作猶太總督，希律作加利利王，他的兄弟腓力作以土利亞和特拉可尼王，呂撒聶作亞比利尼王，[2]亞那和該亞法作大祭司。那時，上帝的話臨到在曠野的撒迦利亞的兒子約翰。[3]約翰走遍了約旦河一帶地區，宣揚說：「你們要悔改，接受洗禮，上帝就赦免你們的罪。」[4]正如先知以賽亞書上所記載：

在曠野裏有人呼喊說：
為主準備他的道路，
修直他要走的路徑。
[5]一切山谷都要填滿；
大小山岡都要削低。
彎曲的路徑要修直；
崎嶇的道路要剷平。
[6]全人類都要看見上帝的救恩。

[7]人羣擁擠，出來要接受約翰的洗禮。約翰對他們說：「你們這些毒蛇！上帝的審判快要到了，你們以為能夠逃避嗎？[8]要用行為證明你們已經悔改。不要自以為亞伯拉罕是你們的祖宗就可以逃避審判。我告訴你

③「在我父親的家裏」或譯「關心我父親的事」。

tor. I tell you that God can take these rocks and make descendants for Abraham! ⁹The ax is ready to cut down the trees at the roots; every tree that does not bear good fruit will be cut down and thrown in the fire."

¹⁰The people asked him, "What are we to do, then?"

¹¹He answered, "Whoever has two shirts must give one to the man who has none, and whoever has food must share it."

¹²Some tax collectors came to be baptized, and they asked him, "Teacher, what are we to do?"

¹³"Don't collect more than is legal," he told them.

¹⁴Some soldiers also asked him, "What about us? What are we to do?"

He said to them, "Don't take money from anyone by force or accuse anyone falsely. Be content with your pay."

¹⁵People's hopes began to rise, and they began to wonder whether John perhaps might be the Messiah. ¹⁶So John said to all of them, "I baptize you with water, but someone is coming who is much greater than I am. I am not good enough even to untie his sandals. He will baptize you with the Holy Spirit and fire. ¹⁷He has his winnowing shovel with him, to thresh out all the grain and gather the wheat into his barn; but he will burn the chaff in a fire that never goes out."

¹⁸In many different ways John preached the Good News to the people and urged them to change their ways. ¹⁹But John reprimanded Governor Herod, because he had married Herodias, his brother's wife, and had done many other evil things. ²⁰Then Herod did an even worse thing by putting John in prison.

The Baptism of Jesus
(Matthew 3.13-17; Mark 1.9-11)

²¹After all the people had been baptized, Jesus also was baptized. While he was praying, heaven was opened, ²²and the Holy Spirit came down upon him in bodily form like a dove. And a voice came from heaven, "You are my own dear Son. I am pleased with you."

The Ancestors of Jesus
(Matthew 1.1-17)

²³When Jesus began his work, he was about thirty years old. He was the son, so people thought, of Joseph, who was the son of Heli, ²⁴the son of Matthat, the son of Levi, the son of Melchi, the son of Jannai, the son of Joseph,

們,上帝能夠拿這些石頭爲亞伯拉罕造出子孫來!⁹斧頭已經擱在樹根上,凡不結好果子的樹都要砍掉,丟在火裏。」

¹⁰ 羣衆問他:「那麼,我們該做甚麼呢?」

¹¹ 約翰回答:「有兩件內衣的,要分一件給沒有的;有食物的,也要這樣。」

¹² 有些稅棍也要來接受洗禮;他們問約翰:「老師,我們該做甚麼呢?」

¹³ 他告訴他們:「不可收取法定以外的稅金。」

¹⁴ 有些當兵的也來問他:「我們呢?該做些甚麼呢?」

他對他們說:「不可强索金錢,不可敲詐;要以所得的糧餉爲足。」

¹⁵ 人民的希望提高了,大家心裏猜想,也許約翰就是基督。¹⁶因此約翰告訴他們:「我用水給你們施洗;可是,有一位能力比我更大的要來,我就是替他脫鞋子也不配。他要用聖靈和火爲你們施洗。¹⁷他手裏拿着簸箕,要揚淨穀物,把麥子收進倉庫;至於糠粃,他要用永不熄滅的火燒掉。」

¹⁸ 約翰向人民傳福音,用許多不同的方法規勸他們。¹⁹但是約翰譴責希律王,因爲希律娶了他的弟婦希羅底,又做了許多的壞事。²⁰以後他做了一件更嚴重的壞事,就是把約翰關在監獄裏。

耶穌接受洗禮
(太 3 · 13—17;可 1 · 9—11)

²¹ 一般人民都接受洗禮,耶穌也來受洗。他在禱告的時候,天開了,²²聖靈有形體的降在他身上,彷彿鴿子。從天上有聲音傳下來,說:「你是我親愛的兒子,我喜愛你。」

耶穌的家譜
(太 1 · 1—17)

²³ 耶穌開始傳道的時候,年紀約三十歲。在人的眼中,他是約瑟的兒子,約瑟是希里的兒子,²⁴希里是瑪塔的兒子,瑪塔是利未的兒子,利未是麥基的兒子,麥基是雅拿的

25the son of Mattathias, the son of Amos, the son of Nahum, the son of Esli, the son of Naggai, 26the son of Maath, the son of Mattathias, the son of Semein, the son of Josech, the son of Joda, 27the son of Joanan, the son of Rhesa, the son of Zerubbabel, the son of Shealtiel, the son of Neri, 28the son of Melchi, the son of Addi, the son of Cosam, the son of Elmadam, the son of Er, 29the son of Joshua, the son of Eliezer, the son of Jorim, the son of Matthat, the son of Levi, 30the son of Simeon, the son of Judah, the son of Joseph, the son of Jonam, the son of Eliakim, 31the son of Melea, the son of Menna, the son of Mattatha, the son of Nathan, the son of David, 32the son of Jesse, the son of Obed, the son of Boaz, the son of Salmon, the son of Nahshon, 33the son of Amminadab, the son of Admin, the son of Arni, the son of Hezron, the son of Perez, the son of Judah, 34the son of Jacob, the son of Isaac, the son of Abraham, the son of Terah, the son of Nahor, 35the son of Serug, the son of Reu, the son of Peleg, the son of Eber, the son of Shelah, 36the son of Cainan, the son of Arphaxad, the son of Shem, the son of Noah, the son of Lamech, 37the son of Methuselah, the son of Enoch, the son of Jared, the son of Mahalaleel, the son of Kenan, 38the son of Enosh, the son of Seth, the son of Adam, the son of God.

兒子，雅拿是約瑟的兒子，25約瑟是瑪他提亞的兒子，瑪他提亞是亞摩斯的兒子，亞摩斯是拿鴻的兒子，拿鴻是以斯利的兒子，以斯利是拿該的兒子，26拿該是瑪押的兒子，瑪押是瑪他提亞的兒子，瑪他提亞是西美的兒子，西美是約色克的兒子，約色克是約大的兒子，27約大是約亞拿的兒子。約亞拿是利撒的兒子，利撒是所羅巴伯的兒子，所羅巴伯是撒拉鐵的兒子，撒拉鐵是尼利的兒子。28尼利是麥基的兒子，麥基是亞底的兒子，亞底是哥桑的兒子，哥桑是以摩當的兒子，以摩當是珥的兒子，29珥是約細的兒子。約細是以利以謝的兒子，以利以謝是約令的兒子，約令是瑪塔的兒子，瑪塔是利未的兒子。30利未是西緬的兒子，西緬是猶大的兒子，猶大是約瑟的兒子，約瑟是約南的兒子，約南是以利亞敬的兒子。31以利亞敬是米利亞的兒子，米利亞是買南的兒子，買南是瑪達他的兒子，瑪達他是拿單的兒子，拿單是大衛的兒子。32大衛是耶西的兒子，耶西是俄備得的兒子，俄備得是波阿斯的兒子，波阿斯是撒門的兒子，撒門是拿順的兒子。33拿順是亞米拿達的兒子，亞米拿達是亞民的兒子，亞民是亞尼的兒子，亞尼是希斯崙的兒子，希斯崙是法勒斯的兒子，法勒斯是猶大的兒子，34猶大是雅各的兒子，雅各是以撒的兒子，以撒是亞伯拉罕的兒子，亞伯拉罕是他拉的兒子，他拉是拿鶴的兒子，35拿鶴是西鹿的兒子，西鹿是拉吳的兒子，拉吳是法勒的兒子，法勒是希伯的兒子，希伯是沙拉的兒子，36沙拉是該南的兒子，該南是亞法撒的兒子，亞法撒是閃的兒子，閃是挪亞的兒子，挪亞是拉麥的兒子，37拉麥是瑪土撒拉的兒子，瑪土撒拉是以諾的兒子，以諾是雅列的兒子，雅列是瑪勒列的兒子，瑪勒列是該南的兒子，38該南是以挪士的兒子，以挪士是塞特的兒子，塞特是亞當的兒子，亞當是上帝的兒子。

The Temptation of Jesus
(Matthew 4.1-11; Mark 1.12-13)

4 Jesus returned from the Jordan full of the Holy Spirit and was led by the Spirit into the desert, 2where he was tempted by the Devil for forty days. In all that time he ate nothing, so that he was hungry when it was over.

耶穌受試探
（太 4・1—11；可 1・12—13）

4 耶穌從約旦河回來，充滿着聖靈。聖靈領他到曠野，2 在那裏四十天之久，受魔鬼試探。那些日子，他甚麼東西都沒有吃，日期一過，他餓了。

3The Devil said to him, "If you are God's Son, order this stone to turn into bread."

4But Jesus answered, "The scripture says, 'Human beings cannot live on bread alone.' "

5Then the Devil took him up and showed him in a second all the kingdoms of the world. 6"I will give you all this power and all this wealth," the Devil told him. "It has all been handed over to me, and I can give it to anyone I choose. 7All this will be yours, then, if you worship me."

8Jesus answered, "The scripture says, 'Worship the Lord your God and serve only him!' "

9Then the Devil took him to Jerusalem and set him on the highest point of the Temple, and said to him, "If you are God's Son, throw yourself down from here. 10For the scripture says, 'God will order his angels to take good care of you.' 11It also says, 'They will hold you up with their hands so that not even your feet will be hurt on the stones.' "

12But Jesus answered, "The scripture says, 'Do not put the Lord your God to the test.' "

13When the Devil finished tempting Jesus in every way, he left him for a while.

Jesus Begins His Work in Galilee
(Matthew 4.12-17; Mark 1.14-15)

14Then Jesus returned to Galilee, and the power of the Holy Spirit was with him. The news about him spread throughout all that territory. 15He taught in the synagogues and was praised by everyone.

Jesus Is Rejected at Nazareth
(Matthew 13.53-58; Mark 6.1-6)

16Then Jesus went to Nazareth, where he had been brought up, and on the Sabbath he went as usual to the synagogue. He stood up to read the Scriptures 17and was handed the book of the prophet Isaiah. He unrolled the scroll and found the place where it is written,

18"The Spirit of the Lord is upon me,
  because he has chosen me to bring good
      news to the poor.
He has sent me to proclaim liberty to the
      captives
  and recovery of sight to the blind,
to set free the oppressed
19 and announce that the time has come
      when the Lord will save his people."

20Jesus rolled up the scroll, gave it back to the attendant, and sat down. All the people in

3 魔鬼對他說:「既然你是上帝的兒子,命令這塊石頭變成麵包吧!」

4 耶穌回答:「聖經說:『人的生存不僅是靠食物。』」

5 魔鬼又帶他到一個很高的地方,轉眼之間讓他看見了天下萬國,對他說:6-7「你若向我下拜,我就把這一切權柄和財富都給你;因為這一切都已交給了我,我願意給誰就給誰。」

8 耶穌說:「聖經說:『要拜主——你的上帝,惟獨敬奉他!』」

9 魔鬼又帶耶穌到耶路撒冷,讓他站在聖殿上的最高處,對他說:「既然你是上帝的兒子,就從這裏跳下去吧;10因為聖經說:『上帝要吩咐他的天使保護你』;11又說:『他們要用手托住你,使你的腳不至於在石頭上碰傷。』」

12 耶穌回答:「聖經說:『不可試探主——你的上帝。』」

13 魔鬼用盡各樣的試探,就暫時離開耶穌。

耶穌開始在加利利傳道
(太4·12—17;可1·14—15)

14 耶穌回到加利利;聖靈的能力與他同在。他的名聲傳遍那一帶地區。15他在各會堂教導人,人人都讚揚他。

耶穌在拿撒勒被厭棄
(太13·53—58;可6·1—6)

16 耶穌來到拿撒勒——他長大的地方。在安息日,他照常到猶太會堂去。他站起來要念聖經,17有人把先知以賽亞書給他。他打開書卷,找到一個地方寫着:

18 主的靈臨到我,
  因為他揀選了我,
  要我向貧窮人傳佳音。
他差遣我宣告:
  被擄的,得釋放;
  失明的,得光明;
  受欺壓的,得自由;
19 並宣告主拯救他子民的恩年。

20 耶穌把書卷捲起來,交還給會堂助理,

the synagogue had their eyes fixed on him, 21as he said to them, "This passage of scripture has come true today, as you heard it being read."

22They were all well impressed with him and marveled at the eloquent words that he spoke. They said, "Isn't he the son of Joseph?"

23He said to them, "I am sure that you will quote this proverb to me, 'Doctor, heal yourself.' You will also tell me to do here in my hometown the same things you heard were done in Capernaum. 24I tell you this," Jesus added, "prophets are never welcomed in their hometown. 25Listen to me: it is true that there were many widows in Israel during the time of Elijah, when there was no rain for three and a half years and a severe famine spread throughout the whole land. 26Yet Elijah was not sent to anyone in Israel, but only to a widow living in Zarephath in the territory of Sidon. 27And there were many people suffering from a dreaded skin disease who lived in Israel during the time of the prophet Elisha; yet not one of them was healed, but only Naaman the Syrian."

28When the people in the synagogue heard this, they were filled with anger. 29They rose up, dragged Jesus out of town, and took him to the top of the hill on which their town was built. They meant to throw him over the cliff, 30but he walked through the middle of the crowd and went his way.

A Man with an Evil Spirit
(Mark 1.21-28)

31Then Jesus went to Capernaum, a town in Galilee, where he taught the people on the Sabbath. 32They were all amazed at the way he taught, because he spoke with authority. 33In the synagogue was a man who had the spirit of an evil demon in him; he screamed out in a loud voice, 34"Ah! What do you want with us, Jesus of Nazareth? Are you here to destroy us? I know who you are: you are God's holy messenger!"

35Jesus ordered the spirit, "Be quiet and come out of the man!" The demon threw the man down in front of them and went out of him without doing him any harm.

36The people were all amazed and said to one another, "What kind of words are these? With authority and power this man gives orders to the evil spirits, and they come out!" 37And the report about Jesus spread everywhere in that region.

然後坐下。全會堂的人都盯着他，21他就對他們說：「今天，你們所聽見的這段經文已經應驗了。」

22 大家對他有深刻的印象，對他所說那動人的話大感驚奇。他們說：「這個人不是約瑟的兒子嗎？」

23 耶穌告訴他們：「無疑地，你們要引用這一句俗語對我說：『醫生啊，治好你自己吧！』你們還要對我說：『我們所聽到你在迦百農做過的事，也該在你自己的家鄉做出來！』」24耶穌又說：「我實在告訴你們，先知在自己的家鄉是從不受人歡迎的。25聽吧，在先知以利亞的時代，以色列中確有許多寡婦。那時，連續三年半天旱無雨，遍地大饑荒。26可是以利亞並沒有奉派去見她們當中任何人，卻只到西頓地方、撒勒法的一個寡婦那裏去。27在先知以利沙的時代，以色列中有許多患痲瘋病的，但是除了敍利亞人乃縵，沒有一個人得到潔淨。」

28 聽了這話，全會堂的人都怒氣填胸。29大家起來，把他拉到城外，帶他到山崖上（他們的城建造在山上），要把他推下去。30耶穌卻從容地從人羣中走出去。

一個污鬼附身的人
（可1‧21-28）

31 耶穌到加利利的迦百農去。安息日，他在那裏教導人。32聽見他教導的人都很驚奇，因為他的話滿有權威。33在會堂裏，有一個污鬼附身的人，大聲喊叫：34「唉！拿撒勒的耶穌，你為甚麼干擾我們？你是來除滅我們的嗎？我知道你是誰；你是上帝的聖者！」

35 耶穌斥責那污鬼說：「住口，快從這個人身上出來！」污鬼在大家面前把那人摔倒，就從他身上出來，一點兒也沒有傷害他。

36 大家驚訝不已，彼此議論說：「這是甚麼話呢？這個人居然有權柄和能力指揮污靈，污靈竟出來了！」37於是耶穌的名聲傳遍了那一帶地區。

Jesus Heals Many People
(Matthew 8.14-17; Mark 1.29-34)

38Jesus left the synagogue and went to Simon's home. Simon's mother-in-law was sick with a high fever, and they spoke to Jesus about her. 39He went and stood at her bedside and ordered the fever to leave her. The fever left her, and she got up at once and began to wait on them.

40After sunset all who had friends who were sick with various diseases brought them to Jesus; he placed his hands on every one of them and healed them all. 41Demons also went out from many people, screaming, "You are the Son of God!"

Jesus gave the demons an order and would not let them speak, because they knew he was the Messiah.

Jesus Preaches in the Synagogues
(Mark 1.35-39)

42At daybreak Jesus left the town and went off to a lonely place. The people started looking for him, and when they found him, they tried to keep him from leaving. 43But he said to them, "I must preach the Good News about the Kingdom of God in other towns also, because that is what God sent me to do."

44So he preached in the synagogues throughout the country.

Jesus Calls the First Disciples
(Matthew 4.18-22; Mark 1.16-20)

5 One day Jesus was standing on the shore of Lake Gennesaret while the people pushed their way up to him to listen to the word of God. 2He saw two boats pulled up on the beach; the fishermen had left them and were washing the nets. 3Jesus got into one of the boats–it belonged to Simon–and asked him to push off a little from the shore. Jesus sat in the boat and taught the crowd.

4When he finished speaking, he said to Simon, "Push the boat out further to the deep water, and you and your partners let down your nets for a catch."

5"Master," Simon answered, "we worked hard all night long and caught nothing. But if you say so, I will let down the nets." 6They let them down and caught such a large number of fish that the nets were about to break. 7So they motioned to their partners in the other boat to come and help them. They came and filled both boats so full of fish that the boats were about to sink. 8When Simon Peter saw what had happened, he fell on his knees before Jesus and said, "Go away from me, Lord! I am a sinful man!"

耶穌治好許多病人
（太 8‧14－17；可 1‧29－34）

38 耶穌離開會堂，到西門家裏去。西門的岳母患病，發高燒；他們向耶穌求助。39耶穌去看她，站在她的旁邊，斥責熱病，熱就退了。她立刻起來，接待他們。

40 太陽下山的時候，許多患各樣疾病的人被親友帶來見耶穌；耶穌一一替他們按手，治好了他們。41又有鬼從好些人身上出來，喊叫：「你是上帝的兒子！」

耶穌斥責他們，不許他們說話，因為他們知道他就是基督。

耶穌在會堂傳道
（可 1‧35－39）

42 破曉的時候，耶穌出城到偏僻的地方去。大家到處找他，找到了，想挽留他，不要他離開。43可是耶穌對他們說：「我也必須到別的城鎮去傳揚有關上帝主權的福音，因為我正是為這工作奉差遣來的。」

44 於是，耶穌到猶太各會堂傳道。

耶穌呼召門徒
（太 4‧18－22；可 1‧16－20）

5 有一次，耶穌站在革尼撒勒湖邊，人羣擁上來，要聽他宣講上帝的話。2他看見兩條船停在湖邊，打魚的人離開船，正在岸上洗網。3耶穌上了西門的那一條船，吩咐西門把船稍微划開。耶穌坐下來，從船上教導羣眾。

4 講完後，他對西門說：「把船划到水深的地方去，然後你跟你的夥伴撒網打魚。」

5 西門說：「老師，我們整夜辛勞，甚麼都沒有打着；既然你這麼說，我就撒網吧！」6於是他們撒網，捕到了一大羣魚，魚網差一點破了。7他們就打手勢，招呼另一條船的夥伴過來幫忙。他們來，把魚裝滿了兩條船，船幾乎沉下去。8西門‧彼得看見這情形，就跪在耶穌面前，說：「主啊，請你離開我吧，我是個罪人！」

9He and the others with him were all amazed at the large number of fish they had caught. 10The same was true of Simon's partners, James and John, the sons of Zebedee. Jesus said to Simon, "Don't be afraid; from now on you will be catching people."

11They pulled the boats up on the beach, left everything, and followed Jesus.

Jesus Heals a Man
(Matthew 8.1-4; Mark 1.40-45)

12Once Jesus was in a town where there was a man who was suffering from a dreaded skin disease. When he saw Jesus, he threw himself down and begged him, "Sir, if you want to, you can make me clean!"c

13Jesus reached out and touched him. "I do want to," he answered. "Be clean!" At once the disease left the man. 14Jesus ordered him, "Don't tell anyone, but go straight to the priest and let him examine you; then to prove to everyone that you are cured, offer the sacrifice as Moses ordered."

15But the news about Jesus spread all the more widely, and crowds of people came to hear him and be healed from their diseases. 16But he would go away to lonely places, where he prayed.

Jesus Heals a Paralyzed Man
(Matthew 9.1-8; Mark 2.1-12)

17One day when Jesus was teaching, some Pharisees and teachers of the Law were sitting there who had come from every town in Galilee and Judea and from Jerusalem. The power of the Lord was present for Jesus to heal the sick. 18Some men came carrying a paralyzed man on a bed, and they tried to carry him into the house and put him in front of Jesus. 19Because of the crowd, however, they could find no way to take him in. So they carried him up on the roof, made an opening in the tiles, and let him down on his bed into the middle of the group in front of Jesus. 20When Jesus saw how much faith they had, he said to the man, "Your sins are forgiven, my friend."

21The teachers of the Law and the Pharisees began to say to themselves, "Who is this man who speaks such blasphemy? God is the only one who can forgive sins!"

22Jesus knew their thoughts and said to them, "Why do you think such things? 23Is it easier to say, 'Your sins are forgiven you,' or to say, 'Get up and walk'? 24I will prove to you, then,

c MAKE ME CLEAN: *This disease was considered to make a person ritually unclean.*

9 他和其他夥伴對打到了這一大網魚都很驚訝。10他的夥伴西庇太的兒子雅各和約翰也一樣驚訝。耶穌對西門說:「不要怕,從今以後,你要得人了。」

11 他們把船靠岸,就撇下所有的,跟從了耶穌。

耶穌治好痲瘋病人
(太 8.1-4;可 1.40-45)

12 有一次,耶穌在一個城裏,那裏有一個全身長了痲瘋的病人。他一看見耶穌,就俯伏在他面前,求他說:「主啊,只要你肯,你能夠使我潔淨!」

13 耶穌伸手摸他,說:「我肯,你潔淨吧!」他身上的痲瘋立刻消除了。14耶穌吩咐他說:「不要把這件事告訴人,直接去見祭司,讓他替你檢查;然後按照摩西的規定獻上祭物,向大家證實你已經潔淨了。」

15 於是,耶穌的名聲越發傳開了。一大羣人聚集,要聽他講道,同時希望他們的疾病得到醫治。16耶穌卻退到僻靜的地方去禱告。

耶穌治好癱瘓病人
(太 9.1-8;可 2.1-12)

17 有一天,耶穌正在教導人,有些從加利利各鄉鎮和猶太、耶路撒冷來的法利賽人和法律教師也坐在旁邊。主的能力與耶穌同在,使他能治好病人。18有幾個人抬來一個躺在牀上的癱瘓病人,想法子要把他抬進屋子裏,放在耶穌面前。19可是,因為人多,他們無法抬他進去,就把他抬上屋頂,拆開瓦片,連人帶牀把他縋下,放在人羣中耶穌的面前。20耶穌看見他們的信心,就對那癱瘓病人說:「朋友,你的罪蒙赦免了。」

21 經學教師和法利賽人議論說:「這個人是誰?竟說出這種狂妄的話!除了上帝,誰有赦罪的權呢?」

22 耶穌看穿了他們的念頭,就對他們說:「你們心裏為甚麼這樣想呢?23對病人說『你的罪蒙赦免了』容易?還是說『起來走』容易呢?24我要你們知道,人子在地上有赦罪

that the Son of Man has authority on earth to forgive sins." So he said to the paralyzed man, "I tell you, get up, pick up your bed, and go home!"

25At once the man got up in front of them all, took the bed he had been lying on, and went home, praising God. 26They were all completely amazed! Full of fear, they praised God, saying, "What marvelous things we have seen today!"

Jesus Calls Levi
(Matthew 9.9-13; Mark 2.13-17)

27After this, Jesus went out and saw a tax collector named Levi, sitting in his office. Jesus said to him, "Follow me." 28Levi got up, left everything, and followed him.

29Then Levi had a big feast in his house for Jesus, and among the guests was a large number of tax collectors and other people. 30Some Pharisees and some teachers of the Law who belonged to their group complained to Jesus' disciples. "Why do you eat and drink with tax collectors and other outcasts?" they asked.

31Jesus answered them, "People who are well do not need a doctor, but only those who are sick. 32I have not come to call respectable people to repent, but outcasts."

The Question about Fasting
(Matthew 9.14-17; Mark 2.18-22)

33Some people said to Jesus, "The disciples of John fast frequently and offer prayers, and the disciples of the Pharisees do the same; but your disciples eat and drink."

34Jesus answered, "Do you think you can make the guests at a wedding party go without food as long as the bridegroom is with them? Of course not! 35But the day will come when the bridegroom will be taken away from them, and then they will fast."

36Jesus also told them this parable: "You don't tear a piece off a new coat to patch up an old coat. If you do, you will have torn the new coat, and the piece of new cloth will not match the old. 37Nor do you pour new wine into used wineskins, because the new wine will burst the skins, the wine will pour out, and the skins will be ruined. 38Instead, new wine must be poured into fresh wineskins! 39And you don't want new wine after drinking old wine. 'The old is better,' you say."

的權。」於是他對癱瘓病人說:「我吩咐你,起來,拿起你的牀,回家去吧!」

25 那個人立刻當着大家面前起來,拿起自己所躺臥的牀回家,頌讚上帝。26 大家都非常驚奇,滿懷敬畏地頌讚上帝說:「今天我們看到不可思議的事了!」

耶穌呼召利未
(太 9．9—13;可 2．13—17)

27 這事以後,耶穌出去,看見一個收稅的人名叫利未,坐在稅關上。耶穌對他說:「來跟從我!」28 利未就起來,撇下所有的,跟從了耶穌。

29 利未在自己家裏為耶穌舉行盛大的宴會;許多稅棍和其他的人都來參加這宴會。30 有些法利賽人和屬於他們一派的經學教師向耶穌的門徒埋怨說:「你們為甚麼跟稅棍和壞人一起吃喝呢?」

31 耶穌對他們說:「健康的人用不着醫生,有病的人才用得着。32 我來的目的不是要召好人,而是要召壞人悔改。」

禁食的問題
(太 9．14—17;可 2．18—22)

33 有人對耶穌說:「約翰的門徒常常禁食禱告,法利賽人的門徒也是一樣,只有你的門徒又吃又喝。」

34 耶穌說:「新郎還在婚宴的時候,你能叫賀喜的客人禁食嗎?當然不能!35 可是日子將到,新郎要從他們當中被帶走,那時候,他們就要禁食了。」

36 耶穌又對他們講一個比喻:「沒有人撕破新衣服,把撕下的布塊補在舊衣上;這樣做的話,新衣撕破了,撕下來的那塊新布又不能跟舊的相稱。37 也沒有人拿新酒裝在舊皮袋裏;這樣做的話,新酒會脹破舊皮袋,酒漏掉,皮袋也損壞了。38 新酒必須裝在新皮袋裏。39 沒有人在喝過陳酒以後,再想喝新酒,他總說陳酒好。」

The Question about the Sabbath

(Matthew 12.1-8; Mark 2.23-28)

6 Jesus was walking through some wheat fields on a Sabbath. His disciples began to pick the heads of wheat, rub them in their hands, and eat the grain. ²Some Pharisees asked, "Why are you doing what our Law says you cannot do on the Sabbath?"

³Jesus answered them, "Haven't you read what David did when he and his men were hungry? ⁴He went into the house of God, took the bread offered to God, ate it, and gave it also to his men. Yet it is against our Law for anyone except the priests to eat that bread."

⁵And Jesus concluded, "The Son of Man is Lord of the Sabbath."

The Man with a Paralyzed Hand

(Matthew 12.9-14; Mark 3.1-6)

⁶On another Sabbath Jesus went into a synagogue and taught. A man was there whose right hand was paralyzed. ⁷Some teachers of the Law and some Pharisees wanted a reason to accuse Jesus of doing wrong, so they watched him closely to see if he would heal on the Sabbath. ⁸But Jesus knew their thoughts and said to the man, "Stand up and come here to the front." The man got up and stood there. ⁹Then Jesus said to them, "I ask you: What does our Law allow us to do on the Sabbath? To help or to harm? To save someone's life or destroy it?" ¹⁰He looked around at them all; then he said*d* to the man, "Stretch out your hand." He did so, and his hand became well again.

¹¹They were filled with rage and began to discuss among themselves what they could do to Jesus.

Jesus Chooses the Twelve Apostles

(Matthew 10.1-4; Mark 3.13-19)

¹²At that time Jesus went up a hill to pray and spent the whole night there praying to God. ¹³When day came, he called his disciples to him and chose twelve of them, whom he named apostles: ¹⁴Simon (whom he named Peter) and his brother Andrew; James and John, Philip and Bartholomew, ¹⁵Matthew and Thomas, James son of Alphaeus, and Simon (who was called the Patriot), ¹⁶Judas son of James, and Judas Iscariot, who became the traitor.

Jesus Teaches and Heals

(Matthew 4.23-25)

¹⁷When Jesus had come down from the hill

d said; some manuscripts have said angrily.

安息日的問題

（太12‧1—8；可2‧23—28）

6 有一個安息日，耶穌經過麥田；他的門徒摘了一些麥穗，用手搓着吃。²有些法利賽人看見了，說：「你們爲甚麼做了在安息日不准做的事呢？」

³耶穌回答：「大衞和他的隨從在飢餓的時候做了甚麼，你們沒有念過嗎？⁴他走進上帝的聖殿，拿了獻給上帝的供餅吃，又給他的隨從吃；這餅，除了祭司以外，任何人吃了都算是違法的。」

⁵於是耶穌說：「人子是安息日的主。」

治好手枯萎的病人

（太12‧9—14；可3‧1—6）

⁶另一個安息日，耶穌到會堂去教導人；那裏有一個人，他的右手枯萎了。⁷有些經學教師和法利賽人想找耶穌的錯處，好控告他，因此在旁邊窺伺，看耶穌在安息日治不治病。⁸耶穌知道他們的念頭，就對那手枯萎的病人說：「起來，站到前面來！」那個人就起來站着。⁹於是耶穌對他們說：「我問你們，關於安息日，我們的法律是怎樣規定的？做好事還是壞事？救命還是害命？」¹⁰他環視周圍所有的人，然後對那個人說④：「把手伸直！」那人一伸手，手就復原了。

¹¹他們非常憤怒，彼此商量要怎樣對付耶穌。

耶穌揀選十二使徒

（太10‧1—4；可3‧13—19）

¹²有一天，耶穌到山上禱告，在那裏整夜祈禱上帝。¹³天亮的時候，他叫門徒到他跟前，從他們當中揀選了十二個人，稱他們爲使徒。¹⁴他們是西門（耶穌又給他取名彼得）和他的弟弟安得烈，雅各和約翰，腓力和巴多羅買，¹⁵馬太和多馬，亞勒腓的兒子雅各和那「激進黨」的西門，¹⁶雅各的兒子猶大和後來成爲出賣耶穌的加略人猶大。

耶穌的教導和治病

（太4‧23—25）

¹⁷耶穌和使徒們一起下了山；他與許多門

④「對那個人說」另有古卷作「對那個人生氣地說」。

with the apostles, he stood on a level place with a large number of his disciples. A large crowd of people was there from all over Judea and from Jerusalem and from the coast cities of Tyre and Sidon; 18they had come to hear him and to be healed of their diseases. Those who were troubled by evil spirits also came and were healed. 19All the people tried to touch him, for power was going out from him and healing them all.

Happiness and Sorrow
(Matthew 5.1-12)

20Jesus looked at his disciples and said,
"Happy are you poor;
    the Kingdom of God is yours!
21 "Happy are you who are hungry now;
    you will be filled!
"Happy are you who weep now;
    you will laugh!

22"Happy are you when people hate you, reject you, insult you, and say that you are evil, all because of the Son of Man! 23Be glad when that happens and dance for joy, because a great reward is kept for you in heaven. For their ancestors did the very same things to the prophets.
24 "But how terrible for you who are rich now;
    you have had your easy life!
25 "How terrible for you who are full now;
    you will go hungry!
"How terrible for you who laugh now;
    you will mourn and weep!

26"How terrible when all people speak well of you; their ancestors said the very same things about the false prophets.

Love for Enemies
(Matthew 5.38-48; 7.12a)

27"But I tell you who hear me: Love your enemies, do good to those who hate you, 28bless those who curse you, and pray for those who mistreat you. 29If anyone hits you on one cheek, let him hit the other one too; if someone takes your coat, let him have your shirt as well. 30Give to everyone who asks you for something, and when someone takes what is yours, do not ask for it back. 31Do for others just what you want them to do for you.

32"If you love only the people who love you, why should you receive a blessing? Even sin-

徒一起站在平地上，擁擠的羣衆從猶太全地、耶路撒冷和沿海城市泰爾、西頓等地集合到那裏，18要聽他講道，也盼望他治好他們的疾病。那些被污靈纏擾的也來了，並且得到醫治。19大家都想要摸他，因爲有能力從他身上發出來，治好了他們。

喜樂和憂傷
（太5‧1—12）

20 耶穌轉向他的門徒，對他們說：
「貧窮的人多麼有福啊；
你們是上帝國的子民！
21 「現在飢餓的人多麼有福啊；
你們要得到飽足！
「現在哭泣的人多麼有福啊；
你們將要歡笑！

22 「爲了人子的緣故，有人懷恨你們，棄絕你們，侮辱你們，把你們當作邪惡的，你們就有福了！23從前他們的祖宗也是這樣對待先知。在那日子，你們要歡欣雀躍，因爲在天上將有豐富的獎賞爲你們保存着。

24 「但是，你們現在富有的人要遭殃了，
因爲你們已經享夠了安樂！
25 「現在飽足的人要遭殃了，
因爲你們將要飢餓，
「現在歡笑的人要遭殃了，
因爲你們將要哀慟哭泣！

26 「人人都稱讚你們的時候，你們有禍了，因爲他們的祖宗對假先知也曾說了同樣的話。」

論愛仇敵
（太5‧38—48；7‧12）

27 「但是，你們這些聽我話的，我告訴你們，要愛你們的仇敵，善待恨惡你們的；28爲詛咒你們的人祝福，爲侮辱你們的人禱告。29有人打你一邊的臉，連另一邊也讓他打吧！有人拿走你的外衣，連內衣也讓他拿走吧！30誰對你有所要求，就給他；有人拿走你的東西，不要去要回來。31你們要別人怎樣待你們，你們也要怎樣待他們。

32 「假如你們只愛那些愛你們的人，有甚麼功德呢？就連罪人也愛那些愛他們的人！

ners love those who love them! 33And if you do good only to those who do good to you, why should you receive a blessing? Even sinners do that! 34And if you lend only to those from whom you hope to get it back, why should you receive a blessing? Even sinners lend to sinners, to get back the same amount! 35No! Love your enemies and do good to them; lend and expect nothing back. You will then have a great reward, and you will be children of the Most High God. For he is good to the ungrateful and the wicked. 36Be merciful just as your Father is merciful.

Judging Others
(Matthew 7.1-5)

37"Do not judge others, and God will not judge you; do not condemn others, and God will not condemn you; forgive others, and God will forgive you. 38Give to others, and God will give to you. Indeed, you will receive a full measure, a generous helping, poured into your hands–all that you can hold. The measure you use for others is the one that God will use for you."

39And Jesus told them this parable: "One blind man cannot lead another one; if he does, both will fall into a ditch. 40No pupils are greater than their teacher; but all pupils, when they have completed their training, will be like their teacher.

41"Why do you look at the speck in your brother's eye, but pay no attention to the log in your own eye? 42How can you say to your brother, 'Please, brother, let me take that speck out of your eye,' yet cannot even see the log in your own eye? You hypocrite! First take the log out of your own eye, and then you will be able to see clearly to take the speck out of your brother's eye.

A Tree and Its Fruit
(Matthew 7.16-20; 12.33-35)

43"A healthy tree does not bear bad fruit, nor does a poor tree bear good fruit. 44Every tree is known by the fruit it bears; you do not pick figs from thorn bushes or gather grapes from bramble bushes. 45A good person brings good out of the treasure of good things in his heart; a bad person brings bad out of his treasure of bad things. For the mouth speaks what the heart is full of.

The Two House Builders
(Matthew 7.24-27)

46"Why do you call me, 'Lord, Lord,' and yet

33假如你們只善待那些善待你們的人，有甚麼功德呢？就連罪人也會這樣做的！34假如你們只借錢給有希望償還的人，又有甚麼功德呢？就連罪人也借錢給罪人，只是要如數收回！35不，你們要愛仇敵，善待他們；借錢給人，而不期望收回。那麼，你們將得到豐富的獎賞，而且將成為至高上帝的兒女，因為他也以仁慈待那些忘恩負義和邪惡的人。36你們要仁慈，正像你們的天父是仁慈的。」

不要評斷別人
（太7‧1—5）

37「不要評斷人，上帝就不審斷你們；不要定人的罪，上帝就不定你們的罪；要饒恕人，上帝就饒恕你們。38施與別人，上帝就會施與你們，並且用大升斗，連搖帶按，盡你們所能携帶的，滿滿地倒給你們。你們用甚麼量器來量，上帝也要用同樣的量器來量還給你們。」

39耶穌也對他們講一個比喻，說：「盲人不能領盲人的路；如果這樣，兩個人都會掉進坑裏去。40學生不高過老師，但是他學成後會像老師一樣。

41「你為甚麼只看見弟兄眼中的木屑，卻不管自己眼中的大樑呢？42你自己眼中有大樑，怎能對弟兄說『弟兄，讓我去掉你眼中的木屑』呢？你這偽善的人，先把自己眼中的大樑移去，才能看得清楚，去把弟兄眼中的木屑挑出來。」

樹和果子
（太7‧16—20；12‧33—35）

43「好樹不結壞果子，壞樹也不結好果子；44樹的好壞從它的果子分辨得出來。你們不會在荊棘裏摘無花果，也不會在蒺藜中採葡萄。45好人從他心裏頭積存的善發出善來；壞人從他積存的惡發出惡來。一個人的心裏充滿着甚麼，嘴就說甚麼。」

兩種基礎
（太7‧24—27）

46「你們為甚麼稱呼我『主啊，主啊』，卻

don't do what I tell you? ⁴⁷Anyone who comes to me and listens to my words and obeys them –I will show you what he is like. ⁴⁸He is like a man who, in building his house, dug deep and laid the foundation on rock. The river flooded over and hit that house but could not shake it, because it was well built. ⁴⁹But anyone who hears my words and does not obey them is like a man who built his house without laying a foundation; when the flood hit that house it fell at once–and what a terrible crash that was!"

Jesus Heals a Roman Officer's Servant
(Matthew 8.5-13)

7 When Jesus had finished saying all these things to the people, he went to Capernaum. ²A Roman officer there had a servant who was very dear to him; the man was sick and about to die. ³When the officer heard about Jesus, he sent some Jewish elders to ask him to come and heal his servant. ⁴They came to Jesus and begged him earnestly, "This man really deserves your help. ⁵He loves our people and he himself built a synagogue for us."

⁶So Jesus went with them. He was not far from the house when the officer sent friends to tell him, "Sir, don't trouble yourself. I do not deserve to have you come into my house, ⁷neither do I consider myself worthy to come to you in person. Just give the order, and my servant will get well. ⁸I, too, am a man placed under the authority of superior officers, and I have soldiers under me. I order this one, 'Go!' and he goes; I order that one, 'Come!' and he comes; and I order my slave, 'Do this!' and he does it."

⁹Jesus was surprised when he heard this; he turned around and said to the crowd following him, "I tell you, I have never found faith like this, not even in Israel!"

¹⁰The messengers went back to the officer's house and found his servant well.

Jesus Raises a Widow's Son

¹¹Soon afterward^e Jesus went to a town named Nain, accompanied by his disciples and a large crowd. ¹²Just as he arrived at the gate of the town, a funeral procession was coming out. The dead man was the only son of a woman who was a widow, and a large crowd from the town was with her. ¹³When the Lord saw her, his heart was filled with pity for her, and he said to her, "Don't cry." ¹⁴Then he walked over

e Soon afterward; some manuscripts have The next day.

不實行我吩咐你們的話呢？⁴⁷我告訴你們，那到我跟前來，聽了我的話而去實行的，是像甚麼樣的人呢？⁴⁸他像一個蓋房子的人，挖深了土，把根基立在磐石上。洪水氾濫沖擊那座房子的時候，房子卻不動搖，因為它建造得好。⁴⁹可是，那聽了我的話而不去實行的，是像一個人把房子蓋在沒有打根基的土地上，河水一沖，房子立刻倒塌，造成了極嚴重的損壞！」

耶穌治好羅馬軍官的僕人
（太8・5—13）

7 耶穌向羣眾說完了這些話，就到迦百農去。²那裏有一個羅馬軍官，他所器重的僕人患重病，快要死了。³軍官聽到耶穌的事，就託幾個猶太人的長老去請求耶穌來治好他的僕人。⁴他們到了耶穌那裏，懇切地求他說：「這個人的確值得你的幫助；⁵他愛護我們猶太人，曾經替我們建造會堂。」

⁶於是耶穌和他們去。他快到那裏的時候，軍官託幾個朋友來告訴耶穌說：「主啊，請不必勞駕。你到舍下來，我不敢當；⁷我自己也不配跟你見面。只要你吩咐一聲，我的僕人就會好的。⁸就像在我上面有指揮我的長官，下面有受我指揮的兵士；我命令這個人去，他就去，命令那個人來，他就來；對我的奴僕說『你做這個』，他就去做。」

⁹耶穌聽見這話，非常驚奇，轉身向跟隨着他的羣眾說：「我告訴你們，像這樣的信心，就是在以色列人當中，我也沒有見過！」

¹⁰那些被差派來的人回到軍官家裏，看見軍官的僕人已經好了。

使寡婦的兒子復活

¹¹過了不久^⑤，耶穌到拿因城去；他的門徒和一大羣人跟着他去。¹²他來到城門口，剛好一隊送殯的行列出來。那死者是一個寡婦的獨生子；從城裏有許多人出來，陪着寡婦送殯。¹³主看見了那寡婦，心裏充滿了悲憫，就對她說：「不要哭！」¹⁴然後上前按

⑤「過了不久」另有古卷作「次日」。

and touched the coffin, and the men carrying it stopped. Jesus said, "Young man! Get up, I tell you!" [15]The dead man sat up and began to talk, and Jesus gave him back to his mother.

16They all were filled with fear and praised God. "A great prophet has appeared among us!" they said; "God has come to save his people!"

17This news about Jesus went out through all the country and the surrounding territory.

The Messengers from John the Baptist
(Matthew 11.2-19)

18When John's disciples told him about all these things, he called two of them [19]and sent them to the Lord to ask him, "Are you the one John said was going to come, or should we expect someone else?"

20When they came to Jesus, they said, "John the Baptist sent us to ask if you are the one he said was going to come, or should we expect someone else?"

21At that very time Jesus healed many people from their sicknesses, diseases, and evil spirits, and gave sight to many blind people. [22]He answered John's messengers, "Go back and tell John what you have seen and heard: the blind can see, the lame can walk, those who suffer from dreaded skin diseases are made clean,f the deaf can hear, the dead are raised to life, and the Good News is preached to the poor. [23]How happy are those who have no doubts about me!"

24After John's messengers had left, Jesus began to speak about him to the crowds: "When you went out to John in the desert, what did you expect to see? A blade of grass bending in the wind? [25]What did you go out to see? A man dressed up in fancy clothes? People who dress like that and live in luxury are found in palaces! [26]Tell me, what did you go out to see? A prophet? Yes indeed, but you saw much more than a prophet. [27]For John is the one of whom the scripture says: 'God said, I will send my messenger ahead of you to open the way for you.' [28]I tell you," Jesus added, "John is greater than anyone who has ever lived. But the one who is least in the Kingdom of God is greater than John."

29All the people heard him; they and especially the tax collectors were the ones who had obeyed God's righteous demands and had been baptized by John. [30]But the Pharisees and the teachers of the Law rejected God's purpose for

f MADE CLEAN: See 5.12.

着抬架，抬的人就站住。耶穌說：「年輕人，我吩咐你起來！」15那死者就坐起來，並且開始說話。耶穌把他交給他的母親。

16 大家都非常驚異；他們頌讚上帝說：「有偉大的先知在我們當中出現了！」又說：「上帝來拯救他的子民了！」

17 關於耶穌這件事的消息傳遍了猶太和附近各地區。

施洗者約翰的門徒來見耶穌
(太11·2-19)

18 約翰的門徒把這一切的事都告訴約翰。約翰叫了兩個門徒來，19差他們去見主，要他們問他：「你就是約翰所說將要來臨的那一位，或是我們還得等待另一位呢？」

20 他們到了耶穌那裏，就說：「施洗者約翰差我們來問你：『你就是他所說將要來臨的那一位，或是我們還得等待另一位呢？』」

21 剛好在那時候耶穌治好了許多患病、患疫症，和邪靈附身的人，並且使許多失明的重見光明。22於是他回答約翰的門徒說：「你們回去，把所看見所聽到的報告約翰，就是失明的看見，跛腳的行走，痲瘋的潔淨，耳聾的聽見，死人復活，窮人聽到福音。23那對我不疑惑的人多麼有福啊！」

24 約翰的使者走了以後，耶穌就向羣眾談起約翰，說：「你們從前到曠野去找約翰的時候，想看的是甚麼呢？是被風吹動的蘆葦嗎？25你們究竟要看甚麼呢？是看衣著華麗的人嗎？衣著考究、起居奢侈的人是住在皇宮裏！26那麼，你們出去看甚麼呢？是看先知嗎？是的，可是我告訴你們，他比先知還大。27他就是聖經上所提到的那一位；上帝說：『看吧，我要差遣我的使者作你的前驅；他要為你開路。』28耶穌又說：「我告訴你們，在人間沒有比約翰更偉大的人；但是在上帝的國裏，最微小的一個都要比約翰偉大呢！」

29 一般羣眾，包括收稅的人，聽見耶穌的話，都順從了上帝公義的要求，因為他們已經接受約翰的洗禮。30但是法利賽人和法律教師們拒絕了上帝為他們安排的計劃，因為

themselves and refused to be baptized by John.

31Jesus continued, "Now to what can I compare the people of this day? What are they like? 32They are like children sitting in the market-place. One group shouts to the other, 'We played wedding music for you, but you wouldn't dance! We sang funeral songs, but you wouldn't cry!' 33John the Baptist came, and he fasted and drank no wine, and you said, 'He has a demon in him!' 34The Son of Man came, and he ate and drank, and you said, 'Look at this man! He is a glutton and wine drinker, a friend of tax collectors and other outcasts!' 35God's wisdom, however, is shown to be true by all who accept it."

Jesus at the Home of Simon the Pharisee

36A Pharisee invited Jesus to have dinner with him, and Jesus went to his house and sat down to eat. 37In that town was a woman who lived a sinful life. She heard that Jesus was eating in the Pharisee's house, so she brought an alabaster jar full of perfume 38and stood behind Jesus, by his feet, crying and wetting his feet with her tears. Then she dried his feet with her hair, kissed them, and poured the perfume on them. 39When the Pharisee saw this, he said to himself, "If this man really were a prophet, he would know who this woman is who is touching him; he would know what kind of sinful life she lives!"

40Jesus spoke up and said to him, "Simon, I have something to tell you."

"Yes, Teacher," he said, "tell me."

41"There were two men who owed money to a moneylender," Jesus began. "One owed him five hundred silver coins, and the other owed him fifty. 42Neither of them could pay him back, so he canceled the debts of both. Which one, then, will love him more?"

43"I suppose," answered Simon, "that it would be the one who was forgiven more."

"You are right," said Jesus. 44Then he turned to the woman and said to Simon, "Do you see this woman? I came into your home, and you gave me no water for my feet, but she has washed my feet with her tears and dried them with her hair. 45You did not welcome me with a kiss, but she has not stopped kissing my feet since I came. 46You provided no olive oil for my head, but she has covered my feet with perfume. 47I tell you, then, the great love she has shown proves that her many sins have been forgiven. But whoever has been forgiven little shows only a little love."

48Then Jesus said to the woman, "Your sins

他們沒有接受約翰的洗禮。

31耶穌又說:「那麼,我要拿甚麼來比擬這世代的人呢?他們究竟像甚麼呢?32他們正像坐在街頭上玩耍的孩子,其中的一羣向另一羣喊說:『我們為你們吹婚禮樂曲,你們不跳舞!我們唱喪禮哀歌,你們也不哭泣。』33施洗者約翰來了,不吃不喝,你們說:『他有鬼附身!』34人子來了,也吃也喝,你們卻說:『他是酒肉之徒,跟稅棍和壞人交朋友!』35但是,上帝的智慧是從所有接受智慧的人身上彰顯出來的。」

罪婦的悔改

36有一個法利賽人請耶穌吃飯,耶穌就到他家裏赴席。37當地有一個女人,一向過着罪惡的生活。她聽說耶穌在那法利賽人家裏吃飯,就帶了一個盛滿着香油膏的玉瓶來。38她在耶穌背後,挨着他的腳哭。她的眼淚滴濕了耶穌的腳,就用自己的頭髮擦乾,並用嘴親吻,然後把香油膏抹上。39請耶穌吃飯的那個法利賽人看見了,心裏想:「這人若真的是先知,他應該知道摸他的是怎樣的一個女人;她是有罪的人!」

40耶穌就對他說:「西門,我有句話跟你說。」

西門回答:「老師請說。」

41耶穌說:「有兩個人同欠一個債主的債,一個欠五百塊銀圓,另一個欠五十塊銀圓。42兩個人都無力償還,債主就把他們的債都取消了。你想,他們哪一個會更愛他呢?」

43西門回答:「我想是那個獲得較多寬免的。」

耶穌說:「你說得對。」44於是他轉向那女人,對西門說:「你看見這個女人嗎?我來到你家,你沒有給我水洗腳,她卻用眼淚洗我的腳,並且用她的頭髮擦乾。45你沒有用接吻禮歡迎我,但是她從我進來就不停地親我的腳。46你沒有用油抹我的頭,她卻用香油膏抹我的腳。47我告訴你,她所表示深厚的愛證明了她許許多多的罪都已經蒙赦免。那少得赦免的,所表示的愛也少。」

48耶穌就對那女人說:「你的罪都蒙赦免

are forgiven."

49The others sitting at the table began to say to themselves, "Who is this, who even forgives sins?"

50But Jesus said to the woman, "Your faith has saved you; go in peace."

Women Who Accompanied Jesus

8 Some time later Jesus traveled through towns and villages, preaching the Good News about the Kingdom of God. The twelve disciples went with him, 2and so did some women who had been healed of evil spirits and diseases: Mary (who was called Magdalene), from whom seven demons had been driven out; 3Joanna, whose husband Chuza was an officer in Herod's court; and Susanna, and many other women who used their own resources to help Jesus and his disciples.

The Parable of the Sower

(Matthew 13.1-9; Mark 4.1-9)

4People kept coming to Jesus from one town after another; and when a great crowd gathered, Jesus told this parable:

5"Once there was a man who went out to sow grain. As he scattered the seed in the field, some of it fell along the path, where it was stepped on, and the birds ate it up. 6Some of it fell on rocky ground, and when the plants sprouted, they dried up because the soil had no moisture. 7Some of the seed fell among thorn bushes, which grew up with the plants and choked them. 8And some seeds fell in good soil; the plants grew and bore grain, one hundred grains each."

And Jesus concluded, "Listen, then, if you have ears!"

The Purpose of the Parables

(Matthew 13.10-17; Mark 4.10-12)

9His disciples asked Jesus what this parable meant, 10and he answered, "The knowledge of the secrets of the Kingdom of God has been given to you, but to the rest it comes by means of parables, so that they may look but not see, and listen but not understand.

Jesus Explains the Parable of the Sower

(Matthew 13.18-23; Mark 4.13-20)

11"This is what the parable means: the seed is the word of God. 12The seeds that fell along the path stand for those who hear; but the Devil comes and takes the message away from their hearts in order to keep them from believing and being saved. 13The seeds that fell on rocky ground stand for those who hear the message

了。」

49 於是同席的人心裏想:「這個人是誰?居然赦免人的罪!」

50 耶穌對那女人說:「你的信心救了你;平安地回去吧!」

跟從耶穌的婦女們

8 過了些時候,耶穌走遍各城市鄉村,傳揚上帝主權的福音;十二使徒跟他同行。2 此外還有些婦女,都是曾被邪靈和疾病纏擾、已經被治好了的;其中有抹大拉的馬利亞,從她身上曾有七個鬼被趕出來;3 還有希律官邸的官員苦撒的妻子約亞娜,和蘇撒娜,以及其他好些婦女。她們都用自己的財物供應耶穌和他的門徒。

撒種的比喻

(太13.1—9;可4.1—9)

4 羣眾從各城各地紛紛來見耶穌。一大羣人聚集的時候,耶穌對他們講下面的比喻:

5 「有一個撒種的出去撒種。他撒的時候,有些種子落在路旁,被人踐踏,鳥兒飛來把它們吃掉了。6 有些落在石地上,種子長苗後就枯乾了,因為得不到水分。7 有些種子落在荊棘裏,荊棘跟着一起生長,把幼苗擠住了。8 另外有些種子落在好的土壤裏,長苗,長大起來,結實百倍。」

耶穌又說:「有耳朵的,都聽吧!」

比喻的目的

(太13.10—17;可4.10—12)

9 耶穌的門徒來問他這比喻的意思。10 他說:「有關上帝國奧祕的知識已經給了你們;至於對其他的人,就用比喻,使他們視而不見,聽而不明。」

解釋撒種的比喻

(太13.18—23;可4.13—20)

11 「這比喻的含意是這樣:種子是指上帝的信息。12 落在路旁的種子是指人聽了信息,魔鬼來了,從他們心裏把這信息奪走,使他們不能因信而得救。13 落在石地上的種子是指人聽了信息後樂意接受,可是信息在

and receive it gladly. But it does not sink deep into them; they believe only for a while but when the time of testing comes, they fall away. [14]The seeds that fell among thorn bushes stand for those who hear; but the worries and riches and pleasures of this life crowd in and choke them, and their fruit never ripens. [15]The seeds that fell in good soil stand for those who hear the message and retain it in a good and obedient heart, and they persist until they bear fruit.

A Lamp under a Bowl
(Mark 4.21-25)

[16]"No one lights a lamp and covers it with a bowl or puts it under a bed. Instead, it is put on the lampstand, so that people will see the light as they come in.

[17]"Whatever is hidden away will be brought out into the open, and whatever is covered up will be found and brought to light.

[18]"Be careful, then, how you listen; because those who have something will be given more, but whoever has nothing will have taken away from them even the little they think they have."

Jesus' Mother and Brothers
(Matthew 12.46-50; Mark 3.31-35)

[19]Jesus' mother and brothers came to him, but were unable to join him because of the crowd. [20]Someone said to Jesus, "Your mother and brothers are standing outside and want to see you."

[21]Jesus said to them all, "My mother and brothers are those who hear the word of God and obey it."

Jesus Calms a Storm
(Matthew 8.23-27; Mark 4.35-41)

[22]One day Jesus got into a boat with his disciples and said to them, "Let us go across to the other side of the lake." So they started out. [23]As they were sailing, Jesus fell asleep. Suddenly a strong wind blew down on the lake, and the boat began to fill with water, so that they were all in great danger. [24]The disciples went to Jesus and woke him up, saying, "Master, Master! We are about to die!"

Jesus got up and gave an order to the wind and to the stormy water; they quieted down, and there was a great calm. [25]Then he said to the disciples, "Where is your faith?"

But they were amazed and afraid, and said to one another, "Who is this man? He gives orders to the winds and waves, and they obey him!"

他們心裏扎根不深;他們一時相信,但一遇到考驗就站立不住。[14]落在荊棘裏的種子是指人聽了信息,可是生活上的憂慮,財富和享樂的誘惑,窒息了這信息的生機,不能結出成熟的果實。[15]落在好土壤裏的種子是指人聽了信息,以善良和誠實的心持守它,恆心等待,直到它結出果實。」

斗底下的燈
(可4·21—25)

[16]「沒有人點了燈,卻用斗把它蓋起來,或是拿來放在牀底下。他一定把燈放在燈臺上,使進來的人看得見亮光。[17]任何隱藏的事總會被張揚出來,任何掩蓋的事也會被揭露出來,爲人所知。

[18]「所以,你們要留心聽;因爲那有的,要給他更多;那沒有的,連他自以爲有的一點點也要奪走。」

耶穌的母親和兄弟
(太12·46—50;可3·31—35)

[19]耶穌的母親和兄弟來看他,可是因爲人多,不能接近他。[20]有人告訴耶穌:「你的母親和兄弟站在外面要見你呢!」

[21]耶穌對他們說:「那些聽了上帝的信息而實行的,就是我的母親和兄弟!」

耶穌平息風浪
(太8·23—27;可4·35—41)

[22]有一天,耶穌同門徒上船,對他們說:「我們到湖的那邊去。」他們就出發。[23]船行的時候,耶穌睡着了。忽然有一陣狂風襲擊湖面,船灌滿了水,非常危險。[24]門徒來叫醒耶穌,說:「老師,老師,我們快沒命啦!」

耶穌醒過來,斥責狂風大浪,風浪就止息,湖面平靜。[25]耶穌問他們:「你們的信心在哪裏呢?」

他們又希奇又驚駭,彼此說:「這個人到底是誰?他向風浪下命令,風浪也聽從他!」

Jesus Heals a Man with Demons

(Matthew 8.28-34; Mark 5.1-20)

26Jesus and his disciples sailed on over to the territory of Gerasa,g which is across the lake from Galilee. 27As Jesus stepped ashore, he was met by a man from the town who had demons in him. For a long time this man had gone without clothes and would not stay at home, but spent his time in the burial caves. 28When he saw Jesus, he gave a loud cry, threw himself down at his feet, and shouted, "Jesus, Son of the Most High God! What do you want with me? I beg you, don't punish me!" 29He said this because Jesus had ordered the evil spirit to go out of him. Many times it had seized him, and even though he was kept a prisoner, his hands and feet tied with chains, he would break the chains and be driven by the demon out into the desert.

30Jesus asked him, "What is your name?"

"My name is 'Mob,' " he answered–because many demons had gone into him. 31The demons begged Jesus not to send them into the abyss.h

32There was a large herd of pigs near by, feeding on a hillside. So the demons begged Jesus to let them go into the pigs, and he let them. 33They went out of the man and into the pigs. The whole herd rushed down the side of the cliff into the lake and was drowned.

34The men who had been taking care of the pigs saw what happened, so they ran off and spread the news in the town and among the farms. 35People went out to see what had happened, and when they came to Jesus, they found the man from whom the demons had gone out sitting at the feet of Jesus, clothed and in his right mind; and they were all afraid. 36Those who had seen it told the people how the man had been cured. 37Then all the people from that territory asked Jesus to go away, because they were terribly afraid. So Jesus got into the boat and left. 38The man from whom the demons had gone out begged Jesus, "Let me go with you."

But Jesus sent him away, saying, 39"Go back home and tell what God has done for you."

The man went through the town, telling what Jesus had done for him.

---

g Gerasa; *some manuscripts have* Gadara (*see* Mt 8.28); *others have* Gergesa.
h ABYSS: *It was thought that the demons were to be imprisoned in the depths of the earth until their final punishment.*

耶穌治好被鬼附身的人

（太 8．28－34；可 5．1－20）

26 他們渡過加利利湖到對岸格拉森地區。27耶穌一上岸，當地有一個被鬼附身的人迎面走過來。這個人已經好久不穿衣服，不住在家裏，卻住在墓穴中。28他一看見耶穌，就喊叫起來，俯伏在耶穌面前，大聲說：「至高上帝的兒子耶穌，你爲甚麼要干擾我呢？我求你不要折磨我！」29他這樣說是因爲耶穌曾命令污靈從那個人身上出來。好多次污靈抓住了他，甚至當他被拘禁、手腳給鎖鍊鎖着的時候，他竟也能夠掙斷鎖鍊，被鬼趕到荒野去。

30 耶穌問他：「你叫甚麼名字？」

他回答：「我叫『大羣』」，因爲有許多鬼曾附着他。31鬼央求耶穌，不要把他們趕進深淵去。

32 在附近山坡上剛好有一大羣豬在吃東西。鬼就央求耶穌，准許他們進入豬羣；耶穌准了他們。33鬼就從那人身上出來，進入豬羣；整羣的豬衝下山崖，竄入湖裏，都淹死了。

34 放豬的人看見這事，就逃跑，到鎮上和鄉下散佈消息。35當地的居民出來，要看發生了甚麼事。他們到耶穌那裏，發現鬼已從他身上出來的那人坐在耶穌腳前，穿着衣服，神智清醒，就害怕起來。36看見這事的放豬人把那個人得到醫治的經過告訴大家。37於是格拉森地區的居民都要求耶穌離開那裏，因爲他們非常害怕。耶穌就上船離開。38鬼已從他身上出來的那人要求耶穌說：「請讓我跟你去！」

可是耶穌打發他回去，說：39「你回家去，述說上帝爲你所做的事。」

他就去了，走遍全鎮，傳揚耶穌爲他所做的事。

Jairus' Daughter and the Woman Who Touched Jesus' Cloak

(Matthew 9.18-26; Mark 5.21-43)

40When Jesus returned to the other side of the lake, the people welcomed him, because they had all been waiting for him. 41Then a man named Jairus arrived; he was an official in the local synagogue. He threw himself down at Jesus' feet and begged him to go to his home, 42because his only daughter, who was twelve years old, was dying.

As Jesus went along, the people were crowding him from every side. 43Among them was a woman who had suffered from severe bleeding for twelve years; she had spent all she had on doctors,*i* but no one had been able to cure her. 44She came up in the crowd behind Jesus and touched the edge of his cloak, and her bleeding stopped at once. 45Jesus asked, "Who touched me?"

Everyone denied it, and Peter said, "Master, the people are all around you and crowding in on you."

46But Jesus said, "Someone touched me, for I knew it when power went out of me." 47The woman saw that she had been found out, so she came trembling and threw herself at Jesus' feet. There in front of everybody, she told him why she had touched him and how she had been healed at once. 48Jesus said to her, "My daughter, your faith has made you well. Go in peace."

49While Jesus was saying this, a messenger came from the official's house. "Your daughter has died," he told Jairus; "don't bother the Teacher any longer."

50But Jesus heard it and said to Jairus, "Don't be afraid; only believe, and she will be well."

51When he arrived at the house, he would not let anyone go in with him except Peter, John, and James, and the child's father and mother. 52Everyone there was crying and mourning for the child. Jesus said, "Don't cry; the child is not dead–she is only sleeping!"

53They all made fun of him, because they knew that she was dead. 54But Jesus took her by the hand and called out, "Get up, child!" 55Her life returned, and she got up at once, and Jesus ordered them to give her something to eat. 56Her parents were astounded, but Jesus commanded them not to tell anyone what had happened.

葉魯的女兒和患血崩的女人

(太 9·18–26；可 5·21–43)

40耶穌回到湖的對岸，羣衆歡迎他，因為大家都在等候他來。41有一個會堂主管，名叫葉魯，也來了。他俯伏在耶穌腳前，求耶穌到他家裏去，42因為他十二歲的獨生女兒快要死了。

耶穌去的時候，人羣前後擁擠着他。43有一個女人患血崩已經十二年；她在醫生手上花盡了她所有的錢⑥，還是沒有人能夠治好她。44她走到耶穌背後，摸了耶穌外袍的衣角，她的血崩立刻止住。45耶穌問：「誰摸了我？」

大家都不承認。彼得說：「老師，你前後左右都是人，大家擁擠着你呢！」

46可是耶穌說：「有人摸了我，因為我知道有能力從我身上出去！」47那女人知道自己被發覺了，就戰戰兢兢地來跪在耶穌面前，當着大家告訴耶穌，她為甚麼摸他，又怎樣立刻好了。48耶穌對她說：「孩子，你的信心救了你！平安地回去吧。」

49耶穌正說這話的時候，有人從會堂主管的家裏趕來，告訴葉魯：「你的女兒已經死了，不必再麻煩老師了。」

50耶穌聽見了就對葉魯說：「不要怕，只要信！她會好起來的。」

51耶穌到了葉魯家裏的時候，除了彼得、約翰、雅各，和女孩子的父母，不許別人跟他一起進去。52在那裏的人都在為這女孩子號咷大哭。耶穌說：「不要哭！這女孩子沒有死，只是睡着了。」

53大家都譏笑他，因為他們知道女孩子已經死了。54耶穌拉着她的手，喊說：「孩子，起來！」55她的魂就回來，立刻起來。耶穌吩咐他們給她一些東西吃。56女孩子的父母非常驚訝，耶穌鄭重地叮囑他們，不要把所發生的事告訴任何人。

---

i Some manuscripts do not have she had spent all she had on doctors.

⑥有些古卷沒有「她在醫生手上花盡了她所有的錢」。

Jesus Sends Out the Twelve Disciples
(Matthew 10.5-15; Mark 6.7-13)

9 Jesus called the twelve disciples together and gave them power and authority to drive out all demons and to cure diseases. ²Then he sent them out to preach the Kingdom of God and to heal the sick, ³after saying to them, "Take nothing with you for the trip: no walking stick, no beggar's bag, no food, no money, not even an extra shirt. ⁴Wherever you are welcomed, stay in the same house until you leave that town; ⁵wherever people don't welcome you, leave that town and shake the dust off your feet as a warning to them."

⁶The disciples left and traveled through all the villages, preaching the Good News and healing people everywhere.

Herod's Confusion
(Matthew 14.1-12; Mark 6.14-29)

⁷When Herod, the ruler of Galilee, heard about all the things that were happening, he was very confused, because some people were saying that John the Baptist had come back to life. ⁸Others were saying that Elijah had appeared, and still others that one of the prophets of long ago had come back to life. ⁹Herod said, "I had John's head cut off; but who is this man I hear these things about?" And he kept trying to see Jesus.

Jesus Feeds Five Thousand
(Matthew 14.13-21; Mark 6.30-44; John 6.1-14)

¹⁰The apostles came back and told Jesus everything they had done. He took them with him, and they went off by themselves to a town named Bethsaida. ¹¹When the crowds heard about it, they followed him. He welcomed them, spoke to them about the Kingdom of God, and healed those who needed it.

¹²When the sun was beginning to set, the twelve disciples came to him and said, "Send the people away so that they can go to the villages and farms around here and find food and lodging, because this is a lonely place."

¹³But Jesus said to them, "You yourselves give them something to eat."

They answered, "All we have are five loaves and two fish. Do you want us to go and buy food for this whole crowd?" ¹⁴(There were about five thousand men there.)

Jesus said to his disciples, "Make the people sit down in groups of about fifty each."

¹⁵After the disciples had done so, ¹⁶Jesus took the five loaves and two fish, looked up to heaven, thanked God for them, broke them,

耶穌派遣十二使徒
（太10‧5—15；可6‧7—13）

9 耶穌召集了十二使徒，賜給他們趕鬼和醫治疾病的權柄，²然後派遣他們出去傳揚上帝國的信息，並且醫治病人。³他對門徒說：「你們在路上的時候，甚麼東西都不用帶：不帶手杖，不帶旅行袋，不帶食物或錢，也不需要有兩件內衣。⁴無論到甚麼地方，哪一家願意接待你們，就住在那裏，直到你們離開那地方。⁵遇到不接待你們的人，你們在離開那市鎮的時候，把腳上的塵土也跺掉，表示對他們的警告。」

⁶ 門徒就出門，走遍各村鎮傳福音，到處治病。

希律的困惑
（太14‧1—12；可6‧14—29）

⁷ 加利利的希律王聽見所發生的一切事，心裏非常困惑，因為有人說：「施洗者約翰復活了。」⁸也有人說是以利亞顯現了；又有人說是古時的一個先知復活了。⁹希律說：「我已經砍了約翰的頭，可是這個人又是誰呢？我竟聽到這許多關於他的事。」於是他一直想見耶穌。

耶穌使五千人吃飽
（太14‧13—21；可6‧30—44；約6‧1—13）

¹⁰ 使徒們一回來，把他們所做的一切事都向耶穌報告。耶穌帶着他們，悄悄地到一個叫伯賽大的城去。¹¹羣眾一知道，就跟着他去。耶穌歡迎他們，向他們講解有關上帝主權的事，又治好需要醫治的人。

¹² 太陽下山的時候，十二使徒來見耶穌，對他說：「請叫羣眾散開，讓他們到附近的村莊去找吃的東西和住的地方，因為這地方很偏僻。」

¹³ 可是耶穌對他們說：「你們給他們東西吃吧！」

他們說：「我們只有五個餅和兩條魚。難道你要我們去買食物給這一大羣人吃嗎？」（¹⁴男人的數目約有五千。）

耶穌對門徒說：「叫羣眾一組一組地坐下來，每組約五十個人。」¹⁵門徒照他的話做了，讓羣眾都坐下來。¹⁶耶穌拿起五個餅和兩條魚，舉目望天，感謝上帝，然後擘

and gave them to the disciples to distribute to the people. [17]They all ate and had enough, and the disciples took up twelve baskets of what was left over.

Peter's Declaration about Jesus
(Matthew 16.13-19; Mark 8.27-29)

[18]One day when Jesus was praying alone, the disciples came to him. "Who do the crowds say I am?" he asked them.

[19]"Some say that you are John the Baptist," they answered. "Others say that you are Elijah, while others say that one of the prophets of long ago has come back to life."

[20]"What about you?" he asked them. "Who do you say I am?"

Peter answered, "You are God's Messiah."

Jesus Speaks about His Suffering and Death
(Matthew 16.20-28; Mark 8.30-9.1)

[21]Then Jesus gave them strict orders not to tell this to anyone. [22]He also told them, "The Son of Man must suffer much and be rejected by the elders, the chief priests, and the teachers of the Law. He will be put to death, but three days later he will be raised to life."

[23]And he said to them all, "If you want to come with me, you must forget yourself, take up your cross every day, and follow me. [24]For if you want to save your own life, you will lose it, but if you lose your life for my sake, you will save it. [25]Will you gain anything if you win the whole world but are yourself lost or defeated? Of course not! [26]If you are ashamed of me and of my teaching, then the Son of Man will be ashamed of you when he comes in his glory and in the glory of the Father and of the holy angels. [27]I assure you that there are some here who will not die until they have seen the Kingdom of God."

The Transfiguration
(Matthew 17.1-8; Mark 9.2-8)

[28]About a week after he had said these things, Jesus took Peter, John, and James with him and went up a hill to pray. [29]While he was praying, his face changed its appearance, and his clothes became dazzling white. [30]Suddenly two men were there talking with him. They were Moses and Elijah, [31]who appeared in heavenly glory and talked with Jesus about the way in which he would soon fulfill God's purpose by dying in Jerusalem. [32]Peter and his companions were sound asleep, but they woke up and saw Jesus' glory and the two men who

開，遞給門徒，門徒就分給羣衆。[17]大家都吃，而且都吃飽了。門徒把剩下的碎屑收拾起來，裝滿了十二個籃子。

彼得認耶穌爲基督
（太16．13—19；可8．27—29）

[18]有一次，耶穌單獨一個人在禱告，門徒們來見他。他問他們說：「一般羣衆說我是誰？」

[19]他們回答：「有的說是施洗者約翰；有的說是以利亞；也有的說是古時的一位先知復活了。」

[20]耶穌問他們：「你們呢？你們說我是誰？」

彼得回答：「上帝所立的基督。」

耶穌預言自己的受難和死
（太16．20—28；可8．30—9．1）

[21]於是，耶穌嚴嚴地命令他們不要把這事告訴任何人。[22]接着他又說：「人子必須遭受許多苦難，被長老、祭司長，和經學教師棄絕，被殺害，第三天將復活。」

[23]耶穌又對大家說：「如果有人要跟從我，就得捨棄自己，天天背負他的十字架來跟從我。[24]因爲那想救自己生命的，反要喪失生命；那爲了我喪失生命的，反要得到生命。[25]一個人就是贏得了全世界，卻失去自己或賠上了自己的生命，有甚麼益處呢？沒有！[26]如果有人以我和我的話爲恥，人子在他的榮耀中，跟在他父親與聖天使們的榮耀中來臨的時候，也要以他爲恥。[27]我鄭重地告訴你們，站在這裏的人，有的在死以前會看見上帝主權的實現。」

改變形像
（太17．1—8；可9．2—8）

[28]說了這些話後約八天，耶穌帶着彼得、約翰，和雅各到山上禱告。[29]耶穌在禱告的時候外貌改變了；他的衣服也變成潔白發光。[30]忽然有兩個人出現跟他說話，這兩個人是摩西和以利亞。[31]他們在榮耀中顯現，跟耶穌談論他將在耶路撒冷以死來完成使命的事。[32]彼得和他的同伴都睡着了；他們一醒過來，看見耶穌的榮耀以及跟他站在一起

were standing with him. ³³As the men were leaving Jesus, Peter said to him, "Master, how good it is that we are here! We will make three tents, one for you, one for Moses, and one for Elijah." (He did not really know what he was saying.)

³⁴While he was still speaking, a cloud appeared and covered them with its shadow; and the disciples were afraid as the cloud came over them. ³⁵A voice said from the cloud, "This is my Son, whom I have chosen–listen to him!"

³⁶When the voice stopped, there was Jesus all alone. The disciples kept quiet about all this and told no one at that time anything they had seen.

Jesus Heals a Boy with an Evil Spirit
(Matthew 17.14-18; Mark 9.14-27)

³⁷The next day Jesus and the three disciples went down from the hill, and a large crowd met Jesus. ³⁸A man shouted from the crowd, "Teacher! I beg you, look at my son–my only son! ³⁹A spirit attacks him with a sudden shout and throws him into a fit, so that he foams at the mouth; it keeps on hurting him and will hardly let him go! ⁴⁰I begged your disciples to drive it out, but they couldn't."

⁴¹Jesus answered, "How unbelieving and wrong you people are! How long must I stay with you? How long do I have to put up with you?" Then he said to the man, "Bring your son here."

⁴²As the boy was coming, the demon knocked him to the ground and threw him into a fit. Jesus gave a command to the evil spirit, healed the boy, and gave him back to his father. ⁴³All the people were amazed at the mighty power of God.

Jesus Speaks Again about His Death
(Matthew 17.22-23; Mark 9.30-32)

The people were still marveling at everything Jesus was doing, when he said to his disciples, ⁴⁴"Don't forget what I am about to tell you! The Son of Man is going to be handed over to the power of human beings." ⁴⁵But the disciples did not know what this meant. It had been hidden from them so that they could not understand it, and they were afraid to ask him about the matter.

Who Is the Greatest?
(Matthew 18.1-5; Mark 9.33-37)

⁴⁶An argument broke out among the disciples as to which one of them was the greatest.

的兩個人。³³那兩個人要離開耶穌的時候，彼得對耶穌說：「老師，我們在這裏真好！讓我們搭三座帳棚，一座給你，一座給摩西，一座給以利亞。」（他實在不知道他在說些甚麼。）

³⁴ 他還在說話的時候，有一朵雲彩出現，籠罩他們，雲彩移近的時候，門徒都很害怕。³⁵忽然有聲音從雲裏傳出來，說：「這是我的兒子，是我所揀選的。你們要聽從他！」

³⁶ 那聲音停止後，只有耶穌一個人在那裏。在那些日子，門徒對這件事守口如瓶，沒有向任何人提起他們所看見的事。

治好被鬼附身的兒童
（太17·14-18；可9·14-27）

³⁷ 第二天，他們從山上下來的時候，有一大羣人來迎接耶穌。³⁸人羣中忽然有人呼喊說：「老師，求你救救我的兒子，他是我的獨子！³⁹邪靈常常襲擊他，使他突然大喊大叫，又使他抽瘋，口吐白沫；邪靈不停地傷害他，不肯罷休！⁴⁰我求你的門徒趕走邪靈，但是他們做不到。」

⁴¹ 耶穌說：「你們這時代的人是多麼沒有信心，多麼腐敗啊！我還得在你們這裏多久呢？還得容忍你們多久呢？」接着他對那個人說：「把你的兒子帶到這裏來。」

⁴² 孩子來的時候，鬼把他摔倒在地上，使他抽瘋。耶穌斥責邪污靈，治好了孩子，把他交給他父親。⁴³大家對上帝的大能都很驚異。

耶穌再預言自己的死
（太17·22-23；可9·30-32）

大家對耶穌所做的一切事還在詫異的時候，耶穌又對他的門徒說：⁴⁴「不要忘記我要告訴你們的話：人子將被交在人手裏。」⁴⁵可是他們不明白這話的意思；因為它的含意隱晦不明，使他們不能了解。他們又不敢問他這件事的究竟。

誰最偉大
（太18·1-5；可9·33-37）

⁴⁶ 門徒在爭論究竟他們當中誰最偉大。

47Jesus knew what they were thinking, so he took a child, stood him by his side, 48and said to them, "Whoever welcomes this child in my name, welcomes me; and whoever welcomes me, also welcomes the one who sent me. For the one who is least among you all is the greatest."

Whoever Is Not against You Is for You
(Mark 9.38-40)

49John spoke up, "Master, we saw a man driving out demons in your name, and we told him to stop, because he doesn't belong to our group."

50"Do not try to stop him," Jesus said to him and to the other disciples, "because whoever is not against you is for you."

A Samaritan Village Refuses to Receive Jesus

51As the time drew near when Jesus would be taken up to heaven, he made up his mind and set out on his way to Jerusalem. 52He sent messengers ahead of him, who went into a village in Samaria to get everything ready for him. 53But the people there would not receive him, because it was clear that he was on his way to Jerusalem. 54When the disciples James and John saw this, they said, "Lord, do you want us to call fire down from heaven to destroy them?"j

55Jesus turned and rebuked them.k 56Then Jesus and his disciples went on to another village.

The Would-Be Followers of Jesus
(Matthew 8.19-22)

57As they went on their way, a man said to Jesus, "I will follow you wherever you go."

58Jesus said to him, "Foxes have holes, and birds have nests, but the Son of Man has no place to lie down and rest."

59He said to another man, "Follow me."

But that man said, "Sir, first let me go back and bury my father."

60Jesus answered, "Let the dead bury their own dead. You go and proclaim the Kingdom of God."

61Someone else said, "I will follow you, sir; but first let me go and say good-bye to my family."

62Jesus said to him, "Anyone who starts to plow and then keeps looking back is of no use for the Kingdom of God."

j Some manuscripts add as Elijah did.
k Some manuscripts add and said, "You don't know what kind of a Spirit you belong to; for the Son of Man did not come to destroy human lives, but to save them."

47耶穌知道他們在想些甚麼，就叫一個小孩子來，讓他站在自己旁邊，48然後對他們說：「那為我的名接待這小孩子的，就是接待我；那接待我的，就是接待差遣我來的那一位。你們當中誰是最微不足道的，誰就是最偉大的。」

反對或贊同
（可9．38-40）

49約翰對耶穌說：「老師，我們看見有人藉着你的名趕鬼，我們就禁止他，因為他不和我們同夥跟從你。」

50耶穌就對他和其他的門徒說：「不要禁止他，因為不反對你們就是贊同你們。」

不接待耶穌的村莊

51耶穌被接升天的日子快到了，他決心朝耶路撒冷去，52於是派人先走。他們來到撒馬利亞的一個村莊，要替耶穌準備一切。53可是那地方的人不歡迎他，因為他顯然是朝着耶路撒冷去的。54他的門徒雅各和約翰看見這情形，就說：「主啊，你要我們呼喚⑦天上的火來燒滅他們嗎？」

55耶穌轉過身來，責備他們⑧。56他們就到別的村莊去。

要跟從耶穌的人
（太8．19-22）

57在他們的旅途中，有一個人對耶穌說：「你無論到哪裏去，我都要跟從你。」

58耶穌告訴他：「狐狸有洞，飛鳥有窩，可是人子連枕頭的地方都沒有。」59他對另一個人說：「來跟從我。」

可是那個人說：「主啊，請讓我先回去埋葬我的父親。」

60耶穌說：「讓死人去埋葬他們的死人吧！至於你，你要去傳上帝國的福音。」

61又有一個人說：「主啊，我要跟從你，但是請讓我先回去向家人告別吧。」

62耶穌對他說：「手扶着耕犁而不斷向後看的人對上帝國是沒有用處的！」

⑦「你要我們呼喚」另有些古卷作「你要我們像以利亞一樣呼喚」。
⑧有些古卷在「責備他們」之後加「說：你們不曉得自己是屬於哪一種靈；因為人子來的目的，不是要毀滅人的生命，而是要拯救他們。」

Jesus Sends Out the Seventy-Two

10 After this the Lord chose another seventy-two[l] men and sent them out two by two, to go ahead of him to every town and place where he himself was about to go. ²"There is a large harvest, but few workers to gather it in. Pray to the owner of the harvest that he will send out workers to gather in his harvest. ³Go! I am sending you like lambs among wolves. ⁴Don't take a purse or a beggar's bag or shoes; don't stop to greet anyone on the road. ⁵Whenever you go into a house, first say, 'Peace be with this house.' ⁶If someone who is peace-loving lives there, let your greeting of peace remain on that person; if not, take back your greeting of peace. ⁷Stay in that same house, eating and drinking whatever they offer you, for workers should be given their pay. Don't move around from one house to another. ⁸Whenever you go into a town and are made welcome, eat what is set before you, ⁹heal the sick in that town, and say to the people there, 'The Kingdom of God has come near you.' ¹⁰But whenever you go into a town and are not welcomed, go out in the streets and say, ¹¹'Even the dust from your town that sticks to our feet we wipe off against you. But remember that the Kingdom of God has come near you!' ¹²I assure you that on the Judgment Day God will show more mercy to Sodom than to that town!

The Unbelieving Towns
(Matthew 11.20-24)

¹³"How terrible it will be for you, Chorazin! How terrible for you too, Bethsaida! If the miracles which were performed in you had been performed in Tyre and Sidon, the people there would have long ago sat down, put on sackcloth, and sprinkled ashes on themselves, to show that they had turned from their sins! ¹⁴God will show more mercy on the Judgment Day to Tyre and Sidon than to you. ¹⁵And as for you, Capernaum! Did you want to lift yourself up to heaven? You will be thrown down to hell!"

¹⁶Jesus said to his disciples, "Whoever listens to you listens to me; whoever rejects you rejects me; and whoever rejects me rejects the one who sent me."

The Return of the Seventy-Two

¹⁷The seventy-two[m] men came back in great

耶穌派遣七十二人

10 過了些時候，主另外揀選了七十二⑨人，派遣他們出去，每組兩個人，先到他所要訪問的每一個市鎮。²他對他們說：「農作物很多，而工人很少。所以，你們要懇求農場的主人多派工人去收割他的農作物。³去吧！我派你們出去，好像把小羊放在狼羣裏。⁴不要帶錢包；不要帶旅行袋；不要帶鞋子；也不要在路上停下來向人打招呼。⁵你們無論到哪一家，先要說：『願你們一家平安！』⁶如果那裏有喜愛和平的人，你們所求的平安就歸他；否則那祝福就歸回你們。⁷你們要住在那一家，吃喝他們所供給的，因為工人獲得工資是合理的。不要從這一家搬到那一家。⁸你們無論到哪一個城市，如果有人歡迎你們，給你們預備甚麼吃的，你們就吃甚麼，⁹並且醫治那地方的病人，告訴他們：『上帝的主權快要在你們當中實現了。』¹⁰但是，如果你們到了一個城市，那裏的人不歡迎你們，你們就到大街上宣佈說：¹¹『連你們這城裏那黏在我們腳上的塵土，我們也要踩掉，表示對你們的警告。但是你們要記住，上帝的主權快要實現了！』¹²我告訴你們，在審判的日子，所多瑪人所遭受的懲罰比那城所受的要輕呢！」

不信的城
（太11‧20—24）

¹³「哥拉汛哪，你要遭殃了！伯賽大呀，你要遭殃了！我在你們當中行過的神蹟要是行在泰爾和西頓，那裏的人早就坐在地上，披麻蒙灰，表示他們已棄邪歸正了！¹⁴在審判的日子，泰爾和西頓所遭受的懲罰比你們所受的要輕呢！¹⁵至於你，迦百農啊，你要把自己捧上天嗎？你會給摔進地獄去！」

¹⁶耶穌又對他的門徒說：「誰聽從你們就是聽從我，拒絕你們就是拒絕我；拒絕我也就是拒絕差我來的那一位。」

七十二人回來

¹⁷那七十二人高高興興地回來，報告說：

---

l seventy-two; *some manuscripts have* seventy.
m seventy-two; *some manuscripts have* seventy *(see verse 1)*.

joy. "Lord," they said, "even the demons obeyed us when we gave them a command in your name!"

18Jesus answered them, "I saw Satan fall like lightning from heaven. 19Listen! I have given you authority, so that you can walk on snakes and scorpions and overcome all the power of the Enemy, and nothing will hurt you. 20But don't be glad because the evil spirits obey you; rather be glad because your names are written in heaven."

Jesus Rejoices
(Matthew 11.25-27; 13.16-17)

21At that time Jesus was filled with joy by the Holy Spirit*n* and said, "Father, Lord of heaven and earth! I thank you because you have shown to the unlearned what you have hidden from the wise and learned. Yes, Father, this was how you were pleased to have it happen.

22"My Father has given me all things. No one knows who the Son is except the Father, and no one knows who the Father is except the Son and those to whom the Son chooses to reveal him."

23Then Jesus turned to the disciples and said to them privately, "How fortunate you are to see the things you see! 24I tell you that many prophets and kings wanted to see what you see, but they could not, and to hear what you hear, but they did not "

The Parable of the Good Samaritan

25A teacher of the Law came up and tried to trap Jesus. "Teacher," he asked, "what must I do to receive eternal life?"

26Jesus answered him, "What do the Scriptures say? How do you interpret them?"

27The man answered, " 'Love the Lord your God with all your heart, with all your soul, with all your strength, and with all your mind'; and 'Love your neighbor as you love yourself.' "

28"You are right," Jesus replied; "do this and you will live."

29But the teacher of the Law wanted to justify himself, so he asked Jesus, "Who is my neighbor?"

30Jesus answered, "There was once a man who was going down from Jerusalem to Jericho when robbers attacked him, stripped him, and beat him up, leaving him half dead. 31It so happened that a priest was going down that road;

---

n *by the Holy Spirit; some manuscripts have* by the Spirit; *others have* in his spirit.

「主啊,我們藉着你的名發命令,連鬼也服從了我們!」

18 耶穌對他們說:「我看見撒但像閃電一樣從天上墜下來。19你們聽吧!我已經賜給你們權柄,能夠踐踏蛇和蠍子,也能勝過仇敵一切的力量,再也沒有甚麼能加害你們。20但是,不要因邪靈向你們降服而高興,卻要因你們的名字記錄在天上而歡樂。」

耶穌的歡樂
(太11.25—27;13.16—17)

21 就在這時候,耶穌在聖靈⑩的感動下充滿着歡樂,說:「天父啊,天地的主,我感謝你;因為你向聰明、有學問的人所隱藏的事,卻向沒有學問的人啓示出來。是的,父親啊,這樣的安排都是出於你的美意!

22「我父親已經把一切都給了我。除了父親,沒有人知道兒子是誰;除了兒子和兒子所願意啓示的人,也沒有人知道父親是誰。」

23 於是耶穌轉身向着門徒,悄悄地對他們說:「你們能看見這一切是多麼幸福啊!24我告訴你們,許多先知和君王想看你們所看見的,卻沒有看到,想聽你們所聽見的,卻沒有聽到。」

好撒馬利亞人的比喻

25 有一個法律教師前來試探耶穌,說:「老師,我該做甚麼才能得到永恆的生命?」

26 耶穌說:「法律書上說的是甚麼?你是怎樣解釋的呢?」

27 那人回答:「你要全心、全情、全力、全意愛主—你的上帝,又要愛鄰人,像愛自己一樣。」

28 耶穌對他說:「你答得對,照這樣做,就可以得到永恆的生命。」

29 那個法律教師為要表示自己有理,就問耶穌:「誰是我的鄰人呢?」

30 耶穌說:「有一個人從耶路撒冷下耶利哥,途中遇到強盜。他們剝掉他的衣服,把他打個半死,丟在那裏。31剛好有一個祭司

---

⑩「聖靈」有些古卷沒有「聖」字;另有些古卷作「自己的靈」。

but when he saw the man, he walked on by on the other side. [32]In the same way a Levite also came there, went over and looked at the man, and then walked on by on the other side. [33]But a Samaritan who was traveling that way came upon the man, and when he saw him, his heart was filled with pity. [34]He went over to him, poured oil and wine on his wounds and bandaged them; then he put the man on his own animal and took him to an inn, where he took care of him. [35]The next day he took out two silver coins and gave them to the innkeeper. 'Take care of him,' he told the innkeeper, 'and when I come back this way, I will pay you whatever else you spend on him.' "

[36]And Jesus concluded, "In your opinion, which one of these three acted like a neighbor toward the man attacked by the robbers?"

[37]The teacher of the Law answered, "The one who was kind to him."

Jesus replied, "You go, then, and do the same."

Jesus Visits Martha and Mary

[38]As Jesus and his disciples went on their way, he came to a village where a woman named Martha welcomed him in her home. [39]She had a sister named Mary, who sat down at the feet of the Lord and listened to his teaching. [40]Martha was upset over all the work she had to do, so she came and said, "Lord, don't you care that my sister has left me to do all the work by myself? Tell her to come and help me!"

[41]The Lord answered her, "Martha, Martha! You are worried and troubled over so many things, [42]but just one is needed. Mary has chosen the right thing, and it will not be taken away from her."

Jesus' Teaching on Prayer
(Matthew 6.9-13; 7.7-11)

11 One day Jesus was praying in a certain place. When he had finished, one of his disciples said to him, "Lord, teach us to pray, just as John taught his disciples."

[2]Jesus said to them, "When you pray, say this:
'Father:
 May your holy name be honored;
 may your Kingdom come.
[3] Give us day by day the food we need.[o]
[4] Forgive us our sins,
  for we forgive everyone who does us
  wrong.

o the food we need; or food for the next day.

從那條路下去;他一看見那個人就從另一邊走開。[32]同樣,有一個利未人經過那裏;他上前看看那人,也從另一邊走開。[33]可是有一個撒馬利亞人路過那人身邊,一看見他,就動了慈心。[34]他上前用油和酒倒在他的傷口,替他包紮,然後把他扶上自己的牲口,帶他到一家客棧,在那裏照顧他。[35]第二天,他拿兩個銀幣交給客棧的主人,說:『請你照顧他,等我回來經過這裏,我會付清所有的費用。』」

[36]於是耶穌問:「依你的看法,這三個人當中,哪一個是遭遇到強盜那人的鄰人呢?」

[37]法律教師回答:「以仁慈待他的那個人。」

耶穌說:「那麼,你去,照樣做吧!」

耶穌探望馬大和馬利亞

[38]耶穌和門徒繼續他們的旅程,來到一個村莊。那裏有一個名叫馬大的女人,接待耶穌到她家裏。[39]馬大有一個妹妹叫馬利亞。馬利亞來坐在主的腳前,聽他講道。[40]可是馬大因為要做的事情多,心裏忙亂,就上前說:「主啊,我妹妹讓我一個人做這許多事,你不介意嗎?請叫她來幫幫我吧!」

[41]主回答:「馬大!馬大!你為許多事操心忙亂,[42]但是只有一件是不可缺少的。馬利亞已經選擇了那最好的;沒有人能從她手中奪走。」

論禱告
(太6‧9—13;7‧7—11)

11 有一次,耶穌在一個地方禱告。禱告完了,有一個門徒對他說:「主啊,請教導我們禱告,像約翰教導他的門徒一樣。」

[2]耶穌對他們說:「你們要這樣禱告:
父親啊:
 願人都尊崇你的聖名;
 願你在世上掌權。
[3]賜給我們每天⑪需要的飲食。
[4]饒恕我們的罪,
 因為我們也饒恕所有得罪我們的人。

⑪「每天」或譯「明天」。

And do not bring us to hard testing.' "

5And Jesus said to his disciples, "Suppose one of you should go to a friend's house at midnight and say, 'Friend, let me borrow three loaves of bread. 6A friend of mine who is on a trip has just come to my house, and I don't have any food for him!' 7And suppose your friend should answer from inside, 'Don't bother me! The door is already locked, and my children and I are in bed. I can't get up and give you anything.' 8Well, what then? I tell you that even if he will not get up and give you the bread because you are his friend, yet he will get up and give you everything you need because you are not ashamed to keep on asking. 9And so I say to you: Ask, and you will receive; seek, and you will find; knock, and the door will be opened to you. 10For those who ask will receive, and those who seek will find, and the door will be opened to anyone who knocks. 11Would any of you who are fathers give your son a snake when he asks for fish? 12Or would you give him a scorpion when he asks for an egg? 13As bad as you are, you know how to give good things to your children. How much more, then, will the Father in heaven give the Holy Spirit to those who ask him!"

Jesus and Beelzebul
(Matthew 12.22-30; Mark 3.20-27)

14Jesus was driving out a demon that could not talk; and when the demon went out, the man began to talk. The crowds were amazed, 15but some of the people said, "It is Beelzebul, the chief of the demons, who gives him the power to drive them out."

16Others wanted to trap Jesus, so they asked him to perform a miracle to show that God approved of him. 17But Jesus knew what they were thinking, so he said to them, "Any country that divides itself into groups which fight each other will not last very long; a family divided against itself falls apart. 18So if Satan's kingdom has groups fighting each other, how can it last? You say that I drive out demons because Beelzebul gives me the power to do so. 19If this is how I drive them out, how do your followers drive them out? Your own followers prove that you are wrong! 20No, it is rather by means of God's power that I drive out demons, and this proves that the Kingdom of God has already come to you.

21"When a strong man, with all his weapons ready, guards his own house, all his belongings are safe. 22But when a stronger man attacks him and defeats him, he carries away all the weapons the owner was depending on and divides up what he stole.

不要讓我們遭受承擔不起的考驗。」

5 接着，耶穌告訴他的門徒：「假如你們當中有人半夜裏到朋友家去，對他說：『朋友，請借三個麵包給我；6因為有一個朋友旅行來到我家，我沒有甚麼吃的好招待他。』7假如你的朋友從裏面回答：『別打擾我，門已經關上了；我和孩子們也上了牀，我不能起來拿甚麼給你。』8怎麼辦呢？我告訴你們，縱使他不因那個人是他的朋友而起來拿麵包給他，也要因那個人一再地懇求而起來，把他所需要的給他。9所以我告訴你們，你們祈求，就得到；尋找，就找到；敲門，就給你們開門。10因為那祈求的，就得到；尋找的，就找到；敲門的，門就開了。11你們當中作父親的，有誰在兒子要魚的時候，拿蛇給他？12要雞蛋的時候，拿蠍子給他呢？13你們雖然邪惡還曉得拿好東西給自己的兒女；那麼，你們的天父豈不更要把聖靈賜給向他祈求的人嗎？」

耶穌和別西卜
（太12‧22-30；可3‧20-27）

14耶穌趕走了一個啞鬼，鬼出去以後，那個人又能夠說話了。羣衆都很驚訝，15可是他們當中有人說：「他是靠鬼王別西卜趕鬼的。」

16也有些人想陷害他，要求他行個神蹟來表明他所做的是出於上帝。17耶穌知道他們在想些甚麼，就對他們說：「任何國家自相紛爭，必然衰敗；一個家庭自相紛爭，也必然破碎。18如果撒但自相紛爭，他的國度又怎能站立得住呢？你們說我趕鬼是靠別西卜，19果然這樣的話，你們的子弟趕鬼又是靠誰呢？你們的子弟要證明你們是錯的！20其實，我趕鬼若是靠上帝的能力，這就證明上帝已經在你們當中掌權了。

21「一個武器齊備的武士守衛自己住宅的時候，他的財物是安全的。22但是一個比他更有力的武士來了，制伏了他，就會把他所倚靠的武器都奪走，而且分了他所盜取的贓物。

23"Anyone who is not for me is really against me; anyone who does not help me gather is really scattering.

The Return of the Evil Spirit
(Matthew 12.43-45)

24"When an evil spirit goes out of a person, it travels over dry country looking for a place to rest. If it can't find one, it says to itself, 'I will go back to my house.' 25So it goes back and finds the house clean and all fixed up. 26Then it goes out and brings seven other spirits even worse than itself, and they come and live there. So when it is all over, that person is in worse shape than at the beginning."

True Happiness

27When Jesus had said this, a woman spoke up from the crowd and said to him, "How happy is the woman who bore you and nursed you!"

28But Jesus answered, "Rather, how happy are those who hear the word of God and obey it!"

The Demand for a Miracle
(Matthew 12.38-42)

29As the people crowded around Jesus, he went on to say, "How evil are the people of this day! They ask for a miracle, but none will be given them except the miracle of Jonah. 30In the same way that the prophet Jonah was a sign for the people of Nineveh, so the Son of Man will be a sign for the people of this day. 31On the Judgment Day the Queen of Sheba will stand up and accuse the people of today, because she traveled all the way from her country to listen to King Solomon's wise teaching; and there is something here, I tell you, greater than Solomon. 32On the Judgment Day the people of Nineveh will stand up and accuse you, because they turned from their sins when they heard Jonah preach; and I assure you that there is something here greater than Jonah!

The Light of the Body
(Matthew 5.15; 6.22-23)

33"No one lights a lamp and then hides it or puts it under a bowl;*p* instead, it is put on the lampstand, so that people may see the light as they come in. 34Your eyes are like a lamp for the body. When your eyes are sound, your whole body is full of light; but when your eyes are no good, your whole body will be in darkness. 35Make certain, then, that the light in you

---

23「那不跟我同夥的就是反對我;那不幫我收聚的便是在拆散。」

污靈回來
(太12・43—45)

24「污靈離開了所附的人,走遍乾旱區域,尋找棲息的地方,都找不到,就說:『我要回原來的屋子去。』25於是他回去,發現那屋子打掃得又乾淨又整齊。26他又出去,帶回七個比自己更邪惡的靈來,跟他住在一起。這樣,那個人後來的景況比從前更壞了。」

眞的有福

27耶穌正說這話的時候,有一個女人從人羣中大聲對他說:「那懷你胎和哺育你的眞有福啊!」

28耶穌說:「那聽見上帝的話而遵守的人才眞有福呢!」

求神蹟
(太12・38—42)

29那時羣衆圍繞着耶穌,耶穌繼續講論說:「這時代的人多麼邪惡呀!他們竟要求看神蹟,可是除了約拿的神蹟,再沒有別的神蹟給他們看了。30約拿怎樣成爲尼尼微人眼中的神蹟,人子也要同樣成爲這一代人眼中的神蹟。31在審判的日子,南方的女王要站起來控告這一代的人,因爲她長途跋涉來聽所羅門王智慧的話。我告訴你們,這裏有比所羅門更重大的事呢!32在審判的日子,尼尼微人要站起來控告你們,因爲他們聽見了約拿的宣道就棄邪歸正了。我告訴你們,這裏有比約拿更重大的事呢!」

身體的燈
(太5・15;6・22—23)

33「沒有人點亮了燈而把它藏在地窖裏或放在斗底下;相反地,他一定把燈放在燈臺上,讓進來的人都看得見亮光。34你的眼睛好比身體的燈。你的眼睛好,全身就光明;你的眼睛壞,全身就黑暗。35所以,要當

---

p *Some manuscripts do not have* or puts it under a bowl.

is not darkness. 36If your whole body is full of light, with no part of it in darkness, it will be bright all over, as when a lamp shines on you with its brightness."

Jesus Accuses the Pharisees and the Teachers of the Law

(Matthew 23.1-36; Mark 12.38-40)

37When Jesus finished speaking, a Pharisee invited him to eat with him; so he went in and sat down to eat. 38The Pharisee was surprised when he noticed that Jesus had not washed before eating. 39So the Lord said to him, "Now then, you Pharisees clean the outside of your cup and plate, but inside you are full of violence and evil. 40Fools! Did not God, who made the outside, also make the inside? 41But give what is in your cups and plates to the poor, and everything will be ritually clean for you.

42"How terrible for you Pharisees! You give to God one tenth of the seasoning herbs, such as mint and rue and all the other herbs, but you neglect justice and love for God. These you should practice, without neglecting the others.

43"How terrible for you Pharisees! You love the reserved seats in the synagogues and to be greeted with respect in the marketplaces. 44How terrible for you! You are like unmarked graves which people walk on without knowing it."

45One of the teachers of the Law said to him, "Teacher, when you say this, you insult us too!"

46Jesus answered, "How terrible also for you teachers of the Law! You put onto people's backs loads which are hard to carry, but you yourselves will not stretch out a finger to help them carry those loads. 47How terrible for you! You make fine tombs for the prophets–the very prophets your ancestors murdered. 48You yourselves admit, then, that you approve of what your ancestors did; they murdered the prophets, and you build their tombs. 49For this reason the Wisdom of God said, 'I will send them prophets and messengers; they will kill some of them and persecute others.' 50So the people of this time will be punished for the murder of all the prophets killed since the creation of the world, 51from the murder of Abel to the murder of Zechariah, who was killed between the altar and the Holy Place. Yes, I tell you, the people of this time will be punished for them all!

52"How terrible for you teachers of the Law! You have kept the key that opens the door to the house of knowledge; you yourselves will not

心，免得你裏面的光變成黑暗。36如果你全身充滿光明，毫無黑暗，就會光輝四射，好像燈的亮光照耀你。」

譴責法利賽人和法律教師

（太23・1—36；可12・38—40）

37耶穌講完了這些話，一個法利賽人來請他吃飯，他就進去坐席。38這個法利賽人看見耶穌飯前不先洗手，非常詫異。39主就對他說：「你們法利賽人把杯盤的外面洗得乾乾淨淨，你們裏面卻盛滿着貪慾和邪惡。40無知的人哪，那造外面的上帝不也造裏面嗎？41只要把杯盤裏面的東西送給窮人，對你們來說，一切都算潔淨了。

42「你們法利賽人要遭殃了！你們把那些調味品，如薄荷、茴香，和其他的香料，奉獻十分之一給上帝，但是忽視了正義和對上帝的愛。其實，這才是你們必須實行的；至於其他的，也不可忽略。

43「你們法利賽人要遭殃了！你們喜歡會堂裏的特別座位，喜歡人家在公共場所向你們致敬問安。44你們要遭殃了！因為你們好像是沒有記號的墳墓，人在上面走過，卻不知道。」

45有一個法律教師對耶穌說：「老師，你這樣說，連我們也侮辱了！」

46耶穌回答：「你們這班法律教師也要遭殃了！你們把難背的重擔擱在別人的肩膀上，自己卻不肯動一根手指頭去減輕他們的負擔。47你們要遭殃了！你們替先知修造墳墓，而那些先知正是你們的祖宗所殺害的。48這樣，你們證明了你們同意祖宗所做的；他們殺害了先知，而你們替先知修造墳墓。49所以，上帝的智者曾經說過：『我要派遣先知和使徒到他們那裏去；有的要被他們殺害，有的要受他們逼迫。』50因此，從創世以來，所有殺害先知的罪，51就是從亞伯的被殺，直到在祭壇和聖所之間被殺的撒迦利亞為止的血債，都要這一時代的人償還。是的，我告訴你們，這時代的人一定會為這一切受到懲罰！

52「你們這班法律教師要遭殃了！你們把持着開啓知識寶庫的鑰匙，自己不願意進

go in, and you stop those who are trying to go in!"

53When Jesus left that place, the teachers of the Law and the Pharisees began to criticize him bitterly and ask him questions about many things, 54trying to lay traps for him and catch him saying something wrong.

A Warning against Hypocrisy
(Matthew 10.26-27)

12As thousands of people crowded together, so that they were stepping on each other, Jesus said first to his disciples, "Be on guard against the yeast of the Pharisees–I mean their hypocrisy. 2Whatever is covered up will be uncovered, and every secret will be made known. 3So then, whatever you have said in the dark will be heard in broad daylight, and whatever you have whispered in private in a closed room will be shouted from the housetops.

Whom to Fear
(Matthew 10.28-31)

4"I tell you, my friends, do not be afraid of those who kill the body but cannot afterward do anything worse. 5I will show you whom to fear: fear God, who, after killing, has the authority to throw into hell. Believe me, he is the one you must fear!

6"Aren't five sparrows sold for two pennies? Yet not one sparrow is forgotten by God. 7Even the hairs of your head have all been counted. So do not be afraid; you are worth much more than many sparrows!

Confessing and Rejecting Christ
(Matthew 10.32-33; 12.32; 10.19-20)

8"I assure you that those who declare publicly that they belong to me, the Son of Man will do the same for them before the angels of God. 9But those who reject me publicly, the Son of Man will also reject them before the angels of God.

10"Whoever says a word against the Son of Man can be forgiven; but whoever says evil things against the Holy Spirit will not be forgiven.

11"When they bring you to be tried in the synagogues or before governors or rulers, do not be worried about how you will defend yourself or what you will say. 12For the Holy Spirit will teach you at that time what you should say."

去，也不讓想進去的人進去！」

53耶穌離開了那裏，經學教師和法利賽人開始激烈地批評他，向他發出許多難題，54要找話柄來陷害他。

警戒偽善
（太10‧26—27）

12那時候，成千上萬的人羣擁擠在一起，甚至彼此踐踏。耶穌先對門徒說：「你們要提防法利賽人的酵母，就是他們的偽善。2一切隱藏的事都會被揭發；秘密的事也會被洩露。3因此，你們在暗中所說的話會在光天化日之下被人聽到；你們在密室中的耳語也會在屋頂上給宣佈出來。」

不要怕
（太10‧28—31）

4「朋友們，我告訴你們，那只能殺害肉體，卻不能進一步傷害你們的，不用害怕。5我要指示你們該怕的是誰：你們要怕那位奪走人的生命以後，又有權把他投入地獄的上帝。是的，我告訴你們，應該懼怕的就是他！

6「五隻麻雀固然用兩個銅錢就買得到，可是上帝一隻也不忘記；7就是你們的頭髮他也都數過了。所以，你們不要怕，你們比許多麻雀要貴重多了！」

宣認基督
（太10‧32—33；12‧32；10‧19—20）

8「我告訴你們，凡在人面前認我的，人子在上帝的天使面前也要認他；9凡在人面前不認我的，人子在上帝的天使面前也不認他。

10「說話冒犯人子的，可以蒙赦免；只是褻瀆聖靈的，不能蒙赦免。

11「人家把你們帶上會堂，或是帶到官長或統治者面前受審問的時候，你們不用擔心要怎樣為自己辯護，或是要說些甚麼話；12因為在那時候，聖靈會指示你們該說的話。」

The Parable of the Rich Fool

13A man in the crowd said to Jesus, "Teacher, tell my brother to divide with me the property our father left us."

14Jesus answered him, "Friend, who gave me the right to judge or to divide the property between you two?" 15And he went on to say to them all, "Watch out and guard yourselves from every kind of greed; because your true life is not made up of the things you own, no matter how rich you may be."

16Then Jesus told them this parable: "There was once a rich man who had land which bore good crops. 17He began to think to himself, 'I don't have a place to keep all my crops. What can I do? 18This is what I will do,' he told himself; 'I will tear down my barns and build bigger ones, where I will store the grain and all my other goods. 19Then I will say to myself, Lucky man! You have all the good things you need for many years. Take life easy, eat, drink, and enjoy yourself!' 20But God said to him, 'You fool! This very night you will have to give up your life; then who will get all these things you have kept for yourself?' "

21And Jesus concluded, "This is how it is with those who pile up riches for themselves but are not rich in God's sight."

Trust in God

(Matthew 6.25-34)

22Then Jesus said to the disciples, "And so I tell you not to worry about the food you need to stay alive or about the clothes you need for your body. 23Life is much more important than food, and the body much more important than clothes. 24Look at the crows: they don't plant seeds or gather a harvest; they don't have storage rooms or barns; God feeds them! You are worth so much more than birds! 25Can any of you live a bit longerq by worrying about it? 26If you can't manage even such a small thing, why worry about the other things? 27Look how the wild flowers grow: they don't work or make clothes for themselves. But I tell you that not even King Solomon with all his wealth had clothes as beautiful as one of these flowers. 28It is God who clothes the wild grass–grass that is here today and gone tomorrow, burned up in the oven. Won't he be all the more sure to clothe you? What little faith you have!

29"So don't be all upset, always concerned about what you will eat and drink. 30(For the pagans of this world are always concerned about all these things.) Your Father knows that you need these things. 31Instead, be concerned with his Kingdom, and he will provide you with these things.

q live a bit longer; or grow a bit taller.

無知的財主

13 羣眾當中有一個人對耶穌說：「老師，請吩咐我的兄弟跟我分父親的遺產。」

14 耶穌回答：「朋友，誰指派我為你們審案或替你們分家產呢？」15於是他繼續向大家說：「你們要謹慎自守，躲避各樣的貪婪；因為，一個人無論怎樣富裕，他的眞生命不在乎他有多少財產。」

16 於是耶穌對他們講一個比喻：「有一個財主，田產豐富，17他心裏盤算着：『我沒有夠大的地方來儲藏所有的穀物，該怎麼辦呢？』18他又自言自語：『對了，我要把原有的倉庫拆了，改建更大的，來存放五穀和別的貨物，19然後我要對自己說，幸運的人哪，你擁有一切好東西，足夠你多年花用，慢慢享受，吃吃喝喝，過舒服的日子吧！』20可是，上帝要對他說：『你這個糊塗人，就在今夜，你得交出你的生命；那麼，你為自己所積存的一切財物要歸給誰呢？』」

21 耶穌結論說：「那為自己積聚財富、在上帝眼中卻不富足的人也是這樣。」

信靠上帝

（太 6，25－34）

22 耶穌又對門徒說：「所以，我告訴你們，不要為生活上所需的食物，或身上所穿的衣服操心。23生命比食物貴重得多；身體也比衣服貴重得多。24看看那些烏鴉吧。牠們不種不收，無倉無庫，上帝尚且飼養牠們，你們比鳥兒貴重多了！25你們當中又有誰能藉着憂慮多活幾天⑫呢？26如果你們連這樣的小事也做不到，又何必為其他的事操心呢？27看看百合花怎樣生長吧。它們既不工作又不縫衣，可是我告訴你們，甚至像所羅門王那樣的榮華顯赫，他的衣飾也比不上一朵野花那樣的美麗。28野地的花草今朝出現，明天枯萎，給扔在火爐裏焚燒，上帝還這樣打扮它們，他豈不更要賜衣服給你們嗎？你們的信心太小了！29所以，你們不要掛慮吃甚麼，喝甚麼，為這些事煩惱。30這些事是世上不信的人所追逐的。你們的天父知道你們需要這一切東西。31你們要追求上帝主權的實現，他就會把這一切都供給你們。」

⑫「多活幾天」或譯「多長高幾寸」。

Riches in Heaven
(Matthew 6.19-21)

32"Do not be afraid, little flock, for your Father is pleased to give you the Kingdom. 33Sell all your belongings and give the money to the poor. Provide for yourselves purses that don't wear out, and save your riches in heaven, where they will never decrease, because no thief can get to them, and no moth can destroy them. 34For your heart will always be where your riches are.

Watchful Servants

35"Be ready for whatever comes, dressed for action and with your lamps lit, 36like servants who are waiting for their master to come back from a wedding feast. When he comes and knocks, they will open the door for him at once. 37How happy are those servants whose master finds them awake and ready when he returns! I tell you, he will take off his coat, have them sit down, and will wait on them. 38How happy they are if he finds them ready, even if he should come at midnight or even later! 39And you can be sure that if the owner of a house knew the time when the thief would come, he would not let the thief break into his house. 40And you, too, must be ready, because the Son of Man will come at an hour when you are not expecting him."

The Faithful or the Unfaithful Servant
(Matthew 24.45-51)

41Peter said, "Lord, does this parable apply to us, or do you mean it for everyone?"

42The Lord answered, "Who, then, is the faithful and wise servant? He is the one that his master will put in charge, to run the household and give the other servants their share of the food at the proper time. 43How happy that servant is if his master finds him doing this when he comes home! 44Indeed, I tell you, the master will put that servant in charge of all his property. 45But if that servant says to himself that his master is taking a long time to come back and if he begins to beat the other servants, both the men and the women, and eats and drinks and gets drunk, 46then the master will come back one day when the servant does not expect him and at a time he does not know. The master will cut him in pieces^r and make him share the fate of the disobedient.

47"The servant who knows what his master wants him to do, but does not get himself ready and do it, will be punished with a heavy whip-

r cut him in pieces; *or* throw him out.

論天上的財寶
（太6‧19-21）

32「你們這小小的一羣，不要害怕，因為你們的父親樂意把他的國賜給你們。33要賣掉你們所有的，把錢賙濟窮人；要為自己預備不會破損的錢袋，把財寶存在天上。在那裏，財寶是使用不盡的；因為盜賊偷不到，也沒有蟲蛀。34你們的財寶在哪裏，你們的心也在那裏。」

警醒的僕人

35「你們要隨時準備好，束緊腰帶，點上燈，36好像僕人等候主人從婚宴上回來。主人回來敲門的時候，他們立刻為他開門。37主人回來，發現這些僕人警醒，他們就有福了！我實在告訴你們，主人要束上腰帶，讓他們坐下來吃飯，親自伺候他們。38甚至主人延遲到半夜或黎明才回來，他若發現僕人警醒，他們就有福了！39要記住這一點：一家的主人要是知道小偷甚麼時候要來，他一定不會讓小偷破門而入。40你們也要隨時準備好，因為人子會在你們料想不到的時候來臨。」

可靠和不可靠的僕人
（太24‧45-51）

41彼得說：「主啊，你這比喻是對我們說的，還是也對大眾說的？」

42主說：「那麼，誰是那又可靠又機智的管家呢？就是受主人指派來管理家務、按時把糧食分配給其他僕人的那個人。43主人回來的時候，看見這僕人這樣忠於職守；這僕人是多麼有福啊！44我實在告訴你們，主人要派他管理他所有的產業。45但是，如果這僕人心裏盤算，『我的主人不會那麼早回來』，於是動手毆打其他的奴僕和婢女，並且吃喝鬧酒，46主人會在他料想不到的日子，在他不知道的時候回來。主人要重重地責打他⑬，使他和其他不可靠的僕人同受懲罰。

47「僕人知道主人要他做些甚麼，卻不準備，也不照主人的意思做；這樣，他會受重

⑬「要重重地責打他」或譯「要把他攆出去」。

ping. [48]But the servant who does not know what his master wants, and yet does something for which he deserves a whipping, will be punished with a light whipping. Much is required from the person to whom much is given; much more is required from the person to whom much more is given.

Jesus the Cause of Division
(Matthew 10.34-36)

[49]"I came to set the earth on fire, and how I wish it were already kindled! [50]I have a baptism to receive, and how distressed I am until it is over! [51]Do you suppose that I came to bring peace to the world? No, not peace, but division. [52]From now on a family of five will be divided, three against two and two against three. [53]Fathers will be against their sons, and sons against their fathers; mothers will be against their daughters, and daughters against their mothers; mothers-in-law will be against their daughters-in-law, and daughters-in-law against their mothers-in-law."

Understanding the Time
(Matthew 16.2-3)

[54]Jesus said also to the people, "When you see a cloud coming up in the west, at once you say that it is going to rain–and it does. [55]And when you feel the south wind blowing, you say that it is going to get hot–and it does. [56]Hypocrites! You can look at the earth and the sky and predict the weather; why, then, don't you know the meaning of this present time?

Settle with Your Opponent
(Matthew 5.25-26)

[57]"Why do you not judge for yourselves the right thing to do? [58]If someone brings a lawsuit against you and takes you to court, do your best to settle the dispute before you get to court. If you don't, you will be dragged before the judge, who will hand you over to the police, and you will be put in jail. [59]There you will stay, I tell you, until you pay the last penny of your fine."

Turn from Your Sins or Die

13 At that time some people were there who told Jesus about the Galileans whom Pilate had killed while they were offering sacrifices to God. [2]Jesus answered them, "Because those Galileans were killed in that way, do you think it proves that they were worse sinners than all other Galileans? [3]No indeed! And I tell you that if you do not turn from your sins, you will

重的鞭打。[48]至於那不知道主人的意思而做了該受鞭打的事的僕人，會受比較輕的鞭打。上帝多給誰，就向誰多取；多付託誰，向誰的要求也大。」

分裂的原因
（太10‧34—36）

[49]「我到地上來是要點燃烽火，我多麼盼望它已經燃燒起來了！[50]我應當受苦難的洗禮。在經歷這苦難以前，我心裏多麼困擾！[51]你們不要以為我是帶和平到世上來的。我告訴你們，我並不是帶來和平，而是帶來分裂。[52]從今以後，五口之家將要分裂，三個跟兩個爭，兩個跟三個鬥。[53]他們將起紛爭：父親跟兒子爭，兒子跟父親鬥；母親跟女兒爭，女兒跟母親鬥；婆婆跟媳婦爭，媳婦跟婆婆鬥。」

洞察時代的徵兆
（太16‧2—3）

[54]耶穌又對羣衆說：「你們一看見西邊有雲彩出現，立刻說『快下雨了』，果然這樣。[55]南風一吹，你們就說『天氣要燥熱了』，果然這樣。[56]僞善的人哪，你們很會觀察天地的顏色，爲甚麼不會洞察這個時代呢？」

跟對頭和解
（太5‧25—26）

[57]「你們爲甚麼不自己判斷甚麼是合宜的事？[58]如果有人控告你，要把你拉上法庭，你就盡所能，趁着還在路上的時候跟他和解，免得他把你交給法官，法官把你交給法警，法警把你關進牢裏去。[59]我告訴你，非等到你繳清罰款的最後一分錢，你是不能從監獄出來的。」

不悔改則死亡

13 當時，在那裏有人告訴耶穌，說有些加利利人在向上帝獻祭的時候被彼拉多殺害。[2]耶穌說：「因為這些加利利人死於非命，你們就以為他們比其他的加利利人更有罪嗎？[3]我告訴你們，不是的；除非你們悔

all die as they did. 4What about those eighteen people in Siloam who were killed when the tower fell on them? Do you suppose this proves that they were worse than all the other people living in Jerusalem? 5No indeed! And I tell you that if you do not turn from your sins, you will all die as they did."

The Parable of the Unfruitful Fig Tree

6Then Jesus told them this parable: "There was once a man who had a fig tree growing in his vineyard. He went looking for figs on it but found none. 7So he said to his gardener, 'Look, for three years I have been coming here looking for figs on this fig tree, and I haven't found any. Cut it down! Why should it go on using up the soil?' 8But the gardener answered, 'Leave it alone, sir, just one more year; I will dig around it and put in some fertilizer. 9Then if the tree bears figs next year, so much the better; if not, then you can have it cut down.' "

Jesus Heals a Crippled Woman on the Sabbath

10One Sabbath Jesus was teaching in a synagogue. 11A woman there had an evil spirit that had kept her sick for eighteen years; she was bent over and could not straighten up at all. 12When Jesus saw her, he called out to her, "Woman, you are free from your sickness!" 13He placed his hands on her, and at once she straightened herself up and praised God.

14The official of the synagogue was angry that Jesus had healed on the Sabbath, so he spoke up and said to the people, "There are six days in which we should work; so come during those days and be healed, but not on the Sabbath!"

15The Lord answered him, "You hypocrites! Any one of you would untie your ox or your donkey from the stall and take it out to give it water on the Sabbath. 16Now here is this descendant of Abraham whom Satan has kept in bonds for eighteen years; should she not be released on the Sabbath?" 17His answer made his enemies ashamed of themselves, while the people rejoiced over all the wonderful things that he did.

The Parable of the Mustard Seed

(Matthew 13.31-32; Mark 4.30-32)

18Jesus asked, "What is the Kingdom of God like? What shall I compare it with? 19It is like this. A man takes a mustard seed and plants it in his field. The plant grows and becomes a tree, and the birds make their nests in its branches."

改，你們也會遭遇到同樣的結局。4西羅亞塔倒塌時所壓死的那十八個人，你們以為他們比其他住在耶路撒冷的人更壞嗎？5我告訴你們，不是的；你們要是不悔改，你們也要同樣死亡。」

不結果子的無花果樹的比喻

6 接着，耶穌對他們講一個比喻：「有一個人在自己的葡萄園裏種了一棵無花果樹。他想在樹上找果子，卻找不着。7於是他對園丁說：『你看，三年來，我在這棵無花果樹上找果子，甚麼也沒有找到。把它砍了吧！何必白佔土地？』8園丁說：『主人，請再寬容一年，等我挖鬆它周圍的泥土，加上肥料。9如果明年結果子便罷；不然，你就把它砍掉。』」

在安息日治好駝背的女人

10一個安息日，耶穌在某會堂裏教導人。11有一個女人被邪靈附着，病了十八年，腰老是彎着，不能站直。12耶穌看見她，就叫她，對她說：「婦人，你的病離開你了！」13耶穌用手按着她，她立刻直起腰來，就頌讚上帝。

14 會堂的主管看見耶穌在安息日治病，十分惱怒，對大家說：「我們有六天好工作，要治病應該在這六天裏，而不該在安息日。」

15 主回答他：「你這偽善的人哪，難道你們在安息日就不解開槽邊的牛、驢，牽去喝水嗎？16這女人是亞伯拉罕的後代，她被撒但捆綁了十八年，難道在安息日就不應該解開她的鎖鍊嗎？」17耶穌這話使他的敵人都覺得慚愧，但是羣衆對他所做一切奇妙的事都很興奮。

芥菜種的比喻

（太13‧31-32；可4‧30-32）

18 耶穌說：「上帝國像甚麼呢？我要拿甚麼來比擬呢？19它好比一粒芥菜種子，有人把它種在自己的園裏。芥菜長大以後，成為一棵樹，連飛鳥也在它的枝子上面搭窩。」

The Parable of the Yeast
(Matthew 13.33)

20Again Jesus asked, "What shall I compare the Kingdom of God with? 21It is like this. A woman takes some yeast and mixes it with a bushel of flour until the whole batch of dough rises."

The Narrow Door
(Matthew 7.13-14, 21-23)

22Jesus went through towns and villages, teaching the people and making his way toward Jerusalem. 23Someone asked him, "Sir, will just a few people be saved?"

Jesus answered them, 24"Do your best to go in through the narrow door; because many people will surely try to go in but will not be able. 25The master of the house will get up and close the door; then when you stand outside and begin to knock on the door and say, 'Open the door for us, sir!' he will answer you, 'I don't know where you come from!' 26Then you will answer, 'We ate and drank with you; you taught in our town!' 27But he will say again, 'I don't know where you come from. Get away from me, all you wicked people!' 28How you will cry and gnash your teeth when you see Abraham, Isaac, and Jacob, and all the prophets in the Kingdom of God, while you are thrown out! 29People will come from the east and the west, from the north and the south, and sit down at the feast in the Kingdom of God. 30Then those who are now last will be first, and those who are now first will be last."

Jesus' Love for Jerusalem
(Matthew 23.37-39)

31At that same time some Pharisees came to Jesus and said to him, "You must get out of here and go somewhere else, because Herod wants to kill you."

32Jesus answered them, "Go and tell that fox: 'I am driving out demons and performing cures today and tomorrow, and on the third day I shall finish my work.' 33Yet I must be on my way today, tomorrow, and the next day; it is not right for a prophet to be killed anywhere except in Jerusalem.

34"Jerusalem, Jerusalem! You kill the prophets, you stone the messengers God has sent you! How many times I wanted to put my arms around all your people, just as a hen gathers her chicks under her wings, but you would not let me! 35And so your Temple will be abandoned. I assure you that you will not see me until the time comes when you say, 'God bless him who comes in the name of the Lord.' "

麵酵的比喻
（太13·33）

20 耶穌又說：「我要拿甚麼來比擬上帝的國呢？21它好比酵母，有女人拿來放在四十公升的麵裏，使全團麵都發起來。」

窄門
（太7·13—14；21—23）

22 耶穌經過許多村鎮，朝耶路撒冷去，沿途教導人。23有人問他：「主啊，得救的人不多吧？」

24 耶穌回答他們：「你們要努力從窄門進去。我告訴你們，有許多人想進去，卻進不去。25等到一家的主人起來關了門，你們才站在門外敲門，說：『先生，請給我們開門！』他要回答：『我不曉得你們是從哪裏來的！』26你們要說：『我們曾經跟你一起吃喝；你也在我們的大街上教導過我們。』27可是，他要說：『我告訴你們，我不曉得你們是從哪裏來的。你們這些作惡的人，走開！』28你們看見亞伯拉罕、以撒、雅各，和先知們都在上帝的國度裏，而你們卻被驅逐在外面的時候，就要哀哭，咬牙切齒了！29從東西南北各地都有人要來參加上帝國裏的筵席。30那些居後的，將要在先，在先的，將要居後。」

為耶路撒冷哀哭
（太23·37—39）

31 就在那時候，有幾個法利賽人來見耶穌，對他說：「你得離開這裏到別的地方去，因為希律想要殺你。」

32 耶穌回答他們說：「你們去告訴那狐狸：『你瞧！今天和明天我要趕鬼治病，第三天我要完成我的工作。』33雖然這樣，今天、明天、後天，我必須向前走，因為先知在耶路撒冷以外的地方被殺是不對的。

34「耶路撒冷啊，耶路撒冷啊，你殺了先知，又用石頭打死了上帝差派到你這裏來的使者！我多少次要保護你的子女，像母雞把小雞聚集在翅膀下一樣。可是你們不願意！35瞧吧，你們的家園將變成一片荒涼。我告訴你們，你們從此再也見不到我，直到你們說：『願上帝賜福給奉主名而來的那位！』」

Jesus Heals a Sick Man

14 One Sabbath Jesus went to eat a meal at the home of one of the leading Pharisees; and people were watching Jesus closely. [2]A man whose legs and arms were swollen came to Jesus, [3]and Jesus spoke up and asked the teachers of the Law and the Pharisees, "Does our Law allow healing on the Sabbath or not?"

[4]But they would not say a thing. Jesus took the man, healed him, and sent him away. [5]Then he said to them, "If any one of you had a child or an ox that happened to fall in a well on a Sabbath, would you not pull it out at once on the Sabbath itself?"

[6]But they were not able to answer him about this.

Humility and Hospitality

[7]Jesus noticed how some of the guests were choosing the best places, so he told this parable to all of them: [8]"When someone invites you to a wedding feast, do not sit down in the best place. It could happen that someone more important than you has been invited, [9]and your host, who invited both of you, would have to come and say to you, 'Let him have this place.' Then you would be embarrassed and have to sit in the lowest place. [10]Instead, when you are invited, go and sit in the lowest place, so that your host will come to you and say, 'Come on up, my friend, to a better place.' This will bring you honor in the presence of all the other guests. [11]For those who make themselves great will be humbled, and those who humble themselves will be made great."

[12]Then Jesus said to his host, "When you give a lunch or a dinner, do not invite your friends or your brothers or your relatives or your rich neighbors—for they will invite you back, and in this way you will be paid for what you did. [13]When you give a feast, invite the poor, the crippled, the lame, and the blind; [14]and you will be blessed, because they are not able to pay you back. God will repay you on the day the good people rise from death."

The Parable of the Great Feast

(Matthew 22.1-10)

[15]When one of the guests sitting at the table heard this, he said to Jesus, "How happy are those who will sit down at the feast in the Kingdom of God!"

[16]Jesus said to him, "There was once a man who was giving a great feast to which he invited many people. [17]When it was time for the feast, he sent his servant to tell his guests, 'Come, everything is ready!' [18]But they all began, one after another, to make excuses. The first one told

耶穌治好病人

14 有一個安息日，耶穌到一個法利賽人領袖的家裏吃飯；有些人窺伺着他。[2]剛好在他面前有一個患水腫病的人，[3]耶穌就問那些法律教師和法利賽人說：「我們的法律准不准許在安息日治病呢？」

[4] 他們都閉口不言。耶穌就扶着那人，治好他，打發他走。[5]於是他對大家說：「你們當中誰有兒子或牛在安息日掉進井裏去，而不立刻把他拉上來？」

[6] 他們對耶穌所問的話無法回答。

謙卑和待客之道

[7] 耶穌注意到有些客人替自己挑選筵席上的首位，就用比喻對大家說：[8]「你被請去參加婚宴的時候，不要坐在首座上，恐怕有比你更受尊重的客人也在被邀請之列。[9]那個邀請你們的主人要上來對你說：『請讓座給這一位吧！』那時候，你會覺得很難為情，不得不退到末座。[10]你被請的時候，就去坐在末座，讓主人來對你說：『朋友，請上座。』這樣，你在賓客面前就有光彩。[11]因為上帝要把自高的人降為卑微，又高舉自甘卑微的人。」

[12] 耶穌又對宴請他的主人說：「你招待午飯或晚餐的時候，不要邀請你的朋友、弟兄、親戚，或是富有的鄰居，恐怕他們要回請你，還了你的人情。[13]你要請客，就請那些貧窮的、殘疾的、跛腳的、失明的；[14]這樣，你就有福了，因為那些人無力報答你。在義人復活的時候，上帝要親自報答你。」

大宴會的比喻

（太22·1—10）

[15] 同席有一個人聽見了這些話，就對耶穌說：「能夠在上帝的國裏享受筵席的人多麼有福啊！」

[16] 耶穌對他說：「有人大開宴會，邀請了許多客人。[17]入席的時候，他差派僕人去向被請的客人說：『請來吧，一切都準備好了！』[18]可是他們開始一個一個地推辭。頭一個說：『我剛買了一塊地皮，不能不去看

the servant, 'I have bought a field and must go and look at it; please accept my apologies.' [19]Another one said, 'I have bought five pairs of oxen and am on my way to try them out; please accept my apologies.' [20]Another one said, 'I have just gotten married, and for that reason I cannot come.' [21]The servant went back and told all this to his master. The master was furious and said to his servant, 'Hurry out to the streets and alleys of the town, and bring back the poor, the crippled, the blind, and the lame.' [22]Soon the servant said, 'Your order has been carried out, sir, but there is room for more.' [23]So the master said to the servant, 'Go out to the country roads and lanes and make people come in, so that my house will be full. [24]I tell you all that none of those who were invited will taste my dinner!' "

The Cost of Being a Disciple
(Matthew 10.37-38)

[25]Once when large crowds of people were going along with Jesus, he turned and said to them, [26]"Those who come to me cannot be my disciples unless they love me more than they love father and mother, wife and children, brothers and sisters, and themselves as well. [27]Those who do not carry their own cross and come after me cannot be my disciples. [28]If one of you is planning to build a tower, you sit down first and figure out what it will cost, to see if you have enough money to finish the job. [29]If you don't, you will not be able to finish the tower after laying the foundation; and all who see what happened will make fun of you. [30]'You began to build but can't finish the job!' they will say. [31]If a king goes out with ten thousand men to fight another king who comes against him with twenty thousand men, he will sit down first and decide if he is strong enough to face that other king. [32]If he isn't, he will send messengers to meet the other king to ask for terms of peace while he is still a long way off. [33]In the same way," concluded Jesus, "none of you can be my disciple unless you give up everything you have.

Worthless Salt
(Matthew 5.13; Mark 9.50)

[34]"Salt is good, but if it loses its saltiness, there is no way to make it salty again. [35]It is no good for the soil or for the manure pile; it is thrown away. Listen, then, if you have ears!"

The Lost Sheep
(Matthew 18.12-14)

15 One day when many tax collectors and other outcasts came to listen to Jesus, [2]the Pharisees and the teachers of the Law started

---

看。請原諒我,我不能來。』[19]另一個說:『我買了五對牛,剛要去試一試。請原諒我,我不能奉陪。』[20]又有一個說:『我才結婚,實在無法分身。』[21]那僕人回去把這情形都報告給主人。這家的主人非常惱怒,就對僕人說:『趕快出去,到城裏的大街小巷,把貧窮的、殘疾的、失明的、跛腳的都帶進來。』[22]不久,僕人來回話說:『主人,你所吩咐的已經辦好了,可是還有許多空位呢!』[23]主人就對僕人說:『到馬路和陋巷裏去,強拉人進來,坐滿我的屋子。』[24]我告訴你們,那些先前所邀請的人絕不能享受我的筵席!』

作門徒的代價
(太10‧37-38)

[25]有許許多多的人跟耶穌一起走。耶穌轉過身來對他們說:[26]「到我這裏來的人要不是愛我勝過愛自己的父母、妻子、兒女、兄弟、姊妹,甚至於他自己,就不能作我的門徒。[27]不願意背起自己的十字架來跟從我的,也不能作我的門徒。[28]你們當中有誰想蓋一座高樓,不先坐下來精打細算一番,看看有沒有完成全部工程的費用?[29]否則,恐怕地基築好以後,樓房無法完成,看見的人都會笑話他,[30]說:『這個人開工建造,卻不能完工!』[31]假使有一個國王領着一支一萬人的隊伍,要去跟另一個擁有兩萬人軍隊的國王打仗,他一定先坐下來估量自己的實力,看看能不能對抗敵軍;[32]如果不能,他就得趁着敵軍還在遠方的時候,派遣使節去跟對方談判和平的條件。[33]同樣,你們無論誰,除非放棄所有的一切,不能作我的門徒。」

無用的鹽
(太5‧13;可9‧50)

[34]「鹽原是好的,但如果失了味,怎能使它再鹹呢?[35]就是把它當土壤或肥料也不適宜,只好丟棄。有耳朵的,都聽吧!」

迷羊的比喻
(太18‧12-14)

15 有一次,好些稅棍和壞人都來聽耶穌講道。[2]法利賽人和經學教師們埋怨說:

grumbling, "This man welcomes outcasts and even eats with them!" [3]So Jesus told them this parable:

[4]"Suppose one of you has a hundred sheep and loses one of them–what do you do? You leave the other ninety-nine sheep in the pasture and go looking for the one that got lost until you find it. [5]When you find it, you are so happy that you put it on your shoulders [6]and carry it back home. Then you call your friends and neighbors together and say to them, 'I am so happy I found my lost sheep. Let us celebrate!' [7]In the same way, I tell you, there will be more joy in heaven over one sinner who repents than over ninety-nine respectable people who do not need to repent.

The Lost Coin

[8]"Or suppose a woman who has ten silver coins loses one of them–what does she do? She lights a lamp, sweeps her house, and looks carefully everywhere until she finds it. [9]When she finds it, she calls her friends and neighbors together, and says to them, 'I am so happy I found the coin I lost. Let us celebrate!' [10]In the same way, I tell you, the angels of God rejoice over one sinner who repents."

The Lost Son

[11]Jesus went on to say, "There was once a man who had two sons. [12]The younger one said to him, 'Father, give me my share of the property now.' So the man divided his property between his two sons. [13]After a few days the younger son sold his part of the property and left home with the money. He went to a country far away, where he wasted his money in reckless living. [14]He spent everything he had. Then a severe famine spread over that country, and he was left without a thing. [15]So he went to work for one of the citizens of that country, who sent him out to his farm to take care of the pigs. [16]He wished he could fill himself with the bean pods the pigs ate, but no one gave him anything to eat. [17]At last he came to his senses and said, 'All my father's hired workers have more than they can eat, and here I am about to starve! [18]I will get up and go to my father and say, 'Father, I have sinned against God and against you. [19]I am no longer fit to be called your son; treat me as one of your hired workers.' [20]So he got up and started back to his father.

"He was still a long way from home when his father saw him; his heart was filled with pity, and he ran, threw his arms around his son, and kissed him. [21]'Father,' the son said, 'I have sinned

「這個人竟接納壞人，並且跟他們一起吃飯！」[3]因此，耶穌給他們講一個比喻：

[4]「假如你們當中有人有一百隻羊，其中的一隻迷失了，怎麼辦呢？他一定把其他的九十九隻留在草場，去找那隻迷失的，直到找着爲止。[5]一旦找着了，他就高興的把羊兒攔在肩膀上，[6]帶回家去，然後邀請朋友鄰居，對他們說：『來跟我一起慶祝吧，我那隻迷失的羊兒已經找着了！』[7]同樣，我告訴你們，一個罪人的悔改，在天上的喜樂要比已經有了九十九個無需悔改的義人所有的喜樂還大呢！」

失錢的比喻

[8]「假如一個女人有十個銀幣，失掉了一個，怎麼辦呢？她一定點起燈來，打掃房子，到處仔細尋找，直到找着爲止。[9]一旦找着了，她就邀請朋友和鄰居來，對她們說：『來跟我一起慶祝吧，我那遺失的銀幣已經找着了！』[10]同樣，我告訴你們，上帝的天使也要爲了一個罪人的悔改而高興。」

仁慈父親的比喻

[11]耶穌繼續說：「某人有兩個兒子。[12]那小兒子對父親說：『爸爸，請你現在就把我應得的產業分給我。』父親就把產業分給兩個兒子。[13]過幾天，小兒子賣掉了分得的產業，帶着錢，離家走了。他到了遙遠的地方，在那裏揮霍無度，過放蕩的生活。[14]當他花盡了所有的一切，那地方發生了嚴重饑荒，他就一貧如洗，[15]只好去投靠當地的一個居民；那人打發他到自己的農場去看豬。[16]他恨不得拿豬吃的豆莢來充飢；可是，沒有人給他任何東西吃。[17]最後，他醒悟過來，說：『我父親那裏有許多雇工，他們糧食充足有餘，我反倒在這裏餓死嗎？[18]我要起來，回到父親那裏去，對他說：爸爸，我得罪了天，也得罪了你。[19]我再也不配作你的兒子；請把我當作你的雇工吧！』[20]於是，他動身回父親那裏去。

「他離家還遠，父親望見了他，就充滿愛憐，奔向前去，緊抱着他，不停地親吻。[21]兒子說：『爸爸，我得罪了天，也得罪了

against God and against you. I am no longer fit to be called your son.' ²²But the father called to his servants. 'Hurry!' he said. 'Bring the best robe and put it on him. Put a ring on his finger and shoes on his feet. ²³Then go and get the prize calf and kill it, and let us celebrate with a feast! ²⁴For this son of mine was dead, but now he is alive; he was lost, but now he has been found.' And so the feasting began.

²⁵"In the meantime the older son was out in the field. On his way back, when he came close to the house, he heard the music and dancing. ²⁶So he called one of the servants and asked him, 'What's going on?' ²⁷'Your brother has come back home,' the servant answered, 'and your father has killed the prize calf, because he got him back safe and sound.' ²⁸The older brother was so angry that he would not go into the house; so his father came out and begged him to come in. ²⁹But he spoke back to his father, 'Look, all these years I have worked for you like a slave, and I have never disobeyed your orders. What have you given me? Not even a goat for me to have a feast with my friends! ³⁰But this son of yours wasted all your property on prostitutes, and when he comes back home, you kill the prize calf for him!' ³¹'My son,' the father answered, 'you are always here with me, and everything I have is yours. ³²But we had to celebrate and be happy, because your brother was dead, but now he is alive; he was lost, but now he has been found.' "

The Shrewd Manager

16 Jesus said to his disciples, "There was once a rich man who had a servant who managed his property. The rich man was told that the manager was wasting his master's money, ²so he called him in and said, 'What is this I hear about you? Turn in a complete account of your handling of my property, because you cannot be my manager any longer.' ³The servant said to himself, 'My master is going to dismiss me from my job. What shall I do? I am not strong enough to dig ditches, and I am ashamed to beg. ⁴Now I know what I will do! Then when my job is gone, I shall have friends who will welcome me in their homes.' ⁵So he called in all the people who were in debt to his master. He asked the first one, 'How much do you owe my master?' ⁶'One hundred barrels of olive oil,' he answered. 'Here is your account,' the manager told him; 'sit down and write fifty.' ⁷Then he asked another one, 'And you–how much do you owe?' 'A thousand bushels of wheat,' he answered. 'Here is your account,' the manager told him; 'write eight hundred.' ⁸As a result the master of this dishonest manager praised him for doing such a shrewd thing; because the

你；我再也不配作你的兒子。』²²可是父親吩咐僕人說：『趕快拿最好的衣服給他穿上，拿戒指給他戴上，拿鞋子替他穿上，²³把那頭小肥牛牽來，宰了，讓我們設宴慶祝！²⁴因為我這個兒子是死而復活、失而復得的。』於是大家歡宴起來。

²⁵「那時候，大兒子正在農場。他回來，離家不遠，聽見音樂和跳舞的聲音。²⁶他叫一個僕人過來，問他怎麼一回事。²⁷僕人回答：『你弟弟回來了，你父親看見他無災無病地回來，把小肥牛宰了。』²⁸大兒子非常生氣，不肯進去；他父親出來勸他。²⁹他卻對父親說：『你看，這些年來，我像奴隸一樣為你工作，沒有違背過你的命令，你給過我甚麼呢？連一頭小山羊讓我跟朋友們熱鬧一番都沒有！³⁰但是你這個兒子，他把你的財產都花在娼妓身上，現在回來，你就為他宰了小肥牛！』³¹父親對他說：『孩子啊，你常跟我在一起；我所有的一切都是你的。³²可是你這個弟弟是死而復活、失而復得的，我們為他設宴慶祝是應該的。』」

機警管家的比喻

16 耶穌對他的門徒說：「某財主有一個管家；有人向他告狀，說這管家浪費主人的財物。²主人就把管家叫來，對他說：『我聽到的是怎麼一回事呢？把你經管的帳簿交出來吧，你不能再擔任管家的職務了。』³那個管家心裏想：『主人要辭退我了，今後我去做甚麼呢？鋤地嗎？沒有力氣；討飯嗎？怕難為情。⁴對了，我曉得怎麼做，好使我在失業的時候有朋友肯接我到他們家裏住。』

⁵「於是他把主人的債戶一一叫了來。他對頭一個說：『你欠我主人多少？』⁶他回答：『一百桶橄欖油。』管家說：『這是你的帳，快坐下來，改寫五十。』⁷他問另一個說：『你呢，你欠多少？』他回答：『一百石麥子。』管家說：『這是你的帳，改寫八十。』

⁸「主人誇獎這個不誠實的管家的機警行

people of this world are much more shrewd in handling their affairs than the people who belong to the light."

9And Jesus went on to say, "And so I tell you: make friends for yourselves with worldly wealth, so that when it gives out, you will be welcomed in the eternal home. 10Whoever is faithful in small matters will be faithful in large ones; whoever is dishonest in small matters will be dishonest in large ones. 11If, then, you have not been faithful in handling worldly wealth, how can you be trusted with true wealth? 12And if you have not been faithful with what belongs to someone else, who will give you what belongs to you?

13"No servant can be the slave of two masters; such a slave will hate one and love the other or will be loyal to one and despise the other. You cannot serve both God and money."

Some Sayings of Jesus

(Matthew 11.12-13; 5.31-32; Mark 10.11-12)

14When the Pharisees heard all this, they made fun of Jesus, because they loved money. 15Jesus said to them, "You are the ones who make yourselves look right in other people's sight, but God knows your hearts. For the things that are considered of great value by people are worth nothing in God's sight.

16"The Law of Moses and the writings of the prophets were in effect up to the time of John the Baptist; since then the Good News about the Kingdom of God is being told, and everyone forces their way in. 17But it is easier for heaven and earth to disappear than for the smallest detail of the Law to be done away with.

18"Any man who divorces his wife and marries another woman commits adultery; and the man who marries a divorced woman commits adultery.

The Rich Man and Lazarus

19"There was once a rich man who dressed in the most expensive clothes and lived in great luxury every day. 20There was also a poor man named Lazarus, covered with sores, who used to be brought to the rich man's door, 21hoping to eat the bits of food that fell from the rich man's table. Even the dogs would come and lick his sores. 22The poor man died and was carried by the angels to sit beside Abraham at the feast in heaven. The rich man died and was buried, 23and in Hades,s where he was in great pain, he looked up and saw Abraham, far away, with Lazarus at his side. 24So he called

s HADES: *The world of the dead.*

為。因為在應付世事方面，俗世的人竟比光明的人更加精明。」

9 耶穌接着又說：「我告訴你們，要用今世的錢財結交朋友，這樣，錢財完了的時候，你可以被接到永久的家鄉去。10一個人在小事上靠得住，在大事上也靠得住；一個人在小事上不誠實，在大事上也不誠實。11如果你們在處理今世的錢財上靠不住，誰又會把那眞實的財富付託你們呢？12如果你們對屬於別人的東西靠不住，誰會把你們自己的東西給你們呢？

13 「沒有僕人能夠伺候兩個主人。他要不是厭惡這個，喜愛那個，就是看重這個，輕看那個。你們不可能同時事上帝的僕人，又作錢財的奴隸。」

其他的教導

（太5．31—32；11．12—13；可10．11—12）

14 那些愛錢的法利賽人聽見這些話，就譏笑耶穌。15耶穌對他們說：「你們在人面前儼然正人君子，但是上帝洞察你們的內心；因為人所看重的，在上帝眼中卻是可憎惡的。

16 「摩西的法律和先知們的書的效用到施洗者約翰為止；從此，上帝國的福音被傳開了，人人都想猛烈地擠進去。17可是，天地消失要比法律的一筆一劃被塗抹還容易呢！

18 「任何人休棄自己的妻子去跟別的女人結合就是犯姦淫；娶了被休棄的女人也是犯姦淫。」

財主和拉撒路

19 「從前有一個財主，每天穿着華麗的衣服，過着窮奢極侈的生活。20同時有一個討飯的，名叫拉撒路，渾身生瘡；他常常被帶到財主家的門口，21希望撿些財主桌子上掉下來的東西充飢；連狗也來舔他的瘡。

22 「後來這窮人死了，天使把他帶到亞伯拉罕身邊。財主也死了，並且埋葬了。23財主在陰間痛苦極了；他抬頭瞧見亞伯拉罕在遙遠的地方，又看見拉撒路在他身邊，24就

out, 'Father Abraham! Take pity on me, and send Lazarus to dip his finger in some water and cool off my tongue, because I am in great pain in this fire!' ²⁵But Abraham said, 'Remember, my son, that in your lifetime you were given all the good things, while Lazarus got all the bad things. But now he is enjoying himself here, while you are in pain. ²⁶Besides all that, there is a deep pit lying between us, so that those who want to cross over from here to you cannot do so, nor can anyone cross over to us from where you are.' ²⁷The rich man said, 'Then I beg you, father Abraham, send Lazarus to my father's house, ²⁸where I have five brothers. Let him go and warn them so that they, at least, will not come to this place of pain.' ²⁹Abraham said, 'Your brothers have Moses and the prophets to warn them; your brothers should listen to what they say.' ³⁰The rich man answered, 'That is not enough, father Abraham! But if someone were to rise from death and go to them, then they would turn from their sins.' ³¹But Abraham said, 'If they will not listen to Moses and the prophets, they will not be convinced even if someone were to rise from death.' "

Sin

(Matthew 18.6-7, 21-22; Mark 9.42)

17 Jesus said to his disciples, "Things that make people fall into sin are bound to happen, but how terrible for the one who makes them happen! ²It would be better for him if a large millstone were tied around his neck and he were thrown into the sea than for him to cause one of these little ones to sin. ³So watch what you do!

"If your brother sins, rebuke him, and if he repents, forgive him. ⁴If he sins against you seven times in one day, and each time he comes to you saying, 'I repent,' you must forgive him."

Faith

⁵The apostles said to the Lord, "Make our faith greater."

⁶The Lord answered, "If you had faith as big as a mustard seed, you could say to this mulberry tree, 'Pull yourself up by the roots and plant yourself in the sea!' and it would obey you.

A Servant's Duty

⁷"Suppose one of you has a servant who is plowing or looking after the sheep. When he comes in from the field, do you tell him to hurry along and eat his meal? ⁸Of course not!

呼叫說：『我的祖宗亞伯拉罕哪，可憐我吧！請打發拉撒路用指尖蘸點水來涼涼我的舌頭吧，因為我在這火燄裏，非常痛苦！』

25 「可是亞伯拉罕說：『孩子啊，你該記得你生前享盡了福，可是拉撒路從來沒有好日子過；現在他在這裏得着安慰，你反而在痛苦中。²⁶而且，在你們和我們之間有深淵隔開，人要從這邊到你們那邊去是不可能的，要從你們那邊到我們這邊來也不可能。』²⁷財主說：『祖宗啊，既然這樣，求你打發拉撒路到我父親家去；²⁸我有五個兄弟，讓他去警告他們，免得他們也到這痛苦的地方來。』

29 「亞伯拉罕說：『你的兄弟有摩西和先知們去警告他們，讓你的兄弟去聽他們吧！』³⁰財主說：『祖宗亞伯拉罕哪，那是不夠的。假如有人從死裏復活，到他們那裏去，他們就會悔改。』³¹可是亞伯拉罕說：『如果他們不聽摩西和先知們的話，即使有人從死裏復活，他們也不會相信的！』」

論罪

（太18‧6-7，21-22；可9‧42）

17 耶穌向他的門徒說：「使人犯罪的事是必然會有的，可是造成這種事的人要遭殃了！²倒不如用大磨石拴在他脖子上，沉到海底去；這樣比讓他使任何一個微不足道的人犯罪還好。³你們總要當心！

「如果你的弟兄犯罪，勸誡他；要是他悔改，饒恕他。⁴如果他在一天裏得罪了你七次，每一次都回頭對你說：『我懊悔了』，你都得原諒他。」

論信

5 使徒們對主說：「請增加我們的信心！」

6 主說：「你們若有像一粒芥菜種子大小的信心，就是對這棵桑樹說：『連根拔起來，去栽在海裏！』它也會聽從你們。」

僕人的責任

7 「假使你們當中某人有一個種田或放羊的僕人，他從農場回來時，你會不會對他說『趕快坐下來吃飯』？⁸當然不會！你會對他

Instead, you say to him, 'Get my supper ready, then put on your apron and wait on me while I eat and drink; after that you may have your meal.' ⁹The servant does not deserve thanks for obeying orders, does he? ¹⁰It is the same with you; when you have done all you have been told to do, say, 'We are ordinary servants; we have only done our duty.' "

Jesus Heals Ten Men

11As Jesus made his way to Jerusalem, he went along the border between Samaria and Galilee. ¹²He was going into a village when he was met by ten men suffering from a dreaded skin disease. They stood at a distance ¹³and shouted, "Jesus! Master! Have pity on us!"

14Jesus saw them and said to them, "Go and let the priests examine you."

On the way they were made clean.ᵗ ¹⁵When one of them saw that he was healed, he came back, praising God in a loud voice. ¹⁶He threw himself to the ground at Jesus' feet and thanked him. The man was a Samaritan. ¹⁷Jesus spoke up, "There were ten who were healed; where are the other nine? ¹⁸Why is this foreigner the only one who came back to give thanks to God?" ¹⁹And Jesus said to him, "Get up and go; your faith has made you well."

The Coming of the Kingdom
(Matthew 24.23-28, 37-41)

20Some Pharisees asked Jesus when the Kingdom of God would come. His answer was, "The Kingdom of God does not come in such a way as to be seen. ²¹No one will say, 'Look, here it is!' or, 'There it is!'; because the Kingdom of God is within you."ᵘ

22Then he said to the disciples, "The time will come when you will wish you could see one of the days of the Son of Man, but you will not see it. ²³There will be those who will say to you, 'Look, over there!' or, 'Look, over here!' But don't go out looking for it. ²⁴As the lightning flashes across the sky and lights it up from one side to the other, so will the Son of Man be in his day. ²⁵But first he must suffer much and be rejected by the people of this day. ²⁶As it was in the time of Noah so shall it be in the days of the Son of Man. ²⁷Everybody kept on eating and drinking, and men and women married, up to the very day Noah went into the boat and the flood came and killed them all. ²⁸It will be

t MADE CLEAN: See 5.12.
u within you; or among you, or will suddenly appear among you.

說：『先替我預備晚飯，繫上圍裙，伺候我，等我吃過了，你才吃。』⁹僕人照着主人的吩咐做事，難道主人還得向他道謝嗎？¹⁰你們也是一樣。當你們做完上帝吩咐你們做的一切事，要說：『我們原是無用的僕人；我們不過盡了本份而已。』」

治好十個痲瘋病人

11耶穌在往耶路撒冷去的旅途中，經過撒馬利亞和加利利中間的地區。¹²他進了一個村莊的時候，有十個痲瘋病人迎着他走過來。他們遠遠地站着，¹³高聲喊說：「耶穌，老師啊，可憐我們吧！」

14耶穌看見了，對他們說：「你們去，讓祭司檢查你們吧！」

他們去的時候已經潔淨了。¹⁵其中有一個人看見自己已經好了，連忙轉回來，大聲頌讚上帝，¹⁶又俯伏在耶穌腳前感謝他。這個人是撒馬利亞人。¹⁷耶穌說：「得到醫治的有十個人，其他的九個在哪裏呢？¹⁸爲甚麼只有這個外族人回來感謝上帝呢？」¹⁹於是耶穌對他說：「起來，去吧！你的信心治好你了。」

上帝主權的實現
（ 太24・23－28，37－41 ）

20有些法利賽人來問耶穌，要知道上帝的主權甚麼時候實現。耶穌回答：「上帝主權的實現並不是眼睛所能看見的。²¹沒有人能說：『看吧，它在這裏！』或『它在那裏！』因為上帝的主權是在你們心裏⑭！」

22接着，他又對門徒說：「日子將到，你們渴望能看見人子當權之日的來臨，卻見不到。²³有人要對你們說：『看吧，在那裏！』『看吧，在這裏！』你們不要出去看，也不要追隨他們。²⁴正像閃電橫掃天空，從天的這邊照射到天的那邊，人子來臨的日子也是這樣。²⁵但是他必須先受許多苦難，被這時代的人棄絕。²⁶正像挪亞的時代，人子來臨的日子也是一樣。²⁷那時代的人照常吃喝嫁娶，一直到了挪亞進方舟那一天，洪水來到，把他們都消滅了。²⁸人子來臨的日子，

⑭「在你們心裏」或譯「在你們當中」或「忽然出現在你們當中」。

as it was in the time of Lot. Everybody kept on eating and drinking, buying and selling, planting and building. ²⁹On the day Lot left Sodom, fire and sulfur rained down from heaven and killed them all. ³⁰That is how it will be on the day the Son of Man is revealed.

³¹"On that day someone who is on the roof of a house must not go down into the house to get any belongings; in the same way anyone who is out in the field must not go back to the house. ³²Remember Lot's wife! ³³Those who try to save their own life will lose it; those who lose their life will save it. ³⁴On that night, I tell you, there will be two people sleeping in the same bed: one will be taken away, the other will be left behind. ³⁵Two women will be grinding meal together: one will be taken away, the other will be left behind."ᵛ

³⁷The disciples asked him, "Where, Lord?"

Jesus answered, "Wherever there is a dead body, the vultures will gather."

The Parable of the Widow and the Judge

18 Then Jesus told his disciples a parable to teach them that they should always pray and never become discouraged. ²"In a certain town there was a judge who neither feared God nor respected people. ³And there was a widow in that same town who kept coming to him and pleading for her rights, saying, 'Help me against my opponent!' ⁴For a long time the judge refused to act, but at last he said to himself, 'Even though I don't fear God or respect people, ⁵yet because of all the trouble this widow is giving me, I will see to it that she gets her rights. If I don't, she will keep on coming and finally wear me out!' "

⁶And the Lord continued, "Listen to what that corrupt judge said. ⁷Now, will God not judge in favor of his own people who cry to him day and night for help? Will he be slow to help them? ⁸I tell you, he will judge in their favor and do it quickly. But will the Son of Man find faith on earth when he comes?"

The Parable of the Pharisee and the Tax Collector

⁹Jesus also told this parable to people who were sure of their own goodness and despised everybody else. ¹⁰"Once there were two men who went up to the Temple to pray: one was a

---

ᵛ *Some manuscripts add verse 36:* Two men will be working in a field: one will be taken away, the other will be left behind *(see Mt 24.40).*

又像羅得的時代;那時代的人吃喝如常,買賣如常,也耕種也建造。²⁹到羅得離開所多瑪的那一天,火和硫磺從天上降下來,把他們都消滅了。³⁰人子顯現的那一天也會這樣。

³¹「那一天,在屋頂上的,不要下來到屋子裏拿他的東西;同樣,在田野工作的,也不要回家。³²要記住羅得妻子的遭遇!³³那想保全自己生命的,要喪失生命;那失掉生命的,要保存生命。³⁴我告訴你們,那天夜裏,兩個人睡在一張牀上,一個被帶走,一個留下;³⁵兩個女人一起推磨,一個被帶走,一個留下。⑮

³⁷門徒問說:「主啊,這些事會在哪裏發生呢?」

耶穌回答說:「屍首在哪裏,禿鷹也會聚在那裏。」

寡婦和法官的比喻

18 耶穌向門徒們講一個比喻,要他們常常禱告,不可灰心。²他說:「某城有一個法官,他既不敬畏上帝,也不尊重人。³那城裏有一個寡婦常常去見他,請求他主持公道,制裁她的冤家。⁴這個法官一直拖延,但後來心裏想:我雖然不敬畏上帝,也不尊重人,⁵可是這個寡婦不斷地煩擾我,不如爲她伸冤,免得她經常上門,糾纏不休。」

⁶主接著說:「你們聽聽那不義的法官所說的話吧!⁷難道上帝不會替那些日夜向他求援的子民伸冤嗎?他會延遲援助他們嗎?⁸我告訴你們,他一定盡快爲他們伸冤。可是,人子來臨的時候,他能在世上找到這樣的信心嗎?」

法利賽人和收稅人的比喻

⁹耶穌又講另一個比喻,是針對那些自以爲義而輕視別人的人說的。他說:¹⁰「有兩個人到聖殿裏禱告:一個是法利賽人,一個

---

⑮有些古卷加36節「兩個人在田裏做工,一個被帶走,一個留下。」

Pharisee, the other a tax collector. [11]The Pharisee stood apart by himself and prayed,[w] 'I thank you, God, that I am not greedy, dishonest, or an adulterer, like everybody else. I thank you that I am not like that tax collector over there. [12]I fast two days a week, and I give you one tenth of all my income.' [13]But the tax collector stood at a distance and would not even raise his face to heaven, but beat on his breast and said, 'God, have pity on me, a sinner!' [14]I tell you," said Jesus, "the tax collector, and not the Pharisee, was in the right with God when he went home. For those who make themselves great will be humbled, and those who humble themselves will be made great."

Jesus Blesses Little Children
(Matthew 19.13-15; Mark 10.13-16)

[15]Some people brought their babies to Jesus for him to place his hands on them. The disciples saw them and scolded them for doing so, [16]but Jesus called the children to him and said, "Let the children come to me and do not stop them, because the Kingdom of God belongs to such as these. [17]Remember this! Whoever does not receive the Kingdom of God like a child will never enter it."

The Rich Man
(Matthew 19.16-30; Mark 10.17-31)

[18]A Jewish leader asked Jesus, "Good Teacher, what must I do to receive eternal life?"

[19]"Why do you call me good?" Jesus asked him. "No one is good except God alone. [20]You know the commandments: 'Do not commit adultery; do not commit murder; do not steal; do not accuse anyone falsely; respect your father and your mother.' "

[21]The man replied, "Ever since I was young, I have obeyed all these commandments."

[22]When Jesus heard this, he said to him, "There is still one more thing you need to do. Sell all you have and give the money to the poor, and you will have riches in heaven; then come and follow me." [23]But when the man heard this, he became very sad, because he was very rich.

[24]Jesus saw that he was sad and said, "How hard it is for rich people to enter the Kingdom of God! [25]It is much harder for a rich person to enter the Kingdom of God than for a camel to go through the eye of a needle."

w stood apart by himself and prayed; *some manuscripts have* stood up and prayed to himself.

是收稅的人。[11]那個法利賽人昂然站立,禱告說[⑩]:『上帝啊,我感謝你,因爲我不像別人那樣貪婪、不義、淫亂,更不像那個稅棍。[12]我每星期禁食兩次,又奉獻全部收入的十分之一。』[13]但是那個收稅的人遠遠地站着,連抬頭望天都不敢,只捶着胸膛說:『上帝啊,可憐我這個罪人!』[14]我告訴你們,這兩個人回去的時候,在上帝眼中的義人是那個收稅的人,而不是那個法利賽人。因爲上帝要把那自高的人降爲卑微,卻高舉自甘卑微的人。」

耶穌祝福小孩子
(太19‧13－15;可10‧13－16)

[15]有人帶着他們的嬰兒來見耶穌,要讓耶穌爲他們按手。門徒看見了,就責備他們。[16]可是耶穌叫孩子們到他跟前來,說:「讓小孩子到我這裏來,不要阻止他們,因爲上帝國的子民正是像他們這樣的人。[17]你們要記住:凡不像小孩子一樣接受上帝主權的人,絕不能成爲他的子民。」

財主的難題
(太19‧16－30;可10‧17－31)

[18]有一個猶太人的領袖來請教耶穌說:「良善的老師,我該做甚麼才能夠得到永恆的生命呢?」

[19]耶穌問他:「你爲甚麼稱我爲良善的呢?除上帝一位以外,再也沒有良善的。[20]你一定曉得誡命所規定的:『不可姦淫;不可殺人;不可偷竊;不可作假證;要孝敬父母。』」

[21]那個人回答:「這一切誡命我從小都遵守了。」

[22]耶穌聽見這話,再對他說:「你還缺少一件。去賣掉你所有的產業,把錢捐給窮人,你就會有財富積存在天上;然後來跟從我。」[23]那個人一聽見這話,就垂頭喪氣,因爲他很富有。

[24]耶穌看着他,就說:「有錢人要成爲上帝國的子民多麼難啊![25]有錢人要成爲上帝國的子民比駱駝穿過針眼還要難!」

⑩「昂然站立,禱告說」另有些古卷作「站着,自言自語地禱告說」。

26The people who heard him asked, "Who, then, can be saved?"

27Jesus answered, "What is humanly impossible is possible for God."

28Then Peter said, "Look! We have left our homes to follow you."

29"Yes," Jesus said to them, "and I assure you that anyone who leaves home or wife or brothers or parents or children for the sake of the Kingdom of God 30will receive much more in this present age and eternal life in the age to come."

Jesus Speaks a Third Time about His Death
(Matthew 20.17-19; Mark 10.32-34)

31Jesus took the twelve disciples aside and said to them, "Listen! We are going to Jerusalem where everything the prophets wrote about the Son of Man will come true. 32He will be handed over to the Gentiles, who will make fun of him, insult him, and spit on him. 33They will whip him and kill him, but three days later he will rise to life."

34But the disciples did not understand any of these things; the meaning of the words was hidden from them, and they did not know what Jesus was talking about.

Jesus Heals a Blind Beggar
(Matthew 20.29-34; Mark 10.46-52)

35As Jesus was coming near Jericho, there was a blind man sitting by the road, begging. 36When he heard the crowd passing by, he asked, "What is this?"

37"Jesus of Nazareth is passing by," they told him.

38He cried out, "Jesus! Son of David! Have mercy on me!"

39The people in front scolded him and told him to be quiet. But he shouted even more loudly, "Son of David! Have mercy on me!"

40So Jesus stopped and ordered the blind man to be brought to him. When he came near, Jesus asked him, 41"What do you want me to do for you?"

"Sir," he answered, "I want to see again."

42Jesus said to him, "Then see! Your faith has made you well."

43At once he was able to see, and he followed Jesus, giving thanks to God. When the crowd saw it, they all praised God.

26 聽見這話的人就問:「這樣說來,誰能得救呢?」

27 耶穌說:「人所不能的,上帝都能。」

28 這時候,彼得說:「你看,我們已經撇下我們的家來跟從你了。」

29 耶穌說:「是的,我實在告訴你們,凡是為上帝的國而撇下自己的房屋、妻子、兄弟、父母,或兒女的,30一定要在今世得到更多,並且在來世享受永恆的生命。」

耶穌第三次預言自己的死
(太20‧17—19;可10‧32—34)

31 耶穌把十二使徒帶到一邊,對他們說:「我們現在上耶路撒冷去;先知所記述關於人子的每一件事都要實現。32他將被交在外邦人的手裏;他們要戲弄他,侮辱他,向他吐口水,33又要鞭打他,殺害他,但第二天,他將復活。」

34 門徒對這些事一樣也不明白,對耶穌所說的話茫然無知,因為那些話的意思是隱藏着的。

耶穌治好失明的乞丐
(太20‧29—34;可10‧46—52)

35 耶穌來到靠近耶利哥的地方,有一個盲人坐在路旁討飯。36他聽見羣衆經過,就查問是甚麼事。

37 有人告訴他:「拿撒勒的耶穌正經過這裏。」

38 他就呼喊:「大衛之子耶穌啊,可憐我吧!」

39 在他前頭走的人責備他,叫他不要作聲。他卻更大聲地喊叫:「大衛之子啊,可憐我吧!」

40 於是耶穌站住,吩咐把盲人帶到他面前來。他近前的時候,耶穌問他:41「你要我為你做甚麼?」

他回答:「主啊,我要能看見!」

42 耶穌對他說:「你就看見吧!你的信心治好你了。」

43 盲人立刻能看見,就跟隨了耶穌,一路頌讚上帝。羣衆看見這事,也都頌讚上帝。

Jesus and Zacchaeus

19 Jesus went on into Jericho and was passing through. ²There was a chief tax collector there named Zacchaeus, who was rich. ³He was trying to see who Jesus was, but he was a little man and could not see Jesus because of the crowd. ⁴So he ran ahead of the crowd and climbed a sycamore tree to see Jesus, who was going to pass that way. ⁵When Jesus came to that place, he looked up and said to Zacchaeus, "Hurry down, Zacchaeus, because I must stay in your house today."

6Zacchaeus hurried down and welcomed him with great joy. 7All the people who saw it started grumbling, "This man has gone as a guest to the home of a sinner!"

8Zacchaeus stood up and said to the Lord, "Listen, sir! I will give half my belongings to the poor, and if I have cheated anyone, I will pay back four times as much."

9Jesus said to him, "Salvation has come to this house today, for this man, also, is a descendant of Abraham. 10The Son of Man came to seek and to save the lost."

The Parable of the Gold Coins
(Matthew 25.14-30)

11While the people were listening to this, Jesus continued and told them a parable. He was now almost at Jerusalem, and they supposed that the Kingdom of God was just about to appear. 12So he said, "There was once a man of high rank who was going to a country far away to be made king, after which he planned to come back home. 13Before he left, he called his ten servants and gave them each a gold coin and told them, 'See what you can earn with this while I am gone.' 14Now, his own people hated him, and so they sent messengers after him to say, 'We don't want this man to be our king.'

15"The man was made king and came back. At once he ordered his servants to appear before him, in order to find out how much they had earned. 16The first one came and said, 'Sir, I have earned ten gold coins with the one you gave me.' 17'Well done,' he said; 'you are a good servant! Since you were faithful in small matters, I will put you in charge of ten cities.' 18The second servant came and said, 'Sir, I have earned five gold coins with the one you gave me.' 19To this one he said, 'You will be in charge of five cities.' 20Another servant came and said, 'Sir, here is your gold coin; I kept it hidden in a handkerchief. 21I was afraid of you, because you are a hard man. You take what is not yours and reap what you did not plant.' 22He said to him, 'You bad servant! I will use

耶穌和撒該

19 耶穌進耶利哥城，正要從那城經過。²當地有一個稅務長，名叫撒該，是個很有錢的人。³撒該很想看看耶穌是怎樣的一個人，可是他身材矮小，在人羣中無法看到耶穌。⁴於是他跑在大家前頭，爬上一棵桑樹，要看看耶穌，因為耶穌就要從這條路經過。⁵耶穌走到那地方，抬頭看撒該，對他說：「撒該，快下來！今天我必須住在你家裏。」

6 撒該急忙下來，非常高興地接待耶穌。7大家看見都埋怨說：「這個人居然到罪人家裏作客！」

8 撒該站起來對主說：「主啊，我要把我財產的一半分給窮人；如果我欺詐過誰，我就還他四倍。」

9 耶穌對他說：「今天救恩來到這一家了，因為這個人同樣是亞伯拉罕的子孫。10人子來是要尋找和拯救迷失的人。」

僕人和金幣的比喻
（太25．14－30）

11 大家正在聽這話，耶穌又告訴他們一個比喻。這時候，耶穌已經快到耶路撒冷，他們以為上帝的主權就要實現。12耶穌說：「有一個貴族到遠方去，要被册封為王，然後回來。13動身以前，他把十個僕人召來，每人給了一個金幣，說：『我不在的時候，你們拿這錢去做生意，看看能賺多少。』14他本國的人一向恨他，打發代表隨後去說：『我們不要這個人作我們的王。』

15 「那貴族被册封為王回來以後，立刻命令那些領過金幣的僕人到他面前來，要知道他們每人做生意賺了多少。16頭一個上來說：『主人，我用你給的那個金幣賺了十個金幣。』17主人說：『很好！你是個好僕人；你既然在小事上可靠，我要委派你管理十座城。』18第二個僕人上來說：『主人，我用你給的那個金幣賺了五個金幣。』19主人對他說：『你也要管五座城。』20又有一個僕人上來說：『主人，你的金幣在這裏；我用手帕把它包起來。21我一向怕你，因為你是個嚴厲的人。沒有存放的，你還要提取；沒有栽種的，你還要收割。』22主人對他說：『你這

your own words to condemn you! You know that I am a hard man, taking what is not mine and reaping what I have not planted. 23Well, then, why didn't you put my money in the bank? Then I would have received it back with interest when I returned.' 24Then he said to those who were standing there, 'Take the gold coin away from him and give it to the servant who has ten coins.' 25But they said to him, 'Sir, he already has ten coins!' 26'I tell you,' he replied, 'that to those who have something, even more will be given; but those who have nothing, even the little that they have will be taken away from them. 27Now, as for those enemies of mine who did not want me to be their king, bring them here and kill them in my presence!' "

The Triumphant Approach to Jerusalem
(Matthew 21.1-11; Mark 11.1-11; John 12.12-19)

28After Jesus said this, he went on in front of them toward Jerusalem. 29As he came near Bethphage and Bethany at the Mount of Olives, he sent two disciples ahead 30with these instructions: "Go to the village there ahead of you; as you go in, you will find a colt tied up that has never been ridden. Untie it and bring it here. 31If someone asks you why you are untying it, tell him that the Master* needs it."

32They went on their way and found everything just as Jesus had told them. 33As they were untying the colt, its owners said to them, "Why are you untying it?"

34"The Master needs it," they answered, 35and they took the colt to Jesus. Then they threw their cloaks over the animal and helped Jesus get on. 36As he rode on, people spread their cloaks on the road.

37When he came near Jerusalem, at the place where the road went down the Mount of Olives, the large crowd of his disciples began to thank God and praise him in loud voices for all the great things that they had seen: 38"God bless the king who comes in the name of the Lord! Peace in heaven and glory to God!"

39Then some of the Pharisees in the crowd spoke to Jesus. "Teacher," they said, "command your disciples to be quiet!"

40Jesus answered, "I tell you that if they keep quiet, the stones themselves will start shouting."

個壞僕人,我要用你自己的話定你的罪!既然你知道我是一個嚴厲的人,提取沒有存放的,收割沒有栽種的,23那麼,你為甚麼不把我的錢存入銀行,讓我回來的時候,可以連本帶利收回呢?』24於是他向侍立在左右的人說:『把他的金幣拿過來,給那個有十個金幣的僕人。』25他們對他說:『主人,他已經有十個金幣了。』26主人說:『我告訴你們,那已經有的,要給他更多;那沒有的,連他所有的也要奪走。27至於不要我作他們的王的那些敵人,把他們帶來,在我面前殺掉吧!』」

光榮進耶路撒冷
(太21.1-11;可11.1-11;約12.12-19)

28 說完這些話,耶穌走在前頭,上耶路撒冷去。29快到伯法其和伯大尼、向着橄欖山去的時候,耶穌打發兩個門徒先走,30吩咐他們說:「你們到前面的村子去,進去的時候,會看見一匹還沒有人騎過的小驢拴在那裏。你們把牠解開,牽到這裏來。31如果有人問你們為甚麼解開小驢,你們就說:『主⑰要用牠。』」

32 他們去了,所遇見的正和耶穌所告訴他們的一樣。33當他們在解開小驢的時候,驢的主人問他們:「你們為甚麼解開小驢呢?」

34 他們回答:「主要用牠。」35然後他們把小驢牽到耶穌跟前,把自己的衣服搭在驢背上,扶着耶穌騎上去。36耶穌前進的時候,大家拿自己的衣服鋪在路上。

37 當他靠近耶路撒冷、到橄欖山下坡那地方時,眾門徒因所看見的這一切奇蹟就都感謝上帝,大聲歡呼:38「願上帝賜福給奉主名來的君王!天上有和平,榮耀歸於至高上帝!」

39 人羣中有幾個法利賽人對耶穌說:「老師,命令你的門徒安靜吧!」

40 耶穌回答:「我告訴你們,他們要是不作聲,這些石頭也會呼喊起來。」

---

x the Master; *or* its owner.

⑰「主」或譯「牠的主人」。

Jesus Weeps over Jerusalem

41He came closer to the city, and when he saw it, he wept over it, 42saying, "If you only knew today what is needed for peace! But now you cannot see it! 43The time will come when your enemies will surround you with barricades, blockade you, and close in on you from every side. 44They will completely destroy you and the people within your walls; not a single stone will they leave in its place, because you did not recognize the time when God came to save you!"

Jesus Goes to the Temple

(Matthew 21.12-17; Mark 11.15-19; John 2.13-22)

45Then Jesus went into the Temple and began to drive out the merchants, 46saying to them, "It is written in the Scriptures that God said, 'My Temple will be a house of prayer.' But you have turned it into a hideout for thieves!"

47Every day Jesus taught in the Temple. The chief priests, the teachers of the Law, and the leaders of the people wanted to kill him, 48but they could not find a way to do it, because all the people kept listening to him, not wanting to miss a single word.

The Question about Jesus' Authority

(Matthew 21.23-27; Mark 11.27-33)

20One day when Jesus was in the Temple teaching the people and preaching the Good News, the chief priests and the teachers of the Law, together with the elders, came 2and said to him, "Tell us, what right do you have to do these things? Who gave you such right?"

3Jesus answered them, "Now let me ask you a question. Tell me, 4did John's right to baptize come from God or from human beings?"

5They started to argue among themselves, "What shall we say? If we say, 'From God,' he will say, 'Why, then, did you not believe John?' 6But if we say, 'From human beings,' this whole crowd here will stone us, because they are convinced that John was a prophet." 7So they answered, "We don't know where it came from."

8And Jesus said to them, "Neither will I tell you, then, by what right I do these things."

The Parable of the Tenants in the Vineyard

(Matthew 21.33-46; Mark 12.1-12)

9Then Jesus told the people this parable: "There was once a man who planted a vineyard, rented it out to tenants, and then left

爲耶路撒冷哀哭

41 耶穌快到耶路撒冷的時候，看見那城，就爲它哀哭，42說：「但願你今日知道那有關你和平的事，可是你現在那樣的盲目。43日子將到，那時候你的仇敵要造土壘包圍你，從四面困住你。44他們要徹底消滅你和你城牆裏面的人民，不留一塊石頭在另一塊石頭上面，因爲你沒有認出上帝拯救的時機。」

潔淨聖殿

（太21·12-17；可11·15-19；約2·13-22）

45 耶穌一進聖殿，就趕出做買賣的人，46對他們說：「聖經上記着上帝的話說：『我的聖殿要作禱告的殿』，你們卻把它變成賊窩了！」

47 耶穌每天在聖殿裏教導人。祭司長、經學教師，和民間的領袖要殺害他，48只是不知道怎樣下手；因爲人民都喜歡聽他，注意他所說的每一句話。

耶穌的權柄

（太21·23-27；可11·27-33）

20 有一天，耶穌在聖殿裏教導人，宣講福音。有祭司長、經學教師，和長老來見他，2問他：「你憑着甚麼權柄做這些事情？是誰給你這權柄？請告訴我們！」

3 耶穌回答他們：「讓我先問你們一句話，告訴我，4約翰施洗的權是從上帝還是從人那裏來的呢？」

5 他們開始爭辯起來，說：「我們該怎樣回答呢？如果我們說『從上帝那裏來的』，他會說：『那麼，你們爲甚麼不相信約翰呢？』6如果我們說『從人那裏來的』，羣眾會拿石頭打我們，因爲他們都相信約翰是個先知。」7於是他們回答：「我們不知道是從甚麼地方來的。」

8 耶穌就對他們說：「那麼，我也不告訴你們，我憑着甚麼權柄做這些事。」

壞佃戶的比喻

（太21·33-46；可12·1-12）

9 接着，耶穌向他們講這個比喻：「有一個人開墾了一個葡萄園，把它租給佃戶，自

home for a long time. 10When the time came to gather the grapes, he sent a slave to the tenants to receive from them his share of the harvest. But the tenants beat the slave and sent him back without a thing. 11So he sent another slave; but the tenants beat him also, treated him shamefully, and sent him back without a thing. 12Then he sent a third slave; the tenants wounded him, too, and threw him out. 13Then the owner of the vineyard said, 'What shall I do? I will send my own dear son; surely they will respect him!' 14But when the tenants saw him, they said to one another, 'This is the owner's son. Let's kill him, and his property will be ours!' 15So they threw him out of the vineyard and killed him.

"What, then, will the owner of the vineyard do to the tenants?" Jesus asked. 16"He will come and kill those men, and turn the vineyard over to other tenants."

When the people heard this, they said, "Surely not!"

17Jesus looked at them and asked, "What, then, does this scripture mean?

'The stone which the builders rejected
      as worthless
      turned out to be the most important of all.'
18Everyone who falls on that stone will be cut to pieces; and if that stone falls on someone, that person will be crushed to dust."

The Question about Paying Taxes
(Matthew 22.15-22; Mark 12.13-17)

19The teachers of the Law and the chief priests tried to arrest Jesus on the spot, because they knew that he had told this parable against them; but they were afraid of the people. 20So they looked for an opportunity. They bribed some men to pretend they were sincere, and they sent them to trap Jesus with questions, so that they could hand him over to the authority and power of the Roman Governor. 21These spies said to Jesus, "Teacher, we know that what you say and teach is right. We know that you pay no attention to anyone's status, but teach the truth about God's will for people. 22Tell us, is it against our Law for us to pay taxes to the Roman Emperor, or not?"

23But Jesus saw through their trick and said to them, 24"Show me a silver coin. Whose face and name are these on it?"

"The Emperor's," they answered.

25So Jesus said, "Well, then, pay to the Emperor what belongs to the Emperor, and pay to God what belongs to God."

26There before the people they could not

己遠行，在外住了一段時間。10收葡萄的季節到了，他打發一個奴僕去向佃戶收他應得的分額。可是他們把那奴僕毆打一頓，叫他空手回去。11園主再派另一個奴僕去；他們照樣毆打他，侮辱他，又叫他空手回去。12第三次園主又派一個奴僕去；佃戶又打傷他，把他趕出園外。13葡萄園主說：『我該怎麼辦呢？我要差派我所疼愛的兒子去，也許他們會尊敬他。』14可是佃戶一看見園主的兒子，彼此說：『這個人是園主的繼承人；我們殺掉他，他的產業就歸我們了！』15因此，他們把他推到葡萄園外去，殺了。

「這樣，葡萄園的主人要怎樣對付那些佃戶呢？16他一定要來殺滅他們，把葡萄園轉租給別人。」

羣眾聽了這話，都說：「絕不可以有這樣的事！」

17耶穌注目看他們，問說：「聖經上說：
泥水匠所丟棄的這塊石頭
已成為最重要的基石。
這話是甚麼意思呢？18誰跌在那塊石頭上，誰就粉身碎骨；那塊石頭掉在誰的身上，也要把誰砸爛。」

納稅給凱撒的問題
（太22.15—22；可12.13—17）

19經學教師和祭司長知道耶穌的比喻是指着他們說的，就想當場逮捕耶穌；但是又怕羣眾，20只好再等機會。他們收買了一些人，假裝善意，向耶穌提出問題，想抓住他的話柄，好把他送交給羅馬總督懲辦。21這些探子對耶穌說：「老師，我們知道你所講所教的都合情合理，也曉得你不看情面，總是忠實地把上帝的道教導人。22請告訴我們，向羅馬皇帝凱撒納稅是不是違背我們的法律呢？」

23耶穌看穿了他們的詭計，對他們說：24「拿一個銀幣給我看！這上面的像和名號是誰的？」

他們回答：「是凱撒的。」

25耶穌對他們說：「那麼，把凱撒的東西給凱撒，把上帝的東西給上帝。」

26他們無法當着民眾從耶穌所說的話抓到

catch him in a thing, so they kept quiet, amazed at his answer.

The Question about Rising from Death
(Matthew 22.23-33; Mark 12.18-27)

27Then some Sadducees, who say that people will not rise from death, came to Jesus and said, 28"Teacher, Moses wrote this law for us: 'If a man dies and leaves a wife but no children, that man's brother must marry the widow so that they can have children who will be considered the dead man's children.' 29Once there were seven brothers; the oldest got married and died without having children. 30Then the second one married the woman, 31and then the third. The same thing happened to all seven–they died without having children. 32Last of all, the woman died. 33Now, on the day when the dead rise to life, whose wife will she be? All seven of them had married her."

34Jesus answered them, "The men and women of this age marry, 35but the men and women who are worthy to rise from death and live in the age to come will not then marry. 36They will be like angels and cannot die. They are the children of God, because they have risen from death. 37And Moses clearly proves that the dead are raised to life. In the passage about the burning bush he speaks of the Lord as 'the God of Abraham, the God of Isaac, and the God of Jacob.' 38He is the God of the living, not of the dead, for to him all are alive."

39Some of the teachers of the Law spoke up, "A good answer, Teacher!" 40For they did not dare ask him any more questions.

The Question about the Messiah
(Matthew 22.41-46; Mark 12.35-37)

41Jesus asked them, "How can it be said that the Messiah will be the descendant of David? 42For David himself says in the book of Psalms,
'The Lord said to my Lord:
Sit here at my right side
43 until I put your enemies as a footstool under your feet.'
44David called him 'Lord'; how, then, can the Messiah be David's descendant?"

Jesus Warns against the Teachers of the Law
(Matthew 23.1-36; Mark 12.38-40)

45As all the people listened to him, Jesus said to his disciples, 46"Be on your guard against the

甚麼把柄；耶穌的對答使他們十分驚訝，就都閉口無言。

復活的問題
（太22‧23－33；可12‧18－27）

27 有些否認有復活這回事的撒都該人來見耶穌，28問他：「老師，摩西爲我們立法：『如果一個人死了，留下妻子，但是沒有孩子，他的弟弟必須娶寡嫂爲妻，替哥哥傳宗接代。』29從前有兄弟七人：老大結了婚，沒有孩子就死了。30老二就娶了寡嫂，31以後老三也娶了她，一直到老七都娶過她，也都沒有孩子，就死了。32最後那女人也死了。33請問在復活的日子，她要算是哪一個人的妻子呢？因爲兄弟七個人都娶過她。」

34 耶穌回答他們說：「今世的男女有娶有嫁；35但是那些配得從死裏復活，並且活在來世的人，也不娶也不嫁。36他們和天使一樣是不會死的。他們是上帝的兒女，因爲他們從死裏復活。37摩西已經證實有死人復活這回事，他在荊棘燃燒的記載上說了：主是『亞伯拉罕的上帝，以撒的上帝，雅各的上帝。』38這意思是說上帝是活人的上帝，不是死人的上帝。因爲在上帝眼中，人都是活着的。」

39 有些經學教師說：「老師，你說得好！」40從此，他們再也不敢向耶穌提出問題。

有關基督的問題
（太22‧41－46；可12‧35－37）

41 可是耶穌對他們說：「人怎麼能說基督是大衛的子孫呢？42大衛在詩篇上自己說過：
主對我主說：
你坐在我的右邊，
43 等我使你的仇敵屈服在你腳下。
44大衛旣然稱他爲『主』，基督又怎麼會是大衛的子孫呢？」

耶穌譴責經學教師
（太23‧1－36；可12‧38－40）

45 羣衆傾聽着的時候，耶穌對他的門徒說：46「要防備那些經學教師。他們喜歡穿

teachers of the Law, who like to walk around in their long robes and love to be greeted with respect in the marketplace; who choose the reserved seats in the synagogues and the best places at feasts; [47]who take advantage of widows and rob them of their homes, and then make a show of saying long prayers! Their punishment will be all the worse!"

The Widow's Offering
(Mark 12.41-44)

21 Jesus looked around and saw rich people dropping their gifts in the Temple treasury, [2]and he also saw a very poor widow dropping in two little copper coins. [3]He said, "I tell you that this poor widow put in more than all the others. [4]For the others offered their gifts from what they had to spare of their riches; but she, poor as she is, gave all she had to live on."

Jesus Speaks of the Destruction of the Temple
(Matthew 24.1-2; Mark 13.1-2)

[5]Some of the disciples were talking about the Temple, how beautiful it looked with its fine stones and the gifts offered to God. Jesus said, [6]"All this you see–the time will come when not a single stone here will be left in its place; every one will be thrown down."

Troubles and Persecutions
(Matthew 24.3-14; Mark 13.3-13)

[7]"Teacher," they asked, "when will this be? And what will happen in order to show that the time has come for it to take place?"

[8]Jesus said, "Watch out; don't be fooled. Many men, claiming to speak for me, will come and say, 'I am he!' and, 'The time has come!' But don't follow them. [9]Don't be afraid when you hear of wars and revolutions; such things must happen first, but they do not mean that the end is near."

[10]He went on to say, "Countries will fight each other; kingdoms will attack one another. [11]There will be terrible earthquakes, famines, and plagues everywhere; there will be strange and terrifying things coming from the sky. [12]Before all these things take place, however, you will be arrested and persecuted; you will be handed over to be tried in synagogues and be put in prison; you will be brought before kings and rulers for my sake. [13]This will be your chance to tell the Good News. [14]Make up your minds ahead of time not to worry about how you will defend yourselves, [15]because I will give

着長袍招搖過市，喜歡人家在公共場所向他們致敬問安，又愛會堂裏的特別座位和宴會上的首座。[47]他們吞沒了寡婦的家產，然後表演長篇的禱告。他們一定受到更嚴厲的懲罰！」

寡婦的奉獻
（可12‧41－44）

21 耶穌抬頭觀看，看見一些有錢人把他們的捐款投進聖殿的奉獻箱裏。[2]他又看見一個窮寡婦投了兩個小銅板。[3]於是他說：「我實在告訴你們，這個窮寡婦所奉獻的比其他的人都多。[4]因為別人是從他們的財富中捐出有餘的；可是她已經很窮，卻把自己全部的生活費用都獻上了。」

預言聖殿的毀滅
（太24‧1－2；可13‧1－2）

[5]有人在談論聖殿，說它是怎樣用精美的石頭和還願的禮物裝飾成的。耶穌說：[6]「你們看見這一切嗎？日子將到，那時候，沒有一塊石頭會留在另一塊上面，每一塊都要被拆下來。」

災難和迫害
（太24‧3－14；可13‧3－13）

[7]他們就問：「老師，幾時會發生這事呢？這一切發生的時候會有甚麼預兆呢？」

[8]耶穌說：「你們要當心，不要受愚弄；因為有許多人要假冒我的名來，說：『我就是基督！』又說：『時機已經成熟了！』可是不要跟從他們。[9]當你們聽見戰爭和叛亂的消息時，不用害怕。這些事必然會先發生；但是這並不是說歷史的終局快到了。」

[10]耶穌接着說：「一個民族要跟另一個民族爭戰，一個國家要攻打另一個國家。[11]到處會有嚴重的地震、饑荒，和瘟疫，又有可怕的奇蹟異象在空中出現。[12]可是在這些事發生以前，你們要被逮捕並遭受迫害；人要把你們交給會堂審問，又使你們坐牢。為我的緣故，你們要被帶到君王和統治者面前。[13]這就是你們為福音作見證的機會了。[14]所以，你們要拿定主意，不必事先考慮怎樣為自己申訴；[15]因為我要賜給你們口才和智

you such words and wisdom that none of your enemies will be able to refute or contradict what you say. [16]You will be handed over by your parents, your brothers, your relatives, and your friends; and some of you will be put to death. [17]Everyone will hate you because of me. [18]But not a single hair from your heads will be lost. [19]Stand firm, and you will save yourselves.

Jesus Speaks of the Destruction of Jerusalem
(Matthew 24.15-21; Mark 13.14-19)

[20]"When you see Jerusalem surrounded by armies, then you will know that it will soon be destroyed. [21]Then those who are in Judea must run away to the hills; those who are in the city must leave, and those who are out in the country must not go into the city. [22]For those will be 'The Days of Punishment,' to make come true all that the Scriptures say. [23]How terrible it will be in those days for women who are pregnant and for mothers with little babies! Terrible distress will come upon this land, and God's punishment will fall on this people. [24]Some will be killed by the sword, and others will be taken as prisoners to all countries; and the heathen will trample over Jerusalem until their time is up.

The Coming of the Son of Man
(Matthew 24.29-31; Mark 13.24-27)

[25]"There will be strange things happening to the sun, the moon, and the stars. On earth whole countries will be in despair, afraid of the roar of the sea and the raging tides. [26]People will faint from fear as they wait for what is coming over the whole earth, for the powers in space will be driven from their courses. [27]Then the Son of Man will appear, coming in a cloud with great power and glory. [28]When these things begin to happen, stand up and raise your heads, because your salvation is near."

The Lesson of the Fig Tree
(Matthew 24.32-35; Mark 13.28-31)

[29]Then Jesus told them this parable: "Think of the fig tree and all the other trees. [30]When you see their leaves beginning to appear, you know that summer is near. [31]In the same way, when you see these things happening, you will know that the Kingdom of God is about to come.

[32]"Remember that all these things will take place before the people now living have all died. [33]Heaven and earth will pass away, but my words will never pass away.

慧，使你們的敵人對你們所說的話無法反對辯駁。[16]甚至有你們的父母、兄弟、親戚、朋友也要出賣你們；你們當中有些人且要被他們治死。[17]因我的緣故，大家要憎恨你們。[18]可是你們連一根頭髮也不至於失掉。[19]你們要堅忍才能夠保全自己的性命。」

預言耶路撒冷的毀滅
（太24‧15-21；可13‧14-19）

[20]「當你們看見耶路撒冷被敵軍圍困時，你們就知道它快要被毀滅了。[21]那時候，住在猶太的，要逃到山上去；住在城裏的，要出來；住在鄉下的，不要進城。[22]因為這是『懲罰的日子』，要使聖經上的話都得應驗。[23]在那些日子裏，孕婦和哺育嬰兒的母親就苦了！嚴重的災難將臨到這地方，上帝的義憤要降在這人民身上。[24]他們要死在刀劍下，或被俘虜到各國去。異教徒要踐踏耶路撒冷，直到他們的期限滿了。」

人子的來臨
（太24‧29-31；可13‧24-27）

[25]「那時候，太陽、月亮、星星都要顯出異象。地上的國家都要因海洋的怒嘯而驚惶失措。[26]人人在等待着那將要臨到世上的事，恐懼戰慄以至於昏厥，因為太空的一切系統都要搖動。[27]那時候，人子要出現，充滿着大能力和榮耀駕雲降臨。[28]這些事發生的時候，你們要昂首挺胸，因為你們得救的日子就到了！」

無花果樹的教訓
（太24‧32-35；可13‧28-31）

[29]耶穌又對他們講一個比喻：「你們看看無花果樹和其他的各種樹。[30]它們一長出新葉，你們就知道夏天快到了。[31]同樣，你們看見這一切的現象就知道上帝的主權快要實現了。

[32]「你們要記住：這一代的人還沒有都去世以前，這一切事就要發生。[33]天地要消失，我的話卻永不消失。」

The Need to Watch

34"Be careful not to let yourselves become occupied with too much feasting and drinking and with the worries of this life, or that Day may suddenly catch you 35like a trap. For it will come upon all people everywhere on earth. 36Be on watch and pray always that you will have the strength to go safely through all those things that will happen and to stand before the Son of Man."

37Jesus spent those days teaching in the Temple, and when evening came, he would go out and spend the night on the Mount of Olives. 38Early each morning all the people went to the Temple to listen to him.

The Plot against Jesus

(Matthew 26.1-5; Mark 14.1-2; John 11.45-53)

22The time was near for the Festival of Unleavened Bread, which is called the Passover. 2The chief priests and the teachers of the Law were afraid of the people, and so they were trying to find a way of putting Jesus to death secretly.

Judas Agrees to Betray Jesus

(Matthew 26.14-16; Mark 14.10-11)

3Then Satan entered into Judas, called Iscariot, who was one of the twelve disciples. 4So Judas went off and spoke with the chief priests and the officers of the Temple guard about how he could betray Jesus to them. 5They were pleased and offered to pay him money. 6Judas agreed to it and started looking for a good chance to hand Jesus over to them without the people knowing about it.

Jesus Prepares to Eat the Passover Meal

(Matthew 26.17-25; Mark 14.12-21; John 13.21-30)

7The day came during the Festival of Unleavened Bread when the lambs for the Passover meal were to be killed. 8Jesus sent Peter and John with these instructions: "Go and get the Passover meal ready for us to eat."

9"Where do you want us to get it ready?" they asked him.

10He answered, "As you go into the city, a man carrying a jar of water will meet you. Follow him into the house that he enters, 11and say to the owner of the house: 'The Teacher says to you, Where is the room where my disciples and I will eat the Passover meal?' 12He will show you a large furnished room upstairs, where you will get everything ready."

13They went off and found everything just as Jesus had told them, and they prepared the Passover meal.

必須警醒

34「你們自己要警醒！不要讓酒肉和生活上的憂慮麻痹你們的心靈，恐怕那日子要忽然臨到你們。因為那日子35像羅網一樣，要臨到全世界所有的人身上。36你們要警醒，不斷地禱告，使你們有力量忍受一切要發生的事，得以站在人子面前。」

37耶穌白天都在聖殿裏教導人，晚上出城，在橄欖山過夜；38羣眾一早就上聖殿，要聽耶穌講道。

殺害耶穌的陰謀

（太26．1－5；可14．1－2；約11．45－53）

22除酵節（又叫逾越節）的節期快到了。2祭司長和經學教師因懼怕羣眾，就想法子秘密地殺害耶穌。

猶大同意出賣耶穌

（太26．14－16；可14．10－11）

3那時候，撒但進入加略人猶大的心。（猶大是耶穌十二使徒之一。）

4猶大去跟祭司長以及聖殿的警衛官商量，要怎樣把耶穌交給他們。5他們很高興，又答應給他錢。6猶大同意了，開始找機會，要在羣眾不注意的時候把耶穌交給他們。

預備逾越節的晚餐

（太26．17－25；可14．12－21；約13．21－30）

7除酵節期內，該宰逾越節羔羊的日子到了。8耶穌差派彼得和約翰出去，吩咐他們說：「你們去為我們預備逾越節的晚餐。」

9他們就問：「你要我們在甚麼地方預備呢？」

10耶穌說：「你們進城，會遇見一個人，拿着一瓶水，你們就跟着他，到他進去的那座房子，11問那家的主人說：『老師問，他和門徒吃逾越節晚餐的那間客房在哪裏？』12他會帶你們去看樓上一間佈置好了的大房間；你們就在那裏預備。」

13他們去了，所遇見的正和耶穌所說的一樣，他們就預備逾越節的晚餐。

The Lord's Supper

(Matthew 26.26-30; Mark 14.22-26; 1 Corinthians 11.23-25)

14When the hour came, Jesus took his place at the table with the apostles. 15He said to them, "I have wanted so much to eat this Passover meal with you before I suffer! 16For I tell you, I will never eat it until it is given its full meaning in the Kingdom of God."

17Then Jesus took a cup, gave thanks to God, and said, "Take this and share it among yourselves. 18I tell you that from now on I will not drink this wine until the Kingdom of God comes."

19Then he took a piece of bread, gave thanks to God, broke it, and gave it to them, saying, "This is my body, which is given for you. Do this in memory of me." 20In the same way, he gave them the cup after the supper, saying, "This cup is God's new covenant sealed with my blood, which is poured out for you.y

21"But, look! The one who betrays me is here at the table with me! 22The Son of Man will die as God has decided, but how terrible for that man who betrays him!"

23Then they began to ask among themselves which one of them it could be who was going to do this.

The Argument about Greatness

24An argument broke out among the disciples as to which one of them should be thought of as the greatest. 25Jesus said to them, "The kings of the pagans have power over their people, and the rulers claim the title 'Friends of the People.' 26But this is not the way it is with you; rather, the greatest one among you must be like the youngest, and the leader must be like the servant. 27Who is greater, the one who sits down to eat or the one who serves? The one who sits down, of course. But I am among you as one who serves.

28"You have stayed with me all through my trials; 29and just as my Father has given me the right to rule, so I will give you the same right. 30You will eat and drink at my table in my Kingdom, and you will sit on thrones to rule over the twelve tribes of Israel.

Jesus Predicts Peter's Denial

(Matthew 26.31-35; Mark 14.27-31; John 13.36-38)

31"Simon, Simon! Listen! Satan has received permission to test all of you, to separate the good from the bad, as a farmer separates the wheat from the bad and the chaff. 32But I have prayed for

y Some manuscripts do not have the words of Jesus after This is my body in verse 19, and all of verse 20.

主的晚餐

（太26·26—30；可14·22—26；林前11·23—25）

14 晚餐的時間到了，耶穌坐席；使徒跟他同坐。15他對他們說：「我一直盼望坐在受難以前和你們一起吃這逾越節的晚餐。16我告訴你們，非等到這晚餐在上帝的國度裏有了眞正的意義，我絕不再吃它。」

17 於是耶穌拿起杯，向上帝感謝了，說：「你們拿這杯，分着喝。18我告訴你們，從今以後，非等到上帝的國度來臨，我絕不再喝這酒。」

19 然後他拿起餅，向上帝感謝了，擘開，分給他們，說：「這是我的身體，是爲你們捨的。你們這樣做來記念我。」20飯後，他照樣拿起杯來，說：「這杯是上帝的新約，是用我爲你們流出的血設立的⑬。

21「你們看，那出賣我的人在這裏和我同桌！22人子固然要照上帝所安排的受死，可是那出賣他的人有禍了！」

23 他們彼此追問：「要幹這事的人到底是誰呢？」

門徒爭論誰最偉大

24 門徒們有了爭論，究竟他們當中誰算是最偉大的。25耶穌對他們說：「世上的君王有管轄人民的權力，而統治者被尊稱爲救星；26但是你們不應該這樣。你們當中那最大的，反而應該像年幼的；作領袖的，應該像僕人。27那坐着吃喝的大，還是那伺候他的大呢？當然是那坐着的大。然而，我在你們當中是伺候人的。

28「我在磨煉中，你們始終跟我在一起。29我現在要把我父親所賜給我的王權也賜給你們。30你們要在我的國度裏跟我同桌吃喝，並且要坐在寶座上審判以色列的十二支族。」

耶穌預言彼得不認他

（太26·31—35；可14·27—31；約13·36—38）

31 耶穌又說：「西門，西門！撒但已得到准許來試探你們，要像農夫篩麥子一樣來篩你們。32但是我已經爲你祈求，使你不至於

⑬有些古卷沒有19節「是爲你們……來記念我」這段話和20節。

you, Simon, that your faith will not fail. And when you turn back to me, you must strengthen your brothers."

33Peter answered, "Lord, I am ready to go to prison with you and to die with you!"

34"I tell you, Peter," Jesus said, "the rooster will not crow tonight until you have said three times that you do not know me."

Purse, Bag, and Sword

35Then Jesus asked his disciples, "When I sent you out that time without purse, bag, or shoes, did you lack anything?"

"Not a thing," they answered.

36"But now," Jesus said, "whoever has a purse or a bag must take it; and whoever does not have a sword must sell his coat and buy one. 37For I tell you that the scripture which says, 'He shared the fate of criminals,' must come true about me, because what was written about me is coming true."

38The disciples said, "Look! Here are two swords, Lord!"

"That is enough!"z he replied.

Jesus Prays on the Mount of Olives
(Matthew 26.36-46; Mark 14.32-42)

39Jesus left the city and went, as he usually did, to the Mount of Olives; and the disciples went with him. 40When he arrived at the place, he said to them, "Pray that you will not fall into temptation."

41Then he went off from them about the distance of a stone's throw and knelt down and prayed. 42"Father," he said, "if you will, take this cup of suffering away from me. Not my will, however, but your will be done." 43An angel from heaven appeared to him and strengthened him. 44In great anguish he prayed even more fervently; his sweat was like drops of blood falling to the ground.a

45Rising from his prayer, he went back to the disciples and found them asleep, worn out by their grief. 46He said to them, "Why are you sleeping? Get up and pray that you will not fall into temptation."

The Arrest of Jesus
(Matthew 26.47-56; Mark 14.43-50; John 18.3-11)

47Jesus was still speaking when a crowd arrived, led by Judas, one of the twelve disciples.

z That is enough; or Enough of this.
a Some manuscripts do not have verses 43-44.

失掉信心。你再回轉歸我以後,就要激勵你的弟兄們。」

33 彼得說:「主啊,我願意跟你一起坐牢,一起死!」

34 耶穌說:「彼得,我告訴你:今天雞叫以前,你會三次說你不認得我。」

錢包、旅行袋、刀

35 耶穌又對他們說:「從前我差遣你們出去,叫你們不帶錢包,不帶旅行袋或鞋子,你們缺少了甚麼沒有?」

他們回答:「沒有。」

36 耶穌說:「但現在那有錢包或旅行袋的,要帶着;沒有刀的,要賣掉衣服去買一把。37我告訴你們,聖經所說『他被列在罪犯中』那句話必須在我身上實現。其實,有關於我的一切記載已經在應驗了。」

38 門徒說:「主啊,你看,這裏有兩把刀。」

耶穌說:「夠了!」

耶穌在橄欖山上禱告
(太26.36—46;可14.32—42)

39 耶穌出城,照常往橄欖山;門徒們跟着他去。40到了那地方,耶穌對他們說:「你們要禱告,免得陷於誘惑。」

41 於是耶穌離開他們,在約扔一塊石子的距離,跪下禱告,42說:「父親哪,若是你願意,就把這苦杯移去;然而,不要照我的意思,而是要成全你的旨意。」〔43有一個天使從天上向他顯現,加強他的力量。44在極度傷痛中,耶穌更懇切地禱告,他的汗珠像大滴的血滴落在地上⑲。〕

45 禱告後,耶穌起來,回到門徒們那裏,發現他們因憂傷過度沉睡了。46他對他們說:「你們為甚麼睡着呢?起來,禱告吧,免得陷於誘惑。」

耶穌被捕
(太26.47—56;可14.43—50;約18.3—11)

47 耶穌還在說話的時候,有一羣人來了。十二使徒之一的猶大帶着他們,他上前去要親耶穌。

⑲有些古卷沒有43—44節。

He came up to Jesus to kiss him. [48]But Jesus said, "Judas, is it with a kiss that you betray the Son of Man?"

[49]When the disciples who were with Jesus saw what was going to happen, they asked, "Shall we use our swords, Lord?" [50]And one of them struck the High Priest's slave and cut off his right ear.

[51]But Jesus said, "Enough of this!" He touched the man's ear and healed him.

[52]Then Jesus said to the chief priests and the officers of the Temple guard and the elders who had come there to get him, "Did you have to come with swords and clubs, as though I were an outlaw? [53]I was with you in the Temple every day, and you did not try to arrest me. But this is your hour to act, when the power of darkness rules."

Peter Denies Jesus
(Matthew 26.57-58, 69-75; Mark 14.53-54, 66-72;
 John 18.12-18, 25-27)

[54]They arrested Jesus and took him away into the house of the High Priest; and Peter followed at a distance. [55]A fire had been lit in the center of the courtyard, and Peter joined those who were sitting around it. [56]When one of the servant women saw him sitting there at the fire, she looked straight at him and said, "This man too was with Jesus!"

[57]But Peter denied it, "Woman, I don't even know him!"

[58]After a little while a man noticed Peter and said, "You are one of them, too!"

But Peter answered, "Man, I am not!"

[59]And about an hour later another man insisted strongly, "There isn't any doubt that this man was with Jesus, because he also is a Galilean!"

[60]But Peter answered, "Man, I don't know what you are talking about!"

At once, while he was still speaking, a rooster crowed. [61]The Lord turned around and looked straight at Peter, and Peter remembered that the Lord had said to him, "Before the rooster crows tonight, you will say three times that you do not know me." [62]Peter went out and wept bitterly.

Jesus Is Mocked and Beaten
(Matthew 26.67-68; Mark 14.65)

[63]The men who were guarding Jesus made fun of him and beat him. [64]They blindfolded him and asked him, "Who hit you? Guess!" [65]And they said many other insulting things to him.

[48]耶穌對他說：「猶大，你用親吻來出賣人子嗎？」

[49]跟耶穌在一起的門徒看見這情形，就說：「主啊，我們可以用刀砍嗎？」[50]其中一個人揮刀向大祭司的奴僕砍去，削掉了他的右耳。

[51]耶穌說：「別再動武！」就伸手摸那個人的耳朵，治好了他。

[52]於是，耶穌對那些來抓他的祭司長、聖殿警衛官，和長老說：「你們帶着刀棒出來抓我，把我當作暴徒嗎？[53]我天天和你們在聖殿裏，你們並沒有下手；但現在是你們橫行的時刻，黑暗掌權了。」

彼得不認耶穌
（太26‧57—58，69—75；可14‧53—54，66—72；
約18‧12—18，25—27）

[54]這時候，他們抓住耶穌，把他帶到大祭司的府邸去；彼得遠遠地跟着。[55]他們在院子裏生了火，大家圍着火坐着，彼得也混在他們中間。[56]有一個婢女看見彼得坐着烤火，就盯着他看，說：「這個人跟他是一夥的！」

[57]彼得否認說：「你這個女人，我不認識他！」

[58]過了不久，又有人注意到他，說：「你也是他們一夥的！」

彼得說：「你這個人，我不是！」

[59]大約再過了一個鐘頭，另一個人一口咬定說：「毫無疑問，這個人跟他是一夥的，因為他也是加利利人！」

[60]可是彼得說：「你這個人，我不懂得你在說些甚麼！」

他的話還沒有說完，雞叫了。[61]主轉過身來，注目看彼得；彼得記起主說過的話：「今天在雞叫以前，你會三次說你不認識我。」[62]彼得就出去，痛哭起來。

耶穌受戲弄侮辱
（太26‧67—68；可14‧65）

[63]看守耶穌的人戲弄他，毆打他。[64]他們蒙着他的眼睛，問他：「猜猜看，是誰打你？」[65]他們又說了許多侮辱他的話。

Jesus before the Council

(Matthew 26.59-66; Mark 14.55-64; John 18.19-24)

66When day came, the elders, the chief priests, and the teachers of the Law met together, and Jesus was brought before the Council. 67"Tell us," they said, "are you the Messiah?"

He answered, "If I tell you, you will not believe me; 68and if I ask you a question, you will not answer. 69But from now on the Son of Man will be seated at the right side of Almighty God."

70They all said, "Are you, then, the Son of God?"

He answered them, "You say that I am."

71And they said, "We don't need any witnesses! We ourselves have heard what he said!"

Jesus before Pilate

(Matthew 27.1-2, 11-14; Mark 15.1-5; John 18.28-38)

23The whole group rose up and took Jesus before Pilate, 2where they began to accuse him: "We caught this man misleading our people, telling them not to pay taxes to the Emperor and claiming that he himself is the Messiah, a king."

3Pilate asked him, "Are you the king of the Jews?"

"So you say," answered Jesus.

4Then Pilate said to the chief priests and the crowds, "I find no reason to condemn this man."

5But they insisted even more strongly, "With his teaching he is starting a riot among the people all through Judea. He began in Galilee and now has come here."

Jesus before Herod

6When Pilate heard this, he asked, "Is this man a Galilean?" 7When he learned that Jesus was from the region ruled by Herod, he sent him to Herod, who was also in Jerusalem at that time. 8Herod was very pleased when he saw Jesus, because he had heard about him and had been wanting to see him for a long time. He was hoping to see Jesus perform some miracle. 9So Herod asked Jesus many questions, but Jesus made no answer. 10The chief priests and the teachers of the Law stepped forward and made strong accusations against Jesus. 11Herod and his soldiers made fun of Jesus and treated him with contempt; then they put a fine robe on him and sent him back to Pilate. 12On that very day Herod and Pilate became friends; before this they had been enemies.

在議會受審

（太26‧59-66；可14‧55-64；約18‧19-24）

66 天亮的時候，猶太人的長老、祭司長，和經學教師都聚集在一起，又把耶穌帶到他們的議會裏。67他們問他：「告訴我們，你是不是基督？」

他回答：「即使我告訴你們，你們也不會相信我；68如果我問你們甚麼問題，你們也不會回答。69但是從今以後，人子要坐在全能上帝的右邊。」

70 他們都說：「這樣，你是上帝的兒子了？」

耶穌回答：「你們說我是！」

71 於是他們說：「我們再也不需要甚麼證據了！我們已經聽見他親口說的話了！」

在彼拉多面前受審

（太27‧1-2，11-14；可15‧1-5；約18‧28-38）

23成羣的人都起來，把耶穌押到彼拉多面前，2在那裏控告他說：「我們發現這個人煽動我們的同胞，反對我們向皇上納稅，又自稱基督，是王。」

3 彼拉多問耶穌：「你是猶太人的王嗎？」

耶穌回答：「這是你說的。」

4 於是彼拉多向祭司長和羣眾說：「我查不出這個人有甚麼罪狀。」

5 但是他們越發堅持說：「他藉着傳教，在猶太全境煽動民衆，從加利利開始，現在到這裏來了。」

在希律面前

6 彼拉多一聽見這話就問：「這個人是加利利人嗎？」7他一知道耶穌是從希律的轄區來的，就把他送到希律那裏。（那時希律也在耶路撒冷。）8希律看見耶穌，非常高興；因為他聽見了關於耶穌的事，早就想要見他，希望看耶穌顯個神蹟。9因此，他問耶穌好些問題，可是耶穌一句話都不回答。10祭司長和經學教師上前，大力控告他。11希律和他的兵士戲弄他，侮辱他。他們替他披上一件華麗的長袍，送他回彼拉多那裏。12就在這一天，希律和彼拉多成了朋友；這以前兩個人是寃家。

Jesus Is Sentenced to Death

(Matthew 27.15-26; Mark 15.6-15; John 18.39–19.16)

13Pilate called together the chief priests, the leaders, and the people, 14and said to them, "You brought this man to me and said that he was misleading the people. Now, I have examined him here in your presence, and I have not found him guilty of any of the crimes you accuse him of. 15Nor did Herod find him guilty, for he sent him back to us. There is nothing this man has done to deserve death. 16So I will have him whipped and let him go."[b]

18The whole crowd cried out, "Kill him! Set Barabbas free for us!" 19(Barabbas had been put in prison for a riot that had taken place in the city, and for murder.)

20Pilate wanted to set Jesus free, so he appealed to the crowd again. 21But they shouted back, "Crucify him! Crucify him!"

22Pilate said to them the third time, "But what crime has he committed? I cannot find anything he has done to deserve death! I will have him whipped and set him free."

23But they kept on shouting at the top of their voices that Jesus should be crucified, and finally their shouting succeeded. 24So Pilate passed the sentence on Jesus that they were asking for. 25He set free the man they wanted, the one who had been put in prison for riot and murder, and he handed Jesus over for them to do as they wished.

Jesus Is Crucified

(Matthew 27.32-44; Mark 15.21-32; John 19.17-27)

26The soldiers led Jesus away, and as they were going, they met a man from Cyrene named Simon who was coming into the city from the country. They seized him, put the cross on him, and made him carry it behind Jesus.

27A large crowd of people followed him; among them were some women who were weeping and wailing for him. 28Jesus turned to them and said, "Women of Jerusalem! Don't cry for me, but for yourselves and your children. 29For the days are coming when people will say, 'How lucky are the women who never had children, who never bore babies, who never nursed them!' 30That will be the time when people will say to the mountains, 'Fall on us!' and to the hills, 'Hide us!' 31For if such things as these are done when the wood is green, what will happen when it is dry?"

被判死刑

（太27‧15—26；可15‧6—15；約18‧39—19‧16）

13 彼拉多召集了祭司長、民間的領袖，和民衆，14對他們說：「你們把這個人押到我這裏來，控告他煽動人民；我在你們面前審問他，卻查不出他犯過你們所控告的任何罪狀。15連希律也查不出他有罪，把他送回這裏來。可見他沒有甚麼該死的行爲。16我要叫人鞭打他，然後把他釋放了。」⑳

18 羣衆卻齊聲喊叫：「殺掉他！釋放巴拉巴給我們！」（19巴拉巴曾在城裏作亂，並且殺過人，因此被下在監獄裏。）

20 彼拉多想要釋放耶穌，就再勸解羣衆。21可是他們更大聲呼喊：「把他釘十字架！把他釘十字架！」

22 彼拉多第三次對他們說：「他究竟犯了甚麼罪呢？我查不出他有該死的罪狀。我要叫人鞭打他，把他釋放了。」

23 羣衆繼續大聲喊叫，堅持把耶穌釘十字架；他們的呼喊終於得勝。24於是彼拉多照着他們的要求宣判。25他把那個作亂殺人、囚在獄中的兇手釋放了，又把耶穌交給他們，任憑他們處置。

耶穌被釘十字架

（太27‧32—44；可15‧21—32；約19‧17—27）

26 兵士把耶穌帶走，途中遇見一個從鄉下進城的古利奈人，名叫西門。他們抓住他，把十字架擱在他肩上，叫他背着，跟在耶穌後面走。

27 一大羣人跟隨着耶穌，其中有些婦女爲他悲傷哀哭。28耶穌轉過身來，對她們說：「耶路撒冷的女子啊，別爲我哭，要爲你們自己和你們的兒女哭。29因爲日子就要到了，人要說：『未生育、未懷過胎、未哺育嬰兒的，多麼幸運哪！』30那時候，人要對大山說：『倒在我們身上吧！』要對小山說：『遮蓋我們吧！』31因爲，要是他們對青綠的樹木做了這樣的事，對枯乾的樹木又將怎樣呢？」

---

b *Some manuscripts add verse 17:* At every Passover Festival Pilate had to set free one prisoner for them *(see Mk 15.6).*

⑳有些古卷加17節「每逢逾越節，彼拉多都照例爲他們釋放一個囚犯。」

32Two other men, both of them criminals, were also led out to be put to death with Jesus. 33When they came to the place called "The Skull," they crucified Jesus there, and the two criminals, one on his right and the other on his left. 34Jesus said, "Forgive them, Father! They don't know what they are doing."c

They divided his clothes among themselves by throwing dice. 35The people stood there watching while the Jewish leaders made fun of him: "He saved others; let him save himself if he is the Messiah whom God has chosen!"

36The soldiers also made fun of him: they came up to him and offered him cheap wine, 37and said, "Save yourself if you are the king of the Jews!"

38Above him were written these words: "This is the King of the Jews."

39One of the criminals hanging there hurled insults at him: "Aren't you the Messiah? Save yourself and us!"

40The other one, however, rebuked him, saying, "Don't you fear God? You received the same sentence he did. 41Ours, however, is only right, because we are getting what we deserve for what we did; but he has done no wrong." 42And he said to Jesus, "Remember me, Jesus, when you come as King!"

43Jesus said to him, "I promise you that to-day you will be in Paradise with me."

The Death of Jesus
(Matthew 27.45-56; Mark 15.33-41; John 19.28-30)

44-45It was about twelve o'clock when the sun stopped shining and darkness covered the whole country until three o'clock; and the curtain hanging in the Temple was torn in two. 46Jesus cried out in a loud voice, "Father! In your hands I place my spirit!" He said this and died.

47The army officer saw what had happened, and he praised God, saying, "Certainly he was a good man!"

48When the people who had gathered there to watch the spectacle saw what happened, they all went back home, beating their breasts in sorrow. 49All those who knew Jesus personally, including the women who had followed him from Galilee, stood at a distance to watch.

---

c Some manuscripts do not have Jesus said, "Forgive them, Father! They don't know what they are doing."

32 他們同時帶來兩個囚犯，要跟耶穌一起處死。33他們到一個地方，叫「髑髏岡」，在那裏把耶穌釘在十字架上，同時又釘了兩個囚犯，一個在他右邊，一個在他左邊。〔34耶穌說：「父親哪，赦免他們，因為他們不曉得自己在做甚麼21。」〕

他們抽籤分了耶穌的衣服。35民眾站着觀看，猶太的領袖卻嗤笑他，說：「他救了別人，要是他真的是上帝所揀選的基督，讓他救救自己吧！」

36 兵士也同樣譏笑他。他們上前，拿酸酒給他，37說：「你若是猶太人的王，救救你自己吧！」

38 在他上面有牌子寫着：「這是猶太人的王。」

39 兩個跟他同釘的囚犯，有一個開口侮辱他說：「你不是基督嗎？救救你自己，也救救我們吧！」

40 另外一個卻責備那囚犯說：「你同樣受刑，你就不怕上帝嗎？41我們受刑是活該；我們所受的不正是我們該得的報應嗎？但是這人並沒有做過一件壞事。」42於是他對耶穌說：「耶穌啊，你作王臨到的時候，求你記得我！」

43 耶穌對他說：「我告訴你，今天你要跟我一起在樂園裏。」

耶穌的死
（太27．45—56；可15．33—41；約19．28—30）

44-45約在中午的時候，日光消失了，黑暗籠罩大地，直到下午三點鐘；懸掛在聖殿裏的幔子裂成兩半。46耶穌大聲呼喊：「父親哪，我把自己的靈魂交在你手裏！」說了這話，他就斷了氣。

47 那軍官看見這事的經過，就頌讚上帝說：「這個人真是義人！」

48 圍觀這景象的民眾看見了這一切，都悲傷地捶着胸膛回去。49所有跟耶穌熟悉的人，和從加利利跟隨他來的婦女，都站在遠處看這些事的經過。

21有些古卷沒有括弧內的字。

The Burial of Jesus

(Matthew 27.57-61; Mark 15.42-47; John 19.38-42)

50-51There was a man named Joseph from Arimathea, a town in Judea. He was a good and honorable man, who was waiting for the coming of the Kingdom of God. Although he was a member of the Council, he had not agreed with their decision and action. 52He went into the presence of Pilate and asked for the body of Jesus. 53Then he took the body down, wrapped it in a linen sheet, and placed it in a tomb which had been dug out of solid rock and which had never been used. 54It was Friday, and the Sabbath was about to begin.

55The women who had followed Jesus from Galilee went with Joseph and saw the tomb and how Jesus' body was placed in it. 56Then they went back home and prepared the spices and perfumes for the body.

On the Sabbath they rested, as the Law commanded.

The Resurrection

(Matthew 28.1-10; Mark 16.1-8; John 20.1-10)

24 Very early on Sunday morning the women went to the tomb, carrying the spices they had prepared. 2They found the stone rolled away from the entrance to the tomb, 3so they went in; but they did not find the body of the Lord Jesus. 4They stood there puzzled about this, when suddenly two men in bright shining clothes stood by them. 5Full of fear, the women bowed down to the ground, as the men said to them, "Why are you looking among the dead for one who is alive? 6He is not here; he has been raised. Remember what he said to you while he was in Galilee: 7'The Son of Man must be handed over to sinners, be crucified, and three days later rise to life.'"

8Then the women remembered his words, 9returned from the tomb, and told all these things to the eleven disciples and all the rest. 10The women were Mary Magdalene, Joanna, and Mary the mother of James; they and the other women with them told these things to the apostles. 11But the apostles thought that what the women said was nonsense, and they did not believe them. 12But Peter got up and ran to the tomb; he bent down and saw the grave cloths but nothing else. Then he went back home amazed at what had happened.d

The Walk to Emmaus

(Mark 16.12-13)

13On that same day two of Jesus' followers were going to a village named Emmaus, about

d Some manuscripts do not have verse 12.

耶穌的安葬

（太27·57—61；可15·42—47；約19·38—42）

50-51有一個從猶太地區亞利馬太城來的人，名叫約瑟。這人良善正直，一向盼望上帝主權的實現。他雖然是議會的議員，卻沒有附和別人的計謀和行為。52他到彼拉多面前要求耶穌的身體，53然後去把身體取下來，用麻紗包好，安放在一個從巖石鑿成的墓穴裏—這墓穴還沒有葬過人。54那天是預備日，安息日就要到了。

55那些從加利利跟隨耶穌來的婦女和約瑟一起去，看見了墓穴，也看見了耶穌的身體怎樣被安放在裏面。56她們就回去，為他的身體預備香料和香油膏。

她們遵照法律的規定，在安息日休息。

耶穌復活

（太28·1—10；可16·1—8；約20·1—10）

24 星期天，天剛亮的時候，那些婦女帶着所預備的香料到墳地去。2她們發現石頭已經從墓門前給滾開了，3就走進墓穴，卻沒有看見主耶穌的身體。4正在疑慮不定的時候，忽然有兩個衣服發光的人站在她們旁邊；5她們非常驚駭，伏在地上。那兩個人對她們說：「你們為甚麼在死人中找活人呢？6他不在這裏；他已經復活了。要記得他在加利利時向你們說過的話；他說：7『人子必須被交在罪人手中，釘在十字架上，在第三天復活。』」

8她們這才記起耶穌的話，9就從墳地回去，把所遇見的一切事向十一使徒和其他的人報告。10向使徒報告這一切的婦女包括抹大拉的馬利亞、約亞娜、雅各的母親馬利亞，和跟她們一起的婦女。11可是使徒以為這些婦女胡說八道，沒有相信她們的話。12彼得卻起來，跑到墳地去，俯身探視墓穴，只看見那塊麻紗，沒有別的。於是他回去，對所發生的事非常驚奇㉒。

以馬忤斯路上

（可16·12—13）

13同一天，門徒中有兩個人要到一個村子去。這村子名叫以馬忤斯，離耶路撒冷約十

㉒有些古卷沒有這一節。

seven miles from Jerusalem, 14and they were talking to each other about all the things that had happened. 15As they talked and discussed, Jesus himself drew near and walked along with them; 16they saw him, but somehow did not recognize him. 17Jesus said to them, "What are you talking about to each other, as you walk along?"

They stood still, with sad faces. 18One of them, named Cleopas, asked him, "Are you the only visitor in Jerusalem who doesn't know the things that have been happening there these last few days?"

19"What things?" he asked.

"The things that happened to Jesus of Nazareth," they answered. "This man was a prophet and was considered by God and by all the people to be powerful in everything he said and did. 20Our chief priests and rulers handed him over to be sentenced to death, and he was crucified. 21And we had hoped that he would be the one who was going to set Israel free! Besides all that, this is now the third day since it happened. 22Some of the women of our group surprised us; they went at dawn to the tomb, 23but could not find his body. They came back saying they had seen a vision of angels who told them that he is alive. 24Some of our group went to the tomb and found it exactly as the women had said, but they did not see him."

25Then Jesus said to them, "How foolish you are, how slow you are to believe everything the prophets said! 26Was it not necessary for the Messiah to suffer these things and then to enter his glory?" 27And Jesus explained to them what was said about himself in all the Scriptures, beginning with the books of Moses and the writings of all the prophets.

28As they came near the village to which they were going, Jesus acted as if he were going farther; 29but they held him back, saying, "Stay with us; the day is almost over and it is getting dark." So he went in to stay with them. 30He sat down to eat with them, took the bread, and said the blessing; then he broke the bread and gave it to them. 31Then their eyes were opened and they recognized him, but he disappeared from their sight. 32They said to each other, "Wasn't it like a fire burning in us when he talked to us on the road and explained the Scriptures to us?"

33They got up at once and went back to Jerusalem, where they found the eleven disciples gathered together with the others 34and saying, "The Lord is risen indeed! He has appeared to Simon!"

35The two then explained to them what had happened on the road, and how they had recog-

一公里。14他們沿路談論所發生的一切事。15正談論的時候,耶穌親自走近他們,同他們一起走;16他們看見他,卻不認得他。17耶穌問他們:「你們一邊走,一邊談論些甚麼呢?」

他們就站住,滿面愁容。18其中一個名叫革流巴的,問耶穌:「難道你是耶路撒冷旅客中惟一不知道這幾天在那邊發生了甚麼事的人嗎?」

19耶穌說:「甚麼事呢?」

他們回答:「是拿撒勒人耶穌的事啊!他是個先知,在上帝和眾人面前,說話做事都有力量;20我們的祭司長和首領竟把他解去,判了死刑,釘在十字架上。21我們原來盼望他就是要來拯救以色列的那一位!不但如此,這事發生已經三天了。22我們當中有幾個婦女很使我們驚奇,她們一早到墓穴那裏去,23沒有看到他的身體。她們回來報告說,她們看見了天使,而天使告訴她們耶穌活着。24我們當中有人到墓穴去看,發現一切都跟婦女們所說的一樣,可是沒有看見他。」

25於是耶穌對他們說:「你們可真蠢哪!對先知所說的話你們為甚麼會覺得那樣的難信呢?26基督不是必須經歷這一切才進入榮耀嗎?」27於是,他根據摩西和先知所寫的,開始向他們解釋聖經上關於自己的一切記載。

28他們走近了所要去的村子,耶穌似乎還要繼續趕路,29他們卻挽留他說:「太陽已經下山,天就黑了,請和我們住下吧!」耶穌就進去,要與他們住下。30當他們坐下來吃飯的時候,耶穌拿起餅,向上帝感謝了,然後擘開餅,遞給他們。31他們的眼睛忽然開了,這才認出他來;但是耶穌忽然不見了。32他們彼此說:「他在路上向我們說話,給我們解釋聖經的時候,我們的心不是像火一樣地燃燒着嗎?」

33他們立刻動身,回耶路撒冷去。在那裏,他們看見十一使徒和另外一些人聚集在一起,34正在說:「主真的復活了;他已經顯現給西門看了!」

35那兩個人也把路上所遇見的,和他們怎

nized the Lord when he broke the bread.

Jesus Appears to His Disciples

(Matthew 28.16-20; Mark 16.14-18; John 20.19-23; Acts 1.6-8)

36While the two were telling them this, suddenly the Lord himself stood among them and said to them, "Peace be with you."[e]

37They were terrified, thinking that they were seeing a ghost. 38But he said to them, "Why are you alarmed? Why are these doubts coming up in your minds? 39Look at my hands and my feet, and see that it is I myself. Feel me, and you will know, for a ghost doesn't have flesh and bones, as you can see I have."

40He said this and showed them his hands and his feet.[f] 41They still could not believe, they were so full of joy and wonder; so he asked them, "Do you have anything here to eat?" 42They gave him a piece of cooked fish, 43which he took and ate in their presence.

44Then he said to them, "These are the very things I told you about while I was still with you: everything written about me in the Law of Moses, the writings of the prophets, and the Psalms had to come true."

45Then he opened their minds to understand the Scriptures, 46and said to them, "This is what is written: the Messiah must suffer and must rise from death three days later, 47and in his name the message about repentance and the forgiveness of sins must be preached to all nations, beginning in Jerusalem. 48You are witnesses of these things. 49And I myself will send upon you what my Father has promised. But you must wait in the city until the power from above comes down upon you."

Jesus Is Taken Up to Heaven

(Mark 16.19-20; Acts 1.9-11)

50Then he led them out of the city as far as Bethany, where he raised his hands and blessed them. 51As he was blessing them, he departed from them and was taken up into heaven.[g] 52They worshiped him and went back into Jerusalem, filled with great joy, 53and spent all their time in the Temple giving thanks to God.

e *Some manuscripts do not have* and said to them, "Peace be with you."

f *Some manuscripts do not have verse 40.*

g *Some manuscripts do not have* and was taken up into heaven.

樣在主擘開餅的時候認出他來的經過，告訴了大家。

耶穌向門徒顯現

（太28・16—20；可16・14—18；約20・19—23；徒1・6—8）

36 他們正在講這些事，忽然，主親自站在他們當中，對他們說：「願你們平安㉓！」

37 他們驚惶戰慄，以為見到了幽靈。38耶穌對他們說：「你們為甚麼煩擾呢？為甚麼心裏疑惑呢？39看看我的手和腳！是我，不是別人！摸一摸我，你們就知道，幽靈沒有肉沒有骨，你們看，我是有的。」

40 他這樣說着，把手和腳給他們看㉔。

41他們還不敢相信，卻是驚喜交集。他問他們：「你們這裏有甚麼吃的沒有？」42他們就拿一片烤魚給他。43他接過來，在他們面前吃了。

44 然後耶穌對他們說：「這一切事就是從前我和你們在一起的時候告訴過你們的：摩西的法律、先知的書，和詩篇所敍述關於我的每一件事必須實現。」

45 於是他開啓他們的心智，使他們明白聖經的話，46又對他們說：「聖經記載：基督要受害，第三天從死裏復活。47你們要奉他的名，把悔改和赦罪的信息傳開，從耶路撒冷遍及萬國。48你們就是這些事的見證人。49我要親自把我父親所應許的賜給你們；你們要在城裏等候，直到那從上面來的能力臨到你們。」

耶穌被接升天

（可16・19—20；徒1・9—11）

50 接着，耶穌領他們出城，到伯大尼去。在那裏，他舉手給他們祝福。51他在祝福他們的時候離開了他們，被接到天上去了㉕。52他們就敬拜他，懷着極喜樂的心回耶路撒冷，53時常在聖殿裏頌讚上帝。

㉓有些古卷沒有「對他們說：『願你們平安！』」。

㉔有些古卷沒有這一節。

㉕有些古卷沒有「被接到天上去了」。

約翰福音
JOHN

INTRODUCTION

The Gospel according to John presents Jesus as 1the eternal Word of God, who "became a human being and lived among us." As the book itself says, this Gospel was written so that its readers might believe that Jesus is the promised Savior, the Son of God, and that through their faith in him they may have life (20.31).

After an introduction that identifies the eternal Word of God with Jesus, the first part of the Gospel presents various miracles which show that Jesus is the promised Savior, the Son of God. These are followed by discourses that explain what is revealed by the miracles. This part of the book tells how some people believed in Jesus and became his followers, while others opposed him and refused to believe. Chapters 13-17 record at length the close fellowship of Jesus with his disciples on the night of his arrest, and his words of preparation and encouragement to them on the eve of his crucifixion. The closing chapters tell of Jesus' arrest and trial, his crucifixion and resurrection, and his appearances to his disciples after the resurrection.

The story of the woman caught in adultery (8.1-11) is placed in brackets because many manuscripts and early translations omit it, while others include it in other places.

John emphasizes the gift of eternal life through Christ, a gift which begins now and which comes to those who respond to Jesus as the way, the truth, and the life. A striking feature of John is the symbolic use of common things from everyday life to point to spiritual realities, such as water, bread, light, the shepherd and his sheep, and the grapevine and its fruit.

Outline of Contents

簡 介

　　約翰福音的主要內容在描寫耶穌是上帝的永恆之道；他「成為人，住在我們當中」。作者的目的是要讀這本書的人信耶穌是基督，是上帝的兒子，並因信這樣信而獲得永恆的生命（20．31）。

　　本書第一章指出上帝的永恆之道成為人，以此作為全書的導論。第二至十二章記述耶穌所行的許多神蹟異能，證明他就是救主，是上帝的兒子。根據這十二章的記載，我們知道有許多人信了他，接受他作救主；但也有些人反對他，不信他。第十三至十七章詳載耶穌和門徒的親密關係，以及他在受難前夕教導他們、鼓勵他們的話，第十八至廿一章記載他被捕，受審，被釘死，復活，以及復活後向門徒顯現。

　　一個女人在行淫時被抓到的故事（8．1 11）加上了〔 〕的符號，因為許多抄本和古譯本沒有這一段記載，也有些抄本把這故事放在其他地方。

　　本書作者特別強調耶穌就是道路、真理、生命。凡信並接受他的人都將得到永恆的生命。約翰福音的顯著特徵在於能用日常生活上的普通事物，好比水、餅、光、牧者和羊羣、葡萄樹和它的果子等，來象徵靈性上的意義。

提要

The Word of Life

1 In the beginning the Word already existed; the Word was with God, and the Word was God. [2]From the very beginning the Word was with God. [3]Through him God made all things; not one thing in all creation was made without him. [4]The Word was the source of life,[a] and this life brought light to people. [5]The light shines in the darkness, and the darkness has never put it out.

[6]God sent his messenger, a man named John, [7]who came to tell people about the light, so that all should hear the message and believe. [8]He himself was not the light; he came to tell about the light. [9]This was the real light–the light that comes into the world and shines on all people.

[10]The Word was in the world, and though God made the world through him, yet the world did not recognize him. [11]He came to his own country, but his own people did not receive him. [12]Some, however, did receive him and believed in him; so he gave them the right to become God's children. [13]They did not become God's children by natural means, that is, by being born as the children of a human father; God himself was their Father.

[14]The Word became a human being and, full of grace and truth, lived among us. We saw his glory, the glory which he received as the Father's only Son.

[15]John spoke about him. He cried out, "This is the one I was talking about when I said, 'He comes after me, but he is greater than I am, because he existed before I was born.'"

[16]Out of the fullness of his grace he has blessed us all, giving us one blessing after another. [17]God gave the Law through Moses, but grace and truth came through Jesus Christ. [18]No one has ever seen God. The only Son, who is the same as God and is at the Father's side, he has made him known.

John the Baptist's Message

(Matthew 3.1-12; Mark 1.1-8; Luke 3.1-18)

[19]The Jewish authorities in Jerusalem sent some priests and Levites to John to ask him, "Who are you?"

[20]John did not refuse to answer, but spoke out openly and clearly, saying: "I am not the Messiah."

[21]"Who are you, then?" they asked. "Are you Elijah?"

"No, I am not," John answered.

a The Word was the source of life; or What was made had life in union with the Word.

生命之道

1 宇宙被造以前,道已經存在。道與上帝同在;道是上帝。[2]在太初,道就與上帝同在。[3]上帝藉着他創造萬有;在整個創造中,沒有一樣不是藉着他造的。[4]道就是生命的根源,這生命把光賜給人類。[5]光照射黑暗,黑暗從沒有勝過光。

[6]有一個人,名叫約翰,是上帝所差遣的使者。[7]他來爲那光作證,爲要使大家聽見他的信息而信。[8]他本身不是那光,而是要爲光作證。[9]那光是真光,來到世上照亮全人類。

[10]道在世上,上帝藉着他創造世界,而世人竟不認識他。[11]他來到自己的地方,自己的人卻不接受他。[12]然而,凡接受他的,就是信他的人,他就賜給他們特權作上帝的兒女。[13]這樣的人不是由血統關係,不是由人的性慾,也不是由男人的意願生的,而是由上帝生的。

[14]道成爲人,住在我們當中,充滿着恩典和真理。我們看見了他的榮耀,這榮耀正是父親的獨子所當得的。

[15]約翰爲他作證,呼喊說:「關於他,我曾經說過:『他在我以後來,卻比我偉大;因爲我出生以前,他已經存在。』」

[16]從他的豐盛裏,我們領受了恩典,而且恩上加恩。[17]上帝藉着摩西頒佈法律,但恩典和真理是藉着耶穌基督來的。[18]沒有人見過上帝,只有獨子①,就是跟父親最親密的那一位,把他啓示出來。

施洗者約翰的信息

(太3·1-12;可1·1-8;路3·1-18)

[19]以下是約翰的見證。當時,耶路撒冷的猶太人派遣祭司和利未人去見約翰,問他:「你是誰?」

[20]約翰沒有拒絕回答,卻坦白承認說:「我並不是基督。」

[21]他們問:「那麼,你是誰?是以利亞嗎?」

約翰回答:「我不是。」

①「只有獨子」另有古卷作「只有與上帝相同的獨子」。

"Are you the Prophet?"[b] they asked.

"No," he replied.

22"Then tell us who you are," they said. "We have to take an answer back to those who sent us. What do you say about yourself?"

23John answered by quoting the prophet Isaiah:

"I am 'the voice of someone shouting in the desert:

Make a straight path for the Lord to travel!'"

24The messengers, who had been sent by the Pharisees, 25then[c] asked John, "If you are not the Messiah nor Elijah nor the Prophet, why do you baptize?"

26John answered, "I baptize with water, but among you stands the one you do not know. 27He is coming after me, but I am not good enough even to untie his sandals."

28All this happened in Bethany on the east side of the Jordan River, where John was baptizing.

The Lamb of God

29The next day John saw Jesus coming to him, and said, "There is the Lamb of God, who takes away the sin of the world! 30This is the one I was talking about when I said, 'A man is coming after me, but he is greater than I am, because he existed before I was born.' 31I did not know who he would be, but I came baptizing with water in order to make him known to the people of Israel."

32And John gave this testimony: "I saw the Spirit come down like a dove from heaven and stay on him. 33I still did not know that he was the one, but God, who sent me to baptize with water, had said to me, 'You will see the Spirit come down and stay on a man; he is the one who baptizes with the Holy Spirit.' 34I have seen it," said John, "and I tell you that he is the Son of God."

The First Disciples of Jesus

35The next day John was standing there again with two of his disciples, 36when he saw Jesus walking by. "There is the Lamb of God!" he said.

37The two disciples heard him say this and went with Jesus. 38Jesus turned, saw them following him, and asked, "What are you looking for?"

They answered, "Where do you live, Rabbi?" (This word means "Teacher.")

b THE PROPHET: *The one who was expected to appear and announce the coming of the Messiah.*

c The messengers, who had been sent by the Pharisees, then; *or* Those who had been sent were Pharisees; they.

他們又問:「是那位先知嗎?」

他再答:「不是。」

22他們接着說:「請告訴我們,你到底是誰,好讓我們回覆派遣我們來的人。你自己說,你是甚麼人?」

23約翰引先知以賽亞的話回答,說:

我就是在曠野呼喊的聲音:

為主修直他要走的道路!

24法利賽人所派來的那些人25質問約翰:「既然你不是基督,不是以利亞,也不是那位先知,那麼,你為甚麼施洗?」

26約翰回答:「我用水施洗;但有一位站在你們當中,是你們所不認識的,27他在我以後來,我就是替他脫鞋子也不配。」

28這些事發生在約旦河對岸的伯大尼,就是約翰正在施洗的地方。

上帝的羔羊

29第二天,約翰看見耶穌向他走過來,就說:「看哪,上帝的羔羊,除掉世人的罪的!30這一位就是我說過『他在我以後來,卻比我偉大;因為我出生以前,他已經存在』的那一位。31我並不認識他;現在我來,用水施洗,為要讓以色列人認識他。」

32約翰又見證說:「我看見聖靈像鴿子從天上降下來,落在他身上。33我還是不認識他,但是那差遣我用水施洗的上帝對我說:『你看見聖靈降下來,落在誰身上,誰就是那要用聖靈施洗的。』34我已經看見了,所以向你們證明他就是上帝的兒子。」

初次選召門徒

35過了一天,約翰和他的兩個門徒又在那裏;36他看見耶穌經過,就說:「看哪,上帝的羔羊!」

37兩個門徒一聽見這話,就跟隨耶穌。38耶穌轉身,看見他們跟着,就問:「你們想要甚麼?」

他們回答:「拉比,你住在哪裏?」(「拉比」的意思是「老師」。)

39"Come and see," he answered. (It was then about four o'clock in the afternoon.) So they went with him and saw where he lived, and spent the rest of that day with him.

40One of them was Andrew, Simon Peter's brother. 41At once he found his brother Simon and told him, "We have found the Messiah." (This word means "Christ.") 42Then he took Simon to Jesus.

Jesus looked at him and said, "Your name is Simon son of John, but you will be called Cephas." (This is the same as Peter and means "a rock.")

Jesus Calls Philip and Nathanael

43The next day Jesus decided to go to Galilee. He found Philip and said to him, "Come with me!" 44(Philip was from Bethsaida, the town where Andrew and Peter lived.) 45Philip found Nathanael and told him, "We have found the one whom Moses wrote about in the book of the Law and whom the prophets also wrote about. He is Jesus son of Joseph, from Nazareth."

46"Can anything good come from Nazareth?" Nathanael asked.

"Come and see," answered Philip.

47When Jesus saw Nathanael coming to him, he said about him, "Here is a real Israelite; there is nothing false in him!"

48Nathanael asked him, "How do you know me?"

Jesus answered, "I saw you when you were under the fig tree before Philip called you."

49"Teacher," answered Nathanael, "you are the Son of God! You are the King of Israel!"

50Jesus said, "Do you believe just because I told you I saw you when you were under the fig tree? You will see much greater things than this!" 51And he said to them, "I am telling you the truth: you will see heaven open and God's angels going up and coming down on the Son of Man."

The Wedding in Cana

2 Two days later there was a wedding in the town of Cana in Galilee. Jesus' mother was there, 2and Jesus and his disciples had also been invited to the wedding. 3When the wine had given out, Jesus' mother said to him, "They are out of wine."

4"You must not tell me what to do," Jesus replied. "My time has not yet come."

39耶穌說：「你們來看吧！」他們跟他一起去，看到了他住的地方，當天就跟他住在一起。（那時候約下午四點鐘。）

40聽見約翰的話而跟從耶穌的那兩個人中，有一個是西門·彼得的弟弟安得烈。41他先去找他的哥哥西門，對他說：「我們已經遇見彌賽亞了。」（「彌賽亞」的意思是「基督」。）42於是他帶西門去見耶穌。

耶穌注視着他，說：「你是約翰的兒子西門，你的名要叫磯法。」（磯法和彼得同義，意思是「磐石」。）

呼召腓力和拿但業

43過了一天，耶穌決定到加利利省去。他遇見腓力，對他說：「來跟從我！」（44腓力是伯賽大人，跟安得烈和彼得同鄉。）45腓力找到拿但業，對他說：「摩西在法律書上所寫和先知們所記載的那一位，我們已經遇見了。他就是約瑟的兒子，拿撒勒人耶穌。」

46拿但業就問：「拿撒勒會出甚麼好的嗎？」

腓力說：「你來看吧！」

47當耶穌看見拿但業向他走過來，就說：「看，他是個地道的以色列人；他心裏毫無詭詐！」

48拿但業問他：「你怎麼認識我呢？」

耶穌回答：「當你在無花果樹下，腓力還沒有招呼你，我已經看見你了。」

拿但業說：49「老師，你是上帝的兒子；你是以色列的君王！」

50耶穌說：「因為我告訴你，我看見你在無花果樹下，你就信了嗎？你要看見比這更大的事呢！」51又對他們說：「我鄭重地告訴你們，你們要看見天敞開，上帝的天使在人子身上，上下往來。」

迦拿的婚宴

2 第三天，在加利利的迦拿城有人舉行婚禮。耶穌的母親在那裏；2耶穌和他的門徒也受邀請參加婚宴。3酒喝光了，耶穌的母親告訴他：「他們沒有酒了。」

4耶穌說：「母親，請別勉強我做甚麼，我的時刻還沒有到呢。」

5Jesus' mother then told the servants, "Do whatever he tells you."

6The Jews have rules about ritual washing, and for this purpose six stone water jars were there, each one large enough to hold between twenty and thirty gallons. 7Jesus said to the servants, "Fill these jars with water." They filled them to the brim, 8and then he told them, "Now draw some water out and take it to the man in charge of the feast." They took him the water, 9which now had turned into wine, and he tasted it. He did not know where this wine had come from (but, of course, the servants who had drawn out the water knew); so he called the bridegroom 10and said to him, "Everyone else serves the best wine first, and after the guests have drunk a lot, he serves the ordinary wine. But you have kept the best wine until now!"

11Jesus performed this first miracle in Cana in Galilee; there he revealed his glory, and his disciples believed in him.

12After this, Jesus and his mother, brothers, and disciples went to Capernaum and stayed there a few days.

Jesus Goes to the Temple
(Matthew 21.12,13; Mark 11.15-17; Luke 19.45,46)

13It was almost time for the Passover Festival, so Jesus went to Jerusalem. 14There in the Temple he found people selling cattle, sheep, and pigeons, and also the moneychangers sitting at their tables. 15So he made a whip from cords and drove all the animals out of the Temple, both the sheep and the cattle; he overturned the tables of the moneychangers and scattered their coins; 16and he ordered those who sold the pigeons, "Take them out of here! Stop making my Father's house a marketplace!" 17His disciples remembered that the scripture says, "My devotion to your house, O God, burns in me like a fire."

18The Jewish authorities came back at him with a question, "What miracle can you perform to show us that you have the right to do this?"

19Jesus answered, "Tear down this Temple, and in three days I will build it again."

20"Are you going to build it again in three days?" they asked him. "It has taken forty-six years to build this Temple!"

21But the temple Jesus was speaking about was his body. 22So when he was raised from death, his disciples remembered that he had said this, and they believed the scripture and what Jesus had said.

5 耶穌的母親卻吩咐僕人：「他要你們做甚麼，就照他的話做。」

6 在那裏有六口石缸，是猶太人行潔淨禮的時候用的，每一口石缸可以盛水約一百公升。7耶穌對僕人說：「把水缸都裝滿水。」他們就倒水入缸，直到缸口。8耶穌又說：「現在可以舀些出來，送給管筵席的。」他們就送了去。9管筵席的嘗了那已經變成酒的水，不知道這酒是從哪裏來的（舀水的僕人卻知道），於是叫新郎來，10對他說：「別人都是先上好酒，等客人喝夠了才上普通的，你倒把最好的酒留到現在！」

11 這是耶穌所行的第一個神蹟，是在加利利的迦拿城行的。這事顯示了他的榮耀；他的門徒都信了他。

12 這事以後，耶穌跟他的母親、弟弟，和門徒到迦百農去，在那裏住了幾天。

耶穌潔淨聖殿
（太21‧12—13；可11‧15—17；路19‧45—46）

13 猶太人的逾越節快到了，耶穌上耶路撒冷去。14在聖殿的外院，他看見有人在販賣牛、羊、鴿子，又有人坐着兌換銀錢。15他就拿繩子做了一條鞭子，把牛羊從聖殿裏都趕出去，把兌換銀錢的桌子推倒，錢幣滾落一地。16他又對賣鴿子的人說：「把東西都搬走，不要把我父親的聖殿當作市場！」17他的門徒想起聖經上的話說：「上帝啊，我對你的聖殿大發熱心，如火燃燒！」

18 那些猶太人的領袖就質問他：「你能顯甚麼神蹟給我們看，好證明你有權做這事呢？」

19 耶穌說：「你們拆毀這聖殿，三天之內，我要把它重建起來。」

20 他們說：「這聖殿用四十六年才造成，你能在三天之內重建它嗎？」

21 其實，耶穌所說的聖殿是指他自己的身體。22耶穌從死裏復活以後，他的門徒記起他曾說過這話，就信聖經和耶穌所說的。

Jesus' Knowledge of Human Nature

23While Jesus was in Jerusalem during the Passover Festival, many believed in him as they saw the miracles he performed. 24But Jesus did not trust himself to them, because he knew them all. 25There was no need for anyone to tell him about them, because he himself knew what was in their hearts.

Jesus and Nicodemus

3 There was a Jewish leader named Nicodemus, who belonged to the party of the Pharisees. 2One night he went to Jesus and said to him, "Rabbi, we know that you are a teacher sent by God. No one could perform the miracles you are doing unless God were with him."

3Jesus answered, "I am telling you the truth: no one can see the Kingdom of God without being born again."*d*

4"How can a grown man be born again?" Nicodemus asked. "He certainly cannot enter his mother's womb and be born a second time!"

5"I am telling you the truth," replied Jesus, "that no one can enter the Kingdom of God without being born of water and the Spirit. 6A person is born physically of human parents, but is born spiritually of the Spirit. 7Do not be surprised because I tell you that you must all be born again.*e* 8The wind blows wherever it wishes; you hear the sound it makes, but you do not know where it comes from or where it is going. It is like that with everyone who is born of the Spirit."

9"How can this be?" asked Nicodemus.

10Jesus answered, "You are a great teacher in Israel, and you don't know this? 11I am telling you the truth: we speak of what we know and report what we have seen, yet none of you is willing to accept our message. 12You do not believe me when I tell you about the things of this world; how will you ever believe me, then, when I tell you about the things of heaven? 13And no one has ever gone up to heaven except the Son of Man, who came down from heaven."*x*

14As Moses lifted up the bronze snake on a pole in the desert, in the same way the Son of Man must be lifted up, 15so that everyone who believes in him may have eternal life. 16For God loved the world so much that he gave his only Son, so that everyone who believes in him may not die but have eternal life. 17For God did not send his Son into the world to be its judge, but to be its savior.

d again; *or* from above.
e again; *or* from above.
x *The quotation may continue through verse 21.*

耶穌洞悉人心

23耶穌在耶路撒冷過逾越節的時候，許多人看見他所行的神蹟，就信了他。24但是耶穌不能使自己信任他們，因為他對所有的人都有深刻的了解。25他不需要人告訴他關於人性的事，因為他洞悉人的內心。

耶穌和尼哥德慕

3 有一個法利賽人，名叫尼哥德慕，是猶太人的領袖。2他在晚上來見耶穌，說：「老師，我們知道你是從上帝那裏來的教師。你所行的神蹟，要不是有上帝同在，沒有人能行。」

3 耶穌回答：「我鄭重地告訴你，人若不重生②就不能看見上帝國的實現。」

4 尼哥德慕問：「一個已經老了的人怎麼能重生呢？他能重進母胎再生下來嗎？」

5 耶穌回答：「我鄭重地告訴你，人若不從水和聖靈重生，就不能成為上帝國的子民。6 人的肉身是父母生的，他的靈性是聖靈生的。7 不要因為我說『你們必須重生③』而驚奇。8 風隨意吹動，你聽見它的聲音，卻不知道它從哪裏來，往哪裏去。凡從聖靈生的，也都是這樣。」

9 尼哥德慕問：「怎麼能有這樣的事呢？」

10 耶穌回答：「你是以色列的教師，連這事都不明白嗎？11我實在告訴你，我們講論我們所確知的，我們見證我們所見到的；可是你們偏偏不願意領受我們的見證。12我告訴你們關於這世上的事，你們尚且不信，我要是告訴你們天上的事，你們又怎麼會信呢？13除了從天上降下來的人子，從來沒有人上過天。」

14 正好像摩西在曠野舉起銅蛇，人子也必須被舉起，15要使所有信他的人都得到永恆的生命。16上帝那麼愛世人，甚至賜下他的獨子，要使所有信他的人不致滅亡，反得永恆的生命。17因為上帝差遣他的兒子到世上來，不是要定世人的罪，而是要藉著他來拯救世人。

②「人若不重生」或譯「人若不從上帝那裏領受新生命」（「重」字在希臘語也有「上面」的意思）。
③「你們必須重生」或譯「你們必須從上帝那裏領受新生命」。

18Those who believe in the Son are not judged; but those who do not believe have already been judged, because they have not believed in God's only Son. 19This is how the judgment works: the light has come into the world, but people love the darkness rather than the light, because their deeds are evil. 20Those who do evil things hate the light and will not come to the light, because they do not want their evil deeds to be shown up. 21But those who do what is true come to the light in order that the light may show that what they did was in obedience to God.

Jesus and John

22After this, Jesus and his disciples went to the province of Judea, where he spent some time with them and baptized. 23John also was baptizing in Aenon, not far from Salim, because there was plenty of water in that place. People were going to him, and he was baptizing them. 24(This was before John had been put in prison.)

25Some of John's disciples began arguing with a Jew*f* about the matter of ritual washing. 26So they went to John and told him, "Teacher, you remember the man who was with you on the east side of the Jordan, the one you spoke about? Well, he is baptizing now, and everyone is going to him!"

27John answered, "No one can have anything unless God gives it. 28You yourselves are my witnesses that I said, 'I am not the Messiah, but I have been sent ahead of him.' 29The bridegroom is the one to whom the bride belongs; but the bridegroom's friend, who stands by and listens, is glad when he hears the bridegroom's voice. This is how my own happiness is made complete. 30He must become more important while I become less important."

He Who Comes from Heaven

31He who comes from above is greater than all. He who is from the earth belongs to the earth and speaks about earthly matters, but he who comes from heaven is above all. 32He tells what he has seen and heard, yet no one accepts his message. 33But whoever accepts his message confirms by this that God is truthful. 34The one whom God has sent speaks God's words, because God gives him the fullness of his Spirit. 35The Father loves his Son and has put everything in his power. 36Whoever believes in the Son has eternal life; whoever disobeys the Son will not have life, but will remain under God's punishment.

18信兒子的人不被定罪；不信的人已經被定罪了，因為他不信上帝的獨子。19光來到世上，世人因為自己的壞行為，不愛光而愛黑暗；他們被定罪的原因就在這裏。20做壞事的，都恨光，不接近光，因為怕他的壞行為被揭露出來。21但是，那依照真理做事的，卻接近光，為要使光顯明他所做的一切都是照着上帝的旨意做的。

耶穌和約翰

22這事以後，耶穌和門徒到猶太地區去。他在那裏和他們住了一些時候，並施洗禮。23約翰也在距離撒冷不遠的哀嫩施洗；因為那地方水多，人家都去受洗。（24那時約翰還沒有被囚禁。）

25約翰的幾個門徒跟一個猶太人為了潔淨禮爭辯。26他們去見約翰，對他說：「老師，你看，從前跟你在約旦河對岸、你為他作見證的那　位，現在也在施洗，大家都找他去了！」

27約翰說：「除非上帝有所賞賜，沒有人能得到甚麼。28我曾經說過，我不是基督；我不過是奉差遣作他的前驅。這話你們可以為我作證。29娶新娘的是新郎；新郎的朋友站在旁邊聽着，一聽見新郎的聲音就歡喜快樂。同樣，我已經得到了完全的喜樂。30他必定興旺，我卻必定衰微。」

從天上來的那一位

31那從上面來的是超越萬有；那從地上來的是屬於地，他所說的也是地上的事。那從天上來的是超越萬有。32他為所看見所聽到的作證，可是沒有人接受他的見證。33那接受他見證的，證明了上帝是信實的。34上帝所差遣的那一位傳講上帝的話，因為上帝無限量地把聖靈賜給他。35父親愛兒子，已經把萬有交在他手中。36信兒子的，有永恆的生命；不信兒子的，不會有真生命，而且上帝的懲罰永不離開他。

---

f a Jew; some manuscripts have some Jews.

Jesus and the Samaritan Woman

4 The Pharisees heard that Jesus was winning and baptizing more disciples than John. [2](Actually, Jesus himself did not baptize anyone; only his disciples did.) [3]So when Jesus heard what was being said, he left Judea and went back to Galilee; [4]on his way there he had to go through Samaria.

[5]In Samaria he came to a town named Sychar, which was not far from the field that Jacob had given to his son Joseph. [6]Jacob's well was there, and Jesus, tired out by the trip, sat down by the well. It was about noon.

[7]A Samaritan woman came to draw some water, and Jesus said to her, "Give me a drink of water." [8](His disciples had gone into town to buy food.)

[9]The woman answered, "You are a Jew, and I am a Samaritan–so how can you ask me for a drink?" (Jews will not use the same cups and bowls that Samaritans use.)[g]

[10]Jesus answered, "If you only knew what God gives and who it is that is asking you for a drink, you would ask him, and he would give you life-giving water."

[11]"Sir," the woman said, "you don't have a bucket, and the well is deep. Where would you get that life-giving water? [12]It was our ancestor Jacob who gave us this well; he and his children and his flocks all drank from it. You don't claim to be greater than Jacob, do you?"

[13]Jesus answered, "Those who drink this water will get thirsty again, [14]but those who drink the water that I will give them will never be thirsty again. The water that I will give them will become in them a spring which will provide them with life-giving water and give them eternal life."

[15]"Sir," the woman said, "give me that water! Then I will never be thirsty again, nor will I have to come here to draw water."

[16]"Go and call your husband," Jesus told her, "and come back."

[17]"I don't have a husband," she answered.

Jesus replied, "You are right when you say you don't have a husband. [18]You have been married to five men, and the man you live with now is not really your husband. You have told me the truth."

[19]"I see you are a prophet, sir," the woman said. [20]"My Samaritan ancestors worshiped God on this mountain, but you Jews say that Jerusalem is the place where we should worship God."

[21]Jesus said to her, "Believe me, woman, the

g Jews will not use the same cups and bowls that Samaritans use;
or Jews will have nothing to do with Samaritans.

耶穌和撒馬利亞的女人

4 法利賽人聽說耶穌招收門徒和施行洗禮比約翰多。（[2]其實，耶穌未曾親自爲任何人施洗，而是他的門徒施洗。）[3]耶穌知道這事就離開猶太，再回加利利去；[4]他必須經過撒馬利亞。

[5] 他來到撒馬利亞的敍加鎭，距離雅各給他兒子約瑟的那塊地不遠；[6]雅各井就在那裏。耶穌因爲趕路疲倦，就坐在井旁；時候約在中午。

[7] 有一個撒馬利亞女人來打水；耶穌對她說：「請給我一點水喝。」（[8]他的門徒已經到鎭上買食物去了。）

[9] 那女人回答：「你是猶太人，而我是撒馬利亞女人，你爲甚麼向我要水喝呢？」（原來猶太人跟撒馬利亞人不相往來。）

[10] 耶穌說：「要是你知道上帝的恩賜和現在向你要水喝的是誰，你就會求他，而他會把活水給你。」

[11] 那女人說：「先生，你沒有打水的器具，井又深，你哪裏去取活水呢？[12]我們的祖先雅各給我們這口井；他、他的兒女，和他的牲畜都喝這口井的水。難道你自以爲比他還大嗎？」

[13] 耶穌回答：「喝了這水的人還會再渴；[14]但是，誰喝了我所給的水，誰就永遠不再渴。我給的水要在他裏面成爲泉源，不斷地湧出活水，使他得到永恆的生命。」

[15] 女人說：「先生，請給我這水，使我永不再渴，也不用再來這裏打水。」

[16] 耶穌對她說：「去叫你的丈夫，然後再到這裏來。」

[17] 女人說：「我沒有丈夫。」

耶穌說：「你說你沒有丈夫，並沒有錯。[18]你曾經有五個丈夫，現在跟你一起的不是你的丈夫。你說的話是對的。」

[19] 女人說：「先生，我看出你是一位先知。[20]我們撒馬利亞人的祖先在這山上敬拜上帝，你們猶太人卻說耶路撒冷才是敬拜上帝的地方。」

[21] 耶穌對她說：「女人，要信我！時刻將

time will come when people will not worship the Father either on this mountain or in Jerusalem. 22You Samaritans do not really know whom you worship; but we Jews know whom we worship, because it is from the Jews that salvation comes. 23But the time is coming and is already here, when by the power of God's Spirit people will worship the Father as he really is, offering him the true worship that he wants. 24God is Spirit, and only by the power of his Spirit can people worship him as he really is."

25The woman said to him, "I know that the Messiah will come, and when he comes, he will tell us everything."

26Jesus answered, "I am he, I who am talking with you."

27At that moment Jesus' disciples returned, and they were greatly surprised to find him talking with a woman. But none of them said to her, "What do you want?" or asked him, "Why are you talking with her?"

28Then the woman left her water jar, went back to the town, and said to the people there, 29"Come and see the man who told me everything I have ever done. Could he be the Messiah?" 30So they left the town and went to Jesus.

31In the meantime the disciples were begging Jesus, "Teacher, have something to eat!"

32But he answered, "I have food to eat that you know nothing about."

33So the disciples started asking among themselves, "Could somebody have brought him food?"

34"My food," Jesus said to them, "is to obey the will of the one who sent me and to finish the work he gave me to do. 35You have a saying, 'Four more months and then the harvest.' But I tell you, take a good look at the fields; the crops are now ripe and ready to be harvested! 36The one who reaps the harvest is being paid and gathers the crops for eternal life; so the one who plants and the one who reaps will be glad together. 37For the saying is true, 'Someone plants, someone else reaps.' 38I have sent you to reap a harvest in a field where you did not work; others worked there, and you profit from their work."

39Many of the Samaritans in that town believed in Jesus because the woman had said, "He told me everything I have ever done." 40So when the Samaritans came to him, they begged him to stay with them, and Jesus stayed there two days.

41Many more believed because of his mess-

到，人不再在這山上或在耶路撒冷敬拜天父。22你們撒馬利亞人不知道你們所拜的是誰，我們猶太人知道我們所拜的是誰，因為救恩是從猶太人來的。23可是時刻將到，現在就是了，那真正敬拜天父的，要用心靈和真誠敬拜。這樣的敬拜就是天父所要的。24上帝是靈，敬拜他的人必須以心靈和真誠敬拜。」

25 女人對他說：「我知道那稱為基督的彌賽亞要來，他來了就會把一切的事都告訴我們。」

26 耶穌回答：「我，正在跟你說話的，就是他！」

27 就在這時候，耶穌的門徒回來了。他們看見他正在跟一個女人說話，覺得很驚奇，可是沒有人問那女人：「你要甚麼？」或問耶穌：「你為甚麼跟她說話？」

28 那女人放下水罐，往鎮上去，向大家說：29「你們來看！有一個人把我生平所做一切的事都說了出來；這個人也許就是基督吧？」30大家就出城去看耶穌。

31 這時候，門徒勸耶穌：「老師，請吃點東西。」

32 耶穌回答：「我有吃的東西，是你們所不知道的。」

33 門徒彼此議論：「難道有人拿東西給他吃嗎？」

34 耶穌對他們說：「我的食物就是實行差我來那一位的旨意，並且完成他交給我的工作。35你們說：『再過四個月才是收割的時候。』我告訴你們，看看那片田地吧，農作物已經成熟，可以收割了！36收割的人得到報賞，為永恆的生命積聚果實，使栽種的和收割的，一同快樂。37『一人栽種，另一人收割』這話是真的。38我差遣你們去收割你們所沒有耕作的田地；別人辛勞，而你們享受他們辛勞的成果。」

39 鎮上有許多撒馬利亞人信了耶穌，因為那女人說：「他把我所做的事都說了出來。」40那些撒馬利亞人來見耶穌，要求他和他們一起住，於是耶穌在那裏住了兩天。

41 有更多的人因耶穌的信息而信了他。

age, ⁴²and they told the woman, "We believe now, not because of what you said, but because we ourselves have heard him, and we know that he really is the Savior of the world."

Jesus Heals an Official's Son

43After spending two days there, Jesus left and went to Galilee. ⁴⁴For he himself had said, "Prophets are not respected in their own country." ⁴⁵When he arrived in Galilee, the people there welcomed him, because they had gone to the Passover Festival in Jerusalem and had seen everything that he had done during the festival.

46Then Jesus went back to Cana in Galilee, where he had turned the water into wine. A government official was there whose son was sick in Capernaum. ⁴⁷When he heard that Jesus had come from Judea to Galilee, he went to him and asked him to go to Capernaum and heal his son, who was about to die. ⁴⁸Jesus said to him, "None of you will ever believe unless you see miracles and wonders."

49"Sir," replied the official, "come with me before my child dies."

50Jesus said to him, "Go; your son will live!"

The man believed Jesus' words and went. ⁵¹On his way home his servants met him with the news, "Your boy is going to live!"

52He asked them what time it was when his son got better, and they answered, "It was one o'clock yesterday afternoon when the fever left him." ⁵³Then the father remembered that it was at that very hour when Jesus had told him, "Your son will live." So he and all his family believed.

54This was the second miracle that Jesus performed after coming from Judea to Galilee.

The Healing at the Pool

5 After this, Jesus went to Jerusalem for a religious festival. ²Near the Sheep Gate in Jerusalem there is a pool*ʰ* with five porches; in Hebrew it is called Bethzatha.ⁱ ³A large crowd of sick people were lying on the porches–the blind, the lame, and the paralyzed.ʲ ⁵A man was there who had been sick for thirty-eight years. ⁶Jesus saw him lying there, and he knew that

h *Near the Sheep Gate ... a pool; or Near the Sheep Pool ... a place.*
i *Bethzatha; some manuscripts have Bethesda.*
j *Some manuscripts add verses 3b-4: They were waiting for the water to move. ⁴because every now and then an angel of the Lord went down into the pool and stirred up the water. The first sick person to go into the pool after the water was stirred up was healed from whatever disease he had.*

⁴²他們告訴那女人:「我們現在信了,不是因為你說的話,而是因為我們親自聽見了他的話,知道他真是世界的救主。」

耶穌治好官員的兒子

43耶穌在那裏住了兩天,然後到加利利去。⁴⁴他自己說過:「先知在本鄉是不受尊重的。」⁴⁵耶穌一到加利利,當地的人都歡迎他;因為他們上耶路撒冷過逾越節的時候,看見了他在節期中所做的一切事。

46耶穌又回到加利利的迦拿,就是從前他變水為酒的地方。那地方有一個官員,他的兒子在迦百農害病。⁴⁷他一聽到耶穌從猶太來到加利利,就去見他,求他去迦百農治好他那病危的兒子。⁴⁸耶穌對他說:「要不是看見神蹟奇事,你們總是不信。」

49那官員回答:「先生,求你在我兒子沒有死以前同我一起去。」

50耶穌對他說:「去吧,你的兒子會活的!」

那人信了耶穌的話就回去。⁵¹在途中,他的僕人迎着他來,對他說:「你的兒子活了!」

52他問他們,兒子是甚麼時候好起來的。他們回答:「昨天下午一點鐘的時候,熱退了。」⁵³那父親想起,就是在那個時間,耶穌對他說「你的兒子會活的」。因此他和他全家都信了。

54這是耶穌從猶太回到加利利後所行的第二個神蹟。

在畢士大池邊治病

5 這事以後,剛好是猶太人的一個節期,耶穌上耶路撒冷去。²在耶路撒冷,靠近羊門地方有一個池子,希伯來話叫畢士大,池邊有五個走廊④。³走廊上躺着成羣的病人,其中有失明的、跛腳的、癱瘓的。⑤ ⁵在那裏有一個已經病了三十八年的病人。⁶耶穌看見他躺着,知道他已患病多

④「靠近羊門地方有一個池子……池邊有五個走廊」或譯「靠近羊池有一個地方……這地方周圍有五個走廊」。
⑤有些古卷加 4 節「他們在等候池水的攪動;因為他們相信每隔一些時候,主的天使會下來攪動池水,水動之後,最先下池的病人,無論害甚麼病,都會得到醫治。」

the man had been sick for such a long time; so he asked him, "Do you want to get well?"

7The sick man answered, "Sir, I don't have anyone here to put me in the pool when the water is stirred up; while I am trying to get in, somebody else gets there first."

8Jesus said to him, "Get up, pick up your mat, and walk." 9Immediately the man got well; he picked up his mat and started walking.

The day this happened was a Sabbath, 10so the Jewish authorities told the man who had been healed, "This is a Sabbath, and it is against our Law for you to carry your mat."

11He answered, "The man who made me well told me to pick up my mat and walk."

12They asked him, "Who is the man who told you to do this?"

13But the man who had been healed did not know who Jesus was, for there was a crowd in that place, and Jesus had slipped away.

14Afterward, Jesus found him in the Temple and said, "Listen, you are well now; so stop sinning or something worse may happen to you."

15Then the man left and told the Jewish authorities that it was Jesus who had healed him. 16So they began to persecute Jesus, because he had done this healing on a Sabbath. 17Jesus answered them, "My Father is always working, and I too must work."

18This saying made the Jewish authorities all the more determined to kill him; not only had he broken the Sabbath law, but he had said that God was his own Father and in this way had made himself equal with God.

The Authority of the Son

19So Jesus answered them, "I tell you the truth: the Son can do nothing on his own; he does only what he sees his Father doing. What the Father does, the Son also does. 20For the Father loves the Son and shows him all that he himself is doing. He will show him even greater things to do than this, and you will all be amazed. 21Just as the Father raises the dead and gives them life, in the same way the Son gives life to those he wants to. 22Nor does the Father himself judge anyone. He has given his Son the full right to judge, 23so that all will honor the Son in the same way as they honor the Father. Whoever does not honor the Son does not honor the Father who sent him.

24"I am telling you the truth: those who hear my words and believe in him who sent me have eternal life. They will not be judged, but have

年，就問他：「你要得到醫治嗎？」

7 那病人回答：「先生，水動的時候沒有人幫我，把我放進池子，等我正想下去，已經有人搶先下去了。」

8 耶穌對他說：「起來，拿起你的褥子走吧！」9那人立刻好了，拿起他的褥子走了。

那天剛好是安息日，10因此猶太人的領袖對那個被治好的人說：「今天是安息日，你拿着褥子是不合法的。」

11 他說：「那個治好我的人吩咐我：『拿起你的褥子走吧！』」

12 他們問：「那個吩咐你拿起褥子走的是誰？」

13 可是那個被治好的人竟不知道是誰；因為那地方人很多，而耶穌又已經避開了。

14 事後，耶穌在聖殿裏找到他，對他說：「你已經完全好了，不可再犯罪，免得招來更大的禍患。」

15 那人走開後，告訴猶太人的領袖，說是耶穌治好他的。16從此，他們開始迫害耶穌，因為他在安息日治病。17耶穌對他們說：「我父親一直在工作，我也該照樣工作。」

18 這話更使猶太人的領袖決意要殺害他；因為他不但破壞了安息日的戒律，而且說上帝是他自己的父親，把自己當作跟上帝平等。

兒子的權柄

19 接着，耶穌對他們說：「我鄭重地告訴你們，兒子憑着自己不能做甚麼；他看見父親做甚麼，才做甚麼。父親所做的，兒子也做。20父親愛兒子，把自己所做的指示兒子。他要把比這更重大的事指示兒子，要使你們驚奇。21父親怎樣使已經死了的人復活，賜生命給他們；同樣，兒子也要隨着自己的意思賜生命給人。22父親自己不審判任何人；他把審判的權交給兒子，23為的要使人都尊敬兒子，像尊敬父親一樣。那不尊敬兒子的，就是不尊敬差遣他來的父親。

24「我鄭重地告訴你們，那聽我話、又信差我來那一位的，就有永恆的生命。他不至

already passed from death to life. ²⁵I am telling you the truth: the time is coming–the time has already come–when the dead will hear the voice of the Son of God, and those who hear it will come to life. ²⁶Just as the Father is himself the source of life, in the same way he has made his Son to be the source of life. ²⁷And he has given the Son the right to judge, because he is the Son of Man. ²⁸Do not be surprised at this; the time is coming when all the dead will hear his voice ²⁹and come out of their graves: those who have done good will rise and live, and those who have done evil will rise and be condemned.

Witnesses to Jesus

³⁰"I can do nothing on my own authority; I judge only as God tells me, so my judgment is right, because I am not trying to do what I want, but only what he who sent me wants.

³¹"If I testify on my own behalf, what I say is not to be accepted as real proof. ³²But there is someone else who testifies on my behalf, and I know that what he says about me is true. ³³John is the one to whom you sent your messengers, and he spoke on behalf of the truth. ³⁴It is not that I must have a human witness; I say this only in order that you may be saved. ³⁵John was like a lamp, burning and shining, and you were willing for a while to enjoy his light. ³⁶But I have a witness on my behalf which is even greater than the witness that John gave: what I do, that is, the deeds my Father gave me to do, these speak on my behalf and show that the Father has sent me. ³⁷And the Father, who sent me, also testifies on my behalf. You have never heard his voice or seen his face, ³⁸and you do not keep his message in your hearts, for you do not believe in the one whom he sent. ³⁹You study the Scriptures, because you think that in them you will find eternal life. And these very Scriptures speak about me! ⁴⁰Yet you are not willing to come to me in order to have life.

⁴¹"I am not looking for human praise. ⁴²But I know what kind of people you are, and I know that you have no love for God in your hearts. ⁴³I have come with my Father's authority, but you have not received me; when, however, someone comes with his own authority, you will receive him. ⁴⁴You like to receive praise from one another, but you do not try to win praise from the one who alone is God; how, then, can you believe me? ⁴⁵Do not think, however, that I am the one who will accuse you to my Father. Moses, in whom you have put your hope, is the very one who will accuse you. ⁴⁶If you had really believed Moses, you would have believed me, because he wrote about me. ⁴⁷But

於被定罪，而是已經出死入生了。²⁵我鄭重地告訴你們，時刻將到，現在就是了，已死的人要聽見上帝兒子的聲音；那聽見的都要活過來。²⁶正如父親本身是生命的根源，他也使兒子成爲生命的根源。²⁷他又把執行審判的權柄賜給兒子，因爲他是人子。²⁸你們不要爲這事驚訝；因爲時刻將到，所有在墳墓裏的人都要聽見他的聲音，²⁹而且要從墳墓裏出來：行善的，復活得生命；作惡的，復活被定罪。」

爲耶穌作見證

³⁰「我憑自己不能做甚麼；我按照上帝的旨意來審判，而我的審判是公正的；因爲我不尋求自己所要的，只要實行差我來那一位的旨意。

³¹「我若見證自己，我的見證就不足信。³²然而，有一位爲我作見證的，我知道他爲我所作的見證是眞實的。³³你們曾派人去見約翰，聽見他見證眞理。³⁴其實，我並不需要人的見證；我說這話是爲了使你們得救。³⁵約翰好比一盞點亮照明的燈，你們願意暫時享受他的亮光。³⁶但是我可以提出比約翰更有力的見證，那便是我的工作－是我父親交給我去完成的工作。這些工作可以證明父親差遣了我。³⁷差遣我來的父親也爲我作見證。你們從來沒有聽見他的聲音，沒有看見他的容貌，³⁸沒有把他的話存在心裏，因爲你們不信他所差來的那一位。³⁹你們研究聖經，認爲從裏面可以找到永恆的生命；其實聖經的話就是爲我作見證的！⁴⁰然而，你們不肯到我這裏來尋求生命。

⁴¹「我不是在求人的稱讚。⁴²但是我看透了你們，你們並沒有愛上帝的心。⁴³我奉我父親的名而來，你們卻不接納我；可是有人奉自己的名來，你們反而會接納他。⁴⁴你們喜歡彼此恭維，卻不追求從獨一無二的上帝那裏來的稱讚；這樣，你們怎麼能信呢？⁴⁵別以爲我要在我父親面前控告你們；要控告你們的，就是你們一向所期望的摩西。⁴⁶要是你們眞的信摩西，你們當然會信我，因爲他在他的書上記載着我的事。⁴⁷你們旣

since you do not believe what he wrote, how can you believe what I say?"

Jesus Feeds Five Thousand
(Matthew 14.13-21; Mark 6.30-44; Luke 9.10-17)

6 After this, Jesus went across Lake Galilee (or, Lake Tiberias, as it is also called). ²A large crowd followed him, because they had seen his miracles of healing the sick. ³Jesus went up a hill and sat down with his disciples. ⁴The time for the Passover Festival was near. ⁵Jesus looked around and saw that a large crowd was coming to him, so he asked Philip, "Where can we buy enough food to feed all these people?" ⁶(He said this to test Philip; actually he already knew what he would do.)

⁷Philip answered, "For everyone to have even a little, it would take more than two hundred silver coins*ᵏ* to buy enough bread."

⁸Another one of his disciples, Andrew, who was Simon Peter's brother, said, ⁹"There is a boy here who has five loaves of barley bread and two fish. But they will certainly not be enough for all these people."

¹⁰"Make the people sit down," Jesus told them. (There was a lot of grass there.) So all the people sat down; there were about five thousand men. ¹¹Jesus took the bread, gave thanks to God, and distributed it to the people who were sitting there. He did the same with the fish, and they all had as much as they wanted. ¹²When they were all full, he said to his disciples, "Gather the pieces left over; let us not waste a bit." ¹³So they gathered them all and filled twelve baskets with the pieces left over from the five barley loaves which the people had eaten.

¹⁴Seeing this miracle that Jesus had performed, the people there said, "Surely this is the Prophet*ˡ* who was to come into the world!" ¹⁵Jesus knew that they were about to come and seize him in order to make him king by force; so he went off again to the hills by himself.

Jesus Walks on the Water
(Matthew 14.22-33; Mark 6.45-52)

¹⁶When evening came, Jesus' disciples went down to the lake, ¹⁷got into a boat, and went back across the lake toward Capernaum. Night came on, and Jesus still had not come to them. ¹⁸By then a strong wind was blowing and stirring up the water. ¹⁹The disciples had rowed about three or four miles when they saw Jesus walking on the water, coming near the boat,

k SILVER COINS: A silver coin was the daily wage of a rural worker (see Mt 20.2).
l THE PROPHET: See 1.21.

耶穌使五千人吃飽
（太14．13—21；可6．30—44；路9．10—17）

6 過了些時候，耶穌渡過加利利湖（又稱提比哩亞湖）。²有一大羣人跟隨他，因為他們看見了他治病的神蹟。³耶穌上山，與他的門徒坐在那裏。⁴那時候猶太人的逾越節快到了。⁵耶穌抬頭，看見一大羣人到他跟前來，就對腓力說：「我們到哪裏去買食物，好讓這些人都吃飽呢？」⁶他說這話是要試驗腓力；他自己已經知道要怎麼做。

⁷腓力回答：「就是花兩百塊銀子去買餅也不夠每人吃一小塊！」

⁸另外一個門徒，就是西門·彼得的弟弟安得烈，上前說：⁹「這裏有一個孩子帶來了五個大麥餅和兩條魚，可是哪裏夠分給這許多人呢？」

¹⁰耶穌吩咐他們：「叫大家坐下。」（那地方草很多。）大家都坐下，單是男人，總數約有五千。¹¹耶穌拿起餅，祝謝了，然後分給坐着的人，魚也是這樣分了；他們都盡量吃。¹²他們吃飽後，耶穌吩咐門徒：「把剩下的零碎都收拾起來，不可糟蹋。」¹³他們就把五個餅的碎塊，就是大家所吃剩的，收拾起來，一共裝滿了十二個籃子。

¹⁴大家看見耶穌所行的神蹟，就說：「這個人一定是那要到世上來的先知！」¹⁵耶穌知道他們要拉住他，強迫他作王，又獨自避到山上去了。

在水上行走
（太14．22—33；可6．45—52）

¹⁶傍晚，耶穌的門徒來到湖邊，¹⁷上了船，向對岸的迦百農出發。那時候天已經黑了，耶穌還沒有來到他們那裏。¹⁸忽然，狂風大作，浪濤翻騰。¹⁹門徒搖櫓，約走了五、六公里，看見耶穌在水上朝着船走過

and they were terrified. 20"Don't be afraid," Jesus told them, "it is I!" 21Then they willingly took him into the boat, and immediately the boat reached land at the place they were heading for.

The People Seek Jesus

22Next day the crowd which had stayed on the other side of the lake realized that there had been only one boat there. They knew that Jesus had not gone in it with his disciples, but that they had left without him. 23Other boats, which were from Tiberias, came to shore near the place where the crowd had eaten the bread after the Lord had given thanks. 24When the crowd saw that Jesus was not there, nor his disciples, they got into those boats and went to Capernaum, looking for him.

Jesus the Bread of Life

25When the people found Jesus on the other side of the lake, they said to him, "Teacher, when did you get here?"

26Jesus answered, "I am telling you the truth: you are looking for me because you ate the bread and had all you wanted, not because you understood my miracles. 27Do not work for food that spoils; instead, work for the food that lasts for eternal life. This is the food which the Son of Man will give you, because God, the Father, has put his mark of approval on him."

28So they asked him, "What can we do in order to do what God wants us to do?"

29Jesus answered, "What God wants you to do is to believe in the one he sent."

30They replied, "What miracle will you perform so that we may see it and believe you? What will you do? 31Our ancestors ate manna in the desert, just as the scripture says, 'He gave them bread from heaven to eat.'"

32"I am telling you the truth," Jesus said. "What Moses gave you was not*m* the bread from heaven; it is my Father who gives you the real bread from heaven. 33For the bread that God gives is he who comes down from heaven and gives life to the world."

34"Sir," they asked him, "give us this bread always."

35"I am the bread of life," Jesus told them. "Those who come to me will never be hungry; those who believe in me will never be thirsty. 36Now, I told you that you have seen me but will not believe. 37Everyone whom my Father

m What Moses gave you was not; *or* It was not Moses who gave you.

來，就很害怕。20耶穌對他們說：「是我，不要怕！」21他們這才歡欣地接他上船；船立刻到達目的地。

羣眾尋找耶穌

22 第二天，留在湖對岸的一羣人看見那裏只有一條小船；他們知道耶穌並沒有與門徒一起上船，而是門徒自己去的。23有幾條從提比哩亞來的小船停靠在岸邊，就是主祝謝後分餅給大家吃的那地方附近。24這羣人發覺耶穌和他的門徒都不在那裏，就上船往迦百農去找他。

耶穌是生命的食糧

25 他們在湖的對岸找到了耶穌，問他：「老師，你幾時到這裏來的？」

26 耶穌回答：「老實說，你們找我，不是因為看見了神蹟，而是因為吃餅吃飽了。27不要為那會腐壞的食物操勞，要為那存到永生的食物努力。這食物就是人子要賜給你們的，因為父上帝已經在人子身上蓋了印記。」

28 他們就問：「我們該做甚麼才算是做上帝的工作呢？」

29 耶穌回答：「信他所差來的那一位，這就是上帝要你們做的工作。」

30 他們又說：「那麼，你會行甚麼神蹟，好讓我們看了就信你呢？你的工作到底是甚麼呢？31我們的祖先在曠野吃了嗎哪，正如聖經所記載的：『他從天上賜食糧給他們吃。』」

32 耶穌說：「我鄭重地告訴你們，摩西並沒有給你們從天上來的食糧⑥；從天上來的真食糧是我父親賜給你們的。33因為上帝所賜的食糧就是那從天上降下來、把生命給了世界的那一位。」

34 他們說：「先生，請時常把這食糧賜給我們！」

35 耶穌對他們說：「我就是生命的食糧；到我這裏來的，永遠不餓；信我的，永遠不渴。36但是我對你們說過，你們已經看見了我，仍然不信。37凡是父親所賜給我的人都

⑥「摩西並沒有給你們從天上來的食糧」或譯「摩西所給你們的，並不是從天上來的食糧」。

gives me will come to me. I will never turn away anyone who comes to me, 38because I have come down from heaven to do not my own will but the will of him who sent me. 39And it is the will of him who sent me that I should not lose any of all those he has given me, but that I should raise them all to life on the last day. 40For what my Father wants is that all who see the Son and believe in him should have eternal life. And I will raise them to life on the last day."

41The people started grumbling about him, because he said, "I am the bread that came down from heaven." 42So they said, "This man is Jesus son of Joseph, isn't he? We know his father and mother. How, then, does he now say he came down from heaven?"

43Jesus answered, "Stop grumbling among yourselves. 44People cannot come to me unless the Father who sent me draws them to me; and I will raise them to life on the last day. 45The prophets wrote, 'Everyone will be taught by God.' Anyone who hears the Father and learns from him comes to me. 46This does not mean that anyone has seen the Father; he who is from God is the only one who has seen the Father. 47I am telling you the truth: he who believes has eternal life. 48I am the bread of life. 49Your ancestors ate manna in the desert, but they died. 50But the bread that comes down from heaven is of such a kind that whoever eats it will not die. 51I am the living bread that came down from heaven. If you eat this bread, you will live forever. The bread that I will give you is my flesh, which I give so that the world may live."

52This started an angry argument among them. "How can this man give us his flesh to eat?" they asked.

53Jesus said to them, "I am telling you the truth: if you do not eat the flesh of the Son of Man and drink his blood, you will not have life in yourselves. 54Those who eat my flesh and drink my blood have eternal life, and I will raise them to life on the last day. 55For my flesh is the real food; my blood is the real drink. 56Those who eat my flesh and drink my blood live in me, and I live in them. 57The living Father sent me, and because of him I live also. In the same way whoever eats me will live because of me. 58This, then, is the bread that came down from heaven; it is not like the bread that your ancestors ate, but then later died. Those who eat this bread will live forever."

59Jesus said this as he taught in the synagogue in Capernaum.

會到我這裏來。到我這裏來的，我絕對不會拒絕他；38因為我從天上下來，不是要憑我自己的意思行事，而是要實行差我來那位的旨意。39差我來那位的旨意就是：他所賜給我的人，一個也不失落，並且在末日要使他們復活。40因為父親的旨意是要使所有看見兒子而信他的人獲得永恆的生命；在末日，我要使他們復活。」

41猶太人的領袖因為耶穌說「我是從天上降下來的食糧」，就竊竊私議：42「這個人不就是約瑟的兒子耶穌嗎？我們認識他的父母。現在他竟說他是從天上降下來的！」

43耶穌說：「你們用不着私下議論。44要不是那差我來的父親吸引了人，沒有人能到我這裏來；到我這裏來的，在末日我要使他復活。45先知的書上說過：『人都要蒙上帝的教導。』所有聽從父親而接受他教導的，都要到我這裏來。46這不是說有誰看見過父親，惟有從上帝那裏來的那一位見過父親。47我鄭重地告訴你們，信的人就有永恆的生命。48我就是生命的食糧。49你們的祖先在曠野吃了嗎哪，還是死了；50但是那從天上降下來的食糧是使人吃了不死的。51我就是從天上降下來那賜生命的食糧；吃了這食糧的人永遠不死。我所要賜給人的食糧就是我的肉，是為使世人得生命而獻出的。」

52這話在猶太人當中引起了劇烈的爭論。他們說：「這個人怎麼能把自己的肉給我們吃呢？」

53耶穌對他們說：「我鄭重地告訴你們，如果你們不吃人子的肉，喝他的血，你們就沒有真生命。54吃我肉，喝我血的，就有永恆的生命；在末日我要使他復活。55我的肉是真正的食物，我的血是真正的飲料。56那吃我的肉，喝我的血的，常在我生命裏，而我也在他生命裏。57永生的父親差遣了我，我也因他而活。同樣，吃我肉的人也要因我而活。58這就是從天上降下來的食糧；那吃這食糧的，要永遠活着。這食糧不像你們祖先吃過的，他們吃了，還是死了。」

59這些話是耶穌在迦百農會堂教導人的時候說的。

The Words of Eternal Life

60Many of his followers heard this and said, "This teaching is too hard. Who can listen to it?"

61Without being told, Jesus knew that they were grumbling about this, so he said to them, "Does this make you want to give up? 62Suppose, then, that you should see the Son of Man go back up to the place where he was before? 63What gives life is God's Spirit; human power is of no use at all. The words I have spoken to you bring God's life-giving Spirit. 64Yet some of you do not believe." (Jesus knew from the very beginning who were the ones that would not believe and which one would betray him.) 65And he added, "This is the very reason I told you that no people can come to me unless the Father makes it possible for them to do so."

66Because of this, many of Jesus' followers turned back and would not go with him any more. 67So he asked the twelve disciples, "And you–would you also like to leave?"

68Simon Peter answered him, "Lord, to whom would we go? You have the words that give eternal life. 69And now we believe and know that you are the Holy One who has come from God."

70Jesus replied, "I chose the twelve of you, didn't I? Yet one of you is a devil!" 71He was talking about Judas, the son of Simon Iscariot. For Judas, even though he was one of the twelve disciples, was going to betray him.

Jesus and His Brothers

7 After this, Jesus traveled in Galilee; he did not want to travel in Judea, because the Jewish authorities there were wanting to kill him. 2The time for the Festival of Shelters was near, 3so Jesus' brothers said to him, "Leave this place and go to Judea, so that your followers will see the things that you are doing. 4People don't hide what they are doing if they want to be well known. Since you are doing these things, let the whole world know about you!" 5(Not even his brothers believed in him.)

6Jesus said to them, "The right time for me has not yet come. Any time is right for you. 7The world cannot hate you, but it hates me, because I keep telling it that its ways are bad. 8You go on to the festival. I am not going[n] to this festival, because the right time has not come for me." 9He said this and then stayed on in Galilee.

永生的話

60好些門徒聽見這些話，就說：「這教導太難了，誰聽得進去呢？」

61耶穌知道他的門徒私下在議論這件事，就對他們說：「這話使你們信心動搖嗎？62假如你們看見人子上升回到他原來所在的地方，又怎樣呢？63給人生命的是聖靈，肉體是無濟於事的；我告訴你們的話就是賜生命的靈。64但是，你們當中有人不信。」（耶穌早就知道哪些人不信，誰會出賣他。）65他又說：「因此，我對你們說過，要不是出於我父親的恩賜，沒有人能到我這裏來。」

66從此，跟從他的人當中有好些人退出，不再跟他一道。67耶穌就問他的十二使徒：「你們呢？你們也要退出嗎？」

68西門・彼得回答：「主啊，你有賜永生的話語，我們還跟從誰呢？69我們信，並且知道你是從上帝那裏來的聖者。」

70耶穌說：「我豈不是選召了你們十二個人嗎？可是你們當中有一個是魔鬼！」71耶穌這話是指加略人西門的兒子猶大說的。猶大是十二使徒之一，就是後來要出賣他的人。

耶穌和他的兄弟

7 事後，耶穌周遊加利利省一帶，不願意在猶太地區來往，因為猶太人的領袖想殺害他。2猶太人的住棚節快到了，3所以耶穌的弟兄對他說：「你離開此地到猶太去吧，好讓你的門徒能看見你所行的事。4人要出名，就不能暗中裏做事。你既然能行這些事，就該在世人面前表現出來！」（5原來連他的兄弟也還沒有信他。）

6耶穌對他們說：「我的時機還沒有成熟；你們卻隨時都方便。7世人不會恨你們，卻憎恨我，因為我不斷地指證他們的行為是邪惡的。8你們自己去過節吧，我現在不上去⑦，因為我的時機還沒有成熟。」9耶穌說了這些話後仍然留在加利利。

---

n I am not going; *some manuscripts have* I am not yet going.

⑦「我現在不上去」有些古卷作「我不去」。

Jesus at the Festival of Shelters

10After his brothers had gone to the festival, Jesus also went; however, he did not go openly, but secretly. 11The Jewish authorities were looking for him at the festival. "Where is he?" they asked.

12There was much whispering about him in the crowd. "He is a good man," some people said. "No," others said, "he fools the people." 13But no one talked about him openly, because they were afraid of the Jewish authorities.

14The festival was nearly half over when Jesus went to the Temple and began teaching. 15The Jewish authorities were greatly surprised and said, "How does this man know so much when he has never been to school?"

16Jesus answered, "What I teach is not my own teaching, but it comes from God, who sent me. 17Whoever is willing to do what God wants will know whether what I teach comes from God or whether I speak on my own authority. 18Those who speak on their own authority are trying to gain glory for themselves. But he who wants glory for the one who sent him is honest, and there is nothing false in him. 19Moses gave you the Law, didn't he? But not one of you obeys the Law. Why are you trying to kill me?"

20"You have a demon in you!" the crowd answered. "Who is trying to kill you?"

21Jesus answered, "I performed one miracle, and you were all surprised. 22Moses ordered you to circumcise your sons (although it was not Moses but your ancestors who started it), and so you circumcise a boy on the Sabbath. 23If a boy is circumcised on the Sabbath so that Moses' Law is not broken, why are you angry with me because I made a man completely well on the Sabbath? 24Stop judging by external standards, and judge by true standards."

Is He the Messiah?

25Some of the people of Jerusalem said, "Isn't this the man the authorities are trying to kill? 26Look! He is talking in public, and they say nothing against him! Can it be that they really know that he is the Messiah? 27But when the Messiah comes, no one will know where he is from. And we all know where this man comes from."

28As Jesus taught in the Temple, he said in a loud voice, "Do you really know me and know where I am from? I have not come on my own authority. He who sent me, however, is truthful. You do not know him, 29but I know him,

耶穌過住棚節

10 耶穌的兄弟走了以後，耶穌也上去過節。他不是公開出門，而是秘密去的。11節期中，猶太人的領袖到處找耶穌，要知道他在哪裏。

12 人羣中對他議論紛紛，有的說：「他是一個好人」；有的說：「不，他在煽惑羣眾。」13只是大家都不敢公開講論他的事，因為他們怕猶太人的領袖。

14 節期過了一半，耶穌就上聖殿去教導人。15猶太人的領袖都很詫異，說：「這個人沒有跟過老師，怎麼會這樣有學問呢？」

16 耶穌說：「我的教導不是我自己的，而是出於那位差我來的。17一個人若決心要實行上帝的旨意就會曉得，我的教導是出於上帝的旨意還是憑着我自己講的。18那憑着自己講的，是想尋求自己的榮耀；但是那尋求差他來那位的榮耀的，才是真實無偽的。19摩西不是把法律頒佈給你們嗎？可是你們沒有一個人遵守法律。你們為甚麼想殺害我呢？」

20 羣眾回答：「你有鬼附身，誰想殺你呢？」

21 耶穌說：「我在安息日行了一件大事，你們都引以為奇。22可是摩西吩咐你們行割禮（其實割禮不是從摩西，而是從你們的祖先開始的），你們就在安息日為嬰兒行割禮。23如果人在安息日行割禮，目的是維護摩西的法律，那麼，我在安息日使一個人完全恢復了健康，你們又為甚麼責怪我呢？24不要根據外表斷定是非，要按照公正的標準來判斷才是。」

他是不是基督

25 有些耶路撒冷人說：「這個人不是我們的領袖們想殺掉的嗎？26你看，他公開講話，竟沒有人出來反對！是不是他們真的知道他就是基督？27可是基督出現的時候，沒有人會知道他從甚麼地方來，而這個人的來歷我們都很清楚。」

28 當時，耶穌在聖殿裏教導人，他高聲說：「你們真的認識我，知道我從哪裏來的嗎？我來，並不是憑着自己的意思。差我來的那一位是真實的。你們不認識他，29我卻

because I come from him and he sent me."

30Then they tried to seize him, but no one laid a hand on him, because his hour had not yet come. 31But many in the crowd believed in him and said, "When the Messiah comes, will he perform more miracles than this man has?"

Guards Are Sent to Arrest Jesus
32The Pharisees heard the crowd whispering these things about Jesus, so they and the chief priests sent some guards to arrest him. 33Jesus said, "I shall be with you a little while longer, and then I shall go away to him who sent me. 34You will look for me, but you will not find me, because you cannot go where I will be."

35The Jewish authorities said among themselves, "Where is he about to go so that we shall not find him? Will he go to the Greek cities where our people live, and teach the Greeks? 36He says that we will look for him but will not find him, and that we cannot go where he will be. What does he mean?"

Streams of Life-Giving Water
37On the last and most important day of the festival Jesus stood up and said in a loud voice, "Whoever is thirsty should come to me, and 38whoever believes in me should drink. As the scripture says, 'Streams of life-giving water will pour out from his side.'"o 39Jesus said this about the Spirit, which those who believed in him were going to receive. At that time the Spirit had not yet been given, because Jesus had not been raised to glory.

Division among the People
40Some of the people in the crowd heard him say this and said, "This man is really the Prophet!"p

41Others said, "He is the Messiah!"

But others said, "The Messiah will not come from Galilee! 42The scripture says that the Messiah will be a descendant of King David and will be born in Bethlehem, the town where David lived." 43So there was a division in the crowd because of Jesus. 44Some wanted to seize him, but no one laid a hand on him.

The Unbelief of the Jewish Authorities
45When the guards went back, the chief

o *Jesus' words in verses 37-38 may be translated:* "Whoever is thirsty should come to me and drink. 38 As the scripture says, 'Streams of life-giving water will pour out from within anyone who believes in me.'"
p THE PROPHET: *See 1.21.*

認識他;因爲我從他那裏來,是他差遣我的。」

30 於是,他們想逮捕他,只是沒有人下手,因爲他的時刻還沒有到。31羣衆當中也有許多人信了他;他們說:「基督來的時候會比這個人行更多的神蹟嗎?」

警衛逮捕耶穌
32 法利賽人聽見羣衆在紛紛議論耶穌的事,他們和祭司長就派警衛去逮捕耶穌。33耶穌說:「我還有一點點時間跟你們在一起,然後要回到差我來的那位那裏去。34你們要尋找我,但是找不着;因爲我要去的地方,你們不能去。」

35 猶太人的領袖們彼此對問:「他想到哪裏去,使我們找不着呢?難道他要到散居在希臘城市的猶太僑民那裏去教導希臘人嗎?36他所說『你們要尋找我,但是找不着』和『我要去的地方,你們不能去』這話是甚麼意思呢?」

活水的河流
37 節期的最後一天是最隆重的一天。耶穌站起來,高聲宣告說:「人要是渴了,就該到我這裏來喝。38聖經上說:『那信我的人有活水的河流要從他心中湧流出來⑧。』」39耶穌這話是指信他的人將要接受的聖靈說的。那時候聖靈還沒有降臨,因爲耶穌還沒有得到榮耀。

羣衆因耶穌紛爭
40 羣衆當中有許多人聽見了這話,就說:「這個人確實是那位先知!」

41 也有人說:「他是基督!」

另有人說:「基督怎麼會來自加利利?42因為聖經記載著:基督是大衛的後代,要降生在大衛的本鄉伯利恆。」43於是羣衆爲了耶穌引起紛爭。44有些人想逮捕他,但是沒有人下手。

猶太人的領袖不信耶穌
45 警衛們回去見祭司長和法利賽人;他們

⑧「人要是渴了……湧流出來」或譯「人要是渴了,就該到我這裏來;人要是信了我,就該來喝。聖經上說:『有活水的河流要從他心中湧流出來』」。

priests and Pharisees asked them, "Why did you not bring him?"

46The guards answered, "Nobody has ever talked the way this man does!"

47"Did he fool you, too?" the Pharisees asked them. 48"Have you ever known one of the authorities or one Pharisee to believe in him? 49This crowd does not know the Law of Moses, so they are under God's curse!"

50One of the Pharisees there was Nicodemus, the man who had gone to see Jesus before. He said to the others, 51"According to our Law we cannot condemn people before hearing them and finding out what they have done."

52"Well," they answered, "are you also from Galilee? Study the Scriptures and you will learn that no prophet ever comes*q* from Galilee."

The Woman Caught in Adultery

8 [Then everyone went home, but Jesus went to the Mount of Olives. 2Early the next morning he went back to the Temple. All the people gathered around him, and he sat down and began to teach them. 3The teachers of the Law and the Pharisees brought in a woman who had been caught committing adultery, and they made her stand before them all. 4"Teacher," they said to Jesus, "this woman was caught in the very act of committing adultery. 5In our Law Moses commanded that such a woman must be stoned to death. Now, what do you say?" 6They said this to trap Jesus, so that they could accuse him. But he bent over and wrote on the ground with his finger. 7As they stood there asking him questions, he straightened up and said to them, "Whichever one of you has committed no sin may throw the first stone at her." 8Then he bent over again and wrote on the ground. 9When they heard this, they all left, one by one, the older ones first. Jesus was left alone, with the woman still standing there. 10He straightened up and said to her, "Where are they? Is there no one left to condemn you?"

11"No one, sir," she answered.

"Well, then," Jesus said, "I do not condemn you either. Go, but do not sin again."]*r*

Jesus the Light of the World

12Jesus spoke to the Pharisees again. "I am the light of the world," he said. "Whoever follows me will have the light of life and will never walk in darkness."

q no prophet ever comes; one manuscript has the Prophet will not come.

r Many manuscripts and early translations do not have this passage (8.1-11); others have it after Jn 21.24; others have it after Lk 21.38; one manuscript has it after Jn 7.36.

問:「為甚麼沒有把耶穌帶來呢?」

46 警衛們回答:「從來沒有人像他那樣講話的!」

47 法利賽人說:「你們也受他愚弄了嗎? 48難道我們的領袖或法利賽人有信他的嗎? 49這些不明白摩西法律的愚民是該受詛咒的!」

50 他們當中有尼哥德慕;他從前去見過耶穌。他警告他們:51「我們的法律容許在沒有聽口供或查明真相之前定人的罪嗎?」

52 他們說:「難道你也是加利利人嗎?去查考聖經就知道,加利利不會出先知②。」

行淫的女人

8 〔大家都回家去了,耶穌卻到橄欖山去。2第二天一早,他回到聖殿;羣衆都來找他,他就坐下,開始教導他們。3經學教師和法利賽人帶來一個女人;她是在行淫時被抓到的。他們叫她站在中間,4問耶穌:「老師,這個女人在行淫時被抓到。5摩西在法律上命令我們,這樣的女人必須用石頭打死。你認為怎樣?」6他們想用這話陷害耶穌,找把柄控告他。但是耶穌彎下身子,用指頭在地上寫字。7他們還是不停地問他,耶穌就直起腰來,對他們說:「你們當中誰沒有犯過罪,誰就先拿石頭打她。」8說過這話,他又彎下身子,在地上寫字。9他們聽見這話,就一個一個溜走,從年紀大的先走,只剩下耶穌和那個還站在那裏的女人。10耶穌就直起腰來,問她說:「婦人,他們都哪裏去了?沒有人留下來定你的罪嗎?」

11 她說:「先生,沒有。」

耶穌說:「好,我也不定你的罪。去吧,別再犯罪!」〕⑩

耶穌是世界的光

12 耶穌又對大家說:「我是世界的光;跟從我的,會得着生命的光,絕不會在黑暗裏走。」

⑨「加利利不會出先知」另有些古卷作「那位先知不可能出自加利利」。
⑩有些古卷沒有括弧內這一段;另有些古卷把這一段放在約翰福音21.24之後;也有些古卷放在路加福音21.38之後;再有古卷放在約翰福音7.36之後。

13The Pharisees said to him, "Now you are testifying on your own behalf; what you say proves nothing."

14"No," Jesus answered, "even though I do testify on my own behalf, what I say is true, because I know where I came from and where I am going. You do not know where I came from or where I am going. 15You make judgments in a purely human way; I pass judgment on no one. 16But if I were to do so, my judgment would be true, because I am not alone in this; the Father who sent me is with me. 17It is written in your Law that when two witnesses agree, what they say is true. 18I testify on my own behalf, and the Father who sent me also testifies on my behalf."

19"Where is your father?" they asked him.

"You know neither me nor my Father," Jesus answered. "If you knew me, you would know my Father also."

20Jesus said all this as he taught in the Temple, in the room where the offering boxes were placed. And no one arrested him, because his hour had not come.

You Cannot Go Where I Am Going

21Again Jesus said to them, "I will go away; you will look for me, but you will die in your sins. You cannot go where I am going."

22So the Jewish authorities said, "He says that we cannot go where he is going. Does this mean that he will kill himself?"

23Jesus answered, "You belong to this world here below, but I come from above. You are from this world, but I am not from this world. 24That is why I told you that you will die in your sins. And you will die in your sins if you do not believe that 'I Am Who I Am'."

25"Who are you?" they asked him.

Jesus answered, "What I have told you from the very beginning.s 26I have much to say about you, much to condemn you for. The one who sent me, however, is truthful, and I tell the world only what I have heard from him."

27They did not understand that Jesus was talking to them about the Father. 28So he said to them, "When you lift up the Son of Man, you will know that 'I Am Who I Am'; then you will know that I do nothing on my own authority, but I say only what the Father has instructed me to say. 29And he who sent me is with me; he has not left me alone, because I always do what pleases him."

s What I have told you from the very beginning; or Why should I speak to you at all?

13 法利賽人對他說:「你在為自己作證;你的證言是無效的。」

14 耶穌說:「即使我為自己作見證,我的證言也是真實的;因為我知道我從那裏來,往哪裏去。你們卻不知道我從哪裏來,往哪裏去。15你們以人的標準來判斷人;我卻不判斷任何人。16即使我判斷人,我的判斷也是正確的;因為我不是獨自判斷,而是那位差我來的父親跟我一起判斷。17你們的法律書上記載着,有兩個人見證相符,他們的見證就算有效。18我為自己作見證;那位差我來的父親也為我作見證。」

19 於是他們問:「你的父親在哪裏?」

耶穌回答:「你們不認識我,也不認識我的父親;如果你們認識我,也就會認識我的父親。」

20 這些話是耶穌在聖殿的庫房裏教導人的時候說的。當時沒有人逮捕他,因為他的時刻還沒有到。

我去的地方你們不能去

21 耶穌又對他們說:「我要走了;你們要尋找我,可是你們將死在自己的罪中。我去的地方,你們不能去。」

22 猶太人的領袖就說:「他說『我去的地方,你們不能去』,難道他要自殺嗎?」

23 耶穌說:「你們是從地上來的,我是從天上來的;你們屬這世界,我不屬這世界。24所以我說,你們將死在自己的罪中。如果你們不信我就是『自有永有』的那一位,你們將死在自己的罪中。」

25 他們就問:「你到底是誰?」

耶穌回答:「我從一開始就告訴過你們了⑪。26關於你們,有許多事我應當說,應當審判。但是,差我來的那一位是真實的;我只是把從他那裏聽到的告訴世人。」

27 他們不明白耶穌所說關於父親的事。28所以耶穌告訴他們:「當你們把人子舉了起來,你們就會知道我就是『自有永有』的,並且知道我不憑着自己做甚麼,我只說父親所教導我的。29差遣我來的那一位跟我同在;他並沒有撇下我,使我孤單,因為我始終做他所喜歡的事。」

⑪「我從一開始就告訴過你們了」或譯「我何必告訴你們」。

30Many who heard Jesus say these things believed in him.

The Truth Will Set You Free

31So Jesus said to those who believed in him, "If you obey my teaching, you are really my disciples; 32you will know the truth, and the truth will set you free."

33"We are the descendants of Abraham," they answered, "and we have never been anybody's slaves. What do you mean, then, by saying, 'You will be free'?"

34Jesus said to them, "I am telling you the truth: everyone who sins is a slave of sin. 35A slave does not belong to a family permanently, but a son belongs there forever. 36If the Son sets you free, then you will be really free. 37I know you are Abraham's descendants. Yet you are trying to kill me, because you will not accept my teaching. 38I talk about what my Father has shown me, but you do what your father has told you."

39They answered him, "Our father is Abraham."

"If you really were Abraham's children," Jesus replied, "you would do[t] the same things that he did. 40All I have ever done is to tell you the truth I heard from God, yet you are trying to kill me. Abraham did nothing like this! 41You are doing what your father did."

"God himself is the only Father we have," they answered, "and we are his true children."

42Jesus said to them, "If God really were your Father, you would love me, because I came from God and now I am here. I did not come on my own authority, but he sent me. 43Why do you not understand what I say? It is because you cannot bear to listen to my message. 44You are the children of your father, the Devil, and you want to follow your father's desires. From the very beginning he was a murderer and has never been on the side of truth, because there is no truth in him. When he tells a lie, he is only doing what is natural to him, because he is a liar and the father of all lies. 45But I tell the truth, and that is why you do not believe me. 46Which one of you can prove that I am guilty of sin? If I tell the truth, then why do you not believe me? 47He who comes from God listens to God's words. You, however, are not from God, and that is why you will not listen."

Jesus and Abraham

48They asked Jesus, "Were we not right in

t If you really were ... you would do; *some manuscripts have* If you are ... do.

自由人和奴隸

30 許多人聽到耶穌這些話就信了他。

31 耶穌對信他的猶太人說:「你們若常常遵守我的教導,就眞的是我的門徒了;32你們會認識眞理,眞理會使你們得自由。」

33 他們回答:「我們是亞伯拉罕的子孫;我們沒作過誰的奴隸,你說『你們會得自由』,這話是甚麼意思呢?」

34 耶穌對他們說:「我鄭重地告訴你們,每個犯罪的人都是罪的奴隸。35奴隸在家庭裏沒有穩固的地位,兒子卻始終屬於家庭。36要是上帝的兒子使你們得自由,你們就眞的是自由人了。37我知道你們是亞伯拉罕的子孫,叫是你們想殺害我,因爲你們不接受我的教導。38我講的是我父親指示我的,而你們是做你們的父親告訴你們的。」

39 他們回答:「我們的祖宗是亞伯拉罕。」

耶穌說:「如果你們眞的是亞伯拉罕的子孫,你們一定會做亞伯拉罕所做的事。40我只不過告訴你們我從上帝那裏聽到的眞理,你們卻想殺我。亞伯拉罕並沒有做過種事啊!41你們是做你們的父親所做的事。」

他們回答:「上帝是我們惟一的父親;我們並不是私生子啊!」

42 耶穌對他們說:「如果上帝眞的是你們的父親,你們一定會愛我,因爲我是從上帝那裏來的,而我已經在這裏了。我不是憑自己來的,而是他差遣我的。43你們爲甚麼不明白我的話呢?因爲我的話你們聽不進去。44你們原是魔鬼的兒女,只想隨從你們父親的慾念行事。從起初他就是謀殺者,從不站在眞理一邊,因爲他根本沒有眞理。他撒謊是出於本性;因爲他本是撒謊者,也是一切虛謊的根源。45正因爲我講眞理,你們就不信我。46你們當中誰能指證我有罪呢?我既然講眞理,你們爲甚麼不信我呢?47凡是上帝的兒女,必然聽上帝的話。你們不是從上帝那裏來的,所以你們不聽。」

耶穌和亞伯拉罕

48 猶太人問耶穌:「我們說你是撒馬利亞

saying that you are a Samaritan and have a demon in you?"

49"I have no demon," Jesus answered. "I honor my Father, but you dishonor me. 50I am not seeking honor for myself. But there is one who is seeking it and who judges in my favor. 51I am telling you the truth: whoever obeys my teaching will never die."

52They said to him, "Now we know for sure that you have a demon! Abraham died, and the prophets died, yet you say that whoever obeys your teaching will never die. 53Our father Abraham died; you do not claim to be greater than Abraham, do you? And the prophets also died. Who do you think you are?"

54Jesus answered, "If I were to honor myself, that honor would be worth nothing. The one who honors me is my Father—the very one you say is your God. 55You have never known him, but I know him. If I were to say that I do not know him, I would be a liar like you. But I do know him, and I obey his word. 56Your father Abraham rejoiced that he was to see the time of my coming; he saw it and was glad."

57They said to him, "You are not even fifty years old—and you have seen Abraham?"u

58"I am telling you the truth," Jesus replied. "Before Abraham was born, 'I Am'."

59Then they picked up stones to throw at him, but Jesus hid himself and left the Temple.

Jesus Heals a Man Born Blind

9 As Jesus was walking along, he saw a man who had been born blind. 2His disciples asked him, "Teacher, whose sin caused him to be born blind? Was it his own or his parents' sin?"

3Jesus answered, "His blindness has nothing to do with his sins or his parents' sins. He is blind so that God's power might be seen at work in him. 4As long as it is day, we must do the work of him who sent me; night is coming when no one can work. 5While I am in the world, I am the light for the world."

6After he said this, Jesus spat on the ground and made some mud with the spittle; he rubbed the mud on the man's eyes 7and told him, "Go and wash your face in the Pool of Siloam." (This name means "Sent.") So the man went, washed his face, and came back seeing.

8His neighbors, then, and the people who

u you have seen Abraham?; *some manuscripts have* has Abraham seen you?

人,並且有鬼附身,難道說錯了嗎?」

49耶穌說:「我並沒有鬼附身;我尊敬我的父親,你們卻侮辱我。50我不求自己的榮耀,但是有一位替我尋求並主持公道的。51我鄭重地告訴你們,遵守我教導的人一定永遠不死。」

52他們對他說:「現在我們更確實知道你有鬼附身!亞伯拉罕死了,先知們也死了,你卻說『遵守我教導的人一定永遠不死』。53你敢說你比我們祖宗亞伯拉罕偉大嗎?亞伯拉罕死了,先知們也死了,你把自己當作甚麼人呢?」

54耶穌回答:「如果我榮耀自己,我的榮耀就毫無價值。那位榮耀我的是我的父親,就是你們所說是你們上帝的那一位。55你們從來不認識他,我卻認識他。如果我說我不認識他,我就跟你們一樣是撒謊者了。可是我認識他,並且遵守他的教導。56你們的祖宗亞伯拉罕曾歡歡喜喜地盼望着我來的日子;一看見了,他就非常快樂。」

57他們對他說:「你還不到五十歲,你見過亞伯拉罕⑫嗎?」

58耶穌回答:「我鄭重地告訴你們,亞伯拉罕出生以前,我就『有』了。」

59於是,他們撿起石頭要打他,耶穌卻躲開,從聖殿走出去。

治好生來失明的

9 耶穌在路上看見一個生下來就失明的人。2他的門徒問他:「老師,這個人生來就失明,是誰的罪造成的?是他自己的罪或是他父母的罪呢?」

3 耶穌回答:「他失明跟他自己或他父母的罪都沒有關係,而是要在他身上彰顯上帝的作爲。4趁着白天,我們必須做差我來那位的工作;黑夜一到,就沒有人能工作。5我在世上的時候,我就是世上的光。」

6 說了這話,耶穌吐口水在地上,用口水和着泥,抹在盲人的眼睛上,7並對他說:「你到西羅亞池子去洗吧。」(西羅亞的意思是「奉差遣」。)他就去洗,回來的時候,能看見了。

8 他的鄰居和經常看見他在討飯的人說:

⑫「你見過亞伯拉罕嗎」另有些古卷作「亞伯拉罕見過你嗎」。

had seen him begging before this, asked, "Isn't this the man who used to sit and beg?"

9Some said, "He is the one," but others said, "No he isn't; he just looks like him."

So the man himself said, "I am the man."

10"How is it that you can now see?" they asked him.

11He answered, "The man called Jesus made some mud, rubbed it on my eyes, and told me to go to Siloam and wash my face. So I went, and as soon as I washed, I could see."

12"Where is he?" they asked.

"I don't know," he answered.

The Pharisees Investigate the Healing

13Then they took to the Pharisees the man who had been blind. 14The day that Jesus made the mud and cured him of his blindness was a Sabbath. 15The Pharisees, then, asked the man again how he had received his sight. He told them, "He put some mud on my eyes; I washed my face, and now I can see."

16Some of the Pharisees said, "The man who did this cannot be from God, for he does not obey the Sabbath law."

Others, however, said, "How could a man who is a sinner perform such miracles as these?" And there was a division among them.

17So the Pharisees asked the man once more, "You say he cured you of your blindness well, what do you say about him?"

"He is a prophet," the man answered.

18The Jewish authorities, however, were not willing to believe that he had been blind and could now see, until they called his parents 19and asked them, "Is this your son? You say that he was born blind; how is it, then, that he can now see?"

20His parents answered, "We know that he is our son, and we know that he was born blind. 21But we do not know how it is that he is now able to see, nor do we know who cured him of his blindness. Ask him; he is old enough, and he can answer for himself!" 22His parents said this because they were afraid of the Jewish authorities, who had already agreed that anyone who said he believed that Jesus was the Messiah would be expelled from the synagogue. 23That is why his parents said, "He is old enough; ask him!"

24A second time they called back the man who had been born blind, and said to him, "Promise before God that you will tell the truth! We know that this man who cured you is a sinner."

「這個人不是一向坐在這裏討飯的嗎？」

9 有的說：「就是他」；也有的說：「不是他，只是像他罷了。」

那個人自己說：「我就是他。」

10 他們問：「你的眼睛是怎樣開的呢？」

11 他回答：「一個名叫耶穌的，和了泥抹我的眼睛，對我說：『你到西羅亞池子去洗。』我去，一洗就能看見。」

12 他們問：「那個人在哪裏？」

他回答：「我不知道。」

法利賽人查究失明人的事

13 他們帶那從前失明的人去見法利賽人。14耶穌和了泥開他眼睛的那一天是安息日。15法利賽人又一次盤問那個人是怎樣得看見的。他告訴他們：「他用泥抹我的眼睛，我一洗就能看見。」

16 有些法利賽人說：「做這事的人不可能是從上帝那裏來的，因為他不守安息日的戒律。」

另有些人說：「一個有罪的人怎能行這樣的神蹟呢？」他們因此爭論起來。

17 於是，法利賽人再次盤問那個人：「既然他開了你的眼睛，你說他是怎樣的人呢？」

他回答：「他是一位先知。」

18 猶太人的領袖不相信他從前失明，現在看得見；等到把他的父母找來，19他們問：「這個人是你們的兒子嗎？你們不是說他生下來就失明嗎？那麼，現在又怎麼會看見呢？」

20 他的父母回答：「他是我們的兒子，他生下來就是失明的，這個我們知道。21至於他現在怎麼會看見，是誰開了他的眼睛，我們都不知道。他已經成人了，你們去問他吧，讓他自己回答你們！」22他的父母這樣說是因為怕猶太人的領袖；當時他們已經商妥，如果有人承認耶穌是基督，就要把他趕出會堂。23因此他的父母回答：「他已經成人了，你們去問他吧！」

24 他們再一次把那生下來就失明的叫來，對他說：「你必須在上帝面前說誠實話！我們知道耶穌是一個罪人。」

25"I do not know if he is a sinner or not," the man replied. "One thing I do know: I was blind, and now I see."

26"What did he do to you?" they asked. "How did he cure you of your blindness?"

27"I have already told you," he answered, "and you would not listen. Why do you want to hear it again? Maybe you, too, would like to be his disciples?"

28They insulted him and said, "You are that fellow's disciple; but we are Moses' disciples. 29We know that God spoke to Moses; as for that fellow, however, we do not even know where he comes from!"

30The man answered, "What a strange thing that is! You do not know where he comes from, but he cured me of my blindness! 31We know that God does not listen to sinners; he does listen to people who respect him and do what he wants them to do. 32Since the beginning of the world nobody has ever heard of anyone giving sight to a person born blind. 33Unless this man came from God, he would not be able to do a thing."

34They answered, "You were born and brought up in sin–and you are trying to teach us?" And they expelled him from the synagogue.

Spiritual Blindness

35When Jesus heard what had happened, he found the man and asked him, "Do you believe in the Son of Man?"

36The man answered, "Tell me who he is, sir, so that I can believe in him!"

37Jesus said to him, "You have already seen him, and he is the one who is talking with you now."

38"I believe, Lord!" the man said, and knelt down before Jesus.

39Jesus said, "I came to this world to judge, so that the blind should see and those who see should become blind."

40Some Pharisees who were there with him heard him say this and asked him, "Surely you don't mean that we are blind, too?"

41Jesus answered, "If you were blind, then you would not be guilty; but since you claim that you can see, this means that you are still guilty."

The Parable of the Shepherd

10 Jesus said, "I am telling you the truth: the man who does not enter the sheep pen by the gate, but climbs in some other way, is a

25 他回答：「他是不是罪人，我不知道；不過我知道一件事：我從前失明，現在能看見了。」

26 他們問：「他替你做了甚麼？他怎樣開了你的眼睛？」

27 他回答：「我已經告訴你們了，你們不肯聽。爲甚麼現在又要聽呢？難道你們也想作他的門徒嗎？」

28 他們辱罵他：「你才是那個傢伙的門徒；我們是摩西的門徒。29我們知道上帝對摩西說過話；至於那傢伙，我們根本不知道他是哪裏來的！」

30 他回答：「這就怪了。他開了我的眼睛，你們卻不知道他是從哪裏來的！31我們知道，上帝不聽罪人的祈求；他只垂聽那敬拜他、並實行他旨意的人。32從創世以來，未曾聽過有人開了生來就是失明的眼睛的。33除非他是從上帝那裏來的，他甚麼都不能做。」

34 他們斥責他：「你這生長在罪中的傢伙，居然教訓起我們來！」於是他們把他從會堂裏趕出去。

靈性的盲目

35 耶穌聽見他們把他趕出會堂。以後耶穌找到他，對他說：「你信人子嗎？」

36 他回答：「先生，請告訴我他是誰，好讓我信他！」

37 耶穌對他說：「你已經見到他，現在跟你講話的就是他。」

38 他說：「主啊，我信！」就向耶穌下拜。

39 耶穌說：「我到這世上來的目的是要審判，使失明的，能看見；能看見的，反而失明。」

40 在那裏的一些法利賽人聽見這話，就問他：「難道你把我們也當作失明的嗎？」

41 耶穌回答：「如果你們是失明的，你們就沒有罪；既然你們說『我們能看見』，那麼，你們仍然是有罪的。」

羊圈的比喻

10 耶穌又說：「我鄭重地告訴你們，那不從門進羊圈，卻從別處爬進去的，是

thief and a robber. 2The man who goes in through the gate is the shepherd of the sheep. 3The gatekeeper opens the gate for him; the sheep hear his voice as he calls his own sheep by name, and he leads them out. 4When he has brought them out, he goes ahead of them, and the sheep follow him, because they know his voice. 5They will not follow someone else; instead, they will run away from such a person, because they do not know his voice."

6Jesus told them this parable, but they did not understand what he meant.

Jesus the Good Shepherd

7So Jesus said again, "I am telling you the truth: I am the gate for the sheep. 8All others who came before me are thieves and robbers, but the sheep did not listen to them 9I am the gate. Those who come in by me will be saved; they will come in and go out and find pasture. 10The thief comes only in order to steal, kill, and destroy. I have come in order that you might have life–life in all its fullness.

11"I am the good shepherd, who is willing to die for the sheep. 12When the hired man, who is not a shepherd and does not own the sheep, sees a wolf coming, he leaves the sheep and runs away; so the wolf snatches the sheep and scatters them. 13The hired man runs away because he is only a hired man and does not care about the sheep. 14-15I am the good shepherd. As the Father knows me and I know the Father, in the same way I know my sheep and they know me. And I am willing to die for them. 16There are other sheep which belong to me that are not in this sheep pen. I must bring them, too; they will listen to my voice, and they will become[v] one flock with one shepherd.

17"The Father loves me because I am willing to give up my life, in order that I may receive it back again. 18No one takes my life away from me. I give it up of my own free will. I have the right to give it up, and I have the right to take it back. This is what my Father has commanded me to do."

19Again there was a division among the people because of these words. 20Many of them were saying, "He has a demon! He is crazy! Why do you listen to him?"

21But others were saying, "A man with a demon could not talk like this! How could a demon give sight to blind people?"

Jesus Is Rejected

22It was winter, and the Festival of the Dedication of the Temple was being celebrated

v they will become; *some manuscripts have* there will be.

賊，是強盜。2那從門進去的，才是羊的牧人。3看門的替他開門；他的羊認得他的聲音。他按名字呼喚自己的羊，領他們出來。4他把自己的羊都領出來，就走在牠們前頭；他的羊跟着他，因為牠們認得他的聲音。5牠們並不跟隨陌生人，反而要逃開，因為不認得陌生人的聲音。」

6 耶穌對他們說了這個比喻，但是他們不明白他所說的是甚麼意思。

好牧人耶穌

7 於是，耶穌又對他們說：「我鄭重地告訴你們，我就是羊的門。8凡在我以前來的都是賊，是強盜；羊不聽從他們。9我是門；那從我進來的，必然安全，並且可以進進出出，也會找到草場。10盜賊進來，無非要偷，要殺，要毀壞。我來的目的是要使他們得生命，而且是豐豐富富的生命。

11「我是好牧人；好牧人願意為羊捨命。12雇工不是牧人，羊也不是他自己的。他一看見豺狼來，就撇下羊逃跑；豺狼抓住羊，趕散了羊羣。13雇工逃掉了，因為他不過是一個雇工，並不關心羊羣。14-15我是好牧人。正如父親認識我，我認識父親。同樣，我認得我的羊；牠們也認得我。我願意為牠們捨命。16我還有其他的羊不在這羊圈裏，我也必須把牠們領來；牠們會聽我的聲音。牠們兩者要合成一羣，同屬於一個牧人。

17「父親愛我；因為我願意犧牲自己的生命，為要再得到生命。18沒有人能奪走我的生命，是我自願犧牲的；我有權犧牲，也有權再得回。這是我父親命令我做的。」

19 猶太人又為了這些話起紛爭。20他們當中有好些人說：「他是鬼附的！他發瘋了！何必聽他？」

21 另有些人說：「鬼附的人不能說出這樣的話！鬼能開盲人的眼睛嗎？」

被猶太人棄絕

22 在耶路撒冷，慶祝獻殿節的時候到了；

in Jerusalem. 23Jesus was walking in Solomon's Porch in the Temple, 24when the people gathered around him and asked, "How long are you going to keep us in suspense? Tell us the plain truth: are you the Messiah?"

25Jesus answered, "I have already told you, but you would not believe me. The deeds I do by my Father's authority speak on my behalf; 26but you will not believe, for you are not my sheep. 27My sheep listen to my voice; I know them, and they follow me. 28I give them eternal life, and they shall never die. No one can snatch them away from me. 29What my Father has given me is greater[w] than everything, and no one can snatch them away from the Father's care. 30The Father and I are one."

31Then the people again picked up stones to throw at him. 32Jesus said to them, "I have done many good deeds in your presence which the Father gave me to do; for which one of these do you want to stone me?"

33They answered, "We do not want to stone you because of any good deeds, but because of your blasphemy! You are only a man, but you are trying to make yourself God!"

34Jesus answered, "It is written in your own Law that God said, 'You are gods.' 35We know that what the scripture says is true forever; and God called those people gods, the people to whom his message was given. 36As for me, the Father chose me and sent me into the world. How, then, can you say that I blaspheme because I said that I am the Son of God? 37Do not believe me, then, if I am not doing the things my Father wants me to do. 38But if I do them, even though you do not believe me, you should at least believe my deeds, in order that you may know once and for all that the Father is in me and that I am in the Father."

39Once more they tried to seize Jesus, but he slipped out of their hands.

40Jesus then went back again across the Jordan River to the place where John had been baptizing, and he stayed there. 41Many people came to him. "John performed no miracles," they said, "but everything he said about this man was true." 42And many people there believed in him.

The Death of Lazarus

11 A man named Lazarus, who lived in Bethany, became sick. Bethany was the town where Mary and her sister Martha lived. 2(This Mary was the one who poured the per-

w What my Father has given me is greater; *some manuscripts have* My Father, who gave them to me, is greater.

那時候是冬天。23耶穌在聖殿裏的所羅門廊下走着;24猶太人圍繞着他,對他說:「你使我們懸疑要到幾時呢?坦白地告訴我們,你是不是基督?」

25 耶穌回答:「我已經告訴過你們,可是你們不信。我奉我父親的名所做的事就是我的證據。26但是,你們不是我的羊,所以你們不信。27我的羊聽我的聲音,我認得牠們;牠們跟隨我。28我賜給他們永恆的生命,他們不至於死亡;無論誰都不能從我手中把他們奪走。29那位把他們賜給我的父親比一切都偉大[13],沒有人能從父親手裏把他們奪走。30父親和我原為一。」

31 這時候,猶太人又拿起石頭要打他。32耶穌對他們說:「我在你們面前做了父親要我做的許多善事;你們究竟為了哪一件事要拿石頭打我?」

33 他們回答:「我們不是為了你所做的善事要拿石頭打你,而是因為你侮辱了上帝!你不過是一個人,竟把自己當作上帝!」

34 耶穌說:「你們的法律不是寫着上帝曾說『你們是神』嗎?35我們知道聖經的話是永不改變的;對那些接受上帝信息的人,上帝尚且稱他們為神。36至於我,我是父親所揀選並差遣到世上來的。我說我是上帝的兒子,你們為甚麼說我侮辱上帝呢?37如果我不是做我父親的事,你們就不必信我;38如果是,你們縱使不信我,也應當相信我的工作,好使你們確實知道父親在我的生命裏,我也在父親的生命裏。」

39 於是他們又想逮捕他,他卻逃脫了他們的手。

40 耶穌又回約旦河的對岸,到約翰從前施洗的地方,住在那裏。41有許多人來找他,說:「約翰沒有行過神蹟,但是他指着這個人所說的一切話都是真實的。」42在那裏,有許多人信了耶穌。

拉撒路的死

11 有一個患病的人名叫拉撒路,住在伯大尼;馬利亞和她的姊妹馬大也住在這個村莊。(2這馬利亞就是那位曾用香油膏抹

⑬「那位把他們賜給我的父親比一切都偉大」另有些古卷作「我父親所賜給我的比一切都偉大」。

fume on the Lord's feet and wiped them with her hair; it was her brother Lazarus who was sick.) [3]The sisters sent Jesus a message: "Lord, your dear friend is sick."

[4]When Jesus heard it, he said, "The final result of this sickness will not be the death of Lazarus; this has happened in order to bring glory to God, and it will be the means by which the Son of God will receive glory."

[5]Jesus loved Martha and her sister and Lazarus. [6]Yet when he received the news that Lazarus was sick, he stayed where he was for two more days. [7]Then he said to the disciples, "Let us go back to Judea."

[8]"Teacher," the disciples answered, "just a short time ago the people there wanted to stone you; and are you planning to go back?"

[9]Jesus said, "A day has twelve hours, doesn't it? So those who walk in broad daylight do not stumble, for they see the light of this world. [10]But if they walk during the night they stumble, because they have no light." [11]Jesus said this and then added, "Our friend Lazarus has fallen asleep, but I will go and wake him up."

[12]The disciples answered, "If he is asleep, Lord, he will get well."

[13]Jesus meant that Lazarus had died, but they thought he meant natural sleep. [14]So Jesus told them plainly, "Lazarus is dead, [15]but for your sake I am glad that I was not with him, so that you will believe. Let us go to him."

[16]Thomas (called the Twin) said to his fellow disciples, "Let us all go along with the Teacher, so that we may die with him!"

Jesus the Resurrection and the Life
[17]When Jesus arrived, he found that Lazarus had been buried four days before. [18]Bethany was less than two miles from Jerusalem, [19]and many Judeans had come to see Martha and Mary to comfort them about their brother's death.

[20]When Martha heard that Jesus was coming, she went out to meet him, but Mary stayed in the house. [21]Martha said to Jesus, "If you had been here, Lord, my brother would not have died! [22]But I know that even now God will give you whatever you ask him for."

[23]"Your brother will rise to life," Jesus told her.

[24]"I know," she replied, "that he will rise to life on the last day."

[25]Jesus said to her, "I am the resurrection

主的腳,用自己的頭髮去擦乾的。患病的拉撒路就是她的弟弟。)[3]那兩姊妹打發人去見耶穌,說:「主啊,你所愛的朋友病了。」

[4]耶穌聽了這消息就說:「拉撒路的病不至於死,而是要榮耀上帝,並且使上帝的兒子因此得榮耀。」

[5]耶穌一向愛馬大和她的妹妹,也愛拉撒路。[6]他接到拉撒路害病的消息後,繼續在所住的地方停留兩天。[7]然後他對門徒說:「我們再到猶太去吧。」

[8]他的門徒說:「老師,前些時候,猶太人要拿石頭打你,你還想再到那裏去嗎?」

[9]耶穌說:「白天不是有十二個鐘頭嗎?人在白天走路,不至於跌倒,因為他看得見這世上的光。[10]人在黑夜走路,就會絆倒,因為他沒有光。」[11]耶穌說了這些話後,又說:「我們的朋友拉撒路睡着了,我要去喚醒他。」

[12]門徒說:「主啊,如果他是睡着了,他會好起來的。」

[13]其實,耶穌的意思是說拉撒路已經死了;他們卻以為他講的是正常的睡眠。[14]於是耶穌明明地告訴他們:「拉撒路死了;[15]為了要使你們相信,我不在他那裏倒是好的。現在我們去看他吧。」

[16]多馬(綽號雙胞胎的)對其他的門徒說:「我們跟老師一道去,跟他 起死吧!」

復活和生命的主
[17]耶穌到了伯大尼,知道拉撒路已經在四天前埋葬了。[18]伯大尼離耶路撒冷還不到三公里;[19]有好些猶太人來探望馬大和馬利亞,為了她們弟弟的死來安慰她們。

[20]馬大聽見耶穌來了,就出來迎接他;馬利亞卻留在家裏。[21]馬大對耶穌說:「主啊,要是你在這裏,我的弟弟就不會死![22]但是我知道,甚至現在,無論你向上帝求甚麼,他一定賜給你。」

[23]耶穌告訴她:「你的弟弟一定會復活的。」

[24]馬大說:「我知道在末日他一定會復活。」

[25]耶穌說:「我就是復活,就是生命。信

and the life. Those who believe in me will live, even though they die; 26and those who live and believe in me will never die. Do you believe this?"

27"Yes, Lord!" she answered. "I do believe that you are the Messiah, the Son of God, who was to come into the world."

Jesus Weeps

28After Martha said this, she went back and called her sister Mary privately. "The Teacher is here," she told her, "and is asking for you." 29When Mary heard this, she got up and hurried out to meet him. 30(Jesus had not yet arrived in the village, but was still in the place where Martha had met him.) 31The people who were in the house with Mary comforting her followed her when they saw her get up and hurry out. They thought that she was going to the grave to weep there.

32Mary arrived where Jesus was, and as soon as she saw him, she fell at his feet. "Lord," she said, "if you had been here, my brother would not have died!"

33Jesus saw her weeping, and he saw how the people with her were weeping also; his heart was touched, and he was deeply moved. 34"Where have you buried him?" he asked them.

"Come and see, Lord," they answered.

35Jesus wept. 36"See how much he loved him!" the people said.

37But some of them said, "He gave sight to the blind man, didn't he? Could he not have kept Lazarus from dying?"

Lazarus Is Brought to Life

38Deeply moved once more, Jesus went to the tomb, which was a cave with a stone placed at the entrance. 39"Take the stone away!" Jesus ordered.

Martha, the dead man's sister, answered, "There will be a bad smell, Lord. He has been buried four days!"

40Jesus said to her, "Didn't I tell you that you would see God's glory if you believed?" 41They took the stone away. Jesus looked up and said, "I thank you, Father, that you listen to me. 42I know that you always listen to me, but I say this for the sake of the people here, so that they will believe that you sent me." 43After he had said this, he called out in a loud voice, "Lazarus, come out!" 44He came out, his hands and feet wrapped in grave cloths, and with a cloth around his face. "Untie him," Jesus told them, "and let him go."

我的人，雖然死了，仍然要活着；26活着信我的人一定永遠不死。你信這一切嗎？」

27馬大回答：「主啊，是的！我信你就是那要到世上來的基督，是上帝的兒子。」

耶穌哭了

28馬大說了這話就回家，輕聲告訴妹妹馬利亞說：「老師來了，他叫你。」29馬利亞聽見這話，立刻起來，去見耶穌。（30當時耶穌還沒有進村子，仍然在馬大迎接他的地方。）31那些到家裏安慰馬利亞的猶太人看見她急忙起身出去，就跟着她，以為她要到墳墓去哭。

32馬利亞來到耶穌那裏，一看見他，就俯伏在他腳前，說：「主啊，要是你在這裏，我的弟弟就不會死！」

33耶穌看見馬利亞哭，也看見跟她一起來的猶太人在哭，心裏非常悲傷，深深地激動，34就問他們：「你們把他葬在哪裏？」

他們回答：「主啊，請來看。」

35耶穌哭了。36因此猶太人說：「你看，他多麼愛這個人！」

37有些人卻說：「他開過盲人的眼睛，難道他不能使拉撒路不死嗎？」

使拉撒路復活

38耶穌心裏又非常激動。他來到墳墓前；那墳墓是一個洞穴，入口的地方有一塊石頭堵住。39耶穌吩咐：「把石頭挪開！」

死者的姊姊馬大說：「主啊，他已經葬了四天，屍體都發臭了！」

40耶穌對她說：「我不是對你說過，你信就會看見上帝的榮耀嗎？」41於是他們把石頭挪開。耶穌舉目望天，說：「父親哪，我感謝你，因為你已經垂聽了我。42我知道你時常垂聽我；但是我說這話是為了周圍這些人，為要使他們信是你差遣我來的。」43說完這話，他大聲喊：「拉撒路，出來！」44那死了的人就出來；他的手腳裹着布條，臉上也包着布。耶穌吩咐他們說：「解開他，讓他走！」

The Plot against Jesus
(Matthew 26.1-5; Mark 14.1,2; Luke 22.1,2)

45Many of the people who had come to visit Mary saw what Jesus did, and they believed in him. 46But some of them returned to the Pharisees and told them what Jesus had done. 47So the Pharisees and the chief priests met with the Council and said, "What shall we do? Look at all the miracles this man is performing! 48If we let him go on in this way, everyone will believe in him, and the Roman authorities will take action and destroy our Temple and our nation!"

49One of them, named Caiaphas, who was High Priest that year, said, "What fools you are! 50Don't you realize that it is better for you to have one man die for the people, instead of having the whole nation destroyed?" 51Actually, he did not say this of his own accord; rather, as he was High Priest that year, he was prophesying that Jesus was going to die for the Jewish people, 52and not only for them, but also to bring together into one body all the scattered people of God.

53From that day on the Jewish authorities made plans to kill Jesus. 54So Jesus did not travel openly in Judea, but left and went to a place near the desert, to a town named Ephraim, where he stayed with the disciples.

55The time for the Passover Festival was near, and many people went up from the country to Jerusalem to perform the ritual of purification before the festival. 56They were looking for Jesus, and as they gathered in the Temple, they asked one another, "What do you think? Surely he will not come to the festival, will he?" 57The chief priests and the Pharisees had given orders that if anyone knew where Jesus was, he must report it, so that they could arrest him.

Jesus Is Anointed at Bethany
(Matthew 26.6-13; Mark 14.3-9)

12 Six days before the Passover, Jesus went to Bethany, the home of Lazarus, the man he had raised from death. 2They prepared a dinner for him there, which Martha helped serve; Lazarus was one of those who were sitting at the table with Jesus. 3Then Mary took a whole pint of a very expensive perfume made of pure nard, poured it on Jesus' feet, and wiped them with her hair. The sweet smell of the perfume filled the whole house. 4One of Jesus' disciples, Judas Iscariot–the one who was going to betray him–said, 5"Why wasn't this perfume sold for three hundred silver coins^x and the money given to the poor?" 6He said this, not because he cared about the poor, but because he was a

x SILVER COINS: See 6.7.

殺害耶穌的陰謀
（太26.1－5；可14.1－2；路22.1－2）

45 許多來探訪馬利亞的猶太人看見耶穌所做的事，就信了他。46但也有些人回去見法利賽人，把耶穌所做的事向他們報告。47因此，法利賽人和祭司長們召開議會，在會上說：「這個人行了這許多神蹟，我們該怎麼辦呢？48要是讓他這樣搞下去，大家都信了他，羅馬人會來擄掠我們的聖殿和民族的！」

49 他們當中有一個人名叫該亞法，就是當年的大祭司。他發言：「你們甚麼都不懂！50讓一個人替全民死，免得整個民族被消滅。難道看不出這對你們是一件合算的事嗎？」51其實，這話不是出於他自己；只因他是當年的大祭司，他在預言耶穌要替猶太人死，52不但替他們死，也要把分散各地的上帝的兒女都召集在一起，合成一羣。

53 從那時候開始，猶太人的領袖們計劃殺害耶穌。54因此耶穌不在猶太地區公開活動。他到一個靠近曠野、叫以法蓮的鎮上去，在那裏和門徒一起住。

55 猶太人的逾越節快到了。節期以前，許多人從鄉下上耶路撒冷去，要在那裏守潔淨禮。56他們到處尋找耶穌；當他們聚在聖殿裏的時候，彼此對問：「你認爲怎樣，他不會來過節吧？」57那些祭司長和法利賽人早已下命令：如果有人知道耶穌在甚麼地方，必須報告，好讓他們去逮捕他。

在伯大尼受膏
（太26.6－13；可14.3－9）

12 逾越節前六天，耶穌到了伯大尼，就是拉撒路住的地方（耶穌曾在這裏使拉撒路復活。）2有人在那裏爲耶穌預備了晚飯；馬大幫忙招待，拉撒路和其他的客人跟耶穌一起用飯。3這時候，馬利亞拿來一瓶極珍貴的純哪噠香油膏，倒在耶穌腳上，然後用自己的頭髮去擦；屋子裏充滿了香氣。4耶穌的一個門徒，就是將出賣他的加略人猶大，說：5「爲甚麼不拿這香油膏去賣三百塊銀子來分給窮人呢？」6他說這話，並不是眞的關心窮人，而是因爲他是賊；他管

thief. He carried the money bag and would help himself from it.

7But Jesus said, "Leave her alone! Let her keep what she has for the day of my burial. 8You will always have poor people with you, but you will not always have me."

The Plot against Lazarus

9A large number of people heard that Jesus was in Bethany, so they went there, not only because of Jesus but also to see Lazarus, whom Jesus had raised from death. 10So the chief priests made plans to kill Lazarus too, 11because on his account many Jews were rejecting them and believing in Jesus.

The Triumphant Entry into Jerusalem

(Matthew 21.1-11; Mark 11.1-11; Luke 19.28-40)

12The next day the large crowd that had come to the Passover Festival heard that Jesus was coming to Jerusalem. 13So they took branches of palm trees and went out to meet him, shouting, "Praise God! God bless him who comes in the name of the Lord! God bless the King of Israel!"

14Jesus found a donkey and rode on it, just as the scripture says,
15"Do not be afraid, city of Zion!
　Here comes your king,
　　riding on a young donkey."

16His disciples did not understand this at the time; but when Jesus had been raised to glory, they remembered that the scripture said this about him and that they had done this for him.

17The people who had been with Jesus when he called Lazarus out of the grave and raised him from death had reported what had happened. 18That was why the crowd met him–because they heard that he had performed this miracle. 19The Pharisees then said to one another, "You see, we are not succeeding at all! Look, the whole world is following him!"

Some Greeks Seek Jesus

20Some Greeks were among those who had gone to Jerusalem to worship during the festival. 21They went to Philip (he was from Bethsaida in Galilee) and said, "Sir, we want to see Jesus."

22Philip went and told Andrew, and the two of them went and told Jesus. 23Jesus answered them, "The hour has now come for the Son of Man to receive great glory. 24I am telling you

錢，常盜用公款。

7 但是耶穌說：「由她吧！這是她留下來爲着我安葬之日用的。8 常常有窮人跟你們一起，但是你們不常有我。」

殺害拉撒路的陰謀

9 一大羣猶太人聽說耶穌在伯大尼，就到那裏去。他們不但是爲着耶穌而去，也是想看看耶穌使他從死裏復活的拉撒路。10因此，祭司長們計謀連拉撒路也要殺，11因爲許多猶太人爲了他的緣故離開他們，信了耶穌。

光榮進耶路撒冷

（太21 · 1－11；可11 · 1－11；路19 · 28－40）

12第二天，一大羣到耶路撒冷過節的人聽說耶穌就要進城。13於是他們拿着棕樹枝出去迎接他，歡呼說：「讚美上帝！願上帝賜福給那位奉主的名而來的！願上帝賜福給以色列的君王！」

14耶穌找到一匹驢，騎上去，正如聖經所記載的：

15錫安城的兒女們哪，
　不要懼怕。
　看哪，你們的君王
　騎着小驢來了！

16 起初，他的門徒不明白這事的意義，到了耶穌得了榮耀以後才想起聖經的話是指着他說的，而且他們果然照所說的做了。

17 當耶穌呼喚拉撒路，使他從死裏復活，走出墓穴時，跟耶穌在一起的那羣人把他們所看見的傳開了。18許多人因爲聽見他行這神蹟，都去迎接他。19法利賽人彼此說：「我們眞是一事無成；你看，全世界都跟他去了！」

希臘人要求見耶穌

20 在節期中，到耶路撒冷禮拜的人當中有些希臘人。21他們來見加利利的伯賽大人腓力，要求他：「先生，我們想見耶穌。」

22 腓力去告訴安得烈，兩個人一起去告訴耶穌。23耶穌說：「人子得榮耀的時刻已經到了。24我鄭重地告訴你們，一粒麥子不落

the truth: a grain of wheat remains no more than a single grain unless it is dropped into the ground and dies. If it does die, then it produces many grains. 25Those who love their own life will lose it; those who hate their own life in this world will keep it for life eternal. 26Whoever wants to serve me must follow me, so that my servant will be with me where I am. And my Father will honor anyone who serves me.

Jesus Speaks about His Death

27"Now my heart is troubled–and what shall I say? Shall I say, 'Father, do not let this hour come upon me'? But that is why I came–so that I might go through this hour of suffering. 28Father, bring glory to your name!"

Then a voice spoke from heaven, "I have brought glory to it, and I will do so again."

29The crowd standing there heard the voice, and some of them said it was thunder, while others said, "An angel spoke to him!"

30But Jesus said to them, "It was not for my sake that this voice spoke, but for yours. 31Now is the time for this world to be judged; now the ruler of this world will be overthrown. 32When I am lifted up from the earth, I will draw everyone to me." 33(In saying this he indicated the kind of death he was going to suffer.)

34The crowd answered, "Our Law tells us that the Messiah will live forever. How, then, can you say that the Son of Man must be lifted up? Who is this Son of Man?"

35Jesus answered, "The light will be among you a little longer. Continue on your way while you have the light, so that the darkness will not come upon you; for the one who walks in the dark does not know where he is going. 36Believe in the light, while you have it, so that you will be the people of the light."

The Unbelief of the People

After Jesus said this, he went off and hid himself from them. 37Even though he had performed all these miracles in their presence, they did not believe in him, 38so that what the prophet Isaiah had said might come true:

"Lord, who believed the message we told?
To whom did the Lord reveal his power?"

39And so they were not able to believe, because Isaiah also said,
40"God has blinded their eyes
and closed their minds,
so that their eyes would not see,

在地裏，死了，仍舊是一粒；如果死了，就結出許多子粒來。25那愛惜自己生命的，要喪失生命；願意犧牲自己在這世上的生命的，反而要保存這生命到永生。26誰要事奉我，就得跟從我；我在哪裏，我的僕人也要在那裏。那事奉我的人，我父親一定重用他。」

耶穌講到自己的死

27「現在我心裏愁煩，我該說甚麼好呢？我該求父親救我脫離這時刻嗎？但我正是為此而來，要經歷這苦難的時刻。28父親哪，願你榮耀你的名！」

當時，有聲音從天上下來，說：「我已經榮耀了我的名，還要再榮耀！」

29站在那裏的羣眾聽見這聲音，就說：「打雷了！」

另有些人說：「有大使在跟他講話！」

30但是耶穌對他們說：「這聲音不是為我，而是為你們發的。31現在這世界要受審判；現在世上的統治者要被推翻。32我從地上被舉起的時候，我要吸引萬人來歸我。」（33他這話是指自己將怎樣死說的。）

34羣眾回答：「我們的法律告訴我們，基督是永世長存的；你為甚麼說人子必須被舉起？這人子是誰呢？」

35耶穌說：「光在你們中間為時不多了，你們該趁着還有光的時候繼續行走，免得黑暗追上你們，因為在黑暗中行走的人不知道他往哪裏去。36趁着你們還有光的時候要信從光，好使你們成為光明的人。」

猶太人的不信

說完了這些話，耶穌離開他們，隱藏起來。37他雖然在他們面前行過許多神蹟，他們還是不信他。38這是要應驗先知以賽亞說過的話：

主啊，有誰信我們所傳的信息呢？
主的權力向誰彰顯呢？

39他們所以不能信的理由，以賽亞也說過：

40上帝使他們的眼睛瞎了，
使他們的心智痲木了，
免得他們的眼睛看見，

and their minds would not understand,
and they would not turn to me, says God,
for me to heal them."

41Isaiah said this because he saw Jesus' glory
and spoke about him.

42Even then, many Jewish authorities believed in Jesus; but because of the Pharisees
they did not talk about it openly, so as not to
be expelled from the synagogue. 43They loved
human approval rather than the approval of
God.

Judgment by Jesus' Words

44Jesus said in a loud voice, "Whoever believes in me believes not only in me but also in
him who sent me. 45Whoever sees me sees also
him who sent me. 46I have come into the world
as light, so that everyone who believes in me
should not remain in the darkness. 47If people
hear my message and do not obey it, I will not
judge them. I came, not to judge the world, but
to save it. 48Those who reject me and do not
accept my message have one who will judge
them. The words I have spoken will be their
judge on the last day! 49This is true, because I
have not spoken on my own authority, but the
Father who sent me has commanded me what I
must say and speak. 50And I know that his command brings eternal life. What I say, then, is
what the Father has told me to say."

Jesus Washes His Disciples' Feet

13It was now the day before the Passover
Festival. Jesus knew that the hour had
come for him to leave this world and go to the
Father. He had always loved those in the world
who were his own, and he loved them to the
very end.
2Jesus and his disciples were at supper. The
Devil had already put into the heart of Judas,
the son of Simon Iscariot, the thought of betraying Jesus.y 3Jesus knew that the Father had
given him complete power; he knew that he
had come from God and was going to God. 4So
he rose from the table, took off his outer garment, and tied a towel around his waist. 5Then
he poured some water into a washbasin and began to wash the disciples' feet and dry them
with the towel around his waist. 6He came to
Simon Peter, who said to him, "Are you going
to wash my feet, Lord?"
7Jesus answered him, "You do not understand now what I am doing, but you will understand later."

y The Devil ... betraying Jesus; or The Devil had already decided
that Judas, the son of Simon Iscariot, would betray Jesus.

他們的心智領悟。
所以上帝說:他們不會轉向我,
讓我治好他們。

41 以賽亞說這些話是因為他看見了耶穌的
榮耀,指着他說的。

42 雖然如此,猶太人的領袖中也有許多信
耶穌的,只因怕法利賽人,不敢公開承認,
免得被趕出會堂。43他們愛人的讚許勝過愛
上帝的讚許。

耶穌的話要審判人

44 耶穌高聲呼喊:「信我的,不僅是信
我,也是信差我來的那位。45看見我的,也
就是看見那差我來的。46我作光,來到世
上,為要使所有信我的人不住在黑暗裏。
47那聽見我的信息而不遵守的人,我不審判
他。我來的目的不在審判世人,而是要拯救
世人。48那拒絕我、不接受我信息的人自有
審判他的;在末日,我所講的話要審判他!
49因為我沒有憑着自己講甚麼,而是那位差
我來的父親命令我說甚麼,講甚麼。50我知
道他的命令會帶來永恆的生命。所以,我講
的正是父親要我講的。」

耶穌為門徒洗腳

13 逾越節前,耶穌知道他離開這世界、回
父親那裏去的時刻到了。他一向愛世上
屬於他自己的人,他始終如一地愛他們。

2 耶穌和他的門徒在吃晚飯的時候,魔鬼
已經控制了加略人西門的兒子猶大的心,使
他決意出賣耶穌。3耶穌知道父親已經把一
切的權力交給他;他知道自己是從上帝那裏
來的,又要回到上帝那裏去。4他從席位上
起來,脫了外衣,拿一條毛巾束在腰間,
5然後倒水在盆裏,開始替門徒們洗腳,又
用毛巾擦乾。6他來到西門·彼得跟前的時
候,彼得說:「主啊,你替我洗腳嗎?」

7 耶穌回答:「我所做的,你現在不知
道,日後你就會明白。」

8Peter declared, "Never at any time will you wash my feet!"

"If I do not wash your feet," Jesus answered, "you will no longer be my disciple."

9Simon Peter answered, "Lord, do not wash only my feet, then! Wash my hands and head, too!"

10Jesus said, "Those who have taken a bath are completely clean and do not have to wash themselves, except for their feet.z All of you are clean–all except one." 11(Jesus already knew who was going to betray him; that is why he said, "All of you, except one, are clean.")

12After Jesus had washed their feet, he put his outer garment back on and returned to his place at the table. "Do you understand what I have just done to you?" he asked. 13"You call me Teacher and Lord, and it is right that you do so, because that is what I am. 14I, your Lord and Teacher, have just washed your feet. You, then, should wash one another's feet. 15I have set an example for you, so that you will do just what I have done for you. 16I am telling you the truth: no slaves are greater than their master, and no messengers are greater than the one who sent them. 17Now that you know this truth, how happy you will be if you put it into practice!

18"I am not talking about all of you; I know those I have chosen. But the scripture must come true that says, 'The man who shared my food turned against me.' 19I tell you this now before it happens, so that when it does happen, you will believe that 'I Am Who I Am.' 20I am telling you the truth: whoever receives anyone I send receives me also; and whoever receives me receives him who sent me."

Jesus Predicts His Betrayal

(Matthew 26.20-25; Mark 14.17-21; Luke 22.21-23)

21After Jesus had said this, he was deeply troubled and declared openly, "I am telling you the truth: one of you is going to betray me."

22The disciples looked at one another, completely puzzled about whom he meant. 23One of the disciples, the one whom Jesus loved, was sitting next to Jesus. 24Simon Peter motioned to him and said, "Ask him whom he is talking about."

25So that disciple moved closer to Jesus' side and asked, "Who is it, Lord?"

26Jesus answered, "I will dip some bread in the sauce and give it to him; he is the man." So

z Some manuscripts do not have except for their feet.

8 彼得說：「我決不讓你洗我的腳！」

耶穌說：「如果我不洗你的腳，你跟我就沒有關係了。」

9 西門・彼得說：「主啊，這樣的話，不只我的腳，連我的手和頭也洗吧！」

10 耶穌說：「洗過澡的人全身都乾淨了，只需要洗腳⑭。你們是乾淨的，但不是每一個人都乾淨。」（11耶穌已經知道誰要出賣他，所以說「不是每一個人都乾淨」。）

12 耶穌洗完了他們的腳，穿上外衣，然後又回到自己的座位。他問門徒們：「我剛才替你們做的，你們明白嗎？13你們尊我為師，為主，這是對的，因為我本來就是。14我是你們的主，你們的老師，我尚且替你們洗腳，你們也應該彼此洗腳。15我為你們立了榜樣，是要你們照着我替你們做的去做。16我鄭重地告訴你們，奴僕不比主人大，奉差遣的也不比差遣他的人重要。17既然明白這事，你們若能夠實行是多麼的有福啊！

18「我這話不是指你們全體說的；我認識我所揀選的人。只是聖經上所說『那跟我一起吃飯的人竟用腳踢我』這話必須實現。19我在事情還沒有發生以前告訴你們，為要使你們在事情發生的時候信我就是那『自有永有』的。20我鄭重地告訴你們，凡接待我所差遣的，就是接待我；凡接待我的，就是接待差遣我的那一位。」

耶穌預言將被出賣

（太26・20—25；可14・17—21；路22・21—23）

21 耶穌說了這話，心裏非常傷痛，就宣佈：「我鄭重地告訴你們，你們當中有一個人要出賣我。」

22 門徒面面相覷，不曉得他是指着誰說的。23門徒中有耶穌所鍾愛的一個人，他坐在耶穌身邊。24西門・彼得向他示意，說：「問問他指的是誰。」

25 於是那門徒挨近耶穌，問他：「主啊，是誰？」

26 耶穌回答：「我蘸一塊餅給誰，誰就是

⑭有些古卷沒有「只需要洗腳」。

he took a piece of bread, dipped it, and gave it to Judas, the son of Simon Iscariot. [27]As soon as Judas took the bread, Satan entered into him. Jesus said to him, "Hurry and do what you must!" [28]None of the others at the table understood why Jesus said this to him. [29]Since Judas was in charge of the money bag, some of the disciples thought that Jesus had told him to go and buy what they needed for the festival, or to give something to the poor.

[30]Judas accepted the bread and went out at once. It was night.

The New Commandment

[31]After Judas had left, Jesus said, "Now the Son of Man's glory is revealed; now God's glory is revealed through him. [32]And if God's glory is revealed through him, then God will reveal the glory of the Son of Man in himself, and he will do so at once. [33]My children, I shall not be with you very much longer. You will look for me; but I tell you now what I told the Jewish authorities, 'You cannot go where I am going.' [34]And now I give you a new commandment: love one another. As I have loved you, so you must love one another. [35]If you have love for one another, then everyone will know that you are my disciples."

Jesus Predicts Peter's Denial
(Matthew 26.31-35; Mark 14.27-31; Luke 22.31-34)

[36]"Where are you going, Lord?" Simon Peter asked him.

"You cannot follow me now where I am going," answered Jesus; "but later you will follow me."

[37]"Lord, why can't I follow you now?" asked Peter. "I am ready to die for you!"

[38]Jesus answered, "Are you really ready to die for me? I am telling you the truth: before the rooster crows you will say three times that you do not know me.

Jesus the Way to the Father

14 "Do not be worried and upset," Jesus told them. "Believe[a] in God and believe also in me. [2]There are many rooms in my Father's house, and I am going to prepare a place for you. I would not tell you this if it were not so.[b] [3]And after I go and prepare a place for you, I will come back and take you to myself, so that

a Believe; or You believe.
b There are ... were not so; or There are many rooms in my Father's house; if it were not so, would I tell you that I am going to prepare a place for you?

了。」說了這話,他拿一塊餅蘸一蘸,給了加略人西門的兒子猶大。[27]猶大一接過餅,撒但就附着他。耶穌對他說:「你要做的,快去做吧!」[28]在座的人都不明白耶穌對他說這話的意思。[29]因為猶大是管錢的,有的門徒以為耶穌吩咐他去買過節要用的東西,或是要他帶點東西去分給窮人。

[30] 猶大吃了那塊餅,立刻出去。那時候正是黑夜。

新的命令

[31] 猶大出去後,耶穌說:「現在人子已經得到榮耀了;上帝的榮耀也在人子身上顯明了。[32]既然上帝的榮耀藉着人子顯明,他自己也要顯明人子的榮耀,而且要立刻榮耀他。[33]孩子們,我和你們在一起的時間不多了。你們將尋找我;但是我現在要告訴你們,正如我告訴過猶太人的領袖:『我去的地方,你們不能去。』[34]我給你們一條新命令:要彼此相愛。我怎樣愛你們,你們也要怎樣彼此相愛。[35]如果你們彼此相愛,世人就知道你們是我的門徒。」

耶穌預言彼得不認主
(太26‧31─35;可14‧27─31;路22‧31─34)

[36] 西門‧彼得問耶穌:「主啊,你到哪裏去?」

耶穌回答:「我所要去的地方,你現在不能跟我去,但是後來你會跟我去的。」

[37] 彼得說:「主啊,為甚麼現在我不能跟你去呢?我願意為你捨命!」

[38] 耶穌說:「你願意為我捨命嗎?我鄭重地告訴你,雞叫以前,你會三次不認我。」

耶穌是道路、真理、生命

14 耶穌又對他們說:「你們心裏不要愁煩;要信上帝[15],也要信我。[2]在我父親家裏有許多住的地方,我去是為你們預備地方;若不是這樣,我就不說這話。[16] [3]我去為你們預備地方以後,要再回來,接你們

[15]「要信上帝」或譯「信上帝」。
[16]「在我父親家裏有許多住的地方,……我就不說這話。」或譯「在我父親家裏有許多住的地方,要不是這樣,我怎麼會告訴你們我是為你們預備地方呢?」

you will be where I am. ⁴You know the way that leads to the place where I am going."

⁵Thomas said to him, "Lord, we do not know where you are going; so how can we know the way to get there?"

⁶Jesus answered him, "I am the way, the truth, and the life; no one goes to the Father except by me. ⁷Now that you have known me," he said to them, "you will know*c* my Father also, and from now on you do know him and you have seen him."

⁸Philip said to him, "Lord, show us the Father; that is all we need."

⁹Jesus answered, "For a long time I have been with you all; yet you do not know me, Philip? Whoever has seen me has seen the Father. Why, then, do you say, 'Show us the Father'? ¹⁰Do you not believe, Philip, that I am in the Father and the Father is in me? The words that I have spoken to you," Jesus said to his disciples, "do not come from me. The Father, who remains in me, does his own work. ¹¹Believe me when I say that I am in the Father and the Father is in me. If not, believe because of the things I do. ¹²I am telling you the truth: those who believe in me will do what I do—yes, they will do even greater things, because I am going to the Father. ¹³And I will do whatever you ask for in my name, so that the Father's glory will be shown through the Son. ¹⁴If you ask me*d* for anything in my name, I will do it.

The Promise of the Holy Spirit

¹⁵"If you love me, you will obey my commandments. ¹⁶I will ask the Father, and he will give you another Helper, who will stay with you forever. ¹⁷He is the Spirit, who reveals the truth about God. The world cannot receive him, because it cannot see him or know him. But you know him, because he remains with you and is*e* in you.

¹⁸"When I go, you will not be left all alone; I will come back to you. ¹⁹In a little while the world will see me no more, but you will see me; and because I live, you also will live. ²⁰When that day comes, you will know that I am in my Father and that you are in me, just as I am in you.

²¹"Those who accept my commandments and obey them are the ones who love me. My Father will love those who love me; I too will

---

到我那裏去,爲要使你們跟我同在一個地方。⁴我要去的地方,那條路你們是知道的。」

⁵ 多馬對他說:「主啊,我們不知道你要到哪裏去,怎麼會知道那條路呢?」

⁶ 耶穌說:「我就是道路、眞理、生命;要不是藉着我,沒有人能到父親那裏去。⁷你們旣然認識我,也會認識我父親的⑰。從此你們認識他,而且已經看見他了。」

⁸ 腓力對耶穌說:「主啊,把父親顯示給我們,我們就滿足了。」

⁹ 耶穌回答:「腓力,我和你們在一起這麼久了,你還不認識我嗎?誰看見我就是看見父親。爲甚麼你還說『把父親顯示給我們』呢?¹⁰我在父親的生命裏,父親在我的生命裏,你不信嗎?我對你們說的話不是出於我自己,而是在我生命裏的父親親自做他的工作。¹¹你們要信我,我在父親的生命裏,父親在我的生命裏;如果不信這話,也要因我的工作而信我。¹²我鄭重地告訴你們,信我的人也會做我所做的事,甚至要做更大的,因爲我到父親那裏去。¹³你們奉我的名,無論求甚麼,我一定成全,爲要使父親的榮耀藉着兒子顯示出來。¹⁴你們奉我的名,無論向我求甚麼,我一定成全。」

應許聖靈的幫助

¹⁵「你們若愛我,就要遵守我的命令。¹⁶我要祈求父親,他就賜給你們另一位慰助者,永遠與你們同在。¹⁷他就是眞理的靈。世人不接受他;因爲他們看不到他,也不認識他。但是你們認識他;因爲他在你們的生命裏,常與你們同在。

¹⁸「我不撇下你們爲孤兒;我要再回到你們這裏來。¹⁹過些時候,世人再也看不見我;但是你們會看見我,而且因爲我活着,你們也要活着。²⁰那一天來到的時候,你們就會知道我在我父親的生命裏,而你們在我的生命裏,像我在你們的生命裏一樣。

²¹「凡接受我命令並且遵守的,就是愛我的人。愛我的,我父親必定愛他;我也愛

---

c Now that you have known me ... you will know; *some manuscripts have* If you had known me ... you would know.
d *Some manuscripts do not have* me.
e is; *some manuscripts have* will be.

⑰「你們旣然認識我,也會認識我父親的」另有些古卷作「如果你們認識我,你們就會認識我父親」。

love them and reveal myself to them."

22Judas (not Judas Iscariot) said, "Lord, how can it be that you will reveal yourself to us and not to the world?"

23Jesus answered him, "Those who love me will obey my teaching. My Father will love them, and my Father and I will come to them and live with them. 24Those who do not love me do not obey my teaching. And the teaching you have heard is not mine, but comes from the Father, who sent me.

25"I have told you this while I am still with you. 26The Helper, the Holy Spirit, whom the Father will send in my name, will teach you everything and make you remember all that I have told you.

27"Peace is what I leave with you; it is my own peace that I give you. I do not give it as the world does. Do not be worried and upset; do not be afraid. 28You heard me say to you, 'I am leaving, but I will come back to you.' If you loved me, you would be glad that I am going to the Father; for he is greater than I. 29I have told you this now before it all happens, so that when it does happen, you will believe. 30I cannot talk with you much longer, because the ruler of this world is coming. He has no power over me, 31but the world must know that I love the Father; that is why I do everything as he commands me.

"Come, let us go from this place.

Jesus the Real Vine

15 "I am the real vine, and my Father is the gardener. 2He breaks off every branch in me that does not bear fruit, and he prunes every branch that does bear fruit, so that it will be clean and bear more fruit. 3You have been made clean already by the teaching I have given you. 4Remain united to me, and I will remain united to you. A branch cannot bear fruit by itself; it can do so only if it remains in the vine. In the same way you cannot bear fruit unless you remain in me.

5"I am the vine, and you are the branches. Those who remain in me, and I in them, will bear much fruit; for you can do nothing without me. 6Those who do not remain in me are thrown out like a branch and dry up; such branches are gathered up and thrown into the fire, where they are burned. 7If you remain in me and my words remain in you, then you will ask for anything you wish, and you shall have it. 8My Father's glory is shown by your bearing much fruit; and in this way you become my disciples. 9I love you just as the Father loves me;

他，並且向他顯明我自己。」

22 猶大（不是加略人猶大）問：「主啊，為甚麼只向我們顯明，而不向世人顯明呢？」

23 耶穌回答：「愛我的人都會遵守我的話。我父親必定愛他，而且我父親和我要到他那裏去，與他同在。24不愛我的人就不遵守我的話。你們所聽到的話不是出於我，而是出於那差遣我來的父親。

25「我還與你們同在的時候，已經把這些話告訴你們了。26但是那慰助者，就是父親因着我的名要差來的聖靈，會把一切的事指示你們，並且使你們記起我對你們所說的一切話。

27「我留下平安給你們，我把我的平安賜給你們。我所給你們的，跟世人所給的不同。你們心裏不要愁煩，也不要害怕。28你們聽見我說過『我去了，但是還要回來』。你們若愛我，就會因着我回到父親那裏去而歡喜，因為他比我大。29我在這些事發生以前先告訴了你們，爲要使你們在事情發生的時候能夠信。30我現在不能再和你們多講，因爲這世界的統治者就要來了。他對我是無能爲力的；31但爲了要世人知道我愛我的父親，所以我遵行他所命令的一切。

「起來，我們走吧！」

耶穌是眞葡萄樹

15 「我是眞葡萄樹；我父親是園丁。2所有連接着我而不結果實的枝子，他就剪掉；能結果實的枝子，他就修剪，使它結更多的果實。3我對你們所講的信息已經使你們潔淨了。4你們要常跟我連結，我就常跟你們連結。要是不跟我連結，你們就不能結出果實，正像枝子不跟葡萄樹連接就不能結果實一樣。

5「我是葡萄樹；你們是枝子。那常跟我連結，而我也常跟他連結的，必定結很多果實；因爲沒有我，你們就甚麼也不能做。6那不跟我連結的人要被扔掉，像枯乾的枝子被扔掉，讓人撿去投在火裏焚燒。7如果你們常跟我連結，而我的話也常存在你們裏面，你們無論要甚麼，求，就會得着。8我父親將因你們結很多果實而得到榮耀，而你們也因此成爲我的門徒。9正如父親愛我，

remain in my love. [10]If you obey my commands, you will remain in my love, just as I have obeyed my Father's commands and remain in his love.

[11]"I have told you this so that my joy may be in you and that your joy may be complete. [12]My commandment is this: love one another, just as I love you. [13]The greatest love you can have for your friends is to give your life for them. [14]And you are my friends if you do what I command you. [15]I do not call you servants any longer, because servants do not know what their master is doing. Instead, I call you friends, because I have told you everything I heard from my Father. [16]You did not choose me; I chose you and appointed you to go and bear much fruit, the kind of fruit that endures. And so the Father will give you whatever you ask of him in my name. [17]This, then, is what I command you: love one another.

The World's Hatred
[18]"If the world hates you, just remember that it has hated me first. [19]If you belonged to the world, then the world would love you as its own. But I chose you from this world, and you do not belong to it; that is why the world hates you. [20]Remember what I told you: 'Slaves are not greater than their master.' If people persecuted me, they will persecute you too; if they obeyed my teaching, they will obey yours too. [21]But they will do all this to you because you are mine; for they do not know the one who sent me. [22]They would not have been guilty of sin if I had not come and spoken to them; as it is, they no longer have any excuse for their sin. [23]Whoever hates me hates my Father also. [24]They would not have been guilty of sin if I had not done among them the things that no one else ever did; as it is, they have seen what I did, and they hate both me and my Father. [25]This, however, was bound to happen so that what is written in their Law may come true: 'They hated me for no reason at all.'

[26]"The Helper will come–the Spirit, who reveals the truth about God and who comes from the Father. I will send him to you from the Father, and he will speak about me. [27]And you, too, will speak about me, because you have been with me from the very beginning.

16 [1]"I have told you this, so that you will not give up your faith. [2]You will be expelled from the synagogues, and the time will come when those who kill you will think that by

我愛你們;你們要常生活在我的愛中。[10]你們若遵守我的命令,你們會常生活在我的愛中,正像我遵守我父親的命令,而常在他的愛中一樣。

[11]「我告訴你們這些事,為要使你們得到我的喜樂,讓你們的喜樂滿溢。[12]你們要彼此相愛,像我愛你們一樣;這是我的命令。[13]人為朋友犧牲自己的性命,人間的愛沒有比這更偉大的了。[14]你們若遵守我的命令,就是我的朋友。[15]我不再把你們當作僕人,因為僕人不知道主人所做的事。我把你們當作朋友,因為我已經把從我父親那裏所聽到的一切都告訴了你們。[16]不是你們揀選了我,而是我揀選了你們,並且指派你們去結那常存的果實。你們奉我的名,無論向父親求甚麼,他一定賜給你們。[17]你們要彼此相愛;這就是我給你們的命令。」

世人的憎恨
[18]「如果世人憎恨你們,你們該曉得,他們已先憎恨了我。[19]如果你們屬於這世界,世人一定愛那屬於他們自己的。可是,我從這世界中把你們揀選了出來,你們不屬於它;因此世人憎恨你們。[20]你們要記住我對你們說過的話:『奴僕不比主人大。』如果他們迫害過我,他們也會迫害你們;如果他們遵從我的話,他們也會遵從你們的話。[21]為了我的緣故,他們要對你們做這一切事,因為他們不認識差遣我來的那位。[22]我若沒有來向他們講解過,他們就沒有罪;如今,他們的罪是無可推諉的了。[23]憎恨我的,也憎恨我的父親。[24]如果我沒有在他們當中做了那從來沒有人做過的事,他們就沒有罪。事實上,他們已經看見我所做的,卻還憎恨我,也憎恨我的父親。[25]但是,這無非要應驗他們的法律書上所寫的:『他們無緣無故地憎恨我!』

[26]「但是,那出自父親的慰助者要來;他就是真理的靈。我從父親那裏差他來的時候,他要為我作證。[27]同樣,你們也要為我作證,因為你們從開始就跟我在一起。」

16 [1]「我把這些事告訴了你們,為要使你們的信心不至於動搖。[2]他們要把你們趕出會堂;而且時刻就要到了,那殺害你們的

doing this they are serving God. [3]People will do these things to you because they have not known either the Father or me. [4]But I have told you this, so that when the time comes for them to do these things, you will remember what I told you.

The Work of the Holy Spirit

"I did not tell you these things at the beginning, for I was with you. [5]But now I am going to him who sent me, yet none of you asks me where I am going. [6]And now that I have told you, your hearts are full of sadness. [7]But I am telling you the truth: it is better for you that I go away, because if I do not go, the Helper will not come to you. But if I do go away, then I will send him to you. [8]And when he comes, he will prove to the people of the world that they are wrong about sin and about what is right and about God's judgment. [9]They are wrong about sin, because they do not believe in me; [10]they are wrong about what is right, because I am going to the Father and you will not see me any more; [11]and they are wrong about judgment, because the ruler of this world has already been judged.

[12]"I have much more to tell you, but now it would be too much for you to bear. [13]When, however, the Spirit comes, who reveals the truth about God, he will lead you into all the truth. He will not speak on his own authority, but he will speak of what he hears and will tell you of things to come. [14]He will give me glory, because he will take what I say and tell it to you. [15]All that my Father has is mine; that is why I said that the Spirit will take what I give him and tell it to you.

Sadness and Gladness

[16]"In a little while you will not see me any more, and then a little while later you will see me."

[17]Some of his disciples asked among themselves, "What does this mean? He tells us that in a little while we will not see him, and then a little while later we will see him; and he also says, 'It is because I am going to the Father.' [18]What does this 'a little while' mean? We don't know what he is talking about!"

[19]Jesus knew that they wanted to question him, so he said to them, "I said, 'In a little while you will not see me, and then a little while later you will see me.' Is this what you are asking about among yourselves? [20]I am telling you the truth: you will cry and weep, but the world will be glad; you will be sad, but

人還以爲做這種事是在事奉上帝。[3]其實，他們這樣做是因爲他們既不認識父親，也不認識我。[4]我告訴你們這些事，爲要讓你們在這時刻來臨時記得我曾經對你們說過了。」

聖靈的工作

「我當初沒有告訴你們這些事，是因爲我一直與你們在一起。[5]現在我要回到那位差我來的那裏去，你們當中沒有人問『你要到哪裏去？』[6]可是，因爲我把這些事告訴了你們，你們心裏竟充滿憂愁。[7]然而，我實在告訴你們，我去，對你們是有益的；我不去，那慰助者就不會到你們這裏來；我去了，就差他來。[8]他來的時候，他要向世人證明，他們對於罪，對於義，對於上帝審判的觀念都錯了。[9]他們對罪的觀念錯了，因爲他們不信我；[10]他們對義的觀念錯了，因爲我往父親那裏去，你們再也看不見我；[11]他們對審判的觀念錯了，因爲這世界的王已經受了審判。

[12]「我還有許多事要告訴你們，可是你們現在擔負不了。[13]等到賜真理的聖靈來了，他要指引你們進到一切的真理中。他不憑着自己說話，而是把他所聽到的告訴你們，並且要說出將來的事。[14]他要榮耀我，因爲他要把我所要說的告訴你們。[15]我父親所有的一切都是我的，所以我說，聖靈要把我所要說的告訴你們。」

憂愁變成喜樂

[16]「過一會兒，你們就看不見我了；然而，再過一會兒，你們還要看見我。」

[17]門徒當中有幾個人彼此說：「他告訴我們『過一會兒，你們就看不見我了；然而，再過一會兒，你們還要看見我』；又說『因爲我要到父親那裏去』；這些話是甚麼意思呢？」[18]也有人問：「他所說的『過一會兒』是指甚麼呢？我們不曉得他在說些甚麼！」

[19]耶穌知道他們想問的，就對他們說：「我說『過一會兒，你們看不見我了；然而，再過一會兒，你們還要看見我』；你們彼此在討論這句話嗎？[20]我鄭重地告訴你們，你們要痛哭哀號，世人卻要歡樂；你們

your sadness will turn into gladness. 21When a woman is about to give birth, she is sad because her hour of suffering has come; but when the baby is born, she forgets her suffering, because she is happy that a baby has been born into the world. 22That is how it is with you: now you are sad, but I will see you again, and your hearts will be filled with gladness, the kind of gladness that no one can take away from you.

23"When that day comes, you will not ask me for anything. I am telling you the truth: the Father will give you whatever you ask of him in my name.f 24Until now you have not asked for anything in my name; ask and you will receive, so that your happiness may be complete.

Victory over the World

25"I have used figures of speech to tell you these things. But the time will come when I will not use figures of speech, but will speak to you plainly about the Father. 26When that day comes, you will ask him in my name; and I do not say that I will ask him on your behalf, 27for the Father himself loves you. He loves you because you love me and have believed that I came from God. 28I did come from the Father, and I came into the world; and now I am leaving the world and going to the Father."

29Then his disciples said to him, "Now you are speaking plainly, without using figures of speech. 30We know now that you know everything; you do not need to have someone ask you questions. This makes us believe that you came from God."

31Jesus answered them, "Do you believe now? 32The time is coming, and is already here, when all of you will be scattered, each of you to your own home, and I will be left all alone. But I am not really alone, because the Father is with me. 33I have told you this so that you will have peace by being united to me. The world will make you suffer. But be brave! I have defeated the world!"

Jesus Prays for His Disciples

17 After Jesus finished saying this, he looked up to heaven and said, "Father, the hour has come. Give glory to your Son, so that the Son may give glory to you. 2For you gave him authority over all people, so that he might give eternal life to all those you gave him. 3And eternal life means to know you, the only true God, and to know Jesus Christ, whom you sent. 4I have shown your glory on earth; I have

f the Father will give you whatever you ask of him in my name; some manuscripts have if you ask the Father for anything, he will give it to you in my name.

要憂愁，可是你們的憂愁將變成喜樂。21女人快要生產的時候憂愁，因為受苦的時刻到了；但是生了嬰兒後就忘掉了痛苦，因為高興有嬰兒出生到世上來。22你們也是這樣：現在你們有憂愁，但是我要再見到你們，你們心裏就會充滿喜樂；你們的喜樂是沒有人能奪走的。

23「在那一天，你們不向我求甚麼。我鄭重地告訴你們，你們奉我的名，無論向父親求甚麼，他一定賜給你們⑱。24直到現在，你們並沒有奉我的名求過甚麼；你們求，就得到，好讓你們的喜樂滿溢。」

勝過世界

25「我用比喻把這些事向你們說了。可是時刻就到，我不再使用比喻，卻要明明地把父親的事告訴你們。26在那一天，你們要奉我的名祈求；我並不是說我要替你們向父親求，27因為父親自己愛你們。他愛你們；因為你們愛我，並且信我是從上帝那裏來的。28我從父親那裏來到這世界；現在我要離開這世界，回到父親那裏去。」

29門徒對他說：「你看，現在你是明明講論，並沒有用甚麼比喻。30我們已經曉得，你無所不知，不需要有人向你發問。因此，我們信你是從上帝那裏來的。」

31耶穌說：「現在你們信了嗎？32時刻到了，現在已經是了，你們都要分散，各人回自己的地方去，只留下我自己一個人。其實，我不是自己一個人，因為有父親與我同在。33我把這件事告訴你們，是要使你們因跟我連結而有平安。在世上，你們有苦難；但是你們要勇敢，我已經勝過了世界！」

耶穌為門徒禱告

17 耶穌講完了這些話，就舉目望天，說：「父親哪，時刻已經到了，求你榮耀你的兒子，好使兒子也榮耀你。2你把管理全人類的權柄給了他，好使他把永恆的生命賜給你所付託給他的人。3認識你是惟一的眞神，並且認識你所差來的耶穌基督，這就是永恆的生命。4我已經在地上榮耀了你；我

⑱「你們奉我的名，無論向父求甚麼，他一定賜給你們」另有些古卷作「如果你們向父親求，他會因着我的名而賜給你們」。

finished the work you gave me to do. [5]Father! Give me glory in your presence now, the same glory I had with you before the world was made.

[6]"I have made you known to those you gave me out of the world. They belonged to you, and you gave them to me. They have obeyed your word, [7]and now they know that everything you gave me comes from you. [8]I gave them the message that you gave me, and they received it; they know that it is true that I came from you, and they believe that you sent me.

[9]"I pray for them. I do not pray for the world but for those you gave me, for they belong to you. [10]All I have is yours, and all you have is mine; and my glory is shown through them. [11]And now I am coming to you; I am no longer in the world, but they are in the world. Holy Father! Keep them safe by the power of your name, the name you gave me,[g] so that they may be one just as you and I are one. [12]While I was with them, I kept them safe by the power of your name, the name you gave me.[h] I protected them, and not one of them was lost, except the man who was bound to be lost–so that the scripture might come true. [13]And now I am coming to you, and I say these things in the world so that they might have my joy in their hearts in all its fullness. [14]I gave them your message, and the world hated them, because they do not belong to the world, just as I do not belong to the world. [15]I do not ask you to take them out of the world, but I do ask you to keep them safe from the Evil One. [16]Just as I do not belong to the world, they do not belong to the world. [17]Dedicate them to yourself by means of the truth; your word is truth. [18]I sent them into the world, just as you sent me into the world. [19]And for their sake I dedicate myself to you, in order that they, too, may be truly dedicated to you.

[20]"I pray not only for them, but also for those who believe in me because of their message. [21]I pray that they may all be one. Father! May they be in us, just as you are in me and I am in you. May they be one, so that the world will believe that you sent me. [22]I gave them the same glory you gave me, so that they may be one, just as you and I are one: [23]I in them and you in me, so that they may be completely one, in order that the world may know that you sent

g Keep them safe by the power of your name, the name you gave me; *some manuscripts have* By the power of your name keep safe those you have given me.

h I kept them safe by the power of your name, the name you gave me; *some manuscripts have* By the power of your name I kept safe those you have given me.

已經完成了你所付託給我的使命。[5]父親哪,現在求你在你自己面前榮耀我,賜給我那創世之前我和你一同享有的榮耀吧!

[6]「我已經把你顯明給那些你從世界選召出來付託給我的人。他們原屬於你,你把他們賜給我;他們也遵守了你的話。[7]現在,他們都知道,你所賜給我的,都是從你那裏來的。[8]我把你所給我的信息給了他們,他們也領受了。他們確實知道我是從你那裏來的,也信是你差遣了我。

[9]「我為他們祈求;我不為世人祈求,而是為你所賜給我的人祈求,因為他們是屬於你的。[10]我所有的,都是你的;你所有的,也都是我的。我的榮耀是藉着他們彰顯出來的。[11]我現在到你那裏去,不再留在世上,他們卻在世上。聖父啊!求你藉着你的名,就是你賜給我的名,保守他們⑲,使他們合而為一,如同你和我是合一的。[12]我與他們同在的時候,我藉着你的名,就是你賜給我的名,保守他們⑳。我保護他們,其中除了註定滅亡的那個人以外,沒有一個失掉的;這正應驗了聖經的話。[13]現在,我到你那裏去,我還在世上的時候說這些話,為要使他們心裏充滿我的喜樂。[14]我把你的信息給了他們;世人憎恨他們,因為他們不屬於這世界,正如我不屬於這世界一樣。[15]我不求你從世上把他們帶走,但我求你使他們脫離那邪惡者。[16]正如我不屬於世界,他們也不屬於世界。[17]求你藉着真理使他們把自己奉獻給你;你的話就是真理。[18]正如你差遣我進入世界,我也差遣他們進入世界。[19]為了他們的緣故,我把自己奉獻給你,好使他們也真誠地奉獻給你。

[20]「我不但為他們祈求,也為那些因接受他們的信息而信我的人祈求。[21]願他們都合而為一。父親哪,願他們在我們的生命裏;正如你在我生命裏,我在你生命裏一樣。願他們都合而為一,為要使世人信是你所差遣的。[22]你給我的榮耀,我也給了他們,為要使他們合而為一,像我們合而為一一樣。[23]我在他們的生命裏,而你在我的生命裏,為要使他們完全合一,好讓世人知道你差遣

⑲「求你藉着你的名,就是你賜給我的名,保守他們」另有些古卷作「求你藉着你的名的權力,保守你所賜給我的那些人」。

⑳「我藉着你的名,就是你賜給我的名,保守他們」另有些古卷作「我藉着你的名的權力,保守了你所賜給我的那些人」。

me and that you love them as you love me.

24"Father! You have given them to me, and I want them to be with me where I am, so that they may see my glory, the glory you gave me; for you loved me before the world was made. 25Righteous Father! The world does not know you, but I know you, and these know that you sent me. 26I made you known to them, and I will continue to do so, in order that the love you have for me may be in them, and so that I also may be in them."

The Arrest of Jesus
(Matthew 26.47-56; Mark 14.43-50; Luke 22.47-53)

18 After Jesus had said this prayer, he left with his disciples and went across Kidron Brook. There was a garden in that place, and Jesus and his disciples went in. 2Judas, the traitor, knew where it was, because many times Jesus had met there with his disciples. 3So Judas went to the garden, taking with him a group of Roman soldiers, and some Temple guards sent by the chief priests and the Pharisees; they were armed and carried lanterns and torches. 4Jesus knew everything that was going to happen to him, so he stepped forward and asked them, "Who is it you are looking for?"

5"Jesus of Nazareth," they answered.

"I am he," he said.

Judas, the traitor, was standing there with them. 6When Jesus said to them, "I am he," they moved back and fell to the ground. 7Again Jesus asked them, "Who is it you are looking for?"

"Jesus of Nazareth," they said.

8"I have already told you that I am he," Jesus said. "If, then, you are looking for me, let these others go." 9(He said this so that what he had said might come true: "Father, I have not lost even one of those you gave me.")

10Simon Peter, who had a sword, drew it and struck the High Priest's slave, cutting off his right ear. The name of the slave was Malchus. 11Jesus said to Peter, "Put your sword back in its place! Do you think that I will not drink the cup of suffering which my Father has given me?"

Jesus before Annas

12Then the Roman soldiers with their commanding officer and the Jewish guards arrested Jesus, tied him up, 13and took him first to Annas. He was the father-in-law of Caiaphas, who was High Priest that year. 14It was Caiaphas who had advised the Jewish auth-

---

我,也知道你愛他們,像你愛我一樣。

24「父親哪,你已經把他們賜給我;我在哪裏,願他們也跟我同在那裏,爲要使他們看見你賜給我的榮耀;因爲在創世之前,你已經愛我了。25公義的父親哪,世人不認識你,但我認識你。這些人知道你差遣了我。26我已經把你顯明給他們;我將繼續這樣做,爲要使你對我的愛能生長在他們的生命裏,我也在他們的生命裏。」

耶穌被捕
(太26‧47–56;可14‧43–50;路22‧47–53)

18 耶穌這樣禱告後,和門徒一道出去,過了汲淪溪。那地方有一個園子,耶穌和門徒都進去。2 出賣耶穌的猶大也知道那地方,因爲耶穌常和他的門徒在那裏聚集。3 猶大引了一隊羅馬兵,會同祭司長和法利賽人所派遣的聖殿警衞隊走進園子裏。他們都帶着武器,也拿着燈籠和火把。4耶穌知道將要發生在他身上的一切事,所以上前問他們:「你們找誰?」

5 他們回答:「拿撒勒人耶穌。」

耶穌說:「我就是。」

那時,出賣耶穌的猶大也跟他們站在一起。6 耶穌一說「我就是」,他們都倒退,跌在地上。7耶穌再一次問:「你們找誰?」

他們回答:「拿撒勒人耶穌。」

8 耶穌說:「我已經告訴你們,我就是。如果你們找的是我,就讓這些人走吧。」9耶穌這樣說,正應驗了他從前說過的話:「父親哪,你賜給我的人,我一個也沒有失落。」

10 西門‧彼得帶着一把刀;他抽出刀來,向大祭司的奴僕馬勒古砍去,砍掉他的右耳。11耶穌對彼得說:「把刀收起來!你以爲我不願意喝我父親給我的苦杯嗎?」

在亞那面前

12 那一隊羅馬兵和隊長,連同猶太人的聖殿警衞拿住耶穌,綁了起來,13先把他解送到亞那面前;亞那是當年的大祭司該亞法的岳父。14這該亞法曾經向猶太人建議,說讓

orities that it was better that one man should die for all the people.

一個人替全民死是一件合算的事。

Peter Denies Jesus

(Matthew 26.69,70; Mark 14.66-68; Luke 22.55-57)

15Simon Peter and another disciple followed Jesus. That other disciple was well known to the High Priest, so he went with Jesus into the courtyard of the High Priest's house, 16while Peter stayed outside by the gate. Then the other disciple went back out, spoke to the girl at the gate, and brought Peter inside. 17The girl at the gate said to Peter, "Aren't you also one of the disciples of that man?"

"No, I am not," answered Peter.

18It was cold, so the servants and guards had built a charcoal fire and were standing around it, warming themselves. So Peter went over and stood with them, warming himself.

The High Priest Questions Jesus

(Matthew 26.59-66; Mark 14.55-64; Luke 22.66-71)

19The High Priest questioned Jesus about his disciples and about his teaching. 20Jesus answered, "I have always spoken publicly to everyone; all my teaching was done in the synagogues and in the Temple, where all the people come together. I have never said anything in secret. 21Why, then, do you question me? Question the people who heard me. Ask them what I told them—they know what I said."

22When Jesus said this, one of the guards there slapped him and said, "How dare you talk like that to the High Priest!"

23Jesus answered him, "If I have said anything wrong, tell everyone here what it was. But if I am right in what I have said, why do you hit me?"

24Then Annas sent him, still tied up, to Caiaphas the High Priest.

Peter Denies Jesus Again

(Matthew 26.71-75; Mark 14.69-72; Luke 22.58-62)

25Peter was still standing there keeping himself warm. So the others said to him, "Aren't you also one of the disciples of that man?"

But Peter denied it. "No, I am not," he said.

26One of the High Priest's slaves, a relative of the man whose ear Peter had cut off, spoke up. "Didn't I see you with him in the garden?" he asked.

27Again Peter said "No"–and at once a rooster crowed.

彼得不認耶穌

(太26‧69－70；可14‧66－68；路22‧55－57)

15 西門‧彼得和另一個門徒跟着耶穌；那門徒是大祭司所熟悉的，所以跟着耶穌進了大祭司的院子。16彼得留在門外。那個跟大祭司相識的門徒再出來，對看門的女孩子說了一聲，然後帶彼得進去。17看門的女孩子指着彼得，說：「你不也是那個人的門徒嗎？」

彼得說：「我不是！」

18 當時天氣寒冷，那些僕人和警衞生了炭火，大家站着取暖；彼得也上前，跟他們一起站着取暖。

大祭司盤問耶穌

(太26‧59－66；可14‧55－64；路22‧66－71)

19 大祭司盤問耶穌有關他的門徒和他的教導等事情。20耶穌回答：「我對人講話一向都是公開的。我常在會堂和聖殿裏，那些猶太人聚會的場所，教導人，從來沒有暗地裏講甚麼。21你爲甚麼盤問我呢？去問那些聽過我說話的人吧，他們知道我講過甚麼。」

22 耶穌說了這話，旁邊的一個警衞打了他一巴掌，說：「你竟敢這樣回答大祭司！」

23 耶穌說：「我若說錯了，你儘管指出我的錯處，若是對，你爲甚麼打我？」

24 這候候耶穌仍然被綁着，亞那又把他解送到大祭司該亞法那裏去。

彼得再不認耶穌

(太26‧71－75；可14‧69－72；路22‧58－62)

25 這時候，西門‧彼得還站着取暖。有人對他說：「你不也是那個人的門徒嗎？」

彼得否認說：「我不是！」

26 有一個大祭司的奴僕，是被彼得砍掉耳朵那人的親戚，說：「我不是看見你跟那個人在園子裏嗎？」

27 彼得又說：「不是！」就在這時候，雞叫了。

Jesus before Pilate

(Matthew 27.1,2, 11-14; Mark 15.1-5; Luke 23.1-5)

28Early in the morning Jesus was taken from Caiaphas' house to the governor's palace. The Jewish authorities did not go inside the palace, for they wanted to keep themselves ritually clean, in order to be able to eat the Passover meal. 29So Pilate went outside to them and asked, "What do you accuse this man of?"

30Their answer was, "We would not have brought him to you if he had not committed a crime."

31Pilate said to them, "Then you yourselves take him and try him according to your own law."

They replied, "We are not allowed to put anyone to death." 32(This happened in order to make come true what Jesus had said when he indicated the kind of death he would die.)

33Pilate went back into the palace and called Jesus. "Are you the king of the Jews?" he asked him.

34Jesus answered, "Does this question come from you or have others told you about me?"

35Pilate replied, "Do you think I am a Jew? It was your own people and the chief priests who handed you over to me. What have you done?"

36Jesus said, "My kingdom does not belong to this world; if my kingdom belonged to this world, my followers would fight to keep me from being handed over to the Jewish authorities. No, my kingdom does not belong here!"

37So Pilate asked him, "Are you a king, then?"

Jesus answered, "You say that I am a king. I was born and came into the world for this one purpose, to speak about the truth. Whoever belongs to the truth listens to me."

38"And what is truth?" Pilate asked.

Jesus Is Sentenced to Death

(Matthew 27.15-31; Mark 15.6-20; Luke 23.13-25)

Then Pilate went back outside to the people and said to them, "I cannot find any reason to condemn him. 39But according to the custom you have, I always set free a prisoner for you during the Passover. Do you want me to set free for you the king of the Jews?"

40They answered him with a shout, "No, not him! We want Barabbas!" (Barabbas was a bandit.)

19Then Pilate took Jesus and had him whipped. 2The soldiers made a crown

在彼拉多面前受審

（太27‧1－2‧11－14；可15‧1－5；路23‧1－5）

28 他們從該亞法的府邸把耶穌押到總督府。那時候天已破曉。猶太人的領袖沒有進總督府裏面去，他們要在節期裏保持潔淨，為了要吃逾越節的筵席。29於是彼拉多出來，問他們：「你們拿甚麼罪名控告這個人？」

30 他們回答：「如果他沒有做壞事，我們不會把他帶到你這裏來。」

31 彼拉多對他們說：「你們自己把他帶走，按照你們的法律審判他好啦。」

他們說：「可是我們沒有權判人死刑。」32這應驗了耶穌所說、自己將怎樣死的那句話。

33 彼拉多又進總督府內，叫耶穌來，問他：「你是猶太人的王嗎？」

34 耶穌回答：「你問這話是出於你自己，或是聽別人談論到我呢？」

35 彼拉多說：「你以為我是猶太人嗎？是你本國的人和祭司長們把你交給我的。你做了甚麼事呢？」

36 耶穌說：「我的國度不屬這世界；如果我的國度屬這世界，我的臣民一定為我爭戰，使我不至於落在猶太人手裏。不，我的國度不屬於這世界！」

37 彼拉多說：「那麼，你是王了？」

耶穌回答：「我是王，這是你說的。我的使命是為真理作證，我為此而生，也為此來到世上。凡是屬於真理的人一定聽我的話。」

38 彼拉多問：「真理是甚麼？」

耶穌被判死刑

（太27‧15－31；可15‧6－20；路23‧13－25）

彼拉多又出來，對猶太人說：「我查不出這個人有甚麼罪名。39但是你們有個慣例，要我在逾越節為你們釋放一個囚犯。你們要我為你們釋放猶太人的王嗎？」

40 他們又大喊：「不要他！我們要巴拉巴！」（巴拉巴是個暴徒。）

19於是，彼拉多命令把耶穌帶去，鞭打了。2兵士用荊棘編成一頂冠冕，戴在

out of thorny branches and put it on his head;
then they put a purple robe on him ³and came
to him and said, "Long live the King of the
Jews!" And they went up and slapped him.

⁴Pilate went back out once more and said to
the crowd, "Look, I will bring him out here to
you to let you see that I cannot find any reason
to condemn him." ⁵So Jesus came out, wearing
the crown of thorns and the purple robe. Pilate
said to them, "Look! Here is the man!"

⁶When the chief priests and the Temple
guards saw him, they shouted, "Crucify him!
Crucify him!"

Pilate said to them, "You take him, then,
and crucify him. I find no reason to condemn
him."

⁷The crowd answered back, "We have a law
that says he ought to die, because he claimed to
be the Son of God."

⁸When Pilate heard this, he was even more
afraid. ⁹He went back into the palace and asked
Jesus, "Where do you come from?"

But Jesus did not answer. ¹⁰Pilate said to
him, "You will not speak to me? Remember, I
have the authority to set you free and also to
have you crucified."

¹¹Jesus answered, "You have authority over
me only because it was given to you by God.
So the man who handed me over to you is
guilty of a worse sin."

¹²When Pilate heard this, he tried to find a
way to set Jesus free. But the crowd shouted
back, "If you set him free, that means that you
are not the Emperor's friend! Anyone who
claims to be a king is a rebel against the
Emperor!"

¹³When Pilate heard these words, he took
Jesus outside and sat down on the judge's seat
in the place called "The Stone Pavement." (In
Hebrew the name is "Gabbatha.") ¹⁴It was then
almost noon of the day before the Passover.
Pilate said to the people, "Here is your king!"

¹⁵They shouted back, "Kill him! Kill him!
Crucify him!"

Pilate asked them, "Do you want me to crucify your king?"

The chief priests answered, "The only king
we have is the Emperor!"

¹⁶Then Pilate handed Jesus over to them to
be crucified.

Jesus Is Crucified
(Matthew 27.32-44; Mark 15.21-32; Luke 23.26-43)

So they took charge of Jesus. ¹⁷He went out,

他頭上,又給他穿上紫色的袍子。³他們上
前對他說:「猶太人的王萬歲!」然後用手
掌打他。

⁴彼拉多又出來對羣眾說:「好!我帶他
出來,讓你們知道,我查不出他有甚麼罪
名。」⁵於是耶穌出來,戴着荊棘的冠冕,
穿着紫色的袍子。彼拉多對他們說:「瞧!
這個人!」

⁶那些祭司長和聖殿警衛一看見耶穌,大
喊:「把他釘十字架!把他釘十字架!」

彼拉多對他們說:「你們自己帶他去釘
十字架吧。我查不出他有甚麼罪名。」

⁷羣眾說:「我們有法律,根據那法律他
是該死的,因為他自命為上帝的兒子。」

⁸彼拉多聽見他們這樣說,更加害怕。
⁹他再一次進總督府內,問耶穌:「你究竟
是從哪裏來的?」

但是耶穌沒有回答。¹⁰彼拉多對他說:
「你不回答我嗎?你要知道,我有權釋放
你,也有權把你釘十字架。」

¹¹耶穌說:「只因上帝給你這權,你才有
權辦我。所以,把我交給你那個人的罪更重
了。」

¹²彼拉多聽見這話,愈想要釋放耶穌。可
是羣眾叫喊說:「你釋放他,你就不是皇上
的朋友!誰自命為王,誰就是皇上的敵人。」

¹³彼拉多聽見他們說這樣的話,就帶耶穌
出來,在名叫「石砌階」(希伯來話叫加巴
大)的地方開庭審問。¹⁴那天是逾越節的預
備日,約在正午,彼拉多對羣眾說:「瞧!
你們的王。」

¹⁵他們就喊叫:「殺掉他!殺掉他!把他
釘十字架!」

彼拉多問他們:「要我把你們的王釘在
十字架上嗎?」

祭司長們回答:「只有凱撒是我們的
王!」

¹⁶於是彼拉多把耶穌交給他們去釘十字
架。

耶穌被釘十字架
(太27‧32—44;可15‧21—32;路23‧26—43)

他們把耶穌帶走。¹⁷耶穌出來,背着自

carrying his cross, and came to "The Place of the Skull," as it is called. (In Hebrew it is called "Golgotha.") [18]There they crucified him; and they also crucified two other men, one on each side, with Jesus between them. [19]Pilate wrote a notice and had it put on the cross. "Jesus of Nazareth, the King of the Jews," is what he wrote. [20]Many people read it, because the place where Jesus was crucified was not far from the city. The notice was written in Hebrew, Latin, and Greek. [21]The chief priests said to Pilate, "Do not write 'The King of the Jews,' but rather, 'This man said, I am the King of the Jews.'"

[22]Pilate answered, "What I have written stays written."

[23]After the soldiers had crucified Jesus, they took his clothes and divided them into four parts, one part for each soldier. They also took the robe, which was made of one piece of woven cloth without any seams in it. [24]The soldiers said to one another, "Let's not tear it; let's throw dice to see who will get it." This happened in order to make the scripture come true:

"They divided my clothes among themselves
    and gambled for my robe."
And this is what the soldiers did.

[25]Standing close to Jesus' cross were his mother, his mother's sister, Mary the wife of Clopas, and Mary Magdalene. [26]Jesus saw his mother and the disciple he loved standing there; so he said to his mother, "He is your son."

[27]Then he said to the disciple, "She is your mother." From that time the disciple took her to live in his home.

The Death of Jesus
(Matthew 27.45-56; Mark 15.33-41; Luke 23.44-49)

[28]Jesus knew that by now everything had been completed; and in order to make the scripture come true, he said, "I am thirsty."

[29]A bowl was there, full of cheap wine; so a sponge was soaked in the wine, put on a stalk of hyssop, and lifted up to his lips. [30]Jesus drank the wine and said, "It is finished!"

Then he bowed his head and gave up his spirit.

Jesus' Side Is Pierced

[31]Then the Jewish authorities asked Pilate to allow them to break the legs of the men who had been crucified, and to take the bodies down from the crosses. They requested this because it was Friday, and they did not want the

己的十字架，到了「髑髏岡」（希伯來話叫各各他。）[18]在那裏，他們把他釘在十字架上；他們另外還釘了兩個人，一邊一個，耶穌在中間。[19]彼拉多寫了一面牌子，叫人釘在十字架上。牌子上寫着：「拿撒勒人耶穌，猶太人的王。」[20]許多人看見這牌子上所寫的，因爲耶穌被釘十字架的地方離城不遠；而且這牌子是用希伯來、拉丁，和希臘三種文字寫的。[21]猶太人的祭司長對彼拉多說：「請不要寫『猶太人的王』，要寫『這個人自稱爲猶太人的王』。」

[22]彼拉多回答：「我所寫的，不再更改！」

[23]兵士把耶穌釘十字架後，拿他的外衣分爲四份，每人一份。他們又拿他的內衣；這件內衣沒有縫線，是用整塊布織成的。[24]所以，兵士彼此商量：「我們不要把它撕開，我們抽籤，看誰得着。」這正應驗了聖經上所說的：

他們分了我的外衣，
又爲我的內衣抽籤。
兵士果然做了這樣的事。

[25]站在耶穌的十字架旁邊的，有耶穌的母親、他的姨母、革羅罷的妻子馬利亞，和抹大拉的馬利亞。[26]耶穌看見他的母親和他所鍾愛的門徒站在旁邊，就對他母親說：「母親，瞧，你的兒子！」

[27]接着，他又對那個門徒說：「瞧，你的母親！」從那時起，那門徒接耶穌的母親到自己的家裏住。

耶穌的死
(太27．45—56；可15．33—41；路23．44—49)

[28]耶穌知道一切事都成就了，爲要應驗聖經上的話，就說：「我口渴。」

[29]在那裏有一個壺，盛滿着酸酒；他們就拿海綿浸了酸酒，綁在牛膝草的桿子上，送到他唇邊。[30]耶穌嘗過後，說：「成了！」

於是他垂下頭，氣就斷了。

肋旁被刺

[31]那天是預備日，就要到的安息日是個大節日；猶太人的領袖爲要避免安息日有屍首

bodies to stay on the crosses on the Sabbath, since the coming Sabbath was especially holy. ³²So the soldiers went and broke the legs of the first man and then of the other man who had been crucified with Jesus. ³³But when they came to Jesus, they saw that he was already dead, so they did not break his legs. ³⁴One of the soldiers, however, plunged his spear into Jesus' side, and at once blood and water poured out. ³⁵(The one who saw this happen has spoken of it, so that you also may believe.[i] What he said is true, and he knows that he speaks the truth.) ³⁶This was done to make the scripture come true: "Not one of his bones will be broken." ³⁷And there is another scripture that says, "People will look at him whom they pierced."

The Burial of Jesus
(Matthew 27.57-61; Mark 15.42-47; Luke 23.50-56)

³⁸After this, Joseph, who was from the town of Arimathea, asked Pilate if he could take Jesus' body. (Joseph was a follower of Jesus, but in secret, because he was afraid of the Jewish authorities.) Pilate told him he could have the body, so Joseph went and took it away. ³⁹Nicodemus, who at first had gone to see Jesus at night, went with Joseph, taking with him about one hundred pounds of spices, a mixture of myrrh and aloes. ⁴⁰The two men took Jesus' body and wrapped it in linen cloths with the spices according to the Jewish custom of preparing a body for burial. ⁴¹There was a garden in the place where Jesus had been put to death, and in it there was a new tomb where no one had ever been buried. ⁴²Since it was the day before the Sabbath and because the tomb was close by, they placed Jesus' body there.

The Empty Tomb
(Matthew 28.1-8; Mark 16.1-8; Luke 24.1-12)

20 Early on Sunday morning, while it was still dark, Mary Magdalene went to the tomb and saw that the stone had been taken away from the entrance. ²She went running to Simon Peter and the other disciple, whom Jesus loved, and told them, "They have taken the Lord from the tomb, and we don't know where they have put him!"

³Then Peter and the other disciple went to the tomb. ⁴The two of them were running, but the other disciple ran faster than Peter and reached the tomb first. ⁵He bent over and saw the linen cloths, but he did not go in. ⁶Behind him came Simon Peter, and he went straight into the tomb. He saw the linen cloths lying there ⁷and the cloth which had been around

i believe; *some manuscripts have* continue to believe.

留在十字架上,就去要求彼拉多叫人打斷受刑者的腿,然後把屍首搬走。³²兵士奉命去,把跟耶穌同釘十字架的頭一個和另一個的腿打斷。³³他們走近耶穌,看見他已經死了,就沒有打斷他的腿。³⁴但是,有一個兵士用槍刺他的肋旁,立刻有血和水流出來。(³⁵這是親眼看見這事的人可靠的見證;他知道他的見證是真實的,為要使你們也信。)³⁶因為這事要應驗聖經上所說的話:「他的骨頭連一根也不可打斷。」³⁷另外有一段經文說:「他們要瞻望自己用槍刺了的人。」

耶穌的安葬
(太27·57-61;可15·42-47;路23·50-56)

³⁸這些事過後,有一個亞利馬太人約瑟向彼拉多請求,准他把耶穌的身體領去。(約瑟是耶穌的門徒,只因怕猶太人的領袖,不敢公開。)彼拉多准了他的請求,約瑟就把耶穌的身體領去。

³⁹那個先前曾在夜間來見耶穌的尼哥德慕跟約瑟一起去。他帶了沒藥和沉香混合的香料,約有三十公斤。⁴⁰兩個人用配着香料的麻紗把耶穌的身體裹好;這是猶太人安葬的規矩。⁴¹在耶穌被釘十字架的地方有一個園子,裏面有一個沒有葬過人的新墓穴。⁴²因為那天正是猶太人的預備日,那墓穴又很近,他們就把耶穌葬在那裏。

空墓
(太28·1-8;可16·1-8;路24·1-12)

20 星期日清晨,天還沒有亮,抹大拉的馬利亞往墳墓去,看見墓門的石頭已經移開了。²她就跑去找西門·彼得和耶穌所鍾愛的另一個門徒,告訴他們:「有人從墓裏把主移走了,我們不知道他們把他放在哪裏!」

³彼得和那個門徒就往墓地去。⁴兩個人一起跑,但那門徒比彼得跑得快,首先到達墓穴。⁵他俯身往裏面看,看見麻紗還在那裏,但是他沒有進去。⁶西門·彼得跟着趕到;他一直走進墓穴,看見麻紗還在那裏,⁷又看見那裹耶穌的頭巾沒有跟麻紗放

Jesus' head. It was not lying with the linen cloths but was rolled up by itself. [8]Then the other disciple, who had reached the tomb first, also went in; he saw and believed. [9](They still did not understand the scripture which said that he must rise from death.) [10]Then the disciples went back home.

Jesus Appears to Mary Magdalene
(Matthew 28.9,10; Mark 16.9-11)

[11]Mary stood crying outside the tomb. While she was still crying, she bent over and looked in the tomb [12]and saw two angels there dressed in white, sitting where the body of Jesus had been, one at the head and the other at the feet. [13]"Woman, why are you crying?" they asked her.

She answered, "They have taken my Lord away, and I do not know where they have put him!"

[14]Then she turned around and saw Jesus standing there; but she did not know that it was Jesus. [15]"Woman, why are you crying?" Jesus asked her. "Who is it that you are looking for?"

She thought he was the gardener, so she said to him, "If you took him away, sir, tell me where you have put him, and I will go and get him."

[16]Jesus said to her, "Mary!"

She turned toward him and said in Hebrew, "Rabboni!" (This means "Teacher.")

[17]"Do not hold on to me," Jesus told her, "because I have not yet gone back up to the Father. But go to my brothers and tell them that I am returning to him who is my Father and their Father, my God and their God."

[18]So Mary Magdalene went and told the disciples that she had seen the Lord and related to them what he had told her.

Jesus Appears to His Disciples
(Matthew 28.16-20; Mark 16.14-18; Luke 24.36-49)

[19]It was late that Sunday evening, and the disciples were gathered together behind locked doors, because they were afraid of the Jewish authorities. Then Jesus came and stood among them. "Peace be with you," he said. [20]After saying this, he showed them his hands and his side. The disciples were filled with joy at seeing the Lord. [21]Jesus said to them again, "Peace be with you. As the Father sent me, so I send you." [22]Then he breathed on them and said, "Receive the Holy Spirit. [23]If you forgive people's sins, they are forgiven; if you do not

在一起，是捲着，放在另一邊。[8]首先到達的那個門徒也跟着走進墓穴；他一看見就信了。（[9]他們還不明白聖經所說他必須從死裏復活那句話的意思。）[10]於是兩個門徒回家去了。

耶穌向抹大拉的馬利亞顯現
（太28·9—10；可16·9—11）

[11]馬利亞還站在墳墓外面哭泣。她一邊哭，一邊低頭往墓裏看，[12]看見兩個穿着白衣的天使，坐在原來安放耶穌身體的地方，一個在頭這邊，一個在腳那邊。

[13]他們問馬利亞：「婦人，你爲甚麼哭呢？」

她回答：「他們把我的主移走，我不知道他們把他放在哪裏！」

[14]說了這話，馬利亞轉身，看見耶穌站在那裏，可是還不知道他就是耶穌。[15]耶穌問她：「婦人，你爲甚麼哭呢？你在找誰？」

馬利亞以爲他是管園子的人，所以對他說：「先生，如果是你把他移走的，請告訴我，你把他放在哪裏，我好去把他移回來。」

[16]耶穌叫她：「馬利亞！」

馬利亞轉身，用希伯來話說：「拉波尼！」（意思就是「老師」。）

[17]耶穌說：「你不要拉住我，因爲我還沒有上到我父親那裏。你往我的弟兄那裏去，告訴他們：『我要上去見我的父親，也就是你們的父親；去見我的上帝，也就是你們的上帝。』」

[18]於是，抹大拉的馬利亞去告訴門徒，說她已經看見了主，又傳達主對她說的話。

耶穌向門徒顯現
（太28·16—20；可16·14—18；路24·36—49）

[19]星期日晚上，耶穌的門徒聚集在一起，門緊緊地關着，因爲他們怕猶太人的領袖。那時候，耶穌顯現，站在他們當中，說：「願你們平安！」[20]說了這話，他把自己的手和肋旁給他們看。門徒看見了主，非常歡喜。[21]耶穌又對他們說：「願你們平安！正如父親差遣了我，我照樣差遣你們。」[22]說完這話，他向他們吹一口氣，說：「領受聖靈吧！[23]你們赦免誰的罪，誰的罪就得赦

forgive them, they are not forgiven."

Jesus and Thomas

24One of the twelve disciples, Thomas (called the Twin), was not with them when Jesus came. 25So the other disciples told him, "We have seen the Lord!"

Thomas said to them, "Unless I see the scars of the nails in his hands and put my finger on those scars and my hand in his side, I will not believe."

26A week later the disciples were together again indoors, and Thomas was with them. The doors were locked, but Jesus came and stood among them and said, "Peace be with you." 27Then he said to Thomas, "Put your finger here, and look at my hands; then reach out your hand and put it in my side. Stop your doubting, and believe!"

28Thomas answered him, "My Lord and my God!"

29Jesus said to him, "Do you believe because you see me? How happy are those who believe without seeing me!"

The Purpose of This Book

30In his disciples' presence Jesus performed many other miracles which are not written down in this book. 31But these have been written in order that you may believe/ that Jesus is the Messiah, the Son of God, and that through your faith in him you may have life.

Jesus Appears to Seven Disciples

21 After this, Jesus appeared once more to his disciples at Lake Tiberias. This is how it happened. 2Simon Peter, Thomas (called the Twin), Nathanael (the one from Cana in Galilee), the sons of Zebedee, and two other disciples of Jesus were all together. 3Simon Peter said to the others, "I am going fishing."

"We will come with you," they told him. So they went out in a boat, but all that night they did not catch a thing. 4As the sun was rising, Jesus stood at the water's edge, but the disciples did not know that it was Jesus. 5Then he asked them, "Young men, haven't you caught anything?"

"Not a thing," they answered.

6He said to them, "Throw your net out on the right side of the boat, and you will catch some." So they threw the net out and could not pull it back in, because they had caught so

j believe; *some manuscripts have* continue to believe.

免;你們不赦免誰的罪,誰的罪就不得赦免。」

耶穌和多馬

24 當耶穌顯現時,十二使徒之一的多馬(綽號雙胞胎的)沒有跟他們在一起。25所以其他的門徒把已經看見了主的事告訴多馬。

多馬對他們說:「除非我親眼看見他手上的釘痕,並用我的指頭摸那釘痕,用我的手摸他的肋旁,我絕對不信。」

26 一星期後,門徒又在屋子裏聚集;多馬也跟他們在一起。門關著,可是耶穌忽然顯現,站在他們當中,說:「願你們平安!」27然後他對多馬說:「把你的指頭放在這裏,看看我的手吧;再伸出你的手,摸摸我的肋旁吧。不要疑惑,只要信!」

28 多馬說:「我的主,我的上帝!」

29 耶穌說:「你因為看見了我才信嗎?那些沒有看見而信的是多麼有福啊!」

本書的目的

30 耶穌在他的門徒面前還行了許多神蹟,可是沒有記錄在這本書裏。31本書記述的目的是要你們信⑳耶穌是基督,是上帝的兒子,並且要你們因信他而獲得生命。

向七個門徒顯現

21 這些事以後,耶穌再一次在提比哩亞湖邊向門徒顯現。這次顯現的經過是這樣的:2當時,西門‧彼得、綽號雙胞胎的多馬、加利利的迦拿人拿但業、西庇太的兩個兒子,和另外兩個門徒都在一起。3西門‧彼得對他們說:「我打魚去。」

大家說:「我們跟你一道去。」於是他們出去,上了船;可是整夜沒有捕到甚麼。4太陽剛出來的時候,耶穌站在水邊,可是門徒不知道他就是耶穌。5耶穌對他們說:「朋友,你們捕到了魚沒有?」

他們回答:「沒有。」

6 耶穌說:「把網撒向船的右邊,那邊有魚。」他們就撒網下去,可是拉不上來,因

⑳「是要你們信」另有些古卷作「是要你們繼續信」。

many fish.

7The disciple whom Jesus loved said to Peter, "It is the Lord!" When Peter heard that it was the Lord, he wrapped his outer garment around him (for he had taken his clothes off) and jumped into the water. 8The other disciples came to shore in the boat, pulling the net full of fish. They were not very far from land, about a hundred yards away. 9When they stepped ashore, they saw a charcoal fire there with fish on it and some bread. 10Then Jesus said to them, "Bring some of the fish you have just caught."

11Simon Peter went aboard and dragged the net ashore full of big fish, a hundred and fifty-three in all; even though there were so many, still the net did not tear. 12Jesus said to them, "Come and eat." None of the disciples dared ask him, "Who are you?" because they knew it was the Lord. 13So Jesus went over, took the bread, and gave it to them; he did the same with the fish.

14This, then, was the third time Jesus appeared to the disciples after he was raised from death.

Jesus and Peter

15After they had eaten, Jesus said to Simon Peter, "Simon son of John, do you love me more than these others do?"

"Yes, Lord," he answered, "you know that I love you."

Jesus said to him, "Take care of my lambs." 16A second time Jesus said to him, "Simon son of John, do you love me?"

"Yes, Lord," he answered, "you know that I love you."

Jesus said to him, "Take care of my sheep." 17A third time Jesus said, "Simon son of John, do you love me?"

Peter became sad because Jesus asked him the third time, "Do you love me?" and so he said to him, "Lord, you know everything; you know that I love you!"

Jesus said to him, "Take care of my sheep. 18I am telling you the truth: when you were young, you used to get ready and go anywhere you wanted to; but when you are old, you will stretch out your hands and someone else will tie you up and take you where you don't want to go." 19(In saying this, Jesus was indicating the way in which Peter would die and bring glory to God.) Then Jesus said to him, "Follow me!"

7 耶穌所鍾愛的那門徒對彼得說:「是主!」西門‧彼得一聽說是主,連忙拿一件外衣披在身上(他那時赤着身子),跳進水裏。8 其餘的門徒搖着小船靠岸,把一整網的魚拖了上來。當時他們離岸不遠,約有一百公尺的距離。9 他們上了岸,看見一堆炭火,上面有魚和餅。10耶穌對他們說:「把你們剛打的魚拿幾條來。」

11 西門‧彼得到船上去,把網拖到岸上;網裏都是大魚,一共有一百五十三條。雖然有這麼多魚,網卻沒有破。12耶穌對他們說:「你們來吃早飯吧。」沒有一個門徒敢問他「你是誰」,因為他們都知道他是主。13耶穌就走過去,拿餅分給他們,也照樣把魚分了。

14 這是耶穌從死裏復活以後,第三次向門徒顯現。

耶穌和彼得

15 他們吃過以後,耶穌問西門‧彼得:「約翰的兒子西門,你愛我勝過這些嗎?」

他回答:「主啊,是的,你知道我愛你。」

耶穌說:「你餵養我的小羊。」16耶穌第二次問:「約翰的兒子西門,你愛我嗎?」

他回答:「主啊,是的,你知道我愛你。」

耶穌對他說:「你牧養我的羊。」17耶穌第三次再問:「約翰的兒子西門,你愛我嗎?」

彼得因為耶穌一連三次問他「你愛我嗎」就難過起來,對耶穌說:「主啊,你無所不知,你知道我愛你。」

耶穌說:「你餵養我的羊。18我鄭重地告訴你,你年輕的時候,自己束上腰帶,隨意往來;但年老的時候,你要伸出手來,別人要把你綁着,帶你到不願意去的地方。」19(耶穌說這話是指明彼得將怎樣死,來榮耀上帝。)接着,耶穌又對他說:「你跟從我吧!」

Jesus and the Other Disciple

20Peter turned around and saw behind him that other disciple, whom Jesus loved–the one who had leaned close to Jesus at the meal and had asked, "Lord, who is going to betray you?" 21When Peter saw him, he asked Jesus, "Lord, what about this man?"

22Jesus answered him, "If I want him to live until I come, what is that to you? Follow me!"

23So a report spread among the followers of Jesus that this disciple would not die. But Jesus did not say he would not die; he said, "If I want him to live until I come, what is that to you?"

24He is the disciple who spoke of these things, the one who also wrote them down; and we know that what he said is true.

Conclusion

25Now, there are many other things that Jesus did. If they were all written down one by one, I suppose that the whole world could not hold the books that would be written.

耶穌和其他的門徒

20 彼得轉身，看見耶穌所鍾愛的那門徒跟在後面（那門徒曾在那晚吃飯的時候挨近耶穌，問他「主啊，要出賣你的是誰」。）。 21彼得看見他，就問耶穌：「主啊，這個人將來怎樣？」

22 耶穌回答：「如果我要他活着等到我來，也不關你的事。你只管跟從我吧！」

23 於是，這話流傳在跟從耶穌的人當中，說那個門徒不會死。其實，耶穌並沒有說他不會死，而是說「如果我要他活着等到我來，也不關你的事」。

24 這個人就是爲這些事作見證的那門徒；他把這些事記錄下來。我們知道他的見證都是眞的。

結語

25 耶穌還做了許多別的事，要是一一記錄下來，我想整個世界也容納不下那麼多的書。

使徒行傳
ACTS

INTRODUCTION

The Acts of the Apostles is a continuation of *The Gospel according to Luke*. Its chief purpose is to tell how Jesus' early followers, led by the Holy Spirit, spread the Good News about him in Jerusalem, in all of Judea and Samaria, and to the ends of the earth" (1.8). It is the story of the Christian movement as it began among the Jewish people and went on to become a faith for the whole world. The writer was also concerned to reassure his readers that the Christians were not a subversive political threat to the Roman Empire, and that the Christian faith was the fulfillment of the Jewish religion.

Acts may be divided into three principal parts, reflecting the ever widening area in which the Good News about Jesus was proclaimed and the church established:

(1) the beginning of the Christian movement in Jerusalem following the ascension of Jesus;

(2) expansion into other parts of Palestine; and

(3) further expansion, into the Mediterranean world as far as Rome.

An important feature of *Acts* is the activity of the Holy Spirit, who comes with power upon the believers in Jerusalem on the day of Pentecost and continues to guide and strengthen the church and its leaders throughout the events reported in the book. The early Christian message is summarized in a number of sermons, and the events recorded in *Acts* show the power of this message in the lives of the believers and in the fellowship of the church.

Outline of Contents

簡 介

使徒行傳是路加福音的續篇，主要目的在記述耶穌早期的門徒怎樣在聖靈引導下「在耶路撒冷、猶太，和撒馬利亞全境，甚至到天涯海角」傳福音（1‧8）。基督教發源於猶太人中，而逐漸成爲世界性的信仰，這是本書的主題。作者鄭重地說明基督教並不是顛覆羅馬帝國的一種政治運動，也强調基督教的信仰成全了猶太教。

使徒行傳可分爲三個主要部分，敍述在日益擴大的地區中耶穌福音的傳開和敎會的建立：

一．耶穌升天後信徒在耶路撒冷推動福音的工作；

二．向猶太及撒馬利亞全境發展；

三．進一步向地中海周圍發展，直到羅馬。

使徒行傳的一個重要特徵就是聖靈的工作。聖靈的大能在五旬節那天降臨在耶路撒冷信徒身上，並且在本書所敍述的各件事蹟上繼續帶領及加添力量給教會和教會的領袖們。初代教會的信息可以從本書中幾篇重要的講章看出。書中所記述的許多重大事件顯示這信息的力量怎樣影響了初期的信徒和教會的團契生活。

提要

1 Dear Theophilus:

In my first book I wrote about all the things that Jesus did and taught from the time he began his work [2]until the day he was taken up to heaven. Before he was taken up, he gave instructions by the power of the Holy Spirit to the men he had chosen as his apostles. [3]For forty days after his death he appeared to them many times in ways that proved beyond doubt that he was alive. They saw him, and he talked with them about the Kingdom of God. [4]And when they came together,[a] he gave them this order: "Do not leave Jerusalem, but wait for the gift I told you about, the gift my Father promised. [5]John baptized with water, but in a few days you will be baptized with the Holy Spirit."

Jesus Is Taken Up to Heaven

[6]When the apostles met together with Jesus, they asked him, "Lord, will you at this time give the Kingdom back to Israel?"

[7]Jesus said to them, "The times and occasions are set by my Father's own authority, and it is not for you to know when they will be. [8]But when the Holy Spirit comes upon you, you will be filled with power, and you will be witnesses for me in Jerusalem, in all of Judea and Samaria, and to the ends of the earth." [9]After saying this, he was taken up to heaven as they watched him, and a cloud hid him from their sight.

[10]They still had their eyes fixed on the sky as he went away, when two men dressed in white suddenly stood beside them [11]and said, "Galileans, why are you standing there looking up at the sky? This Jesus, who was taken from you into heaven, will come back in the same way that you saw him go to heaven."

Judas' Successor

[12]Then the apostles went back to Jerusalem from the Mount of Olives, which is about half a mile away from the city. [13]They entered the city and went up to the room where they were staying: Peter, John, James and Andrew, Philip and Thomas, Bartholomew and Matthew, James son of Alphaeus, Simon the Patriot, and Judas son of James. [14]They gathered frequently to pray as a group, together with the women and with Mary the mother of Jesus and with his brothers.

[15]A few days later there was a meeting of the believers, about a hundred and twenty in all, and Peter stood up to speak. [16]"My friends," he said, "the scripture had to come true in which

a when they came together; or while he was staying with them, or while he was eating with them.

1 提阿非羅閣下：

在我所寫的第一部書裏，我已經把耶穌的一切事蹟和教導，從他開始工作[2]到他被接升天那日，都敍述過了。在升天以前，他藉着聖靈的力量給自己所選召的使徒許多指示。[3]受害後四十天當中，他曾經向他們顯現許多次，用不同的方法證明自己是活着的；他讓他們看見自己，又向他們講論上帝國的事。[4]當他們在一起的時候[1]，他吩咐他們：「不要離開耶路撒冷，照我對你們說過的，要等候我父親的應許。[5]約翰用水施洗，你們卻要在幾天後受聖靈的洗禮。」

耶穌被接升天

[6]使徒們跟耶穌聚集的時候，問耶穌：「主啊，你是不是要在這時候恢復以色列國的主權？」

[7]耶穌對他們說：「那時間和日期是我父親憑着自己的權柄定下的，不是你們應該知道的。[8]可是聖靈臨到你們的時候，你們會充滿着能力，要在耶路撒冷、猶太、和撒馬利亞全境，甚至到天涯海角，為我作見證。」[9]說完了這話，耶穌在他們的注視中被接升天；有一朵雲彩把他們的視綫遮住了。

[10]他離去的時候，他們正定睛望着天空。忽然，有兩個穿着白衣的人站在他們旁邊，[11]說：「加利利人哪，為甚麼站在這裏望着天空呢？這位離開你們、被接升天的耶穌，你們看見他怎樣升天，他也要怎樣回來。」

接替猶大的人

[12]於是，使徒從橄欖山回耶路撒冷城去；橄欖山離城約有一公里。[13]他們一進城，上了他們住宿的樓房；在那裏有彼得、約翰、雅各和安得烈、腓力和多馬、巴多羅買和馬太、亞勒腓的兒子雅各、激進黨的西門，和雅各的兒子猶大。[14]他們常在一起同心禱告；當中也有幾個婦女和耶穌的母親馬利亞，以及他的兄弟們。

[15]過了幾天有信徒的聚會，約有一百二十人參加。彼得站起來，說：[16]「朋友們！聖靈藉着大衛的口在聖經上預言有關猶大帶人

①「當他們在一起的時候」或譯「當他跟他們吃飯的時候」。

the Holy Spirit, speaking through David, made a prediction about Judas, who was the guide for those who arrested Jesus. [17]Judas was a member of our group, for he had been chosen to have a part in our work."

[18]With the money that Judas got for his evil act he bought a field, where he fell to his death; he burst open and all his insides spilled out. [19]All the people living in Jerusalem heard about it, and so in their own language they call that field Akeldama, which means "Field of Blood.")

[20]"For it is written in the book of Psalms,
'May his house become empty;
    may no one live in it.'
It is also written,
'May someone else take his place of service.'

[21-22]"So then, someone must join us as a witness to the resurrection of the Lord Jesus. He must be one of the men who were in our group during the whole time that the Lord Jesus traveled about with us, beginning from the time John preached his message of baptism[b] until the day Jesus was taken up from us to heaven."

[23]So they proposed two men: Joseph, who was called Barsabbas (also known as Justus), and Matthias. [24]Then they prayed, "Lord, you know the thoughts of everyone, so show us which of these two you have chosen [25]to serve as an apostle in the place of Judas, who left to go to the place where he belongs." [26]Then they drew lots to choose between the two men, and the one chosen was Matthias, who was added to the group of eleven apostles.

The Coming of the Holy Spirit

2 When the day of Pentecost came, all the believers were gathered together in one place. [2]Suddenly there was a noise from the sky which sounded like a strong wind blowing, and it filled the whole house where they were sitting. [3]Then they saw what looked like tongues of fire which spread out and touched each person there. [4]They were all filled with the Holy Spirit and began to talk in other languages, as the Spirit enabled them to speak.

[5]There were Jews living in Jerusalem, religious people who had come from every country in the world. [6]When they heard this noise, a large crowd gathered. They were all excited, because all of them heard the believers talking in their own languages. [7]In amazement and wonder they exclaimed, "These people who are talking like this are Galileans! [8]How is it, then, that all of us hear them speaking in our own native languages? [9]We are from Parthia, Media,

b John preached his message of baptism; or John baptized him.

逮捕耶穌的事是必須實現的。[17]猶大本來被揀選來分擔我們的事奉,是我們當中的一員。」

([18]猶大用他作惡賺來的錢買了一塊地皮;就在那裏,他墜下,五臟迸裂而死。[19]住在耶路撒冷的人都聽見這件事,所以用他們的語言叫那塊地為亞革大馬,意思就是「血田」。)

[20]正如詩篇上寫的:
願他的住宅荒涼,
    沒有人住在裏面。
又有一處寫着:
    願別人取代他的職份。

[21-22]彼得接着說:「因此,必須有另外一個人加入我們的行列,一起作主耶穌復活的見證人。這個人必須是當主耶穌在我們當中出入時—從約翰施洗開始到耶穌被接升天為止那一段期間—始終跟我們在一起的人。」

[23]於是,大家推選兩個人,就是約瑟(別號巴撒巴,又名猶士都)和馬提亞。[24]他們禱告說:「主啊,你知道每一個人的心;求你指示我們,這兩位當中哪一位是你所揀選[25]來取代這使徒職份的。這職份猶大已經捨棄,到他該去的地方去了。」[26]說完這話,他們抽籤,在兩個名字中抽出馬提亞來;他就加入十一個使徒的行列。

聖靈的降臨

2 五旬節那一天,信徒都聚集在一個地方。[2]忽然有聲音從天上下來,彷彿一陣大風颳過的聲音,充滿了他們坐着的整個屋子。[3]他們又看見形狀像火燄的舌頭,散開,停落在每一個人身上。[4]他們都被聖靈充滿,照着聖靈所賜的才能開始說起別種語言來。

[5]那時候,有從世界各國來的虔誠的猶太人住在耶路撒冷。[6]一聽見這響聲,一大羣人就都聚集在一個地方。大家非常興奮,因為每一個人都聽見信徒用他本地的語言說話。[7]在驚訝詫異中,他們說:「你看,這樣說話的人不都是加利利人嗎?[8]為甚麼我們個個都聽見他們用我們自己的母語說話呢?[9]我們當中有帕提亞人、米底亞人、以

and Elam; from Mesopotamia, Judea, and Cappadocia; from Pontus and Asia, [10]from Phrygia and Pamphylia, from Egypt and the regions of Libya near Cyrene. Some of us are from Rome, [11]both Jews and Gentiles converted to Judaism, and some of us are from Crete and Arabia–yet all of us hear them speaking in our own languages about the great things that God has done!" [12]Amazed and confused, they kept asking each other, "What does this mean?"

[13]But others made fun of the believers, saying, "These people are drunk!"

Peter's Message

[14]Then Peter stood up with the other eleven apostles and in a loud voice began to speak to the crowd: "Fellow Jews and all of you who live in Jerusalem, listen to me and let me tell you what this means. [15]These people are not drunk, as you suppose; it is only nine o'clock in the morning. [16]Instead, this is what the prophet Joel spoke about:

[17]"This is what I will do in the last days,
    God says:
    I will pour out my Spirit on everyone.
    Your sons and daughters will proclaim
        my message;
    your young men will see visions,
        and your old men will have dreams.
[18]Yes, even on my servants, both men and
        women,
    I will pour out my Spirit in those days,
        and they will proclaim my message.
[19]I will perform miracles in the sky above
        and wonders on the earth below.
    There will be blood, fire, and thick smoke;
[20]   the sun will be darkened,
        and the moon will turn red as blood,
    before the great and glorious Day of the
        Lord comes.
[21]And then, whoever calls out to the Lord for
    help will be saved.'

[22]"Listen to these words, fellow Israelites! Jesus of Nazareth was a man whose divine authority was clearly proven to you by all the miracles and wonders which God performed through him. You yourselves know this, for it happened here among you. [23]In accordance with his own plan God had already decided that Jesus would be handed over to you; and you killed him by letting sinful men crucify him. [24]But God raised him from death, setting him

攔人；還有從美索不達米亞、猶太、加帕多家、本都、亞細亞、[10]弗呂家、旁非利亞、埃及，和靠近古利奈的利比亞一帶地方來的人，也有從羅馬來的，[11]包括猶太人和皈依猶太教的外邦人；此外有克里特人和阿拉伯人。我們竟然都聽見他們用我們本地的語言述說上帝偉大的作為！」[12]他們又驚奇又困惑，彼此你問我，我問你；「這是怎麼回事？」

[13] 有些人竟取笑信徒說：「這些人不過是喝醉罷了！」

彼得的信息

[14] 這時候，彼得和其他十一個使徒站起來。他高聲向大家說：「猶太同胞和所有住在耶路撒冷的人哪，你們要明白，要留心聽我的話。[15]你們以為這些人是喝醉了嗎？不是的，因為現在才早晨九點鐘。[16]這情形正是先知約珥所說的：

[17] 上帝說：

    這是我在世界的末期所要做的：
    我要把我的靈傾注給每一個人。
    你們的兒女要宣告我的信息；
    你們的年輕人要看見異象；
    你們的老年人要作奇異的夢。
[18] 在那些日子，
    我要把我的靈傾注出來，
    甚至給我的奴僕和婢女；
    他們要宣告我的信息。
[19] 我要在天上顯神蹟，
    在地上行奇事；
    有血，有火，有濃煙；
[20] 太陽要昏暗無光；
    月亮像血一般的紅；
    在主那偉大榮耀的日子來到以前，
    這一切都要發生。
[21] 那時，凡呼求主名的人必然得救。

[22] 「以色列同胞啊，你們要聽我的話。拿撒勒人耶穌的神聖使命，很清楚地由上帝藉着他所行的神蹟、異能、奇事，向你們顯示出來了。這事你們自己都知道，因為是發生在你們當中的。[23]上帝按照自己的旨意和先見早已決定把耶穌交給你們；而你們藉着不法的人把他釘在十字架上，殺了他。[24]但是上帝使他從死裏復活，把死亡的痛苦解除

free from its power, because it was impossible that death should hold him prisoner. ²⁵For David said about him,

'I saw the Lord before me at all times;
  he is near me, and I will not be troubled.
²⁶And so I am filled with gladness,
  and my words are full of joy.
And I, mortal though I am,
  will rest assured in hope,
²⁷because you will not abandon me in the world
    of the dead;
  you will not allow your faithful servant to
    rot in the grave.
²⁸You have shown me the paths that lead
    to life,
  and your presence will fill me with joy.'

²⁹"My friends, I must speak to you plainly about our famous ancestor King David. He died and was buried, and his grave is here with us to this very day. ³⁰He was a prophet, and he knew what God had promised him: God had made a vow that he would make one of David's descendants a king, just as David was. ³¹David saw what God was going to do in the future, and so he spoke about the resurrection of the Messiah when he said,

'He was not abandoned in the world of the
    dead;
  his body did not rot in the grave.'

³²God has raised this very Jesus from death, and we are all witnesses to this fact. ³³He has been raised to the right side of God, his Father, and has received from him the Holy Spirit, as he had promised. What you now see and hear is his gift that he has poured out on us. ³⁴For it was not David who went up into heaven; rather he said,

'The Lord said to my Lord:
  Sit here at my right side
³⁵until I put your enemies as a footstool under
    your feet.'

³⁶"All the people of Israel, then, are to know for sure that this Jesus, whom you crucified, is the one that God has made Lord and Messiah!"

³⁷When the people heard this, they were deeply troubled and said to Peter and the other apostles, "What shall we do, brothers?"

³⁸Peter said to them, "Each one of you must turn away from your sins and be baptized in the name of Jesus Christ, so that your sins will be forgiven; and you will receive God's gift, the Holy Spirit. ³⁹For God's promise was made to you and your children, and to all who are far away–all whom the Lord our God calls to himself."

了，因為死亡囚禁不了他。²⁵大衛曾經指着他說：

我時常看見主在我面前；
他在我右邊，我不至於動搖。
²⁶因此，我心歡喜，
我的言語充滿快樂；
而我必朽之軀仍要棲息在盼望中。
²⁷因為你不會讓我下陰間，
也不會容許你忠心的僕人腐爛。
²⁸你已經指示我生命的道路；
你的同在使我充滿喜樂。

²⁹「同胞們，關於先祖大衛的事，我必須坦白向你們說明。他不但死了，也埋葬了；他的墳墓到今天還在我們這裏。³⁰他是先知，他知道上帝對他的應許：上帝曾發誓要從他的子孫中立一個王來坐在他的寶座上。³¹大衛預知上帝的計劃，所以當他講到關於基督的復活，他說：

他沒有被撇下在陰間；
他的肉體也沒有腐爛。

³²這位耶穌，上帝已經使他復活了；我們都是這事的見證人。³³他已經被高升在上帝的右邊，並從他父親接受了所應許的聖靈。你們現在所看見所聽到的，就是上帝傾注給我們的恩賜。³⁴大衛自己並沒有升到天上，可是他說：

主對我主說：
你坐在我右邊，
³⁵等我使你的仇敵
屈服在你腳下。

³⁶「所以，以色列全體同胞啊，你們要確實知道，你們釘在十字架上的這位耶穌，上帝已經立他為主，為基督了！」

³⁷大家聽到了這話，覺得很扎心，向彼得和其他的使徒說：「弟兄們，我們該做甚麼呢？」

³⁸彼得告訴他們：「你們每一個人都要悔改，並且要奉耶穌基督的名受洗，好使你們的罪得到赦免，你們就會領受上帝所賜的聖靈。³⁹因為上帝的應許是給所有我們的主上帝所呼召的人，就是你們、你們的兒女，和一切在遠方的人。」

40Peter made his appeal to them and with many other words he urged them, saying, "Save yourselves from the punishment coming on this wicked people!" 41Many of them believed his message and were baptized, and about three thousand people were added to the group that day. 42They spent their time in learning from the apostles, taking part in the fellowship, and sharing in the fellowship meals and the prayers.

Life among the Believers

43Many miracles and wonders were being done through the apostles, and everyone was filled with awe. 44All the believers continued together in close fellowship and shared their belongings with one another. 45They would sell their property and possessions, and distribute the money among all, according to what each one needed. 46Day after day they met as a group in the Temple, and they had their meals together in their homes, eating with glad and humble hearts, 47praising God, and enjoying the good will of all the people. And every day the Lord added to their group those who were being saved.

A Lame Beggar Is Healed

3 One day Peter and John went to the Temple at three o'clock in the afternoon, the hour for prayer. 2There at the Beautiful Gate, as it was called, was a man who had been lame all his life. Every day he was carried to the gate to beg for money from the people who were going into the Temple. 3When he saw Peter and John going in, he begged them to give him something. 4They looked straight at him, and Peter said, "Look at us!" 5So he looked at them, expecting to get something from them. 6But Peter said to him, "I have no money at all, but I give you what I have: in the name of Jesus Christ of Nazareth I order you to get up and walk!" 7Then he took him by his right hand and helped him up. At once the man's feet and ankles became strong; 8he jumped up, stood on his feet, and started walking around. Then he went into the Temple with them, walking and jumping and praising God. 9The people there saw him walking and praising God, 10and when they recognized him as the beggar who had sat at the Beautiful Gate, they were all surprised and amazed at what had happened to him.

Peter's Message in the Temple

11As the man held on to Peter and John in Solomon's Porch, as it was called, the people were amazed and ran to them. 12When Peter saw the people, he said to them, "Fellow Israelites, why are you surprised at this, and why do you stare at us? Do you think that it

40 彼得又用許多話向他們作見證,勸勉他們說:「你們要救自己脫離這些邪惡的人所要遭受的懲罰!」41許多人領受了他的信息,並接受洗禮;那一天信徒約增加了三千人。42他們專心向使徒們領教,參加團契生活,分享愛筵,一起禱告。

團契的生活

43 使徒們行了許多神蹟奇事;人人都因此起了敬畏的心。44全體信徒繼續在一起過團契的生活,所有的東西大家公用。45他們又賣掉田產家業,按照各人的需要把錢分給大家。46他們同心合意,天天在聖殿裏聚會,又分別在各人的家裏分享愛筵,以歡喜純潔的心一起用飯,47頌讚上帝,跟人人保持和睦的關係。主天天把得救的人數加給他們。

彼得和約翰醫好跛腳的人

3 有一天,下午三點禱告的時間,彼得和約翰上聖殿去。2 在那叫美門的地方有一個生來跛腳的人;他天天被人抬來放在門口,向進聖殿的人求乞。3 他看見彼得和約翰要進聖殿,就求他們施捨。4 他們注目看他;彼得說:「你看我們!」5 他就留神看他們,希望得些甚麼。6 彼得對他說:「金銀我都沒有,但是我要給你我所有的:我奉拿撒勒人耶穌基督的名命令你,起來走!」7 於是彼得拉着他的右手,扶他起來。那個人的腳和踝骨立刻有了力氣,8 就跳起來,站直了,開始走路。然後他跟他們一起進聖殿,邊走邊跳,頌讚上帝。9 大家看見他一面走路,一面頌讚上帝;10他們一認出他就是坐在聖殿的美門口求乞的那個乞丐,就對所發生的事大感驚異。

彼得在聖殿裏傳揚信息

11 在所羅門廊下,那個人緊緊地拉着彼得和約翰;在場的人很驚訝,都跑去看他們。12彼得看見這許多人,就對他們說:「以色列同胞們,何必為這一件事驚奇呢?為甚麼

was by means of our own power or godliness that we made this man walk? [13]The God of Abraham, Isaac, and Jacob, the God of our ancestors, has given divine glory to his Servant Jesus. But you handed him over to the authorities, and you rejected him in Pilate's presence, even after Pilate had decided to set him free. [14]He was holy and good, but you rejected him, and instead you asked Pilate to do you the favor of turning loose a murderer. [15]You killed the one who leads to life, but God raised him from death–and we are witnesses to it. [16]It was the power of his name that gave strength to this lame man. What you see and know was done by faith in his name; it was faith in Jesus that has made him well, as you can all see.

[17]"And now, my friends, I know that what you and your leaders did to Jesus was due to your ignorance. [18]God announced long ago through all the prophets that his Messiah had to suffer; and he made it come true in this way. [19]Repent, then, and turn to God, so that he will forgive your sins. If you do, [20]times of spiritual strength will come from the Lord, and he will send Jesus, who is the Messiah he has already chosen for you. [21]He must remain in heaven until the time comes for all things to be made new, as God announced through his holy prophets of long ago. [22]For Moses said, 'The Lord your God will send you a prophet, just as he sent me,[c] and he will be one of your own people. You are to obey everything that he tells you to do. [23]Anyone who does not obey that prophet shall be separated from God's people and destroyed.' [24]And all the prophets who had a message, including Samuel and those who came after him, also announced what has been happening these days. [25]The promises of God through his prophets are for you, and you share in the covenant which God made with your ancestors. As he said to Abraham, 'Through your descendants I will bless all the people on earth.' [26]And so God chose his Servant and sent him to you first, to bless you by making every one of you turn away from your wicked ways."

Peter and John before the Council

4 Peter and John were still speaking to the people when some priests,[d] the officer in charge of the Temple guards, and some Sadducees arrived. [2]They were annoyed because the two apostles were teaching the people that Jesus had risen from death, which proved that the dead will rise to life. [3]So they arrested them

c just as he sent me; or like me.
d priests; some manuscripts have chief priests.

直盯着我們呢？你們以為我們是憑着自己的能力或虔誠使這個人走路嗎？[13]亞伯拉罕、以撒、雅各的上帝，就是我們祖先的上帝，已經榮耀了他的僕人耶穌；這耶穌你們把他交給官府，彼拉多決定要釋放他，你們反而在彼拉多面前背棄他。[14]他是聖潔公義的，你們卻棄絕他，要求彼拉多把一個殺人犯釋放給你們。[15]這樣，你們殺了生命之主；但是上帝使他從死裏復活了。我們就是這事的見證人。[16]這耶穌的名所發出的能力使這跛腳的有了力氣。你們所看見所知道發生在這個人身上的事都是由於信了他的名。因為他信耶穌才使他完全好了起來；你們大家也都看見了。

[17]「那麼，朋友們，我曉得你們和你們的長官那樣對待耶穌是出於無知。[18]上帝早已藉着先知們預言基督必須受苦；這預言果然實現了。[19]所以，你們要悔改，轉向上帝，他就赦免你們的罪。[20]這樣，主會賜給你們靈力更新的日子；同時，他會差遣耶穌，就是他已經為你們選定的基督來。[21]基督必須留在天上，直到萬物更新的時候；這是上帝在古時藉着他的聖先知所宣佈的。[22]摩西說過：『主—你們的上帝要從你們同胞中為你們興起一位先知，像他興起我一樣[2]。他向你們說的話，你們都得聽從。[23]不聽從這位先知的話的人要從上帝的子民中除滅。』[24]所有傳信息的先知們，包括撒母耳和他的後繼者，都宣佈這些日子所要發生的事。[25]你們是先知的繼承人；你們承接上帝與你們的祖先所立的約。上帝對亞伯拉罕說過：『我要藉着你的後代賜福給地上萬民。』[26]所以，上帝興起他的僕人，先差遣他到你們這裏來，賜福給你們，使你們每一個人都回頭，離開邪惡的道路。」

彼得和約翰在議會受審

4 彼得和約翰還在向眾人講話的時候，有些祭司[3]、聖殿的警衞官，和撒都該人忽然來了。[2]因為這兩位使徒教導人有關復活的事，宣講耶穌從死裏復活，這些人非常惱怒，[3]所以拘捕他們，把他們囚禁在監獄

[2]「為你們興起一位先知，像他興起我一樣」或譯「為你們興起一位像我一樣的先知」。
[3]「祭司」另有些古卷作「祭司長」。

and put them in jail until the next day, since it was already late. 4But many who heard the message believed; and the number grew to about five thousand.

5The next day the Jewish leaders, the elders, and the teachers of the Law gathered in Jerusalem. 6They met with the High Priest Annas and with Caiaphas, John, Alexander, and the others who belonged to the High Priest's family. 7They made the apostles stand before them and asked them, "How did you do this? What power do you have or whose name did you use?"

8Peter, full of the Holy Spirit, answered them, "Leaders of the people and elders: 9if we are being questioned today about the good deed done to the lame man and how he was healed, 10then you should all know, and all the people of Israel should know, that this man stands here before you completely well through the power of the name of Jesus Christ of Nazareth–whom you crucified and whom God raised from death. 11Jesus is the one of whom the scripture says,

'The stone that you the builders despised
    turned out to be the most important of all.'
12Salvation is to be found through him alone; in all the world there is no one else whom God has given who can save us."

13The members of the Council were amazed to see how bold Peter and John were and to learn that they were ordinary men of no education. They realized then that they had been companions of Jesus. 14But there was nothing that they could say, because they saw the man who had been healed standing there with Peter and John. 15So they told them to leave the Council room, and then they started discussing among themselves. 16"What shall we do with these men?" they asked. "Everyone in Jerusalem knows that this extraordinary miracle has been performed by them, and we cannot deny it. 17But to keep this matter from spreading any further among the people, let us warn these men never again to speak to anyone in the name of Jesus."

18So they called them back in and told them that under no condition were they to speak or to teach in the name of Jesus. 19But Peter and John answered them, "You yourselves judge which is right in God's sight–to obey you or to obey God. 20For we cannot stop speaking of what we ourselves have seen and heard." 21So the Council warned them even more strongly and then set them free. They saw that it was impossible to punish them, because the people were all praising God for what had happened. 22The man on whom this miracle of healing had been performed was over forty years old.

裏到隔日,因為那時天色黑了。4但是聽見信息的人有許多信了,光是男人,數目將近五千。

5 第二天,猶太人的領袖、長老,和經學教師在耶路撒冷聚會。6大祭司亞那和該亞法、約翰、亞歷山大,以及大祭司的親屬都在座。7他們叫使徒站在他們面前,問:「你們靠甚麼能力,奉誰的名做這事呢?」

8 彼得被聖靈充滿,回答說:「民間領袖和長老們,9如果我們今天被查問是關於這跛腳的人怎樣被治好這一件善事,10那麼,你們大家和一切以色列人都應該知道:這個人,站在你們面前,完全康復了;這是由於拿撒勒人耶穌的名所發出的能力。他被你們釘在十字架上,而上帝已經使他從死裏復活了。11關於這位耶穌,聖經說過:

你們的泥水匠所丟棄的這塊石頭
已成為最重要的基石。
12拯救只從他而來;因為天下人間,上帝並沒有賜下任何其他的名,使我們藉着它得救。」

13議員們看見彼得和約翰那麼勇敢,又曉得他們是沒有受過甚麼教育的平常人,十分希奇,就理會到這兩人原是跟隨過耶穌的。14可是,他們沒有甚麼話好講,因為他們看見那個被治好了的人跟彼得和約翰站在一起。15議員們只好命令他們兩人從議會出去,然後商議,16說:「我們該怎樣處置他們呢?住在耶路撒冷的人都知道他們行了這奇異的神蹟,我們也沒有辦法否認。17可是,為了避免這事在民間越傳越廣,我們來警告他們,叫他們不可再藉耶穌的名對任何人講論甚麼。」

18於是,他們把兩人叫回來,警告他們無論如何不得再藉耶穌的名發表言論或教導人。19可是,彼得和約翰回答他們:「在上帝面前,聽從你們對,或是聽從上帝對呢?你們自己判斷吧!20我們所看見所聽到的,不能不說出來。」21於是議會再嚴厲地警告一番,然後釋放了他們,因為找不出理由來處罰他們。羣衆都為所發生的事頌讚上帝。22在這個神蹟中被治好的那個人已經四十多歲。

The Believers Pray for Boldness

23As soon as Peter and John were set free, they returned to their group and told them what the chief priests and the elders had said. 24When the believers heard it, they all joined together in prayer to God: "Master and Creator of heaven, earth, and sea, and all that is in them! 25By means of the Holy Spirit you spoke through our ancestor David, your servant, when he said,

'Why were the Gentiles furious;
why did people make their useless plots?
26The kings of the earth prepared themselves,
and the rulers met together
against the Lord and his Messiah.'

27For indeed Herod and Pontius Pilate met together in this city with the Gentiles and the people of Israel against Jesus, your holy Servant, whom you made Messiah. 28They gathered to do everything that you by your power and will had already decided would happen. 29And now, Lord, take notice of the threats they have made, and allow us, your servants, to speak your message with all boldness. 30Reach out your hand to heal, and grant that wonders and miracles may be performed through the name of your holy Servant Jesus." 31When they finished praying, the place where they were meeting was shaken. They were all filled with the Holy Spirit and began to proclaim God's message with boldness.

The Believers Share Their Possessions

32The group of believers was one in mind and heart. None of them said that any of their belongings were their own, but they all shared with one another everything they had. 33With great power the apostles gave witness to the resurrection of the Lord Jesus, and God poured rich blessings on them all. 34There was no one in the group who was in need. Those who owned fields or houses would sell them, bring the money received from the sale, 35and turn it over to the apostles; and the money was distributed according to the needs of the people.

36And so it was that Joseph, a Levite born in Cyprus, whom the apostles called Barnabas (which means "One who Encourages"), 37sold a field he owned, brought the money, and turned it over to the apostles.

Ananias and Sapphira

5 But there was a man named Ananias, who with his wife Sapphira sold some property that belonged to them. 2But with his wife's agreement he kept part of the money for him-

信徒同心禱告

23 彼得和約翰一被釋放，立刻回到自己的人那裏，把祭司長和長老所說的話都向大家報告。24他們聽見了，就同心高聲禱告上帝說：「創造天、地、海，和其中萬物的主宰啊！25你曾藉着聖靈，用你的僕人—我們先祖大衞的口說：

外邦為甚麼吼叫？
萬民為甚麼妄圖虛幻的事？
26 地上的君王都披掛上陣；
統治者也都結集在一起，
要攻擊主和他的受膏者基督。

27果然這樣，希律和龐修·彼拉多在本城跟外邦人和以色列人勾結，要攻擊你神聖的僕人耶穌，就是你所選立的基督。28他們勾結起來，要做你的權力和旨意早就預定要實現的一切事。29主啊，他們的恐嚇，現在求你鑒察，並且使我們，就是你的僕人，能夠勇敢地傳講你的信息。30求你伸手醫治疾病，又使我們能藉着你神聖的僕人耶穌的名行神蹟奇事。」

31 他們禱告完了，聚會的地方震動。他們都被聖靈充滿，開始勇敢地傳講上帝的信息。

財物公用

32 這一羣信徒都同心合意，沒有一個人說他的財物是屬自己的；所有的東西大家公用。33使徒們大有能力地見證主耶穌的復活；上帝大大降福給他們每一個人。34在他們中間，沒有人缺乏甚麼。那些擁有田產房屋的，都賣了，35把賣產業的錢交給使徒，照各人的需要分給各人。

36 有一個出生在塞浦路斯的利未人，名叫約瑟，使徒們叫他巴拿巴（巴拿巴的意思是鼓勵者）；37他賣掉了自己的一塊田地，把錢拿來，交給使徒。

亞拿尼亞和撒非喇

5 另外有一個人，叫亞拿尼亞；他和他的妻子撒非喇賣了一些田產。2他留下一部分錢，把剩下的交給使徒；這事他的妻子

self and turned the rest over to the apostles.
[3]Peter said to him, "Ananias, why did you let
Satan take control of you and make you lie to
the Holy Spirit by keeping part of the money
you received for the property? [4]Before you sold
the property, it belonged to you; and after you
sold it, the money was yours. Why, then, did
you decide to do such a thing? You have not
lied to people–you have lied to God!" [5]As soon
as Ananias heard this, he fell down dead; and
all who heard about it were terrified. [6]The
young men came in, wrapped up his body,
carried him out, and buried him.

[7]About three hours later his wife, not knowing what had happened, came in. [8]Peter asked
her, "Tell me, was this the full amount you and
your husband received for your property?"

"Yes," she answered, "the full amount."

[9]So Peter said to her, "Why did you and your
husband decide to put the Lord's Spirit to the
test? The men who buried your husband are at
the door right now, and they will carry you out
too!" [10]At once she fell down at his feet and
died. The young men came in and saw that she
was dead, so they carried her out and buried
her beside her husband. [11]The whole church
and all the others who heard of this were
terrified.

Miracles and Wonders

[12]Many miracles and wonders were being
performed among the people by the apostles.
All the believers were together in Solomon's
Porch. [13]Nobody outside the group dared join
them, even though the people spoke highly of
them. [14]But more and more people were added
to the group–a crowd of men and women who
believed in the Lord. [15]As a result of what the
apostles were doing, sick people were carried
out into the streets and placed on beds and
mats so that at least Peter's shadow might fall
on some of them as he passed by. [16]And crowds
of people came in from the towns around
Jerusalem, bringing those who were sick or who
had evil spirits in them; and they were all healed.

The Apostles Are Persecuted

[17]Then the High Priest and all his companions, members of the local party of the
Sadducees, became extremely jealous of the apostles; so they decided to take action. [18]They
arrested the apostles and put them in the public
jail. [19]But that night an angel of the Lord
opened the prison gates, led the apostles out,
and said to them, [20]"Go and stand in the
Temple, and tell the people all about this new
life." [21]The apostles obeyed, and at dawn they
entered the Temple and started teaching.

也同意。[3]彼得對他說:「亞拿尼亞,為甚
麼讓撒但控制了你的心,使你欺騙聖靈,把
賣田產所得來的錢留下一部分呢?[4]田產沒
有賣出,是你的,賣了以後,錢也是你的;
你為甚麼存心這樣做呢?你不是欺騙人,是
欺騙上帝!」[5]亞拿尼亞一聽見這話,就倒
下去,死了;聽見這事的人都非常害怕。
[6]有些年輕人進來,把他的屍體裹起來,抬
出去埋葬了。

[7]約過了三個鐘頭,他的妻子進來,還不
知道已經發生了的事。[8]彼得對她說:「告
訴我,你們賣田產的錢都在這裏嗎?」

她回答:「是的,都在這裏。」

[9]彼得就說:「你們為甚麼串通來試探主
的靈呢?你看,埋葬你丈夫的人就在門口,
他們也要把你抬出去!」[10]她立刻倒在彼得
腳前,死了。那些年輕人進來,看見她已經
死了,就把她抬出去,葬在她丈夫旁邊。
[11]全教會和其他聽見這事的人都非常害怕。

神蹟奇事

[12]使徒們在民間行了許多神蹟奇事;所有
信徒都同心合意地在所羅門廊下聚集。[13]雖
然一般民眾尊重他們,但是信徒以外的人都
不敢接近他們。[14]當時信主的人越來越多,
男女都有。[15]由於使徒們行了許多神蹟,有
人把病人抬到街上來,放在牀上、褥子上,
希望彼得走過的時候,他的影子會投在他們
一些人身上。[16]還有一大羣人帶着病人和污
靈附身的人從耶路撒冷附近的市鎮來;這些
病人都得到了醫治。

使徒受迫害

[17]大祭司和他的黨羽,就是當地的撒都該
人,對使徒非常嫉妒,因此決定採取行動。
[18]他們下手逮捕使徒,把他們囚禁在拘留所
裏。[19]但是當夜,主的天使打開監門,把使
徒領了出來,對他們說:[20]「你們去,站在
聖殿裏,向人民宣講有關這新生命的道
理。」[21]使徒聽從這話,在天快亮的時候進
了聖殿,開始教導人。

The High Priest and his companions called together all the Jewish elders for a full meeting of the Council; then they sent orders to the prison to have the apostles brought before them. 22But when the officials arrived, they did not find the apostles in prison, so they returned to the Council and reported, 23"When we arrived at the jail, we found it locked up tight and all the guards on watch at the gates; but when we opened the gates, we found no one inside!" 24When the chief priests and the officer in charge of the Temple guards heard this, they wondered what had happened to the apostles. 25Then a man came in and said to them, "Listen! The men you put in prison are in the Temple teaching the people!" 26So the officer went off with his men and brought the apostles back. They did not use force, however, because they were afraid that the people might stone them.

27They brought the apostles in, made them stand before the Council, and the High Priest questioned them. 28"We gave you strict orders not to teach in the name of this man," he said; "but see what you have done! You have spread your teaching all over Jerusalem, and you want to make us responsible for his death!"

29Peter and the other apostles answered, "We must obey God, not men. 30The God of our ancestors raised Jesus from death, after you had killed him by nailing him to a cross. 31God raised him to his right side as Leader and Savior, to give the people of Israel the opportunity to repent and have their sins forgiven. 32We are witnesses to these things—we and the Holy Spirit, who is God's gift to those who obey him."

33When the members of the Council heard this, they were so furious that they wanted to have the apostles put to death. 34But one of them, a Pharisee named Gamaliel, who was a teacher of the Law and was highly respected by all the people, stood up in the Council. He ordered the apostles to be taken out for a while, 35and then he said to the Council, "Fellow Israelites, be careful what you do to these men. 36You remember that Theudas appeared some time ago, claiming to be somebody great, and about four hundred men joined him. But he was killed, all his followers were scattered, and his movement died out. 37After that, Judas the Galilean appeared during the time of the census; he drew a crowd after him, but he also was killed, and all his followers were scattered. 38And so in this case, I tell you, do not take any action against these men. Leave them alone! If what they have planned and done is of human origin, it will disappear, 39but if it comes from

大祭司和他的黨羽召集議會裏所有的猶太長老舉行全體會議，然後下令到監獄裏把使徒提出來。22但是警衞到達的時候，發現使徒們不在監獄裏，就回議會報告說：23「我們到了監獄，看見監門牢牢地鎖住，獄警都守在門外；但我們開了監門，發現裏面連一個人也沒有！」24聖殿的警衞官和祭司長們聽見這報告，非常驚異，不知道使徒們遇到了甚麼事。25這時候，有一個人進來報告：「你們拘禁在監獄裏的人正站在聖殿裏教導民衆呢！」26於是那警衞官領着侍從去，把使徒們帶來。他們沒有使用暴力，因為怕人民用石頭打他們。

27他們把使徒們帶來後，叫他們站在議會面前。大祭司開始審問他們。28他說：「我們嚴嚴地禁止過你們，不得藉着這個人的名敎導人，你們反而把你們那一套道理傳遍耶路撒冷，而且想把殺這個人的血債歸在我們身上！」

29彼得和其他的門徒回答：「我們必須服從上帝，不是服從人。30你們所釘死在十字架上的耶穌，我們祖先的上帝已經使他復活了。31上帝高舉他，使他在自己的右邊作元首，作救主，爲要給以色列人有悔改的機會，讓他們的罪得到赦免。32我們就是這些事的見證人；上帝對服從他的人所賜的聖靈也與我們一同作證。」

33議會的議員聽見了這話，非常惱怒，決定要殺害使徒們。34可是，他們中間有一個法利賽人，名叫迦瑪列，是一向受人尊敬的法律敎師；他在議會中站起來，吩咐人把使徒們帶出去，35然後向議員發言：「以色列同胞們，你們處理這些人的事必須謹愼！36從前這時候，杜達起來，自吹自擂，約有四百人附從了他。他終於被殺，附從的人作鳥獸散，亂事歸於消滅。37以後又有加利利的猶大在戶口調查的時候起來，也引誘了好些人跟從他；他也被殺，附從他的人也被趕散。38對於現在這件事，我告訴你們，不要跟他們作對，由他們去吧！如果他們所計劃、所做的是出於人，一定失敗；39如果是

God, you cannot possibly defeat them. You could find yourselves fighting against God!"

The Council followed Gamaliel's advice. [40]They called the apostles in, had them whipped, and ordered them never again to speak in the name of Jesus; and then they set them free. [41]As the apostles left the Council, they were happy, because God had considered them worthy to suffer disgrace for the sake of Jesus. [42]And every day in the Temple and in people's homes they continued to teach and preach the Good News about Jesus the Messiah.

The Seven Helpers

6 Some time later, as the number of disciples kept growing, there was a quarrel between the Greek-speaking Jews and the native Jews. The Greek-speaking Jews claimed that their widows were being neglected in the daily distribution of funds. [2]So the twelve apostles called the whole group of believers together and said, "It is not right for us to neglect the preaching of God's word in order to handle finances. [3]So then, friends, choose seven men among you who are known to be full of the Holy Spirit and wisdom, and we will put them in charge of this matter. [4]We ourselves, then, will give our full time to prayer and the work of preaching."

[5]The whole group was pleased with the apostles' proposal, so they chose Stephen, a man full of faith and the Holy Spirit, and Philip, Prochorus, Nicanor, Timon, Parmenas, and Nicolaus, a Gentile from Antioch who had earlier been converted to Judaism. [6]The group presented them to the apostles, who prayed and placed their hands on them.

[7]And so the word of God continued to spread. The number of disciples in Jerusalem grew larger and larger, and a great number of priests accepted the faith.

The Arrest of Stephen

[8]Stephen, a man richly blessed by God and full of power, performed great miracles and wonders among the people. [9]But he was opposed by some men who were members of the synagogue of the Freedmen[e] (as it was called), which had Jews from Cyrene and Alexandria. They and other Jews from the provinces of Cilicia and Asia started arguing with Stephen. [10]But the Spirit gave Stephen such wisdom that when he spoke, they could not refute him. [11]So they bribed some men to say, "We heard him speaking against Moses and against God!" [12]In this way they stirred up the

e FREEDMEN: These were Jews who had been slaves, but had bought or been given their freedom.

出於上帝，你們就不能夠擊敗他們。你們所做的，恐怕是在敵對上帝了！」

議會接納迦瑪列的意見，[40]於是把使徒叫進來，鞭打他們，又命令他們不得再藉着耶穌的名講道，然後釋放他們。[41]使徒離開議會，因配得為耶穌的名受凌辱，心裏非常高興。[42]他們仍然天天在聖殿和個人的家裏不停地教導人，傳揚有關基督耶穌的福音。

七個助手

6 這些時候，門徒的數目日日增加；那些說希臘話的猶太人和說希伯來土話的猶太人之間發生了爭執。說希臘話的猶太人埋怨使徒在分配每日的生活費這事上疏忽了他們當中的寡婦。[2]因此，十二使徒召集全體門徒，對他們說：「叫我們放下傳講上帝信息的工作，去辦膳食，這是不應該的。[3]所以，主內朋友們，要從你們當中選出七個有名望、受聖靈充滿、又有智慧的人，讓他們來負責這事務。[4]至於我們，我們要專心於禱告和傳道的任務。」

[5]使徒的建議得到全體的贊同。於是大家推選司提反；他是一個信心堅定、被聖靈充滿的人；又選出腓利、伯羅哥羅、尼迦挪、提門、巴米拿，和改宗加入過猶太教的安提阿人尼哥拉。[6]大家請他們站在使徒面前；使徒禱告後，就給他們行按手禮。

[7]上帝的信息繼續傳開；在耶路撒冷的門徒數目增加很多，許多祭司也接受了這信仰。

司提反被捕

[8]司提反充滿着上帝的恩賜和能力，在民間行了大奇事和神蹟。[9]但是有些人反對他；這些人是所謂『自由人』會堂的會員，包括從古利奈和亞歷山大來的猶太人。他們和其他從基利家和亞細亞來的猶太人跟司提反辯論。[10]聖靈賜下智慧給司提反，所以他們無法辯駁他所說的話。[11]於是他們收買了一些人出來誣告他說：「我們聽見這人說了毀謗摩西和褻瀆上帝的話！」[12]他們用這種方

people, the elders, and the teachers of the Law. They seized Stephen and took him before the Council. [13]Then they brought in some men to tell lies about him. "This man," they said, "is always talking against our sacred Temple and the Law of Moses. [14]We heard him say that this Jesus of Nazareth will tear down the Temple and change all the customs which have come down to us from Moses!" [15]All those sitting in the Council fixed their eyes on Stephen and saw that his face looked like the face of an angel.

Stephen's Speech

7 The High Priest asked Stephen, "Is this true?"

[2]Stephen answered, "Brothers and fathers, listen to me! Before our ancestor Abraham had gone to live in Haran, the God of glory appeared to him in Mesopotamia [3]and said to him, 'Leave your family and country and go to the land that I will show you.' [4]And so he left his country and went to live in Haran. After Abraham's father died, God made him move to this land where you now live. [5]God did not then give Abraham any part of it as his own, not even a square foot of ground, but God promised to give it to him, and that it would belong to him and to his descendants. At the time God made this promise, Abraham had no children. [6]This is what God said to him: 'Your descendants will live in a foreign country, where they will be slaves and will be badly treated for four hundred years. [7]But I will pass judgment on the people that they will serve, and afterward your descendants will come out of that country and will worship me in this place.' [8]Then God gave to Abraham the ceremony of circumcision as a sign of the covenant. So Abraham circumcised Isaac a week after he was born; Isaac circumcised his son Jacob, and Jacob circumcised his twelve sons, the famous ancestors of our race.

[9]"Jacob's sons became jealous of their brother Joseph and sold him to be a slave in Egypt. But God was with him [10]and brought him safely through all his troubles. When Joseph appeared before the king of Egypt, God gave him a pleasing manner and wisdom, and the king made Joseph governor over the country and the royal household. [11]Then there was a famine all over Egypt and Canaan, which caused much suffering. Our ancestors could not find any food, [12]and when Jacob heard that there was grain in Egypt, he sent his sons, our ancestors, on their first visit there. [13]On the second visit Joseph made himself known to his brothers, and the king of Egypt came to know

法煽動羣衆、長老，和經學教師。他們來找司提反，抓住他，把他帶到議會去。[13]他們所收買的假證人出來說：「這個人常常說話反對我們的聖殿和摩西的法律。[14]我們聽見他說這個拿撒勒人耶穌要拆毀聖殿，要改變摩西所傳給我們的一切傳統！」[15]所有在議會裏面坐着的人都注目看着司提反，看見他的面貌好像是天使的面貌。

司提反直言不諱

7 大祭司問司提反：「果眞有這樣的事嗎？」

[2]司提反回答：「諸位父老弟兄們，請聽！當我們的先祖亞伯拉罕住在美索不達米西，還沒有移居哈蘭的時候，榮耀的上帝向他顯現，[3]對他說：『你要離開你的故鄉和親族，到我所要指示你去的地方。』[4]於是亞伯拉罕離開了迦勒底人的地方，去住在哈蘭。他父親死了以後，上帝把他遷移到本地來，就是你們現在所住的地方。[5]當時上帝並沒有給亞伯拉罕甚麼產業，連立足地也沒有；但是上帝應許要把這土地賜給他，作爲他和他後代的產業，雖然那時候他還沒有兒子。[6]上帝對他這樣說：『你的後代要寄居外國，在那裏作奴隸，受虐待四百年。[7]但是，我要懲罰奴役他們的那一國。以後他們要離開那地方，在這裏敬拜我。』[8]於是上帝和亞伯拉罕立約，以割禮爲記號。所以，亞伯拉罕在以撒出生後第八天給他行割禮，照樣以撒給雅各行割禮，雅各給十二個族長行割禮。

[9]「族長們嫉妒約瑟，把他賣到埃及去。但是上帝與他同在，[10]救他脫離了一切的災難。當他站在埃及王法老面前的時候，上帝賜給他風度和智慧。法老立他爲國家的首相和王室的總管。[11]不久，埃及和迦南全境有嚴重的饑荒，造成很大的災害；我們的祖先絕了糧。[12]雅各聽見了埃及有食糧，便差遣他的兒子們，就是我們的祖先，到那裏去；這是第一次。[13]第二次他們去的時候，約瑟和他的兄弟們相認；法老由此認識了約瑟的

about Joseph's family. ¹⁴So Joseph sent a message to his father Jacob, telling him and the whole family, seventy-five people in all, to come to Egypt. ¹⁵Then Jacob went to Egypt, where he and his sons died. ¹⁶Their bodies were taken to Shechem, where they were buried in the grave which Abraham had bought from the clan of Hamor for a sum of money.

¹⁷"When the time drew near for God to keep the promise he had made to Abraham, the number of our people in Egypt had grown much larger. ¹⁸At last a king who did not know about Joseph began to rule in Egypt. ¹⁹He tricked our ancestors and was cruel to them, forcing them to put their babies out of their homes, so that they would die. ²⁰It was at this time that Moses was born, a very beautiful child. He was cared for at home for three months, ²¹and when he was put out of his home, the king's daughter adopted him and brought him up as her own son. ²²He was taught all the wisdom of the Egyptians and became a great man in words and deeds.

²³"When Moses was forty years old, he decided to find out how his fellow Israelites were being treated. ²⁴He saw one of them being mistreated by an Egyptian, so he went to his help and took revenge on the Egyptian by killing him.(²⁵He thought that his own people would understand that God was going to use him to set them free, but they did not understand.) ²⁶The next day he saw two Israelites fighting, and he tried to make peace between them. 'Listen, men,' he said, 'you are fellow Israelites; why are you fighting like this?' ²⁷But the one who was mistreating the other pushed Moses aside. 'Who made you ruler and judge over us?' he asked. ²⁸'Do you want to kill me, just as you killed that Egyptian yesterday?' ²⁹When Moses heard this, he fled from Egypt and went to live in the land of Midian. There he had two sons.

³⁰"After forty years had passed, an angel appeared to Moses in the flames of a burning bush in the desert near Mount Sinai. ³¹Moses was amazed by what he saw, and went near the bush to get a better look. But he heard the Lord's voice: ³²'I am the God of your ancestors, the God of Abraham, Isaac, and Jacob.' Moses trembled with fear and dared not look. ³³The Lord said to him, 'Take your sandals off, for the place where you are standing is holy ground. ³⁴I have seen the cruel suffering of my people in Egypt. I have heard their groans, and I have come down to set them free. Come now; I will send you to Egypt.'

³⁵"Moses is the one who was rejected by the people of Israel. 'Who made you ruler and

家族。¹⁴約瑟派人去見他的父親雅各，請他跟全家到埃及來；來的親族一共有七十五人。¹⁵雅各南下到埃及；他和其他的祖先死在那裏。¹⁶他們的遺體被送到示劍，葬在亞伯拉罕用一筆錢向哈抹的子孫買來的墳地裏。

¹⁷「上帝要向亞伯拉罕實行諾言的日子快到的時候，以色列族在埃及的人口已經增加很多。¹⁸後來有一個完全不認識約瑟的新王開始統治埃及。¹⁹這王用詭計剝削我們的同胞，虐待我們的祖先，強迫他們丟棄嬰兒，不讓他們活下去。²⁰就在這時候摩西出生了；他長得非常可愛，在家裏被撫養了三個月，²¹到了他被丟棄時，法老的女兒收養了他，把他當作自己的兒子帶大。²²他接受了埃及文化的薰陶，很有說話和辦事的能力。

²³「摩西四十歲的時候，決心要了解以色列同胞的情況。²⁴有一次，他看見一個同胞受埃及人的欺負，就上前保護他，為他伸冤，把那埃及人殺了。²⁵他以為同胞會明白上帝要用他來解救他們，可是他們竟不明白。²⁶第二天，他看見兩個以色列人在打架，想替他們調解，就說：『你們是同胞，為甚麼自相傷害呢？』²⁷那欺負同胞的把摩西推開，說：『誰指定你作領袖、作法官來管我們呢？²⁸你也要殺我，像你昨天殺了那埃及人一樣嗎？』²⁹摩西一聽見這話就逃離埃及，去寄居在米甸。在那裏，他生了兩個兒子。

³⁰「過了四十年，在西奈山附近的曠野，有一位天使從荊棘的火燄中向摩西顯現。³¹摩西看見了這景象非常驚駭，走上前去，要看個究竟。這時候，他聽見主的聲音說：³²『我是你祖先的上帝，就是亞伯拉罕、以撒、雅各的上帝。』摩西恐懼戰慄，不敢注視。³³主又對他說：『脫掉你的鞋子！因為你所站的地方是聖地。³⁴我的子民在埃及所受的苦難我都清楚地看見了；我也聽見他們的呻吟，我下來要解救他們。你來！我要差遣你到埃及去。』

³⁵「這位摩西就是以色列人所拒絕、質問說『誰指定你作領袖、作法官來管我們呢』的

judge over us?' they asked. He is the one whom God sent to rule the people and set them free with the help of the angel who appeared to him in the burning bush. [36]He led the people out of Egypt, performing miracles and wonders in Egypt and at the Red Sea and for forty years in the desert. [37]Moses is the one who said to the people of Israel, 'God will send you a prophet, just as he sent me,*f* and he will be one of your own people.' [38]He is the one who was with the people of Israel assembled in the desert; he was there with our ancestors and with the angel who spoke to him on Mount Sinai, and he received God's living messages to pass on to us.

[39]"But our ancestors refused to obey him; they pushed him aside and wished that they could go back to Egypt. [40]So they said to Aaron, 'Make us some gods who will lead us. We do not know what has happened to that man Moses, who brought us out of Egypt.' [41]It was then that they made an idol in the shape of a bull, offered sacrifice to it, and had a feast in honor of what they themselves had made. [42]So God turned away from them and gave them over to worship the stars of heaven, as it is written in the book of the prophets:

'People of Israel! It was not to me
   that you slaughtered and sacrificed animals
   for forty years in the desert.
[43]It was the tent of the god Molech that you
   carried,
   and the image of Rephan, your star god;
   they were idols that you had made to
   worship.
And so I will send you into exile beyond
   Babylon.'

[44]"Our ancestors had the Tent of God's presence with them in the desert. It had been made as God had told Moses to make it, according to the pattern that Moses had been shown. [45]Later on, our ancestors who received the tent from their fathers carried it with them when they went with Joshua and took over the land from the nations that God drove out as they advanced. And it stayed there until the time of David. [46]He won God's favor and asked God to allow him to provide a dwelling place for the God of Jacob.*g* [47]But it was Solomon who built him a house.

[48]"But the Most High God does not live in houses built by human hands; as the prophet says,

[49]"Heaven is my throne, says the Lord,
   and the earth is my footstool.

---

f *just as he sent me; or* like me.
g *the God of Jacob; some manuscripts have* the people of Israel.

那個人。藉着在荊棘中顯現的天使,上帝差派他作領袖、作解救者。[36]他帶領人民從埃及出來,在埃及,在紅海,和在曠野的四十年間,行了許多神蹟奇事。[37]也就是這位摩西告訴以色列人民說:『上帝要從你們的同胞中為你們興起一位先知,正像他興起我一樣④。』[38]他在曠野跟以色列會眾在一起;他和我們的祖先以及在西奈山跟他說話的天使在一起;他領受了上帝永恆的信息,把信息傳給我們。

[39]「但是,我們的祖先不聽從他,也不理會他,寧願再回到埃及去。[40]他們對亞倫說:『請替我們造些神像,好在我們前面帶路。我們不曉得把我們從埃及領出來的那個摩西遭遇到甚麼事。』[41]於是他們造了一個小牛像,向它獻祭,為自己的手所造出來的東西歡樂慶祝。[42]但是,上帝轉面不看他們,任憑他們去拜天上的星辰,正如先知書上所說:

以色列人民哪,在曠野的四十年間,
   你們並沒有為我獻上犧牲和祭物呀!
[43]你們抬着摩洛神的聖幕,
   又抬着理番神的星像,
   就是你們造來拜的偶像。
因此,我要把你們遷移到巴比倫外去。

[44]「我們的祖先在曠野有象徵上帝臨在的聖幕,是上帝吩咐摩西依照他所指示的模型造成的。[45]後來我們的祖先繼承了這聖幕;當上帝在他們前頭趕走外邦人、佔據那片土地時,約書亞和他們把聖幕搬到那裏去,直到大衛的時代。[46]大衛蒙上帝喜悅,要求准許他為上帝─就是雅各的上帝─建造一座殿宇⑤;[47]可是,後來為上帝建造殿宇的卻是所羅門。

[48]「其實,至高的上帝並不住在人所建造的殿宇裏,正如先知所說:

[49]主說:天是我的寶座;
   地是我的腳凳。

---

④「為你們興起一位先知,正像他興起我一樣」或譯「為你們興起像我一樣的先知」。
⑤「為上帝─就是雅各的上帝─建造一座殿宇」另有古卷作「為以色列人建造一座殿宇」。

What kind of house would you build for me?
Where is the place for me to live in?
[50]Did not I myself make all these things?'

[51]"How stubborn you are!" Stephen went on to say. "How heathen your hearts, how deaf you are to God's message! You are just like your ancestors: you too have always resisted the Holy Spirit! [52]Was there any prophet that your ancestors did not persecute? They killed God's messengers, who long ago announced the coming of his righteous Servant. And now you have betrayed and murdered him. [53]You are the ones who received God's law, that was handed down by angels–yet you have not obeyed it!"

The Stoning of Stephen

[54]As the members of the Council listened to Stephen, they became furious and ground their teeth at him in anger. [55]But Stephen, full of the Holy Spirit, looked up to heaven and saw God's glory and Jesus standing at the right side of God. [56]"Look!" he said. "I see heaven opened and the Son of Man standing at the right side of God!"

[57]With a loud cry the Council members covered their ears with their hands. Then they all rushed at him at once, [58]threw him out of the city, and stoned him. The witnesses left their cloaks in the care of a young man named Saul. [59]They kept on stoning Stephen as he called out to the Lord, "Lord Jesus, receive my spirit!" [60]He knelt down and cried out in a loud voice, "Lord! Do not remember this sin against them!" He said this and died.

8 And Saul approved of his murder.

Saul Persecutes the Church

That very day the church in Jerusalem began to suffer cruel persecution. All the believers, except the apostles, were scattered throughout the provinces of Judea and Samaria. [2]Some devout men buried Stephen, mourning for him with loud cries.

[3]But Saul tried to destroy the church; going from house to house, he dragged out the believers, both men and women, and threw them into jail.

The Gospel Is Preached in Samaria

[4]The believers who were scattered went everywhere, preaching the message. [5]Philip went to the principal city[h] in Samaria and preached the Messiah to the people there. [6]The

h the principal city; *some manuscripts have* a city.

你們要爲我建造哪一種殿宇呢？
何處是我安息的地方呢？
50 這一切不都是我親自創造的嗎？

51「你們這些頑固的人哪，你們心胸閉塞，充耳不聞上帝的信息！你們和你們的祖先一樣，總是跟聖靈作對。52哪一個先知沒有受過你們祖先的迫害呢？先知們宣告那公義的僕人要來臨，你們的祖先卻把他們殺了；現在你們竟又出賣那僕人，殺害了他。53你們是接受了上帝法律的人；這法律是由天使傳下的，而你們卻不遵守法律！」

司提反殉道

54 議會的議員聽了司提反這一些話，非常惱怒，向他咬牙切齒。55司提反被聖靈充滿，舉目望天，看見上帝的榮耀，又看見耶穌站在上帝的右邊，56就說：「我看見天門開了，人子站在上帝的右邊！」

57 他們就大聲喊叫，用手掩耳，又一擁上前，抓住司提反，58把他推出城外，用石頭打他。那些證人把自己的外衣交給一個名叫掃羅的青年看管。59司提反在石頭紛紛襲擊下，向主呼求說：「主耶穌啊，求你接納我的靈魂！」60他又跪下來，大聲喊說：「主啊，不要把這罪歸給他們！」他說完這話就死了。

8 殺害司提反這件事，掃羅是贊同的。

掃羅迫害教會

從那一天開始，耶路撒冷的教會遭受極殘酷的迫害。使徒以外，所有的信徒都分散到猶大和撒馬利亞各地區去。2 有些虔誠的人把司提反埋葬了，並且爲他大聲哀哭。

3 這時候，掃羅進行摧殘教會的工作；他挨家挨戶搜捕男女信徒，把他們關進牢裏。

福音傳到撒馬利亞

4 那些分散的信徒到各地傳福音。5 腓利到撒馬利亞去，向當地的人宣講基督的事。6 羣衆都聚精會神地聽腓利所說的話。他們

crowds paid close attention to what Philip said, as they listened to him and saw the miracles that he performed. [7]Evil spirits came out from many people with a loud cry, and many paralyzed and lame people were healed. [8]So there was great joy in that city.

[9]A man named Simon lived there, who for some time had astounded the Samaritans with his magic. He claimed that he was someone great, [10]and everyone in the city, from all classes of society, paid close attention to him. "He is that power of God known as 'The Great Power'," they said. [11]They paid this attention to him because for such a long time he had astonished them with his magic. [12]But when they believed Philip's message about the good news of the Kingdom of God and about Jesus Christ, they were baptized, both men and women. [13]Simon himself also believed; and after being baptized, he stayed close to Philip and was astounded when he saw the great wonders and miracles that were being performed.

[14]The apostles in Jerusalem heard that the people of Samaria had received the word of God, so they sent Peter and John to them. [15]When they arrived, they prayed for the believers that they might receive the Holy Spirit. [16]For the Holy Spirit had not yet come down on any of them; they had only been baptized in the name of the Lord Jesus. [17]Then Peter and John placed their hands on them, and they received the Holy Spirit.

[18]Simon saw that the Spirit had been given to the believers when the apostles placed their hands on them. So he offered money to Peter and John, [19]and said, "Give this power to me too, so that anyone I place my hands on will receive the Holy Spirit."

[20]But Peter answered him, "May you and your money go to hell, for thinking that you can buy God's gift with money! [21]You have no part or share in our work, because your heart is not right in God's sight. [22]Repent, then, of this evil plan of yours, and pray to the Lord that he will forgive you for thinking such a thing as this. [23]For I see that you are full of bitter envy and are a prisoner of sin."

[24]Simon said to Peter and John, "Please pray to the Lord for me, so that none of these things you spoke of will happen to me."

[25]After they had given their testimony and proclaimed the Lord's message, Peter and John went back to Jerusalem. On their way they preached the Good News in many villages of Samaria.

一邊聽，一邊觀看他所行的神蹟。[7]污靈大聲呼叫，從許多所依附的人身上出來；許多癱瘓的、跛腳的也都獲得醫治。[8]撒馬利亞城裏充滿着喜樂。

[9]有一個人，名叫西門，他的邪術曾經轟動了撒馬利亞居民。他也自以為了不起；[10]城裏各階層的人都很喜歡聽他。大家說：「這個人有上帝的能力，是『大能者』。」[11]因為他長久用邪術迷惑他們，所以他們聽從他。[12]但是，他們相信了腓利所傳關於上帝主權的福音和耶穌基督的名時，男男女女都接受了洗禮。[13]西門自己也相信了；他受洗後常常跟腓利在一起。他看見了腓利所行的大異能和神蹟，很覺得驚奇。

[14]在耶路撒冷的使徒聽見撒馬利亞人領受了上帝的信息，就派彼得和約翰到他們那裏去。[15]兩人一到，就替信徒們禱告，要使他們領受聖靈。[16]因為當時聖靈還沒有臨到他們當中的任何人；他們只是奉主耶穌的名接受洗禮。[17]於是彼得和約翰給他們按手，他們就領受了聖靈。

[18]西門看見使徒所按手的人都領受了聖靈，就拿錢給使徒，[19]說：「請把這能力也給我，使我替誰按手，誰就領受聖靈。」

[20]彼得卻對他說：「你跟你的金錢一起滅亡吧！你居然妄想能夠用錢買上帝的恩賜！[21]你在我們的工作上沒有份；因為在上帝面前，你的心術不正。[22]所以，你要悔改，離棄邪惡，祈求主赦免你心中這種意念。[23]我看出你正在啃着嫉妒的苦果，作罪的囚徒。」

[24]西門對彼得和約翰說：「請你們為我向主祈求，使你們所說的這事不至於發生在我身上。」

[25]彼得和約翰在那裏作了見證，宣講主的信息，然後回耶路撒冷去。歸途中，他們在撒馬利亞的許多村鎮傳福音。

Philip and the Ethiopian Official

26An angel of the Lord said to Philip, "Get ready and go south[i] to the road that goes from Jerusalem to Gaza." (This road is not used nowadays.)[j] 27-28So Philip got ready and went. Now an Ethiopian eunuch, who was an important official in charge of the treasury of the queen of Ethiopia, was on his way home. He had been to Jerusalem to worship God and was going back home in his carriage. As he rode along, he was reading from the book of the prophet Isaiah. 29The Holy Spirit said to Philip, "Go over to that carriage and stay close to it." 30Philip ran over and heard him reading from the book of the prophet Isaiah. He asked him, "Do you understand what you are reading?"

31The official replied, "How can I understand unless someone explains it to me?" And he invited Philip to climb up and sit in the carriage with him. 32The passage of scripture which he was reading was this:

"He was like a sheep that is taken to be
    slaughtered,
  like a lamb that makes no sound when its
    wool is cut off.
He did not say a word.
33He was humiliated, and justice was denied him.
  No one will be able to tell about his
    descendants,
  because his life on earth has come to an end."

34The official asked Philip, "Tell me, of whom is the prophet saying this? Of himself or of someone else?" 35Then Philip began to speak; starting from this passage of scripture, he told him the Good News about Jesus. 36As they traveled down the road, they came to a place where there was some water, and the official said, "Here is some water. What is to keep me from being baptized?"[k]

38The official ordered the carriage to stop, and both Philip and the official went down into the water, and Philip baptized him. 39When they came up out of the water, the Spirit of the Lord took Philip away. The official did not see him again, but continued on his way, full of joy. 40Philip found himself in Azotus; he went on to Caesarea, and on the way he preached the Good News in every town.

The Conversion of Saul

(Acts 22.6-16; 26.12-18)

9 In the meantime Saul kept up his violent threats of murder against the followers of the Lord. He went to the High Priest 2and

i south; *or* at midday.
j This road is not used nowadays; *or* This is the desert road.
k *Some manuscripts add verse 37:* Philip said to him, "You may be baptized if you believe with all your heart." "I do," he answered; "I believe that Jesus Christ is the Son of God."

腓利和衣索匹亞的太監

26 有主的一個天使告訴腓利：「你動身向南走，到那條從耶路撒冷通往迦薩的路上去。」（這條路已經荒廢了⑥。）27-28腓利就動身前往。在途中，他遇見一個衣索匹亞的太監。這個人是一位高級官員，在衣索匹亞女王甘大基手下經管財務。他上耶路撒冷去敬拜上帝；歸途中，他坐在自己的馬車上誦讀先知以賽亞的書。29聖靈對腓利說：「你過去，靠近那車子走。」30腓利跑過去，聽見太監正在誦讀先知以賽亞的書，就問他：「你所讀的，你明白嗎？」

31 他回答：「除非有人開導，我怎能明白呢？」於是他邀請腓利上車，跟他坐在一起。32他所誦讀的那一段經文是：

他像一隻被牽去屠宰的羊，
像一隻在剪毛人手下的羔羊默默無聲；
同樣，他也一言不發。
33 他忍受恥辱；
沒有人替他主持正義，
也沒有人能指出他的世系，
因為他在世上的生命已到了盡頭。

34 太監問腓利：「請指教我，先知這段話是指着誰說的？是指他自己呢，還是指着別人？」35腓利就開口，從這一段經文開始，向他講解關於耶穌的福音的事。36他們經過一個地方，路旁有水，太監說：「這裏有水，我不可以就在這裏接受洗禮嗎？」⑦

38 太監就吩咐停車；腓利跟他一同下到水裏，為他施行洗禮。39他們從水裏上來的時候，主的靈把腓利帶走；太監再也看不見他了。他繼續趕路，滿心快樂。40後來有人在亞鎮都遇見腓利；他走遍那一帶地方，在各村鎮宣講福音，直到他來到凱撒利亞。

掃羅信主

（徒22‧6—16；26‧12—18）

9 掃羅繼續用凶煞的口氣恐嚇主的門徒。他去見大祭司，2要求發給致大馬士革

⑥「（這條路已經荒廢了）」或譯「（這條路經過曠野）」。
⑦有些古卷加37節「腓利對他說：『你如果真心相信，就可以接受洗禮。』他回答：『我信耶穌基督是上帝的兒子。』」

asked for letters of introduction to the synagogues in Damascus, so that if he should find there any followers of the Way of the Lord, he would be able to arrest them, both men and women, and bring them back to Jerusalem.

3As Saul was coming near the city of Damascus, suddenly a light from the sky flashed around him. 4He fell to the ground and heard a voice saying to him, "Saul, Saul! Why do you persecute me?"

5"Who are you, Lord?" he asked.

"I am Jesus, whom you persecute," the voice said. 6"But get up and go into the city, where you will be told what you must do."

7The men who were traveling with Saul had stopped, not saying a word; they heard the voice but could not see anyone. 8Saul got up from the ground and opened his eyes, but could not see a thing. So they took him by the hand and led him into Damascus. 9For three days he was not able to see, and during that time he did not eat or drink anything.

10There was a believer in Damascus named Ananias. He had a vision, in which the Lord said to him, "Ananias!"

"Here I am, Lord," he answered.

11The Lord said to him, "Get ready and go to Straight Street, and at the house of Judas ask for a man from Tarsus named Saul. He is praying, 12and in a vision he has seen a man named Ananias come in and place his hands on him so that he might see again."

13Ananias answered, "Lord, many people have told me about this man and about all the terrible things he has done to your people in Jerusalem. 14And he has come to Damascus with authority from the chief priests to arrest all who worship you."

15The Lord said to him, "Go, because I have chosen him to serve me, to make my name known to Gentiles and kings and to the people of Israel. 16And I myself will show him all that he must suffer for my sake."

17So Ananias went, entered the house where Saul was, and placed his hands on him. "Brother Saul," he said, "the Lord has sent me –Jesus himself, who appeared to you on the road as you were coming here. He sent me so that you might see again and be filled with the Holy Spirit." 18At once something like fish scales fell from Saul's eyes, and he was able to see again. He stood up and was baptized; 19and after he had eaten, his strength came back.

Saul Preaches in Damascus

Saul stayed for a few days with the believers in Damascus. 20He went straight to the

各猶太會堂的文件，准許他搜捕跟從主道路的人，無論男女，都押解到耶路撒冷去。

3 在往大馬士革去的途中，快到城裏的時候，忽然有一道光從天上下來，四面照射着他。4他仆倒在地上，聽見有聲音對他說：「掃羅，掃羅！你為甚麼迫害我？」

5 他就問：「主啊，你是誰？」那聲音回答：「我就是你所迫害的耶穌。6起來，進城裏去，有人會把你所該做的事告訴你。」

7 跟掃羅同行的人都站住，說不出話來；他們聽見聲音，卻看不見人。8掃羅從地上爬起來，睜開眼睛，甚麼都看不見；同行的人就拉着他的手，帶他進大馬士革城。9他三天看不見甚麼；沒有吃，也沒有喝。

10 在大馬士革有一個門徒，名叫亞拿尼亞。他得了一個異象；在異象中主叫他：「亞拿尼亞！」他回答：「主啊，我在這裏。」

11 主說：「你立刻往直街去，在猶大家裏找一個大數人，名叫掃羅。他正在禱告，12在異象中看見了一個人，名叫亞拿尼亞，進來給他按手，使他恢復視覺。」

13 亞拿尼亞回答：「主啊，許多人告訴過我，這個人怎樣在耶路撒冷殘酷地迫害你的信徒。14現在他到大馬士革來，帶着祭司長授給他的權，要拘捕所有敬拜你的人。」

15 主對他說：「你只管去吧！因為我揀選他來事奉我，要他在外邦人、君王，以及以色列人當中宣揚我的名。16我要親自指示他，他必須為我的緣故遭受種種的苦難。」

17 於是亞拿尼亞去了。他進了那家，按手在掃羅身上，說：「掃羅弟兄啊，在你到這裏來的路上向你顯現的主耶穌親自差我來，要使你再看得見，並且受聖靈充滿。」18立刻，有魚鱗似的東西從掃羅的眼睛掉下來，他的視覺又恢復了。於是他起來，接受洗禮；19吃過東西後，體力就恢復過來。

掃羅在大馬士革傳道

掃羅在大馬士革跟門徒一起住了一些時候。20他馬上到各會堂去宣講耶穌，說：

synagogues and began to preach that Jesus was the Son of God.

21All who heard him were amazed and asked, "Isn't he the one who in Jerusalem was killing those who worship that man Jesus? And didn't he come here for the very purpose of arresting those people and taking them back to the chief priests?"

22But Saul's preaching became even more powerful, and his proofs that Jesus was the Messiah were so convincing that the Jews who lived in Damascus could not answer him.

23After many days had gone by, the Jews met together and made plans to kill Saul, 24but he was told of their plan. Day and night they watched the city gates in order to kill him. 25But one night Saul's followers took him and let him down through an opening in the wall, lowering him in a basket.

Saul in Jerusalem

26Saul went to Jerusalem and tried to join the disciples. But they would not believe that he was a disciple, and they were all afraid of him. 27Then Barnabas came to his help and took him to the apostles. He explained to them how Saul had seen the Lord on the road and that the Lord had spoken to him. He also told them how boldly Saul had preached in the name of Jesus in Damascus. 28And so Saul stayed with them and went all over Jerusalem, preaching boldly in the name of the Lord. 29He also talked and disputed with the Greek-speaking Jews, but they tried to kill him. 30When the believers found out about this, they took Saul to Caesarea and sent him away to Tarsus.

31And so it was that the church throughout Judea, Galilee, and Samaria had a time of peace. Through the help of the Holy Spirit it was strengthened and grew in numbers, as it lived in reverence for the Lord.

Peter in Lydda and Joppa

32Peter traveled everywhere, and on one occasion he went to visit God's people who lived in Lydda. 33There he met a man named Aeneas, who was paralyzed and had not been able to get out of bed for eight years. 34"Aeneas," Peter said to him, "Jesus Christ makes you well. Get up and make your bed." At once Aeneas got up. 35All the people living in Lydda and Sharon saw him, and they turned to the Lord.

36In Joppa there was a woman named Tabitha, who was a believer. (Her name in Greek is Dorcas, meaning "a deer.") She spent all her time doing good and helping the poor.

「他就是上帝的兒子。」

21 所有聽見的人都很驚奇,說:「這個人不就是在耶路撒冷殘害耶穌信徒的那個人嗎?他到這裏來,不就是要拘捕信徒、把他們押交給祭司長的嗎?」

22 但是,掃羅的講道反而更有力量;他用堅強的論據證明耶穌是基督,使大馬士革的猶太人無法辯駁。

23 過了一些時候,猶太人陰謀要把掃羅殺掉。24 有人把他們的陰謀告訴掃羅。為了要殺掃羅,他們日夜守在城門口。25 可是,有一個晚上,他的門徒用大籃子把他從城牆上縋了下去。

掃羅在耶路撒冷

26 掃羅到了耶路撒冷,想跟門徒來往。可是,他們不相信他是門徒;大家都怕他,27 只有巴拿巴來協助他,帶他去見使徒,向他們解釋掃羅怎樣在路上遇見了主,主怎樣向他說話。他又告訴他們掃羅怎樣勇敢地在大馬士革奉主的名講道。28 於是掃羅跟使徒出入來往,在耶路撒冷奉主的名大膽地傳道。29 他也跟講希臘話的猶太人講解,辯論,他們卻想殺他。30 信徒們知道了這件事,就帶他到凱撒利亞,送他往大數去。

31 當時,猶大、加利利、撒馬利亞各地的教會有了一段平安的時期。教會在敬畏主,在聖靈的扶助下建立了起來,人數日日增加。

彼得在呂大和約帕

32 彼得走遍各地方;有一次,他訪問住在呂大的信徒。33 在那裏,他遇見一個人,名叫以尼雅;這個人患癱瘓症,在牀上躺了八年。34 彼得對他說:「以尼雅,耶穌基督治好你了。起來,收拾鋪蓋吧!」以尼雅立刻起來。35 所有住在呂大和沙崙的人都看見了他,他們就都歸信了主。

36 在約帕有一個女門徒名叫大比大(希臘文的名字是多加,意思是羚羊)。她做了許

³⁷At that time she got sick and died. Her body was washed and laid in a room upstairs. ³⁸Joppa was not very far from Lydda, and when the believers in Joppa heard that Peter was in Lydda, they sent two men to him with the message, "Please hurry and come to us." ³⁹So Peter got ready and went with them. When he arrived, he was taken to the room upstairs, where all the widows crowded around him, crying and showing him all the shirts and coats that Dorcas had made while she was alive. ⁴⁰Peter put them all out of the room, and knelt down and prayed; then he turned to the body and said, "Tabitha, get up!" She opened her eyes, and when she saw Peter, she sat up. ⁴¹Peter reached over and helped her get up. Then he called all the believers, including the widows, and presented her alive to them. ⁴²The news about this spread all over Joppa, and many people believed in the Lord. ⁴³Peter stayed on in Joppa for many days with a tanner of leather named Simon.

Peter and Cornelius

10 There was a man in Caesarea named Cornelius, who was a captain in the Roman army regiment called "The Italian Regiment." ²He was a religious man; he and his whole family worshiped God. He also did much to help the Jewish poor people and was constantly praying to God. ³It was about three o'clock one afternoon when he had a vision, in which he clearly saw an angel of God come in and say to him, "Cornelius!"

⁴He stared at the angel in fear and said, "What is it, sir?"

The angel answered, "God is pleased with your prayers and works of charity, and is ready to answer you. ⁵And now send some men to Joppa for a certain man whose full name is Simon Peter. ⁶He is a guest in the home of a tanner of leather named Simon, who lives by the sea." ⁷Then the angel went away, and Cornelius called two of his house servants and a soldier, a religious man who was one of his personal attendants. ⁸He told them what had happened and sent them off to Joppa.

⁹The next day, as they were on their way and coming near Joppa, Peter went up on the roof of the house about noon in order to pray. ¹⁰He became hungry and wanted something to eat; while the food was being prepared, he had a vision. ¹¹He saw heaven opened and something coming down that looked like a large sheet being lowered by its four corners to the earth. ¹²In it were all kinds of animals, reptiles, and wild birds. ¹³A voice said to him, "Get up, Peter; kill and eat!"

¹⁴But Peter said, "Certainly not, Lord! I have

多好事，樂意幫助貧窮的人。³⁷有一天，她害病，死了。人家把她的屍體洗過，放在樓上一間房裏。³⁸約帕離呂大不遠，在約帕的門徒聽見彼得在呂大，就派兩個人去見他，要求他：「請你快點到我們這裏來。」³⁹彼得立刻動身，跟他們一道去。彼得一到，有人領他到樓上的房間去。所有的寡婦圍着彼得哭，又把多加生前所縫製的內衣、外衣給他看。⁴⁰彼得吩咐大家都出去，就跪下禱告，然後轉向屍體，說：「大比大，起來！」她睜開眼睛，看見彼得，就坐起來。⁴¹彼得走過去扶她起來，又叫信徒和寡婦們進去，把多加活活的交給他們。⁴²這消息傳遍了約帕，有許多人信了主。⁴³彼得在約帕一個皮革匠[畫門]的家裏住了好些日子。

彼得傳福音給哥尼流

10 凱撒利亞有一個人，名叫哥尼流，是羅馬軍「意大利營」的軍官。²他是一個虔誠的人；他跟他一家人都敬畏上帝，常常慷慨賙濟貧窮的猶太人，又時常熱心向上帝禱告。³有一天下午，在三點鐘左右，他得了一個異象；在異象中他清楚地看見上帝的一個使者進來，叫他：「哥尼流！」

⁴ 他注目看着天使，非常驚惶，就說：「主啊，甚麼事？」

天使說：「上帝已經聽了你的禱告，也看見你所做賙濟的善事。⁵現在你要派人到約帕去，邀請那個名叫西門·彼得的人來。⁶他在一個皮革匠西門的家裏作客；西門的家就在海邊。」⁷那對他說話的天使離去後，哥尼流叫了兩個家僕和平常伺候他的一個敬虔的侍衞來，⁸把所遇到的事告訴他們，然後差他們到約帕去。

⁹ 第二天，他們趕路將近約帕。約在中午，彼得到屋頂上禱告。¹⁰他餓了，想吃東西。那家人在預備午飯的時候，他得了一個異象，¹¹看見天開了，有一件東西降下來，好像一大塊布，布的四角綁住，縋到地上，¹²裏面有地上的各種飛禽走獸，又有爬蟲。¹³有聲音對他說：「彼得，起來，宰了吃！」

¹⁴ 可是彼得說：「主啊，絕對不可！我從

never eaten anything ritually unclean or defiled."

15The voice spoke to him again, "Do not consider anything unclean that God has declared clean." 16This happened three times, and then the thing was taken back up into heaven.

17While Peter was wondering about the meaning of this vision, the men sent by Cornelius had learned where Simon's house was, and they were now standing in front of the gate. 18They called out and asked, "Is there a guest here by the name of Simon Peter?"

19Peter was still trying to understand what the vision meant, when the Spirit said, "Listen! Three*l* men are here looking for you. 20So get ready and go down, and do not hesitate to go with them, for I have sent them." 21So Peter went down and said to the men, "I am the man you are looking for. Why have you come?"

22"Captain Cornelius sent us," they answered. "He is a good man who worships God and is highly respected by all the Jewish people. An angel of God told him to invite you to his house, so that he could hear what you have to say." 23Peter invited the men in and had them spend the night there.

The next day he got ready and went with them; and some of the believers from Joppa went along with him. 24The following day he arrived in Caesarea, where Cornelius was waiting for him, together with relatives and close friends that he had invited. 25As Peter was about to go in, Cornelius met him, fell at his feet, and bowed down before him. 26But Peter made him rise. "Stand up," he said, "I myself am only a man." 27Peter kept on talking to Cornelius as he went into the house, where he found many people gathered. 28He said to them, "You yourselves know very well that a Jew is not allowed by his religion to visit or associate with Gentiles. But God has shown me that I must not consider any person ritually unclean or defiled. 29And so when you sent for me, I came without any objection. I ask you, then, why did you send for me?"

30Cornelius said, "It was about this time three days ago that I was praying*m* in my house at three o'clock in the afternoon. Suddenly a man dressed in shining clothes stood in front of me 31and said: 'Cornelius! God has heard your prayer and has taken notice of your works of charity. 32Send someone to Joppa for a man whose full name is Simon Peter. He is a guest in the home of Simon the tanner of leather,

l Three; *some manuscripts have* Some; *one manuscript has* Two.
m praying; *some manuscripts have* fasting and praying.

來沒有吃過任何污穢不潔的東西。」

15那聲音第二次對他說:「上帝認爲潔淨的,你不可當作污穢。」16這樣一連三次,那件東西就被收回天上去了。

17彼得正在猜疑,不知道所看見的異象是甚麼意思;這時候,哥尼流所差來的人已經找到西門的家,站在門外,18高聲問:「有沒有一位名叫西門·彼得的客人住在這裏?」

19彼得還在尋思那異象究竟是甚麼意思的時候,聖靈對他說:「有三個人⑧來找你呢!20你起來,下去,跟他們一道去,不要疑惑,因爲是我差遣他們來的。」21於是彼得下去,對那些人說:「我就是你們所要找的人。你們來是爲着甚麼呢?」

22他們回答:「是我們的長官哥尼流差我們來的;他是一位敬畏上帝的義人,一向受全體猶太人民的尊敬。有一位聖天使指示他,要他來請你到他家裏去,好領受你的教導。」23彼得就請他們進去,招待他們在那裏過夜。

第二天,彼得動身跟他們一道去;從約帕來的幾位信徒也跟他同行。24再過一天,他們到了凱撒利亞。哥尼流已經邀請他的親朋好友在家裏迎候。25彼得剛要進去,哥尼流上前,俯伏在他腳前拜他。26彼得連忙扶他起來,說:「請起來,我自己也是人。」27彼得一邊說跟哥尼流說話,一邊走進屋裏去。他看見裏面有許多人聚集,28就對他們說:「你們都知道,按照我們的規矩,猶太人是不許跟異族人密切來往的;但是上帝已經指示我,不可以把任何人當作不潔淨或凡俗的。29所以,當你們差人來邀請我時,我沒有推辭就來了。現在請問,你們請我來是爲着甚麼?」

30哥尼流說:「四天前,大約下午三點鐘的時候,我在家裏禱告。忽然有一個穿着光亮衣服的人站在我面前,31說:『哥尼流!上帝垂聽了你的禱告,也記得你所做賙濟的善事。32你要派人到約帕去,邀請名叫西門·彼得的那人來。他在皮革匠西門的家裏

⑧「有三個人」有古卷作「有兩個人」;另有些古卷作「有一些人」。

who lives by the sea.' ³³And so I sent for you at once, and you have been good enough to come. Now we are all here in the presence of God, waiting to hear anything that the Lord has instructed you to say."

Peter's Speech

³⁴Peter began to speak: "I now realize that it is true that God treats everyone on the same basis. ³⁵Those who fear him and do what is right are acceptable to him, no matter what race they belong to. ³⁶You know the message he sent to the people of Israel, proclaiming the Good News of peace through Jesus Christ, who is Lord of all. ³⁷You know of the great event that took place throughout the land of Israel, beginning in Galilee after John preached his message of baptism. ³⁸You know about Jesus of Nazareth and how God poured out on him the Holy Spirit and power. He went everywhere, doing good and healing all who were under the power of the Devil, for God was with him. ³⁹We are witnesses of everything that he did in the land of Israel and in Jerusalem. Then they put him to death by nailing him to a cross. ⁴⁰But God raised him from death three days later and caused him to appear, ⁴¹not to everyone, but only to the witnesses that God had already chosen, that is, to us who ate and drank with him after he rose from death. ⁴²And he commanded us to preach the gospel to the people and to testify that he is the one whom God has appointed judge of the living and the dead. ⁴³All the prophets spoke about him, saying that all who believe in him will have their sins forgiven through the power of his name."

The Gentiles Receive the Holy Spirit

⁴⁴While Peter was still speaking, the Holy Spirit came down on all those who were listening to his message. ⁴⁵The Jewish believers who had come from Joppa with Peter were amazed that God had poured out his gift of the Holy Spirit on the Gentiles also. ⁴⁶For they heard them speaking in strange tongues and praising God's greatness. Peter spoke up: ⁴⁷"These people have received the Holy Spirit, just as we also did. Can anyone, then, stop them from being baptized with water?" ⁴⁸So he ordered them to be baptized in the name of Jesus Christ. Then they asked him to stay with them for a few days.

Peter's Report to the Church at Jerusalem

11 The apostles and the other believers throughout Judea heard that the Gentiles also had received the word of God. ²When Peter went to Jerusalem, those who were in favor

作客;西門的家就在海邊。」³³因此,我立刻差人去請你;你肯光臨,真是再好沒有了。現在我們都在上帝面前,要聽主吩咐你說的一切話。」

彼得講道

³⁴彼得開始說:「現在我確實知道,上帝對所有的人都平等看待。³⁵只要是敬畏他、行為正直的人,無論屬哪一種族,他都喜歡。³⁶你們知道,他藉着萬人之主耶穌基督傳給以色列人的信息是和平的福音。³⁷約翰宣講洗禮的福音以來,那從加利利開始傳遍猶太全境的大事你們都知道。³⁸你們也知道拿撒勒人耶穌;上帝怎樣以聖靈和大能傾注在他身上,使他走遍各地,廣行善事,治好一切受魔鬼控制的人,因為上帝與他同在。³⁹我們就是他在耶路撒冷和其他猶太人的地方所做一切事的見證人。他們把他釘死在十字架上。⁴⁰但是,第三天,上帝使他復活,而且向人顯現;⁴¹不是顯現給大家看,只是顯現給我們這些被上帝揀選來作見證的人看。他從死裏復活之後,我們曾跟他同吃同喝。⁴²他命令我們把福音傳給人民,證明他就是上帝所立、作為活人和死人的審判者的。⁴³所有的先知也都為他作見證;他們都說,凡信他的,都可以藉着他的名蒙赦罪。」

外邦人接受聖靈

⁴⁴彼得還在講道的時候,聖靈降臨在所有領受信息的人身上。⁴⁵那些跟着彼得從約帕來的猶太信徒,看見上帝把聖靈的恩賜也傾注給外邦人,都很驚訝;⁴⁶因為他們聽見了這些人說靈語,並且頌讚上帝的偉大。於是彼得說:⁴⁷「這些人已經領受了聖靈,跟我們一樣,有誰能阻止他們領受水的洗禮呢?」⁴⁸因此,他吩咐他們奉耶穌基督的名領受洗禮。他們又要求彼得跟他們一起多住幾天。

彼得向耶路撒冷教會報告

11 使徒和在猶太全境的信徒們聽見了有些外邦人也接受上帝的道這件事。²因此,當彼得到了耶路撒冷的時候,主張外邦

of circumcising Gentiles criticized him, saying,
[3]"You were a guest in the home of uncircumcised Gentiles, and you even ate with them!" [4]So Peter gave them a complete account of what had happened from the very beginning:

[5]"While I was praying in the city of Joppa, I had a vision. I saw something coming down that looked like a large sheet being lowered by its four corners from heaven, and it stopped next to me. [6]I looked closely inside and saw domesticated and wild animals, reptiles, and wild birds. [7]Then I heard a voice saying to me, 'Get up, Peter; kill and eat!' [8]But I said, 'Certainly not, Lord! No ritually unclean or defiled food has ever entered my mouth.' [9]The voice spoke again from heaven, 'Do not consider anything unclean that God has declared clean.' [10]This happened three times, and finally the whole thing was drawn back up into heaven. [11]At that very moment three men who had been sent to me from Caesarea arrived at the house where I was[n] staying. [12]The Spirit told me to go with them without hesitation. These six fellow believers from Joppa accompanied me to Caesarea, and we all went into the house of Cornelius. [13]He told us how he had seen an angel standing in his house, who said to him, 'Send someone to Joppa for a man whose full name is Simon Peter. [14]He will speak words to you by which you and all your family will be saved.' [15]And when I began to speak, the Holy Spirit came down on them just as on us at the beginning. [16]Then I remembered what the Lord had said: 'John baptized with water, but you will be baptized with the Holy Spirit.' [17]It is clear that God gave those Gentiles the same gift that he gave us when we believed in the Lord Jesus Christ; who was I, then, to try to stop God!"

[18]When they heard this, they stopped their criticism and praised God, saying, "Then God has given to the Gentiles also the opportunity to repent and live!"

The Church at Antioch

[19]Some of the believers who were scattered by the persecution which took place when Stephen was killed went as far as Phoenicia, Cyprus, and Antioch, telling the message to Jews only. [20]But other believers, who were from Cyprus and Cyrene, went to Antioch and proclaimed the message to Gentiles[o] also, telling them the Good News about the Lord Jesus. [21]The Lord's power was with them, and a great number of people believed and turned to the Lord.

n I was; *some manuscripts have* we were.
o Gentiles; *some manuscripts have* Greek-speaking Jews *or* Greek-speaking people.

人也必須領受割禮的人批評他說：[3]「你竟在沒有受割禮的外邦人家裏作客，甚至跟他們一起吃飯！」[4]彼得就把整個事情的經過一一向他們解釋。

[5]他說：「在約帕城裏禱告的時候，我得到一個異象。我看見有一件東西從天上降下來，好像一大塊布，布的四角綁住，停落在我身邊；[6]我仔細察看，裏面有飛禽走獸，又有爬蟲。[7]接著，我聽見有聲音對我說：『彼得，起來，宰了吃！』[8]我說：『主啊，絕對不可！任何污穢不潔的東西，我都沒有吃過。』[9]從天上來的聲音又說：『上帝認為潔淨的，你不可當作污穢。』[10]這樣一連三次。最後，那件東西就被收回天上去了。[11]剛好在這時候，奉派從凱撒利亞來找我的三個人到了我居住那家的門口。[12]聖靈指示我跟他們一道去，不必猶疑。從約帕來的六個信徒也跟我一道去。我們都到了哥尼流家裏。[13]哥尼流告訴我們，他怎樣看見一個天使站在他的屋子裏，對他說：『你要打發人到約帕去，邀請一個名叫西門·彼得的人來。[14]他有話要對你說，使你和你的全家得救。』[15]當我開始講話的時候，聖靈降臨在他們身上，正如當初降臨在我們身上一樣。[16]於是我記起主曾經說過：『約翰用水施洗，但你們要領受聖靈的洗禮。』[17]很顯然地，上帝把這恩賜也賜給這些外邦人，如同我們信了主耶穌基督時，他賜給我們的一樣。我是誰，能夠阻擋上帝的工作嗎？」

[18]他們聽見了這話，就不再批評，都頌讚上帝說：「上帝把因悔改而得生命的機會也賜給外邦人了！」

安提阿的教會

[19]這時候，信徒們因司提反被殺事件所引起的迫害而分散到各地去，有的遠走腓尼基、塞浦路斯，和安提阿；他們只把信息傳給猶太人。[20]但是，另有一些塞浦路斯和古利奈的信徒到了安提阿；他們也向希臘人傳講有關主耶穌的福音。[21]主的能力跟他們同在；有許許多多的人信了，歸向主。

22The news about this reached the church in Jerusalem, so they sent Barnabas to Antioch. 23When he arrived and saw how God had blessed the people, he was glad and urged them all to be faithful and true to the Lord with all their hearts. 24Barnabas was a good man, full of the Holy Spirit and faith, and many people were brought to the Lord.

25Then Barnabas went to Tarsus to look for Saul. 26When he found him, he took him to Antioch, and for a whole year the two met with the people of the church and taught a large group. It was at Antioch that the believers were first called Christians.

27About that time some prophets went from Jerusalem to Antioch. 28One of them, named Agabus, stood up and by the power of the Spirit predicted that a severe famine was about to come over all the earth. (It came when Claudius was emperor.) 29The disciples decided that they each would send as much as they could to help their fellow believers who lived in Judea. 30They did this, then, and sent the money to the church elders by Barnabas and Saul.

More Persecution

12About this time King Herod[p] began to persecute some members of the church. 2He had James, the brother of John, put to death by the sword. 3When he saw that this pleased the Jews, he went ahead and had Peter arrested. (This happened during the time of the Festival of Unleavened Bread.) 4After his arrest Peter was put in jail, where he was handed over to be guarded by four groups of four soldiers each. Herod planned to put him on trial in public after Passover. 5So Peter was kept in jail, but the people of the church were praying earnestly to God for him.

Peter Is Set Free from Prison

6The night before Herod was going to bring him out to the people, Peter was sleeping between two guards. He was tied with two chains, and there were guards on duty at the prison gate. 7Suddenly an angel of the Lord stood there, and a light shone in the cell. The angel shook Peter by the shoulder, woke him up, and said, "Hurry! Get up!" At once the chains fell off Peter's hands. 8Then the angel said, "Tighten your belt and put on your sandals." Peter did so, and the angel said, "Put your cloak around you and come with me." 9Peter followed him out of the prison, not knowing, however, if what the angel was doing was real; he thought he was seeing a vision. 10They

p KING HEROD: *Herod Agrippa I, ruler of all Palestine.*

22 這消息傳到了耶路撒冷的教會，他們就派巴拿巴到安提阿去。23巴拿巴到達的時候，看見上帝賜福給那邊的人，就很高興；他勸勉他們，要大家專心一意地信靠主。24巴拿巴是個好人，被聖靈充滿，有堅強的信心。於是有許多人信了主。

25 後來，巴拿巴到大數去找掃羅，26找到了，就帶他到安提阿。有一整年的時間，兩人跟教會的會友相聚，教導許多人。門徒被稱為「基督徒」是從安提阿開始的。

27 在這時候，有幾個先知從耶路撒冷下安提阿去。28其中有一個人叫亞迦布；他得到聖靈的指示，站起來預言天下將有嚴重的饑荒。（這事到克勞第在位年間果然發生。）29於是門徒決定每人按照自己的能力，捐錢救濟住在猶太的信徒們。30他們就這樣做了，託巴拿巴和掃羅把捐款帶給教會的長老們。

教會受更多的迫害

12 約在這時候，希律王下手迫害教會的一些會友。2他把約翰的哥哥雅各殺了。3他知道猶太人喜歡他這樣做，又去拘捕彼得。（這事發生在除酵節期間。）4他抓到彼得後，把他關在監獄裏，交給四班警衛看守，每班有四名兵士。希律計劃在逾越節後把他提出來，當眾審他。5因此，彼得在監獄裏受到嚴密的監視；教會的弟兄姊妹為着他懇切向上帝禱告。

彼得獲救出獄

6 希律要把彼得提出來公審的前一夜，彼得睡在兩名警衛中間，有兩條鐵鍊鎖住他，門外又有警衛把守着。7忽然，有主的一位天使站在那裏；有一道光射進牢房。天使拍一拍彼得的肩膀，把他叫醒了，說：「快點起來！」那鐵鍊立刻從彼得手上掉下。8天使對他說：「繫上帶子，把鞋子穿好。」彼得照他的話做了。天使又說：「披上外衣，跟我來。」9彼得跟着他走出監獄，卻不知道天使所做的是真有其事，以為是看見了異象。10他們通過了第一重和第二重的警衛崗

passed by the first guard station and then the second, and came at last to the iron gate that opens into the city. The gate opened for them by itself, and they went out. They walked down a street, and suddenly the angel left Peter.

11Then Peter realized what had happened to him, and said, "Now I know that it is really true! The Lord sent his angel to rescue me from Herod's power and from everything the Jewish people expected to happen."

12Aware of his situation, he went to the home of Mary, the mother of John Mark, where many people had gathered and were praying. 13Peter knocked at the outside door, and a servant named Rhoda came to answer it. 14She recognized Peter's voice and was so happy that she ran back in without opening the door, and announced that Peter was standing outside. 15"You are crazy!" they told her. But she insisted that it was true. So they answered, "It is his angel."

16Meanwhile Peter kept on knocking. At last they opened the door, and when they saw him, they were amazed. 17He motioned with his hand for them to be quiet, and he explained to them how the Lord had brought him out of prison. "Tell this to James and the rest of the believers," he said; then he left and went somewhere else.

18When morning came, there was a tremendous confusion among the guards–what had happened to Peter? 19Herod gave orders to search for him, but they could not find him. So he had the guards questioned and ordered them put to death.

After this, Herod left Judea and spent some time in Caesarea.

The Death of Herod
20Herod was very angry with the people of Tyre and Sidon, so they went in a group to see him. First they convinced Blastus, the man in charge of the palace, that he should help them. Then they went to Herod and asked him for peace, because their country got its food supplies from the king's country.

21On a chosen day Herod put on his royal robes, sat on his throne, and made a speech to the people. 22"It isn't a man speaking, but a god!" they shouted. 23At once the angel of the Lord struck Herod down, because he did not give honor to God. He was eaten by worms and died.

24Meanwhile the word of God continued to spread and grow.

25Barnabas and Saul finished their mission and returned from*q* Jerusalem, taking John Mark with them.

q from; *some manuscripts have* to.

位,最後來到通往城裏去的一道鐵門,門自動地開了。他們出來,走過一條街;突然,天使離開了彼得。

11 這時候,彼得才明白過來,就說:「現在我知道這是眞的;主差遣他的天使,救我脫離希律的手和猶太人要加給我的一切災害。」

12 他看淸楚這個情勢,就往約翰‧馬可的母親馬利亞家裏去;有好些人聚集在那裏禱告。13彼得敲了外門,就有一個名叫羅大的婢女應聲出來。14她認出是彼得的聲音,大喜過望,顧不得開門就跑回去告訴大家,說彼得站在門外。15他們說:「你發瘋了!」那婢女堅持眞有這回事。他們就說:「那一定是他的天使。」

16 這時候,彼得不停地敲門。他們開了門,看見果然是他,都很驚奇。17他做手勢,叫他們安靜下來,向他們解釋主怎樣帶他出了監獄。彼得又吩咐他們把消息告訴雅各和信徒們,然後離開,往別的地方去了。

18 天亮的時候,警衛們亂成一團,不知道彼得出了甚麼事。19希律下令搜查,可是不見彼得的蹤跡;他就審訊警衛,下令把他們處死。

這事以後,希律離開猶太,去凱撒利亞,在那裏住了一些時候。

希律的死
20 希律向泰爾和西頓的人民大發脾氣,所以,他們推派代表團去見希律。他們首先說服了宮廷總管伯拉斯都,然後去向希律求和,因爲他們需要從王的轄區獲得糧食的供應。

21 在特定的日子,希律穿上他的王服,坐在王位上,向人民訓話。22他們呼喊說:「這不是凡人的聲音,而是神明的聲音!」23主的天使立刻擊打希律,因爲他沒有把榮耀歸給上帝。他被蟲咬而死。

24 上帝的道繼續擴展,日見興旺。

25 巴拿巴和掃羅完成任務以後,離開耶路撒冷回去⑨;他們帶着約翰‧馬可同行。

⑨「離開耶路撒冷回去」另有些古卷作「就回到耶路撒冷去」。

Barnabas and Saul Are Chosen and Sent

13 In the church at Antioch there were some prophets and teachers: Barnabas, Simeon (called the Black), Lucius (from Cyrene), Manaen (who had been brought up with Governor Herod[r]) and Saul. [2]While they were serving the Lord and fasting, the Holy Spirit said to them, "Set apart for me Barnabas and Saul, to do the work to which I have called them."

[3]They fasted and prayed, placed their hands on them, and sent them off.

In Cyprus

[4]Having been sent by the Holy Spirit, Barnabas and Saul went to Seleucia and sailed from there to the island of Cyprus. [5]When they arrived at Salamis, they preached the word of God in the synagogues. They had John Mark with them to help in the work.

[6]They went all the way across the island to Paphos, where they met a certain magician named Bar-Jesus, a Jew who claimed to be a prophet. [7]He was a friend of the governor of the island, Sergius Paulus, who was an intelligent man. The governor called Barnabas and Saul before him because he wanted to hear the word of God. [8]But they were opposed by the magician Elymas (that is his name in Greek), who tried to turn the governor away from the faith. [9]Then Saul–also known as Paul–was filled with the Holy Spirit; he looked straight at the magician [10]and said, "You son of the Devil! You are the enemy of everything that is good. You are full of all kinds of evil tricks, and you always keep trying to turn the Lord's truths into lies! [11]The Lord's hand will come down on you now; you will be blind and will not see the light of day for a time."

At once Elymas felt a dark mist cover his eyes, and he walked around trying to find someone to lead him by the hand. [12]When the governor saw what had happened, he believed; for he was greatly amazed at the teaching about the Lord.

In Antioch in Pisidia

[13]Paul and his companions sailed from Paphos and came to Perga, a city in Pamphylia, where John Mark left them and went back to Jerusalem. [14]They went on from Perga and arrived in Antioch in Pisidia, and on the Sabbath they went into the synagogue and sat down. [15]After the reading from the Law of Moses and from the writings of the prophets, the officials

r HEROD: *Herod Antipas, ruler of Galilee (see Lk 3.1).*

聖靈選派巴拿巴和掃羅

13 在安提阿教會中，有幾位先知和教師，就是巴拿巴，西面（別號「黑漢」），古利奈人路求，跟希律王一起長大的馬念，還有掃羅。[2]當他們在敬拜主、禁食的時候，聖靈對他們說：「你們要為我指派巴拿巴和掃羅，去做我呼召他們來擔任的工作。」

[3]於是他們禁食禱告，給他們按手，派遣他們出去。

在塞浦路斯

[4]巴拿巴和掃羅已經奉聖靈差遣，就下西流基去，從那裏坐船到塞浦路斯。[5]他們一到撒拉米，就在各猶太人的會堂傳講上帝的道。約翰·馬可在那裏協助他們的工作。

[6]他們走遍全島，一直到了帕弗，在那裏遇到一個名叫巴·耶穌的術士，是一個猶太人，自稱為先知。[7]他和本島的總督士求·保羅頗有交情。總督為人明達；他邀請巴拿巴和掃羅來，要聽上帝的道。[8]可是，術士以呂馬（以呂馬是他的希臘名字）反對；他想阻止總督接受這信仰。[9]這時候，掃羅一也就是保羅一被聖靈充滿，就瞪着眼看那術士，[10]對他說：「你這個魔鬼的兒子！你是一切正義的仇敵，充滿着各樣的邪惡詭詐，故意歪曲主的真理！[11]現在主的懲罰要臨到你；你要瞎了，暫時看不見日光。」

立刻，以呂馬覺得一片黑霧遮住他的眼睛；他到處摸索，求人牽他的手，替他領路。[12]總督看見所發生的事，就成為信徒；他對有關主的教導覺得很希奇。

在彼西底的安提阿

[13]保羅和他的同伴從帕弗開船，到了旁非利亞的別加；約翰·馬可在那裏離開他們，回耶路撒冷去。[14]他們從別加繼續他們的行程，到了彼西底的安提阿。在安息日，他們到猶太人的會堂去，坐下。[15]讀過了摩西的法律和先知的書後，會堂的主管們派人去告

of the synagogue sent them a message: "Friends, we want you to speak to the people if you have a message of encouragement for them." [16]Paul stood up, motioned with his hand, and began to speak:

"Fellow Israelites and all Gentiles here who worship God: hear me! [17]The God of the people of Israel chose our ancestors and made the people a great nation during the time they lived as foreigners in Egypt. God brought them out of Egypt by his great power, [18]and for forty years he endured[s] them in the desert. [19]He destroyed seven nations in the land of Canaan and made his people the owners of the land. [20]All of this took about 450 years.

"After this[t] he gave them judges until the time of the prophet Samuel. [21]And when they asked for a king, God gave them Saul son of Kish from the tribe of Benjamin, to be their king for forty years. [22]After removing him, God made David their king. This is what God said about him: 'I have found that David son of Jesse is the kind of man I like, a man who will do all I want him to do.' [23]It was Jesus, a descendant of David, whom God made the Savior of the people of Israel, as he had promised. [24]Before Jesus began his work, John preached to all the people of Israel that they should turn from their sins and be baptized. [25]And as John was about to finish his mission, he said to the people, 'Who do you think I am? I am not the one you are waiting for. But listen! He is coming after me, and I am not good enough to take his sandals off his feet.'

[26]"My fellow Israelites, descendants of Abraham, and all Gentiles here who worship God: it is to us that this message of salvation has been sent! [27]For the people who live in Jerusalem and their leaders did not know that he is the Savior, nor did they understand the words of the prophets that are read every Sabbath. Yet they made the prophets' words come true by condemning Jesus. [28]And even though they could find no reason to pass the death sentence on him, they asked Pilate to have him put to death. [29]And after they had done everything that the Scriptures say about him, they took him down from the cross and placed him in a tomb. [30]But God raised him from death, [31]and for many days he appeared to those who had traveled with him from Galilee to Jerusalem. They are now witnesses for him to the people of Israel. [32-33]And we are here to bring the Good News to you: what God promised our

s he endured; *some manuscripts have* he took care of.

t All of this took about 450 years. After this; *or* Some 450 years later.

訴他們：「兄長們，如果你們有話要勸勉大家，請說吧。」[16]保羅就站起來，做個手勢，說：

「以色列同胞和所有敬畏上帝的外邦人哪，請聽！[17]以色列人的上帝揀選了我們的祖先。當他們寄居在埃及的時候，上帝使他們成為一個偉大的民族，用大能的手領他們出了埃及，[18]在曠野他容忍[10]他們約有四十年之久。[19]他消滅了迦南地區的七個民族，把他們的土地交給他的子民；[20]這些事歷時約四百五十年。

「以後，上帝又給他們設立士師，直到先知撒母耳的時候。[21]後來，他們要求有一個王，上帝就從便雅憫支族選出基士的兒子掃羅，立他作他們的王，前後四十年。[22]掃羅被廢後，上帝又替他們立大衛為王。關於大衛，上帝說：『我已經找到耶西的兒子大衛；他是合我心意、事事遵從我旨意的人。』[23]從他的後代中，上帝照着他的應許為以色列立了一位救主，就是耶穌。[24]耶穌開始工作以前，約翰向全體以色列人民傳道，要他們悔改，接受洗禮。[25]約翰的使命快要完成的時候，他向以色列人民說：『你們想我是誰？我並不是你們所期待的那一位。但是，那位隨後來的，我連替他脫鞋子都不配。』

[26]「諸位同胞──亞伯拉罕的子孫和所有敬畏上帝的外邦人哪，這拯救的信息是傳給我們的！[27]可是，住在耶路撒冷的人和他們的領袖不知道他是救主，也不明白每安息日所宣讀先知的經文。他們把耶穌定了罪，倒應驗了先知的預言。[28]雖然他們找不到定他死罪的理由，仍然要求彼拉多處死他。[29]他們做了先知書所記載關於耶穌的一切事情以後，就從十字架上把他取下來，安放在墓穴裏。[30]可是，上帝使他從死裏復活，[31]而且在一段時間裏，他好多次向那些曾經跟他一道從加利利到耶路撒冷去的人顯現。這些人如今在以色列民間成為他的見證人。[32-33]我們現在把這福音傳給你們：藉着耶穌的復

⑩「容忍」另有些古卷作「照顧」。

ancestors he would do, he has now done for us, who are their descendants, by raising Jesus to life. As it is written in the second Psalm,

'You are my Son;

today I have become your Father.'

[34]And this is what God said about raising him from death, never to rot away in the grave:

'I will give you the sacred and sure blessings that I promised to David.'

[35]As indeed he says in another passage,

'You will not allow your faithful servant to rot in the grave.'

[36]For David served God's purposes in his own time, and then he died, was buried with his ancestors, and his body rotted in the grave. [37]But this did not happen to the one whom God raised from death. [38-39]All of you, my fellow Israelites, are to know for sure that it is through Jesus that the message about forgiveness of sins is preached to you; you are to know that everyone who believes in him is set free from all the sins from which the Law of Moses could not set you free. [40]Take care, then, so that what the prophets said may not happen to you:[u]

[41]'Look, you scoffers! Be astonished and die!

For what I am doing today

is something that you will not believe,

even when someone explains it to you!' "

[42]As Paul and Barnabas were leaving the synagogue, the people invited them to come back the next Sabbath and tell them more about these things. [43]After the people had left the meeting, Paul and Barnabas were followed by many Jews and by many Gentiles who had been converted to Judaism. The apostles spoke to them and encouraged them to keep on living in the grace of God.

[44]The next Sabbath nearly everyone in the town came to hear the word of the Lord. [45]When the Jews saw the crowds, they were filled with jealousy; they disputed what Paul was saying and insulted him. [46]But Paul and Barnabas spoke out even more boldly: "It was necessary that the word of God should be spoken first to you. But since you reject it and do not consider yourselves worthy of eternal life, we will leave you and go to the Gentiles. [47]For this is the commandment that the Lord has given us:

'I have made you a light for the Gentiles, so that all the world may be saved.' "

[48]When the Gentiles heard this, they were glad and praised the Lord's message; and those

u *Some manuscripts do not have* to you.

活,上帝應許要為我們祖先成就的,已經向我們作子孫的實現了。正如詩篇第二篇所說:

你是我的兒子;

我今天作了你的父親。

[34]關於使他從死裏復活、永不再死的事,上帝這樣說過:

我要把應許給大衞

那神聖可靠的恩典賜給你們。

[35]在另一處,詩篇的作者也說:

你不會容許你忠心的僕人腐爛。

[36]「大衞在世的時候實現了上帝的計劃,死後被葬在祖先的旁邊,腐爛了;[37]但是,上帝使他從死裏復活的那一位卻沒有腐爛。[38-39]同胞們,你們都應該明白,那赦罪的信息就是耶穌傳給你們的。你們要知道,摩西的法律不能使你們解脫一切罪;可是每一個信耶穌的人都能從罪得釋放。[40]所以,你們要謹慎,免得先知所說的發生在你們身上:

[41]藐視上帝的人哪,

瞧吧,你們要驚駭,要死亡!

因為我在你們的時代所做的事,

即使有人向你們說明,

你們總是不信!」

[42]保羅和巴拿巴正要離開會堂的時候,大家邀請他們下一個安息日再來向他們講解這些事。[43]散會後,許多猶太人和皈依了猶太教的外邦人跟隨着保羅和巴拿巴。兩位使徒鼓勵他們要繼續倚靠上帝的恩典。

[44]下一個安息日,幾乎全城的人都來了,要聽主的道。[45]猶太人看見這一大羣人,心裏充滿嫉妒;他們辯駁保羅所說的話,並且侮辱他。[46]可是,保羅和巴拿巴更加勇敢地宣講說:「上帝的道必須先傳給你們。但是,你們不接受它,自以為不配得到永恆的生命。所以,我們要離開你們,到外邦人當中去;[47]因為主已經吩咐我們說:

我已經指定你們作外邦人的光,

要你們把拯救帶到天涯海角。」

[48]外邦人聽見了這話都很高興,頌讚主的道;那些已經被上帝揀選來接受永恆生命的

who had been chosen for eternal life became believers.

49The word of the Lord spread everywhere in that region. 50But the Jews stirred up the leading men of the city and the Gentile women of high social standing who worshiped God. They started a persecution against Paul and Barnabas and threw them out of their region. 51The apostles shook the dust off their feet in protest against them and went on to Iconium. 52The believers in Antioch were full of joy and the Holy Spirit.

In Iconium

14The same thing happened in Iconium: Paul and Barnabas went to the synagogue and spoke in such a way that a great number of Jews and Gentiles became believers. 2But the Jews who would not believe stirred up the Gentiles and turned them against the believers. 3The apostles stayed there for a long time, speaking boldly about the Lord, who proved that their message about his grace was true by giving them the power to perform miracles and wonders. 4The people of the city were divided: some were for the Jews, others for the apostles.

5Then some Gentiles and Jews, together with their leaders, decided to mistreat the apostles and stone them. 6When the apostles learned about it, they fled to the cities of Lystra and Derbe in Lycaonia and to the surrounding territory. 7There they preached the Good News.

In Lystra and Derbe

8In Lystra there was a crippled man who had been lame from birth and had never been able to walk. 9He sat there and listened to Paul's words. Paul saw that he believed and could be healed, so he looked straight at him 10and said in a loud voice, "Stand up straight on your feet!" The man jumped up and started walking around. 11When the crowds saw what Paul had done, they started shouting in their own Lycaonian language, "The gods have become like men and have come down to us!" 12They gave Barnabas the name Zeus, and Paul the name Hermes, because he was the chief speaker. 13The priest of the god Zeus, whose temple stood just outside the town, brought bulls and flowers to the gate, for he and the crowds wanted to offer sacrifice to the apostles.

14When Barnabas and Paul heard what they were about to do, they tore their clothes and ran into the middle of the crowd, shouting, 15"Why are you doing this? We ourselves are only human beings like you! We are here to announce the Good News, to turn you away from these worthless things to the living God,

人都成為信徒。

49主的道在那一帶地方傳遍了。50可是，猶太人煽動當地有地位的人士和外邦上流社會那些歸信上帝的婦女，開始迫害保羅和巴拿巴，把他們驅逐出境。51兩人跺掉了腳上的塵土，警告他們，然後往以哥念去了。52安提阿的門徒們心裏充滿了喜樂和聖靈。

在以哥念

14同樣的事也發生在以哥念。保羅跟巴拿巴到猶太人的會堂去；他們的言論使許多猶太人和外邦人成為信徒。2可是，那些不信的猶太人煽動外邦人，使他們厭惡信徒。3兩人在那裏住了好些日子；他們大膽地談論主的事。主賜給他們行神蹟奇事的能力，藉此證明他們所傳有關他恩典的信息是真實的。4城裏的羣眾為此分裂，有的站在猶太人一邊，有的卻擁護使徒。

5可是，猶太人和外邦人連同他們的領袖決心要傷害使徒，用石頭打死他們。6他們知道了這事，就避往呂高尼的路司得和特庇兩城以及附近一帶地區，7在那些地方繼續傳福音。

在路司得和特庇

8路司得城裏有一個殘疾的人，生下來就跛腳，從沒有行走過。9他坐在那裏，聽保羅講道。保羅看出他有信心，可以得到醫治，就定睛看他，10大聲說：「起來，兩腳站直！」那個人跳了起來，開始行走。11羣眾看見保羅所做的，就用呂高尼話高聲喊說：「有神明化身為人，降臨在我們中間了！」12他們稱巴拿巴為宙斯，稱保羅為希耳米，因為帶頭說話的是他。13城郊有一個宙斯廟的祭司，牽着牛，帶着花，來到城門口，要跟羣眾向使徒獻祭。

14巴拿巴和保羅聽見他們想做的事，就撕破衣服，衝進羣眾當中，大聲說：15「諸位，為甚麼做這種事呢？我們不過是人，人性上跟你們一樣。我們到這裏來傳福音，為要使你們離棄虛幻的偶像，歸向那位創造

who made heaven, earth, sea, and all that is in them. ¹⁶In the past he allowed all people to go their own way. ¹⁷But he has always given evidence of his existence by the good things he does: he gives you rain from heaven and crops at the right times; he gives you food and fills your hearts with happiness." ¹⁸Even with these words the apostles could hardly keep the crowd from offering a sacrifice to them.

¹⁹Some Jews came from Antioch in Pisidia and from Iconium; they won the crowds over to their side, stoned Paul and dragged him out of the town, thinking that he was dead. ²⁰But when the believers gathered around him, he got up and went back into the town. The next day he and Barnabas went to Derbe.

The Return to Antioch in Syria
²¹Paul and Barnabas preached the Good News in Derbe and won many disciples. Then they went back to Lystra, to Iconium, and on to Antioch in Pisidia. ²²They strengthened the believers and encouraged them to remain true to the faith, "We must pass through many troubles to enter the Kingdom of God," they taught. ²³In each church they appointed elders, and with prayers and fasting they commended them to the Lord, in whom they had put their trust.

²⁴After going through the territory of Pisidia, they came to Pamphylia. ²⁵There they preached the message in Perga and then went to Attalia, ²⁶and from there they sailed back to Antioch, the place where they had been commended to the care of God's grace for the work they had now completed.

²⁷When they arrived in Antioch, they gathered the people of the church together and told them about all that God had done with them and how he had opened the way for the Gentiles to believe. ²⁸And they stayed a long time there with the believers.

The Meeting at Jerusalem
15Some men came from Judea to Antioch and started teaching the believers, "You cannot be saved unless you are circumcised as the Law of Moses requires." ²Paul and Barnabas got into a fierce argument with them about this, so it was decided that Paul and Barnabas and some of the others in Antioch should go to Jerusalem and see the apostles and elders about this matter.

³They were sent on their way by the church; and as they went through Phoenicia and Samaria, they reported how the Gentiles had turned to God; this news brought great joy to all the believers. ⁴When they arrived in Jerusalem,

天、地、海、和其中萬物的永生上帝。¹⁶在以往，他任憑萬民各行其道。¹⁷然而，他時常藉着各樣善事來證明自己的存在，例如：從天上降雨給你們，使你們按時豐收；他賜食物給你們，使你們心裏充滿喜樂。」¹⁸雖然使徒說了這些話，也幾乎無法阻止羣眾向他們獻祭。

¹⁹但是，有些猶太人從彼西底的安提阿和以哥念來；他們唆使羣眾用石頭打保羅，以為他死了，就把他拖出城外。²⁰當門徒們環繞着他時，他站立起來，走回城裏去。第二天，他跟巴拿巴一道往特庇去。

回到安提阿
²¹保羅和巴拿巴在特庇傳福音，使許多人成為門徒。他們回到路司得，然後到以哥念，又到彼西底的安提阿。²²他們到處堅固門徒的心，鼓勵他們堅守信仰，又告訴他們：「我們必須經歷許多苦難才能成為上帝國的子民。」²³兩人又為各教會按立長老，禱告和禁食後，把他們交託給他們所信靠的主。

²⁴兩人經過彼西底地區，到了旁非利亞。²⁵他們在別加傳佈信息，然後去亞大利，²⁶從那裏坐船回安提阿。當初，就是在這地方，他們被交託在上帝的恩典中來從事現在已經完成的工作。

²⁷他們回到安提阿，就召集教會的弟兄姊妹，向他們報告上帝怎樣藉着他們工作，怎樣為外邦人開了信仰之門。²⁸他們在那裏跟信徒一起住了好些日子。

耶路撒冷會議
15有些人從猶太來到安提阿，開始教導信徒們說：「除非你們遵照摩西的法律接受割禮，你們不能得救。」²為了這個問題，保羅和巴拿巴兩個人跟他們發生了劇烈的爭辯。因此，大家決定派保羅、巴拿巴，和當地教會的幾個人上耶路撒冷去，向使徒和長老們請示這件事。

³於是教會為他們送行。旅途中，他們經過腓尼基和撒馬利亞，到處報告外邦人歸信上帝的事。所有的信徒聽到這消息都很欣慰。⁴他們到了耶路撒冷時，受到教會、使

they were welcomed by the church, the apostles, and the elders, to whom they told all that God had done through them. [5]But some of the believers who belonged to the party of the Pharisees stood up and said, "The Gentiles must be circumcised and told to obey the Law of Moses."

[6]The apostles and the elders met together to consider this question. [7]After a long debate Peter stood up and said, "My friends, you know that a long time ago God chose me from among you to preach the Good News to the Gentiles, so that they could hear and believe. [8]And God, who knows the thoughts of everyone, showed his approval of the Gentiles by giving the Holy Spirit to them, just as he had to us. [9]He made no difference between us and them; he forgave their sins because they believed. [10]So then, why do you now want to put God to the test by laying a load on the backs of the believers which neither our ancestors nor we ourselves were able to carry? [11]No! We believe and are saved by the grace of the Lord Jesus, just as they are."

[12]The whole group was silent as they heard Barnabas and Paul report all the miracles and wonders that God had performed through them among the Gentiles. [13]When they had finished speaking, James spoke up: "Listen to me, my friends! [14]Simon has just explained how God first showed his care for the Gentiles by taking from among them a people to belong to him. [15]The words of the prophets agree completely with this. As the scripture says,

[16]'After this I will return, says the Lord,
and restore the kingdom of David.
I will rebuild its ruins
and make it strong again.
[17]And so all the rest of the human race will
come to me,
all the Gentiles whom I have called to be
my own.
[18]So says the Lord, who made this known
long ago.'

[19]"It is my opinion," James went on, "that we should not trouble the Gentiles who are turning to God. [20]Instead, we should write a letter telling them not to eat any food that is ritually unclean because it has been offered to idols; to keep themselves from sexual immorality; and not to eat any animal that has been strangled, or any blood. [21]For the Law of Moses has been read for a very long time in the synagogues every Sabbath, and his words are preached in every town."

徒，和長老們的接待。他們向大家報告上帝藉着他們所做的一切事。[5]可是有些法利賽派的信徒站起來說：「外邦人必須接受割禮，也必須遵守摩西的法律。」

[6]於是，使徒和長老們開會討論這個問題。[7]經過長時間的辯論，彼得站起來，說：「諸位主內朋友，你們知道，上帝早已從你們當中選召了我，要我把福音的信息傳給外邦人，好使他們聽見而相信。[8]那洞察人心的上帝把聖靈賜給外邦人，如同賜給我們一樣，以此來表明他也接納外邦人。[9]在我們和他們之間，上帝不做任何區別，卻因為他們信而潔淨了他們的心。[10]既然這樣，你們現在為甚麼要試探上帝，把我們的祖先和我們自己所挑不起的擔子，放在外邦門徒的肩膀上呢？[11]這是不對的！我們相信我們得救是藉着主耶穌的恩典，是跟他們一樣的。」

[12]大家默默地聽着巴拿巴和保羅報告上帝藉着他們在外邦人當中所行的一切神蹟奇事。[13]他們講完後，雅各也說：「諸位主內朋友，請聽！[14]剛才西門說明了上帝怎樣眷顧外邦人，從他們當中選召人來歸屬自己。[15]先知所說的話完全跟這個相符。聖經這樣記載：

[16]主說：此後我要回來，
重建大衛倒塌了的家。
我要從廢墟中重新建造，
把它建立起來。
[17]這樣，所有其餘的人，
我所選召歸向我的外邦人，
都要尋求主。
[18]那位從遠古就指示這事的主這樣宣佈了。」

[19]雅各繼續說：「所以照我的看法，我們不應該為難那些歸向上帝的外邦人。[20]我們應該寫信，吩咐他們不可吃因祭過偶像而不潔淨的食物，不可有淫亂的行為，不可吃勒死的牲畜和血。[21]因為自古以來，每逢安息日，在各會堂裏都有人宣讀摩西的法律，在各城裏都有人宣揚他的教導。」

The Letter to the Gentile Believers

22Then the apostles and the elders, together with the whole church, decided to choose some men from the group and send them to Antioch with Paul and Barnabas. They chose two men who were highly respected by the believers, Judas, called Barsabbas, and Silas, 23and they sent the following letter by them:

"We, the apostles and the elders, your brothers, send greetings to all our brothers of Gentile birth who live in Antioch, Syria, and Cilicia. 24We have heard that some who went from our group have troubled and upset you by what they said; they had not, however, received any instruction from us. 25And so we have met together and have all agreed to choose some messengers and send them to you. They will go with our dear friends Barnabas and Paul, 26who have risked their lives in the service of our Lord Jesus Christ. 27We send you, then, Judas and Silas, who will tell you in person the same things we are writing. 28The Holy Spirit and we have agreed not to put any other burden on you besides these necessary rules: 29eat no food that has been offered to idols; eat no blood; eat no animal that has been strangled; and keep yourselves from sexual immorality. You will do well if you take care not to do these things. With our best wishes."

30The messengers were sent off and went to Antioch, where they gathered the whole group of believers and gave them the letter. 31When the people read it, they were filled with joy by the message of encouragement. 32Judas and Silas, who were themselves prophets, spoke a long time with them, giving them courage and strength. 33After spending some time there, they were sent off in peace by the believers and went back to those who had sent them.ᵛ

35Paul and Barnabas spent some time in Antioch, and together with many others they taught and preached the word of the Lord.

Paul and Barnabas Separate

36Some time later Paul said to Barnabas, "Let us go back and visit the believers in every town where we preached the word of the Lord, and let us find out how they are getting along." 37Barnabas wanted to take John Mark with them, 38but Paul did not think it was right to take him, because he had not stayed with them to the end of their mission, but had turned back and left them in Pamphylia. 39There was a sharp argument, and they separated: Barnabas took Mark and sailed off for Cyprus, 40while Paul chose Silas and left, commended by the believers to the care of the Lord's grace. 41He

ᵛ *Some manuscripts add verse 34: But Silas decided to stay there.*

致外邦信徒的信

22 這時候，使徒和長老們以及全教會決定要推選代表，派他們跟保羅、巴拿巴一道去安提阿。他們選出別號巴撒巴的猶大和西拉。這兩個人一向爲信徒們所尊重。23他們帶去的信這樣寫着：

「使徒和作長老的弟兄們問候在安提阿、敍利亞、基利家所有的外邦信徒們！24我們聽說有些人從我們這裏出去；他們所說的話使你們徬徨困惑。其實，我們並沒有吩咐他們去說那些話。25所以我們一起商議，大家同意選派代表到你們那裏去。他們要跟我們親愛的朋友巴拿巴和保羅同行；26這兩人曾爲着事奉我們的主耶穌基督而不惜冒生命的危險。27所以我們選派猶大和西拉；他們要當面告訴你們信中所提起的事。28因爲聖靈贊同我們，除了一些必要的規例，不要把其他的重擔加給你們。29你們不可吃祭過偶像的食物；不可吃血和被勒死的牲畜；也不可有淫亂的行爲。你們能夠不犯這幾件就好了。願你們平安！」

30 代表們奉命動身到安提阿去，在那裏召集了全體信徒，把信件交給他們。31他們宣讀信件的時候，因着信上鼓勵的話而非常欣慰。32猶大和西拉也是代上帝發言的先知；他們向信徒們說了許多話，激勵他們，堅固他們的信心。33在那裏住了一些日子後，信徒們就歡送他們，祝他們平安地回去。⑪

35 保羅和巴拿巴暫時住在安提阿；他們跟其他好些人一起教導並傳講主的道。

保羅和巴拿巴分手

36 過了些日子，保羅對巴拿巴說：「讓我們回到從前傳佈主道的各村鎮去，看看信徒們的情況。」37巴拿巴想帶約翰‧馬可一起去，38可是保羅不同意；因爲前次他不肯留下來跟他們一起工作，在旁非利亞離開了他們。39他們兩人爲了這件事劇烈地爭執，終於分手。巴拿巴帶着馬可坐船到塞浦路斯去，40保羅卻選擇西拉，蒙信徒們把他們交託在主恩典的眷顧中後，也離開了。41他走

⑪有些古卷加34節「可是，西拉決定留在那裏。」

went through Syria and Cilicia, strengthening the churches.

Timothy Goes with Paul and Silas

16 Paul traveled on to Derbe and Lystra, where a Christian named Timothy lived. His mother, who was also a Christian, was Jewish, but his father was a Greek. [2]All the believers in Lystra and Iconium spoke well of Timothy. [3]Paul wanted to take Timothy along with him, so he circumcised him. He did so because all the Jews who lived in those places knew that Timothy's father was Greek. [4]As they went through the towns, they delivered to the believers the rules decided upon by the apostles and elders in Jerusalem, and they told them to obey those rules. [5]So the churches were made stronger in the faith and grew in numbers every day.

In Troas: Paul's Vision

[6]They traveled through the region of Phrygia and Galatia because the Holy Spirit did not let them preach the message in the province of Asia. [7]When they reached the border of Mysia, they tried to go into the province of Bithynia, but the Spirit of Jesus did not allow them. [8]So they traveled right on through[w] Mysia and went to Troas. [9]That night Paul had a vision in which he saw a Macedonian standing and begging him, "Come over to Macedonia and help us!" [10]As soon as Paul had this vision, we got ready to leave for Macedonia, because we decided that God had called us to preach the Good News to the people there.

In Philippi: the Conversion of Lydia

[11]We left by ship from Troas and sailed straight across to Samothrace, and the next day to Neapolis. [12]From there we went inland to Philippi, a city of the first district of Macedonia;[x] it is also a Roman colony. We spent several days there. [13]On the Sabbath we went out of the city to the riverside, where we thought there would be a place where Jews gathered for prayer. We sat down and talked to the women who gathered there. [14]One of those who heard us was Lydia from Thyatira, who was a dealer in purple cloth. She was a woman who worshiped God, and the Lord opened her mind to pay attention to what Paul was saying. [15]After she and the people of her house had been baptized, she invited us, "Come and stay in my house if you have decided that I am a true

w traveled right on through; *or* passed by.
x a city of the first district of Macedonia; *some manuscripts have* a leading city of the district of Macedonia, *or* a leading city of that district in Macedonia.

遍了敍利亞和基利家，堅固各地教會弟兄姊妹們的信心。

提摩太跟保羅、西拉同工

16 保羅來到特庇和路司得。在路司得有一個門徒，名叫提摩太；他的母親是猶太人，也是信徒，父親是希臘人。[2]在路司得和以哥念的信徒們都稱讚提摩太。[3]保羅要帶他一起走，就替他行了割禮，因為這一帶的猶太人都知道他的父親是希臘人。[4]他們經過那些村鎮，把耶路撒冷的使徒和長老們所定下的規例交給他們，吩咐他們遵守。[5]因此，各教會在信心方面得以堅固，人數也一天比一天多起來。

馬其頓的呼聲

[6]他們取道弗呂家和加拉太地區，因為聖靈不准許他們在亞細亞省傳佈信息。[7]當他們到了每西亞邊界時，想進入庇推尼省，可是耶穌的靈禁止他們。[8]於是他們繞過[12]每西亞，到特羅亞去。[9]當天晚上，保羅得到一個異象，在異象中他看見一個馬其頓人，站著懇求他說：「請到馬其頓來幫助我們！」[10]保羅一有了這個異象，我們立刻準備往馬其頓去，因為我們知道上帝呼召我們去傳福音給當地的人。

呂底亞歸主

[11]我們坐船從特羅亞出發，直開撒摩特喇，第二天到尼亞坡里。[12]從那裏我們往內地走，來到馬其頓第一區的一個城市[13]腓立比；這城也是羅馬的殖民區。我們在這裏住了幾天。[13]安息日，我們出城到了河邊，心裏想，那裏可能有一個猶太人禱告的地方。我們坐下，向聚集在那裏的婦女們講道。[14]聽眾中有一個從推雅推喇城來的婦人，名叫呂底亞，以販賣紫色布疋為業。她一向敬拜上帝；主敞開了她的心，使她留心聆聽保羅所講的話。[15]她和她一家的人都受洗禮。隨後，她請求我們：「如果你們認為我是真

⑫「繞過」或譯「經過」。
⑬「馬其頓第一區的一個城市」另有些古卷作「馬其頓區的主要城市」或「馬其頓一帶，一個行政區的主要城市」。

believer in the Lord." And she persuaded us to go.

In Prison at Philippi

16One day as we were going to the place of prayer, we were met by a young servant woman who had an evil spirit that enabled her to predict the future. She earned a lot of money for her owners by telling fortunes. 17She followed Paul and us, shouting, "These men are servants of the Most High God! They announce to you how you can be saved!" 18She did this for many days, until Paul became so upset that he turned around and said to the spirit, "In the name of Jesus Christ I order you to come out of her!" The spirit went out of her that very moment.

19When her owners realized that their chance of making money was gone, they seized Paul and Silas and dragged them to the authorities in the public square. 20They brought them before the Roman officials and said, "These men are Jews, and they are causing trouble in our city. 21They are teaching customs that are against our law; we are Roman citizens, and we cannot accept these customs or practice them." 22And the crowd joined in the attack against Paul and Silas.

Then the officials tore the clothes off Paul and Silas and ordered them to be whipped. 23After a severe beating, they were thrown into jail, and the jailer was ordered to lock them up tight. 24Upon receiving this order, the jailer threw them into the inner cell and fastened their feet between heavy blocks of wood.

25About midnight Paul and Silas were praying and singing hymns to God, and the other prisoners were listening to them 26Suddenly there was a violent earthquake, which shook the prison to its foundations. At once all the doors opened, and the chains fell off all the prisoners. 27The jailer woke up, and when he saw the prison doors open, he thought that the prisoners had escaped; so he pulled out his sword and was about to kill himself. 28But Paul shouted at the top of his voice, "Don't harm yourself! We are all here!"

29The jailer called for a light, rushed in, and fell trembling at the feet of Paul and Silas. 30Then he led them out and asked, "Sirs, what must I do to be saved?"

31They answered, "Believe in the Lord Jesus, and you will be saved–you and your family." 32Then they preached the word of the Lord to him and to all the others in the house. 33At that very hour of the night the jailer took them and washed their wounds; and he and all his family

---

心信主，請到我家裏來住。」於是她堅決把我們留下。

在腓立比獄中

16 有一天，我們到那禱告的地方去，一個女奴迎着我們走來。這個女奴有邪靈附身，能夠占卜將來的事，因此替她主人賺了好多錢。17她一路跟着保羅和我們，大喊說：「這些人是至高上帝的僕人，要對你們宣佈那得救的道路！」18她一連好幾天這樣喊叫；保羅覺得不勝其煩，就轉過身來，對那邪靈說：「我奉耶穌基督的名，命令你從她身上出去！」那邪靈立刻出去了。

19 那女奴的主人知道他們的財源從此斷絕，便揪住保羅和西拉，把他們拖到廣場上見官，20帶他們到羅馬官長面前，指控說：「這些人是猶太人，竟來擾亂我們的城。21他們提倡違法的規矩，是我們羅馬人所不能接受、不能實行的！」22羣衆也附和着攻擊他們，官長就吩咐剝了他們的衣服，鞭打他們。23兵士們狠狠地把保羅和西拉打了一頓後，把他們關進牢裏，並命令看守的人嚴密看管。24看守領命，把他們關在內監，兩腳上了足枷。

25 約在半夜，保羅和西拉在禱告、唱詩頌讚上帝，其他的囚犯都側耳聽着。26忽然有劇烈的地震，連監獄的地基也搖動了；一下子所有的監門都開了，囚犯的鎖鍊也都掉落。27看守醒了過來，看見監門都敞開，以為所有的囚犯都逃掉了，就拔出刀來，想要自殺。28保羅一看見，大聲呼喊：「不要傷害自己，我們都在這裏！」

29 看守叫人拿燈來，衝了進去，戰戰兢兢地俯伏在保羅和西拉腳前，30接着領他們出來，問說：「兩位先生，我該做甚麼才能得救呢？」

31 他們說：「信主耶穌，你和你一家人就會得救。」32兩人又向他和他全家的人講解主的道。33當夜，就在那個時候，看守把他們帶去洗滌傷口；他和他的一家立刻都受了

were baptized at once. [34]Then he took Paul and Silas up into his house and gave them some food to eat. He and his family were filled with joy, because they now believed in God.

[35]The next morning the Roman authorities sent police officers with the order, "Let those men go."

[36]So the jailer told Paul, "The officials have sent an order for you and Silas to be released. You may leave, then, and go in peace."

[37]But Paul said to the police officers, "We were not found guilty of any crime, yet they whipped us in public–and we are Roman citizens! Then they threw us in prison. And now they want to send us away secretly? Not at all! The Roman officials themselves must come here and let us out."

[38]The police officers reported these words to the Roman officials; and when they heard that Paul and Silas were Roman citizens, they were afraid. [39]So they went and apologized to them; then they led them out of the prison and asked them to leave the city. [40]Paul and Silas left the prison and went to Lydia's house. There they met the believers, spoke words of encouragement to them, and left.

In Thessalonica

17 Paul and Silas traveled on through Amphipolis and Apollonia and came to Thessalonica, where there was a synagogue. [2]According to his usual habit Paul went to the synagogue. There during three Sabbaths he held discussions with the people, quoting [3]and explaining the Scriptures, and proving from them that the Messiah had to suffer and rise from death. "This Jesus whom I announce to you," Paul said, "is the Messiah." [4]Some of them were convinced and joined Paul and Silas; so did many of the leading women and a large group of Greeks who worshiped God.

[5]But some Jews were jealous and gathered worthless loafers from the streets and formed a mob. They set the whole city in an uproar and attacked the home of a man named Jason, in an attempt to find Paul and Silas and bring them out to the people. [6]But when they did not find them, they dragged Jason and some other believers before the city authorities and shouted, "These men have caused trouble everywhere! Now they have come to our city, [7]and Jason has kept them in his house. They are all breaking the laws of the Emperor, saying that there is another king, whose name is Jesus." [8]With these words they threw the crowd and the city authorities in an uproar. [9]The authorities made Jason and the others pay the required amount of money to be released, and then let them go.

洗禮。[34]他請保羅和西拉上自己的家，讓他們吃了東西。他和全家滿有喜樂，因為他們都信了上帝。

[35] 第二天一早，羅馬的官長派警官去說：「把那兩個人放了吧！」

[36] 看守就對保羅說：「官長有令釋放你和西拉，你們現在可以出獄，安心地去吧。」

[37] 可是，保羅對警官說：「我們是羅馬公民，並沒有被定罪，他們卻當眾鞭打我們，又把我們關進牢裏。現在他們想把我們偷偷地送走；這是不行的！叫羅馬官長親自來領我們出去吧！」

[38] 警官把這些話報告官長。他們一聽見保羅和西拉是羅馬公民，心裏害怕，[39]就到監獄裏向他們道歉，領他們出來，請他們離開那城。[40]保羅和西拉出了監門，就往呂底亞的家去，在那裏見到信徒們，勸慰他們一番，然後離開。

在帖撒羅尼迦

17 保羅和西拉繼續他們的旅程，經過暗妃坡里、亞波羅尼亞，來到帖撒羅尼迦，在那裏有猶太人的會堂。[2]保羅照習慣進會堂，連續三個安息日，根據聖經跟人家辯論，[3]講解並證明基督必須受害，然後從死裏復活。他說：「我對你們傳揚的這位耶穌，就是基督。」[4]其中有些人信了，成為保羅和西拉的同道；有好些敬拜上帝的希臘人和婦女界的領袖也信了。

[5] 可是，當地的猶太人心裏嫉妒，召集了一些市井無賴，糾合成羣，在城裏引起暴動。他們闖進耶孫的家，要找保羅和西拉，把他們拉去交給暴民；[6]可是找不着，竟把耶孫和其他幾個信徒拉去見地方官，控訴說：「這班擾亂天下的人，現在來到本城，[7]耶孫竟收留他們在家裏！他們違反皇上的諭令，說是另有一個王，名叫耶穌。」[8]這些話使羣眾和地方官起了一場騷動。[9]地方官命令耶孫和其他的人繳款具保，然後釋放他們。

In Berea

10As soon as night came, the believers sent Paul and Silas to Berea. When they arrived, they went to the synagogue. 11The people there were more open-minded than the people in Thessalonica. They listened to the message with great eagerness, and every day they studied the Scriptures to see if what Paul said was really true. 12Many of them believed; and many Greek women of high social standing and many Greek men also believed. 13But when the Jews in Thessalonica heard that Paul had preached the word of God in Berea also, they came there and started exciting and stirring up the mobs. 14At once the believers sent Paul away to the coast; but both Silas and Timothy stayed in Berea. 15The men who were taking Paul went with him as far as Athens and then returned to Berea with instructions from Paul that Silas and Timothy should join him as soon as possible.

In Athens

16While Paul was waiting in Athens for Silas and Timothy, he was greatly upset when he noticed how full of idols the city was. 17So he held discussions in the synagogue with the Jews and with the Gentiles who worshiped God, and also in the public square every day with the people who happened to come by. 18Certain Epicurean and Stoic teachers also debated with him. Some of them asked, "What is this ignorant show-off trying to say?"

Others answered, "He seems to be talking about foreign gods." They said this because Paul was preaching about Jesus and the resurrection.y 19So they took Paul, brought him before the city council, the Areopagus, and said, "We would like to know what this new teaching is that you are talking about. 20Some of the things we hear you say sound strange to us, and we would like to know what they mean." (21For all the citizens of Athens and the foreigners who lived there liked to spend all their time telling and hearing the latest new thing.)

22Paul stood up in front of the city council and said, "I see that in every way you Athenians are very religious. 23For as I walked through your city and looked at the places where you worship, I found an altar on which is written, 'To an Unknown God.' That which you worship, then, even though you do not know it, is what I now proclaim to you. 24God, who made the world and everything in it, is Lord of heaven and earth and does not live in temples made by human hands. 25Nor does he need anything that we can supply by working for him,

---

y JESUS AND THE RESURRECTION: *In Greek, the feminine noun "resurrection" could be understood to be the name of a goddess.*

在庇哩亞

10 一到晚上，信徒們立刻送保羅和西拉往庇哩亞去。他們到了那裏，就進猶太人的會堂。11這裏的人比帖撒羅尼迦人開明。他們熱心地傾聽信息，每天查考聖經，要知道保羅所說的是不是真實。12他們當中有許多人信了；有許多希臘上流社會的婦女和希臘男子也信了。13可是，帖撒羅尼迦的猶太人一聽說保羅也在庇哩亞傳上帝的道，就到那裏去搗亂，煽動羣衆。14信徒們立刻送保羅往沿海地方去；西拉和提摩太卻留在庇哩亞。15護送保羅的人一直把他送到雅典，然後回到庇哩亞，帶來保羅所交代的話，要西拉和提摩太儘快趕到他那裏，跟他會合。

在雅典

16 保羅在雅典等候西拉和提摩太的時候，看見滿城都是偶像，心裏非常難過。17他在會堂裏跟猶太人和敬拜上帝的外邦人辯論，又每天在廣場上跟偶然遇到的人辯論。18有些伊壁鳩魯派和斯多亞派的哲學家也來跟他爭論。有的說：「這走江湖的在胡吹些甚麼？」

也有的說：「他好像在傳講外國的鬼神。」他們這樣說是因爲保羅在傳耶穌和他復活的福音。19他們就帶保羅到亞略·巴古的議會上，說：「我們可以知道一些你所講論的新學說嗎？20有些事我們聽來覺得非常奇異，很想知道究竟是甚麼意思。」(21原來雅典人和所有旅居在那裏的外國人都喜歡把時間全花在談論新聞、打聽消息上面。)

22 保羅站立在亞略·巴古議會上，說：「雅典的居民們！我知道你們在各方面都表現出濃厚的宗教熱情。23我在城裏到處走動，觀看你們崇拜的場所，竟發現有一座祭壇，上面刻着『獻給不認識的神』。我現在要告訴你們的就是這位你們不認識、卻在敬拜着的神。24這位創造天、地，和其中萬物的上帝乃是天地的主。他不住人所建造的殿宇，25也不需要人的任何供奉；因爲他自己

since it is he himself who gives life and breath and everything else to everyone. [26]From one human being he created all races of people and made them live throughout the whole earth. He himself fixed beforehand the exact times and the limits of the places where they would live. [27]He did this so that they would look for him, and perhaps find him as they felt around for him. Yet God is actually not far from any one of us; [28]as someone has said,

'In him we live and move and exist.'

It is as some of your poets have said,

'We too are his children.'

[29]Since we are God's children, we should not suppose that his nature is anything like an image of gold or silver or stone, shaped by human art and skill. [30]God has overlooked the times when people did not know him, but now he commands all of them everywhere to turn away from their evil ways. [31]For he has fixed a day in which he will judge the whole world with justice by means of a man he has chosen. He has given proof of this to everyone by raising that man from death!"

[32]When they heard Paul speak about a raising from death, some of them made fun of him, but others said, "We want to hear you speak about this again." [33]And so Paul left the meeting. [34]Some men joined him and believed, among whom was Dionysius, a member of the council; there was also a woman named Damaris, and some other people.

In Corinth

18 After this, Paul left Athens and went on to Corinth. [2]There he met a Jew named Aquila, born in Pontus, who had recently come from Italy with his wife Priscilla, for Emperor Claudius had ordered all the Jews to leave Rome. Paul went to see them, [3]and stayed and worked with them, because he earned his living by making tents, just as they did. [4]He held discussions in the synagogue every Sabbath, trying to convince both Jews and Greeks.

[5]When Silas and Timothy arrived from Macedonia, Paul gave his whole time to preaching the message, testifying to the Jews that Jesus is the Messiah. [6]When they opposed him and said evil things about him, he protested by shaking the dust from his clothes and saying to them, "If you are lost, you yourselves must take the blame for it! I am not responsible. From now on I will go to the Gentiles." [7]So he left them and went to live in the house of a Gentile named Titius Justus, who worshiped God; his house was next to the synagogue. [8]Crispus, who

把生命、氣息，和萬物賜給人類。[26]他從一人造出萬族，使他們散居在整個地面上，而且為他們預先定下了年限和居住的疆界。[27]他這樣做是要他們尋求上帝，或者能夠在摸索中找到他。其實，上帝與我們每一個人相距不遠。[28]有人說：『我們的生活、行動、存在都在於他。』又如你們當中某詩人說的：『我們也是他的兒女。』[29]既然我們是他的兒女，我們就不應該幻想上帝的本性是可以用人的技巧，用金銀或石頭所雕製的偶像來比擬的。[30]當人類處在蒙昧無知的時候，上帝不加深究，但現在他命令全人類要離棄邪惡的道路。[31]因為他已經定下日子，要藉着他所揀選的一個人，用公義來審判全世界；由於使這一個人從死裏復活，他已經把憑據給了全人類。」

[32]他們一聽見保羅說起死人復活的事，有人就譏笑他；另有些人說：「我們希望再聽你講講這件事。」[33]於是保羅離開了議會。[34]有些人成為他的同道，作了信徒；其中有亞略·巴古的議員杜尼修，又有一個名叫大馬哩的婦人，和另外一些人。

在哥林多

18 這事以後，保羅離開雅典，來到哥林多。[2]他在那裏遇到一個在本都出生的猶太人，名叫亞居拉，新近跟妻子百基拉從意大利來，因為皇帝克勞第命令所有的猶太人離開羅馬。保羅去看他們，[3]留下來跟他們一起工作；因為保羅一向靠製造帳棚維持生活，跟他們是同業。[4]每逢安息日，保羅都到會堂去，跟人家辯論，勸導猶太人和希臘人歸信。

[5]西拉和提摩太從馬其頓來到的時候，保羅就用全部的時間傳講信息，向猶太人見證耶穌是基督。[6]可是，當他們反對他、毀謗他的時候，他就抖掉衣服上的灰塵，對他們說：「要是你們滅亡，罪不在我，你們自己負責吧！從今以後，我要到外邦人那裏去了。」[7]於是保羅離開他們，去住在一個敬畏上帝、名叫提多·猶士都的家裏，他的家靠近會堂。[8]會堂的主管基利司布和全家都

was the leader of the synagogue, believed in the Lord, together with all his family; and many other people in Corinth heard the message, believed, and were baptized.

9One night Paul had a vision in which the Lord said to him, "Do not be afraid, but keep on speaking and do not give up, 10for I am with you. No one will be able to harm you, for many in this city are my people." 11So Paul stayed there for a year and a half, teaching the people the word of God.

12When Gallio was made the Roman governor of Achaia, Jews there got together, seized Paul, and took him into court. 13"This man," they said, "is trying to persuade people to worship God in a way that is against the law!"

14Paul was about to speak when Gallio said to the Jews, "If this were a matter of some evil crime or wrong that has been committed, it would be reasonable for me to be patient with you Jews. 15But since it is an argument about words and names and your own law, you yourselves must settle it. I will not be the judge of such things!" 16And he drove them out of the court. 17They all grabbed Sosthenes, the leader of the synagogue, and beat him in front of the court. But that did not bother Gallio a bit.

The Return to Antioch

18Paul stayed on with the believers in Corinth for many days, then left them and sailed off with Priscilla and Aquila for Syria. Before sailing from Cenchreae he had his head shaved because of a vow he had taken.z 19They arrived in Ephesus, where Paul left Priscilla and Aquila. He went into the synagogue and held discussions with the Jews. 20The people asked him to stay longer, but he would not consent. 21Instead, when he left them as he left, "If it is the will of God, I will come back to you." And so he sailed from Ephesus.

22When he arrived at Caesarea, he went to Jerusalem and greeted the church, and then went to Antioch. 23After spending some time there, he left and went through the region of Galatia and Phrygia, strengthening all the believers.

Apollos in Ephesus and Corinth

24At that time a Jew named Apollos, who had been born in Alexandria, came to Ephesus. He was an eloquent speaker and had a thorough knowledge of the Scriptures. 25He had been instructed in the Way of the Lord, and

信了主;還有許多哥林多人聽了信息也信了,並接受洗禮。

9 有一個晚上,保羅得了一個異象。主在異象中對他說:「你別害怕,只管講,不要緘默,10有我與你同在,沒有人能傷害你,而且這城裏有許多我的子民。」11保羅就在那裏住了一年半,把上帝的道教導他們。

12當迦流出任亞該亞總督的時候,猶太人集合起來攻擊保羅,把他拉上法庭,13控告他:「這個人教唆別人用不合法的方式敬拜上帝!」

14保羅剛要開口,迦流對猶太人說:「假如這是一件寃枉或犯法的事,我當然要耐着性子聽你們;15旣然所爭論的是你們法律上的一些字眼名詞,你們自己去解決吧。我不願意審判這樣的事!」16於是把他們趕出法庭。17大家就揪着會堂的主管所提尼,在庭前毆打他。這事迦流也不過問。

保羅回到安提阿

18保羅在哥林多和信徒們又住了好些日子,然後離開他們,跟百基拉和亞居拉一道坐船到敍利亞去。動身以前,他在堅革哩把頭髮剪掉了,因為他曾經許下一個願。19他們到了以弗所,在那裏,保羅向百基拉和亞居拉告別,自己到會堂去跟猶太人辯論。20大家請他留下來多住些日子,但保羅不答應。21臨別的時候,他對他們說:「如果是上帝的旨意,我會再回到你們這裏來。」於是保羅又從以弗所上船。

22保羅一到凱撒利亞,就上耶路撒冷探望教會,然後去安提阿,23在那裏住了一些日子才走。他走遍了加拉太和弗呂家一帶地方,到處堅固門徒的信心。

亞波羅在以弗所和哥林多

24 有一個猶太人名叫亞波羅,來到以弗所。他生在亞歷山大,是個很有口才的人,對聖經有非常豐富的知識。25他在主所指示的道路上面,已經受過相當的訓練,而且心

z A VOW HE TAKEN: *This refers to the Jewish custom of shaving the head as a sign that a vow has been kept.*

with great enthusiasm he proclaimed and taught correctly the facts about Jesus. However, he knew only the baptism of John. [26]He began to speak boldly in the synagogue. When Priscilla and Aquila heard him, they took him home with them and explained to him more correctly the Way of God. [27]Apollos then decided to go to Achaia, so the believers in Ephesus helped him by writing to the believers in Achaia, urging them to welcome him. When he arrived, he was a great help to those who through God's grace had become believers. [28]For with his strong arguments he defeated the Jews in public debates by proving from the Scriptures that Jesus is the Messiah.

Paul in Ephesus

19 While Apollos was in Corinth, Paul traveled through the interior of the province and arrived in Ephesus. There he found some disciples [2]and asked them, "Did you receive the Holy Spirit when you became believers?"

"We have not even heard that there is a Holy Spirit," they answered.

[3]"Well, then, what kind of baptism did you receive?" Paul asked.

"The baptism of John," they answered.

[4]Paul said, "The baptism of John was for those who turned from their sins; and he told the people of Israel to believe in the one who was coming after him–that is, in Jesus."

[5]When they heard this, they were baptized in the name of the Lord Jesus. [6]Paul placed his hands on them, and the Holy Spirit came upon them; they spoke in strange tongues and also proclaimed God's message. [7]They were about twelve men in all.

[8]Paul went into the synagogue and for three months spoke boldly with the people, holding discussions with them and trying to convince them about the Kingdom of God. [9]But some of them were stubborn and would not believe, and before the whole group they said evil things about the Way of the Lord. So Paul left them and took the believers with him, and every day[a] he held discussions in the lecture hall of Tyrannus. [10]This went on for two years, so that all the people who lived in the province of Asia, both Jews and Gentiles, heard the word of the Lord.

The Sons of Sceva

[11]God was performing unusual miracles through Paul. [12]Even handkerchiefs and aprons he had used were taken to the sick, and their

a *Some manuscripts add* from 11:00 a.m. until 4:00 p.m.

中火熱，常常把耶穌的事正確地向人講解。可是，他只曉得有約翰的洗禮。[26]亞波羅開始在會堂裏大膽地講論；百基拉和亞居拉聽到了，就請他到家裏去，更加準確地把上帝的道路向他解釋。[27]以後亞波羅決定到亞該亞去，以弗所的信徒就幫助他，寫信給亞該亞的門徒，請他們接待他。他到了那裏，對那些蒙恩信主的人大有幫助。[28]他屢次在公開的辯論中有力地駁倒了猶太人，根據聖經證明耶穌是基督。

保羅在以弗所

19 亞波羅在哥林多的時候，保羅旅行經過內陸地區，來到以弗所。在那裏，他遇見一些門徒，[2]就問他們：「你們信主的時候，有沒有領受聖靈？」

他們回答：「我們從來沒有聽過有聖靈這回事。」

[3]保羅又問：「那麼，你們受的是甚麼洗禮呢？」

他們回答：「是約翰的洗禮。」

[4]保羅說：「約翰的洗禮是為那些悔改了的人行的；他告訴以色列人民要信在他以後來的那一位，就是耶穌。」

[5]他們一聽見這話，就奉主耶穌的名領受洗禮。[6]保羅為他們按手，聖靈降臨在他們身上，他們就講靈語，又宣講上帝的信息。[7]他們一共約有十二個人。

[8]一連三個月，保羅照常到會堂去，大膽地講道，跟人家辯論上帝國的事，勸人歸信。[9]他們當中有些人頑固不肯相信；在會眾面前公然毀謗主的道路。於是保羅帶着門徒離開他們，天天[14]在推喇奴講堂進行討論。[10]這樣的工作繼續了兩年，因此所有住在亞細亞省的人，無論猶太人或外邦人，都聽見主的道。

士基瓦的兒子

[11]上帝藉着保羅行了些奇異的神蹟；[12]甚至有人把他用過的手巾或圍裙拿去放在病人

[14]「天天」另有些古卷作「每天從早上十一點到下午四點」。

diseases were driven away, and the evil spirits would go out of them. ¹³Some Jews who traveled around and drove out evil spirits also tried to use the name of the Lord Jesus to do this. They said to the evil spirits, "I command you in the name of Jesus, whom Paul preaches." ¹⁴Seven brothers, who were the sons of a Jewish High Priest named Sceva, were doing this.

¹⁵But the evil spirit said to them, "I know Jesus, and I know about Paul; but you–who are you?"

¹⁶The man who had the evil spirit in him attacked them with such violence that he over-powered them all. They ran away from his house, wounded and with their clothes torn off. ¹⁷All the Jews and Gentiles who lived in Ephesus heard about this; they were all filled with fear, and the name of the Lord Jesus was given greater honor. ¹⁸Many of the believers came, publicly admitting and revealing what they had done. ¹⁹Many of those who had practiced magic brought their books together and burned them in public. They added up the price of the books, and the total came to fifty thousand silver coins.[b] ²⁰In this powerful way the word of the Lord[c] kept spreading and growing stronger.

The Riot in Ephesus

²¹After these things had happened, Paul made up his mind[d] to travel through Macedonia and Achaia and go on to Jerusalem. "After I go there," he said, "I must also see Rome." ²²So he sent Timothy and Erastus, two of his helpers, to Macedonia, while he spent more time in the province of Asia.

²³It was at this time that there was serious trouble in Ephesus because of the Way of the Lord. ²⁴A certain silversmith named Demetrius made silver models of the temple of the god-dess Artemis, and his business brought a great deal of profit to the workers. ²⁵So he called them all together with others whose work was like theirs and said to them, "Men, you know that our prosperity comes from this work. ²⁶Now, you can see and hear for yourselves what this fellow Paul is doing. He says that hand-made gods are not gods at all, and he has succeeded in convincing many people, both here in Ephesus and in nearly the whole prov-ince of Asia. ²⁷There is the danger, then, that this business of ours will get a bad name. Not only that, but there is also the danger that the

身上，會使疾病消除，也使邪靈從附着的人身上出來。¹³有些到處招搖、驅邪趕鬼的猶太人也想假借主耶穌的名來做這種事。他們對邪靈說：「我奉保羅所傳的耶穌的名，命令你們出來。」¹⁴做這種事的是猶太祭司長士基瓦的七個兒子。

¹⁵但是，邪靈回答他們：「我認識耶穌，也知道保羅是誰；可是，你們是誰？」

¹⁶那個邪靈附身的人就猛烈地襲擊他們，制伏了他們。他們都受傷，衣服給撕碎了，狼狽地逃出屋子。¹⁷所有住在以弗所的猶太人和外邦人聽見這事，都很害怕；主耶穌的名從此更受尊崇。¹⁸有許多信徒開始把他們以往所做過的事公開坦白地承認出來。¹⁹許多行邪術的人帶來他們的書，堆在一起，當眾焚燒。他們計算這些書的價錢，總共約值五萬銀幣。²⁰這樣，主的道普遍傳開，大大興旺。

以弗所的騷動

²¹這些事情過後，保羅決定⑮取道馬其頓和亞該亞，到耶路撒冷去。他說：「到了那裏以後，我也必須訪問羅馬。」²²於是他打發他的兩個助手—提摩太和以拉都—到馬其頓去，自己暫時留在亞細亞省。

²³就在這時候，為了主的道路，以弗所發生了一件嚴重的亂事。²⁴有一個名叫底米特的銀匠，一向以製造銀質的亞底米女神廟模型為業；這行業使許多匠人獲得厚利。²⁵底米特召集了這些工人和所有的同業，對他們說：「各位，你們知道我們的繁榮是靠這一行業的。²⁶現在你們已經聽見，也看到這個保羅在搞些甚麼。他說：『人手所造的神都不是神。』這話已經使以弗所和幾乎全亞細亞省的許許多多人相信了。²⁷看來我們這一行業有蒙受惡名的危險。不但這樣，連大女

---

b SILVER COINS: *A silver coin was the daily wage of a rural worker (see Mt 20.2).*

c In this … Lord; *or* And so, by the power of the Lord, the message.

d Paul made up his mind; *or* Paul, led by the Spirit, decided.

⑮「保羅決定」或譯「保羅蒙受聖靈的指示，決定」。

temple of the great goddess Artemis will come to mean nothing and that her greatness will be destroyed–the goddess worshiped by everyone in Asia and in all the world!"

28As the crowd heard these words, they became furious and started shouting, "Great is Artemis of Ephesus!" 29The uproar spread throughout the whole city. The mob grabbed Gaius and Aristarchus, two Macedonians who were traveling with Paul, and rushed with them to the theater. 30Paul himself wanted to go before the crowd, but the believers would not let him. 31Some of the provincial authorities, who were his friends, also sent him a message begging him not to show himself in the theater. 32Meanwhile the whole meeting was in an uproar: some people were shouting one thing, others were shouting something else, because most of them did not even know why they had come together. 33Some of the people concluded that Alexander was responsible, since the Jews made him go up to the front. Then Alexander motioned with his hand for the people to be silent, and he tried to make a speech of defense. 34But when they recognized that he was a Jew, they all shouted together the same thing for two hours: "Great is Artemis of Ephesus!"

35At last the city clerk was able to calm the crowd. "Fellow Ephesians!" he said. "Everyone knows that the city of Ephesus is the keeper of the temple of the great Artemis and of the sacred stone that fell down from heaven. 36Nobody can deny these things. So then, you must calm down and not do anything reckless. 37You have brought these men here even though they have not robbed temples or said evil things about our goddess. 38If Demetrius and his workers have an accusation against anyone, we have the authorities and the regular days for court; charges can be made there. 39But if there is something more that you want, it will have to be settled in a legal meeting of citizens. 40For after what has happened today, there is the danger that we will be accused of a riot. There is no excuse for all this uproar, and we would not be able to give a good reason for it." 41After saying this, he dismissed the meeting.

To Macedonia and Achaia

20 After the uproar died down, Paul called together the believers and with words of encouragement said good-bye to them. Then he left and went on to Macedonia. 2He went through those regions and encouraged the people with many messages. Then he came to Achaia, 3where he stayed three months. He was getting ready to go to Syria when he discovered that there were Jews plotting against him; so he

---

神亞底米的廟也要被輕視，一向在亞細亞省和普天下受崇拜的女神的尊榮也要遭受破壞！」

28 羣眾一聽見這些話就狂怒起來，大嚷說：「以弗所人的亞底米女神多麼偉大啊！」29於是騷動蔓延全城。暴民抓住跟保羅同行的兩個馬其頓人——該猶和亞里達古——一起衝進戲院裏去。30保羅想走到羣眾前面，但是門徒們不讓他進去。31還有亞細亞省的幾位領袖，是保羅的朋友，也派人去勸阻保羅，叫他別冒險到戲院裏去。32這時候，整個會場亂哄哄的，有的喊這個，有的喊那個，多數的人不曉得他們聚在那裏是幹甚麼的。33猶太人把亞歷山大推向前去，有些人以為這件事該由他負責。於是亞歷山大做個手勢，要發言向羣眾分訴。34可是，當大家認出他是猶太人，就一齊呼喊：「以弗所人的亞底米女神多麼偉大啊！」這樣一直呼喊了兩個鐘頭。

35 最後，那城裏的書記官把羣眾安撫下來。他說：「以弗所人哪，誰不知道以弗所城是守護大亞底米女神廟和那塊從天上降下來的聖石的？36既然沒有人能否認這些事，你們就應該安靜下來，不可有鹵莽的行動。37你們把這些人帶到這裏來，可是，他們並沒有盜取廟中的東西，也沒有褻瀆我們的女神。38如果底米特和他的同業要控告甚麼人，自有規定的開庭日子和聽訴訟的官長，他們可以對質。39如果有其他的事，也可以在合法的會議中解決。40像今天的暴動，我們難免要被追究責任的。這一切的紛擾是不對的，我們自己也說不出甚麼理由來。」41說了這些話，他就把聚會解散了。

保羅再訪問馬其頓和希臘

20 騷動平息後，保羅召集信徒，鼓勵他們，同時向他們告別。於是他離開那裏，往馬其頓去。2他走遍了那一帶地區，對信徒們說許多鼓勵的話，然後他到了希臘，3在那裏住了三個月。保羅準備坐船到敍利亞去的時候，發現猶太人陰謀要殺害

decided to go back through Macedonia. [4]Sopater son of Pyrrhus, from Berea, went with him; so did Aristarchus and Secundus, from Thessalonica; Gaius, from Derbe; Tychicus and Trophimus, from the province of Asia; and Timothy. [5]They went ahead and waited for us in Troas. [6]We sailed from Philippi after the Festival of Unleavened Bread, and five days later we joined them in Troas, where we spent a week.

Paul's Last Visit to Troas

[7]On Saturday[e] evening we gathered together for the fellowship meal. Paul spoke to the people and kept on speaking until midnight, since he was going to leave the next day. [8]Many lamps were burning in the upstairs room where we were meeting. [9]A young man named Eutychus was sitting in the window, and as Paul kept on talking, Eutychus got sleepier and sleepier, until he finally went sound asleep and fell from the third story to the ground. When they picked him up, he was dead. [10]But Paul went down and threw himself on him and hugged him. "Don't worry," he said, "he is still alive!" [11]Then he went back upstairs, broke bread, and ate. After talking with them for a long time, even until sunrise, Paul left. [12]They took the young man home alive and were greatly comforted.

From Troas to Miletus

[13]We went on ahead to the ship and sailed off to Assos, where we were going to take Paul aboard. He had told us to do this, because he was going there by land. [14]When he met us in Assos, we took him aboard and went on to Mitylene. [15]We sailed from there and arrived off Chios the next day. A day later we came to Samos, and the following day we reached Miletus. [16]Paul had decided to sail on by Ephesus, so as not to lose any time in the province of Asia. He was in a hurry to arrive in Jerusalem by the day of Pentecost, if at all possible.

Paul's Farewell Speech to the Elders of Ephesus

[17]From Miletus Paul sent a message to Ephesus, asking the elders of the church to meet him. [18]When they arrived, he said to them, "You know how I spent the whole time I was with you, from the first day I arrived in the province of Asia. [19]With all humility and many tears I did my work as the Lord's servant during the hard times that came to me because of the plots of some Jews. [20]You know that I did not hold back anything that would be of help to

e Saturday; *or* Sunday.

他，因此決定取道馬其頓回去。[4]跟他同行的有庇哩亞人畢羅斯的兒子所巴特，有帖撒羅尼迦人亞里達古和西公都，特庇人該猶，還有提摩太和亞細亞人推基古和特羅非摩。[5]他們一行先走，在特羅亞等候我們。[6]過了除酵節，我們從肺立比開船，五天後到達特羅亞，跟他們會合，在那裏住了一星期。

保羅最後一次訪問特羅亞

[7]星期六晚上[⑩]，我們在一起聚會，分享愛筵。保羅向大家講道，因爲他第二天就要動身，所以一直講下去，到了半夜。[8]我們聚會的樓上房間有許多燈火。[9]有一個名叫猶推古的年輕人坐在窗口，當保羅繼續講話的時候，他漸漸困倦，終於沉沉入睡，從三層樓上掉了下去。大家扶他起來，發現他已經死了。[10]保羅下樓，伏在他身上，擁抱着他，說：「不要慌亂，他還有氣息呢！」[11]他接着又上樓，擘開餅吃了。他繼續談論許久，到天亮才離開。[12]他們把那年輕人活活的送回家，大家都大受安慰。

從特羅亞到米利都

[13]我們先上船，開往亞朔，準備在那裏接保羅。這是他所安排的，因爲他自己要走陸路。[14]他在亞朔跟我們會合，我們就接他上船，然後向米推利尼出發。[15]我們從那裏再開船，第二天抵達基阿的對岸；再過一天，在撒摩靠岸，又次日到了米利都。[16]保羅早已決定不在以弗所停留，免得在亞細亞省耽擱時日。他急着要趕到耶路撒冷，希望盡可能在五旬節前抵達。

保羅臨別贈言

[17]保羅從米利都派人去找以弗所教會的長老們，請他們來見他。[18]他們來了，保羅對他們說：「你們知道，自從我來到亞細亞省的第一天，我一直怎樣和你們相處，[19]在謙卑和憂傷中事奉主，又由於猶太人的謀害而經歷許多磨煉。[20]你們也都知道，無論在公共場所，或在你們個別的家裏，在我宣講和

⑩「星期六晚上」或譯「星期日晚上」。

you as I preached and taught in public and in your homes. ²¹To Jews and Gentiles alike I gave solemn warning that they should turn from their sins to God and believe in our Lord Jesus. ²²And now, in obedience to the Holy Spirit I am going to Jerusalem, not knowing what will happen to me there. ²³I only know that in every city the Holy Spirit has warned me that prison and troubles wait for me. ²⁴But I reckon my own life to be worth nothing to me; I only want to complete my mission and finish the work that the Lord Jesus gave me to do, which is to declare the Good News about the grace of God.

²⁵"I have gone about among all of you, preaching the Kingdom of God. And now I know that none of you will ever see me again. ²⁶So I solemnly declare to you this very day: if any of you should be lost, I am not responsible. ²⁷For I have not held back from announcing to you the whole purpose of God. ²⁸So keep watch over yourselves and over all the flock which the Holy Spirit has placed in your care. Be shepherds of the church of God,^f which he made his own through the blood of his Son.^g ²⁹I know that after I leave, fierce wolves will come among you, and they will not spare the flock. ³⁰The time will come when some men from your own group will tell lies to lead the believers away after them. ³¹Watch, then, and remember that with many tears, day and night, I taught every one of you for three years.

³²"And now I commend you to the care of God and to the message of his grace, which is able to build you up and give you the blessings God has for all his people. ³³I have not wanted anyone's silver or gold or clothing. ³⁴You yourselves know that I have worked with these hands of mine to provide everything that my companions and I have needed. ³⁵I have shown you in all things that by working hard in this way we must help the weak, remembering the words that the Lord Jesus himself said, 'There is more happiness in giving than in receiving.' "

³⁶When Paul finished, he knelt down with them and prayed. ³⁷They were all crying as they hugged him and kissed him good-bye. ³⁸They were especially sad because he had said that they would never see him again. And so they went with him to the ship.

Paul Goes to Jerusalem

21 We said good-bye to them and left. After sailing straight across, we came to Cos; the next day we reached Rhodes, and from there

f God; *some manuscripts have* the Lord.
g through the blood of his Son; *or* through the sacrificial death of his Son; *or* through his own blood.

教導你們的時候,只要是對你們有益的,我都沒有保留。²¹無論對猶太人或外邦人,我都鄭重地勸告他們,要他們悔改,轉向上帝,並且信我們的主耶穌。²²現在,為着順服聖靈,我要上耶路撒冷去。我不知道在那裏要遇到甚麼事;²³我只知道,在各城市聖靈都指示我,有監獄和災難等着我。²⁴但是,我並不珍惜自己的性命,為的是要完成我的使命,成就主耶穌交給我的工作,就是見證上帝恩典的福音。

²⁵「我在各位當中跟大家來往,宣揚上帝的主權。現在我知道,今後你們都不能再見到我。²⁶所以,我今天鄭重地告訴你們,如果你們當中有人沉淪,罪不在我;²⁷因為我已經毫無保留地把上帝的旨意傳給你們了。²⁸你們自己要謹慎,也要為聖靈所付託你們照顧的全羣謹慎。要牧養上帝的教會^⑰—就是他藉着自己兒子的死^⑱所換來的。²⁹我知道在我離開後,有凶暴的豺狼要混入你們中間來傷害羊羣。³⁰就是在你們中間,也有人會造謠撒謊,誘惑門徒去跟從他們。³¹所以,你們要警醒,要記得,在三年的歲月裏,我怎樣日夜用眼淚勸誡、教導你們每一個人。

³²「現在我把你們交託在上帝的手裏和他恩典的信息中;他能夠堅定你們的信心,又把他為自己的子民所預備的福澤賜給你們。³³我從來沒有貪圖任何人的金銀或衣服。³⁴你們自己知道,我用我這雙手工作,來供給我和同工們的需要。³⁵我在各種事上給你們留下榜樣,告訴你們應該這樣勤勞工作來幫助軟弱的人。要記得主耶穌親自說過的話:『施比受更為有福。』」

³⁶說完了這些話,保羅就跟他們全體跪下來祈禱。³⁷大家都哭了,抱着他親吻,跟他道別。³⁸他們為了保羅所說此後不能再見到他這一句話特別傷心。他們就送他上船。

保羅上耶路撒冷

21 我們向他們告別後就開船。船直航哥士島,第二天抵達羅底,從那裏到帕大

⑰「上帝的教會」另有些古卷作「主的教會」。
⑱「他藉着自己兒子的死」或譯「他藉着自己的死」。

we went on to Patara. [2]There we found a ship that was going to Phoenicia, so we went aboard and sailed away. [3]We came to where we could see Cyprus, and then sailed south of it on to Syria. We went ashore at Tyre, where the ship was going to unload its cargo. [4]There we found some believers and stayed with them a week. By the power of the Spirit they told Paul not to go to Jerusalem. [5]But when our time with them was over, we left and went on our way. All of them, together with their wives and children, went with us out of the city to the beach, where we all knelt and prayed. [6]Then we said good-bye to one another, and we went on board the ship while they went back home.

[7]We continued our voyage, sailing from Tyre to Ptolemais, where we greeted the believers and stayed with them for a day. [8]On the following day we left and arrived in Caesarea. There we stayed at the house of Philip the evangelist, one of the seven men who had been chosen as helpers in Jerusalem. [9]He had four unmarried daughters who proclaimed God's message. [10]We had been there for several days when a prophet named Agabus arrived from Judea. [11]He came to us, took Paul's belt, tied up his own feet and hands with it, and said, "This is what the Holy Spirit says: The owner of this belt will be tied up in this way by the Jews in Jerusalem, and they will hand him over to the Gentiles."

[12]When we heard this, we and the others there begged Paul not to go to Jerusalem. [13]But he answered, "What are you doing, crying like this and breaking my heart? I am ready not only to be tied up in Jerusalem but even to die there for the sake of the Lord Jesus."

[14]We could not convince him, so we gave up and said, "May the Lord's will be done."

[15]After spending some time there, we got our things ready and left for Jerusalem. [16]Some of the disciples from Caesarea also went with us and took us to the house of the man we were going to stay with[h]—Mnason, from Cyprus, who had been a believer since the early days.

Paul Visits James

[17]When we arrived in Jerusalem, the believers welcomed us warmly. [18]The next day Paul went with us to see James; and all the church elders were present. [19]Paul greeted them and gave a complete report of everything that God had done among the Gentiles through his work. [20]After hearing him, they all praised God. Then they said, "Brother Paul, you can see how

[h] and took us to the house of the man we were going to stay with; *or* bringing with them the man at whose house we were going to stay.

喇。[2]在帕大喇遇着一條要開往腓尼基去的船，我們就上船起航。[3]航行到望見塞浦路斯，船就繞過南邊，朝着敍利亞走。我們在泰爾上岸，因為船要在這裏卸貨。[4]我們在這裏找到了一些信徒，就跟他們一起住了七天。他們得到聖靈的指示，勸保羅不要上耶路撒冷去。[5]可是，我們逗留的時間到了，就繼續我們的旅程。信徒和他們的妻子兒女都送我們到城外。大家都在沙灘上跪下來祈禱，[6]然後彼此道別。我們上船，他們回家去了。

[7]我們繼續航行，從泰爾到了多利買，向當地的信徒們問安，跟他們住了一天。[8]第二天我們離開那裏，到了凱撒利亞，就到傳道人腓利的家去，跟他住在一起。他是在耶路撒冷被選出的那七位助手之一。[9]他有四個沒有結婚的女兒，都有傳講上帝信息的恩賜。[10]我們在那裏住了幾天後，有一個先知名叫亞迦布，從猶太來。[11]他來看我們，拿起保羅的腰帶，把自己的手腳綁了起來，說：「聖靈這麼說：這腰帶的主人會在耶路撒冷受猶太人這樣的捆綁，然後被交給外邦人。」

[12]我們一聽見這話就跟當地的人一起懇切地勸告保羅不要上耶路撒冷去。[13]可是，他說：「你們為甚麼這樣痛哭，使我心碎呢？我為着主耶穌的緣故，不但在耶路撒冷被捆綁，就是死在那裏也是心甘情願的。」

[14]我們無法說服他，就都住口，只說：「願主的旨意成就。」

[15]在那裏住了幾天，我們就收拾行李，上耶路撒冷去。[16]有些從凱撒利亞來的門徒跟我們同行，把我們帶到一個塞浦路斯人拿孫的家裏去住⑲；這個人是早期的門徒。

保羅訪問雅各

[17]我們到了耶路撒冷，信徒們熱誠地接待我們。[18]第二天，保羅跟我們一道去見雅各；所有教會的長老也都在場。[19]保羅向他們問安，然後把上帝怎樣使用他在外邦人當中的事奉都向他們報告。[20]他們聽見了都頌讚上帝，又對保羅說：「弟兄啊，情形是這

⑲「把我們帶到一個塞浦路斯人拿孫的家裏去住」或譯「他們帶着一個塞浦路斯人拿孫同行，我們要住在這個人家裏」。

many thousands of Jews have become believers, and how devoted they all are to the Law. [21]They have been told that you have been teaching all the Jews who live in Gentile countries to abandon the Law of Moses, telling them not to circumcise their children or follow the Jewish customs. [22]They are sure to hear that you have arrived. What should be done, then? [23]This is what we want you to do. There are four men here who have taken a vow. [24]Go along with them and join them in the ceremony of purification and pay their expenses; then they will be able to shave their heads.[i] In this way everyone will know that there is no truth in any of the things that they have been told about you, but that you yourself live in accordance with the Law of Moses. [25]But as for the Gentiles who have become believers, we have sent them a letter telling them we decided that they must not eat any food that has been offered to idols, or any blood, or any animal that has been strangled, and that they must keep themselves from sexual immorality."

[26]So Paul took the men and the next day performed the ceremony of purification with them. Then he went into the Temple and gave notice of how many days it would be until the end of the period of purification, when a sacrifice would be offered for each one of them.

Paul Is Arrested in the Temple

[27]But just when the seven days were about to come to an end, some Jews from the province of Asia saw Paul in the Temple. They stirred up the whole crowd and grabbed Paul. [28]"People of Israel!" they shouted. "Help! This is the man who goes everywhere teaching everyone against the people of Israel, the Law of Moses, and this Temple. And now he has even brought some Gentiles into the Temple and defiled this holy place!"([29]They said this because they had seen Trophimus from Ephesus with Paul in the city, and they thought that Paul had taken him into the Temple.)

[30]Confusion spread through the whole city, and the people all ran together, grabbed Paul, and dragged him out of the Temple. At once the Temple doors were closed. [31]The mob was trying to kill Paul, when a report was sent up to the commander of the Roman troops that all of Jerusalem was rioting. [32]At once the commander took some officers and soldiers and rushed down to the crowd. When the people saw him with the soldiers, they stopped beating Paul. [33]The commander went over to Paul, arrested him, and ordered him to be bound with two chains. Then he asked, "Who is this man, and what has he done?" [34]Some in the crowd

i SHAVE THEIR HEADS: See 18.18.

樣的：在猶太人當中有數以萬計的信徒，他們都是嚴守摩西法律的。[21]他們聽見你曾經教導僑居外邦的猶太人放棄摩西的法律，不要替孩子行割禮，也不必遵守猶太人一般的規矩。[22]他們一定會聽到你已來此地的消息，我們該怎麼辦呢？[23]現在請你照我們的話做吧！這裏有四個許下了願的人；[24]你帶着他們，跟他們一道去行潔淨禮，替他們繳費。這樣，他們就可以剃掉頭髮。你這樣做，大家就會知道，他們所聽見關於你的事不是事實，並且知道你自己也是遵守摩西法律的。[25]至於對外邦人中的信徒，我們已經寫信吩咐他們不可吃任何祭過偶像的食物，不可吃血或被勒死的牲畜，也不可有淫亂的行為。」

[26]於是，保羅帶着那些人，在第二天跟他們一起行了潔淨禮。他又到聖殿去報告潔淨期屆滿的日子，等候祭司為他們每一個人獻上祭物。

保羅在聖殿裏被捕

[27]那七天的期間快要結束的時候，有些從亞細亞來的猶太人看見保羅在聖殿裏。他們就煽動羣眾，抓住保羅，[28]呼喊說：「以色列人哪，來幫一手吧！這個人到處說教，反對以色列人民和摩西的法律，也反對這聖殿，現在他居然帶着希臘人進入聖殿，污辱了神聖的地方！」（[29]他們這樣說是因為看見了以弗所人特羅非摩跟保羅一起在城裏，以為保羅曾經帶他進聖殿去。）

[30]這時候，全城騷動，羣眾都跑過來，抓住保羅，把他從聖殿裏拖出去；殿門立刻都關閉起來。[31]暴民正想把保羅殺掉的時候，有人向羅馬駐軍的指揮官報告，說全耶路撒冷在騷動中。[32]指揮官連忙帶領軍隊和幾個軍官，趕到羣眾那裏。他們一看見指揮官和軍隊，就停止毆打保羅。[33]指揮官上前拘捕保羅，吩咐用兩條鐵鍊把他鎖起來。他問：「這個人是誰？他做了些甚麼事呢？」[34]人

shouted one thing, others something else. There was such confusion that the commander could not find out exactly what had happened, so he ordered his men to take Paul up into the fort. 35They got as far as the steps with him, and then the soldiers had to carry him because the mob was so wild. 36They were all coming after him and screaming, "Kill him!"

Paul Defends Himself

37As the soldiers were about to take Paul into the fort, he spoke to the commander: "May I say something to you?"

"You speak Greek, do you?" the commander asked. 38"Then you are not that Egyptian fellow who some time ago started a revolution and led four thousand armed terrorists out into the desert?"

39Paul answered, "I am a Jew, born in Tarsus in Cilicia, a citizen of an important city. Please let me speak to the people."

40The commander gave him permission, so Paul stood on the steps and motioned with his hand for the people to be silent. When they were quiet, Paul spoke to them in Hebrew:

22"My fellow Jews, listen to me as I make my defense before you!" 2When they heard him speaking to them in Hebrew, they became even quieter; and Paul went on:

3"I am a Jew, born in Tarsus in Cilicia, but brought up here in Jerusalem as a student of Gamaliel. I received strict instruction in the Law of our ancestors and was just as dedicated to God as are all of you who are here today. 4I persecuted to the death the people who followed this Way. I arrested men and women and threw them into prison. 5The High Priest and the whole Council can prove that I am telling the truth. I received from them letters written to fellow Jews in Damascus, so I went there to arrest these people and bring them back in chains to Jerusalem to be punished.

Paul Tells of His Conversion

(Acts 9.1-19; 26.12-18)

6"As I was traveling and coming near Damascus, about midday a bright light from the sky flashed suddenly around me. 7I fell to the ground and heard a voice saying to me, 'Saul, Saul! Why do you persecute me?' 8'Who are you, Lord?' I asked. 'I am Jesus of Nazareth, whom you persecute,' he said to me. 9The men with me saw the light, but did not hear the voice of the one who was speaking to me. 10I asked, 'What shall I do, Lord?' and the Lord

臺當中有的喊這個，有的喊那個，亂成一團，叫指揮官無法查出真相，於是命令把保羅帶進營房。35保羅剛走上台階，因為臺眾非常凶暴，兵士們只好把保羅抬了過去。36臺眾都跟在後面，大喊：「殺掉他！」

保羅為自己辯護

37快要被帶進營房的時候，保羅對指揮官說：「可不可以讓我向你講一句話？」

指揮官問：「你也懂希臘話！38那麼，你就不是前些時候作亂、率領四千個暴徒往曠野逃去的那個埃及人啦？」

39保羅回答：「我是猶太人，出生在基利家的大數，是一個著名城市的公民。請你准許我向臺眾講話。」

40指揮官准了他。於是保羅站在台階上，向臺眾做個手勢。大家都靜了下來，保羅就用希伯來語向他們講話。

22保羅說：「各位父老弟兄們，請聽我為自己辯護的話。」2他們一聽見保羅用希伯來語向他們講話，就都更加安靜。保羅繼續說下去：

3「我是猶太人，出生在基利家的大數，卻在耶路撒冷長大，在迦瑪列門下受教，接受過祖先一切律法的嚴格訓練，熱心事奉上帝，跟今天在場的各位一樣。4我曾迫害遵行這道路的人，置他們於死地。我也搜捕男女信徒，把他們關在監獄裏。5大祭司和全議會都能夠證明我所說的話是實在的。我從他們取得了給大馬士革的猶太同胞的信件，因此我到那裏去，要逮捕那些人，把他們綁起來，帶回耶路撒冷受刑。」

保羅敘述歸主經過

(徒9．1—19；26．12—18)

6「當我趕路快到大馬士革的時候，約在中午，忽然有一道強烈的光從天空照射在我的周圍。7我仆倒在地上，聽見有聲音對我說：『掃羅，掃羅！你為甚麼迫害我？』8我就問：『主啊，你是誰？』他說：『我是你所迫害的拿撒勒人耶穌。』9那些跟我同行的人看見了那光，但沒有聽見那向我說話的聲音。10我又問：『主啊，我該做甚麼？』主對

said to me, 'Get up and go into Damascus, and there you will be told everything that God has determined for you to do.' [11]I was blind because of the bright light, and so my companions took me by the hand and led me into Damascus.

[12]"In that city was a man named Ananias, a religious man who obeyed our Law and was highly respected by all the Jews living there. [13]He came to me, stood by me, and said, 'Brother Saul, see again!' At that very moment I saw again and looked at him. [14]He said, 'The God of our ancestors has chosen you to know his will, to see his righteous Servant, and to hear him speaking with his own voice. [15]For you will be a witness for him to tell everyone what you have seen and heard. [16]And now, why wait any longer? Get up and be baptized and have your sins washed away by praying to him.'

Paul's Call to Preach to the Gentiles

[17]"I went back to Jerusalem, and while I was praying in the Temple, I had a vision, [18]in which I saw the Lord, as he said to me, 'Hurry and leave Jerusalem quickly, because the people here will not accept your witness about me.' [19]'Lord,' I answered, 'they know very well that I went to the synagogues and arrested and beat those who believe in you. [20]And when your witness Stephen was put to death, I myself was there, approving of his murder and taking care of the cloaks of his murderers.' [21]'Go,' the Lord said to me, 'for I will send you far away to the Gentiles.' "

[22]The people listened to Paul until he said this; but then they started shouting at the top of their voices, "Away with him! Kill him! He's not fit to live!" [23]They were screaming, waving their clothes, and throwing dust up in the air. [24]The Roman commander ordered his men to take Paul into the fort, and he told them to whip him in order to find out why the Jews were screaming like this against him. [25]But when they had tied him up to be whipped, Paul said to the officer standing there, "Is it lawful for you to whip a Roman citizen who hasn't even been tried for any crime?"

[26]When the officer heard this, he went to the commander and asked him, "What are you doing? That man is a Roman citizen!"

[27]So the commander went to Paul and asked him, "Tell me, are you a Roman citizen?"

"Yes," answered Paul.

[28]The commander said, "I became one by paying a large amount of money."

我說:『起來,進大馬士革城去,在那裏有人會告訴你上帝要你做的一切事。』[11]由於那強烈的光,我的眼睛不能看見,跟我同行的人就牽著我的手,帶我進大馬士革。

[12]「在那裏有一個人名叫亞拿尼亞。他一向虔誠,嚴守法律,深得大馬士革所有猶太人的尊重。[13]他來看我,站在我旁邊,說:『掃羅弟兄啊,願你恢復視覺!』就在那時候,我的視覺恢復,我看見了他。[14]他說:『我們祖先的上帝已經揀選了你,使你明白他的旨意,得以看見他公義的僕人,又聽見他口裏發出的聲音。[15]因為你要為他作見證,把你所看見所聽到的告訴萬民。[16]那麼,你還耽擱甚麼呢?起來,呼求他的名,領受洗禮,好潔淨你的罪!』」

保羅奉召向外邦人傳道

[17]「後來,我回到耶路撒冷;我在聖殿裏祈禱的時候得了一個異象,[18]在異象中我看見主。他對我說:『趕快離開耶路撒冷,因為這裏的人不接受你為我所作的見證。』[19]我說:『主啊,他們都知道我到各地的會堂去,逮捕並毆打信你的人。[20]當你的見證人司提反被處死的時候,我也在場,贊同那暴行,還替殺他的暴徒看守衣服。』[21]主對我說:『去吧!我要差你到遠方,到外邦人那裏去。』」

[22]羣眾一直聽著保羅述說;他們聽到這句話就大喊大叫:「除掉他!殺掉他!他是該死的!」[23]他們一面喧嚷,一面拋衣服,撒灰塵。[24]羅馬的指揮官命令把保羅帶進營房去,吩咐兵士鞭打他,拷問他,要查出羣眾為甚麼對他這樣喊叫。[25]當他們把他捆起來要打的時候,保羅向站在旁邊的一個軍官說:「對一個羅馬公民,沒有判罪就下手鞭打是合法的嗎?」

[26]那軍官一聽見這句話就去見指揮官,對他說:「你想怎麼辦?那個人是羅馬公民呢!」

[27]指揮官去見保羅,問他:「告訴我,你是羅馬公民嗎?」

保羅回答:「是的。」

[28]指揮官說:「我花了一大筆錢,才取得公民身份。」

"But I am one by birth," Paul answered.

29At once the men who were going to question Paul drew back from him; and the commander was frightened when he realized that Paul was a Roman citizen and that he had put him in chains.

Paul before the Council

30The commander wanted to find out for sure what the Jews were accusing Paul of; so the next day he had Paul's chains taken off and ordered the chief priests and the whole Council to meet. Then he took Paul and made him stand before them.

23 Paul looked straight at the Council and said, "My fellow Israelites! My conscience is perfectly clear about the way in which I have lived before God to this very day." 2The High Priest Ananias ordered those who were standing close to Paul to strike him on the mouth. 3Paul said to him, "God will certainly strike you–you whitewashed wall! You sit there to judge me according to the Law, yet you break the Law by ordering them to strike me!"

4The men close to Paul said to him, "You are insulting God's High Priest!"

5Paul answered, "My fellow Israelites, I did not know that he was the High Priest. The scripture says, 'You must not speak evil of the ruler of your people.' "

6When Paul saw that some of the group were Sadducees and the others were Pharisees, he called out in the Council, "Fellow Israelites! I am a Pharisee, the son of Pharisees. I am on trial here because of the hope I have that the dead will rise to life!"

7As soon as he said this, the Pharisees and Sadducees started to quarrel, and the group was divided.(8For the Sadducees say that people will not rise from death and that there are no angels or spirits; but the Pharisees believe in all three.) 9The shouting became louder, and some of the teachers of the Law who belonged to the party of the Pharisees stood up and protested strongly: "We cannot find a thing wrong with this man! Perhaps a spirit or an angel really did speak to him!"

10The argument became so violent that the commander was afraid that Paul would be torn to pieces. So he ordered his soldiers to go down into the group, get Paul away from them, and take him into the fort.

11That night the Lord stood by Paul and said, "Don't be afraid! You have given your witness for me here in Jerusalem, and you must also do the same in Rome."

保羅說:「我生下來就是。」

29 於是那些要拷問保羅的人馬上閃開。指揮官也恐慌起來;因為知道保羅是羅馬公民,而且捆綁過他。

保羅在議會申訴

30 那指揮官想確實知道猶太人控告保羅的理由,因此,在第二天,他解開保羅的鎖鍊,召集祭司長和全議會在一起,然後把保羅帶出來,讓他站在他們面前。

23 保羅定睛注視議會的人,說:「同胞們,我生平行事為人,在上帝面前良心清白,直到今天。」2大祭司亞拿尼亞吩咐侍從打保羅的嘴巴。3保羅對他說:「你這粉飾的牆,上帝要擊打你!你坐在那裏是要根據法律審判我,而你竟違背法律,吩咐他們打我!」

4 站在旁邊的人說:「你竟侮辱上帝的大祭司!」

5 保羅說:「同胞們,我不知道他是大祭司;聖經說過:『不可毀謗治理人民的長官。』」

6 保羅看出這一羣人當中有些是撒都該黨的人,另有些是法利賽派的人;於是他在議會裏高聲說:「同胞們,我是一個法利賽人,是法利賽人的兒子。我今天在這裏受審問是因為我盼望死人復活!」

7 他這話一出口,法利賽人和撒都該人就爭吵起來,會眾也分成兩派。8因為撒都該人不相信復活,也不信有天使和神靈,但是法利賽人三樣都信。9喧嚷的聲音越來越大,有些法利賽派的經學教師站起來,強烈地抗議說:「我們找不出這個人有任何錯處!可能真的有神靈或天使向他說話呢!」

10 爭吵越來越劇烈,指揮官怕保羅被他們撕碎了,於是命令兵士下去,從人羣中把保羅搶出來,帶進營房。

11 當夜,主站在保羅旁邊,說:「你要有勇氣!你已經在耶路撒冷為我作了見證,你同樣必須在羅馬作見證。」

The Plot against Paul's Life

12The next morning some Jews met together and made a plan. They took a vow that they would not eat or drink anything until they had killed Paul. 13There were more than forty who planned this together. 14Then they went to the chief priests and elders and said, "We have taken a solemn vow together not to eat a thing until we have killed Paul. 15Now then, you and the Council send word to the Roman commander to bring Paul down to you, pretending that you want to get more accurate information about him. But we will be ready to kill him before he ever gets here."

16But the son of Paul's sister heard about the plot; so he went to the fort and told Paul. 17Then Paul called one of the officers and said to him, "Take this young man to the commander; he has something to tell him." 18The officer took him, led him to the commander, and said, "The prisoner Paul called me and asked me to bring this young man to you, because he has something to say to you."

19The commander took him by the hand, led him off by himself, and asked him, "What do you have to tell me?"

20He said, "The Jewish authorities have agreed to ask you tomorrow to take Paul down to the Council, pretending that the Council wants to get more accurate information about him. 21But don't listen to them, because there are more than forty men who will be hiding and waiting for him. They have taken a vow not to eat or drink until they have killed him. They are now ready to do it and are waiting for your decision."

22The commander said, "Don't tell anyone that you have reported this to me." And he sent the young man away.

Paul Is Sent to Governor Felix

23Then the commander called two of his officers and said, "Get two hundred soldiers ready to go to Caesarea, together with seventy horsemen and two hundred spearmen, and be ready to leave by nine o'clock tonight. 24Provide some horses for Paul to ride and get him safely through to Governor Felix." 25Then the commander wrote a letter that went like this:

26"Claudius Lysias to His Excellency, Governor Felix: Greetings. 27The Jews seized this man and were about to kill him. I learned that he is a Roman citizen, so I went with my soldiers and rescued him. 28I wanted to know what they were accusing him of, so I took him down to their Council. 29I found out that he had not done a thing for which he deserved to die or be

殺害保羅的陰謀

12第二天早上,猶太人在一起計謀,發誓非殺掉保羅不吃不喝。13同謀的有四十多人。14他們去見祭司長和長老們,說:「我們已經發了重誓:不殺保羅不吃東西!15現在,你們和議會要請求羅馬指揮官,把保羅帶到這裏來,假裝要更詳細地審查他的事;我們會佈置好,在他到達以前殺掉他。」

16保羅的外甥聽見了這個陰謀,就進營房去告訴保羅。17於是保羅請來一個軍官,對他說:「請帶這個年輕人去見指揮官;他有事向他報告。」18那軍官就帶這個年輕人去見指揮官,說:「囚犯保羅請我過去,要求我帶這個年輕人來見你,他有事向你報告。」

19指揮官就拉着他的手,把他帶到一邊,問他:「你有甚麼事報告?」

20他回答:「猶太人已經商量好,要請求你明天把保羅帶到議會去,假裝要詳細地審查他的事。21請你不要答應他們,因爲有四十多人要埋伏等着他。他們都發過誓,非殺掉保羅不吃不喝。現在他們都準備好了,只等你決定。」

22指揮官吩咐他說:「不要讓人家知道你已經把這事報告我了」,然後打發他走。

保羅被解交腓力斯總督

23於是,指揮官召來了兩個軍官,吩咐說:「預備好步兵兩百,騎兵七十,長槍手兩百,今晚九點鐘出發往凱撒利亞去;24同時要爲保羅預備坐騎,護送他到腓力斯總督那裏去。」25指揮官又寫好公文,內容如下:

26「克勞第·呂西亞上書總督腓力斯大人臺前,敬謹請安:27猶太人抓住了這個人,正要殺害他,我發現他是羅馬公民,就帶軍隊前往搶救。28我想查明他們控告他的理由,因此把他帶到他們的議會去。29我發現他並沒有甚麼該死或該囚禁的罪行;他們對

put in prison; the accusation against him had to do with questions about their own law. ³⁰And when I was informed that there was a plot against him, at once I decided to send him to you. I told his accusers to make their charges against him before you."

³¹The soldiers carried out their orders. They got Paul and took him that night as far as Antipatris. ³²The next day the foot soldiers returned to the fort and left the horsemen to go on with him. ³³They took him to Caesarea, delivered the letter to the governor, and turned Paul over to him. ³⁴The governor read the letter and asked Paul what province he was from. When he found out that he was from Cilicia, ³⁵he said, "I will hear you when your accusers arrive." Then he gave orders for Paul to be kept under guard in the governor's headquarters.

The Case Against Paul

24 Five days later the High Priest Ananias went to Caesarea with some elders and a lawyer named Tertullus. They appeared before Governor Felix and made their charges against Paul. ²Then Paul was called in, and Tertullus began to make his accusation, as follows: "Your Excellency! Your wise leadership has brought us a long period of peace, and many necessary reforms are being made for the good of our country. ³We welcome this everywhere and at all times, and we are deeply grateful to you. ⁴I do not want to take up too much of your time, however, so I beg you to be kind and listen to our brief account. ⁵We found this man to be a dangerous nuisance; he starts riots among Jews all over the world and is a leader of the party of the Nazarenes. ⁶He also tried to defile the Temple, and we arrested him.ʲ ⁸If you question this man, you yourself will be able to learn from him all the things that we are accusing him of." ⁹The Jews joined in the accusation and said that all this was true.

Paul's Defense before Felix

¹⁰The governor then motioned to Paul to speak, and Paul said, "I know that you have been a judge over this nation for many years, and so I am happy to defend myself before you. ¹¹As you can find out for yourself, it was no more than twelve days ago that I went to Jerusalem to worship. ¹²The Jews did not find me arguing with anyone in the Temple, nor did they find me stirring up the people, either in the synagogues or any-

ʲ *Some manuscripts add verses 6b-8a:* We planned to judge him according to our own law, 7Wbut when the commander Lysias came, and with great violence took him from us. 8Then Lysias gave orders that his accusers should come before you.

他的控告無非牽涉到他們法律上的問題。³⁰後來有人向我報告猶太人圖謀殺害他,我立刻決定把他解到你那裏去,同時吩咐各原告到你面前控訴。」

³¹兵士們執行命令,把保羅帶去,連夜解往安提帕底。³²第二天,步兵回營,讓騎兵護送保羅。³³他們到了凱撒利亞,把公文呈給總督,又把保羅交給他。³⁴總督閱讀公文,並問保羅是哪一省人,發現他是基利家籍的人,³⁵就說:「等你的原告到達,我就處理你的案件。」於是他命令把保羅拘禁在希律的公署裏。

猶太人控告保羅

24 過了五天,大祭司亞拿尼亞和幾個長老,連同一個名叫帖土羅的律師,來到凱撒利亞。他們在總督腓力斯面前控告保羅。²保羅被傳出庭;帖土羅控告他說:

「腓力斯大人!由於你賢明的治理,我們得以享受長期的太平,國中的陋政獲得改革。³對於你的德政,我們隨時隨地感戴無已。⁴我不敢過份煩擾你,只求你垂聽我們簡短的控訴;⁵我們看清楚了,這個人是危險人物。他在全世界猶太人當中製造亂事,又是拿撒勒教派的一個頭目,⁶連聖殿也要褻瀆,我們就把他抓住。⑳ ⁸你審問這個人就會明白我們所控告他的一切事由。」⁹在場的猶太人也都同聲控告,認為所指出的都是事實。

保羅為自己辯護

¹⁰這時候,總督向保羅示意,要他說話。保羅就說:「我知道你在本國執掌法政多年,因此,我樂意在你面前為自己辯護。¹¹你不難查明,從我上耶路撒冷去禮拜到現在只不過十二天。¹²他們並沒有看見我在聖殿裏跟任何人辯論,也沒有看見我在會堂或

⑳有些古卷加第 6 節下半節至第 8 節上半節「我們原想要按照我們的法律審判他,7 不料指揮官呂西亞橫加十詞,從我們手中把他搶走,8 並命令各原告都到你這裏來。」

where else in the city. [13]Nor can they give you proof of the accusations they now bring against me. [14]I do admit this to you: I worship the God of our ancestors by following that Way which they say is false. But I also believe in everything written in the Law of Moses and the books of the prophets. [15]I have the same hope in God that these themselves have, namely, that all people, both the good and the bad, will rise from death. [16]And so I do my best always to have a clear conscience before God and people.

[17]"After being away from Jerusalem for several years, I went there to take some money to my own people and to offer sacrifices. [18]It was while I was doing this that they found me in the Temple after I had completed the ceremony of purification. There was no crowd with me and no disorder. [19]But some Jews from the province of Asia were there; they themselves ought to come before you and make their accusations if they have anything against me. [20]Or let these who are here tell what crime they found me guilty of when I stood before the Council— [21]except for the one thing I called out when I stood before them: 'I am being tried by you today for believing that the dead will rise to life.'"

[22]Then Felix, who was well informed about the Way, brought the hearing to a close. "When the commander Lysias arrives," he told them, "I will decide your case." [23]He ordered the officer in charge of Paul to keep him under guard, but to give him some freedom and allow his friends to provide for his needs.

Paul before Felix and Drusilla

[24]After some days Felix came with his wife Drusilla, who was Jewish. He sent for Paul and listened to him as he talked about faith in Christ Jesus. [25]But as Paul went on discussing about goodness, self-control, and the coming Day of Judgment, Felix was afraid and said, "You may leave now. I will call you again when I get the chance." [26]At the same time he was hoping that Paul would give him some money; and for this reason he would call for him often and talk with him.

[27]After two years had passed, Porcius Festus succeeded Felix as governor. Felix wanted to gain favor with the Jews so he left Paul in prison.

Paul Appeals to the Emperor

25 [1]Three days after Festus arrived in the province, he went from Caesarea to Jerusalem, [2]where the chief priests and the Jewish leaders brought their charges against Paul. They

城裏其他地方煽動羣眾。[13]他們無法向你提出控告我的證據。[14]然而，有一件事我要承認：我是根據他們所認為異端的那道路來敬拜我們祖先的上帝的。我也相信在摩西的法律和先知書上所記載的一切。[15]我對上帝存着跟他們相同的盼望，就是盼望所有的人，無論善惡，都要從死裏復活。[16]因此，我常常勉勵自己，在上帝和人面前，常保持着清白的良心。

[17]「我離開耶路撒冷已經有好幾年。我這回上去是帶着賙濟同胞的款項，同時要獻祭物。[18]他們在聖殿裏發現我的時候，我已經行了潔淨禮，正在獻祭；我並沒有聚眾，也沒有作亂。[19]不過有幾個從亞細亞省來的猶太人在那裏，這些人若有控告我的事，應該到你面前控訴。[20]再不然，就讓這些在場的人指出，當我在議會申訴的時候有甚麼犯罪的行為。[21]我站在他們面前只高聲說過一句話，就是：『今天我受你們審判，無非是為了相信死人復活的道理。』」

[22]腓力斯對這道路原有相當的認識，於是停止了聽訟，對他們說：「且等指揮官呂西亞來到，我就為你們判決。」[23]他命令那軍官看守保羅，寬待他，准許親友供應他日常的需要。

保羅在腓力斯和土西拉面前

[24]過了幾天，腓力斯和他的夫人—猶太女子土西拉——一起來到。他把保羅叫來，聽他講論對基督耶穌的信仰。[25]保羅又談論關於良善、節制、將來的審判等教訓；腓力斯覺得很恐懼，對保羅說：「你現在去吧，等我有空再叫你來。」[26]他又盼望保羅送錢給他，所以常常叫他來，跟他談論。

[27]過了兩年，波求·非斯都替代了腓力斯，出任總督。腓力斯為了要討好猶太人，仍舊把保羅留在監獄裏。

保羅上訴於羅馬皇帝

25 [1]非斯都到任後三天，從凱撒利亞上耶路撒冷去。[2]祭司長和猶太人的領袖向他

begged Festus ³to do them the favor of having Paul come to Jerusalem, for they had made a plot to kill him on the way. ⁴Festus answered, "Paul is being kept a prisoner in Caesarea, and I myself will be going back there soon. ⁵Let your leaders go to Caesarea with me and accuse the man if he has done anything wrong."

⁶Festus spent another eight or ten days with them and then went to Caesarea. On the next day he sat down in the judgment court and ordered Paul to be brought in. ⁷When Paul arrived, the Jews who had come from Jerusalem stood around him and started making many serious charges against him, which they were not able to prove. ⁸But Paul defended himself: "I have done nothing wrong against the Law of the Jews or against the Temple or against the Roman Emperor."

⁹But Festus wanted to gain favor with the Jews, so he asked Paul, "Would you be willing to go to Jerusalem and be tried on these charges before me there?"

¹⁰Paul said, "I am standing before the Emperor's own judgment court, where I should be tried. I have done no wrong to the Jews, as you yourself well know. ¹¹If I have broken the law and done something for which I deserve the death penalty, I do not ask to escape it. But if there is no truth in the charges they bring against me, no one can hand me over to them I appeal to the Emperor."

¹²Then Festus, after conferring with his advisers, answered, "You have appealed to the Emperor, so to the Emperor you will go."

Paul before Agrippa and Bernice

¹³Some time later King Agrippa and Bernice came to Caesarea to pay a visit of welcome to Festus. ¹⁴After they had been there several days, Festus explained Paul's situation to the king: "There is a man here who was left a prisoner by Felix; ¹⁵and when I went to Jerusalem, the Jewish chief priests and elders brought charges against him and asked me to condemn him. ¹⁶But I told them that we Romans are not in the habit of handing over any who are accused of a crime before they have met their accusers face-to-face and have had the chance of defending themselves against the accusation. ¹⁷When they came here, then, I lost no time, but on the very next day I sat in the judgment court and ordered the man to be brought in. ¹⁸His opponents stood up, but they did not accuse him of any of the evil crimes that I thought they would. ¹⁹All they had were some arguments with him about their own religion

控告保羅。他們請求非斯都，³要求他送保羅到耶路撒冷，陰謀在路上埋伏殺他。⁴非斯都回答他們：「保羅現在被拘禁在凱撒利亞，我不久要回到那裏去。⁵你們的領袖可以跟我一道去，如果那個人有甚麼不法的行為，就在那裏控告他。」

⁶非斯都在他們那裏又住了十天八天，然後回凱撒利亞去。第二天他就開庭，命令把保羅帶來。⁷保羅來了，那些從耶路撒冷來的猶太人在他周圍站着，用許多嚴重的罪名控告他，可是都無法提出證據。⁸保羅為自己辯護，說：「我沒有做過任何事違反猶太人的法律，褻瀆聖殿，或冒犯羅馬皇帝。」

⁹可是非斯都為了討好猶太人，就問保羅：「你願意上耶路撒冷，在那裏接受我對這案件的審判嗎？」

¹⁰保羅說：「我現在站在皇帝的法庭上；這裏就是我應該受審的地方。你自己也知道，我並沒有得罪過猶太人。¹¹如果我犯法，有甚麼該死的罪行，我絕不逃避懲罰。如果他們對我的控告都不是事實，誰也不能把我交給他們。我要向皇帝上訴。」

¹²腓斯都跟他的參謀商量之後，就說：「既然你向皇帝上訴，你就到皇帝那裏去。」

非斯都向亞基帕王敍述保羅的事

¹³過了些日子，亞基帕王和貝妮絲到凱撒利亞來迎候非斯都。¹⁴在那裏住了幾天之後，非斯都把保羅的事告訴亞基帕王，說：「這裏有一個人，是腓力斯留下的囚犯。¹⁵前次我上耶路撒冷，那邊的猶太祭司長和長老控告他，要求我定他的罪。¹⁶我告訴他們，按照羅馬人的規矩，在被告沒有跟原告對質，還沒有機會為自己辯護之前是不能夠判罪的。¹⁷等他們都到這裏之後，我沒有耽誤時間，第二天就開庭，命令把那個人提出來應訊。¹⁸原告都站起來控告他，但所告的並不是我想像中的那種罪。¹⁹他們跟他爭論的是有關宗教上的問題，以及一個名叫耶穌

and about a man named Jesus, who has died; but Paul claims that he is alive. 20I was undecided about how I could get information on these matters, so I asked Paul if he would be willing to go to Jerusalem and be tried there on these charges. 21But Paul appealed; he asked to be kept under guard and to let the Emperor decide his case. So I gave orders for him to be kept under guard until I could send him to the Emperor."

22Agrippa said to Festus, "I would like to hear this man myself."

"You will hear him tomorrow," Festus answered.

23The next day Agrippa and Bernice came with great pomp and ceremony and entered the audience hall with the military chiefs and the leading men of the city. Festus gave the order, and Paul was brought in. 24Festus said, "King Agrippa and all who are here with us: You see this man against whom all the Jewish people, both here and in Jerusalem, have brought complaints to me. They scream that he should not live any longer. 25But I could not find that he had done anything for which he deserved the death sentence. And since he himself made an appeal to the Emperor, I have decided to send him. 26But I have nothing definite about him to write to the Emperor. So I have brought him here before you–and especially before you, King Agrippa!–so that, after investigating his case, I may have something to write. 27For it seems unreasonable to me to send a prisoner without clearly indicating the charges against him."

Paul Defends Himself before Agrippa

26 Agrippa said to Paul, "You have permission to speak on your own behalf." Paul stretched out his hand and defended himself as follows:

2"King Agrippa! I consider myself fortunate that today I am to defend myself before you from all the things these Jews accuse me of, 3particularly since you know so well all the Jewish customs and disputes. I ask you, then, to listen to me with patience.

4"All the Jews know how I have lived ever since I was young. They know how I have spent my whole life, at first in my own country and then in Jerusalem. 5They have always known, if they are willing to testify, that from the very first I have lived as a member of the strictest party of our religion, the Pharisees. 6And now I stand here to be tried because of the hope I have in the promise that God made to our ancestors– 7the very thing that the twelve tribes of our people hope to receive, as they worship

的人；這人已經死了，保羅卻說他還活着。 20對這案件我簡直不知道該怎麼辦。我問保羅是否願意上耶路撒冷去，在那裏受審。 21可是，保羅請求把他留下，由皇上審判。因此我命令把他留在牢裏，等着解他到皇上那裏去。」

22亞基帕對非斯都說：「我自己也想聽聽這個人講論。」

非斯都說：「明天你可以聽。」

23第二天，亞基帕和貝妮絲大排儀仗，浩浩蕩蕩地進入大廳；跟他同來的有各指揮官和城裏的顯貴。非斯都一聲令下，保羅就被帶進來。24非斯都說：「亞基帕王和在座各位！請看這個人；他就是所有猶太人在這裏和耶路撒冷向我控告，要求處死的。25但是，我查不出他犯了甚麼該判死刑的罪；而且他既然要向皇帝上訴，我決定把他解去。26只是關於這個人，我並沒有具體資料可以奏明皇上，因此我帶他到各位面前來，尤其是亞基帕王面前，好在查明案情之後有所陳奏。27因為依我看，解送囚犯而不詳具案由是不合理的。」

保羅在亞基帕王面前自辯

26 亞基帕對保羅說：「准你為自己申辯。」

保羅就伸手為自己申辯：

2「亞基帕王啊，我今天得以在你面前，為猶太人所控告我的一切事申辯，實在覺得萬幸！3更可幸的是你對於猶太人的規矩和爭論的問題都很熟悉。因此，我求你耐心垂聽我的申訴。

4「我自幼至今是怎樣的一個人，猶太人沒有不知道的。有生以來我就生活在本國人民當中，居住在耶路撒冷。5如果他們肯為我作證，他們知道我從起初就屬於我們宗教中最嚴格的法利賽派。6現在我站在這裏受審，是因為我對上帝向我們祖先所應許的存着盼望。7這應許是我們十二個支族的全體

God day and night. And it is because of this hope, Your Majesty, that I am being accused by these Jews! [8]Why do you who are here find it impossible to believe that God raises the dead?

[9]"I myself thought that I should do everything I could against the cause of Jesus of Nazareth. [10]That is what I did in Jerusalem. I received authority from the chief priests and put many of God's people in prison; and when they were sentenced to death, I also voted against them. [11]Many times I had them punished in the synagogues and tried to make them deny their faith. I was so furious with them that I even went to foreign cities to persecute them.

Paul Tells of His Conversion
(Acts 9.1-19; 22.6-16)

[12]"It was for this purpose that I went to Damascus with authority and orders from the chief priests. [13]It was on the road at midday, Your Majesty, that I saw a light much brighter than the sun, coming from the sky and shining around me and the men traveling with me. [14]All of us fell to the ground, and I heard a voice say to me in Hebrew, 'Saul, Saul! Why are you persecuting me? You are hurting yourself by hitting back, like an ox kicking against its owner's stick.' [15]'Who are you, Lord?' I asked. And the Lord answered, 'I am Jesus, whom you persecute. [16]But get up and stand on your feet. I have appeared to you to appoint you as my servant. You are to tell others what you have seen of me[k] today and what I will show you in the future. [17]I will rescue you from the people of Israel and from the Gentiles to whom I will send you. [18]You are to open their eyes and turn them from the darkness to the light and from the power of Satan to God, so that through their faith in me they will have their sins forgiven and receive their place among God's chosen people.'

Paul Tells of His Work

[19]"And so, King Agrippa, I did not disobey the vision I had from heaven. [20]First in Damascus and in Jerusalem and then in the whole country of Israel and among the Gentiles, I preached that they must repent of their sins and turn to God and do the things that would show they had repented. [21]It was for this reason that these Jews seized me while I was in the Temple, and they tried to kill me. [22]But to this very day I have been helped by God, and so I stand here giving my witness to all, to small and great alike. What I say is the very same thing

k Some manuscripts do not have of me.

同胞日夜敬拜上帝盼望得着的。王啊,正是為了這個盼望,我才被猶太人控告! [8]可是,你們這些猶太人為甚麼不相信上帝使死人復活是一件可能的事呢?

[9]「我從前也相信應該盡力反對拿撒勒人耶穌。[10]我在耶路撒冷就這樣做了。我從祭司長得了權柄,把許多信徒抓來坐牢;不但這樣,他們被判處死刑,我也贊成。[11]此外,我在各會堂多次對他們用刑,強迫他們放棄信仰。我非常厭恨他們,甚至到國外的城市去迫害他們。」

保羅敍述歸主經過
(徒9·1—19;22·6—16)

[12]「有一次,我帶着祭司長給我的權柄和命令住大馬士革去。[13]王啊,約當正午,我在途中看見一道光,比太陽的光還要強烈,從天空照射在我和同行的人周圍。[14]我們都仆倒地上。我聽見一個聲音,用希伯來話對我說:『掃羅,掃羅!你為甚麼迫害我?你像牛用腳踢主人的刺棒,反而傷了自己。』[15]我就問:『主啊,你是誰?』主說:『我是你所迫害的耶穌。[16]起來,站着。我向你顯現,是要指派你作我的僕人。你要見證今天所看見有關於我以及將來我要指示你的事。[17]我要從以色列人和外邦人手中救你出來,差遣你到他們中間去。[18]你要開啟他們的眼睛,使他們從黑暗轉向光明,從撒但權勢下歸向上帝,好使他們因信了我而蒙赦罪,並且在上帝的子民中有他們的地位。』」

保羅敍述他的工作

[19]「因此,亞基帕王啊,我沒有違背從天上來的異象。[20]我先在大馬士革和耶路撒冷,然後在全猶太和外邦人當中勸勉他們必須悔改,歸向上帝,所作所為要符合他們悔改的心志。[21]為了這個緣故,當我在聖殿裏的時候,猶太人抓住我,想要殺我。[22]可是,直到今天,我蒙上帝幫助,能夠站在這裏,向所有高貴和低微的人作見證。我所說

which the prophets and Moses said was going to happen: 23that the Messiah must suffer and be the first one to rise from death, to announce the light of salvation to the Jews and to the Gentiles."

24As Paul defended himself in this way, Festus shouted at him, "You are mad, Paul! Your great learning is driving you mad!"

25Paul answered, "I am not mad, Your Excellency! I am speaking the sober truth. 26King Agrippa! I can speak to you with all boldness, because you know about these things. I am sure that you have taken notice of every one of them, for this thing has not happened hidden away in a corner. 27King Agrippa, do you believe the prophets? I know that you do!"

28Agrippa said to Paul, "In this short time do you think you will make me a Christian?"

29"Whether a short time or a long time," Paul answered, "my prayer to God is that you and all the rest of you who are listening to me today might become what I am–except, of course, for these chains!"

30Then the king, the governor, Bernice, and all the others got up, 31and after leaving they said to each other, "This man has not done anything for which he should die or be put in prison." 32And Agrippa said to Festus, "This man could have been released if he had not appealed to the Emperor."

Paul Sails for Rome

27 When it was decided that we should sail to Italy, they handed Paul and some other prisoners over to Julius, an officer in the Roman army regiment called "The Emperor's Regiment." 2We went aboard a ship from Adramyttium, which was ready to leave for the seaports of the province of Asia, and we sailed away. Aristarchus, a Macedonian from Thessalonica, was with us. 3The next day we arrived at Sidon. Julius was kind to Paul and allowed him to go and see his friends, to be given what he needed. 4We went on from there, and because the winds were blowing against us, we sailed on the sheltered side of the island of Cyprus. 5We crossed over the sea off Cilicia and Pamphylia and came to Myra in Lycia. 6There the officer found a ship from Alexandria that was going to sail for Italy, so he put us aboard.

7We sailed slowly for several days and with great difficulty finally arrived off the town of Cnidus. The wind would not let us go any farther in that direction, so we sailed down the sheltered side of the island of Crete, passing by Cape Salmone. 8We kept close to the coast and

的也就是先知和摩西所說將要發生的事，23就是基督必須受害，並且首先從死裏復活，向猶太人和外邦人宣佈拯救的亮光已經臨到。」

24保羅這樣為自己申辯；非斯都大聲對他喊叫：「保羅，你瘋了；你的大學問使你神經失常了！」

25保羅說：「非斯都大人！我並沒有發瘋；我所說的話是真實無偽的。26王也知道這些事，所以我對王大膽直言；相信每一件事王都注意到了，因為這些事是人人都知道的。27亞基帕王啊，你相信先知嗎？我知道你是相信的！」

28亞基帕對保羅說：「你想用幾句話就會說服我作基督徒嗎？」

29保羅回答：「無論話多話少，我向上帝所求的是你和所有今天在這裏聽我說話的人都會像我一樣，只是別像我帶着這些鎖鍊！」

30於是王、總督、貝妮絲，和其他的人都起來。31他們退出之後，彼此說：「這個人並沒有犯甚麼該死或該囚禁的罪。」32亞基帕對非斯都說：「要是這個人沒有向皇上上訴，他早就被釋放了。」

保羅乘船往羅馬

27 既然決定要我們從水路往意大利去，他們就把保羅和其他囚犯交給「御營」的羅馬軍官猶流。2我們上了一條從亞大米田來的船；這條船就要起航，沿着亞細亞省的幾個港口航行。有一個馬其頓的帖撒羅尼迦人，名叫亞里達古，跟我們同行。3第二天到了西頓，猶流寬待保羅，准許他去找朋友，受朋友招待。4我們又從那裏起航，因為遇到逆風，船就靠塞浦路斯背風的一面航行。5我們渡過基利家、旁非利亞一帶海面，到了呂家的每拉。6在那裏，猶流找到一條從亞歷山大來的船，要開往意大利去，就叫我們都上了船。

7一連好幾天，船行得很慢，好不容易才開到革尼土附近。因為風的攔阻，我們不能繼續照原來的方向往前行，就靠着克里特島背風的一面航行，從撒摩尼角過去。8我們

with great difficulty came to a place called Safe Harbors, not far from the town of Lasea.

9We spent a long time there, until it became dangerous to continue the voyage, for by now the Day of Atonement[l] was already past. So Paul gave them this advice: 10"Men, I see that our voyage from here on will be dangerous; there will be great damage to the cargo and to the ship, and loss of life as well." 11But the army officer was convinced by what the captain and the owner of the ship said, and not by what Paul said. 12The harbor was not a good one to spend the winter in; so almost everyone was in favor of putting out to sea and trying to reach Phoenix, if possible, in order to spend the winter there. Phoenix is a harbor in Crete that faces southwest and northwest.[m]

The Storm at Sea

13A soft wind from the south began to blow, and the men thought that they could carry out their plan, so they pulled up the anchor and sailed as close as possible along the coast of Crete. 14But soon a very strong wind–the one called "Northeaster"–blew down from the island. 15It hit the ship, and since it was impossible to keep the ship headed into the wind, we gave up trying and let it be carried along by the wind. 16We got some shelter when we passed to the south of the little island of Cauda. There, with some difficulty we managed to make the ship's boat secure. 17They pulled it aboard and then fastened some ropes tight around the ship. They were afraid that they might run into the sandbanks off the coast of Libya, so they lowered the sail and let the ship be carried by the wind. 18The violent storm continued, so on the next day they began to throw some of the ship's cargo overboard, 19and on the following day they threw part of the ship's equipment overboard. 20For many days we could not see the sun or the stars, and the wind kept on blowing very hard. We finally gave up all hope of being saved.

21After everyone had gone a long time without food, Paul stood before them and said, "You should have listened to me and not have sailed from Crete; then we would have avoided all this damage and loss. 22But now I beg you, take courage! Not one of you will lose your life; only the ship will be lost. 23For last night an angel of the God to whom I belong and whom I worship came to me 24and said, 'Don't be afraid, Paul! You must stand before the Emperor.

---

l DAY OF ATONEMENT: *This was celebrated toward the end of September or beginning of October, at which time bad weather made sailing dangerous.*

m south-west and north-west; *or* north-east and south-east.

傍着海岸前進，費盡力氣才到達距離拉西亞城不遠的一個佳澳港。

9 我們耽誤了好些時間，已經過了禁食的節期，不適合繼續航行。於是保羅勸告大家，10說：「各位，我看從這裏繼續航行是很危險的；不但貨物和船將受損壞，連我們的生命也難保。」11可是，軍官寧願相信船長和船主的話，而不相信保羅的。12這港口也不是過冬的理想地方；因此大多數的人贊成開船，盡可能趕到菲尼基去過冬。菲尼基是克里特島的一個港口，朝向西南和西北㉑。

海上風暴

13 當時，有一陣柔和的南風吹來，大家以爲可照原有計劃航行，就起錨開船，緊靠着克里特島行。14不久，有一種叫「東北風」的巨風從島上撲過來。15船被風襲擊，擋不住，我們無法可施，任由颶風把船颳着走。16當船靠着那名叫高大的小島南面航行時，我們好不容易才保住了救生艇。17水手們把它拖上大船，用纜索綁住。他們又怕船撞在賽耳底的沙洲上，就落下大帆，讓它隨着風飄流。18風暴繼續襲擊，第二天，他們開始把貨物拋入海中，19再過一天，連船上的器具也都扔掉了。20好些日子我們看不見太陽和星星；風浪繼續催逼，我們終於放棄了獲救的希望。

21 船上的人已有許多天沒有吃甚麼東西，保羅站在他們面前說：「各位，你們要是早聽我的話，不從克里特島開船，就不致遭受這一切損失。22現在我勸你們放心，你們中間不會有人喪失性命，只是會損失這條船。23昨夜，我所屬、所敬拜的上帝差他的天使對我說：24『保羅，不要害怕！你必須站在皇帝面前。而且，由於上帝的慈愛，他已經

㉑「西南和西北」或譯「東北和東南」。

And God in his goodness to you has spared the lives of all those who are sailing with you.' 25So take courage, men! For I trust in God that it will be just as I was told. 26But we will be driven ashore on some island."

27It was the fourteenth night, and we were being driven in the Mediterranean by the storm. About midnight the sailors suspected that we were getting close to land. 28So they dropped a line with a weight tied to it and found that the water was one hundred and twenty feet deep; a little later they did the same and found that it was ninety feet deep. 29They were afraid that the ship would go on the rocks, so they lowered four anchors from the back of the ship and prayed for daylight. 30Then the sailors tried to escape from the ship; they lowered the boat into the water and pretended that they were going to put out some anchors from the front of the ship. 31But Paul said to the army officer and soldiers, "If the sailors don't stay on board, you have no hope of being saved." 32So the soldiers cut the ropes that held the boat and let it go.

33Just before dawn, Paul begged them all to eat some food: "You have been waiting for fourteen days now, and all this time you have not eaten a thing. 34I beg you, then, eat some food; you need it in order to survive. Not even a hair of your heads will be lost." 35After saying this, Paul took some bread, gave thanks to God before them all, broke it, and began to eat. 36They took courage, and every one of them also ate some food. 37There was a total of 276[n] of us on board. 38After everyone had eaten enough, they lightened the ship by throwing all the wheat into the sea.

The Shipwreck

39When day came, the sailors did not recognize the coast, but they noticed a bay with a beach and decided that, if possible, they would run the ship aground there. 40So they cut off the anchors and let them sink in the sea, and at the same time they untied the ropes that held the steering oars. Then they raised the sail at the front of the ship so that the wind would blow the ship forward, and we headed for shore. 41But the ship hit a sandbank and went aground; the front part of the ship got stuck and could not move, while the back part was being broken to pieces by the violence of the waves.

42The soldiers made a plan to kill all the prisoners, in order to keep them from swimming ashore and escaping. 43But the army officer wanted to save Paul, so he stopped them from

n 276; *some manuscripts have* 275; *others have about* 76.

定意保守所有跟你同船的人的性命。」25所以，各位可以放心；我相信上帝必定實現他對我說的話。26不過我們會給飄到一個島上去。」

27到了第十四天夜裏，我們的船仍然在亞得里亞海飄來飄去。到了半夜，水手以為我們已靠近陸地，28就拋下測繩，探測水的深淺，得四十公尺；稍往前再探，得三十公尺。29他們怕船觸了暗礁，就從船尾拋下四個錨，盼望天亮。30水手們想逃出這條船，把救生艇縋下海裏，假裝要從船頭拋錨。31保羅對軍官和兵士們說：「這些人不留在船上，你們就不能獲救。」32兵士就砍斷救生艇的繩子，由它飄去。

33天快亮的時候，保羅勸大家吃點東西。他說：「你們懸心焦慮，不吃不喝，已經十四天了。34所以我勸你們，吃點東西才能夠支持下去，因為你們每一個人連一根頭髮都不至於損失。」35說了這話，保羅拿出麵包，在大家面前向上帝獻上感謝，然後擘開來吃。36大家都覺得放心，也就吃了。37我們同船的共有兩百七十六人㉒。38大家吃飽後，為了減輕船的載重，又把船上的麥子拋進海裏。

船擱淺了

39天亮了，水手不認識那地方，但是發現一個海灣，而且有沙灘，就決定想法子把船攏上去。40他們先砍斷纜索，把錨丟在海裏，同時鬆開舵繩，拉起船頭的帆，讓風把船推向岸去。41但是，船因衝到沙洲擱淺，船頭膠住，不能轉動，船尾被大浪猛力衝擊，破損不堪。

42兵士想把囚犯都殺了，避免有潛水逃脫的。43但是軍官要救保羅，不准他們妄動，

㉒「兩百七十六人」有些古卷作「兩百七十五人」；另有些古卷作「大約有七十六人」。

doing this. Instead, he ordered everyone who could swim to jump overboard first and swim ashore; ⁴⁴the rest were to follow, holding on to the planks or to some broken pieces of the ship. And this was how we all got safely ashore.

In Malta

28When we were safely ashore, we learned that the island was called Malta. ²The natives there were very friendly to us. It had started to rain and was cold, so they built a fire and made us all welcome. ³Paul gathered up a bundle of sticks and was putting them on the fire when a snake came out on account of the heat and fastened itself to his hand. ⁴The natives saw the snake hanging on Paul's hand and said to one another, "This man must be a murderer, but Fate will not let him live, even though he escaped from the sea." ⁵But Paul shook the snake off into the fire without being harmed at all. ⁶They were waiting for him to swell up or suddenly fall down dead. But after waiting for a long time and not seeing anything unusual happening to him, they changed their minds and said, "He is a god!"

⁷Not far from that place were some fields that belonged to Publius, the chief of the island. He welcomed us kindly and for three days we were his guests. ⁸Publius' father was in bed, sick with fever and dysentery. Paul went into his room, prayed, placed his hands on him, and healed him. ⁹When this happened, all the other sick people on the island came and were healed. ¹⁰They gave us many gifts, and when we sailed, they put on board what we needed for the voyage.

From Malta to Rome

¹¹After three months we sailed away on a ship from Alexandria, called "The Twin Gods," which had spent the winter in the island. ¹²We arrived in the city of Syracuse and stayed there for three days. ¹³From there we sailed on and arrived in the city of Rhegium. The next day a wind began to blow from the south, and in two days we came to the town of Puteoli. ¹⁴We found some believers there who asked us to stay with them a week. And so we came to Rome. ¹⁵The believers in Rome heard about us and came as far as the towns of Market of Appius and Three Inns to meet us. When Paul saw them, he thanked God and was greatly encouraged.

In Rome

¹⁶When we arrived in Rome, Paul was allowed to live by himself with a soldier guarding him.

於是下令會游泳的人先跳下水去，游泳上岸；⁴⁴其餘的人利用木板和船上的斷木上岸。這樣，大家都獲救上岸。

在馬耳他島

28我們獲救上岸後才知道那島叫馬耳他。²島上的居民對我們很友善。當時因下雨，天氣又冷，他們就生火，接待我們。³保羅撿來了一把柴，放在火中。有一條毒蛇受不住熱，鑽了出來，纏住他的手。⁴島上的人看見那條蛇懸在保羅手上，彼此說：「這個人一定是殺人犯，雖然從海裏被救了上來，天理還是不容他活着。」⁵可是保羅把那條蛇抖在火裏，自己沒受絲毫傷害。⁶大家等着要看他的手腫起來，或是突然仆倒死去；可是等了好久，看不出他有甚麼異樣，就改變念頭，說：「他是神明！」

⁷距離那地方不遠，酋長部百流有一片田產。他歡迎我們，誠意款待我們三天。⁸當時，部百流的父親患熱病和痢疾，躺在牀上，保羅到他的臥室去，為他禱告，按手，治好了他。⁹這一來，島上所有的病人都來了，也都得到醫治。¹⁰他們送給我們許多禮物；開船的時候又把我們途中所需要的東西送到船上。

從馬耳他到羅馬

¹¹過了三個月，我們搭上一條從亞歷山大來的船；這條船名叫「雙神號」，是停在那海島過冬的。¹²船到了敍拉古，我們在那裏停留三天，¹³然後再開船，到了利基翁。第二天有南風，所以兩天內我們就到了部丟利，¹⁴在那裏遇見一些信徒；他們邀請我們停留了七天。就這樣，我們到了羅馬。¹⁵羅馬的信徒們聽到我們抵達的消息，就到亞比烏市場和三館來迎接我們。保羅一看見他們就感謝上帝，更加壯膽。

保羅在羅馬

¹⁶我們到了羅馬之後，保羅得到准許，跟看守他的那個兵士住另外一個地方。

17After three days Paul called the local Jewish leaders to a meeting. When they had gathered, he said to them, "My fellow Israelites, even though I did nothing against our people or the customs that we received from our ancestors, I was made a prisoner in Jerusalem and handed over to the Romans. 18After questioning me, the Romans wanted to release me, because they found that I had done nothing for which I deserved to die. 19But when the Jews opposed this, I was forced to appeal to the Emperor, even though I had no accusation to make against my own people. 20That is why I asked to see you and talk with you. As a matter of fact, I am bound in chains like this for the sake of him for whom the people of Israel hope."

21They said to him, "We have not received any letters from Judea about you, nor have any of our people come from there with any news or anything bad to say about you. 22But we would like to hear your ideas, because we know that everywhere people speak against this party to which you belong."

23So they set a date with Paul, and a large number of them came that day to the place where Paul was staying. From morning till night he explained to them his message about the Kingdom of God, and he tried to convince them about Jesus by quoting from the Law of Moses and the writings of the prophets. 24Some of them were convinced by his words, but others would not believe. 25So they left, disagreeing among themselves, after Paul had said this one thing: "How well the Holy Spirit spoke through the prophet Isaiah to your ancestors! 26For he said,

'Go and say to this people:

You will listen and listen, but not understand;
   you will look and look, but not see,
27because this people's minds are dull,
   and they have stopped up their ears
   and closed their eyes.
Otherwise, their eyes would see,
   their ears would hear,
   their minds would understand,
and they would turn to me, says God,
   and I would heal them.' "

28And Paul concluded: "You are to know, then, that God's message of salvation has been sent to the Gentiles. They will listen!"o

30For two years Paul lived in a place he rented for himself, and there he welcomed all who came to see him. 31He preached about the Kingdom of God and taught about the Lord Jesus Christ, speaking with all boldness and freedom.

o Some manuscripts add verse 29: After Paul said this, the Jews left, arguing violently among themselves.

17過了三天，保羅約當地猶太人的領袖相見。他們來了，保羅對他們說：「同胞們，雖然我沒有做甚麼冒犯同胞，或是違背祖宗規矩的事，我竟在耶路撒冷被囚禁，又被解交羅馬當局。18他們審問我，可是找不出我有甚麼該死的罪，有意要釋放我。19但是猶太人反對，迫不得已，我只好上訴於皇帝，並不是我對同胞有甚麼要控告的。20為了這個緣故，我要求跟諸位見面談談。我之所以帶着這鎖鍊，原是為了以色列人所盼望的那一位。」

21他們對保羅說：「關於你的事，我們並沒有從猶太接到任何信件，也沒有同道從那裏帶甚麼消息來，或是說你甚麼壞話。22但是，我們想聽聽你的意見，因為我們知道，你所屬的這一門教派是到處受人攻擊的。」

23於是，他們跟保羅約定聚會的日子。那天到保羅住處來的人很多；從早到晚，他向他們講解上帝國的信息。他引證摩西法律和先知書，要他們信耶穌。24對於他所說的話，有的信，有的不信。25他們彼此不能同意，就散開了。未散之前，保羅說了一句話：「聖靈藉着先知以賽亞向你們的祖宗說過的話是不錯的！26以賽亞說：

你去告訴這人民：

你們聽了又聽，卻不明白，
看了又看，卻看不見。
27因為這人民心智閉塞；
他們塞住了耳朵，
閉上了眼睛。
不然，他們的眼睛就會看見，
耳朵也會聽見，
心裏領悟，回心轉意，
我就治好他們。」

28於是保羅說：「所以，你們應當知道，上帝拯救的信息已經傳給外邦人了。他們倒是會聽的！」㉓

30保羅在自己所租的房子住了兩年。凡來訪問的人，他都接待。31他大膽地宣揚上帝國的信息，教導有關主耶穌基督的事，沒有受到甚麼阻礙。

㉓有些古卷加29節「保羅說了這話後，那些猶太人就走了；他們中間發生了劇烈的爭辯。」

羅馬書
ROMANS

INTRODUCTION

Paul's Letter to the Romans was written to prepare the way for a visit Paul planned to make to the church at Rome. His plan was to work among the Christians there for a while and then, with their support, to go on to Spain. He wrote to explain his understanding of the Christian faith and its practical implications for the lives of Christians. The book contains Paul's most complete statement of his message.

After greeting the people of the church at Rome and telling them of his prayers for them, Paul states the theme of the letter: "The gospel reveals how God puts people right with himself: it is through faith from beginning to end" (1.17).

Paul then develops this theme. All people, both Jews and Gentiles, need to be put right with God, for all alike are under the power of sin. People are put right with God through faith in Jesus Christ. Next Paul describes the new life in union with Christ that results from this new relation with God. The believer has peace with God and is set free by God's Spirit from the power of sin and death. In chapters 5-8 Paul also discusses the purpose of the Law of God and the power of God's Spirit in the believer's life. Then the apostle wrestles with the question of how Jews and Gentiles fit into the plan of God for all people. He concludes that the Jewish rejection of Jesus is part of God's plan for bringing all people within the reach of God's grace in Jesus Christ, and he believes that the Jews will not always reject Jesus. Finally Paul writes about how the Christian life should be lived, especially about the way of love in relations with others. He takes up such themes as service to God, the duty of Christians to the state and to one another, and questions of conscience. He ends the letter with personal messages and with words of praise to God.

Outline of Contents

簡介

保羅寫羅馬書是為訪問羅馬教會的事作準備。保羅的計劃是先在羅馬信徒中工作一段時期,然後在他們幫助下繼續前往西班牙。他寫這封信來解釋他對基督信仰的了解,和這信仰應如何在信徒生活上實踐出來。這是保羅對他所傳的信息解釋得最詳盡的一本書。

保羅首先問候羅馬教會的信徒,告訴他們,他常常為他們禱告。接着,他指出這信的重點在於說明:「因為這福音啓示上帝怎樣使人跟他有合宜的關係:是起於信,止於信。」(1.17)

保羅進一步發揮這一主題。他認為,全人類,不管是猶太人或外邦人,都必須跟上帝有合宜的關係。世上的人都處在罪的權勢下,只有信耶穌基督才得以跟上帝有合宜的關係。接着,保羅描寫人和上帝有了這種新關係後將獲得與基督連結的新生命。信的人與上帝有合宜的關係;上帝的靈使他從罪和死的權勢下得到釋放。在第五至第八章,保羅也討論上帝法律的目的,以及上帝的靈在信徒生命中的功效。然後,保羅討論猶太人和外邦人在上帝對人類的計劃中所扮演的角色。他的結論是:猶太人拒絕耶穌是上帝對人類計劃的一部分——上帝要藉着耶穌基督使全人類都得到他的恩典。保羅相信猶太人不至於永遠拒絕耶穌。最後他討論基督徒應有的生活態度,特別強調要以愛心跟人相處。他也提到基督徒事奉上帝、對國家對別人的責任,以及良心等問題。他以個人的問候和頌讚上帝的話結束這封信。

提要

1 From Paul, a servant of Christ Jesus and an apostle chosen and called by God to preach his Good News.

2The Good News was promised long ago by God through his prophets, as written in the Holy Scriptures. 3It is about his Son, our Lord Jesus Christ: as to his humanity, he was born a descendant of David; 4as to his divine holiness, he was shown with great power to be the Son of God by being raised from death. 5Through him God gave me the privilege of being an apostle for the sake of Christ, in order to lead people of all nations to believe and obey. 6This also includes you who are in Rome, whom God has called to belong to Jesus Christ.

7And so I write to all of you in Rome whom God loves and has called to be his own people:

May God our Father and the Lord Jesus Christ give you grace and peace.

Prayer of Thanksgiving

8First, I thank my God through Jesus Christ for all of you, because the whole world is hearing about your faith. 9God is my witness that what I say is true–the God whom I serve with all my heart by preaching the Good News about his Son. God knows that I remember you 10every time I pray. I ask that God in his good will may at last make it possible for me to visit you now. 11For I want very much to see you, in order to share a spiritual blessing with you to make you strong. 12What I mean is that both you and I will be helped at the same time, you by my faith and I by yours.

13You must remember, my friends, that many times I have planned to visit you, but something has always kept me from doing so. I want to win converts among you also, as I have among other Gentiles. 14For I have an obligation to all peoples, to the civilized and to the savage, to the educated and to the ignorant. 15So then, I am eager to preach the Good News to you also who live in Rome.

The Power of the Gospel

16I have complete confidence in the gospel; it is God's power to save all who believe, first the Jews and also the Gentiles. 17For the gospel reveals how God puts people right with himself: it is through faith from beginning to end. As the scripture says, "The person who is put right with God through faith shall live."*a*

---

a put right with God through faith shall live; or put right with God shall live through faith.

1 我是基督耶穌的僕人保羅；上帝選召我作使徒，特派我傳他的福音。

2-4 這福音是上帝在很久以前藉着他的先知在聖經上所應許的，內容有關他的兒子——我們的主耶穌基督。從身世來說，他是大衛的後代；從聖潔的神性說，因上帝使他從死裏復活，以大能顯示他是上帝的兒子。5 藉着他，我得到特別恩賜，為他的名作使徒，來帶領各國的人信從他。6 這當然包括你們這些在羅馬、蒙上帝選召歸屬於耶穌基督的人。

7 我問候所有在羅馬、上帝所愛、所選召作他子民的人。

願我們的父上帝和主耶穌基督賜恩典平安給你們！

感謝的禱告

8 首先，藉着耶穌基督，我為你們大家感謝我的上帝，因為你們的信心已經傳遍天下。9 上帝知道我常常在禱告中想念你們。我全心全意事奉他，傳揚有關他兒子的福音；他可以證明我所說的話是真的。10我懇求上帝，按照他美好的意思為我開路，讓我終於有機會去訪問你們。11我很希望見到你們，跟你們分享屬靈的恩賜，好使你們堅強起來。12或者我應該說，由於你的信心，我們可以互相獲得鼓勵。

13 弟兄姊妹們，我要你們知道，有好幾次我計劃訪問你們，可是總有一些事阻撓，不能成行。我的目的是要在你們當中領人歸主，好像在其他外邦人當中一樣。14因為無論對甚麼人，開化的，沒有開化的，有學問的，沒有學問的，我都欠他們的債。15所以，我迫切地要把這福音也傳給你們在羅馬的人。

福音的大能

16 我不以福音為恥；這福音是上帝的大能，要拯救一切信的人，先是猶太人，而後外邦人。17因為這福音啟示上帝怎樣使人跟他有合宜的關係：是起於信，止於信。正如聖經所說的：「因信而得以跟上帝有合宜關係的人將得生命①。」

---

① 「因信而得以跟上帝有合宜關係的人將得生命」或譯「得以跟上帝有合宜關係的人將因信而得生命」。

Human Guilt

18God's anger is revealed from heaven against all the sin and evil of the people whose evil ways prevent the truth from being known. 19God punishes them, because what can be known about God is plain to them, for God himself made it plain. 20Ever since God created the world, his invisible qualities, both his eternal power and his divine nature, have been clearly seen; they are perceived in the things that God has made. So those people have no excuse at all! 21They know God, but they do not give him the honor that belongs to him, nor do they thank him. Instead, their thoughts have become complete nonsense, and their empty minds are filled with darkness. 22They say they are wise, but they are fools; 23instead of worshiping the immortal God, they worship images made to look like mortals or birds or animals or reptiles.

24And so God has given those people over to do the filthy things their hearts desire, and they do shameful things with each other. 25They exchange the truth about God for a lie; they worship and serve what God has created instead of the Creator himself, who is to be praised forever! Amen.

26Because they do this, God has given them over to shameful passions. Even the women pervert the natural use of their sex by unnatural acts. 27In the same way the men give up natural sexual relations with women and burn with passion for each other. Men do shameful things with each other, and as a result they bring upon themselves the punishment they deserve for their wrongdoing.

28Because those people refuse to keep in mind the true knowledge about God, he has given them over to corrupted minds, so that they do the things that they should not do. 29They are filled with all kinds of wickedness, evil, greed, and vice; they are full of jealousy, murder, fighting, deceit, and malice. They gossip 30and speak evil of one another; they are hateful to God, insolent,*b* proud, and boastful; they think of more ways to do evil; they disobey their parents; 31they have no conscience; they do not keep their promises, and they show no kindness or pity for others. 32They know that God's law says that people who live in this way deserve death. Yet, not only do they continue to do these very things, but they even approve of others who do them.

God's Judgment

2 Do you, my friend, pass judgment on others? You have no excuse at all, whoever you are. For when you judge others and then

b are hateful to God, insolent; *or* hate God, and are insolent.

人類的罪過

18 人的不虔不義蒙蔽了真理,上帝就從天上啓示他的義憤。19上帝懲罰他們;因為關於他的事,人可以知道的,已經清清楚楚地擺在他們眼前,是上帝親自向他們顯明的。20上帝那看不見的特性,就是他永恆的大能和神性,其實從創世以來都看得見,是由他所造的萬物來辨認出來的。所以人沒有甚麼藉口。21他們雖然知道上帝,卻不把榮耀歸給他,也不感謝他;他們的思想荒唐,心智暗昧。22他們自以為聰明,其實是愚蠢。23他們不敬拜永生的上帝,反而去拜偶像,就是那些仿照必死的人、飛禽、走獸、爬蟲等形狀所製造出來的。

24 所以,上帝任憑他們隨着心裏的慾念做下流的事,彼此玷污自己的身體。25他們放棄了上帝的真理,寧願接受虛謊;他們敬奉被造之物,而不敬奉造物之主—他是永遠該受讚美的,阿們!

26 因為這樣,上帝任憑他們放縱自己的情慾;不但女人以反自然的性行為替代自然的性關係,27男人也放棄跟女人自然的性關係,彼此慾火中燒,男人跟男人做可恥的事,結果招來這種敗行所應得的懲罰。

28 既然人認為不必承認上帝,上帝就任憑他們存着敗壞的心,做那些不該做的事。29他們充滿着各樣的不義、邪惡、貪婪、毒行;也充滿着嫉妒、凶殺、爭鬥、詭詐,和陰謀。他們造謠,30彼此毀謗。他們憎恨上帝②,互相侮辱,傲慢,自誇,惹是生非,不孝順父母,31喪盡天良,言而無信,沒有愛心,沒有同情心。32他們知道,按照上帝的命令,凡做這種事的人是該死的;可是,他們不但自己這樣做,也贊同別人這樣做。

上帝的審判

2 朋友啊,你評斷別人,不管你是誰,都是不可原諒的。你評斷別人,而自己所

②「他們憎恨上帝」或譯「他們是上帝所憎恨的」。

do the same things which they do, you condemn yourself. [2]We know that God is right when he judges the people who do such things as these. [3]But you, my friend, do those very things for which you pass judgment on others! Do you think you will escape God's judgment? [4]Or perhaps you despise his great kindness, tolerance, and patience. Surely you know that God is kind, because he is trying to lead you to repent. [5]But you have a hard and stubborn heart, and so you are making your own punishment even greater on the Day when God's anger and righteous judgments will be revealed. [6]For God will reward each of us according to what we have done. [7]Some people keep on doing good, and seek glory, honor, and immortal life; to them God will give eternal life. [8]Other people are selfish and reject what is right, in order to follow what is wrong; on them God will pour out his anger and fury. [9]There will be suffering and pain for all those who do what is evil, for the Jews first and also for the Gentiles. [10]But God will give glory, honor, and peace to all who do what is good, to the Jews first and also to the Gentiles. [11]For God judges everyone by the same standard.

[12]The Gentiles do not have the Law of Moses; they sin and are lost apart from the Law. The Jews have the Law; they sin and are judged by the Law. [13]For it is not by hearing the Law that people are put right with God, but by doing what the Law commands. [14]The Gentiles do not have the Law; but whenever they do by instinct what the Law commands, they are their own law, even though they do not have the Law. [15]Their conduct shows that what the Law commands is written in their hearts. Their consciences also show that this is true, since their thoughts sometimes accuse them and sometimes defend them. [16]And so, according to the Good News I preach, this is how it will be on that Day when God through Jesus Christ will judge the secret thoughts of all.

The Jews and the Law

[17]What about you? You call yourself a Jew; you depend on the Law and boast about God; [18]you know what God wants you to do, and you have learned from the Law to choose what is right; [19]you are sure that you are a guide for the blind, a light for those who are in darkness, [20]an instructor for the foolish, and a teacher for the ignorant. You are certain that in the Law you have the full content of knowledge and of truth. [21]You teach others–why don't you teach yourself? You preach, "Do not steal"–but do you yourself steal? [22]You say, "Do not commit adultery"–but do you commit adultery? You de-

做的卻跟他們一樣，你就是定自己的罪了。[2]我們知道，上帝審判做這種事的人是沒有錯的。[3]可是，朋友啊，你用來評斷別人的事正是你自己所做的！你想你能夠逃避上帝的審判嗎？[4]是不是你輕視他的仁慈、寬容、和忍耐？你應該曉得上帝是仁慈的，因為他要你悔改！[5]可是你的心頑固剛硬，為自己招來更多的忿怒，以致在上帝的義憤和公義的審判來到的日子受更重的刑罰。[6]因為上帝要按照每一個人的行為報應他。[7]有些人恆心行善，追求從上帝來的尊貴、榮耀、和不朽的生命；這樣的人，上帝將以永恆的生命賜給他們。[8]至於那些自私、拒絕真理、反而隨從不義的人，上帝的義憤和懲罰要臨到他們。[9]所有作惡的人將逃不了患難和痛苦，先是猶太人，然後外邦人。[10]但是，所有行善的人，他要賜給他們尊貴、榮耀、和平安，先是猶太人，然後外邦人。[11]因為上帝是不偏待人的。

[12]外邦人沒有摩西的法律，他們犯罪就不在法律下滅亡；猶太人有法律，他們犯罪就按照法律受審判。[13]因為上帝宣判為無罪的，不是單聽法律的人，而是實行法律的人。[14]外邦人沒有法律；但是當他們本着天性做了合乎法律的事，他們就是自己的法律，雖然他們並沒有法律。[15]他們的行為顯明了法律的要求是寫在他們心裏的。他們的良知也證明這是對的；因為他們的思想有時候譴責自己，有時候為自己辯護。[16]所以，按照我所傳的福音，上帝在末日要藉着基督耶穌，針對着人心中的隱祕，實行審判。

猶太人和法律

[17]那麼，你怎麼樣呢？你自稱為猶太人，倚靠法律，又誇口你跟上帝有特殊關係。[18]你已經受法律的薰陶，知道上帝的旨意，也能夠辨別是非。[19]你自以為是瞎子的嚮導，是在黑暗中之人的亮光，[20]是無知之人的指導，又是年輕人的老師。你又認為，因為你有摩西的法律，你就掌握了知識和真理。[21]你教導別人，為甚麼不教導自己呢？你教人不可偷竊，你自己偷竊嗎？[22]你說不可姦淫，你自己姦淫嗎？你憎惡偶像，你自

test idols–but do you rob temples? [23]You boast about having God's law–but do you bring shame on God by breaking his law? [24]The scripture says, "Because of you Jews, the Gentiles speak evil of God."

[25]If you obey the Law, your circumcision is of value; but if you disobey the Law, you might as well never have been circumcised. [26]If the Gentile, who is not circumcised, obeys the commands of the Law, will not God regard him as though he were circumcised? [27]And so you Jews will be condemned by the Gentiles because you break the Law, even though you have it written down and are circumcised; but they obey the Law, even though they are not physically circumcised. [28]After all, who is a real Jew, truly circumcised? It is not the man who is a Jew on the outside, whose circumcision is a physical thing. [29]Rather, the real Jew is the person who is a Jew on the inside, that is, whose heart has been circumcised, and this is the work of God's Spirit, not of the written Law. Such a person receives praise from God, not from human beings.

3 Do the Jews then have any advantage over the Gentiles? Or is there any value in being circumcised? [2]Much, indeed, in every way! In the first place, God trusted his message to the Jews. [3]But what if some of them were not faithful? Does this mean that God will not be faithful? [4]Certainly not! God must be true, even though all human beings are liars. As the scripture says,

"You must be shown to be right when you speak;
   you must win your case when you are being tried."

[5]But what if our doing wrong serves to show up more clearly God's doing right? Can we say that God does wrong when he punishes us? (This would be the natural question to ask.) [6]By no means! If God is not just, how can he judge the world?

[7]But what if my untruth serves God's glory by making his truth stand out more clearly? Why should I still be condemned as a sinner? [8]Why not say, then, "Let us do evil so that good may come"? Some people, indeed, have insulted me by accusing me of saying this very thing! They will be condemned, as they should be.

No One Is Righteous

[9]Well then, are we Jews in any better condition than the Gentiles? Not at all![c] I have already shown that Jews and Gentiles alike are

c any better condition than the Gentiles? Not at all!; or any worse condition than the Gentiles? Not altogether.

己盜取寺廟裏的東西嗎？[23]你誇口你有上帝的法律，你有沒有破壞上帝的法律而羞辱了他？[24]聖經上說：「為了你們猶太人的緣故，上帝的名受到外邦人的侮辱。」

[25]如果你遵守法律，你的割禮就有價值；你違反法律，你的割禮就一點作用都沒有。[26]這樣看來，一個沒有受割禮的人若遵守法律的命令，上帝豈不把他當作是受過割禮的嗎？[27]你們猶太人要被外邦人定罪；因為你們雖然擁有法律經典，也受了割禮，可是你們破壞了法律。他們縱使身體上沒有受割禮，卻遵守法律。[28]其實，誰才算是真猶太人，真受割禮的人呢？並不是在外表上作猶太人、接受過身體上的割禮的。[29]真猶太人是從內心開始的；換句話說，他心裏受了割禮，是上帝的靈的工作，而不是藉着法律經典。這樣的人所受的稱讚不是從人來的，而是從上帝來的。

3 照這樣說，猶太人有甚麼地方勝過外邦人呢？割禮又有甚麼價值呢？[2]事實上各方面都有。第一，上帝把他的信息交託給猶太人。[3]即使他們當中有背信的，上帝就因此不信實了嗎？[4]當然不！甚至人人都虛謊，上帝還是真實的；正像聖經所說：

你發言的時候無懈可擊；
你受指控的時候必然勝訴。

[5]如果我們的不義能夠顯明上帝的公義，我們要怎麼說呢？上帝懲罰我們，是他不義嗎？（我是照人的想法講的。）[6]當然不是！如果上帝是不義的，他怎麼能審判世界呢？

[7]如果我的虛謊能夠使上帝的真實更加顯明，更得榮耀，我要怎麼說呢？為甚麼我還要被判為罪人呢？[8]為甚麼不說：「讓我們作惡以成善呢？」有些人指控我說過這樣的話；他們被定罪是應該的。

沒有義人

[9]那麼，我們猶太人比外邦人強③嗎？沒有這回事！我已經指出，猶太人和外邦人同

③「強」或譯「弱」。

all under the power of sin. [10]As the Scriptures say:

"There is no one who is righteous,
[11]   no one who is wise
    or who worships God.
[12]All have turned away from God;
    they have all gone wrong;
    no one does what is right, not even one.
[13]Their words are full of deadly deceit;
    wicked lies roll off their tongues,
    and dangerous threats, like snake's poison,
      from their lips;
[14]   their speech is filled with bitter curses.
[15]They are quick to hurt and kill;
[16]   they leave ruin and destruction wherever
    they go.
[17]They have not known the path of peace,
[18]   nor have they learned reverence for God."

[19]Now we know that everything in the Law applies to those who live under the Law, in order to stop all human excuses and bring the whole world under God's judgment. [20]For no one is put right in God's sight by doing what the Law requires; what the Law does is to make us know that we have sinned.

How We Are Put Right with God

[21]But now God's way of putting people right with himself has been revealed. It has nothing to do with law, even though the Law of Moses and the prophets gave their witness to it. [22]God puts people right through their faith in Jesus Christ. God does this to all who believe in Christ, because there is no difference at all: [23]everyone has sinned and is far away from God's saving presence. [24]But by the free gift of God's grace all are put right with him through Christ Jesus, who sets them free. [25-26]God offered him, so that by his blood[d] he should become the means by which people's sins are forgiven through their faith in him. God did this in order to demonstrate that he is righteous. In the past he was patient and overlooked people's sins; but in the present time he deals with their sins, in order to demonstrate his righteousness. In this way God shows that he himself is righteous and that he puts right everyone who believes in Jesus.

[27]What, then, can we boast about? Nothing! And what is the reason for this? Is it that we obey the Law? No, but that we believe. [28]For we conclude that a person is put right with God only through faith, and not by doing what the

d by his blood; *or* by his sacrificial death.

樣處在罪惡的權勢下。[10]正像聖經所說：

沒有義人，連一個也沒有。
[11] 沒有明智的人，
  也沒有尋求上帝的人。
[12] 人人背離上帝，
  一齊走入歧途；
  沒有行善的人，
  連一個也沒有。
[13] 他們的喉嚨像敞開的墳墓；
  他們的舌頭儘說詭詐的話；
  蛇一般的毒氣從他們的嘴唇發出；
[14] 他們滿口惡毒和咒罵。
[15] 他們的腳奔跑如飛，到處傷害殘殺，
[16] 所到的地方留下破壞和悲慘的痕跡。
[17] 他們不知道有平安的路；
[18] 他們也不曉得敬畏上帝。

[19]我們知道，法律的命令是向在法律下的人說的，爲要全世界的人都伏在上帝的審判下，使人不能再有甚麼藉口。[20]因爲沒有人能夠靠遵守法律得以在上帝面前被宣佈爲義。法律的效用不過使人知道自己有罪罷了。

上帝使人跟他有正確合宜的關係

[21] 但現在，上帝已經顯示怎樣使人跟他有正確合宜的關係；這是跟法律沒有關係的。摩西的法律和先知們都這樣見證。[22]上帝使他們跟他有合宜的關係是基於他們信耶穌基督。上帝這樣對待所有信基督的人，任何差別都沒有：[23]因爲人人都犯罪，虧欠了上帝的榮耀。[24]然而，上帝白白地賜恩典，藉着基督耶穌救贖他們，使他們跟他有合宜的關係。[25]上帝不惜犧牲基督，以他爲贖罪祭，藉着他的死，使人由於信他而蒙赦罪。上帝這樣做是要顯明自己的公義。[26]因爲他忍耐，寬容人過去的罪。但在這時刻，他以除罪來顯明自己的公義。這樣，上帝顯示了他自己是公義的，也使一切信耶穌的人跟他有合宜的關係。

[27] 那麼，我們有甚麼可誇口的呢？一點兒也沒有！甚麼理由呢？是由於遵守法律嗎？不是！是由於信。[28]我們的結論是：人得以跟上帝有合宜的關係只藉着信，而不藉着遵

Law commands. [29]Or is God the God of the Jews only? Is he not the God of the Gentiles also? Of course he is. [30]God is one, and he will put the Jews right with himself on the basis of their faith, and will put the Gentiles right through their faith. [31]Does this mean that by this faith we do away with the Law? No, not at all; instead, we uphold the Law.

The Example of Abraham

4 What shall we say, then, of Abraham, the father of our race? What was his experience? [2]If he was put right with God by the things he did, he would have something to boast about—but not in God's sight. [3]The scripture says, "Abraham believed God, and because of his faith God accepted him as righteous." [4]A person who works is paid wages, but they are not regarded as a gift; they are something that has been earned. [5]But those who depend on faith, not on deeds, and who believe in the God who declares the guilty to be innocent, it is this faith that God takes into account in order to put them right with himself. [6]This is what David meant when he spoke of the happiness of the person whom God accepts as righteous, apart from anything that person does:

[7]"Happy are those whose wrongs are forgiven,
   whose sins are pardoned!
[8]Happy is the person whose sins the Lord will
   not keep account of!"

[9]Does this happiness that David spoke of belong only to those who are circumcised? No indeed! It belongs also to those who are not circumcised. For we have quoted the scripture, "Abraham believed God, and because of his faith God accepted him as righteous." [10]When did this take place? Was it before or after Abraham was circumcised? It was before, not after. [11]He was circumcised later, and his circumcision was a sign to show that because of his faith God had accepted him as righteous before he had been circumcised. And so Abraham is the spiritual father of all who believe in God and are accepted as righteous by him, even though they are not circumcised. [12]He is also the father of those who are circumcised, that is, of those who, in addition to being circumcised, also live the same life of faith that our father Abraham lived before he was circumcised.

God's Promise Is Received through Faith

[13]When God promised Abraham and his descendants that the world would belong to him, he did so, not because Abraham obeyed the Law, but because he believed and was accepted as righteous by God. [14]For if what God promises is to be given to those who obey the Law,

守法律的要求。[29]難道上帝只是猶太人的上帝？他不也是外邦人的上帝嗎？當然是！[30]上帝只有一位，他要猶太人基於信，外邦人也是藉着信而跟他有合宜的關係。[31]這樣說來，我們的信使摩西的法律失去效力嗎？當然不！相反地，我們使法律更為鞏固。

以亞伯拉罕為例

4 至於在血統上作為我們先祖的亞伯拉罕的事，我們該怎麼說呢？[2]如果他得以被稱為義人是由於他的行為，他就有所誇口的，但在上帝面前不能。[3]聖經上說：「亞伯拉罕信上帝，因他的信，上帝認他為義人。」[4]做工的人得工資，不算恩典，而是他應得的。[5]但是那信宣判罪人為無罪的上帝的人，上帝要因着他的信，而不是他的行為，使他跟自己有合宜的關係，[6]大衛所說，那不靠行為而蒙上帝認為義人的人有福了，就是這個意思。他說：

[7] 那違犯蒙寬恕、罪被赦免的人有福了！
[8] 那罪過不被主計算的人有福了！

[9] 大衛所說的這福澤只是屬於受割禮的人嗎？不是的。它也屬於沒有受割禮的人；因為我們已經引證聖經的話，說：「亞伯拉罕信上帝，因他的信，上帝認他為義人。」[10]這是在哪一種情形下發生的呢？在亞伯拉罕受割禮以前，還是以後呢？是在以前，不是以後。[11]他後來受了割禮；這是一種表徵，證明他在受割禮前已經因信而成為義人了。所以，對所有未受割禮、但因信而被上帝認為義的人來說，亞伯拉罕是屬靈的父親。[12]他也是已經受割禮的人的父親，不但因為他們受了割禮，也因為他們跟隨了我們先祖亞伯拉罕在未受割禮時的那種信心生活。

上帝的應許因信實現

[13] 上帝應許亞伯拉罕和他的子孫，說他將承受這世界。這應許不是因為亞伯拉罕遵守法律，而是由於他因信而被稱為義人。[14]如果上帝的應許是給遵守摩西法律的人，人的

then faith means nothing and God's promise is worthless. [15]The Law brings down God's anger; but where there is no law, there is no disobeying of the law.

[16]And so the promise was based on faith, in order that the promise should be guaranteed as God's free gift to all of Abraham's descendants –not just to those who obey the Law, but also to those who believe as Abraham did. For Abraham is the spiritual father of us all; [17]as the scripture says, "I have made you father of many nations." So the promise is good in the sight of God, in whom Abraham believed–the God who brings the dead to life and whose command brings into being what did not exist. [18]Abraham believed and hoped, even when there was no reason for hoping, and so became "the father of many nations." Just as the scripture says, "Your descendants will be as many as the stars." [19]He was then almost one hundred years old; but his faith did not weaken when he thought of his body, which was already practically dead, or of the fact that Sarah could not have children. [20]His faith did not leave him, and he did not doubt God's promise; his faith filled him with power, and he gave praise to God. [21]He was absolutely sure that God would be able to do what he had promised. [22]That is why Abraham, through faith, "was accepted as righteous by God." [23]The words "he was accepted as righteous" were not written for him alone. [24]They were written also for us who are to be accepted as righteous, who believe in him who raised Jesus our Lord from death. [25]Because of our sins he was given over to die, and he was raised to life in order to put us right with God.

Right with God

5 Now that we have been put right with God through faith, we have[e] peace with God through our Lord Jesus Christ. [2]He has brought us by faith into this experience of God's grace, in which we now live. And so we boast[f] of the hope we have of sharing God's glory! [3]We also boast[g] of our troubles, because we know that trouble produces endurance, [4]endurance brings God's approval, and his approval creates hope. [5]This hope does not disappoint us, for God has poured out his love into our hearts by means of the Holy Spirit, who is God's gift to us.

[6]For when we were still helpless, Christ died for the wicked at the time that God chose. [7]It is a difficult thing for someone to die for a righteous person. It may even be that someone

e we have; *some manuscripts have* let us have.
f we boast; *or* let us boast.
g We also boast; *or* Let us also boast.

信就是空的，而上帝的應許也是無效的。 [15]上帝的義憤是從法律而來的；沒有法律，就沒有違犯法律的事。

[16]因此，應許是以信為根據的；這是要保證上帝的應許白白地賜給亞伯拉罕所有的子孫，不僅是遵守法律的，也包括那些像亞伯拉罕一樣信上帝的人。因為亞伯拉罕是我們大家屬靈之父。[17]正如聖經所說：「我立了你作許多民族之父。」在上帝面前，這應許是有效的；亞伯拉罕所信的就是那位使死人復活、從無有創造萬有的上帝。[18]在沒有盼望的時候，亞伯拉罕仍然盼望，仍然信，因此成為「許多民族之父」。正如聖經所說：「你必定會有許多子孫。」[19]當時亞伯拉罕快要一百歲了。他自己的身體如同已死，而莎拉生育的機能也已經喪失，可是，他並不因此削弱了信心。[20]他沒有失去信心，也沒有懷疑上帝的應許；他的信心反而更堅固，把榮耀歸給上帝。[21]他堅決信上帝一定成就他所應許的。[22]這就是為甚麼亞伯拉罕因信而「被上帝認為義人」。[23]可是「他被認為義人」這句話並不單是為他說的，[24]也是為我們說的。因為我們信那使我們的主耶穌從死裏復活的上帝，因而被認為是義人。[25]主耶穌被交在人手裏，為我們的罪死；上帝使他復活，使我們得以跟上帝有合宜的關係。

跟上帝有和睦的關係

5 既然我們因信得以被稱為義人，就藉着我們的主耶穌基督跟上帝有了和睦的關係。[2]藉着信，基督使我們得以活在上帝的恩典裏④，因此我們歡歡喜喜地⑤盼望着分享上帝的榮耀！[3]不但如此，在患難中，我們仍然喜樂⑥；因為我們知道患難培養忍耐，[4]忍耐蒙上帝嘉許，上帝的嘉許帶來盼望。[5]這盼望不至於落空；因為上帝藉着他賜給我們的聖靈，已把他的愛澆灌在我們心裏。

[6]當我們還軟弱的時候，基督就按照上帝特定的時機為罪人死。[7]為義人死是罕有

④「藉着信……恩典裏」或譯「藉着基督，我們得以進入現在所享有的恩典裏」。
⑤「我們歡歡喜喜地」或譯「我們要歡歡喜喜地」。
⑥「我們仍然喜樂」或譯「我們仍然要喜樂」。

might dare to die for a good person. ⁸But God has shown us how much he loves us–it was while we were still sinners that Christ died for us! ⁹By his blood*ʰ* we are now put right with God; how much more, then, will we be saved by him from God's anger! ¹⁰We were God's enemies, but he made us his friends through the death of his Son. Now that we are God's friends, how much more will we be saved by Christ's life! ¹¹But that is not all; we rejoice because of what God has done through our Lord Jesus Christ, who has now made us God's friends.

Adam and Christ

¹²Sin came into the world through one man, and his sin brought death with it. As a result, death has spread to the whole human race because everyone has sinned. ¹³There was sin in the world before the Law was given; but where there is no law, no account is kept of sins. ¹⁴But from the time of Adam to the time of Moses, death ruled over all human beings, even over those who did not sin in the same way that Adam did when he disobeyed God's command.

Adam was a figure of the one who was to come. ¹⁵But the two are not the same, because God's free gift is not like Adam's sin. It is true that many people died because of the sin of that one man. But God's grace is much greater, and so is his free gift to so many people through the grace of the one man, Jesus Christ. ¹⁶And there is a difference between God's gift and the sin of one man. After the one sin, came the judgment of "Guilty"; but after so many sins, comes the undeserved gift of "Not guilty!" ¹⁷It is true that through the sin of one man death began to rule because of that one man. But how much greater is the result of what was done by the one man, Jesus Christ! All who receive God's abundant grace and are freely put right with him will rule in life through Christ.

¹⁸So then, as the one sin condemned all people, in the same way the one righteous act sets all people free and gives them life. ¹⁹And just as all people were made sinners as the result of the disobedience of one man, in the same way they will all be put right with God as the result of the obedience of the one man.

²⁰Law was introduced in order to increase wrongdoing; but where sin increased, God's grace increased much more. ²¹So then, just as sin ruled by means of death, so also God's grace rules by means of righteousness, leading us to eternal life through Jesus Christ our Lord.

---

h By his blood; *or* By his sacrificial death.

的；爲好人死，或者有人敢做。⁸但是上帝對我們顯示了無比的愛：當我們還是罪人的時候，基督已經爲我們死了！⁹由於他的死，我們現在得以跟上帝有合宜的關係；他的死更要救我們脫離上帝的義憤。¹⁰我們原是上帝的仇敵，但是藉着他兒子的死叫我們得以跟他和好。既然跟他和好，我們豈不更藉着基督的生命而得拯救嗎？¹¹不但這樣，我們已經得以跟上帝和好，不也藉着我們的主耶穌基督以上帝爲樂嗎？

亞當與基督

¹²罪從一個人進入世界，因着罪，死接踵而來；於是死亡臨到了全人類，因爲人人都犯罪。¹³在法律頒佈以前，世界就有了罪；但是沒有法律，人就不在法律的標準下被懲罰。¹⁴然而，從亞當到摩西，死亡支配了人類，甚至不像亞當犯了不服從上帝的罪的人，也不免一死。

亞當是預表以後要來的那一位。¹⁵然而，兩者並不相同，因爲上帝白白的恩賜和亞當的罪大有差別。固然有許多人因亞當一人的罪而死；但是上帝的恩典更為浩大，他藉着耶穌基督一人白白賜給許多人的恩典也一樣浩大。¹⁶上帝的恩賜和一個人的過犯是截然不同的。一個人犯罪，被判「有罪」；但是許多人犯罪，卻得到那不配得的恩賜，而被判「無罪」！¹⁷固然死亡因一個人犯罪開始支配世人，但是耶穌基督一個人所成就的更為浩大！所有領受上帝豐富恩典和白白地得以跟他有合宜關係的人，都要藉着基督而生，而掌權。

¹⁸這樣，因一個人犯罪，衆人都被定罪；同樣，因一個人的義行，衆人都得到赦罪而獲得生命。¹⁹正如一個人違背命令，衆人成爲罪人；同樣，一個人順服，衆人成爲義人。²⁰法律的制訂使過犯增多；但是罪越增多，上帝的恩典也更加豐富。²¹正如罪藉着死亡來管轄，上帝的恩典也藉着公義來統治，使我們藉着我們的主耶穌基督得到永恆的生命。

Dead to Sin but Alive in Union with Christ

6 What shall we say, then? Should we continue to live in sin so that God's grace will increase? [2]Certainly not! We have died to sin–how then can we go on living in it? [3]For surely you know that when we were baptized into union with Christ Jesus, we were baptized into union with his death. [4]By our baptism, then, we were buried with him and shared his death, in order that, just as Christ was raised from death by the glorious power of the Father, so also we might live a new life.

[5]For since we have become one with him in dying as he did, in the same way we shall be one with him by being raised to life as he was. [6]And we know that our old being has been put to death with Christ on his cross, in order that the power of the sinful self might be destroyed, so that we should no longer be the slaves of sin. [7]For when we die, we are set free from the power of sin. [8]Since we have died with Christ, we believe that we will also live with him. [9]For we know that Christ has been raised from death and will never die again–death will no longer rule over him. [10]And so, because he died, sin has no power over him; and now he lives his life in fellowship with God. [11]In the same way you are to think of yourselves as dead, so far as sin is concerned, but living in fellowship with God through Christ Jesus.

[12]Sin must no longer rule in your mortal bodies, so that you obey the desires of your natural self. [13]Nor must you surrender any part of yourselves to sin to be used for wicked purposes. Instead, give yourselves to God, as those who have been brought from death to life, and surrender your whole being to him to be used for righteous purposes. [14]Sin must not be your master; for you do not live under law but under God's grace.

Slaves of Righteousness

[15]What, then? Shall we sin, because we are not under law but under God's grace? By no means! [16]Surely you know that when you surrender yourselves as slaves to obey someone, you are in fact the slaves of the master you obey–either of sin, which results in death, or of obedience, which results in being put right with God. [17]But thanks be to God! For though at one time you were slaves to sin, you have obeyed with all your heart the truths found in the teaching you received. [18]You were set free from sin and became the slaves of righteousness. [19](I use everyday language because of the weakness of your natural selves.) At one time you surrendered yourselves entirely as slaves to

向罪而死，在基督裏活

6 那麼，我們該怎麼說呢？我們該繼續生活在罪裏，好讓上帝的恩典顯得更豐富嗎？[2]當然不！從罪這一方面來說，我們已經是死了。我們怎麼能繼續生活在罪裏呢？[3]你們一定知道，我們受洗跟基督耶穌合而爲一，也就是受洗跟他同死。[4]藉着洗禮，我們已經跟他同歸於死，一起埋葬；正如天父以他榮耀的大能使基督從死裏復活，我們同樣也要過着新的生活。

[5]如果我們跟基督合而爲一，經歷了他的死，我們同樣也要經歷他的復活。[6]我們知道，我們的舊我已經跟基督同釘十字架，爲的是要摧毀罪性的自我，使我們不再作罪的奴隸。[7]因爲人死了就脫離罪的權勢。[8]如果我們跟基督同死，我們信，我們也要跟基督同活。[9]因爲我們知道，基督已經從死裏復活，他不再死；死也不能再控制他。[10]他的死，是跟罪決絕，一舉而竟全功；他現在活着，是爲上帝而活。[11]同樣，從罪這方面來說，你們也要把自己當作死了，但是在基督耶穌的生命裏，你們是爲上帝而活。

[12]所以，不可再讓罪支配你們必朽的身體，使你們順服本性的情慾。[13]也不可讓你們自己的肢體向罪投降，作了邪惡的工具。相反地，你們要把自己奉獻給上帝，像一個從死裏被救活起來的人，把自己的整體奉獻給他，作爲公義的器皿。[14]從此，你們不可再受罪的管轄；因爲你們已不在法律之下，而是在上帝恩典之下。

義的奴僕

[15]這樣說來，因爲我們不在法律之下而是在上帝的恩典之下，我們就可以犯罪嗎？絕對不可！[16]你們當然知道，當你們作人的奴僕去服從主人時，你們就是他的奴僕。這就是說，你們作罪的奴僕，結果就是死；你們順服上帝，就得以成爲義人。[17]感謝上帝！雖然你們曾經是罪的奴僕，現在你們卻一心順從所傳授給你們的教訓。[18]你們已經從罪中被釋放出來，而成爲義的奴僕。[19]我怕你們難以了解我的意思，所以用很普通的例子對你們說。從前你們放縱自己的肢體，爲非

impurity and wickedness for wicked purposes. In the same way you must now surrender yourselves entirely as slaves of righteousness for holy purposes.

20When you were the slaves of sin, you were free from righteousness. 21What did you gain from doing the things that you are now ashamed of? The result of those things is death! 22But now you have been set free from sin and are the slaves of God. Your gain is a life fully dedicated to him, and the result is eternal life. 23For sin pays its wage–death; but God's free gift is eternal life in union with Christ Jesus our Lord.

An Illustration from Marriage

7 Certainly you will understand what I am about to say, my friends, because all of you know about law. The law rules over people only as long as they live. 2A married woman, for example, is bound by the law to her husband as long as he lives; but if he dies, then she is free from the law that bound her to him. 3So then, if she lives with another man while her husband is alive, she will be called an adulteress; but if her husband dies, she is legally a free woman and does not commit adultery if she marries another man. 4That is how it is with you, my friends. As far as the Law is concerned, you also have died because you are part of the body of Christ; and now you belong to him who was raised from death in order that we might be useful in the service of God. 5For when we lived according to our human nature, the sinful desires stirred up by the Law were at work in our bodies, and all we did ended in death. 6Now, however, we are free from the Law, because we died to that which once held us prisoners. No longer do we serve in the old way of a written law, but in the new way of the Spirit.

Law and Sin

7Shall we say, then, that the Law itself is sinful? Of course not! But it was the Law that made me know what sin is. If the Law had not said, "Do not desire what belongs to someone else," I would not have known such a desire. 8But by means of that commandment sin found its chance to stir up all kinds of selfish desires in me. Apart from law, sin is a dead thing. 9I myself was once alive apart from law; but when the commandment came, sin sprang to life, 10and I died. And the commandment which was meant to bring life, in my case brought death. 11Sin found its chance, and by means of the

作歹，作罪的奴僕。現在你們要奉獻自己的整體，作義的奴僕，成為聖潔的器皿。

20你們作罪的奴僕的時候，不受義的管束。21你們現在認為可恥的事，當時做了，到底得到些甚麼好處呢？不過是死罷了！22現在，你們已經從罪中被釋放出來，作上帝的奴僕；你們把生命完全奉獻給他，所收穫的就是永恆的生命。23因為罪的代價是死亡；但是上帝所賜白白的恩典是讓我們在主基督耶穌的生命裏得到永恆的生命。

以婚姻關係為例

7 弟兄姊妹們，你們都是懂法律的人，所以你們一定會明白我所要說明的：法律對人的約束是人活着的時候才有效力。2舉例說，一個已婚的女人，只要丈夫活着，就在法律的約束之下；丈夫死了，她就不再受這種法律的限制。3因此，丈夫活着的時候，她要是跟別的男人同居就要被當作淫婦；如果丈夫死了，她在法律上是一個自由的人，要是再跟別的男人結婚，並不算犯姦淫。4弟兄姊妹們，你們的情形也是這樣。在法律上說，你們已經死了，因為你們是基督身體的一部分；現在你們是屬於那位從死裏復活的主，使我們能夠好好地為上帝工作。5當我們還照着人的本性生活時，摩西的法律激起了我們罪的慾念，在我們的肢體中發作，結果是死亡。6但是，現在法律已經不拘束我們；因為從管束我們的法律來說，我們已經死了。我們不再依照法律條文的舊方式，而是依照聖靈的新指示來事奉上帝。

法律和罪

7 那麼，我們可以說法律本身是罪嗎？當然不可！然而，藉着法律，我才知道罪是甚麼。要不是法律說「不可貪心」，我就不知道貪心是甚麼。8罪藉着法律的命令，尋找機會，在我心裏激發各種貪慾。沒有法律，罪就無機可乘。9我從前生活在法律之外；後來有了法律的命令，罪就活躍起來，10結果我在罪中死了。原來法律的命令是要使人得生命的；可是，對我來講，它反而帶來死亡。11因為罪藉着法律的命令找機會誘騙

commandment it deceived me and killed me.

12So then, the Law itself is holy, and the commandment is holy, right, and good. 13But does this mean that what is good caused my death? By no means! It was sin that did it; by using what is good, sin brought death to me, in order that its true nature as sin might be revealed. And so, by means of the commandment sin is shown to be even more terribly sinful.

The Conflict in Us

14We know that the Law is spiritual; but I am a mortal, sold as a slave to sin. 15I do not understand what I do; for I don't do what I would like to do, but instead I do what I hate. 16Since what I do is what I don't want to do, this shows that I agree that the Law is right. 17So I am not really the one who does this thing; rather it is the sin that lives in me. 18I know that good does not live in me–that is, in my human nature. For even though the desire to do good is in me, I am not able to do it. 19I don't do the good I want to do; instead, I do the evil that I do not want to do. 20If I do what I don't want to do, this means that I am no longer the one who does it; instead, it is the sin that lives in me.

21So I find that this law is at work: when I want to do what is good, what is evil is the only choice I have. 22My inner being delights in the law of God. 23But I see a different law at work in my body–a law that fights against the law which my mind approves of. It makes me a prisoner to the law of sin which is at work in my body. 24What an unhappy man I am! Who will rescue me from this body that is taking me to death? 25Thanks be to God, who does this through our Lord Jesus Christ!

This, then, is my condition: on my own I can serve God's law only with my mind, while my human nature serves the law of sin.

Life in the Spirit

8 There is no condemnation now for those who live in union with Christ Jesus. 2For the law of the Spirit, which brings us life in union with Christ Jesus, has set me*i* free from the law of sin and death. 3What the Law could not do, because human nature was weak, God did. He condemned sin in human nature by sending his own Son, who came with a nature like our

---

我，也藉着法律的命令置我於死地。

12摩西的法律本身是神聖的；法律的命令是神聖、公平，和良善的。13這樣說來，是那良善的使我死亡嗎？當然不是！是罪！只是罪藉着那良善的，帶來死亡，為要使罪的眞面目更加明顯。藉着法律的命令，罪的惡性就變本加厲了。

人的自我分裂

14我們知道，摩西的法律是屬靈的；但是我是必朽的人，已經賣給罪作奴隸。15我竟不明白我所做的；因為我所願意的，我偏不去做；我所恨惡的，我反而去做。16我若做了我不願意做的事，我就不得不承認法律是對的。17既然這樣，我所做的並不眞的是我在做，而是在我裏面的罪做的。18我也知道，在我裏面，就是在我的本性裏面，沒有良善。因為，我有行善的意願，卻沒有行善的能力。19我所願意的善，我偏不去做；我所不願意的惡，我反而去做。20如果我做了我不願意做的，就表示這不是我做的，而是那在我裏面的罪做的。

21因此，我發覺有一個法則在作祟：當我願意行善的時候，邪惡老是糾纏着我。22我的內心原喜愛上帝的法則，23我的身體卻受另一個法則的驅使—這法則跟我內心所喜愛的法則交戰，使我不能脫離那束縛我的罪的法則；這法則在我身體裏作祟。24我眞苦啊！誰能救我脫離這使我死亡的身體呢？25感謝上帝，藉着我們的主耶穌基督，他能夠救我。

我的情況就是這樣：我自己只能在心靈上順服上帝的法則，而我的肉體卻服從罪的法則。

意向於聖靈的生活

8 如今，那些活在基督耶穌生命裏的人就不被定罪。2因為聖靈的法則，就是那使我們⑦跟基督耶穌聯合而得生命的，已經從罪和死的法則下把我們釋放出來。3摩西的法律因人性的軟弱而不能成就的，上帝卻親自成就了。上帝差遣自己的兒子，使他有了跟我們人相同的罪性⑧，為要宣判人性裏

⑦「我們」有些古卷作「我」，也有些古卷作「你」。
⑧「使他……罪性」或譯「取了跟我們相似的罪的肉身」。

---

i me; some manuscripts have you; others have us.

sinful nature, to do away with sin. ⁴God did this so that the righteous demands of the Law might be fully satisfied in us who live according to the Spirit, and not according to human nature. ⁵Those who live as their human nature tells them to, have their minds controlled by what human nature wants. Those who live as the Spirit tells them to, have their minds controlled by what the Spirit wants. ⁶To be controlled by human nature results in death; to be controlled by the Spirit results in life and peace. ⁷And so people become enemies of God when they are controlled by their human nature; for they do not obey God's law, and in fact they cannot obey it. ⁸Those who obey their human nature cannot please God.

⁹But you do not live as your human nature tells you to; instead, you live as the Spirit tells you to–if, in fact, God's Spirit lives in you. Whoever does not have the Spirit of Christ does not belong to him. ¹⁰But if Christ lives in you, the Spirit is life for you[j] because you have been put right with God, even though your bodies are going to die because of sin. ¹¹If the Spirit of God, who raised Jesus from death, lives in you, then he who raised Christ from death will also give life to your mortal bodies by the presence of his Spirit in you.

¹²So then, my friends, we have an obligation, but it is not to live as our human nature wants us to. ¹³For if you live according to your human nature, you are going to die; but if by the Spirit you put to death your sinful actions, you will live. ¹⁴Those who are led by God's Spirit are God's children. ¹⁵For the Spirit that God has given you does not make you slaves and cause you to be afraid; instead, the Spirit makes you God's children, and by the Spirit's power we cry out to God, "Father! my Father!" ¹⁶God's Spirit joins himself to our spirits to declare that we are God's children. ¹⁷Since we are his children, we will possess the blessings he keeps for his people, and we will also possess with Christ what God has kept for him; for if we share Christ's suffering, we will also share his glory.

The Future Glory

¹⁸I consider that what we suffer at this present time cannot be compared at all with the glory that is going to be revealed to us. ¹⁹All of creation waits with eager longing for God to reveal his children. ²⁰For creation was condemned to lose its purpose, not of its own will, but because God willed it to be so. Yet there was the hope ²¹that creation itself would one day be set free from its slavery to decay and would share

j the Spirit is life for you; or your spirit is alive.

面的罪，把罪除去。⁴上帝這樣做是要使法律的正當要求實現在我們這些不服從本性、只順服聖靈的人身上。⁵因為，服從本性的人意向於本性的事；順服聖靈的人意向於聖靈的事。⁶意向於本性就是死；意向於聖靈就有生命和平安。⁷所以，意向於本性的人就是跟上帝為敵；因為他不順服上帝的法則，事實上也不能順服。⁸服從本性的人不能夠得到上帝的喜歡。

⁹至於你們，既然上帝的靈住在你們裏面，你們的生活就不受本性的支配，只受聖靈的管束。沒有基督的靈的人就不屬於基督。¹⁰可是，基督若住在你們裏面，縱使你們的身體將因罪而死，上帝的靈要使你們活⑨，因為上帝已經使你們成為義人了。¹¹上帝的靈使耶穌從死裏復活；如果這靈住在你們裏面，那麼，這位使基督從死裏復活的上帝，也要藉着住在你們裏面的聖靈，把生命賜給你們那必朽的身體。

¹²因此，弟兄姊妹們，我們是負債的，但不是欠本性的債，得受本性的支配。¹³你們若服從本性，一定死亡；你們若依靠聖靈治死罪行，一定存活。¹⁴凡是被上帝的靈導引的人都是上帝的兒女。¹⁵因為，上帝所賜的靈不是要奴役你們，使你們仍在恐懼中，而是要使你們有上帝兒女的名份。藉着聖靈，我們向上帝呼叫：「阿爸！我的父親！」¹⁶上帝的靈和我們的靈一同證實我們是上帝的兒女。¹⁷既然是上帝的兒女，我們就享有上帝為他的子民所預備的福澤，也要跟基督同享上帝所為他保留的；因為，只要我們分擔基督的苦難，我們也要分享他的榮耀。

將來的榮耀

¹⁸我認為，我們現在的苦難跟將來要顯明給我們的榮耀相比是算不了甚麼的。¹⁹一切被造的都熱切地盼望着上帝的榮耀從他的兒女們顯示出來。²⁰因為整個被造的變成虛空，不是出於本意，而是出於上帝的旨意。然而，被造的仍然盼望着，²¹有一天能擺脫那會朽壞的枷鎖，得以跟上帝的兒女分享光

⑨「上帝的靈要使你們活」或譯「你們的靈要活着」。

the glorious freedom of the children of God. [22]For we know that up to the present time all of creation groans with pain, like the pain of childbirth. [23]But it is not just creation alone which groans; we who have the Spirit as the first of God's gifts also groan within ourselves as we wait for God to make us his children and[k] set our whole being free. [24]For it was by hope that we were saved; but if we see what we hope for, then it is not really hope. For who of us hopes for something we see? [25]But if we hope for what we do not see, we wait for it with patience.

[26]In the same way the Spirit also comes to help us, weak as we are. For we do not know how we ought to pray; the Spirit himself pleads with God for us in groans that words cannot express. [27]And God, who sees into our hearts, knows what the thought of the Spirit is; because the Spirit pleads with God on behalf of his people and in accordance with his will.

[28]We know that in all things God works for good with those who love him,[l] those whom he has called according to his purpose. [29]Those whom God had already chosen he also set apart to become like his Son, so that the Son would be the first among many believers. [30]And so those whom God set apart, he called; and those he called, he put right with himself, and he shared his glory with them.

God's Love in Christ Jesus

[31]In view of all this, what can we say? If God is for us, who can be against us? [32]Certainly not God, who did not even keep back his own Son, but offered him for us all! He gave us his Son –will he not also freely give us all things? [33]Who will accuse God's chosen people? God himself declares them not guilty! [34]Who, then, will condemn them? Not Christ Jesus, who died, or rather, who was raised to life and is at the right side of God, pleading with him for us! [35]Who, then, can separate us from the love of Christ? Can trouble do it, or hardship or persecution or hunger or poverty or danger or death? [36]As the scripture says,

"For your sake we are in danger of death at
    all times;
    we are treated like sheep that are going to
    be slaughtered."

[37]No, in all these things we have complete vic-

k *Some manuscripts do not have* make us his children and.
l in all things God works for good with those who love him; *some manuscripts have* all things work for good for those who love God.

榮的自由。[22]我們知道,直到現在,一切被造的都在呻吟,好像經歷生產的陣痛。[23]不只被造的是這樣,我們這些得到初熟果子,就是得到聖靈的人,也在心裏歎息呻吟,等候上帝收養我們作他的兒女⑩,使整個的自我得自由。[24]因為,由於盼望,我們得救。那看得見的盼望不算是盼望。誰盼望他所看得見的呢?[25]如果我們盼望那看不見的,我們就會忍耐等候。

[26]同樣,我們的軟弱有聖靈幫助。我們原不知道該怎樣禱告;可是聖靈親自用言語所不能表達的歎息為我們向上帝祈求。[27]洞察人心的上帝知道聖靈的意思,因為聖靈依照上帝的旨意,替他的子民祈求。

[28]我們知道,上帝使萬事互相效力,叫愛上帝的人——就是他按照自己的旨意呼召的人都得益處⑪。[29]因為上帝預知他們,把他們預先揀選出來,使他們跟他的兒子有相同的特質,好讓他的兒子在信徒大家庭中居首位。[30]上帝預先揀選的人,他呼召他們;他呼召的人,他宣佈他們為義人;他宣佈為義人的人,他讓他們分享榮耀。

上帝的愛從耶穌表現出來

[31]既然這樣,我們該怎麼說呢?只要上帝在我們這一邊,誰能敵對我們呢?[32]他連自己的兒子都不顧惜,給了我們眾人。既然這樣,他不會也把萬物白白地賜給我們嗎?[33]誰會控告上帝所揀選的人呢?上帝已經宣佈他們無罪了?[34]那麼,誰還會定他們的罪呢?不是基督耶穌!他是那位死了,其實,我應該說是那位已經復活、現在正在上帝的右邊替我們向上帝祈求的![35]既然這樣,誰能夠使我們跟基督的愛隔絕呢?是患難嗎?困苦嗎?迫害嗎?飢餓嗎?貧窮嗎?危險嗎?刀劍嗎?[36]像聖經所說:

為了你的緣故,我們整天被置於死地;
人把我們當作待宰的羊。

[37]都不是。在這一切事情上面,我們靠著

⑩有些古卷沒有「收養我們作他的兒女」。
⑪「上帝……益處」或譯「上帝與愛他的人,就是他按照自己的旨意呼召的,一同工作,使萬事都有益處」;另有些古卷作「萬事互相效力,使那些愛上帝的人,就是他按照自己旨意呼召的人,都有益處」。

tory through him who loved us! [38]For I am certain that nothing can separate us from his love: neither death nor life, neither angels nor other heavenly rulers or powers, neither the present nor the future, [39]neither the world above nor the world below–there is nothing in all creation that will ever be able to separate us from the love of God which is ours through Christ Jesus our Lord.

God and His People

9 I am speaking the truth; I belong to Christ and I do not lie. My conscience, ruled by the Holy Spirit, also assures me that I am not lying [2]when I say how great is my sorrow, how endless the pain in my heart [3]for my people, my own flesh and blood! For their sake I could wish that I myself were under God's curse and separated from Christ. [4]They are God's people; he made them his children and revealed his glory to them; he made his covenants[m] with them and gave them the Law; they have the true worship; they have received God's promises; [5]they are descended from the famous Hebrew ancestors; and Christ, as a human being, belongs to their race. May God, who rules over all, be praised forever![n] Amen.

[6]I am not saying that the promise of God has failed; for not all the people of Israel are the people of God. [7]Nor are all of Abraham's descendants the children of God. God said to Abraham, "It is through Isaac that you will have the descendants I promised you." [8]This means that the children born in the usual way[o] are not the children of God; instead, the children born as a result of God's promise are regarded as the true descendants. [9]For God's promise was made in these words: "At the right time[p] I will come back, and Sarah will have a son."

[10]And this is not all. For Rebecca's two sons had the same father, our ancestor Isaac. [11-12]But in order that the choice of one son might be completely the result of God's own purpose, God said to her, "The older will serve the younger." He said this before they were born, before they had done anything either good or bad; so God's choice was based on his call, and not on anything they had done. [13]As the scripture says, "I loved Jacob, but I hated Esau."

[14]Shall we say, then, that God is unjust? Not

m covenants; *some manuscripts have* covenant.

n May God, who rules over all, be praised forever!; *or* And may he, who is God ruling over all, be praised forever!

o CHILDREN BORN IN THE USUAL WAY: *This refers to the descendants Abraham had through Ishmael, his son by Hagar (see Ga 4.22-23).*

p At the right time; *or* At this time next year.

愛我們的主已經獲得完全的勝利！[38]因為我確信，甚麼都不能夠使我們跟上帝的愛隔絕。不管是死，是活；是天使，是靈界的掌權者；是現在，是將來；[39]是高天，是深淵；在整個被造的宇宙中，沒有任何事物能夠把我們跟上帝藉着我們的主基督耶穌所給我們的愛隔絕起來。

上帝和他的選民

9 我說真實的話；我屬於基督，我不撒謊。我的良心在聖靈的光照下也證實我沒有撒謊：[2]我的憂愁多麼沉重，我心裏無限傷痛！[3]為了我的同胞，我骨肉之親，縱使我自己被上帝詛咒，跟基督隔絕，我也願意。[4]他們是上帝的選民；上帝使他們有兒女的名份，分享他的榮耀。上帝與他們立約，賜給他們法律；他們有敬拜上帝的知識，也接受了他的應許。[5]他們是族長們的子孫，按照身世說，基督和他們是同一族的。願那統治萬有的上帝[12]永遠得到頌讚，阿們！

[6]我並不是說上帝的應許已經落空。因為，以色列人不都是上帝的選民；[7]亞伯拉罕的子孫也不都是他的真兒女。上帝曾對亞伯拉罕說：「惟有從以撒生的才算是你的子孫。」[8]這就是說，從自然的生育過程所生的，不就是上帝的兒女；惟有從上帝的應許所生的才算是上帝的兒女。[9]因為上帝的應許是這樣說的：「在時機成熟的時候[13]，我要回來，莎拉要生一個兒子。」

[10]不但這樣，麗百加的兩個兒子都是從同一個父親，就是我們的祖先以撒生的。[11-12]然而，為了要表示他確實根據自己的旨意揀選了其中的一個兒子，上帝對麗百加說：「那大兒子要服事小兒子。」他說這話的時候，他們還沒有出生，還沒有行善或作惡；可見上帝的揀選是出於自己的旨意，跟他們的行為沒有關係。[13]正像聖經所說：「我愛雅各，勝過愛以掃。」

[14]那麼，我們可以說上帝不公平嗎？當然

[12]「願那統治萬有的上帝」或譯「願基督，就是那統治萬有的上帝」。

[13]「時機成熟的時候」或譯「明年這個時候」。

at all. ¹⁵For he said to Moses, "I will have mercy on anyone I wish; I will take pity on anyone I wish." ¹⁶So then, everything depends, not on what we humans want or do, but only on God's mercy. ¹⁷For the scripture says to the king of Egypt, "I made you king in order to use you to show my power and to spread my fame over the whole world." ¹⁸So then, God has mercy on anyone he wishes, and he makes stubborn anyone he wishes.

God's Anger and Mercy

¹⁹But one of you will say to me, "If this is so, how can God find fault with anyone? Who can resist God's will?" ²⁰But who are you, my friend, to talk back to God? A clay pot does not ask the man who made it, "Why did you make me like this?" ²¹After all, the man who makes the pots has the right to use the clay as he wishes, and to make two pots from the same lump of clay, one for special occasions and the other for ordinary use.

²²And the same is true of what God has done. He wanted to show his anger and to make his power known. But he was very patient in enduring those who were the objects of his anger, who were doomed to destruction. ²³And he also wanted to reveal his abundant glory, which was poured out on us who are the objects of his mercy, those of us whom he has prepared to receive his glory. ²⁴For we are the people he called, not only from among the Jews but also from among the Gentiles. ²⁵This is what he says in the book of Hosea:

"The people who were not mine
   I will call 'My People.'
The nation that I did not love
   I will call 'My Beloved.'
²⁶And in the very place where they were told,
    'You are not my people,'
   there they will be called the children of the
    living God."

²⁷And Isaiah exclaims about Israel: "Even if the people of Israel are as many as the grains of sand by the sea, yet only a few of them will be saved; ²⁸for the Lord will quickly settle his full account with the world." ²⁹It is as Isaiah had said before, "If the Lord Almighty had not left us some descendants, we would have become like Sodom, we would have been like Gomorrah."

Israel and the Gospel

³⁰So we say that the Gentiles, who were not trying to put themselves right with God, were put right with him through faith; ³¹while God's people, who were seeking a law that would put them right with God, did not find it. ³²And why

不可以。¹⁵因為他對摩西說過:「我要憐憫誰就憐憫誰,要體恤誰就體恤誰。」¹⁶可見上帝的揀選不是根據人的意志或努力,而是出於他的憐憫。¹⁷聖經中,上帝對法老說:「我立你作王,為要用你來彰顯我的權能,使我的名傳遍天下。」¹⁸這樣說來,上帝要憐憫誰就憐憫誰;要使誰頑固就使誰頑固。

上帝的義憤和憐憫

¹⁹或許你會對我說:「既然這樣,上帝怎麼能責怪人?誰能抗拒他的旨意呢?」²⁰可是朋友啊,你是誰,竟敢跟上帝頂嘴呢?一個瓦器怎麼能對造它的人說:「為甚麼把我造成這樣子呢?」²¹陶匠畢竟有權拿泥土來造他所要造的;他可以用同一團泥土製造兩個器皿,一個貴重的,一個普通的。

²²上帝所做的也是這樣。他要顯示他的義憤,彰顯他的權能。因此他以耐心寬容他發怒的對象,就是那些本來應該被擊碎的器皿。²³他也要把他豐富的榮耀向我們顯明出來。我們是他憐憫的對象,而且是他所預備來接受他的榮耀的人。²⁴因為我們不但是他從猶太人中,也是從外邦人中,呼召出來的。²⁵這就是他在何西阿書上所說:

本來不是我子民的,
我要稱他們為「我的子民」;
本來我所不愛的邦國,
我要稱它為「我所愛的」。
²⁶在哪地方我曾經對他們說:
你們不是我的子民;
也在那地方他們要被稱為:
永生上帝的兒女!

²⁷關於以色列人,以賽亞曾經呼喊:「雖然以色列人像海沙那麼多,但只有剩餘的少數得救,²⁸因為主將迅速而徹底地審判全人類。」²⁹正如以賽亞從前說過:「要是主—萬軍的統帥不為我們留下一些後代,我們早已像所多瑪、蛾摩拉那樣了。」

以色列人和福音

³⁰那麼,我們該怎麼說呢?那些本來不尋求上帝的義的外邦人,卻因信而得以成為義人;³¹而那些尋求藉着法律得以成為義人的選民,反而不能達到目的。³²為甚麼呢?因

not? Because they did not depend on faith but on what they did. And so they stumbled over the "stumbling stone" [33]that the scripture speaks of:

"Look, I place in Zion a stone
that will make people stumble,
a rock that will make them fall.
But whoever believes in him will not be
disappointed."

10My friends, how I wish with all my heart that my own people might be saved! How I pray to God for them! [2]I can assure you that they are deeply devoted to God; but their devotion is not based on true knowledge. [3]They have not known the way in which God puts people right with himself, and instead, they have tried to set up their own way; and so they did not submit themselves to God's way of putting people right. [4]For Christ has brought the Law to an end, so that everyone who believes is put right with God.

Salvation Is for All

[5]Moses wrote this about being put right with God by obeying the Law: "Whoever obeys the commands of the Law will live." [6]But what the scripture says about being put right with God through faith is this: "You are not to ask yourself, Who will go up into heaven?" (that is, to bring Christ down). [7]"Nor are you to ask, Who will go down into the world below?" (that is, to bring Christ up from death). [8]What it says is this: "God's message is near you, on your lips and in your heart"–that is, the message of faith that we preach. [9]If you confess that Jesus is Lord and believe that God raised him from death, you will be saved. [10]For it is by our faith that we are put right with God; it is by our confession that we are saved. [11]The scripture says, "Whoever believes in him will not be disappointed." [12]This includes everyone, because there is no difference between Jews and Gentiles; God is the same Lord of all and richly blesses all who call to him. [13]As the scripture says, "Everyone who calls out to the Lord for help will be saved."

[14]But how can they call to him for help if they have not believed? And how can they believe if they have not heard the message? And how can they hear if the message is not proclaimed? [15]And how can the message be proclaimed if the messengers are not sent out? As the scripture says, "How wonderful is the coming of messengers who bring good news!" [16]But not all have accepted the Good News. Isaiah himself said, "Lord, who believed our message?" [17]So then, faith comes from hearing the message, and the message comes through

為他們不倚靠信心,而倚靠行為,結果正跌在那「絆腳石」上面。[33]正像聖經所說:

瞧!我在錫安放着一塊絆腳的石頭,
是絆倒他們的石塊!
然而,信靠他的人不至於失望。

10弟兄姊妹們,我多麼熱切地盼望我的同胞能夠得救,也為着這件事不斷地向上帝懇求![2]我可以證明他們對上帝確實很熱心,可是他們的熱心並不是以真知識為基礎。[3]他們不明白上帝的義,想自找門路,而沒有順服上帝的義。[4]其實,基督已經終止了法律的功效,使一切信他的人都得以成為義人。

救恩給全人類

[5]關於藉着遵守法律得以成為義人這件事,摩西曾經這樣寫:「那遵守法律命令的人將因法律而存活。」[6]但是,因信得以成為義人這件事,聖經這樣說:「你不要自問:誰要到天上去?(也就是說,去帶基督下來。)[7]也不要問:誰要到陰間去?(也就是說,把基督從死人中領上來。)」[8]這些話的意思是:「上帝的信息離你不遠,就在你口裏,就在你心裏。」換句話說,就是在我們所宣講信的信息裏面。[9]如果你口裏宣認耶穌為主,心裏信上帝使他從死裏復活,你就會得救。[10]因為我們心裏這樣信,就得以成為義人,口裏這樣宣認,就會得救。[11]聖經上說:「信他的人不至於失望。」[12]這話是指所有的人說的,因為沒有猶太人跟外邦人的區別;上帝是萬人的主,他要豐豐富富地賜福給所有呼求他的人。[13]正像聖經所說:「凡呼求主名的人必定得救。」

[14]可是,他們沒有信,怎能呼求他呢?沒有聽,怎能信呢?沒有傳,怎能聽呢?[15]沒有奉差派,怎能傳呢?正像聖經所說:「傳福音的人,他們的腳蹤多麼佳美!」[16]然而,並不是每一個人都接受福音。以賽亞曾經說過:「主啊,誰相信我們所傳的信息呢?」[17]可見信是從聽而來的,而聽是從基

preaching Christ.

18But I ask: Is it true that they did not hear the message? Of course they did–for as the scripture says:

"The sound of their voice went out to all the world;

their words reached the ends of the earth."

19Again I ask: Did the people of Israel not understand? Moses himself is the first one to answer:

"I will use a so-called nation to make my people jealous;

and by means of a nation of fools I will make my people angry."

20And Isaiah is even bolder when he says,

"I was found by those who were not looking for me;

I appeared to those who were not asking for me."

21But concerning Israel he says, "All day long I held out my hands to welcome a disobedient and rebellious people."

God's Mercy on Israel

11 I ask, then: Did God reject his own people? Certainly not! I myself am an Israelite, a descendant of Abraham, a member of the tribe of Benjamin. 2God has not rejected his people, whom he chose from the beginning. You know what the scripture says in the passage where Elijah pleads with God against Israel: 3"Lord, they have killed your prophets and torn down your altars; I am the only one left, and they are trying to kill me." 4What answer did God give him? "I have kept for myself seven thousand men who have not worshiped the false god Baal." 5It is the same way now: there is a small number left of those whom God has chosen because of his grace. 6His choice is based on his grace, not on what they have done. For if God's choice were based on what people do, then his grace would not be real grace.

7What then? The people of Israel did not find what they were looking for. It was only the small group that God chose who found it; the rest grew deaf to God's call. 8As the scripture says, "God made their minds and hearts dull; to this very day they cannot see or hear." 9And David says,

"May they be caught and trapped at their feasts;

may they fall, may they be punished!

10May their eyes be blinded so that they cannot see;

and make them bend under their troubles at all times."

11I ask, then: When the Jews stumbled, did

督的話語來的。

18 可是我要問：他們眞的沒有聽見過信息嗎？當然聽見過。正像聖經所說：

他們的聲音已傳遍人間；

他們的言語已傳佈天涯。

19我要再問：以色列人眞的不知道嗎？首先，摩西用上帝的話回答了這個問題：

我要以「不算爲民」的民引起你們的嫉妒，

用愚昧的國來激動你們的怒氣。

20以賽亞更大膽地說過：

我讓沒有尋找我的人找到，

向沒有求問我的人顯現。

21但關於以色列人，他說：

我整天伸出手，

要那悖逆剛愎的人民跟我言歸於好。

上帝對以色列人的慈愛

11 那麼，我要問：上帝棄絕了他的子民嗎？當然沒有！我自己也是一個以色列人，是亞伯拉罕的後代，屬於便雅憫支族的。2上帝沒有棄絕他從遠古就揀選了的子民。你們知道，聖經記載：當以利亞向上帝控告以色列人的時候，3他說：「主啊，他們殺了你的先知，拆了你的祭壇；只剩下我一個人，他們還想殺我。」4上帝怎樣回答他呢？他說：「我爲我自己留下七千人，他們都沒有跪拜過假神巴力。」5現在的情形也是一樣：上帝出於自己的恩典所揀選的人只剩下少數。6上帝的揀選是出於恩典，而不是根據人的行爲；如果是根據人的行爲，所謂恩典就不是眞的恩典了。

7 結果怎樣呢？結果是以色列人得不到他們所尋求的，倒是上帝所揀選的少數人找到了；其餘的人對上帝的呼召充耳不聞。8正如聖經所說：「上帝使他們的心靈痲木；直到現在，他們的眼睛不能看，耳朶不能聽。」9大衛也說過：

願他們在宴會上陷入圈套，給抓住了；

願他們絆倒了，遭受懲罰！

10 願他們的眼睛昏暗，不能看見；

願他們彎腰駝背，無休無止！

11 那麼，我要問：猶太人失足跌倒，就完

they fall to their ruin? By no means! Because they sinned, salvation has come to the Gentiles, to make the Jews jealous of them. [12]The sin of the Jews brought rich blessings to the world, and their spiritual poverty brought rich blessings to the Gentiles. Then, how much greater the blessings will be when the complete number of Jews is included!

The Salvation of the Gentiles

[13]I am speaking now to you Gentiles: As long as I am an apostle to the Gentiles, I will take pride in my work. [14]Perhaps I can make the people of my own race jealous, and so be able to save some of them. [15]For when they were rejected, all other people were changed from God's enemies into his friends. What will it be, then, when they are accepted? It will be life for the dead!

[16]If the first piece of bread is given to God, then the whole loaf is his also; and if the roots of a tree are offered to God, the branches are his also. [17]Some of the branches of the cultivated olive tree have been broken off, and a branch of a wild olive tree has been joined to it. You Gentiles are like that wild olive tree, and now you share the strong spiritual life of the Jews. [18]So then, you must not despise those who were broken off like branches. How can you be proud? You are just a branch, you don't support the roots–the roots support you.

[19]But you will say, "Yes, but the branches were broken off to make room for me." [20]That is true. They were broken off because they did not believe, while you remain in place because you do believe. But do not be proud of it; instead, be afraid. [21]God did not spare the Jews, who are like natural branches; do you think he will spare you? [22]Here we see how kind and how severe God is. He is severe toward those who have fallen, but kind to you–if you continue in his kindness. But if you do not, you too will be broken off. [23]And if the Jews abandon their unbelief, they will be put back in the place where they were; for God is able to do that. [24]You Gentiles are like the branch of a wild olive tree that is broken off and then, contrary to nature, is joined to a cultivated olive tree. The Jews are like this cultivated tree; and it will be much easier for God to join these broken-off branches to their own tree again.

God's Mercy on All

[25]There is a secret truth, my friends, which I want you to know, for it will keep you from thinking how wise you are. It is that the stubbornness of the people of Israel is not perma-

全毀滅了嗎?當然不!由於他們的過犯,拯救便臨到了外邦人,使猶太人嫉妒發憤起來。[12]猶太人的過犯給世界帶來了豐富的福澤;他們靈性上的貧乏反而使外邦人富足。那麼,如果猶太人全體都包括在上帝的拯救裏面,這豈不帶來更豐富的福澤嗎?

上帝拯救外邦人

[13]現在我向你們外邦人說話:既然我是外邦人的使徒,我當然看重我事奉的職務。[14]或者我也可以激發同胞的嫉妒發憤的心,藉此拯救他們當中的一些人。[15]如果他們被遺棄反而使世人成為上帝的朋友,那麼,他們被接納的時候,已死的人不是會重獲生命嗎?

[16]如果把麵團的頭一塊獻給了上帝,那麼,全團也就是獻給他了。如果把樹根獻給了上帝,那麼,連樹的枝子也是獻給他了。[17]有些橄欖樹的枝子給折了下來,而野生的橄欖樹的枝子被接上去。你外邦人就像野橄欖樹,現在分享著猶太人的豐富的生命力。[18]所以,你不可輕看那些像枝子給折下來的人。你不過是枝子,怎麼可以自誇呢?不是你在支持樹根,而是樹根在支持你!

[19]也許你要說:「枝子給折了下來,為的是讓我能接上去。」[20]這話不錯。他們給折下來,因為他們不信;你站立得住,因為你信。但是你不可驕傲,要存著警戒的心。[21]猶太人是原有的枝子;上帝既然沒有饒恕他們,你以為他會饒恕你嗎?[22]從這裏我們看出,上帝既仁慈又嚴厲。對於那些失足跌倒的人,他是嚴厲的;對於你,他是仁慈的,只要你繼續生活在他的慈愛中;否則,你也會被折下來的。[23]至於猶太人,如果他們不固執他們的不信,就可以被恢復到原來的地位上,因為上帝能夠把他們再接上去。[24]你外邦人好比給折下來的野橄欖樹的枝子,不自然地被接在好橄欖樹上。猶太人就像經過培植的樹;上帝把從這樹折下來的枝子再接在原來的樹上,不是更容易嗎?

上帝的慈愛普及萬民

[25]弟兄姊妹們,有一個奧祕的真理,我希望你們知道,免得你們老是覺得自己聰明。這真理是:部分的以色列人頑固,只是要等

nent, but will last only until the complete number of Gentiles comes to God. ²⁶And this is how all Israel will be saved. As the scripture says,

> "The Savior will come from Zion
> and remove all wickedness from the
> descendants of Jacob.
²⁷I will make this covenant with them
> when I take away their sins."

²⁸Because they reject the Good News, the Jews are God's enemies for the sake of you Gentiles. But because of God's choice, they are his friends because of their ancestors. ²⁹For God does not change his mind about whom he chooses and blesses. ³⁰As for you Gentiles, you disobeyed God in the past; but now you have received God's mercy because the Jews were disobedient. ³¹In the same way, because of the mercy that you have received, the Jews now disobey God, in order that they also may now^q receive God's mercy. ³²For God has made all people prisoners of disobedience, so that he might show mercy to them all.

Praise to God

³³How great are God's riches! How deep are his wisdom and knowledge! Who can explain his decisions? Who can understand his ways? ³⁴As the scripture says,

> "Who knows the mind of the Lord?
> Who is able to give him advice?
³⁵Who has ever given him anything,
> so that he had to pay it back?"

³⁶For all things were created by him, and all things exist through him and for him. To God be the glory forever! Amen.

Life in God's Service

12So then, my friends, because of God's great mercy to us I appeal to you: Offer yourselves as a living sacrifice to God, dedicated to his service and pleasing to him. This is the true worship that you should offer. ²Do not conform yourselves to the standards of this world, but let God transform you inwardly by a complete change of your mind. Then you will be able to know the will of God–what is good and is pleasing to him and is perfect.

³And because of God's gracious gift to me I say to every one of you: Do not think of yourself more highly than you should. Instead, be modest in your thinking, and judge yourself according to the amount of faith that God has given you. ⁴We have many parts in the one body, and all these parts have different func-

q *Some manuscripts do not have* now.

到外邦人全數都歸向上帝⑭。²⁶到那時全部的以色列人終必得救。正如聖經所說：

> 拯救者要從錫安出來；
> 他要除掉雅各子孫的罪惡。
²⁷ 上帝說：
> 這就是我要與他們訂立的約；
> 那時候，我要赦免他們的罪。

²⁸ 猶太人拒絕了福音，成為上帝的敵人，結果使你們外邦人得到益處。但是，由於上帝的選擇，又根據上帝對族長們的應許，猶太人仍然是上帝的朋友。²⁹因為上帝的選召和恩典是從不改變的。³⁰從前你們外邦人不順從上帝；現在因猶太人的不順服，你們倒得了上帝的慈愛。³¹同樣，因為你們得了慈愛，猶太人現在不順服，為的是他們也能夠在這時候得到上帝的慈愛。³²上帝使全人類被囚禁在不順服當中，好對他們顯示他的慈愛。

頌讚上帝

³³ 上帝的恩典多麼豐富！他的智慧和知識多麼深奧！誰能解釋他的決斷？誰能探測他的道路？³⁴正像聖經所說：

> 誰知道主的心意？
> 誰能夠替他出主意？
³⁵ 誰給過他甚麼，
> 使他不得不償還？

³⁶ 因為萬物都出自他，藉着他，歸於他。願榮耀歸於上帝，直到永遠！阿們。

事奉上帝的生活

12所以，弟兄姊妹們，既然上帝這樣憐恤我們，我勸你們把自己當作活的祭物獻給上帝，專心事奉他，蒙他喜悅。這就是你們應該獻上的真實敬拜。²不要被這世界同化，要讓上帝改造你們，更新你們的心思意念，好明察甚麼是他的旨意，知道甚麼是良善、完全，可蒙悅納的。

³ 憑着上帝給我的恩惠，我要對你們各位說：不要把自己看得太高，倒要謙恭自守，各人按照上帝所賜給他的信心來衡量自己。⁴一個身體是由好些肢體構成的，而每一個

⑭「全數都歸向上帝」或譯「歸向上帝的數目滿了」。

tions. [5]In the same way, though we are many, we are one body in union with Christ, and we are all joined to each other as different parts of one body. [6]So we are to use our different gifts in accordance with the grace that God has given us. If our gift is to speak God's message, we should do it according to the faith that we have; [7]if it is to serve, we should serve; if it is to teach, we should teach; [8]if it is to encourage others, we should do so. Whoever shares with others should do it generously; whoever has authority should work hard; whoever shows kindness to others should do it cheerfully.

[9]Love must be completely sincere. Hate what is evil, hold on to what is good. [10]Love one another warmly as Christians, and be eager to show respect for one another. [11]Work hard and do not be lazy. Serve the Lord with a heart full of devotion. [12]Let your hope keep you joyful, be patient in your troubles, and pray at all times. [13]Share your belongings with your needy fellow Christians, and open your homes to strangers.

[14]Ask God to bless those who persecute you—yes, ask him to bless, not to curse. [15]Be happy with those who are happy, weep with those who weep. [16]Have the same concern for everyone. Do not be proud, but accept humble duties.[r] Do not think of yourselves as wise.

[17]If someone has done you wrong, do not repay him with a wrong. Try to do what everyone considers to be good. [18]Do everything possible on your part to live in peace with everybody. [19]Never take revenge, my friends, but instead let God's anger do it. For the scripture says, "I will take revenge, I will pay back, says the Lord." [20]Instead, as the scripture says: "If your enemies are hungry, feed them; if they are thirsty, give them a drink; for by doing this you will make them burn with shame." [21]Do not let evil defeat you; instead, conquer evil with good.

Duties toward State Authorities

13 Everyone must obey state authorities, because no authority exists without God's permission, and the existing authorities have been put there by God. [2]Whoever opposes the existing authority opposes what God has ordered; and anyone who does so will bring judgment on himself. [3]For rulers are not to be feared by those who do good, but by those who do evil. Would you like to be unafraid of those in authority? Then do what is good, and they will praise you, [4]because they are God's servants working for your own good. But if you do evil, then be afraid of them, because their

r accept humble duties; *or* make friends with humble people.

肢體有它不同的功用。[5]同樣,雖然我們有許多人,我們在基督裏成為一體,各自彼此聯絡,構成身體不同的部分。[6]所以,我們要按照上帝給我們的恩惠,好好地運用不同的恩賜,做應該做的事。如果我們的恩賜是傳講信息,應該照着信心的程度傳講;[7]是服務,應該服務;是教導,應該教導;[8]是勸勉,應該勸勉;是施與,應該慷慨;作領袖,應該不辭辛勞;是憐憫人,應該高高興興。

[9]愛人要真誠。要厭棄邪惡,持守良善。[10]要以手足之情相親相愛;要竭誠互相敬重。[11]不要懶惰,要努力工作,以火熱的心事奉主。[12]在盼望中要喜樂,在患難中要忍耐,禱告要恆切。[13]要讓貧窮的弟兄分享你所有的;要接待異鄉人。

[14]要祝福迫害你的人;是的,要祝福,不要詛咒。[15]要跟喜樂的人同喜樂,跟哭泣的人同哭泣。[16]無論對甚麼人,要同心彼此關懷。不要心驕氣傲,倒要俯就卑微;也不要自以為聰明。

[17]不要以惡報惡;人家看為美好的事,要踴躍去做。[18]要盡你的全力跟大家和睦相處。[19]朋友們,不可為自己復仇,寧可讓上帝的忿怒替你伸寃,因為聖經說:「主說:伸寃在我;我必報應。」[20]聖經又說:「如果你的仇敵餓了,就給他吃,渴了,就給他喝;你這樣做會使他羞慚交加。」[21]所以,不要被惡所勝,要以善勝惡。

對政府的責任

13 人人都應該服從國家的權力機構,因為權力的存在是上帝所准許的;當政者的權力是從上帝來的。[2]所以,抗拒當政者就是抗拒上帝的命令;這樣的人難免受審判。[3]統治者不是要使行善的人懼怕,而是要使作惡的人懼怕。你要不怕當政者,就得行善,他就會嘉許你;[4]因為他是上帝所使用的人,他的工作是對你有益處的。如果你作惡,你就得怕他,因為他的懲罰並非兒戲。

power to punish is real. They are God's servants and carry out God's punishment on those who do evil. 5For this reason you must obey the authorities–not just because of God's punishment, but also as a matter of conscience.

6That is also why you pay taxes, because the authorities are working for God when they fulfill their duties. 7Pay, then, what you owe them; pay them your personal and property taxes, and show respect and honor for them all.

Duties toward One Another

8Be under obligation to no one–the only obligation you have is to love one another. Whoever does this has obeyed the Law. 9The commandments, "Do not commit adultery; do not commit murder; do not steal; do not desire what belongs to someone else"–all these, and any others besides, are summed up in the one command, "Love your neighbor as you love yourself." 10If you love others, you will never do them wrong; to love, then, is to obey the whole Law.

11You must do this, because you know that the time has come for you to wake up from your sleep. For the moment when we will be saved is closer now than it was when we first believed. 12The night is nearly over, day is almost here. Let us stop doing the things that belong to the dark, and let us take up weapons for fighting in the light. 13Let us conduct ourselves properly, as people who live in the light of day–no orgies or drunkenness, no immorality or indecency, no fighting or jealousy. 14But take up the weapons of the Lord Jesus Christ, and stop paying attention to your sinful nature and satisfying its desires.

Do Not Judge Others

14 Welcome those who are weak in faith, but do not argue with them about their personal opinions. 2Some people's faith allows them to eat anything, but the person who is weak in the faith eats only vegetables. 3The person who will eat anything is not to despise the one who doesn't; while the one who eats only vegetables is not to pass judgment on the one who will eat anything; for God has accepted that person. 4Who are you to judge the servants of someone else? It is their own Master who will decide whether they succeed or fail. And they will succeed, because the Lord is able to make them succeed.

5Some people think that a certain day is more important than other days, while others think that all days are the same. We each

他是上帝所使用的人,要執行上帝對那些作惡的人的懲罰。5所以,你們必須服從當政者,不但是爲了怕上帝的懲罰,也是爲了良心。

6 你們納稅,也是爲了同樣的理由,因爲當政者在執行任務的時候是爲上帝工作。7所以,要還清一切所虧欠的:該貢獻的,要貢獻;該繳納的,要繳納;該懼怕的,要懼怕;該尊敬的,要尊敬。

對別人的責任

8 千萬不要負債!只有彼此相愛是你們該負的債。那愛別人的,就是成全了法律。9法律的命令規定:「不可姦淫;不可殺人;不可盜竊;不可貪心。」這一切以及其他的命令都包括在「愛人如己」這一條命令裏面了。10一個愛別人的人,不會做出傷害他人的事。所以,愛成全了全部的法律。

11 你們必須這樣做,因爲你們知道這是甚麼時候;這是你們該從睡眠中醒過來的時候。現在我們比剛信的時候更接近上帝的拯救。12黑夜快要過去,白天就要來臨。我們不可再做暗昧的事;要拿起武器,準備在日光下作戰。13我們行事爲人要光明正大,就像生活在白晝中的人一樣。不可縱慾醉酒,不可邪淫放蕩,不可紛爭嫉妒。14但是,你們要以主耶穌基督裝備自己;不要只顧滿足肉體的情慾!

不可評斷人

14 信心軟弱的人,你們要接納他,即使他有不同的見解,也不要跟他爭辯。2有信心的人甚麼東西都吃;信心軟弱的人只吃蔬菜。3甚麼東西都吃的人不要輕視那不吃的;只吃蔬菜的人也不要評斷甚麼都吃的,因爲上帝已經接納了他。4你是誰,竟去評斷人家的僕人?他的主人不能判斷他的成敗得失嗎?何況,主能夠幫助他,使他有所成就。

5 有人認爲這一天比另一天重要;也有人認爲所有的日子都同樣重要。每一個人都應

should firmly make up our own minds. [6]Those who think highly of a certain day do so in honor of the Lord; those who will eat anything do so in honor of the Lord, because they give thanks to God for the food. Those who refuse to eat certain things do so in honor of the Lord, and they give thanks to God. [7]We do not live for ourselves only, and we do not die for ourselves only. [8]If we live, it is for the Lord that we live, and if we die, it is for the Lord that we die. So whether we live or die, we belong to the Lord. [9]For Christ died and rose to life in order to be the Lord of the living and of the dead. [10]You then, who eat only vegetables –why do you pass judgment on others? And you who eat anything–why do you despise other believers? All of us will stand before God to be judged by him. [11]For the scripture says,

"As surely as I am the living God, says the Lord,
      everyone will kneel before me,
      and everyone will confess that I am God."
[12]Every one of us, then, will have to give an account to God.

Do Not Make Others Fall

[13]So then, let us stop judging one another. Instead, you should decide never to do anything that would make others stumble or fall into sin. [14]My union with the Lord Jesus makes me certain that no food is of itself ritually unclean; but if you believe that some food is unclean, then it becomes unclean for you. [15]If you hurt others because of something you eat, then you are no longer acting from love. Do not let the food that you eat ruin the person for whom Christ died! [16]Do not let what you regard as good get a bad name. [17]For God's Kingdom is not a matter of eating and drinking, but of the righteousness, peace, and joy which the Holy Spirit gives. [18]And when you serve Christ in this way, you please God and are approved by others.

[19]So then, we must always aim[s] at those things that bring peace and that help strengthen one another. [20]Do not, because of food, destroy what God has done. All foods may be eaten, but it is wrong to eat anything that will cause someone else to fall into sin. [21]The right thing to do is to keep from eating meat, drinking wine, or doing anything else that will make other believers fall. [22]Keep what you believe about this matter, then, between yourself and God. Happy are those who do not feel guilty when they do something they judge is right! [23]But if they have doubts about what they eat, God condemns them when they eat it, because their action is not based on faith. And anything

s we must always aim; *some manuscripts have* we always aim.

該有他自己的見解。[6]有人特別重視某一天，表示他對主的尊崇；有人甚麼東西都吃，也是表示他對主的尊崇，因為他為所吃的食物感謝上帝。有人不吃某種食物，同樣是表示他對主的尊崇，也感謝上帝。[7]我們當中沒有人只為自己活，也沒有人只為自己死；[8]我們活著，是為主而活，死了，是為主而死。所以，活也好，死也好，我們都是屬主的人。[9]為此，基督死了又復活，目的是要作活人和死人的主。[10]那麼，你這個人，為甚麼評斷你的弟兄姊妹呢？為甚麼輕視你的弟兄姊妹呢？我們都要站在上帝面前接受他的審判；[11]因為聖經說：

主說：我指著我的生命發誓，
      人人要向我屈膝下拜；
      人人要宣認我是上帝。
[12]這樣說來，我們每一個人都得向上帝交帳。

不可使人跌倒

[13]所以，我們不可再彼此評斷；應該立下決心，不做任何使人跌倒犯罪的事。[14]我憑著跟主耶穌的密切關係確實知道，食物本身都是潔淨的；如果有人以為它不潔淨，那麼，對這個人來說，它就是不潔淨的了。[15]如果你因食物傷了弟兄姊妹的心，你所做的就不是出於愛心。不可因你的食物毀了一個基督已經為他死的人！[16]不可使你認為好的事得了壞名。[17]因為上帝的主權不在於飲食，而在於聖靈所賜的公正、和平、喜樂。[18]這樣事奉基督的人必定得到上帝的喜歡和人的讚許。

[19]所以，我們要追求那促進和睦、彼此建立群體生活的事。[20]不要因食物而破壞上帝的工作。一切食物都可以吃，但如果你所吃的使別人跌倒，那就不對了。[21]所以，最好不吃肉，不喝酒，不做任何使你弟兄姊妹跌倒的事。[22]你對這問題的看法怎樣，是你跟上帝之間的事。一個人能夠在自己所認為對的事上不自責是多麼有福啊！[23]可是，如果他對所吃的食物心懷疑惑，那麼，他吃的時候，上帝要定他的罪，因為他不憑著信心

that is not based on faith is sin.

Please Others, Not Yourselves

15 We who are strong in the faith ought to help the weak to carry their burdens. We should not please ourselves. [2]Instead, we should all please other believers for their own good, in order to build them up in the faith. [3]For Christ did not please himself. Instead, as the scripture says, "The insults which are hurled at you have fallen on me." [4]Everything written in the Scriptures was written to teach us, in order that we might have hope through the patience and encouragement which the Scriptures give us. [5]And may God, the source of patience and encouragement, enable you to have the same point of view among yourselves by following the example of Christ Jesus, [6]so that all of you together may praise with one voice the God and Father of our Lord Jesus Christ.

The Gospel to the Gentiles

[7]Accept one another, then, for the glory of God, as Christ has accepted you. [8]For I tell you that Christ's life of service was on behalf of the Jews, to show that God is faithful, to make his promises to their ancestors come true, [9]and to enable even the Gentiles to praise God for his mercy. As the scripture says,

> "And so I will praise you among the Gentiles;
> I will sing praises to you."

[10]Again it says,

> "Rejoice, Gentiles, with God's people!"

[11]And again,

> "Praise the Lord, all Gentiles;
> praise him, all peoples!"

[12]And again, Isaiah says,

> "A descendant of Jesse will appear;
> he will come to rule the Gentiles,
> and they will put their hope in him."

[13]May God, the source of hope, fill you with all joy and peace by means of your faith in him, so that your hope will continue to grow by the power of the Holy Spirit.

Paul's Reason for Writing So Boldly

[14]My friends: I myself feel sure that you are full of goodness, that you have all knowledge, and that you are able to teach one another. [15]But in this letter I have been quite bold about certain subjects of which I have reminded you. I have been bold because of the privilege God

吃。任何不憑着信心而做的事都是罪。

不求滿足自己

15 我們信心堅強的人應該幫助信心軟弱的人，分擔他們的重擔，而不求滿足自己。[2]我們每人要為其他信徒的益處着想，來建立共同的信心生活。[3]因為基督並不求滿足自己，倒是像聖經所說：「辱罵你的人的辱罵都落在我身上。」[4]聖經裏面的話都是為教導我們而寫的，目的是要我們能夠藉着忍耐和聖經所給與的鼓勵獲得希望。[5]願那位賜忍耐和鼓勵的上帝幫助你們有同樣的見解，學習基督耶穌的榜樣，[6]好使大家在一起，同聲頌讚我們的主耶穌基督的父上帝。

向外邦人傳福音

[7]所以，為了榮耀上帝，你們要彼此接納，如同基督接納你們一樣。[8]我告訴你們，基督為着要顯明上帝的信實，作了猶太人的僕人，為要使上帝對族長們的許諾得以實現，[9]同時使外邦人也能夠頌讚上帝的慈愛。正像聖經所說：

> 因此，我要在外邦人中頌揚你；
> 我要歌頌你的名。

[10]聖經又說：

> 外邦人哪！要跟上帝的子民一同歡樂。

[11]再說：

> 所有的外邦人哪！要頌讚主；
> 萬民哪！你們要頌讚他。

[12]以賽亞也說：

> 有耶西的後代要出來，
> 他要起來統治外邦；
> 外邦人都要仰望他！

[13]願上帝，就是那希望的泉源，因着你們對他的信心，讓你們充滿各樣喜樂、平安，使你們的希望，藉着聖靈的能力，不斷增加。

保羅直言無諱

[14]弟兄姊妹們，我自己確實知道你們滿有良善的品德，也具備着豐富的知識，能夠彼此勸導。[15]但是，在這封信裏，對於某些問題，我仍然大膽地提醒你們。我這樣直言無

has given me [16]of being a servant of Christ Jesus to work for the Gentiles. I serve like a priest in preaching the Good News from God, in order that the Gentiles may be an offering acceptable to God, dedicated to him by the Holy Spirit. [17]In union with Christ Jesus, then, I can be proud of my service for God. [18]I will be bold and speak only about what Christ has done through me to lead the Gentiles to obey God. He has done this by means of words and deeds, [19]by the power of miracles and wonders, and by the power of the Spirit of God. And so, in traveling all the way from Jerusalem to Illyricum, I have proclaimed fully the Good News about Christ. [20]My ambition has always been to proclaim the Good News in places where Christ has not been heard of, so as not to build on a foundation laid by someone else. [21]As the scripture says,

"Those who were not told about him will see, and those who have not heard will understand."

Paul's Plan to Visit Rome

[22]And so I have been prevented many times from coming to you. [23]But now that I have finished my work in these regions and since I have been wanting for so many years to come to see you, [24]I would like to do so now. I would like to see you on my way to Spain, and be helped by you to go there, after I have enjoyed visiting you for a while. [25]Right now, however, I am going to Jerusalem in the service of God's people there. [26]For the churches in Macedonia and Achaia have freely decided to give an offering to help the poor among God's people in Jerusalem. [27]That decision was their own, but, as a matter of fact, they have an obligation to help them. Since the Jews shared their spiritual blessings with the Gentiles, the Gentiles ought to use their material blessings to help the Jews. [28]When I have finished this task and have turned over to them all the money that has been raised for them, I shall leave for Spain and visit you on my way there. [29]When I come to you, I know that I shall come with a full measure of the blessing of Christ.

[30]I urge you, friends, by our Lord Jesus Christ and by the love that the Spirit gives: join me in praying fervently to God for me. [31]Pray that I may be kept safe from the unbelievers in Judea and that my service in Jerusalem may be acceptable to God's people there. [32]And so I will come to you full of joy, if it is God's will, and enjoy a refreshing visit with you. [33]May God, our source of peace, be with all of you. Amen.

諱,是因為上帝給我特權,[16]使我成為基督耶穌的僕人,在外邦人當中工作。我像祭司一樣宣講上帝的福音,為要使外邦人成為聖靈所獻上的祭物,是上帝所悅納的。[17]這樣,因為我在基督耶穌裏,我可以因着事奉上帝而覺得光榮。[18-19]我所要大膽講的只是這一句話:基督藉着我的言語行為,又用神蹟奇事和上帝之靈的能力使外邦人順服上帝。因此,從耶路撒冷一直到以利哩古一帶地方,我到處傳揚關於基督的福音。[20]我一向的抱負是在還沒有聽見基督的地方傳福音,免得我的工作建立在別人的基礎上。[21]聖經說過:

不曾認識他的人要看見;
沒有聽見過他的人要領悟。

保羅計劃訪問羅馬

[22]可是,我多次遇到阻撓,不能夠到你們那裏去。[23]但現在,既然我已經完成了在這一帶的工作,而且多年來一直想去訪問你們,[24]我希望現在就去,在我往西班牙去的途中,順便去看你們,在你們那裏歡聚一些時候,然後讓你們幫我成行。[25]可是,為了接濟信徒的事,我現在必須上耶路撒冷去。[26]因為馬其頓和亞該亞的教會樂意捐出一筆錢,來幫助耶路撒冷信徒中窮苦的人。[27]這固然是他們樂意做的,事實上也是他們的義務。既然猶太的基督徒讓外邦人分享屬靈的恩賜,外邦人也應該在物質上幫助他們。[28]等我辦完了這件事,把他們所募捐的錢都交付清楚以後,我就要取道你們那裏,到西班牙去。[29]我知道,我去探望你們的時候也要把基督豐富的恩典帶給你們。

[30]弟兄姊妹們,憑着我們的主耶穌基督,又憑着聖靈所賜的愛心,我請求你們,為着我的緣故跟我一起懇切地祈求上帝,[31]使我不至於受到在猶太那些不信的人的危害,又使我在耶路撒冷辦理的救濟工作得到信徒的滿意。[32]上帝若准許,我就可以高高興興地去看你們,在你們當中休息一些時候。

[33]願賜平安的上帝與你們各位同在!阿們。

Personal Greetings

16¹I recommend to you our sister Phoebe, who serves the church at Cenchreae. ²Receive her in the Lord's name, as God's people should, and give her any help she may need from you; for she herself has been a good friend to many people and also to me.

³I send greetings to Priscilla and Aquila, my fellow workers in the service of Christ Jesus; ⁴they risked their lives for me. I am grateful to them—not only I, but all the Gentile churches as well. ⁵Greetings also to the church that meets in their house.

Greetings to my dear friend Epaenetus, who was the first in the province of Asia to believe in Christ. ⁶Greetings to Mary, who has worked so hard for you. ⁷Greetings also to Andronicus and Junia,ᶠ fellow Jews who were in prison with me; they are well known among the apostles, and they became Christians before I did.

⁸My greetings to Ampliatus, my dear friend in the fellowship of the Lord. ⁹Greetings also to Urbanus, our fellow worker in Christ's service, and to Stachys, my dear friend. ¹⁰Greetings to Apelles, whose loyalty to Christ has been proved. Greetings to those who belong to the family of Aristobulus. ¹¹Greetings to Herodion, a fellow Jew, and to the Christians in the family of Narcissus.

¹²My greetings to Tryphaena and Tryphosa, who work in the Lord's service, and to my dear friend Persis, who has done so much work for the Lord. ¹³I send greetings to Rufus, that outstanding worker in the Lord's service, and to his mother, who has always treated me like a son. ¹⁴My greetings to Asyncritus, Phlegon, Hermes, Patrobas, Hermas, and all the other Christians with them. ¹⁵Greetings to Philologus and Julia, to Nereus and his sister, to Olympas and to all of God's people who are with them.

¹⁶Greet one another with the kiss of peace. All the churches of Christ send you their greetings.

Final Instructions

¹⁷I urge you, my friends: watch out for those who cause divisions and upset people's faith and go against the teaching which you have received. Keep away from them! ¹⁸For those who do such things are not serving Christ our Lord, but their own appetites. By their fine words and flattering speech they deceive innocent people. ¹⁹Everyone has heard of your loyalty to the gospel, and for this reason I am happy about you. I want you to be wise about what is good, but

ᶠ Junia; *or* Junias; *some manuscripts have* Julia.

保羅問候信徒

16我向你們介紹我們的姊妹菲比；她是堅革哩教會的執事。²請為主的緣故，依照信徒的本份好好地接待她。無論她有甚麼需要，請你們幫助她。她曾熱心地幫助了許多人，我自己也得過她的幫助。

³ 請問候事奉基督耶穌的同工百基拉和亞居拉；⁴他們為了我冒生命的危險。不但我感謝他們，外邦的各教會也都感謝他們。⁵也請問候在他們家裏聚集的教會。

請問候我親愛的朋友以拜尼土；他是亞細亞省第一個歸信基督的人。⁶也向為你們辛勞工作的馬利亞致意。⁷請問候曾經跟我一起坐牢的猶太同胞安多尼古和猶尼亞。他們在使徒中頗有名望，也是比我先歸信基督的。

⁸ 請問候主內親愛的朋友暗伯利；⁹也問候事奉基督的同工耳巴努和我親愛的朋友士大古。¹⁰請問候經歷過考驗、對基督始終忠心的亞比利；也問候亞利多布一家人。¹¹請問候猶太同胞希羅天；也問候拿其數一家信主的弟兄們。

¹² 請問候主內的同工土非拿和土富撒；也問候為主勤勞工作的親愛朋友彼息。¹³請問候魯孚；他是主內一位傑出的工人；也問候他的母親—她一向待我像自己的兒子一樣。¹⁴請問候亞遜其土、弗勒干、黑米、八羅巴、黑馬，和其他跟他們在一起的弟兄姊妹們。¹⁵請問候非羅羅古和猶利亞，尼利亞和他的姊妹，阿林巴以及跟他們在一起的信徒們。

¹⁶ 你們要用聖潔的親吻互相問安。基督的各教會都向你們問安。

最後的勸導

¹⁷ 弟兄姊妹們，我勸告你們，要防備那些製造分裂、動搖別人的信心、背棄你們所受的教導的人；要遠離他們。¹⁸因為這樣的人不在事奉我們的主基督，是在滿足自己的肚子。他們用花言巧語迷惑老實人的心。¹⁹大家都曉得你們對福音的信從，因此我很為你們高興。我要你們在好事上聰明，在壞事上

innocent in what is evil. [20]And God, our source of peace, will soon crush Satan under your feet.

The grace of our Lord Jesus be with you.[u]

[21]Timothy, my fellow worker, sends you his greetings; and so do Lucius, Jason, and Sosipater, fellow Jews.

[22]I, Tertius, the writer of this letter, send you Christian greetings.

[23]My host Gaius, in whose house the church meets, sends you his greetings; Erastus, the city treasurer, and our brother Quartus send you their greetings.[v]

Concluding Prayer of Praise

[25]Let us give glory to God! He is able to make you stand firm in your faith, according to the Good News I preach about Jesus Christ and according to the revelation of the secret truth which was hidden for long ages in the past. [26]Now, however, that truth has been brought out into the open through the writings of the prophets; and by the command of the eternal God it is made known to all nations, so that all may believe and obey.

[27]To the only God, who alone is all-wise, be glory through Jesus Christ forever! Amen.[w]

u *Some manuscripts omit this sentence.*
v *Some manuscripts add verse 24: The grace of our Lord Jesus Christ be with you all. Amen; others add this after verse 27.*
w *Some manuscripts have verses 25-27 here and after 14.23; others have them only after 14.23; one has them after 15.33.*

無知。[20]賜平安的上帝就要摧毀撒但,使他屈服在你們腳下。

願我們的主耶穌賜恩典給你們!

[21] 我的同工提摩太,以及猶太同胞路求、耶孫、所西巴德,都問候你們。[22]我一代寫這封信的德提,也在主內問候你們。[23]那接待我、又讓教會在他家聚集的該猶問候你們。本城司庫以拉都和我們的弟兄括土也問候你們。⑮

結束的禱告和頌讚

[25] 願榮耀歸於上帝!他能夠照我所傳的福音堅定你們的信心。這福音是關於耶穌基督的信息,啓示了自古以來隱藏着的奧祕。[26]這奧祕已經藉着先知們的書顯明出來,並且按照永生上帝的命令昭示萬國,好使萬民信服。

[27] 願榮耀藉着耶穌基督歸與獨一全智的上帝,直到永遠!阿們。⑯

⑮有些古卷加24節「願我們的主耶穌基督賜恩典給你們各位!阿們。」
⑯有些古卷16.25-27也在14.23後出現;有些古卷只在14.23後出現;有一古卷在15.33後出現。

哥林多前書
1 CORINTHIANS

INTRODUCTION

Paul's First Letter to the Corinthians was written to deal with problems of Christian life and faith that had arisen in the church which Paul had established at Corinth. At that time Corinth was a great cosmopolitan Greek city, the capital of the Roman province of Achaia. It was noted for its thriving commerce, proud culture, widespread immorality, and variety of religions.

The apostle's chief concerns are with problems such as divisions and immorality in the church, and with questions about sex and marriage, matters of conscience, church order, gifts of the Holy Spirit, and the resurrection. With deep insight he shows how the Good News speaks to these questions.

Chapter 13, which presents love as the best of God's gifts to his people, is probably the most widely known passage in the book.

Outline of Contents

簡　介

哥林多前書是保羅解釋基督徒生活和信仰問題的書信；這些問題發生在他所建立的哥林多教會。

當時，哥林多是希臘的一個大都市——羅馬治下亞該亞省的首府。這城以繁盛的商業和高度的文明著稱；但風氣敗壞，道德低落，人民信奉多種宗教。

保羅最關心的是教會分裂和內部道德敗壞的問題。他也論到淫亂和婚姻、良心、教會的組織、聖靈的恩賜，和復活等問題。對這些問題，他都根據福音提出明智的指示。

「愛之歌」（十三章）是保羅書信中最重要最受歡迎的經文之一。

提要

1 From Paul, who was called by the will of God to be an apostle of Christ Jesus, and from our brother Sosthenes–

2To the church of God which is in Corinth, to all who are called to be God's holy people, who belong to him in union with Christ Jesus, together with all people everywhere who worship our Lord Jesus Christ, their Lord and ours:

3May God our Father and the Lord Jesus Christ give you grace and peace.

Blessings in Christ

4I always give thanks to my God for you because of the grace he has given you through Christ Jesus. 5For in union with Christ you have become rich in all things, including all speech and all knowledge. 6The message about Christ has become so firmly established in you 7that you have not failed to receive a single blessing, as you wait for our Lord Jesus Christ to be revealed. 8He will also keep you firm to the end, so that you will be faultless on the Day of our Lord Jesus Christ. 9God is to be trusted, the God who called you to have fellowship with his Son Jesus Christ, our Lord.

Divisions in the Church

10By the authority of our Lord Jesus Christ I appeal to all of you, my friends, to agree in what you say, so that there will be no divisions among you. Be completely united, with only one thought and one purpose. 11For some people from Chloe's family have told me quite plainly, my friends, that there are quarrels among you. 12Let me put it this way: each one of you says something different. One says, "I follow Paul"; another, "I follow Apollos"; another, "I follow Peter"; and another, "I follow Christ." 13Christ has been divided[a] into groups! Was it Paul who died on the cross for you? Were you baptized as Paul's disciples?

14I thank God that I did not baptize any of you except Crispus and Gaius. 15No one can say, then, that you were baptized as my disciples. 16(Oh yes, I also baptized Stephanas and his family; but I can't remember whether I baptized anyone else.) 17Christ did not send me to baptize. He sent me to tell the Good News, and to tell it without using the language of human wisdom, in order to make sure that Christ's death on the cross is not robbed of its power.

Christ the Power and the Wisdom of God

18For the message about Christ's death on

a Christ has been divided; *some manuscripts have* Christ cannot be divided.

1 我是保羅;由於上帝的旨意,我蒙召作基督耶穌的使徒。我和所提尼弟兄 2寫信給哥林多城上帝教會的信徒們。你們和在各地呼求我們主耶穌基督的名的人,同樣是在基督耶穌裏蒙召作信徒而歸屬上帝的。基督是他們的主,也是我們的主。 3願我們的父上帝和主耶穌基督賜恩典、平安給你們!

在基督裏的福澤

4 我常常替你們感謝我的上帝,因為他藉着基督耶穌賜恩給你們, 5使你們在基督裏樣樣富足,具備充分的知識和口才。 6有關基督的見證已經堅立在你們當中, 7以致你們在等待着我們的主耶穌基督顯現的時候,沒有缺少任何一樣恩賜。 8主必定始終幫助你們,使你們在我們的主耶穌基督降臨的日子無可指責。 9上帝是信實的;他呼召你們,使你們跟他的兒子—我們的主耶穌基督有了團契。

教會的分裂

10 弟兄姊妹們,我奉我們的主耶穌基督的名勸你們大家,說話要一致,不可分裂,要團結,有一致的想法,有共同的目標。 11我的弟兄姊妹們,有革來家的人坦白告訴過我,說你們中間有紛爭。 12我的意思是,你們來說紛紛。有的說:「我是保羅的人」;有的說:「我是亞波羅的人」;有的說:「我是屬彼得的」;有的說:「我是屬基督的。」13基督耶穌被分割了!難道替你們死在十字架上的是保羅嗎?你們是奉保羅的名受洗的嗎?

14 感謝上帝,除了基利司布和該猶,我並沒有給你們任何人施洗, 15所以沒有人能說,你們是奉我的名受洗的。(16對了,我也給司提法那和他家的人施洗過,此外還給誰施洗沒有,我倒記不清了。)17基督差遣我不是為了施洗,而是要我傳福音,不用智慧的言論,免得基督在十字架上的死失去了效力。

基督是上帝的大能和智慧

18 基督死在十字架上的信息,在那些走向

the cross is nonsense to those who are being lost; but for us who are being saved it is God's power. [19]The scripture says,

"I will destroy the wisdom of the wise
and set aside the understanding of the
scholars."

[20]So then, where does that leave the wise? or the scholars? or the skillful debaters of this world? God has shown that this world's wisdom is foolishness!

[21]For God in his wisdom made it impossible for people to know him by means of their own wisdom. Instead, by means of the so-called "foolish" message we preach, God decided to save those who believe. [22]Jews want miracles for proof, and Greeks look for wisdom. [23]As for us, we proclaim the crucified Christ, a message that is offensive to the Jews and nonsense to the Gentiles; [24]but for those whom God has called, both Jews and Gentiles, this message is Christ, who is the power of God and the wisdom of God. [25]For what seems to be God's foolishness is wiser than human wisdom, and what seems to be God's weakness is stronger than human strength.

[26]Now remember what you were, my friends, when God called you. From the human point of view few of you were wise or powerful or of high social standing. [27]God purposely chose what the world considers nonsense in order to shame the wise, and he chose what the world considers weak in order to shame the powerful. [28]He chose what the world looks down on and despises and thinks is nothing, in order to destroy what the world thinks is important. [29]This means that no one can boast in God's presence. [30]But God has brought you into union with Christ Jesus, and God has made Christ to be our wisdom. By him we are put right with God; we become God's holy people and are set free. [31]So then, as the scripture says, "Whoever wants to boast must boast of what the Lord has done."

The Message about the Crucified Christ

2 When I came to you, my friends, to preach God's secret truth,[b] I did not use big words and great learning. [2]For while I was with you, I made up my mind to forget everything except Jesus Christ and especially his death on the cross. [3]So when I came to you, I was weak and trembled all over with fear, [4]and my teaching and message were not delivered with 'skillful words of human wisdom, but with convincing proof of the power of God's Spirit. [5]Your faith,

b God's secret truth; *some manuscripts have* the testimony about God.

滅亡的人看來是愚拙的；對我們這些得救的人來說，卻是上帝的大能。[19]因為聖經說：

我要摧毀聰明人的智慧；
我要廢除博學者的學問。

[20]那麼，聰明人在哪裏呢？博學者在哪裏呢？世上的雄辯家在哪裏呢？上帝已經使這世界的智慧成為愚拙了！

[21]上帝運用他的智慧，使世人不能夠藉着自己的智慧去認識他；相反地，上帝決定藉着我們所傳那「愚拙」的信息來拯救信他的人。[22]猶太人要求神蹟，希臘人尋求智慧，[23]我們卻宣揚被釘十字架的基督。這信息在猶太人看來是侮辱，在外邦人看來是荒唐。[24]可是在蒙上帝選召的人眼中，不管是猶太人或是希臘人，這信息是基督；他是上帝的大能，上帝的智慧。[25]因為所謂「上帝的愚拙」總勝過人的智慧，所謂「上帝的軟弱」也勝過人的堅強。

[26]弟兄姊妹們，要記得上帝呼召你們的時候，你們是處在哪一種景況中。從人的觀點看，你們很少是聰明的，很少是有能力的，很少是有高貴地位的。[27]上帝偏要揀選世人所認為愚拙的，來使聰明人羞愧；上帝揀選世人所認為軟弱的，來使堅強的人羞愧。[28]上帝也揀選世人所輕視、厭惡、認為不足輕重的，來推翻一向被認為重要的，[29]使人在上帝面前無可誇口。[30]然而，上帝使你們得以跟基督耶穌聯合，又使他成為我們的智慧；藉着他，我們得以跟上帝有合宜的關係，成為上帝聖潔的子民，並且得到自由。[31]正像聖經上說：「誰要誇口，就該誇耀主的作為。」

基督十字架的信息

2 弟兄姊妹們，我從前到你們那裏去，並沒有用甚麼華麗的詞藻或高深的學問對你們宣講上帝的奧祕①。[2]因為我拿定了主意，當我跟你們在一起的時候，除了耶穌基督和他死在十字架上的事以外，甚麼都不提。[3]因此，我到你們那裏去的時候十分軟弱，又害怕又戰戰兢兢。[4]我所講的道，所傳的福音，都不是用委婉動聽的智言，而是倚靠聖靈的大能來證實的，[5]使你們的信仰

①「上帝的奧祕」另有些古卷作「上帝的見證」。

then, does not rest on human wisdom but on God's power.

God's Wisdom

6Yet I do proclaim a message of wisdom to those who are spiritually mature. But it is not the wisdom that belongs to this world or to the powers that rule this world–powers that are losing their power. 7The wisdom I proclaim is God's secret wisdom, which is hidden from human beings, but which he had already chosen for our glory even before the world was made. 8None of the rulers of this world knew this wisdom. If they had known it, they would not have crucified the Lord of glory. 9However, as the scripture says,

> "What no one ever saw or heard,
> what no one ever thought could happen,
> is the very thing God prepared for those
> who love him."

10But*c* it was to us that God made known his secret by means of his Spirit. The Spirit searches everything, even the hidden depths of God's purposes. 11It is only our own spirit within us that knows all about us; in the same way, only God's Spirit knows all about God. 12We have not received this world's spirit; instead, we have received the Spirit sent by God, so that we may know all that God has given us.

13So then, we do not speak in words taught by human wisdom, but in words taught by the Spirit, as we explain spiritual truths to those who have the Spirit.*d* 14Whoever does not have the Spirit cannot receive the gifts that come from God's Spirit. Such a person really does not understand them, and they seem to be non sense, because their value can be judged only on a spiritual basis. 15Whoever has the Spirit, however, is able to judge the value of everything, but no one is able to judge him. 16As the scripture says,

> "Who knows the mind of the Lord?
> Who is able to give him advice?"

We, however, have the mind of Christ.

Servants of God

3 As a matter of fact, my friends, I could not talk to you as I talk to people who have the Spirit; I had to talk to you as though you belonged to this world, as children in the Christian faith. 2I had to feed you milk, not solid food, because you were not ready for it. And even now you are not ready for it, 3because you still live as the people of this

---

c But; *some manuscripts have* For.

d to those who have the Spirit; *or* with words given by the Spirit.

不根據人的智慧,而是以上帝的大能為基礎。

上帝的智慧

6 然而,對那些靈性成熟的人,我也講智慧;只是不講屬於這世界的智慧,也不講那些即將沒落的世界統治者的智慧。7我所講的智慧是上帝奧祕的智慧,是那向人隱藏着、卻在創世之前已經預定要使我們得榮耀的智慧。8世上的統治者沒有一個懂得這智慧,如果懂得,他們就不會把榮耀的主釘在十字架上了。9正如聖經所說:

> 上帝為愛他的人所預備的,
> 正是眼睛沒有見過,
> 耳朵沒有聽過,
> 也從來沒有人想到的!

10但是,上帝藉着他的靈把他的奧祕啟示我們。聖靈細察萬事,連上帝深藏的旨意也能細察。11至於人,只有他自己裏面的靈才知道關於他一切的事。同樣,只有上帝的靈才知道上帝一切的事。12我們沒有領受這世界的靈,而是領受上帝所差來的聖靈,為要使我們能夠知道上帝所給我們的一切恩賜。

13 所以,我們講的道不是用人的智慧所教導的言論來講,而是用聖靈所教導的言語,向屬聖靈的人②講解屬靈的真理。14但是,那沒有上帝的靈的人不能夠領受上帝的靈所給的恩賜。這樣的人不能明白這些事,認為這是荒唐的,因為這些事的價值必須用屬靈的眼光才能領悟。15屬聖靈的人能判斷萬事的價值,可是沒有人能夠評斷他。16正如聖經所說:

> 誰知道主的心?
> 誰能替他出主意?

然而,我們屬聖靈的人是有基督的心的。

上帝的同工

3 弟兄姊妹們,老實說,我一向對你們說話,不能把你們當作是屬聖靈的,而是把你們當作屬世的,是基督信仰上的嬰兒。2我只能用奶餵你們,不能用飯,因為你們還不會吃飯。就是現在,你們也還不會吃飯,3因為你們仍然照着人的標準生活。你

---

②「向屬聖靈的人」或譯「用聖靈所賜的言語」。

world live. When there is jealousy among you and you quarrel with one another, doesn't this prove that you belong to this world, living by its standards? 4When one of you says, "I follow Paul," and another, "I follow Apollos"–aren't you acting like worldly people?

5After all, who is Apollos? And who is Paul? We are simply God's servants, by whom you were led to believe. Each one of us does the work which the Lord gave him to do: 6I planted the seed, Apollos watered the plant, but it was God who made the plant grow. 7The one who plants and the one who waters really do not matter. It is God who matters, because he makes the plant grow. 8There is no difference between the one who plants and the one who waters; God will reward each one according to the work each has done. 9For we are partners working together for God, and you are God's field.

You are also God's building. 10Using the gift that God gave me, I did the work of an expert builder and laid the foundation, and someone else is building on it. But each of you must be careful how you build. 11For God has already placed Jesus Christ as the one and only foundation, and no other foundation can be laid. 12Some will use gold or silver or precious stones in building on the foundation; others will use wood or grass or straw. 13And the quality of each person's work will be seen when the Day of Christ exposes it. For on that Day fire will reveal everyone's work; the fire will test it and show its real quality. 14If what was built on the foundation survives the fire, the builder will receive a reward. 15But if your work is burnt up, then you will lose it; but you yourself will be saved, as if you had escaped through the fire.

16Surely you know that you are God's temple and that God's Spirit lives in you! 17God will destroy anyone who destroys God's temple. For God's temple is holy, and you yourselves are his temple.

18You should not fool yourself. If any of you think that you are wise by this world's standards, you should become a fool, in order to be really wise. 19For what this world considers to be wisdom is nonsense in God's sight. As the scripture says, "God traps the wise in their cleverness"; 20and another scripture says, "The Lord knows that the thoughts of the wise are worthless." 21No one, then, should boast about what human beings can do. Actually everything belongs to you: 22Paul, Apollos, and Peter; this world, life and death, the present and the future–all these are yours, 23and you belong to Christ, and Christ belongs to God.

們當中有嫉妒，有紛爭；難道這不是證明你們是屬世的，是依照人的標準生活的嗎？ 4你們當中有人說：「我是保羅的人」；也有人說：「我是亞波羅的人。」這樣，你們跟屬世的人有甚麼不同呢？

5 到底亞波羅算甚麼？保羅算甚麼？我們不過是上帝的僕人，要引導你們歸信上帝。我們每一個人都按照主所分派的工作去做：6我栽種，亞波羅灌漑，可是使它生長的卻是上帝。7栽種的和灌漑的都算不了甚麼；一切在於使它生長的上帝。8栽種的和灌漑的沒有甚麼差別，上帝會按照每一個人的工作酬報他。9我們是上帝的同工；你們是上帝的園地。

你們也是上帝的建築物。10我用上帝給我的恩賜，像一個內行的建築師立好根基，別人在它上面建造。可是每一個人都要謹愼自己怎樣在根基上建造。11因為上帝已經立耶穌基督作惟一的根基，沒有人能夠立其他的根基。12在這根基上，有人要用金銀，或寶石建造；也有人要用木料、草、禾稭建造。13到了審判的日子，每一個人的工程好壞都會顯露出來；因為大火將顯露並試驗每一個人的工程，使那眞的品質出現。14如果他所建造的工程經得起火的考驗，他就得獎賞。15如果他的工程被火燒毀，他就虧損，而他自己卻會得救，像從火裏逃出來一樣。

16 你們一定曉得，你們是上帝的殿，上帝的靈住在你們裏面。17因此，要是有人毀壞了上帝的殿，上帝一定要毀滅他；因為上帝的殿是神聖的，你們自己就是上帝的殿。

18 人不可自欺。要是你們中間有人按照世人的標準自以為有智慧，他倒應該成為愚拙，好成為眞有智慧的。19因為這世界所認為有智慧的，在上帝眼中卻是愚拙的。正像聖經所說：「上帝使智慧的人中了自己的詭計。」20另一處經文說：「主知道智慧者的思想不過是一種妄想。」21所以，無論誰都不應該誇耀人所能做到的事。其實，一切都是你們的：22保羅、亞波羅、彼得、這個世界、生或死、現在或將來，這一切全是你們的；23你們卻是基督的，而基督是上帝的。

Apostles of Christ

4 You should think of us as Christ's servants, who have been put in charge of God's secret truths. [2]The one thing required of such servants is that they be faithful to their master. [3]Now, I am not at all concerned about being judged by you or by any human standard; I don't even pass judgment on myself. [4]My conscience is clear, but that does not prove that I am really innocent. The Lord is the one who passes judgment on me. [5]So you should not pass judgment on anyone before the right time comes. Final judgment must wait until the Lord comes; he will bring to light the dark secrets and expose the hidden purposes of people's minds. And then all will receive from God the praise they deserve.

[6]For your sake, my friends, I have applied all this to Apollos and me, using the two of us as an example, so that you may learn what the saying means, "Observe the proper rules." None of you should be proud of one person and despise another. [7]Who made you superior to others? Didn't God give you everything you have? Well, then, how can you boast, as if what you have were not a gift?

[8]Do you already have everything you need? Are you already rich? Have you become kings, even though we are not? Well, I wish you really were kings, so that we could be kings together with you. [9]For it seems to me that God has given the very last place to us apostles, like people condemned to die in public as a spectacle for the whole world of angels and of human beings. [10]For Christ's sake we are fools; but you are wise in union with Christ! We are weak, but you are strong! We are despised, but you are honored! [11]To this very moment we go hungry and thirsty; we are clothed in rags; we are beaten; we wander from place to place; [12]we wear ourselves out with hard work. When we are cursed, we bless; when we are persecuted, we endure; [13]when we are insulted, we answer back with kind words. We are no more than this world's garbage; we are the scum of the earth to this very moment!

[14]I write this to you, not because I want to make you feel ashamed, but to instruct you as my own dear children. [15]For even if you have ten thousand guardians in your Christian life, you have only one father. For in your life in union with Christ Jesus I have become your father by bringing the Good News to you. [16]I beg you, then, to follow my example. [17]For this purpose I am sending to you Timothy, who is my own dear and faithful son in the Christian life. He will remind you of the principles which I follow in the new life in union with Christ

基督的使徒

4 你們應該把我們看作是基督的僕人，受命作上帝之奧祕的管家。[2]主人對管家所要求的就是忠心。[3]我被你們，或任何人評斷，都認為是一件小事；我自己並不評斷自己。[4]我覺得自己良心清白，但不能因此證明我沒有罪。惟有主才是審斷我的。[5]所以，時機還沒有到的時候，你們不要評斷任何人。要等到主再來的時候才有最後的審判；那時候，他要暴露藏在黑暗中的祕密，揭發人心裏的動機。那時候，每一個人會從上帝得到應得的稱讚。

[6]弟兄姊妹們，為了你們的緣故，我把這些事情應用到亞波羅和我身上，當作例子，好使你們學到「循規蹈矩」這話的意思。你們無論誰都不可自高，看重這個，輕視那個。[7]誰使你勝過別人呢？難道你所有的不都是上帝所賜的嗎？那麼，為甚麼自誇，好像你所有的並不是上帝的恩賜呢？

[8]你們已經甚麼都有了！你們已經富足了！你們在作王，把我們撇在一邊。好吧！我倒願意你們真的作王，好讓我們也跟你們一起作王。[9]因為，據我看來，上帝顯然是把我們這些作使徒的列在最末後，好像判了死刑的囚犯，在天地間成了一齣戲，讓天使和世人觀看。[10]我們為基督的緣故成了愚笨的人，而你們在基督裏倒很聰明；我們軟弱，你們倒堅強；我們被輕視，你們倒受尊重。[11]直到現在，我們還是飢渴交迫，衣不蔽體，常常挨打，到處流浪，[12]並且雙手辛勞工作來養活自己。被人咒罵，我們就說祝福的話；受人逼迫，我們就忍耐；[13]被侮辱，我們就用好話回答。直到現在，我們還被看作是世上的垃圾，人間的渣滓。

[14]我寫這樣的話，不是要使你們覺得慚愧，是要教導你們，把你們當作自己親愛的兒女一樣。[15]儘管你們在基督徒的生活上有上萬的導師，你們卻只有一個父親。因為我把福音傳給你們，我在基督耶穌裏就成了你們的父親。[16]所以，我勸你們要學我的榜樣。[17]為了這個緣故，我差遣提摩太到你們那裏去；在主裏他是我親愛而又忠心的兒子。他要提醒你們，我在基督耶穌裏的新生

Jesus and which I teach in all the churches everywhere.

18Some of you have become proud because you have thought that I would not be coming to visit you. 19If the Lord is willing, however, I will come to you soon, and then I will find out for myself the power which these proud people have, and not just what they say. 20For the Kingdom of God is not a matter of words but of power. 21Which do you prefer? Shall I come to you with a whip, or in a spirit of love and gentleness?

Immorality in the Church

5 Now, it is actually being said that there is sexual immorality among you so terrible that not even the heathen would be guilty of it. I am told that a man is sleeping with his stepmother! 2How, then, can you be proud? On the contrary, you should be filled with sadness, and the man who has done such a thing should be expelled from your fellowship. 3-4And even though I am far away from you in body, still I am there with you in spirit; and as though I were there with you, I have in the name of our Lord Jesus already passed judgment on the man who has done this terrible thing. As you meet together, and I meet with you in my spirit, by the power of our Lord Jesus present with us, 5you are to hand this man over to Satan for his body to be destroyed, so that his spirit may be saved in the Day of the Lord.

6It is not right for you to be proud! You know the saying, "A little bit of yeast makes the whole batch of dough rise." 7You must remove the old yeast of sin so that you will be entirely pure. Then you will be like a new batch of dough without any yeast, as indeed I know you actually are. For our Passover Festival is ready, now that Christ, our Passover lamb, has been sacrificed. 8Let us celebrate our Passover, then, not with bread having the old yeast of sin and wickedness, but with the bread that has no yeast, the bread of purity and truth.

9In the letter that I wrote you I told you not to associate with immoral people. 10Now I did not mean pagans who are immoral or greedy or are thieves, or who worship idols. To avoid them you would have to get out of the world completely. 11What I meant was that you should not associate with a person who calls himself a believer but is immoral or greedy or worships idols or is a slanderer or a drunkard or a thief. Don't even sit down to eat with such a person.

12-13After all, it is none of my business to judge outsiders. God will judge them. But should you not judge the members of your own

活所遵行的道路,也就是我在各地教會所教導的。

18你們當中,有些人以為我不會到你們那裏去,就自高自大起來。19其實,如果主准許,我不久就會來看你們。那時候,我不但要聽那些傲慢的人在說些甚麼,也要看看他們究竟能做些甚麼。20因為上帝的主權不在於言詞,而是在於權能。21你們願意選擇哪一個呢?要我帶着鞭子去,還是要我帶着慈愛溫柔的心去呢?

教會中淫亂的事

5 我確實聽說你們當中有淫亂的事;這種淫亂在異教徒中也是不能容忍的。我聽說有人跟他的繼母同居!2你們還有甚麼好誇口的呢?你們倒應該覺得痛心,把做這種事的人從你們當中開除。3-4至於我,雖然我身體離開你們很遠,我的心卻跟你們在一起。我已經奉主耶穌的名判定了那犯這種淫亂罪行的人,好像我是在你們那裏一樣。你們聚會的時候,我的心跟你們在一起。靠着我們的主耶穌的權能,5你們應該把這個人交給撒但,讓撒但毀滅他的身體,好使他的靈,在主再來的日子,能夠得救。

6你們自誇是不對的!你們知道有句話說:「一點點酵母可以使全團的麵發起來。」7要把罪的舊酵除掉,你們才能完全潔淨。這樣,你們就像沒有酵母的新麵團;其實,你們本應該是沒有酵的。我們逾越節的筵席已經預備好了,逾越節的羔羊基督已經作為犧牲獻上了。8所以,我們守這節,不要用舊酵,就是含有邪惡的酵,卻要用無酵餅,就是含有純潔和真理的餅。

9從前給你們的信裏,我告誡過你們不可跟淫亂的人來往。10我並不是指異教徒中那些淫亂、貪婪、盜竊,或拜偶像的人;除非離開這世界,要跟這樣的人隔絕是做不到的。11我的意思是:不可跟那自稱為信徒,卻淫亂、貪婪、拜偶像、辱罵別人、酒醉,或盜竊的人來往;就是跟這樣的人同桌吃飯也不可以。

12-13我的責任不在於審判教外的人,上帝自然會審判他們。然而,你們不是應該審判

fellowship? As the scripture says, "Remove the evil person from your group."

Lawsuits against Fellow Christians

6 If any of you have a dispute with another Christian, how dare you go before heathen judges instead of letting God's people settle the matter? ²Don't you know that God's people will judge the world? Well, then, if you are to judge the world, aren't you capable of judging small matters? ³Do you not know that we shall judge the angels? How much more, then, the things of this life! ⁴If such matters come up, are you going to take them to be settled by people who have no standing in the church? ⁵Shame on you! Surely there is at least one wise person in your fellowship who can settle a dispute between fellow Christians. ⁶Instead, one Christian goes to court against another and lets unbelievers judge the case!

⁷The very fact that you have legal disputes among yourselves shows that you have failed completely. Would it not be better for you to be wronged? Would it not be better for you to be robbed? ⁸Instead, you yourselves wrong one another and rob one another, even other believers! ⁹Surely you know that the wicked will not possess God's Kingdom. Do not fool yourselves; people who are immoral or who worship idols or are adulterers or homosexual perverts ¹⁰or who steal or are greedy or are drunkards or who slander others or are thieves –none of these will possess God's Kingdom. ¹¹Some of you were like that. But you have been purified from sin; you have been dedicated to God; you have been put right with God by the Lord Jesus Christ and by the Spirit of our God.

Use Your Bodies for God's Glory

¹²Someone will say, "I am allowed to do anything." Yes; but not everything is good for you. I could say that I am allowed to do anything, but I am not going to let anything make me its slave. ¹³Someone else will say, "Food is for the stomach, and the stomach is for food." Yes; but God will put an end to both. The body is not to be used for sexual immorality, but to serve the Lord; and the Lord provides for the body. ¹⁴God raised the Lord from death, and he will also raise us by his power.

¹⁵You know that your bodies are parts of the body of Christ. Shall I take a part of Christ's body and make it part of the body of a prostitute? Impossible! ¹⁶Or perhaps you don't know that the man who joins his body to a prostitute becomes physically one with her? The scripture

教內的人嗎？正如聖經上說：「要從你們當中把那邪惡的人開除！」

信徒間的爭論

6 你們信徒間，如果有爭論的事，怎麼敢告到不信主的法官面前去，而不讓信徒替你們解決呢？²難道你們不知道信徒要審判世界嗎？你們既然要審判世界，難道沒有能力解決那些小事情嗎？³你們不知道我們要審判天使嗎？何況世上的事呢？⁴那麼，如果有這一類的糾紛，你們要讓那些不足為教會所重視的人來處理嗎？⁵多麼可恥啊！難道在你們當中竟然沒有一個智慧人能夠替信徒們解決糾紛嗎？⁶你們當中竟然有信徒控告信徒的事，而且告到不信主的人面前去！

⁷你們彼此告狀，這證明你們是完全失敗的。為甚麼不寧願受點冤枉？為甚麼不甘心吃點虧？⁸你們竟彼此冤枉人，互相虧負，連對自己的同道們也是這樣。⁹難道你們不知道邪惡的人不能作上帝國的子民嗎？不要欺騙自己呀！凡是淫亂，拜偶像，姦淫，作變童，親男色，¹⁰盜竊，貪婪，酒醉，毀謗人，或勒索人的，都不能作上帝國的子民。¹¹你們當中，有些人從前正是這樣。但是，你們已經被洗淨，已經被聖化歸上帝，已經藉着主耶穌基督的名和我們上帝的靈得以跟上帝有合宜的關係了。

用你們的身體榮耀上帝

¹²也許有人要說：「甚麼事我都可以做。」不錯，但不是每件事都對你有益處。我可以說：「甚麼事我都可以做」，但我不要受任何一件事的奴役。¹³有人要說：「食物是為肚子，肚子是為食物。」不錯，但上帝會把這兩樣都毀壞的。我們的身體不是為着行淫，是為主存在的，而主供應我們身體的需要。¹⁴上帝使主從死裏復活，他也同樣要憑着自己的大能使我們復活。

¹⁵你們一定知道，你們的身體就是基督的肢體。我可以把基督的肢體當作娼妓的肢體嗎？絕對不可！¹⁶你們也一定知道，誰跟娼妓苟合，誰就是跟她成為一體了。因為聖經

says quite plainly, "The two will become one body." 17But he who joins himself to the Lord becomes spiritually one with him.

18Avoid immorality. Any other sin a man commits does not affect his body; but the man who is guilty of sexual immorality sins against his own body. 19Don't you know that your body is the temple of the Holy Spirit, who lives in you and who was given to you by God? You do not belong to yourselves but to God; 20he bought you for a price. So use your bodies for God's glory.

Questions about Marriage

7 Now, to deal with the matters you wrote about.

A man does well not to marry.[e] 2But because there is so much immorality, every man should have his own wife, and every woman should have her own husband. 3A man should fulfill his duty as a husband, and a woman should fulfill her duty as a wife, and each should satisfy the other's needs. 4A wife is not the master of her own body, but her husband is; in the same way a husband is not the master of his own body, but his wife is. 5Do not deny yourselves to each other, unless you first agree to do so for a while in order to spend your time in prayer; but then resume normal marital relations. In this way you will be kept from giving in to Satan's temptation because of your lack of self-control.

6I tell you this not as an order, but simply as a permission. 7Actually I would prefer that all of you were as I am; but each one has a special gift from God, one person this gift, another one that gift.

8Now, to the unmarried and to the widows I say that it would be better for you to continue to live alone as I do. 9But if you cannot restrain your desires, go ahead and marry–it is better to marry than to burn with passion.

10For married people I have a command which is not my own but the Lord's: a wife must not leave her husband; 11but if she does, she must remain single or else be reconciled to her husband; and a husband must not divorce his wife.

12To the others I say (I, myself, not the Lord): if a Christian man has a wife who is an unbeliever and she agrees to go on living with him, he must not divorce her. 13And if a Christian woman is married to a man who is an unbeliever and he agrees to go on living with her, she must not divorce him. 14For the unbelieving

e A man does well not to marry; or You say that a man does well not to marry.

上說了：「兩個人要成為一體。」17但是，誰跟主聯合，誰就在靈性上跟主合而為一了。

18所以，你們要避免淫亂。人無論犯甚麼罪都不影響自己的身體，惟有犯淫亂的人是害了自己的身體，19你們不知道你們的身體就是聖靈的殿嗎？這聖靈住在你們裏面，是上帝所賜的。你們不屬於自己，而是屬於上帝，20因為他用重價買了你們。所以，你們要用身體來榮耀上帝。

婚姻問題

7 現在來討論你們信中所提的事。你們說，一個男人能夠不結婚倒是好的。
2不過，既然有那麼多淫亂的事發生，每一個男人應該有自己的妻子；每一個女人也應該有自己的丈夫。3丈夫要對妻子盡夫妻間的責任；妻子也要對丈夫盡夫妻間的責任。4妻子對自己的身體沒有主權，主權在丈夫；同樣，丈夫對自己的身體也沒有主權，主權在妻子。5夫妻不要忽略對方的需要，除非為了要專心禱告，彼此同意暫時分房；但以後還是要恢復正常的關係，免得你們因節制不了而受撒但的誘惑。6我這樣說不是對你們下命令，而是勉強同意罷了。7事實上，我願意大家都像我一樣不結婚。但是，每一個人都從上帝領受了不同的恩賜，有人是這樣，有人是那樣。

8 現在，我要向沒有結婚的人和寡婦說：能夠像我一樣過獨身生活倒是不錯的。9如果你們不能抑制慾念，那就結婚好啦。與其慾火中燒，不如嫁有娶。

10 對於已經結婚的人，我也有所吩咐；其實不是我的意思，而是主的命令：妻子不可離開丈夫，11要是離開了，就不可再嫁；不然，她必須再跟丈夫和好。丈夫也不可離棄妻子。

12 對其他的人我自己也有話要說（不是主說的）：如果一個信徒已經娶了非信徒作妻子，而妻子願意繼續跟他一起生活，他就不可以離棄妻子。13如果有一個女信徒已經跟非信徒結了婚，而丈夫願意繼續跟她一起生活，她也不可以離棄丈夫。14因為那沒有信

husband is made acceptable to God by being united to his wife, and the unbelieving wife is made acceptable to God by being united to her Christian husband. If this were not so, their children would be like pagan children; but as it is, they are acceptable to God. 15However, if the one who is not a believer wishes to leave the Christian partner, let it be so. In such cases the Christian partner, whether husband or wife, is free to act. God has called you to live in peace. 16How can you be sure, Christian wife, that you will not save*f* your husband? Or how can you be sure, Christian husband, that you will not save*f* your wife?

Live As God Called You

17Each of you should go on living according to the Lord's gift to you, and as you were when God called you. This is the rule I teach in all the churches. 18If a circumcised man has accepted God's call, he should not try to remove the marks of circumcision; if an uncircumcised man has accepted God's call, he should not get circumcised. 19For whether or not a man is circumcised means nothing; what matters is to obey God's commandments. 20Each of you should remain as you were when you accepted God's call. 21Were you a slave when God called you? Well, never mind; but if you have a chance to become free, use it.*g* 22For a slave who has been called by the Lord is the Lord's free person, in the same way a free person who has been called by Christ is his slave. 23God bought you for a price; so do not become slaves of people. 24My friends, each of you should remain in fellowship with God in the same condition that you were when you were called.

Questions about the Unmarried and the Widows

25Now, concerning what you wrote about unmarried people: I do not have a command from the Lord, but I give my opinion as one who by the Lord's mercy is worthy of trust.

26Considering the present distress, I think it is better for a man to stay as he is. 27Do you have a wife? Then don't try to get rid of her. Are you unmarried? Then don't look for a wife. 28But if you do marry, you haven't committed a sin; and if an unmarried woman marries, she hasn't committed a sin. But I would rather spare you the everyday troubles

主的丈夫是因信了主的妻子而蒙上帝悅納的；同樣，那沒有信主的妻子也是因信主的丈夫而為上帝所悅納的。要不是這樣，他們的兒女就算不蒙悅納了；事實上，他們是上帝所悅納的。15然而，如果沒有信主的一方要離開信主的伴侶，就由他去吧。在這種情形下，那信主的，無論是丈夫或是妻子，都可以自由了。上帝呼召了你們，要你們和睦相處。16信主的妻子啊，你怎麼能肯定救不了自己的丈夫呢？信主的丈夫啊，你怎麼能肯定救不了自己的妻子呢？

保持蒙召時的身份

17 每一個人的生活應該按照主的恩賜，並且符合上帝呼召他的目的。這是我教導各教會的原則。18那受割禮後接受呼召的人不必除掉割禮的印記；那接受呼召時未受割禮的人也用不着受割禮。19因為受不受割禮都算不了甚麼；重要的是服從上帝的命令。20每一個人應該保持蒙召時的身份。21要是你蒙召時是奴隸的身份，那也沒有關係；可是一有獲得自由的機會，你就爭取自由。22一個奴隸蒙主呼召便是主所釋放的人；一個自由的人蒙召就成為基督的奴隸。23你們是上帝用重價買來的，所以不要作人的奴隸。24弟兄姊妹們，你們每一個人，在上帝面前，都要保持蒙召時的身份。

獨身和寡居的問題

25 關於獨身的問題，我沒有從主那裏得到甚麼指示。但是我蒙上帝憐憫，成為可信託的人。我就以這樣的身份向各位提供我的意見。

26 想到目前處境的艱難，我認為人最好能夠安於現狀。27如果你已經有了妻子，不要想擺脫；如果你還沒有結婚，也無需追求家室。28你要是結婚，不算犯罪；未婚的女子結婚，也沒有甚麼不對。可是，我寧願你們不像這樣的人，在日常生活上遭受種種的拖

that married people will have.

29What I mean, my friends, is this: there is not much time left, and from now on married people should live as though they were not married; 30those who weep, as though they were not sad; those who laugh, as though they were not happy; those who buy, as though they did not own what they bought; 31those who deal in material goods, as though they were not fully occupied with them. For this world, as it is now, will not last much longer.

32I would like you to be free from worry. An unmarried man concerns himself with the Lord's work, because he is trying to please the Lord. 33But a married man concerns himself with worldly matters, because he wants to please his wife; 34and so he is pulled in two directions. An unmarried woman or a virgin concerns herself with the Lord's work, because she wants to be dedicated both in body and spirit; but a married woman concerns herself with worldly matters, because she wants to please her husband.

35I am saying this because I want to help you. I am not trying to put restrictions on you. Instead, I want you to do what is right and proper, and to give yourselves completely to the Lord's service without any reservation.

36In the case of an engaged couple who have decided not to marry: if the man feels that he is not acting properly toward the young woman and if his passions are too strong and he feels that they ought to marry, then they should get married, as he wants to.[h] There is no sin in this. 37But if a man, without being forced to do so, has firmly made up his mind not to marry,[i] and if he has his will under complete control and has already decided in his own mind what to do–then he does well not to marry the young woman.[j] 38So the man who marries[k] does well, but the one who doesn't marry[l] does even better.

39A married woman is not free as long as her husband lives; but if her husband dies, then she is free to be married to any man she wishes, but only if he is a Christian. 40She will be happier, however, if she stays as she is. That is my opinion, and I think that I too have God's Spirit.

---

h an engaged couple ... as he wants to; or a man and his unmarried daughter: if he feels that he is not acting properly toward her, and if she is at the right age to marry, then he should do as he wishes and let her get married.

i not to marry; or not to let his daughter get married.

j marry the young woman; or let her get married.

k marries; or lets his daughter get married.

l doesn't marry; or doesn't let her get married.

累。

29 弟兄姊妹們，我想告訴你們的是：時候不多了，從今以後，有妻子的，要像沒有妻子；30哭泣的，像不哭泣；歡笑的，像不歡笑；購置的，像未擁有甚麼；31享受世上財富的，像沒有盡情享受。因為現有的這個世界快要過去了。

32 我希望你們無所掛慮。沒有結婚的人是專心以主的事為念，因為他想討主的喜悅。33結了婚的人所關心的是世上的事；因為他要取悅自己的妻子，34難免分心。沒有丈夫和守獨身的女人所關心的是主的工作，因為她願意奉獻自己的身體和心靈。結了婚的女人所關心的是世上的事，因為她要取悅自己的丈夫。

35 我這樣說是要幫助你們，不是要限制你們。我要你們做得對，做得合適，並且為主的工作完全奉獻自己，毫無保留。

36 至於那已經訂了婚卻決定不結婚的人，如果男的覺得對女的有不適當的行為，自己又有旺盛的性慾，覺得應該結婚，他們就結婚好啦③；這樣做不算有罪。37可是，一個人若有堅定的意志不結婚④，（不是由於外來的壓力，而是出於自己的決心），並且能夠自制，那麼，不跟未婚妻結婚⑤倒是好的。38這樣說來，那跟未婚妻結婚的固然好，不結婚的更好⑥。

39 一個已婚的女人在丈夫活着的時候是受約束的；要是丈夫死了，她有自由跟她所喜歡的男人結婚，只是應該以信徒為對象。40但是，她若不再嫁就更有福氣。這是我個人的意見；可是我想，有上帝的靈在指引我。

---

③「至於那已經訂了婚……他們就結婚好啦」或譯「至於一個人跟他守獨身女兒的關係，如果他覺得待自己的女兒不合宜，女兒已經過了結婚的年齡，他就可以照自己的意思做，叫她結婚」。

④「不結婚」或譯「不讓守獨身的女兒結婚」。

⑤「不跟未婚妻結婚」或譯「不讓女兒結婚」。

⑥「這樣說來……不結婚的更好」或譯「這樣說來，那讓女兒結婚的固然好，不讓女兒結婚的更好」。

The Question about Food Offered to Idols

8 Now, concerning what you wrote about food offered to idols.

It is true, of course, that "all of us have knowledge," as they say. Such knowledge, however, puffs a person up with pride; but love builds up. [2]Those who think they know something really don't know as they ought to know. [3]But the person who loves God is known by him.

[4]So then, about eating the food offered to idols: we know that an idol stands for something that does not really exist; we know that there is only the one God. [5]Even if there are so-called "gods," whether in heaven or on earth, and even though there are many of these "gods" and "lords," [6]yet there is for us only one God, the Father, who is the Creator of all things and for whom we live; and there is only one Lord, Jesus Christ, through whom all things were created and through whom we live.

[7]But not everyone knows this truth. Some people have been so used to idols that to this day when they eat such food they still think of it as food that belongs to an idol; their conscience is weak, and they feel they are defiled by the food. [8]Food, however, will not improve our relation with God; we shall not lose anything if we do not eat, nor shall we gain anything if we do eat.

[9]Be careful, however, not to let your freedom of action make those who are weak in the faith fall into sin. [10]Suppose a person whose conscience is weak in this matter sees you, who have so-called "knowledge," eating in the temple of an idol; will not this encourage him to eat food offered to idols? [11]And so this weak person, your brother for whom Christ died, will perish because of your "knowledge"! [12]And in this way you will be sinning against Christ by sinning against other Christians and wounding their weak conscience. [13]So then, if food makes a believer sin, I will never eat meat again, so as not to make a believer fall into sin.

Rights and Duties of an Apostle

9 Am I not a free man? Am I not an apostle? Haven't I seen Jesus our Lord? And aren't you the result of my work for the Lord? [2]Even if others do not accept me as an apostle, surely you do! Because of your life in union with the Lord you yourselves are proof of the fact that I am an apostle.

[3]When people criticize me, this is how I defend myself: [4]Don't I have the right to be given food and drink for my work? [5]Don't I have the right to follow the example of the other

論祭偶像的食物

8 關於祭過偶像的食物這一個問題，我們以爲「我們都有這方面的知識」。其實，這一類的知識只會使人自高自大，惟有愛心才能夠造就人。[2]那自以爲知道一些甚麼的，實際上還不知道他所該知道的。[3]可是，那愛上帝的人是上帝所認識的。

[4]那麼，關於吃祭過偶像的食物這個問題，我們知道，偶像並不代表一種眞實的存在；我們也知道，上帝只有一位。[5]雖然天上人間也有所謂「神」的，（有許許多多的「神」和許許多多的「主」），[6]但是對我們來說，只有一位上帝，就是天父，萬物的創造者；我們是爲他而活的。並且，只有一位主，就是耶穌基督；萬物都藉着他而造，而我們也藉着他生存。

[7]然而，並不是人人都有這知識。有些人一向習慣於拜偶像，所以直到今天，每逢吃這種食物，總覺得是吃偶像的食物。他們的良心本來就軟弱，更因爲吃了這種食物覺得受汚染了。[8]其實，食物並不能改善我們跟上帝的關係；不吃沒有甚麼損失，吃了也沒有甚麼收穫。

[9]但是，要小心哪，不要因你們運用個人的自由而使信心軟弱的人犯罪。[10]假如有人在這件事上良心軟弱，看見你這些「知識豐富」的人在偶像的廟裏吃喝，這不等於鼓勵他去吃那祭偶像的食物嗎？[11]那麼，這個軟弱的信徒，也就是基督爲他死的人，將因你的「知識」而滅亡了！[12]你們這樣做，得罪了信徒，傷害他們軟弱的良心，就是得罪基督。[13]所以，如果食物會使信徒犯罪，我就永遠不再吃肉，免得使信徒犯罪。

使徒的權利和責任

9 我不是自由的人嗎？我不是使徒嗎？我沒有見過我們的主耶穌嗎？你們不是我爲主工作所結的果實嗎？[2]儘管別人不把我當作使徒，你們總會把我當作使徒！因爲你們成爲主的信徒這一事實正是我作使徒的證據。

[3]人家批評我的時候，我就這樣辯護：[4]難道我沒有權利靠賴福音吃飯嗎？[5]難道我不能像其他的使徒，像主的兄弟，像彼得

apostles and the Lord's brothers and Peter, by taking a Christian wife with me on my trips? [6]Or are Barnabas and I the only ones who have to work for our living? [7]What soldiers ever have to pay their own expenses in the army? What farmers do not eat the grapes from their own vineyard? What shepherds do not use the milk from their own sheep?

[8]I don't have to limit myself to these everyday examples, because the Law says the same thing. [9]We read in the Law of Moses, "Do not muzzle an ox when you are using it to thresh grain." Now, is God concerned about oxen? [10]Didn't he really mean us when he said that? Of course that was written for us. Anyone who plows and anyone who reaps should do their work in the hope of getting a share of the crop. [11]We have sown spiritual seed among you. Is it too much if we reap material benefits from you? [12]If others have the right to expect this from you, don't we have an even greater right?

But we haven't made use of this right. Instead, we have endured everything in order not to put any obstacle in the way of the Good News about Christ. [13]Surely you know that the men who work in the Temple get their food from the Temple and that those who offer the sacrifices on the altar get a share of the sacrifices. [14]In the same way, the Lord has ordered that those who preach the gospel should get their living from it.

[15]But I haven't made use of any of these rights, nor am I writing this now in order to claim such rights for myself. I would rather die first! Nobody is going to turn my rightful boast into empty words! [16]I have no right to boast just because I preach the gospel. After all, I am under orders to do so. And how terrible it would be for me if I did not preach the gospel! [17]If I did my work as a matter of free choice, then I could expect to be paid; but I do it as a matter of duty, because God has entrusted me with this task. [18]What pay do I get, then? It is the privilege of preaching the Good News without charging for it, without claiming my rights in my work for the gospel.

[19]I am a free man, nobody's slave; but I make myself everybody's slave in order to win as many people as possible. [20]While working with the Jews, I live like a Jew in order to win them; and even though I myself am not subject to the Law of Moses, I live as though I were when working with those who are, in order to win them. [21]In the same way, when working with Gentiles, I live like a Gentile, outside the Jewish Law, in order to win Gentiles. This does not mean that I don't obey God's law; I am

一樣，帶着信主的妻子一起旅行嗎？[6]難道說只有巴拿巴和我非得爲自己的衣食工作不可嗎？[7]有誰當兵而自備糧餉呢？有誰栽種葡萄而不吃自己園裏出產的葡萄呢？有誰牧養羊羣而不喝自己羊羣的奶呢？

[8]我所說的不必只限於日常的例子，法律不也這樣說嗎？[9]摩西的法律規定：「牛在場上踹穀的時候，不可籠住牠的嘴。」上帝所關心的難道是牛嗎？[10]他說這話不就是爲着我們說的嗎？當然這是爲我們寫的！因爲耕種的跟收割的出去工作，都盼望分到他們所應得的穀物。[11]我們在你們當中撒了屬靈的種子，就算是從你們得到物質上的供給，這算過份嗎？[12]如果別人有權利這樣期待你們，我們不是更有這樣的權利嗎？

但是，我們從來沒有利用過這種權利，反而忍受一切，免得基督的福音受到阻礙。[13]你們當然知道，在聖殿裏供職的人從聖殿得到食物；在祭壇邊侍候的人也分到壇上的祭物。[14]同樣，主也這樣吩咐：凡從事傳福音的人都應該倚靠傳福音維持生活。

[15]但是，我並沒有利用過這些權利；我現在寫這些也不是爲着爭取這種權利。我寧死也不願使我所誇耀的落空！[16]我沒有理由爲着傳福音而誇口；我不過是奉命去傳的。我不傳福音就有禍了！[17]如果我傳福音是出於自願，我就可以獲得報酬；但是，上帝既然把這任務交給我，我就認爲這是一種責任。[18]那麼，我所得的報酬是甚麼呢？就是我有傳福音而不叫人花錢的榮幸，就是說不享受傳福音應得的權利。

[19]我是自由的人，不受任何人的奴役；但是我卻甘心作大衆的僕人，爲要爭取更多的人。[20]跟猶太人一起工作，我就像猶太人，爲的要爭取猶太人。雖然我不處在摩西法律的控制下，我卻像生活在法律下的人，爲要爭取法律下的人。[21]同樣，跟法律外的人在一起的時候，我就像法律外的人，不受猶太法律的拘束，爲要爭取法律外的人。然而，這不是說我不服從上帝的法律；其實我是受

really under Christ's law. 22Among the weak in faith I become weak like one of them, in order to win them. So I become all things to all people, that I may save some of them by whatever means are possible.

23All this I do for the gospel's sake, in order to share in its blessings. 24Surely you know that many runners take part in a race, but only one of them wins the prize. Run, then, in such a way as to win the prize. 25Every athlete in training submits to strict discipline, in order to be crowned with a wreath that will not last; but we do it for one that will last forever. 26That is why I run straight for the finish line; that is why I am like a boxer who does not waste his punches. 27I harden my body with blows and bring it under complete control, to keep myself from being disqualified after having called others to the contest.

Warnings against Idols

10 I want you to remember, my friends, what happened to our ancestors who followed Moses. They were all under the protection of the cloud, and all passed safely through the Red Sea. 2In the cloud and in the sea they were all baptized as followers of Moses. 3All ate the same spiritual bread 4and drank the same spiritual drink. They drank from the spiritual rock that went with them, and that rock was Christ himself. 5But even then God was not pleased with most of them, and so their dead bodies were scattered over the desert.

6Now, all of this is an example for us, to warn us not to desire evil things, as they did, 7nor to worship idols, as some of them did. As the scripture says, "The people sat down to a feast which turned into an orgy of drinking and sex." 8We must not be guilty of sexual immorality, as some of them were–and in one day twenty-three thousand of them fell dead. 9We must not put the Lord[m] to the test, as some of them did–and they were killed by snakes. 10We must not complain, as some of them did–and they were destroyed by the Angel of Death.

11All these things happened to them as examples for others, and they were written down as a warning for us. For we live at a time when the end is about to come.

12If you think you are standing firm you had better be careful that you do not fall. 13Every test that you have experienced is the kind that normally comes to people. But God keeps his promise, and he will not allow you to be tested beyond your power to remain firm; at the time you are put to the test, he will give you the

基督法律約束的。22在信心軟弱的人當中，我就作軟弱的人，為要爭取他們。所以，在甚麼樣的人當中，我就作甚麼樣的人；無論用甚麼方法，我總要救一些人。23我為了福音的緣故做這些事，目的是在跟別人分享福音的好處。

24你們一定知道，在運動場上賽跑的人很多，但是只有一個得獎。所以，你們要抱着奪標的心來跑。25每一個運動員接受嚴格的訓練，為要爭取那會朽壞的華冠；但是我們所求的卻是那不朽的冠冕。26所以，我只向着目標直奔；我又像鬥拳的人每一拳都不落空。27我嚴格地對付自己的身體，為要完全控制它，免得我召喚別人參加競賽，自己反而被淘汰了。

警戒拜偶像的事

10 弟兄姊妹們，我要你們記得，我們的祖宗跟隨摩西在曠野所經歷的事。他們都在雲彩的保護下平安過了紅海。2在雲中，在海裏，他們都受洗歸於摩西。3他們都吃了一樣的靈糧，4喝了一樣的靈泉。這泉是從跟他們同行的屬靈磐石上湧流出來的；那磐石就是基督。5但是，他們當中，大多數人不為上帝所喜悅，因此都倒斃在荒野間。

6這一切事都是我們的鑑戒，警告我們不可像他們那樣貪婪邪惡的事，7不可像他們當中一些人那樣去拜偶像。正像聖經所說：「這人民坐下吃喝，站起來跳舞。」8我們不可像他們當中一些人那樣荒淫無恥：他們因犯淫亂的罪，一天之內，有兩萬三千人倒斃。9我們不可像他們當中一些人那樣試探基督⑦：他們因試探他而被蛇咬死。10我們不可像他們某些人口出怨言：他們因口出怨言而被執行毀滅的天使殺了。

11他們所遭遇的這些事成為別人的鑑戒，也都記載下來，作為我們的警戒，因為我們正是處在末世的時代。

12所以，誰自以為站得穩，誰就該小心，免得跌倒。13你們所遭遇的每一個試探無非是一般人所受得了的。上帝是信實的；他絕不讓你們遭遇到無力抵抗的試探。當試探來的時候，他會給你們力量，使你們擔當得

m the Lord; *some manuscripts have Christ.*

⑦「基督」另有古卷作「主」。

strength to endure it, and so provide you with a way out.

14So then, my dear friends, keep away from the worship of idols. 15I speak to you as sensible people; judge for yourselves what I say. 16The cup we use in the Lord's Supper and for which we give thanks to God: when we drink from it, we are sharing in the blood of Christ. And the bread we break: when we eat it, we are sharing in the body of Christ. 17Because there is the one loaf of bread, all of us, though many, are one body, for we all share the same loaf.

18Consider the people of Israel; those who eat what is offered in sacrifice share in the altar's service to God. 19Do I imply, then, that an idol or the food offered to it really amounts to anything? 20No! What I am saying is that what is sacrificed on pagan altars is offered to demons, not to God. And I do not want you to be partners with demons. 21You cannot drink from the Lord's cup and also from the cup of demons; you cannot eat at the Lord's table and also at the table of demons. 22Or do we want to make the Lord jealous? Do we think that we are stronger than he?

23"We are allowed to do anything," so they say. That is true, but not everything is good. "We are allowed to do anything"–but not everything is helpful. 24None of you should be looking out for your own interests, but for the interests of others.

25You are free to eat anything sold in the meat market, without asking any questions because of your conscience. 26For, as the scripture says, "The earth and everything in it belong to the Lord."

27If an unbeliever invites you to a meal and you decide to go, eat what is set before you, without asking any questions because of your conscience. 28But if someone tells you, "This food was offered to idols," then do not eat that food, for the sake of the one who told you and for conscience' sake– 29that is, not your own conscience, but the other person's conscience.

"Well, then," someone asks, "why should my freedom to act be limited by another person's conscience? 30If I thank God for my food, why should anyone criticize me about food for which I give thanks?"

31Well, whatever you do, whether you eat or drink, do it all for God's glory. 32Live in such a way as to cause no trouble either to Jews or Gentiles or to the church of God. 33Just do as I do; I try to please everyone in all that I do, not thinking of my own good, but of the good of

起，替你們打開一條出路。

14 所以，親愛的朋友們，你們要遠避拜偶像的事。15我是向你們這些明白事理的人說話；你們自己可以判斷我所說的對不對。16我們喝祝謝了的杯，不是分享基督的血嗎？我們吃擘開了的餅，不是分享基督的身體嗎？17因為我們只有一個餅，也都分享同一個餅；所以，我們人數雖多，仍然是一體。

18 請看看以色列人吧，那些吃過祭物的，就跟祭壇有了關係。19我這樣說是甚麼意思呢？是真的以為偶像和祭物本身那麼重要嗎？20不是的！我是說，那獻在異教祭壇上的祭物是獻給鬼，不是獻給上帝的。我不願意你們跟鬼同夥。21你們不能喝主的杯又喝鬼的杯，不能參加主的筵席又參加鬼的筵席。22我們要惹主發怒嗎？我們比他強嗎？

23 有人說：「我們有自由做任何事。」這話不錯。然而，並不是每一件事都有益處。「我們有自由做任何事。」然而，並不是每一件事都會幫助人。24每一個人都不應該為自己的利益着想，而應該關心別人的利益。

25 肉市場上所賣的，你們都可以吃，不要為良心的緣故查問甚麼。26因為聖經上說：「地上和其中的萬物都屬於主。」

27 如果有不信主的人請你們吃飯，你們也願意去，那麼，只管吃桌上所擺的食物，不必為着良心的緣故猶豫。28但是，如果有人告訴你們，說那些食物是祭過偶像的，你們就為了那告訴你們的人，也是為了良心的緣故，不要吃這食物—29我不是指你們自己的良心，而是指那個人的良心。

也許有人要問：「那麼，為甚麼我的自由要受別人的良心所拘束呢？30如果我存着感恩的心領受了食物，別人怎能批評我吃那祝謝了的食物呢？」

31 那麼，你們無論做甚麼，或吃或喝，都要為榮耀上帝而做。32你們無論對猶太人、希臘人，或是對上帝的教會，都不可以使人跌倒。33你們要照我所做的去做；我是要使大家歡喜，從來沒有為自己的好處着想，而

all, so that they might be saved.

11 Imitate me, then, just as I imitate Christ.

Covering the Head in Worship

2I praise you because you always remember me and follow the teachings that I have handed on to you. 3But I want you to understand that Christ is supreme over every man, the husband is supreme over his wife, and God is supreme over Christ. 4So a man who prays or proclaims God's message in public worship with his head covered disgraces Christ. 5And any woman who prays or proclaims God's message in public worship with nothing on her head disgraces her husband; there is no difference between her and a woman whose head has been shaved. 6If the woman does not cover her head, she might as well cut her hair. And since it is a shameful thing for a woman to shave her head or cut her hair, she should cover her head. 7A man has no need to cover his head, because he reflects the image and glory of God. But woman reflects the glory of man; 8for man was not created from woman, but woman from man. 9Nor was man created for woman's sake, but woman was created for man's sake. 10On account of the angels, then, a woman should have a covering over her head to show that she is under her husband's authority. 11In our life in the Lord, however, woman is not independent of man, nor is man independent of woman. 12For as woman was made from man, in the same way man is born of woman; and it is God who brings everything into existence.

13Judge for yourselves whether it is proper for a woman to pray to God in public worship with nothing on her head. 14Why, nature itself teaches you that long hair on a man is a disgrace, 15but on a woman it is a thing of beauty. Her long hair has been given her to serve as a covering. 16But if anyone wants to argue about it, all I have to say is that neither we nor the churches of God have any other custom in worship.

The Lord's Supper

(Matthew 26.26-29; Mark 14.22-25; Luke 22.14-20)

17In the following instructions, however, I do not praise you, because your meetings for worship actually do more harm than good. 18In the first place, I have been told that there are opposing groups in your meetings; and this I believe is partly true. 19(No doubt there must be divisions among you so that the ones who are in the right may be clearly seen.) 20When you meet together as a group, it is not the Lord's

是關心大家的好處，爲要使他們得救。

11 你們要效法我，像我效法基督一樣。

敬拜的禮儀

2 我稱讚你們；因爲你們常常記得我，並且遵從我傳授給你們的教訓。

3 但是，我希望你們明白，基督是每一個男人的頭；丈夫是妻子的頭；上帝是基督的頭。4 男人在公共場所禱告或宣講上帝信息的時候，要是把頭蒙着就是羞辱基督。5 可是，妻子在公共場所禱告或宣講上帝信息的時候，要是不蒙着頭就是羞辱自己的丈夫。這樣的女人和剃了頭髮的女人沒有甚麼區別。6 女人要是不蒙頭，倒不如剪掉頭髮；既然認爲剃頭或剪頭髮是可恥的事，她就應該蒙着頭。7 男人不應該蒙頭，因爲他反映上帝的形像和榮耀。但女人是反映男人的榮耀；8 因爲男人不是從女人造的，女人卻是從男人造的；9 男人不是爲着女人造的，女人卻是爲着男人造的。

10 爲此，因着天使的緣故，女人的頭上應該有權威的記號。11重要的是：在主裏，男女互相倚賴，彼此需要。12因爲女人是從男人造的，男人是從女人生的，而萬物都是從上帝來的。

13 你們自己判斷吧！女人在公共場所禱告不蒙頭是合宜的嗎？14你們的本性不是指示你們，男人留長頭髮是他的羞辱，15女人留長頭髮卻是她的榮耀嗎？因爲長頭髮可以做女人的遮蓋。16如果有人要辯駁，我只能說，我們和上帝的諸教會在敬拜的事上沒有其他的規矩。

主的聖餐

（太26‧26—29；可14‧22—25；路22‧14—20）

17 我現在要吩咐的話不是要稱讚你們，因爲你們的聚會實在是有損無益的。18第一，有人告訴我，你們在聚會的時候結黨分派。我相信這話有一部分是眞的。19你們當中有分裂是不可避免的；這可以使人看出誰有正確的主張。

20 你們聚集的時候，並不是來守主的聖

Supper that you eat. 21For as you eat, you each go ahead with your own meal, so that some are hungry while others get drunk. 22Don't you have your own homes in which to eat and drink? Or would you rather despise the church of God and put to shame the people who are in need? What do you expect me to say to you about this? Shall I praise you? Of course I don't!

23For I received from the Lord the teaching that I passed on to you: that the Lord Jesus, on the night he was betrayed, took a piece of bread, 24gave thanks to God, broke it, and said, "This is my body, which is for you. Do this in memory of me." 25In the same way, after the supper he took the cup and said, "This cup is God's new covenant, sealed with my blood. Whenever you drink it, do so in memory of me."

26This means that every time you eat this bread and drink from this cup you proclaim the Lord's death until he comes. 27It follows that if one of you eats the Lord's bread or drinks from his cup in a way that dishonors him, you are guilty of sin against the Lord's body and blood. 28So then, you should each examine yourself first, and then eat the bread and drink from the cup. 29For if you do not recognize the meaning of the Lord's body when you eat the bread and drink from the cup, you bring judgment on yourself as you eat and drink. 30That is why many of you are sick and weak, and several have died. 31If we would examine ourselves first, we would not come under God's judgment. 32But we are judged and punished by the Lord, so that we shall not be condemned together with the world.

33So then, my friends, when you gather together to eat the Lord's Supper, wait for one another. 34And if any of you are hungry, you should eat at home, so that you will not come under God's judgment as you meet together. As for the other matters, I will settle them when I come.

Gifts from the Holy Spirit

12 Now, concerning what you wrote about the gifts from the Holy Spirit.

I want you to know the truth about them, my friends. 2You know that while you were still heathen, you were led astray in many ways to the worship of lifeless idols. 3I want you to know that no one who is led by God's Spirit can say "A curse on Jesus!" and no one can confess "Jesus is Lord," without being guided by the Holy Spirit.

4There are different kinds of spiritual gifts, but the same Spirit gives them. 5There are different ways of serving, but the same Lord is

餐。21因為你們各人都急着吃自己帶來的東西,以致有的捱餓,有的醉飽。22難道你們沒有家可以吃喝嗎?還是你們故意輕視上帝的教會,並且使窮人難堪呢?我對你們該怎麼說呢?稱讚你們嗎?我不能稱讚你們!

23我所傳授給你們的是我從主所領受的:主耶穌被出賣的那一夜,拿起餅,24感謝上帝,擘開,說:「這是我的身體,是為你們犧牲的;你們應該這樣做,來記念我。」25吃過後,他照樣拿起杯,說:「這杯是上帝用我的血所立的新約。你們每次喝的時候,應該這樣做,來記念我。」26所以,直到主再來,每逢吃這餅喝這杯的時候,你們是在宣告主的死。

27所以,無論誰,要是不用敬虔的心吃主的餅,喝主的杯,他就冒犯了主的身體和血。28每一個人必須先省察自己,然後吃這餅,喝這杯。29如果他不辨認所吃所喝的跟主身體的關係,他吃這餅喝這杯就是自招審判。30為了這緣故,你們當中才有好些衰弱的、患病的,也有些死了的。31如果我們先省察自己,我們就不至於受審判。32可是,我們受主的審判,是主在管教我們,使我們不至於跟世人同被定罪。

33所以,我的弟兄姊妹們,你們聚集守主的聖餐時,應該彼此等候。34有誰餓了,應該在家裏先吃,免得聚會的時候受上帝審判。至於其他的事,等我來了再解決吧。

聖靈的恩賜

12 弟兄姊妹們,關於聖靈的恩賜,我希望你們都明白。2從前你們信從異教的時候,往往被引入歧途,受那些沒有生命的偶像轄制。3我告訴你們,凡是被上帝的靈感動的人一定不說「耶穌是該受詛咒的」。同樣,除非被聖靈引導,也沒有人能承認「耶穌是主」。

4恩賜有多種,卻是同一位聖靈所賜;5事

served. ⁶There are different abilities to perform service, but the same God gives ability to all for their particular service. ⁷The Spirit's presence is shown in some way in each person for the good of all. ⁸The Spirit gives one person a message full of wisdom, while to another person the same Spirit gives a message full of knowledge. ⁹One and the same Spirit gives faith to one person, while to another person he gives the power to heal. ¹⁰The Spirit gives one person the power to work miracles; to another, the gift of speaking God's message; and to yet another, the ability to tell the difference between gifts that come from the Spirit and those that do not. To one person he gives the ability to speak in strange tongues, and to another he gives the ability to explain what is said. ¹¹But it is one and the same Spirit who does all this; as he wishes, he gives a different gift to each person.

One Body with Many Parts

¹²Christ is like a single body, which has many parts; it is still one body, even though it is made up of different parts. ¹³In the same way, all of us, whether Jews or Gentiles, whether slaves or free, have been baptized into the one body by the same Spirit, and we have all been given the one Spirit to drink.

¹⁴For the body itself is not made up of only one part, but of many parts. ¹⁵If the foot were to say, "Because I am not a hand, I don't belong to the body," that would not keep it from being a part of the body. ¹⁶And if the ear were to say, "Because I am not an eye, I don't belong to the body," that would not keep it from being a part of the body. ¹⁷If the whole body were just an eye, how could it hear? And if it were only an ear, how could it smell? ¹⁸As it is, however, God put every different part in the body just as he wanted it to be. ¹⁹There would not be a body if it were all only one part! ²⁰As it is, there are many parts but one body.

²¹So then, the eye cannot say to the hand, "I don't need you!" Nor can the head say to the feet, "Well, I don't need you!" ²²On the contrary, we cannot do without the parts of the body that seem to be weaker; ²³and those parts that we think aren't worth very much are the ones which we treat with greater care; while the parts of the body which don't look very nice are treated with special modesty, ²⁴which the more beautiful parts do not need. God himself has put the body together in such a way as to give greater honor to those parts that need it. ²⁵And so there is no division in the body, but all its different parts have the same concern for one another. ²⁶If one part of the body suffers, all the other parts suffer with it; if one part is

奉有多種，卻是同一位主所賜；⁶工作有多種，卻是同一位上帝賜給每人工作的能力。⁷爲了使大家都得到好處，聖靈在我們每一個人身上所彰顯的也各不相同。⁸聖靈把智慧的信息賜給一個人，同一位聖靈把知識的信息賜給另一個人。⁹同一位聖靈把信心賜給一個人，把治病的能力賜給另一個人。¹⁰聖靈賜給這個人行神蹟的能力，給那個人傳講上帝信息的恩賜，給某人有辨別諸靈的能力，給另一個人有講靈語的能力，又給另一個人有解釋靈語的能力。¹¹可是，這一切都是從同一位、惟一的聖靈來的；他按照自己的旨意，把不同的恩賜給每一個人。

一個身體有許多肢體

¹²基督就像一個身體，有許多肢體；雖然身體有許多肢體，到底還是一個身體。¹³同樣，我們無論是猶太人或希臘人，作奴隸的或自由的，都從同一位聖靈受洗，成了一個身體，而且共享這一位聖靈。

¹⁴身體不是只有一個肢體，而是由許多肢體構成的。¹⁵如果腳說：「我不是手，所以不屬於身體」，它不能因此就不是身體的一部分。¹⁶如果耳朶說：「我不是眼睛，所以不屬於身體」，它也不能因此就不是身體的一部分。¹⁷如果全身是眼睛，怎麼能聽呢？如果全身是耳朶，怎麼能嗅呢？¹⁸然而，上帝按照自己的旨意把那些不同的肢體都安置在人的身體上。¹⁹如果全身體只有一個肢體，怎麼能算是身體呢？²⁰其實，肢體有許多，身體卻只是一個。

²¹所以，眼睛不能對手說：「我不需要你！」頭也不能對腳說：「我用不着你！」²²相反地，身體上那些似乎比較軟弱的肢體，更是我們所不能缺少的。²³在我們的身體上，那些看來不太重要的部分，卻是我們所特別愛護的；那些不太好看的部分尤其爲我們所關注，²⁴那些比較美觀的部分就不需要特別加以裝飾。上帝這樣安置我們身體的各部分，把更大的光榮分給那些比較不美觀的肢體，²⁵好使整個身體不至於分裂，各不同肢體能互相關懷。²⁶一個肢體受苦，所有的肢體就一同受苦；一個肢體得榮耀，所有

praised, all the other parts share its happiness.

27All of you are Christ's body, and each one is a part of it. 28In the church God has put all in place: in the first place apostles, in the second place prophets, and in the third place teachers; then those who perform miracles, followed by those who are given the power to heal or to help others or to direct them or to speak in strange tongues. 29They are not all apostles or prophets or teachers. Not everyone has the power to work miracles 30or to heal diseases or to speak in strange tongues or to explain what is said. 31Set your hearts, then, on the more important gifts.

Best of all, however, is the following way.

Love

13I may be able to speak the languages of human beings and even of angels, but if I have no love, my speech is no more than a noisy gong or a clanging bell. 2I may have the gift of inspired preaching; I may have all knowledge and understand all secrets; I may have all the faith needed to move mountains–but if I have no love, I am nothing. 3I may give away everything I have, and even give up my body to be burned[n]–but if I have no love, this does me no good.

4Love is patient and kind; it is not jealous or conceited or proud; 5love is not ill-mannered or selfish or irritable; love does not keep a record of wrongs; 6love is not happy with evil, but is happy with the truth. 7Love never gives up; and its faith, hope, and patience never fail.

8Love is eternal. There are inspired messages, but they are temporary; there are gifts of speaking in strange tongues, but they will cease; there is knowledge, but it will pass. 9For our gifts of knowledge and of inspired messages are only partial; 10but when what is perfect comes, then what is partial will disappear. 11When I was a child, my speech, feelings, and thinking were all those of a child; now that I am an adult, I have no more use for childish ways. 12What we see now is like a dim image in a mirror; then we shall see face-to-face. What I know now is only partial; then it will be complete–as complete as God's knowledge of me.

13Meanwhile these three remain: faith, hope, and love; and the greatest of these is love.

的肢體就一同快樂。

27 你們就是基督的身體,而每一個人都是肢體。28在教會裏,上帝使人各得其所;他所安排的:第一是使徒,第二是先知,第三是教師;其次是行神蹟的,再次是有治病能力的;此外還有能夠幫助別人,能夠管理事務,能夠講靈語的。29他們並不都是使徒,不都是先知,不都是教師;也不都能行神蹟,30不都能治病,不都能講靈語,不都能解釋靈語。31可是,你們要追求那更重要的恩賜。

我現在要指示你們那至善的道路。

論愛

13我即使會講人間各種話,甚至於天使的話,要是沒有愛,我的話就像吵鬧的鑼和響亮的鈸一樣。2我即使有講道的才能,也能夠洞悉各種知識、各種奧祕,甚至有堅強的信心能夠移山倒海,要是沒有愛,就算不了甚麼。3我即使把所有的財產都捐給人,甚至犧牲自己的身體被人焚燒⑧,要是沒有愛,我所做的仍然沒有益處。

4 愛是堅忍的,仁慈的;有愛就不嫉妒,不自誇,不驕傲,5不做鹵莽的事,不自私,不輕易動怒,不記住別人的過錯,6不喜歡不義,只喜愛真理。7愛能包容一切,對一切有信心,對一切有盼望,能忍受一切。

8 愛是永恆的。講道的才能是暫時的;講靈語的恩賜總有一天會終止;知識也會成為過去。9因為我們的知識有限,講道的恩賜也有限。10可是,那完全的一到,有限的就會消失了。

11 我作孩子的時候,說話像孩子,情感像孩子,想法也像孩子。現在我已長大成人,我把孩子氣的事都丟棄了。12我們現在所看見的是間接從鏡子裏看見的影像,模糊不清,將來就會面對面看得清清楚楚。我現在對上帝的認識不完全,將來就會完全,正像上帝完全認識我一樣。

13 然而,信心、盼望,和愛這三樣是永存的,而其中最重要的是愛。

---

n to be burned; *some manuscripts have* in order to boast.

⑧「被人焚燒」有些古卷作「讓人誇讚」。

More about Gifts from the Spirit

14It is love, then, that you should strive for. Set your hearts on spiritual gifts, especially the gift of proclaiming God's message. ²Those who speak in strange tongues do not speak to others but to God, because no one understands them. They are speaking secret truths by the power of the Spirit. ³But those who proclaim God's message speak to people and give them help, encouragement, and comfort. ⁴Those who speak in strange tongues help only themselves, but those who proclaim God's message help the whole church.

⁵I would like for all of you to speak in strange tongues; but I would rather that you had the gift of proclaiming God's message. For the person who proclaims God's message is of greater value than the one who speaks in strange tongues—unless there is someone present who can explain what is said, so that the whole church may be helped. ⁶So when I come to you, my friends, what use will I be to you if I speak in strange tongues? Not a bit, unless I bring you some revelation from God or some knowledge or some inspired message or some teaching.

⁷Take such lifeless musical instruments as the flute or the harp—how will anyone know the tune that is being played unless the notes are sounded distinctly? ⁸And if the one who plays the bugle does not sound a clear call, who will prepare for battle? ⁹In the same way, how will anyone understand what you are talking about if your message given in strange tongues is not clear? Your words will vanish in the air! ¹⁰There are many different languages in the world, yet none of them is without meaning. ¹¹But if I do not know the language being spoken, those who use it will be foreigners to me and I will be a foreigner to them. ¹²Since you are eager to have the gifts of the Spirit, you must try above everything else to make greater use of those which help to build up the church.

¹³The person who speaks in strange tongues, then, must pray for the gift to explain what is said. ¹⁴For if I pray in this way, my spirit prays indeed, but my mind has no part in it. ¹⁵What should I do, then? I will pray with my spirit, but I will pray also with my mind; I will sing with my spirit, but I will sing also with my mind. ¹⁶When you give thanks to God in spirit only, how can ordinary people taking part in the meeting say "Amen" to your prayer of thanksgiving? They have no way of knowing what you are saying. ¹⁷Even if your prayer of thanks to God is quite good, other people are not helped at all.

¹⁸I thank God that I speak in strange tongues

再論聖靈的恩賜

14你們要追求愛。要渴慕屬靈的恩賜，尤其是宣講上帝信息的恩賜。²那講靈語的不是對人講，而是對上帝講，因為沒有人聽得懂他的話。他是藉着聖靈在講述奧祕的真理。³可是，那宣講上帝信息的是對人講，是要造就，鼓勵，和安慰他們。⁴講靈語的人只造就自己，宣講上帝信息的人是造就全教會。

⁵我希望你們都會講靈語，可是我更希望你們都有宣講上帝信息的恩賜。因為，除非有人能把靈語翻譯出來，使全教會得到造就，否則，宣講上帝信息的就比講靈語的更重要。⁶所以，弟兄姊妹們，我到你們那裏去，如果只講靈語，不帶給你們從上帝來的啓示、知識、預言，或教導，那對你們有甚麼益處呢？

⁷甚至那些沒有生命的樂器，就像笛子或豎琴吧，如果它們發出的聲音沒有高低的分別，怎麼能使人知道所吹所彈的是甚麼曲調呢？⁸要是吹號的吹不出準確的音，誰能準備打仗呢？⁹同樣，你們所講的靈語若不清楚，誰能明白裏頭的信息呢？你們就是向空氣說話罷了！¹⁰世界上有許多不同的語言，而沒有一種語言是不表達意思的。¹¹要是我不明白那種語言，那麼，使用那種語言的人對我來說是外國人，我在他眼中也是一個外國人。¹²同樣，既然你們熱切希望有屬靈的恩賜，就應該多多追求那能夠造就教會的恩賜。

¹³所以，講靈語的人應該祈求特別的恩賜，好解釋靈語的意思。¹⁴如果我用靈語禱告，就是我的靈在禱告，可是我的理智不發生作用。¹⁵這怎麼辦呢？我要用靈禱告，也要用理智禱告；我要用靈歌唱，也要用理智歌唱。¹⁶要不然，當你只用靈向上帝感謝的時候，在聚會中不通靈語的人不懂得你說的是甚麼，怎能跟你同心說「阿們」呢？他無法知道你在說甚麼。¹⁷這樣，即使你向上帝感謝的禱告是好的，別人也不能夠得到造就。

¹⁸我感謝上帝，我講靈語比你們當中任何

much more than any of you. [19]But in church worship I would rather speak five words that can be understood, in order to teach others, than speak thousands of words in strange tongues.

[20]Do not be like children in your thinking, my friends; be children so far as evil is concerned, but be grown up in your thinking. [21]In the Scriptures it is written,

"By means of people speaking strange
     languages
  I will speak to my people, says the Lord.
I will speak through lips of foreigners,
  but even then my people will not listen to
     me."

[22]So then, the gift of speaking in strange tongues is proof for unbelievers, not for believers, while the gift of proclaiming God's message is proof for believers, not for unbelievers.

[23]If, then, the whole church meets together and everyone starts speaking in strange tongues–and if some ordinary people or unbelievers come in, won't they say that you are all crazy? [24]But if everyone is proclaiming God's message when some unbelievers or ordinary people come in, they will be convinced of their sin by what they hear. They will be judged by all they hear, [25]their secret thoughts will be brought into the open, and they will bow down and worship God, confessing, "Truly God is here among you!"

Order in the Church

[26]This is what I mean, my friends. When you meet for worship, one person has a hymn, another a teaching, another a revelation from God, another a message in strange tongues, and still another the explanation of what is said. Everything must be of help to the church. [27]If someone is going to speak in strange tongues, two or three at the most should speak, one after the other, and someone else must explain what is being said. [28]But if no one is there who can explain, then the one who speaks in strange tongues must be quiet and speak only to himself and to God. [29]Two or three who are given God's message should speak, while the others are to judge what they say. [30]But if someone sitting in the meeting receives a message from God, the one who is speaking should stop. [31]All of you may proclaim God's message, one by one, so that everyone will learn and be encouraged. [32]The gift of proclaiming God's message should be under the speaker's control, [33]because God does not want us to be in disorder but in harmony and peace.

As in all the churches of God's people, [34]the women should keep quiet in the meetings. They are not allowed to speak; as the Jewish Law

一個人都多。[19]可是,在教會的聚會中,我寧願說五句使人明白、能夠教導人的話,而不講千萬句靈語。

[20]弟兄姊妹們,你們在思想上不要像小孩子;在壞事上要像嬰孩。你們在思想上要成熟。[21]聖經上說過:

主說:我要藉着說奇異語言的人,
    藉着外國人的嘴唇向這人民說話;
    可是,他們還是不聽從我。

[22]這樣看來,講靈語的恩賜不是為着信徒,而是給不信的人作憑據的。可是,傳講上帝信息的恩賜不是為着不信的人,而是給信徒作憑據的。

[23]那麼,如果全教會聚會的時候,大家都講靈語,一般外人或不信的人進來,不是要說你們都發瘋了嗎?[24]如果大家在傳講上帝的信息,有不信的或外人進來,他會從所聽見的話省悟到自己的罪,感覺到耳心不安,[25]隱密的意念顯露出來,他不能不俯伏敬拜上帝,承認說:「上帝實在與你們同在。」

教會該守的規矩

[26]弟兄姊妹們,我的意思是甚麼呢?你們聚會敬拜的時候,有人獻詩歌,有人教導,有人得到從上帝來的啟示,有人講靈語,又有人翻譯靈語。要知道,所做的一切都應該對教會有造就才對。[27]如果有人要講靈語,最多讓兩三個人輪流着講,而且需要別人把所講的翻譯出來。[28]要是沒有翻譯的人,那講靈語的就應當緘默,只對自己和上帝講好了。[29]至於宣講上帝信息,可以由兩三個人發言,其餘的人小心辨察他們所說的。[30]在座的,要是另外有人從上帝得了啟示,那先說話的人就應該停止。[31]你們每一個人都可以輪流宣講上帝的信息,讓大家學習,都得到鼓勵。[32]宣講上帝信息的人應該約束自己的恩賜;[33]因為上帝不要紛亂,而是要我們和諧。

就跟上帝子民的各教會一樣,[34]婦女在聚會中要安靜。她們不可以發言;就像猶太

says, they must not be in charge. [35]If they want to find out about something, they should ask their husbands at home. It is a disgraceful thing for a woman to speak in a church meeting.

[36]Or could it be that the word of God came from you? Or are you the only ones to whom it came? [37]If anyone supposes he is God's messenger or has a spiritual gift, he must realize that what I am writing to you is the Lord's command. [38]But if he does not pay attention to this, pay no attention to him.

[39]So then, my friends, set your heart on proclaiming God's message, but do not forbid the speaking in strange tongues. [40]Everything must be done in a proper and orderly way.

The Resurrection of Christ

15And now I want to remind you, my friends, of the Good News which I preached to you, which you received, and on which your faith stands firm. [2]That is the gospel, the message that I preached to you. You are saved by the gospel if you hold firmly to it–unless it was for nothing that you believed.

[3]I passed on to you what I received, which is of the greatest importance: that Christ died for our sins, as written in the Scriptures; [4]that he was buried and that he was raised to life three days later, as written in the Scriptures; [5]that he appeared to Peter and then to all twelve apostles. [6]Then he appeared to more than five hundred of his followers at once, most of whom are still alive, although some have died. [7]Then he appeared to James, and afterward to all the apostles.

[8]Last of all he appeared also to me–even though I am like someone whose birth was abnormal.[o] [9]For I am the least of all the apostles–I do not even deserve to be called an apostle, because I persecuted God's church. [10]But by God's grace I am what I am, and the grace that he gave me was not without effect. On the contrary, I have worked harder than any of the other apostles, although it was not really my own doing, but God's grace working with me. [11]So then, whether it came from me or from them, this is what we all preach, and this is what you believe.

Our Resurrection

[12]Now, since our message is that Christ has been raised from death, how can some of you say that the dead will not be raised to life? [13]If that is true, it means that Christ was not raised; [14]and if Christ has not been raised from death, then we have nothing to preach and you have

o whose birth was abnormal; or who was born at the wrong time.

人的法律所規定的,她們要安於本份。[35]如果她們想知道甚麼,可以在家裏問丈夫。婦女在聚會中說話是不體面的事。

[36]甚麼話?上帝的道豈是從你們來的?豈是單單傳授給你們的?[37]如果有人自以為是傳講上帝信息的人,或以為他有屬靈的恩賜,他應該知道我寫給你們的是出於主的命令。[38]要是他忽視這個,你們可以不理他。

[39]所以,我的弟兄姊妹們,你們應該追求宣講上帝信息的恩賜,但也不要禁止講靈語。[40]凡事要做得恰當而有次序。

基督的復活

15弟兄姊妹們,我要你們記住我以前所傳給你們的福音;這福音你們領受了,並且用它作信心的基礎。[2]如果你們持守這福音,不是空空洞洞地相信,一定會因着它而得救。

[3]我曾經把我所領受那最重要的信息傳授給你們,就是:按照聖經所說的,基督為我們的罪死了;[4]又按照聖經所說的,他被埋葬了,在第三天復活了。[5]他向彼得顯現,又向十二使徒顯現。[6]以後他又一次向五百多個跟從他的人顯現;這些人多數還活着,雖然也有些已經死了。[7]後來,他向雅各顯現,又向所有的使徒顯現。

[8]最後,他也向我顯現;我好像是一個在不正常[9]的情況下出生的人。[9]我在使徒中原是最微小的,不配稱為使徒,因為我迫害過上帝的教會。[10]但是,由於上帝的恩典,我才成了今天的我,他所賜給我的恩典沒有落空。相反地,我比其他所有的使徒更加辛勞地工作;其實,不是我自己在工作,而是上帝的恩典與我一同工作。[11]那麼,無論是我還是別的使徒,我們都這樣傳,你們也都這樣信。

信徒的復活

[12]既然我們所傳的信息是基督已經從死裏復活了,為甚麼你們當中有人說沒有死人復活的事呢?[13]要是沒有復活的事,那等於說,基督沒有復活了;[14]如果基督沒有從死裏復活,我們就沒有甚麼好傳的,你們也沒

⑨「不正常」或譯「不適時」。

nothing to believe. [15]More than that, we are shown to be lying about God, because we said that he raised Christ from death–but if it is true that the dead are not raised to life, then he did not raise Christ. [16]For if the dead are not raised, neither has Christ been raised. [17]And if Christ has not been raised, then your faith is a delusion and you are still lost in your sins. [18]It would also mean that the believers in Christ who have died are lost. [19]If our hope in Christ is good for this life only and no more,[p] then we deserve more pity than anyone else in all the world.

[20]But the truth is that Christ has been raised from death, as the guarantee that those who sleep in death will also be raised. [21]For just as death came by means of a man, in the same way the rising from death comes by means of a man. [22]For just as all people die because of their union with Adam, in the same way all will be raised to life because of their union with Christ. [23]But each one will be raised in proper order: Christ, first of all; then, at the time of his coming, those who belong to him. [24]Then the end will come; Christ will overcome all spiritual rulers, authorities, and powers, and will hand over the Kingdom to God the Father. [25]For Christ must rule until God defeats all enemies and puts them under his feet. [26]The last enemy to be defeated will be death. [27]For the scripture says, "God put *all* things under his feet." It is clear, of course, that the words "all things" do not include God himself, who puts all things under Christ. [28]But when all things have been placed under Christ's rule, then he himself, the Son, will place himself under God, who placed all things under him; and God will rule completely over all.

[29]Now, what about those people who are baptized for the dead? What do they hope to accomplish? If it is true, as some claim, that the dead are not raised to life, why are those people being baptized for the dead? [30]And as for us–why would we run the risk of danger every hour? [31]My friends, I face death every day! The pride I have in you, in our life in union with Christ Jesus our Lord, makes me declare this. [32]If I have, as it were, fought "wild beasts" here in Ephesus simply from human motives, what have I gained? But if the dead are not raised to life, then, as the saying goes, "Let us eat and drink, for tomorrow we will die."

[33]Do not be fooled. "Bad companions ruin good character." [34]Come back to your right senses and stop your sinful ways. I declare to your shame that some of you do not know

p If our hope in Christ is good for this life only and no more; *or* If all we have in this life is our hope in Christ.

有甚麼好信的。[15]這樣，我們顯然在爲上帝作假證；因爲我們見證，說他使基督從死裏復活了。如果眞的沒有死人復活的事，上帝就沒有使基督復活了。[16]死人若沒有復活，那等於說，基督沒有復活了。[17]基督若沒有復活，你們的信仰就是幻想，你們仍然迷失在罪中。[18]這樣的話，死了的基督徒就都算滅亡了。[19]如果我們信基督的人只在今生有希望⑩，我們就比世界上任何人更可憐了。

[20]然而，事實上基督已經從死裏復活；這是要保證已經死了的人也要復活。[21]因爲死亡是從一人來的，死人的復活也是從一人來的。[22]正如衆人的死亡是因爲他們跟亞當連結，同樣，衆人的復活是因爲他們跟基督連結。[23]不過，每一個人要按照適當的次序復活：最先是基督，其次是，他再來時，屬於他的人。[24]然後末期到了；那時候，基督要消滅一切靈界的執政者、掌權者，和有能者，把王權交還給父上帝。[25]因爲基督必須統治，直到上帝打敗一切仇敵，使他們都屈服在他腳下。[26]他所要毀滅的最後仇敵就是死亡。[27]因爲聖經上說：「上帝使萬物都服在他腳下。」很明顯地，這裏所說的「萬物」並不包括上帝本身，因爲他就是那使萬物屈服在基督腳下的。[28]到了萬物都屈服於基督時，兒子本身也要屈服在那位使萬物都順服他的上帝，好讓上帝在萬物之上統御一切。

[29]要不是這樣，那些代死人受洗禮的又有甚麼意思呢？他們所希望的是甚麼呢？要是沒有死人復活這回事，那他們爲甚麼還代死人受洗呢？[30]我們又何必時時刻刻冒險呢？[31]弟兄姊妹們，我天天面對着死！我敢這樣說，是因爲我們同在我們的主基督耶穌的生命裏，我以你們爲榮。[32]如果我在以弗所跟那些野獸格鬥純粹是出於人的動機，這對我有甚麼益處呢？如果死人不復活，那麼，就像俗語所說的：「讓我們吃吃喝喝吧，反正我們明天就要死了。」

[33]不要受愚弄了。「壞友伴敗壞品德！」[34]要醒悟，不要再犯罪了。我說這話是要你們覺得羞愧，因爲你們當中有人不認識

⑩「如果我們信基督的人只在今生有希望」或譯「如果我們對基督的希望只限於今生」。

God.

The Resurrection Body

35Someone will ask, "How can the dead be raised to life? What kind of body will they have?" 36You fool! When you plant a seed in the ground, it does not sprout to life unless it dies. 37And what you plant is a bare seed, perhaps a grain of wheat or some other grain, not the full-bodied plant that will later grow up. 38God provides that seed with the body he wishes; he gives each seed its own proper body.

39And the flesh of living beings is not all the same kind of flesh; human beings have one kind of flesh, animals another, birds another, and fish another.

40And there are heavenly bodies and earthly bodies; the beauty that belongs to heavenly bodies is different from the beauty that belongs to earthly bodies. 41The sun has its own beauty, the moon another beauty, and the stars a different beauty; and even among stars there are different kinds of beauty.

42This is how it will be when the dead are raised to life. When the body is buried, it is mortal; when raised, it will be immortal. 43When buried, it is ugly and weak; when raised, it will be beautiful and strong. 44When buried, it is a physical body; when raised, it will be a spiritual body. There is, of course, a physical body, so there has to be a spiritual body. 45For the scripture says, "The first man, Adam, was created a living being"; but the last Adam is the life-giving Spirit. 46It is not the spiritual that comes first, but the physical, and then the spiritual. 47The first Adam, made of earth, came from the earth; the second Adam came from heaven. 48Those who belong to the earth are like the one who was made of earth; those who are of heaven are like the one who came from heaven. 49Just as we wear the likeness of the man made of earth, so we will wear*q* the likeness of the Man from heaven.

50What I mean, friends, is that what is made of flesh and blood cannot share in God's Kingdom, and what is mortal cannot possess immortality. 51-52Listen to this secret truth: we shall not all die, but when the last trumpet sounds, we shall all be changed in an instant, as quickly as the blinking of an eye. For when the trumpet sounds, the dead will be raised, never to die again, and we shall all be changed. 53For what is mortal must be changed into what is immortal; what will die must be changed into what cannot die. 54So when this takes place, and the mortal has been changed into the immortal,

q we will wear; some manuscripts have let us wear.

復活的身體

35 有人要問：「死人怎麼能復活呢？他們會有甚麼樣的形體呢？」36無知的人哪，你種在地裏的種子，要不是死了就不能發芽生長。37你們所種的是麥子，或是別的種子，都是一顆光光的子粒，並不是那將來要長成的形體。38上帝照着自己的意思給種子一個形體；他使各樣的種子各有適當的形體。

39 各種動物的肉體也都不相同：人有人體，獸有獸體，鳥有鳥體，魚有魚體。

40 還有天上的形體，也有地上的形體；天上的形體有一種美，地上的形體有另一種美。41太陽有太陽的光輝，月亮有月亮的光輝，星星有星星的光輝；甚至這顆星和那顆星所發的光也不一樣。

42 死人復活也是這樣。身體埋葬後會朽壞；復活後是不朽壞的。43被埋葬的是醜陋衰弱的；復活的是完美健壯的。44被埋葬的是血肉的身體；復活的是屬靈的身體。既然有血肉的身體，也就有屬靈的身體。45因為聖經上說：「頭一個人亞當被造成爲有生命的人」；可是末後的亞當是賜生命的靈。46先有的不是屬靈的；是先有血肉的，然後才有屬靈的。47頭一個亞當是從地上的塵土造成的；第二個亞當是從天上來的。48屬塵土的人是像那由塵土造成的人；屬天的人是像那從天上來的人。49我們已經有了屬塵土的人的形像，將來也會⑪有那從天上來的人的形像。

50 弟兄姊妹們，我要說的是：血肉造成的身體不能承受上帝的國，那會朽壞的不能承受不朽壞的。

51-52你們要注意這一件奧祕的事：我們並不是都要死，而是在一刹那、一眨眼間，最後的號角響的時候，都要改變。最後的號角一響，死人要復活而成爲不朽壞的；我們也要改變。53因爲那會朽壞的必須變成不朽壞的，會死的必須變成不會死的。54到了那會朽壞的已經變成不朽壞的，那會死的已經變

⑪有些古卷是「讓我們也……」。

then the scripture will come true: "Death is destroyed; victory is complete!"

55"Where, Death, is your victory?

Where, Death, is your power to hurt?"

56Death gets its power to hurt from sin, and sin gets its power from the Law. 57But thanks be to God who gives us the victory through our Lord Jesus Christ!

58So then, my dear friends, stand firm and steady. Keep busy always in your work for the Lord, since you know that nothing you do in the Lord's service is ever useless.

The Offering for Needy Believers

16 Now, concerning what you wrote about the money to be raised to help God's people in Judea. You must do what I told the churches in Galatia to do. 2Every Sunday each of you must put aside some money, in proportion to what you have earned, and save it up, so that there will be no need to collect money when I come. 3After I come, I shall give letters of introduction to those you have approved, and send them to take your gift to Jerusalem. 4If it seems worthwhile for me to go, then they can go along with me.

Paul's Plans

5I shall come to you after I have gone through Macedonia–for I have to go through Macedonia. 6I shall probably spend some time with you, perhaps the whole winter, and then you can help me to continue my trip, wherever it is I shall go next. 7I want to see you more than just briefly in passing; I hope to spend quite a long time with you, if the Lord allows.

8I will stay here in Ephesus until the day of Pentecost. 9There is a real opportunity here for great and worthwhile work, even though there are many opponents.

10If Timothy comes your way, be sure to make him feel welcome among you, because he is working for the Lord, just as I am. 11No one should look down on him, but you must help him continue his trip in peace, so that he will come back to me; for I am expecting him back with the believers.

12Now, about brother Apollos. I have often encouraged him to visit you with the other believers, but he is not completely convinced[r] that he should go at this time. When he gets the chance, however, he will go.

成不會死的，聖經上的話就實現了：

死亡被消滅了；

勝利已經達成了！

55 死亡啊！你的勝利在哪裏？

死亡啊！你的毒刺在哪裏？

56死亡的毒刺是從罪來的，而罪的權勢是從法律來的。57但是，感謝上帝，他使我們藉着我們的主耶穌基督得勝了！

58 所以，親愛的弟兄姊妹們，你們要站穩，不可動搖。要不辭勞苦地為主工作；因為你們知道，為主工作絕不會是徒然的。

捐助信徒

16 關於籌款幫助信徒的事，你們可以依照我從前吩咐加拉太各教會的辦法去做。2 每星期天，你們每一個人應當按自己的收入照比例撥出一些錢，積存起來，不必等我來時才現湊。3 我到的時候，會派你們所信任的人，給他們介紹信，讓他們把你們的捐款帶到耶路撒冷去。4 如果需要我親自走一趟，他們可以跟我一起去。

保羅的計劃

5 我現在正要路過馬其頓。我訪問了馬其頓以後，就到你們那裏去。6 我可能在你們那裏住些時候，也許在那裏過冬，再繼續我的旅程。這樣，我無論上哪裏去，你們可以給我送行。7 我不願意只在路過時訪問你們；主若准許，我希望跟你們多住一些時候。

8 可是，我還要留在以弗所，一直到五旬節；9 因為，儘管有許多反對的人，這裏的門大開，有很好的工作機會。

10 如果提摩太到你們那裏，我希望你們好好地接待他，使他安心，因為他跟我一樣在為主工作。11誰都不要輕看他；要送他平安地繼續他的旅程，讓他回到我這裏來，因為我正等着他跟信徒們一起來。

12 至於亞波羅弟兄，我常常鼓勵他跟其他信徒一起去訪問你們，可是他總覺得現在去不合適[12]，等有機會，他會去的。

---

r he is not completely convinced; *or* it is not at all God's will.

⑫「不合適」或譯「不是上帝的意思」。

Final Words

13Be alert, stand firm in the faith, be brave, be strong. 14Do all your work in love.

15You know about Stephanas and his family; they are the first Christian converts in Achaia and have given themselves to the service of God's people. I beg you, my friends, 16to follow the leadership of such people as these, and of anyone else who works and serves with them.

17I am happy about the coming of Stephanas, Fortunatus, and Achaicus; they have made up for your absence 18and have cheered me up, just as they cheered you up. Such men as these deserve notice.

19The churches in the province of Asia send you their greetings; Aquila and Priscilla and the church that meets in their house send warm Christian greetings. 20All the believers here send greetings.

Greet one another with the kiss of peace.

21With my own hand I write this: *Greetings from Paul.*

22Whoever does not love the Lord–a curse on him!

Marana tha–Our Lord, come!

23The grace of the Lord Jesus be with you.

24My love be with you all in Christ Jesus.

末了的話

13你們要警醒,要在信仰上站穩,要勇敢,要剛強。14一切工作都要憑着愛心去做。

15弟兄姊妹們,我有話勸你們。你們認得司提法那和他一家人;他們是亞該亞最早成爲基督徒的一家,並且在服事信徒的事上非常熱心。16你們要聽從這樣的人,以及跟他們一起辛勞工作的人。

17司提法那、福徒拿都,和亞該古能夠到這裏來,我很高興。他們正好補償你們不在這裏的遺憾。18他們使我覺得快慰,就像使你們快慰一樣。這樣的人是值得你們敬重的。

19亞細亞省的各教會都向你們問安;亞居拉和百基拉,以及在他們家裏的教會,在主裏面熱切向你們問安。20這裏的弟兄姊妹們都向你們問安。

你們要以聖潔的親吻彼此問安。

21我親手寫:「保羅祝你們好!」

22如果有不愛主的人,他是該受詛咒的。

主啊,願你來!

23願主耶穌賜恩典給你們!

24在基督⑬耶穌裏,我深愛你們大家!⑭

⑬有些古卷沒有「基督」。
⑭有些古卷加「阿們。」

哥林多後書
2 CORINTHIANS

INTRODUCTION

Paul's Second Letter to the Corinthians was written during a difficult period in his relation with the church at Corinth. Some members of the church had evidently made strong attacks against Paul, but he shows his deep longing for reconciliation and expresses his great joy when this is brought about.

In the first part of the letter Paul discusses his relationship with the church at Corinth, explaining why he had responded with severity to insult and opposition in the church and expressing his joy that this severity had resulted in repentance and reconciliation. Then he appeals to the church for a generous offering to help the needy Christians in Judea. In the final chapters Paul defends his apostleship against a few people at Corinth who had set themselves up as true apostles, while accusing Paul of being a false one.

Outline of Contents

簡　介

哥林多後書是當保羅跟哥林多教會之間發生裂痕時寫的。當時，哥林多教會的某些會友多方攻擊保羅，但是他始終盼望跟他們和解。他終於能夠跟哥林多教會和解，爲此他表示十分欣慰。

在本書信的前部，保羅討論他和哥林多教會的關係，解釋他爲甚麼要嚴厲地對付教會裏說侮慢話和站在反對立場的人。他對採取這種態度而促成的悔悟與和解覺得欣慰。接着，他勸勉哥林多教會努力捐獻，接濟在猶太貧窮的信徒。最後幾章，保羅爲他自己的使徒職份辯護，因爲當時哥林多教會有少數人自認是眞使徒，而指責保羅爲假使徒。

提要

1 From Paul, an apostle of Christ Jesus by God's will, and from our brother Timothy–
To the church of God in Corinth, and to all God's people throughout Achaia:
2May God our Father and the Lord Jesus Christ give you grace and peace.

Paul Gives Thanks to God

3Let us give thanks to the God and Father of our Lord Jesus Christ, the merciful Father, the

1 我是保羅；我奉上帝的旨意作基督耶穌的使徒。我和我們的弟兄提摩太寫信給在哥林多上帝的教會和全亞該亞所有的信徒。2願我們的父上帝和主耶穌基督賜恩典、平安給你們！

保羅感謝上帝

3 我們要感謝我們的主耶穌基督的父上帝！他是慈愛的天父，也是一切安慰的來

God from whom all help comes! [4]He helps us in all our troubles, so that we are able to help others who have all kinds of troubles, using the same help that we ourselves have received from God. [5]Just as we have a share in Christ's many sufferings, so also through Christ we share in God's great help. [6]If we suffer, it is for your help and salvation; if we are helped, then you too are helped and given the strength to endure with patience the same sufferings that we also endure. [7]So our hope in you is never shaken; we know that just as you share in our sufferings, you also share in the help we receive.

[8]We want to remind you, friends, of the trouble we had in the province of Asia. The burdens laid upon us were so great and so heavy that we gave up all hope of staying alive. [9]We felt that the death sentence had been passed on us. But this happened so that we should rely, not on ourselves, but only on God, who raises the dead. [10]From such terrible dangers of death[a] he saved us, and will save us; and we have placed our hope in him that he will save us again, [11]as you help us by means of your prayers for us. So it will be that the many prayers for us will be answered, and God will bless us; and many will raise their voices to him in thanksgiving for us.

The Change in Paul's Plans

[12]We are proud that our conscience assures us that our lives in this world, and especially our relations with you, have been ruled by God-given frankness[b] and sincerity, by the power of God's grace and not by human wisdom. [13-14]We write to you only what you can read and understand. But even though you now understand us only in part, I hope that you will come to understand us completely, so that in the Day of our Lord Jesus you can be as proud of us as we shall be of you.

[15]I was so sure of all this that I made plans at first to visit you, in order that you might be blessed twice. [16]For I planned to visit you on my way to Macedonia and again on my way back, in order to get help from you for my trip to Judea. [17]In planning this, did I appear fickle? When I make my plans, do I make them from selfish motives, ready to say "Yes, yes" and "No, no" at the same time? [18]As surely as God speaks the truth, my promise to you was not a "Yes" and a "No." [19]For Jesus Christ, the Son of God, who was preached among you by Silas, Timothy, and myself, is not one who is "Yes" and "No." On the contrary, he is God's "Yes";

---

a terrible dangers of death; *some manuscripts have* terrible death.
b frankness; *some manuscripts have* holiness.

源。[4]在我們的各種患難中,他安慰我們,使我們能夠用他所賜給我們的安慰去安慰遭遇各種患難的人。[5]正像我們跟基督同受許多苦難,我們也藉着基督得到許多安慰。[6]如果我們遭遇苦難,那是為要使你們得到安慰,得到拯救;如果我們得了安慰,你們也同樣得到安慰,並且得到力量來忍受我們所遭受的苦難。[7]我們對你們的信心從不動搖;我們知道,你們分擔了我們的苦難,也要分享我們所得到的安慰。

[8] 弟兄姊妹們,我們希望你們知道,我們從前在亞細亞省所遭遇的患難。那壓在我們身上的擔子是多麼大,多麼沉重,連生存的希望都沒有了。[9]我們只覺得已經被判死刑。這樣的情形使我們知道不能倚靠自己,只能倚靠那使死人復活的上帝。[10-11]他曾經從死亡的危險中拯救了我們,將來仍要拯救;只要你們用禱告幫助我們,我們確信這位上帝將來還要施行拯救。這樣,有許多人為我們禱告,使我們蒙恩,也必定有許多人要為我們感謝上帝。

保羅改變計劃

[12]我們所誇耀的是:我們的良知證明我們在世為人,尤其是我們跟你們的關係,都受上帝所賜的坦率①和誠懇所支配,而這是由於上帝恩典的力量,不是出於屬世的智慧。[13-14]我們寫給你們的,只限於你們所能讀、所能領會的。你們現在領會的只是一部分,我希望你們以後會完全明白。這樣,在我們的主耶穌再來的日子,你們會誇耀我們,正像我們誇耀你們一樣。

[15]既然有了這樣的確信,我就計劃先去訪問你們,使你們加倍獲得欣慰。[16]我往馬其頓去的時候,計劃先經過你們那裏,回來的時候再去一次,好讓你們幫助我前往猶太。[17]這樣的計劃,有誰能批評我輕率呢?難道我計劃這件事是出於自私的動機,是是非非,反覆無常嗎?[18]我指着信實的上帝說,我的諾言並不是「是」而又「非」的。[19]因為西拉、提摩太,和我傳給你們的那位上帝的兒子耶穌基督並不是一位是而又非的。相

---

①「坦率」另有些古卷作「聖潔」。

²⁰for it is he who is the "Yes" to all of God's promises. This is why through Jesus Christ our "Amen" is said to the glory of God. ²¹It is God himself who makes us, together with you, sure of our life in union with Christ; it is God himself who has set us apart, ²²who has placed his mark of ownership upon us, and who has given us the Holy Spirit in our hearts as the guarantee of all that he has in store for us.

²³I call God as my witness–he knows my heart! It was in order to spare you that I decided not to go to Corinth. ²⁴We are not trying to dictate to you what you must believe; we know that you stand firm in the faith. Instead, we are working with you for your own happiness.

2 So I made up my mind not to come to you again to make you sad. ²For if I were to make you sad, who would be left to cheer me up? Only the very persons I had made sad. ³That is why I wrote that letter to you–I did not want to come to you and be made sad by the very people who should make me glad. For I am convinced that when I am happy, then all of you are happy too. ⁴I wrote you with a greatly troubled and distressed heart and with many tears; my purpose was not to make you sad, but to make you realize how much I love you all.

Forgiveness for the Offender

⁵Now, if anyone has made somebody sad, he has not done it to me but to all of you–in part, at least. (I say this because I do not want to be too hard on him.) ⁶It is enough that this person has been punished in this way by most of you. ⁷Now, however, you should forgive him and encourage him, in order to keep him from becoming so sad as to give up completely. ⁸And so I beg you to let him know that you really do love him. ⁹I wrote you that letter because I wanted to find out how well you had stood the test and whether you are always ready to obey my instructions. ¹⁰When you forgive people for what they have done, I forgive them too. For when I forgive–if, indeed, I need to forgive anything–I do it in Christ's presence because of you, ¹¹in order to keep Satan from getting the upper hand over us; for we know what his plans are.

Paul's Anxiety in Troas

¹²When I arrived in Troas to preach the Good News about Christ, I found that the Lord had opened the way for the work there. ¹³But I was deeply worried, because I could not find our brother Titus. So I said good-bye to the people there and went on to Macedonia.

反地,他就是上帝的「是」字。²⁰上帝一切的應許在基督身上都成為「是」了。因此,我們藉着他說「阿們」來榮耀上帝。²¹上帝向你我保證,我們生活在基督裏面;他把我們分別出來,²²在我們身上蓋上了他的印記,並且賜下聖靈在我們心裏,作為他為我們所預備的一切的擔保。

²³我祈求上帝為我作證;如果我撒謊,他會懲罰我。我決定不去哥林多是為你們着想。²⁴我們不是要命令你們該信甚麼,因為你們在信仰上已經站穩了。我們倒願意跟你們同工合作,為要使你們有喜樂。

2 因此,我下了決心,在下次訪問你們的時候不再使你們憂愁。²如果我使你們憂愁,有誰能夠使我快樂呢?只有因我而引起憂愁的你們能使我快樂。³所以,我寫了那封信給你們,為要避免我到你們那裏去的時候,那些應該使我快樂的人反而使我憂愁。我也確信,我的喜樂就是你們大家的喜樂。⁴我在憂傷痛苦中流着許多眼淚給你們寫信,不是要使你們憂愁,而是要你們都知道我多麼愛你們!

赦免犯過失的人

⁵那麼,如果有人使別人憂愁,他不是使我,而是使你們大家憂愁,至少使你們當中的某些人憂愁。我這樣說,是因為我不願意使這樣的人太難堪。⁶他受大多數人的譴責已經夠了。⁷你們應該寬恕他,勸慰他,免得他過份傷心而絕望。⁸所以,我要求你們讓他知道,你們確實愛他。⁹我以前給你們寫那封信,目的是要知道你們是否經得起考驗,是不是願意一切都服從我。¹⁰你們寬恕誰,我就寬恕誰。如果我有所寬恕,是代表基督為你們寬恕的,¹¹免得撒但佔了優勢,因為我們對撒但的詭計知道得很清楚。

保羅的焦慮

¹²我到特羅亞傳基督福音的時候,主已經為我開了工作的門。¹³可是,因為沒有遇見我們的弟兄提多,我心裏非常焦慮。於是我向當地的人告別,到馬其頓去。

Victory through Christ

14But thanks be to God! For in union with Christ we are always led by God as prisoners in Christ's victory procession. God uses us to make the knowledge about Christ spread everywhere like a sweet fragrance. 15For we are like a sweet-smelling incense offered by Christ to God, which spreads among those who are being saved and those who are being lost. 16For those who are being lost, it is a deadly stench that kills; but for those who are being saved, it is a fragrance that brings life. Who, then, is capable for such a task? 17We are not like so many others, who handle God's message as if it were cheap merchandise; but because God has sent us, we speak with sincerity in his presence, as servants of Christ.

Servants of the New Covenant

3 Does this sound as if we were again boasting about ourselves? Could it be that, like some other people, we need letters of recommendation to you or from you? 2You yourselves are the letter we have, written on our hearts for everyone to know and read. 3It is clear that Christ himself wrote this letter and sent it by us. It is written, not with ink but with the Spirit of the living God, and not on stone tablets but on human hearts.

4We say this because we have confidence in God through Christ. 5There is nothing in us that allows us to claim that we are capable of doing this work. The capacity we have comes from God; 6it is he who made us capable of serving the new covenant, which consists not of a written law but of the Spirit. The written law brings death, but the Spirit gives life.

7The Law was carved in letters on stone tablets, and God's glory appeared when it was given. Even though the brightness on Moses' face was fading, it was so strong that the people of Israel could not keep their eyes fixed on him. If the Law, which brings death when it is in force, came with such glory, 8how much greater is the glory that belongs to the activity of the Spirit? 9The system which brings condemnation was glorious; how much more glorious is the activity which brings salvation! 10We may say that because of the far brighter glory now the glory that was so bright in the past is gone. 11For if there was glory in that which lasted for a while, how much more glory is there in that which lasts forever!

12Because we have this hope, we are very bold. 13We are not like Moses, who had to put a veil over his face so that the people of Israel would not see the brightness fade and dis-

靠基督得勝

14 但是，感謝上帝！因爲他時常率領我們，使作爲基督俘虜的我們②得以參加基督凱旋的行列。他又使用我們到處散播那因認識基督而有的香氣。15我們好比基督獻給上帝的馨香之氣，散播在那些得救和失喪的人身上。16對於那些失喪的人，這氣味成爲致死的臭氣；對於那些得救的人，這氣味卻成爲得生命的香氣。誰能擔當這重大的任務呢？17我們不像許許多多的人，把上帝的信息當商品叫賣；因爲上帝指派我們，讓我們在他面前以基督奴僕的身份誠誠懇懇地宣揚信息。

新約的僕人

3 我們又在高抬自己了嗎？難道我們也像某些人需要給你們或向你們要推薦書嗎？2你們就是我們的推薦書，寫在我們心裏，給大家知道，給大家誦讀。3很明顯地，基督自己寫了這封信，由我們傳送。這封信不是用墨寫在石版上的，而是用永生上帝的靈寫在人心裏的。

4 我們這樣說，因爲我們藉着基督對上帝有這樣的信心。5這不是說，我們憑着自己的才幹做這工作；我們的才幹是從上帝來的。6他使我們有才幹作新約的僕人；這約不是字面上的法律，而是聖靈的約。字面上的法律帶來死亡，但是聖靈賜生命。

7 這法律是用文字刻在石版上的，頒佈的時候，上帝的榮耀顯現出來。雖然照射在摩西臉上的光漸漸褪色，那光輝還是那麼強烈，以致以色列人不能定睛看他。如果那使人死亡的法律尚且帶來榮耀，8那麼，聖靈的功用豈不更有榮耀嗎？9如果定罪的功用會帶來榮耀，那宣佈人無罪的功用就帶來更大的榮耀了！10其實，我們可以這樣說，既然現在有了更輝煌的榮耀，從前的光輝就黯然失色了。11如果那漸漸褪色的尚且有榮耀，那長存的一定有更大的榮耀。

12 因爲我們有這樣的盼望，我們有無比的勇氣。13我們不像摩西，他必須拿帕子蒙着自己的臉，使以色列人不能看見那光輝漸漸

②「作爲基督俘虜的我們」或譯「我們」。

appear. [14]Their minds, indeed, were closed; and to this very day their minds are covered with the same veil as they read the books of the old covenant. The veil is removed only when a person is joined to Christ. [15]Even today, whenever they read the Law of Moses, the veil still covers their minds. [16]But it can be removed, as the scripture says about Moses: "His veil was removed when he turned to the Lord."[c] [17]Now, "the Lord" in this passage is the Spirit; and where the Spirit of the Lord is present, there is freedom. [18]All of us, then, reflect the glory of the Lord with uncovered faces; and that same glory, coming from the Lord, who is the Spirit, transforms us into his likeness in an ever greater degree of glory.

Spiritual Treasure in Clay Pots

4 God in his mercy has given us this work to do, and so we do not become discouraged. [2]We put aside all secret and shameful deeds; we do not act with deceit, nor do we falsify the word of God. In the full light of truth we live in God's sight and try to commend ourselves to everyone's good conscience. [3]For if the gospel we preach is hidden, it is hidden only from those who are being lost. [4]They do not believe, because their minds have been kept in the dark by the evil god of this world. He keeps them from seeing the light shining on them, the light that comes from the Good News about the glory of Christ, who is the exact likeness of God. [5]For it is not ourselves that we preach; we preach Jesus Christ as Lord, and ourselves as your servants for Jesus' sake. [6]The God who said, "Out of darkness the light shall shine!" is the same God who made his light shine in our hearts, to bring us the knowledge of God's glory shining in the face of Christ.

[7]Yet we who have this spiritual treasure are like common clay pots, in order to show that the supreme power belongs to God, not to us. [8]We are often troubled, but not crushed; sometimes in doubt, but never in despair; [9]there are many enemies, but we are never without a friend; and though badly hurt at times, we are not destroyed. [10]At all times we carry in our mortal bodies the death of Jesus, so that his life also may be seen in our bodies. [11]Throughout our lives we are always in danger of death for Jesus' sake, in order that his life may be seen in this mortal body of ours. [12]This means that death is at work in us, but life is at work in you.

[13]The scripture says, "I spoke because I believed." In the same spirit of faith we also

c *Verse 16 may be translated:* But the veil is removed whenever someone turns to the Lord.

褪色。[14]可是他們的心智被阻塞了。直到今天,當他們誦讀舊約諸書的時候,心裏還蒙着同樣的帕子。因為只有當人跟基督連結的時候,這帕子才被揭去。[15]甚至在今天,他們每逢誦讀摩西律法,那帕子還蒙着他們的心。[16]但是,正如聖經所說的:「當摩西轉向主的時候,他臉上的帕子就被挪掉了[3]。」[17]這裏所說的「主」就是聖靈。主的靈在哪裏,那裏就有自由。[18]我們大家都用沒有蒙着帕子的臉反映主的榮耀;那從主—就是聖靈—所發出這榮耀在改變我們,使我們成為他的樣式,有更輝煌的榮耀。

瓦器中的寶物

4 既然上帝憐憫我們,把這任務交給我們,我們就不灰心。[2]我們放棄了一切暗昧可恥的事,不做詭詐的事,也不曲解上帝的話。在上帝面前,我們公開顯明真理,以自己的行為來啟發每一個人的良心。[3]即使我們所傳的福音難以明白,那是只有走向滅亡的人才不明白。[4]這些人不信,因為這世界的神明把他們的心眼弄瞎了,使他們看不見福音的光;這福音是關於基督的榮耀,而基督是上帝的真像。[5]我們所宣揚的不是自己,我們只宣揚「耶穌基督是主」;為了耶穌的緣故,我們作了你們的僕人。[6]那位吩咐「要有光從黑暗裏照出來」的上帝也就是用光照亮我們內心的上帝;他使我們認識上帝的榮耀,照耀在耶穌基督臉上。

[7]可是,擁有這屬靈寶物的我們不過是像普通的瓦器,為的要證明這無上的能力是屬於上帝,不是屬於我們。[8]我們遭遇各樣的困難,卻沒有被壓碎;常有疑慮,卻未嘗絕望;[9]有許多仇敵,但總有朋友;常被打倒,卻沒有喪亡。[10]我們必朽的身體時常帶着耶穌的死,為要使耶穌的生命也同時顯明在我們身上。[11]我們的一生,常常為了耶穌的緣故冒着死亡的危險,為要使他的生命能夠在我們這必朽的身上顯明出來。[12]這就是說,我們常常面對死亡,你們卻因此得生命。

[13]聖經上說:「我信,所以我宣揚。」基於同樣的信心,我們信,所以我們也宣揚。

③「但是……就被挪掉了」或譯「無論甚麼時候,當人轉向主時,那帕子就被挪掉了」。

speak because we believe. 14We know that God, who raised the Lord Jesus to life, will also raise us up with Jesus and take us, together with you, into his presence. 15All this is for your sake; and as God's grace reaches more and more people, they will offer to the glory of God more prayers of thanksgiving.

Living by Faith

16For this reason we never become discouraged. Even though our physical being is gradually decaying, yet our spiritual being is renewed day after day. 17And this small and temporary trouble we suffer will bring us a tremendous and eternal glory, much greater than the trouble. 18For we fix our attention, not on things that are seen, but on things that are unseen. What can be seen lasts only for a time, but what cannot be seen lasts forever.

5 For we know that when this tent we live in-our body here on earth-is torn down, God will have a house in heaven for us to live in, a home he himself has made, which will last forever. 2And now we sigh, so great is our desire that our home which comes from heaven should be put on over us; 3by being clothed with it we shall not be without a body. 4While we live in this earthly tent, we groan with a feeling of oppression; it is not that we want to get rid of our earthly body, but that we want to have the heavenly one put on over us, so that what is mortal will be transformed by life 5God is the one who has prepared us for this change, and he gave us his Spirit as the guarantee of all that he has in store for us.

6So we are always full of courage. We know that as long as we are at home in the body we are away from the Lord's home. 7For our life is a matter of faith, not of sight. 8We are full of courage and would much prefer to leave our home in the body and be at home with the Lord. 9More than anything else, however, we want to please him, whether in our home here or there. 10For all of us must appear before Christ, to be judged by him. We will each receive what we deserve, according to everything we have done, good or bad, in our bodily life.

Friendship with God through Christ

11We know what it means to fear the Lord, and so we try to persuade others. God knows us completely, and I hope that in your hearts you know me as well. 12We are not trying again to recommend ourselves to you; rather, we are trying to give you a good reason to be proud of us, so that you will be able to answer those who boast about people's appearance and not about

14我們知道,那使主耶穌復活的上帝也必定使我們跟耶穌一同復活,並且帶我們跟你們一起到他面前。15這一切都是爲了你們,好叫上帝的恩典臨到更多的人,使更多的人獻上他們的感謝,來彰顯上帝的榮耀。

靠信心生活

16因此,我們從不灰心。雖然我們外在的軀體漸漸衰敗,我們內在的生命卻日日更新。17我們所遭受這短暫的痛苦要爲我們帶來無可比擬的永久榮耀。18我們並不關心看得見的事物,而是關心看不見的事物。看得見的是暫時的;看不見的是永恆的。

5 我們知道,如果我們所住的這地上的帳棚拆去了,上帝會給我們天上的住宅,是他親自建造、永遠存在的。2我們現在歎息着,切切地盼望住進那天上的住宅,好像穿上衣服;3穿上了,我們就不至於赤身露體。4我們住在這地上的帳棚裏,像是背負重擔而歎息着;這並不是說我們要脫下地上的身體,而是要穿上屬天的身體,好使那必朽的被生命取代。5上帝親自準備我們來適應這變化;他把聖靈賜給我們,作爲擔保。

6所以,我們常有充分的勇氣。我們知道,只要還住在這身體裏,我們便遠離了主爲我們預備的住處。7因爲我們活着是憑信心,而不是憑眼見。8我們有充分的勇氣,情願離開這地上的身體,跟主一同居住。9更重要的是,無論在這地上的身體裏,還是穿上屬天的身體,我們都要討主的喜悅。10因爲我們都必須站在基督面前,受他審判。每一個人會按照肉身的行爲,或善或惡,接受報應。

藉着基督跟上帝和好

11我們旣然曉得怎樣敬畏主,就以此勸導人。上帝完全認識我們;我希望你們也從心裏認識我。12我們不是想再向你們推薦自己,而是要你們覺得有理由以我們爲榮,好讓你們有話回答那些只重外貌、不重品格的

their character. 13Are we really insane? It is for God's sake. Or are we sane? Then it is for your sake. 14We are ruled by the love of Christ, now that we recognize that one man died for everyone, which means that they all share in his death. 15He died for all, so that those who live should no longer live for themselves, but only for him who died and was raised to life for their sake.

16No longer, then, do we judge anyone by human standards. Even if at one time we judged Christ according to human standards, we no longer do so. 17Anyone who is joined to Christ is a new being; the old is gone, the new has come. 18All this is done by God, who through Christ changed us from enemies into his friends and gave us the task of making others his friends also. 19Our message is that God was making all human beings his friends through Christ.*d* God did not keep an account of their sins, and he has given us the message which tells how he makes them his friends.

20Here we are, then, speaking for Christ, as though God himself were making his appeal through us. We plead on Christ's behalf: let God change you from enemies into his friends! 21Christ was without sin, but for our sake God made him share our sin in order that in union with him we might share the righteousness of God.

6 In our work together with God, then, we beg you who have received God's grace not to let it be wasted. 2Hear what God says:

"When the time came for me to show you favor,
    I heard you;
when the day arrived for me to save you,
    I helped you."

Listen! This is the hour to receive God's favor; today is the day to be saved!

3We do not want anyone to find fault with our work, so we try not to put obstacles in anyone's way. 4Instead, in everything we do we show that we are God's servants by patiently enduring troubles, hardships, and difficulties. 5We have been beaten, jailed, and mobbed; we have been overworked and have gone without sleep or food. 6By our purity, knowledge, patience, and kindness we have shown ourselves to be God's servants–by the Holy Spirit, by our true love, 7by our message of truth, and by the power of God. We have righteousness as our weapon, both to attack and to defend ourselves. 8We are honored and disgraced; we are insulted and praised. We are treated as liars, yet we speak the truth; 9as unknown, yet

d God was making all human beings his friends through Christ; *or* God was in Christ making all human beings his friends.

人。13如果我們真的是瘋了的話，那是為着上帝的緣故；如果我們神志清醒，那是為着你們。14基督的愛支配着我們，因為我們明白，一個人為眾人死，也就是說眾人都死了。15他為眾人死，是要使那些活着的人不再為自己活，而是為那位替他們死而復活的基督活。

16所以，我們從此不再根據人的標準來估量人。雖然我們曾經根據人的標準來看基督，現在我們不再這樣做了。17無論誰，一旦有了基督的生命就是新造的人；舊的已經過去，新的已經來臨。18這一切都是上帝的作為；他藉着基督使我們得以跟上帝和好，又給我們傳和好福音的職份。19我們所傳的信息就是：上帝藉着基督與人類建立和好的關係①。他不追究他們的過犯，並且把他與人和好的信息付託了我們。

20因此，我們作了基督的特使。上帝親自藉着我們勸勉你們；我們替基督請求你們，讓上帝使你們跟他和好。21基督是無罪的，可是為了我們，上帝讓他擔負我們的罪，使我們藉着他得以跟上帝有合宜的關係。

6 我們是上帝的同工；我們要勸勉你們：既然已經接受了上帝的恩典，你們不可使這恩典落空。2因為上帝說：

在接納的時刻，我垂聽你；
在拯救的日子，我幫助你。

聽啊，現在就是接納上帝恩惠的時刻！今天就是上帝拯救的日子！

3我們不願意別人毀謗我們的事奉，所以我們也不妨礙別人。4為了在一切事上表明我們是上帝的僕人，我們忍受各種患難、貧窮、困苦。5我們曾遭受鞭打、監禁、暴民的騷擾；我們勞苦，失眠，和捱餓。6我們以純潔、知識、忍耐、仁慈，更藉着聖靈、真摯的愛、7真理的信息，和上帝的大能，來表明我們是上帝的僕人。我們以正義作武器，攻擊敵人，也保衛自己。8我們受尊敬，也被侮辱；受責罵，也被稱讚。人家說我們是騙子，其實我們說的是誠實話；9說

①「上帝藉着基督與人類建立和好的關係」或譯「上帝在基督裏與人類建立和好的關係」。

we are known by all; as though we were dead, but, as you see, we live on. Although punished, we are not killed; [10]although saddened, we are always glad; we seem poor, but we make many people rich; we seem to have nothing, yet we really possess everything.

[11]Dear friends in Corinth! We have spoken frankly to you; we have opened our hearts wide. [12]It is not we who have closed our hearts to you; it is you who have closed your hearts to us. [13]I speak now as though you were my children: show us the same feelings that we have for you. Open your hearts wide!

Warning against Pagan Influences

[14]Do not try to work together as equals with unbelievers, for it cannot be done. How can right and wrong be partners? How can light and darkness live together? [15]How can Christ and the Devil agree? What does a believer have in common with an unbeliever? [16]How can God's temple come to terms with pagan idols? For we are the temple of the living God! As God himself has said,

"I will make my home with my people
  and live among them;
I will be their God,
  and they shall be my people."

[17]And so the Lord says,

"You must leave them
  and separate yourselves from them.
Have nothing to do with what is unclean,
  and I will accept you.
[18]I will be your father,
  and you shall be my sons and daughters,
  says the Lord Almighty."

7 All these promises are made to us, my dear friends. So then, let us purify ourselves from everything that makes body or soul unclean, and let us be completely holy by living in awe of God.

Paul's Joy

[2]Make room for us in your hearts. We have wronged no one; we have ruined no one, nor tried to take advantage of anyone. [3]I do not say this to condemn you; for, as I have said before, you are so dear to us that we are always together, whether we live or die. [4]I am so sure of you; I take such pride in you! In all our troubles I am still full of courage; I am running over with joy.

[5]Even after we arrived in Macedonia, we did not have any rest. There were troubles everywhere, quarrels with others, fears in our hearts. [6]But God, who encourages the downhearted,

我們寂寂無聞,其實是家喻戶曉;說我們死了,其實都好好地活着。我們受刑罰,卻沒有被殺;[10]憂傷,卻常有喜樂;貧窮,卻使許多人富足;好像一無所有,卻樣樣都有。

[11] 哥林多的朋友們,我們向你們推心置腹,坦白說話。[12]不是我們褊狹,而是你們心胸狹窄。[13]我對你們說話,像對自己的兒女說話一樣;你們要寬宏大量,用我們待你們的器量來對待我們。

防備異教的影響

[14] 不要跟不信的人同負一軛。正和邪怎能合作呢?光明和黑暗怎能共存呢?[15]基督和魔鬼怎能協調呢?信和不信的人有甚麼共同的地方呢?[16]上帝的聖殿和偶像怎能並立呢?我們是永生上帝的聖殿。正如上帝說:

    我要與我的子民同住,
    在他們當中往來。
    我要作他們的上帝;
    他們要作我的子民。

[17]因此主說:

    你們要離開他們,
    從他們當中分離出來。
    不要沾染不潔之物,
    我就接納你們。
[18] 我要作你們的父親;
    你們要作我的兒女。
    這話是我—全能的主說的。

7 親愛的朋友們,既然我們得到這些應許,我們應該潔淨自己,除去一切使身體和心靈污染的事物,在敬畏上帝的生活中達到聖潔。

保羅的喜樂

[2] 請你們以寬大的胸懷容納我們。我們沒有做過對不起人的事;沒有破壞誰,也沒有佔過誰的便宜。[3]我這樣說,不是在譴責你們。我已經說過了,我們多麼愛你們;我們願意跟你們同生共死。[4]我絕對信任你們,十分誇耀你們。在一切患難中,我深受安慰,充滿快樂。

[5] 到馬其頓以後,我們還是不能安定。我們到處遭遇困難,遇到衝突紛爭,也有內心的恐懼。[6]但是,那位鼓勵灰心喪志的人的

encouraged us with the coming of Titus. [7]It was not only his coming that cheered us, but also his report of how you encouraged him. He told us how much you want to see me, how sorry you are, how ready you are to defend me; and so I am even happier now.

[8]For even if that letter of mine made you sad, I am not sorry I wrote it. I could have been sorry when I saw that it made you sad for a while. [9]But now I am happy–not because I made you sad, but because your sadness made you change your ways. That sadness was used by God, and so we caused you no harm. [10]For the sadness that is used by God brings a change of heart that leads to salvation–and there is no regret in that! But sadness that is merely human causes death. [11]See what God did with this sadness of yours: how earnest it has made you, how eager to prove your innocence! Such indignation, such alarm, such feelings, such devotion, such readiness to punish wrongdoing! You have shown yourselves to be without fault in the whole matter.

[12]So, even though I wrote that letter, it was not because of the one who did wrong or the one who was wronged. Instead, I wrote it to make plain to you, in God's sight, how deep your devotion to us really is. [13]That is why we were encouraged.

Not only were we encouraged; how happy Titus made us with his happiness over the way in which all of you helped to cheer him up! [14]I did boast of you to him, and you have not disappointed me. We have always spoken the truth to you, and in the same way the boast we made to Titus has proved true. [15]And so his love for you grows stronger, as he remembers how all of you were ready to obey his instructions, how you welcomed him with fear and trembling. [16]How happy I am that I can depend on you completely!

Christian Giving

8 Our friends, we want you to know what God's grace has accomplished in the churches in Macedonia. [2]They have been severely tested by the troubles they went through; but their joy was so great that they were extremely generous in their giving, even though they are very poor. [3]I can assure you that they gave as much as they could, and even more than they could. Of their own free will [4]they begged us and pleaded for the privilege of having a part in helping God's people in Judea. [5]It was more than we could have hoped for! First they gave themselves to the Lord; and then, by God's will they gave themselves to us as well. [6]So we

上帝藉着提多來鼓勵我們。[7]他不但到這裏來，還向我們報告他怎樣在你們得到鼓勵，以及你們怎樣渴望見到我，怎樣地憂傷，並且懇切地為我辯護；這一切都使我更加欣慰。

[8]關於從前我給你們的那封信，即使它使你們心裏難過，我也不後悔。我可能因知道那封信在你們當中引起一時的憂愁而有點後悔。[9]但是，現在我很高興，不是因為我使你們憂愁，而是因為憂愁改變了你們的心。上帝善用你們的憂愁，因此可說我們所做的並沒有傷害你們。[10]上帝用憂愁改變人心，使人得救；這是用不着後悔的！可是屬世的憂愁會使人死亡。[11]你們看，上帝這樣地善用了你們的憂愁，使你們急切地為自己辯護，而且顯出義憤，又警惕，又熱望，又忠心，又懲罰不義！在各方面你們都證明自己是清白的。

[12]因此，我雖然寫了那一封信，但並不是為了犯過錯的人寫的，也不是為受虧負的人寫的。相反地，我寫那封信的目的是要表明你們在上帝面前對我們的熱情是多麼深切。[13]我們因此得到了鼓勵。

不但這樣，提多的喜樂更增加了我們的喜樂；因為你們都幫助他，使他快樂。[14]我曾在他面前誇獎你們，你們並沒有使我慚愧。我們一向對你們說實在話；同樣，我們對提多誇獎你們的話也證明是實在的。[15]所以，當提多想起你們怎樣地順服，怎樣地用恐懼戰兢的心接待他，他對你們的愛心就更增加了。[16]現在我多麼高興，因為我可以完全信任你們！

基督徒的捐助

8 弟兄姊妹們，我們希望你們知道上帝怎樣恩待馬其頓的各教會。[2]他們從所經歷的患難受到嚴重的考驗；但是他們充滿着快樂，在極度的貧困中仍然慷慨捐助。[3]我敢證明，他們的捐助是竭盡所能的，甚至超過了他們的力量。自願地，[4]他們向我們懇求，讓他們在接濟猶太的信徒這一件善事上有份。[5]這實在遠超過我們所期待的。首先，他們把自己奉獻給主，然後又按照上帝的旨意幫助我們。[6]因此，我們鼓勵提多繼

urged Titus, who began this work, to continue it and help you complete this special service of love. ⁷You are so rich in all you have: in faith, speech, and knowledge, in your eagerness to help and in your love for us.ᵉ And so we want you to be generous also in this service of love.

8I am not laying down any rules. But by showing how eager others are to help, I am trying to find out how real your own love is. ⁹You know the grace of our Lord Jesus Christ; rich as he was, he made himself poor for your sake, in order to make you rich by means of his poverty.

10My opinion is that it is better for you to finish now what you began last year. You were the first, not only to act, but also to be willing to act. ¹¹On with it, then, and finish the job! Be as eager to finish it as you were to plan it, and do it with what you now have. ¹²If you are eager to give, God will accept your gift on the basis of what you have to give, not on what you don't have.

13-14I am not trying to relieve others by putting a burden on you; but since you have plenty at this time, it is only fair that you should help those who are in need. Then, when you are in need and they have plenty, they will help you. In this way both are treated equally. ¹⁵As the scripture says, "The one who gathered much did not have too much, and the one who gathered little did not have too little."

Titus and His Companions

16How we thank God for making Titus as eager as we are to help you! ¹⁷Not only did he welcome our request; he was so eager to help that of his own free will he decided to go to you. ¹⁸With him we are sending the brother who is highly respected in all the churches for his work in preaching the gospel. ¹⁹And besides that, he has been chosen and appointed by the churches to travel with us as we carry out this service of love for the sake of the Lord's glory and in order to show that we want to help.

20We are being careful not to stir up any complaints about the way we handle this generous gift. ²¹Our purpose is to do what is right, not only in the sight of the Lord, but also in the sight of others.

22So we are sending our brother with them; we have tested him many times and found him always very eager to help. And now that he has so much confidence in you, he is all the more eager to help. ²³As for Titus, he is my partner

ᵉ your love for us; *some manuscripts have* our love for you.

續協助你們，完成他所開始的這一件善事。⁷無論是信心、口才、知識、幫助別人的熱誠，和對我們⑤的愛心，你們都那麼豐富，我希望你們在這件善事上也格外慷慨。

8 我不是要定下甚麼規則，只是要你們知道別人怎樣熱心幫助人，以此來考驗你們的愛心。⁹你們已經知道我們的主耶穌基督的恩典：他本來是富足的，卻爲了你們的緣故使自己成爲貧窮，目的是要你們由於他的貧窮而成爲富足。

10 對於這件事，我認爲：你們最好在這時候完成去年所開始的募捐。你們不但是最先有這行動的，也是最先有意願這樣做的。¹¹那麼，堅持下去，完成這件工作吧！你們應該用當初計劃時那樣的熱心去完成這件工作，而且要按照你們現在所有的去進行。¹²如果你們眞心捐助，上帝一定悅納；他要你們獻上你們所有的，而不是所沒有的。

13-14我不是想加重你們的負擔，來減輕別人的負擔。既然你們現在富足，就應該幫助那些貧窮的。到了他們富足而你們有需要的時候，他們也會幫助你們。這樣雙方面都有機會互相幫助。¹⁵正如聖經上說：

多收的，沒有餘；
少收的，沒有缺。

提多和他的同工

16 感謝上帝，他使提多跟我們同樣熱心地協助你們。¹⁷他不只是因爲我們的鼓勵，也是出於自願，更熱切盼望到你們那裏去。¹⁸我們另外派一位弟兄跟他一道去；這位弟兄在傳福音的工作上爲各地教會所尊重。¹⁹不但這樣，在我們爲主的榮耀而進行的這件善事上，他被各教會選派，作我們的旅伴，也表示我們大家都樂意援助。

20 我們經管這一筆慷慨的捐款，始終十分謹愼，免得引起人家的挑剔；²¹因爲我們定意做善事，不但在主面前這樣，在人面前也是這樣。

22 我們又派另一位弟兄跟他們同行。這位弟兄經過我們多次的考驗，我們知道他在許多事上熱心幫助別人。現在，他深深地信任你們，就更渴望去幫助你們了。²³至於提

⑤「我們」有些抄本作「你們」。

and works with me to help you; as for the other brothers who are going with him, they represent the churches and bring glory to Christ. 24Show your love to them, so that all the churches will be sure of it and know that we are right in boasting about you.

Help for Needy Believers

9 There is really no need for me to write you about the help being sent to God's people in Judea. 2I know that you are willing to help, and I have boasted of you to the people in Macedonia. "The believers in Achaia," I said, "have been ready to help since last year." Your eagerness has stirred up most of them. 3Now I am sending these believers, so that our boasting about you in this matter may not turn out to be empty words. But, just as I said, you will be ready with your help. 4However, if the people from Macedonia should come with me and find out that you are not ready, how ashamed we would be–not to speak of your shame–for feeling so sure of you! 5So I thought it was necessary to urge these believers to go to you ahead of me and get ready in advance the gift you promised to make. Then it will be ready when I arrive, and it will show that you give because you want to, not because you have to.

6Remember that the person who plants few seeds will have a small crop; the one who plants many seeds will have a large crop. 7You should each give, then, as you have decided, not with regret or out of a sense of duty; for God loves the one who gives gladly. 8And God is able to give you more than you need, so that you will always have all you need for yourselves and more than enough for every good cause. 9As the scripture says,

"He gives generously to the needy;
   his kindness lasts forever."

10And God, who supplies seed for the sower and bread to eat, will also supply you with all the seed you need and will make it grow and produce a rich harvest from your generosity. 11He will always make you rich enough to be generous at all times, so that many will thank God for your gifts which they receive from us. 12For this service you perform not only meets the needs of God's people, but also produces an outpouring of gratitude to God. 13And because of the proof which this service of yours brings, many will give glory to God for your loyalty to the gospel of Christ, which you profess, and for your generosity in sharing with them and everyone else. 14And so with deep affection they will pray for you because of the extraordinary grace God has shown you. 15Let us thank God for his priceless gift!

多，他是我的同伴，在協助你們的工作上跟我同工。另外跟他一起去的兩位弟兄是各教會的代表，是基督的光榮。24所以，你們要在各教會面前證明對他們的愛心，並且讓各教會知道，我們對你們的誇獎是沒有錯的。

幫助同道

9 關於接濟猶太信徒的事，我不必給你們寫信。2我知道你們是願意出力的，因此曾向馬其頓人誇耀你們的慷慨。我說：「亞該亞的信徒們從去年就有了準備。」你們的熱心已經感動了許多人。3現在我派這幾位弟兄去，希望你們正像我所說的早已把捐款準備好了，使我們在這件事上稱讚你們的話不是空話。4假如有馬其頓人跟我們一起去，發現你們並沒有準備好，我們就會很難爲情，因爲對你們太相信了。至於你們會覺得慚愧，那就更不用說了！5因此，我認爲必須派這幾位弟兄先到你們那裏去，把你們所答應的捐款先湊齊，等我到的時候都預備好了；這可以表示你們的捐助是出於甘心樂意，而不是出於勉強。

6 要記住：少種的少收；多種的多收。7所以，每一個人都應該按照自己的心願捐助，不猶豫，不勉強，因爲上帝喜愛樂意奉獻的人。8上帝會更加豐富地賜給你們，使你們不但自己充足有餘，還能夠在各樣慈善的事上出力。9正如聖經上說：

他慷慨救濟窮苦人；
他的仁義存到永遠。

10那位賜種子給農撒種的，又賜食物給人吃的上帝，也必定把你們所需要的種子賜給你們，又使它長大，讓你們的義舉結出豐豐富富的果子。11他也要使你們富足，隨時有慷慨施捨的能力，使許多人因爲從我們手上接受你們的禮物而感謝上帝。12因爲你們的捐助不但供應了信徒的需要，也使許多人更加流露對上帝的感謝。13這件慈善工作是一種證據，使許多人知道你們對基督順服，對所宣認的福音忠誠，也能慷慨地救濟別人，他們就會將一切榮耀都歸給上帝。14他們也要因上帝將非凡的恩典賜給你們而更愛慕你們，熱切地爲你們禱告。

15我們要感謝上帝！他有無法形容的恩典！

Paul Defends His Ministry

10 I, Paul, make a personal appeal to you–I who am said to be meek and mild when I am with you, but harsh with you when I am away. By the gentleness and kindness of Christ ²I beg you not to force me to be harsh when I come; for I am sure I can deal harshly with those who say that we act from worldly motives. ³It is true that we live in the world, but we do not fight from worldly motives. ⁴The weapons we use in our fight are not the world's weapons but God's powerful weapons, which we use to destroy strongholds. We destroy false arguments; ⁵we pull down every proud obstacle that is raised against the knowledge of God; we take every thought captive and make it obey Christ. ⁶And after you have proved your complete loyalty, we will be ready to punish any act of disloyalty.

⁷You are looking at the outward appearance of things. Are there some there who reckon themselves to belong to Christ? Well, let them think again about themselves, because we belong to Christ just as much as they do. ⁸For I am not ashamed, even if I have boasted somewhat too much about the authority that the Lord has given us–authority to build you up, not to tear you down. ⁹I do not want it to appear that I am trying to frighten you with my letters. ¹⁰Someone will say, "Paul's letters are severe and strong, but when he is with us in person, he is weak, and his words are nothing!" ¹¹Such a person must understand that there is no difference between what we write in our letters when we are away and what we will do when we are there with you.

¹²Of course we would not dare classify ourselves or compare ourselves with those who rate themselves so highly. How stupid they are! They make up their own standards to measure themselves by, and they judge themselves by their own standards! ¹³As for us, however, our boasting will not go beyond certain limits; it will stay within the limits of the work which God has set for us, and this includes our work among you. ¹⁴And since you are within those limits, we were not going beyond them when we came to you, bringing the Good News about Christ. ¹⁵So we do not boast about the work that others have done beyond the limits God set for us. Instead, we hope that your faith may grow and that we may be able to do a much greater work among you, always within the limits that God has set. ¹⁶Then we can preach the Good News in other countries beyond you and shall not have to boast about work already done in someone else's field.

¹⁷But as the scripture says, "Whoever wants

保羅爲工作辯護

10 我一保羅親自勸勉你們。你們認爲我跟你們在一起的時候很謙和，不在的時候卻很嚴厲；現在我以基督的溫柔和慈祥要求你們：² 當我去的時候，請不要逼着我對你們不客氣。對於那些批評我們是憑着屬世的動機做事的人，我是會不客氣的。³ 我們固然是生活在這世上，但我們的爭戰並不是出於屬世的動機。⁴ 我們作戰的武器不是屬世的，而是上帝大能的武器，能夠摧毀堅固的堡壘。我們要攻破一切荒謬的辯論，⁵ 推倒那阻礙別人認識上帝的每一種高傲的言論。我們要掠取每一個人的心思來歸順基督。⁶ 等你們完全順服的時候，我們就懲罰那些不順服的人。

⁷ 你們是從外表觀看事物。如果有人認爲自己是屬基督的，他應該再想 想，他屬於基督，我們也一樣屬於基督。⁸ 主所賜給我們的職權是要造就你們，不是要摧毀你們；所以，即使我有點過份地誇耀這職權，我也不以爲恥。⁹ 你們別以爲我寫這封信是想嚇你們。¹⁰ 有人說：「保羅寫信時，既嚴厲又強硬，他本人卻顯得外表平凡，言語粗俗！」¹¹ 說這種話的人應該知道，我們不在你們那裏的時候，在信上所說的話，跟到了你們那裏時所要做的是一致的。

¹² 我們當然不敢跟那些自命不凡的人同列或相比。他們實在是糊塗，拿自己的尺度衡量自己，自己跟自己比較！¹³ 至於我們，我們的誇口不會超過限度，是在上帝劃定給我們的範圍裏；這範圍也包括在你們當中的工作。¹⁴ 既然你們是在這範圍內，我們把基督的福音傳給你們，就不算越過了界限。¹⁵ 對於在我們範圍以外、別人做完了的工作，我們不敢誇口。我們只希望你們的信心增長，使我們能夠在上帝所劃定的範圍內繼續擴展在你們中間的工作。¹⁶ 這樣，我們可以把福音傳到你們以外的其他地區，而不以他人的園地所成就的工作誇口。

¹⁷ 正如聖經所說：「誰要誇口，就該誇耀

to boast must boast about what the Lord has done." [18]For it is when the Lord thinks well of us that we are really approved, and not when we think well of ourselves.

Paul and the False Apostles

11 I wish you would tolerate me, even when I am a bit foolish. Please do! [2]I am jealous for you, just as God is; you are like a pure virgin whom I have promised in marriage to one man only, Christ himself. [3]I am afraid that your minds will be corrupted and that you will abandon your full and pure devotion to Christ–in the same way that Eve was deceived by the snake's clever lies. [4]For you gladly tolerate anyone who comes to you and preaches a different Jesus, not the one we preached; and you accept a spirit and a gospel completely different from the Spirit and the gospel you received from us!

[5]I do not think that I am the least bit inferior to those very special so-called "apostles" of yours! [6]Perhaps I am an amateur in speaking, but certainly not in knowledge; we have made this clear to you at all times and in all conditions.

[7]I did not charge you a thing when I preached the Good News of God to you; I humbled myself in order to make you important. Was that wrong of me? [8]While I was working among you, I was paid by other churches. I was robbing them, so to speak, in order to help you. [9]And during the time I was with you I did not bother you for help when I needed money; the believers who came from Macedonia brought me everything I needed. As in the past, so in the future: I will never be a burden to you! [10]By Christ's truth in me, I promise that this boast of mine will not be silenced anywhere in all of Achaia. [11]Do I say this because I don't love you? God knows I love you!

[12]I will go on doing what I am doing now, in order to keep those other "apostles" from having any reason for boasting and saying that they work in the same way that we do. [13]Those men are not true apostles–they are false apostles, who lie about their work and disguise themselves to look like real apostles of Christ. [14]Well, no wonder! Even Satan can disguise himself to look like an angel of light! [15]So it is no great thing if his servants disguise themselves to look like servants of righteousness. In the end they will get exactly what their actions deserve.

Paul's Sufferings as an Apostle

[16]I repeat: no one should think that I am a

主的作為！」[18]因為，真正值得稱讚的是主所稱讚的人，而不是自吹自擂的人。

保羅和假使徒

11 我希望你們會容忍我，就算我有一點蠢，相信你們還是會容忍的！[2]我愛你們到了嫉妒的程度，像上帝對你們一樣。因為你們好像貞潔的童女，我只把你們許配給一個丈夫，就是基督。[3]我只怕你們的心被腐化，放棄了對基督純潔專一的愛，像夏娃被蛇的詭詐所誘惑一樣。[4]因為，隨便甚麼人來傳另一個耶穌，不是我們所傳的那一位，你們竟然都容忍；有另外的靈和另一種福音，跟我們所傳授給你們的不同，你們也樂意接受！

[5]我相信我沒有哪一點比不上你們的那些「超等使徒」！[6]我或許不善言令，可是在知識上並不比別人差；這一點，我在各樣事上隨時都向你們表明過了。

[7]我傳上帝的福音給你們，未曾向你們索取甚麼；我貶低自己，好使你們高升。難道這是我的過錯嗎？[8]當我在你們當中工作的時候，有別的教會供給我；我似乎是剝削了別的教會來服務你們。[9]我跟你們在一起的時候，無論有甚麼需要，從來沒有求你們幫助。我需要的一切都是從馬其頓來的信徒們供給的。過去是這樣，將來還是這樣。我絕不會成為你們的負擔！[10]我敢指著在我心中的基督的真理說，我所誇的口將在亞該亞全境傳開。[11]為甚麼我這樣說呢？難道我不愛你們嗎？上帝知道，我是愛你們的！

[12]我要繼續現在的工作，為要讓那些所謂「使徒」的人再也無法誇口，以為他們所做的都跟我們所做的一樣。[13]這班人不是真使徒；他們行為詭詐，偽裝作基督的使徒。[14]其實這也不足為奇，連撒但也會把自己化裝成光明的天使！[15]所以，要是撒但的爪牙化裝為仁義的僕人，這也沒有甚麼好希奇的。他們的結局一定跟他們的行為相符。

保羅遭受的苦難

[16]我再說：誰都不應該把我當作蠢材。假

fool. But if you do, at least accept me as a fool, just so I will have a little to boast of. ¹⁷Of course what I am saying now is not what the Lord would have me say; in this matter of boasting I am really talking like a fool. ¹⁸But since there are so many who boast for merely human reasons, I will do the same. ¹⁹You yourselves are so wise, and so you gladly tolerate fools! ²⁰You tolerate anyone who orders you around or takes advantage of you or traps you or looks down on you or slaps you in the face. ²¹I am ashamed to admit that we were too timid to do those things!

But if anyone dares to boast about something–I am talking like a fool–I will be just as daring. ²²Are they Hebrews? So am I. Are they Israelites? So am I. Are they Abraham's descendants? So am I. ²³Are they Christ's servants? I sound like a madman–but I am a better servant than they are! I have worked much harder, I have been in prison more times, I have been whipped much more, and I have been near death more often. ²⁴Five times I was given the thirty-nine lashes by the Jews; ²⁵three times I was whipped by the Romans; and once I was stoned. I have been in three shipwrecks, and once I spent twenty-four hours in the water. ²⁶In my many travels I have been in danger from floods and from robbers, in danger from my own people and from Gentiles; there have been dangers in the cities, dangers in the wilds, dangers on the high seas, and dangers from false friends. ²⁷There has been work and toil; often I have gone without sleep; I have been hungry and thirsty; I have often been without enough food, shelter, or clothing. ²⁸And not to mention other things, every day I am under the pressure of my concern for all the churches. ²⁹When someone is weak, then I feel weak too; when someone is led into sin, I am filled with distress.

³⁰If I must boast, I will boast about things that show how weak I am. ³¹The God and Father of the Lord Jesus–blessed be his name forever!–knows that I am not lying. ³²When I was in Damascus, the governor under King Aretas placed guards at the city gates to arrest me. ³³But I was let down in a basket through an opening in the wall and escaped from him.

Paul's Visions and Revelations

12 I have to boast, even though it doesn't do any good. But I will now talk about visions and revelations given me by the Lord. ²I know a certain Christian man who fourteen years ago was snatched up to the highest heaven (I do not know whether this actually happened or

如你們要把我當作蠢材，就把我當作蠢材吧，好讓我稍微誇口一下。¹⁷我現在所說的話並不是主要我說的；我這樣誇口只不過像一個蠢材在胡吹。¹⁸既然有那麼多人拿屬世的事來誇口，我也不妨誇口一下。¹⁹你們都那麼聰明，居然樂意容忍蠢材！²⁰無論誰奴役你們，佔你們的便宜，陷害你們，輕視你們，還是打你們耳光，你們都能容忍。²¹讓我說句慚愧的話，這樣的事，我們沒有勇氣去做。

但是，假如有人敢在甚麼事上大膽誇口，讓我說句不用頭腦的話，我也會有同樣的膽量。²²他們是希伯來人嗎？我也是。他們是以色列人嗎？我也是。他們是亞伯拉罕的子孫嗎？我也是。²³他們是基督的僕人嗎？說句狂話，我更是！我的工作更辛苦，坐牢的次數更多，更常受鞭打，更多冒生命的危險。²⁴我被猶太人鞭打過五次，每次照例打三十九下；²⁵被羅馬人用棍子打過三次，被人用石頭打過一次，三次遭遇海難，一次在水裏掙扎過二十四小時。²⁶在屢次旅行中，我經歷過洪水的危險，盜賊的危險，來自猶太人和來自外邦人的危險，又有都市裏的危險、荒野間的危險、海洋上的危險，和假弟兄姊妹所造成的危險。²⁷我又有工作上的勞碌困苦，常常徹夜不眠，忍受飢渴，缺乏食物，沒有住處，衣不蔽體。²⁸這且不說，我還為各教會的事掛慮，像重擔一樣天天壓在我的身上。²⁹有誰軟弱，我不軟弱？有誰失足犯罪，我不滿懷焦慮呢？

³⁰如果我必須誇口，我寧願誇耀那些顯示我自己軟弱的事。³¹我們的主耶穌的父上帝是那位永遠當受頌讚的；他知道我不撒謊。³²當我在大馬士革的時候，亞哩達王手下的總督派警衛把守各城門，要逮捕我。³³但是有人用大籃子從城牆的窗口把我縋下，使我逃脫了他的手。

保羅見異象和啟示

12 雖然自誇沒有好處，但是我必須誇一誇口。現在我要說主所賜給我的異象和啟示。²我知道有一個基督徒，他在十四年前被提到第三層天（我不知道是他的身體上

whether he had a vision–only God knows). ³⁻⁴I repeat, I know that this man was snatched to Paradise (again, I do not know whether this actually happened or whether it was a vision–only God knows), and there he heard things which cannot be put into words, things that human lips may not speak. ⁵So I will boast about this man–but I will not boast about myself, except the things that show how weak I am. ⁶If I wanted to boast, I would not be a fool, because I would be telling the truth. But I will not boast, because I do not want any of you to have a higher opinion of me than you have as a result of what you have seen me do and heard me say.

⁷But to keep me from being puffed up with pride because of the many wonderful things I saw, I was given a painful physical ailment, which acts as Satan's messenger to beat me and keep me from being proud. ⁸Three times I prayed to the Lord about this and asked him to take it away. ⁹But his answer was: "My grace is all you need, for my power is greatest when you are weak." I am most happy, then, to be proud of my weaknesses, in order to feel the protection of Christ's power over me. ¹⁰I am content with weaknesses, insults, hardships, persecutions, and difficulties for Christ's sake. For when I am weak, then I am strong.

Paul's Concern for the Corinthians

¹¹I am acting like a fool–but you have made me do it. You are the ones who ought to show your approval of me. For even if I am nothing, I am in no way inferior to those very special "apostles" of yours. ¹²The many miracles and wonders that prove that I am an apostle were performed among you with much patience. ¹³How were you treated any worse than the other churches, except that I did not bother you for financial help? Please forgive me for being so unfair!

¹⁴This is now the third time that I am ready to come to visit you–and I will not make any demands on you. It is you I want, not your money. After all, children should not have to provide for their parents, but parents should provide for their children. ¹⁵I will be glad to spend all I have, and myself as well, in order to help you. Will you love me less because I love you so much?

¹⁶You will agree, then, that I was not a burden to you. But someone will say that I was tricky, and trapped you with lies. ¹⁷How? Did I take advantage of you through any of the messengers I sent? ¹⁸I begged Titus to go, and I sent the other believer with him. Would you say that Titus took advantage of you? Do not

去，還是他得了異象，只有上帝知道）。³我再說，這個人被提到樂園（是他的身體上去，還是他得了異象，我也不知道，只有上帝知道）。⁴在那裏，他聽見了不能用言語表達、也不能用口舌描述的事。⁵我要為這個人誇口；但是除了有關我軟弱的事，我不為自己誇口。⁶其實，我自誇也不算是愚蠢，因為我說的是實話。但是我不自誇，因為我不願意有人把我捧得太高，超過了他在我身上所看到或聽到的。

⁷為了使我不至於因得到許多奇特的啟示而趾高氣揚，有一種病痛像刺糾纏在我身上，如同撒但的使者刺痛我，使我不敢驕傲。⁸為了這件事，我曾經三次祈求主把這刺移去，⁹他卻回答我：「你只要有我的恩典就夠了；因為我的能力在你軟弱的時候顯得最剛強。」因此，我特別喜歡誇耀我的軟弱，好使我覺得基督的能力在保護着我。¹⁰為了基督的緣故，我樂意忍受軟弱、侮慢、困苦、艱難，和迫害；因為我甚麼時候軟弱，甚麼時候就剛強。

保羅關心哥林多教會

¹¹我竟像一個蠢材，是你們逼着我這樣的。你們原應該讚許我的。縱使我算不了甚麼，我也沒有不如那些「超等使徒」的地方。¹²在你們當中，我用各樣的忍耐，又藉着奇事、異能，和神蹟向你們證明我的使徒身份。¹³除了我不曾拖累過你們這一事實，你們所受的待遇有哪一樣不及其他的教會呢？這是我不公道的地方，請原諒我吧！

¹⁴現在我準備第三次訪問你們，我對你們沒有甚麼要求。我要的是你們，不是你們的金錢。其實，兒女不必為父母積蓄，父母倒應該為兒女積蓄。¹⁵為了幫助你們，我願意支付我所有的一切，甚至我本身。難道我越愛你們就越少得你們的愛嗎？

¹⁶那麼，你們得承認，我不曾拖累過你們；可是還有人說我詭詐，用謊言籠絡你們。¹⁷我利用過派到你們那裏去的人佔你們的便宜嗎？¹⁸我鼓勵提多去訪問你們，又派另一個弟兄同去。提多佔過你們的便宜嗎？

he and I act from the very same motives and behave in the same way?

19Perhaps you think that all along we have been trying to defend ourselves before you. No! We speak as Christ would have us speak in the presence of God, and everything we do, dear friends, is done to help you. 20I am afraid that when I get there I will find you different from what I would like you to be and you will find me different from what you would like me to be. I am afraid that I will find quarreling and jealousy, hot tempers and selfishness, insults and gossip, pride and disorder. 21I am afraid that the next time I come my God will humiliate me in your presence, and I shall weep over many who sinned in the past and have not repented of the immoral things they have done–their lust and their sexual sins.

Final Warnings and Greetings

13This is now the third time that I am coming to visit you. "Any accusation must be upheld by the evidence of two or more witnesses"–as the scripture says. 2I want to tell those of you who have sinned in the past, and all the others; I said it before during my second visit to you, but I will say it again now that I am away: the next time I come nobody will escape punishment. 3You will have all the proof you want that Christ speaks through me. When he deals with you, he is not weak; instead, he shows his power among you. 4For even though it was in weakness that he was put to death on the cross, it is by God's power that he lives. In union with him we also are weak; but in our relations with you we shall share God's power in his life.

5Put yourselves to the test and judge yourselves, to find out whether you are living in faith. Surely you know that Christ Jesus is in you?–unless you have completely failed. 6I trust you will know that we are not failures. 7We pray to God that you will do no wrong–not in order to show that we are a success, but so that you may do what is right, even though we may seem to be failures. 8For we cannot do a thing against the truth, but only for it. 9We are glad when we are weak but you are strong. And so we also pray that you will become perfect. 10That is why I write this while I am away from you; it is so that when I arrive I will not have to deal harshly with you in using the authority that the Lord has given me–authority to build you up, not to tear you down.

11And now, my friends, good-bye! Strive for perfection; listen to my appeals; agree with one

他跟我所做的不是出自同樣的動機嗎？我們的步伐不是一致的嗎？

19 或者，你們以為我們一向都在替自己辯護，其實不然；在上帝面前我們只說基督要我們說的話。親愛的朋友們，我們所做的一切無非想造就你們。20我怕當我去的時候，看見你們不符合我的期望，而你們看見我，也不符合你們的期望。我也怕看見了紛爭、嫉妒、鬧脾氣、自私、毀謗、流言、傲慢，和騷擾。21我又怕下次去的時候，我的上帝要使我在你們面前蒙羞，而我難免會為着許多從前犯罪，淫亂，放蕩，到現在還沒有悔改的人悲傷哭泣。

警告和問候

13這是我第二次要來訪問你們。聖經上說過：「任何控告都必須要兩個或三個證人才能成立。」2對那些從前犯過罪的，和其餘的人，我在第二次訪問你們時已經警告過了，現在我不在你們那裏，再次警告你們，下一次我去的時候，我一定不寬容他們。3你們會有你們所要的憑據，可證明基督在藉着我說話。基督對付你們的時候並不是軟弱的，相反地，他在你們當中顯出能力。4雖然他在軟弱中被釘死在十字架上，可是，靠着上帝的能力他仍然活着。我們跟他連結，也成為軟弱，但是為了你們的益處，我們要靠着上帝的大能跟他一同活着。

5 你們要考驗自己，省察自己，看看你們是否過着信心的生活。除非你們完全經不起考驗，你們應該知道耶穌基督在你們的生命裏。6我希望你們知道，我們並不是經不起考驗的。7我們祈求上帝，使你們不做任何壞事；這不是要表彰我們經得起考驗，而是要你們有正直的行為，即使我們被當作是失敗的。8我們絕對不能做任何敵對真理的事，只能維護真理。9我們軟弱而你們剛強，這是我們應該高興的。我們所祈求的，是你們會成為完全。10因此，我在遠離你們時寫這封信，好使我跟你們見面的時候，不必使用主給我的職權嚴厲地對待你們。主給我的職權是要建立你們，不是要拆毀你們。

11 末了，弟兄姊妹們，再見。你們要努力作完全人。接受我的勸告；大家要同心，和

another; live in peace. And the God of love and peace will be with you.

12 Greet one another with the kiss of peace. All of God's people send you their greetings.

13 The grace of the Lord Jesus Christ, the love of God, and the fellowship of the Holy Spirit be with you all.

睦相處。願慈愛和賜平安的上帝與你們同在！

12 你們要用聖潔的親吻彼此問安！

所有的信徒都向你們問安！

13 願主耶穌基督的恩典、上帝的慈愛、聖靈的團契，與你們每一位同在！

加拉太書
GALATIANS

INTRODUCTION

As the good news about Jesus began to be preached and welcomed among people who were not Jews, the question arose as to whether a person must obey the Law of Moses in order to be a true Christian. Paul had argued that this was not necessary—that in fact, the only sound basis for life in Christ was faith, by which all are put right with God. But among the churches of Galatia, a Roman province in Asia Minor, there had come people who opposed Paul and claimed that one must also observe the Law of Moses in order to be right with God.

Paul's Letter to the Galatians was written in order to bring back to true faith and practice those people who were being misled by this false teaching. Paul begins by defending his right to be called an apostle of Jesus Christ. He insists that his call to be an apostle came from God, not from any human authority, and that his mission was especially to the non-Jews. Then he develops the argument that it is by faith alone that people are put right with God. In the concluding chapters Paul shows that Christian conduct flows naturally from the love that results from faith in Christ.

Outline of Contents

簡 介

當耶穌的福音開始在非猶太人中傳佈並廣受歡迎時，教會中開始討論是否必須遵守摩西的法律才能成為眞基督徒。保羅認為沒有這必要。他指出：要在基督裏得生命的惟一可靠的根基是信；由於信，人得以跟上帝有合宜的關係。但是，當時羅馬治下小亞細亞有一個加拉太省，省裏的幾個教會中，有人反對保羅的主張，聲言一個人必須同時遵守摩西的法律才能夠跟上帝有合宜的關係。

保羅寫加拉太書的目的是要把那些接受謬誤教訓的信徒們帶回到正確的信仰和生活中來。保羅先為自己有權稱爲使徒一事辯護。他堅持他蒙召作使徒是出於上帝，不是出於人的權柄，並且他對非猶太人有特別的使命。接着，他發揮他的主張，指出只有藉着信，人才得以跟上帝有合宜正確的關係。最後，保羅強調：惟有藉着信，基督徒才有眞自由，而這自由應該藉着愛的行為在日常生活上表現出來。

提要

1 From Paul, whose call to be an apostle did not come from human beings or by human means, but from Jesus Christ and God the Father, who raised him from death. [2]All the believers who are here join me in sending greetings to the churches of Galatia:

[3]May God our Father and the Lord Jesus Christ give you grace and peace.

[4]In order to set us free from this present evil age, Christ gave himself for our sins, in obedience to the will of our God and Father. [5]To God be the glory forever and ever! Amen.

The One Gospel

[6]I am surprised at you! In no time at all you are deserting the one who called you by the grace of Christ,[a] and are accepting another gospel. [7]Actually, there is no "other gospel," but I say this because there are some people who are upsetting you and trying to change the gospel of Christ. [8]But even if we or an angel from heaven should preach to you a gospel that is different from the one we preached to you, may he be condemned to hell! [9]We have said it before, and now I say it again: if anyone preaches to you a gospel that is different from the one you accepted, may he be condemned to hell!

[10]Does this sound as if I am trying to win human approval? No indeed! What I want is God's approval! Am I trying to be popular with people? If I were still trying to do so, I would not be a servant of Christ.

How Paul Became an Apostle

[11]Let me tell you, my friends, that the gospel I preach is not of human origin. [12]I did not receive it from any human being, nor did anyone teach it to me. It was Jesus Christ himself who revealed it to me.

[13]You have been told how I used to live when I was devoted to the Jewish religion, how I persecuted without mercy the church of God and did my best to destroy it. [14]I was ahead of most other Jews of my age in my practice of the Jewish religion, and was much more devoted to the traditions of our ancestors.

[15]But God in his grace chose me even before I was born, and called me to serve him. And when he decided [16]to reveal his Son to me, so that I might preach the Good News about him to the Gentiles, I did not go to anyone for advice, [17]nor did I go to Jerusalem to see those who were apostles before me. Instead, I went

a by the grace of Christ; some manuscripts have by his grace.

1 我是使徒保羅。我作使徒不是由於人的選召，也不是受人的委派，而是耶穌基督和那使他從死裏復活的父上帝指派的。[2]我和跟我一起的信徒們寫信給加拉太的各教會。

[3] 願我們的父上帝和主耶穌基督賜恩典、平安給你們！

[4] 基督為了要救我們脫離這邪惡的時代，遵照我們父上帝的旨意，為我們的罪獻上了自己。[5]願榮耀歸於上帝，世世無窮！阿們。

惟一的福音

[6] 我很驚奇，你們竟然這麼輕易地離棄了藉基督的[①]恩典選召你們的上帝，而去隨從另一種福音！[7]其實，並沒有另一種福音。我這樣說，因為有人前來騷擾你們，想要改變基督的福音。[8]其實，任何一個人，即使是我們，或是天上來的天使，要是向你們宣傳另一種福音，跟我們以前所傳給你們的不同，他應受詛咒！[9]我們已經說過了，現在我再說：無論誰，要是向你們宣傳另一種福音，跟你們從前所領受的不同，他應受詛咒！

[10] 我這樣說是要贏得人的稱讚嗎？不是！是要上帝的嘉許！難道我想討人喜歡嗎？如果我仍然想討人喜歡，我就不是基督的僕人了。

保羅怎樣成為使徒

[11] 弟兄姊妹們，我要你們知道，我所傳的福音不是人想出來的。[12]我沒有從任何人接受這福音，也沒有向任何人求教過，而是耶穌基督親自向我啟示的。

[13] 我從前信奉猶太教時的行為為人，你們都很清楚。我不留情地迫害上帝的教會，極力摧殘它。[14]在同輩猶太人中，我比別人更積極地遵行猶太教規，更熱心遵奉祖宗的傳統教訓。

[15] 但是，由於上帝的恩典，在我出生以前，他已經揀選了我，召我來事奉他。[16]當他決定向我啟示他的兒子，使我在外邦人當中宣揚有關基督的福音時，我並沒有向任何人求教，[17]也沒有上耶路撒冷去見那些比我

①有些古卷沒有「基督的」三字。

at once to Arabia, and then I returned to Damascus. [18]It was three years later that I went to Jerusalem to obtain information from Peter, and I stayed with him for two weeks. [19]I did not see any other apostle except James,[b] the Lord's brother.

[20]What I write is true. God knows that I am not lying!

[21]Afterward I went to places in Syria and Cilicia. [22]At that time the members of the churches in Judea did not know me personally. [23]They knew only what others were saying: "The man who used to persecute us is now preaching the faith that he once tried to destroy!" [24]And so they praised God because of me.

Paul and the Other Apostles

2 Fourteen years later I went back to Jerusalem with Barnabas, taking Titus along with me. [7]I went because God revealed to me that I should go. In a private meeting with the leaders I explained the gospel message that I preach to the Gentiles. I did not want my work in the past or in the present to be a failure. [3]My companion Titus, even though he is Greek, was not forced to be circumcised, [4]although some wanted it done. Pretending to be believers, these men slipped into our group as spies, in order to find out about the freedom we have through our union with Christ Jesus. They wanted to make slaves of us, [5]but in order to keep the truth of the gospel safe for you, we did not give in to them for a minute.

[6]But those who seemed to be the leaders–I say this because it makes no difference to me what they were; God does not judge by outward appearances–those leaders, I say, made no new suggestions to me. [7]On the contrary, they saw that God had given me the task of preaching the gospel to the Gentiles, just as he had given Peter the task of preaching the gospel to the Jews. [8]For by God's power I was made an apostle to the Gentiles, just as Peter was made an apostle to the Jews. [9]James, Peter, and John, who seemed to be the leaders, recognized that God had given me this special task; so they shook hands with Barnabas and me, as a sign that we were all partners. We agreed that Barnabas and I would work among the Gentiles and they among the Jews. [10]All they asked was that we should remember the needy in their group, which is the very thing I have[c] been eager to do.

b any other apostle except James; or any other apostle; the only other person I saw was James.
c have; or had.

先作使徒的人，卻立刻到阿拉伯去，然後返回大馬士革。[18]過了三年，我才上耶路撒冷去會見彼得，跟他住了十五天。[19]除了主的兄弟雅各，我沒有見過其他的使徒。

[20]我說的都是實話；上帝知道，我不撒謊。

[21]後來，我到了敘利亞和基利家境內各地。[22]那時，猶太省各教會的基督徒都還不認識我。[23]他們只聽到別人說：「那從前迫害我們的人，現在卻在傳揚他過去所要摧毀的信仰！」[24]因此，他們為了我的緣故頌讚上帝。

保羅和其他使徒

2 十四年後，我跟巴拿巴回到耶路撒冷去，並帶著提多同行。[2]我上耶路撒冷去是遵照主的啟示；在私下會見那些領袖的時候，我向他們說明我在外邦人中所傳的福音。我不願意我過去或目前的工作落空。[3]跟我同去的提多，雖然是希臘人，也沒有被迫接受割禮。[4]但有些人假裝信徒，偷偷地加入教會，要他接受割禮；這些人像偵探似的混進來，要偵察我們因信基督耶穌而享有的自由，為的是想奴役我們。[5]可是，為了要替你們保存福音的真理，我們對這班人毫不讓步。

[6]但是，那些被認為有名望的領袖（他們地位高低，我不在乎，因為上帝是不以外表來判斷人的），我是說，那些有名望的人並沒有給我甚麼新的指示。[7]相反地，他們看出上帝把傳福音給外邦人的任務交給了我，正像他把傳福音給猶太人的任務交給彼得一樣。[8]因為，上帝以他的大能使我成為外邦人的使徒，正像他使彼得成為猶太人的使徒一樣。[9]雅各、彼得、約翰，這三位有名望的教會柱石，既然知道上帝把這特別的使命交給我，就跟巴拿巴和我握手；既然成為同工，我們就同意：巴拿巴跟我應該到外邦人中工作，而他們在猶太人中工作。[10]他們只要求我們記得猶太人中窮人的需要；這件事正是我一向努力在做的。

Paul Rebukes Peter at Antioch

11But when Peter came to Antioch, I opposed him in public, because he was clearly wrong. 12Before some men who had been sent by James arrived there, Peter had been eating with the Gentile believers. But after these men arrived, he drew back and would not eat with the Gentiles, because he was afraid of those who were in favor of circumcising them. 13The other Jewish believers also started acting like cowards along with Peter; and even Barnabas was swept along by their cowardly action. 14When I saw that they were not walking a straight path in line with the truth of the gospel, I said to Peter in front of them all, "You are a Jew, yet you have been living like a Gentile, not like a Jew. How, then, can you try to force Gentiles to live like Jews?"

Jews and Gentiles Are Saved by Faith

15Indeed, we are Jews by birth and not "Gentile sinners," as they are called. 16Yet we know that a person is put right with God only through faith in Jesus Christ, never by doing what the Law requires. We, too, have believed in Christ Jesus in order to be put right with God through our faith in Christ, and not by doing what the Law requires. For no one is put right with God by doing what the Law requires. 17If, then, as we try to be put right with God by our union with Christ, we are found to be sinners, as much as the Gentiles are–does this mean that Christ is serving the cause of sin? By no means! 18If I start to rebuild the system of Law that I tore down, then I show myself to be someone who breaks the Law. 19So far as the Law is concerned, however, I am dead–killed by the Law itself–in order that I might live for God. I have been put to death with Christ on his cross, 20so that it is no longer I who live, but it is Christ who lives in me. This life that I live now, I live by faith in the Son of God, who loved me and gave his life for me. 21I refuse to reject the grace of God. But if a person is put right with God through the Law, it means that Christ died for nothing!

Law or Faith

3 You foolish Galatians! Who put a spell on you? Before your very eyes you had a clear description of the death of Jesus Christ on the cross! 2Tell me this one thing: did you receive God's Spirit by doing what the Law requires or by hearing the gospel and believing it? 3How can you be so foolish! You began by God's Spirit; do you now want to finish by your own

保羅在安提阿責備彼得

11以後，彼得到安提阿來；因為他有明顯的錯誤，我就公開指責他。12原來，在雅各所派來的人沒有到達以前，彼得跟外邦的信徒一起吃飯。可是那些人一到，他就退縮，不敢再一起吃飯，因為怕那些主張外邦人必須接受割禮的人。13其他的猶太信徒也跟着彼得，像沒有原則的人一樣；連巴拿巴也受了他們的影響。14我一看出他們不遵循福音真理，就當眾對彼得說：「你是猶太人，而你的生活卻像外邦人，不像猶太人。這樣，你怎麼可以勉強外邦人過猶太化的生活呢？」

猶太人和外邦人都因信得救

15不錯，我們這些人生下來就是猶太人，不是外邦罪人。16然而，我們知道，一個人得以跟上帝有合宜的關係是藉着信耶穌基督，而不是靠遵行摩西的法律。我們也信了基督耶穌，為要因信基督而得以跟上帝有合宜的關係，不是靠遵行法律。因為沒有人能夠靠遵行法律而得以跟上帝有合宜的關係。17這樣，如果我們這些尋求因信基督得以跟上帝有合宜關係的人還跟外邦人一樣，都是罪人，這不等於說基督是支持罪嗎？絕對不是！18因為，如果我重新建造自己所拆毀的，就是證明我破壞法律。19就法律來說，我已經死了，是被法律處死的，為要使我能為上帝而活。我已經跟基督一同被釘在十字架上，20這樣，現在活着的不再是我自己，而是基督在我生命裏活着。我現在活着，是藉着信上帝的兒子而活；他愛我，為我捨命。21我不拒絕上帝的恩典。如果人得以跟上帝有合宜的關係是藉着法律，那麼，基督不是白死了嗎？

法律或信心

3 無知的加拉太人哪，誰又迷惑了你們呢？耶穌基督被釘死在十字架上的事，你們眼前不是有一幅清楚的圖畫嗎？2你們只要告訴我一件事：你們受了上帝的靈是靠遵行法律，還是藉着聽信福音呢？3你們怎麼會那樣無知呢？你們是從接受上帝的靈開始的，現在竟要靠自己的能力去完成嗎？

power? ⁴Did all your experience mean nothing at all? Surely it meant something! ⁵Does God give you the Spirit and work miracles among you because you do what the Law requires or because you hear the gospel and believe it?

⁶Consider the experience of Abraham; as the scripture says, "He believed God, and because of his faith God accepted him as righteous." ⁷You should realize, then, that the real descendants of Abraham are the people who have faith. ⁸The scripture predicted that God would put the Gentiles right with himself through faith. And so the scripture announced the Good News to Abraham: "Through you God will bless all people." ⁹Abraham believed and was blessed; so all who believe are blessed as he was.

¹⁰Those who depend on obeying the Law live under a curse. For the scripture says, "Whoever does not always obey everything that is written in the book of the Law is under God's curse!" ¹¹Now, it is clear that no one is put right with God by means of the Law, because the scripture says, "Only the person who is put right with God through faith shall live."ᵈ ¹²But the Law has nothing to do with faith. Instead, as the scripture says, "Whoever *does* everything the Law requires will live."

¹³But by becoming a curse for us Christ has redeemed us from the curse that the Law brings; for the scripture says, "Anyone who is hanged on a tree is under God's curse." ¹⁴Christ did this in order that the blessing which God promised to Abraham might be given to the Gentiles by means of Christ Jesus, so that through faith we might receive the Spirit promised by God.

The Law and the Promise
¹⁵My friends, I am going to use an everyday example: when two people agree on a matter and sign an agreement, no one can break it or add anything to it. ¹⁶Now, God made his promises to Abraham and to his descendant. The scripture does not use the plural "descendants," meaning many people, but the singular "descendant," meaning one person only, namely, Christ. ¹⁷What I mean is that God made a covenant with Abraham and promised to keep it. The Law, which was given four hundred and thirty years later, cannot break that covenant and cancel God's promise. ¹⁸For if God's gift depends on the Law, then it no longer depends on his promise. However, it was because of his promise that God gave that gift to Abraham.

¹⁹What, then, was the purpose of the Law? It

ᵈ put right with God through faith shall live; *or* put right with God shall live through faith.

⁴你們以往一切的經驗是徒然的嗎?絕對不是!⁵上帝賜給你們聖靈,又在你們當中行各樣神蹟,是因為你們遵行法律,還是因為你們聽信福音呢?

⁶ 正如聖經提到亞伯拉罕的時候說:「他信上帝,因他的信,上帝認他為義人。」⁷所以,你們知道,有了信的人就是亞伯拉罕的真子孫。⁸聖經預先看到,上帝要使外邦人因信而跟他有合宜的關係,所以早已把這福音傳給亞伯拉罕,說:「萬民都要藉着你蒙上帝賜福!」⁹亞伯拉罕信了,因而蒙福;這樣,一切信了的人也要跟他一同蒙福。

¹⁰ 以遵守法律為憑藉的人都是活在詛咒之下。因為聖經上說:「凡不事事遵行法律書上一切規條的人都要受上帝詛咒。」¹¹可見沒有人能靠遵守法律而得以跟上帝有合宜的關係;因為聖經上說:「因信而得以跟上帝有合宜關係的人將得生命②。」¹²但是,法律並不是以信為憑藉的,而是像聖經所說:「那遵守法律的人將因法律而存活。」

¹³ 基督已經為我們承擔詛咒,藉此救贖我們脫離了法律的詛咒;因為聖經上說:「凡被掛在木頭上的人都受上帝詛咒。」¹⁴基督這樣做的目的是要使外邦人藉着基督耶穌獲得上帝應許給亞伯拉罕的福澤;這樣,我們能藉着信而領受上帝所應許的聖靈。

法律和應許
¹⁵ 弟兄姊妹們,讓我從日常生活中舉一個例子:當兩個人同意某一件事,並且簽訂了契約,沒有人能有所增減。¹⁶同樣,上帝已經向亞伯拉罕和他的子孫立了應許。聖經並不是用「向子子孫孫」,指多數的人,而是用「向你的子孫」,指一個人,就是基督。¹⁷我的意思是:上帝立了約,並答應持守這約。那在四百三十年後才出現的法律不能夠破壞這約,以致取消了上帝的應許。¹⁸如果上帝賜產業是根據法律,那就不是靠應許了;然而,上帝賜產業給亞伯拉罕是靠應許的。

¹⁹ 那麼,法律的目的是甚麼呢?法律是為

---

② 「因信而得以跟上帝有合宜關係的人將得生命」或譯「跟上帝有合宜關係的人將因信而得生命」。

was added in order to show what wrongdoing is, and it was meant to last until the coming of Abraham's descendant, to whom the promise was made. The Law was handed down by angels, with a man acting as a go-between. 20But a go-between is not needed when only one person is involved; and God is one.e

The Purpose of the Law

21Does this mean that the Law is against God's promises? No, not at all! For if human beings had received a law that could bring life, then everyone could be put right with God by obeying it. 22But the scripture says that the whole world is under the power of sin; and so the gift which is promised on the basis of faith in Jesus Christ is given to those who believe.

23But before the time for faith came, the Law kept us all locked up as prisoners until this coming faith should be revealed. 24And so the Law was in charge of us until Christ came, in order that we might then be put right with God through faith. 25Now that the time for faith is here, the Law is no longer in charge of us.

26It is through faith that all of you are God's children in union with Christ Jesus. 27You were baptized into union with Christ, and now you are clothed, so to speak, with the life of Christ himself. 28So there is no difference between Jews and Gentiles, between slaves and free people, between men and women; you are all one in union with Christ Jesus. 29If you belong to Christ, then you are the descendants of Abraham and will receive what God has promised.

4 But now to continue–the son who will receive his father's property is treated just like a slave while he is young, even though he really owns everything. 2While he is young, there are men who take care of him and manage his affairs until the time set by his father. 3In the same way, we too were slaves of the ruling spirits of the universe before we reached spiritual maturity. 4But when the right time finally came, God sent his own Son. He came as the son of a human mother and lived under the Jewish Law, 5to redeem those who were under the Law, so that we might become God's children.

6To show that you aref his children, God sent the Spirit of his Son into our hearts, the Spirit

了指出甚麼是過犯而設的,直到那應許給亞伯拉罕的子孫來臨才結束。法律是由天使藉着一位中間人頒佈的。20可是,屬於單方的事就無需中間人,而上帝是單方的③。

法律的目的

21 這樣說來,法律跟上帝的應許相抵觸嗎?絕對不是!如果法律的頒佈能夠給人帶來生命,人就可以靠法律而得以跟上帝有合宜的關係。22然而,聖經說,全世界都處在罪的權勢下,爲要以信耶穌基督作爲領受上帝應許的根據;這應許是賜給所有信的人的。

23 但是,「信」的時代沒有來臨以前,法律看守着我們,像看守囚犯一樣,直到「信」被顯示出來。24這樣,法律成爲我們的監護人,指引我們歸向基督④,目的是要使我們因「信」得以跟上帝有合宜的關係。25既然現在是「信」的時代,法律就不再監護我們了。

26 你們大家都藉着「信」跟基督耶穌合而爲一,成爲上帝的兒女。27你們受洗跟基督合而爲一,正像穿上基督,有他的生命。28不分猶太人或外邦人,奴隸或自由人,男人或女人,在基督耶穌的生命裏,你們都成爲一體了。29如果你們是屬基督的,你們就是亞伯拉罕的後代,會承受上帝給亞伯拉罕的應許。

4 還有,繼承人在未成年時,雖然所有的產業都是他的,但他跟奴僕沒有甚麼分別。2在他年幼的時候,有人照顧他,替他管理業務,等候他父親爲他所定的日子來到。3同樣,在靈性幼稚的時候,我們也受宇宙間所謂星宿之靈的支配。4但是時機成熟,上帝就差遣了自己的兒子,爲女子所生,活在法律下,5爲要救贖在法律下的人,使我們獲得上帝兒女的名份。

6 因爲我們⑤是他的兒女,上帝就差遣他兒子的靈進入我們的心,呼叫:「阿爸!我

---

e and God is one; or and God acts alone.
f To show that you are; or Because you are.

③「而上帝是單方的」原文是「上帝卻是一位」。
④「指引我們歸向基督」或譯「直到基督來了」。
⑤「我們」原文是「你們」。

who cries out, "Father, my Father." [7]So then, you are no longer a slave but a child. And since you are his child, God will give you all that he has for his children.

Paul's Concern for the Galatians

[8]In the past you did not know God, and so you were slaves of beings who are not gods. [9]But now that you know God–or, I should say, now that God knows you–how is it that you want to turn back to those weak and pitiful ruling spirits? Why do you want to become their slaves all over again? [10]You pay special attention to certain days, months, seasons, and years. [11]I am worried about you! Can it be that all my work for you has been for nothing?

[12]I beg you, my friends, be like me. After all, I am like you. You have not done me any wrong. [13]You remember why I preached the gospel to you the first time; it was because I was sick. [14]But even though my physical condition was a great trial to you, you did not despise or reject me. Instead, you received me as you would an angel from heaven; you received me as you would Christ Jesus. [15]You were so happy! What has happened? I myself can say that you would have taken out your own eyes, if you could, and given them to me. [16]Have I now become your enemy by telling you the truth?

[17]Those other people show a deep interest in you, but their intentions are not good. All they want is to separate you from me, so that you will have the same interest in them as they have in you. [18]Now, it is good to have such a deep interest if the purpose is good–this is true always, and not merely when I am with you. [19]My dear children! Once again, just like a mother in childbirth, I feel the same kind of pain for you until Christ's nature is formed in you. [20]How I wish I were with you now, so that I could take a different attitude toward you. I am so worried about you!

The Example of Hagar and Sarah

[21]Let me ask those of you who want to be subject to the Law: do you not hear what the Law says? [22]It says that Abraham had two sons, one by a slave woman, the other by a free woman. [23]His son by the slave woman was born in the usual way, but his son by the free woman was born as a result of God's promise. [24]These things can be understood as a figure: the two women represent two covenants. The one whose children are born in slavery is Hagar, and she represents the covenant made at Mount Sinai. [25]Hagar, who stands for Mount Sinai in

的父親!」[7]這樣,你不再是奴僕,而是兒子;既然是上帝的兒子,上帝就以你爲繼承人。

保羅關懷加拉太人

[8] 過去你們不認識上帝,被那些不是神的神明所奴役。[9]現在你們認識上帝(或者說,已經被上帝所認識),爲甚麼又要回去找那些無能無用的星宿之靈呢?爲甚麼要重新去作他們的奴隸呢?[10]你們竟死守着某些日子、月份、節期、年份![11]我很替你們擔憂,只怕從前我在你們當中的工作全都落空了。

[12] 弟兄姊妹們,我懇求你們,要認同我的立場,畢竟我曾認同過你們的立場。你們並沒有做過對不起我的事。[13]你們知道,因爲我身體有病,我才有初次向你們傳福音的機會。[14]雖然我的病況使你們困擾,但是你們並沒有厭煩我,丟棄我。相反地,你們接待我,像接待上帝的天使,像接待基督耶穌。[15]當時你們多麼高興,現在又怎樣呢?我可以這麼說,那時候,你們即使把自己的眼睛挖出來給我也是願意的![16]現在我對你們說實話,倒成爲你們的敵人了嗎?

[17] 那些人對你們表示熱情,原是不懷好意的。他們的目的是要把我孤立起來,好叫你們也對他們表示熱情。[18]在善事上熱心原是好的,但不可只限於我跟你們在一起的時候才這樣。[19]我的孩子們,我再一次像母親爲你們忍受生產的痛苦,直到基督的特性在你們的生命中成形。[20]我多麼渴望現在就跟你們在一起,好讓我用另一種態度來對待你們。爲着你們,我心裏多麼困惑不安!

夏甲和莎拉的例子

[21] 讓我向那些願意生活在法律下的人提出一個問題:你們沒有聽見摩西的法律嗎?[22]法律書上記載,亞伯拉罕有兩個兒子,一個是從女奴生的,另一個是從自由的女子生的。[23]從女奴生的是循着自然生的;從自由的女子生的卻是出於上帝的應許。[24]這可以當作一種寓意:那兩個女人代表兩種約。其中之一是夏甲,她來自西奈山,所生的都是奴隸。[25]夏甲是指在阿拉伯的西

Arabia, is[g] a figure of the present city of Jerusalem, in slavery with all its people. [26]But the heavenly Jerusalem is free, and she is our mother. [27]For the scripture says,

"Be happy, you childless woman!
    Shout and cry with joy, you who never felt the pains of childbirth!
For the woman who was deserted will have more children
    than the woman whose husband never left her."

[28]Now, you, my friends, are God's children as a result of his promise, just as Isaac was. [29]At that time the son who was born in the usual way persecuted the one who was born because of God's Spirit; and it is the same now. [30]But what does the scripture say? It says, "Send the slave woman and her son away; for the son of the slave woman will not have a part of the father's property along with the son of the free woman." [31]So then, my friends, we are not the children of a slave woman but of a free woman.

Preserve Your Freedom

5 Freedom is what we have–Christ has set us free! Stand, then, as free people, and do not allow yourselves to become slaves again.

[2]Listen! I, Paul, tell you that if you allow yourselves to be circumcised, it means that Christ is of no use to you at all. [3]Once more I warn any man who allows himself to be circumcised that he is obliged to obey the whole Law. [4]Those of you who try to be put right with God by obeying the Law have cut yourselves off from Christ. You are outside God's grace. [5]As for us, our hope is that God will put us right with him; and this is what we wait for by the power of God's Spirit working through our faith. [6]For when we are in union with Christ Jesus, neither circumcision nor the lack of it makes any difference at all; what matters is faith that works through love.

[7]You were doing so well! Who made you stop obeying the truth? How did he persuade you? [8]It was not done by God, who calls you. [9]"It takes only a little yeast to make the whole batch of dough rise," as they say. [10]But I still feel confident about you. Our life in union with the Lord makes me confident that you will not

g Hagar ... is; *some manuscripts have* Sinai is a mountain in Arabia, and it is.

奈山⑥，象徵今天的耶路撒冷；她和她的兒女生活在奴役中。[26]但是那天上的耶路撒冷卻是自由的；她是我們的母親。[27]因爲聖經上記載：

那不能懷孕、沒有生產過的女子啊，
你要歡樂！
那沒有經歷過生產痛苦的女子啊，
你要高聲歡呼！
因爲被冷落的女人
比那跟丈夫一起生活的，
會有更多的兒女！

[28]弟兄姊妹們，正如以撒一樣，你們是由於上帝的應許而成爲他的兒女的。[29]當時，那循着自然生的迫害那聖靈所生的；現在也是這樣。[30]但是聖經怎麼說呢？聖經說：「把女奴趕她的兒子趕出去，因爲女奴的兒子不可以跟自由的女子所生的兒子一同繼承產業。」[31]所以，弟兄姊妹們，我們並不是女奴的兒女，而是自由的女子所生的。

基督徒的自由

5 爲了要使我們得自由，基督已經釋放了我們。所以，你們要挺起胸膛，不要再讓奴隸的軛控制你們。

[2] 我—保羅鄭重地告訴你們，如果你們接受割禮，基督對你們就毫無益處。[3] 現在我再次警告你們，任何一個接受割禮的人必須遵守全部的法律。[4] 想倚靠遵守法律而得以跟上帝有合宜關係的人就是跟基督切斷了關係，自絕於上帝的恩典。[5] 至於我們所熱切盼望着的，是上帝會使我們跟他有合宜的關係；這是聖靈的力量藉着我們的信心達成的。[6] 因爲，當我們在基督耶穌的生命裏的時候，受割禮或不受割禮都沒有甚麼關係，惟有那以愛的行動表現出來的信心才算重要。

[7] 你們一向都表現得很好！是誰阻擋了你們，使你們不再服從眞理呢？[8] 這種勸誘當然不會出於那呼召你們的上帝。[9] 俗語說：「一點點酵母可以使全團的麵發起來。」[10] 可是我仍然信任你們；因爲我們同在主的生命裏，我深信你們一定不至於跟我有不同

⑥「夏甲是指……西奈山」另有些古卷作「西奈是在阿拉伯的一座山」。

take a different view and that whoever is upsetting you will be punished by God.

11But as for me, my friends, if I continue to preach that circumcision is necessary, why am I still being persecuted? If that were true, then my preaching about the cross of Christ would cause no trouble. 12I wish that the people who are upsetting you would go all the way; let them go on and castrate themselves!

13As for you, my friends, you were called to be free. But do not let this freedom become an excuse for letting your physical desires control you. Instead, let love make you serve one another. 14For the whole Law is summed up in one commandment: "Love your neighbor as you love yourself." 15But if you act like wild animals, hurting and harming each other, then watch out, or you will completely destroy one another.

The Spirit and Human Nature

16What I say is this: let the Spirit direct your lives, and you will not satisfy the desires of the human nature. 17For what our human nature wants is opposed to what the Spirit wants, and what the Spirit wants is opposed to what our human nature wants. These two are enemies, and this means that you cannot do what you want to do. 18If the Spirit leads you, then you are not subject to the Law.

19What human nature does is quite plain. It shows itself in immoral, filthy, and indecent actions; 20in worship of idols and witchcraft. People become enemies and they fight; they become jealous, angry, and ambitious. They separate into parties and groups; 21they are envious, get drunk, have orgies, and do other things like these. I warn you now as I have before: those who do these things will not possess the Kingdom of God.

22But the Spirit produces love, joy, peace, patience, kindness, goodness, faithfulness, 23humility, and self-control. There is no law against such things as these. 24And those who belong to Christ Jesus have put to death their human nature with all its passions and desires. 25The Spirit has given us life; he must also control our lives. 26We must not be proud or irritate one another or be jealous of one another.

Bear One Another's Burdens

6 My friends, if someone is caught in any kind of wrongdoing, those of you who are spiritual should set him right; but you must do it in a gentle way. And keep an eye on yourselves, so that you will not be tempted,

的見解。只是那擾亂你們的，無論是誰，將受上帝的懲罰。

11 弟兄姊妹們，我若繼續宣傳割禮，為甚麼還受迫害呢？我若這樣做的話，即使傳基督的十字架也不至於成為他們的障礙了。12我倒希望那些擾亂你們的人自己去閹割！

13 弟兄姊妹們，上帝選召你們，要你們成為自由人。只是不可用這自由作放縱情慾的藉口，卻要以愛心互相服事。14因為全部法律都綜合在「愛人如己」這條命令裏面。15要當心哪，如果你們像禽獸一樣相咬相吞，你們一定同歸於盡。

聖靈和人的本性

16 我要強調的是：你們的言行要順從聖靈的引導，不要滿足自己本性的慾望。17因為本性的慾望跟聖靈互相敵對，彼此對立，使你們不能做自己所願意做的。18但是，如果聖靈引導你們，你們就不受法律的拘束了。

19 人本性的慾望是顯而易見的；它表現在淫亂、穢行、邪蕩、20偶像崇拜、巫術、仇恨、爭鬥、忌恨、惱怒、好爭、分派、結黨、21嫉妒、酗酒、狂歡宴樂，和其他類似的事。我從前警告過你們，現在又警告你們：做這種事的人一定不能成為上帝國的子民。

22 至於聖靈所結的果子，就是：博愛、喜樂、和平、忍耐、仁慈、良善、忠信、23溫柔、節制。這些事是沒有任何法律會加以禁止的。24那些屬於基督耶穌的人已經把他們本性上的一切邪情慾望都釘死在十字架上了。25既然聖靈賜給我們新生命，我們就該讓他引導我們的生活。26我們不可驕傲，不可彼此激怒，互相嫉妒。

分擔重擔

6 弟兄姊妹們，如果有人偶然犯了過錯，你們這些屬靈的人就要用溫和的方法糾正他。你們自己也要小心，免得也受引誘。

too. ²Help carry one another's burdens, and in this way you will obey[h] the law of Christ. ³If you think you are something when you really are nothing, you are only deceiving yourself. ⁴You should each judge your own conduct. If it is good, then you can be proud of what you yourself have done, without having to compare it with what someone else has done. ⁵For each of you have to carry your own load.

⁶If you are being taught the Christian message, you should share all the good things you have with your teacher.

⁷Do not deceive yourselves; no one makes a fool of God. You will reap exactly what you plant. ⁸If you plant in the field of your natural desires, from it you will gather the harvest of death; if you plant in the field of the Spirit, from the Spirit you will gather the harvest of eternal life. ⁹So let us not become tired of doing good; for if we do not give up, the time will come when we will reap the harvest. ¹⁰So then, as often as we have the chance, we should do good to everyone, and especially to those who belong to our family in the faith.

Final Warning and Greeting

¹¹See what big letters I make as I write to you now with my own hand! ¹²The people who are trying to force you to be circumcised are the ones who want to show off and boast about external matters. They do it, however, only so that they may not be persecuted for the cross of Christ. ¹³Even those who practice circumcision do not obey the Law; they want you to be circumcised so that they can boast that you submitted to this physical ceremony. ¹⁴As for me, however, I will boast only about the cross of our Lord Jesus Christ; for by means of his cross the world is dead to me, and I am dead to the world. ¹⁵It does not matter at all whether or not one is circumcised; what does matter is being a new creature. ¹⁶As for those who follow this rule in their lives, may peace and mercy be with them–with them and with all of God's people!

¹⁷To conclude: let no one give me any more trouble, because the scars I have on my body show that I am the slave of Jesus.

¹⁸May the grace of our Lord Jesus Christ be with you all, my friends. Amen.

---

h you will obey; *some manuscripts have* obey.

² 要彼此分擔重擔,這樣就是成全基督的命令。³ 一無所有而自以爲了不起的人只是欺騙自己罷了。⁴ 每一個人都應該省察自己的行爲;如果有好行爲,他可以引以爲榮,不需要跟別人的成就相較量。⁵ 每一個人應該肩負自己的擔子。

⁶ 那在基督正道上受教導的人應該和教導他的老師分享一切美好的東西。

⁷ 你們不要自欺,也不要欺騙上帝。一個人種甚麼,就收甚麼。⁸ 他若爲着滿足自己的情慾而撒種,他會從情慾收取死亡;他若爲着得聖靈的喜悅而撒種,他會從聖靈收穫永恆的生命。⁹ 所以,我們行善,不可喪志;我們若不灰心,時候到了就有收成。¹⁰ 因此,無論甚麼時候,一有機會就該爲公衆做有益的事,對那些在信仰上同屬一家的人更應該這樣。

警告和問候

¹¹ 你們看,這些大的字是我親筆寫給你們的!¹² 那些喜歡在外表上炫耀的人就是勉強你們接受割禮的人。他們這樣做,無非是怕爲基督的十字架遭受迫害。¹³ 其實,連那些接受割禮的人也不遵守律法;他們勉強你們受割禮,是要誇耀他們在外表的儀式上已經屈服了。¹⁴ 至於我,我不誇耀別的,我只誇耀我們的主耶穌基督的十字架。因爲,藉着這十字架,世界對我已經釘死了;我於世界也已經釘死了。¹⁵ 受割禮或是不受割禮都算不了甚麼;重要的是我們要成爲新造的人。¹⁶ 願所有遵照這原則的人,和一切上帝的子民,都同樣得到平安和憐憫!

¹⁷ 從今以後,別在這些事上找我的麻煩,因爲我身上帶着耶穌的傷痕。

¹⁸ 弟兄姊妹們,願我們的主耶穌基督賜恩典給你們大家!阿們。

以弗所書
EPHESIANS

INTRODUCTION

Paul's Letter to the Ephesians is concerned first of all with "God's plan ... to bring all creation together, everything in heaven and on earth, with Christ as head" (1.10). It is also an appeal to God's people to live out the meaning of this great plan for the unity of the whole human race through oneness with Jesus Christ.

In the first part of *Ephesians* the writer develops the theme of unity by speaking of the way in which God the Father has chosen his people, how they are forgiven and set free from their sins through Jesus Christ the Son, and how God's great promise is guaranteed by the Holy Spirit. In the second part he appeals to the readers to live in such a way that their oneness in Christ may become real in their life together.

Several figures of speech are used to show the oneness of God's people in union with Christ: the church is like a body, with Christ as the head; or like a building, with Christ as the cornerstone; or like a wife, with Christ as the husband. This letter rises to great heights of expression as the writer is moved by the thought of God's grace in Christ. Everything is seen in the light of Christ's love, sacrifice, forgiveness, grace, and purity.

Outline of Contents

簡 介

以弗所書的主題是：「上帝在時機成熟的時候要完成的計劃就是：要使天上和地上一切被造的都歸屬基督，以他爲首。」（1．10）作者也要求上帝的子民在生活上力求符合上帝這一個偉大的計劃—全人類在耶穌基督的生命裏合而爲一。

在本書的前部，作者闡述合一的理論，說明父上帝選召他的子民，藉着他的兒子耶穌基督赦免他們，使他們從罪的束縛中得到釋放，並且說明上帝的偉大應許是以聖靈爲保證的。在後半部，作者勸勉讀者，要他們在團契生活中實現與基督的合一。

作者用好些比喩說明上帝子民在基督生命裏的合一：敎會好比人的身體，而基督是頭；敎會好比一所建築物，而基督是基石；敎會好比妻子，而基督是丈夫。作者深受上帝在基督裏所賜的恩典的激勵，而用深奧的言詞把它表達出來。他以基督的愛、犧牲、赦免、恩典，和聖潔爲標準來判斷一切事物。

提要

1 From Paul, who by God's will is an apostle of Christ Jesus–

To God's people in Ephesus,[a] who are faithful in their life in union with Christ Jesus:

2May God our Father and the Lord Jesus Christ give you grace and peace.

Spiritual Blessings in Christ

3Let us give thanks to the God and Father of our Lord Jesus Christ! For in our union with Christ he has blessed us by giving us every spiritual blessing in the heavenly world. 4Even before the world was made, God had already chosen us to be his through our union with Christ, so that we would be holy and without fault before him.

Because of his love 5God[b] had already decided that through Jesus Christ he would make us his children–this was his pleasure and purpose. 6Let us praise God for his glorious grace, for the free gift he gave us in his dear Son! 7For by the blood of Christ[c] we are set free, that is, our sins are forgiven. How great is the grace of God, 8which he gave to us in such large measure!

In all his wisdom and insight 9God did what he had purposed, and made known to us the secret plan he had already decided to complete by means of Christ. 10This plan, which God will complete when the time is right, is to bring all creation together, everything in heaven and on earth, with Christ as head.

11All things are done according to God's plan and decision; and God chose us to be his own people in union with Christ because of his own purpose, based on what he had decided from the very beginning. 12Let us, then, who were the first to hope in Christ, praise God's glory!

13And you also became God's people when you heard the true message, the Good News that brought you salvation. You believed in Christ, and God put his stamp of ownership on you by giving you the Holy Spirit he had promised. 14The Spirit is the guarantee that we shall receive what God has promised his people, and this assures us that God will give complete freedom to those who are his. Let us praise his glory!

Paul's Prayer

15For this reason, ever since I heard of your faith in the Lord Jesus and your love for all of

a *Some manuscripts do not have* in Ephesus.
b before him. Because of his love God; *or* before him, and to live in love. God.
c by the blood of Christ; *or* by the sacrificial death of Christ.

---

1 我是保羅;我奉上帝的旨意作基督耶穌的使徒。我寫信給以弗所地方①那些在基督耶穌裏真忠心的信徒們:

2 願我們的父上帝和主耶穌基督賜恩典、平安給你們!

基督裏的屬靈恩賜

3 感謝我們的主耶穌基督的父上帝!因為他藉着基督把天上各樣屬靈的福氣賜給我們。4 在創世以前,他已經藉着基督揀選我們,使我們在他面前成為聖潔、沒有絲毫缺點的人。

5 上帝愛我們,預先決定藉着耶穌基督使我們歸屬於他,使我們有作他兒女的名份;這是他所喜悅的,是他的旨意。6 讓我們頌讚上帝這榮耀的恩典,因為他把他親愛的兒子白白地賜給我們!7 由於基督的死,我們得到自由,我們的罪蒙赦免。這是出於上帝豐富的恩典。8 他賜給我們的恩典是多麼充足啊!

上帝用聰明智慧 9 完成了他的旨意,又使我們知道他已經決定要藉着基督去完成的奧祕。10 上帝在時機成熟的時候要完成的計劃就是:要使天上和地上一切被造的都歸屬基督,以他為首。

11 宇宙萬物都要按照上帝的計劃和決定來完成。上帝根據他原始定下的旨意,藉着基督揀選了我們作他的子民。12 他的旨意是要我們這些首先把希望寄託於基督的人都頌讚上帝的榮耀!

13 你們也是這樣:當你們聽見了真理的信息,就是聽見那使你們得救的福音時,你們信了基督,上帝就把他所應許的聖靈賜給你們,作為你們歸屬於他的印記。14 聖靈保證我們要承受上帝的應許,把完全的自由賜給屬他的人。我們要頌讚他的榮耀!

保羅的禱告

15 因此,自從我聽到了你們對主耶穌有信

① 有些古卷沒有「以弗所地方」。

God's people, [16]I have not stopped giving thanks to God for you. I remember you in my prayers [17]and ask the God of our Lord Jesus Christ, the glorious Father, to give you the Spirit, who will make you wise and reveal God to you, so that you will know him. [18]I ask that your minds may be opened to see his light, so that you will know what is the hope to which he has called you, how rich are the wonderful blessings he promises his people, [19]and how very great is his power at work in us who believe. This power working in us is the same as the mighty strength [20]which he used when he raised Christ from death and seated him at his right side in the heavenly world. [21]Christ rules there above all heavenly rulers, authorities, powers, and lords; he has a title superior to all titles of authority in this world and in the next. [22]God put all things under Christ's feet and gave him to the church as supreme Lord over all things. [23]The church is Christ's body, the completion of him who himself completes all things everywhere.[d]

From Death to Life

2 In the past you were spiritually dead because of your disobedience and sins. [2]At that time you followed the world's evil way; you obeyed the ruler of the spiritual powers in space, the spirit who now controls the people who disobey God. [3]Actually all of us were like them and lived according to our natural desires, doing whatever suited the wishes of our own bodies and minds. In our natural condition we, like everyone else, were destined to suffer God's anger.

[4]But God's mercy is so abundant, and his love for us is so great, [5]that while we were spiritually dead in our disobedience he brought us to life with Christ. It is by God's grace that you have been saved. [6]In our union with Christ Jesus he raised us up with him to rule with him in the heavenly world. [7]He did this to demonstrate for all time to come the extraordinary greatness of his grace in the love he showed us in Christ Jesus. [8-9]For it is by God's grace that you have been saved through faith. It is not the result of your own efforts, but God's gift, so that no one can boast about it. [10]God has made us what we are, and in our union with Christ Jesus he has created us for a life of good deeds, which he has already prepared for us to do.

One in Christ

[11]You Gentiles by birth–called "the uncircumcised" by the Jews, who call themselves the

d who himself completes all things everywhere; or who is himself completely filled with God's fullness.

心,以及對信徒們有愛心,[16]我就不斷地為你們感謝上帝。我在禱告中提到你們,[17]求我們主耶穌基督的上帝,榮耀的天父,把聖靈賜給你們。這聖靈會給你們智慧,啟示你們認識上帝。[18]我也求上帝開啟你們的心眼,好使你們知道:他呼召你們來得的盼望是甚麼;他所應許給他子民的產業是多麼豐富;[19-20]他在我們信他的人當中所運行的大能是多麼強大。這大能與他使基督從死裏復活、使基督在天上坐在自己右邊的大力量是相同的。[21]在那裏,基督的統治超越了一切靈界邪惡的執政者、掌權者、統治者,和主宰;他超越了現世和來世一切的名號。[22]上帝又使宇宙萬物屈服在基督腳下,以他為教會的元首,統御一切。[23]教會是基督的身體,是充滿宇宙萬物的那位基督所充滿的[②]。

出死入生

2 從前,你們因犯罪違抗上帝的命令,你們在靈性上是死了。[2]那時候,你們隨從這世界的邪風惡俗,順服天界的掌權者,就是管轄着那些違抗上帝命令的人的邪靈。[3]其實,我們每一個人從前也都跟他們一樣,放縱本性的慾望,隨從肉體的私慾意念。因此,我們跟別人沒有差別,都注定了要受上帝的懲罰。

[4]但是,上帝有豐盛的憐憫;他對我們的愛浩大無窮。[5]我們的靈性在違命的罪中死了的時候,他使我們跟基督一同復活;是他的恩典救了你們的。[6]上帝已經使我們在基督耶穌的生命裏跟基督一同復活,一同在天上掌權。[7]他這樣做是要向世世代代表明他極大的恩典,就是他從基督耶穌向我們顯示出來的慈愛。[8]你們是靠上帝的恩典、憑信心而得救的;這不是出於你們自己的行為,而是上帝的恩賜。[9]既然不是靠行為,你們就沒有甚麼好誇口的。[10]上帝是我們的創造者;他藉着基督耶穌改造了我們,要我們行善;這是他早已計劃要我們去做的。

在基督的生命裏合而為一

[11]你們生而為外邦人的,要記得過去的情

②「是充滿宇宙⋯⋯的」或譯「是被上帝完全充滿的那位基督所充滿的」或「是充滿着上帝的那位基督所充滿的」。

circumcised (which refers to what men do to their bodies)–remember what you were in the past. [12]At that time you were apart from Christ. You were foreigners and did not belong to God's chosen people. You had no part in the covenants, which were based on God's promises to his people, and you lived in this world without hope and without God. [13]But now, in union with Christ Jesus you, who used to be far away, have been brought near by the blood of Christ.[e] [14]For Christ himself has brought us peace by making Jews and Gentiles one people. With his own body he broke down the wall that separated them and kept them enemies. [15]He abolished the Jewish Law with its commandments and rules, in order to create out of the two races one new people in union with himself, in this way making peace. [16]By his death on the cross Christ destroyed their enmity; by means of the cross he united both races into one body and brought them back to God. [17]So Christ came and preached the Good News of peace to all–to you Gentiles, who were far away from God, and to the Jews, who were near to him. [18]It is through Christ that all of us, Jews and Gentiles, are able to come in the one Spirit into the presence of the Father.

[19]So then, you Gentiles are not foreigners or strangers any longer; you are now citizens together with God's people and members of the family of God. [20]You, too, are built upon the foundation laid by the apostles and prophets,[f] the cornerstone being Christ Jesus himself. [21]He is the one who holds the whole building together and makes it grow into a sacred temple dedicated to the Lord. [22]In union with him you too are being built together with all the others into a place where God lives through his Spirit.

Paul's Work for the Gentiles

3 For this reason I, Paul, the prisoner of Christ Jesus for the sake of you Gentiles, pray to God. [2]Surely you have heard that God in his grace has given me this work to do for your good. [3]God revealed his secret plan and made it known to me. (I have written briefly about this, [4]and if you will read what I have written, you can learn about my understanding of the secret of Christ.) [5]In past times human beings were not told this secret, but God has revealed it now by the Spirit to his holy apostles and prophets. [6]The secret is that by means of the gospel the Gentiles have a part with the Jews in God's blessings; they are members of the same body and share in the

況：你們被那些自稱受過割禮的人—就是那些在自己身體上動過刀的猶太人—稱你們為沒有受過割禮的。[12]那時候，你們跟基督沒有關係，是外人，不在上帝選民的行列裏。你們在上帝應許給他子民的約上無份，在世上沒有盼望，沒有上帝。[13]你們這些從前遠離上帝、現在卻跟基督耶穌結合的人，藉着他的死，已經接近上帝。[14]基督親自把和平賜給我們；他使猶太人和外邦人合而為一，以自己的身體推倒那使他們互相敵對、使他們分裂的牆。[15]他廢除了猶太法律的誡命規條，為要使兩種人藉着他的生命成為一種新人，得以和平相處。[16]藉着在十字架上的死，基督終止了這種敵對的形勢，藉着十字架使兩者結為一體，得以跟上帝和好。[17]這樣，基督來的目的是要傳和平的福音給所有的人，包括你們這些從前遠離上帝的外邦人和接近上帝的猶太人。[18]藉着基督，不管是猶太人或是外邦人，我們都能夠在同一位聖靈裏來到天父面前。

[19]這樣看來，你們外邦人不再是外人或陌生人；你們是上帝子民的同胞，是上帝一家的人。[20]跟猶太人一樣，你們也是建立在使徒和先知的基礎上，而基督耶穌自己是這家的基石。[21]倚靠他，整座建築得以互相連接，逐漸擴大成為聖殿獻給上主。[22]倚靠他，你們也同被建造，成為上帝藉着聖靈居住的地方。

保羅向外邦人傳福音

3 因此，我這為你們外邦人作了基督耶穌囚徒的保羅替你們向上帝祈求。[2]你們一定知道，為了你們的好處，上帝賜恩典，把一項職務付託給我。[3]他啟示我，使我知道他的奧祕。（我已經簡略地把這奧祕寫下來；[4]你們讀了就會知道我對基督的奧祕所領悟的是甚麼。）[5]以往，上帝沒有向任何人顯示這奧祕，現在他藉着聖靈向他的聖使徒和先知啟示了。[6]這奧祕的內容是這樣：藉着福音，外邦人得以跟猶太人同享上帝的福澤。他們是同一身體的肢體，並且分享上

e by the blood of Christ; or by the sacrificial death of Christ.
f the foundation laid by the apostles and prophets; or the foundation, that is, the apostles and prophets.

Promise that God made through Christ Jesus.

7I was made a servant of the gospel by God's special gift, which he gave me through the working of his power. 8I am less than the least of all God's people; yet God gave me this privilege of taking to the Gentiles the Good News about the infinite riches of Christ, 9and of making all people see how God's secret plan is to be put into effect. God, who is the Creator of all things, kept his secret hidden through all the past ages, 10in order that at the present time, by means of the church, the angelic rulers and powers in the heavenly world might learn of his wisdom in all its different forms. 11God did this according to his eternal purpose, which he achieved through Christ Jesus our Lord. 12In union with Christ and through our faith in him we have the boldness to go into God's presence with all confidence. 13I beg you, then, not to be discouraged because I am suffering for you; it is all for your benefit.

The Love of Christ

14For this reason I fall on my knees before the Father, 15from whom every family in heaven and on earth receives its true name. 16I ask God from the wealth of his glory to give you power through his Spirit to be strong in your inner selves, 17and I pray that Christ will make his home in your hearts through faith. I pray that you may have your roots and foundation in love, 18so that you, together with all God's people, may have the power to understand how broad and long, how high and deep, is Christ's love, 19Yes, may you come to know his love–although it can never be fully known–and so be completely filled with the very nature of God.

20To him who by means of his power working in us is able to do so much more than we can ever ask for, or even think of: 21to God be the glory in the church and in Christ Jesus for all time, forever and ever! Amen.

The Unity of the Body

4 I urge you, then–I who am a prisoner because I serve the Lord: live a life that measures up to the standard God set when he called you. 2Be always humble, gentle, and patient. Show your love by being tolerant with one another. 3Do your best to preserve the unity which the Spirit gives by means of the peace that binds you together. 4There is one body and one Spirit, just as there is one hope to which God has called you. 5There is one Lord, one faith, one baptism; 6there is one God and Father of all people, who is Lord of all, works

帝藉着在基督耶穌裏實現了的應許。

7 由於上帝特別的恩賜，我作了這福音的僕人；這是按照他大能的運作賜給我的。8 雖然我是所有信徒中最微不足道的，我竟蒙上帝賜給我這特權，得以把基督那無限豐富的福音傳給外邦人，9 使全人類知道上帝怎樣實行他奧祕的計劃。以往的世代，萬物的創造主─上帝把這奧祕隱藏起來，10 目的是要在現今的世代，藉着教會，使在天界執政的、掌權的都能夠知道上帝各樣的智慧。11 上帝這樣做是根據他永恆的旨意；這旨意已經在我們的主基督耶穌身上實現了。12 藉着基督，信靠他③，我們得以坦然無懼地來到上帝面前。13 所以，我請求你們，不要因為我為你們受苦難而灰心，倒要以此為榮。

基督的愛

14 因此，我在天父面前跪下。15 天上地下所有的家族都是從他而有的。16 我祈求上帝，依照他榮耀的豐富，藉着聖靈賜給你們力量，使你們內在的生命強壯起來。17 我又祈求基督，藉着你們的信心，住在你們心裏，使你們在他的愛中有根有基，18 好使你們能夠跟所有上帝的子民一同體會基督的愛是多麼的長闊高深。19 願你們能理解基督那超越知識所能領悟的愛，好使你們能完全被上帝的完美所充滿。

20 上帝能以運行在我們當中的大能成就一切，遠超過我們所求所想的。21 願他在教會中，並在基督耶穌裏得到頌讚，世世代代，直到永遠！阿們。

教會的合一

4 所以，我勸你們─我是因事奉主而成為囚徒的─你們行事為人都應該符合上帝呼召你們時所立的標準。2 你們要謙遜、溫柔、忍耐，以愛心互相寬容，3 以和平彼此聯繫，盡力保持聖靈所賜合一的心。4 惟有一個身體，惟有一位聖靈，正如上帝呼召你們來享有同一個盼望。5 惟有一位主，一個信仰，一個洗禮。6 惟有一位上帝，就是人類的父親；他在萬有之中，統御萬有，貫徹

---

③「藉着基督，信靠他」或譯「在基督裏面，藉着他的信實」。

through all, and is in all.

7Each one of us has received a special gift in proportion to what Christ has given. 8As the scripture says,

"When he went up to the very heights,
　he took many captives with him;
　he gave gifts to people."

9Now, what does "he went up" mean? It means that first he came down to the lowest depths of the earth.*g* 10So the one who came down is the same one who went up, above and beyond the heavens, to fill the whole universe with his presence. 11It was he who "gave gifts to people"; he appointed some to be apostles, others to be prophets, others to be evangelists, others to be pastors and teachers. 12He did this to prepare all God's people for the work of Christian service, in order to build up the body of Christ. 13And so we shall all come together to that oneness in our faith and in our knowledge of the Son of God; we shall become mature people, reaching to the very height of Christ's full stature. 14Then we shall no longer be children, carried by the waves and blown about by every shifting wind of the teaching of deceitful people, who lead others into error by the tricks they invent. 15Instead, by speaking the truth in a spirit of love, we must grow up in every way to Christ, who is the head. 16Under his control all the different parts of the body fit together, and the whole body is held together by every joint with which it is provided. So when each separate part works as it should, the whole body grows and builds itself up through love.

The New Life in Christ

17In the Lord's name, then, I warn you: do not continue to live like the heathen, whose thoughts are worthless 18and whose minds are in the dark. They have no part in the life that God gives, for they are completely ignorant and stubborn. 19They have lost all feeling of shame; they give themselves over to vice and do all sorts of indecent things without restraint.

20That was not what you learned about Christ! 21You certainly heard about him, and as his followers you were taught the truth that is in Jesus. 22So get rid of your old self, which made you live as you used to–the old self that was being destroyed by its deceitful desires. 23Your hearts and minds must be made completely new, 24and you must put on the new self, which is created in God's likeness and reveals itself in the true life that is upright and holy.

25No more lying, then! Each of you must tell

---

g the lowest depths of the earth; *or* the lower depths, the earth itself.

萬有。

7 我們每一個人都按照基督所分配的，領受特別的恩賜。8 正如聖經所說：

他升上到至高之處的時候，
帶去了無數的俘虜；
他賜恩賜給人。

9 「他升上」這話是甚麼意思呢？這是說：他曾經先降下，到了地的最深處。10那「降下」的就是「升上」到諸天之上的那一位；他這樣做是要充滿萬有。11他也是「賜恩賜給人」的那一位；他指定有些人作使徒，有些人作先知，有些人傳福音，有些人作牧師或教師；12目的是要準備上帝的子民爲他工作，建立教會—就是基督的身體。13最後，我們將對上帝的兒子有一致的信仰和認識；我們將長大成熟，達到基督那完整的境界。14這樣，我們才不至於再像小孩子，中了人所編造巧妙的詭計，隨着各樣學風飄來飄去。15相反地，我們要以愛心說誠實話，在各方面向着基督不斷長進。他是頭；16整個身體都倚靠他，藉着各關節筋絡互相配合，彼此連結。這樣，當各肢體發揮功用時，身體就會在愛中漸漸長大，建立起來。

基督裏的新生命

17我現在奉主的名鄭重地勸告你們：不要再過着像外邦人那樣的生活。他們的思想虛妄，18心地黑暗，跟上帝所賜的生命隔絕了；因爲他們全然無知，剛愎自用。19他們喪盡了羞恥之心，縱情恣慾，無拘束地做各種敗德的事。

20但是，你們從基督所學的卻不是這樣！21你們無疑聽見過他的事，作了他的門徒，學到在耶穌裏才有的眞理。22那麼，你們要脫下那一向使你們生活在腐敗中的「舊我」；那舊我是由於私慾的誘惑而腐化了的。23你們的心思意念要更新，24要穿上「新我」；這新我是照着上帝的形像造的，表現在眞理所產生的正義和聖潔上。

25所以，你們不可再撒謊！每一個人必須

the truth to the other believer, because we are all members together in the body of Christ. 26If you become angry, do not let your anger lead you into sin, and do not stay angry all day. 27Don't give the Devil a chance. 28If you used to rob, you must stop robbing and start working, in order to earn an honest living for yourself and to be able to help the poor. 29Do not use harmful words, but only helpful words, the kind that build up and provide what is needed, so that what you say will do good to those who hear you. 30And do not make God's Holy Spirit sad; for the Spirit is God's mark of ownership on you, a guarantee that the Day will come when God will set you free. 31Get rid of all bitterness, passion, and anger. No more shouting or insults, no more hateful feelings of any sort. 32Instead, be kind and tender-hearted to one another, and forgive one another, as God has forgiven you through Christ.

Living in the Light

5 Since you are God's dear children, you must try to be like him. 2Your life must be controlled by love, just as Christ loved us and gave his life for us as a sweet-smelling offering and sacrifice that pleases God.

3Since you are God's people, it is not right that any matters of sexual immorality or indecency or greed should even be mentioned among you. 4Nor is it fitting for you to use language which is obscene, profane, or vulgar. Rather you should give thanks to God. 5You may be sure that no one who is immoral, indecent, or greedy (for greed is a form of idolatry) will ever receive a share in the Kingdom of Christ and of God.

6Do not let anyone deceive you with foolish words; it is because of these very things that God's anger will come upon those who do not obey him. 7So have nothing at all to do with such people. 8You yourselves used to be in the darkness, but since you have become the Lord's people, you are in the light. So you must live like people who belong to the light, 9for it is the light[h] that brings a rich harvest of every kind of goodness, righteousness, and truth. 10Try to learn what pleases the Lord. 11Have nothing to do with the worthless things that people do, things that belong to the darkness. Instead, bring them out to the light. 12(It is really too shameful even to talk about the things they do in secret.) 13And when all things are brought out to the light, then their true nature is clearly revealed; 14for anything that is clearly revealed becomes light.[i] That is why it is said,

h the light; *some manuscripts have the Spirit.*
i anything that is clearly revealed becomes light; *or it is light that clearly reveals everything.*

向弟兄說誠實話，因為我們都是基督身體上的肢體。26你們若發脾氣，不可因這脾氣而犯罪；也不可生一整天的氣，27不可讓魔鬼有機可乘。28從前偷竊的，不可再偷竊；要靠雙手誠實工作才能夠幫助貧窮的人。29不要在言語上傷害別人，只要說幫助人、造就人的話，使聽見的人得益處。30不要使上帝的聖靈憂傷；因為聖靈是上帝擁有了你們的印記，保證上帝釋放你們的日子就要來到。31你們要除掉一切怨恨、暴戾、忿怒。不要再喧擾或毀謗；不要再有任何的仇恨。32要親切仁慈相對待，彼此饒恕，正如上帝藉着基督饒恕了你們一樣。

生活在光明中

5 既然你們是上帝所愛的兒女，你們必須效法他。2你們的生活要處處表現愛心，正如基督愛我們，為我們捨命，作為馨香的供物和祭品獻給上帝。

3至於那些淫亂、污穢，和貪婪的事，在你們當中連提都不可提，因為你們是上帝的子民。4你們也不可以說淫猥、愚妄，或下流的話；倒要說感謝上帝的話。5無可懷疑地，淫亂、污穢，或貪婪的人（貪婪等於拜偶像）絕對不能成為基督和上帝國的子民。

6不要讓任何人用空口白話欺騙你們；正是為了這些事，上帝的忿怒要臨到悖逆的人身上。7所以，不要跟這些人來往。8你們原是在黑暗中，可是自從成為主的信徒，你們就在光明中。你們的生活必須像光明的人。9光明結出一切豐盛的果實，就是良善、正義，和真理。10要明辨甚麼是主所喜悅的事。11不可做別人在黑暗中所做那些無益的事，反而要把這種事揭發出來。12他們暗地裏所幹的勾當，連提一提都是很可恥的！13當一切的事被公開出來的時候，真相就顯露了，14因為凡顯明出來的就是光④。所以詩中這樣說：

④「因為凡顯明出來的就是光」或譯「因為光顯明一切」。

> "Wake up, sleeper,
> and rise from death,
> and Christ will shine on you."

15So be careful how you live. Don't live like ignorant people, but like wise people. 16Make good use of every opportunity you have, because these are evil days. 17Don't be fools, then, but try to find out what the Lord wants you to do.

18Do not get drunk with wine, which will only ruin you; instead, be filled with the Spirit. 19Speak to one another with the words of psalms, hymns, and sacred songs; sing hymns and psalms to the Lord with praise in your hearts. 20In the name of our Lord Jesus Christ, always give thanks for everything to God the Father.

Wives and Husbands

21Submit yourselves to one another because of your reverence for Christ.

22Wives, submit yourselves to your husbands as to the Lord. 23For a husband has authority over his wife just as Christ has authority over the church; and Christ is himself the Savior of the church, his body. 24And so wives must submit themselves completely to their husbands just as the church submits itself to Christ.

25Husbands, love your wives just as Christ loved the church and gave his life for it. 26He did this to dedicate the church to God by his word, after making it clean by washing it in water, 27in order to present the church to himself in all its beauty–pure and faultless, without spot or wrinkle or any other imperfection. 28Men ought to love their wives just as they love their own bodies. A man who loves his wife loves himself. 29(None of us ever hate our own bodies. Instead, we feed them, and take care of them, just as Christ does the church; 30for we are members of his body.) 31As the scripture says, "For this reason a man will leave his father and mother and unite with his wife, and the two will become one." 32There is a deep secret truth revealed in this scripture, which I understand as applying to Christ and the church. 33But it also applies to you: every husband must love his wife as himself, and every wife must respect her husband.

Children and Parents

6 Children, it is your Christian duty to*j* obey your parents, for this is the right thing to do. 2"Respect your father and mother" is the first commandment that has a promise added: 3"so that all may go well with you, and you may

j Some manuscripts do not have it is your Christian duty to.

醒過來吧，睡着的人，
從死人中起來！
基督要光照你們。

15 所以，你們的行為要謹慎。不要像無知的人，要像智慧的人。16要善用每一個機會，因為目前的日子很險惡。17因此，不要做糊塗人，要明白主的旨意是甚麼。

18 不要酗酒，那是會敗壞人的；要被聖靈充滿。19要用詩篇、聖詩、靈歌對唱；要從心底發出音樂，頌讚主，向他歌唱。20要奉我們主耶穌基督的名常常為各樣的事感謝父上帝。

夫妻的關係

21 你們要彼此順服，因為你們是敬畏基督的。

22 作妻子的，你們要順服自己的丈夫，好像順服主。23因為丈夫是妻子的頭，正如基督是教會—他的身體—的頭，也是教會的救主。24正如教會順服基督，妻子也應該凡事順服丈夫。

25 作丈夫的，你們要愛自己的妻子，好像基督愛教會，為教會捨命一樣。26他這樣做是要藉着他的話、用水來潔淨教會，27使她榮美、聖潔、沒有瑕疵、沒有任何污點或皺紋，好獻給自己。28丈夫應該愛自己的妻子，好像愛自己的身體一樣；愛妻子就是愛自己。29沒有人恨惡自己的身體；他總是保養、照顧它，正如基督對待教會一樣；30因為我們是他身上的肢體。31聖經上說：「因此，人要離開父母，跟妻子結合，兩個人成為一體。」32這經文啟示了極大的奧祕；我是指着基督和教會的關係說的，33可是也可以應用在你們身上；丈夫必須愛妻子，像愛自己一樣，而妻子必須敬重丈夫。

父母和兒女的關係

6 作兒女的，你們要聽從父母；這是基督徒的⑤本份。2-3「要孝敬父母，你就事事亨通，在世上享長壽。」這是第一條帶

⑤有些古卷沒有「基督徒的」幾字。

live a long time in the land."

4Parents, do not treat your children in such a way as to make them angry. Instead, raise them with Christian discipline and instruction.

Slaves and Masters

5Slaves, obey your human masters with fear and trembling; and do it with a sincere heart, as though you were serving Christ. 6Do this not only when they are watching you, because you want to gain their approval; but with all your heart do what God wants, as slaves of Christ. 7Do your work as slaves cheerfully, as though you served the Lord, and not merely human beings. 8Remember that the Lord will reward each of us, whether slave or free, for the good work we do.

9Masters, behave in the same way toward your slaves and stop using threats. Remember that you and your slaves belong to the same Master in heaven, who judges everyone by the same standard.

The Whole Armor of God

10Finally, build up your strength in union with the Lord and by means of his mighty power. 11Put on all the armor that God gives you, so that you will be able to stand up against the Devil's evil tricks. 12For we are not fighting against human beings but against the wicked spiritual forces in the heavenly world, the rulers, authorities, and cosmic powers of this dark age. 13So put on God's armor now! Then when the evil day comes, you will be able to resist the enemy's attacks; and after fighting to the end, you will still hold your ground.

14So stand ready, with truth as a belt tight around your waist, with righteousness as your breastplate, 15and as your shoes the readiness to announce the Good News of peace. 16At all times carry faith as a shield; for with it you will be able to put out all the burning arrows shot by the Evil One. 17And accept salvation as a helmet, and the word of God as the sword which the Spirit gives you. 18Do all this in prayer, asking for God's help. Pray on every occasion, as the Spirit leads. For this reason keep alert and never give up; pray always for all God's people. 19And pray also for me, that God will give me a message when I am ready to speak, so that I may speak boldly and make known the gospel's secret. 20For the sake of this gospel I am an ambassador, though now I am in prison. Pray that I may be bold in speaking about the gospel as I should.

Final Greetings

21Tychicus, our dear brother and faithful ser-

着應許的誡命。

4 作父親的，你們不要激怒兒女，要用主的教導來養育栽培他們。

主僕的關係

5 作奴僕的，你們要戰戰兢兢，專心服從世上的主人，像事奉基督一樣；6 不只在他們注意的時候這樣做，想討他們的喜歡，而是作為基督的奴僕，要從心裏來遵行上帝的旨意。7 你們要甘心樂意地盡奴僕的本份，像是在服事主，不是服事人。8 要知道，無論是奴僕或是自由人，主都要照各人的好行為報答他。

9 作主人的，你們也要好好地對待奴僕，不要威嚇他們。要知道，你們和你們的奴僕同有一位在天上的主人；他要用同樣的標準來對待每一個人。

上帝所賜的全副裝備

10 最後，你們要倚靠主的大能力作堅強的人。11 你們要穿戴上帝所賜的全副軍裝，好使你們能站穩，來抵禦魔鬼的詭計。12 因為我們不是對抗有血有肉的人，而是對天界的邪靈，就是這黑暗世代的執政者、掌權者，和宇宙間邪惡的勢力作戰。13 因此，你們要以上帝所賜的武器裝備自己，好在險惡的日子裏能夠抵抗敵人的攻擊，戰鬥到底，始終守住陣地。

14 所以，你們要準備好。要以真理作腰帶，以正義作護胸甲，15 以隨時宣揚和平的福音作鞋子穿上。16 要常常拿着信心的盾牌，好使你們能夠抵禦那邪惡者所射出的一切火箭。17 你們要以救恩作頭盔，以上帝的話作聖靈所賜的寶劍。18 你們要在禱告中祈求上帝的幫助，常常隨從聖靈的帶領禱告。要事事警醒，不可放鬆；要不斷地為信徒們禱告。19 也要為我禱告，求上帝賜給我適當的話，在我該講的時候，能夠大膽地開口傳揚福音的奧祕。20 雖然我帶着鎖鍊，我卻是為這福音的緣故作特使的。你們要祈求主賜給我勇氣講應該講的話。

問候和祝福

21 推基古會把一切有關我的事都告訴你

vant in the Lord's work, will give you all the news about me, so that you may know how I am getting along. 22That is why I am sending him to you–to tell you how all of us are getting along and to encourage you.

23May God the Father and the Lord Jesus Christ give to all Christians peace and love with faith. 24May God's grace be with all those who love our Lord Jesus Christ with undying love.

們，讓你們知道我的情況。他是我們所親愛、忠心事奉主的弟兄。22我派他到你們那裏去的目的是要你們知道我們這裏的情況，使你們得到鼓勵。

23願父上帝和主耶穌基督賜平安、仁愛，和信心給所有的信徒。24願上帝賜恩典給所有恆心愛我們的主耶穌基督的人！

腓立比書
PHILIPPIANS

INTRODUCTION

Paul's Letter to the Philippians was written to the first church that Paul established on European soil, in the Roman province of Macedonia. It was written while the apostle was in prison, and at a time when he was troubled by the opposition of other Christian workers toward himself and was distressed by false teaching in the church at Philippi. Yet this letter breathes a joy and confidence that can be explained only by Paul's deep faith in Jesus Christ.

The immediate reason for writing the letter was to thank the Philippian Christians for the gift which they had sent to help him in his time of need. He uses this opportunity to reassure them, so that they may have courage and confidence in spite of all his troubles and their own as well. He pleads with them to have the humble attitude of Jesus, rather than to be controlled by selfish ambition and pride. He reminds them that their life in union with Christ is a gift of God's grace which they have received through faith, not through obedience to the ceremonies of the Jewish Law. He writes of the joy and peace that God gives to those who live in union with Christ.

This letter is marked by its emphasis on joy, confidence, unity, and perseverance in the Christian faith and life. It also reveals the deep affection Paul had for the church at Philippi.

Outline of Contents

簡 介

腓立比書是保羅寫給他在歐洲建立的第一個教會的信。腓立比在羅馬治下的馬其頓省。這封信是保羅在監獄裏寫的。那時候，他正遭受其他同工的攻擊，又因腓立比教會有異端而深感困擾。可是，這封信依然洋溢着喜樂和確信，顯出他對耶穌基督有堅定不移的信心。

保羅寫這封信的主要目的是向腓立比的信徒們道謝；因爲在他缺乏的時候，他們接濟他。現在他要趁這機會鼓勵他們，堅定他們的信心，讓他們看見，雖然他遭受患難，而他們自己也在困難中，但仍然能保持勇氣和信心。保羅勸勉他們要學習耶穌的謙卑，不要被自私和驕傲所支配。他提醒他們；他們生活在基督的生命裏是出於上帝的恩典；這恩典是他們藉着信心領受的，不是靠順從猶太人的法律而得到的。他也提到上帝賜給在基督生命裏的人所享有的喜樂和平安。

本書的特徵是强調喜樂、合一，和堅忍不拔的信心和生活。信中處處流露出保羅對腓立比教會的熱愛。

提要

1 From Paul and Timothy, servants of Christ Jesus–

To all God's people in Philippi who are in union with Christ Jesus, including the church leaders and helpers:

2May God our Father and the Lord Jesus Christ give you grace and peace.

Paul's Prayer for His Readers

3I thank my God for you every time I think of you; 4and every time I pray for you all, I pray with joy 5because of the way in which you have helped me in the work of the gospel from the very first day until now. 6And so I am sure that God, who began this good work in you, will carry it on until it is finished on the Day of Christ Jesus. 7You are always in my heart! And so it is only right for me to feel as I do about you. For you have all shared with me in this privilege that God has given me, both now that I am in prison and also while I was free to defend the gospel and establish it firmly. 8God is my witness that I tell the truth when I say that my deep feeling for you all comes from the heart of Christ Jesus himself.

9I pray that your love will keep on growing more and more, together with true knowledge and perfect judgment, 10so that you will be able to choose what is best. Then you will be free from all impurity and blame on the Day of Christ. 11Your lives will be filled with the truly good qualities which only Jesus Christ can produce, for the glory and praise of God.

To Live Is Christ

12I want you to know, my friends, that the things that have happened to me have really helped the progress of the gospel. 13As a result, the whole palace guard and all the others here know that I am in prison because I am a servant of Christ. 14And my being in prison has given most of the believers more confidence in the Lord, so that they grow bolder all the time to preach the message*a* fearlessly.

15Of course some of them preach Christ because they are jealous and quarrelsome, but others from genuine good will. 16These do so from love, because they know that God has given me the work of defending the gospel. 17The others do not proclaim Christ sincerely, but from a spirit of selfish ambition; they think that they will make more trouble for me while I am in prison.

18It does not matter! I am happy about it–just so Christ is preached in every way possible, whether from wrong or right motives. And I

a the message; *some manuscripts have* God's message.

1 我—保羅和提摩太是基督耶穌的僕人。我們寫信給所有住在腓立比的上帝的子民，就是屬於基督耶穌的信徒，以及教會領袖和助手們①。

2 願我們的父上帝和主耶穌基督賜恩典、平安給你們！

保羅為收信人禱告

3 每逢想到你們，我就感謝我的上帝，4 每次為你們大家禱告都懷着喜樂的心；5 因為從開始的一天到現在，你們在傳福音的工作上一直都協助我。6 我深信，那位在你們當中開始了這美好工作的上帝一定會繼續這工作，在基督耶穌再來的日子完成它。7 你們大家常常在我心裏！我想念你們大家是當然的；因為，無論我現在在獄中，或是從前自由地在為福音辯護和作證的時候，你們大家都分享了上帝所賜給我的特權。8 上帝知道，我說我用基督耶穌的愛心深切地想念你們，這話是實在的。

9 我為你們禱告的是：你們的愛心會不斷地跟真知識和判斷力一齊增進，10使你們能夠選擇那最好的。這樣，在基督再來的日子，你們會純潔無可指責。11你們的生活會充滿着憑藉耶穌基督才能有的仁義果子，來榮耀讚美上帝。

為基督而活

12 弟兄姊妹們，我要你們知道，我的遭遇反而幫助了福音的進展。13結果，王宮警衛隊全體，和在這裏所有其他的人，都知道我是因着基督的緣故被囚禁的。14我坐牢，卻使多半的信徒對主更有信心，更加勇敢，毫無畏懼地傳講上帝的信息。

15 當然，有些人傳揚基督是出於嫉妒和好鬥的心理，但也有些是出於誠意的。16後者出於愛心而這樣做，因為他們知道上帝交給我為福音辯護的使命。17前者傳基督的動機不純，是出於野心，想趁着我坐牢的時候給我製造更多的麻煩。18可是，這有甚麼關係呢？不管他們的動機對不對，只要基督被傳開了，我就會高興。

①「教會領袖和助手們」或譯「監督和執事們」。

will continue to be happy, [19]because I know that by means of your prayers and the help which comes from the Spirit of Jesus Christ I shall be set free. [20]My deep desire and hope is that I shall never fail in my duty, but that at all times, and especially right now, I shall be full of courage, so that with my whole being I shall bring honor to Christ, whether I live or die. [21]For what is life? To me, it is Christ. Death, then, will bring more. [22]But if by continuing to live I can do more worthwhile work, then I am not sure which I should choose. [23]I am pulled in two directions. I want very much to leave this life and be with Christ, which is a far better thing; [24]but for your sake it is much more important that I remain alive. [25]I am sure of this, and so I know that I will stay. I will stay on with you all, to add to your progress and joy in the faith, [26]so that when I am with you again, you will have even more reason to be proud of me in your life in union with Christ Jesus.

[27]Now, the important thing is that your way of life should be as the gospel of Christ requires, so that, whether or not I am able to go and see you, I will hear that you are standing firm with one common purpose and that with only one desire you are fighting together for the faith of the gospel. [28]Don't be afraid of your enemies; always be courageous, and this will prove to them that they will lose and that you will win, because it is God who gives you the victory. [29]For you have been given the privilege of serving Christ, not only by believing in him, but also by suffering for him. [30]Now you can take part with me in the battle. It is the same battle you saw me fighting in the past, and as you hear, the one I am fighting still.

Christ's Humility and Greatness

2 Your life in Christ makes you strong, and his love comforts you. You have fellowship with the Spirit,[b] and you have kindness and compassion for one another. [2]I urge you, then, to make me completely happy by having the same thoughts, sharing the same love, and being one in soul and mind. [3]Don't do anything from selfish ambition or from a cheap desire to boast, but be humble toward one another, always considering others better than yourselves. [4]And look out for one another's interests, not just for your own. [5]The attitude you should have is the one that Christ Jesus had:
[6]He always had the nature of God,
   but he did not think that by force he
      should try to remain[c] equal with God.
[7]Instead of this, of his own free will he gave up

b You have fellowship with the Spirit; or The Spirit has brought you into fellowship with one another.
c remain; or become.

我還要繼續高興;[19]因為知道藉着你們的禱告和耶穌基督的靈的幫助,我一定會恢復自由。[20]我迫切期待和盼望的是:我不至於在責任上有所虧負,反而能時時刻刻,尤其是現在,具有充分的勇氣,無論生死,用整個的我來榮耀基督。[21]因為對我來說,我活着,是為基督;死了,更有收穫![22]可是,如果我沽着能夠多做些有益的工作,那我就不曉得該怎樣選擇了。[23]我處在兩難之間。我很願意離開這世界,去跟基督在一起,那是再好沒有了。[24]可是,為了你們的緣故,我更該活下去。[25]對這一點,我深信無疑;我知道我還要活下去,而且要繼續跟你們大家在一起,幫助你們在信仰上更長進,更有喜樂,[26]目的是我跟你們再見面的時候,你們在基督耶穌裏將更加以我為榮!

[27]最重要的是:你們的生活應該符合基督福音的要求。這樣,無論我能不能親自來看你們,我都會知道你們抱着共同的目標,堅定不移,同心協力為福音的信仰爭戰。[28]在任何事上都不受反對你們的人的恐嚇;要勇敢,以此向他們證明,他們一定滅亡,而你們一定得救,因為這是上帝的作為。[29]你們得到特權來事奉基督,不只是信他,也要為他受苦。[30]現在,你們可以跟我並肩作戰,這仗,你們看見我打過,你們一定聽見,我仍然在從事同樣的戰鬥。

以基督為榜樣

2 究竟你們在基督裏的生命有沒有使你們堅強起來?他的愛有沒有鼓勵了你們?你們和聖靈有沒有團契?你們彼此間有沒有親愛同情的心?[2]如果有,我要求你們,要有共同的目標,同樣的愛心,相同的情感,和一致的想法,好讓我充滿喜樂。[3]不要自私自利,不要貪圖虛名,要彼此謙讓,看別人比自己高明。[4]不要只顧自己,也要關心別人的利益。[5]你們要以基督耶穌的心為心:
6 他原有上帝的本質,
   卻沒有濫用[②]跟上帝同等的特權。
7 相反地,他自願放棄一切,

②「卻沒有濫用」或譯「卻沒有牢牢地抓住」或「卻沒有用力爭取」。

all he had,
and took the nature of a servant.
He became like a human being
and appeared in human likeness.
[8]He was humble and walked the path of
obedience all the way to death–
his death on the cross.
[9]For this reason God raised him to the highest
place above
and gave him the name that is greater than
any other name.
[10]And so, in honor of the name of Jesus
all beings in heaven, on earth, and in the
world below[d]
will fall on their knees,
[11]and all will openly proclaim that Jesus Christ
is Lord,
to the glory of God the Father.

Shining as Lights in the World

[12]So then, dear friends, as you always
obeyed me when I was with you, it is even
more important that you obey me now while I
am away from you. Keep on working with fear
and trembling to complete your salvation,
[13]because God is always at work in you to make
you willing and able to obey his own purpose.

[14]Do everything without complaining or
arguing, [15]so that you may be innocent and pure
as God's perfect children, who live in a world
of corrupt and sinful people. You must shine
among them like stars lighting up the sky, [16]as
you offer them the message of life. If you do
so, I shall have reason to be proud of you on
the Day of Christ, because it will show that all
my effort and work have not been wasted.

[17]Perhaps my life's blood is to be poured out
like an offering on the sacrifice that your faith
offers to God. If that is so, I am glad and share
my joy with you all. [18]In the same way, you too
must be glad and share your joy with me.

Timothy and Epaphroditus

[19]If it is the Lord's will, I hope that I will be
able to send Timothy to you soon, so that I
may be encouraged by news about you. [20]He is
the only one who shares my feelings and who
really cares about you. [21]Everyone else is concerned only with their own affairs, not with the
cause of Jesus Christ. [22]And you yourselves
know how he has proved his worth, how he and
I, like a son and his father, have worked
together for the sake of the gospel. [23]So I hope
to send him to you as soon as I know how

d WORLD BELOW: *It was thought that the dead continued to
exist in a dark world under the ground.*

取了奴僕的本質。
他成為人,
以人的形體出現。
8 他自甘卑微,
順服至死,
且死在十字架上。
9 因此,上帝高舉他,及於至高,
賜給他那超越萬名的名號。
10 為要尊崇耶穌的名,
天上、人間,和地底下的眾生
都得向他下拜,
11 眾口要宣認:
耶穌基督是主,
同頌父上帝的榮耀。

世上的光

12 那麼,親愛的朋友們,我跟你們一起的
時候你們常常聽從我;現在我不在你們那
裏,你們更應該聽從我。要戰戰兢兢,不斷
努力來完成你們自己的得救;13因為上帝常
常在你們心裏工作,使你們既願意又能夠實
行他美善的旨意。

14 你們無論做甚麼事都不要埋怨或爭論,
15好使你們在這腐敗、彎曲的世代中純潔無
邪,作上帝沒有缺點的兒女。你們要在世人
當中發光,像星星照耀天空,16堅守生命的
道③。你們這樣做的話,在基督再來的日
子,我就有所誇口了,因為這可以證明我一
切的辛勞不是徒勞無功的。

17 即使我必須以自己的血作為奠祭,澆在
你們用信心獻給上帝的祭品上,我也喜樂,
而且要跟你們大家分享我的喜樂。18同樣,
你們要喜樂,也讓我分享你們的喜樂。

提摩太和以巴弗提

19 我仰賴主耶穌,希望不久能夠差提摩太
到你們那裏去,使我能聽到你們的消息而獲
得安慰。20他是惟一跟我同心,並且真心關
懷你們的人。21別人只為自己圖謀,不關心
耶穌基督的事。22但是提摩太的為人,你們
都很清楚,他跟我的關係就像兒子和父親,
為着福音的工作一起勞苦。23我希望,當我
一知道我的事情有甚麼結局,就立刻差他去

③「堅守……道」或譯「把生命的道傳給他們」。

things are going to turn out for me. 24And I trust in the Lord that I myself will be able to come to you soon.

25I have thought it necessary to send to you our brother Epaphroditus, who has worked and fought by my side and who has served as your messenger in helping me. 26He is anxious to see you all and is very upset because you had heard that he was sick. 27Indeed he was sick and almost died. But God had pity on him, and not only on him but on me, too, and spared me an even greater sorrow. 28I am all the more eager, then, to send him to you, so that you will be glad again when you see him, and my own sorrow will disappear. 29Receive him, then, with joy, as a believer in the Lord. Show respect to all such people as he, 30because he risked his life and nearly died for the sake of the work of Christ, in order to give me the help that you yourselves could not give.

The True Righteousness

3 In conclusion, my friends, be joyful in your union with the Lord. I don't mind repeating what I have written before, and you will be safer if I do so. 2Watch out for those who do evil things, those dogs, those who insist on cutting the body. 3It is we, not they, who have received the true circumcision, for we worship God by means of his Spirit and rejoice in our life in union with Christ Jesus. We do not put any trust in external ceremonies. 4I could, of course, put my trust in such things. If any of you think you can trust in external ceremonies, I have even more reason to feel that way. 5I was circumcised when I was a week old. I am an Israelite by birth, of the tribe of Benjamin, a pure-blooded Hebrew. As far as keeping the Jewish Law is concerned, I was a Pharisee, 6and I was so zealous that I persecuted the church. As far as a person can be righteous by obeying the commands of the Law, I was without fault. 7But all those things that I might count as profit I now reckon as loss for Christ's sake. 8Not only those things; I reckon everything as complete loss for the sake of what is so much more valuable, the knowledge of Christ Jesus my Lord. For his sake I have thrown everything away; I consider it all as mere garbage, so that I may gain Christ 9and be completely united with him. I no longer have a righteousness of my own, the kind that is gained by obeying the Law. I now have the righteousness that is given through faith in Christ, the righteousness that comes from God and is based on faith. 10All I want is to know Christ and to experience the power of his resurrection, to share in his sufferings and become like him in his death,

看你們。24我深信主會讓我也在短期內親自來看你們。

25 我想，我應該送我們的弟兄以巴弗提回到你們那裏去。你們選派他來幫助我，跟我一起工作，一同作戰。26他很想念你們各位，並且知道了你們聽到他生病的消息，非常難過。27他真的害過病，幾乎死了。可是上帝憐憫他，不但憐憫他，也憐憫我，使我沒有遭受更大的憂傷。28所以，我更想盡速送他回去，使你們得以高高興興地跟他團聚；這也可以消除我的憂傷。29我希望你們在主裏歡歡喜喜地接待他。你們要尊重像他這樣的人；30因為他為基督的工作冒生命的危險，幾乎死了，為了要彌補你們未能服事我的地方。

真正的義

3 弟兄姊妹們，我還有話說。願你們在主裏有喜樂！向你們重複我從前說過的話，對我沒有麻煩，對你們卻有益處。2你們要提防那些作惡的人，那些狐羣狗黨，就是那些堅持要割自己身體的人。3其實，接受真割禮的，不是他們，是我們。因為我們藉着上帝的靈來敬拜；我們所誇耀的是基督耶穌。我不倚靠任何外表的禮儀。4若有人以為他可以倚靠外表的禮儀，我更可以這樣做。5我出生第八天就受割禮。我生來就是以色列人，屬於便雅憫支族，是血統純粹的希伯來人。就遵守猶太教規這一點說，我屬於法利賽派；6就熱心說，我曾經迫害過教會。所以，如果遵守摩西法律就算是義的話，我並沒有甚麼可指責的地方。7但是，我一向認為有盈利的，現在為了基督的緣故，我把這些看作虧損。8不只這樣，我更把萬事看作虧損的，因為我以認識我主基督耶穌為至寶。為了他，我損失了一切，當作垃圾，為要贏得基督，9完全跟他連結。我不再有那種因遵守法律而有的義。我現在有的義是因信基督而有的，是上帝所賜的，是以信為根據的。10我只渴望認識基督，體驗他復活的大能，分擔他的苦難，經歷他的

[11]in the hope that I myself will be raised from death to life.

Running toward the Goal

[12]I do not claim that I have already succeeded or have already become perfect. I keep striving to win the prize for which Christ Jesus has already won me to himself. [13]Of course, my friends, I really do not[e] think that I have already won it; the one thing I do, however, is to forget what is behind me and do my best to reach what is ahead. [14]So I run straight toward the goal in order to win the prize, which is God's call through Christ Jesus to the life above.

[15]All of us who are spiritually mature should have this same attitude. But if some of you have a different attitude, God will make this clear to you. [16]However that may be, let us go forward according to the same rules we have followed until now.

[17]Keep on imitating me, my friends. Pay attention to those who follow the right example that we have set for you. [18]I have told you this many times before, and now I repeat it with tears: there are many whose lives make them enemies of Christ's death on the cross. [19]They are going to end up in hell, because their god is their bodily desires. They are proud of what they should be ashamed of, and they think only of things that belong to this world. [20]We, however, are citizens of heaven, and we eagerly wait for our Savior, the Lord Jesus Christ, to come from heaven. [21]He will change our weak mortal bodies and make them like his own glorious body, using that power by which he is able to bring all things under his rule.

Instructions

4 So then, my friends, how dear you are to me and how I miss you! How happy you make me, and how proud I am of you!--this, dear friends, is how you should stand firm in your life in the Lord.

[2]Euodia and Syntyche, please, I beg you, try to agree as sisters in the Lord. [3]And you too, my faithful partner, I want you to help these women; for they have worked hard with me to spread the gospel, together with Clement and all my other fellow workers, whose names are in God's book of the living.

[4]May you always be joyful in your union with the Lord. I say it again: rejoice!

[5]Show a gentle attitude toward everyone. The Lord is coming soon. [6]Don't worry about anything, but in all your prayers ask God for

e not; *some manuscripts have* not yet.

死，[11]希望我自己也得以從死裏復活。

向着目標直奔

[12] 這不是說我已經成功，或已經完全了。我繼續奔跑，只求贏得那獎賞；其實，爲要使我達到這目標，基督耶穌已經先贏得了我。[13]弟兄姊妹們，我並不認爲我已經贏得了這獎賞；我只專心一件事：就是忘記背後，全力追求前面的事。[14]我向着目標直奔，爲要得到獎賞；這獎賞就是屬天的新生命，是上帝藉着基督耶穌呼召我去領受的。

[15] 所以，我們當中所有靈性成熟的人都要有這樣的想法；如果你們有不同的想法，上帝會清楚地指示你們。[16]無論如何，我們要依照我們一向所遵循的規矩向前走。

[17] 弟兄姊妹們，你們要繼續效法我。我們已經爲你們立了榜樣；你們要學習那些效法我們的人。[18]我已經多次勸告你們，現在再一次流淚勸告你們：有些人的行爲使他們成爲基督十字架的仇敵。[19]他們的結局是滅亡，因爲他們的神就是自己的肚子。他們以可恥的事爲榮，念念不忘世上的東西。[20]然而，我們是天上的公民；我們一心等候着我們的救主，就是主耶穌基督從天上降臨。[21]他要運用那使萬有歸服於他的大能，來改變我們這脆弱必死的身體，使我們跟他一樣，有榮耀的身體。

保羅的勸導

4 弟兄姊妹們，你們是我所親愛的，我多麼想念你們！你們是我的喜樂，我的華冠。親愛的朋友們，你們要倚靠主站得穩。

[2] 友阿蝶和循都基兩位姊妹啊，我勸你們要在主裏同心。[3]我忠實的伙伴啊，我也要求你幫助她們兩位；因爲她們在福音的工作上跟我、革利免，以及其他同工一起勞苦過；這些人的名字已經都記在上帝的生命册上。

[4] 你們要因爲跟主連結而常常喜樂。我再說，你們要喜樂！

[5] 你們也要向大家表現謙讓。主就要來了。[6]你們應該一無掛慮；要在禱告中把你

what you need, always asking him with a thankful heart. 7And God's peace, which is far beyond human understanding, will keep your hearts and minds safe in union with Christ Jesus.

8In conclusion, my friends, fill your minds with those things that are good and that deserve praise: things that are true, noble, right, pure, lovely, and honorable. 9Put into practice what you learned and received from me, both from my words and from my actions. And the God who gives us peace will be with you.

Thanks for the Gift

10In my life in union with the Lord it is a great joy to me that after so long a time you once more had the chance of showing that you care for me. I don't mean that you had stopped caring for me—you just had no chance to show it. 11And I am not saying this because I feel neglected, for I have learned to be satisfied with what I have. 12I know what it is to be in need and what it is to have more than enough. I have learned this secret, so that anywhere, at any time, I am content, whether I am full or hungry, whether I have too much or too little. 13I have the strength to face all conditions by the power that Christ gives me.

14But it was very good of you to help me in my troubles. 15You Philippians know very well that when I left Macedonia in the early days of preaching the Good News, you were the only church to help me; you were the only ones who shared my profits and losses. 16More than once when I needed help in Thessalonica, you sent it to me. 17It is not that I just want to receive gifts; rather, I want to see profit added to your account. 18Here, then, is my receipt for everything you have given me—and it has been more than enough! I have all I need now that Epaphroditus has brought me all your gifts. They are like a sweet-smelling offering to God, a sacrifice which is acceptable and pleasing to him. 19And with all his abundant wealth through Christ Jesus, my God will supply all your needs. 20To our God and Father be the glory forever and ever! Amen.

Final Greetings

21Greetings to each one of God's people who belong to Christ Jesus. The believers here with me send you their greetings. 22All God's people here send greetings, especially those who belong to the Emperor's palace.

23May the grace of the Lord Jesus Christ be with you all.

們所需要的告訴上帝，用感謝的心祈求。 7 上帝所賜那超越人所能理解的平安，會藉着基督耶穌，保守你們的心懷意念。

8 末了，弟兄姊妹們，你們要常常留意那些美善和值得讚揚的事。一切眞實、高尚、公正、純潔、可愛，和光榮的事都應該重視。 9 你們從我所學習，領受，或聽到，看到的言行，都要實行出來。那賜平安的上帝就會與你們同在。

感謝的話

10 我在主的生命裏有極大的喜樂。因爲過了一段時間，現在你們再一次來供應我。其實，你們向來關心我，只是沒有機會表示罷了。11 我這樣說，不是因爲我缺少甚麼；我已經學會對現狀滿足。12 我知道怎樣過貧困的生活，也知道怎樣過富裕的生活。我已經得到祕訣，隨時隨地，飽足好，飢餓也好，豐富好，缺乏也好，我都知足。13 藉着基督所賜的力量，我能夠適應任何情況。

14 但是，在我困難的時候，你們來幫助我，我很感激。15 你們腓立比人都知道，在我傳福音的初期，我離開了馬其頓；那時候只有你們的教會幫助我，有份於我的盈虧得失。16 在帖撒羅尼迦的時候，不只一次，我有需要，你們就來幫助我。17 不是我貪圖甚麼餽贈，而是希望你們多得盈餘，歸入你們自己的帳上。18 這就是你們送給我一切禮物的收據；你們所送的超過了我的需要。以巴弗提替你們帶來了這許多豐富的禮物，正像是芬芳的香氣，是上帝所悅納的祭品。19 我的上帝會照着他在基督耶穌裏那豐富的福澤把你們所需要的一切賜給你們。

20 願榮耀歸於我們的父上帝，世世無窮！阿們。

最後問安

21 請向各位屬基督耶穌的信徒問安。跟我在一起的信徒們向你們問安。22 所有的信徒，特別是皇宮裏的人，都向你們問安。

23 願主耶穌基督賜恩典給你們！

歌羅西書
COLOSSIANS

INTRODUCTION

Paul's Letter to the Colossians was written to the church at Colossae, a town in Asia Minor east of Ephesus. This church had not been established by Paul, but was in an area for which Paul felt responsible, as he sent out workers from Ephesus, the capital of the Roman province of Asia. Paul had learned that there were false teachers in the church at Colossae who insisted that in order to know God and have full salvation one must worship certain "spiritual rulers and authorities." In addition, these teachers said, one must submit to special rites such as circumcision and must observe strict rules about foods and other matters.

Paul writes to oppose these teachings with the true Christian message. The heart of his reply is that Jesus Christ is able to give full salvation and that these other beliefs and practices actually lead away from him. Through Christ, God created the world and through him he is bringing it back to himself. Only in union with Christ is there hope of salvation for the world. Paul then spells out the implications of this great teaching for the lives of believers.

It is noteworthy that Tychicus, who took this letter to Colossae for Paul, was accompanied by Onesimus, the slave on whose behalf Paul wrote *Philemon*.

Outline of Contents

簡 介

歌羅西書是保羅寫給歌羅西教會的信。歌羅西是小亞細亞省以弗所東邊的一個市鎮。這裏的教會不是保羅創立的，但他覺得對這一地區的教會負有相當的責任，因為他曾從以弗所（羅馬治下亞細亞省的首府）派遣同工到那裏工作。保羅聽見歌羅西教會出現假教師；他們堅持人若要認識上帝，獲得完全的拯救，必須崇拜某些「靈界的執政者和掌權者」。他們又主張：人必須遵守特別的禮儀，如割禮，也必須嚴格遵守有關食物和其他的一些規例。

保羅根據福音的信息寫信反對這種教訓。他認為耶穌基督有完全的救恩，其他的理論或方法反而把人引入歧途，離開了基督。上帝藉基督創造世界，也藉基督使世界歸回於他。只有生活在基督的生命裏，世界才有獲得拯救的希望。最後，保羅說明這重要教訓在信徒生活上的意義。

值得注意的是，替保羅送信往歌羅西去的推基古有阿尼西謀跟他結伴同行。阿尼西謀是一個奴隸；保羅曾經為着他寫信給腓利門。

提 要

1 From Paul, who by God's will is an apostle of Christ Jesus, and from our brother Timothy–

2To God's people in Colossae, who are our faithful friends in union with Christ:

May God our Father give you grace and peace.

Prayer of Thanksgiving

3We always give thanks to God, the Father of our Lord Jesus Christ, when we pray for you. 4For we have heard of your faith in Christ Jesus and of your love for all God's people. 5When the true message, the Good News, first came to you, you heard about the hope it offers. So your faith and love are based on what you hope for, which is kept safe for you in heaven. 6The gospel keeps bringing blessings and is spreading throughout the world, just as it has among you ever since the day you first heard about the grace of God and came to know it as it really is. 7You learned of God's grace from Epaphras, our dear fellow servant, who is Christ's faithful worker on our[a] behalf. 8He has told us of the love that the Spirit has given you.

9For this reason we have always prayed for you, ever since we heard about you. We ask God to fill you with the knowledge of his will, with all the wisdom and understanding that his Spirit gives. 10Then you will be able to live as the Lord wants and will always do what pleases him. Your lives will produce all kinds of good deeds, and you will grow in your knowledge of God. 11-12May you be made strong with all the strength which comes from his glorious power, so that you may be able to endure everything with patience. And with joy give thanks to[b] the Father, who has made you fit to have your share of what God has reserved for his people in the kingdom of light. 13He rescued us from the power of darkness and brought us safe into the kingdom of his dear Son, 14by whom we are set free, that is, our sins are forgiven.

The Person and Work of Christ

15Christ is the visible likeness of the invisible God. He is the first-born Son, superior to all created things. 16For through him God created everything in heaven and on earth, the seen and the unseen things, including spiritual powers, lords, rulers, and authorities. God created the whole universe through him and for him. 17Christ existed before all things, and in union

a our; *some manuscripts have* your.
b with patience. And with joy give thanks to; *or* with patience and joy. And give thanks to.

1 我是保羅；我奉上帝的旨意作基督耶穌的使徒。我和提摩太弟兄 2 寫信給你們在歌羅西的信徒，就是在基督裏忠心的弟兄姊妹們。

願我們的父上帝賜恩典、平安給你們！

感謝的禱告

3 在替你們禱告的時候，我們常常感謝上帝，就是我們的主耶穌基督的父親；4 因為我們聽見你們對基督耶穌有信心，對所有信徒有愛心。5 起初，福音真道傳到你們那裏的時候，你們就聽見了這福音所帶來的盼望。這樣，你們的信心和愛心都是以那為你們保存在天上的盼望為根據的。6 這福音不但傳到你們那裏，也傳遍全世界，不斷地生長，結果子，正像當初你們聽見而且真正認識上帝的恩典時，生長，結果子一樣。7 你們是從我們親愛的同工以巴弗學習到這福音的；他為我們① 作了基督忠心的僕人。8 有關聖靈賜給你們愛心的消息是他告訴我們的。

9 因此，自從聽到了有關你們的消息，我們不斷地為你們禱告，求上帝使你們從聖靈得到各樣的智慧和理解力，能夠充分地認識他的旨意。10 這樣，你們的生活就會合乎主的要求，凡事使他喜歡。同時，你們會在生活上結出各種美好的果子，對上帝的認識也會增進。11 願你們從他榮耀的權能中得到堅強的力量，有耐心忍受一切。要以快樂的心 12 感謝天父②，因為他使你們③ 有資格分享他為信徒們在那光明的國度裏所保留的福澤。13 他救我們脫離了黑暗的權勢，使我們生活在他愛子的主權下。14 藉着他的愛子，我們得到自由—我們的罪得赦免。

基督和他的工作

15 基督是那看不見的上帝的形像，是超越萬有的長子。16 藉着他，上帝創造了天地萬有：看得見和看不見的，包括靈界的在位者、主宰者、執政者，和掌權者。藉着他，也為着他，上帝創造了整個宇宙。17 基督在

①有些古卷是「你們……」。
②「有耐心……感謝天父」或譯「以耐心和喜樂忍受一切。12要感謝上帝」。
③有些古卷是「我們……」。

with him all things have their proper place.
[18]He is the head of his body, the church; he is
the source of the body's life. He is the first-
born Son, who was raised from death, in order
that he alone might have the first place in all
things. [19]For it was by God's own decision that
the Son has in himself the full nature of God.
[20]Through the Son, then, God decided to bring
the whole universe back to himself. God made
peace through his Son's blood[c] on the cross and
so brought back to himself all things, both on
earth and in heaven.

[21]At one time you were far away from God
and were his enemies because of the evil things
you did and thought. [22]But now, by means of
the physical death of his Son, God has made
you his friends, in order to bring you, holy,
pure, and faultless, into his presence. [23]You
must, of course, continue faithful on a firm and
sure foundation, and must not allow yourselves
to be shaken from the hope you gained when
you heard the gospel. It is of this gospel that I,
Paul, became a servant–this gospel which has
been preached to everybody in the world.

Paul's Work as a Servant of the Church

[24]And now I am happy about my sufferings
for you, for by means of my physical sufferings
I am helping to complete what still remains of
Christ's sufferings on behalf of his body, the
church. [25]And I have been made a servant of
the church by God, who gave me this task to
perform for your good. It is the task of fully
proclaiming his message, [26]which is the secret
he hid through all past ages from all human
beings but has now revealed to his people.
[27]God's plan is to make known his secret to his
people, this rich and glorious secret which he
has for all peoples. And the secret is that Christ
is in you, which means that you will share in
the glory of God. [28]So we preach Christ to
everyone. With all possible wisdom we warn
and teach them in order to bring each one into
God's presence as a mature individual in union
with Christ. [29]To get this done I toil and
struggle, using the mighty strength which Christ
supplies and which is at work in me.

2 Let me tell you how hard I have worked
for you and for the people in Laodicea and
for all others who do not know me personally.
[2]I do this in order that they may be filled with
courage and may be drawn together in love,
and so have the full wealth of assurance which
true understanding brings. In this way they will
know God's secret, which is Christ himself.[d]

c his Son's blood; or his Son's sacrificial death.
d God's secret, which is Christ himself; some manuscripts have
God's secret; others have the secret of God the Father of Christ;
others have the secret of the God and Father, and of Christ.

萬有之先就存在；萬有也藉着他各得其所。
[18]他是教會的頭，也就是他身體的頭；他是
新生命的源頭。他是長子，首先從死裏復
活，目的是要在萬有中居首位。[19]上帝親自
決定使兒子有他自己完整的特質。[20]藉着兒
子，上帝決定使全宇宙再跟自己和好。上帝
藉着他兒子死在十字架上成就了和平，使天
地萬有再歸屬他。

[21] 從前，你們由於邪惡的行為和思想遠離
上帝，作了他的仇敵。[22]現在，藉着他兒子
肉體的死，上帝使你們成為他的朋友，為了
要你們在他面前聖潔，沒有缺點，無可指
責。[23]你們必須持守信仰，堅立在鞏固的基
礎上；不要放棄當初領受福音時所得到的盼
望。現在，這福音已經傳遍了全世界；我—
保羅就是這福音的僕人。

保羅的任務

[24] 我現在覺得為你們受苦是一件快樂的
事；因為我在肉體上受苦，等於繼續在擔受
基督為着他的身體—就是他的教會所忍受而
未完成的苦難。[25]為了你們的益處，上帝把
這任務交給我，使我作教會的僕人。這任務
是要我充分地把上帝的信息傳開，[26]就是他
歷代以來向人類隱藏着的奧祕；這奧祕現在
已經向他的子民顯明出來了。[27]上帝的計劃
是要他的子民知道，這豐盛而榮耀的奧祕是
要顯示給全人類的。這奧祕是：基督在你們
的生命裏，也就是說，你們要分享上帝的榮
耀。[28]因此，我們向所有的人傳揚基督，用
各樣的智慧勸誡教導大家，為要使每一個人
成為成熟的基督徒，把他們帶到上帝面前。
[29]為了這目的，我運用基督賜給我的大能
力，不辭勞苦，竭力工作。

2 我希望你們知道，為着你們和老底嘉
人，以及許多還沒有見過面的人，我盡
心竭力地工作。[2]我要使他們得到鼓勵，能
夠以愛心團結，有那從真知灼見所產生充足
的信心來認識上帝的奧祕；這奧祕就是基督

[3]He is the key that opens all the hidden treasures of God's wisdom and knowledge.

[4]I tell you, then, do not let anyone deceive you with false arguments, no matter how good they seem to be. [5]For even though I am absent in body, yet I am with you in spirit, and I am glad as I see the resolute firmness with which you stand together in your faith in Christ.

Fullness of Life in Christ

[6]Since you have accepted Christ Jesus as Lord, live in union with him. [7]Keep your roots deep in him, build your lives on him, and become stronger in your faith, as you were taught. And be filled with thanksgiving.

[8]See to it, then, that no one enslaves you by means of the worthless deceit of human wisdom, which comes from the teachings handed down by human beings and from the ruling spirits of the universe, and not from Christ. [9]For the full content of divine nature lives in Christ, in his humanity, [10]and you have been given full life in union with him. He is supreme over every spiritual ruler and authority.

[11]In union with Christ you were circumcised, not with the circumcision that is made by human beings, but with the circumcision made by Christ, which consists of being freed from the power of this sinful self. [12]For when you were baptized, you were buried with Christ, and in baptism you were also raised with Christ through your faith in the active power of God, who raised him from death. [13]You were at one time spiritually dead because of your sins and because you were Gentiles without the Law. But God has now brought you to life with Christ. God forgave us all our sins; [14]he canceled the unfavorable record of our debts with its binding rules and did away with it completely by nailing it to the cross. [15]And on that cross Christ freed himself from the power of the spiritual rulers and authorities;[e] he made a public spectacle of them by leading them as captives in his victory procession.

[16]So let no one make rules about what you eat or drink or about holy days or the New Moon Festival or the Sabbath. [17]All such things are only a shadow of things in the future; the reality is Christ. [18]Do not allow yourselves to be condemned by anyone who claims to be superior because of special visions and who insists on false humility and the worship of angels. For no reason at all, such people are all puffed up by their human way of thinking [19]and have stopped

---

e Christ freed himself from the power of the spiritual rulers and authorities; or Christ stripped the spiritual rulers and authorities of their power.

本身。[3]他是開啓上帝所儲藏着的一切智慧和知識的鑰匙。

[4]我說這話，免得你們被任何人用花言巧語把你們引入歧途。[5]雖然我的身體不在你們那裏，我的心卻跟你們在一起。我很高興，能夠看見你們循規蹈矩，並且對基督的信仰有堅固的基礎。

在基督裏完整的生命

[6]既然你們接受基督耶穌爲主，你們的行爲必須以他爲中心，[7]在他裏面扎根，生長，建立信心；你們就是這樣受教的。你們也要充滿着感謝的心。

[8]你們要謹慎，不要被虛妄的哲學迷住了；因爲那種學說是人所傳授的，是根據宇宙間所謂星宿之靈，而不是根據基督。[9]因爲上帝完整的神件具體地在基督裏，[10]而你們跟基督連結，也得到了豐盛的生命。他是元首，超越一切靈界的執政者和掌權者。

[11]你們已經在基督的生命裏受了割禮；這割禮不是人爲的，而是他使你們擺脫肉身罪性的割禮。[12]因爲，你們受洗禮的時候，你們是跟基督一同埋葬；你們受洗禮的時候，也藉着信那使他復活的上帝的作爲跟他一同復活。[13]從前，因爲你們有罪性，又是沒有法律的外邦人，你們在靈性上是死的。但是，上帝使你們跟基督一同再活過來。他赦免了我們一切的過犯，[14]取消了那對我們不利、法律上束縛我們的罪債記錄，把它釘在十字架上，毀掉了它。[15]在十字架上，基督親自解除了[①]那些靈界執政者和掌權者的權勢，把他們當作凱旋行列中的俘虜，公開示衆。

[16]所以，不要讓人在你們的飲食、節期、月朔，或安息日這些問題上用條例束縛你們。[17]這一切不過是將來之事的影兒；基督才是實體。[18]不要讓那些堅持有特殊遠見、故作謙虛、崇拜天使的人使你們喪失了得獎的機會。他們隨着人的幻想，無故狂妄自大，[19]跟元首基督斷了聯繫。其實，只有從

---

①「基督親自解除了」或譯「基督親自脫離了」。「基督」原文是「他」，也可能指上帝。

holding on to Christ, who is the head of the body. Under Christ's control the whole body is nourished and held together by its joints and ligaments, and it grows as God wants it to grow.

Dying and Living with Christ

20You have died with Christ and are set free from the ruling spirits of the universe. Why, then, do you live as though you belonged to this world? Why do you obey such rules as 21"Don't handle this," "Don't taste that," "Don't touch the other"? 22All these refer to things which become useless once they are used; they are only human rules and teachings. 23Of course such rules appear to be based on wisdom in their forced worship of angels, and false humility, and severe treatment of the body; but they have no real value in controlling physical passions.

3 You have been raised to life with Christ, so set your hearts on the things that are in heaven, where Christ sits on his throne at the right side of God. 2Keep your minds fixed on things there, not on things here on earth. 3For you have died, and your life is hidden with Christ in God. 4Your real life is Christ and when he appears, then you too will appear with him and share his glory!

The Old Life and the New

5You must put to death, then, the earthly desires at work in you, such as sexual immorality, indecency, lust, evil passions, and greed (for greed is a form of idolatry). 6Because of such things God's anger will come upon those who do not obey him.*f* 7At one time you yourselves used to live according to such desires, when your life was dominated by them.

8But now you must get rid of all these things: anger, passion, and hateful feelings. No insults or obscene talk must ever come from your lips. 9Do not lie to one another, for you have put off the old self with its habits 10and have put on the new self. This is the new being which God, its Creator, is constantly renewing in his own image, in order to bring you to a full knowledge of himself. 11As a result, there is no longer any distinction between Gentiles and Jews, circumcised and uncircumcised, barbarians, savages, slaves, and free, but Christ is all, Christ is in all.

12You are the people of God; he loved you and chose you for his own. So then, you must clothe yourselves with compassion, kindness, humility, gentleness, and patience. 13Be tolerant

f Some manuscripts do not have upon those who do not obey him.

身體的頭,就是基督,整個身體才能夠得到滋養,藉著關節筋絡,互相連結,按照上帝的旨意逐漸生長。

與基督同生死

20-21既然你們跟基督同死,擺脫了那些星宿之靈,你們為甚麼仍然跟世俗的人一樣生活,繼續守「不可動這個,不可嘗那個,不可摸這個」這一類的禁忌呢?22這類東西一經使用就完了,因為它們無非是人的規例和教訓的產物。23從表面看,崇拜天使、故作謙虛、苦待自己的身體等等,似乎是明智之舉,究其實,對於抑制肉體的情慾是毫無價值的。

3 你們已經跟基督一起復活,你們必須追求天上的事;在那裏,基督坐在上帝右邊的寶座上。2你們要專心於天上的事,而不是地上的事。3因為你們已經跟基督一起死了,你們的生命跟他一同藏在上帝裏面。4基督是你們的真生命;當他顯現的時候,你們也要跟他一起顯現,分享他的榮耀。

舊的和新的生命

5所以,你們必須治死在你們身上作崇的那些屬世的慾望,就如淫亂、污穢、邪情、惡慾,和貪婪(貪婪是一種偶像崇拜)。6由於這些事,上帝的義憤將臨到那些不順從他的人⑤。7你們從前也曾經生活在這一類的慾望中,受它們的支配。

8 但是,現在你們必須根絕這些事:不可再有忿怒、暴戾,和仇恨;不可說毀謗、污穢的話。9不可彼此欺騙,因為你們已經脫掉舊我和舊習慣,10換上了新我。這新我,由創造主上帝按照自己的形像不斷地加以更新,能夠完全地認識他。11這樣說來,不再有希臘人或猶太人的區分;也不再有受割禮、不受割禮,野蠻的、未開化的,奴隸或自由人等的分別。基督就是一切,基督貫徹一切。

12上帝愛你們,揀選了你們作他的子民。所以,你們要有憐憫、慈愛、謙遜、溫柔,和忍耐的心。13有糾紛的時候要互相寬容,

⑤有些古卷沒有「那些不順從他的人」。

with one another and forgive one another whenever any of you has a complaint against someone else. You must forgive one another just as the Lord has forgiven you. [14]And to all these qualities add love, which binds all things together in perfect unity. [15]The peace that Christ gives is to guide you in the decisions you make; for it is to this peace that God has called you together in the one body. And be thankful. [16]Christ's message in all its richness must live in your hearts. Teach and instruct one another with all wisdom. Sing psalms, hymns, and sacred songs; sing to God with thanksgiving in your hearts. [17]Everything you do or say, then, should be done in the name of the Lord Jesus, as you give thanks through him to God the Father.

Personal Relations in the New Life

[18]Wives, submit yourselves to your husbands, for that is what you should do as Christians.

[19]Husbands, love your wives and do not be harsh with them.

[20]Children, it is your Christian duty to obey your parents always, for that is what pleases God.

[21]Parents, do not irritate your children, or they will become discouraged.

[22]Slaves, obey your human masters in all things, not only when they are watching you because you want to gain their approval; but do it with a sincere heart because of your reverence for the Lord. [23]Whatever you do, work at it with all your heart, as though you were working for the Lord and not for people. [24]Remember that the Lord will give you as a reward what he has kept for his people. For Christ is the real Master you serve. [25]And all wrongdoers will be repaid for the wrong things they do, because God judges everyone by the same standard.

4 Masters, be fair and just in the way you treat your slaves. Remember that you too have a Master in heaven.

Instructions

[2]Be persistent in prayer, and keep alert as you pray, giving thanks to God. [3]At the same time pray also for us, so that God will give us a good opportunity to preach his message about the secret of Christ. For that is why I am now in prison. [4]Pray, then, that I may speak, as I should, in such a way as to make it clear.

[5]Be wise in the way you act toward those who are not believers, making good use of every opportunity you have. [6]Your speech should

彼此饒恕；主怎樣饒恕你們，你們也要怎樣饒恕別人。[14]在這一切之上，要加上愛，因為愛是聯繫一切德行的關鍵。[15]基督所賜的和平要在你們心裏作主；為了使你們有這和平，上帝選召你們，歸於一體。你們要感謝。[16]你們要讓基督的信息豐豐富富地長住在你們心裏。要用各樣的智慧互相教導、規勸，用詩篇、聖詩、靈歌從心底發出感謝的聲音來頌讚上帝。[17]無論做甚麼，說甚麼，你們都要奉主耶穌的名，藉着他感謝父上帝。

新的人際關係

[18]作妻子的，你們要服從丈夫，因為這是基督徒的本份。

[19]作丈夫的，你們要愛妻子，不可虐待她們。

[20]作兒女的，你們要事事聽從父母；因為這是主所喜歡的。

[21]作父母的⑥，你們不要激怒兒女，免得他們灰心喪志。

[22]作奴僕的，你們要事事聽從世上的主人。你們所做的不僅是做給主人看，討他們的喜歡，而是出於真心誠意，因為你們敬畏主。[23]無論做甚麼，你們都要專心一意，像是為主工作，不是為人工作。[24]要知道主會把他為自己的子民所保存的賞賜給你。你們事奉的是主基督。[25]那作惡的，無論是誰，都要受應得的報應，因為上帝用一樣的標準對待每一個人。

4 作主人的，你們要公平合理地對待奴僕，因為你們知道，你們在天上也有一位主人。

勸導的話

[2]你們禱告要恆切，且要警醒，對上帝存感謝的心。[3]也要為我們禱告，求上帝賜給我們傳佈信息的好機會，得以宣揚基督的奧祕。我現在就是為了這工作坐牢的。[4]請為我禱告，使我能盡責任把這奧祕闡明出來。

[5]你們跟非信徒來往要有智慧，要把握機會。[6]講話要溫和風趣，要知道該怎樣回答

⑥原文是「作父親的」。

always be pleasant and interesting, and you should know how to give the right answer to everyone.

Final Greetings

7Our dear friend Tychicus, who is a faithful worker and fellow servant in the Lord's work, will give you all the news about me. 8That is why I am sending him to you, in order to cheer you up by telling you how all of us are getting along. 9With him goes Onesimus, that dear and faithful friend, who belongs to your group. They will tell you everything that is happening here.

10Aristarchus, who is in prison with me, sends you greetings, and so does Mark, the cousin of Barnabas. (You have already received instructions to welcome Mark if he comes your way.) 11Joshua, also called Justus, sends greetings too. These three are the only Jewish believers who work with me for the Kingdom of God, and they have been a great help to me.

12Greetings from Epaphras, another member of your group and a servant of Christ Jesus. He always prays fervently for you, asking God to make you stand firm, as mature and fully convinced Christians, in complete obedience to God's will. 13I can personally testify to his hard work for you and for the people in Laodicea and Hierapolis. 14Luke, our dear doctor, and Demas send you their greetings.

15Give our best wishes to the believers in Laodicea and to Nympha and the church that meets in her house.*g* 16After you read this letter, make sure that it is read also in the church at Laodicea. At the same time, you are to read the letter that the believers in Laodicea will send you. 17And tell Archippus, "Be sure to finish the task you were given in the Lord's service."

18With my own hand I write this: *Greetings from Paul.* Do not forget my chains!

May God's grace be with you.

g Nympha ... her house; *some manuscripts have* Nymphas ... his house.

每一個人所提出的問題。

最後問安

7 我在這裏的一切情形,我們親愛的弟兄推基古會詳細地告訴你們。他是一位忠心的僕人,在事奉主的工作上和我同作僕人。8我特意派他到你們那裏去,報告我們這裏的情況,好使你們得到鼓勵。9跟他一起去的有一位忠心親愛的弟兄阿尼西謀;他是你們那裏的人。他們兩人會把這裏一切的事都告訴你們。

10跟我一起坐牢的亞里達古向你們問安。巴拿巴的表弟馬可也問候你們。(關於馬可,我已經吩咐過,如果他上你們那裏去,請接待他。)11別號猶士都的耶穌也向你們問安。在猶太人的信徒中,只有上面這三位為了上帝國的工作跟我同工,對我有很大的幫助。

12 從你們那裏來的以巴弗問候你們;他也是基督耶穌的僕人。他常常為你們懇切禱告,求上帝使你們的信心堅定,作為成熟的基督徒,完全順服他的旨意。13他為着你們,也為着老底嘉以及希拉坡里的信徒們辛勞工作;這是我個人可以作證的。14我們親愛的路加醫生和底馬兩人也問候你們。

15 請替我們向老底嘉的弟兄姊妹們、寧法,和在她家裏的教會問安。16你們宣讀了這封信以後,請轉交給老底嘉教會宣讀;同時,你們也要宣讀從老底嘉教會轉給你們的信。17要告訴亞基布,他所領受那事奉主的任務一定要盡力完成。

18 我親手寫:「保羅祝你們好!」別忘了我是帶着鎖鍊的。

願上帝賜恩典給你們!

帖撒羅尼迦前書
1 THESSALONIANS

INTRODUCTION

Thessalonica was the capital city of the Roman province of Macedonia. Paul established a church there after he left Philippi. Soon, however, there was opposition from Jews who were jealous of Paul's success in preaching the Christian message among the non-Jews who had become interested in Judaism. Paul was forced to leave Thessalonica and go on to Berea. Later on, after he reached Corinth, Paul received a personal report from his companion and fellow worker Timothy about the situation in the church at Thessalonica.

Paul's First Letter to the Thessalonians was then written to encourage and reassure the Christians there. He gives thanks for the news about their faith and love; he reminds them of the kind of life he had lived while he was with them, and then answers questions that had arisen in the church about the return of Christ: Could a believer who died before Christ's return still share in the eternal life that his return will bring? And when will Christ come again? Paul takes this occasion to tell them to go on working quietly while waiting in hope for Christ's return.

Outline of Contents

簡　介

帖撒羅尼迦是羅馬治下馬其頓的首府。保羅離開腓立比後，在那裏建立了教會。可是不久，當地的猶太人因嫉妒保羅在非猶太人中傳佈基督的信息、成功地轉移了他們對猶太教的興趣而起來反對保羅。保羅被迫離開帖撒羅尼迦，往庇哩亞去。他到了哥林多以後，他的同工提摩太來看他，向他報告帖撒羅尼迦教會的情況。

保羅寫這封信的目的在鼓勵帖撒羅尼迦的基督徒，堅定他們的信心。他為了所聽到有關他們的愛心和信心的消息而感謝上帝。他提到他跟他們在一起時的生活情況，然後回答他們所提出關於基督再來的一些問題，例如：一個信耶穌的人在基督再來以前死了，能否分享基督再來時所帶來的永恆生命？基督甚麼時候再來？保羅乘這個機會勸勉他們，要繼續靜默地工作，在盼望中等候基督的再來。

提要

1 From Paul, Silas, and Timothy–
To the people of the church in Thessalonica, who belong to God the Father and the Lord Jesus Christ:
May grace and peace be yours.

The Life and Faith of the Thessalonians

2We always thank God for you all and always mention you in our prayers. 3For we remember before our God and Father how you put your faith into practice, how your love made you work so hard, and how your hope in our Lord Jesus Christ is firm. 4Our friends, we know that God loves you and has chosen you to be his own. 5For we brought the Good News to you, not with words only, but also with power and the Holy Spirit, and with complete conviction of its truth. You know how we lived when we were with you; it was for your own good. 6You imitated us and the Lord; and even though you suffered much, you received the message with the joy that comes from the Holy Spirit. 7So you became an example to all believers in Macedonia and Achaia. 8For not only did the message about the Lord go out from you throughout Macedonia and Achaia, but the news about your faith in God has gone everywhere. There is nothing, then, that we need to say. 9All those people speak about how you received us when we visited you, and how you turned away from idols to God, to serve the true and living God 10and to wait for his Son to come from heaven–his Son Jesus, whom he raised from death and who rescues us from God's anger that is coming.

Paul's Work in Thessalonica

2 Our friends, you yourselves know that our visit to you was not a failure. 2You know how we had already been mistreated and insulted in Philippi before we came to you in Thessalonica. And even though there was much opposition, our God gave us courage to tell you the Good News that comes from him. 3Our appeal to you is not based on error or impure motives, nor do we try to trick anyone. 4Instead, we always speak as God wants us to, because he has judged us worthy to be entrusted with the Good News. We do not try to please people, but to please God, who tests our motives. 5You know very well that we did not come to you with flattering talk, nor did we use words to cover up greed–God is our witness! 6We did not try to get praise from anyone, either from you or from others, 7even though as apostles of Christ we could have made demands

1 我是保羅；我跟西拉和提摩太寫信給帖撒羅尼迦教會—屬於父上帝和主耶穌基督的信徒們。
願你們都得到恩典和平安！

帖撒羅尼迦人的生活和信心

2 我們常常為你們大家感謝上帝，在禱告中不斷地提起你們，3 在我們的父上帝面前記念你們怎樣把所信的實行出來，怎樣以愛心辛勞工作，又怎樣堅守對我們的主耶穌基督的盼望。4 弟兄姊妹們，我們知道上帝愛你們，揀選了你們。5 我們把這福音傳給你們，不僅是用言語，也是倚靠聖靈的大能，並且是根據對福音的確信。你們都知道，我們在你們那裏時的生活是怎樣的；一切無非是為了你們的好處。6 你們效法了我們，也效法主；雖然你們遭受大難，仍然在聖靈所賜的喜樂中領受信息。7 因此，你們成為馬其頓和亞該亞所有信徒的模範。8 主的信息不僅從你們那裏傳開到馬其頓和亞該亞，你們對上帝的信心也傳到遠近各處；這實在用不着我們多說。9 大家都在傳講：在我們訪問你們的時候，你們怎樣接待我們，又怎樣離棄偶像，歸向上帝，事奉這位又活又真的上帝，10 並且盼望着他的兒子耶穌從天上降臨。這位耶穌就是上帝使他從死裏復活的那一位；他使我們脫離那將要臨到的上帝的義憤。

保羅在帖撒羅尼迦工作

2 弟兄姊妹們，你們自己知道，我們去訪問你們並不是沒有效果的。2 你們知道，我們到你們那裏去以前，在腓立比已經受了傷害，受了侮辱。可是，我們的上帝給我們勇氣，在激烈的反對下仍然把他的福音傳給你們。3 我們的勸勉不是出於幻想或不良的動機，也不是想欺詐甚麼人。4 相反地，上帝信任我們，把傳福音的任務付託我們。因此，我們只說他要我們說的話。我們不討好人，只求取悅那位察驗我們內心的上帝。5 你們知道，我們從來不向你們說諂媚的話，也沒有藏着貪婪的念頭；這是上帝可以為我們作證的。6 我們不求任何人的稱讚，沒有求你們的，也沒有求別人的。7 我們身為基督的使徒，本來有權要求你們的尊

on you. But we were gentle when we were with you, like a mother*a* taking care of her children. [8]Because of our love for you we were ready to share with you not only the Good News from God but even our own lives. You were so dear to us! [9]Surely you remember, our friends, how we worked and toiled! We worked day and night so that we would not be any trouble to you as we preached to you the Good News from God.

[10]You are our witnesses, and so is God, that our conduct toward you who believe was pure, right, and without fault. [11]You know that we treated each one of you just as parents treat their own children. [12]We encouraged you, we comforted you, and we kept urging you to live the kind of life that pleases God, who calls you to share in his own Kingdom and glory.

[13]And there is another reason why we always give thanks to God. When we brought you God's message, you heard it and accepted it, not as a message from human beings but as God's message, which indeed it is. For God is at work in you who believe. [14]Our friends, the same things happened to you that happened to the churches of God in Judea, to the people there who belong to Christ Jesus. You suffered the same persecutions from your own people that they suffered from the Jews, [15]who killed the Lord Jesus and the prophets, and persecuted us. How displeasing they are to God! How hostile they are to everyone! [16]They even tried to stop us from preaching to the Gentiles the message that would bring them salvation. In this way they have brought to completion all the sins they have always committed. And now God's anger has at last come down on them!

Paul's Desire to Visit Them Again

[17]As for us, friends, when we were separated from you for a little while–not in our thoughts, of course, but only in body–how we missed you and how hard we tried to see you again! [18]We wanted to return to you. I myself tried to go back more than once, but Satan would not let us. [19]After all, it is you–you, no less than others!–who are our hope, our joy, and our reason for boasting of our victory in the presence of our Lord Jesus when he comes. [20]Indeed, you are our pride and our joy!

3 Finally, we could not bear it any longer. So we decided to stay on alone in Athens [2]while we sent Timothy, our brother who works

---

重；可是在你們那裏的時候,我們溫柔地待你們,像母親乳養兒女一般。[8]爲了愛你們,我們不但願意跟你們分享從上帝來的福音,連我們的生命也願意給你們,因爲你們是我們所疼愛的。[9]弟兄姊妹們,你們一定記得,我們怎樣日夜辛勤工作,爲的是在向你們傳上帝福音的時候,不至於成爲你們的負擔。

[10]對你們這些信徒,我們的言行都是純潔、公正、無可責備的。這一點,你們自己和上帝都可以作證。[11]你們知道,我們待你們每一個人,像父親待自己的兒女一樣。[12]我們鼓勵你們,安慰你們;我們不斷地勸勉你們要在生活上蒙上帝喜悅—他呼召你們來分享他的主權和榮耀。

[13]我們也常常感謝上帝;因爲我們所傳的信息,你們聽見了,領受了,並不以爲是領受人的信息,而是領受那確確實實出自上帝的信息;因爲上帝①在你們信的人當中工作。[14]弟兄姊妹們,你們的遭遇跟猶太地區上帝的各教會—就是屬於基督耶穌的信徒們—所遭遇到的一樣。你們受到自己同胞的迫害,正如他們受過猶太同胞的迫害一樣。[15]那些猶太人殺了主耶穌和先知們,又驅逐我們。他們冒犯了上帝,也跟全人類爲敵![16]他們甚至要阻止我們向外邦人傳講那會使外邦人得救的信息。這樣,他們不斷地累積自己的罪,惡貫滿盈;上帝的義憤終於臨到他們的身上。

保羅希望再訪問帖撒羅尼迦教會

[17]弟兄姊妹們,我們跟你們暫時分離,不過是身體的分離,我們的心並沒有離開過你們。我們非常想念你們,迫切盼望再見到你們![18]我們很想再到你們那裏去。我—保羅不只一次想回去探望你們,可是撒但阻撓了我們。[19]你們是我們的希望,我們的喜樂。在我們的主耶穌再來的時候,我們所要誇耀的冠冕不正是你們嗎?[20]你們的確是我們的光榮和喜樂!

3 所以,我們不能再等下去,終於決定繼續留在雅典,[2]派我們的弟兄提摩太到你們那裏去;他是我們爲上帝傳揚基督福

---

a we were gentle when we were with you, like a mother; *some manuscripts have* we were like children when we were with you; we were like a mother.

①「上帝」或譯「上帝的信息」。

with us for God in preaching the Good News about Christ. We sent him to strengthen you and help your faith, [3]so that none of you should turn back because of these persecutions. You yourselves know that such persecutions are part of God's will for us. [4]For while we were still with you, we told you ahead of time that we were going to be persecuted; and as you well know, that is exactly what happened. [5]That is why I had to send Timothy. I could not bear it any longer, so I sent him to find out about your faith. Surely it could not be that the Devil had tempted you and all our work had been for nothing!

[6]Now Timothy has come back, and he has brought us the welcome news about your faith and love. He has told us that you always think well of us and that you want to see us just as much as we want to see you. [7]So, in all our trouble and suffering we have been encouraged about you, friends. It was your faith that encouraged us, [8]because now we really live if you stand firm in your life in union with the Lord. [9]Now we can give thanks to our God for you. We thank him for the joy we have in his presence because of you. [10]Day and night we ask him with all our heart to let us see you personally and supply what is needed in your faith.

[11]May our God and Father himself and our Lord Jesus prepare the way for us to come to you! [12]May the Lord make your love for one another and for all people grow more and more and become as great as our love for you. [13]In this way he will strengthen you, and you will be perfect and holy in the presence of our God and Father when our Lord Jesus comes with all who belong to him.[b]

A Life That Pleases God

4 Finally, our friends, you learned from us how you should live in order to please God. This is, of course, the way you have been living. And now we beg and urge you in the name of the Lord Jesus to do even more. [2]For you know the instructions we gave you by the authority of the Lord Jesus. [3]God wants you to be holy and completely free from sexual immorality. [4]Each of you should know how to live with your wife[c] in a holy and honorable way, [5]not with a lustful desire, like the heathen who do not know God. [6]In this matter, then, none of you should do wrong to other Christians or take advantage of them. We have told you this before, and we strongly warned you that the Lord will punish those who do that. [7]God did not call us to live in immorality, but in holiness.

b all who belong to him; *or* all his angels.
c live with your wife; *or* control your body.

音的同工。我們派他去的目的是要堅固和幫助你們的信心，[3]使你們當中不會有人因受迫害而退縮。你們知道，這迫害也是我們所必須經歷的。[4]跟你們在一起的時候，我們已經預先告訴你們關於我們將受迫害的事。現在所發生的跟預料的正相符；這是你們所知道的。[5]因此，我才派提摩太去；我不能再等了。我派他去，為要知道你們的信心到底怎樣。我不相信魔鬼已經誘惑了你們，而我們的工作落了空！

[6] 現在，提摩太已經從你們那裏回來了；他帶來有關你們信心和愛心的好消息。他說你們常常在想念我們，迫切希望見到我們，正像我們迫切希望見到你們一樣。[7]所以，弟兄姊妹們，我們在一切患難困苦中，因着你們的信心而得到鼓勵。[8]如果你們對主有堅定的信心，我們現在可真的是在喘氣了。[9]我們可以為你們感謝上帝。我們感謝他，因為你們使我們在他面前得到喜樂。[10]我們日夜向他懇切祈求，讓我們能夠親自去看你們，來補足你們在信心上的需要。

[11] 願上帝—我們的天父，和我們的主耶穌親自開路，讓我們能夠到你們那裏去！[12]願主使你們有彼此相愛和愛人類的心，並且日益增長，正像我們熱切地愛你們一樣。[13]這樣，他會使你們心志堅定，在我們的主耶穌和他的信徒們來臨的時候，能夠在我們的父上帝面前聖潔，沒有缺點。

上帝所嘉許的生活

4 末了，弟兄姊妹們，你們已經從我們學到了怎樣在生活上討上帝的喜歡—其實，你們一向都這樣做；現在，我們奉主耶穌的名勸勉你們，要求你們必須更加努力。[2]你們都知道，我們藉着主耶穌所教導你們的是甚麼。[3]上帝的旨意是要你們聖潔，絕對沒有淫亂的事。[4]每一個人要曉得依照聖潔合宜的方法控制自己的身體②，[5]而不是憑着情慾，像不認識上帝的異教徒那樣。[6] 在這種事上，不可以有對不起同道或佔他便宜的行為。我們已經向你們說過，警告過你們：主一定要懲罰那些犯這種過錯的人。[7] 上帝選召我們，不是要我們生活在污穢

②「控制自己的身體」或譯「與自己的妻子相處」。

[8]So then, whoever rejects this teaching is not rejecting a human being, but God, who gives you his Holy Spirit.

[9]There is no need to write you about love for each other. You yourselves have been taught by God how you should love one another. [10]And you have, in fact, behaved like this toward all the believers in all of Macedonia. So we beg you, our friends, to do even more. [11]Make it your aim to live a quiet life, to mind your own business, and to earn your own living, just as we told you before. [12]In this way you will win the respect of those who are not believers, and you will not have to depend on anyone for what you need.

The Lord's Coming

[13]Our friends, we want you to know the truth about those who have died, so that you will not be sad, as are those who have no hope. [14]We believe that Jesus died and rose again, and so we believe that God will take back with Jesus those who have died believing in him.

[15]What we are teaching you now is the Lord's teaching: we who are alive on the day the Lord comes will not go ahead of those who have died. [16]There will be the shout of command, the archangel's voice, the sound of God's trumpet, and the Lord himself will come down from heaven. Those who have died believing in Christ will rise to life first; [17]then we who are living at that time will be gathered up along with them in the clouds to meet the Lord in the air. And so we will always be with the Lord. [18]So then, encourage one another with these words.

Be Ready for the Lord's Coming

5 There is no need to write you, friends, about the times and occasions when these things will happen. [2]For you yourselves know very well that the Day of the Lord will come as a thief comes at night. [3]When people say, "Everything is quiet and safe," then suddenly destruction will hit them! It will come as suddenly as the pains that come upon a woman in labor, and people will not escape. [4]But you, friends, are not in the darkness, and the Day should not take you by surprise like a thief. [5]All of you are people who belong to the light, who belong to the day. We do not belong to the night or to the darkness. [6]So then, we should not be sleeping like the others; we should be awake and sober. [7]It is at night when people sleep; it is at night when they get drunk. [8]But we belong to the day, and we should be sober. We must wear faith and love as a breastplate, and our

中，而是要我們聖潔。[8]所以那拒絕這種教導的，不是拒絕人，而是拒絕那賜聖靈給你們的上帝。

[9] 關於彼此相愛的事，我用不着寫信跟你們討論；上帝已經教導你們怎樣彼此相愛，[10]而你們也照着這教導對待全馬其頓所有的信徒。但弟兄姊妹們，我仍然勸你們要更加努力，[11]立志安份守己，親手做工來維持自己的生活，正像我們從前勸導你們的，[12]好使你們得到非信徒的尊敬，也用不着倚賴別人的供給。

主要再來

[13] 弟兄姊妹們，關於已經死了的人，我們希望你們知道一些事，免得你們憂傷，像那些沒有盼望的人。[14]我們相信耶穌死而復活，所以相信上帝也要把那些已經死了的信徒跟耶穌一起帶去。

[15] 我們現在照主的教導告訴你們：我們這些在主再臨那一天還活着的人，不會比那些已經死了的人先跟主相會。[16]因為，主的命令一下，天使長一喊，上帝的號筒一響，主本身要從天上降下。那時，那些信基督而已經死了的人要先復活；[17]接着，我們這些還活着的人都要跟他們一起被提到雲裏，在空中跟主相會。從此，我們就永遠跟主在一起了。[18]所以，你們要用這些話彼此安慰。

準備迎接主再來

5 弟兄姊妹們，關於這事發生的時間日期，不需要人家寫信告訴你們；[2]因為你們自己知道，主再來的日子就像小偷在夜裏忽然來到一樣。[3]當大家正說「一切平安無事」的時候，災禍會突然臨到，正像陣痛突然臨到快生產的女人一樣。他們一定是逃脫不了的。[4]但是，弟兄姊妹們，你們並不生活在黑暗中；那日子不會像小偷一樣突然來到。[5]你們都是光明的人，是屬於白晝的。我們不屬於黑夜，不生活在黑暗中。[6]所以，我們不應該像別人那樣沉睡；我們要警醒戒備。[7]睡覺的人在夜裏睡覺；酒徒在夜裏酗酒。[8]既然我們屬於白晝，就應該戒備。我們要以信和愛作護胸甲穿上，以得

hope of salvation as a helmet. ⁹God did not choose us to suffer his anger, but to possess salvation through our Lord Jesus Christ, ¹⁰who died for us in order that we might live together with him, whether we are alive or dead when he comes. ¹¹And so encourage one another and help one another, just as you are now doing.

Final Instructions and Greetings

¹²We beg you, our friends, to pay proper respect to those who work among you, who guide and instruct you in the Christian life. ¹³Treat them with the greatest respect and love because of the work they do. Be at peace among yourselves.

¹⁴We urge you, our friends, to warn the idle, encourage the timid, help the weak, be patient with everyone. ¹⁵See that no one pays back wrong for wrong, but at all times make it your aim to do good to one another and to all people.

¹⁶Be joyful always, ¹⁷pray at all times, ¹⁸be thankful in all circumstances. This is what God wants from you in your life in union with Christ Jesus.

¹⁹Do not restrain the Holy Spirit; ²⁰do not despise inspired messages. ²¹Put all things to the test: keep what is good ²²and avoid every kind of evil.

²³May the God who gives us peace make you holy in every way and keep your whole being–spirit, soul, and body–free from every fault at the coming of our Lord Jesus Christ. ²⁴He who calls you will do it, because he is faithful.

²⁵Pray also for us, friends.

²⁶Greet all the believers with the kiss of peace.

²⁷I urge you by the authority of the Lord to read this letter to all the believers.

²⁸The grace of our Lord Jesus Christ be with you.

救的盼望作頭盔戴上。⁹上帝不是揀選我們來受他的懲罰，而是要我們藉着我們的主耶穌基督得拯救。¹⁰基督為我們死，為要使我們，無論是死了的或是活着的，都能夠在他再來的時候跟他一同活着。¹¹因此，你們要互相鼓勵，彼此幫助，像你們現在所做的一樣。

最後的指示和問候

¹²弟兄姊妹們，我們求你們，要尊重那些在你們當中辛勞工作—那些主所揀選召來勸誡你們的人。¹³為了他們的工作，你們應該用最大的敬意和愛心對待他們。你們自己也要和睦相處。

¹⁴弟兄姊妹們，我們勸你們，要警告懶惰的人，鼓勵灰心的人，扶助軟弱的人，耐心待每一個人。¹⁵要謹慎，誰都不可以惡報惡，要常常彼此關心，為別人的好處着想。

¹⁶要常常喜樂，¹⁷常常禱告，¹⁸在任何環境中都要感謝。這是上帝為你們這些屬於基督耶穌的人所定的旨意。

¹⁹不要抑制聖靈的工作；²⁰不要輕視信息的傳講。²¹要詳細察驗每一件事，持守那美善的，²²棄絕一切邪惡。

²³願上帝賜平安給我們的上帝使你們完全聖潔！願他保守你們的靈、魂、體，在我們的主耶穌基督再來的時候完整無缺！²⁴那選召你們的上帝是信實可靠的；他一定成全這事。

²⁵弟兄姊妹們，請為我們禱告。

²⁶要以聖潔的親吻向弟兄姊妹們問安。

²⁷我奉主的名吩咐你們，要向所有的信徒宣讀這一封信。

²⁸願我們的主耶穌基督賜恩典給你們！

帖撒羅尼迦後書
2 THESSALONIANS

INTRODUCTION

Confusion over the expected return of Christ continued to cause disturbances in the church at Thessalonica. *Paul's Second Letter to the Thessalonians* deals with the belief that the day of the Lord's coming had already arrived. Paul corrects this idea, pointing out that before Christ returns, evil and wickedness will reach a climax under the leadership of a mysterious figure called "the Wicked One," who would be opposed to Christ.

The apostle emphasizes the need for his readers to remain steady in their faith in spite of trouble and suffering, to work for a living as did Paul and his fellow workers, and to persevere in doing good.

Outline of Contents

簡　介

　　基督再來的問題不斷地困擾着帖撒羅尼迦的教會。保羅給帖撒羅尼迦人的第二封信提起他們所相信、認爲基督再來那日子已經到了的問題。他糾正他們的錯誤，指出：基督再來以前，由於敵基督那神祕的「不法者」的誘惑，世上的罪惡將發展到最高峯。

　　保羅極力勸勉信徒，無論在任何困難環境中都要堅守信仰，像他和他的同工們一樣，靠自己做工來維持生活，並盡力行善。

提要

1

From Paul, Silas, and Timothy–
　　To the people of the church in Thessalonica, who belong to God our Father and the Lord Jesus Christ:

2May God our Father and the Lord Jesus Christ give you grace and peace.

The Judgment at Christ's Coming

3Our friends, we must thank God at all times for you. It is right for us to do so, because your faith is growing so much and the love each of you has for the others is becoming greater. 4That is why we ourselves boast about you in the churches of God. We boast about the way

1

我是保羅；我跟西拉和提摩太寫信給帖撒羅尼迦教會—屬於我們的父上帝和主耶穌基督的信徒們。

2 願我們的父上帝和主耶穌基督賜恩典、平安給你們！

基督再來時的審判

3 弟兄姊妹們，我們應該常常爲你們感謝上帝。這是當然的；因爲你們的信心大有進步，彼此相愛的心也大爲增進。4因此，我們在上帝的各教會裏誇獎你們。你們經歷一

you continue to endure and believe through all the persecutions and sufferings you are experiencing.

5All of this proves that God's judgment is just and as a result you will become worthy of his Kingdom, for which you are suffering. 6God will do what is right: he will bring suffering on those who make you suffer, 7and he will give relief to you who suffer and to us as well. He will do this when the Lord Jesus appears from heaven with his mighty angels, 8with a flaming fire, to punish those who reject God and who do not obey the Good News about our Lord Jesus. 9They will suffer the punishment of eternal destruction, separated from the presence of the Lord and from his glorious might, 10when he comes on that Day to receive glory from all his people and honor from all who believe. You too will be among them, because you have believed the message that we told you.

11That is why we always pray for you. We ask our God to make you worthy of the life he has called you to live. May he fulfill by his power all your desire for goodness and complete your work of faith. 12In this way the name of our Lord Jesus will receive glory from you, and you from him, by the grace of our God and of the Lord*e* Jesus Christ.

The Wicked One

2 Concerning the coming of our Lord Jesus Christ and our being gathered together to be with him: I beg you, my friends, 2not to be so easily confused in your thinking or upset by the claim that the Day of the Lord has come. Perhaps it is thought that we said this while prophesying or preaching, or that we wrote it in a letter. 3Do not let anyone deceive you in any way. For the Day will not come until the final Rebellion takes place and the Wicked One appears, who is destined to hell. 4He will oppose every so-called god or object of worship and will put himself above them all. He will even go in and sit down in God's Temple and claim to be God.

5Don't you remember? I told you all this while I was with you. 6Yet there is something that keeps this from happening now, and you know what it is. At the proper time, then, the Wicked One will appear. 7The Mysterious Wickedness is already at work, but what is going to happen will not happen until the one who holds it back is taken out of the way. 8Then the Wicked One will be revealed, but when the Lord Jesus comes, he will kill him

a our God and of the Lord; *or* our God and Lord.

切迫害、患難，仍然相信，仍然忍耐；這就是我們所誇耀的。

5 這正是上帝公義審判的證據，證明你們配得享受上帝國的福澤。你們就是為了這個國度繼續在忍受苦難。6 上帝要執行公義。他要使那些迫害你們的人遭受患難；7 他要使你們這些受苦的人跟我們一同得到釋放。主耶穌和他大能的天使從天上顯現在火燄中的時候，上帝就要執行這一件事。8 他要懲罰不承認他、不聽從有關我們主耶穌福音的那些人。9 主再來的日子，那些人要受懲罰，永遠滅亡，從主面前被隔絕，離開他榮耀的大能。10 在那一天，他要從信徒們得榮耀，並受他們的頌讚。你們也要在他們的行列中，因為你們相信了我們所傳的福音。

11 為了這目的，我們常常為你們禱告，求我們的上帝使你們不至於辜負他的呼召。願他用他的大能來幫助你們，實現一切向善的志願，成就你們憑信心所做的工作。12 這樣，我們主耶穌的名會從你們得榮耀，而你們也要從他得榮耀；這是藉着我們的上帝和主耶穌基督的恩典而來的。

那不法者

2 弟兄姊妹們，關於我們的主耶穌基督的再來，以及他要聚集我們跟他相會的事，我要求你們，2 不要輕易被「主再來的日子到了」這種說法所困惑，所煩擾。也許有人說這說法是我們傳講信息或傳道時說的，或甚至有人說是我們在信上這樣寫着的。3 不要讓任何人用任何手段欺騙你們。因為，那日子來到以前必定先有最後的反叛；那註定滅亡的不法者要出現。4 那不法者要反對一切被人稱為神明或崇拜的對象，把自己高抬在一切之上；他甚至去坐在上帝的聖殿裏，自稱為上帝。

5 你們不記得嗎？我跟你們一起的時候已經把這事告訴你們了。6 那阻止這事在現在發生的是甚麼，你們是知道的。時機一到，那不法者就要出現。7 那神祕的不法者已經開始工作；但是，等到阻止這事的手移去後，這事才會發生。8 那時，不法者要出現，可是主耶穌再來的時候要用口吹氣殺死

with the breath from his mouth and destroy him with his dazzling presence. [9]The Wicked One will come with the power of Satan and perform all kinds of false miracles and wonders, [10]and use every kind of wicked deceit on those who will perish. They will perish because they did not welcome and love the truth so as to be saved. [11]And so God sends the power of error to work in them so that they believe what is false. [12]The result is that all who have not believed the truth, but have taken pleasure in sin, will be condemned.

You Are Chosen for Salvation

[13]We must thank God at all times for you, friends, you whom the Lord loves. For God chose you as the first[b] to be saved by the Spirit's power to make you his holy people and by your faith in the truth. [14]God called you to this through the Good News we preached to you; he called you to possess your share of the glory of our Lord Jesus Christ. [15]So then, our friends, stand firm and hold on to those truths which we taught you, both in our preaching and in our letter.

[16]May our Lord Jesus Christ himself and God our Father, who loved us and in his grace gave us unfailing courage and a firm hope, [17]encourage you and strengthen you to always do and say what is good.

Pray for Us

3 Finally, our friends, pray for us that the Lord's message may continue to spread rapidly and be received with honor, just as it was among you. [2]Pray also that God will rescue us from wicked and evil people; for not everyone believes the message.

[3]But the Lord is faithful, and he will strengthen you and keep you safe from the Evil One. [4]And the Lord gives us confidence in you, and we are sure that you are doing and will continue to do what we tell you.

[5]May the Lord lead you into a greater understanding of God's love and the endurance that is given by Christ.

The Obligation to Work

[6]Our friends, we command you in the name of our Lord Jesus Christ to keep away from all believers who are living a lazy life and who do not follow the instructions that we gave them. [7]You yourselves know very well that you should do just what we did. We were not lazy when we

b as the first; *some manuscripts have* from the beginning.

他，並以光輝的顯現消滅他。[9]那不法者要帶着撒但的權力來到，行各種奇蹟異能，顯假的預兆，[10]並且對那些將要滅亡的人使用各種詭計，因為他們不接受、不喜愛那會使他們得救的真理。[11]因此，上帝給他們一種強烈的錯覺，讓他們去信從虛謊。[12]結果，一切不信真理、以罪惡為樂的人將被定罪。

被揀選接受救恩

[13]主所愛的弟兄姊妹們，我們應該常常為你們感謝上帝；因為上帝揀選了你們，藉着聖靈成聖的工作和你們對真理的信仰，使你們先得救①。[14]藉着我們所傳給你們的福音，上帝呼召了你們；他呼召你們來分享我們的主耶穌基督的榮耀。[15]所以，弟兄姊妹們，要有堅定的信心，對我們所教導的真理，無論是傳講的或是在書信中所寫的，你們都要堅守。

[16]上帝愛我們，由於他的恩典，他賜給我們永恆的毅力和美好的盼望。願這位父上帝和我們的主耶穌基督，[17]激勵你們，使你們有勇氣來宣傳和實行一切美善的事。

為我們禱告

3 末了，弟兄姊妹們，請為我們禱告，好使主的信息快快傳開，並且得到尊重，好像在你們中間被傳開、得尊重一樣。[2]也請你們祈求上帝救我們脫離邪惡的人，因為並不是人人都信從主。

[3]但是，主是信實的；他會使你們堅強，使你們不受那邪惡者的侵害。[4]主使我們對你們有信心，我們確信你們是在實行，並且要繼續實行我們所吩咐的。

[5]願主引導你們，使你們對上帝的愛有更深的體驗，並且有基督所賜的耐心。

盡工作的義務

[6]弟兄姊妹們，我們奉主耶穌基督的名命令你們：要遠離所有游手好閒、不遵守我們教導的信徒。[7]你們自己知道得很清楚，應該怎樣效法我們。我們跟你們在一起的時

① 「上帝揀選……使你們先得救」有些古卷是「上帝從起初揀選……使你們得救」。

were with you. ⁸We did not accept anyone's support without paying for it. Instead, we worked and toiled; we kept working day and night so as not to be an expense to any of you. ⁹We did this, not because we do not have the right to demand our support; we did it to be an example for you to follow. ¹⁰While we were with you, we used to tell you, "Whoever refuses to work is not allowed to eat."

¹¹We say this because we hear that there are some people among you who live lazy lives and who do nothing except meddle in other people's business. ¹²In the name of the Lord Jesus Christ we command these people and warn them to lead orderly lives and work to earn their own living.

¹³But you, friends, must not become tired of doing good. ¹⁴It may be that some there will not obey the message we send you in this letter. If so, take note of them and have nothing to do with them, so that they will be ashamed. ¹⁵But do not treat them as enemies; instead, warn them as believers.

Final Words

¹⁶May the Lord himself, who is our source of peace, give you peace at all times and in every way. The Lord be with you all.

¹⁷With my own hand I write this: *Greetings from Paul.* This is the way I sign every letter; this is how I write.

¹⁸May the grace of our Lord Jesus Christ be with you all.

候，並不偷懶，⁸也沒有白吃別人的飯，倒是辛苦勞碌，日夜做工，為的是不要連累你們。⁹我們這樣做，不是說我們無權要求生活上的供給，而是要你們學習我們的榜樣。¹⁰我們在你們那裏的時候說過：「不做工的人不得吃飯。」

¹¹我們說這話，是因為聽見你們當中有人過着游手好閒的生活，整天甚麼事都不做，專管別人的閒事。¹²這樣的人，我們奉主耶穌基督的名警告他們，命令他們，要安靜下來，親手做工來維持生活。

¹³但是，弟兄姊妹們，你們要不鬆懈地行善。¹⁴也許有人不肯服從我們在這封信上所吩咐的話；這樣的人，你們要提防，不要跟他同夥，使他覺得慚愧。¹⁵可是，不要把他當作敵人，要像對待信徒一樣勸導他。

祝福

¹⁶願賜平安的主隨時用各種方法賜平安給你們！願主與你們大家同在！

¹⁷我親筆寫：「保羅祝你們好。」我每一封信都這樣簽字；這是我的筆跡。

¹⁸願我們的主耶穌基督賜恩典給你們大家！

提摩太前書
1 TIMOTHY

INTRODUCTION

Timothy, a young Christian from Asia Minor, was the son of a Jewish mother and a Greek father. He became a companion and assistant to Paul in his missionary work. *Paul's First Letter to Timothy* deals with three main concerns.

The letter is first of all a warning against false teaching in the church. This teaching, a mixture of Jewish and non-Jewish ideas, was based on the belief that the physical world is evil and that one can attain salvation only by special secret knowledge and by practices such as avoiding certain foods and not marrying. The letter also contains instructions about church administration and worship, with a description of the kind of character that church leaders and helpers should have. Finally, Timothy is advised how to be a good servant of Jesus Christ and about the responsibilities that he has toward various groups of believers.

Outline of Contents

Introduction 1.1-2
Instructions concerning the church and its officers 1.3–3.16
Instructions to Timothy about his work 4.1-6.21

簡 介

提摩太是小亞細亞的一個青年基督徒；他的母親是猶太人，父親是希臘人。在保羅的宣道工作上，提摩太成為他的同工和助手。保羅致提摩太前書的主要內容有三點：

一．警告教會要提防虛偽的教義。這種教義混合着猶太和非猶太的思想，相信物質世界是邪惡的；人要獲得拯救必須只依靠特殊的祕密知識，以及禁戒某些食物和守獨身。

二．對教會行政和禮拜秩序的指示，討論教會領袖和助手們應有的品德。

三．指導提摩太怎樣作耶穌基督忠心的僕人，怎樣對各種不同的信徒盡勸戒教導的責任。

提要

1. 序言（1.1-2）
2. 對教會和教會領袖們的指示（1.3-3.16）
3. 指導提摩太怎樣作忠心的僕人（4.1-6.21）

---

1 From Paul, an apostle of Christ Jesus by order of God our Savior and Christ Jesus our hope–
²To Timothy, my true son in the faith:

May God the Father and Christ Jesus our Lord give you grace, mercy, and peace.

Warnings against False Teaching

³I want you to stay in Ephesus, just as I urged you when I was on my way to Macedonia. Some people there are teaching false

1 我是保羅；我奉我們的救主上帝和我們的盼望基督耶穌的命令，作基督耶穌的使徒。²我寫信給你—提摩太，就是我在信仰上的真兒子：

願父上帝和我們的主基督耶穌賜恩典、憐憫、平安給你！

譴責虛偽的教訓

³ 我希望你留在以弗所；我在往馬其頓去的時候曾經這樣吩咐過你。有些人在那裏傳

doctrines, and you must order them to stop. [4]Tell them to give up those legends and those long lists of ancestors, which only produce arguments; they do not serve God's plan, which is known by faith. [5]The purpose of this order is to arouse the love that comes from a pure heart, a clear conscience, and a genuine faith. [6]Some people have turned away from these and have lost their way in foolish discussions. [7]They want to be teachers of God's law, but they do not understand their own words or the matters about which they speak with so much confidence.

[8]We know that the Law is good if it is used as it should be used. [9]It must be remembered, of course, that laws are made, not for good people, but for lawbreakers and criminals, for the godless and sinful, for those who are not religious or spiritual, for those who kill their fathers or mothers, for murderers, [10]for the immoral, for sexual perverts, for kidnappers, for those who lie and give false testimony or who do anything else contrary to sound doctrine. [11]That teaching is found in the gospel that was entrusted to me to announce, the Good News from the glorious and blessed God.

Gratitude for God's Mercy

[12]I give thanks to Christ Jesus our Lord, who has given me strength for my work. I thank him for considering me worthy and appointing me to serve him, [13]even though in the past I spoke evil of him and persecuted and insulted him. But God was merciful to me because I did not yet have faith and so did not know what I was doing. [14]And our Lord poured out his abundant grace on me and gave me the faith and love which are ours in union with Christ Jesus. [15]This is a true saying, to be completely accepted and believed: Christ Jesus came into the world to save sinners. I am the worst of them, [16]but God was merciful to me in order that Christ Jesus might show his full patience in dealing with me, the worst of sinners, as an example for all those who would later believe in him and receive eternal life. [17]To the eternal King, immortal and invisible, the only God—to him be honor and glory forever and ever! Amen.

[18]Timothy, my child, I entrust to you this command, which is in accordance with the words of prophecy spoken in the past about you. Use those words as weapons in order to fight well, [19]and keep your faith and a clear conscience. Some people have not listened to their conscience and have made a ruin of their faith. [20]Among them are Hymenaeus and Alexander, whom I have punished by handing

不正確的教義，你必須命令他們停止。[4]叫他們要放棄那些荒唐的傳說和冗長的族譜；因為這些東西只會引起爭論，絲毫不能幫助了解上帝的計劃，這計劃是藉着信心才能了解的。[5]這命令的目的是要激發愛；這愛是從純潔的心、清白的良知，和純真的信心所產生的。[6]有些人離棄了這些，迷失在虛無的談論中。[7]他們想作上帝法律的導師，可是連自己所說的話都不明白，連自己那麼肯定主張的事都不清楚。

[8]我們知道，只要人能夠合宜地使用法律，法律原是好的。[9]當然，我們要了解這一點：法律不是為好人制定的，而是為那些不法、不受管束、不敬虔、犯罪、藐視宗教、貪戀世俗、弒父殺母、謀殺、[10]淫亂、親男色的、拐騙、撒謊、作假證、違反健全教義等一類的人。[11]這健全的教義是根據福音，就是那榮耀、可稱頌的上帝所交託我宣佈的。

感謝上帝的憐憫

[12]我感謝我們的主基督耶穌；因為他賜給我力量，以我為可信任的，指派我來事奉他。[13]雖然我從前毀謗過他，逼迫侮辱他。可是上帝憐憫我；因為那時候我不信他，不知道我在做些甚麼。[14]我們的主賜給我格外的恩典，使我有信心和愛心，這是因跟基督耶穌連結而有的。[15]「基督耶穌降世的目的是要拯救罪人」這話是可靠、值得完全接受的。我是罪人中最壞的一個，[16]可是這正是上帝憐憫我的原因，好使基督耶穌對我這罪人中最壞的一個顯示他充分的忍耐，使我得以作那些以後要信他、接受永恆生命的人的榜樣。[17]願尊貴、榮耀永遠歸於萬世的君王—那不朽、看不見、獨一無二的上帝！阿們。

[18]我兒提摩太啊，根據從前那有關你的預言，我把這命令付託給你。這些話要作為你上陣打美好的仗的武器。[19]要持守信仰和清白的良知。有些人不聽從自己的良知，因此他們的信仰觸了礁，[20]其中有舒米乃和亞歷山大；我已經把他們交在撒但手中，使他們

them over to the power of Satan; this will teach them to stop their blasphemy.

Church Worship

2 First of all, then, I urge that petitions, prayers, requests, and thanksgivings be offered to God for all people; [2]for kings and all others who are in authority, that we may live a quiet and peaceful life with all reverence toward God and with proper conduct. [3]This is good and it pleases God our Savior, [4]who wants everyone to be saved and to come to know the truth. [5]For there is one God, and there is one who brings God and human beings together, the man Christ Jesus, [6]who gave himself to redeem the whole human race. That was the proof at the right time that God wants everyone to be saved, [7]and that is why I was sent as an apostle and teacher of the Gentiles, to proclaim the message of faith and truth. I am not lying; I am telling the truth!

[8]In every church service I want the men to pray, men who are dedicated to God and can lift up their hands in prayer without anger or argument. [9]I also want the women to be modest and sensible about their clothes and to dress properly; not with fancy hair styles or with gold ornaments or pearls or expensive dresses, [10]but with good deeds, as is proper for women who claim to be religious. [11]Women should learn in silence and all humility. [12]I do not allow them to teach or to have authority over men; they must keep quiet. [13]For Adam was created first, and then Eve. [14]And it was not Adam who was deceived; it was the woman who was deceived and broke God's law. [15]But a woman will be saved through having children,[a] if she perseveres[b] in faith and love and holiness, with modesty.

Leaders in the Church

3 This is a true saying: If a man is eager to be a church leader, he desires an excellent work. [2]A church leader must be without fault; he must have only one wife,[c] be sober, self-controlled, and orderly; he must welcome strangers in his home; he must be able to teach; [3]he must not be a drunkard or a violent man, but gentle and peaceful; he must not love money; [4]he must be able to manage his own family well and make his children obey him with all respect. [5]For if a man does not know how to manage his own family, how can he take care of the church of God? [6]He must be mature in

a will be saved through having children; *or* will be kept safe through childbirth.
b if she perseveres; *or* if they persevere.
c have only one wife; *or* be married only once.

學會不再毀謗上帝。

教會裏的敬拜

2 首先，我勸你，要為所有的人向上帝祈求，禱告，代求，感恩；[2]也要為君王和所有在位的人禱告，使我們能過着安寧、和平、端正、虔敬的生活。[3]這是好的，是我們的救主上帝所喜歡的。[4]上帝要人人得救，都認識真理。[5]這真理就是說：只有一位上帝，在上帝和人之間有一位中間人，就是成為人的基督耶穌；[6]他犧牲自己為要使人類得自由，證明了在時機成熟的時候，上帝要人人得救。[7]為了這目的，我奉差遣作外邦人的傳道者和使徒，作教師來使他們相信並認識真理。我沒有撒謊；我所說的都是真的！

[8]在各地方的聚會，我希望男人禱告，虔誠地舉起手來禱告，不發怒，不爭論。

[9]我也希望女人穿戴樸素大方的衣飾；不要以奇異的髮型、金飾珠寶，或高價的衣裳為裝飾。[10]要有好行為，跟自己所表白的信仰相稱。[11]女人要默默地學習，事事謙卑。[12]我不准女人教導人，或管轄男人；她們要沉默。[13]因為上帝先造亞當，然後夏娃。[14]被誘惑的不是亞當，而是女人；她被誘惑，違背了上帝的法律。[15]但是，女人若安份守己，持守信心、愛心、聖潔，就會因生兒育女而得救。

教會的領袖

3 這話是可靠的。[1]有人說：誰有作教會領袖[2]的抱負，誰就是羨慕一件美好的工作。[2]教會領袖必須無可指責。他只能有一個妻子[3]；他為人要嚴肅，能管束自己，生活有規律，樂意款待異鄉人。他必須善於教導，[3]不酗酒，不好鬥，性情溫和良善，不貪愛錢財。[4]他必須善於處理自己家裏的事，使兒女知道順從，事事敬重。[5]一個人不知道處理自己的家，怎能看顧上帝的教會呢？[6]教會領袖也不應該是初參加教會的

[1]有些解經家認為這句話應緊接 2、15 節。
[2]「教會領袖」或譯「監督」。
[3]「他只能有一個妻子」或譯「他只能結一次婚」。

the faith, so that he will not swell up with pride and be condemned, as the Devil was. [7]He should be a man who is respected by the people outside the church, so that he will not be disgraced and fall into the Devil's trap.

Helpers in the Church

[8]Church helpers must also have a good character and be sincere; they must not drink too much wine or be greedy for money; [9]they should hold to the revealed truth of the faith with a clear conscience. [10]They should be tested first, and then, if they pass the test, they are to serve. [11]Their wives[d] also must be of good character and must not gossip; they must be sober and honest in everything. [12]A church helper must have only one wife,[e] and be able to manage his children and family well. [13]Those helpers who do their work well win for themselves a good standing and are able to speak boldly about their faith in Christ Jesus.

The Great Secret

[14]As I write this letter to you, I hope to come and see you soon. [15]But if I delay, this letter will let you know how we should conduct ourselves in God's household, which is the church of the living God, the pillar and support of the truth. [16]No one can deny how great is the secret of our religion:

He appeared in human form,
  was shown to be right by the Spirit,[f]
  · and was seen by angels.
He was preached among the nations,
  was believed in throughout the world,
    and was taken up to heaven.

False Teachers

4 The Spirit says clearly that some people will abandon the faith in later times; they will obey lying spirits and follow the teachings of demons. [2]Such teachings are spread by deceitful liars, whose consciences are dead, as if burnt with a hot iron. [3]Such people teach that it is wrong to marry and to eat certain foods. But God created those foods to be eaten, after a prayer of thanks, by those who are believers and have come to know the truth. [4]Everything that God has created is good; nothing is to be rejected, but everything is to be received with a prayer of thanks, [5]because the word of God and the prayer make it acceptable to God.

d Their wives; or Women helpers.
e have only one wife; or be married only once.
f was shown to be right by the Spirit; or and, in spiritual form, was shown to be right.

人，免得這人心高氣傲，蹈魔鬼的覆轍而被定罪。[7]他在教外也必須有好聲望，免得受毀謗，陷入魔鬼的圈套。

教會領袖的助手

[8]教會領袖的助手④也必須有好品格。他們必須說話誠實，不貪杯，不貪財；[9]應該以清白的良知持守信仰的奧祕。[10]他們應該先受考驗，証明無可指責才可以擔任職務。[11]他們的妻子⑤也得有好品行，不說閒話，要莊重，事事都誠實可靠。[12]教會領袖的助手只能有一個妻子⑥，而且必須善於管教兒女和治理家庭。[13]那些在工作上有好成績的助手會得到好聲譽，能夠坦然講論他們對基督耶穌的信仰。

極大的奧祕

[14]我一面寫這封信，一面希望快點來看你們；[15]如果躭擱了，這封信要告訴你們，我們在上帝的家應該怎樣生活。這個家就是永生上帝的教會，是眞理的柱石和基礎。[16]大家都宣認，我們信仰的奧祕是多麼的高深：
    他以人的形體顯現，
    由聖靈證明爲義，
    被天使們看見。
    他被萬邦傳揚，
    被世人信仰，
    被接到天上。

假教師

4 聖靈明明說了，在末後的時期，有些人會放棄信仰，去順從欺騙的靈和邪魔的道理。[2]這一套道理是從騙子的伎倆來的；他們的良心像是給熱鐵烙死了。[3]他們禁止嫁娶；他們禁吃某些食物，可是上帝造這些食物是要給信而明白眞理的人在感謝後吃的。[4]上帝所造的一切都是好的，都應該用感謝的心領受，不可拒絕，[5]因爲上帝的話和人的祈禱使這些食物成爲聖潔了。

④「教會領袖的助手」或譯「執事」。
⑤「他們的妻子」或譯「女助手」。
⑥「教會領袖的助手只能有一個妻子」或譯「教會領袖的助手只能結一次婚」。

A Good Servant of Christ Jesus

6If you give these instructions to the believers, you will be a good servant of Christ Jesus, as you feed yourself spiritually on the words of faith and of the true teaching which you have followed. 7But keep away from those godless legends, which are not worth telling. Keep yourself in training for a godly life. 8Physical exercise has some value, but spiritual exercise is valuable in every way, because it promises life both for the present and for the future. 9This is a true saying, to be completely accepted and believed. 10We struggleg and work hard, because we have placed our hope in the living God, who is the Savior of all and especially of those who believe.

11Give them these instructions and these teachings. 12Do not let anyone look down on you because you are young, but be an example for the believers in your speech, your conduct, your love, faith, and purity. 13Until I come, give your time and effort to the public reading of the Scriptures and to preaching and teaching. 14Do not neglect the spiritual gift that is in you, which was given to you when the prophets spoke and the elders laid their hands on you. 15Practice these things and devote yourself to them, in order that your progress may be seen by all. 16Watch yourself and watch your teaching. Keep on doing these things, because if you do, you will save both yourself and those who hear you.

Responsibilities toward Believers

5 Do not rebuke an older man, but appeal to him as if he were your father. Treat the younger men as your brotheis, 2the older women as mothers, and the younger women as sisters, with all purity.

3Show respect for widows who really are all alone. 4But if a widow has children or grandchildren, they should learn first to carry out their religious duties toward their own family and in this way repay their parents and grandparents, because that is what pleases God. 5A widow who is all alone, with no one to take care of her, has placed her hope in God and continues to pray and ask him for his help night and day. 6But a widow who gives herself to pleasure has already died, even though she lives. 7Give them these instructions, so that no one will find fault with them. 8But if any do not take care of their relatives, especially the members of their own family, they have denied the faith and are worse than an unbeliever.

9Do not add any widow to the list of widows unless she is over sixty years of age. In addi-

g struggle; *some manuscripts have* are reviled.

基督耶穌的好僕人

6 如果你把這些事指示弟兄姊妹們，你就是基督耶穌的好僕人；同時那信心的話和你一向跟從的正確道理會幫助你自己在靈性上長進。7 至於那些不值一談的荒唐傳說都應該避免；要為着敬度的生活鍛鍊自己。8 身體的鍛鍊固然有些益處，靈性的鍛鍊在各方面對你都有益處，因為後者帶來今生和來生的盼望。9 這話是可靠、值得完全接受的。10因此，我們辛勤努力⑦，把盼望寄託於永生的上帝；他是萬人的救主，更是信他的人的救主。

11 你要把這些事指示他們，教導他們。12別讓人小看你年輕。無論在言語、行為、愛心、信心，和純潔各方面，都要作信徒的榜樣。13你要在宣讀聖經、講道，和教導等工作上多下工夫，直到我來。14不要忽略了你屬靈的恩賜；這恩賜是藉着先知的預言和長老們的按手賜給你的。15這些事你要專心一意去做，讓大家看出你的長進。16你要謹慎自己，對你的教導也得小心。要有恆心做這些事；這樣，你不但能救自己，也能救你的聽眾。

對信徒的責任

5 不可斥責老年人；要勸他像勸自己的父親一樣。待年輕人要像待兄弟一樣；2 待年老的婦人要像待母親一樣；待年輕婦人要有純潔的心，像待姊妹一樣。

3 要尊敬真在守寡的婦女。4 如果一個寡婦有兒女或孫兒女，這些後輩就得先學習怎樣在家中盡孝道，來報答父母和祖父母，因為這是上帝所喜歡的。5 真在守寡的婦女無依無靠，只仰望上帝，日夜禱告，祈求他的幫助。6 至於專想享樂的寡婦，雖然活着，其實已經死了。7 你要這樣教導她們，免得她們受指責。8 如果有人不照顧親戚，尤其是自己家裏的人，他就是背棄信仰，比不信的人還要壞。

9 關於寡婦的登記，六十歲以上的才登

⑦有些古卷是「遭受譴責」。

tion, she must have been married only once[h] [10]and have a reputation for good deeds: a woman who brought up her children well, received strangers in her home, performed humble duties for other Christians, helped people in trouble, and devoted herself to doing good.

[11]But do not include younger widows in the list; because when their desires make them want to marry, they turn away from Christ, [12]and so become guilty of breaking their earlier promise to him. [13]They also learn to waste their time in going around from house to house; but even worse, they learn to be gossips and busy-bodies, talking of things they should not. [14]So I would prefer that the younger widows get married, have children, and take care of their homes, so as to give our enemies no chance of speaking evil of us. [15]For some widows have already turned away to follow Satan. [16]But if any Christian woman has widows in her family, she must take care of them and not put the burden on the church, so that it may take care of the widows who are all alone.

[17]The elders who do good work as leaders should be considered worthy of receiving double pay, especially those who work hard at preaching and teaching. [18]For the scripture says, "Do not muzzle an ox when you are using it to thresh grain" and "Workers should be given their pay." [19]Do not listen to an accusation against an elder unless it is brought by two or more witnesses. [20]Rebuke publicly all those who commit sins, so that the rest may be afraid.

[21]In the presence of God and of Christ Jesus and of the holy angels I solemnly call upon you to obey these instructions without showing any prejudice or favor to anyone in anything you do. [22]Be in no hurry to lay hands on people to dedicate them to the Lord's service. Take no part in the sins of others; keep yourself pure.

[23]Do not drink water only, but take a little wine to help your digestion, since you are sick so often.

[24]The sins of some people are plain to see, and their sins go ahead of them to judgment; but the sins of others are seen only later. [25]In the same way good deeds are plainly seen, and even those that are not so plain cannot be hidden.

6 Those who are slaves must consider their masters worthy of all respect, so that no one will speak evil of the name of God and of our teaching. [2]Slaves belonging to Christian masters must not despise them, for they are believers too. Instead, they are to serve them even better, because those who benefit from their work are believers whom they love.

h married only once; *or* faithful to her husband.

記；她們必須是只結過一次婚的，[10]而且必須有善行的聲譽，好比：善於養育兒女，接待遠客，洗信徒的腳，扶難濟急，盡力做各樣善事。

[11]至於年輕的寡婦，不要登記；因為她們性慾衝動，離棄基督，就想再嫁，[12]違背當初所許的願，因而取罪。[13]她們又學會了浪費光陰，挨家挨戶串門子。更糟的是，她們說長道短，專管閒事，說些不應說的話。[14]所以，我寧願年輕的寡婦再嫁，生兒育女，照顧自己的家，使敵對我們的人沒有攻擊的把柄。[15]因為已經有些寡婦改變初衷，隨着撒但去了。[16]如果信主的婦女家裏有寡婦，她就得照顧她們，不可把擔子推給教會；這樣，教會才能照顧那些無依無靠的寡婦。

[17]善於領導的長老們，尤其是在講道和教導上特別努力的，應該得到加倍的酬報。[18]因為聖經上說：「牛在踹穀的時候，不可籠住牠的嘴」；又說：「工人應得工錢。」[19]如果有人控告長老的事，除非有兩個或三個證人，就不必理會。[20]要公開譴責所有犯罪的人，好讓其他的人有所警惕。

[21]我在上帝、基督耶穌，和蒙揀選的天使面前，鄭重地吩咐你遵守這些教訓，不可在任何事上有成見或偏私的心。[22]不可隨便給人行按手禮。不可捲入別人的罪行中；要保守自己的純潔。

[23]因為你的身體常有毛病，不要只喝水，也喝點酒來幫助消化。

[24]有些人的罪是顯而易見的，他們早已受了審判；也有些人的罪是後來才顯露的。[25]同樣，善行是顯而易見的，即使不明顯也隱藏不了。

6 負軛為奴的，應當尊敬自己的主人，免得有人藉口毀謗上帝的名和我們的教導。[2]如果主人是信徒，作奴僕的不要因他們是信徒便怠慢他們，反要更殷勤伺候，因為那些受伺候得益處的人正是他們所愛的信徒。

False Teaching and True Riches

You must teach and preach these things. [3]Whoever teaches a different doctrine and does not agree with the true words of our Lord Jesus Christ and with the teaching of our religion [4]is swollen with pride and knows nothing. He has an unhealthy desire to argue and quarrel about words, and this brings on jealousy, disputes, insults, evil suspicions, [5]and constant arguments from people whose minds do not function and who no longer have the truth. They think that religion is a way to become rich.

[6]Well, religion does make us very rich, if we are satisfied with what we have. [7]What did we bring into the world? Nothing! What can we take out of the world? Nothing! [8]So then, if we have food and clothes, that should be enough for us. [9]But those who want to get rich fall into temptation and are caught in the trap of many foolish and harmful desires, which pull them down to ruin and destruction. [10]For the love of money is a source of all kinds of evil. Some have been so eager to have it that they have wandered away from the faith and have broken their hearts with many sorrows.

Personal Instructions

[11]But you, man of God, avoid all these things. Strive for righteousness, godliness, faith, love, endurance, and gentleness. [12]Run your best in the race of faith, and win eternal life for yourself; for it was to this life that God called you when you firmly protessed your faith before many witnesses. [13]Before God, who gives life to all things, and before Christ Jesus, who firmly professed his faith before Pontius Pilate, I command you [14]to obey your orders and keep them faithfully until the Day when our Lord Jesus Christ will appear. [15]His appearing will be brought about at the right time by God, the blessed and only Ruler, the King of kings and the Lord of lords. [16]He alone is immortal; he lives in the light that no one can approach. No one has ever seen him; no one can ever see him. To him be honor and eternal power! Amen.

[17]Command those who are rich in the things of this life not to be proud, but to place their hope, not in such an uncertain thing as riches, but in God, who generously gives us everything for our enjoyment. [18]Command them to do good, to be rich in good works, to be generous and ready to share with others. [19]In this way they will store up for themselves a treasure which will be a solid foundation for the future. And then they will be able to win the life which

假教義和眞財富

你應該教訓和勸導這些事：[3]如果有人宣講不同的教義，跟我們主耶穌基督那健全的信息以及敬虔的教義不相符合，[4]就是自高自大，極端的無知。這種人顯然喜歡辯論，喜歡在字句上吹毛求疵，因而造成嫉妒、紛爭、毀謗、猜疑，[5]引起那些心術不正、喪失眞理的人無休無止地爭吵。在他們的心目中，宗教不過是發財的門徑罷了。

[6]是的，一個人若知足，宗教的確可以使他富有。[7]我們到這世界，沒有帶來甚麼；我們又能從這世界帶走甚麼呢？[8]如果我們有得吃，有得穿，就該知足。[9]那些想發財的人是掉在誘惑裏，被許多無知和有害的慾望抓住，終於沉沒毀滅了。[10]貪財是萬惡的根源。有些人因貪慕錢財而背離了信仰，飽嘗痛苦，心靈破碎。

給提摩太的指示

[11]至於你，你是上帝所重用的人，你要遠避這一切。要追求正義、敬虔、信心、愛心、忍耐，和溫柔。[12]在信仰的競賽上要盡力奔跑，爲自己贏得永恆的生命；就是爲了這個目的，你蒙上帝呼召，在許多證人面前公開宣認了那美好的信仰。[13]其實，基督耶穌在龐修·彼拉多面前作證時，也同樣做過美好的宣認。在賜生命給萬物的上帝和這位耶穌面前，我吩咐你：[14]要忠誠，無可指責地遵守所受的命令，直到我們的主耶穌基督顯現的那一天。[15]上帝要在時機成熟的時候使他顯現；上帝是可受頌讚、獨一無二的全能者，萬王的王，萬主的主。[16]惟有他是不朽不滅的。他住在人所不能靠近的光裏；沒有人見過他，也沒有人能看見他。願尊貴和永恆的主權都歸於他！阿們。

[17]對那些今世富足的人，你要警戒他們不可驕傲。不要把希望寄託在不可靠的財物上，而要倚靠那把萬物豐豐富富地賜給我們享受的上帝。[18]要吩咐他們行善，多做好事，慷慨施捨，隨時濟助。[19]這樣，他們就是在爲自己積存財寶，爲將來建立堅固的根

is true life.

20Timothy, keep safe what has been entrusted to your care. Avoid the profane talk and foolish arguments of what some people wrongly call "Knowledge." 21For some have claimed to possess it, and as a result they have lost the way of faith.

God's grace be with you all.

基，好把握生命，那眞正的生命。

20 提摩太啊，你要好好地持守你所接受的託付。要避免那些不敬虔的空談和所謂「知識」的荒謬爭論。21有些人以爲他們已經有了這種知識，以致在信仰上迷失了方向。

願上帝賜恩典給你們！

提摩太後書
2 TIMOTHY

INTRODUCTION

Paul's Second Letter to Timothy consists largely of personal advice to Timothy, as a younger colleague and assistant. The main theme is endurance. Timothy is advised and encouraged to keep on witnessing faithfully to Jesus Christ, to hold to the true teaching of the Good News and the Old Testament, and to do his duty as teacher and evangelist, all in the face of suffering and opposition.

Timothy is especially warned about the dangers of becoming involved in "foolish and ignorant arguments" that do no good, but only ruin the people who listen to them.

In all this, Timothy is reminded of the example of the writer's own life and purpose-his faith, patience, love, endurance, and suffering in persecution.

Outline of Contents

Introduction 1.1-2
Praise and exhortation 1.3-2.13
Counsel and warning 2.14-4.5
Paul's own situation 4.6-18
Conclusion 4.19-22

簡　介

提摩太後書多半是保羅個人指導他年輕同工和助手的話。主要的論題是堅忍。保羅勸勉提摩太，要不畏懼任何艱難，始終忠心見證耶穌基督，堅守基督福音和舊約的純正教義，負起教師和傳道人的責任。

保羅特別告誡提摩太，要棄絕「愚拙無知的辯論」；因爲那種辯論毫無益處，只會腐化聽之人。

保羅希望提摩太能以他自己的生平爲榜樣，學習他的信心、忍耐、愛心、堅忍，並忍受壓迫的痛苦。

提要

1. 序言（1.1－2）
2. 稱讚和勸勉（1.3－2.13）
3. 指導和警告（2.14－4.5）
4. 保羅自己的處境（4.6－18）
5. 結語（4.19－22）

---

1 From Paul, an apostle of Christ Jesus by God's will, sent to proclaim the promised life which we have in union with Christ Jesus– 2To Timothy, my dear son:

May God the Father and Christ Jesus our Lord give you grace, mercy, and peace.

Thanksgiving and Encouragement
3I give thanks to God, whom I serve with a clear conscience, as my ancestors did. I thank

1 我是保羅；我奉上帝的旨意作基督耶穌的使徒，來宣佈他藉着基督耶穌所應許的新生命。2我寫信給你—我親愛的兒子提摩太：

願父上帝和我們的主基督耶穌賜恩典、憐憫、平安給你！

感謝和鼓勵
3 我感謝上帝，就是那位我跟祖宗一樣用

him as I remember you always in my prayers night and day. [4]I remember your tears, and I want to see you very much, so that I may be filled with joy. [5]I remember the sincere faith you have, the kind of faith that your grandmother Lois and your mother Eunice also had. I am sure that you have it also. [6]For this reason I remind you to keep alive the gift that God gave you when I laid my hands on you. [7]For the Spirit that God has given us does not make us timid; instead, his Spirit fills us with power, love, and self-control.

[8]Do not be ashamed, then, of witnessing for our Lord; neither be ashamed of me, a prisoner for Christ's sake. Instead, take your part in suffering for the Good News, as God gives you the strength for it. [9]He saved us and called us to be his own people, not because of what we have done, but because of his own purpose and grace. He gave us this grace by means of Christ Jesus before the beginning of time, [10]but now it has been revealed to us through the coming of our Savior, Christ Jesus. He has ended the power of death and through the gospel has revealed immortal life.

[11]God has appointed me as an apostle and teacher to proclaim the Good News, [12]and it is for this reason that I suffer these things. But I am still full of confidence, because I know whom I have trusted, and I am sure that he is able to keep safe until that Day what he has entrusted to me.[a] [13]Hold firmly to the true words that I taught you, as the example for you to follow, and remain in the faith and love that are ours in union with Christ Jesus. [14]Through the power of the Holy Spirit, who lives in us, keep the good things that have been entrusted to you.

[15]You know that everyone in the province of Asia, including Phygelus and Hermogenes, has deserted me. [16]May the Lord show mercy to the family of Onesiphorus, because he cheered me up many times. He was not ashamed that I am in prison, [17]but as soon as he arrived in Rome, he started looking for me until he found me. [18]May the Lord grant him his mercy on that Day! And you know very well how much he did for me in Ephesus.

A Loyal Soldier of Christ Jesus

2 As for you, my son, be strong through the grace that is ours in union with Christ Jesus. [2]Take the teachings that you heard me proclaim in the presence of many witnesses,

---

清白的良心所敬拜的上帝。我日夜在禱告中懷念着你，[4]一想起你惜別時所流的眼淚，我就急切地想要見你；見到你，我就會滿心快樂。[5]我記得你那純真的信心，就是你外祖母羅綺和你母親友妮基所有的那種信心。她們的信心，我相信你也有了。[6]所以，我提醒你：那在我為你按手時上帝所賜給你的恩賜，你要使它像火一樣燃燒不熄。[7]因為，上帝所賜給我們的靈不使我們膽怯；相反地，他的靈會使我們充滿力量、愛心，和自制。

[8]因此，你不要把為我們的主作證當作一件羞恥的事，也不要因我為了主的緣故成為囚犯而覺得羞恥。你要按照上帝所賜的力量，為福音分擔苦難。[9]上帝拯救我們，呼召我們作他的子民，並不是因為我們有甚麼好行為，而是出於他的旨意和恩典。他在萬世以前就藉着基督耶穌把這恩典賜給了我們，[10]現在由於我們的救主基督耶穌的來臨而實現了。基督已經毀滅了死亡的權勢，更藉着福音把不朽的生命彰顯出來。

[11]為了這福音，上帝指派我作傳道者、使徒，和教師。[12]因此，我才受這些苦難。但是，我仍然滿懷確信；因為我知道我所信靠的是誰，也深信他能夠保守他所付託給我的①，直到主再來的日子。[13]你要堅守我所給你的那健全的信息，作為你的規範，也要守住我們跟基督耶穌連結所得到的信心和愛心。[14]要藉着住在我們內心的聖靈持守那付託給你的美善。

[15]你知道，在亞細亞省的人都離棄了我，包括腓吉路和黑摩其尼在內。[16]願主憐憫阿尼色弗一家；因為他屢次鼓勵我，使我精神愉快。他不因我作囚犯而覺得羞恥，[17]一到羅馬就四處尋找我，終於找到了。[18]願主使他在那日子得到主的憐憫！至於他在以弗所為我做的許多事，你是清楚知道的。

基督的忠勇戰士

2 我兒啊，你要藉着基督耶穌所賜的恩典剛強起來。[2]你在許多證人面前從我領受了的教導，你也應該交付給你所信任而能

---

a what he has entrusted to me; *or* what I have entrusted to him.

①「他所付託給我的」或譯「我所付託給他的」。

and entrust them to reliable people, who will be able to teach others also.

³Take your part in suffering, as a loyal soldier of Christ Jesus. ⁴A soldier on active duty wants to please his commanding officer and so does not get mixed up in the affairs of civilian life. ⁵An athlete who runs in a race cannot win the prize unless he obeys the rules. ⁶The farmer who has done the hard work should have the first share of the harvest. ⁷Think about what I am saying, because the Lord will enable you to understand it all.

⁸Remember Jesus Christ, who was raised from death, who was a descendant of David, as is taught in the Good News I preach. ⁹Because I preach the Good News, I suffer and I am even chained like a criminal. But the word of God is not in chains, ¹⁰and so I endure everything for the sake of God's chosen people, in order that they too may obtain the salvation that comes through Christ Jesus and brings eternal glory. ¹¹This is a true saying:

"If we have died with him,
    we shall also live with him.
¹² If we continue to endure,
    we shall also rule with him.
If we deny him,
    he also will deny us.
¹³ If we are not faithful,
    he remains faithful,
    because he cannot be false to himself."

An Approved Worker

¹⁴Remind your people of this, and give them a solemn warning in God's presence not to fight over words. It does no good, but only ruins the people who listen. ¹⁵Do your best to win full approval in God's sight, as a worker who is not ashamed of his work, one who correctly teaches the message of God's truth. ¹⁶Keep away from profane and foolish discussions, which only drive people farther away from God. ¹⁷Such teaching is like an open sore that eats away the flesh. Two men who have taught such things are Hymenaeus and Philetus. ¹⁸They have left the way of truth and are upsetting the faith of some believers by saying that our resurrection has already taken place. ¹⁹But the solid foundation that God has laid cannot be shaken; and on it are written these words: "The Lord knows those who are his" and "Those who say that they belong to the Lord must turn away from wrongdoing."

²⁰In a large house there are dishes and bowls of all kinds: some are made of silver and gold,

夠教導別人的人。

³ 作為基督耶穌的忠勇戰士，你要分擔苦難。⁴ 一個入伍的兵士要爭取長官的嘉許就不能讓營外的事務纏擾他。⁵ 一個賽跑的人在競賽的時候不遵守規則就不能得獎。⁶ 辛勤耕作的農夫應該首先享受所收成的穀物。⁷ 你要思想我所說的話，因為主必定使你能領悟一切的事。

⁸ 你要記得耶穌基督，他是大衛的後代，上帝使他從死裏復活；這就是我所傳的福音。⁹ 我因為傳這福音而遭受苦難，甚至被捆綁，像囚犯一樣。但是，上帝的話是不受捆綁的。¹⁰ 因此，我為了上帝所揀選的子民忍受這一切，好使他們也能得到那從基督耶穌來的拯救和永恆的榮耀。¹¹ 以下這話是可靠的：

    如果我們已跟他同死，
    我們也會跟他同活。
¹² 如果我們忍耐到底，
    我們也會跟他一同掌權。
    如果我們不認他，
    他也會不認我們。
¹³ 如果我們失信，
    他依然信實可靠，
    因為他不違背自己。

蒙嘉許的工人

¹⁴ 你要提醒大家，在上帝面前鄭重地勸誡他們：不要在言詞上爭辯；那是毫無益處的，只會腐化聽的人。¹⁵ 要努力在上帝面前作一個經得起考驗、問心無愧的工人，正確地講解真理的信息。¹⁶ 要遠避荒唐無稽的空談，因為這一類的談話使人遠離上帝；¹⁷ 他們所談的是像那腐蝕肌肉的毒瘡。這些人當中有舒米乃和腓理徒；¹⁸ 他們離開了真理，竟說復活的事已成為過去，因而動搖了某些人的信心。¹⁹ 可是，上帝所建立那鞏固的根基是不動搖的；在這基石上面刻著：「主認得屬他的人」，又刻著：「那自稱為屬主的人必須離棄邪惡。」

²⁰ 每一個大屋子裏都有許多器皿，不僅有

others of wood and clay; some are for special occasions, others for ordinary use. ²¹Those who make themselves clean from all those evil things, will be used for special purposes, because they are dedicated and useful to their Master, ready to be used for every good deed. ²²Avoid the passions of youth, and strive for righteousness, faith, love, and peace, together with those who with a pure heart call out to the Lord for help. ²³But keep away from foolish and ignorant arguments; you know that they end up in quarrels. ²⁴As the Lord's servant, you must not quarrel. You must be kind toward all, a good and patient teacher, ²⁵who is gentle as you correct your opponents, for it may be that God will give them the opportunity to repent and come to know the truth. ²⁶And then they will come to their senses and escape from the trap of the Devil, who had caught them and made them obey his will.

The Last Days

3 Remember that there will be difficult times in the last days. ²People will be selfish, greedy, boastful, and conceited; they will be insulting, disobedient to their parents, ungrateful, and irreligious; ³they will be unkind, merciless, slanderers, violent, and fierce; they will hate the good; ⁴they will be treacherous, reckless, and swollen with pride; they will love pleasure rather than God; ⁵they will hold to the outward form of our religion, but reject its real power. Keep away from such people. ⁶Some of them go into people's houses and gain control over weak women who are burdened by the guilt of their sins and driven by all kinds of desires, ⁷women who are always trying to learn but who can never come to know the truth. ⁸As Jannes and Jambres were opposed to Moses, so also these people are opposed to the truth–people whose minds do not function and who are failures in the faith. ⁹But they will not get very far, because everyone will see how stupid they are. That is just what happened to Jannes and Jambres.

Last Instructions

¹⁰But you have followed my teaching, my conduct, and my purpose in life; you have observed my faith, my patience, my love, my endurance, ¹¹my persecutions, and my sufferings. You know all that happened to me in Antioch, Iconium, and Lystra, the terrible persecutions I endured! But the Lord rescued me from them all. ¹²Everyone who wants to live a godly life in union with Christ Jesus will be persecuted; ¹³and evil persons and impostors will keep on going from bad to worse, deceiving others and being deceived themselves. ¹⁴But as

金器、銀器,也有木器、瓦器;有的用在特別的場合,有的用在普通的場合。²¹人如果自潔,脫離一切邪惡的事,就能夠被主所器重;因為他已獻給主,為主所重用,來做各樣善事。

²²你不要像少年人意氣用事;要跟那些心地純潔、祈求主幫助的人一同追求正義、信心、愛心,與和平。²³要棄絕那種愚拙無知的辯論;你知道,這種辯論往往會引起爭吵。²⁴主的僕人不可爭吵;他應該和氣待人,殷勤善導,處處忍耐,²⁵用溫柔規勸敵對的人。也許上帝會給他們悔改的機會,使他們認識真理。²⁶這樣,雖然他們被魔鬼抓去,被迫順服了他,他們也會醒悟,從他的羅網中掙脫出來。

世界的末期

3 你要知道,世界的末期會有種種苦難。²那時候,人只顧自己,貪財,自誇,狂傲,毀謗,忤逆父母,忘恩負義,不聖潔,³沒有親情,殘忍,散播謠言,蠻橫,凶暴,恨惡良善。⁴他們出賣師友,任意妄為,狂妄自大,愛享樂過於愛上帝。⁵他們披着宗教的外衣,卻拒絕宗教的實質。這一類的人,你們要躲避他們。⁶他們當中有些人穿門入戶,到別人家裏去,迷惑意志薄弱、被罪過所壓制、被各種慾望所支配的婦女們。⁷這些婦女雖然常常想要學習,卻無法認識真理。⁸就像從前雅尼和洋布雷怎樣反對摩西,現在這些人照樣在反對真理。他們心思敗壞,在信仰上經不起考驗,⁹再也發生不了甚麼作用;因為他們的愚昧會在眾人面前暴露無遺,正像雅尼和洋布雷一樣。

最後的指示

¹⁰但是,你已經跟隨了我的教導和人生觀,仿效了我的行為、信心、寬容、愛心、忍耐,¹¹並分擔了我所受的迫害和痛苦。我在安提阿、以哥念、路司得這些地方所遭遇、所忍受的迫害,你都知道;但是,主救我脫離了這一切。¹²凡是立志跟從基督耶穌、過敬虔生活的人,都會遭受迫害。¹³邪惡的人和騙子們也會一天比一天壞;他們欺騙別人,自己也被欺騙了。¹⁴至於你,你要

for you, continue in the truths that you were taught and firmly believe. You know who your teachers were, [15]and you remember that ever since you were a child, you have known the Holy Scriptures, which are able to give you the wisdom that leads to salvation through faith in Christ Jesus. [16]All Scripture is inspired by God and is useful[b] for teaching the truth, rebuking error, correcting faults, and giving instruction for right living, [17]so that the person who serves God may be fully qualified and equipped to do every kind of good deed.

4 In the presence of God and of Christ Jesus, who will judge the living and the dead, and because he is coming to rule as King, I solemnly urge you [2]to preach the message, to insist upon proclaiming it (whether the time is right or not), to convince, reproach, and encourage, as you teach with all patience. [3]The time will come when people will not listen to sound doctrine, but will follow their own desires and will collect for themselves more and more teachers who will tell them what they are itching to hear. [4]They will turn away from listening to the truth and give their attention to legends. [5]But you must keep control of yourself in all circumstances; endure suffering, do the work of a preacher of the Good News, and perform your whole duty as a servant of God.

[6]As for me, the hour has come for me to be sacrificed; the time is here for me to leave this life. [7]I have done my best in the race, I have run the full distance, and I have kept the faith.[c] [8]And now there is waiting for me the victory prize of being put right with God, which the Lord, the righteous Judge, will give me on that Day–and not only to me, but to all those who wait with love for him to appear.

Personal Words

[9]Do your best to come to me soon. [10]Demas fell in love with this present world and has deserted me, going off to Thessalonica. Crescens went to Galatia, and Titus to Dalmatia. [11]Only Luke is with me. Get Mark and bring him with you, because he can help me in the work. [12]I sent Tychicus to Ephesus. [13]When you come, bring my coat that I left in Troas with Carpus; bring the books too, and especially the ones made of parchment.

[14]Alexander the metalworker did me great harm; the Lord will reward him according to what he has done. [15]Be on your guard against

b All Scripture is inspired by God and is useful; or Every scripture inspired by God is also useful.
c kept the faith; or been true to my promise.

持守你所接受和確信的眞理。你曉得誰是你的導師；[15]你也記得你從小就明白聖經，就是能給你智慧、指引你藉着信基督耶穌而獲得拯救的那本書。[16]全部聖經是受上帝靈感而寫的[②]，對於教導眞理，指責謬誤，糾正過錯，指示人生正路，都有益處，[17]要使事奉上帝的人得到充分的準備，能做各種善事。

4 在上帝和那位要審判所有活人死人的基督耶穌面前，憑着他的顯現和他的主權，我迫切地勸告你：[2]要傳福音，不管時機理想不理想都要傳，用最大的耐心勸勉，督責，鼓勵，教導。[3]時候將到，那時人要拒絕健全的教義，隨從自己的慾望，到處拜人爲師，好來滿足他們發癢的耳朵。[4]他們掩耳不聽眞理的話，卻傾向荒唐的傳說。[5]至於你，無論在任何情況下都要謹慎；要忍受苦難，做傳道人應做的工作，忠心履行你事奉的職務。

[6]至於我，我犧牲自己的時候到了；現在就是我離開人世的時刻。[7]那值得競爭的賽跑，我已經跑過；該跑的全程，我已經跑完；該守的信仰，我已經守住。[8]從今以後，有公義的華冠等着我，就是那以公義施行審判的主在基督再來的日子要賜給我的，不但賜給我，也要賜給所有愛慕他顯現的人。

私事的囑咐

[9]你要盡快到我這裏來。[10]底馬貪愛現世，離開我到帖撒羅尼迦去了。革勒士到加拉太去，提多到撻馬太去，[11]只有路加跟我在一起。你要去找馬可，帶他一起來，因爲他會幫助我的工作。[12]我已經派推基古到以弗所去。[13]你來的時候，要把我在特羅亞時留在加布家裏那一件外衣帶來；同時要把那些書，尤其是那幾本羊皮書卷也一起帶來。

[14]銅匠亞歷山大害我不淺；主會照他所做的報應他。[15]你自己也得提防他，因爲他極

②「全部聖經是受上帝靈感而寫的」或譯「受上帝靈感而寫的每一卷聖經」。

him yourself, because he was violently opposed to our message.

16No one stood by me the first time I defended myself; all deserted me. May God not count it against them! 17But the Lord stayed with me and gave me strength, so that I was able to proclaim the full message for all the Gentiles to hear; and I was rescued from being sentenced to death. 18And the Lord will rescue me from all evil and take me safely into his heavenly Kingdom. To him be the glory forever and ever! Amen.

Final Greetings

19I send greetings to Priscilla and Aquila and to the family of Onesiphorus. 20Erastus stayed in Corinth, and I left Trophimus in Miletus, because he was sick. 21Do your best to come before winter.

Eubulus, Pudens, Linus, and Claudia send their greetings, and so do all the other Christians.

22The Lord be with your spirit.

God's grace be with you all.

力反對我們所傳的信息。

16我第一次為自己辯護的時候，沒有人在我身邊，大家都離棄了我。願上帝不加罪於他們！17主在旁支持我，給我力量，使我能夠把信息完整地傳給所有的外邦人；我也從獅子口裏被救了出來。18主一定會救我脫離一切邪惡，接我安全地到他的天國去。願榮耀永永遠遠歸於他！阿們。

最後問安

19請替我向百基拉、亞居拉，和阿尼色弗一家問安。20以拉都在哥林多住下了。特羅非摩害病，我讓他留在米利都。21你要盡可能在冬季以前來。

友布羅、布田、利努、喀勞底雅，和其他所有的弟兄姊妹們都向你問安。

22願主與你同在！願上帝賜恩典給你們！

提多書
TITUS

INTRODUCTION

Titus was a Gentile convert to Christianity who became a fellow worker and assistant to Paul in his missionary work. *Paul's Letter to Titus* is addressed to his young helper in Crete, who had been left there to supervise the work of the church. The letter expresses three main concerns.

First, Titus is reminded of the kind of character that church leaders should have, especially in view of the bad character of many Cretans. Next, Titus is advised how to teach the various groups in the church, the older men, the older women (who are, in turn, to teach the younger women), the young men, and the slaves. Finally, the writer gives Titus advice regarding Christian conduct, especially the need to be peaceful and friendly, and to avoid hatred, argument, and division in the church.

Outline of Contents

Introduction 1.1-4
Church officers 1.5-16
Duties of various groups in the church 2.1-15
Exhortations and warning 3.1-11
Conclusion 3.12-15

簡　介

提多是一個皈依基督教的外邦人，以後成為保羅宣教工作的同工和助手。保羅致提多的信就是寫給這位當時在克里特的年輕助手；他曾留在那裏指導教會的工作。這封信討論三件重要的事：

一．保羅提醒提多，處在道德低落的克里特人中，教會領袖所應具備的品格和條件。

二．保羅告訴提多怎樣教導教會中各種類型的人──老年人、年老的婦女（讓她們再去教導年輕婦女）、青年人，和奴隸。

三．保羅指示一般基督徒應有的品行，特別注重要以和平友善的態度待人，以及避免憤恨、爭辯，或在教會裏製造紛爭。

提要

1. 序言（1.1-4）
2. 教會領袖（1.5-16）
3. 教會各成員的責任（2.1-15）
4. 勸勉和警告（3.1-11）
5. 結語（3.12-15）

---

1 From Paul, a servant of God and an apostle of Jesus Christ.

I was chosen and sent to help the faith of God's chosen people and to lead them to the truth taught by our religion, [2]which is based on the hope for eternal life. God, who does not lie, promised us this life before the beginning of time, [3]and at the right time he revealed it in his message. This was entrusted to me, and I proclaim it by order of God our Savior.

[4]I write to Titus, my true son in the faith that

1 我──保羅是上帝的僕人，耶穌基督的使徒。我蒙召、奉差遣去幫助上帝選民的信仰，引領他們認識我們的信仰所教導的真理；[2]這真理是以盼望永恆的生命為根據的。那不撒謊的上帝，在萬世以前，已經應許把這永恆的生命賜給我們，[3]在時機成熟的時候，便藉着信息的宣揚顯明出來。我受了付託，奉上帝──我們救主的命令負起傳揚這信息的任務。

[4] 提多，我現在寫信給你；你在我們共同

we have in common.

May God the Father and Christ Jesus our Savior give you grace and peace.

Titus' Work in Crete

⁵I left you in Crete, so that you could put in order the things that still needed doing and appoint church elders in every town. Remember my instructions: ⁶an elder must be without fault; he must have only one wife,ᵃ and his children must be believers and not have the reputation of being wild or disobedient. ⁷For since a church leader is in charge of God's work, he should be without fault. He must not be arrogant or quick-tempered, or a drunkard or violent or greedy for money. ⁸He must be hospitable and love what is good. He must be self-controlled, upright, holy, and disciplined. ⁹He must hold firmly to the message which can be trusted and which agrees with the doctrine. In this way he will be able to encourage others with the true teaching and also to show the error of those who are opposed to it.

¹⁰For there are many, especially the converts from Judaism, who rebel and deceive others with their nonsense. ¹¹It is necessary to stop their talk, because they are upsetting whole families by teaching what they should not, and all for the shameful purpose of making money. ¹²⁻¹³It was a Cretan himself, one of their own prophets, who spoke the truth when he said, "Cretans are always liars, wicked beasts, and lazy gluttons." For this reason you must rebuke them sharply, so that they may have a healthy faith ¹⁴and no longer hold on to Jewish legends and to human commandments which come from people who have rejected the truth. ¹⁵Everything is pure to those who are themselves pure; but nothing is pure to those who are defiled and unbelieving, for their minds and consciences have been defiled. ¹⁶They claim that they know God, but their actions deny it. They are hateful and disobedient, not fit to do anything good.

Sound Doctrine

2 But you must teach what agrees with sound doctrine. ²Instruct the older men to be sober, sensible, and self-controlled; to be sound in their faith, love, and endurance. ³In the same way instruct the older women to behave as women should who live a holy life. They must not be slanderers or slaves to wine. They must teach what is good, ⁴in order to train the younger women to love their husbands and children, ⁵to be self-controlled and pure, and to be good

a have only one wife; or be married only once.

的信仰上是我的真兒子。

願父上帝和我們的救主基督耶穌賜恩典、平安給你！

提多在克里特的工作

⁵ 我把你留在克里特，目的是要你處理那些還沒有辦完的事務，並且在各城市設立長老。我曾經吩咐過：⁶ 當長老的必須是無可指責的人。他只能有一個妻子①；他的兒女都應該是信徒，沒有放蕩或不受管教的事。⁷ 他既然作教會的領袖②，作上帝的管家，就應該是無可指責的。他必須不傲慢，不暴躁，不酗酒，不好鬥，不貪財；⁸ 要樂意接待人，喜歡做好事，莊敬自重，要正直，聖潔，能管束自己。⁹ 他必須堅守那可靠、符合教義的教訓。這樣，他就能夠用健全的教義來感化別人，同時糾正那些反對的人的錯誤。

¹⁰ 因為有許多人叛道，用荒唐無稽的話欺騙別人，尤其是那些主張受割禮的猶太基督徒。¹¹ 你必須禁止這些人說話；因為，他們為了貪圖錢財，已經用不該傳講的學說破壞了許多家庭。¹² 他們克里特人自己有一個先知說過這樣的話：「克里特人總是撒謊，是惡獸，好吃懶做。」¹³ 他這話沒有講錯。所以，你必須嚴厲地責備他們，好使他們有健全的信仰，¹⁴ 不再聽猶太人那些荒唐的傳說和那些背棄真理的人所堅持的規例。¹⁵ 對潔淨的人來說，一切都是潔淨的；但對那些污穢和不信的人來說，沒有一件東西是潔淨的，因為他們的心地和良知都污穢不堪。¹⁶ 他們宣稱認識上帝，卻在行為上否認他。他們是可惡的，是叛徒，做不出甚麼好事來。

健全的教義

2 至於你，你的教導必須合乎健全的教義。² 你要勸老年人，要他們嚴肅，有好品格，管束自己，要有健全的信心、愛心，和耐心。³ 你也要勸年老的婦女，要行為謹慎。不可搬弄是非，不作酒的奴隸。要作好榜樣，⁴ 善導年輕婦女，訓練她們怎樣愛丈夫和兒女，⁵ 怎樣管束自己，要貞潔，

① 「他只能有一個妻子」或譯「他只能結一次婚」。
② 「教會的領袖」或「監督」。

housewives who submit themselves to their husbands, so that no one will speak evil of the message that comes from God.

6In the same way urge the young men to be self-controlled. 7In all things you yourself must be an example of good behavior. Be sincere and serious in your teaching. 8Use sound words that cannot be criticized, so that your enemies may be put to shame by not having anything bad to say about us.

9Slaves are to submit themselves to their masters and please them in all things. They must not talk back to them 10or steal from them. Instead, they must show that they are always good and faithful, so as to bring credit to the teaching about God our Savior in all they do.

11For God has revealed his grace for the salvation of all people. 12That grace instructs us to give up ungodly living and worldly passions, and to live self-controlled, upright, and godly lives in this world, 13as we wait for the blessed Day we hope for, when the glory of our great God and Savior Jesus Christ[b] will appear. 14He gave himself for us, to rescue us from all wickedness and to make us a pure people who belong to him alone and are eager to do good.

15Teach these things and use your full authority as you encourage and rebuke your hearers. Let none of them look down on you.

Christian Conduct

3 Remind your people to submit to rulers and authorities, to obey them, and to be ready to do good in every way. 2Tell them not to speak evil of anyone, but to be peaceful and friendly, and always to show a gentle attitude toward everyone. 3For we ourselves were once foolish, disobedient, and wrong. We were slaves to passions and pleasures of all kinds. We spent our lives in malice and envy; others hated us and we hated them. 4But when the kindness and love of God our Savior was revealed, 5he saved us. It was not because of any good deeds that we ourselves had done, but because of his own mercy that he saved us, through the Holy Spirit, who gives us new birth and new life by washing us. 6God poured out the Holy Spirit abundantly on us through Jesus Christ our Savior, 7so that by his grace we might be put right with God and come into possession of the eternal life we hope for. 8This is a true saying.

I want you to give special emphasis to these matters, so that those who believe in God may

b our great God and Savior Jesus Christ; or the great God and our Savior Jesus Christ.

勤於家務，慈善，順服丈夫，免得上帝的道受毀謗。

6 同樣，你也要勸年輕人，要他們管束自己。7你自己呢，無論在甚麼事上都要有好行為，作別人的模範。教導人要誠懇、嚴肅，8言語要恰當，讓人家沒有批評的餘地。這樣，那些敵對的人，因為找不到我們的錯處，就會覺得慚愧，無話可說。

9 你們要勸作奴僕的，要他們服從主人，事事討主人的喜歡，不可頂撞他們，10也不可偷竊，卻要事事表現忠厚可靠，好使在所做的一切事上，讓有關我們救主上帝的教義更受尊重。

11 因為上帝拯救全人類的恩典已經顯明出來了。12這恩典訓練我們棄絕不敬虔的行為和屬世的私慾，在世上過着自制、正直，和敬虔的生活，13等待我們所盼望那蒙恩的日子來臨；那時候，至尊的上帝和我們的救主耶穌基督③的榮耀要顯現。14基督為我們獻上自己，救贖我們，脫離一切邪惡，使我們成為他純潔的子民，歸屬於他，熱心行善。

15 你要講論這些事，充分運用你的職權來勸勉人或責備人。不要讓人輕看你。

基督徒的行為

3 你要提醒大家，要他們服從執政者和當權者，聽從命令，隨時隨地做各樣好事。2勸他們不要毀謗別人，不要爭吵；要和氣友善，以謙讓的態度對待所有的人。3我們從前也是無知、悖逆，和迷失的；我們作了各種情慾和享樂的奴隸，生活在惡毒和嫉妒中，互相仇恨。4-5但是，我們的救主上帝已經顯出他的慈悲和仁愛，藉着聖靈所施重生和更新的洗禮，拯救了我們；這並不是因為我們自己有甚麼好行為，而是因為他憐憫我們。6藉着我們的救主耶穌基督，上帝把聖靈豐豐富富地傾注在我們身上；7由於他的恩典，我們得以跟上帝有合宜的關係，而得到所盼望那永恆的生命。8這話是可靠的。

我希望你特別強調這些事，好使那些信

③「至尊的上帝和我們的救主耶穌基督」或譯「我們的至尊上帝和救主耶穌基督」。

be concerned with giving their time to doing good deeds, which are good and useful for everyone. [9]But avoid stupid arguments, long lists of ancestors, quarrels, and fights about the Law. They are useless and worthless. [10]Give at least two warnings to those who cause divisions, and then have nothing more to do with them. [11]You know that such people are corrupt, and their sins prove that they are wrong.

Final Instructions

[12]When I send Artemas or Tychicus to you, do your best to come to me in Nicopolis, because I have decided to spend the winter there. [13]Do your best to help Zenas the lawyer and Apollos to get started on their travels, and see to it that they have everything they need. [14]Our people must learn to spend their time doing good, in order to provide for real needs; they should not live useless lives.

[15]All who are with me send you greetings. Give our greetings to our friends in the faith.

God's grace be with you all.

上帝的人熱心行善；這些事都是美好的，是對人有益的。[9]要避免無知的辯論和有關族譜名錄以及法律上的爭執；這些都是沒有益處、沒有價值的。[10]對那製造紛爭的人，至少給他兩次警告，以後就不再跟他來往。[11]你知道，這樣的人是腐化的；他的罪行證明自己是錯誤的。

最後的指示

[12]我差亞提馬或推基古到你那裏去的時候，你要盡可能趕到尼哥城里來見我，因為我已決定在那裏過冬。[13]要盡力促成律師西納和亞波羅旅行的計劃，幫助他們，使他們不至於有甚麼缺乏。[14]讓我們自己的人學習努力行善，來供給生活上的需要；不要作閒散無用的人。

[15]跟我在一起的人都問候你。請向同一信仰的朋友們問安。

願上帝賜恩典給你們大家！

腓利門書
PHILEMON

INTRODUCTION

Philemon was a prominent Christian, probably a member of the church at Colossae and the owner of a slave named Onesimus. This slave had run away from his master, and then somehow he had come in contact with Paul, who was then in prison. Through Paul, Onesimus became a Christian. *Paul's Letter to Philemon* is an appeal to Philemon to be reconciled to his slave, whom Paul is sending back to him, and to welcome him not only as a forgiven slave but as a Christian brother.

Outline of Contents

簡 介

腓利門是一個有聲望的基督徒，可能是歌羅西教會的會友。他也是奴隸阿尼西謀的主人。阿尼西謀從主人那裏逃出來，跟正在囚禁中的保羅有了來往。阿尼西謀受保羅的影響成為基督徒。保羅寫信給腓利門，送阿尼西謀回到他那裏去，請他原諒這個奴隸，歡迎阿尼西謀回去，不但寬恕這個出走的奴隸，也要以同屬於基督的弟兄關係看待他。

提要

---

¹From Paul, a prisoner for the sake of Christ Jesus, and from our brother Timothy–

To our friend and fellow worker Philemon, ²and the church that meets in your house, and our sister Apphia, and our fellow soldier Archippus:

³May God our Father and the Lord Jesus Christ give you grace and peace.

Philemon's Love and Faith

⁴Brother Philemon, every time I pray, I mention you and give thanks to my God. ⁵For I hear of your love for all of God's people and the faith you have in the Lord Jesus. ⁶My prayer is that our fellowship with you as believers will bring about a deeper understanding of every blessing which we have in our life in union with Christ. ⁷Your love, dear brother, has

¹ 我是保羅；我為了基督耶穌的緣故成為囚犯。我和提摩太弟兄寫信給你—我們親愛的同工腓利門，² 和在你家裏聚會的教會，也給亞腓亞姊妹以及跟我們一起服役的亞基布。

³ 願我們的父上帝和主耶穌基督賜恩典、平安給你們！

腓利門的愛心和信心

⁴ 腓利門弟兄啊，我每次禱告的時候都提到你，常常為你感謝我的上帝；⁵ 因為我聽到你對所有的信徒都有愛心，對主耶穌有信心。⁶ 我求上帝使我們能夠藉着在同一信仰裏的團契，更深刻地體會到與基督連結而有的一切好處。⁷ 親愛的弟兄啊，你的愛心給

brought me great joy and much encouragement!
You have cheered the hearts of all of God's
people.

A Request for Onesimus

8For this reason I could be bold enough, as
your brother in Christ, to order you to do what
should be done. 9But because I love you, I
make a request instead. I do this even though I
am Paul, the ambassador of Christ Jesus, and at
present also a prisoner for his sake.*a 10So I
make a request to you on behalf of Onesimus,
who is my own son in Christ; for while in prison I
have become his spiritual father. 11At one
time he was of no use to you, but now he is
useful*b both to you and to me.

12I am sending him back to you now, and
with him goes my heart. 13I would like to keep
him here with me, while I am in prison for the
gospel's sake, so that he could help me in your
place. 14However, I do not want to force you to
help me; rather, I would like for you to do it of
your own free will. So I will not do anything
unless you agree.

15It may be that Onesimus was away from
you for a short time so that you might have him
back for all time. 16And now he is not just a
slave, but much more than a slave: he is a dear
brother in Christ. How much he means to me!
And how much more he will mean to you, both
as a slave and as a brother in the Lord!

17So, if you think of me as your partner, welcome him back just as you would welcome me.
18If he has done you any wrong or owes you
anything, charge it to my account. 19Here, I will
write this with my own hand: *I, Paul, will pay
you back.* (I should not have to remind you, of
course, that you owe your very self to me.)
20So, my brother, please do me this favor for
the Lord's sake; as a brother in Christ, cheer
me up!

21I am sure, as I write this, that you will do
what I ask–in fact I know that you will do even
more. 22At the same time, get a room ready for
me, because I hope that God will answer the
prayers of all of you and give me back to you.

了我極大的喜樂和鼓勵;所有的信徒也因你
而覺得愉快。

爲阿尼西謀請求

8 旣然我是你在基督裏的弟兄,我本來可
以大膽地吩咐你做應該做的事;9可是,愛
心催逼我向你提出請求。雖然我—保羅,身
爲基督耶穌的大使,現在又因他的緣故成爲
囚犯①,還是願意這樣做。10我對你的請求
是爲了阿尼西謀。他是我在基督裏的兒子;
我在監獄裏的時候作了他靈性上的父親。
11從前他對於你沒有甚麼用處,現在他對
你、對我都有用處②。

12 現在我送他回到你那裏去,等於把我自
己的心送去。13我本來想留他在我身邊,讓
他在我爲福音坐牢的時候替你伺候我;14不
過,我希望一切都是出於你甘心樂意,而不
是勉強。沒有你的同意,我甚麼都不願意
做。

15 阿尼西謀暫時離開了你,也許是要使你
永久留着他。16現在,他不再是一個奴隸,
而是遠高過奴隸;因爲他已經是基督裏親愛
的弟兄。對我來說,他確是如此,何況對
你!因爲你們旣有主僕的關係,又是主內的
弟兄。

17 所以,如果你把我當作親密的朋友,你
就接他回去,像接納我一樣。18要是他做了
對不起你的事,或者虧欠了你甚麼,都記在
我的帳上好了。19我在這裏親筆寫下:我—
保羅負責償還。(當然,我用不着提醒你,
你欠我的竟是你自己的生命呢!)20所以,
弟兄啊,爲了主的緣故,讓我向你求這個
情,好解除我精神上的負擔!我們都是基督
裏的弟兄。

21 我深信你會聽從我,我才寫這封信。其
實,我知道,你所做的會超過我的要求。
22同時,請替我預備一個房間;我希望上帝
會答應你們大家的禱告,讓我回到你們那裏
去。

---

a the ambassador of Christ Jesus, and at present also a prisoner for
his sake; or an old man, and at present a prisoner for the sake of
Christ Jesus.
b *The Greek name Onesimus means "useful."*

①「我……囚犯」或譯「我這上了年紀的保羅,現在又因基督耶
穌的緣故成爲囚犯」。
②「有用處」:這正是阿尼西謀這名字的意思。

Final Greetings

23Epaphras, who is in prison with me for the sake of Christ Jesus, sends you his greetings, 24and so do my co-workers Mark, Aristarchus, Demas, and Luke.

25May the grace of the Lord Jesus Christ be with you all.

最後問安

23 為了基督耶穌而跟我一起坐牢的以巴弗問候你。24我的同工馬可、亞里達古、底馬、路加也都問候你。

25 願主耶穌基督賜恩典給你們大家！

Final Greetings
Aristarchus, who is in prison with me for the
sake of Christ Jesus, sends you his greetings,
and so do my co-workers Mark, Aristarchus,
Demas, and Luke.
25May the grace of the Lord Jesus Christ be
with you all.

希伯來書
HEBREWS

INTRODUCTION

The Letter to the Hebrews was written to a group of Christians who, faced with increasing opposition, were in danger of abandoning the Christian faith. The writer encourages them in their faith primarily by showing that Jesus Christ is the true and final revelation of God. In doing this he emphasizes three truths:

(1) Jesus is the eternal Son of God, who learned true obedience to the Father through the suffering that he endured. As the Son of God, Jesus is superior to the prophets of the Old Testament, to the angels, and to Moses himself.

(2) Jesus has been declared by God to be an eternal priest, superior to the priests of the Old Testament.

(3) Through Jesus the believer is saved from sin, fear, and death; and Jesus, as High Priest, provides the true salvation, which was only foreshadowed by the rituals and animal sacrifices of the Hebrew religion.

By citing the example of the faith of some famous persons in Israel's history (chapter 11), the writer appeals to his readers to remain faithful, and in chapter 12 he urges his readers to continue faithful to the end, with eyes fixed on Jesus, and to endure whatever suffering and persecution may come to them. The book closes with words of advice and warning.

Outline of Contents

簡 介

希伯來書是作者寫給一羣面臨困難的信徒的信。他們受到反對者日益增加的壓力，有放棄原有信仰的危險。作者為要堅定他們的信心，鄭重地向他們指出：耶穌基督是上帝最真確、最完整的啟示。作者特別強調下列三方面：

一. 耶穌是上帝的永恆兒子；他忍受一切苦難，始終順服父親的旨意。作為上帝的兒子，耶穌的地位比舊約的衆先知高，也比天使和摩西高。

二. 上帝立耶穌為永遠的祭司，高過舊約的祭司們。

三. 藉着耶穌，信徒得以從罪惡、恐懼，和死亡中被拯救出來。作為大祭司的耶穌給人真的拯救；他在天上聖所獻上的祭遠超過猶太教的禮儀和牲祭。

作者引述以色列史上好些著名人物的信心榜樣（第十一章），勸勉讀者們要堅守信仰。在第十二章，他要求讀者們守信到底，始終仰望耶穌，忍受各種可能臨到他們身上的災難和迫害。最後，他用勸導和警告的話結束。

提要

God's Word through His Son

1 In the past God spoke to our ancestors many times and in many ways through the prophets, [2]but in these last days he has spoken to us through his Son. He is the one through whom God created the universe, the one whom God has chosen to possess all things at the end. [3]He reflects the brightness of God's glory and is the exact likeness of God's own being, sustaining the universe with his powerful word. After achieving forgiveness for the sins of all human beings, he sat down in heaven at the right side of God, the Supreme Power.

The Greatness of God's Son

[4]The Son was made greater than the angels, just as the name that God gave him is greater than theirs. [5]For God never said to any of his angels,

"You are my Son;
   today I have become your Father."
Nor did God say about any angel,
   "I will be his Father,
   and he will be my Son."
[6]But when God was about to send his first-born Son into the world, he said,
   "All of God's angels must worship him."
[7]But about the angels God said,
   "God makes his angels winds,
   and his servants flames of fire."
[8]About the Son, however, God said:
   "Your kingdom, O God, will last[a] forever and ever!
   You rule over your[b] people with justice.
[9]You love what is right and hate what is wrong.
   That is why God, your God, has chosen you
   and has given you the joy of an honor far greater
   than he gave to your companions."
[10]He also said,
   "You, Lord, in the beginning created the earth,
   and with your own hands you made the heavens.
[11]They will disappear, but you will remain;
   they will all wear out like clothes.
[12]You will fold them up like a coat,
   and they will be changed like clothes.
   But you are always the same,
   and your life never ends."
[13]God never said to any of his angels:
   "Sit here at my right side
   until I put your enemies
   as a footstool under your feet."

a Your kingdom, O God, will last; or God is your kingdom.
b your; some manuscripts have his.

上帝藉着他的兒子說話

1 在古時候,上帝多次用多種方法,藉着先知向我們的祖先說話; [2]但是在這末後的日子,他藉着自己的兒子向我們說話。這兒子,上帝曾藉着他創造宇宙,而且揀選他來承受萬有。 [3]他反照着上帝的光輝,也完全反映上帝的本體;他用他大能的話托住萬有。他清除了人的罪惡以後,就坐在天上至高權力者的右邊。

兒子位居天使之上

[4]這兒子的地位遠比天使崇高,正如上帝所賜給他的名遠比天使的名高貴。 [5]上帝從來沒有對任何一個天使說:

你是我的兒子;
今天我作你的父親。
他也從來沒有指着任何一個天使說:
我要作他的父親;
他要作我的兒子。
[6]上帝要差遣他的長子到世上的時候,又說:
上帝所有的天使都必須拜他。
[7]關於天使,他說:
上帝使他的大使成為風,
使他的僕役成為火燄。
[8]關於兒子,他卻說:
上帝啊,你的寶座世世長存!
你①以公平掌權。
[9]你喜愛正義,憎恨不義;
因此上帝—你的上帝選立了你;
他賜給你的喜樂
遠超過賜給你同伴的。
[10]他又說:
主啊,起初你創造了地;
你又親手創造了天。
[11]天地都要消失,而你卻要常存;
天地要像衣服一樣破舊。
[12]你要把天地捲起來,
像更換舊衣服,
你卻始終如一,永不改變。
[13]上帝從來沒有對任何天使說:
你來坐在我的右邊,
等我使你的仇敵屈服在你腳下。

①有些古卷是「他」。

14What are the angels, then? They are spirits who serve God and are sent by him to help those who are to receive salvation.

The Great Salvation

2 That is why we must hold on all the more firmly to the truths we have heard, so that we will not be carried away. 2The message given to our ancestors by the angels was shown to be true, and those who did not follow it or obey it received the punishment they deserved. 3How, then, shall we escape if we pay no attention to such a great salvation? The Lord himself first announced this salvation, and those who heard him proved to us that it is true. 4At the same time God added his witness to theirs by performing all kinds of miracles and wonders and by distributing the gifts of the Holy Spirit according to his will.

The One Who Leads Us to Salvation

5God has not placed the angels as rulers over the new world to come–the world of which we speak. 6Instead, as it is said somewhere in the Scriptures:

"What are human beings, O God, that you
    should think of them;
  mere human beings, that you should care
    for them?
7You made them for a little while lower than
    the angels;
  you crowned them with glory and honor,c
8   and made them rulers over all things."

It says that God made them "rulers over all things"; this clearly includes everything. We do not, however, see human beings ruling over all things now. 9But we do see Jesus, who for a little while was made lower than the angels, so that through God's grace he should die for everyone. We see him now crowned with glory and honor because of the death he suffered. 10It was only right that God, who creates and preserves all things, should make Jesus perfect through suffering, in order to bring many children to share his glory. For Jesus is the one who leads them to salvation.

11He purifies people from their sins, and both he and those who are made pure all have the same Father. That is why Jesus is not ashamed to call them his family. 12He says to God,

"I will tell my people what you have done;
  I will praise you in their meeting."

13He also says, "I will put my trust in God." And he also says, "Here I am with the children

c *Many manuscripts add:* You made them rulers over everything you made *(see Ps 8.6).*

14 那麼,天使是甚麼呢?他們都是事奉上帝的靈;上帝派遣他們來幫助那些要承受拯救的人。

偉大的拯救

2 因此,我們必須更加堅守所聽到的眞理,免得被潮流沖走。2天使所傳給我們的信息已經證實都有效力,所有不遵從這信息的人已經受到應得的懲罰。3既然這樣,如果我們忽略這麼偉大的拯救,怎能逃避懲罰呢?主本身首先宣告了這拯救;那些聽見的人也已經向我們證實。4同時,上帝自己用異能、奇事,和各樣的神蹟來加強他們的見證。他又按照自己的旨意,把聖靈的恩賜分給我們。

爲人類的拯救開路

5 上帝並沒有把他將要創造的世界,就是我們所說的那個世界,置於天使的管轄下。6相反地,正如聖經上某處所說的:

上帝啊,人算甚麼,你竟顧念他;
  世人算甚麼,你竟關懷他。
7 你使他一時比天使低微;
  你用榮耀、尊貴作他的華冠;
8 你使他統轄萬有。

這裏說,上帝使人「統轄萬有」,這明顯地是包括一切。可是,我們現在並沒有看見人統轄萬有。9我們倒是看見耶穌,他一時被置於比天使低微的地位上,好藉著上帝的恩典,爲萬人死。如今,我們看見他經過了死的痛苦而獲得榮耀、尊貴的華冠。10那位創造和維持萬有的上帝使耶穌經歷苦難,成爲完全,爲要使許多兒子一起享受他的榮耀;上帝這樣做是適當的。因爲耶穌原是帶領他們進入拯救的先鋒。

11 他洗淨人的罪;他和那些得到潔淨的人同有一位父親。所以,耶穌不以認他們作一家人爲恥。12他說:

上帝啊,我要向我的弟兄姊妹們傳揚你的名;
我要在全會眾面前歌頌你。

13他也說:

我要信靠上帝;

又說:

that God has given me."

14Since the children, as he calls them, are people of flesh and blood, Jesus himself became like them and shared their human nature. He did this so that through his death he might destroy the Devil, who has the power over death, 15and in this way set free those who were slaves all their lives because of their fear of death. 16For it is clear that it is not the angels that he helps. Instead, he helps the descendants of Abraham. 17This means that he had to become like his people in every way, in order to be their faithful and merciful High Priest in his service to God, so that the people's sins would be forgiven. 18And now he can help those who are tempted, because he himself was tempted and suffered.

Jesus Is Greater than Moses

3 My Christian friends, who also have been called by God! Think of Jesus, whom God sent to be the High Priest of the faith we profess. 2He was faithful to God, who chose him to do this work, just as Moses was faithful in his work in God's house. 3A man who builds a house receives more honor than the house itself. In the same way Jesus is worthy of much greater honor than Moses. 4Every house, of course, is built by someone–and God is the one who has built all things 5Moses was faithful in God's house as a servant, and he spoke of the things that God would say in the future. 6But Christ is faithful as the Son in charge of God's house. We are his house if we keep up our courage and our confidence in what we hope for.

A Rest for God's People

7So then, as the Holy Spirit says,
"If you hear God's voice today,
8 　do not be stubborn, as your ancestors were
　　when they rebelled against God,
　as they were that day in the desert when
　　they put him to the test.
9There they put me to the test and tried me,
　says God,
　although they had seen what I did for forty
　　years.
10And so I was angry with those people and said,
'They are always disloyal
and refuse to obey my commands.'
11I was angry and made a solemn promise:
'They will never enter the land where I
would have given them rest!'"

12My friends, be careful that none of you

看哪，我和上帝所賜給我的兒女都在這裏！

14 既然這些兒女都是有血肉的人，耶穌本身也同樣有了人性。這樣，由於他的死，他能夠毀滅那掌握死亡權勢的魔鬼，15並釋放了那些因為怕死而一生處在奴役下的人。16很明顯地，他不是幫助天使，而是幫助亞伯拉罕的子孫。17所以，他必須在各方面與他的弟兄姊妹們相同，在上帝面前作他們仁慈而可靠的祭司，好使人的罪得到赦免。18因為他親自經歷過被考驗、受折磨的痛苦；他現在能夠幫助那些被考驗的人。

耶穌超越摩西

3 蒙上帝選召的信徒朋友們，你們應該思想耶穌；他是我們信仰宣認的使者和大祭司。2他忠心於選召他來工作的上帝，正像摩西忠心為上帝之家工作一樣。3蓋房子的人所得的榮耀超過了他所蓋的房子。同樣，耶穌比摩西配得更多的榮耀。4每一所房子都是人所建造的，但是上帝創造萬物。5摩西在上帝之家作忠心的僕人，為上帝在將來所要說的話作證。6然而，基督以兒子的身份忠心治理上帝之家。如果我們堅持所盼望的信念和勇氣，我們就是上帝一家的人了。

上帝子民的安息

7 所以，正像聖靈所說的：
今天，如果你們聽見上帝的聲音，
8 你們不要頑固，
像從前背叛上帝、
在曠野裏試探他一樣。
9 上帝說：雖然四十年當中，
你們的祖宗曾看見了我的作為，
他們還是在那裏試探我，考驗我。
10 因此，我向那時代的人發怒；
我說：他們都不忠心，
又違背了我的命令。
11 我在忿怒中發誓：
他們永不能享受我所賜的安息！
12 我的弟兄姊妹們，你們要謹慎，免得你

have a heart so evil and unbelieving that you will turn away from the living God. [13]Instead, in order that none of you be deceived by sin and become stubborn, you must help one another every day, as long as the word "Today" in the scripture applies to us. [14]For we are all partners with Christ if we hold firmly to the end the confidence we had at the beginning.

[15]This is what the scripture says:
"If you hear God's voice today,
  do not be stubborn, as your ancestors were
  when they rebelled against God."

[16]Who were the people who heard God's voice and rebelled against him? All those who were led out of Egypt by Moses. [17]With whom was God angry for forty years? With the people who sinned, who fell down dead in the desert. [18]When God made his solemn promise, "They will never enter the land where I would have given them rest"–of whom was he speaking? Of those who rebelled. [19]We see, then, that they were not able to enter the land, because they did not believe.

4 Now, God has offered us the promise that we may receive that rest he spoke about. Let us take care, then, that none of you will be found to have failed to receive that promised rest. [2]For we have heard the Good News, just as they did. They heard the message, but it did them no good, because when they heard it, they did not accept it with faith. [3]We who believe, then, do receive that rest which God promised. It is just as he said,
"I was angry and made a solemn promise:
  'They will never enter the land where I
    would have given them rest!' "
He said this even though his work had been finished from the time he created the world. [4]For somewhere in the Scriptures this is said about the seventh day: "God rested on the seventh day from all his work." [5]This same matter is spoken of again: "They will never enter that land where I would have given them rest." [6]Those who first heard the Good News did not receive that rest, because they did not believe. There are, then, others who are allowed to receive it. [7]This is shown by the fact that God sets another day, which is called "Today." Many years later he spoke of it through David in the scripture already quoted:
"If you hear God's voice today,
  do not be stubborn."

[8]If Joshua had given the people the rest that God had promised, God would not have spoken later about another day. [9]As it is, however, there still remains for God's people a

們當中有人心思敗壞，不肯相信，背離了永生的上帝。[13]但是，為了避免你們當中有人為罪所迷惑，心腸剛硬，你們要趁着還有所謂「今天」的時候，天天互相勸勉。[14]如果我們能夠堅持當初的信念，始終不變，我們就是基督的同工。

[15]聖經上這樣說：
  今天，如果你們聽見上帝的聲音，
  你們不要頑固，
  像從前背叛上帝一樣。

[16]誰聽見上帝的聲音而背叛了他？豈不是摩西從埃及帶領出來的人民嗎？[17]在那四十年，上帝向誰發怒呢？豈不是那犯罪、倒斃在曠野的人民嗎？[18]當上帝發誓說：「他們不能享受我給他們的安息」，這是向誰發的？豈不是向那背叛的人民發的嗎？[19]這樣看來，他們不能享受到安息是因為他們不信。

4 既然上帝應許我們享受他所賜的安息，我們就應該有畏懼的心，免得你們當中有人被認為是失敗了，無法享受他的安息。[2]我們已經跟他們一樣聽見福音。他們聽了信息，並沒有得到益處，因為他們聽見的時候沒有用信心去領受。[3]我們相信的人可以享受上帝的安息，正如他所說的：
  我在忿怒中發誓：
  他們永不能享受我所賜的安息！

雖然上帝從創世以來已經完成了他的工作，他仍然說了這樣的話。[4]聖經有一處論到第七天，說：「在第七天，上帝歇了他一切的工作。」[5]在同一件事上所引的經文又說：「他們永不能享受我所賜的安息。」[6]那些先聽到福音的人不能享受到安息，因為他們不信；可是另有些人得以享受他的安息。[7]這說明了上帝為甚麼另外定了一天，稱為「今天」。他在許多年後藉着大衛說的話，聖經上已經有了記載：
  今天，如果你們聽見上帝的聲音，
  你們不要頑固。

[8]如果約書亞已經帶領人民進入上帝所應許的安息，上帝在後來就不會再提那另外的一天。[9]這樣看來，還有另外的「安息

rest like God's resting on the seventh day. [10]For those who receive that rest which God promised will rest from their own work, just as God rested from his. [11]Let us, then, do our best to receive that rest, so that no one of us will fail as they did because of their lack of faith.

[12]The word of God is alive and active, sharper than any double-edged sword. It cuts all the way through, to where soul and spirit meet, to where joints and marrow come together. It judges the desires and thoughts of the heart. [13]There is nothing that can be hid from God; everything in all creation is exposed and lies open before his eyes. And it is to him that we must all give an account of ourselves.

Jesus the Great High Priest

[14]Let us, then, hold firmly to the faith we profess. For we have a great High Priest who has gone into the very presence of God–Jesus, the Son of God. [15]Our High Priest is not one who cannot feel sympathy for our weaknesses. On the contrary, we have a High Priest who was tempted in every way that we are, but did not sin. [16]Let us have confidence, then, and approach God's throne, where there is grace. There we will receive mercy and find grace to help us just when we need it.

5 Every high priest is chosen from his fellow-men and appointed to serve God on their behalf, to offer sacrifices and offerings for sins. [2]Since he himself is weak in many ways, he is able to be gentle with those who are ignorant and make mistakes. [3]And because he is himself weak, he must offer sacrifices not only for the sins of the people but also for his own sins. [4]No one chooses for himself the honor of being a high priest. It is only by God's call that a man is made a high priest–just as Aaron was.

[5]In the same way, Christ did not take upon himself the honor of being a high priest. Instead, God said to him,

"You are my Son;
　　today I have become your Father."
[6]He also said in another place,

"You will be a priest forever,
　　in the priestly order of Melchizedek."[d]

[7]In his life on earth Jesus made his prayers and requests with loud cries and tears to God, who could save him from death. Because he was humble and devoted, God heard him. [8]But even though he was God's Son, he learned

d in the priestly order of Melchizedek; or like Melchizedek; or in the line of succession to Melchizedek.

日」，是爲上帝子民的安息保留着的。[10]因爲，凡進入上帝所應許的安息的人，就是歇了自己的工作，正像上帝歇了他的工作一樣。[11]所以，我們應該努力進入那安息；這樣，無論誰都不至於像那些違背命令的人跌倒失敗。

[12]上帝的話活潑有效，比雙刃的劍還要鋒利，連靈和魂，關節和骨髓，都能刺透。它能判斷人心中的慾望和意念。[13]沒有一件事能向上帝隱瞞；一切被造的都赤裸裸地暴露在他眼前。我們都必須向他交帳。

大祭司耶穌

[14]那麼，我們應該持守我們所宣認的信仰。因爲我們有一位偉大的大祭司，就是上帝的兒子耶穌；他已經進到上帝的面前。[15]我們的大祭司並不是不能同情我們的軟弱。相反地，我們的大祭司曾經像我們一樣在各方面經歷過試探，只是他沒有犯罪。[16]所以，我們應該大膽地來到上帝恩典的寶座前，好領受慈愛和恩典，作爲我們及時的幫助。

5 每一個大祭司都是從民間選出來，被指定替人民事奉上帝，爲他們的罪獻上禮物和祭品。[2]大祭司自己在許多地方是軟弱的，因此他能夠溫和地對待那些無知和犯錯誤的人。[3]並且，因爲他自己的軟弱，他不但必須爲人民的罪獻祭，也必須爲自己的罪獻祭。[4]沒有人能爲自己取得大祭司的尊貴地位，惟有上帝選召的人才能夠作大祭司，像亞倫一樣。

[5]同樣，基督沒有爲自己爭取作大祭司的尊貴地位；相反地，上帝對他說：

你是我的兒子；
　　今天我作你的父親。
[6]他又在另一處說：

你要依照麥基洗德一系
　　永遠作祭司。

[7]耶穌在世的時候，曾經向那位能救他脫離死亡的上帝大聲禱告，流淚祈求。因爲他謙虛虔誠，上帝聽了他的祈求。[8]雖然他是上帝的兒子，仍然從他所受的苦難學習順

through his sufferings to be obedient. ⁹When he was made perfect, he became the source of eternal salvation for all those who obey him, ¹⁰and God declared him to be high priest, in the priestly order of Melchizedek.ᵉ

Warning against Abandoning the Faith

¹¹There is much we have to say about this matter, but it is hard to explain to you, because you are so slow to understand. ¹²There has been enough time for you to be teachers—yet you still need someone to teach you the first lessons of God's message. Instead of eating solid food, you still have to drink milk. ¹³Anyone who has to drink milk is still a child, without any experience in the matter of right and wrong. ¹⁴Solid food, on the other hand, is for adults, who through practice are able to distinguish between good and evil.

6 Let us go forward, then, to mature teaching and leave behind us the first lessons of the Christian message. We should not lay again the foundation of turning away from useless works and believing in God; ²of the teaching about baptismsᶠ and the laying on of hands; of the resurrection of the dead and the eternal judgment. ³Let us go forward! And this is what we will do, if God allows.

⁴For how can those who abandon their faith be brought back to repent again? They were once in God's light; they tasted heaven's gift and received their share of the Holy Spirit; ⁵they knew from experience that God's word is good, and they had felt the powers of the coming age. ⁶And then they abandoned their faith! It is impossible to bring them back to repent again, because they are again crucifying the Son of God and exposing him to public shame.

⁷God blesses the soil which drinks in the rain that often falls on it and which grows plants that are useful to those for whom it is cultivated. ⁸But if it grows thorns and weeds, it is worth nothing; it is in danger of being cursed by God and will be destroyed by fire.

⁹But even if we speak like this, dear friends, we feel sure about you. We know that you have the better blessings that belong to your salvation. ¹⁰God is not unfair. He will not forget the work you did or the love you showed for him in the help you gave and are still giving to other Christians. ¹¹Our great desire is that each of you keep up your eagerness to the end, so that the things you hope for will come true. ¹²We do not want you to become lazy, but to be like those who believe and are patient, and so receive what God has promised.

e in the priestly order of Melchizedek; *or* like Melchizedek; *or* in the line of succession to Melchizedek.

f baptisms; *or* purification ceremonies.

服。⁹ 既然上帝使他達到完全的地步,他就成為所有服從他的人永遠得救的根源。¹⁰ 上帝宣佈他依照麥基洗德一系作大祭司。

警誡叛道的人

11 關於這事,還有許多可說的,但是不容易對你們解釋,因為你們的聽覺遲鈍。¹² 你們早就應該為人師表了,可是你們竟還需要別人用上帝信息的第一課來教你們。你們還需要吃奶,不能吃乾飯。¹³ 凡是吃奶的都是嬰兒,還不會辨別是非。¹⁴ 從另一方面說,只有成年人才吃乾飯。他們已經有了豐富的經驗,能辨別好壞。

6 那麼,我們應該把關於基督的初步信息拋在背後,朝著更成熟的信仰前進。我們不要老是在信仰的初步階段下功夫,如懊悔腐朽的習俗、信上帝、² 不同的洗禮、按手禮、死人復活、永遠的審判等道理。³ 讓我們朝著成熟的信仰前進!上帝若准許,這就是我們所要做的。

⁴ 至於那些離棄正道的人,怎能使他們重新悔改呢?他們曾經有了上帝的光照,嘗到了屬天恩賜的滋味,又已分享到聖靈,⁵ 且體驗到上帝的話是佳美的,也感受到末世的能力,⁶ 竟然還離棄正道。這樣的人無法使他們回頭,重新悔改;因為他們再一次把上帝的兒子釘在十字架上,公然羞辱他。

⁷ 一塊田地經常吸收雨水,生長蔬菜,對耕種的人大有用處,這是上帝所賜的福澤。⁸ 可是,如果這塊田地長出來的是無用的荊棘和蒺藜,它就有被詛咒的危險,且要被火燒毀。

⁹ 然而,親愛的朋友們,即使這樣說,我們仍然確信你們的景況更好,更接近拯救。¹⁰ 上帝是公道的;他不會忘記你們為他所做的工作和愛心,就是從你們繼續不斷地幫助其他的信徒所表現出來的。¹¹ 我們最大的願望是:你們每一個人自始至終熱心,好使你們所盼望的一切事都能實現。¹² 不要懶惰,要仿效那些信而有恆的人,來領受上帝的應許。

God's Sure Promise

13When God made his promise to Abraham, he made a vow to do what he had promised. Since there was no one greater than himself, he used his own name when he made his vow. 14He said, "I promise you that I will bless you and give you many descendants." 15Abraham was patient, and so he received what God had promised. 16When we make a vow, we use the name of someone greater than ourselves, and the vow settles all arguments. 17To those who were to receive what he promised, God wanted to make it very clear that he would never change his purpose; so he added his vow to the promise. 18There are these two things, then, that cannot change and about which God cannot lie. So we who have found safety with him are greatly encouraged to hold firmly to the hope placed before us. 19We have this hope as an anchor for our lives. It is safe and sure, and goes through the curtain of the heavenly temple into the inner sanctuary. 20On our behalf Jesus has gone in there before us and has become a high priest forever, in the priestly order of Melchizedek.g

The Priest Melchizedek

7 This Melchizedek was king of Salem and a priest of the Most High God. As Abraham was coming back from the battle in which he defeated the four kings, Melchizedek met him and blessed him, 2and Abraham gave him one tenth of all he had taken. (The first meaning of Melchizedek's name is "King of Righteousness"; and because he was king of Salem, his name also means "King of Peace.") 3There is no record of Melchizedek's father or mother or of any of his ancestors; no record of his birth or of his death. He is like the Son of God; he remains a priest forever.

4You see, then, how great he was. Abraham, our famous ancestor, gave him one tenth of all he got in the battle. 5And those descendants of Levi who are priests are commanded by the Law to collect one tenth from the people of Israel, that is, from their own people, even though they are also descendants of Abraham. 6Melchizedek was not descended from Levi, but he collected one tenth from Abraham and blessed him, the man who received God's promises. 7There is no doubt that the one who blesses is greater than the one who is blessed. 8In the case of the priests the tenth is collected by men who die; but as for Melchizedek the tenth was collected by one who lives, as the scripture says. 9And, so to speak, when Abraham paid the tenth, Levi (whose descendants collect the

g in the priestly order of Melchizedek (see 5.6).

上帝確切的應許

13 上帝向亞伯拉罕立下應許的時候，他曾發誓。因為沒有比他自己大的，他就指着自己的名發誓。14他說：「我一定要賜福給你，使你多子多孫。」15亞伯拉罕耐心等待，終於得到上帝所應許的。16當人發誓的時候，他指着比自己大的發誓；這誓言做擔保結束了人和人當中一切的爭執。17對那些要領受應許的人，上帝要明明白白地指示，他永遠不會改變自己的計劃，於是在應許上面加上誓言。18這兩件事是不能改變的，因為上帝不會撒謊。因此，我們這些尋求他庇護的人深受激勵，要抓住那擺在我們前面的盼望。19我們有這盼望，正像生命之錨，又安全又可靠，通過了天上聖殿的幔子，直到裏面的聖所。20為了我們，耶穌作了先驅，先到了那裏；他已經按照麥基洗德一系永遠作大祭司。

祭司麥基洗德

7 這麥基洗德是撒冷王，也是至高上帝的祭司。在亞伯拉罕殺了諸王，從戰陣回來時，麥基洗德去迎接他，並給他祝福。2 亞伯拉罕把自己所取得的都拿十分之一給他。（首先，麥基洗德名字的意思是「正義的王」；又因為他是撒冷王，他的名字也有「和平的王」的意思。）3 麥基洗德沒有父親，沒有母親，沒有身世族譜，也沒有生死的記錄。他跟上帝的兒子相似，永遠作祭司。

4 你們想一想，他是多麼偉大呀！族長亞伯拉罕把所有戰利品的十分之一給了他。5 那些作祭司的利未子孫，是按照法律的規定，向以色列人民，就是他們自己的同胞，收取十分之一，雖然他們同樣是亞伯拉罕的子孫。6 可是，麥基洗德不屬於利未的世系，他卻從亞伯拉罕收取十分之一，並且為那領受了上帝應許的亞伯拉罕祝福。7 給人家祝福的比那受祝福的人大，這是無可懷疑的。8 就祭司們來說，他們是收取十分之一的人，是必死的；但是，就麥基洗德來說，他也收取十分之一，卻是活着的，正如聖經所說的一樣。9 因此，當亞伯拉罕繳納十分之一時，我們可以說，利未也繳納十分之一

tenth) also paid it. [10]For Levi had not yet been born, but was, so to speak, in the body of his ancestor Abraham when Melchizedek met him.

[11]It was on the basis of the levitical priesthood that the Law was given to the people of Israel. Now, if the work of the levitical priests had been perfect, there would have been no need for a different kind of priest to appear, one who is in the priestly order of Melchizedek,[g] not of Aaron. [12]For when the priesthood is changed, there also has to be a change in the law. [13]And our Lord, of whom these things are said, belonged to a different tribe, and no member of his tribe ever served as a priest. [14]It is well known that he was born a member of the tribe of Judah; and Moses did not mention this tribe when he spoke of priests.

Another Priest, like Melchizedek

[15]The matter becomes even plainer; a different priest has appeared, who is like Melchizedek. [16]He was made a priest, not by human rules and regulations, but through the power of a life which has no end. [17]For the scripture says, "You will be a priest forever, in the priestly order of Melchizedek."[g] [18]The old rule, then, is set aside, because it was weak and useless. [19]For the Law of Moses could not make anything perfect. And now a better hope has been provided through which we come near to God.

[20]In addition, there is also God's vow. There was no such vow when the others were made priests. [21]But Jesus became a priest by means of a vow when God said to him,

"The Lord has made a solemn promise
     and will not take it back:
'You will be a priest forever.' "

[22]This difference, then, also makes Jesus the guarantee of a better covenant.

[23]There is another difference: there were many of those other priests, because they died and could not continue their work. [24]But Jesus lives on forever, and his work as priest does not pass on to someone else. [25]And so he is able, now and always, to save those who come to God through him, because he lives forever to plead with God for them.

[26]Jesus, then, is the High Priest that meets our needs. He is holy; he has no fault or sin in him; he has been set apart from sinners and raised above the heavens. [27]He is not like other high priests; he does not need to offer sacrifices every day for his own sins first and then for the sins of the people. He offered one sacrifice,

g in the priestly order of Melchizedek (see 5.6).

（本來利未的子孫是收取十分之一的）。
[10]其實，麥基洗德迎見亞伯拉罕的時候，利未還沒有出生，可是我們可以說，他已經在他的祖先亞伯拉罕的身體裏面。

[11]從前頒給以色列人民的法律是根據利未的祭司制度的。那麼，要是利未祭司制度的工作是完全的，就用不着有另一種麥基洗德——不是亞倫一制度的祭司出現。[12]既然祭司制度改變，法律也得改變。[13]我們的主，就是現在所討論的那一位，是屬於另一支族的；這一支族從來沒有人當過祭司，在祭壇前供職。[14]大家知道，我們的主是屬於猶大支族的；摩西講到祭司的時候，並沒有提起這一支族。

像麥基洗德的另一個祭司

[15]現在事情更加明顯了，因為另一個像麥基洗德的祭司已經出現。[16]他成為祭司，並不是由於世系承襲下來的條例，而是由於那無窮生命的大能。[17]因為聖經見証說：「你要依照麥基洗德一系永遠作祭司。」[18]這樣，舊的條例被廢棄；因為它軟弱無能，沒有用處。[19]摩西的法律不能夠使任何事達到完全。現在我們有了更好的盼望，藉着它，我們可以接近上帝。

[20]此外，還有上帝的誓言，別的祭司被封立的時候並沒有這種誓言。[21]但是耶穌是藉着誓言成為祭司的；上帝曾對他說：

主曾經發誓，決不改變心意：
你要永遠作祭司。

[22]這樣的差別使耶穌成為那更美好的約的保證。

[23]另外有一個差別，從前被立為祭司的很多；因為他們死了，不能夠繼續工作。[24]但是，耶穌永遠活着；他的祭司工作不由別人繼承。[25]所以，他始終能夠拯救那些藉着他親近上帝的人；因為他永遠活着，替他們求告上帝。

[26]這樣，耶穌正是我們所需要的大祭司。他是聖潔、沒有過錯、沒有罪；他從罪人當中被分別出來，提升到諸天之上。[27]他跟其他的大祭司不同，不需要每天先為自己的罪獻祭，然後再為人民的罪獻祭。他只獻過一

once and for all, when he offered himself. [28]The Law of Moses appoints men who are imperfect to be high priests; but God's promise made with the vow, which came later than the Law, appoints the Son, who has been made perfect forever.

Jesus Our High Priest

8 The whole point of what we are saying is that we have such a High Priest, who sits at the right of the throne of the Divine Majesty in heaven. [2]He serves as high priest in the Most Holy Place, that is, in the real tent which was put up by the Lord, not by human hands.

[3]Every high priest is appointed to present offerings and animal sacrifices to God, and so our High Priest must also have something to offer. [4]If he were on earth, he would not be a priest at all, since there are priests who offer the gifts required by the Jewish Law. [5]The work they do as priests is really only a copy and a shadow of what is in heaven. It is the same as it was with Moses. When he was about to build the Sacred Tent, God told him, "Be sure to make everything according to the pattern you were shown on the mountain." [6]But now, Jesus has been given priestly work which is superior to theirs, just as the covenant which he arranged between God and his people is a better one, because it is based on promises of better things.

[7]If there had been nothing wrong with the first covenant, there would have been no need for a second one. [8]But God finds fault with his people when he says,

"The days are coming, says the Lord,
    when I will draw up a new covenant with the people of Israel and with the people of Judah.
[9]It will not be like the covenant that I made with their ancestors
    on the day I took them by the hand and led them out of Egypt.
They were not faithful to the covenant I made with them,
    and so I paid no attention to them.
[10]Now, this is the covenant that I will make with the people of Israel
    in the days to come, says the Lord:
I will put my laws in their minds
    and write them on their hearts.
I will be their God,
    and they will be my people.
[11]None of them will have to teach their friends
    or tell their neighbors,
    'Know the Lord.'
For they will all know me,
    from the least to the greatest.

次祭;他把自己獻上,一舉而竟全功。[28]摩西的法律封立不完全的人為大祭司;但是,上帝在有了法律後發誓應許,立了他那永遠完全的兒子。

我們的大祭司耶穌

8 我們所討論的重點是這樣:我們有這樣的一位大祭司;他坐在天上至高權力者的寶座右邊。[2]他在至聖所供職當大祭司;這聖所不是人所造,而是主所建立的真聖幕。

[3]每個大祭司是被任命來向上帝獻禮物和祭品的;因此我們的大祭司也應該有所奉獻。[4]如果他是在地上,他就不可能作祭司,因為已經有按照猶太法律來獻禮物的祭司。[5]這些祭司所做的不過是天上聖幕的副本和影像。正如摩西要建造聖幕的時候,上帝對他說:「你所造的都要依照在山上所指示你的模式。」[6]但現在,基督所接受的祭司職務比他們的優越多了,正如他在上帝與人之間作中間人的約是更好的,因為這約是根據那更好的應許而立的。

[7]如果第一個約沒有缺點,就不需要有第二個約。[8]可是上帝指責他的子民,說:

主說:日子要到了,
  我要與以色列人民
  和猶大人民另立新的約。
[9]這約不像從前我與他們祖宗所立的約;
  在那日子我拉著他們的手,
  帶領他們離開埃及。
他們卻沒有遵守我與他們所立的約。
  因此主說:我也不理會他們。
[10]主又說:在往後的日子,
  我要與以色列人民立這樣的約:
我要把我的法律放在他們的頭腦裏,
  寫在他們的心坎上。
我要作他們的上帝;
  他們要作我的子民。
[11]他們無須教導自己的鄉鄰,
  或告訴自己的同胞說:
  你們該認識上帝;
因為從最小到最大,
  他們全都認識我。

[12]I will forgive their sins
   and will no longer remember their
      wrongs."

[13]By speaking of a new covenant, God has made the first one old; and anything that becomes old and worn out will soon disappear.

Earthly and Heavenly Worship

9 The first covenant had rules for worship and a place made for worship as well. [2]A tent was put up, the outer one, which was called the Holy Place. In it were the lampstand and the table with the bread offered to God. [3]Behind the second curtain was the tent called the Most Holy Place. [4]In it were the gold altar for the burning of incense and the Covenant Box all covered with gold and containing the gold jar with the manna in it, Aaron's stick that had sprouted leaves, and the two stone tablets with the commandments written on them. [5]Above the Box were the winged creatures representing God's presence, with their wings spread over the place where sins were forgiven. But now is not the time to explain everything in detail.

[6]This is how those things have been arranged. The priests go into the outer tent every day to perform their duties, [7]but only the high priest goes into the inner tent, and he does so only once a year. He takes with him blood which he offers to God on behalf of himself and for the sins which the people have committed without knowing they were sinning. [8]The Holy Spirit clearly teaches from all these arrangements that the way into the Most Holy Place has not yet been opened as long as the outer tent still stands. [9]This is a symbol which points to the present time. It means that the offerings and animal sacrifices presented to God cannot make the worshiper's heart perfect, [10]since they have to do only with food, drink, and various purification ceremonies. These are all outward rules, which apply only until the time when God will establish the new order.

[11]But Christ has already come as the High Priest of the good things that are already here.[h] The tent in which he serves is greater and more perfect; it is not a tent made by human hands, that is, it is not a part of this created world. [12]When Christ went through the tent and entered once and for all into the Most Holy Place, he did not take the blood of goats and bulls to offer as a sacrifice; rather, he took his own blood and obtained eternal salvation for us. [13]The blood of goats and bulls and the ashes of a burnt calf are sprinkled on the people who are ritually unclean, and this purifies them by

h already here; *some manuscripts have* coming.

[12]我要寬恕他們的過犯，
   不再記住他們的罪惡。

[13]既然上帝提到新的約，可見他已經把頭一個約當作無效的；任何無效逐漸陳舊的，必然急速消逝。

地上和天上的禮拜

9 頭一個約有禮拜的規例和人造的禮拜場所。[2]那個造成了的聖幕，外部叫做聖所，裏面有燈臺、桌子，和供餅。[3]第二層幔子後面的聖幕叫做至聖所，[4]裏面有燒香用的金香壇和整個用金包裹着的約櫃，櫃裏放着盛嗎哪的金罐，又有亞倫那根發過芽的杖和兩塊寫着十誡的石版。[5]約櫃上面有基路伯，象徵着上帝的臨在；基路伯的翅膀覆蓋着赦罪座。關於這些事現在不能一一說明。

[6]這些物件是這樣安排的。祭司們每天到聖幕的外層舉行禮拜儀式；[7]只有大祭司進到聖幕的內層，但每年也只有一次，每次都得帶着血進去，為自己和人民因無知而犯的罪獻給上帝。[8]聖靈藉着這些安排來指明，只要外層的聖幕還在的時候，那通往至聖所的路就不開放。[9]外層的聖幕象徵現今的時代。這就是說獻給上帝的禮物和祭品都不能使敬拜的人內心完全。[10]這些只牽涉到飲食和不同的潔淨儀式罷了，是屬於外表的規例；它們的功效只到上帝改革一切的時候為止。

[11]但是基督已經來了；他作大祭司，實現了②那些美事。他的聖幕更大更完全，不是人手所造的；就是說，不是這被造的世界的一部分。[12]當基督通過了聖幕，一舉而竟全功地進到至聖所的時候，他並沒有用山羊和小牛的血作祭物，卻用他自己的血為我們取得了永恆的救贖。[13]如果把山羊和公牛的血，和焚燒了的母牛的灰，灑在那些在禮儀上不潔淨的人身上，能夠清除他們的污穢，

②「實現了」有些古卷是「將要實現」。

taking away their ritual impurity. [14]Since this is true, how much more is accomplished by the blood of Christ! Through the eternal Spirit he offered himself as a perfect sacrifice to God. His blood will purify our consciences from useless rituals, so that we may serve the living God.

[15]For this reason Christ is the one who arranges a new covenant, so that those who have been called by God may receive the eternal blessings that God has promised. This can be done because there has been a death which sets people free from the wrongs they did while the first covenant was in effect.

[16]In the case of a will it is necessary to prove that the person who made it has died, [17]for a will means nothing while the person who made it is alive; it goes into effect only after his death. [18]That is why even the first covenant[i] went into effect only with the use of blood. [19]First, Moses proclaimed to the people all the commandments as set forth in the Law. Then he took the blood of bulls and goats, mixed it with water, and sprinkled it on the book of the Law and all the people, using a sprig of hyssop and some red wool. [20]He said, "This is the blood which seals the covenant that God has commanded you to obey." [21]In the same way Moses also sprinkled the blood on the Sacred Tent and over all the things used in worship. [22]Indeed, according to the Law almost everything is purified by blood, and sins are forgiven only if blood is poured out.

Christ's Sacrifice Takes Away Sins

[23]Those things, which are copies of the heavenly originals, had to be purified in that way. But the heavenly things themselves require much better sacrifices. [24]For Christ did not go into a Holy Place made by human hands, which was a copy of the real one. He went into heaven itself, where he now appears on our behalf in the presence of God. [25]The Jewish high priest goes into the Most Holy Place every year with the blood of an animal. But Christ did not go in to offer himself many times, [26]for then he would have had to suffer many times ever since the creation of the world. Instead, now when all ages of time are nearing the end, he has appeared once and for all, to remove sin through the sacrifice of himself. [27]Everyone must die once, and after that be judged by God. [28]In the same manner Christ also was offered in sacrifice once to take away the sins of many. He will appear a second time, not to deal with sin, but to save those who are waiting for him.

i COVENANT: *In Greek the same word means "will" and "covenant."*

使他們淨化，[14]那麼，基督的血所能成就的豈不是更多嗎？藉着那永恆的靈，他把自己當作完整的祭物獻給上帝。他的血要淨化我們③的良心，除掉我們的腐敗行為，使我們得以事奉永活的上帝。

[15]因此，基督成為這新約的中間人，為要使上帝所呼召的人能夠領受他所應許永恆的福澤。這事的成就是藉着死；這死釋放了他們在頭一個約下所犯的罪過。

[16]凡遺囑必須證明立遺囑的人已經死了；[17]因為立遺囑的人還活着，遺囑就沒有功效，只有在他死後，遺囑才能生效。[18]所以，連頭一個約也是用血訂立才生效的。[19]當初，摩西按照法律先把所有的誡命傳給人民，然後拿小牛和山羊的血，摻着水，用深紅色的絨和牛膝草蘸上，灑在法律書上和所有的人民身上。[20]他說：「這血印證了上帝命令你們遵守的約。」[21]同樣，摩西也把血灑在聖幕和禮拜及禮儀上所用的各樣器皿上面。[22]按照法律，幾乎各樣器皿都是用血潔淨的；沒有流血，就沒有赦罪。

基督的犧牲潔淨了罪

[23]這些仿照天上的樣式所造的器皿，必須用這方法潔淨。但是，天上的器皿必須用更好的祭物去潔淨。[24]基督並沒有進入人手所造的聖所；那不過是真的聖所的副本。他進到天上，替我們站在上帝面前。[25]猶太人的大祭司每年帶着牲畜的血進到至聖所。但是，基督無須多次獻上自己，[26]否則，從創世以來，他就得多次忍受苦難了。基督一次獻上而竟全功，在這末世，把自己當作祭物獻上，來潔淨罪。[27]到了時候，人人必有一死，死後有上帝的審判。[28]同樣，基督也一次獻上，除掉了許多人的罪。他要再一次顯現，不是來對付罪，而是來拯救迫切等候他的人。

③有些古卷是「你們」。

10 The Jewish Law is not a full and faithful model of the real things; it is only a faint outline of the good things to come. The same sacrifices are offered forever, year after year. How can the Law, then, by means of these sacrifices make perfect the people who come to God? ²If the people worshiping God had really been purified from their sins, they would not feel guilty of sin any more, and all sacrifices would stop. ³As it is, however, the sacrifices serve year after year to remind people of their sins. ⁴For the blood of bulls and goats can never take away sins.

⁵For this reason, when Christ was about to come into the world, he said to God:

"You do not want sacrifices and offerings,
    but you have prepared a body for me.
⁶You are not pleased with animals burned
      whole on the altar
    or with sacrifices to take away sins.
⁷Then I said, 'Here I am,
    to do your will, O God,
    just as it is written of me in the book of
      the Law.' "

⁸First he said, "You neither want nor are you pleased with sacrifices and offerings or with animals burned on the altar and the sacrifices to take away sins." He said this even though all these sacrifices are offered according to the Law. ⁹Then he said, "Here I am, O God, to do your will." So God does away with all the old sacrifices and puts the sacrifice of Christ in their place. ¹⁰Because Jesus Christ did what God wanted him to do, we are all purified from sin by the offering that he made of his own body once and for all.

¹¹Every Jewish priest performs his services every day and offers the same sacrifices many times; but these sacrifices can never take away sins. ¹²Christ, however, offered one sacrifice for sins, an offering that is effective forever, and then he sat down at the right side of God. ¹³There he now waits until God puts his enemies as a footstool under his feet. ¹⁴With one sacrifice, then, he has made perfect forever those who are purified from sin.

¹⁵And the Holy Spirit also gives us his witness. First he says,

¹⁶"This is the covenant that I will make with
    them
    in the days to come, says the Lord:
 I will put my laws in their hearts
    and write them on their minds."

¹⁷And then he says, "I will not remember their sins and evil deeds any longer." ¹⁸So when these have been forgiven, an offering to take away

10 法律並不是真事物的完整和確實的模型，只是將來美好事物的影子。同樣的祭物年年不停地獻上，法律又怎能藉着這些祭物使來到上帝面前的人達到完全呢？²如果敬拜上帝的人的罪真的都得到潔淨，他們就不會再有罪的意識，一切獻祭的事也就可以停止。³其實，年年獻祭只是使人記起自己的罪，⁴因為公牛和山羊的血都無法除掉人的罪。

⁵因此，基督要到世上來的時候，向上帝說：

你不要牲祭和供物；
你已經為我預備了身體。
⁶你不喜歡祭壇上的燒化祭，
也不喜歡贖罪祭。
⁷於是我說：
上帝啊，我來了，
為要遵行你的旨意，
正如法律書上所載，有關於我的事。

⁸首先他說：「你不要，也不喜歡牲祭和供物，或祭壇上燒化祭和贖罪祭。」雖然這些祭物是按照法律獻上的，他還是這樣說。⁹他接着說：「上帝啊，我來了，為要遵行你的旨意。」因此，上帝取消了一切先前的獻祭，為要以基督的犧牲替代。¹⁰耶穌基督遵行了上帝的旨意，獻上自己的身體，一舉而竟全功，使我們聖化歸主。

¹¹猶太的祭司天天站着事奉上帝，多次獻上同樣的祭物；可是這些祭物永遠不能替人除罪。¹²但是，基督獻上一次永遠有效的贖罪祭，然後坐在上帝的右邊，¹³在那裏等着上帝使他的敵人屈服在他腳下。¹⁴他一次的犧牲，使那些聖化歸主的人永遠成為完全。

¹⁵聖靈也曾經對我們作證。首先他說：
¹⁶主這樣說：在往後的日子，
我要與他們立這樣的約：
我要把我的法律放在他們的心坎上，
寫在他們的頭腦裏。

¹⁷他接着說：「我不再記住他們的罪惡和過犯。」¹⁸所以，既然這些罪得到寬赦，再也

sins is no longer needed.

Let Us Come Near to God

19We have, then, my friends, complete freedom to go into the Most Holy Place by means of the death of Jesus. 20He opened for us a new way, a living way, through the curtain–that is, through his own body. 21We have a great priest in charge of the house of God. 22So let us come near to God with a sincere heart and a sure faith, with hearts that have been purified from a guilty conscience and with bodies washed with clean water. 23Let us hold on firmly to the hope we profess, because we can trust God to keep his promise. 24Let us be concerned for one another, to help one another to show love and to do good. 25Let us not give up the habit of meeting together, as some are doing. Instead, let us encourage one another all the more, since you see that the Day of the Lord is coming nearer.

26For there is no longer any sacrifice that will take away sins if we purposely go on sinning after the truth has been made known to us. 27Instead, all that is left is to wait in fear for the coming Judgment and the fierce fire which will destroy those who oppose God! 28Anyone who disobeys the Law of Moses is put to death without any mercy when judged guilty from the evidence of two or more witnesses. 29What, then, of those who despise the Son of God? who treat as a cheap thing the blood of God's covenant which purified them from sin? who insult the Spirit of grace? Just think how much worse is the punishment they will deserve! 30For we know who said, "I will take revenge, I will repay"; and who also said, "The Lord will judge his people." 31It is a terrifying thing to fall into the hands of the living God!

32Remember how it was with you in the past. In those days, after God's light had shone on you, you suffered many things, yet were not defeated by the struggle. 33You were at times publicly insulted and mistreated, and at other times you were ready to join those who were being treated in this way. 34You shared the sufferings of prisoners, and when all your belongings were seized, you endured your loss gladly, because you knew that you still possessed something much better, which would last forever. 35Do not lose your courage, then, because it brings with it a great reward. 36You need to be patient, in order to do the will of God and receive what he promises. 37For, as the scripture says,

"Just a little while longer,
　and he who is coming will come;
　he will not delay.

不需要贖罪的祭物了。

讓我們親近上帝

19那麼，弟兄姊妹們，我們藉着耶穌的死可以坦然無懼地進到至聖所。20他為我們開闢了一條新路，一條通過幔子，就是通過他的身體的活路。21既然我們有一位偉大的祭司在掌管上帝的家，22那麼，我們應該用誠實的心和堅定的信心，用已經蒙潔淨、無虧的良心，和清水洗過的身體，來親近上帝。23讓我們堅定不移地持守我們所宣認的盼望，因為上帝的應許是可靠的。24讓我們彼此關懷，激發愛心，勉勵行善。25不要像某些人放棄了聚會的習慣，卻要彼此勸勉；既然知道主的日子快到，你們更應該這樣。

26如果我們認識了真理後仍然故意犯罪，就不再有任何可以贖罪的祭物了。27我們只有戰戰兢兢地等候着審判和那要燒滅敵對上帝之人的烈火！28那違犯摩西法律的，只要有兩個或三個證人證明他的過犯，就必須處死，不蒙寬恕。29那麼，對於蔑視上帝的兒子，輕看上帝的約的血—就是那潔淨了他的罪的血，並且侮辱恩典之靈的那人又該怎麼辦呢？想想看，他不該受更嚴厲的懲罰嗎？30我們知道誰說過：「伸寃在我，我必報應」；又說：「主要審判他的子民。」31落在永生上帝的手裏是多麼可怕呀！

32要記得以往的日子。上帝光照你們以後，你們遭受許多痛苦，但是並沒有在爭戰中失敗。33有時候，你們當衆受人侮辱和虐待；有時候，你們跟遭受這些苦難的人站在一邊。34你們跟囚犯一同受苦。當你們所有的財物都被奪走的時候，你們甘心忍受；因為你們知道，你們還保有那更美好而長存的產業。35所以，你們不要喪失了勇氣；這勇氣要帶給你們極大的報賞。36為了實行上帝的旨意和領受他的應許，你們必須忍耐。37因為聖經上說：

　再過一會兒，
　　那將要來的會來，不遲延。

[38]My righteous people, however, will believe
    and live;
  but if any of them turns back,
    I will not be pleased with them."
[39]We are not people who turn back and are
lost. Instead, we have faith and are saved.

Faith

11 To have faith is to be sure of the things we
hope for, to be certain of the things we
cannot see. [2]It was by their faith that people of
ancient times won God's approval.

[3]It is by faith that we understand that the
universe was created by God's word, so that
what can be seen was made out of what cannot
be seen.

[4]It was faith that made Abel offer to God a
better sacrifice than Cain's. Through his faith
he won God's approval as a righteous man, because God himself approved of his gifts. By
means of his faith Abel still speaks, even
though he is dead.

[5]It was faith that kept Enoch from dying. Instead, he was taken up to God, and nobody
could find him, because God had taken him up.
The scripture says that before Enoch was taken
up, he had pleased God. [6]No one can please
God without faith, for whoever comes to God
must have faith that God exists and rewards
those who seek him.

[7]It was faith that made Noah hear God's
warnings about things in the future that he
could not see. He obeyed God and built a boat
in which he and his family were saved. As a result, the world was condemned, and Noah received from God the righteousness that comes
by faith.

[8]It was faith that made Abraham obey when
God called him to go out to a country which
God had promised to give him. He left his own
country without knowing where he was going.
[9]By faith he lived as a foreigner in the country
that God had promised him. He lived in tents,
as did Isaac and Jacob, who received the same
promise from God. [10]For Abraham was waiting
for the city which God has designed and built,
the city with permanent foundations.

[11]It was faith that made Abraham able to become a father, even though he was too old and
Sarah herself could not have children. He[j]
trusted God to keep his promise. [12]Though
Abraham was practically dead, from this one
man came as many descendants as there are

---

j It was faith . . . children. He; *some manuscripts have* It was faith
that made Sarah herself able to conceive, even though she was too
old to have children. She.

---

[38]我的義人將因信而得生命。
  但是,若有人退卻,
  我就不喜歡他。
[39]我們並不是退卻而沉淪的人;我們是有
信心而且得救的人。

論信

11 那麼,信心是甚麼呢?信心是對所盼望
的事有把握,對不能看見的事能肯定。
[2]古人能夠贏得上帝的贊許就是由於他們相
信上帝。

[3] 由於信心,我們知道宇宙是藉着上帝的
話造成的;這樣,那看得見的是從那看不見
的造出來的。

[4] 由於信心,亞伯比該隱獻了更好的祭物
給上帝。他藉着信心,贏得上帝的贊許,被
稱爲義人,因爲上帝親自悅納他的禮物。他
雖然死了,仍舊藉着這信心說話。

[5] 由於信心,以諾得以不死。他被提升到
上帝那裏去,沒有人能找到他,因爲上帝接
了他去。聖經上說,他被提升以前已經得到
了上帝的歡心。[6]人沒有信心就不能得到上
帝的歡心。凡是到上帝面前來的人都必須信
上帝的存在,而且信他要報賞尋求他的人。

[7] 由於信心,挪亞在還沒有見到的事上聽
從上帝的警告,造了一條方舟,救了他和他
一家。這樣,他定了那世代的罪,自己也從
上帝領受了因信而有的義。

[8] 由於信心,亞伯拉罕順服上帝的召喚,
去到上帝應許要賜給他的地方。他離開本國
的時候,並不知道要到哪裏去。[9]藉着信
心,他居住在上帝所應許的地方,異地作
客,跟領受上帝同樣應許的以撒和雅各住在
帳棚。[10]因爲亞伯拉罕盼望着那座上帝所設
計建造、根基永固的城。

[11] 由於信心,雖然莎拉不孕,也過了生育
的年齡,她仍然得到生育的能力,因爲她④
相信上帝會持守他的應許。[12]雖然亞伯拉罕
似乎已經死了,從他一個人所傳下來的子孫

---

④「雖然莎拉……因爲她」或譯「雖然亞伯拉罕已經老了,莎拉
也過了生育的年齡,亞伯拉罕仍然能作父親,因爲他」。

stars in the sky, as many as the numberless grains of sand on the seashore.

13It was in faith that all these persons died. They did not receive the things God had promised, but from a long way off they saw them and welcomed them, and admitted openly that they were foreigners and refugees on earth. 14Those who say such things make it clear that they are looking for a country of their own. 15They did not keep thinking about the country they had left; if they had, they would have had the chance to return. 16Instead, it was a better country they longed for, the heavenly country. And so God is not ashamed for them to call him their God, because he has prepared a city for them.

17It was faith that made Abraham offer his son Isaac as a sacrifice when God put Abraham to the test. Abraham was the one to whom God had made the promise, yet he was ready to offer his only son as a sacrifice. 18God had said to him, "It is through Isaac that you will have the descendants I promised." 19Abraham reckoned that God was able to raise Isaac from death–and, so to speak, Abraham did receive Isaac back from death.

20It was faith that made Isaac promise blessings for the future to Jacob and Esau.

21It was faith that made Jacob bless each of the sons of Joseph just before he died. He leaned on the top of his walking stick and worshiped God

22It was faith that made Joseph, when he was about to die, speak of the departure of the Israelites from Egypt, and leave instructions about what should be done with his body.

23It was faith that made the parents of Moses hide him for three months after he was born. They saw that he was a beautiful child, and they were not afraid to disobey the king's order.

24It was faith that made Moses, when he had grown up, refuse to be called the son of the king's daughter. 25He preferred to suffer with God's people rather than to enjoy sin for a little while. 26He reckoned that to suffer scorn for the Messiah was worth far more than all the treasures of Egypt, for he kept his eyes on the future reward.

27It was faith that made Moses leave Egypt without being afraid of the king's anger. As though he saw the invisible God, he refused to turn back. 28It was faith that made him establish the Passover and order the blood to be sprinkled on the doors, so that the Angel of Death would not kill the first-born sons of the Israelites.

卻像天上的星星和海邊無數的沙粒那麼多。

13 這些人是至死有信心的人。他們並沒有領受到上帝所應許的；可是從遠處觀望，心裏歡喜，又承認他們在世上不過是異鄉人和旅客。14說這話的人顯然表示他們在替自己尋求一個家鄉。15他們並不懷念已經離開了的地方，否則，他們還有回去的機會。16他們所渴慕的是那在天上更美好的家鄉；所以，上帝並不因他們稱他為上帝而覺得恥辱，因為他已經為他們預備了一座城。

17 由於信心，亞伯拉罕在上帝考驗他的時候，把兒子以撒獻上，當作祭物。亞伯拉罕乃是領受上帝應許的人，可是他情願把自己的獨子作為祭物獻上。18上帝曾對他說：「你要從以撒得到我所應許的子孫。」19他認為上帝能夠使以撒從死裏復活。其實，我們也可以說，亞伯拉罕的確曾經把以撒從死裏領了回來。

20 由於信心，以撒為了將來的事給雅各和以掃祝福。

21 由於信心，雅各在臨終的時候分別為約瑟的兩個兒子祝福；他扶着自己的拐杖敬拜上帝。

22 由於信心，約瑟在臨終的時候提起以色列族將來要離開埃及的事，並對自己遺體的埋葬有所囑咐。

23 由於信心，摩西出生後，他的父母看見嬰兒俊美，把他隱藏了三個月；他們不怕王的命令。

24 由於信心，摩西長大後，拒絕被稱為埃及公主的兒子。25他寧願跟上帝的子民一同受苦，不願在罪惡中享受片刻的歡樂。26在他的眼中，為彌賽亞受凌辱比埃及所有的財寶更可貴，因為他盼望着將來的獎賞。

27 由於信心，摩西離開了埃及，不怕王的震怒；因為他似乎看見了眼睛所看不見的上帝，堅忍到底，不肯回去。28由於信心，他設立逾越節，並吩咐將血灑在門上，使那執行毀滅的天使不至於殺了以色列人的長子。

29It was faith that made the Israelites able to cross the Red Sea as if on dry land; when the Egyptians tried to do it, the water swallowed them up.

30It was faith that made the walls of Jericho fall down after the Israelites had marched around them for seven days. 31It was faith that kept the prostitute Rahab from being killed with those who disobeyed God, for she gave the Israelite spies a friendly welcome.

32Should I go on? There isn't enough time for me to speak of Gideon, Barak, Samson, Jephthah, David, Samuel, and the prophets. 33Through faith they fought whole countries and won. They did what was right and received what God had promised. They shut the mouths of lions, 34put out fierce fires, escaped being killed by the sword. They were weak, but became strong; they were mighty in battle and defeated the armies of foreigners. 35Through faith women received their dead relatives raised back to life.

Others, refusing to accept freedom, died under torture in order to be raised to a better life. 36Some were mocked and whipped, and others were put in chains and taken off to prison. 37They were stoned, they were sawed in two, they were killed by the sword. They went around clothed in skins of sheep or goats–poor, persecuted, and mistreated. 38The world was not good enough for them! They wandered like refugees in the deserts and hills, living in caves and holes in the ground.

39What a record all of these have won by their faith! Yet they did not receive what God had promised, 40because God had decided on an even better plan for us. His purpose was that only in company with us would they be made perfect.

God Our Father

12As for us, we have this large crowd of witnesses around us. So then, let us rid ourselves of everything that gets in the way, and of the sin which holds on to us so tightly, and let us run with determination the race that lies before us. 2Let us keep our eyes fixed on Jesus, on whom our faith depends from beginning to end. He did not give up because of the cross! On the contrary, because of the joy that was waiting for him, he thought nothing of the disgrace of dying on the cross, and he is now seated at the right side of God's throne.

3Think of what he went through; how he put up with so much hatred from sinners! So do not let yourselves become discouraged and give up. 4For in your struggle against sin you have not yet had to resist to the point of being killed. 5Have you forgotten the encouraging words

29 由於信心,以色列人得以渡過紅海,好像走在乾地上;埃及人一試,水就把他們淹沒了。

30 由於信心,以色列人繞着耶利哥城走了七天以後,城牆倒塌了。31由於信心,妓女喇合不至於跟那些不服從上帝的人一起被殺,因為她友善地接待了探子。

32 我還得說下去嗎?我沒有足夠的時間去提基甸、巴拉、參孫、耶弗他、大衞、撒母耳,和先知們的事蹟呢。33他們藉着信心,戰勝了周圍的國家。他們施行正義,領受上帝的應許。他們堵住獅子的口,34撲滅了烈火,逃脫了刀劍的殺戮。他們變軟弱為剛強,在戰陣上發揮威力,擊敗了外國的軍隊。35藉着信心,有些婦女接納那些從死裏復活的親人。

另有些人拒絕被釋放,寧願死在酷刑下,為要得到更美好的新生命。36又有人忍受戲弄,鞭打;也有人被捆綁,被囚禁。37還有人被石頭擊斃,被鋸子鋸斷,被刀劍殺死。再有人披着綿羊山羊的皮,到處奔跑,忍受窮困,迫害,和虐待。38這世界不值得他們居留!他們像難民一樣在荒野和山嶺間流浪,在山洞和地穴裏棲身。

39 這些人的信心都有着很不平凡的記錄;可是他們並沒有領受到上帝所應許的,40因為上帝決定給我們作更美好的安排。他的旨意是:他們必須跟我們一道才能達到完全。

我們的父上帝

12既然我們有這麼多見證人,像雲彩一樣圍繞着我們,就應該排除一切的障礙和跟我們糾纏不休的罪,堅忍地奔跑我們前面的路程。2我們要注視耶穌,因為他是我們信心的創始者和完成者。他不在十字架前退縮;相反地,為了那等待着他的喜樂,他不把死在十字架上的羞辱當作一回事。現在他已經坐在上帝寶座的右邊。

3 想一想他的經歷。他怎樣忍受罪人的憎恨!所以你們不要灰心喪志。4你們跟罪惡鬥爭,還沒有抵抗到流血的地步。5難道你們忘記了上帝怎樣用勸勉兒子的話勸勉你

which God speaks to you as his children?

"My child, pay attention when the Lord
   corrects you,
   and do not be discouraged when
   he rebukes you.
[6]Because the Lord corrects everyone he loves,
   and punishes everyone he accepts as a
   child."

[7]Endure what you suffer as being a father's
punishment; your suffering shows that God is
treating you as his children. Was there ever a
child who was not punished by his father? [8]If
you are not punished, as all his children are, it
means you are not real children, but bastards.
[9]In the case of our human fathers, they
punished us and we respected them. How much
more, then, should we submit to our spiritual
Father and live! [10]Our human fathers punished
us for a short time, as it seemed right to them;
but God does it for our own good, so that we
may share his holiness. [11]When we are
punished, it seems to us at the time something
to make us sad, not glad. Later, however, those
who have been disciplined by such punishment
reap the peaceful reward of a righteous life.

Instructions and Warnings

[12]Lift up your tired hands, then, and
strengthen your trembling knees! [13]Keep
walking on straight paths, so that the lame foot
may not be disabled, but instead be healed.

[14]Try to be at peace with everyone, and try
to live a holy life, because no one will see the
Lord without it. [15]Guard against turning back
from the grace of God. Let no one become like
a bitter plant that grows up and causes many
troubles with its poison. [16]Let no one become
immoral or unspiritual like Esau, who for a
single meal sold his rights as the older son.
[17]Afterward, you know, he wanted to receive
his father's blessing; but he was turned back,
because he could not find any way to change
what he had done, even though in tears he
looked for it.[k]

[18]You have not come, as the people of Israel
came, to what you can feel, to Mount Sinai
with its blazing fire, the darkness and the
gloom, the storm, [19]the blast of a trumpet, and
the sound of a voice. When the people heard
the voice, they begged not to hear another
word, [20]because they could not bear the order
which said, "If even an animal touches the
mountain, it must be stoned to death." [21]The
sight was so terrifying that Moses said, "I am
trembling and afraid!"

k he looked for it; *or* he tried to get the blessing.

們?他說:

　　我的兒子啊,要留心主的管教,
　　不要因他的責備而灰心;
　 [6] 因為主管教他所愛的每一個人,
　　鞭打他所收納的每一個兒子。

　[7] 你們要忍受管教,因為你們受管教是表
示上帝待你們像兒子一樣。豈有兒子不受父
親管教的? [8] 如果你們不像其他的兒子接受
管教的話,你們就不是真兒子,而是私生
的。[9] 對於肉體的父親,我們接受管教,仍
然尊敬他們。那麼,對於靈性的父親,我們
豈不是要更加順服,以求得到生命嗎? [10] 肉
體的父親隨著自己的意思暫時管教我們;但
是,上帝的管教是為了我們的好處,要使我
們有份於他的聖潔。[11] 我們受管教的時候,
悶悶不樂;可是後來,那些因受管教而經歷
過鍛鍊的人能夠結出平安的果子,過著正直
的生活。

教導和規勸

　[12] 因此,你們要把無力的手舉起來,把發
抖的腿伸直! [13] 要時常走在筆直的路上,使
跛了的腳不至於完全殘廢,反而重新得到力
量。

　[14] 要努力跟人和睦,過聖潔的生活;沒有
聖潔的生活就沒有人能見到主。[15] 要謹慎,
免得有人失去了上帝的恩典。要謹慎,免得
有人像一株有毒的植物,長大起來,遺害人
羣。[16] 要謹慎,免得有人淫亂,或像以掃一
樣不虔,為了一點點食物把長子的名份都出
賣了。[17] 後來,你們知道,他想得到父親的
祝福,可是被拒絕了;雖然他流著眼淚想尋
找補救的辦法,卻無法改變他已經做了的
事。

　[18] 你們並沒有來到一個可觸摸的西奈山,
像以色列人民所到過的;那裏有火燄、密
雲、黑暗,和風暴,[19] 有號筒的響聲和說話
的聲音。人民聽見這聲音的時候,就要求不
再讓他們聽見別的話;[20] 因為他們承擔不起
那命令,說:「接觸到這山的,即使是牲畜
也必須用石頭把牠打死。」[21] 那景象是多麼
的可怕,以致摩西說:「我戰慄恐懼!」

22Instead, you have come to Mount Zion and to the city of the living God, the heavenly Jerusalem, with its thousands of angels. 23You have come to the joyful gathering of God's first-born, whose names are written in heaven. You have come to God, who is the judge of all people, and to the spirits of good people made perfect. 24You have come to Jesus, who arranged the new covenant, and to the sprinkled blood that promises much better things than does the blood of Abel.

25Be careful, then, and do not refuse to hear him who speaks. Those who refused to hear the one who gave the divine message on earth did not escape. How much less shall we escape, then, if we turn away from the one who speaks from heaven! 26His voice shook the earth at that time, but now he has promised, "I will once more shake not only the earth but heaven as well." 27The words "once more" plainly show that the created things will be shaken and re-moved, so that the things that cannot be shaken will remain.

28Let us be thankful, then, because we re-ceive a kingdom that cannot be shaken. Let us be grateful and worship God in a way that will please him, with reverence and awe; 29because our God is indeed a destroying fire.

How to Please God

13 Keep on loving one another as Christians. 2Remember to welcome strangers in your homes. There were some who did that and wel-comed angels without knowing it. 3Remember those who are in prison, as though you were in prison with them. Remember those who are suffering, as though you were suffering as they are.

4Marriage is to be honored by all, and hus-bands and wives must be faithful to each other. God will judge those who are immoral and those who commit adultery.

5Keep your lives free from the love of money, and be satisfied with what you have. For God has said, "I will never leave you; I will never abandon you." 6Let us be bold, then, and say,

"The Lord is my helper,
I will not be afraid.
What can anyone do to me?"

7Remember your former leaders, who spoke God's message to you. Think back on how they lived and died, and imitate their faith. 8Jesus Christ is the same yesterday, today, and for-ever. 9Do not let all kinds of strange teachings lead you from the right way. It is good to re-ceive inner strength from God's grace, and not by obeying rules about foods; those who obey

22 可是，你們是來到錫安山，是來到永活上帝的城，是天上的耶路撒冷，有千千萬萬的天使。23你們是來到上帝的長子們歡聚的場所，這些長子們的名字已經寫在天上。你們是來到審判萬人的上帝面前，是來到已經達到完全的義人的靈那裏。24你們是來到新約的中間人耶穌面前，是來到所灑的血那裏；這血所表達的比亞伯的血更為美好。

25 那麼，你們要謹慎，不要拒絕那向你們說話的。那些拒絕了在地上把神聖的信息傳給他們的人尚且不能逃罪，要是我們拒絕從天上向我們說話的那位，就更不能脫罪了！26當時，他的聲音震動了地，但現在他答應：「再一次，我不但要震動地，也要震動天。」27「再一次」這話明顯地表示被造之物要被震動，被移開，好讓那些未被震動的留下來。

28 所以，我們要為了承受那不能震動的國度感恩。我們要按照上帝所喜悅的，用虔誠敬畏的心事奉他，29因為我們的上帝是毀滅的火。

怎樣得上帝的歡心

13 你們要常有手足相愛之情。2要接待異鄉人到你們家裏。曾經有人這樣做，竟在無意中接待了天使。3要記得那些坐牢的人，好像你們也跟他們一起坐牢。要記得那些在患難中的人，好像你們也在患難中一樣。

4 人人應該尊重婚姻的關係；夫妻必須忠實相待。上帝要審判放蕩和淫亂的人。

5 不要貪慕錢財，要滿足於自己所有的。因為上帝說過：「我永不離開你，永不丟棄你。」6那麼，我們應該大膽地說：

主是我的幫助，
我不懼怕；
人能把我怎麼樣呢？

7 你們要記念從前帶領你們、向你們傳上帝信息的人。回想他們生前怎樣生活，怎樣死；要效法他們的信心。8耶穌基督，昨天、今天、直到永遠，都是一樣。9不要讓各種怪異的學說把你們引入歧途。應該倚靠上帝的恩典，來健全你們的心。不要倚靠食

these rules have not been helped by them.

10The priests who serve in the Jewish place of worship have no right to eat any of the sacrifice on our altar. 11The Jewish high priest brings the blood of the animals into the Most Holy Place to offer it as a sacrifice for sins; but the bodies of the animals are burned outside the camp. 12For this reason Jesus also died outside the city, in order to purify the people from sin with his own blood. 13Let us, then, go to him outside the camp and share his shame. 14For there is no permanent city for us here on earth; we are looking for the city which is to come. 15Let us, then, always offer praise to God as our sacrifice through Jesus, which is the offering presented by lips that confess him as Lord. 16Do not forget to do good and to help one another, because these are the sacrifices that please God.

17Obey your leaders and follow their orders. They watch over your souls without resting, since they must give to God an account of their service. If you obey them, they will do their work gladly; if not, they will do it with sadness, and that would be of no help to you.

18Keep on praying for us. We are sure we have a clear conscience, because we want to do the right thing at all times. 19And I beg you even more earnestly to pray that God will send me back to you soon.

Closing Prayer

20-21God has raised from death our Lord Jesus, who is the Great Shepherd of the sheep as the result of his blood,*l* by which the eternal covenant is sealed. May the God of peace provide you with every good thing you need in order to do his will, and may he, through Jesus Christ, do in us what pleases him. And to Christ be the glory forever and ever! Amen.

Final Words

22I beg you, my friends, to listen patiently to this message of encouragement; for this letter I have written you is not very long. 23I want you to know that our brother Timothy has been let out of prison. If he comes soon enough, I will have him with me when I see you.

24Give our greetings to all your leaders and to all God's people. The believers from Italy send you their greetings.
25May God's grace be with you all.

l his blood; or his sacrificial death.

物的規例；倚靠那些規例的人並沒有得到幫助。

10 在聖幕裏事奉的猶太祭司沒有權吃我們祭壇上的祭物。11猶太大祭司把牲畜的血帶進至聖所，把它當作贖罪的祭物獻上；牲畜的身體卻在營外焚燒。12因此，耶穌也死在城外，為要用自己的血去潔淨人的罪。13那麼，我們應該到營外去找他，分擔他所受的凌辱。14在地上，我們沒有永久的城；我們是在尋求那將來的城。15我們應該憑藉耶穌，常常以頌讚為祭，獻給上帝，就是用我們的嘴唇來宣認他的名。16不可忘記行善和幫助別人，因為這樣的祭物是上帝所喜歡的。

17 要服從帶領你們的人，聽他們的話。他們常常看顧你們的靈魂，因為他們將來要向上帝交帳。你們聽從他們，他們就會高高興興工作，否則，他們會灰心，這對你們又有甚麼益處呢？

18 請不斷地替我們禱告。我們自信有清白的良心，願意時時走正路。19我更懇切要求你們替我禱告，求上帝使我能夠回到你們那裏去。

禱告

20-21上帝已經使我們的主耶穌從死裏復活。他憑藉耶穌所流的血印證了永恆的約，使他成為羣羊的大牧人。願賜平安的上帝在你們所做各樣善事上成全你們，使你們能夠遵行他的旨意！願他藉著耶穌基督在我們身上成就他所喜歡的事！願榮耀歸於基督，世世無窮！阿們。

最後的話

22 我的弟兄姊妹們，我求你們耐心領受這勸勉的話；我並沒有把這封信寫得太長。23我要讓你們知道，我們的弟兄提摩太已經出獄了。如果他早一點來，他會跟我一道去看你們。

24 請向帶領你們的人和所有信徒問安。從意大利來的信徒向你們問安。

25 願上帝賜恩典給你們各位！

雅各書
JAMES

INTRODUCTION

The Letter from James is a collection of practical instructions, written to "all God's people scattered over the whole world." The writer uses many vivid figures of speech to present instructions regarding practical wisdom and guidance for Christian attitudes and conduct. From the Christian perspective he deals with a variety of topics such as riches and poverty, temptation, good conduct, prejudice, faith and actions, the use of the tongue, wisdom, quarreling, pride and humility, judging others, boasting, patience, and prayer.

The letter emphasizes the importance of actions along with faith, in the practice of the Christian religion.

Outline of Contents

簡 介

雅各書搜集一些實際的指導，收信者是「散居在全世界的上帝的子民」。作者引用好些生動的辭藻和比擬，對基督徒應有的態度和行為提出實際的勸勉和指導。他從基督徒的立場討論貧富、試誘、善行、偏見、信心和行為、言語、智慧、爭論、驕傲和謙虛、評斷別人、自誇、忍耐、禱告等許多不同的題目。

本書強調行為和信心兩者在基督信仰上同樣重要。

提要

---

1 From James, a servant of God and of the Lord Jesus Christ:

Greetings to all God's people scattered over the whole world.

Faith and Wisdom

2My friends, consider yourselves fortunate when all kinds of trials come your way, 3for you know that when your faith succeeds in facing

1 我—雅各是上帝和主耶穌基督的僕人；我問候散居在全世界的上帝的子民。

信心和智慧

2 弟兄姊妹們，你們遭遇各種試煉，應該認為是可慶幸的事，3因為知道你們的信心

such trials, the result is the ability to endure. [4]Make sure that your endurance carries you all the way without failing, so that you may be perfect and complete, lacking nothing. [5]But if any of you lack wisdom, you should pray to God, who will give it to you; because God gives generously and graciously to all. [6]But when you pray, you must believe and not doubt at all. Whoever doubts is like a wave in the sea that is driven and blown about by the wind. [7-8]If you are like that, unable to make up your mind and undecided in all you do, you must not think that you will receive anything from the Lord.

Poverty and Riches

[9]Those Christians who are poor must be glad when God lifts them up, [10]and the rich Christians must be glad when God brings them down. For the rich will pass away like the flower of a wild plant. [11]The sun rises with its blazing heat and burns the plant; its flower falls off, and its beauty is destroyed. In the same way the rich will be destroyed while they go about their business.

Testing and Tempting

[12]Happy are those who remain faithful under trials, because when they succeed in passing such a test, they will receive as their reward the life which God has promised to those who love him. [13]If we are tempted by such trials, we must not say, "This temptation comes from God." For God cannot be tempted by evil, and he himself tempts no one. [14]But we are tempted when we are drawn away and trapped by our own evil desires. [15]Then our evil desires conceive and give birth to sin; and sin, when it is full-grown, gives birth to death.

[16]Do not be deceived, my dear friends! [17]Every good gift and every perfect present comes from heaven; it comes down from God, the Creator of the heavenly lights, who does not change or cause darkness by turning. [18]By his own will he brought us into being through the word of truth, so that we should have first place among all his creatures.

Hearing and Doing

[19]Remember this, my dear friends! Everyone must be quick to listen, but slow to speak and slow to become angry. [20]Human anger does not achieve God's righteous purpose. [21]So get rid of every filthy habit and all wicked conduct. Submit to God and accept the word that he plants in your hearts, which is able to save you.

[22]Do not deceive yourselves by just listening

經過了考驗就會產生忍耐。 [4]你們要忍耐到底才能達到十全十美，沒有任何缺欠。 [5]如果你們當中有缺少智慧的，應該向上帝祈求，他會賜智慧給你們，因為他樂意豐豐富富地賜給每一個人。 [6]不過，你們要憑着信心求，不可有絲毫疑惑；疑惑的人好像海中的波浪，被風吹動，翻騰不已。 [7-8]這樣的人三心兩意，搖擺不定，別想從主那裏得到甚麼。

貧賤和富貴

[9]貧賤的信徒蒙上帝提升，應該高興； [10]富貴的人被貶低，也該這樣。富有的人要像野花 樣凋謝。 [11]烈日一出，熱風一吹，草木枯乾，花朵凋謝，所有的美就消失了。同樣，富有的人在事業上孜孜經營，也會消失。

考驗和試誘

[12]遭受試煉而忍耐到底的人有福了；因為通過考驗之後，他將領受上帝向愛他的人所應許那生命的冠冕。 [13]人如果經歷這種試煉，不可以說：「上帝在試誘我」；因為上帝不受邪惡的試誘，也不試誘人。 [14]一個人受試誘，是被自己的慾望勾引去的。 [15]他的慾望懷了胎，生出罪惡，罪惡一旦長成就產生死亡。

[16]我親愛的弟兄姊妹們，不要被愚弄了！ [17]一切美善的事物和各樣完美的恩賜都是從天上來的，是從天父來的；他是一切光的創造主。他沒有改變，也沒有轉動的影子。 [18]他按照自己的旨意，藉着真理的話創造了我們，使我們在他所造的萬物中居首位。

聽和行

[19]我親愛的弟兄姊妹們，你們每一個人都應該隨時聆聽別人的意見，不急於發言，更不要輕易動怒。 [20]人的怒氣並不能達成上帝公義的目的。 [21]所以，你們要掙脫一切不良的習慣和邪惡的行為，用順服的心接受上帝種在你們心裏的道，就是那能夠拯救你們的道。

[22]但是，你們不要欺騙自己，以為只要聽

to his word; instead, put it into practice. [23]If you listen to the word, but do not put it into practice you are like people who look in a mirror and see themselves as they are. [24]They take a good look at themselves and then go away and at once forget what they look like. [25]But if you look closely into the perfect law that sets people free, and keep on paying attention to it and do not simply listen and then forget it, but put it into practice–you will be blessed by God in what you do.

[26]Do any of you think you are religious? If you do not control your tongue, your religion is worthless and you deceive yourself. [27]What God the Father considers to be pure and genuine religion is this: to take care of orphans and widows in their suffering and to keep oneself from being corrupted by the world.

Warning against Prejudice

2 My friends, as believers in our Lord Jesus Christ, the Lord of glory, you must never treat people in different ways according to their outward appearance. [2]Suppose a rich man wearing a gold ring and fine clothes comes to your meeting, and a poor man in ragged clothes also comes. [3]If you show more respect to the well-dressed man and say to him, "Have this best seat here," but say to the poor man, "Stand over there, or sit here on the floor by my feet," [4]then you are guilty of creating distinctions among yourselves and of making judgments based on evil motives.

[5]Listen, my dear friends! God chose the poor people of this world to be rich in faith and to possess the kingdom which he promised to those who love him. [6]But you dishonor the poor! Who are the ones who oppress you and drag you before the judges? The rich! [7]They are the ones who speak evil of that good name which has been given to you.

[8]You will be doing the right thing if you obey the law of the Kingdom, which is found in the scripture, "Love your neighbor as you love yourself." [9]But if you treat people according to their outward appearance, you are guilty of sin, and the Law condemns you as a lawbreaker. [10]Whoever breaks one commandment is guilty of breaking them all. [11]For the same one who said, "Do not commit adultery," also said, "Do not commit murder." Even if you do not commit adultery, you have become a lawbreaker if you commit murder. [12]Speak and act as people who will be judged by the law that sets us free. [13]For God will not show mercy when he judges the person who has not been merciful; but mercy triumphs over judgment.

道就夠了;相反地,你們必須行道。[23]那聽道而不去實行的,正像一個人對着鏡子,看看自己的面目,[24]端詳了一會兒,然後走開,立刻忘了自己的長相。[25]但是,嚴密查考那完整又使人得自由的法則而謹守的人,不是聽了就忘掉,而是切實行道的人;這樣的人在他所做的事上一定蒙上帝賜福。

[26]誰自以為虔誠,卻不管束自己的舌頭,便是欺騙自己;他的虔誠毫無價值。[27]在父上帝眼中,那純潔沒有缺點的虔誠便是:照顧苦難中的孤兒寡婦和保守自己不受世界的腐化。

譴責偏見

2 我的弟兄姊妹們,既然你們是我們榮耀的主耶穌基督的信徒,就不可憑着人的外表,用不同的態度對待人。[2]假定有一個有錢人手戴金戒指,身穿華麗衣服,來到你們聚會的地方,同時有一個衣著破爛的窮人也來了,[3]你要是對那個穿華麗衣服的人特別客氣,對他說:「請上座」,卻對那窮人說:「站在一邊」,或是說:「坐在我腳凳旁」,[4]你就是偏心,是惡意歧視人。

[5]我親愛的弟兄姊妹們,你們要聽:上帝揀選世上的窮人,使他們在信心上富足,又讓他們承受他應許給愛他的人的新國度。[6]你們竟侮辱窮人!其實,欺壓你們、把你們拉去見官的,正是這班有錢人![7]毀謗你們所領受那尊貴名稱的,也就是他們。

[8]你們若遵從聖經上所記載「愛人如己」那新國度的法則,那就對了。[9]但是,你們若憑人的外表待人,就是犯罪;法律要判定你們是犯法的。[10]誰違背了法律中的一條誡命,就等於違背全部法律。[11]因為那位命令說「不可姦淫」的,也說「不可殺人」。儘管你不犯姦淫,你殺人就是違背法律。[12]既然你們要受那使人得自由的法則所審判,你們的言行就要符合這標準。[13]因為上帝審判的時候,不會以仁慈待那些不仁慈的人。然而,仁慈是勝過審判的。

Faith and Actions

14My friends, what good is it for one of you to say that you have faith if your actions do not prove it? Can that faith save you? 15Suppose there are brothers or sisters who need clothes and don't have enough to eat. 16What good is there in your saying to them, "God bless you! Keep warm and eat well!"–if you don't give them the necessities of life? 17So it is with faith: if it is alone and includes no actions, then it is dead.

18But someone will say, "One person has faith, another has actions." My answer is, "Show me how anyone can have faith without actions. I will show you my faith by my actions." 19Do you believe that there is only one God? Good! The demons also believe–and tremble with fear. 20You fool! Do you want to be shown that faith without actions is useless?" 21How was our ancestor Abraham put right with God? It was through his actions, when he offered his son Isaac on the altar. 22Can't you see? His faith and his actions worked together; his faith was made perfect through his actions. 23And the scripture came true that said, "Abraham believed God, and because of his faith God accepted him as righteous." And so Abraham was called God's friend. 24You see, then, that it is by our actions that we are put right with God, and not by our faith alone.

25It was the same with the prostitute Rahab. She was put right with God through her actions, by welcoming the Israelite spies and helping them to escape by a different road.

26So then, as the body without the spirit is dead, also faith without actions is dead.

The Tongue

3 My friends, not many of you should become teachers. As you know, we teachers will be judged with greater strictness than others. 2All of us often make mistakes. But if a person never makes a mistake in what he says, he is perfect and is also able to control his whole being. 3We put a bit into the mouth of a horse to make it obey us, and we are able to make it go where we want. 4Or think of a ship: big as it is and driven by such strong winds, it can be steered by a very small rudder, and it goes wherever the pilot wants it to go. 5So it is with the tongue: small as it is, it can boast about great things.

Just think how large a forest can be set on fire by a tiny flame! 6And the tongue is like a fire. It is a world of wrong, occupying its place in our bodies and spreading evil through our whole being. It sets on fire the entire course of

a useless; *some manuscripts have* dead.

信心和行爲

14我的弟兄姊妹們，如果有人說他有信心，卻不能用他的行爲證明出來，有甚麼用處呢？那信心能救他嗎？15你們當中有弟兄或姊妹沒得穿，沒得吃，16你們卻對他說：「平安！平安！願你們穿得暖，吃得飽！」而不供給他們所需要的，那有甚麼用呢？17同樣，信心沒有行爲就是死的。

18但是，有人要說：「這個人有信心，那個人有行爲。」我要回答：「你給我看那沒有行爲的信心；我要用行爲給你看我的信心。」19你相信上帝只有一位，那很好！邪靈也這樣相信，而且非常怕他。20愚蠢的人哪，你們要知道沒有行爲的信心是無用的嗎？21我們的祖宗<u>亞伯拉罕</u>是怎樣得以跟上帝有合宜的關係呢？是由於他把兒子<u>以撒</u>在祭壇上這一行爲。22可見，他的信心跟行爲相輔並行，信心是藉着行爲而達到完全的。23聖經上說：「<u>亞伯拉罕</u>信上帝，因他的信，上帝認他爲義人。」這話實現了；他稱爲上帝的朋友。24所以，人得以跟上帝有合宜的關係是藉着行爲，不僅僅是藉着信心。25妓女<u>喇合</u>的情形也是一樣。她得以跟上帝有合宜的關係是由於行爲；她接待<u>猶太</u>人的使者，又幫助他們從另一條路逃走。

26所以，正如身體沒有氣息是死的，信心沒有行爲也是死的。

控制自己的舌頭

3 我的弟兄姊妹們，你們不應該個個都想當教師，因爲，你們知道當教師的要比別人受更嚴重的裁判。2我們常常犯錯誤。那在言語上沒有過錯的便是一個完全人；他能夠控制整個自己。3我們把嚼環放在馬嘴裏，就能使牠馴服，驅使牠到我們要去的地方。4再看，一條船雖然那麼大，在大風的吹襲下，只用一個小小的舵操縱，就可以隨着舵手的意思，使船朝目的地走。5同樣，舌頭雖然很小，卻能夠說大話。

試想，星星之火不是可以燎原嗎？6舌頭正像火一樣，在我們的肢體中是邪惡的世界，會污染全身；它藉着地獄的火燒毀我們

our existence with the fire that comes to it from hell itself. [7]We humans are able to tame and have tamed all other creatures–wild animals and birds, reptiles and fish. [8]But no one has ever been able to tame the tongue. It is evil and uncontrollable, full of deadly poison. [9]We use it to give thanks to our Lord and Father and also to curse other people, who are created in the likeness of God. [10]Words of thanksgiving and cursing pour out from the same mouth. My friends, this should not happen! [11]No spring of water pours out sweet water and bitter water from the same opening. [12]A fig tree, my friends, cannot bear olives; a grapevine cannot bear figs, nor can a salty spring produce sweet water.

The Wisdom from Above

[13]Are there any of you who are wise and understanding? You are to prove it by your good life, by your good deeds performed with humility and wisdom. [14]But if in your heart you are jealous, bitter, and selfish, don't sin against the truth by boasting of your wisdom. [15]Such wisdom does not come down from heaven; it belongs to the world, it is unspiritual and demonic. [16]Where there is jealousy and selfishness, there is also disorder and every kind of evil. [17]But the wisdom from above is pure first of all; it is also peaceful, gentle, and friendly; it is full of compassion and produces a harvest of good deeds; it is free from prejudice and hypocrisy. [18]And goodness is the harvest that is produced from the seeds the peacemakers plant in peace.

Friendship with the World

4 Where do all the fights and quarrels among you come from? They come from your desires for pleasure, which are constantly fighting within you. [2]You want things, but you cannot have them, so you are ready to kill; you strongly desire things, but you cannot get them, so you quarrel and fight. You do not have what you want because you do not ask God for it. [3]And when you ask, you do not receive it, because your motives are bad; you ask for things to use for your own pleasures. [4]Unfaithful people! Don't you know that to be the world's friend means to be God's enemy? If you want to be the world's friend, you make yourself God's enemy. [5]Don't think that there is no truth in the scripture that says, "The spirit that God placed in us is filled with fierce desires."[b] [6]But the grace that God gives is even stronger. As the scripture says, "God resists the proud,

b The spirit … fierce desires; or God yearns jealously over the spirit that he placed in us.

整個人生的路程。[7]人能夠制伏野獸、飛禽、爬蟲、和水族;其實,他已經制伏了各類動物。[8]但是,人從來不能制伏舌頭;它是控制不了的邪惡,充滿着致命的毒氣。[9]我們用舌頭頌讚我們的主、我們的天父,也用舌頭詛咒上帝按照自己的形像所造出來的人。[10]頌讚和詛咒都是從同一張嘴巴出來!弟兄姊妹們,這是不應該的![11]從同一泉源能夠湧出甜和苦兩種水來嗎?[12]弟兄姊妹們,無花果樹不能結橄欖;葡萄樹不能結無花果;鹹澀的水源也流不出甘甜的水來。

從天上來的智慧

[13]你們當中有聰明智慧的人嗎?如果有,他就應該以充滿着謙卑和智慧的好行為,來表現他有美好的生活。[14]既然你們心裏有惡毒的嫉妒和自私,你們就不可以自誇,不可以撒謊敵對真理。[15]你們的所謂智慧不是從天上來的,而是屬世,屬情慾,屬魔鬼的。[16]凡是有嫉妒和自私的地方,就有紛亂和各種邪惡的行為。[17]但是,從上面來的智慧有幾樣特徵;第一是純潔,其次是和平、謙和、友善,充滿着仁慈,能結出豐富的善果,沒有偏私,沒有虛偽。[18]一切正義的果子都是從播種和平的人、為和平努力所撒的種子產生出來的。

不要與世界為友

4 你們當中的衝突爭吵是哪裏來的呢?是從你們當中爭戰着的慾望來的![2]你們要抓取奪取,得不到就殺人;你們要貪婪婪,得不到手就爭就鬥。你們得不到所要的,是因為你們沒有向上帝求。[3]你們求仍然得不到,是因為你們的動機不好;你們所求的不過是要揮霍享樂罷了![4]你們這班不忠不信的人哪,難道不曉得跟世界做朋友就是敵對上帝嗎?誰要跟世界做朋友,誰就是上帝的敵人![5]聖經上說:「上帝安置在我們裏面的靈有強烈的慾望[①]。」你們以為這話沒有意思嗎?[6]然而,上帝所賜的恩典更為豐富,正如聖經所說:「上帝敵對驕傲的人,

[①]「上帝安置在我們裏面的靈有強烈的慾望」或譯「上帝強烈地戀慕他安置在我們裏面的靈」。

but gives grace to the humble."

7So then, submit yourselves to God. Resist the Devil, and he will run away from you. 8Come near to God, and he will come near to you. Wash your hands, you sinners! Purify your hearts, you hypocrites! 9Be sorrowful, cry, and weep; change your laughter into crying, your joy into gloom! 10Humble yourselves before the Lord, and he will lift you up.

Warning against Judging One Another

11Do not criticize one another, my friends. If you criticize or judge another Christian, you criticize and judge the Law. If you judge the Law, then you are no longer one who obeys the Law, but one who judges it. 12God is the only lawgiver and judge. He alone can save and destroy. Who do you think you are, to judge someone else?

Warning against Boasting

13Now listen to me, you that say, "Today or tomorrow we will travel to a certain city, where we will stay a year and go into business and make a lot of money." 14You don't even know what your life tomorrow will be! You are like a puff of smoke, which appears for a moment and then disappears. 15What you should say is this: "If the Lord is willing, we will live and do this or that." 16But now you are proud, and you boast; all such boasting is wrong.

17So then, if we do not do the good we know we should do, we are guilty of sin.

Warning to the Rich

5 And now, you rich people, listen to me! Weep and wail over the miseries that are coming upon you! 2Your riches have rotted away, and your clothes have been eaten by moths. 3Your gold and silver are covered with rust, and this rust will be a witness against you and will eat up your flesh like fire. You have piled up riches in these last days. 4You have not paid any wages to those who work in your fields. Listen to their complaints! The cries of those who gather in your crops have reached the ears of God, the Lord Almighty. 5Your life here on earth has been full of luxury and pleasure. You have made yourselves fat for the day of slaughter. 6You have condemned and murdered innocent people, and they do not resist you.c

c people, and they do not resist you; or people. Will God not resist you?

賜恩典給謙卑的人。」

7 所以，你們要順服上帝；要抗拒魔鬼，魔鬼就會逃避。8你們親近上帝，上帝就親近你們。有罪的人哪，要潔淨你們的手！僞善的人哪，要潔淨你們的心！9你們要悲傷，哀慟，哭泣；要把歡笑變爲哀哭，喜樂變爲悲愁。10要在主面前謙卑，他就提升你們。

不要評斷

11 弟兄姊妹們，不要互相批評。誰批評或評斷弟兄姊妹，就是批評和評斷摩西的法律。如果你評斷法律，你就不是服從法律，而是評斷它。12只有上帝是立法者、審判者；只有他能拯救，能毀滅。你是誰，竟敢評斷你的鄰人！

不要自誇

13 有人說：「今天或明天，我們要到某某城去，在那裏住一年，做生意，賺大錢。」可是，聽我說，14你們連明天還活着沒有都不曉得！你們不過像一層霧，出現一會兒就不見了。15你們應該這樣說：「如果主願意，我們就可以活着，做這事，做那事。」16可是，你們竟那麼驕傲自大；這樣的驕傲全是邪惡的。

17 所以，那知道應該行善而不去行的就是罪。

警告有錢的人

5 那麼，你們有錢的人，聽我說。你們要爲那就要臨到的災難痛哭哀號！2你們的財富喪失了，衣裳給蟲蛀了。3你們的金銀都生銹了；這銹要作爲控告你們的證據，又像火一樣吞滅你們的身體。在這世界的末期，你們只知道積蓄財物。4你們剝削在田裏替你們做工的工人，剋扣他們的工錢，他們在控訴你們呢！那些收割工人喊冤的聲音已經進到主─萬軍的統帥的耳朵了。5你們在世上奢侈享樂，把自己養胖了，等待屠宰的日子。6你們定無辜者的罪，殺害了他們；他們並沒有抵抗。②

②「他們並沒有抵抗。」或譯「上帝豈不阻止你們？」

Patience and Prayer

7Be patient, then, my friends, until the Lord comes. See how patient farmers are as they wait for their land to produce precious crops. They wait patiently for the autumn and spring rains. 8You also must be patient. Keep your hopes high, for the day of the Lord's coming is near.

9Do not complain against one another, my friends, so that God will not judge you. The Judge is near, ready to appear. 10My friends, remember the prophets who spoke in the name of the Lord. Take them as examples of patient endurance under suffering. 11We call them happy because they endured. You have heard of Job's patience, and you know how the Lord provided for him in the end. For the Lord is full of mercy and compassion.

12Above all, my friends, do not use an oath when you make a promise. Do not swear by heaven or by earth or by anything else. Say only "Yes" when you mean yes, and "No" when you mean no, and then you will not come under God's judgment.

13Are any among you in trouble? They should pray. Are any among you happy? They should sing praises. 14Are any among you sick? They should send for the church elders, who will pray for them and rub olive oil on them in the name of the Lord. 15This prayer made in faith will heal the sick; the Lord will restore them to health, and the sins they have committed will be forgiven. 16So then, confess your sins to one another and pray for one another, so that you will be healed. The prayer of a good person has a powerful effect. 17Elijah was the same kind of person as we are. He prayed earnestly that there would be no rain, and no rain fell on the land for three and a half years. 18Once again he prayed, and the sky poured out its rain and the earth produced its crops.

19My friends, if any of you wander away from the truth and another one brings you back again, 20remember this: whoever turns a sinner back from the wrong way will save that sinner's soul[d] from death and bring about the forgiveness of many sins.

d that sinner's soul; or his own soul.

忍耐和禱告

7 所以，弟兄姊妹們，你們要忍耐，等到主再來。看吧，農夫多麼耐心地等待着田裏寶貴的產物，耐心地盼望着春霖秋雨。8 你們也必須忍耐。你們要抱着堅定的希望，因為主再來的日子快到了。

9 弟兄姊妹們，不要互相埋怨，免得上帝審判你們。審判的主快要來了，就在門口了。10弟兄姊妹們，要記得奉主名說話的先知們，要學習他們受苦和忍耐的榜樣。11因為他們忍耐到底，我們認為他們是有福了。你們聽見過約伯的忍耐，也知道主後來怎樣看顧他，因為主充滿着憐憫和慈愛。

12我的弟兄姊妹們，最主要的是：不可發誓，不可指天指地，或指任何東西發誓。是，就說是；不是，就說不是。這樣，你們就不至於受上帝的審判。

13 你們當中有有遭遇痛苦的嗎？他應該禱告；有喜樂的嗎？他應該歌頌；14有害病的嗎？他應該請教會的長老替他禱告，奉主的名替他抹油。15這禱告若是出於信心，就能夠治好病人；主會恢復他的健康，病人所犯的罪會得到赦免。16所以，你們要互相認罪，彼此代禱，使你們得醫治。義人的禱告有很大的功效。17以利亞和我們同樣是人；他懇切禱告，求上帝不下雨，果然有三年半之久沒有下雨。18他再禱告，天就下了大雨，大地生產五穀。

19 我的弟兄姊妹們，你們當中若有迷失而離開了眞理的人，有人把他找回來，20你們要知道：那使迷失的罪人回頭的，會把罪人的靈魂從死裏搶救回來，並使許許多多的罪得到寬赦。

彼得前書
1 PETER

INTRODUCTION

The First Letter from Peter was addressed to Christians, here called "God's chosen people," who were scattered throughout the northern part of Asia Minor. The main purpose of the letter is to encourage the readers, who were facing persecution and suffering for their faith. The writer does this by reminding his readers of the Good News about Jesus Christ, whose death, resurrection, and promised coming gave them hope. In the light of this they are to accept and endure their suffering, confident that it is a test of the genuineness of their faith and that they will be rewarded on "the Day when Jesus Christ is revealed."

Along with his encouragement in time of trouble, the writer also urges his readers to live as people who belong to Christ.

Outline of Contents

簡 介

彼得前書是寫給散居在小亞細亞北部一帶的基督徒的，書中稱他們爲「上帝的選民」。本書的主要目的在鼓勵那些爲了信仰遭受苦難和迫害的信徒。作者一再以耶穌基督的福音—他的死、復活，和再來的應許—勸勉他們，給他們希望。因此，他們必須忍受苦難，確信苦難是對他們信心的考驗，並且會使他們在「耶穌基督顯現的日子」得到獎賞。

作者不但鼓勵這些信徒怎樣面對患難，同時也勸告他們在生活上表現出他們是屬於基督的人。

提要

1 From Peter, apostle of Jesus Christ–
To God's chosen people who live as refugees scattered throughout the provinces of Pontus, Galatia, Cappadocia, Asia, and Bithynia. [2]You were chosen according to the purpose of God the Father and were made a holy people by his Spirit, to obey Jesus Christ and be purified by his blood.

May grace and peace be yours in full measure.

1 我—彼得是耶穌基督的使徒。我寫信給上帝所選召的子民：那些因避難散居在本都、加拉太、加帕多家、亞細亞、庇推尼各地的信徒們。 [2]你們蒙選召是按照父上帝預定的旨意，是藉著聖靈而成爲聖潔的，爲要順服耶穌基督，並受他的血的潔淨。

願上帝豐豐富富地賜恩典、平安給你們！

A Living Hope

3Let us give thanks to the God and Father of our Lord Jesus Christ! Because of his great mercy he gave us new life by raising Jesus Christ from death. This fills us with a living hope, 4Oand so we look forward to possessing the rich blessings that God keeps for his people. He keeps them for you in heaven, where they cannot decay or spoil or fade away. 5They are for you, who through faith are kept safe by God's power for the salvation which is ready to be revealed at the end of time.

6Be glad about this, even though it may now be necessary for you to be sad for a while because of the many kinds of trials you suffer. 7Their purpose is to prove that your faith is genuine. Even gold, which can be destroyed, is tested by fire; and so your faith, which is much more precious than gold, must also be tested, so that it may endure. Then you will receive praise and glory and honor on the Day when Jesus Christ is revealed. 8You love him, although you have not seen him, and you believe in him, although you do not now see him. So you rejoice with a great and glorious joy which words cannot express, 9because you are receiving the salvation of your souls, which is the purpose of your faith in him.

10It was concerning this salvation that the prophets made careful search and investigation, and they prophesied about this gift which God would give you. 11They tried to find out when the time would be and how it would come.[a] This was the time to which Christ's Spirit in them was pointing, in predicting the sufferings that Christ would have to endure and the glory that would follow. 12God revealed to these prophets that their work was not for their own benefit, but for yours, as they spoke about those things which you have now heard from the messengers who announced the Good News by the power of the Holy Spirit sent from heaven. These are things which even the angels would like to understand.

A Call to Holy Living

13So then, have your minds ready for action. Keep alert and set your hope completely on the blessing which will be given you when Jesus Christ is revealed. 14Be obedient to God, and do not allow your lives to be shaped by those desires you had when you were still ignorant. 15Instead, be holy in all that you do, just as God who called you is holy. 16The scripture says, "Be holy because I am holy."

17You call him Father, when you pray to

活的盼望

3 我們要感謝我們的主耶穌基督的父上帝！由於他無限的仁慈，藉着耶穌基督從死裏復活，把新的生命賜給我們，使我們有活的盼望，4 來承受上帝為他的子民保留在天上的福澤；這福澤是不敗壞、不污損、不衰殘的，5 是要給你們這些因信上帝而蒙他大能保守的人，好使你們獲得那已經預備好、將在歷史的終點實現的拯救。

6 因此，你們要喜樂，雖然現在因種種的試煉或許必須暫時受苦；7 這種經歷無非要證明你們的確有堅定的信心。甚至那能毀壞的金子也得經過火煉；你們的信心比金子貴重多了，更必須受考驗，好使你們在耶穌基督顯現的日子得到稱讚、光榮，和尊貴。8 你們雖然沒有見過他，卻愛他；雖然現在看不見他，卻信他。你們有言語所不能表達的那無限的喜樂；9 因為你們正在領受信心的效果，就是你們靈魂的得救。

10 論到這拯救，先知們已經有了詳細的尋求和探究，並預言關於上帝要賜給你們的這恩典。11 他們探索，要知道基督的靈在他們裏面所指示的─就是預言基督必須受苦難，後來必定得榮耀這事─會在甚麼時候，在哪一種情況下實現①。12 上帝讓先知們知道，他們的工作並不是為自己，而是為你們。他們所說的這些事，現在已經藉着福音的使者們，靠着從天上來的聖靈的能力，傳給你們了；這些事連天使也希望明白呢！

聖潔的生活

13 所以，你們的心要準備好，時時警惕，把希望完全寄託在耶穌基督顯現時所要賜給你們的恩典上。14 要順服上帝，不可讓私慾支配你們，像從前你們愚昧無知的時候那樣。15 那位呼召你們的上帝是聖潔的；你們也必須在所做的一切事上聖潔。16 聖經上說：「你們要聖潔，因為我是聖潔的。」

17 你們禱告的時候，稱那位按照人的行

---

a when the time would be and how it would come; or who the person would be and when he would come.

① 「會在甚麼時候，在哪一種情況下實現」或譯「是指誰，會在甚麼時候來」。

God, who judges all people by the same stand-ard, according to what each one has done; so then, spend the rest of your lives here on earth in reverence for him. [18]For you know what was paid to set you free from the worthless manner of life handed down by your ancestors. It was not something that can be destroyed, such as silver or gold; [19]it was the costly sacrifice of Christ, who was like a lamb without defect or flaw. [20]He had been chosen by God before the creation of the world and was revealed in these last days for your sake. [21]Through him you believe in God, who raised him from death and gave him glory; and so your faith and hope are fixed on God.

[22]Now that by your obedience to the truth you have purified yourselves and have come to have a sincere love for other believers, love one another earnestly with all your heart.[b] [23]For through the living and eternal word of God you have been born again as the children of a parent who is immortal, not mortal. [24]As the scripture says,

"All human beings are like grass,
    and all their glory is like wild flowers.
The grass withers, and the flowers fall,

[25]   but the word of the Lord remains forever."
This word is the Good News that was proclaimed to you.

The Living Stone and the Holy Nation

2 Rid yourselves, then, of all evil; no more lying or hypocrisy or jealousy or insulting language. [2]Be like newborn babies, always thirsty for the pure spiritual milk, so that by drinking it you may grow up and be saved. [3]As the scripture says, "You have found out for yourselves how kind the Lord is."

[4]Come to the Lord, the living stone rejected by people as worthless but chosen by God as valuable. [5]Come as living stones, and let yourselves be used in building the spiritual temple, where you will serve as holy priests to offer spiritual and acceptable sacrifices to God through Jesus Christ. [6]For the scripture says,

"I chose a valuable stone,
    which I am placing as the cornerstone in
        Zion;
    and whoever believes in him will never be
        disappointed."

[7]This stone is of great value for you that believe; but for those who do not believe:
"The stone which the builders rejected as
        worthless
    turned out to be the most important of
        all."

b with all your heart; *some manuscripts have* with a pure heart.

為,用同一標準來審判人的上帝為父親;那麼,你們寄居世上的日子應該敬畏他。[18]你們知道,你們得以從祖傳的敗壞中釋放出來是付上了甚麼代價的。並不是那些會失掉價值的東西,好像金子銀子,[19]而是憑着基督所流寶貴的血,就像那無瑕疵無汚點的羔羊的血。[20]基督是上帝在創世以前預先揀選,而在這歷史的末期為你們的緣故顯現的。[21]藉着他,你們信了那使他從死裏復活、並賜給他榮耀的上帝;因此,你們的信心和盼望都集中於上帝。

[22]現在,因為你們順服眞理,你們已經潔淨了自己,並且跟其他信徒有手足之情,從心底熱切彼此相愛。[23]你們已經重生,不是從那會朽壞的種子生的,而是從那不朽壞的種子─就是上帝活潑永恆的道所生的。[24]正如聖經所說:

人人像野草一般,
    一切榮華有如野花;
    草會枯乾,花會凋謝,
[25]但是主的道永遠長存!
這道就是所傳給你們的福音。

活的石頭和聖潔的國度

2 所以,你們要排除一切壞事,不再撒謊,偽善,嫉妒,或說人壞話;[2]要像新生的嬰兒,時時渴慕那純淨的靈奶,好藉着它長大,得救。[3]正像聖經所說:「你們嘗過了主的恩慈。」

[4]要親近主─活的石頭;雖然他被人厭棄,但上帝揀選他,珍惜他。[5]你們也要像活的石頭,用來建造屬靈的聖殿,在那裏作聖潔的祭司,藉着耶穌基督獻上為上帝所悅納的屬靈祭物。[6]因為聖經上說:

我選了一塊貴重的石頭
    作為錫安的牆角石;
    凡信靠他的,
    都不至於失望。
[7]對你們信的人來說,這石頭是很寶貴的;可是,對於那些不信的人:
泥水匠所丟棄的這塊石頭
    已成為最重要的基石!

8And another scripture says,

"This is the stone that will make people
stumble,

the rock that will make them fall."

They stumbled because they did not believe in the word; such was God's will for them.

9But you are the chosen race, the King's priests, the holy nation, God's own people, chosen to proclaim the wonderful acts of God, who called you out of darkness into his own marvelous light. 10At one time you were not God's people, but now you are his people; at one time you did not know God's mercy, but now you have received his mercy.

Slaves of God

11I appeal to you, my friends, as strangers and refugees in this world! Do not give in to bodily passions, which are always at war against the soul. 12Your conduct among the heathen should be so good that when they accuse you of being evildoers, they will have to recognize your good deeds and so praise God on the Day of his coming.

13For the sake of the Lord submit yourselves to every human authority: to the Emperor, who is the supreme authority, 14and to the governors, who have been appointed by him to punish the evildoers and to praise those who do good. 15For God wants you to silence the ignorant talk of foolish people by the good things you do. 16Live as free people; do not, however, use your freedom to cover up any evil, but live as God's slaves. 17Respect everyone, love other believers, honor God, and respect the Emperor.

The Example of Christ's Suffering

18You servants must submit yourselves to your masters and show them complete respect, not only to those who are kind and considerate, but also to those who are harsh. 19God will bless you for this, if you endure the pain of undeserved suffering because you are conscious of his will. 20For what credit is there if you endure the beatings you deserve for having done wrong? But if you endure suffering even when you have done right, God will bless you for it. 21It was to this that God called you, for Christ himself suffered for you and left you an example, so that you would follow in his steps. 22He committed no sin, and no one ever heard a lie come from his lips. 23When he was insulted, he did not answer back with an insult; when he suffered, he did not threaten, but placed his hopes in God, the righteous Judge. 24Christ

8 在聖經的另一處說：

這一塊絆腳的石頭

是使人絆倒的石塊。

他們絆倒了，因爲他們不信眞道；這也是出於上帝的旨意。

9 但是，你們是蒙揀選的種族，是王家的祭司，聖潔的國度，上帝的子民。上帝選召你們離別黑暗，進入他輝煌的光明，來宣揚他奇妙的作爲。10從前你們不是上帝的子民，現在是他的子民；從前沒有得到上帝的憐憫，現在已經得到他的憐憫。

上帝的奴僕

11 親愛的朋友們，你們在世上是寄居的，是旅客。我勸你們，不要放縱肉體的情慾；這種情慾老在跟靈魂爭戰。12在外邦人當中，你們應該有端正的品行，使那些說你們壞話、指責你們做壞事的人，因看見你們的好行爲，就在主再來的日子，歸榮耀給上帝。

13 爲了主的緣故，你們要順從人間的掌權者：就是在上的君王14和他所委派執行獎善罰惡的長官。15因爲上帝的旨意是要你們以好行爲來堵住那班糊塗人的無知之口。16你們是自由人，但不要用自由來掩蓋任何邪惡；要作上帝的奴僕。17你們要尊重每一個人；要愛信主的弟兄姊妹；要敬畏上帝；要尊敬君王。

基督忍受苦難的榜樣

18 作奴僕的，你們要恭敬服從主人，不但對良善溫和的主人這樣，對嚴酷的主人也要這樣。19如果你們因領會這是上帝的旨意，願意忍受不當受的痛苦，上帝就會賜福給你們。20如果你們是因犯過錯而忍受責打，那有甚麼光榮呢？只有因行善而忍受苦難的人才能蒙上帝賜福。21上帝呼召你們的目的就在這裏；因爲基督爲你們受苦，給你們留下榜樣，爲要使你們能夠跟隨他的腳步走。22他沒有犯過罪；沒有人聽見過他撒謊。23他受辱罵不還口，受虐待也不說恐嚇的話，只仰望公義的審判者。24基督親身把我

himself carried our sins in his body to the cross, so that we might die to sin and live for righteousness. It is by his wounds that you have been healed. 25You were like sheep that had lost their way, but now you have been brought back to follow the Shepherd and Keeper of your souls.

Wives and Husbands

3 In the same way you wives must submit yourselves to your husbands, so that if any of them do not believe God's word, your conduct will win them over to believe. It will not be necessary for you to say a word, 2because they will see how pure and reverent your conduct is. 3You should not use outward aids to make yourselves beautiful, such as the way you fix your hair, or the jewelry you put on, or the dresses you wear. 4Instead, your beauty should consist of your true inner self, the ageless beauty of a gentle and quiet spirit, which is of the greatest value in God's sight. 5For the devout women of the past who placed their hope in God used to make themselves beautiful by submitting themselves to their husbands. 6Sarah was like that; she obeyed Abraham and called him her master. You are now her daughters if you do good and are not afraid of anything.

7In the same way you husbands must live with your wives with the proper understanding that they are more delicate than you. Treat them with respect, because they also will receive, together with you, God's gift of life. Do this so that nothing will interfere with your prayers.

Suffering for Doing Right

8To conclude: you must all have the same attitude and the same feelings; love one another, and be kind and humble with one another. 9Do not pay back evil with evil or cursing with cursing; instead, pay back with a blessing, because a blessing is what God promised to give you when he called you. 10As the scripture says,

"If you want to enjoy life
and wish to see good times,
you must keep from speaking evil
and stop telling lies.
11You must turn away from evil and do good;
you must strive for peace with all your
heart.
12For the Lord watches over the righteous
and listens to their prayers;
but he opposes those who do evil."

13Who will harm you if you are eager to do what is good? 14But even if you should suffer for doing what is right, how happy you are! Do

們的罪帶到十字架上，使我們不再生活在罪中，只為公義而活。由於他所受的創傷，你們得到了醫治。25從前你們都像迷失的羊，現在已經歸回，跟隨著你們靈魂的牧人和監護者了。

妻子和丈夫

3 同樣，作妻子的，你們也應該順服自己的丈夫，好使沒有接受真道的丈夫能因你們的好品行受感化。你們用不着多說話，2因為他們會看見你們的純潔和端莊的品行。3你們不要藉打扮來妝飾自己，不要講究怎樣鬈頭髮、戴甚麼金飾、穿甚麼衣服。4你們應該有內在的美，以那不會衰退的溫柔嫻靜為妝飾；這在上帝眼中是最有價值的。5因為，從前那些仰望上帝的聖潔婦女也都以服從丈夫來妝飾自己。6莎拉也是這樣；她服從亞伯拉罕，稱呼他「主人」。你們有好行為，不畏懼甚麼，你們就都是莎拉的女兒了。

7同樣，作丈夫的，你們跟妻子一同生活，也應該體貼她們在性別上比較軟弱。要尊重她們，因為她們跟你們一樣都要領受上帝所賜的新生命。能夠這樣，你們的禱告就不至於受阻礙。

為義受苦難

8總括來說：你們都要同心，互相同情，親愛如手足，以仁慈謙讓相待。9不要以惡報惡，以辱罵還辱罵；相反地，要以祝福回報，因為上帝呼召你們的目的是要賜福給你們。10正像聖經所說的：

誰要享受人生的樂趣，
希望過好日子，
就得禁止舌頭說壞話，
禁止嘴唇撒謊。
11他應該避惡行善，
一心追求和平。
12因為上帝看顧義人，
垂聽他們的禱告；
但他要向作惡的人變臉。
13如果你們熱心行善，誰會危害你們呢？
14即使為義受苦，也多麼有福啊！不要怕人

not be afraid of anyone, and do not worry. [15]But have reverence for Christ in your hearts, and honor him as Lord. Be ready at all times to answer anyone who asks you to explain the hope you have in you, [16]but do it with gentleness and respect. Keep your conscience clear, so that when you are insulted, those who speak evil of your good conduct as followers of Christ will become ashamed of what they say. [17]For it is better to suffer for doing good, if this should be God's will, than for doing evil. [18]For Christ died[c] for sins once and for all, a good man on behalf of sinners, in order to lead you to God. He was put to death physically, but made alive spiritually, [19]and in his spiritual existence he went and preached to the imprisoned spirits. [20]These were the spirits of those who had not obeyed God when he waited patiently during the days that Noah was building his boat. The few people in the boat–eight in all–were saved by the water, [21]which was a symbol pointing to baptism, which now saves you. It is not the washing off of bodily dirt, but the promise made to God from a good conscience. It saves you through the resurrection of Jesus Christ, [22]who has gone to heaven and is at the right side of God, ruling over all angels and heavenly authorities and powers.

Changed Lives

4 Since Christ suffered physically, you too must strengthen yourselves with the same way of thinking that he had; because whoever suffers physically is no longer involved with sin. [2]From now on, then, you must live the rest of your earthly lives controlled by God's will and not by human desires. [3]You have spent enough time in the past doing what the heathen like to do. Your lives were spent in indecency, lust, drunkenness, orgies, drinking parties, and the disgusting worship of idols. [4]And now the heathen are surprised when you do not join them in the same wild and reckless living, and so they insult you. [5]But they will have to give an account of themselves to God, who is ready to judge the living and the dead. [6]That is why the Good News was preached also to the dead, to those who had been judged in their physical existence as everyone is judged; it was preached to them so that in their spiritual existence they may live as God lives.

Good Managers of God's Gifts

[7]The end of all things is near. You must be self-controlled and alert, to be able to pray. [8]Above everything, love one another earnestly,

c died; *many manuscripts have* suffered.

的威脅,也不要驚慌。[15]要有敬畏基督的心,以他爲主。有人要求你們解釋心裏的盼望,要隨時準備答辯;[16]可是要以謙恭溫和的態度回答。要有清白的良心,讓那些侮辱你們、對你們作爲基督徒所表現的好品行妄加毀謗的人,自己覺得慚愧。[17]如果行善而受苦是出於上帝的旨意,這總比作惡而受苦强多了。[18]因爲基督也曾一舉而竟全功地爲罪而死[2],是義的代替不義的,爲要把你們帶到上帝面前。他的肉體被處死,他的靈卻被救活[3]。[19]他曾以這靈去向那些被囚禁的靈傳道。[20]這些靈不信從上帝—就是在挪亞造方舟時上帝耐心等待着的靈。當時進入方舟的人不多,只有八個人,他們從水裏獲救;[21]這水就是預表洗禮。這洗禮現在拯救了你們,不是洗滌你們身體的污垢,而是以清白的良心向上帝許願;這洗禮藉着耶穌基督的復活拯救了你們。[22]耶穌基督已經到天上去,如今在上帝右邊,統轄所有的天使和天界的執政者和掌權者。

改變了的生活

4 既然基督在肉體上受苦,你們也應該用同樣的意志裝備自己,因爲在肉體上受過苦的人已經跟罪惡絕緣。[2]從今以後,你們在世上所剩下的日子要受上帝旨意的管束,不再被人的慾望所控制。[3]從前你們浪費光陰,做異教徒喜歡做的事,生活在淫亂、縱慾、酗酒、宴樂、狂飲,和可憎惡的偶像崇拜中。[4]現在你們不再跟他們過那放蕩、沒有節制的生活,他們覺得很奇怪,因而侮辱你們。[5]可是,他們一定要向那位將審判活人和死人的上帝交帳。[6]爲了這理由,福音也曾傳給死人,給那些跟其他的人一樣在肉體上受了審判的人,好使他們的靈得以跟上帝一樣活着。

上帝恩賜的好管家

[7]萬事的終局就要到了。你們要謹慎自守,警醒禱告。[8]最重要的是要彼此眞誠相

[2]「死」有些古卷作「受苦」。
[3]「他的肉體⋯⋯被救活」或譯「按着肉體,他被處死;按着靈,他復活了」。

because love covers over many sins. ⁹Open your homes to each other without complaining. ¹⁰Each one, as a good manager of God's different gifts, must use for the good of others the special gift he has received from God. ¹¹Those who preach must preach God's messages; those who serve must serve with the strength that God gives them, so that in all things praise may be given to God through Jesus Christ, to whom belong glory and power forever and ever. Amen.

Suffering as a Christian

¹²My dear friends, do not be surprised at the painful test you are suffering, as though something unusual were happening to you. ¹³Rather be glad that you are sharing Christ's sufferings, so that you may be full of joy when his glory is revealed. ¹⁴Happy are you if you are insulted because you are Christ's followers; this means that the glorious Spirit, the Spirit of God, is resting on you. ¹⁵If you suffer, it must not be because you are a murderer or a thief or a criminal or a meddler in other people's affairs. ¹⁶However, if you suffer because you are a Christian, don't be ashamed of it, but thank God that you bear Christ's name.

¹⁷The time has come for judgment to begin, and God's own people are the first to be judged. If it starts with us, how will it end with those who do not believe the Good News from God? ¹⁸As the scripture says,

"It is difficult for good people to be saved; what, then, will become of godless sinners?"

¹⁹So then, those who suffer because it is God's will for them, should by their good actions trust themselves completely to their Creator, who always keeps his promise.

The Flock of God

5 I, who am an elder myself, appeal to the church elders among you. I am a witness of Christ's sufferings, and I will share in the glory that will be revealed. I appeal to you ²to be shepherds of the flock that God gave you and to take care of it willingly, as God wants you to, and not unwillingly. Do your work, not for mere pay, but from a real desire to serve. ³Do not try to rule over those who have been put in your care, but be examples to the flock. ⁴And when the Chief Shepherd appears, you will receive the glorious crown which will never lose its brightness.

⁵In the same way you younger people must submit yourselves to your elders. And all of you must put on the apron of humility, to serve one another; for the scripture says, "God resists

愛，因為愛能夠消除許多罪過。⁹要彼此殷勤接待，不要埋怨。¹⁰既然每一個人都是上帝各樣恩賜的好管家，就要照着從上帝所領受的種種恩賜，彼此服事。¹¹誰宣講，就得宣講上帝的話；誰服事，就得本着上帝所賜的力量服事，好使萬事都藉着耶穌基督歸榮耀給上帝。願榮耀和權能都歸於他，世世無窮！阿們。

忍受苦難

¹²親愛的朋友們，你們遇到火一樣的考驗，不要驚怪，好像所遇到的是很不平常似的。¹³你們應該以分擔基督的苦難為一件樂事，好在他榮耀顯現的時候得到充分的喜樂。¹⁴你們若因跟從基督而受凌辱，就有福了；這表示榮耀的聖靈，就是上帝的靈，在你們身上。¹⁵但是，你們當中有人受苦，不可是因凶殺，作賊，犯刑案，或好管閒事而受的。¹⁶如果受苦是由於作基督徒，不要引以為恥，卻要因披戴着基督的名號而榮耀上帝。

¹⁷審判的時候到了，上帝家的兒女要先受審判。如果審判要從我們開始，那麼，不信上帝福音的人會有甚麼結局呢？¹⁸正如聖經所說的：

義人得救已不容易，
不虔的罪人又怎樣呢？

¹⁹所以，那由於上帝的旨意而受苦難的人，應該不斷地以好行為來表示完全信賴那始終信實的創造主。

上帝的羊羣

5 我現在以一個長老的身份向各位同作長老的提出請求。我是見證基督受苦的人，要分享將來所顯示的榮耀。我請求你們，²要牧養上帝所付託你們的羊羣，甘心樂意地按照上帝的旨意照顧他們，不是出於勉強；不是為酬報而工作，而是自動自發的事奉。³不要轄制你們所牧養的羊羣，卻要作羊羣的榜樣。⁴這樣，那大牧人來臨的時候，你們就會領受那永不失去光彩的華冠。

⁵同樣，你們年輕人應該服從長輩。大家要繫上謙卑的圍裙，彼此服事；因為聖經上說：「上帝敵對驕傲的人，賜恩典給謙卑的

the proud, but shows favor to the humble." [6]Humble yourselves, then, under God's mighty hand, so that he will lift you up in his own good time. [7]Leave all your worries with him, because he cares for you.

[8]Be alert, be on watch! Your enemy, the Devil, roams around like a roaring lion, looking for someone to devour. [9]Be firm in your faith and resist him, because you know that other believers in all the world are going through the same kind of sufferings. [10]But after you have suffered for a little while, the God of all grace, who calls you to share his eternal glory in union with Christ, will himself perfect you and give you firmness, strength, and a sure foundation. [11]To him be the power forever! Amen.

Final Greetings

[12]I write you this brief letter with the help of Silas, whom I regard as a faithful Christian. I want to encourage you and give my testimony that this is the true grace of God. Stand firm in it.

[13]Your sister church in Babylon,[d] also chosen by God, sends you greetings, and so does my son Mark. [14]Greet one another with the kiss of Christian love.

May peace be with all of you who belong to Christ.

d BABYLON: *As in the book of Revelation, this probably refers to Rome.*

人。」[6]所以，你們要在上帝大能的手下謙卑，這樣，他會在適當的時機提升你們。[7]要把一切憂慮都卸給他，因為他關心你們。

[8] 要警醒戒備！你們的仇敵一魔鬼正像咆哮的獅子走來走去，搜索可吞吃的人。[9]你們要信心堅定，抗拒他，因為你們知道全世界信主的弟兄姊妹們也都在經歷同樣的苦難。[10]但是，你們受了短暫的苦難以後，那位賜一切恩典的上帝，就是呼召你們藉着跟基督耶穌連結來分享他永遠的榮耀的上帝，必定親自重建你們，堅定你們，賜力量和鞏固的根基給你們。[11]願權能歸於他，世世無窮！阿們。

最後問安

[12] 在忠誠的弟兄西拉的幫助下，我寫這封短信給你們。我要勸勉你們，並且見證這是上帝真實的恩典。你們要在這恩典上堅立不移。

[13] 跟你們同蒙揀選的巴比倫④教會向你們問安；我的兒子馬可也問候你們。[14]你們要用愛心彼此親吻問安。

願你們每一個屬基督的人都得到平安！

④「巴比倫」在這裏可能指羅馬。

彼得後書
2 PETER

INTRODUCTION

The Second Letter from Peter is addressed to a wide circle of early Christians. Its main concern is to combat the work of false teachers and the immorality which results from such teaching. The answer to these problems is found in holding to the true knowledge of God and of the Lord Jesus Christ, knowledge which has been conveyed by persons who themselves have seen Jesus and have heard him teach. The writer is especially concerned with the teaching of those who claim that Christ will not return again. He says that the apparent delay in Christ's return is due to the fact that God "does not want anyone to be destroyed, but wants all to turn away from their sins."

Outline of Contents

簡 介

彼得後書是寫給早期的一般信徒的，主要目的在科正一些假教師們的言論和他們在教會中造成的腐敗現象。要解決這些問題，必須對上帝和主耶穌基督有眞正的認識，這種知識是那些曾經親眼看見耶穌和聽見他教誨的人所傳授的。作者特別指出：那認爲基督不會再來的言論是錯誤的；基督之所以遲遲未來是因爲上帝「不願意有一個人沉淪，卻要人人悔改」。

提要

---

1 From Simon Peter, a servant and apostle of Jesus Christ–

To those who through the righteousness of our God and Savior Jesus Christ have been given a faith as precious as ours:

2 May grace and peace be yours in full measure through your knowledge of God and of Jesus our Lord.

God's Call and Choice

3 God's divine power has given us everything we need to live a truly religious life through·our knowledge of him who called us to share in his own[a] glory and goodness. 4 In this way he

a to share in his own; *some manuscripts have* through his.

1 我—西門・彼得是耶穌基督的僕人和使徒。我寫信給那些藉着我們的上帝和救主耶穌基督的義、跟我們分享了同樣寶貴信仰的人：

2 願你們藉着認識上帝和我們的主耶穌得到豐豐富富的恩典和平安！

上帝的呼召和揀選

3 上帝的神能已經把我們過敬虔生活所需的一切給了我們；這賜是藉着認識那位呼召我們來分享他自己的榮耀和善德的上帝而得的。4 這樣，他把他所應許那最大和最寶

has given us the very great and precious gifts he promised, so that by means of these gifts you may escape from the destructive lust that is in the world, and may come to share the divine nature. [5]For this very reason do your best to add goodness to your faith; to your goodness add knowledge; [6]to your knowledge add self-control; to your self-control add endurance; to your endurance add godliness; [7]to your godliness add Christian affection; and to your Christian affection add love. [8]These are the qualities you need, and if you have them in abundance, they will make you active and effective in your knowledge of our Lord Jesus Christ. [9]But if you do not have them, you are so shortsighted that you cannot see and have forgotten that you have been purified from your past sins.

[10]So then, my friends, try even harder to make God's call and his choice of you a permanent experience; if you do so, you will never abandon your faith.[b] [11]In this way you will be given the full right to enter the eternal Kingdom of our Lord and Savior Jesus Christ.

[12]And so I will always remind you of these matters, even though you already know them and are firmly grounded in the truth you have received. [13]I think it only right for me to stir up your memory of these matters as long as I am still alive. [14]I know that I shall soon put off this mortal body, as our Lord Jesus Christ plainly told me. [15]I will do my best, then, to provide a way for you to remember these matters at all times after my death.

Eyewitnesses of Christ's Glory

[16]We have not depended on made-up stories in making known to you the mighty coming of our Lord Jesus Christ. With our own eyes we saw his greatness. [17]We were there when he was given honor and glory by God the Father, when the voice came to him from the Supreme Glory, saying, "This is my own dear Son, with whom I am pleased!" [18]We ourselves heard this voice coming from heaven, when we were with him on the holy mountain.

[19]So we are even more confident of the message proclaimed by the prophets. You will do well to pay attention to it, because it is like a lamp shining in a dark place until the Day dawns and the light of the morning star shines in your hearts. [20]Above all else, however, remember that none of us can explain by ourselves a prophecy in the Scriptures. [21]For no prophetic message ever came just from the human will, but people were under the control of the Holy Spirit as they spoke the message that came from God.

b abandon your faith; or fall into sin.

貴的恩賜給了我們;藉着這恩賜,你們得以逃避世上那毀滅性的慾望,而分享上帝的神性。 [5]為了這緣故,你們要盡力在信心上加上美德,美德加上知識, [6]知識加上節制,節制加上忍耐,忍耐加上敬虔, [7]敬虔加上手足之愛,手足之愛加上博愛。 [8]這些就是你們應該培養的品德;如果你們都具備了,你們就會更積極、更有效地認識我們的主耶穌基督。 [9]但是,缺少這些品德的人是短視,是瞎眼,忘記了他們的舊罪已經被洗淨了。

[10]所以,弟兄姊妹們,你們要更加努力,使上帝的呼召和揀選成為你們永久的經驗;有了這些經驗,你們就不至於墮落。 [11]這樣,你們會獲得充分的權利,得以進入我們的主和救主耶穌基督永恆的國度裏。

[12]因此,雖然你們已經知道這些事,而且在所領受的真理上站穩了,我仍然要不斷地提醒你們。 [13]我想,只要我活着一天,我應該常常幫助你們記得這些事。 [14]我知道,我不久會脫離這必朽的軀體;這是我們的主耶穌基督指示我的。 [15]我要盡量想法子使你們在我死後還能常常記得這些事。

見證基督的榮耀

[16]我們所告訴你們那有關我們的主耶穌基督的大能和再臨的事,並不是根據捏造出來那些荒唐的傳說;我們曾親眼看見他的偉大。 [17]他從父上帝接受尊貴、榮耀的時候,我們也都在場。那時,至高榮耀的上帝對他說:「這是我親愛的兒子,我喜愛他。」 [18]我們跟他一起在聖山上,親耳聽見這天上來的聲音。

[19]這樣,我們對先知們所宣佈的信息更加確信。你們要好好地留意這信息;因為它像一盞燈照耀黑暗的地方,直到天亮,到晨星在你們心中發出光輝的那一天。 [20]最重要的是,你們要記住:聖經裏的一切預言都不可按照自己的意思解釋。 [21]因為,從來沒有預言是出於人的意思,而是先知受聖靈的感動把上帝的信息傳達出來的。

False Teachers

2 False prophets appeared in the past among the people, and in the same way false teachers will appear among you. They will bring in destructive, untrue doctrines, and will deny the Master who redeemed them, and so they will bring upon themselves sudden destruction. ²Even so, many will follow their immoral ways; and because of what they do, others will speak evil of the Way of truth. ³In their greed these false teachers will make a profit out of telling you made-up stories. For a long time now their Judge has been ready, and their Destroyer has been wide awake!

⁴God did not spare the angels who sinned, but threw them into hell, where they are kept chained in darkness,ᶜ waiting for the Day of Judgment. ⁵God did not spare the ancient world, but brought the flood on the world of godless people; the only ones he saved were Noah, who preached righteousness, and seven other people. ⁶God condemned the cities of Sodom and Gomorrah, destroying them with fire, and made them an example of what will happen to the godless. ⁷He rescued Lot, a good man, who was distressed by the immoral conduct of lawless people. ⁸That good man lived among them, and day after day he suffered agony as he saw and heard their evil actions. ⁹And so the Lord knows how to rescue godly people from their trials and how to keep the wicked under punishment for the Day of Judgment, ¹⁰especially those who follow their filthy bodily lusts and despise God's authority.

These false teachers are bold and arrogant, and show no respect for the glorious beings above; instead, they insult them. ¹¹Even the angels, who are so much stronger and mightier than these false teachers, do not accuse them with insults in the presence of the Lord. ¹²But these people act by instinct, like wild animals born to be captured and killed; they attack with insults anything they do not understand. They will be destroyed like wild animals, ¹³and they will be paid with suffering for the suffering they have caused. Pleasure for them is to do anything in broad daylight that will satisfy their bodily appetites; they are a shame and a disgrace as they join you in your meals, all the while enjoying their deceitful ways! ¹⁴They want to look for nothing but the chance to commit adultery; their appetite for sin is never satisfied. They lead weak people into a trap. Their hearts are trained to be greedy. They are under God's curse! ¹⁵They have left the straight path and have lost their way; they have followed the path taken by Balaam son of Beor, who loved the

c chained in darkness; *some manuscripts have* in dark pits.

假先知

2 從前有假先知在以色列民間出現；同樣也將有假教師在你們當中出現。他們偷偷地輸入毀滅性的異端，不承認救贖他們的主宰，迅速地自取滅亡。²雖然這樣，仍然有許多人要隨從他們邪惡的行為，以致真理因他們的行為遭受毀謗。³這些假先知為了滿足自己的貪婪，用捏造的故事向你們榨取財物。自古以來，上帝的審判總是在等着這種人；他們是逃不了毀滅的！

⁴上帝並沒有寬容犯罪的天使，卻把他們丟進地獄，囚禁在黑暗中，等候審判。⁵上帝也沒有寬容遠古的世代，卻用洪水淹沒那些心目中沒有上帝的人，只拯救了傳揚正義的挪亞和其他七個人。⁶上帝懲罰所多瑪和蛾摩拉兩個城，降火燒毀，作為不敬虔的人的鑑戒。⁷他搶救了好人羅得；羅得為着壞人的淫亂行為大大地憂傷。⁸那好人住在壞人當中，天天看見，天天聽見那些邪惡的事，心裏非常痛苦。⁹⁻¹⁰主知道如何拯救敬虔的人脫離試探，也知道如何把壞人留下來，尤其是那些放縱肉體情慾、藐視上帝權威的人，好在審判的日子懲罰他們。

這班假教師膽大妄為，不但不尊敬天上的尊榮者，反而侮辱他們；¹¹連那些力量和權能強過這班假教師的天使也不用侮辱的話在主面前控告他們。¹²可是，這班人像野獸，生來就是要被捕捉屠殺的；他們憑着本能行動，毀謗自己所不了解的事。他們將像野獸一樣被毀滅。¹³他們製造苦難，必然自食其果。對他們來說，所謂快樂便是在光天化日之下做滿足肉體慾望的事。他們污穢骯髒；他們跟你們同桌吃飯①，始終以詭詐為樂！¹⁴他們好色的眼睛專看淫婦，犯罪的慾望從來得不到滿足。他們誘惑軟弱的人；他們的心習慣於貪婪；他們是被上帝詛咒的！¹⁵他們離開正路，走入歧途，跟比珥的兒子巴蘭走同一條路。巴蘭貪愛不義的錢財，

①「他們跟……吃飯」另有些古卷作「他們在愛筵上」。

money he would get for doing wrong ¹⁶and was rebuked for his sin. His donkey spoke with a human voice and stopped the prophet's insane action.

¹⁷These people are like dried-up springs, like clouds blown along by a storm; God has reserved a place for them in the deepest darkness. ¹⁸They make proud and stupid statements, and use immoral bodily lusts to trap those who are just beginning to escape from among people who live in error. ¹⁹They promise them freedom while they themselves are slaves of destructive habits–for we are slaves of anything that has conquered us. ²⁰If people have escaped from the corrupting forces of the world through their knowledge of our Lord and Savior Jesus Christ, and are again caught and conquered by them, such people are in worse condition at the end than they were at the beginning. ²¹It would have been much better for them never to have known the way of righteousness than to know it and then turn away from the sacred command that was given them. ²²What happened to them shows that the proverbs are true: "A dog goes back to what it has vomited" and "A pig that has been washed goes back to roll in the mud."

The Promise of the Lord's Coming

3 My dear friends, this is now the second letter I have written you. In both letters I have tried to arouse pure thoughts in your minds by reminding you of these things. ²I want you to remember the words that were spoken long ago by the holy prophets, and the command from the Lord and Savior which was given you by your apostles. ³First of all, you must understand that in the last days some people will appear whose lives are controlled by their own lusts. They will make fun of you ⁴and will ask, "He promised to come, didn't he? Where is he? Our ancestors have already died, but everything is still the same as it was since the creation of the world!" ⁵They purposely ignore the fact that long ago God gave a command, and the heavens and earth were created. The earth was formed out of water and by water, ⁶and it was also by water, the water of the flood, that the old world was destroyed. ⁷But the heavens and the earth that now exist are being preserved by the same command of God, in order to be destroyed by fire. They are being kept for the day when godless people will be judged and destroyed.

⁸But do not forget one thing, my dear friends! There is no difference in the Lord's sight between one day and a thousand years; to him the two are the same. ⁹The Lord is not slow to do what he has promised, as some

¹⁶因自己所犯的罪受了譴責。那頭不會說話的驢竟發出人的聲音，阻止了先知的妄為。

¹⁷這些人像乾涸的泉源，像暴風吹散的雲霧；上帝已經為他們在黑暗的深淵裏留了地方。¹⁸他們說狂傲愚蠢的話，用肉體的情慾誘惑那些剛剛逃脫生活糜爛之輩的人。¹⁹他們答應給人自由，自己卻作了腐敗生活的奴隸；因為人給甚麼控制住，就是甚麼的奴隸。²⁰如果人藉着認識我們的主—救主耶穌基督，從這世界腐敗的勢力下逃脫出來，以後又被抓去，被制伏，這種人的結局比先前的更壞了。²¹他們知道有正義的道路，竟又離開他們所承受那神聖的命令；這種人不知道有正義的道路倒好。²²俗語說得對，他們的情況正像「狗回頭吃牠吐出來的東西」，也像「豬洗乾淨了，又回到泥沼裏打滾。」

主應許再來

3 親愛的朋友們，我現在寫給你們的是第二封信。在兩封信裏面，我都提醒你們這些事，來激發你們純潔的思想。²我要你們記得古時候聖先知們所說的話，以及我們的主—救主藉着使徒所傳給你們的命令。³最重要的是，你們必須知道，在這末後的日期，有些人受私慾的支配，會出來譏笑你們，⁴說：「他不是應許要再來嗎？他在哪裏呢？我們的祖先都死了，一切還不是跟創世之初一樣嗎？」⁵他們故意不理會上帝在太初用他的話創造了天地這一事實。地是從水和藉着水而形成的；⁶舊的世界也是由水，就是洪水所消滅的。⁷現在的天和地也同樣是憑着上帝的話保留下來的，要等着不信的人被審判、被消滅那天，好用火燒毀。

⁸可是，親愛的朋友們，有一件事你們不可忘記：在主眼中，千年如一日，一日如千年。⁹主並不像一般人所想的，遲遲不實現他的應許。相反地，他寬容你們；因為他不

think. Instead, he is patient with you, because he does not want anyone to be destroyed, but wants all to turn away from their sins.

10But the Day of the Lord will come like a thief. On that Day the heavens will disappear with a shrill noise, the heavenly bodies will burn up and be destroyed, and the earth with everything in it will vanish.*d* 11Since all these things will be destroyed in this way, what kind of people should you be? Your lives should be holy and dedicated to God, 12as you wait for the Day of God and do your best to make it come soon–the Day when the heavens will burn up and be destroyed, and the heavenly bodies will be melted by the heat. 13But we wait for what God has promised: new heavens and a new earth, where righteousness will be at home.

14And so, my friends, as you wait for that Day, do your best to be pure and faultless in God's sight and to be at peace with him. 15Look on our Lord's patience as the opportunity he is giving you to be saved, just as our dear friend Paul wrote to you, using the wisdom that God gave him. 16This is what he says in all his letters when he writes on the subject. There are some difficult things in his letters which ignorant and unstable people explain falsely, as they do with other passages of the Scriptures. So they bring on their own destruction.

17But you, my friends, already know this. Be on your guard, then, so that you will not be led away by the errors of lawless people and fall from your safe position. 18But continue to grow in the grace and knowledge of our Lord and Savior Jesus Christ. To him be the glory, now and forever! Amen.

d vanish; some manuscripts have be found; others have be burned up; one has be found destroyed.

願意有一個人沉淪，卻要人人悔改。

10 但是，主再來的日子就像小偷忽然來到一樣。在那日，諸天要在巨大的響聲中消失，天體在烈燄中燒毀，大地和萬物都會消滅②。11既然這一切要這樣地毀滅，你們應該作哪一種人呢？你們應該過着聖潔、虔誠的生活，12等候上帝的日子，竭力加速它的臨到。在那日，諸天要被燒毀，天體在烈燄中鎔化。13但是，我們在等候上帝所應許的新天新地；在那裏，正義常住。

14 所以，親愛的朋友們，既然你們等候着那日子，就應該在上帝面前竭力追求聖潔，過無可指責的生活，跟他和好。15要以我們的主的容忍作爲你們得救的機會，正如我們親愛的弟兄保羅用上帝所賜的智慧寫信勸勉你們一樣。16他在所有的書信裏都談到這事。他信中有些難懂的地方，被那些無知和反覆無常的人隨便曲解，正如他們曲解其他經文一樣，結果是自取滅亡。

17 但是，親愛的朋友們，你們已經先知道這些事，就該防備，免得被那些壞人用荒謬的言論把你們引入歧途，便你們離開穩固的立場。18你們要在我們的主—救主耶穌基督的恩典中，以及對他的認識上，繼續長進。願榮耀歸於他，從現在一直到永遠！阿們。

②「消滅」有些古卷作「消失」；另有些古卷作「燒毀了」；又有些古卷作「暴露無遺」。

約翰一書
1 JOHN

INTRODUCTION

The First Letter of John has two main purposes: to encourage its readers to live in fellowship with God and with his Son, Jesus Christ, and to warn them against following false teaching that would destroy this fellowship. This teaching was based on the belief that evil results from contact with the physical world, and so Jesus, the Son of God, could not really have been a human being. Those teachers claimed that to be saved was to be set free from concern with life in this world; and they also taught that salvation had nothing to do with matters of morality or of love for others.

In opposition to this teaching the writer clearly states that Jesus Christ was a real human being, and he emphasizes that all who believe in Jesus and love God must also love one another.

Outline of Contents

Introduction 1.1-4
Light and darkness 1.5-2.29
Children of God and children of the Devil 3.1-24
Truth and error 4.1-6
The duty of love 4.7-21
Victorious faith 5.1-21

簡 介

約翰一書有兩個主要的目的；

一. 鼓勵讀者跟上帝和他的兒子耶穌基督保持親密的團契；

二. 警告讀者不可聽信那會破壞這種團契的謬論。這種謬論認為：邪惡是因跟物質世界接觸而產生的，因此，上帝的兒子耶穌不可能真的是人。這些假教師主張：拯救便是擺脫對今世生活的一切關懷；得救跟道德生活或愛鄰人等並沒有關係。

為反對這種言論，作者清楚地指出：耶穌基督是真實的人，同時強調一切信耶穌、愛上帝的人都必須彼此相愛。

提 要

1. 序言（1.1-4）
2. 光明和黑暗（1.5-2.29）
3. 上帝的兒女和魔鬼的兒女（3.1-24）
4. 真理和謬誤（4.1-6）
5. 愛的責任（4.7-21）
6. 得勝的信心（5.1-21）

The Word of Life

1 We write to you about the Word of life, which has existed from the very beginning. We have heard it, and we have seen it with our eyes; yes, we have seen it, and our hands have touched it. ²When this life became visible, we saw it; so we speak of it and tell you about the eternal life which was with the Father and was made known to us. ³What we have seen and heard we announce to you also, so that you will

生命之道

1 我們寫這封信向你們陳述那從起初就存在的生命之道。這生命之道，我們聽見了，親眼看見了；是的，我們已經看見，而且親手摸過。²這生命出現的時候，我們見到了；因此，我們向你們見證，並傳揚那原來與天父同在、而且已經向我們顯現了的永恆生命。³我們把所看見、所聽見的也傳給你們，好使你們能跟我們共享團契；這團契

join with us in the fellowship that we have with the Father and with his Son Jesus Christ. [4]We write this in order that our[a] joy may be complete.

God Is Light

[5]Now the message that we have heard from his Son and announce is this: God is light, and there is no darkness at all in him. [6]If, then, we say that we have fellowship with him, yet at the same time live in the darkness, we are lying both in our words and in our actions. [7]But if we live in the light–just as he is in the light–then we have fellowship with one another, and the blood of Jesus, his Son, purifies us from every sin.

[8]If we say that we have no sin, we deceive ourselves, and there is no truth in us. [9]But if we confess our sins to God, he will keep his promise and do what is right: he will forgive us our sins and purify us from all our wrongdoing. [10]If we say that we have not sinned, we make a liar out of God, and his word is not in us.

Christ Our Helper

2 I am writing this to you, my children, so that you will not sin; but if anyone does sin, we have someone who pleads with the Father on our behalf–Jesus Christ, the righteous one. [2]And Christ himself is the means by which our sins are forgiven, and not our sins only, but also the sins of everyone.

[3]If we obey God's commands, then we are sure that we know him. [4]If we say that we know him, but do not obey his commands, we are liars and there is no truth in us. [5]But if we obey his word, we are the ones whose love for God has really been made perfect. This is how we can be sure that we are in union with God: [6]if we say that we remain in union with God, we should live just as Jesus Christ did.

The New Command

[7]My dear friends, this command I am writing you is not new; it is the old command, the one you have had from the very beginning. The old command is the message you have already heard. [8]However, the command I now write you is new, because its truth is seen in Christ and also in you. For the darkness is passing away, and the real light is already shining.

[9]If we say that we are in the light, yet hate others, we are in the darkness to this very hour. [10]If we love others, we live in the light, and so

a our; *some manuscripts have* your.

就是我們跟天父和他的兒子耶穌基督所共有的。[4]我們寫這些是要讓我們①大家的喜樂滿溢。

上帝是光

[5] 現在我們要先從上帝的兒子所聽到的信息傳給你們:上帝是光,他完全沒有黑暗。[6]那麼,如果我們說我們跟他有團契,卻仍然生活在黑暗中,我們就是撒謊,行為不合真理。[7]但是,如果我們生活在光明中,正如上帝在光明中,我們就彼此有團契,而他的兒子耶穌的血洗淨我們一切的罪。

[8] 如果我們說自己沒有罪,便是欺騙自己,真理就跟我們沒有關係。[9]如果我們向上帝認罪,他是信實公義的,他要赦免我們的罪,洗淨我們所犯的各種過錯。[10]如果我們說自己沒有犯過罪,我們等於把上帝當作撒謊者,他的道就跟我們沒有關係。

基督為我們陳情

2 我的孩子們,我寫這些是要使你們不犯罪;如果有人犯罪,我們有一位公義的耶穌基督,替我們向天父陳情。[2]基督犧牲自己,贖了我們的罪;他不但為我們的罪,也為全人類的罪,犧牲自己。

[3] 如果我們遵守上帝的命令,我們就知道我們認識他。[4]若有人說「我認識他」,卻不遵守他的命令,這樣的人是撒謊的,真理跟他沒有關係。[5-6]但那遵守上帝的道的人,他對上帝的愛就達到完全。那說他有上帝的生命的,應該照耶穌基督的言行生活;這樣,我們才有把握說,我們有他的生命。

新的命令

[7] 親愛的朋友們,我寫給你們的,不是新的命令,而是舊的命令,是你們一開始就領受的。這舊的命令是你們已經聽過了的信息。[8]然而,我寫給你們的,也是新的命令;這命令的真理在基督身上,也在你們當中表現出來。因為黑暗正在消逝,真光已開始照耀。

[9] 如果有人說他生活在光明中,卻恨自己的弟兄或姊妹,他仍然是在黑暗中。[10]愛弟

①「我們」有些古卷作「你們」。

there is nothing in us that will cause someone else[b] to sin. 11But if we hate others, we are in the darkness; we walk in it and do not know where we are going, because the darkness has made us blind.

12I write to you, my children, because your sins are forgiven for the sake of Christ. 13I write to you, fathers, because you know him who has existed from the beginning. I write to you, young people, because you have defeated the Evil One.

14I write to you, my children, because you know the Father. I write to you, fathers, because you know him who has existed from the beginning. I write to you, young people, because you are strong; the word of God lives in you, and you have defeated the Evil One.

15Do not love the world or anything that belongs to the world. If you love the world, you do not love the Father. 16Everything that belongs to the world–what the sinful self desires, what people see and want, and everything in this world that people are so proud of–none of this comes from the Father; it all comes from the world. 17The world and everything in it that people desire is passing away; but those who do the will of God live forever.

The Enemy of Christ

18My children, the end is near! You were told that the Enemy of Christ would come; and now many enemies of Christ have already appeared, and so we know that the end is near. 19These people really did not belong to our fellowship, and that is why they left us; if they had belonged to our fellowship, they would have stayed with us. But they left so that it might be clear that none of them really belonged to us.

20But you have had the Holy Spirit poured out on you by Christ, and so all of you know the truth. 21I write to you, then, not because you do not know the truth; instead, it is because you do know it, and you also know that no lie ever comes from the truth.

22Who, then, is the liar? It is those who say that Jesus is not the Messiah. Such people are the Enemy of Christ–they reject both the Father and the Son. 23For those who reject the Son reject also the Father; those who accept the Son have the Father also.

24Be sure, then, to keep in your hearts the message you heard from the beginning. If you keep that message, then you will always live in union with the Son and the Father. 25And this is what Christ himself promised to give us–eternal life.

b someone else; or us.

兄姊妹的,就是生活在光明中,他不會使別人失足犯罪。11可是,那恨弟兄或姊妹的,就是在黑暗中;他在黑暗中走,不知道自己往哪裏去,因爲黑暗使他眼睛瞎了。

12孩子們,我寫信給你們,因爲你們的罪已經藉着基督得到赦免。13父老們,我寫信給你們,因爲你們認識那位從太初就已經存在的。青年們,我寫信給你們,因爲你們已經勝過了那邪惡者。

14孩子們,我寫信給你們,因爲你們認識天父。父老們,我寫信給你們,因爲你們認識那位從太初就已經存在的。青年們,我寫信給你們,因爲你們强壯;上帝的道活在你們的生命中,而你們已經勝過了那邪惡者。

15不要愛世界,或任何屬世的東西。如果你們愛世界,你們就沒有愛天父的心。16一切屬世的事物,好比肉體的慾望、眼目的慾望,和人的一切虛榮,都不是從天父來的,而是從世界來的。17這世界和一切屬世的慾望都正在消逝;但是,實行上帝旨意的人要永遠生存。

敵對基督者

18孩子們,世界的終局就要到了!你們曾聽說那敵對基督者要來;現在基督的許多仇敵已經出現,因此我們知道終局就要到了。19這班人並不是屬於我們的,所以離開了我們;如果他們是屬於我們的,他們就會跟我們在一起。可是,他們走開了,可見他們都不是眞的屬於我們的。

20你們已經受了那聖者的恩膏②,所以你們都認識眞理。21我寫信給你們,不是因爲你們不認識眞理,而是因爲你們都認識了,而且知道一切虛謊都不是出自眞理。22那麼,誰是那撒謊的呢?不就是那否認耶穌是基督的嗎?這樣的人就是那敵對基督者;他拒絕了聖父,也拒絕聖子。23因爲,凡拒絕聖子的,也是拒絕聖父;凡公開承認聖子的,也得着了聖父。

24那麼,你們必須謹守當初所聽到的信息。如果你們謹守當初所聽到的信息,你們就會常常活在聖子和聖父的生命裏。25這就是基督親自應許給我們的永恆生命。

②「受了……恩膏」或譯「從基督領受了聖靈」。

26I am writing this to you about those who are trying to deceive you. 27But as for you, Christ has poured out his Spirit on you. As long as his Spirit remains in you, you do not need anyone to teach you. For his Spirit teaches you about everything, and what he teaches is true, not false. Obey the Spirit's teaching, then, and remain in union with Christ.

28Yes, my children, remain in union with him, so that when he appears we may be full of courage and need not hide in shame from him on the Day he comes. 29You know that Christ is righteous; you should know, then, that everyone who does what is right is God's child.

Children of God

3 See how much the Father has loved us! His love is so great that we are called God's children–and so, in fact, we are. This is why the world does not know us: it has not known God. 2My dear friends, we are now God's children, but it is not yet clear what we shall become. But we know that when Christ appears, we shall be like him, because we shall see him as he really is. 3Everyone who has this hope in Christ keeps himself pure, just as Christ is pure.

4Whoever sins is guilty of breaking God's law, because sin is a breaking of the law. 5You know that Christ appeared in order to take away sins,^{c} and that there is no sin in him. 6So everyone who lives in union with Christ does not continue to sin; but whoever continues to sin has never seen him or known him.

7Let no one deceive you, my children! Whoever does what is right is righteous, just as Christ is righteous. 8Whoever continues to sin belongs to the Devil, because the Devil has sinned from the very beginning. The Son of God appeared for this very reason, to destroy what the Devil had done.

9Those who are children of God do not continue to sin, for God's very nature is in them; and because God is their Father, they cannot continue to sin. 10Here is the clear difference between God's children and the Devil's children: those who do not do what is right or do not love others are not God's children.

Love One Another

11The message you heard from the very beginning is this: we must love one another. 12We must not be like Cain; he belonged to the Evil One and murdered his own brother Abel. Why

c sins; *some manuscripts have* our sins.

26我寫這些事是指着那些想欺騙你們的人說的。27至於你們,基督已經把他的靈賜給你們。只要他的靈與你們同在,你們就不需要別人的教導;因為他的靈要把一切事教導你們,而他的教導都是真的,不是假的。所以,你們要順從聖靈的教導,始終活在基督的生命裏。

28是的,孩子們,你們要活在他的生命裏;這樣,在他顯現、再來的日子,我們可以坦然無懼,用不着躲藏。29你們曉得基督是公義的;所以,你們應該知道,遵行公義的人就是上帝的兒女。

上帝的兒女

3 你們看,天父多麼愛我們!甚至稱我們為上帝的兒女;事實上,我們就是他的兒女。世人所以不認識我們,是因為他們還不認識上帝。2親愛的朋友們,現在我們是上帝的兒女,將來會變成怎樣,還沒有顯明。可是,我們知道,基督顯現的時候,我們都會像他,因為我們將看見他的真相。3每一個盼望基督顯現的人都會保持自己的純潔,正像基督是純潔的一樣。

4那犯罪的,就是違背上帝的法律,因為罪就是違背法律。5你們知道,基督顯現的目的是要除罪;他自己並沒有罪。6所以,那活在基督生命裏的人都不犯罪;那繼續犯罪的人沒有見過基督,也不曾認識他。

7孩子們,不要被人家欺騙了。遵行公義的,才是義人,正如基督是公義的。8繼續犯罪的,是屬於魔鬼,因為魔鬼從起初就犯罪。為了這個緣故,上帝的兒子顯現了,目的是要毀滅魔鬼的工作。

9上帝的兒女都不繼續犯罪,因為上帝的生命在他們裏面。既然上帝是他們的父親,他們就不會繼續犯罪。10上帝的兒女和魔鬼的兒女有很明顯的區別:那不遵行公義、不愛自己弟兄姊妹的,就不是上帝的兒女。

彼此相愛

11你們從起初所聽到的信息就是:我們要彼此相愛。12我們不要像該隱。他屬於那邪惡者;他殺死了自己的弟弟。他為甚麼殺死

did Cain murder him? Because the things he himself did were wrong, and the things his brother did were right.

13So do not be surprised, my friends, if the people of the world hate you. 14We know that we have left death and come over into life; we know it because we love others. Those who do not love are still under the power of death. 15Those who hate others are murderers, and you know that murderers do not have eternal life in them. 16This is how we know what love is: Christ gave his life for us. We too, then, ought to give our lives for others! 17If we are rich and see others in need, yet close our hearts against them, how can we claim that we love God? 18My children, our love should not be just words and talk; it must be true love, which shows itself in action.

Courage before God

19This, then, is how we will know that we belong to the truth; this is how we will be confident in God's presence. 20If our conscience condemns us, we know that God is greater than our conscience and that he knows everything. 21And so, my dear friends, if our conscience does not condemn us, we have courage in God's presence. 22We receive from him whatever we ask, because we obey his commands and do what pleases him. 23What he commands is that we believe in his Son Jesus Christ and love one another, just as Christ commanded us. 24Those who obey God's commands live in union with God and God lives in union with them. And because of the Spirit that God has given us we know that God lives in union with us.

The True Spirit and the False Spirit

4 My dear friends, do not believe all who claim to have the Spirit, but test them to find out if the spirit they have comes from God. For many false prophets have gone out everywhere. 2This is how you will be able to know whether it is God's Spirit: anyone who acknowledges that Jesus Christ came as a human being has the Spirit who comes from God. 3But anyone who denies this about Jesus does not have the Spirit from God. The spirit that he has is from the Enemy of Christ; you heard that it would come, and now it is here in the world already.

4But you belong to God, my children, and have defeated the false prophets, because the Spirit who is in you is more powerful than the

弟弟呢？因為他的行為邪惡，而他弟弟的行為正直。

13 所以，弟兄姊妹們，要是這世界的人恨你們，你們不必驚奇。14我們知道我們已經出死入生了；我們所以知道是因為我們愛弟兄姊妹。那沒有愛心的，仍然處在死的權勢下。15凡恨自己弟兄或姊妹的，就是殺人的；你們知道，凡殺人的，就沒有永恆的生命。16基督為我們犧牲生命，從這一點，我們知道甚麼是愛。那麼，我們也應該為弟兄姊妹犧牲生命！17一個富有的人看見自己的弟兄或姊妹缺乏，卻硬着心不理，怎能說他愛上帝呢？18孩子們，我們的愛不應該只是口頭上的愛，必須是真實的愛，用行為證明出來！

在上帝面前坦然無懼

19 那麼，從這一點我們知道，我們是屬真理的；我們在上帝面前心安理得。20即使良心自責，我們仍然知道上帝比我們的心大；他洞察一切。21所以，親愛的朋友們，如果我們的良心不責備我們，我們在上帝面前就可以坦然無懼。22我們無論向他求甚麼，他都會賜給我們；因為我們遵從他的命令，做他所喜歡的事。23他的命令就是：我們必須信他的兒子耶穌基督的名，而且照基督的命令彼此相愛。24那遵從上帝命令的，就有上帝的生命，而上帝也在他的生命裏。我們怎樣知道上帝在我們的生命裏呢？是由於他所賜給我們的聖靈。

真靈和假靈

4 親愛的朋友們，對於自稱有聖靈的，你們不要都相信，總要察驗他們的靈是不是出於上帝，因為已經有許多假先知到處出現了。2你們怎麼辨認上帝的靈呢？誰公開承認耶穌基督降世為人，誰就有從上帝來的靈。3誰不公開承認耶穌，誰就沒有從上帝來的靈；他所有的是敵對基督者的靈。你們聽見過這靈要來，現在已經在世上了。

4 可是，孩子們，你們是屬上帝的，而且已經勝過了假先知，因為在你們裏面的靈比

spirit in those who belong to the world. ⁵Those false prophets speak about matters of the world, and the world listens to them because they belong to the world. ⁶But we belong to God. Whoever knows God listens to us; whoever does not belong to God does not listen to us. This, then, is how we can tell the difference between the Spirit of truth and the spirit of error.

God Is Love

⁷Dear friends, let us love one another, because love comes from God. Whoever loves is a child of God and knows God. ⁸Whoever does not love does not know God, for God is love. ⁹And God showed his love for us by sending his only Son into the world, so that we might have life through him. ¹⁰This is what love is: it is not that we have loved God, but that he loved us and sent his Son to be the means by which our sins are forgiven.

¹¹Dear friends, if this is how God loved us, then we should love one another. ¹²No one has ever seen God, but if we love one another, God lives in union with us, and his love is made perfect in us.

¹³We are sure that we live in union with God and that he lives in union with us, because he has given us his Spirit. ¹⁴And we have seen and tell others that the Father sent his Son to be the Savior of the world. ¹⁵If we declare that Jesus is the Son of God, we live in union with God and God lives in union with us. ¹⁶And we ourselves know and believe the love which God has for us.

God is love, and those who live in love live in union with God and God lives in union with them. ¹⁷Love is made perfect in us in order that we may have courage on the Judgment Day; and we will have it because our life in this world is the same as Christ's. ¹⁸There is no fear in love; perfect love drives out all fear. So then, love has not been made perfect in anyone who is afraid, because fear has to do with punishment.

¹⁹We love because God first loved us. ²⁰If we say we love God, but hate others, we are liars. For we cannot love God, whom we have not seen, if we do not love others, whom we have seen. ²¹The command that Christ has given us is this: whoever loves God must love others also.

Our Victory over the World

5 Whoever believes that Jesus is the Messiah is a child of God; and whoever loves a

那在屬世界的人裏面的靈更有力量。⁵他們講論世上的事，世人聽從他們，因爲他們是屬世的。⁶但是，我們是屬上帝的。認識上帝的人聽從我們；不屬上帝的人不聽從我們。憑着這一點，我們知道怎樣辨別眞理的靈和謬誤的靈。

上帝是愛

⁷親愛的朋友們，我們要彼此相愛，因爲愛是從上帝來的。那有愛的，是上帝的兒女，也認識上帝。⁸那沒有愛的，不認識上帝，因爲上帝是愛。⁹上帝差他的獨子到世上來，使我們藉着他得到生命；上帝用這方法顯示他愛我們。¹⁰這就是愛：不是我們愛上帝，而是上帝愛我們，差了他的兒子，爲我們犧牲，贖了我們的罪。

¹¹親愛的朋友們，既然上帝那麼愛我們，我們也應該彼此相愛。¹²沒有人看見過上帝，但我們若彼此相愛，上帝就在我們的生命裏，而他的愛藉着我們完全實現了。

¹³上帝把他的靈賜給了我們，因此我們知道，我們有他的生命，而他在我們的生命裏。¹⁴天父差他的兒子來作世界的救主；這事我們看見了，也向別人見證。¹⁵那公開承認耶穌是上帝的兒子的，上帝就在他的生命裏，他也有上帝的生命。¹⁶所以，我們知道，並且相信上帝愛我們。

上帝是愛；那有了愛在他的生命裏的人就是有上帝的生命，而上帝在他的生命裏。¹⁷這樣，愛就藉着我們完全實現了，使我們在審判的日子能夠坦然無懼；我們確能這樣，因爲我們在這世上有跟基督一樣的生命。¹⁸有了愛就沒有恐懼；完全的愛驅除一切的恐懼。所以，那有恐懼的就沒有完全的愛，因爲恐懼和懲罰是相關連的。

¹⁹我們愛，因爲上帝先愛了我們。²⁰若有人說「我愛上帝」，卻恨自己的弟兄或姊妹，他就是撒謊的；他既然不愛那看得見的弟兄或姊妹，怎麼能愛那看不見的上帝呢？²¹所以，基督這樣命令我們：那愛上帝的，也必須愛自己的弟兄和姊妹。

勝過世界

5 凡信耶穌是基督的都是上帝的兒女。如果我們愛一個作父親的，也一定愛他的

father loves his child also. [2]This is how we know that we love God's children: it is by loving God and obeying his commands. [3]For our love for God means that we obey his commands. And his commands are not too hard for us, [4]because every child of God is able to defeat the world. And we win the victory over the world by means of our faith. [5]Who can defeat the world? Only the person who believes that Jesus is the Son of God.

The Witness about Jesus Christ

[6]Jesus Christ is the one who came with the water of his baptism and the blood of his death. He came not only with the water, but with both the water and the blood. And the Spirit himself testifies that this is true, because the Spirit is truth. [7]There are three witnesses: [8]the Spirit, the water, and the blood; and all three give the same testimony. [9]We believe human testimony; but God's testimony is much stronger, and he has given this testimony about his Son. [10]So those who believe in the Son of God have this testimony in their own heart; but those who do not believe God, have made a liar of him, because they have not believed what God has said about his Son. [11]The testimony is this: God has given us eternal life, and this life has its source in his Son. [12]Whoever has the Son has this life; whoever does not have the Son of God does not have life.

Eternal Life

[13]I am writing this to you so that you may know that you have eternal life–you that believe in the Son of God. [14]We have courage in God's presence, because we are sure that he hears us if we ask him for anything that is according to his will. [15]He hears us whenever we ask him; and since we know this is true, we know also that he gives us what we ask from him.

[16]If you see a believer commit a sin that does not lead to death, you should pray to God, who will give that person life. This applies to those whose sins do not lead to death. But there is sin which leads to death, and I do not say that you should pray to God about that. [17]All wrongdoing is sin, but there is sin which does not lead to death.

[18]We know that no children of God keep on sinning, for the Son of God keeps them safe, and the Evil One cannot harm them.

[19]We know that we belong to God even though the whole world is under the rule of the Evil One.

兒女。[2]由於我們愛上帝,並遵守他的命令,我們就知道我們愛他的兒女。[3]遵守上帝的命令就是愛上帝;他的命令並不難於遵守,[4]因為上帝的每一個兒女都能夠勝過世界。使我們勝過世界的,是我們的信心。[5]誰能夠勝過世界呢?只有信耶穌是上帝的兒子的人才能勝過世界。

見證耶穌基督

[6] 耶穌基督到世上是藉着洗禮的水和犧牲的血;不僅僅用水,而是用水和血。聖靈也親自見證這是真實的,因為聖靈就是真理。[7-8]聖靈、水、和血三者都作證,而三者都一致。[9]既然我們接受人的見證,上帝的見證當然更有效力,而這見證是上帝為他兒子所作的。[10]所以,誰信上帝的兒子,誰心裏就有這見證;誰不信上帝,就是把上帝當作撒謊的,因為他不信上帝曾經為他的兒子作見證。[11]這見證就是:上帝賜給我們永恆的生命,而這生命的源頭是他的兒子。[12]誰有上帝的兒子,誰就有這生命;誰沒有上帝的兒子,誰就沒有這生命。

永恆的生命

[13]我寫這些給你們,要你們知道,你們信奉上帝兒子的人有永恆的生命。[14]我們在上帝面前坦然無懼;因為我們確實知道,如果我們照着他的旨意求,他都會垂聽。[15]既然我們知道他垂聽我們一切的祈求,也就知道我們向他所求的,他一定賜給我們。

[16] 若有人看見弟兄或姊妹犯了不至於死的罪,他應該向上帝祈求,上帝會賜生命給他們。這是指那些犯了不至於死的罪的人說的。但是,有些罪會導致死亡,我認為你們不必為這種罪祈求。[17]一切不義的行為都是罪,但也有不至於死的罪。

[18]我們知道,上帝的兒女不會繼續犯罪,因為上帝的兒子保守他,使那邪惡者不能加害於他。

[19]我們知道,雖然全世界都處在那邪惡者的轄制下,我們仍然屬於上帝。

20We know that the Son of God has come and has given us understanding, so that we know the true God. We live in union with the true God–union with his Son Jesus Christ. This is the true God, and this is eternal life.

21My children, keep yourselves safe from false gods!

20 我們知道，上帝的兒子已經來了，而且賜給我們理解力，好使我們認識真神。我們在真神的生命裏，就是在他的兒子耶穌基督的生命裏。他就是真神，就是永恆的生命。

21 孩子們，你們要遠避假神！

2³We know that he is the Son of God has come
and have given us understanding, so that we
know the true God. We live in union with the
true God in union with his Son Jesus Christ.
This is the true God, and this is eternal life.
2¹My Children, keep yourselves safe from
idols.

約翰二書
2 JOHN

INTRODUCTION

The Second Letter of John was written by "the Elder" to "the dear Lady and to her children," probably meaning a local church and its members. The brief message is an appeal to love one another and a warning against false teachers and their teachings.

Outline of Contents

Introduction 1-3
The primacy of love 4-6
Warning against false doctrine 7-11
Conclusion 12-13

簡 介

　　約翰二書由一位「長老」寫給「蒙揀選的夫人」和她的兒女｜可能是指某地方教會和教會的會友們。寫這封信的目的是勸勉信徒彼此相愛，同時警告信徒要提防假教師和他們的言論。

提要

1. 序言（ 1－3 ）
2. 愛的首要性（ 4－6 ）
3. 提防謬論（ 7－11 ）
4. 結語（ 12－13 ）

---

¹ From the Elder–
To the dear Lady and to her children,*a* whom I truly love. And I am not the only one, but all who know the truth love you, ²because the truth remains in us and will be with us forever.

³May God the Father and Jesus Christ, the Father's Son, give us grace, mercy, and peace; may they be ours in truth and love.

Truth and Love
⁴How happy I was to find that some of your children live in the truth, just as the Father commanded us. ⁵And so I ask you, dear Lady: let us all love one another. This is no new command I am writing you; it is the command which we have had from the beginning. ⁶This love I speak of means that we must live in

¹我是長老；我寫信給你｜蒙揀選的夫人，也給你的兒女：

　　你們是我誠心所愛的。不但我愛你們，所有認識真理的人也愛你們；²因為真理在我們心裏，而且要永遠與我們同在。

³ 願父上帝和他的兒子耶穌基督賜恩典、憐憫、平安給我們，使我們始終生活在真理和愛中！

真理和愛
⁴ 我很高興，因為我知道在你的兒女當中有遵從天父命令、生活在真理中的人。⁵ 所以，親愛的夫人，我求你，我們要彼此相愛。我向你提的並不是一條新的命令，而是我們從起初就領受了的。⁶ 我說的愛就是：我們必須遵從上帝的命令。你們從起初所聽

a LADY AND...HER CHILDREN: *This probably refers to a church and its members (also in verses 4,5).*

obedience to God's commands. The command, as you have all heard from the beginning, is that you must all live in love.

7Many deceivers have gone out over the world, people who do not acknowledge that Jesus Christ came as a human being. Such a person is a deceiver and the Enemy of Christ. 8Be on your guard, then, so that you will not lose what we[b] have worked for, but will receive your reward in full.

9Anyone who does not stay with the teaching of Christ, but goes beyond it, does not have God. Whoever does stay with the teaching has both the Father and the Son. 10So then, if some come to you who do not bring this teaching, do not welcome them in your homes; do not even say, "Peace be with you." 11For anyone who wishes them peace becomes their partner in the evil things they do.

Final Words

12I have so much to tell you, but I would rather not do it with paper and ink; instead, I hope to visit you and talk with you personally, so that we shall be completely happy.

13The children of your dear Sister[c] send you their greetings.

b we; *some manuscripts have* you.
c CHILDREN OF YOUR DEAR SISTER: *This probably refers to the members of the church to which the writer belonged.*

到的命令就是：你們要以這命令為生活的中心。

7 許多騙子已經在世界上到處活動，他們公開否認耶穌基督降世為人這事實。這樣的人是騙子，是敵對基督者。8你們要小心才不至於失掉你們所成就的，而是要得到全部的獎賞。

9 要是有人不持守基督的教訓，反而偏離了，就是眼中沒有上帝；那持守教訓的，就得着了聖父和聖子。10要是有人到你們那裏，不傳授這個教訓，就不要接待他到你們家裏去，也不要向他問安；11因為向他問安，等於在壞事上成為他的夥伴。

末了的話

12我還有許多話要告訴你們，但我不想藉筆墨傳達。我希望親自去探望你們，跟你們當面傾談，好讓我們的喜樂滿溢。

13 你那蒙揀選的姊妹的兒女①向你問安。

①「蒙揀選的姊妹的兒女」可能指作者所屬教會的信徒。

約翰三書
3 JOHN

INTRODUCTION

The Third Letter of John was written by "the Elder" to a church leader named Gaius. The writer praises Gaius because of his help to other Christians, and warns against a man named Diotrephes.

Outline of Contents

簡 介

約翰三書由一位「長老」寫給一位名該猶的教會領袖。作者稱讚該猶，因為他熱心幫助其他信徒。同時，他譴責一個名叫狄特腓的人；因為他想作教會領袖，卻不行善。

提要

---

1 From the Elder–
To my dear Gaius, whom I truly love.

2My dear friend, I pray that everything may go well with you and that you may be in good health–as I know you are well in spirit. 3I was so happy when some Christians arrived and told me how faithful you are to the truth–just as you always live in the truth. 4Nothing makes me happier than to hear that my children live in the truth.

Gaius Is Praised

5My dear friend, you are so faithful in the work you do for other Christians, even when they are strangers. 6They have spoken to the church here about your love. Please help them to continue their trip in a way that will please God. 7For they set out on their trip in the service of Christ without accepting any help from unbelievers. 8We Christians, then, must help

1 我是長老；我寫信給親愛的該猶—我誠心所愛的朋友：

2 親愛的朋友，我祝你事事順利，身體健康，正如你靈性健全一樣。3 有些信徒到這裏來，告訴我，你對真理忠誠，一向以真理為生活的中心，使我非常高興。4 沒有別的事比聽到我的孩子們都生活在真理中更能使我快樂的了。

稱讚該猶

5 親愛的朋友，你那麼真誠地為你信徒們做事，甚至對陌生的信徒們也一樣。6 他們曾向這裏的教會提起你的愛心。請你照上帝所喜歡的，幫助他們繼續他們的旅程。7 他們為了基督的緣故出外工作，不接受非信徒的幫助。8 所以，我們必須接待這樣的人，

these people, so that we may share in their work for the truth.

Diotrephes and Demetrius

9I wrote a short letter to the church; but Diotrephes, who likes to be their leader, will not pay any attention to what I say. 10When I come, then, I will bring up everything he has done: the terrible things he says about us and the lies he tells! But that is not enough for him; he will not receive the Christians when they come, and even stops those who want to receive them and tries to drive them out of the church!

11My dear friend, do not imitate what is bad, but imitate what is good. Whoever does good belongs to God; whoever does what is bad has not seen God.

12Everyone speaks well of Demetrius; truth itself speaks well of him. And we add our testimony, and you know that what we say is true.

Final Greetings

13I have so much to tell you, but I do not want to do it with pen and ink. 14I hope to see you soon, and then we will talk personally.

15Peace be with you.

All your friends send greetings. Greet all our friends personally.

跟他們一同為真理工作。

狄特腓和底米特

9 我曾寫了一封信給教會；可是，想作領袖的狄特腓不理會我所說的話。10我來的時候，要揭發他所做的事。他用壞話攻擊我們，造謠毀謗。這還不夠，他自己不接待外來的信徒，甚至阻止那些願意接待的人，要把他們趕出教會！

11 親愛的朋友，不要學壞，要學好。誰有好行為，誰就是屬上帝；誰作惡，誰就是沒有見過上帝。

12 大家都稱讚底米特。真理為他作證；我們也為他作證。你知道我們所說的話是真的。

最後問安

13 我還有許多話要告訴你，但我不想藉筆墨傳達。14我希望不久能見到你，當面跟你傾談。

15 願你平安！

你的朋友們都問候你。請替我向各位朋友一一問安。

猶大書
JUDE

INTRODUCTION

The Letter from Jude was written to warn against false teachers who claimed to be believers. In this brief letter, which is similar in content to *2 Peter,* the writer encourages his readers "to fight on for the faith which once and for all God has given to his people."

Outline of Contents

Introduction 1-2
Character, teaching, and doom of the false teachers 3-16
Admonition to keep the faith 17-23
Benediction 24-25

簡 介

猶大書的目的是在警告那些自稱爲信徒的假教師。在這封內容跟彼得後書相似的短信中,作者鼓勵讀者們「繼續爲上帝只一次就完整地傳授給信徒們的信仰爭戰」。(3)

提要

1. 序言(1 - 2)
2. 假教師的性格、言論,和終局(3 -16)
3. 勸勉持守信仰(17-23)
4. 祝福(24-25)

---

1 From Jude, servant of Jesus Christ, and brother of James–

To those who have been called by God, who live in the love of God the Father and the protection of Jesus Christ:

2May mercy, peace, and love be yours in full measure.

False Teachers

3My dear friends, I was doing my best to write to you about the salvation we share in common, when I felt the need of writing at once to encourage you to fight on for the faith which once and for all God has given to his people. 4For some godless people have slipped in unnoticed among us, persons who distort the message about the grace of our God in order to excuse their immoral ways, and who reject Jesus Christ, our only Master and Lord. Long ago the Scriptures predicted the condemnation they have received.

1我是耶穌基督的僕人,雅各的兄弟猶大。我寫信給蒙上帝選召、生活在父上帝的愛中、並蒙耶穌基督保守的人。

2 願上帝豐豐富富地賜給你們憐憫、平安,和慈愛。

假教師

3 親愛的朋友們,我一直很想寫信跟你們談談與我們大家都有關係的救恩問題,可是我覺得有必要立刻向你們提出勸告,要你們繼續爲上帝只一次就完整地傳授給信徒們的信仰爭戰。4因爲,有些不敬虔的人偷偷地混進我們中間,以曲解上帝恩典的信息來掩飾自己腐敗的行爲。他們拒絕了惟一的主宰—我們的主耶穌基督。在很久以前,聖經已經預言他們必須受懲罰。

5For even though you know all this, I want to remind you of how the Lord*a* once rescued the people of Israel from Egypt, but afterward destroyed those who did not believe. 6Remember the angels who did not stay within the limits of their proper authority, but abandoned their own dwelling place: they are bound with eternal chains in the darkness below, where God is keeping them for that great Day on which they will be condemned. 7Remember Sodom and Gomorrah, and the nearby towns, whose people acted as those angels did and indulged in sexual immorality and perversion: they suffer the punishment of eternal fire as a plain warning to all.

8In the same way also, these people have visions which make them sin against their own bodies; they despise God's authority and insult the glorious beings above. 9Not even the chief angel Michael did this. In his quarrel with the Devil, when they argued about who would have the body of Moses, Michael did not dare condemn the Devil with insulting words, but said, "The Lord rebuke you!" 10But these people attack with insults anything they do not understand; and those things that they know by instinct, like wild animals, are the very things that destroy them. 11How terrible for them! They have followed the way that Cain took. For the sake of money they have given themselves over to the error that Balaam committed. They have rebelled as Korah rebelled, and like him they are destroyed. 12With their shameless carousing they are like dirty spots in your fellowship meals. They take care only of themselves. They are like clouds carried along by the wind, but bringing no rain. They are like trees that bear no fruit, even in autumn, trees that have been pulled up by the roots and are completely dead. 13They are like wild waves of the sea, with their shameful deeds showing up like foam. They are like wandering stars, for whom God has reserved a place forever in the deepest darkness.

14It was Enoch, the seventh*b* direct descendant from Adam, who long ago prophesied this about them: "The Lord will come with many thousands of his holy angels 15to bring judgment on all, to condemn them all for the godless deeds they have performed and for all the terrible words that godless sinners have spoken against him!"

16These people are always grumbling and blaming others; they follow their own evil desires; they brag about themselves and flatter

5 雖然你們都知道這一切，我仍然要提醒你們：主①怎樣救以色列人民脫離埃及，然後消滅那些不信的人。6不要忘記那些不守本份、離開崗位的天使們，他們被永遠解不開的鎖鍊鎖在黑暗的深淵裏；上帝把他們囚禁在那裏，等待審判的大日子。7還有住在所多瑪、蛾摩拉，和附近城市的人民，像那些大使一樣，他們行為淫亂，放縱反自然的性慾，因此受那永不熄滅之火的懲罰。這事可作為人人的鑑戒。

8 這些不敬虔的人也是一樣。他們淫穢的幻想驅使他們犯罪，污損自己的身體；他們輕慢上帝的權威，侮辱在天上的尊榮者。9甚至天使長米迦勒，為了摩西的屍體跟魔鬼爭辯時，也不敢用侮辱的話責罵他，只說：「主要譴責你！」10可是，這些人竟毀謗他們所不了解的事，像野獸一樣隨着本能去做那些毀滅自己的事。11這些人要遭殃啦！他們跟該隱走同一條路。為着錢財，他們掉進了巴蘭所犯的錯誤中，像可拉一樣背叛，一樣滅亡。12這些人在你們的愛筵上無恥地狂飲，污穢了自己，像牧人只曉得滿足自己的肚子。他們像雲塊被風吹逐，下不了雨，又像在秋天也結不出果子的樹，連根拔掉，完全枯死。13他們可恥的行為像海裏的狂浪激起泡沫。他們像脫軌的星星掉進上帝永遠保留給他們的幽暗深淵。

14 亞當的第七代孫以諾對這些人早就有了預言，他說：「看哪，主帶着千萬的聖天使一同來。15他要審判所有的人，懲罰所有不敬虔的罪人；因為他們的行為不敬虔，又用不敬虔的話冒犯上帝。」

16 這些人常常埋怨別人，責怪別人；他們隨從自己邪惡的慾望，說誇張的話，為着自

---

a the Lord; *some manuscripts have* Jesus, *which in Greek is the same as Joshua.*
b SEVENTH: *This numbering includes both the first and the last in the series of seven names from Adam to Enoch.*

①「主」有些古卷作「上帝」；另有些古卷作「耶穌」。

others in order to get their own way.

Warnings and Instructions

17But remember, my friends, what you were told in the past by the apostles of our Lord Jesus Christ. 18They said to you, "When the last days come, people will appear who will make fun of you, people who follow their own godless desires." 19These are the people who cause divisions, who are controlled by their natural desires, who do not have the Spirit. 20But you, my friends, keep on building yourselves up on your most sacred faith. Pray in the power of the Holy Spirit, 21and keep yourselves in the love of God, as you wait for our Lord Jesus Christ in his mercy to give you eternal life.

22Show mercy toward those who have doubts; 23save others by snatching them out of the fire; and to others show mercy mixed with fear, but hate their very clothes, stained by their sinful lusts.

Prayer of Praise

24To him who is able to keep you from falling and to bring you faultless and joyful before his glorious presence– 25to the only God our Savior, through Jesus Christ our Lord, be glory, majesty, might, and authority, from all ages past, and now, and forever and ever! Amen.

己的利益諂媚別人。

警告和教導

17 可是，親愛的朋友們，不要忘記我們主耶穌基督的使徒們所說的話。18他們對你們說：「在歷史的末期有人要出來，隨從自己邪惡和不敬虔的慾念嘲弄你們。」19這些人製造紛爭，受本性的支配，沒有聖靈。20至於你們，親愛的朋友們，你們應該始終堅立在至聖的信仰上，藉着聖靈的力量禱告，21常常生活在上帝的愛裏，仰望我們的主耶穌基督憐憫你們，賜給你們永恆的生命。

22 對那些猶疑不定的人，你們要憐憫他們。23有些人，你們要從火中搶救他們；另有些人，你們要憐憫他們，但要戒懼，連他們那沾染情慾的衣服也要厭惡。

頌讚的禱告

24 上帝能保守你們不至於跌倒，使你們沒有缺點，能夠歡歡喜喜地來到他榮耀的面前。25這位獨一無二的上帝，藉着我們的主耶穌基督拯救了我們。願他得到榮耀、威嚴、能力，和權柄，從萬世到現在，直到永遠。阿們！

啓示錄
REVELATION

INTRODUCTION

The Revelation to John was written at a time when Christians were being persecuted because of their faith in Jesus Christ as Lord. The writer's main concern is to give his readers hope and encouragement, and to urge them to remain faithful during times of suffering and persecution.

For the most part the book consists of several series of revelations and visions presented in symbolic language that would have been understood by Christians of that day, but would have remained a mystery to all others. As with the themes of a symphony, the themes of this book are repeated again and again in different ways through the various series of visions. Although there are differences of opinion regarding the details of interpretation of the book, the central theme is clear: through Christ the Lord, God will finally and totally defeat all of his enemies, including Satan, and will reward his faithful people with the blessings of a new heaven and a new earth when this victory is complete.

Outline of Contents

簡 介

約翰寫啓示錄的時候，正值基督徒因信耶穌基督、承認耶穌爲主而慘遭迫害。作者寫本書的主要目的在於給他的讀者希望和鼓勵，勸勉他們在遭受苦難和迫害的時候仍要堅守信仰。

本書多半包含一些默示和異象，用象徵性的語言表達作者的信息。它的內容對當時的信徒來說不難領會，但對未信人士和後世讀者就很難明白。正如交響樂一樣，本書的主題用種種的異象，以不同的方法，重複出現。雖然這些異象的細節有不同的解釋，中心意義卻很明顯：就是藉着主耶穌基督，上帝最後將徹底擊敗一切仇敵，包括撒但在內，而且要在勝利之日獎賞他忠心的子民，賜給他們新天新地。

本書作爲聖經的最後一卷是非常適當的。因爲，最後幾章正描寫世界的末日和上帝拯救大業的完成。

提要

1 This book is the record of the events that Jesus Christ revealed. God gave him this revelation in order to show to his servants what must happen very soon. Christ made these things known to his servant John by sending his angel to him, [2]and John has told all that he has seen. This is his report concerning the message from God and the truth revealed by Jesus Christ. [3]Happy is the one who reads this book, and happy are those who listen to the words of this prophetic message and obey what is written in this book! For the time is near when all these things will happen.

Greetings to the Seven Churches

[4]From John to the seven churches in the province of Asia:

Grace and peace be yours from God, who is, who was, and who is to come, and from the seven spirits in front of his throne, [5]and from Jesus Christ, the faithful witness, the first to be raised from death and who is also the ruler of the kings of the world.

He loves us, and by his sacrificial death he has freed us from our sins [6]and made us a kingdom of priests to serve his God and Father. To Jesus Christ be the glory and power forever and ever! Amen.

[7]Look, he is coming on the clouds! Everyone will see him, including those who pierced him. All peoples on earth will mourn over him. So shall it be!

[8]"I am the first and the last," says the Lord God Almighty, who is, who was, and who is to come.

A Vision of Christ

[9]I am John, your brother, and as a follower of Jesus I am your partner in patiently enduring the suffering that comes to those who belong to his Kingdom. I was put on the island of Patmos because I had proclaimed God's word and the truth that Jesus revealed. [10]On the Lord's day the Spirit took control of me, and I heard a loud voice, that sounded like a trumpet, speaking behind me. [11]It said, "Write down what you see, and send the book to the churches in these seven cities: Ephesus, Smyrna, Pergamum, Thyatira, Sardis, Philadelphia, and Laodicea."

[12]I turned around to see who was talking to me, and I saw seven gold lampstands, [13]and among them there was what looked like a human being, wearing a robe that reached to his feet, and a gold band around his chest. [14]His hair was white as wool, or as snow, and his eyes blazed like fire; [15]his feet shone like brass

1 本書是記載耶穌基督的啟示。上帝給他這啟示,要他把短期內必定發生的事指示給上帝的僕人們。基督差遣天使向他的僕人約翰顯示這些事,[2]約翰就把所看見的告訴大家,為上帝的信息和耶穌基督所啟示的真理作見證。[3]讀這本書的人多麼有福啊!聽見這預言並遵守書中所記載的人多麼有福啊!因為這一切事實現的日子快要到了。

向七教會問安

[4-5]我一約翰寫信給亞細亞省的七個教會:願那位昔在、今在、將來永在的上帝,以及他寶座前的七個靈,和那忠誠的見證者、首先從死裏復活、作地上諸王統治者的耶穌基督,賜恩典、平安給你們!

他愛我們,為我們犧牲流血,從罪中把我們釋放了出來,[6]使我們成為祭司的國度,來事奉他的父上帝。願榮耀和權能歸於耶穌基督,世世無窮!阿們。

[7]看哪,他駕着雲來了!每一個人都要看見他,連槍刺他的那些人也要看見他。他來的時候,地上萬民要為他悲傷痛哭。這事必然發生!阿們。

[8]昔在、今在、將來永在的主一全能的上帝說:「我是阿爾法,就是開始,是亞米茄,就是終結。」

基督向約翰顯現

[9]我是約翰一你們的弟兄。我在耶穌裏跟你們分擔患難,一同忍耐,也要分享他的主權。為了傳揚上帝的道和耶穌所啟示的真理,我曾被囚禁在名叫拔摩的海島上。[10]有一個主日,聖靈支配着我,我聽見了一個大聲音,好像吹號的響聲,在我背後向我說:[11]「把你所看見的寫下來,然後把這書卷寄給以弗所、士每拿、別迦摩、推雅推喇、撒狄、非拉鐵非、老底嘉七個教會。」

[12]我轉身要看誰在向我說話,我看見了七個金燈臺。[13]燈臺中間有一位像人子的,站在那裏,身上穿着垂到腳跟的長袍,胸前繫着金帶。[14]他的頭髮像雪,也像羊毛一樣的潔白;他的眼睛像火燄那樣閃耀;[15]他的腳

1 This book is the record of the events that Jesus Christ revealed. God gave him this revelation in order to show to his servants what must happen very soon. Christ made these things known to his servant John by sending his angel to him, ²and John has told all that he has seen. This is his report concerning the message from God and the truth revealed by Jesus Christ. ³Happy is the one who reads this book, and happy are those who listen to the words of this prophetic message and obey what is written in this book! For the time is near when all these things will happen.

Greetings to the Seven Churches

⁴From John to the seven churches in the province of Asia:

Grace and peace be yours from God, who is, who was, and who is to come, and from the seven spirits in front of his throne, ⁵and from Jesus Christ, the faithful witness, the first to be raised from death and who is also the ruler of the kings of the world.

He loves us, and by his sacrificial death he has freed us from our sins ⁶and made us a kingdom of priests to serve his God and Father. To Jesus Christ be the glory and power forever and ever! Amen.

⁷Look, he is coming on the clouds! Everyone will see him, including those who pierced him. All peoples on earth will mourn over him. So shall it be!

⁸"I am the first and the last," says the Lord God Almighty, who is, who was, and who is to come.

A Vision of Christ

⁹I am John, your brother, and as a follower of Jesus I am your partner in patiently enduring the suffering that comes to those who belong to his Kingdom. I was put on the island of Patmos because I had proclaimed God's word and the truth that Jesus revealed. ¹⁰On the Lord's day the Spirit took control of me, and I heard a loud voice, that sounded like a trumpet, speaking behind me. ¹¹It said, "Write down what you see, and send the book to the churches in these seven cities: Ephesus, Smyrna, Pergamum, Thyatira, Sardis, Philadelphia, and Laodicea."

¹²I turned around to see who was talking to me, and I saw seven gold lampstands, ¹³and among them there was what looked like a human being, wearing a robe that reached to his feet, and a gold band around his chest. ¹⁴His hair was white as wool, or as snow, and his eyes blazed like fire; ¹⁵his feet shone like brass

1 本書是記載耶穌基督的啓示。上帝給他這啓示,要他把短期內必定發生的事指示給上帝的僕人們。基督差遣天使向他的僕人約翰顯示這些事,²約翰就把所看見的告訴大家,為上帝的信息和耶穌基督所啓示的真理作見證。³讀這本書的人多麼有福啊!聽見這預言並遵守書中所記載的人多麼有福啊!因為這一切事實現的日子快要到了。

向七教會問安

⁴⁻⁵我—約翰寫信給亞細亞省的七個教會:願那位昔在、今在、將來永在的上帝,以及他寶座前的七個靈,和那忠誠的見證者、首先從死裏復活、作地上諸王統治者的耶穌基督,賜恩典、平安給你們!

他愛我們,為我們犧牲流血,從罪中把我們釋放了出來,⁶使我們成為祭司的國度,來事奉他的父上帝。願榮耀和權能歸於耶穌基督,世世無窮!阿們。

⁷看哪,他駕着雲來了!每一個人都要看見他,連槍刺他的那些人也要看見他。他來的時候,地上萬民要為他悲傷痛哭。這事必然發生!阿們。

⁸昔在、今在、將來永在的主—全能的上帝說:「我是阿爾法,就是開始,是亞米茄,就是終結。」

基督向約翰顯現

⁹我是約翰—你們的弟兄。我在耶穌裏跟你們分擔患難,一同忍耐,也要分享他的主權。為了傳揚上帝的道和耶穌所啓示的真理,我曾被囚禁在名叫拔摩的海島上。¹⁰有一個主日,聖靈支配着我,我聽見了一個大聲音,好像吹號的響聲,在我背後向我說:¹¹「把你所看見的寫下來,然後把這書卷寄給以弗所、士每拿、別迦摩、推雅推喇、撒狄、非拉鐵非、老底嘉七個教會。」

¹²我轉身要看誰在向我說話,我看見了七個金燈臺。¹³燈臺中間有一位像人子的,站在那裏,身上穿着垂到腳跟的長袍,胸前繫着金帶。¹⁴他的頭髮像雪,也像羊毛一樣的潔白;他的眼睛像火燄那樣閃耀;¹⁵他的腳

啟示錄
REVELATION

INTRODUCTION

The Revelation to John was written at a time when Christians were being persecuted because of their faith in Jesus Christ as Lord. The writer's main concern is to give his readers hope and encouragement, and to urge them to remain faithful during times of suffering and persecution.

For the most part the book consists of several series of revelations and visions presented in symbolic language that would have been understood by Christians of that day, but would have remained a mystery to all others. As with the themes of a symphony, the themes of this book are repeated again and again in different ways through the various series of visions. Although there are differences of opinion regarding the details of interpretation of the book, the central theme is clear: through Christ the Lord, God will finally and totally defeat all of his enemies, including Satan, and will reward his faithful people with the blessings of a new heaven and a new earth when this victory is complete.

Outline of Contents

簡 介

約翰寫啟示錄的時候，正值基督徒因信耶穌基督、承認耶穌爲主而慘遭迫害。作者寫本書的主要目的在於給他的讀者希望和鼓勵，勸勉他們在遭受苦難和迫害的時候仍要堅守信仰。

本書多半包含一些默示和異象，用象徵性的語言表達作者的信息。它的內容對當時的信徒來說不難領會，但對未信人士和後世讀者就很難明白。正如交響樂一樣，本書的主題用種種的異象，以不同的方法，重複出現。雖然這些異象的細節有不同的解釋，中心意義卻很明顯：就是藉着主耶穌基督，上帝最後將徹底擊敗一切仇敵，包括撒但在內，而且要在勝利之日獎賞他忠心的子民，賜給他們新天新地。

本書作爲聖經的最後一卷是非常適當的。因爲，最後幾章正描寫世界的末日和上帝拯救大業的完成。

提要

the wicked things they did with her. 23I will also kill her followers, and then all the churches will know that I am the one who knows everyone's thoughts and wishes. I will repay each of you according to what you have done.

24"But the rest of you in Thyatira have not followed this evil teaching; you have not learned what the others call 'the deep secrets of Satan.' I say to you that I will not put any other burden on you. 25But until I come, you must hold firmly to what you have. 26-28To those who win the victory, who continue to the end to do what I want, I will give the same authority that I received from my Father: I will give them authority over the nations, to rule them with an iron rod and to break them to pieces like clay pots. I will also give them the morning star.

29"If you have ears, then, listen to what the Spirit says to the churches!

The Message to Sardis

3 "To the angel of the church in Sardis write: "This is the message from the one who has the seven spirits of God and the seven stars. I know what you are doing; I know that you have the reputation of being alive, even though you are dead! 2So wake up, and strengthen what you still have before it dies completely. For I find that what you have done is not yet perfect in the sight of my God. 3Remember, then, what you were taught and what you heard; obey it and turn from your sins. If you do not wake up, I will come upon you like a thief, and you will not even know the time when I will come. 4But a few of you there in Sardis have kept your clothes clean. You will walk with me, clothed in white, because you are worthy to do so. 5Those who win the victory will be clothed like this in white, and I will not remove their names from the book of the living. In the presence of my Father and of his angels I will declare openly that they belong to me.

6"If you have ears, then, listen to what the Spirit says to the churches!

The Message to Philadelphia

7"To the angel of the church in Philadelphia write:

"This is the message from the one who is holy and true. He has the key that belonged to David, and when he opens a door, no one can close it, and when he closes it, no one can open it. 8I know what you do; I know that you have a little power; you have followed my teaching and have been faithful to me. I have opened a

大苦難。23我也要擊殺跟從她的人,各教會就會知道,我洞悉人的思想和意念。我要按照你們每一個人所做的報應你們。

24『然而,你們在推雅推喇其餘的人沒有跟從邪說,沒有學習所謂撒但的奧祕。我告訴你們,我不會再把其他的重擔加給你們。25但是,你們要持守你們已經有了的,直到我來。26-28至於那得勝、能夠繼續進行我命令到最後的人,我要賜給他權柄,跟我父親所給我的一樣;我要賜給他權柄來統治萬國,用鐵杖治理它們,像擊碎陶器一樣粉碎它們。我也要把晨星賜給得勝的人。

29『聖靈向各教會所說的話,有耳朵的,都聽吧!』」

給撒狄教會的信息

3 「 你要寫信給撒狄教會的天使,說:
『那位有上帝的七個靈和七顆星的,這樣說:我知道你所做的;我知道有人以為你是活着的,實際上你是死的! 2所以,你要醒過來,堅固你所剩下的一點點生機;因為我看出你所做的,在我上帝眼中還不完全。3所以,你要記住你所聽、所接受的教訓,要切實遵守,要悔改。你若不醒悟,我要像小偷一樣突然來到,而你絕不會知道我要來到的那時刻。4但是,在撒狄,你們還有些人把衣服保持得很乾淨;這些人配得穿上白袍,跟我同行。5得勝的人也要穿同樣穿上白袍;我絕不會從生命冊上把他的名字除掉。在我父親和他的天使面前,我要公開承認他是屬於我的。

6『聖靈向各教會所說的話,有耳朵的,都聽吧!』」

給非拉鐵非教會的信息

7 「 你要寫信給非拉鐵非教會的天使,說:

『那位神聖而信實、執掌着大衞的鑰匙、開了門就沒有人能關、關了門就沒有人能開的,這樣說: 8我知道你所做的;我知道你只有一點兒能力,可是你遵守了我的話,也對我忠誠。我已經在你前面開了一個

door in front of you, which no one can close.
⁹Listen! As for that group that belongs to
Satan, those liars who claim that they are Jews
but are not, I will make them come and bow
down at your feet. They will all know that I
love you. ¹⁰Because you have kept my command to endure, I will also keep you safe from
the time of trouble which is coming upon the
world to test all the people on earth. ¹¹I am
coming soon. Keep safe what you have, so that
no one will rob you of your victory prize. ¹²I
will make those who are victorious pillars in the
temple of my God, and they will never leave it.
I will write on them the name of my God and
the name of the city of my God, the new
Jerusalem, which will come down out of
heaven from my God. I will also write on them
my new name.

¹³"If you have ears, then, listen to what the
Spirit says to the churches!

The Message to Laodicea

¹⁴"To the angel of the church in Laodicea
write:

"This is the message from the Amen, the
faithful and true witness, who is the origin*a* of
all that God has created. ¹⁵I know what you
have done; I know that you are neither cold
nor hot. How I wish you were either one or the
other! ¹⁶But because you are lukewarm, neither
hot nor cold, I am going to spit you out of my
mouth! ¹⁷You say, 'I am rich and well off; I
have all I need.' But you do not know how mis-
erable and pitiful you are! You are poor,
naked, and blind. ¹⁸I advise you, then, to buy
gold from me, pure gold, in order to be rich.
Buy also white clothing to dress yourself and
cover up your shameful nakedness. Buy also
some ointment to put on your eyes, so that you
may see. ¹⁹I rebuke and punish all whom I love.
Be in earnest, then, and turn from your sins.
²⁰Listen! I stand at the door and knock; if any
hear my voice and open the door, I will come
into their house and eat with them, and they
will eat with me. ²¹To those who win the victory
I will give the right to sit beside me on my
throne, just as I have been victorious and now
sit by my Father on his throne.

²²"If you have ears, then, listen to what the
Spirit says to the churches!"

Worship in Heaven

4 At this point I had another vision and saw
an open door in heaven.

And the voice that sounded like a trumpet,

a origin; *or* ruler.

門,是沒有人能夠關上的。⁹看吧,那些撒
但的黨羽,自稱為猶太人而其實不是猶太人
的那些騙子,我要使他們來,在你腳前下
拜,讓他們知道我愛你。¹⁰因為你遵守了我
的命令,忍耐到底,所以在患難臨到全世
界、全人類受試煉的時候,我要保守你。
¹¹我就要來了。你要持守你所有的,不要讓
人奪去你勝利的華冠。¹²那得勝的人,我要
使他成為我上帝聖殿中的柱子;他永遠不再
離開。我要在他身上刻我上帝的名和我上帝
之城的名,就是那要從天上我上帝那裏降下
的新耶路撒冷;我又要在他身上刻上我的新
名。

¹³『聖靈向各教會所說的話,有耳朵的,
都聽吧!』」

給老底嘉教會的信息

¹⁴「你要寫信給老底嘉教會的天使,說:

『那位「阿們」,就是忠實可靠的見證
者,那位上帝創造之根源,這樣說:¹⁵我知
道你所做的;我知道你不冷不熱。我倒願意
你或冷或熱!¹⁶因為你像溫水一樣,既不冷
也不熱,我要從我口中把你吐出去!¹⁷你
說:我富足寬裕,毫無缺乏。然而,你不知
道你自己是多麼悲慘可憐!你貧窮、失明,
又赤身露體。¹⁸所以,我勸你向我買精煉的
金子,好使你富足;又買白袍穿上,好遮蓋
你那可羞恥的裸體;也買眼藥擦你的眼睛,
好使你能夠看見。¹⁹對我所愛的人,我都責
備管教。所以,你要熱心,要悔改。²⁰聽
吧,我站在門外敲門;若有人聽見我的聲音
而開門,我要進去。我要和他一起吃飯,他
也要跟我一起吃飯。²¹至於那得勝的人,我
要賜特權給他,在我寶座上跟我同坐,正如
我已經得勝,現在與我父親同坐在他的寶座
上一樣。

²²『聖靈向各教會所說的話,有耳朵的,
都聽吧!』」

天上的敬拜

4 接著,我得到另一個異象,看見天上有
開著的門。

我從前聽見的那好像吹號的聲音又對我

which I had heard speaking to me before, said, "Come up here, and I will show you what must happen after this." [2]At once the Spirit took control of me. There in heaven was a throne with someone sitting on it. [3]His face gleamed like such precious stones as jasper and carnelian, and all around the throne there was a rainbow the color of an emerald. [4]In a circle around the throne were twenty-four other thrones, on which were seated twenty-four elders dressed in white and wearing crowns of gold. [5]From the throne came flashes of lightning, rumblings, and peals of thunder. In front of the throne seven lighted torches were burning, which are the seven spirits of God. [6]Also in front of the throne there was what looked like a sea of glass, clear as crystal.

Surrounding the throne on each of its sides, were four living creatures covered with eyes in front and behind. [7]The first one looked like a lion; the second looked like a bull; the third had a face like a human face; and the fourth looked like an eagle in flight. [8]Each one of the four living creatures had six wings, and they were covered with eyes, inside and out. Day and night they never stop singing:

"Holy, holy, holy, is the Lord God Almighty, who was, who is, and who is to come."

[9]The four living creatures sing songs of glory and honor and thanks to the one who sits on the throne, who lives forever and ever. When they do so, [10]the twenty-four elders fall down before the one who sits on the throne, and worship him who lives forever and ever. They throw their crowns down in front of the throne and say,

[11]"Our Lord and God! You are worthy
    to receive glory, honor, and power.
    For you created all things,
        and by your will they were given existence
        and life."

The Scroll and the Lamb

5 I saw a scroll in the right hand of the one who sits on the throne; it was covered with writing on both sides and was sealed with seven seals. [2]And I saw a mighty angel, who announced in a loud voice, "Who is worthy to break the seals and open the scroll?" [3]But there was no one in heaven or on earth or in the world below[b] who could open the scroll and look inside it. [4]I cried bitterly because no one could be found who was worthy to open the scroll or look inside it. [5]Then one of the elders said to me, "Don't cry. Look! The Lion from Judah's tribe, the great descendant of David,

b WORLD BELOW: *The world of the dead (see 1.18).*

說：「你上這裏來，我要指示你以後必定發生的事。」立刻，聖靈支配着我。我看見天上有一個寶座；有一位坐在寶座上。[3]他的面貌像碧玉和紅玉髓一樣閃耀。寶座四周有彩虹圍繞着，顏色像翡翠。[4]寶座周圍有二十四個座位，上面坐着二十四個長老，身上穿着白袍，頭上戴着金冠。[5]從寶座發出閃電、響聲、和雷轟。有七枝點燃着的火把在寶座前；那就是上帝的七個靈。[6]寶座前有一片像水晶一樣光潔的玻璃海。

寶座的四邊有四個活物，前後都長滿了眼睛。[7]第一個活物像獅子；第二個像小牛；第三個有一副人的臉孔；第四個像飛鷹。[8]那四個活物，每一個都有六隻翅膀，裏面外面都長滿了眼睛。他們日夜不停地唱着：

聖哉！聖哉！聖哉！
主——全能的上帝，
昔在，今在，將來永在！

[9]四個活物唱着榮耀、尊貴、感謝的歌，獻給坐在寶座上、永遠活着的那一位。[10]這時候，二十四個長老俯伏敬拜坐在寶座上、永遠活着的那一位。他們把自己的冠冕放在寶座前，說：

[11]我們的主，我們的上帝！
你配接受榮耀、尊貴、和權能。
你創造了萬物；
萬物被造、得以生存，
全憑你的旨意。

羔羊的書卷

5 我看見坐在寶座上的那位，右手拿着書卷；這書卷的兩面都寫滿了字，用七個印封着。[2]我又看見一個大力的天使，高聲宣佈：「誰配揭開這些印、展開這書卷呢？」[3]可是，無論在天上、地下，或地底下，都沒有一個能展開書卷或閱讀的。[4]我放聲大哭，因為沒有人配展開或閱讀這書卷。[5]於是，長老中的一個對我說：「不要哭！看吧，那從猶大支族出來的獅子——大衛

has won the victory, and he can break the seven seals and open the scroll."

6Then I saw a Lamb standing in the center of the throne, surrounded by the four living creatures and the elders. The Lamb appeared to have been killed. It had seven horns and seven eyes, which are the seven spirits of God that have been sent through the whole earth. 7The Lamb went and took the scroll from the right hand of the one who sits on the throne. 8As he did so, the four living creatures and the twenty-four elders fell down before the Lamb. Each had a harp and gold bowls filled with incense, which are the prayers of God's people. 9They sang a new song:
"You are worthy to take the scroll
    and to break open its seals.
For you were killed, and by your sacrificial
        death you bought for God
    people from every tribe, language, nation,
        and race.
10You have made them a kingdom of priests to
        serve our God,
    and they shall rule on earth."

11Again I looked, and I heard angels, thousands and millions of them! They stood around the throne, the four living creatures, and the elders, 12and sang in a loud voice:
"The Lamb who was killed is worthy
    to receive power, wealth, wisdom, and
        strength,
    honor, glory, and praise!"
13And I heard every creature in heaven, on earth, in the world below, and in the sea–all living beings in the universe–and they were singing:
"To him who sits on the throne and to the
        Lamb,
    be praise and honor, glory and might,
    forever and ever!"
14The four living creatures answered, "Amen!" And the elders fell down and worshiped.

The Seals

6 Then I saw the Lamb break open the first of the seven seals, and I heard one of the four living creatures say in a voice that sounded like thunder, "Come!" 2I looked, and there was a white horse. Its rider held a bow, and he was given a crown. He rode out as a conqueror to conquer.

3Then the Lamb broke open the second seal; and I heard the second living creature say, "Come!" 4Another horse came out, a red one. Its rider was given the power to bring war on the earth, so that people should kill each other.

的後代已經得勝了;他能夠揭開七個印,展開書卷。」

6 接着,我看見那被四個活物和長老們圍繞着的寶座中,有羔羊站着。羔羊像是被宰殺過的,有七個角,七個眼睛,就是上帝的七個靈,是被差派到世上各地去的。7那羔羊上前,從坐在寶座上那位的右手中把書卷接過來。8他這樣做的時候,四個活物和二十四個長老就俯伏在羔羊面前。每一個長老都拿着豎琴和盛滿着香的金爐;這香就是信徒們的禱告。9他們唱着一首新歌:

　　惟有你配接受那書卷,
　　揭開上面的印;
　　因為你曾被殺!
　　由於你的犧牲流血,
　　你從各部落、各語言、各民族、各國家
　　　把人贖回來,歸給上帝。
10　你使他們成為祭司的國度,
　　來事奉我們的上帝;
　　他們將在地上掌權。

11 我又觀看;我聽見了千千萬萬天使的聲音。他們環立在寶座、四個活物,和長老們的四周,12高聲唱:

　　被宰殺的羔羊,
　　配接受權能、豐富、智慧、力量、
　　　尊貴、榮耀,和頌讚!

13 我又聽見天上、地下,和地底下的生物,海裏的生物,宇宙中的萬有,都在歌唱:

　　願頌讚、尊貴、榮耀,和權柄,
　　都歸於坐在寶座上那位和羔羊,
　　世世無窮!

14 四個活物就應答:「阿們!」長老都俯伏敬拜。

開印

6 我看見羔羊揭開七印的第一個印。那時候,我聽見四活物中的一個發出好像雷轟的響聲,說:「來吧!」2我一看,看見一匹白馬;那騎馬的拿弓,接受了所賜給他的冠冕,就出發征戰,得勝又得勝。

3 羔羊揭開第二個印的時候,我聽見第二個活物說:「來吧!」4於是另一匹馬出來,是紅色的。那騎馬的得了權,使地上發生爭戰,人與人互相殘殺;他又接受了一把

He was given a large sword.

5Then the Lamb broke open the third seal; and I heard the third living creature say, "Come!" I looked, and there was a black horse. Its rider held a pair of scales in his hand. 6I heard what sounded like a voice coming from among the four living creatures, which said, "A quart of wheat for a day's wages, and three quarts of barley for a day's wages. But do not damage the olive trees and the vineyards!"

7Then the Lamb broke open the fourth seal; and I heard the fourth living creature say, "Come!" 8I looked, and there was a pale-colored horse. Its rider was named Death, and Hades*c* followed close behind. They were given authority over one fourth of the earth, to kill by means of war, famine, disease, and wild animals.

9Then the Lamb broke open the fifth seal. I saw underneath the altar the souls of those who had been killed because they had proclaimed God's word and had been faithful in their witnessing. 10They shouted in a loud voice, "Almighty Lord, holy and true! How long will it be until you judge the people on earth and punish them for killing us?" 11Each of them was given a white robe, and they were told to rest a little while longer, until the complete number of other servants and believers were killed, as they had been.

12And I saw the Lamb break open the sixth seal. There was a violent earthquake, and the sun became black like coarse black cloth, and the moon turned completely red like blood. 13The stars fell down to the earth, like unripe figs falling from the tree when a strong wind shakes it. 14The sky disappeared like a scroll being rolled up, and every mountain and island was moved from its place. 15Then the kings of the earth, the rulers and the military chiefs, the rich and the powerful, and all other people, slave and free, hid themselves in caves and under rocks on the mountains. 16They called out to the mountains and to the rocks, "Fall on us and hide us from the eyes of the one who sits on the throne and from the anger of the Lamb! 17The terrible day of their anger is here, and who can stand up against it?"

The 144,000 People of Israel

7 After this I saw four angels standing at the four corners of the earth, holding back the four winds so that no wind should blow on the earth or the sea or against any tree. 2And I saw another angel coming up from the east with the seal of the living God. He called out in a loud voice to the four angels to whom God had

c HADES: *The world of the dead (see 1.18).*

大劍。

5 羔羊揭開第三個印的時候，我聽見第三個活物說：「來吧！」我一看，看見一匹黑馬；那騎馬的手中拿着一個天平。6 我聽見似乎有聲音從四個活物中發出說：「一天的工資只能買一公升小麥；一天的工資只能買三公升大麥。橄欖油和酒不可糟蹋！」

7 羔羊揭開第四個印的時候，我聽見第四個活物說：「來吧！」8 我一看，看見一匹灰色的馬；那騎馬的名叫「死亡」，陰間緊跟着他。他們得了權，管轄四分之一的土地，要用戰爭、饑荒、瘟疫，和地上的野獸殺人。

9 羔羊揭開第五個印的時候，我看見在祭壇下有那些曾經爲了傳揚上帝的道、忠心作證而被殺的人的靈魂。10他們高聲呼喊：「神聖而信實的主宰啊！甚麼時候你才審判地上的人、爲我們所流的血伸冤呢？」11於是，他們每一個人接受了一件白袍，又聽見有話吩咐他們，要他們再歇一會兒，等到跟他們一同事奉主的人和信徒們也像他們一樣被殺，數目湊滿了的時候。

12我又看見羔羊揭開了第六個印。那時候，大地劇烈地震動；太陽變黑，好像一塊黑麻布；月亮整個變爲紅色，像血一般；13星星從天空隆落在地上，好像還沒有成熟的無花果被暴風從樹上吹落一樣。14天空像書卷被捲起來，不見了；山嶺和海島從原處被移開。15地上的君王、統治者、將領、有錢有勢的、奴隸，和自由人，都去躲在山洞和巖穴裏。16他們向山嶺和巖石呼喊：「倒在我們身上吧！把我們藏起來，好躲避坐在寶座上那位的臉和羔羊的義怒！17因爲他們震怒的大日子到了；誰能站得住呢？」

十四萬四千以色列人

7 後來，我看見四個天使站在地的四極，擋住地上四面的風，不使風吹在地上、海上，或樹上。2 我又看見另外一個天使，捧着永生上帝的印，從東方上來。他高聲向那領受了上帝所賜權柄、能夠破壞地和海的

given the power to damage the earth and the sea. ³The angel said, "Do not harm the earth, the sea, or the trees, until we mark the servants of our God with a seal on their foreheads." ⁴And I was told that the number of those who were marked with God's seal on their foreheads was 144,000. They were from the twelve tribes of Israel, ⁵⁻⁸twelve thousand from each tribe: Judah, Reuben, Gad, Asher, Naphtali, Manasseh, Simeon, Levi, Issachar, Zebulun, Joseph, and Benjamin.

The Enormous Crowd

9After this I looked, and there was an enormous crowd–no one could count all the people! They were from every race, tribe, nation, and language, and they stood in front of the throne and of the Lamb, dressed in white robes and holding palm branches in their hands. ¹⁰They called out in a loud voice: "Salvation comes from our God, who sits on the throne, and from the Lamb!" ¹¹All the angels stood around the throne, the elders, and the four living creatures. Then they threw themselves face downward in front of the throne and worshiped God, ¹²saying, "Amen! Praise, glory, wisdom, thanksgiving, honor, power, and might belong to our God forever and ever! Amen!"

¹³One of the elders asked me, "Who are these people dressed in white robes, and where do they come from?"

¹⁴"I don't know, sir. You do," I answered.

He said to me, "These are the people who have come safely through the terrible persecution. They have washed their robes and made them white with the blood of the Lamb. ¹⁵That is why they stand before God's throne and serve him day and night in his temple. He who sits on the throne will protect them with his presence. ¹⁶Never again will they hunger or thirst; neither sun nor any scorching heat will burn them, ¹⁷because the Lamb, who is in the center of the throne, will be their shepherd, and he will guide them to springs of life-giving water. And God will wipe away every tear from their eyes."

The Seventh Seal

8 When the Lamb broke open the seventh seal, there was silence in heaven for about half an hour. ²Then I saw the seven angels who stand before God, and they were given seven trumpets.

³Another angel, who had a gold incense con-

四個天使呼喊：³「不要傷害地、海，或樹木，等我們在上帝僕人的額上先蓋了印。」⁴我聽見說，在以色列各支族中被蓋印的，總數共十四萬四千人；⁵猶大支族中被蓋印的，一萬二千人；呂便支族中，一萬二千人；迦得支族中，一萬二千人；⁶亞設支族中，一萬二千人；拿弗他利支族中，一萬二千人；瑪拿西支族中，一萬二千人；⁷西緬支族中，一萬二千人；利未支族中，一萬二千人；以薩迦支族中，一萬二千人；⁸西布倫支族中，一萬二千人；約瑟支族中，一萬二千人；便雅憫支族中，一萬二千人。

來自各地的羣衆

9 後來，我一看，看見一大羣人，數目難以計算。他們是從各國家、各部落、各民族、各語言來的，都站在寶座和羔羊面前，穿着白袍，手上拿着棕樹枝。¹⁰他們高聲呼喊：「救恩是從坐在寶座上、我們的上帝和羔羊來的！」¹¹所有的天使都站在寶座、長老，和四活物的周圍。他們在寶座前俯伏地上，敬拜上帝，¹²說：「阿們！願頌讚、榮耀、智慧、感謝、尊貴、權能、力量都歸於我們的上帝，世世無窮！阿們。」

¹³有一個長老問我：「那些穿白袍的是誰？他們是從哪裏來的？」

¹⁴我回答：「先生，你才知道。」他對我說：「這些人是經歷過大災難的。他們用羔羊的血把自己的衣服洗得乾淨潔白了。¹⁵因此，他們侍立在上帝的寶座前，日夜在他的聖殿中事奉他。那位坐在寶座上的上帝要親自庇護他們。¹⁶他們不再飢，不再渴；太陽或任何炎熱都不能燒灼他們。¹⁷因為寶座中的羔羊要牧養他們，領他們到生命的水源；上帝也要擦乾他們每一滴眼淚。

第七個印

8 羔羊揭開第七個印的時候，天上寂靜無聲，約半小時。²然後，我看見站在上帝面前的七個天使；他們接受了七枝號筒。

³ 另外有一個天使出來，拿着金香爐，站

tainer, came and stood at the altar. He was given a lot of incense to add to the prayers of all God's people and to offer it on the gold altar that stands before the throne. ⁴The smoke of the burning incense went up with the prayers of God's people from the hands of the angel standing before God. ⁵Then the angel took the incense container, filled it with fire from the altar, and threw it on the earth. There were rumblings and peals of thunder, flashes of lightning, and an earthquake.

The Trumpets

⁶Then the seven angels with the seven trumpets prepared to blow them.

⁷The first angel blew his trumpet. Hail and fire, mixed with blood, came pouring down on the earth. A third of the earth was burned up, a third of the trees, and every blade of green grass.

⁸Then the second angel blew his trumpet. Something that looked like a huge mountain on fire was thrown into the sea. A third of the sea was turned into blood, ⁹a third of the living creatures in the sea died, and a third of the ships were destroyed.

¹⁰Then the third angel blew his trumpet. A large star, burning like a torch, dropped from the sky and fell on a third of the rivers and on the springs of water. ¹¹(The name of the star is "Bitterness.") A third of the water turned bitter, and many people died from drinking the water, because it had turned bitter.

¹²Then the fourth angel blew his trumpet. A third of the sun was struck, and a third of the moon, and a third of the stars, so that their light lost a third of its brightness; there was no light during a third of the day and a third of the night also.

¹³Then I looked, and I heard an eagle that was flying high in the air say in a loud voice, "O horror! horror! How horrible it will be for all who live on earth when the sound comes from the trumpets that the other three angels must blow!"

9 Then the fifth angel blew his trumpet. I saw a star which had fallen down to the earth, and it was given the key to the abyss.ᵈ ²The star opened the abyss, and smoke poured out of it, like the smoke from a large furnace; the sunlight and the air were darkened by the smoke from the abyss. ³Locusts came down out of the smoke upon the earth, and they were given the same kind of power that scorpions

d ABYSS: *The place in the depths of the earth where the demons were imprisoned until their final punishment.*

在祭壇前。他接受了許多香，就連同信徒們的禱告一起獻在寶座前的金祭壇上。⁴那香所發出的煙和信徒們的禱告從天使手中升到上帝面前。⁵接着，天使拿着香爐，把香爐裝滿了祭壇上的火，扔到地上去。於是就有了雷轟、響聲、閃電，和地震。

號筒

⁶ 然後，那七個拿着七枝號筒的天使準備要吹號。

⁷ 第一個天使一吹號，有冰雹和火，攙着血，傾倒在地上。於是地的三分之一，樹木的三分之一，都燒掉了；所有的青草也都燒掉了。

⁸ 第二個天使一吹號，有一座看來像着了火的大山被扔到海中。海的三分之一變成了血，⁹海中的生物死了三分之一，船隻也損壞了三分之一。

¹⁰第三個天使一吹號，有一顆大星，像燃燒着的火把一樣，從天上墜下來，掉在三分之一的河流和一切的水源上。¹¹（這星名叫「苦澀」。）於是水的三分之一變苦了。因為水變苦，許多人喝了這水都死了。

¹²第四個天使一吹號，太陽的三分之一、月亮的三分之一，和星辰的三分之一都被襲擊。於是太陽、月亮、星辰失去了三分之一的光輝；白天的三分之一沒有光，夜晚的三分之一也沒有光。

¹³我觀看，又聽見一隻在高空飛翔的鷹高聲說：「慘啦！慘啦！地上的人都慘啦！另外三個天使就要吹號了！」

9 第五個天使一吹號，我看見一顆星從天空墜下來，掉在地上。這星接受了無底深淵的鑰匙。²它開了無底的深淵，裏面就冒出煙來，好像從大火爐冒出來的；太陽和天空都因深淵冒出來的煙而變為昏暗。³有蝗蟲從煙裏出來，落在地上；牠們接受能

have. 4They were told not to harm the grass or the trees or any other plant; they could harm only the people who did not have the mark of God's seal on their foreheads. 5The locusts were not allowed to kill these people, but only to torture them for five months. The pain caused by the torture is like the pain caused by a scorpion's sting. 6During those five months they will seek death, but will not find it; they will want to die, but death will flee from them.

7The locusts looked like horses ready for battle; on their heads they had what seemed to be crowns of gold, and their faces were like human faces. 8Their hair was like women's hair, their teeth were like lions' teeth. 9Their chests were covered with what looked like iron breastplates, and the sound made by their wings was like the noise of many horse-drawn chariots rushing into battle. 10They have tails and stings like those of a scorpion, and it is with their tails that they have the power to hurt people for five months. 11They have a king ruling over them, who is the angel in charge of the abyss. His name in Hebrew is Abaddon; in Greek the name is Apollyon (meaning "The Destroyer").

12The first horror is over; after this there are still two more horrors to come.

13Then the sixth angel blew his trumpet. I heard a voice coming from the four corners of the gold altar standing before God. 14The voice said to the sixth angel, "Release the four angels who are bound at the great Euphrates River!" 15The four angels were released; for this very hour of this very day of this very month and year they had been kept ready to kill a third of all the human race. 16I was told the number of the mounted troops: it was two hundred million. 17And in my vision I saw the horses and their riders: they had breastplates red as fire, blue as sapphire, and yellow as sulfur. The horses' heads were like lions' heads, and from their mouths came out fire, smoke, and sulfur. 18A third of the human race was killed by those three plagues: the fire, the smoke, and the sulfur coming out of the horses' mouths. 19For the power of the horses is in their mouths and also in their tails. Their tails are like snakes with heads, and they use them to hurt people.

20The rest of the human race, all those who had not been killed by these plagues, did not turn away from what they themselves had made. They did not stop worshiping demons, nor the idols of gold, silver, bronze, stone, and wood, which cannot see, hear, or walk. 21Nor did they repent of their murders, their magic, their sexual immorality, or their stealing.

力,像地上的蠍子所有的能力一樣。4牠們奉命不可傷害地上的草、樹木,或其他的植物,只可傷害那些額上沒有蓋着上帝的印的人。5蝗蟲無權殺死這些人,只可使他們受痛苦五個月。這種痛苦就像人被蠍子刺傷一樣。6在這五個月中,他們求死不得,想死卻死不了。

7蝗蟲的樣子像要上陣的戰馬。牠們頭上所戴的好像金冠;牠們的臉像人的臉。8牠們的頭髮像女人的頭髮,牙齒像獅子的牙齒。9牠們前胸所掛着的,好像鐵的護胸甲,從翅膀發出的聲音像許多車馬奔馳上陣的響聲。10牠們長着尾巴和刺,像蠍子的一樣,就是這尾巴有能力使人受五個月的痛苦。11有一個王管轄牠們;那王就是管那無底深淵的天使。他的名字希伯來話叫亞巴頓,希臘話叫亞玻倫①。

12頭一種災難過去了;等着吧,以後還有兩種災要來。

13第六個天使一吹號,我聽見有聲音從上帝面前那金祭壇的四角發出。14這聲音對吹號的第六個天使說:「把那關在幼發拉底大河的四個天使放出來!」15那四個天使就被釋放了。他們早就被安排好,要在此年、此月、此日、此時殺滅全人類的三分之一。16我聽見騎兵隊的數目有兩億。17在異象中,我看見了那些馬和騎兵。騎兵的護胸甲紅得像火,藍得像藍寶石,黃得像硫磺。馬的頭像獅子的頭,從牠們口中有火、煙、和硫磺噴出來。18人類的三分之一被馬口中所噴出的火、煙、和硫磺三樣災害所殺滅。19馬的能力就在牠們的口中和尾巴上。牠們的尾巴像蛇,上面有頭;牠們就是用這頭來傷害人。

20其餘沒有在這些災害中被殺的人仍然不悔改,不拋棄他們親手所造的偶像。他們照常拜魔鬼,和金、銀、銅、石、木所造的那些不能看、不能聽、不能走的東西。21他們犯了凶殺、邪術、淫亂、偷竊等罪行,也沒有悔改。

---

①「亞玻倫」的意思是「毀滅者」。

The Angel and the Little Scroll

10 Then I saw another mighty angel coming down out of heaven. He was wrapped in a cloud and had a rainbow around his head; his face was like the sun, and his legs were like columns of fire. ²He had a small scroll open in his hand. He put his right foot on the sea and his left foot on the land, ³and called out in a loud voice that sounded like the roar of lions. After he had called out, the seven thunders answered with a roar. ⁴As soon as they spoke, I was about to write. But I heard a voice speak from heaven, "Keep secret what the seven thunders have said; do not write it down!"

⁵Then the angel that I saw standing on the sea and on the land raised his right hand to heaven ⁶and took a vow in the name of God, who lives forever and ever, who created heaven, earth, and the sea, and everything in them. The angel said, "There will be no more delay! ⁷But when the seventh angel blows his trumpet, then God will accomplish his secret plan, as he announced to his servants, the prophets."

⁸Then the voice that I had heard speaking from heaven spoke to me again, saying, "Go and take the open scroll which is in the hand of the angel standing on the sea and on the land."

⁹I went to the angel and asked him to give me the little scroll. He said to me, "Take it and eat it; it will turn sour in your stomach, but in your mouth it will be sweet as honey."

¹⁰I took the little scroll from his hand and ate it, and it tasted sweet as honey in my mouth. But after I swallowed it, it turned sour in my stomach. ¹¹Then I was told, "Once again you must proclaim God's message about many nations, races, languages, and kings."

The Two Witnesses

11 I was then given a stick that looked like a measuring-rod, and was told, "Go and measure the temple of God and the altar, and count those who are worshiping in the temple. ²But do not measure the outer courts, because they have been given to the heathen, who will trample on the Holy City for forty-two months. ³I will send my two witnesses dressed in sackcloth, and they will proclaim God's message during those 1,260 days."

⁴The two witnesses are the two olive trees and the two lamps that stand before the Lord of the earth. ⁵If anyone tries to harm them, fire comes out of their mouths and destroys their enemies; and in this way whoever tries to harm them will be killed. ⁶They have authority to shut up the sky so that there will be no rain

天使和小書卷

10 我又看見一個大力的天使從天下降。他披着雲彩，頭的上面有一條彩虹；他的臉像太陽，腿像火柱。²他手上拿着展開着的小書卷。他的右腳踏在海上，左腳踏在地上。³他高聲呼喊，好像獅子吼叫；他一呼喊就有七個雷發出回響。⁴我正要把七個雷所說的話寫下來，有聲音從天上來，說：「七個雷所說的話，你要嚴守祕密，不可記錄！」

⁵ 這事以後，我所見過站在海上和地上的那天使向天舉起右手，⁶指着那創造天、地、海，和其中萬物的永生上帝發誓說：「不會再遲延了！⁷第七個天使吹號的時候，上帝就要實現他向自己的僕人─先知們宣告過的奧祕。」

⁸ 後來，我聽見先前從天上來的聲音又對我說：「你去，把站在海上和地上那天使手裏展開着的書卷拿來。」

⁹ 我走過去，請那天使把小書卷給我。他對我說：「拿去，吞下！你的肚子會感覺到苦，嘴裏卻像蜜一樣的甜。」¹⁰我從他手上把小書卷拿過來，吃了，嘴裏果然甘甜像蜜一樣，可是等我把它吞下去，肚子就真的感覺到苦。

¹¹ 天使又對我說：「你必須再次宣佈上帝對各民族、各國家、說各種語言的人和君王們所發的預言。」

兩個見證人

11 我接受了一根像杖一樣的尺，有聲音對我說：「起來，量一量上帝的聖殿和祭壇，並數一數在殿裏敬拜的人。²可是，不要量聖殿的外院，因為這外院已經給了外邦人；他們要踐踏聖城四十二個月。³我要差遣兩個穿着麻衣的見證人；他們要傳講上帝的信息一千兩百六十天。」

⁴ 那兩個見證人就是站在世界之主面前的兩棵橄欖樹和兩個燈臺。⁵如果有人想傷害他們，他們會從口中吐出火燄，燒死敵人。所以，誰想傷害他們，誰就被殺。⁶他們有權封閉天空，在他們宣佈上帝信息的日子，

during the time they proclaim God's message. They have authority also over the springs of water, to turn them into blood; they have authority also to strike the earth with every kind of plague as often as they wish.

7When they finish proclaiming their message, the beast that comes up out of the abyss will fight against them. He will defeat them and kill them, 8and their bodies will lie in the street of the great city, where their Lord was crucified. The symbolic name of that city is Sodom, or Egypt. 9People from all nations, tribes, languages, and races will look at their bodies for three and a half days and will not allow them to be buried. 10The people of the earth will be happy because of the death of these two. They will celebrate and send presents to each other, because those two prophets brought much suffering upon the whole human race. 11After three and a half days a life-giving breath came from God and entered them, and they stood up; and all who saw them were terrified. 12Then the two prophets heard a loud voice say to them from heaven, "Come up here!" As their enemies watched, they went up into heaven in a cloud. 13At that very moment there was a violent earthquake; a tenth of the city was destroyed, and seven thousand people were killed. The rest of the people were terrified and praised the greatness of the God of heaven.

14The second horror is over, but the third horror will come soon!

The Seventh Trumpet

15Then the seventh angel blew his trumpet, and there were loud voices in heaven, saying, "The power to rule over the world belongs now to our Lord and his Messiah, and he will rule forever and ever!" 16Then the twenty-four elders who sit on their thrones in front of God threw themselves face downward and worshiped God, 17saying:

"Lord God Almighty, the one who is and who was!
We thank you that you have taken your great power
and have begun to rule!
18The heathen were filled with rage,
because the time for your anger has come,
the time for the dead to be judged.
The time has come to reward your servants,
the prophets,
and all your people, all who have reverence for you,
great and small alike.
The time has come to destroy those who destroy the earth!"

19God's temple in heaven was opened, and

叫天不下雨。他們也有權掌管各水源，使水變成血，也有權隨時隨意用各種災難打擊大地。

7 他們宣佈了信息之後，那從無底深淵出來的獸要對他們作戰，擊敗他們，把他們殺了。8 他們的屍首將倒在大城的街上，就是他們的主被釘十字架的地方。這城的象徵名字叫所多瑪或埃及。9 從各民族、各部落、各語言，和各國家，有人要來看他們的屍首三天半，不准人安葬他們。10地上的人要因他們的死而歡樂。大家慶祝，交換禮物，因為這兩個先知曾經使地上的人受大苦難。11過了三天半，有生命的氣息從上帝那裏來，進入他們裏面，他們就站立起來；看見的人大大驚惶。12兩個先知聽見從天上來的大聲音對他們說：「上這裏來！」他們就在敵人的注視下駕雲升天。13正在那時，地大震動，那城倒塌了十分之一，因地震而死的達七千人。剩下的人非常害怕，都頌讚天上上帝的偉大。

14第二種災難過去了；第三種災難就到了！

第七枝號筒

15第七個天使一吹號，天上就有大聲音說：「統治宇宙的大權已經屬於我們的主和他所立的基督了；他要掌權，世世無窮！」16那在上帝面前、坐在自己位上的二十四個長老都俯伏在地上，敬拜上帝，17說：

昔在、今在的主──全能的上帝啊，
我們感謝你；
因為你運用了大權能，
行使統治。
18列國狂怒，
但是，你的義怒臨到了。
時機已經成熟，
死人要受審判；
你的僕人──先知們，
你的子民和所有敬畏你的人，
不論尊卑，都要得獎賞。
那些毀滅大地的人要被毀滅！

19這時候，上帝在天上的聖殿開了；他的

the Covenant Box was seen there. Then there were flashes of lightning, rumblings and peals of thunder, an earthquake, and heavy hail.

The Woman and the Dragon

12 Then a great and mysterious sight appeared in the sky. There was a woman, whose dress was the sun and who had the moon under her feet and a crown of twelve stars on her head. ²She was soon to give birth, and the pains and suffering of childbirth made her cry out.

³Another mysterious sight appeared in the sky. There was a huge red dragon with seven heads and ten horns and a crown on each of his heads. ⁴With his tail he dragged a third of the stars out of the sky and threw them down to the earth. He stood in front of the woman, in order to eat her child as soon as it was born. ⁵Then she gave birth to a son, who will rule over all nations with an iron rod. But the child was snatched away and taken to God and his throne. ⁶The woman fled to the desert, to a place God had prepared for her, where she will be taken care of for 1,260 days.

⁷Then war broke out in heaven. Michael and his angels fought against the dragon, who fought back with his angels; ⁸but the dragon was defeated, and he and his angels were not allowed to stay in heaven any longer. ⁹The huge dragon was thrown out–that ancient serpent, named the Devil, or Satan, that deceived the whole world. He was thrown down to earth, and all his angels with him.

¹⁰Then I heard a loud voice in heaven saying, "Now God's salvation has come! Now God has shown his power as King! Now his Messiah has shown his authority! For the one who stood before our God and accused believers day and night has been thrown out of heaven. ¹¹They won the victory over him by the blood of the Lamb and by the truth which they proclaimed; and they were willing to give up their lives and die. ¹²And so be glad, you heavens, and all you that live there! But how terrible for the earth and the sea! For the Devil has come down to you, and he is filled with rage, because he knows that he has only a little time left."

¹³When the dragon realized that he had been thrown down to the earth, he began to pursue the woman who had given birth to the boy. ¹⁴She was given the two wings of a large eagle in order to fly to her place in the desert, where she will be taken care of for three and a half years, safe from the dragon's attack. ¹⁵And then from his mouth the dragon poured out a flood of water after the woman, so that it would carry her away. ¹⁶But the earth helped the woman; it opened its mouth and swallowed the water that

約櫃在殿裏出現。接着有閃電、雷轟、響聲、地震，和大冰雹。

女人和戾龍

12 這時候，天上出現了一個又大又神祕的景象。有一個女人身披太陽，腳踏月亮，頭上戴着一頂有十二顆星的冠冕。²她快要生產，生產的陣痛使她呼叫起來。

³天上又出現了另一個神祕的景象。有一條紅色的大戾龍，長着七個頭，十個角，每一個頭上都戴着王冠。⁴牠用尾巴捲起天上三分之一的星辰，摔在地上。牠站在那快要生產的女人面前，等嬰兒一生下，就要把他吞下去。⁵那女人生了一個男孩子；這孩子將來要用鐵杖統治萬國。但是，這孩子被提到上帝的寶座上去。⁶那女人逃往荒野，到了上帝為她預備的地方；在那裏，她要受照顧一千兩百六十天。

⁷後來，天上發生了戰爭。米迦勒和他的天使對戾龍作戰，戾龍和牠的使者也起來應戰。⁸但是，戾龍被擊敗了；牠和牠的使者不得再留在天上。⁹於是，那條大戾龍被摔下來；牠就是那條古蛇，名叫魔鬼或撒但，是迷惑全人類的。牠被摔在地上；牠的使者也都跟着被摔下來。

¹⁰我又聽見天上有大聲音說：「現在就是上帝拯救的時刻！上帝已彰顯了他的權能和統治。他所立的基督也顯示了他的權威。那日夜在我們的上帝面前控告信徒的，已經從天上被摔下來了。¹¹信徒們已經藉着羔羊的血和他們所宣佈的真理勝過了戾龍；他們甚至願意犧牲自己的生命。¹²所以，諸天和住在其中的，你們都應該歡欣！但是，地和海慘啦！魔鬼已經滿懷忿恨地下到你們那裏去了，因為他知道自己來日無多。」

¹³那條戾龍一知道自己被摔在地上，就去追擊那生了男孩子的女人。¹⁴那女人得到了大鷹的兩個翅膀，能夠飛到荒野，到她自己的地方去。在那裏，她要受照顧三年半，使她不致受蛇的攻擊。¹⁵那條蛇在女人背後，從口中噴出一股洪水，要把她沖走。¹⁶可是，地幫助了那女人，張開口把那條戾龍噴

had come from the dragon's mouth. ¹⁷The dragon was furious with the woman and went off to fight against the rest of her descendants, all those who obey God's commandments and are faithful to the truth revealed by Jesus. ¹⁸And the dragon stood*e* on the seashore.

The Two Beasts

13 Then I saw a beast coming up out of the sea. It had ten horns and seven heads; on each of its horns there was a crown, and on each of its heads there was a name that was insulting to God. ²The beast looked like a leopard, with feet like a bear's feet and a mouth like a lion's mouth. The dragon gave the beast his own power, his throne, and his vast authority. ³One of the heads of the beast seemed to have been fatally wounded, but the wound had healed. The whole earth was amazed and followed the beast. ⁴Everyone worshiped the dragon because he had given his authority to the beast. They worshiped the beast also, saying, "Who is like the beast? Who can fight against it?"

⁵The beast was allowed to make proud claims which were insulting to God, and it was permitted to have authority for forty-two months. ⁶It began to curse God, his name, the place where he lives, and all those who live in heaven. ⁷It was allowed to fight against God's people and to defeat them, and it was given authority over every tribe, nation, language, and race. ⁸All people living on earth will worship it, except those whose names were written before the creation of the world in the book of the living which belongs to the Lamb that was killed.

⁹"Listen, then, if you have ears! ¹⁰Whoever is meant to be captured will surely be captured; whoever is meant to be killed by the sword will surely be killed by the sword. This calls for endurance and faith on the part of God's people."

¹¹Then I saw another beast, which came up out of the earth. It had two horns like a lamb's horns, and it spoke like a dragon. ¹²It used the vast authority of the first beast in its presence. It forced the earth and all who live on it to worship the first beast, whose wound had healed. ¹³This second beast performed great miracles; it made fire come down out of heaven to earth in the sight of everyone. ¹⁴And it deceived all the people living on earth by means of the miracles which it was allowed to perform in the presence of the first beast. The beast told them to build an image in honor of the beast that had been wounded by the sword and yet lived. ¹⁵The second beast was allowed to breathe life into the image of the first beast, so

e And the dragon stood; some manuscripts have And I stood, connecting this verse with what follows.

出來的水吞下去。¹⁷戾龍向女人發怒,去跟她其餘的子孫爭戰,就是跟所有服從上帝命令、信守耶穌所啓示眞理的人爭戰。¹⁸那條戾龍站在海灘上②。

兩隻獸

13 接着,我看見一隻獸從海裏上來。牠長着十個角和七個頭,每一個角上戴着王冠,每一個頭上寫着侮辱上帝的名號。²我所看見的獸像一隻豹;牠的腳像熊的腳,口像獅子的口。戾龍把自己的能力、王座,和大權都交給了那隻獸。³獸的一個頭似乎受過致命重傷,可是那傷已經好了。全世界都很驚奇,跟在那獸的背後。⁴大家都拜那條戾龍,因爲戾龍把牠的權交給了獸。他們也拜那獸,說:「誰能跟這獸相比?誰敵得過牠呢?」

⁵那隻獸得到一張誇大褻瀆的嘴巴,又被授權可隨意行事四十二個月。⁶那獸開口侮辱上帝,褻瀆他的名、他的居所,和所有住在天上的。⁷牠被准許攻擊上帝的子民,擊敗他們;也被授權可轄制各部落、各民族、各國家,和說各種語言的人。⁸所有地上的居民,名字在創世之前沒有登記在那被殺羔羊的生命册上的,都要拜牠。

⁹「有耳朶的,都聽吧!¹⁰那該被俘虜的,一定會被俘虜;那該在刀下喪生的,一定會在刀下喪生。因此,上帝的子民都需要有耐心和信心。」

¹¹我又看見另一隻獸從地裏出來。牠有兩個角,像羊的角,可是說話像戾龍。¹²牠在頭一隻獸面前,行使頭一隻獸的一切大權。牠强迫大地和所有住在地上的,都去拜那曾受過致命重傷又好了的頭一隻獸。¹³這第二隻獸又行大奇蹟;牠在人面前使火從天降在地上。¹⁴牠得了權,在頭一隻獸面前行奇蹟,因而迷惑了所有住在地上的人。牠吩咐世上的人爲那受了刀傷而還活着的獸造一座像。¹⁵第二隻獸又得了權,可以把氣息吹進那頭一隻獸的像裏去,使那像能夠說話,並

②「那條戾龍站在海灘上」另有些古卷作「我站在海灘上」,又把這一節當作下一段的開始。

that the image could talk and put to death all those who would not worship it. 16The beast forced all the people, small and great, rich and poor, slave and free, to have a mark placed on their right hands or on their foreheads. 17No one could buy or sell without this mark, that is, the beast's name or the number that stands for the name.

18This calls for wisdom. Whoever is intelligent can figure out the meaning of the number of the beast, because the number stands for the name of someone. Its number is 666.

The Lamb and His People

14 Then I looked, and there was the Lamb standing on Mount Zion; with him were 144,000 people who have his name and his Father's name written on their foreheads. 2And I heard a voice from heaven that sounded like a roaring waterfall, like a loud peal of thunder. It sounded like the music made by musicians playing their harps. 3The 144,000 people stood before the throne, the four living creatures, and the elders; they were singing a new song, which only they could learn. Of the whole human race they are the only ones who have been redeemed. 4They are the men who have kept themselves pure by not having sexual relations with women; they are virgins. They follow the Lamb wherever he goes. They have been redeemed from the rest of the human race and are the first ones to be offered to God and to the Lamb. 5They have never been known to tell lies; they are faultless.

The Three Angels

6Then I saw another angel flying high in the air, with an eternal message of Good News to announce to the peoples of the earth, to every race, tribe, language, and nation. 7He said in a loud voice, "Honor God and praise his greatness! For the time has come for him to judge all people. Worship him who made heaven, earth, sea, and the springs of water!"

8A second angel followed the first one, saying, "She has fallen! Great Babylon has fallen! She made all peoples drink her wine–the strong wine of her immoral lust!"

9A third angel followed the first two, saying in a loud voice, "Those who worship the beast and its image and receive the mark on their forehead or on their hand 10will themselves drink God's wine, the wine of his fury, which he has poured at full strength into the cup of his anger! All who do this will be tormented in fire and sulfur before the holy angels and the Lamb. 11The smoke of the fire that torments them goes up forever and ever. There is no re-

且殺害所有不拜獸像的人。16這獸又強迫所有的人,無論大小、貧窮富貴、奴隸或自由人,在他們的右手和額上打了印記。17這印記就是那獸的名字或代表名字的數字;沒有這印記的,就不能做買賣。

18 這裏需要有智慧。凡是聰明人都能夠算出獸的數字,因為這數字代表一個人。這數字是六百六十六。

救贖之歌

14 我再看,看見羔羊站在錫安山上,跟他一起的有十四萬四千人;他們的額上都寫着他和他父親的名字。2我聽見有聲音從天上來,好像大瀑布的吼聲,也像雷轟。我所聽見的這聲音又像豎琴師彈奏的琴聲。3他們站在寶座和四個活物以及長老們前面,唱了一首新歌;這首歌只有從地上被救贖的十四萬四千人會唱。4這些人都是沒有親近過女人的童男。羔羊走到哪裏,他們就跟到那裏。他們是從人類中被贖出來,首先用來獻給上帝和羔羊的。5他們從不撒謊,是沒有玷污的。

三個天使

6 我又看見另一個天使在空中飛着;他有永恆的福音要向世上各國家、各部落、各民族、和說各種語言的人宣佈。7他大聲說:「要敬畏上帝,頌讚他的偉大!因為他審判人類的時候到了。要敬拜那位創造天、地、海,和一切泉源的主!」

8 第二個天使跟着說:「倒塌了!大巴比倫倒塌了!她拿那淫蕩的烈酒給萬民喝。」

9 第三個天使跟着前兩個天使大聲說:「誰拜那獸和獸像,在額上或手上受了印記的,10也得喝上帝的烈酒;這酒是未經沖淡、倒在他義憤的杯中的。他們要在聖天使和羔羊面前受烈火和硫磺的酷刑。11那折磨他們的煙永遠不停地往上冒。那些拜那獸和

lief day or night for those who worship the beast and its image, for anyone who has the mark of its name."

12This calls for endurance on the part of God's people, those who obey God's commandments and are faithful to Jesus.

13Then I heard a voice from heaven saying, "Write this: Happy are those who from now on die in the service of the Lord!"

"Yes indeed!" answers the Spirit. "They will enjoy rest from their hard work, because the results of their service go with them."

The Harvest of the Earth

14Then I looked, and there was a white cloud, and sitting on the cloud was what looked like a human being, with a crown of gold on his head and a sharp sickle in his hand. 15Then another angel came out from the temple and cried out in a loud voice to the one who was sitting on the cloud, "Use your sickle and reap the harvest, because the time has come; the earth is ripe for the harvest!" 16Then the one who sat on the cloud swung his sickle on the earth, and the earth's harvest was reaped.

17Then I saw another angel come out of the temple in heaven, and he also had a sharp sickle.

18Then another angel, who is in charge of the fire, came from the altar. He shouted in a loud voice to the angel who had the sharp sickle, "Use your sickle, and cut the grapes from the vineyard of the earth, because the grapes are ripe!" 19So the angel swung his sickle on the earth, cut the grapes from the vine, and threw them into the wine press of God's furious anger. 20The grapes were squeezed out in the wine press outside the city, and blood came out of the wine press in a flood two hundred miles long and about five feet deep.

The Angels with the Last Plagues

15 Then I saw in the sky another mysterious sight, great and amazing. There were seven angels with seven plagues, which are the last ones, because they are the final expression of God's anger.

2Then I saw what looked like a sea of glass mixed with fire. I also saw those who had won the victory over the beast and its image and over the one whose name is represented by a number. They were standing by the sea of glass, holding harps that God had given them 3and singing the song of Moses, the servant of God, and the song of the Lamb:

"Lord God Almighty,
 how great and wonderful are your deeds!

獸像,以及額上有牠名號的印記的,日夜不得安寧。」

12 因此,那些服從上帝命令、忠於耶穌的上帝子民需要有耐心。

13 我又聽見從天上有聲音說:「你要把這話寫下來:從今以後,為主而死的人有福了!」

聖靈回答:「是的!他們將結束勞苦而享安息,因為工作的成果隨着他們。」

地上的農作物

14 我再看,看見一片白雲,雲上坐着一位彷彿人子的,頭上戴着金冠,手裏拿着鋒利的鐮刀。15 另外有一個天使從聖殿出來,向坐在雲上的那位高聲呼喊:「時候已經到了,地上的農作物成熟了!用你的鐮刀收割吧!」16 於是坐在雲上的那位向地面揮動鐮刀,地上的農作物就被收割了。

17 我又看見另一個天使從天上的聖殿出來;他也有一把鋒利的鐮刀。

18 接着,又有一個管理火的天使從祭壇那裏出來,向那拿着鋒利鐮刀的天使高聲呼喊:「用你的鐮刀割取地上的葡萄,因為葡萄已經熟了!」19 於是那天使向地面揮動鐮刀,割下地上的葡萄,把它扔在上帝烈怒的大榨酒池裏。20 葡萄在城外的榨酒池裏被踐踏,就有血從榨酒池湧流出來,淹沒了三百公里,深約兩公尺。

天使和末後的災難

15 我又看見天上有另一個神祕的景象,又大又奇。有七個天使掌管着最後的七種災難,因為上帝要在這些災難中貫徹他的忿怒。

2 我又看見一片好像玻璃的海,攙雜着火。我也看見一些人;他們已經勝過了那獸、獸像,和以數字代表名字的那人。他們都站在玻璃海邊,拿着上帝給他們的豎琴,3 唱上帝僕人摩西的歌和羔羊的歌:

主—全能的上帝啊,
 你的作為多麼宏偉奇妙!

King of the nations,*f*
how right and true are your ways!
⁴Who will not stand in awe of you, Lord?
Who will refuse to declare your greatness?
You alone are holy.
All the nations will come
and worship you,
because your just actions are seen by all."

⁵After this I saw the temple in heaven open, with the Sacred Tent in it. ⁶The seven angels who had the seven plagues came out of the temple, dressed in clean shining linen and with gold bands tied around their chests. ⁷Then one of the four living creatures gave the seven angels seven gold bowls full of the anger of God, who lives forever and ever. ⁸The temple was filled with smoke from the glory and power of God, and no one could go into the temple until the seven plagues brought by the seven angels had come to an end.

The Bowls of God's Anger

16 Then I heard a loud voice speaking from the temple to the seven angels: "Go and pour out the seven bowls of God's anger on the earth!"

²The first angel went and poured out his bowl on the earth. Terrible and painful sores appeared on those who had the mark of the beast and on those who had worshiped its image.

³Then the second angel poured out his bowl on the sea. The water became like the blood of a dead person, and every living creature in the sea died.

⁴Then the third angel poured out his bowl on the rivers and the springs of water, and they turned into blood. ⁵I heard the angel in charge of the waters say, "The judgments you have made are just, O Holy One, you who are and who were! ⁶They poured out the blood of God's people and of the prophets, and so you have given them blood to drink. They are getting what they deserve!" ⁷Then I heard a voice from the altar saying, "Lord God Almighty! True and just indeed are your judgments!"

⁸Then the fourth angel poured out his bowl on the sun, and it was allowed to burn people with its fiery heat. ⁹They were burned by the fierce heat, and they cursed the name of God, who has authority over these plagues. But they would not turn from their sins and praise his greatness.

¹⁰Then the fifth angel poured out his bowl on the throne of the beast. Darkness fell over the beast's kingdom, and people bit their tongues

f nations; *some manuscripts have* ages.

萬國③的王啊,
你的道路多麼公正真實!
⁴ 主啊,誰敢不敬畏你?
誰不頌讚你的名?
只有你是神聖的。
萬國都要來,在你面前敬拜,
因為你公義的作為已經彰顯出來。

⁵ 這以後,我看見天上的聖殿開了,裏面有上帝臨在的聖幕。⁶那掌管七種災難的七個天使從聖殿裏出來,穿着光潔的麻紗衣服,胸前繫着金帶。⁷四活物中的一個把盛滿着永生上帝忿怒的七個金碗交給那七個天使。⁸聖殿中充滿着從上帝的榮耀和權能而來的煙,在那七個天使降完七種災難以前,沒有人能進入聖殿。

上帝忿怒之碗

16 我聽見從聖殿裏有大聲音向七個天使說:「你們去,把那盛滿七碗的上帝的忿怒倒在地上!」

² 第一個天使去了,把他那一碗倒在地上;於是有既臭且毒的瘡長在那些有獸的印記和拜過獸像的人身上。

³ 第二個天使把他那一碗倒在海上;海水就變成像死人的血一樣,海裏的生物全都死了。

⁴ 第三個天使把他那一碗倒在河流和水源裏,水就變成了血。⁵我聽見那管理水的天使說:「昔在、今在的至聖者啊,你是公義的審判者。⁶他們曾流了上帝子民和先知們的血,現在你給他們血喝;這是他們所應得的!」⁷我又聽見從祭壇發出聲音說:「主——全能的上帝啊,你的審判的確是真實公義的!」

⁸ 第四個天使把他那一碗倒在太陽上面,使太陽可以用它的炎熱燒灼人。⁹人被炎熱燒灼,就褻瀆那位有權支配這些災難的上帝。他們仍然不悔改,不願意頌讚上帝的偉大。

¹⁰ 第五個天使把他那一碗倒在獸的王座上。於是黑暗籠罩了獸的國度,人因痛苦

③「萬國」另有些古卷作「萬世」。

because of their pain, [11]and they cursed the God of heaven for their pains and sores. But they did not turn from their evil ways.

[12]Then the sixth angel poured out his bowl on the great Euphrates River. The river dried up, to provide a way for the kings who come from the east. [13]Then I saw three unclean spirits that looked like frogs. They were coming out of the mouth of the dragon, the mouth of the beast, and the mouth of the false prophet. [14]They are the spirits of demons that perform miracles. These three spirits go out to all the kings of the world, to bring them together for the battle on the great Day of Almighty God.

[15]"Listen! I am coming like a thief! Happy is he who stays awake and guards his clothes, so that he will not walk around naked and be ashamed in public!"

[16]Then the spirits brought the kings together in the place that in Hebrew is called Armageddon.

[17]Then the seventh angel poured out his bowl in the air. A loud voice came from the throne in the temple, saying, "It is done!" [18]There were flashes of lightning, rumblings and peals of thunder, and a terrible earthquake. There has never been such an earthquake since the creation of human beings; this was the worst earthquake of all! [19]The great city was split into three parts, and the cities of all countries were destroyed. God remembered great Babylon and made her drink the wine from his cup–the wine of his furious anger. [20]All the islands disappeared, all the mountains vanished. [21]Huge hailstones, each weighing as much as a hundred pounds, fell from the sky on people, who cursed God on account of the plague of hail, because it was such a terrible plague.

The Famous Prostitute

17 Then one of the seven angels who had the seven bowls came to me and said, "Come, and I will show you how the famous prostitute is to be punished, that great city that is built near many rivers. [2]The kings of the earth practiced sexual immorality with her, and the people of the world became drunk from drinking the wine of her immorality."

[3]The Spirit took control of me, and the angel carried me to a desert. There I saw a woman sitting on a red beast that had names insulting to God written all over it; the beast had seven heads and ten horns. [4]The woman was dressed in purple and scarlet, and covered with gold ornaments, precious stones, and pearls. In her hand she held a gold cup full of obscene and filthy things, the result of her immorality. [5]On her forehead was written a name that has a se-

咬自己的舌頭。[11]他們因所受的痛苦和身上所長的瘡而褻瀆天上的上帝,仍然不離棄他們邪惡的行為。

[12]第六個天使把他那一碗倒在幼發拉底大河上,河水就乾了,為要給從東方來的諸王預備一條路。[13]接著,我看見三個邪靈,好像青蛙,分別從戾龍的口、獸的口,和假先知的口出來。[14]他們是邪魔的靈,會行奇蹟。這些邪靈出去找全世界的王,把他們集合在一起,準備在全能上帝那偉大的日子裏作戰。

[15]「留心吧,我要像小偷一樣突然來到!那警醒、隨時都穿着衣服的人多麼有福啊!他不至於裸體行走,在人前蒙羞。」

[16]於是,那些邪靈把諸王集合在一個地方;那地方希伯來話叫哈米吉多頓。

[17]第七個天使把他那一碗倒在空中。有大聲音從聖殿的寶座上發出,說:「成了!」[18]於是有閃電、響聲、雷轟,和可怕的地震。自從地上有人類以來,沒有過這樣劇烈的地震。[19]那大城巴比倫裂為三段;各國的城市也都倒塌了。上帝記得大巴比倫的罪惡,叫它喝上帝杯中那義憤的烈酒。[20]所有的島嶼都不見了;所有的山嶺也消失了。[21]從天上有大冰雹掉落在人身上,每一塊重約四十公斤。為了這慘重的雹災,人就褻瀆上帝。

大淫婦

17 那七個拿七個碗的天使當中,有一個上前對我說:「你來,我要讓你看那大淫婦所要受的懲罰;她就是那建造在河流邊的大城。[2]地上諸王都跟那大淫婦行過淫;世上的人也喝醉了她淫亂的酒。」

[3]我受聖靈的支配;天使把我帶到荒野。我看見一個女人騎着一隻朱紅色的獸;那獸遍體寫滿了褻瀆的名號,長着七個頭和十個角。[4]那女人穿着朱紅和紫色的衣服,戴滿了金飾、寶石,和珍珠。她手拿金杯,杯中盛滿了她淫亂可憎的穢物。[5]她額上寫着一個隱祕的名號:「大巴比倫——世上淫婦和一

cret meaning: "Great Babylon, the mother of all prostitutes and perverts in the world." ⁶And I saw that the woman was drunk with the blood of God's people and the blood of those who were killed because they had been loyal to Jesus.

When I saw her, I was completely amazed. ⁷"Why are you amazed?" the angel asked me. "I will tell you the secret meaning of the woman and of the beast that carries her, the beast with seven heads and ten horns. ⁸That beast was once alive, but lives no longer; it is about to come up from the abyss and will go off to be destroyed. The people living on earth whose names have not been written before the creation of the world in the book of the living, will all be amazed as they look at the beast. It was once alive; now it no longer lives, but it will reappear.

⁹"This calls for wisdom and understanding. The seven heads are seven hills, on which the woman sits. They are also seven kings: ¹⁰five of them have fallen, one still rules, and the other one has not yet come; when he comes, he must rule only a little while. ¹¹And the beast that was once alive, but lives no longer, is itself an eighth king who is one of the seven and is going off to be destroyed.

¹²"The ten horns you saw are ten kings who have not yet begun to rule, but who will be given authority to rule as kings for one hour with the beast. ¹³These ten all have the same purpose, and they give their power and authority to the beast. ¹⁴They will fight against the Lamb, but the Lamb, together with his called, chosen, and faithful followers, will defeat them, because he is Lord of lords and King of kings."

¹⁵The angel also said to me, "The waters you saw, on which the prostitute sits, are nations, peoples, races, and languages. ¹⁶The ten horns you saw and the beast will hate the prostitute; they will take away everything she has and leave her naked; they will eat her flesh and destroy her with fire. ¹⁷For God has placed in their hearts the will to carry out his purpose by acting together and giving to the beast their power to rule until God's words come true.

¹⁸"The woman you saw is the great city that rules over the kings of the earth."

The Fall of Babylon

18 After this I saw another angel coming down out of heaven. He had great authority, and his splendor brightened the whole earth. ²He cried out in a loud voice: "She has fallen! Great Babylon has fallen! She is now haunted by demons and unclean spirits; all

切可憎之物的母！」⁶我又看見那女人喝醉了上帝子民的血，和那些爲耶穌作證而殉道的人的血。

我看到她的時候，大大驚奇。⁷天使問我：「你爲甚麼驚奇？我要把那女人和她所騎的那隻長着七頭十角的獸的隱祕告訴你。⁸你看見的那獸曾經活過、現在不再活着，不久要從無底深淵上來，走向滅亡。地上的人，凡是名字在創世以來沒有被登記在生命冊上的，一看見那曾經活過、現在不再活着、將來又要出現的獸，都會大感驚奇。

⁹「這裏需要有聰明智慧。七個頭是指那女人所坐的七座山，也是指七個王。¹⁰其中五個已經倒了，一個還在；另一個還沒有來，來的時候只能停留一會兒。¹¹那曾經活過、現在不再活着的獸，就是第八個王；他也是七王中的一個，正在走向滅亡。

¹²「你看見的那十個角是指十個還沒有開始統治的王；但是他們要承受王權，跟那獸一同統治一個鐘頭。¹³這十個王有相同的目標：他們要把自己的能力權柄交給那獸。¹⁴他們要跟羔羊作戰；但是羔羊要擊敗他們，因爲他是萬主之主，萬王之王。他所選召、忠心隨從他的人也要得勝。

¹⁵天使又對我說：「你看見那淫婦坐着的水流就是指各民族、各種族、各國家，和說各種語言的人。¹⁶你所看見的十個角和那獸都要憎恨那淫婦，要奪走她所有的一切，使她赤身露體；牠們要吃她的肉，用火焚燒她。¹⁷因爲上帝把執行他旨意的意念放在那十個王心裏，使他們有相同的目標，把統治權交給那獸，直到上帝的話實現。

¹⁸「你所看見的那女人就是統治地上諸王的那個大城。」

巴比倫的覆滅

18 這以後，我看見另一個天使從天上下來。他掌握大權；他的光輝照耀大地。²他大聲呼喊：「倒塌了！大巴比倫倒塌了！她成爲邪魔的窩，邪靈的穴，污穢可憎

kinds of filthy and hateful birds live in her. [3]For all the nations have drunk her wine–the strong wine of her immoral lust. The kings of the earth practiced sexual immorality with her, and the merchants of the world grew rich from her unrestrained lust."

[4]Then I heard another voice from heaven, saying,

"Come out, my people! Come out from her!
    You must not take part in her sins;
    you must not share in her punishment!
[5]For her sins are piled up as high as heaven,
    and God remembers her wicked ways.
[6]Treat her exactly as she has treated you;
    pay her back double for all she has done.
Fill her cup with a drink twice as strong
    as the drink she prepared for you.
[7]Give her as much suffering and grief
    as the glory and luxury she gave herself.
For she keeps telling herself:
    'Here I sit, a queen!
    I am no widow,
    I will never know grief!'
[8]Because of this, in one day she will be struck with plagues–
    disease, grief, and famine.
And she will be burned with fire,
    because the Lord God, who judges her, is mighty."

[9]The kings of the earth who took part in her immorality and lust will cry and weep over the city when they see the smoke from the flames that consume her. [10]They stand a long way off, because they are afraid of sharing in her suffering. They say, "How terrible! How awful! This great and mighty city Babylon! In just one hour you have been punished!"

[11]The merchants of the earth also cry and mourn for her, because no one buys their goods any longer; [12]no one buys their gold, silver, precious stones, and pearls; their goods of linen, purple cloth, silk, and scarlet cloth; all kinds of rare woods and all kinds of objects made of ivory and of expensive wood, of bronze, iron, and marble; [13]and cinnamon, spice, incense, myrrh, and frankincense; wine and oil, flour and wheat, cattle and sheep, horses and carriages, slaves, and even human lives. [14]The merchants say to her, "All the good things you longed to own have disappeared, and all your wealth and glamor are gone, and you will never find them again!" [15]The merchants, who became rich from doing business in that city, will stand a long way off, because they are afraid of

的鳥類的巢。[3]因為列國都喝了這大淫婦淫亂的烈酒,地上諸王跟她行淫,世上的商人從她的淫蕩發了大財。」

[4]我又聽見另一個聲音從天上來,說:
出來吧,我的子民!
從那城出來吧!
不然,你們會分沾她的罪行,
分受她的災難!
[5]因為她罪惡滔天,
上帝記得她邪惡的行為。
[6]她怎樣待你們,就怎樣待她,
照她所做的加倍報應她。
她怎樣調酒給你們,
就用雙倍濃烈的酒倒滿她的杯!
[7]她怎樣奢侈,炫耀自己,
就怎樣折磨她,叫她受盡痛苦。
因為她不斷地對自己說:
我是坐在寶座上的王后,
我不是寡婦,我絕不會有悲愁!
[8]正因為這樣,
在同一天裏,災難要臨到她:
有饑荒、哀傷、死亡!
她要在火中被焚燒,
因為審判她的主上帝大有能力!

[9]跟她縱慾行淫的地上諸王一看見那焚燒着她的煙就為她痛哭哀號。[10]他們怕看到她受折磨,遠遠地站着,說:「慘啦!慘啦!這大城。雄壯的巴比倫城啊,還不到一個鐘頭,你已經遭受懲罰了!」

[11]地上的商人也為她悲哀痛哭,因為再也沒有人來買他們的貨物了。[12]沒有人買他們的金、銀、寶石、珍珠;也沒有人買他們的麻紗、絲綢、高貴的紫色和朱紅色衣料、各種香木、各樣象牙製品、貴重的木器、銅器、鐵器,和大理石製品;[13]也沒有人買肉桂、香料、香、香水、乳香、酒、油、麵粉、麥子、牛、羊、馬、馬車、奴隸、人口等。[14]這些商人對她說:「你所貪愛的各種美物都不見了;一切的榮華富貴消失了,再也找不回來了!」[15]在那城做這些生意、發了大財的商人,為了怕看到她受折磨,遠遠

sharing in her suffering. They will cry and mourn, [16]and say, "How terrible! How awful for the great city! She used to dress herself in linen, purple, and scarlet, and cover herself with gold ornaments, precious stones, and pearls! [17]And in one hour she has lost all this wealth!"

All the ships' captains and passengers, the sailors and all others who earn their living on the sea, stood a long way off, [18]and cried out as they saw the smoke from the flames that consumed her: "There never has been another city like this great city!" [19]They threw dust on their heads, they cried and mourned, saying, "How terrible! How awful for the great city! She is the city where all who have ships sailing the seas became rich on her wealth! And in one hour she has lost everything!"

[20]Be glad, heaven, because of her destruction! Be glad, God's people and the apostles and prophets! For God has condemned her for what she did to you!

[21]Then a mighty angel picked up a stone the size of a large millstone and threw it into the sea, saying, "This is how the great city Babylon will be violently thrown down and will never be seen again. [22]The music of harps and of human voices, of players of the flute and the trumpet, will never be heard in you again! No workman in any trade will ever be found in you again; and the sound of the millstone will be heard no more! [23]Never again will the light of a lamp be seen in you; no more will the voices of brides and grooms be heard in you. Your merchants were the most powerful in all the world, and with your false magic you deceived all the peoples of the world!"

[24]Babylon was punished because the blood of prophets and of God's people was found in the city; yes, the blood of all those who have been killed on earth.

19 After this I heard what sounded like the roar of a large crowd of people in heaven, saying, "Praise God! Salvation, glory, and power belong to our God! [2]True and just are his judgments! He has condemned the prostitute who was corrupting the earth with her immorality. God has punished her because she killed his servants." [3]Again they shouted, "Praise God! The smoke from the flames that consume the great city goes up forever and ever!" [4]The twenty-four elders and the four living creatures fell down and worshiped God, who was seated on the throne. They said, "Amen! Praise God!"

The Wedding Feast of the Lamb

[5]Then there came from the throne the sound of a voice, saying, "Praise our God, all his ser-

地站着。他們悲哀痛哭，[16]說：「慘啦！慘啦！這大城啊，她一向穿麻紗、高貴的大紫大紅的衣服，戴着金子、寶石、珍珠等飾物。[17]還不到一個鐘頭，這一切財富竟都喪失了！」

所有的船長、旅客、水手，和所有靠海謀生的人遠遠地站着。[18]他們看見了那焚燒着她的煙，就喊叫：「哪一座城可跟這大城相比！」[19]他們拿灰塵撒在自己頭上，哀哭着說：「慘啦！慘啦！這大城啊，凡有船航行海上的人都靠她發財。還不到一個鐘頭，她所有的一切竟都喪失了！」

[20]天哪，要歡喜！因爲她毀滅了！上帝的子民、使徒和先知們哪，要歡喜！因爲上帝已經替你們伸冤，懲罰她了。

[21]接着，有一個强壯的天使舉起一塊像大磨石那樣大的石頭，拋到海裏去，說：「大城巴比倫也要這樣被猛烈投下，永遠不再出現。[22]你再也聽不到琴師樂手的音樂和吹笛吹號的聲音。各種手藝的技工再也找不到了；推磨的聲音再也聽不到了。[23]燈光再也不發亮了；新郎新娘的輕言細語再也聽不到了。你的商人都是世上最有勢力的人；世上的人也都被你的邪術迷惑了。」

[24]巴比倫受懲罰了，因爲在這城裏發現了先知和上帝子民的血；是的，所有在地上被殺的人的血都在這城裏發現了。

19 這以後，我聽見有大聲音，好像天上有一大羣人在呼喊：「哈利路亞，讚美上主！救恩、榮耀、權能都是從我們的上帝來的！[2]他的審判是眞實公義的！因爲他審判了那以淫行敗壞世界的大淫婦，懲罰了她殺害上帝僕人的罪。」[3]他們又一次呼喊：「哈利路亞，讚美上主！焚燒那大城的煙不斷地往上冒，永不停止！」[4]於是，二十四個長老和四個活物俯伏敬拜那坐在寶座上的上帝，說：「阿們！哈利路亞！」

羔羊的婚宴

[5]接着，有聲音從寶座發出，說：「所有

vants and all people, both great and small, who have reverence for him!" 6Then I heard what sounded like a crowd, like the sound of a roaring waterfall, like loud peals of thunder. I heard them say, "Praise God! For the Lord, our Almighty God, is King! 7Let us rejoice and be glad; let us praise his greatness! For the time has come for the wedding of the Lamb, and his bride has prepared herself for it. 8She has been given clean shining linen to wear." (The linen is the good deeds of God's people.)

9Then the angel said to me, "Write this: Happy are those who have been invited to the wedding feast of the Lamb." And the angel added, "These are the true words of God."

10I fell down at his feet to worship him, but he said to me, "Don't do it! I am a servant together with you and with other believers, all those who hold to the truth that Jesus revealed. Worship God!"

For the truth that Jesus revealed is what inspires the prophets.

The Rider on the White Horse

11Then I saw heaven open, and there was a white horse. Its rider is called Faithful and True; it is with justice that he judges and fights his battles. 12His eyes were like a flame of fire, and he wore many crowns on his head. He had a name written on him, but no one except himself knows what it is. 13The robe he wore was covered with blood. His name is "The Word of God." 14The armies of heaven followed him, riding on white horses and dressed in clean white linen. 15Out of his mouth came a sharp sword, with which he will defeat the nations. He will rule over them with a rod of iron, and he will trample out the wine in the wine press of the furious anger of the Almighty God. 16On his robe and on his thigh was written the name: "King of kings and Lord of lords."

17Then I saw an angel standing on the sun. He shouted in a loud voice to all the birds flying in midair: "Come and gather together for God's great feast! 18Come and eat the flesh of kings, generals, and soldiers, the flesh of horses and their riders, the flesh of all people, slave and free, great and small!"

19Then I saw the beast and the kings of the earth and their armies gathered to fight against the one who was riding the horse and against his army. 20The beast was taken prisoner, together with the false prophet who had performed miracles in his presence. (It was by those miracles that he had deceived those who had the mark of the beast and those who had

上帝的僕人,凡敬畏他的,不論尊貴卑微,都要讚美我們的上主!」6我又聽見好像是一大羣人的聲音,像大瀑布和雷轟的響聲,說:「哈利路亞,讚美上主!因為我們的主——全能的上帝作王了!7我們要歡呼快樂,頌讚他的偉大!因為羔羊的婚期到了;他的新娘準備好了。8上帝已經賜給她潔白光亮的麻紗衣裳。」(麻紗衣裳是指上帝子民的義行。)

9於是,天使對我說:「你要寫下來:被邀請參加羔羊婚宴的人有福了!」天使又說:「這都是上帝真實的話。」

10我俯伏在他腳前,要拜他,但是他對我說:「千萬不可這樣!我和你,以及其他的信徒,所有守住耶穌所啓示的真理的,都同樣是僕人。你應該敬拜上帝!」

因為耶穌所啓示的真理也就是那感動先知們的真理。

騎白馬的人

11後來,我看見天開了。看哪,有一匹白馬,騎馬的那位稱為「真實」和「可靠」;他根據正義來審判和作戰。12他的眼睛像火燄,頭上戴着許多冠冕。他身上寫着一個名字,但是除了他自己,沒有人知道那是甚麼意思。13他所穿的袍子染滿了血。他的名字稱為「上帝的道」。14天上的軍隊騎着白馬,穿着潔白的麻紗衣服,跟隨着他。15從他口中吐出一把鋒利的劍;他要用這劍來擊敗列國。他要用鐵杖治理他們,並且要在全能上帝那忿怒的榨酒池中榨出烈酒來。16在他的袍子和腿上寫着「萬王之王,萬主之主」這名號。

17我又看見一個天使站在太陽裏。他大聲向空中所有的飛鳥呼喊:「來吧,一起來參加上帝的大筵席!18來吃君王、將領,和士兵們的肉,也吃馬和騎士的肉,又吃奴隸、自由人、尊貴卑微各色各樣人的肉!」

19我又看見那獸和地上諸王,以及他們的軍隊集合起來,跟騎馬的那位和他的軍隊爭戰。20那獸被俘了;在他面前行過奇蹟的假先知也一起被俘了。(這假先知曾經藉奇蹟迷惑了那些有獸的印記和拜獸像的人。)那

worshiped the image of the beast.) The beast and the false prophet were both thrown alive into the lake of fire that burns with sulfur. ²¹Their armies were killed by the sword that comes out of the mouth of the one who was riding the horse; and all the birds ate all they could of their flesh.

The Thousand Years

20 Then I saw an angel coming down from heaven, holding in his hand the key of the abyss and a heavy chain. ²He seized the dragon, that ancient serpent–that is, the Devil, or Satan–and chained him up for a thousand years. ³The angel threw him into the abyss, locked it, and sealed it, so that he could not deceive the nations any more until the thousand years were over. After that he must be set loose for a little while.

⁴Then I saw thrones, and those who sat on them were given the power to judge. I also saw the souls of those who had been executed because they had proclaimed the truth that Jesus revealed and the word of God. They had not worshiped the beast or its image, nor had they received the mark of the beast on their foreheads or their hands. They came to life and ruled as kings with Christ for a thousand years. ⁵(The rest of the dead did not come to life until the thousand years were over.) This is the first raising of the dead. ⁶Happy and greatly blessed are those who are included in this first raising of the dead. The second death has no power over them; they shall be priests of God and of Christ, and they will rule with him for a thousand years.

The Defeat of Satan

⁷After the thousand years are over, Satan will be set loose from his prison, ⁸and he will go out to deceive the nations scattered over the whole world, that is, Gog and Magog. Satan will bring them all together for battle, as many as the grains of sand on the seashore. ⁹They spread out over the earth and surrounded the camp of God's people and the city that he loves. But fire came down from heaven and destroyed them. ¹⁰Then the Devil, who deceived them, was thrown into the lake of fire and sulfur, where the beast and the false prophet had already been thrown; and they will be tormented day and night forever and ever.

The Final Judgment

¹¹Then I saw a great white throne and the one who sits on it. Earth and heaven fled from his presence and were seen no more. ¹²And I saw the dead, great and small alike, standing

獸和假先知被活生生地扔進那燃燒着硫磺的火湖裏。²¹他們的軍隊都被那騎士口中所吐出的劍所殺；所有的鳥都飛來，吃盡了他們的肉。

一千年

20 然後，我看見一個天使從天上下來，手裏拿着無底深淵的鑰匙和一條粗大的鍊子。²他捉住了那條戾龍，就是那古蛇，是魔鬼，又叫撒但，把牠捆綁一千年。³天使把牠扔進無底深淵去，關閉起來，加上封印，使牠不再去迷惑列國，直到過了這一千年。期限過後，牠要暫時被釋放。

⁴我又看見一些寶座；那些坐在上面的人都得到審判的權。我也看見了那些因承認耶穌所啟示的真理和上帝的道而被殺害的人的靈魂。他們沒有拜過那獸或獸像，額上或手上也沒有那獸的名號。他們都復活了，跟基督一同作王一千年。⁵（其餘死了的人要等這一千年滿了才復活。）這是頭一次的復活。⁶那得以包括在頭一次復活中的人是聖潔有福的。第二次的死無權轄制他們；他們要作上帝和基督的祭司，要跟基督一同作王一千年。

擊敗撒但

⁷這一千年後，撒但要從囚禁中被釋放出來；⁸他要去迷惑地上四方的國家，就是歌革和瑪各。撒但要把他們集合起來，出去打仗；他們的人數像海灘上的沙那麼多。⁹他們遍滿全地，圍困上帝子民的營和他所愛的城。但是有火從天上④降下，吞滅了他們。¹⁰那迷惑他們的魔鬼被扔到火與硫磺的湖裏去；那隻獸和假先知早已在那地方了。在那裏，他們要日夜受折磨，永不休止。

最後審判

¹¹接着，我看見一個白色的大寶座和坐在上面的那位。天和地都從他面前逃避，再也看不見了。¹²我又看見死了的人，無論尊貴

④「從天上」有些古卷加「一上帝那裏」。

before the throne. Books were opened, and then another book was opened, the book of the living. The dead were judged according to what they had done, as recorded in the books. [13]Then the sea gave up its dead. Death and the world of the dead also gave up the dead they held. And all were judged according to what they had done. [14]Then death and the world of the dead were thrown into the lake of fire. (This lake of fire is the second death.) [15]Those who did not have their name written in the book of the living were thrown into the lake of fire.

The New Heaven and the New Earth

21 Then I saw a new heaven and a new earth. The first heaven and the first earth disappeared, and the sea vanished. [2]And I saw the Holy City, the new Jerusalem, coming down out of heaven from God, prepared and ready, like a bride dressed to meet her husband. [3]I heard a loud voice speaking from the throne: "Now God's home is with people! He will live with them, and they shall be his people. God himself will be with them, and he will be their God. [4]He will wipe away all tears from their eyes. There will be no more death, no more grief or crying or pain. The old things have disappeared."

[5]Then the one who sits on the throne said, "And now I make all things new!" He also said to me, "Write this, because these words are true and can be trusted." [6]And he said, "It is done! I am the first and the last, the beginning and the end. To anyone who is thirsty I will give the right to drink from the spring of the water of life without paying for it. [7]Those who win the victory will receive this from me: I will be their God, and they will be my children. [8]But cowards, traitors, perverts, murderers, the immoral, those who practice magic, those who worship idols, and all liars–the place for them is the lake burning with fire and sulfur, which is the second death."

The New Jerusalem

[9]One of the seven angels who had the seven bowls full of the seven last plagues came to me and said, "Come, and I will show you the Bride, the wife of the Lamb." [10]The Spirit took control of me, and the angel carried me to the top of a very high mountain. He showed me Jerusalem, the Holy City, coming down out of heaven from God [11]and shining with the glory of God. The city shone like a precious stone, like a jasper, clear as crystal. [12]It had a great, high wall with twelve gates and with twelve angels in charge of the gates. On the gates were written the names of the twelve tribes of the

卑微，都站在寶座前。案卷都展開了；另外有一本生命冊也展開了。死了的人都是照着他們的行爲，根據這些案卷所記錄的，接受審判。[13]於是，海把死人交出來；死亡和陰間也把所拘禁的死人交出來。這些人都照着他們的行爲接受審判。[14]死亡和陰間也被扔進火湖裏。（這火湖就是第二次的死。）[15]凡是名字沒有記錄在生命冊上的，都被扔進火湖裏。

新天新地

21 接着，我看見一個新天新地。那先前的天和地不見了，海也消失了。[2]我又看見聖城，就是新耶路撒冷，由上帝那裏，從天上降下來，像打扮好了的新娘來迎接她的丈夫。[3]我聽見有大聲音從寶座上發出，說：「上帝的家在人間了！他要和人住在一起，而他們要作他的子民。上帝要親自與他們同在，要作他們的上帝。[4]他要擦乾他們每一滴眼淚；不再有死亡，也沒有悲傷、哭泣，或痛苦。以往的事都已經過去了。」

[5]這時候，坐在寶座上的那位說：「看哪，我更新一切！」他又說：「要寫下來，因爲這些話是真實可靠的。」[6]他又對我說：「成了！我是阿爾法和亞米茄，是開始和終結。我要把生命的泉水白白地賜給口渴的人喝。[7]得勝的人可以領受這些，就是：我要作他的上帝；他也要作我的兒子。[8]但是那些膽怯、背信、腐敗、殺人、淫亂、行邪術、拜偶像，和所有說謊的人，有火和硫磺燃燒着的湖在等着他們；那就是第二次的死。」

新耶路撒冷

[9]那拿着七個碗，盛滿着末後七種災難的七個天使當中，有一個過來對我說：「你來，我要讓你看見新娘，就是羔羊的妻。」[10]聖靈支配着我；天使把我帶到高山的頂峯上去，讓我看見由上帝那裏、從天降下來的聖城耶路撒冷。[11]那城充滿着上帝的榮光，閃耀像碧玉寶石，光潔像水晶，[12]有高大的城牆，城牆有十二個門，由十二個天使把守着，門上寫着以色列十二支族的名字。

people of Israel. [13]There were three gates on each side: three on the east, three on the south, three on the north, and three on the west. [14]The city's wall was built on twelve foundation stones, on which were written the names of the twelve apostles of the Lamb. [15]The angel who spoke to me had a gold measuring stick to measure the city, its gates, and its wall. [16]The city was perfectly square, as wide as it was long. The angel measured the city with his measuring stick: it was fifteen hundred miles long and was as wide and as high as it was long. [17]The angel also measured the wall, and it was 216 feet high,[g] according to the standard unit of measure which he was using.[h] [18]The wall was made of jasper, and the city itself was made of pure gold, as clear as glass. [19]The foundation stones of the city wall were adorned with all kinds of precious stones. The first foundation stone was jasper, the second sapphire, the third agate, the fourth emerald, [20]the fifth onyx, the sixth carnelian, the seventh yellow quartz, the eighth beryl, the ninth topaz, the tenth chalcedony, the eleventh turquoise, the twelfth amethyst. [21]The twelve gates were twelve pearls; each gate was made from a single pearl. The street of the city was of pure gold, transparent as glass.

[22]I did not see a temple in the city, because its temple is the Lord God Almighty and the Lamb. [23]The city has no need of the sun or the moon to shine on it, because the glory of God shines on it, and the Lamb is its lamp. [24]The peoples of the world will walk by its light, and the kings of the earth will bring their wealth into it. [25]The gates of the city will stand open all day, they will never be closed, because there will be no night there. [26]The greatness and the wealth of the nations will be brought into the city. [27]But nothing that is impure will enter the city, nor anyone who does shameful things or tells lies. Only those whose names are written in the Lamb's book of the living will enter the city.

22 The angel also showed me the river of the water of life, sparkling like crystal, and coming from the throne of God and of the Lamb [2]and flowing down the middle of the city's street. On each side of the river was the tree of life, which bears fruit twelve times a year, once each month; and its leaves are for the healing of the nations. [3]Nothing that is under God's curse will be found in the city.

The throne of God and of the Lamb will be in the city, and his servants will worship him. [4]They will see his face, and his name will be

g high; or thick.
h In verses 16 and 17 the Greek text speaks of "12,000 furlongs" and "144 cubits" which may have symbolic significance.

[13]每一邊各有三個門：東邊三個，西邊三個，南邊三個，北邊三個。[14]城牆建立在十二塊基石上，基石上寫着羔羊的十二個使徒的名字。

[15]對我說話的那天使拿着一根金的量尺要量那城和那城的門與牆。[16]城是四方的，長寬相等；天使用尺量那城：共兩千四百公里，長、寬、高相等。[17]天使按照人的尺寸標準來量城牆，高⑤有六十公尺⑥。[18]城牆是用碧玉造的，而城本身是用透明像玻璃的純金造的。[19]城牆的基石用各種寶石裝飾：第一塊基石是碧玉，第二是藍寶石，第三是瑪瑙，第四是翡翠，[20]第五是紅紋瑪瑙，第六是紅玉髓，第七是貴橄欖石，第八是綠玉石，第九是黃玉，第十是綠玉髓，第十一是紫玉，第十二是紫晶。[21]那十二個門是十二顆珍珠，每一個門用一顆珍珠造成。城裏的街道是純金的，像玻璃一樣的透明。

[22]我沒有看見城裏有聖殿，因為主—全能的上帝和羔羊就是這城的聖殿。[23]這城不需要太陽或月亮的光；因為有上帝的榮光熙耀着，而羔羊就是這城的燈。[24]世上各國都要藉着這光行走；地上的君王要把他們的榮華帶到這城來。[25]城門要整天開着，永不關閉，因為那裏沒有黑夜。[26]列國都要把尊貴榮耀帶到這城。[27]但是，那不潔淨、行為可憎或撒謊的，都不能進去；只有名字寫在羔羊生命冊上的才可以進去。

22 天使又讓我看一道生命水的河流，閃耀像水晶，從上帝和羔羊的寶座流出來，[2]通過城中心的街道。河的兩邊有生命樹，每年結果子十二次，每月一次；樹的葉子能夠醫治萬國。[3]城裏不再有上帝所詛咒的事。

上帝和羔羊的寶座要在這城裏；他的僕人都要敬拜他。[4]他們要朝見上帝，而他的

⑤「高」或譯「厚」。
⑥在16、17節原文數字是一萬兩千「斯塔狄」和一百四十四肘，可能有象徵性意義。

written on their foreheads. [5]There shall be no more night, and they will not need lamps or sunlight, because the Lord God will be their light, and they will rule as kings forever and ever.

The Coming of Jesus

[6]Then the angel said to me, "These words are true and can be trusted. And the Lord God, who gives his Spirit to the prophets, has sent his angel to show his servants what must happen very soon."

[7]"Listen!" says Jesus. "I am coming soon! Happy are those who obey the prophetic words in this book!"

[8]I, John, have heard and seen all these things. And when I finished hearing and seeing them, I fell down at the feet of the angel who had shown me these things, and I was about to worship him. [9]But he said to me, "Don't do it! I am a servant together with you and with your brothers the prophets and of all those who obey the words in this book. Worship God!" [10]And he said to me, "Do not keep the prophetic words of this book a secret, because the time is near when all this will happen. [11]Whoever is evil must go on doing evil, and whoever is filthy must go on being filthy; whoever is good must go on doing good, and whoever is holy must go on being holy."

[12]"Listen!" says Jesus. "I am coming soon! I will bring my rewards with me, to give to each one according to what he has done. [13]I am the first and the last, the beginning and the end."

[14]Happy are those who wash their robes clean and so have the right to eat the fruit from the tree of life and to go through the gates into the city. [15]But outside the city are the perverts and those who practice magic, the immoral and the murderers, those who worship idols and those who are liars both in words and deeds.

[16]"I, Jesus, have sent my angel to announce these things to you in the churches. I am descended from the family of David; I am the bright morning star."

[17]The Spirit and the Bride say, "Come!"

Everyone who hears this must also say, "Come!"

Come, whoever is thirsty; accept the water of life as a gift, whoever wants it.

Conclusion

[18]I, John, solemnly warn everyone who hears the prophetic words of this book: if any add anything to them, God will add to their punishment the plagues described in this book. [19]And

名要寫在他們的額上。[5]那裏不再有黑夜；他們不需要燈光或日光，因爲主上帝是他們的光。他們要作王統治，直到永遠。

耶穌來臨

[6]天使對我說：「這些話是眞實可靠的。那賜下聖靈給先知們的主上帝差遣他的使者，把必定在短期內要發生的事指示給他的僕人們。」

[7]耶穌說：「看吧，我快要來了！那遵守這書上預言的人有福了！」

[8]我—約翰聽見並且看見了這一切事。我聽見看見之後，俯伏在指示我這些事的天使腳前要拜他。[9]但是他對我說：「千萬不可這樣！我和你，以及你的同道們，就是那些先知和所有遵守這書上的話的，同樣都是僕人。你應該敬拜上帝！」[10]他又對我說：「不要把這書上的預言封閉起來，因爲這一切事情實現的時刻快要到了。[11]作惡的必然繼續作惡；汚穢的仍然汚穢。行善的必然繼續行善；聖潔的仍然聖潔。」

[12]耶穌說：「看吧，我快要來了！我要帶來報賞，按照每一個人的行爲賜給每一個人。[13]我是阿爾法和亞米茄，是首先和末後，是開始和終結。」

[14]那洗淨自己衣服的人多麼有福啊！他們有權吃生命樹上的果子，並且可以從城門進入城裏。[15]但是那些犬類、行邪術的、淫亂的、殺人的、拜偶像的、在言語和行爲上虛僞的人，則都留在城外。

[16]「我—耶穌差遣我的天使，在各教會向你們宣佈這些事。我就是大衞家族的後代；我就是明亮的晨星。」

[17]聖靈和新娘都說：「來！」

所有聽見的人也該應聲說：「來！」

來吧，口渴的人都來；願意的人都可以白白地來接受生命的水。

結語

[18]我—約翰鄭重警告那些聽見這書上預言的人：如果有人在這些話上加添甚麼，上帝要把這書上所寫的災難加給他；[19]如果有人

if any take anything away from the prophetic words of this book, God will take away from them their share of the fruit of the tree of life and of the Holy City, which are described in this book.

20He who gives his testimony to all this says, "Yes indeed! I am coming soon!"

So be it. Come, Lord Jesus!

21May the grace of the Lord Jesus be with everyone.*i*

i everyone; *some manuscripts have* God's people; *others have* all of God's people.

從這書上的預言刪掉甚麼，上帝要把他除名，使他不能享受這書上所記載那生命樹和聖城的福澤。

20 爲這一切事作證的那一位說：「是的，我快要來了！」

阿們。主耶穌啊，請來吧！

21 願主耶穌賜恩典給你們大家⑦！

⑦「你們大家」有些古卷作「上帝的子民」；另有些古卷作「所有上帝的子民」。